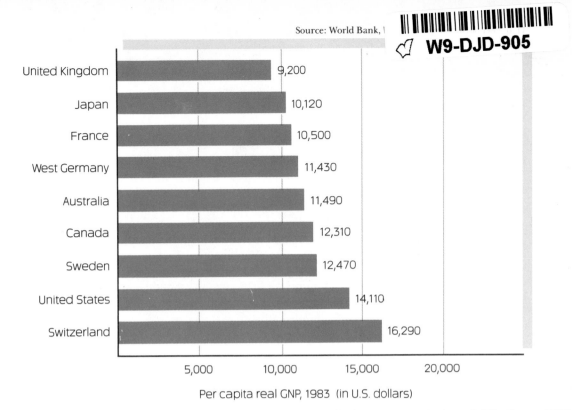

Source: World Bank,

EXHIBIT C: The Gross National Product per Person of Nine Western Industrial Nations, 1983

Per capita real GNP, 1983 (in U.S. dollars)

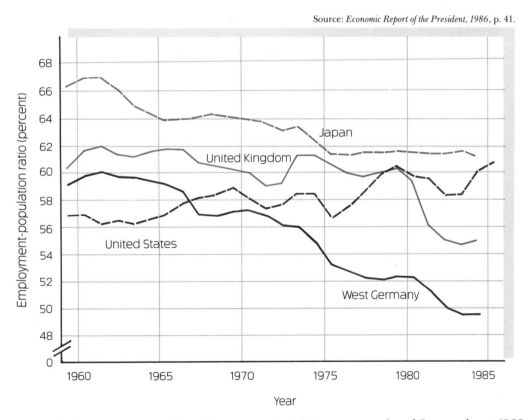

Source: *Economic Report of the President, 1986*, p. 41.

EXHIBIT D: Percent of the Population Employed—An International Comparison, 1960–1985

The employment ratio in the United States and Japan is higher than that in the United Kingdom and West Germany.

FOURTH EDITION

ECONOMICS
PRIVATE AND PUBLIC CHOICE

FOURTH EDITION

ECONOMICS
PRIVATE AND PUBLIC CHOICE

JAMES D. GWARTNEY
Florida State University

RICHARD L. STROUP
Montana State University

with the assistance of
A. H. STUDENMUND
Occidental College

Harcourt Brace Jovanovich, Publishers
and its subsidiary, Academic Press

San Diego   New York   Chicago   Austin   Washington, D.C.
London   Sydney   Tokyo   Toronto

PREFACE

This is an exciting time to study and teach economics. Economic events and advancements in economic theory are changing the introductory economics course. In some cases, recent theoretical contributions have supplemented our previous knowledge. In other instances, they have enlightened it; in still others, they have corrected it. Since the real world is the experimental laboratory of the economist, events often contribute to our understanding of issues. The bitter experience of the 1970s illustrates that economic problem solving is a far more complex and demanding task than was envisioned 15 years ago. A modern principles course must explain why this is so and what lessons we should learn from the recent economic instability that has plagued western economies.

THE FOURTH EDITION

As in previous editions, our approach emphasizes the economic way of thinking. Like Keynes, we believe economics is "an apparatus of the mind." We reject the idea that a principles text should merely teach students *what* economists think. Rather our goal is to teach *how* economists think—to equip students with the tools that will permit them to think like economists.

CHANGES IN THE CORE MACROECONOMICS

During the last 15 years, enormous changes have occurred in macro-economics. Relative prices in aggregated markets and interrelationships among the basic macroeconomic markets now play a central role in macro-economic analysis. Modern macroeconomists stress the importance of whether a change is anticipated or unanticipated. The importance of expectations and how they are developed is a central element of our modern analysis. A consensus view has emerged that there is considerably more to macroeconomics than aggregate demand. All of these elements are a central part of intermediate and advanced macroeconomic analysis.

In prior editions of our text, we stressed the mechanics of the simple Keynesian-cross model. Unfortunately, the Keynesian-cross framework makes it difficult for students to (a) visualize interrelationships among basic macroeconomic markets, (b) incorporate the importance of price changes and expectations into their thought process, and (c) understand alternative macroeconomic theories with regard to monetary and fiscal policy. Furthermore, texts (and courses) built round the Keynesian 45 degree model spend an enormous amount of time on mechanical exercises under highly restrictive assumptions. Secondary effects are often concealed. Of course, most principles texts eventually relax the restrictive assumptions and attach a footnote with regard to the potential secondary effects. However, we believe that this approach generally leaves students with a misleading picture of modern macroeconomics.

As the core macroeconomics sections of this edition indicate, we think there is a better way. Following the lead of successful intermediate macroeconomic texts, the macroeconomic theory of this edition is presented within the framework of a central multi-market model—including aggregate demand and aggregate supply (AD/AS) within the price–quantity framework. We integrate the basic aggregate markets—resources and loanable funds, as well as goods and services—from the beginning. We have gone to great pains to develop and explain the basic multi-market model in a manner that is both logical and understandable to college sophomores.

The multi-market and AD/AS framework make it much easier to visualize the importance of price changes in aggregate markets, interrelationships among markets, and the role of expectations. Our analysis incorporates differences between anticipated and unanticipated changes at an early stage (see Chapter 9). The model also makes it easier to comprehend alternative macroeconomic theories. For example, our approach permits us to present the Keynesian, crowding-out, and new classical theories of fiscal policy in a single chapter (11) and to show that these alternative theories are merely modified forms of the basic AD/AS model. Since the importance of whether a change is anticipated or unanticipated is discussed prior to the full integration of the market for money balances, when this topic is discussed in the monetary theory chapter, students are better prepared to differentiate between the effects of an expected increase in the money supply and a monetary shock. Our method of presentation lays a firm foundation for the discussion of alternative theories of how expectations are formed, shifts in the Phillips curve, short-run versus long-run effects of macroeconomic policy (Chapter 14) and stabilization policy (Chapter 15).

In contrast with prior efforts, we believe this edition does a superior job of communicating the reality of modern macroeconomics—and it does so in a manner understandable to college sophomores. A short list of the features of the macroeconomic section includes:

- The use of the aggregate demand/aggregate supply model to develop the core macroeconomic theory.
- The use of *microeconomic foundations* in the development and analysis of the basic macroeconomic markets.
- The development of macroeconomics within the framework of an *open economy*.
- Stress on *both* changes in the price level and changes in output in the achievement of equilibrium in the aggregate goods and services market.
- Integration of the natural unemployment rate and long-run aggregate supply concepts.
- Presentation of Keynesian, monetarist, new classical, and supply-side theories not just as differences of opinion, but as debates concerning the structure of the central macroeconomic model.
- Comprehensive discussion of the *activism versus nonactivism* stabilization policy debate.

Recent theoretical developments in macroeconomics cannot merely be tacked on to the traditional approach. The new must be *integrated* with the old. This is precisely our goal—to integrate the "new macroeconomics" and preserve the important elements of the traditional approach, while providing the student with an understandable but thorough introduction to modern macroeconomics.

CHANGES IN THE CORE MICROECONOMICS

As in previous editions, we utilize applications and case studies to buttress the core microeconomic theory. The structure of the microeconomic theory is similar to that in the last edition. However, we have included several new features which increase the breadth of coverage and reflect recent developments in the profession. The following brief list indicates the major areas in which our coverage of microeconomic topics is either expanded or substantially revised in this edition.

- The importance of property rights, transaction costs, and middlemen is now more fully integrated into our coverage of exchange theory and gains from trade.
- Recent developments on the significance of low barriers to entry and the theory of contestable markets are incorporated into our theory of the firm analysis.
- Our coverage of deregulation is expanded in light of recent developments in the transportation and communications industries.
- Recent empirical work on employment discrimination and earnings according to race and sex is incorporated into our expanded coverage of these topics.
- The focus of the income distribution chapter is restructured in light of recent findings emanating from the Michigan Panel data, which provide us with substantially improved information on the dynamics of income differences.
- Our expanded coverage of poverty and the analysis of income transfers reflects recent developments in this area.

- Finally, a chapter on natural resources (rather than energy economics) provides greater generality and additional coverage of resource markets, including the analysis of misconceptions that seem to abound in this area.

In this revision, we sought to strengthen and expand the analysis set forth in earlier editions. We have aimed to maximize the pedagogical usefulness of *Economics: Private and Public Choice*, Fourth Edition, by elucidating concepts in greater depth without sacrificing the breadth and clarity that distinguished the prior editions.

DISTINGUISHING FEATURES OF OUR APPROACH

Most of all, we believe that economics is a way of thinking. We seek to emphasize those points that will challenge students to think like economists. The following points are of specific interest in this regard:

1. *Economic Principles Are Presented in a Highly Readable Fashion.* Difficult language and terminology can often hinder successful learning, particularly of economic concepts. Without sacrificing accuracy, we have sought to employ simple language. Simplicity, however, has not been substituted for depth. Rather, our aim is to highlight the power and accessibility of economic concepts. Where complex ideas are essential to our analysis, they are developed fully. We believe that the economics required for the 1980s can be comprehensible to the student as well as challenging and applicable to the real world.

2. *Economic Reasoning and Its Applications Are Emphasized.* Although models, theories, and exercises are important, they are only tools with which to develop the economic way of thinking. Abstractions and mechanics are not stressed so as to obscure major concepts. We consistently emphasize the basics and their real-world applications.

3. *Microeconomic Reasoning Is a Fundamental Component of Macroeconomic Analysis.* The central principle of economics is that incentives matter. The microstructure of an economy does have macroeconomic ramifications. Microincentives influence such macrofactors as the rate of unemployment, the level of current spending, saving, and aggregate output. In this book, the importance of the microincentive structure that is the foundation of our macroeconomic markets is highlighted.

4. *Economic Tools Are Applied to Both the Market and the Political Process.* Most textbooks tell students how an *ideal* market economy would operate, how real-world markets differ from the hypothetical ideal, and how ideal public policy can correct the shortcomings of the market. In addition to discussing these three basic issues, we analyze what real-world public policy is *likely to do*. This central focus emphasizes both the power and the relevance of modern economics. Built on the pioneering work of Kenneth Arrow, Duncan Black, James Buchanan, Gordon Tullock, and others, the economic analysis of both public and private choice fills a void many other textbooks fail even to acknowledge.

5. *The Role of the Human Decision-Maker Is Stressed.* Students often feel that economists exclude human beings from the economic process. In most economics textbooks, business decision-makers are depicted as having perfect knowledge of demand and cost. Like computers, they always arrive at the maximum-profit solution. Likewise, government planners, knowing precisely the deficiency in aggregate demand and the size of the multiplier, simply increase government spending by the right amount to restore full employment. The employer, knowing the marginal productivity of each resource, utilizes each in exactly the proper proportion. Decision-making is treated as a mechanical exercise, removed from the real world. Throughout this book, we stress the importance of information, uncertainty, trial-and-error decision-making, expectations, and other factors that influence real-world choices. Economics is more than a set of guidelines. If students are to be convinced of its applicability, we must delineate the dynamic factors that influence and motivate human beings.

ORGANIZATIONAL FEATURES

We have employed several organizational features designed to make the presentation more understandable and interesting.

1. *Myths of Economics* In a series of boxed articles, commonly held fallacies of economic reasoning are dispelled. Each myth is followed by a concise explanation of why it is incorrect and is presented within a chapter containing closely related material.
2. *Applications in Economics* These boxed features apply economic theory to real-world issues and controversies. They add breadth on topics of special interest and illustrate the relevance of basic principles to the world in which we live.
3. *Measures of Economic Activity* Measurement is an important element of economics. These features explain how important economic indicators such as the Consumer Price Index, unemployment rate, and index of leading indicators are assembled.
4. *Outstanding Economists* These brief profiles stress the contributions of several economists, both current and historical, whose work has been important in development of the field. This series is designed both to enhance the student's appreciation of economic history and to provide depth on the contributions of several present-day economists.
5. *Chapter Focus Questions and Closing Summaries* Each chapter begins with several questions which summarize the focus of the chapter. A summary which provides the student with a concise statement of the material (chapter learning objectives) appears at the end of each chapter. Reviewing the focus questions and chapter summaries will help the student better understand the material and integrate it into the broader economic picture.
6. *Key Terms* The terminology of economics is often confusing to introductory students. Key terms are introduced in the text in boldface type; simultaneously, each term is defined in the margin opposite the first

reference to the term. A glossary containing the key terms also appears at the end of the book.

7. *Discussion Questions*   Intended to test the student's grasp of the economic way of thinking, a set of discussion questions concludes each chapter. These questions, and the discussions they provoke, provide students with the opportunity for self-testing and the review of important material.

SUPPLEMENTARY MATERIALS

The textbook is accompanied by a *Coursebook*. More than just a study guide, the *Coursebook* contains numerous true–false, multiple-choice, and discussion questions. The problems and projects feature of each chapter in the *Coursebook* has been expanded. Almost every chapter of the *Coursebook* also contains a short article designed to supplement the classroom teaching of the important concepts presented in the text. In this series of readings, contrasting positions are often presented. Discussion questions follow each article, challenging students to demonstrate their understanding of the material and to distinguish a sound argument from economic nonsense. As in the textbook, our intent is to help the student to develop the economic way of thinking.

A Test Book for instructors is also available. Approximately 2,600 multiple-choice test questions, many of which have been pretested extensively, are included in the Test Book. Within each chapter, the questions are grouped to correspond to the major headings of the text. The Test Book is also available on computer tape.

An *Instructor's Manual* is available on request. It is divided into two parts. The first part is a detailed outline of each chapter in lecture note form. It is designed to help instructors organize and structure their current lecture notes to accompany this textbook. The second part contains teaching tips, sources of supplementary materials, and other information likely to be of assistance to instructors.

ACKNOWLEDGMENTS

A project of this type is truly a team effort. The suggestions of several people were particularly helpful in the development of this text. In particular, Ron Brandolini (Valencia Community College) played a central role in the development of the macroeconomics material. His clear and precise thoughts, based on extensive teaching experience and familiarity with other texts, initially convinced us of the need to restructure the section on macroeconomic theory. Later, his review comments on our earlier drafts substantially improved our organization of this material. Given the magnitude of his influence on our thought process, we can only hope that our efforts at least partially fulfill his lofty expectations.

Once again, Woody Studenmund provided valuable direction and helped us get some of the early bugs out of the macro material. Often his comments made so much sense, we wondered why we had not incorporated them in the first place. As in the past, his positive attitude was an inspiration to us.

More than ever before we found the comments of reviewers to be extremely helpful. Many areas were rewritten in light of reviewer comments. In fact, the final version bears only a slight resemblance to some of the early draft material. We would like to express our appreciation to the following reviewers for their assistance: Jack Adams (University of Arkansas, Little Rock); John Beck (Case Western University); Wallace Broome (Community College of Rhode Island); Shirley Cassing (University of Pittsburgh); Tom Cate (Northern Kentucky University); Marsha Courchane (North Carolina State University); Eleanor Craig (University of Delaware); David Culp (Slippery Rock University); Thomas Duchesneau (University of Maine); Fred Goddard (University of Florida); Nicolas Grunt (Tarrant

County Junior College); Richard Hansen (University of Northern Iowa); Bruce Harger (Lake Superior State College); Charles Hegji (Auburn University, Montgomery); Thomas Holmstrom (Northern Michigan University); Willard Howard (Phoenix College); Vance Hughey (Western Nevada Community College); Jerry Knarr (Hillsboro Community College); Joe Lammert (University of Cincinnati); Jerry Manahan (Midwestern State University); Drew Mattson (Anoka-Ramsey Community College); James McGowen (Belleville Area College); John Pisciotta (Baylor University); Robert Puth (University of New Hampshire); Stephen Sacks (University of Connecticut); Jim Sheib (Denver Community College); Don Tailby (University of New Mexico); Robert Thomas (Iowa State University); Terry Thornton (Albany Junior College); Roger Trenary (Kansas State University); and William Wood (University of Virginia).

We have also benefited from review comments and discussions with Terry Anderson, John Baden, P. J. Hill, William Laird, Milton Marquis, Brian McGavin, Tom McCaleb, and Charles Rockwood. Amy Dickinson assisted us with the preparation of supplementary materials.

In the planning and development stage, both Bill Bayer and Steven Dowling of Academic Press provided us with valuable direction. Sheila Korman edited the manuscript. Marguerite L. Egan (Acquisitions Editor), Jack Thomas (Managing Editor), and Parma Yarkin (Production Editor) of Harcourt Brace Jovanovich provided us with guidance, editorial assistance, and encouragement. We would also like to thank Lynne Bush (Production Manager), Geri Davis, and Jane Carey (Designers) for their contributions. As has been true for all previous editions, Linda Zingale provided us with superlative word processing assistance. Her special efforts to help us meet the various deadlines are particularly appreciated.

Finally, we would like to acknowledge the assistance of Amy Gwartney and Jane Stroup, both of whom contributed in numerous ways to the success of this project. Without their assistance and encouragement, our mental stability would have been threatened. We dedicate this edition to them.

A NOTE TO STUDENTS

This text contains several features that we think will help you maximize (a good economics term) the returns derived from your study effort. Our past experience indicates that awareness of the following points will help you to use the book more effectively.

- Each chapter begins with a series of focus questions which communicate the central issues of the chapter. Before you read the chapter, briefly think about the focus questions, why they are important, and how they relate to the material of prior chapters.
- The textbook is organized in the form of an outline. The headings within the text are the major points of the outline. Minor headings (contained in the margins) are subpoints under the major headings. In addition, important subpoints within sections are often set off and numbered. Sometimes thumbnail sketches are used to help the reader better organize important points. Careful use of the headings and thumbnail sketches will help you better visualize the organization of the material.
- A summary appears at the end of each chapter. Use the summary as a checklist to determine whether or not you understand the major points of the chapter.
- Review of the exhibits will also provide you with a summary of each chapter. The accompanying legend briefly describes the content and analysis of each exhibit. After studying the chapter, briefly review the exhibits to ensure that you have mastered the central points.
- The key terms introduced in each chapter are defined in the margins. As you study the chapter, go over the marginal definition of each key

term as it is introduced. Later, you may also find it useful to review the marginal definitions. If you have forgotten the meaning of a term introduced earlier, consult the glossary at the end of the book.

• The boxed features provide additional depth on various topics without disrupting the flow of the text. In general, the topics of the boxed features have been chosen because of their relevance as an application of the theory or because of past student interest in the topic. Reading the boxed features will supplement the text and enhance your understanding of important economic concepts.

• If you are having trouble, be sure to obtain a *Coursebook* and work the questions and problems for each chapter. The *Coursebook* also contains the answers to the multiple-choice questions and a brief explanation of why an answer is correct (and other choices incorrect). In most cases, if you master the concepts of the test items in the *Coursebook,* you will do well on the quizzes and examinations of your instructor.

CONTENTS IN BRIEF

CONTENTS

**PART FOUR:
FACTOR MARKETS
AND INCOME
DISTRIBUTION**

MYTHS OF ECONOMICS

MEASURES OF ECONOMIC ACTIVITY

APPLICATIONS IN ECONOMICS

THE ECONOMIC WAY OF THINKING— AN INTRODUCTION

CHAPTER
FOCUS

The ideas of economists and political philosophers, both when they are right and when they are wrong, are more powerful than is commonly understood. Indeed, the world is ruled by little else. Practical men, who believe themselves to be quite exempt from any intellectual influences, are usually slaves of some defunct economist. [1]

JOHN MAYNARD KEYNES

- Why is scarcity a key economic concept, even in an affluent economy?

- How does scarcity differ from poverty?

- What are the basics underlying the economic way of thinking? What is different about the way economists look at choices and human decision-making?

- What is the difference between positive and normative economics?

1 THE ECONOMIC APPROACH

As the strong influence of Professor Keynes's own work has since proved, ideas have consequences. They influence events in the real world. In turn, ideas are influenced by real-world experience. Economic ideas are no exception. The events and patterns of the last 20 years—inflation rates that soared and declined, high unemployment, recession and recovery—have made a dramatic impact on the economics profession. They have also generated additional interest in the subject matter of economics. People are now trying to more fully understand these continually unfolding economic events.

This book will help you understand the recent upheavals in economic thinking and the policies suggested by various theories. Your ability to analyze new policy directions will be increased. This is not to imply that economics provides the answers to the problems of the world. Economics is not an answer, but rather a way of thinking. In fact, economics is more likely to provide an appreciation of the limitations of "grand design" proposals than it is to offer utopian solutions. Nevertheless, we believe that "economic thinking" is a powerful tool capable of illuminating a broad range of real-world events. Our goals are to communicate the basics of economics and to illustrate their power.

WHAT IS ECONOMICS ABOUT?

Economics is about people and the choices they make. The unit of analysis in economics is the individual. Of course, individuals group together to form collective organizations such as corporations, labor unions, and governments. Individual choices, however, still underlie and direct these organizations. Thus, even when we study collective organizations, we will focus on the ways in which their operation is affected by the choices of individuals.

Scarcity: Fundamental concept of economics which indicates that less of a good is freely available than consumers would like.

Economic theory evolves from fundamental postulates about how individual human beings behave, struggle with the problem of scarcity, and respond to change. The reality of life on our planet is that productive resources—resources used to produce goods—are limited. Therefore, goods and services are also limited. In contrast, the desires of human beings are virtually unlimited. These facts confront us with the two basic ingredients of an economic topic—scarcity and choice. **Scarcity** is the term used by economists to indicate that people's desire for a "thing" exceeds the amount of it that is freely available from Nature. Nature has always dealt grudgingly with us; the Garden of Eden has continually eluded our grasp.

Economic Good: A good that is scarce. The desire for economic goods exceeds the amount that is freely available from Nature.

A good that is scarce is an **economic good.** The first column of Exhibit 1 contains a partial listing of scarce or economic goods. The list includes food, clothing, and many of the items that all of us commonly recognize as material goods. It also includes some items, however, that may surprise you.

---

[1]John Maynard Keynes (1883–1946) was an English economist whose writings during the 1920s and 1930s exerted an enormous impact on both economic theory and policy. Keynes established the terminology and the economic framework that are still widely used today when economists study problems of unemployment and inflation.

EXHIBIT 1 • A General Listing of Desired Economic Goods and Limited Resources	
Economic Goods	Limited Resources
Food (bread, milk, meat, eggs, vegetables, coffee, etc.) Clothing (shirts, pants, blouses, shoes, socks, coats, sweaters, etc.) Household goods (tables, chairs, rugs, beds, dressers, television sets, etc.) Space exploration Education National defense Recreation Leisure time Entertainment Clean air Pleasant environment (trees, lakes, rivers, open spaces, etc.) Pleasant working conditions More productive resources	Land (various degrees of fertility) Natural resources (rivers, trees, minerals, oceans, etc.) Machines and other man-made physical resources Nonhuman animal resources Technology (physical and scientific "recipes" of history) Human resources (the knowledge, skill, and talent of individual human beings)

Our history is a record of our struggle to transform available, but limited, resources into things that we would like to have—economic goods.

Is leisure a good? Would you like to have more leisure time than is currently available to you? Most of us would. Therefore, leisure time is a scarce good. What about clean air? A few years ago many economics texts classified clean air as a free good, made available by Nature in such abundant supply that everyone could have all of it they wanted. No longer. Our utilization of air to dispose of wastes has created a scarcity of clean air. Many of the residents of Los Angeles, New York, and other large cities would like to have more clean air.

Few of us usually think of such environmental conditions as economic goods. However, if you would like to have more open spaces, green areas, or dogwood trees, you will recognize that these things are scarce. They, too, are economic goods.

Since scarcity of productive resources, time, and income limit the alternatives available to us, we must make choices. **Choice** is the act of selecting among restricted alternatives. A major focus of economics concerns how people choose when the alternatives open to them are restricted. The choices of the family shopper are restricted by the household budget, market prices, and the shopper's own imagination about ways to satisfy wants. The choices of business decision-makers are restricted by competition from other firms, the cost of productive resources, technology, and their own entrepreneurial ability to open new markets or use new techniques to satisfy customers' wants. The spending choices of political decision-makers are restricted by the taxable income of the citizenry and voter opposition to taxes. The selection of one alternative generally necessitates doing without others. If you choose to spend $10 going to a football game, you will have $10 less to spend on other things. Similarly, if you choose to spend an

Choice: **The act of selecting among alternatives.**

evening watching a movie, you must forgo spending the evening playing Ping-Pong (or participating in some other activity). You cannot have your cake and eat it, too.

Each day, we all make hundreds of economic choices, even though we are not normally aware of doing so. Choosing when to get up in the morning, what to eat for breakfast, how to travel to work, what television program to watch—all of these are economic decisions. They are economic decisions because they involve the utilization of scarce resources (for example, time and income). We all are constantly involved in making choices that relate to economics.

OUR CONSTANT STRUGGLE WITH SCARCITY

Resource: An input used to produce economic goods. Land, labor skills, natural resources, and capital are examples.

Scarcity restricts us. How can we overcome it? **Resources,** including our own skills, can be used to produce economic goods. Human effort and ingenuity can be combined with machines, land, natural resources, and other productive factors (see the second column of Exhibit 1) to increase the availability of economic goods. These are "tools" in our struggle with scarcity. It is important to note that most economic goods are not like manna from heaven. Human energy is nearly always an ingredient in the production of economic goods.

The lessons of history confirm that our desire for economic goods far outstrips our resources to produce them. Are we destined to lead hopeless lives of misery and drudgery because we are involved in a losing battle with scarcity? Some might answer "Yes," pointing out that a substantial proportion of the world's population go to bed hungry each night. The annual income of a typical worker in countries such as Pakistan and India is less than $400. Moreover, the population in these and other areas is increasing almost as rapidly as their output of material goods.

At the same time, the grip of scarcity has been loosened in most of North America, Western Europe, Japan, and the Soviet Union. Most Americans, Japanese, and Europeans have an adequate caloric intake and sufficient housing and clothing. Many own luxuries such as dishwashers, video cassette recorders, and sophisticated audio equipment. Over the last century, the average number of hours worked per week has fallen from 60 to about 40 in most Western nations. From a material viewpoint, life is certainly more pleasant for these people than it was for their ancestors 250 years ago. Despite this progress, though, scarcity is still a fact of life, even in relatively affluent countries. Most of us have substantially fewer goods and resources and less time than we would like to have.

It is important to note that scarcity and poverty are not the same thing. Poverty implies some basic level of need, either in absolute or relative terms. Absence of poverty means that the basic level has been attained. In contrast, the absence of scarcity means that we have not merely attained some basic level, but have acquired as much of all goods as we desire. Poverty is at least partially subjective, but there is an objective test for scarcity. If people are willing to pay—give up something—for a good, that good is scarce. Even though the battle against poverty may ultimately be won, the outcome of the battle against scarcity is already painfully obvious. Our productive capabilities and material desires are such that goods and services will always be scarce.

THE ECONOMIC WAY OF THINKING

It [economics] is a method rather than a doctrine, an apparatus of the mind, a technique of thinking which helps its possessor to draw correct conclusions. [J. M. Keynes]

Reflecting on a television appearance with economist Paul Samuelson and other social scientists (noneconomists), Milton Friedman stated that he was amazed to find that economists, although differing in their ideological viewpoints, usually find themselves to be allies in discussions with other social scientists.[2] One does not have to spend much time around economists to recognize that there is an "economic way of thinking." Admittedly, economists, like others, differ widely in their ideological views. A news commentator once remarked that "any half-dozen economists will normally come up with about six different policy prescriptions." Yet, in spite of their philosophical differences, there is a common ground to the approach of economists.

Economic Theory: A set of definitions, postulates, and principles assembled in a manner that makes clear the "cause and effect" relationships of economic data.

That common ground is **economic theory,** developed from basic postulates of human behavior. Theory has a reputation for being abstract and difficult, but this need not be the case. Economic theory, like a road map or a guidebook, establishes reference points indicating what to look for and what can be considered significant in economic issues. It helps us understand the relationships among complex and often seemingly unrelated events in the real world. A better understanding of cause-and-effect relationships will enhance our ability to accurately predict the likely consequences of alternative policy choices. Economics has sometimes been called the "science of common sense." This is as it should be. After all, common sense is nothing more than a set of beliefs based on sound theories that have been tested over a long period of time and found to be accurate.

EIGHT GUIDEPOSTS TO ECONOMIC THINKING

The economic way of thinking involves the incorporation of certain guidelines—some would say the building blocks of basic economic theory—into one's thought process. Once these guidelines are incorporated, we believe that economics can be a relatively easy subject to master.

Students who have difficulty with economics almost always do so because they fail to develop the economic way of thinking. Their thought processes are not consistently directed by a few simple economic concepts or guideposts. Students who do well in economics learn to use these basic concepts and allow their thought processes to reflect them. We will outline and discuss eight principles that characterize economic thinking and that are essential to the understanding of the economic approach.

1. Scarce Goods Have A Cost—There Are No Free Lunches. The benefits of scarce goods can be obtained only if someone is willing to exert personal effort or give up something. Using the terms of economics, scarce goods cost someone something. The cost of many scarce goods is obvious. The

---

[2]The philosophical views of Professor Friedman and Professor Samuelson differ considerably. They are often on opposite sides of economic policy issues.

purchaser of a new car must give up $11,000 of purchasing power over other goods to own the car. Similarly, the cost to the purchaser of a delightful meal, new clothes, or a Las Vegas weekend is obvious. But, what about a good such as public elementary education? Even though the education is usually free to students, it is not free to the community. Buildings, books, and teachers' salaries must be paid for from tax revenues. The taxpayer incurs the cost. If these scarce resources were not used to produce elementary education, they could be used to produce more recreation, entertainment, housing, and other goods. Providing for public education means that some of these other scarce goods must be forgone. Similarly, provision of free medical service, recreation areas, tennis courts, and parking lots involves the use of scarce resources. Again, something must be given up if we are to produce these goods. Taxpayers usually bear the cost of "free" medical services and tennis courts. Consumers often bear the cost of "free" parking lots in the form of higher prices in areas where this service is provided.

By now the central point should be obvious. Economic thinking recognizes that the provision of a scarce good, any scarce good, involves a cost. We must give up other things if we are to have more of a scarce good. Economic goods are not free.

2. Decision-Makers Choose Purposefully. Therefore, They Will Economize. Since resources are scarce, it is all the more important that decisions be made in a purposeful manner. Decision-makers do not deliberately make choices in a manner that wastes valuable resources. Recognizing the restrictions imposed by their limited resources (income, time, talent, and so on), they seek to choose wisely; they try to select the options that best advance their own personal objectives. In turn, the objectives or preferences of individuals are revealed by the choices they make. **Economizing behavior** results directly from purposeful decision-making. Economizing individuals will seek to accomplish an objective at the least possible cost. When choosing among things that yield equal benefit, an economizer will select the cheapest option. For example, if a hamburger, a fish dinner, and a New York sirloin steak are expected to yield identical benefits, economizing behavior implies that the cheapest of the three alternatives, probably the hamburger, will be chosen. Correspondingly, when choosing among alternatives of equal cost, economizing decision-makers will select the option that yields the greatest benefit. Purposeful decision-makers will not deliberately pay more for something than is necessary.

Purposeful choosing implies that decision-makers have some basis for their evaluation of alternatives. Economists refer to this evaluation as utility. **Utility** is the benefit or satisfaction that an individual expects from the choice of a specific alternative. The utility of an alternative is highly subjective, often differing widely from person to person.

3. Incentives Matter—Human Choice Is Influenced In A Predictable Way By Changes In Economic Incentives. This guidepost to clear economic thinking might be called the basic postulate of all economics. As the personal benefits from choosing an option increase, other things constant,

Economizing Behavior: Choosing the objective of gaining a specific benefit at the least possible cost. A corollary of economizing behavior implies that when choosing among items of equal cost, individuals will choose the option that yields the greatest benefit.

Utility: The benefit or satisfaction expected from a choice or course of action.

a person will be more likely to choose that option. In contrast, as the costs associated with the choice of an item increase, the person will be less likely to choose that option. For a group, this basic economic postulate suggests that making an option more attractive will influence more people to choose it. In contrast, as the cost of a selection to the members of a group increases, fewer of them will make this selection.

This basic economic concept provides a powerful tool with which to analyze various types of human behavior. If laws, taxes, prices, or other "rules of the game" change and alter the costs facing individuals, then people will change their behavior in predictable ways. According to this postulate, what would happen to the birthrate if the U.S. government (a) removed the income tax deduction for dependents, (b) imposed a $1,500 "birth tax" on parents, and (c) made birth-control pills available, free of charge, to all? The birthrate would fall—that's what. In fact, several governments around the world recognize this, and provide economic inducements to increase or decrease birthrates. Canada, for example, provides payments to couples with larger families to encourage population growth, while China penalizes couples who have more than one child.

What would happen if the government imposed a $5,000 tax on smokestacks, required automobile owners to pay a larger license fee for cars with

MYTHS OF ECONOMICS

"Economic analysis assumes people act only out of selfish motives. It rejects the humanitarian side of humankind."

Probably because economics focuses on the efforts of individuals to satisfy material desires, many casual observers of the subject argue that its relevance hinges on the selfish nature of humankind. Some have even charged that economists, and the study of economics, encourage people to be materialistic rather than humanitarian.

This point of view stems from a fundamental misunderstanding of personal decision-making. Obviously, people act for a variety of reasons, some selfish and some humanitarian. The economist merely assumes that actions will be influenced by costs and benefits, as

viewed by the decision-maker. As an activity becomes more costly, it is less likely that a decision-maker will choose it. As the activity becomes more attractive, it is more likely that it will be chosen.

The choices of both the humanitarian and the egocentric individual will be influenced by changes in personal costs and benefits. For example, both will be more likely to try to save the life of a small child in a three-foot swimming pool than in the rapid currents approaching Niagara Falls. Both will be more likely to give a needy person their hand-me-downs rather than their best clothes. Why? Because in both cases, the latter alternative is more costly than the former.

Observation would suggest that the right to control one's destiny is an "economic" good for most per-

sons. Most of us would prefer to make our own choices rather than have someone else decide for us. But, is this always greedy and selfish? If so, why do people often make choices in a way that is charitable toward others? After all, many people freely choose to give a portion of their wealth to the sick, the needy, the less fortunate, religious organizations, and charitable institutions. Economics does not imply that these choices are irrational. It does imply that if you make it more (less) costly to act charitably, fewer (more) persons will do so.

Economics deals with people as they are—not as we would like to remake them. Should people act more charitably? Perhaps so. But this is not the subject matter of economics.

higher exhaust levels, and gave a 10 percent tax reduction to all corporations that did not use the air for waste disposal purposes? Answer: There would be a decline in air pollution levels. Economics suggests that any policy shift that increases the cost and/or reduces the benefits of a specific activity will reduce the frequency of that activity.

Our analysis indicates that an instructor could influence the incidence of cheating on an examination simply by changing the payoffs to students. There would be little cheating on a closely monitored, individualized, essay examination. Why? Because it would be difficult (that is, costly) to cheat on such an exam. Suppose, however, that an instructor gave an objective "take-home" exam, basing students' course grades entirely on the results. More students would be likely to cheat because the benefits of doing so would be great and the risk (cost) minimal.

Economic reasoning recognizes that many factors help determine how people make decisions. Morality, for example, might be a strong factor in the situations discussed above. Incentives, though, will also be important. The economic way of thinking never loses sight of the fact that changes in incentives exert a powerful and predictable influence on human decisions. (The boxed feature "Do Incentives Matter?" gives yet another application of this principle.)

Marginal: Term used to describe the effects of a change, given the current situation. For example, the marginal cost is the cost of producing an additional unit of a product, given the producer's current facility and production rate.

4. Economic Thinking Is Marginal Thinking. Fundamental to economic reasoning and economizing behavior are the effects of decisions made to change the status quo. Economists refer to such decisions as **marginal.** Marginal choices always involve the effects of net additions to or subtractions *from the current conditions.* In fact, the word "additional" is often used as a substitute for marginal. For example, we might ask, "What is the marginal (or additional) cost of producing one more automobile?" Or,

APPLICATIONS IN ECONOMICS

Do Incentives Matter?

How generally can we apply the "incentives matter" principle? Does it apply, for example, to drinking and driving? Will changing the incentives with regard to drinking and driving change behavior? Consider the case of Norway, the country that has the toughest drunk-driving laws in the Western world.[3] Drinking a single can of beer before driving can put a first offender in jail for a minimum sentence of three weeks. These drivers generally lose their licenses for up to two years and often get stiff fines as well. Repeat offenders are treated even more harshly.

These laws are far more Draconian than those of the United States. And the results?

1. One out of three Norwegians arrives at parties in a taxi, while nearly all Americans drive their own cars.
2. One out of ten Norwegian party-goers spends the night at the host's home; Americans seldom do.
3. In Norway, 78 percent of drivers totally avoid drinking at parties, compared to only 17 percent of American drivers.

Norwegians do like to drink, though they consume only half as much alcohol as Americans. The strong incentives built into Norwegian law, however, clearly make a difference in the incidence of drunken driving in that country. Once again, incentives do matter, and matter in a big way.

----

[3]The information in this feature is taken from L. Erik Calonius, "Just a Bottle of Beer Can Land a Motorist in Prison in Norway," *Wall Street Journal,* August 16, 1985, p. 1.

"What is the marginal (or additional) benefit derived from one more glass of water?"

Marginal decisions need not always involve small changes. The "one more unit" can be large or small. For example, the decision to build a new plant is a marginal decision. It is marginal because it involves additional costs and additional benefits. *Given the current situation*, what marginal benefits (additional sales revenues, for example) can be expected from the plant, and what will be the marginal cost of constructing the facility? The answers to these questions will determine whether or not building the new plant is a good decision.

It is important to distinguish between "average" and "marginal." Even though a manufacturer's current average cost (total cost divided by total number of cars produced) of producing automobiles may be $10,000, for example, the marginal cost of producing an additional automobile (or an additional 1,000 automobiles) might be much lower; say, $5,000 per car. Costs associated with research, testing, design, molds, heavy equipment, and similar factors of production must be incurred whether the manufacturer is going to produce 1,000 units, 10,000 units, or 100,000 units. Such costs will clearly contribute to the average cost of an automobile. However, since these activities have already been undertaken to produce the manufacturer's current output level, they may *add little* to the cost of producing *additional* units. Thus, the manufacturer's marginal cost may be substantially less than the average cost. When determining whether to expand or reduce the production of a good, the choice should be based on marginal costs, not the current average cost.

We often confront decisions involving a possible change from the current situation. The marginal benefits and marginal costs associated with the choice will determine the wisdom of our decisions. What happens at the margin is therefore an important part of economic analysis.

5. Information, Like Other Resources, Is Scarce. Therefore, Knowledge About The Future Is Scarce. It is difficult, if not impossible, to anticipate the results of many decisions. Would a different car be better than the one we now use? Is the new movie release worth our time and money? It is difficult even to recognize what all the relevant options are, let alone be sure of a choice among them. Rational decision-makers recognize that it is costly to obtain information and make complex calculations. Although additional information and techniques that improve one's decision-making capabilities are valuable, often the potential benefit is less than its expected cost. Sensible consumers will conserve on these limited resources, therefore, just as they conserve on other scarce resources.

Secondary Effects: Economic consequences of an initial economic change, even though they are not immediately identifiable. Secondary effects will be felt only with the passage of time.

6. Remember The Secondary Effects—Economic Actions Often Generate Secondary Effects In Addition To Their Immediate Effects. Frederic Bastiat, a nineteenth-century French economist, stated that the difference between a good and a bad economist is that the bad economist considers only the immediate, visible effects, whereas the good economist is also aware of the **secondary effects,** effects that are indirectly related to the initial policy and whose influence might only be seen or felt with the passage of time.

Secondary effects are important in areas outside of economics. The immediate effect of an aspirin is a bitter taste in one's mouth. The indirect effect, which is not immediately observable, is relief from a headache. The immediate effect of drinking six quarts of beer might be a warm, jolly feeling. The indirect effect, for many, would be a pounding headache the next morning. In economics, too, the secondary effects of an action may be quite different from the initial impact. According to the economic way of thinking, the significant questions are: In addition to the initial result of this policy, what other factors will be affected? How will future actions be influenced by the changes in economic incentives that have resulted from policy A?

An economic system is much like an ecological system. An ecological action sometimes generates indirect and perhaps unintended secondary effects. For example, the heavy use of a pesticide on a field to kill a specific population of insects may have an undesirable effect on other creatures. Economic actions can generate similar results. For example, price controls on natural gas have the desired effect of reducing heating expenditures for some consumers, but they also reduce both conservation of gas by those consumers and the incentive of producers to bring more natural gas to the market. Other consumers will therefore be forced to rely more heavily on other, more expensive energy sources, pushing the prices of these energy sources upward. Thus, the controls also generate an unintended result: an increase in the energy costs for some consumers. Good economic thinking demands that we recognize the secondary effects, which will often be observed only with the passage of time.

7. The Value of a Good or a Service Is Subjective. Preferences differ, sometimes dramatically, between individuals. How much is a ticket to see tonight's performance of the Bolshoi Ballet worth? *Different people will have very different answers!* Some would be willing to pay a high price indeed, while others might even be willing to pay to avoid the ballet if attendance were mandatory. Even for a given individual, circumstances can change from day to day. Alice, who usually would value the ballet ticket at $20, is invited to a party, and suddenly becomes uninterested in the ballet tonight. Now what is the ticket worth? If she knows a friend who would give her $5 for the ticket, it is worth at least that much. If she advertises on a bulletin board and gets $10 for it, a higher value is created. *One thing is certain: the value of the ticket depends on many things, among them who uses it and when.*

Seldom will one individual know how others value an item. Consider how difficult it often is to know what would make a good gift, even for a close friend or family member! So, arranging trades or otherwise moving items to higher-valued users and uses can be very valuable, but is not a simple task. In fact, how society promotes such coordination in the behavior of individuals is a key subject in many of the chapters that follow.

8. The Test of a Theory Is Its Ability to Predict. Economic Thinking is *Scientific Thinking.* The proof of the pudding is in the eating. The usefulness of an economic theory is revealed by its ability to predict the future consequences of economic action. Economists develop economic theory

Scientific Thinking: Development of theory from basic postulates and the testing of the implications of that theory as to their consistency with events in the real world. Good theories are consistent with and help explain real-world events. Theories that are inconsistent with the real world are invalid and must be rejected.

from analyzing how incentives will affect decision-makers. The theory is then tested against events in the real world. Through testing, we either confirm the theory or recognize the need for amending or rejecting it. If the events in the real world are consistent with a theory, we say that the theory has predictive value. In contrast, theories that are inconsistent with real-world data must be rejected.

If it is impossible to test the theoretical relationships of a discipline, the discipline does not qualify as a science. Since economics deals with human beings, who can think and respond in a variety of ways, can economic theories really be tested? The answer to this question is yes, if, *on average,* human beings respond in predictable and consistent ways to changes in economic conditions. The economist believes that this is the case. Note that this does not necessarily imply that *all* individuals will respond in a specified manner. Economics usually does not seek to predict the behavior of a specific individual; instead, it focuses on the general behavior of a large number of individuals.

How can we test economic theory when, for the most part, controlled experiments are not feasible? This is a problem, but economics is no different from astronomy in this respect. Astronomers also must deal with the world as it is. They cannot change the course of the stars or planets to see what impact the changes would have on the gravitational pull of the earth.

So it is with economists. They cannot arbitrarily institute changes in the price of cars or unskilled labor services just to observe the effect on quantity purchased or level of employment. Still, economic theory can be tested. Economic conditions (for example, prices, production costs, technology, transportation cost, and so on), like the location of the planets, do change from time to time. As actual conditions change, economic theory can be tested by comparing its predictions with real-world outcomes. Just as the universe is the laboratory of the astronomer, the real world is the laboratory of the economist.

In some cases, observations of the real world may be consistent with two (or more) economic theories. Given the current state of our knowledge, we will sometimes be unable to distinguish between competitive theories. Much of the work of economists remains to be done, but in many areas substantial empirical work has been completed. Throughout this book, we will refer to this evidence in an effort to provide information with which we can judge the validity of various economic theories. We must not lose sight of the scientific method of thinking, because it is a requisite for sound economic thinking.

POSITIVE AND NORMATIVE ECONOMICS

Positive Economics: The scientific study of "what is" among economic relationships.

Economics as a social science is concerned with predicting or determining the impact of changes in economic variables on the actions of human beings. Scientific economics, commonly referred to as **positive economics,** attempts to determine "what is." Positive economic statements postulate a relationship that is potentially verifiable or refutable. For example: "If the price of butter were higher, people would buy less." Or, "As the money supply increases, the price level will go up." We can statistically investigate (and estimate) the relationship between butter prices and sales, or between the supply of money and the general price level. We can analyze the facts to determine the correctness of a statement about positive economics.

Normative Economics: Judgments about "what ought to be" in economic matters. Normative economic views cannot be proved false, because they are based on value judgments.

Normative economics involves the advocacy of specific policy alternatives, because it uses ethical judgments as well as knowledge of positive economics. Normative economic statements concern "what ought to be," given the philosophical views of the advocate. Value judgments may be the source of disagreement about normative economic matters. Two persons may differ on a policy matter because one is a socialist and the other a libertarian, one a liberal and the other a conservative, or one a traditionalist and the other a radical. They may agree as to the expected outcome of altering an economic variable (that is, the positive economics of an issue), but disagree as to whether that outcome is "good" or "bad."

In contrast with positive economic statements, normative economic statements cannot be tested and proved false (or confirmed to be correct). "The government *should* increase defense expenditures." "Business firms *should not* maximize profits." "Unions *should not* increase wages more rapidly than the cost of living." These normative statements cannot be scientifically tested, since their validity rests on value judgments.

Positive economics does not tell us which policy is best. The purpose of positive economics is to increase our knowledge of all policy alternatives, thereby eliminating one source of disagreement about policy matters. The knowledge that we gain from positive economics also serves to reduce a potential source of disappointment with policy. Those who do not understand how the economy operates may advocate policies that are actually inconsistent with their philosophical views. Sometimes what one thinks will happen if a policy is instituted may be a very unlikely result in the real world.

Our normative economic views can sometimes influence our attitude toward positive economic analysis. When we agree with the objectives of a policy, it is easy to overlook its potential liabilities. Desired objectives, though, are not the same as workable solutions. The actual effects of policy alternatives often differ dramatically from the objectives of their proponents. A new law forcing employers to double all wage rates might be intended to help workers, but the resulting drop in the number of workers employed would be disastrous despite the good intentions. Proponents of such a law, of course, would not want to believe the economic analysis that predicted the unfortunate outcome.

Sound positive economics will help us evaluate more accurately whether or not a policy alternative will, in fact, accomplish a desired objective. The task of the professional economist is to expand our knowledge of how the real world operates. If we do not fully understand the implications, including the secondary effects, of alternative policies, we will not be able to choose intelligently among the alternatives. It is not always easy to isolate the impact of a change in an economic variable or policy. Let us consider some of the potential pitfalls that retard the growth of economic knowledge.

PITFALLS TO AVOID IN ECONOMIC THINKING

VIOLATION OF THE *CERETIS PARIBUS* CONDITION

Economists often preface their statements with the words *ceteris paribus*, meaning "other things constant." "Other things constant, an increase in the price of housing will cause buyers to reduce their purchases." Unfortunately for the economic researcher, we live in a dynamic world. Other things seldom remain constant. For example, as the price of housing rises, the income of consumers may simultaneously be increasing. Both of these factors, higher housing prices and an expansion in consumer income, will have an impact on housing purchases. In fact, we would generally expect them to exert opposite effects—higher prices retarding housing purchases but the rise in consumer income stimulating the demand for housing. The task of sorting out the specific effects of interrelated variables thus becomes more complex when several changes take place simultaneously.

Economic theory acts as a guide, suggesting the probable linkages among economic variables. However, the relationships suggested by economic theory must be tested for consistency with events in the real world. Statistical procedures are often used by economists to correctly identify and more accurately measure relationships among economic variables. In fact, the major portion of the day-to-day work of many professional economists consists of statistical research.

ASSOCIATION IS NOT CAUSATION

In economics, causation is very important. The incorrect identification of causation is a potential source of error. Statistical association alone, though, does not establish causation. Perhaps an extreme example will illustrate the point. Suppose that each November a witch doctor performs a voodoo dance designed to arouse the cold-weather gods of winter and that soon after the dance is performed, the weather in fact begins to turn cold. The witch doctor's dance is *associated with* the arrival of winter, but does it cause the arrival of winter? Most of us would answer in the negative, even though the two are linked statistically.

Unfortunately, cause-and-effect relationships in economics are not always self-evident. For example, it is sometimes difficult to know whether a rise in income has caused people to buy more or, conversely, whether an increase in people's willingness to buy more has created more business and caused incomes to rise. Similarly, economists sometimes argue whether rising money wages are a cause or an effect of inflation. Economic theory, if rooted to the basic postulates, can often help to determine the source of causation, even though competitive theories may sometimes suggest differing directions of causation.

THE FALLACY OF COMPOSITION

What is true for the individual (or subcomponent) may not be true for the group (or the whole). If you stand up for an exciting play during a football game, you will be better able to see. But, what happens if everyone stands up at the same time? What benefits the individual does not benefit the group as a whole. When everyone stands up, the view for individual spectators fails to improve; in fact, it probably becomes even worse.

Fallacy of Composition: Erroneous view that what is true for the individual (or the part) will also be true for the group (or the whole).

People who argue that what is true for the part is also true for the whole may err because of the **fallacy of composition.** Consider an example from economics. If you have an extra $10,000 in your bank account, you will be better off. But, what if everyone suddenly has an additional $10,000? This increase in the money supply will result in higher prices, as people with more money bid against each other for the existing supply of goods. Without an increase in the availability (or production) of scarce economic goods, the additional money will not make everyone better off. What is true for the individual is misleading and often fallacious when applied to the entire economy.

Potential error associated with the fallacy of composition highlights the importance of considering both a micro- and a macroview in the study of economics. Since individual human decision-makers are the moving force behind all economic action, the foundations of economics are clearly rooted in a microview. Analysis that focuses on a single consumer, producer, product, or productive resource is referred to as **microeconomics.** As Professor Abba Lerner puts it, "Microeconomics consists of looking at the economy through a microscope, as it were, to see how the millions of cells in the body economic—the individuals or households as consumers, and the individuals or firms as producers—play their part in the working of the whole organism."[4]

Microeconomics: The branch of economics that focuses on how human behavior affects the conduct of affairs within narrowly defined units, such as individual households or business firms.

Macroeconomics: The branch of economics that focuses on how human behavior affects outcomes in highly aggregated markets, such as the markets for labor or consumer products.

As we have seen, however, what is true for a small unit may not be true in the aggregate. **Macroeconomics** focuses on how the aggregation of individual microunits affects our analysis. Macroeconomics, like microeconomics, is concerned with incentives, prices, and output. In macroeconomics, however, the markets are highly aggregated. In our study of macroeconomics, the 90 million households in this country will be lumped together when we consider such topics as the importance of consumption spending, saving, and employment. Similarly, the nation's 18 million firms will be lumped together into something we call "the business sector."

What factors determine the level of aggregate output, the rate of inflation, the amount of unemployment, and interest rates? These are macroeconomic questions. In short, macroeconomics examines the forest rather than the individual trees. As we move from the microcomponents to a macroview of the whole, it is important that we bear in mind the potential pitfalls of the fallacy of composition.

WHAT DO ECONOMISTS DO?

The primary functions of economists are to teach, conduct research, and formulate policies. Approximately one half of all professional economists are affiliated with academic institutions. Many of these academicians are involved both in teaching and in scientific research.

---

[4]Abba P. Lerner, "Microeconomy Theory," in *Perspectives in Economics*, ed. A. A. Brown, E. Neuberger, and M. Palmatier (New York: McGraw-Hill, 1968), p. 29.

The job of the research economist is to increase our understanding of economic matters. The tools of statistics and mathematics help the researcher carry out this task. Government agencies and private business firms generate a vast array of economic statistics on such matters as income, employment, prices, and expenditure patterns. A two-way street exists between statistical data and economic theory. Statistics can be used to test the consistency of economic theory and measure the responsiveness of economic variables to changes in policy. At the same time, economic theory helps to explain *which* economic variables are likely to be related and *why* they are linked. Statistics do not tell their own story. We must utilize economic theory to properly interpret and better understand the actual statistical relationships among economic variables.

Economics is a social science. The fields of political science, sociology, psychology, and economics often overlap. Because of the abundance of economic data and the ample opportunity for scientific research in the real world, economics has sometimes been called the "queen of the social sciences." Reflecting the scientific nature of economics, the Swedish Academy of Science in 1969 instituted the Nobel Prize in Economic Science. The men and women of genius in economics now take their place alongside those in physics, chemistry, physiology and medicine, peace and literature.

A knowledge of economics is essential for wise policy-making. Policy-makers who do not understand the consequences of their actions will not likely reach their goals. Recognizing the link between economic analysis and policy, Congress in 1946 established the Council of Economic Advisers. The purpose of the council is to provide the president with analyses of how the activities of the federal government influence the economy. The chairmanship of the Council of Economic Advisers is a cabinet-level position.

FINAL WORD

The primary purpose of this book is to encourage you to develop the economic way of thinking so that you can differentiate sound reasoning from economic nonsense. Once you have developed the economic way of thinking, economics will be relatively easy. Using the economic way of thinking can also be fun. Moreover, it will help you become a better citizen. It will give you a different and fascinating perspective on what motivates people, why they act the way they do, and why their actions are sometimes in conflict with the best interest of the community or nation. It will also give you some valuable insight into how people's actions can be rechanneled for the benefit of the community at large.

Economics is a relatively young science. Current-day economists owe an enormous debt to their predecessors. The Outstanding Economist feature analyzes the contribution of Adam Smith, the father of economics.

CHAPTER SUMMARY

1. Scarcity and choice are the two essential ingredients of an economic topic. Goods are scarce because desire for them far outstrips their availability from Nature. Since scarcity prevents us from having as much of everything as we would like, we must choose among the alternatives available to us. Any choice involving the use of scarce resources requires an economic decision.

2. Scarcity and poverty are not the same thing. Absence of poverty implies that some basic level of need has been met. Absence of scarcity would mean that all of our desires for goods have been met. We may someday be able to eliminate poverty, but scarcity will always be with us.

3. Economics is a method of approach, a way of thinking. The economic way of thinking emphasizes the following:

    (a) Among economic goods, there are no free lunches. Someone must give up something if we are to have more scarce goods.

    (b) Individuals make decisions purposefully, always seeking to choose the option they expect to be most consistent with their personal goals. Purposeful decision-making leads to economizing behavior.

    (c) Incentives matter. People will be more likely to choose an option as the benefits expected from that option increase. In contrast, higher costs will make an alternative less attractive, reducing the likelihood that it will be chosen.

    (d) Marginal costs and marginal benefits (utility) are fundamental to economizing behavior. Economic reasoning focuses on the impact of marginal changes.

    (e) Since information is scarce, uncertainty will be present when decisions are made.

    (f) In addition to their initial impact, economic events often alter personal incentives in a manner that leads to important secondary effects that may be felt only with the passage of time.

Adam Smith (1723–1790) and the Historical Roots of Economics

OUTSTANDING ECONOMIST

The foundation of economics as a systematic area of study was laid in 1776, when Adam Smith published his monumental work, *An Inquiry Into the Nature and Causes of the Wealth of Nations*. Perhaps the most influential book since the Bible, *The Wealth of Nations* was nothing less than a revolutionary attack on the existing orthodoxy. Smith declared that the wealth of a nation did not lie in gold and silver, but rather was determined by the goods and services—whether produced at home or abroad—available to the people.

To increase the nation's hoard of gold and silver, the political and intellectual leaders of Smith's time placed numerous constraints on economic freedoms. Political institutions encouraged citizens to sell their produce abroad in exchange for gold and silver, and discouraged or restrained the purchase of foreign-made goods. Monopolies and guild associations were protected from competition. People thought then that economic activities motivated by private gain were anti-social.

In his book, Smith argued that free exchange, motivated by self-interest, is actually very socially productive. Individuals, if left to pursue their own gains, would employ their own abilities where they performed best. For example, skilled hunters would provide game in exchange for other goods. Skilled tradesmen would specialize in their craft and trade the fruits of their labor for other requirements of life. Smith believed that if freed from

(g) The value of a good or service is subjective, and will differ among individuals.

(h) The test of an economic theory is its ability to predict and to explain events in the real world.

4. Economic science is positive. It attempts to explain the actual consequences of economic actions and alternative policies. Positive economics alone does not state that one policy is superior to another. Normative economics is advocative; using value judgments, it makes suggestions about "what ought to be."

5. Testing economic theory is not an easy task. When several economic variables change simultaneously, it is often difficult to determine the relative importance of each. The direction of economic causation is sometimes difficult to ascertain. Economists consult economic theory as a guide and use statistical techniques as tools to improve our knowledge of positive economics.

6. Microeconomics focuses on narrowly defined units, such as individual consumers or business firms. Macroeconomics is concerned with highly aggregated units, such as the markets for labor or goods and services. When shifting focus from micro- to macrounits, one must be careful not to commit the fallacy of composition. Both micro- and macroeconomics use the same postulates and tools. The level of aggregation is the distinction between the two.

---

government regulation, buyers and sellers would find it in their own interest to work, produce, and exchange goods and services in a manner that promoted the public interest. If kings and politicians would remove legal restrictions that retarded productive activity and exchange, individual self-interest would be harnessed and directed by the "invisible hand" of competitive market prices. Production and the nation's wealth would be increased in the process.

As Keynes noted 160 years later, the world is ruled by ideas. Even though Smith's thinking conflicted with the social environment of his time, his idea that self-interest, economic freedom, and national wealth were all in harmony eventually changed the world. En-

glish historian Henry Thomas Buckle declared that *The Wealth of Nations* represented "the most valuable contribution ever made by a single man towards establishing the principles on which government should be based." It has been said that with this single book, Smith established the principles by which the next several generations would be governed.

Smith's ideas greatly influenced those who mapped out the structure of the United States government. By the end of the eighteenth century, institutional reform had lifted the hand of government from many areas of economic activity in England and throughout Europe. The nineteenth century, the "era of economic freedom," was one of industrialization and growing

prosperity in the Western world. Adam Smith, more than anyone else, established the intellectual climate in which this could happen.

By the time of Smith's death in 1790, five editions of *The Wealth of Nations* had been published, and it had been translated into several foreign languages. The study of the relationship between production, exchange, and wealth began to occupy the time of an increasing number of intellectuals. Political economy—later divided into economics and political science—became a new and widely accepted field of study in major universities throughout the world.

7. The origin of economics as a systematic method of analysis dates back to the publication of *The Wealth of Nations* by Adam Smith in 1776. Even though legal restraints on economic activity abounded at the time, Smith argued that production and wealth would increase if individuals were left free to work, produce, and exchange goods and services. Smith believed that individuals pursuing their own interests would be led by the "invisible hand" of market incentives (prices) to employ their productive talents in a manner "most advantageous to the society." Smith's central message is that when markets are free—when there are no legal restraints limiting the entry of producer-sellers—individual self-interest and the public interest are brought into harmony.

THE ECONOMIC WAY
OF THINKING—
**DISCUSSION
QUESTIONS**

1. Indicate how each of the following changes would influence the incentive of a decision-maker to undertake the action described.
    (a) A reduction in the temperature from 80° to 50° on one's decision to go swimming.
    (b) A change in the meeting time of the introductory economics course from 11:00 A.M. to 7:30 A.M. on one's decision to attend the lectures.
    (c) A reduction in the number of exam questions that relate to the text on the student's decision to read the text.
    (d) An increase in the price of beef on one's decision to have steak every night this week.
    (e) An increase in the rental price of apartments on one's decision to build additional housing units.
2. What does it mean to economize? Do you attempt to economize? Why or why not?
3. Write a couple of paragraphs, explaining in your own words the meaning and essential ingredients of the economic way of thinking.
4. **What's Wrong with This Economic Experiment?**
    A researcher hypothesizes that the medical attention received by U.S. citizens is inadequate because many people cannot afford medical care. The researcher interviews 100 randomly selected individuals and asks them, "Would you use physician services or hospital and nursing-home medical facilities more if they were not so expensive?" Ninety-six of the 100 answer in the affirmative. The researcher concludes that there is a critical need to allocate more resources to the provision of free medical care for all citizens.
5. "Reasonable rental housing could be brought within the economic means of all if the government would prevent landlords from charging more than $200 per month rent for a quality three-bedroom house." Use the economic way of thinking to evaluate this view.
6. SENATOR DOGOODER: I favor an increase in the minimum wage because it would help the unskilled worker.
    SENATOR DONOTHING: I oppose an increase in the minimum wage because it would cause the unemployment rate among the young and unskilled to rise.
    Is the disagreement between Senator Dogooder and Senator Donothing positive or normative? Explain.

ADDENDUM

Understanding Graphs

Economists often use graphs to illustrate economic relations. Graphs are like pictures. They are visual aids that can communicate valuable information in a small amount of space. It has been said that a good picture is worth a thousand words. But, one must understand the picture (and the graph) if it is to be enlightening.

This addendum is designed to illustrate the use of simple graphs as an instrument of communication. Many students, particularly those with an elementary mathematics background, are already familiar with this material, and they may safely ignore it. This addendum is for those who need to be assured that they have the ability to understand graphic economic illustrations.

THE SIMPLE BAR GRAPH

A simple bar graph can often help one better visualize comparative relationships. It can be used to illustrate how an economic indicator varies among countries, time periods, or under alternative economic conditions. A bar graph is nothing more than a visual aid. Nevertheless, it is sometimes a valuable illustrative tool.

Exhibit A-1 shows how a bar graph can be used to illustrate economic data. Exhibit A-1a presents tabular data on the income per person in 1983 for several countries. Exhibit A-1b (next page) uses a bar graph to illustrate the same data. The horizontal scale of the graph indicates the total income per person in 1983. A bar is constructed indicating the income level of each country. The length of each bar is in proportion to the per person income of the country. Thus, the length of the bars makes it easy to see how the per

EXHIBIT A-1 • International Comparison of Income per Person

(a) Chart Presentation

Country	Total Income Per Person, 1983
Switzerland	16,290
United States	14,110
Sweden	12,470
Canada	12,320
France	10,500
Japan	10,120
United Kingdom	9,200
Hong Kong	6,000
Mexico	2,340
Egypt	700
India	260

Source: *World Development Report, 1985.*

(b) Bar Graph Presentation

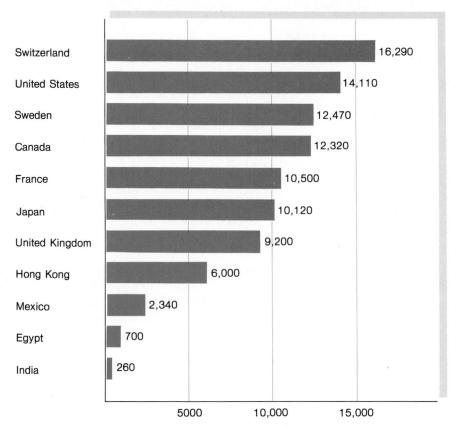

Total income per person, 1983

capita income varies across the countries. For example, the extremely short bar for India makes it easy to visualize that income per person in India is only a small fraction of the comparable figure for Switzerland, the United States, and several other countries.

LINEAR GRAPHIC PRESENTATION

Economists are often interested in illustrating variations in economic variables with the passage of time. A linear graph with time on the horizontal axis and an economic variable on the vertical axis is a useful tool to indicate variations over time. Exhibit A-2 illustrates a simple linear graph of changes in consumer prices (the inflation rate) in the United States between 1960 and 1985. The table of the exhibit presents data on the percent change in consumer prices for each year. Beginning with 1960, the horizontal axis indicates the time period (year). The inflation rate for a country is plotted vertically above each year. Of course, the height of the plot (line) indicates the inflation rate during that year. For example, in 1975, the inflation rate was 7.0 percent. This point is plotted at the 7.0 percent vertical distance directly above the year 1975. In 1976, the inflation rate fell to 4.8 percent. Thus, the vertical plot of the 1976 inflation rate is lower than for 1975. The inflation rate for each year (frame a) is plotted at the corresponding height

EXHIBIT A-2 • Changes in the Level of Prices in the United States, 1960–1985

The tabular data (a) of the inflation rate is presented in graphic form in (b).

(a) Chart Presentation			
Year	Percent Change in Consumer Prices	Year	Percent Change in Consumer Prices
1960	1.5	1973	8.8
1961	0.7	1974	12.2
1962	1.2		
1963	1.6	1975	7.0
1964	1.2	1976	4.8
		1977	6.8
1965	1.9	1978	9.0
1966	3.4	1979	13.3
1967	3.0		
1968	4.7	1980	12.4
1969	6.1	1981	8.9
		1982	3.9
1970	5.5	1983	3.8
1971	3.4	1984	4.0
1972	3.4		
		1985	3.8

Source: *Economic Report of the President, 1986*, Table B-59.

(b) Running Linear Graph

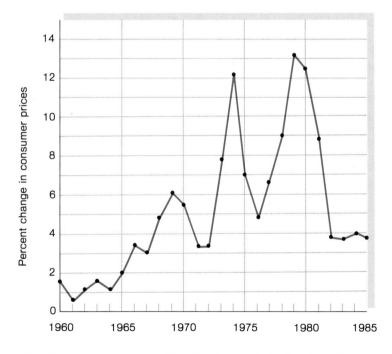

directly above the year. The linear graph is simply a line connecting the points plotted for each of the years 1960 through 1985.

The linear graph makes it easy to visualize what happens to the inflation rate during the period. As the graph shows, the inflation rate rose sharply between 1965 and 1969, in 1973–1974 and again in 1977–1979. It was substantially higher during the 1970s than it was in the early 1960s. While the linear graph does not communicate any information not in the table, it does make it easier to see the pattern of the data. Thus, economists often use simple graphics rather than tables to communicate information.

DIRECT AND INVERSE RELATIONSHIPS

Economic logic often suggests that two variables are linked in a specific way. Suppose an investigation reveals that, other things constant, farmers supply more wheat as the price of wheat increases. Exhibit A-3a presents hypothetical data indicating the relationship between the price of wheat and the quantity supplied by farmers.

The information contained in Exhibit A-3a can also be illustrated with a simple two-dimensional graph. Suppose we measure the quantity of wheat supplied by farmers on the x-axis (the horizontal axis) and the price of wheat on the y-axis (the vertical axis). Points indicating the value of x (quan-

EXHIBIT A-3 • A Direct Relationship Between Variables (hypothetical data)

As the table (a) indicates, farmers are willing to supply more wheat at a higher price. Thus, there is a direct relation between the price of wheat and the quantity supplied. When the x and y variables are directly related, a curve mapping the relationship between the two will slope upward to the right like SS.

Price	Amount of Wheat Supplied by Farmers Per Year (millions of bushels)
$1	45
2	75
3	100
4	120
5	140

(a)

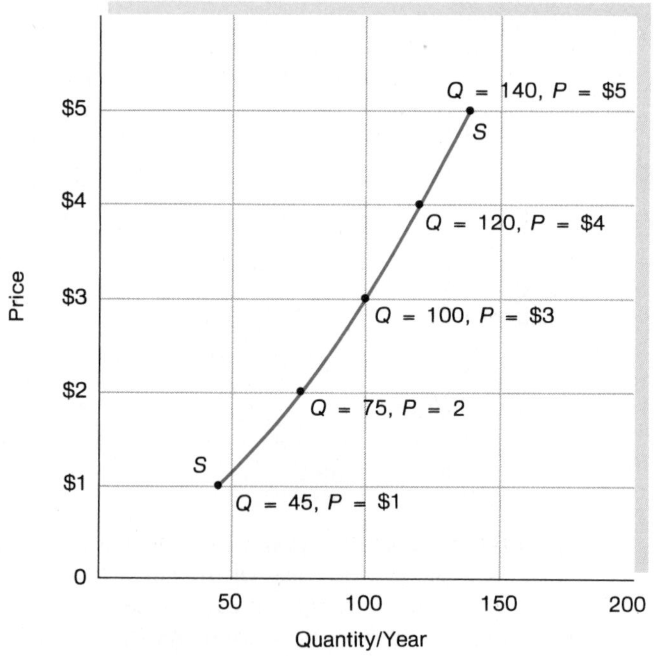

(b)

tity supplied) at alternative values of y (price of wheat) can then be plotted. The line (or curve) linking the points together illustrates the relationship between the price of wheat and amount supplied by farmers.

In the case of price and quantity supplied of wheat, the two variables are *directly related*. When the y-variable increases, so does the x-variable. When two variables are directly related, the graph illustrating the linkage between the two will slope upward to the right (as in the case of SS of Exhibit A-3b).

Sometimes the x-variable and the y-variable are *inversely related*. A decline in the y-variable is associated with an increase in the x-variable. Therefore, a curve picturing the inverse relationship between x and y slopes downward to the right.

Exhibit A-4 illustrates this case. As the data of the table indicate, consumers purchase *less* as the price of wheat increases. Measuring the price of wheat on the y-axis (by convention, economists always place price on the

EXHIBIT A-4 · An Inverse Relationship Between Variables (hypothetical data)

As the table (a) shows, consumers will demand (purchase) more wheat as the price declines. Thus, there is an inverse relationship between the price of wheat and the quantity demanded. When the x and y variables are inversely related, a curve showing the relationship between the two will slope downward to the right like *DD*.

Price	Amount of Wheat Demanded by Consumers Per Year (millions of bushels)
$1	170
$2	130
$3	100
$4	75
$5	60

(a)

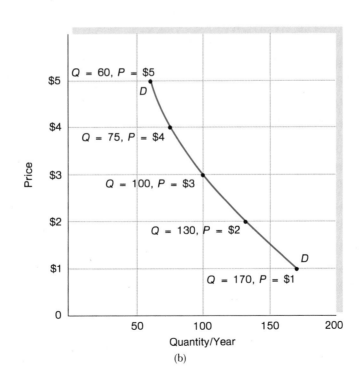

(b)

y-axis) and the quantity of wheat purchased on the *x*-axis, the relationship between these two variables can also be illustrated graphically. If the price of wheat was $5 per bushel, only 60 million bushels would be purchased by consumers. As the price declines to $4 per bushel, annual consumption increases to 75 million bushels. At still lower prices, the quantity purchased by consumers will expand to larger and larger amounts. As Exhibit A-4b illustrates, the inverse relationship between price and quantity of wheat purchased generates a curve that slopes downward to the right.

COMPLEX RELATIONSHIPS

Sometimes the initial relationship between the *x*- and *y*-variables will change. Exhibit A-5 illustrates more complex relations of this type. Frame *a* shows the typical relationship between annual earnings and age. As a young person acquires work experience and develops skills, earnings usually expand. Thus, *initially,* age and annual earnings are directly related; annual earnings increase with age. However, beyond a certain age (approximately age 55), annual earnings generally decline as workers approach retirement. As a result, the initial direct relationship between age and earnings changes to an inverse relation. When this is the case, annual income expands to a maximum (at age 55) and then begins to decline with years of age.

Exhibit A-5b illustrates an initial inverse relation that later changes to a direct relationship. Consider the impact of travel speed on gasoline consumption per mile. At low speeds, the automobile engine will not be used efficiently. As speed increases from 5 mph to 10 mph and on to a speed of 40 mph, gasoline consumption *per mile* declines. In this range, there is an inverse relationship between speed of travel (*x*) and gasoline consumption per mile (*y*). However, as speed increases beyond 40 mph, more gasoline per mile is required to achieve the additional acceleration. At very high speeds, gasoline consumption per mile increases substantially with speed of travel. Thus, gasoline consumption per mile reaches a minimum and a direct relationship between the *x*- and *y*-variables emerges beyond the minimum point (40 mph).

EXHIBIT A-5 • Complex Relationships

At first, an increase in age (and work experience) leads to a higher income but later earnings decline as the worker approaches retirement (a). Thus, age and annual income are initially directly related but at approximately age 55 an inverse relation emerges. Frame b illustrates the relationship between travel speed and gasoline consumption per mile. Initially, gasoline consumption per mile declines as speed increases (an inverse relation), but as speed increases above 40 miles per hour, gasoline consumption per mile increases with the speed of travel (direct relation).

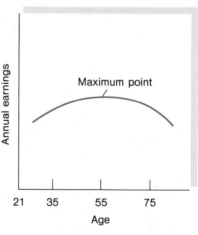

(a) A direct relation changing to inverse

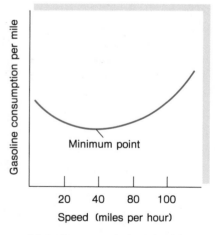

(b) An inverse relation changing to direct

SLOPE OF A STRAIGHT LINE

In economics, we are often interested in how much the y-variable changes in response to a change in the x-variable. The slope of the line or curve reveals this information. Mathematically, the slope of a line or curve is equal to the change in the y-variable divided by the change in the x-variable.

Exhibit A-6 illustrates the calculation of the slope for a straight line. The exhibit shows how the daily earnings (y-variable) of a worker change with hours worked (the x-variable). The wage rate of the worker is $5 per hour. Thus, when 1 hour is worked earnings are equal to $5; for 2 hours of work, earnings jump to $10, and so on. A one-hour change in hours worked leads to a $5 change in earnings. Thus, the slope of the line ($\Delta Y/\Delta X$) is equal to 5. (The symbol Δ means "change in.") In the case of a straight line, the change in y per unit change in x is equal for all points on the line. Thus, the slope of a straight line is constant for all points along the line.

Exhibit A-6 illustrates a case in which there is a direct relation between the x- and y-variable. For an inverse relation, the y-variable decreases as the x-variable increases. So, when x and y are inversely related, the slope of the line will be negative.

SLOPE OF A CURVE

In contrast with a straight line, the slope of a curve is different at each point along the curve. The slope of a curve at a specific point is equal to the slope of a line tangent to the curve at the point. (A tangent is a line that just touches the curve.) Exhibit A-7 illustrates how the slope of a curve at a specific point is determined. First, let us consider the slope of the curve at point A. A line tangent to the curve at point A indicates that y changes by 1 unit when x changes by 2 units at point A. Thus, the slope ($\Delta Y/\Delta X$) of the curve at A is equal to $1/2$.

EXHIBIT A-6 • The Slope of a Straight Line

The slope of a line is equal to change in y divided by the change in x. The line above illustrates the case in which daily earnings increase by $5 per hour worked. Thus, the slope of the earnings function is 5 ($5 ÷ 1 hr). For a straight line, the slope is constant at each point on the line.

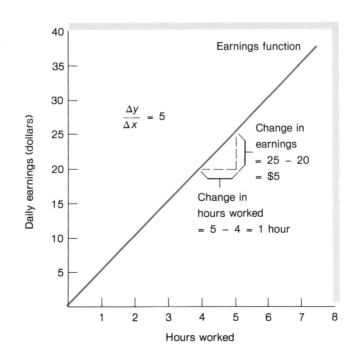

Now, consider the slope of the curve at point B. The line tangent to the curve at B indicates that y changes by 2 units for each one unit change in x at point B. Thus, at B the slope ($\Delta Y/\Delta X$) is equal to 2. At point B, a change in the x-variable leads to a much larger change in y than was true at point A. The greater slope of the curve at B reflects this greater change in y per unit change in x at B relative to A.

GRAPHS ARE NOT A SUBSTITUTE FOR ECONOMIC THINKING

By now you should have a fairly good understanding of how to read a graph. If you still feel uncomfortable with graphs, try drawing (graphing) the relationship between several things with which you are familiar. If you work, try graphing the relationship between *your* hours worked (x-axis) and *your* weekly earnings (y-axis). If need be, refer to Exhibit A-6 to help guide you with this exercise. Can you graph the relationship between the price of gasoline and your expenditures on gasoline? Graphing these simple relationships will give you greater confidence in your ability to grasp more complex economic relationships presented in graphs.

This text uses only simple graphs. Thus, there is no reason for you to be intimidated. Graphs look much more complex than they really are. In fact, they are nothing more than a simple device to communicate information quickly and concisely. One cannot communicate anything with a graph that cannot be communicated verbally.

Most important, graphs are not a substitute for economic thinking. While a graph may illustrate that two variables are related, it tells us nothing about the cause and effect relationship between the variables. To determine probable cause and effect, we must rely on economic theory. Thus, the economic way of thinking, not graphs, is the power station of economic analysis.

EXHIBIT A-7 • The Slope of a Nonlinear Curve

The slope of a curve at any point is equal to the slope of the straight line tangent to the curve at the point. As the lines tangent to the above curve at points A and B illustrate, the slope of a curve will change from point to point along the curve.

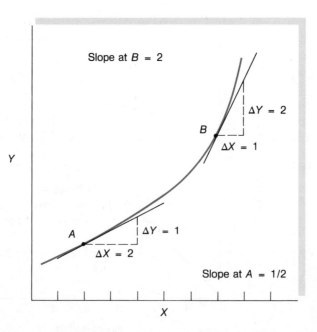

- What is an "opportunity cost"? Why do economists place so much emphasis on opportunity cost?

- What does a production possibilities frontier demonstrate?

- How do specialization and exchange create value?

- What three economizing decisions are faced by every economy?

- How do the two major methods of economic decision-making—the market and government planning—compare?

The goods people sell usually are made by processes using a high proportion of the skills they are gifted in, whereas the goods people buy usually are made by processes they are comparatively ungifted in. [1]

ROBERT A. MUNDELL

2 SOME TOOLS OF THE ECONOMIST

In the last chapter, you were introduced to the economic approach. In this chapter, we discuss a few important tools that will help you develop the economic way of thinking.

WHAT SHALL WE GIVE UP?

Scarcity calls the tune in economics. We cannot have as much of everything as we would like. Most of us would like to have more time for leisure, recreation, vacations, hobbies, education, and skill development. We would also like to have more wealth, a larger savings account, and more consumable goods. However, all of these things either are scarce or require the use of scarce resources. They are in conflict with one another. We can have more leisure time if we sacrifice some wealth. We can increase our current consumption if we reduce our rate of saving. Choosing one requires us to give up something of the other.

OPPORTUNITY COST IS THE HIGHEST VALUED OPPORTUNITY LOST

An unpleasant fact of economics is that the choice to do one thing is, at the same time, a choice not to do something else. Your choice to spend time reading this book is a choice not to play tennis, go out on a date, listen to a math lecture, or attend a party. These things must be given up because of your decision to read. The highest valued alternative that must be sacrificed because one chooses an option is the **opportunity cost** of the choice.

Opportunity Cost: The highest valued benefit that must be sacrificed (forgone) as the result of choosing an alternative.

Note that the cost of an event is not the drudgery and undesirable aspects that may be associated with that event. The distinction between (a) the undesirable attributes of option A and (b) the highest valued opportunity forgone (option B) in order to realize option A, is fundamental because only option B is considered a cost by the economist.[2] Of course if option B is more pleasant, the opportunity cost of A is larger. Cost, in economics, has to do with comparing options, not with evaluating a single option by itself.

Costs are subjective. (So are benefits. After all, a cost is a sacrificed benefit!) A cost exists in the mind of the decision-maker. It is based on expectation—the expected value of the forgone alternative. Cost can never be directly measured by someone other than the decision-maker because only the decision-maker can place a value on what is given up.[3] In fact, this is one reason that voluntary trade is so critical in the creation of value, as we discussed in the last chapter. Only individuals are in a position to evaluate

---

[1]Robert A. Mundell, *Man And Economics: The Science of Choice* (New York: McGraw-Hill, 1968), p. 19.

[2]For an excellent in-depth discussion of this subject, see A. A. Alchian, "Cost," in *International Encyclopedia of the Social Sciences* (New York: Macmillan, 1969), 3:404–415.

[3]See James M. Buchanan, *Cost and Choice* (Chicago: Markham, 1969), for an analysis of the relationship between cost and choice.

options for themselves, and to decide whether a possible trade is personally a good thing.

Cost, however, often has a monetary component that enables us to approximate its value. For example, the cost of attending a ballet is the highest valued opportunity lost due to: (a) the time necessary to attend and (b) the purchasing power (that is, money) necessary to obtain a ticket. The monetary component is, of course, objective and can be measured. When there is good reason to expect that nonmonetary considerations are relatively unimportant, the monetary component will approximate the total cost of an option.

OPPORTUNITY COST AND THE REAL WORLD

Is real-world decision-making influenced by opportunity cost? Remember, the basic economic postulate states that an option is more likely to be chosen when its cost to the decision-maker is less. So, economic theory does imply that differences (or changes) in opportunity cost will influence how decisions are made.

Some examples will demonstrate the real-world application of the opportunity cost concept. Poor people are more likely to travel long distances by bus, whereas the wealthy are more likely to travel by airplane. Why? A simple answer would be that the bus is cheaper; therefore, the poor will be more likely to purchase the cheaper good. But, is the bus cheaper for a relatively well-off individual whose opportunity cost of travel time is high? Suppose that a round-trip airline ticket from Kansas City to Denver costs $150, whereas a bus ticket costs only $110. The bus requires ten hours of travel time, however, and the airplane only two hours. Which would be cheaper? It depends on one's opportunity cost of time. If one's opportunity cost is evaluated at less than $5 per hour, the bus is cheaper, but if one's time is valued at more than $5 per hour, the airplane is clearly the cheaper option. Since the opportunity cost of the travel time will usually be greater for the wealthy than for the poor, the airplane is likely to be much cheaper for those with high incomes.

The concept of opportunity cost also helps us understand labor allocation and wage differences. Setting aside the nonmonetary aspects of a job for the moment, workers whose skills make them valuable to other employers will have to be paid enough to compensate them for what they could be making elsewhere—their highest valued employment alternatives. Thus, a filling station owner is unlikely to hire a physician to pump gas because the physician would have to be paid at least his or her opportunity cost— perhaps $100 per hour or more for delivering babies or performing surgery. Similarly, since the job opportunities forgone on other jobs will be greater for a skilled carpenter than for an unskilled worker, an employer must pay the skilled carpenter a higher wage. Skills and abilities, if they create more valuable alternatives, increase one's earning capability.

Elderly retirees watch considerably more television than high-income lawyers, accountants, and other professionals. Why? Is it because the elderly can better afford the money cost of a TV? Clearly, this is not the case. The time cost, though, is another matter. Consider the difference in the opportunity cost of time between the retirees and the professionals. In terms of lost earnings, watching television costs the professional a lot more than it costs the elderly. The professional watches less TV because it is an expensive good in terms of time.

Why do students watch less television and spend less time at the movies or on the beach during final exam week? Recreation is more costly then, that's why. Using valuable study time to go to the beach might well mean losing better grades in several classes, although a student's grade in economics might be unaffected if he or she kept up during the semester and developed the economic way of thinking!

By now you should have the idea. Choosing one thing means giving up others that might have been chosen. Opportunity cost is the highest valued option sacrificed as the result of choosing an alternative.

TRADE CREATES VALUE

We learned in the last chapter that preferences are subjective, are known only to the individual, and differ among individuals. This means that merely trading—rearranging goods and services among people—can create value. In our Chapter 1 example, the value to Alice of a ticket to attend the Bolshoi ballet performance was zero once she received the party invitation, but the value to other individuals was greater. Suppose the value of the ticket to Jim, who bought it at the advertised price of $10, was $11. An unforeseen change in Alice's schedule had destroyed the value of the performance that evening for her, but trading (selling) the ticket to Jim created $10 in value for her, and it netted $1 in value for Jim—the $11 value he placed on the performance minus the $10 he gave to Alice. The performance remained the same, and the seats available remained the same, but value had been created just as surely as if an additional seat had been made available. *It is wrong to assume that a particular good or service has value just because it exists, independently of the circumstances and who uses it.*[4] As the example of the ballet ticket illustrates, the value of goods and services depends on who uses them, when they are used, and where they are used; as well as on their own physical characteristics.

TRANSACTION COSTS—A BARRIER TO TRADE

Unfortunately, Alice did not know about Andrew, another ballet fan, who would have been willing to pay $15 for the ticket. Andrew lives off campus and failed to see the bulletin board ad, so the potential for another $4 increase in value failed to materialize. A trade to achieve the additional value by putting the ticket into Andrew's hands was overlooked. Still, if Jim and Andrew happen to meet and talk about the ballet before the show, the additional $4 in value for the ticket could be created by another transaction: Jim trading the ticket to Andrew. Such a transaction is unlikely, though, because it would be costly to arrange by other than pure chance. Andrew would have to learn that Jim has the ticket, which seat and what per-

---

[4]An illuminating discussion of this, the "physical fallacy," is found in Thomas Sowell, *Knowledge and Decisions* (New York: Basic Books, 1980), pp. 67–72.

formance the ticket is for, and finally, a price would have to be agreed on. Given the cost of acquiring the necessary information and conducting the trade, the potential exchange between Andrew and Jim will probably not take place.

While exchange creates value, it is also costly. The costs of the time, effort, and other resources necessary to search out, negotiate, and conclude an exchange are called **transaction costs.** Transaction costs reduce our ability to gain from mutually advantageous potential trades.

Since exchange is costly, we should not expect all potentially valuable trades to take place, any more than we expect all useful knowledge to be learned, all safety measures to be taken, or all potential "A" grades to be earned. Frequent fliers know that if they never miss a flight, they are probably spending too much time waiting in airports. Similarly, the seller of a car, a house, or a ballet ticket knows that to find that single person in the world who would be willing to pay the most money is not worth the enormous effort required to locate that buyer. The cost of perfection in exchange, as in other endeavors, is just too high.

Transaction Costs: The time, effort, and other resources needed to search out, negotiate, and consummate an exchange.

THE MIDDLEMAN AS COST REDUCER

Middleman: A person who buys and sells, or who arranges trades. A middleman reduces transactions costs, usually for a fee or a markup in price.

Since there are gains from exchange, some people specialize in providing information and arranging trades. Such a specialist is commonly called a **middleman.** Often, people believe that middlemen are unnecessary; that they simply add to the buyer's expense without benefitting the seller. Now that we recognize transactions costs, however, we can see the fallacy of this view. The auto dealer, for example, can help both the makers and the buyers of cars. By keeping an inventory of autos, and by hiring knowledgeable sales people, the dealer helps the car shopper learn about the many cars offered, and how each car looks, performs, and "feels." (Don't forget that preferences are subjective; they are not objectively known to others.) Car buyers also like to know that the local dealer will honor the warranty, and provide parts and service for the car when they are needed. The car maker, by using the dealer as a middleman, is able to concentrate on designing and making cars, leaving to middlemen—dealers—the task of marketing and servicing them in each community.

Grocers are another provider of middleman services. Each of us could deal with food producers directly, buying in large quantities, perhaps shopping through catalogues to choose what we want. If we did, though, we wouldn't be able to squeeze the tomatoes! Besides, we would each need giant refrigerators, freezers, and storerooms at home to hold huge quantities of food. Or, perhaps we could form consumer cooperatives, banding together to eliminate the middleman, using our own warehouses and our own volunteer labor to order, receive, display, redistribute, and collect payment for the food. In fact, some cooperatives like this do exist, but most people prefer instead to hire the space, and do the planning, record keeping, and labor through the grocer, paying the usual markup for middleman services.

Stockbrokers, publishers of the yellow pages, and merchants of all sorts are middlemen—specialists in selling, guaranteeing, and servicing the items traded. For a fee, they reduce transaction costs both for the shopper and for the seller.

Transaction costs hinder the gain realized from trade; middlemen reduce transaction costs. Simply by making exchange cheaper and more convenient, middlemen cause more efficient trades to happen. In so doing, they themselves create value.

WHAT IS TRADED—PROPERTY RIGHTS

Property Rights: The rights to use, control, and obtain the benefits from a good or service.

Private Property Rights: Property rights that are exclusively held by an owner, and that can be transferred to others at the owner's discretion.

The buyer of an automobile or an apple may take the item home. The buyer of a steamship or an office building, though, might never touch it. When exchange occurs, it is really the rights—the **property rights**—to the item that change hands. It is ownership and control that count, rather than physical possession.

Private property rights exist when property rights are (a) exclusively controlled by one owner and (b) transferable to others. Private ownership of property rights gives owners a chance to act selfishly. However, since they link responsibility to authority, they also make owners accountable for their actions. There are four major reasons why accountability provides an owner with a strong incentive to use resources wisely and consider seriously the wishes of others.

1. *Private owners can gain by employing their resources in ways that are beneficial to others. On the other hand, owners bear the opportunity cost of ignoring the wishes of others.* If someone values an asset more than its current owner, the current owner can gain by paying heed to the wishes of others. For example, suppose Ed owns a car that others would also like to have. What incentive is there for Ed to pay attention to the desires of the others? If someone else values the car at $1,000, while Ed values it at only $800, then Ed can gain by selling the car at any price higher than $800. To turn down the offer of $1,000 costs Ed $200 more than the $800 the car is worth to him. In fact, if transaction costs are low (if search is cheap and easy), Ed might gain by searching for people (potential buyers) who want the car more than he does. If he fails to yield to the desires of others, Ed "pays" the opportunity cost for continued ownership of the car by not receiving the $1,000. Failing to consider the wishes of others may penalize the potential buyer, but it would also hurt Ed. When potential buyers and sellers know that cars are privately owned and thus easily transferable, each has every incentive to search out mutually advantageous trades. After all, if they find such a trade, only the buyer and seller have to approve the deal, and both will gain.

As a second example, suppose Ed owns a house and will be out of town all summer. Will the house stay vacant, or will Ed let someone else use it during those months? We don't know, but we do know that Ed can rent the house to someone else if he chooses, and that if he does not, he will pay the opportunity cost—the rental payments he could get, minus any damages, added upkeep, and transaction costs. Ownership of the private property rights has again faced Ed with the opportunity costs of his actions, making him responsible for whether or not he grants the wishes of others regarding the use of his property.

"Their house looks so nice. They must be getting ready to sell it."

PEPPER ... AND SALT © THE WALL STREET JOURNAL

2. *The private owner has a strong incentive to properly care for the item he or she owns.* Will Ed change the oil in his car? Will he take care to see that the seats do not get torn? Probably so, since not being careful about these things would reduce the car's value, both to him and to any future owner. The car and its value—the sale price if he sells it—belong just to Ed, so he would bear the burden of a fall in the car's value if the oil ran low and ruined the engine, or if the seats were torn. As the owner, Ed has both the authority and the incentive to protect the car against harm or neglect. Private property rights give the owner a strong incentive for good stewardship.

3. *The private owner has an incentive to conserve for the future, if the item is expected to be worth more then.* Suppose our man Ed owns a case of very good red wine, which is only two years old. Age will improve it substantially if he puts it in his cellar for another five years. Will he do so? Well, if he does not, he will personally bear the consequences. He (and presumably his friends) will drink wine sooner, but they will sacrifice quality. Also, Ed will forgo the chance to sell the wine later for much more than its current worth. The opportunity cost of drinking the wine now is its unavailability later. Ed bears that cost. Private property rights assure that Ed has the authority to preserve the wine, and that he bears the cost if he does not. If the greater quality is expected to be worth the wait, then Ed can capture the benefits of not serving the wine "before its time."

4. *With private property rights, a negligent owner can be held accountable for damage to others through misuse of property.* Ed, the car owner, has a right to drive his car, but he has no right to drive in a drunken or reckless way that injures Alice. A chemical company has control over its products, but exactly for that reason, it is legally liable for damages if it mishandles the chemicals. Courts of law recognize and enforce the authority granted by ownership, but they also enforce the responsibility that goes with that authority. Once again, property rights hold accountable the person (owner) with authority over property.

These characteristics of property rights are very useful. When private property rights are not present or are not enforced, other methods must be found to provide the incentives for good stewardship of property, and for proper concern for others by the users of property. For example, when the owner of an automobile or a factory pollutes the air, and is not made to pay for damage done to the property of others, property rights are not being enforced. Without effective property rights, other measures may be necessary to control polluting behavior. We will return to this problem in Chapter 4.

THE PRODUCTION POSSIBILITIES CURVE: SEPARATING THE POSSIBLE FROM THE IMPOSSIBLE

The resources of every individual are limited. Purposeful decision-making and economizing behavior imply that individuals seek to get the most from their limited resources. They do not deliberately waste resources.

Production Possibilities Curve: A curve that outlines all possible combinations of total output that could be produced, assuming (a) the utilization of a fixed amount of productive resources, (b) full and efficient use of those resources, and (c) a specific state of technical knowledge.

The nature of the economizing problem can be made clear by the use of a production possibilities diagram. A **production possibilities curve** reveals the maximum amount of any two products that can be produced from a fixed set of resources.

Exhibit 1 illustrates the production possibilities curve for Susan, an intelligent economics major. This curve indicates the combinations of grades possibile for two alternative amounts of study time—six hours and eight hours. If Susan uses her six hours of study time efficiently, she can choose any grade combination along the six-hour production possibilities curve. When her study time is limited to six hours per week, though, Susan is able to raise her grade in one of the subjects only by accepting a lower grade in the other. If she wants to improve her overall performance (raise at least one grade without lowering the other), she will have to spend more time on academic endeavors. For example, she might increase her weekly study time from six to eight hours. Of course, this would require her to give up something else—leisure.

Can the production possibilities concept be applied to the entire economy? The answer is yes. Having more guns means having less butter, as the old saying goes. Beefing up the military requires the use of resources that otherwise could be used to produce nonmilitary goods. If scarce resources are being used efficiently, more of one thing means the sacrifice of others. Exhibit 2 shows a production possibilities curve for an economy producing only two goods: food and clothing.

What restricts the ability of an economy, once resources are fully utilized, from producing more of everything? The same thing that kept Susan from making a higher grade in both English and economics—lack of resources. There will be various maximum combinations of goods that an economy will be able to produce when:

1. it uses some fixed quantity of resources,
2. the resources are not unemployed or used inefficiently, and
3. the level of technology is constant.

EXHIBIT 1 • The Production Possibilities Curve for Grades in English and Economics

The production possibilities for Susan, in terms of grades, are illustrated for two alternative quantities of total study time. If Susan studied six hours per week, she could attain (a) an F in English and an A in economics, (b) a D in English and a B in economics, (c) a C in both, (d) a B in English and a D in economics, or (e) an F in economics and an A in English.

Could she make higher grades in both? Yes, if she were willing to apply more resources, thereby giving up some leisure. The colored line indicates her production possibilities curve if she studied eight hours per week.

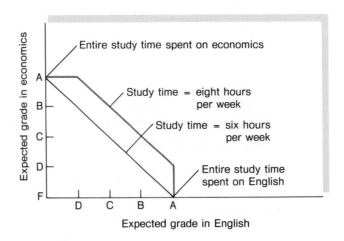

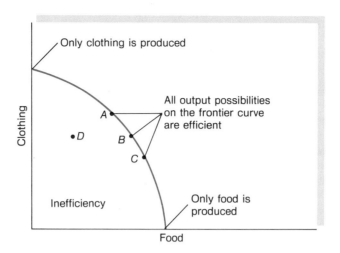

SHIFTING THE PRODUCTION POSSIBILITIES CURVE OUTWARD

When these three conditions are met, the economy will be at the perimeter of its production possibilities frontier (points such as *A, B,* and *C,* Exhibit 2). Producing more of one good, such as clothing, will necessitate less production of other goods (for example, food).

When the resources of an economy are unemployed or used inefficiently, the economy is operating at a point inside the production possibilities curve—point *D,* for example. Why might this happen? It happens because the economy is not properly solving the economizing problem. A major function of economics is to help us get the most use out of available resources, to move us out to the production possibilities frontier. We will return to this problem again and again.

Could an economy ever have more of all goods? Could the production possibilities curve be shifted outward? The answer is yes, under certain circumstances. There are three major methods.

1. An Increase in the Economy's Resource Base Would Expand Our Ability to Produce Goods and Services. If we had more and better resources, we could produce a greater amount of all goods. Many resources are human-made. If we were willing to give up some current consumption, we could invest more of today's resources into the production of long-lasting physical structures, machines, education, and the development of human skills. This **capital formation** would provide us with better tools and skills in the future and thereby increase our ability to produce goods and services. Exhibit 3 illustrates the link between capital formation and the future production possibilities of an economy. The two economies illustrated start with the same production possibilities curve (*RS*). However, since Economy A (Exhibit 3a) allocates more of its resources to investment than does Economy B, A's production possibilities curve shifts outward with the passage of time by a greater amount. The growth rate of A—the expansion rate of the economy's ability to produce goods—is enhanced because the economy allocates a larger share of its output to investment. Of course,

Capital Formation: The production of buildings, machinery, tools, and other equipment that will enhance the ability of future economic participants to produce. The term can also be applied to efforts to upgrade the knowledge and skill of workers and thereby increase their ability to produce in the future.

EXHIBIT 3 • Investment and Production Possibilities in the Future

Here we illustrate two economies that initially confront identical production possibilities curves (*RS*). The economy illustrated on the left allocates a larger share of its output to investment (*I*ₐ, compared to *I*_b for the economy on the right). As a result, the production possibilities of the high-investment economy will shift outward by a larger amount than will be true for the low-investment economy.

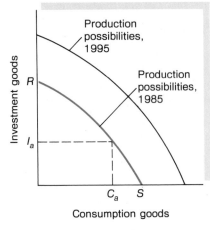
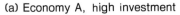

(a) Economy A, high investment

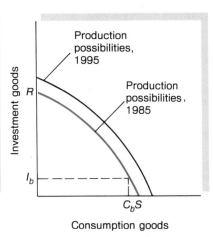

(b) Economy B, low investment

more investment in machines and human skills will necessitate less current consumption.

Technology: The body of skills and technological knowledge available at any given time. The level of technology establishes the relationship between inputs and the maximum output they can generate.

Invention: The discovery of a new product or process, often facilitated by the knowledge of engineering and scientific relationships.

Innovation: The successful introduction and adoption of a new product or process; the economic application of inventions.

Entrepreneur: A profit-seeking decision-maker who decides which projects to undertake and how they should be undertaken. A successful entrepreneur's actions will increase the value of resources.

2. Advancements in Technology Can Expand the Economy's Production Possibilities. Technology determines the maximum physical output obtainable from any particular set of resource inputs. New technology can make it possible to get more from our given base of resources.[5] An important form of technological change is **invention,** the use of science and engineering to discover new products or processes. Sending information instantly and cheaply by satellite, getting more oil from a well, and growing more corn from newly developed hybrid seed are all examples of technological advances resulting from inventions. Each one has pushed our production possibilities curve outward.

An economy can also benefit from technological change through **innovation,** the practical and effective adoption of new techniques. Such innovation is commonly carried out by an **entrepreneur**—one who seeks profit by looking for projects that produce a new product, a better or cheaper one, or simply products that are better located so as to be more valuable.[6] To

---

[5]Without modern technical knowledge, it would be impossible to produce the vast array of goods and services responsible for our standard of living. Thomas Sowell make this point clear when he notes:

The cavemen had the same natural resources at their disposal as we have today, and the difference between their standard of living and ours is a difference between the knowledge they could bring to bear on those resources and the knowledge used today.

See Thomas Sowell, *Knowledge and Decisions* (New York: Basic Books, 1980), p. 47.

[6]This French-origin word literally means "one who undertakes." The entrepreneur is the person who is ultimately responsible. Of course, this responsibility may be shared with others (partners or stockholders, for example) or it may be partially delegated to technical experts. Nevertheless, the success or failure of the entrepreneur is dependent on the outcome of the choices he or she makes.

prosper, an entrepreneur must convert and rearrange resources in a manner that will increase their value, thus expanding our production possibilities. Some examples will help us explain.

One entrepreneur, Henry Ford, changed car-making technology by pioneering the assembly line for making cars. With the same amount of labor and materials, Ford made more cars, more cheaply. Another entrepreneur, the late Ray Kroc, founded the McDonald's hamburger chain. In addition to a popular restaurant menu, he provided information to potential customers. By carefully designing a limited menu that could be prepared according to strict formulas, setting up a training school (Hamburger University, outside of Chicago) for managers, and providing for a regular inspection program, he could guarantee uniformity (known products and quality level) to each customer. Once the McDonald's reputation spread, hungry people knew what to expect at the "golden arches" without even having to enter the restaurant. Trying McDonald's in one location provides information on thousands of others. Nationwide franchises and quality control make it easy for McDonald's fans to find these quick, cheap meals. The same information makes it easy for those who dislike the formula to avoid it. In both cases, we benefit from Mr. Kroc's entrepreneurship—an innovative way to guarantee quality and to transmit instant information cheaply.

Another type of entrepreneur takes inventions produced by others and applies them more effectively. Steven Jobs, co-founder of the Apple Computer Corporation, is an example. He and his firm used the new computer technology to create personal- and small-business computers, and arranged for the "user friendly" software needed by most of us to use such machines. Selling the combination helped make computers useful to millions of people, both at home and on the job, and brought the new technology within their financial reach. Once again, entrepreneurship has expanded our production possibilities.

3. By Working Harder and Giving Up Current Leisure, We Could Increase Our Production of Goods and Services. Strictly speaking, this is not an expansion in the production frontier because leisure is also a good. We are giving up some of that good to have more of other things.

The work effort of individuals depends not only on their personal preferences but also on public policy. For example, high tax rates may induce individuals to reduce their work time. The basic economic postulate implies that as high tax rates reduce the personal payoff from working (and earning taxable income), individuals will shift more of their time to other, untaxed activities, including the consumption of leisure, moving the production possibilities curve for material goods inward.

It is apparent that the production possibilities curve for material goods is not fixed. It is influenced both by individual preferences and by public policy. We will discuss this topic more thoroughly as we proceed.

DIVISION OF LABOR AND PRODUCTION POSSIBILITIES

In a modern economy, individuals do not produce most of the items we consume. Instead, we sell our labor services (usually agreeing to do specified productive work) and use the income we get in exchange to buy what we

Division of Labor: A method that breaks down the production of a commodity into a series of specific tasks, each performed by a different worker.

want. We do this because the **division of labor,** together with exchange, allow us to produce far more goods and services through cooperative effort than we could if each household produced its own food, clothing, shelter, transportation, and other desired goods.

Observing the operation of a pin manufacturer more than 200 years ago, Adam Smith noted that specialization and division of labor permitted far more output. When each worker specialized in a productive function, ten workers were able to produce 48,000 pins per day, or 4,800 pins per worker. Without specialization and division of labor, Smith doubted an individual worker would have been able to produce as many as 20 pins per day.[7]

The division of labor separates production tasks into a series of related operations. Each worker performs a single task, only one of perhaps hundreds of tasks necessary to produce a commodity. There are several reasons why the division of labor often leads to enormous gains in output per worker. First, specialization permits individuals to take advantage of their existing abilities and skills. (Put another way, specialization permits an economy to take advantage of the fact that individuals have different skills.) Productive assignments can be undertaken by those individuals who are able to accomplish them most efficiently. Second, a worker who specializes in just one task (or one narrow area) becomes more experienced and more skilled in that task with the passage of time. Most importantly, the division of labor lets us adopt complex, large-scale production techniques unthinkable for an individual household. As our knowledge of technology and the potential of machinery expand, capital-intensive production procedures and the division of labor permit us to attain living standards undreamed of just a few decades ago.

TRADE, COMPARATIVE ADVANTAGE, AND REALIZING OUR PRODUCTION POSSIBILITIES

Economizing means getting the most out of our available resources. How can this be accomplished? How can we reach our production possibilities frontier and get more value from our productive activities? To answer these questions, we must understand several important principles.

First, let us consider the economizing problem of Woodward and Mason, individuals in the construction business. Exhibit 4 presents certain facts about the abilities of Woodward and Mason. Woodward is highly skilled, fast, and reliable. During one month, Woodward can build either four frame houses or two brick houses. Mason is less skilled, and is slower than

[7]See Adam Smith, *An Inquiry into the Nature and Causes of the Wealth of Nations* (1776; Cannan's ed., Chicago: University of Chicago Press, 1976), pp. 7–16, for additional detail on the importance of the division of labor.

EXHIBIT 4 • Comparative Advantage and Increasing Output

The monthly production possibilities of Woodward and Mason are:

Frame Houses per Month		Brick houses per Month	
Woodward	Mason	Woodward	Mason
4	1	2	1

Initially each produced an equal quantity of both frame and brick houses. Annually, Woodward could produce 16 of each, and Mason only 6 of each. Thus, their total output could reach 22 frame and 22 brick units.

After each specialized in his area of greatest comparative advantage, Mason produced only brick houses, building 12 of them (one each month). Woodward spent 6 months building frame houses, and 6 months building brick houses, producing 24 frame (4 per month) and 12 brick units (2 per month). As the chart shows, after specialization, their total output of both frame houses and brick houses increased from 22 to 24.

If Mason trades 5 brick houses to Woodward for 7 frame houses, Woodward would end up with 17 brick and 17 frame houses, one more of each than he could achieve without specialization and trade. Similarly, Mason would be left with 7 brick and 7 frame (received in the trade with Woodward) houses. Specialization and exchange permit both parties to gain.

	Annual Output Before Specialization		Annual Output After Specialization	
	Frame Houses	Brick Houses	Frame Houses	Brick Houses
Woodward	16	16	24	12
Mason	6	6	0	12
Total	22	22	24	24

Woodward at building both kinds of houses. It takes Mason an entire month to build either a frame or a brick house.

Last year, Woodward spent 8 months producing 16 brick houses and the other 4 months producing 16 frame houses. Mason was able to produce only 6 frame and 6 brick houses during the year. Their joint output was 22 frame and 22 brick houses.

Since Woodward has an absolute advantage (Woodward can build both frame and brick houses more rapidly than Mason) in the production of houses, few observers would believe that Woodward and Mason could gain from specialization and trade of products. Potential gain, though, is clearly present. Suppose Mason specialized in the production of brick houses, while Woodward spent 6 months producing both types of house. Woodward could produce 24 frame houses (4 per month) in those 6 months, and 12 brick houses (2 per month) in another 6 months. After they became more specialized, Mason and Woodward could produce 24 frame houses (all by Woodward) and 24 brick houses (12 each) in the same 12-month period. Together, the builders would be better off. If 5 of Mason's 12 brick houses were traded to Woodward for 7 frame houses, then Mason would have 7 frame and 7 brick houses to show for his efforts, compared to last year's individual output rate of 6 frame and 6 brick. Similarly, upon receipt of the 5 brick houses from Mason in exchange for 7 frame ones, Woodward would also be left with 17 frame and 17 brick houses, definitely an improvement over last year's output of 16 frame and 16 brick. Thus, specialization and exchange could allow both Woodward and Mason to surpass last year's production rate.

Despite the fact that Woodward was better than Mason at producing both frame and brick houses, the two were able to gain from trade and specialization.[8] Was it magic? What is happening here? Our old friend, opportunity cost, will help us unravel this seemingly paradoxical result. In what sense is Woodward better at producing brick houses than Mason? True, in one month, Woodward can produce twice as many brick houses as Mason, but what is Woodward's opportunity cost of producing a brick house? Two frame ones, right? In the same time required to produce a single brick house, Woodward can produce two frame houses.

Consider Mason's opportunity cost of producing a brick house. It is only one frame house. So, who is the cheaper producer of brick houses? Mason is, because Mason's opportunity cost of producing a brick house is one frame house, compared to Woodward's opportunity cost of two frame houses.

The reason that Woodward and Mason could both gain is that their exchange allowed each of them to specialize in the production of the product that, comparatively speaking, they could produce most cheaply. Mason was the cheaper producer of brick houses. Woodward was the cheaper producer of the frame ones. They were able to economize—get more out of their resources—by trading and specializing in the thing that each did better, comparatively speaking.

This simple example demonstrates a basic truth known as the law of comparative advantage, which lies at the heart of economizing behavior for any economy. Initially developed in the early 1800's by the great English economist David Ricardo, the **law of comparative advantage** states that the total output of a group of individuals, an entire economy, or a group of nations will be greatest when the output of each good is produced by the person (or firm) with the lowest opportunity cost.

If a product, any product made, could be produced by someone else with a lower opportunity cost, the economy is giving up more than necessary. It is not economizing. Economizing, or economic efficiency, requires that output always be generated by the producer who has the lowest opportunity cost.

Law of Comparative Advantage: A principle that states that individuals, firms, regions, or nations can gain by specializing in the production of goods that they produce cheaply (that is, at a low opportunity cost) and exchanging those goods for other desired goods for which they are high opportunity cost producers.

---

[8]Throughout this section we will assume that individuals are equally content to produce either product. Dropping this assumption would add to the complexity of the analysis, but it would not change the basic principle.

Perhaps one additional example will help to drive home the implications of the law of comparative advantage. Consider the situation of an attorney who can type 120 words per minute. The attorney is trying to decide whether or not to hire a secretary, who types only 60 words per minute, to complete some legal documents. If the lawyer does the typing job, it will take four hours; if a secretary is hired, the typing job will take eight hours. Thus, the lawyer has an absolute advantage in typing compared to the prospective employee. The attorney's time, though, is worth $50 per hour when working as a lawyer, whereas the typist's time is worth $5 per hour as a typist. Although a fast typist, the attorney is also a high opportunity cost producer of typing service. If the lawyer types the documents, the job will cost $200, which is the opportunity cost of four hours of lost time as a lawyer. Alternatively, if the typist is hired, the cost of having the documents typed is only $40 (eight hours of typing service at $5 per hour). The lawyer's comparative advantage thus lies in practicing law. The attorney will gain by hiring the typist and spending the additional time specializing in the area of comparative advantage.

DIVISION OF LABOR, SPECIALIZATION, AND EXCHANGE IN ACCORDANCE WITH THE LAW OF COMPARATIVE ADVANTAGE

It is difficult to exaggerate the gains derived from specialization, division of labor, and exchange in accordance with the law of comparative advantage. These factors are the primary source of our modern standard of living. Can you imagine the difficulty involved in producing one's own housing, clothing, and food, to say nothing of radios, television sets, dishwashers, automobiles, and telephone services? Yet, most families in North America, Western Europe, Japan, and Australia enjoy these conveniences. They are able to do so largely because their economies are organized in such a way that individuals can cooperate, specialize, and trade, thereby reaping the benefits of the enormous increases in output—both in quantity and diversity—thus produced. An economy not realizing the gains from specialization and division of labor is ignoring the law of comparative advantage. It is operating inside of its production possibilities curve, at a point such as D of Exhibit 2. This is the case for most of the less-developed economies. For various reasons, production in these economies is centered primarily in the individual household. Therefore, the output level per worker of these economies falls well below the attainable level.

When one stops to think about it, the law of comparative advantage is almost common sense. Stated in layman's terms, it simply means that if we want to accomplish a task with the least effort, each of us should specialize in that component of the task that we do best, comparatively speaking.

The principle of comparative advantage is universal. It is just as valid in socialist countries as it is in capitalist countries. Socialist planners, to get the most out of available resources, must also apply the principle of comparative advantage.

DEPENDENCE, SPECIALIZATION, AND EXCHANGE

Specialization and mutual dependence are directly related. If the United States specializes in the production of agricultural products and Middle East countries specialize in the production of oil, the two countries become interdependent. Similarly, if Texas specializes in the production of cotton and Kansas specializes in the production of wheat, interdependence results. In some cases, this dependence can have serious consequences for one or both of the parties. The potential costs of mutual dependence (for example, vulnerability to economic pressure applied by a trading partner who supplies an important economic good) and its potential benefits (for example, economic interaction that may well increase international understanding and reduce the likelihood of war) should be weighed along with the mutual consumption gains when one is evaluating the merits of specialization.

SPECIALIZATION AND WORKER ALIENATION

Specialization clearly makes it possible to produce more goods, but it may also result in many workers performing simple, boring, and monotonous functions. Our friend Woodward may get tired of building frame houses, and Mason's life may lose a certain zest because he produces only brick ones. On a more practical level, specialization often results in assembly-line production techniques. Workers may become quite skilled because they perform identical tasks over and over again, but they may also become bored if the work is personally unrewarding. Thus, strictly speaking, some of the gains associated with the expansion of physical output may result in worker dissatisfaction.

You may be thinking that economists consider only material goods and ignore the importance of human beings. It may seem that they do not care if a worker hates a job because it is repetitive, unchallenging, and boring. Our initial approach to the topic of specialization is vulnerable to this charge. We stressed only physical production because it makes the principle simpler to communicate. However, specialization could be considered strictly from the viewpoint of utility, in which both output and job satisfaction are economic goods.

An individual's opportunity cost of producing a good (or performing a service) includes the sacrifice of both physical production of other goods and any change in the desirability of working conditions. This approach considers both material goods for one's satisfaction and any difference in job satisfaction. It does not alter the basic principle. Individuals could still gain by producing and selling those things for which they have a comparatively low opportunity cost, including the job satisfaction component, while buying other things for which their opportunity cost is high. They would tend to specialize in the provision of those things they both do well and enjoy most. People with a strong aversion to monotonous work would be less likely to choose such work even though they might be skilled at it. Those with a smaller comparative advantage, measured strictly in terms of physical goods, might have a lower opportunity cost because they find the work more rewarding.

The consideration of working conditions and job preferences does not invalidate the basic concept. It is still true that maximum economic efficiency, in the utility sense, requires that each productive activity be performed by those persons with the lowest opportunity cost, including satisfaction given up by turning down other jobs.

PERSONAL MOTIVATION AND THE GAINS FROM SPECIALIZATION AND EXCHANGE

What motivates people to act? How does the purposeful decision-maker choose? Economic thinking implies that people will choose an option only if they expect the benefits (utility) of the choice to exceed its opportunity cost. Purposeful decision-makers will be motivated by the pursuit of personal gain. They will never knowingly choose an alternative when they expect the opportunity cost to exceed the benefits. To do so would be to make a choice with the full awareness that it meant the sacrifice of another, preferred course of action. That simply would not make sense. To say that people are motivated by personal gain does not, of course, mean that they are inconsiderate of others. Other people's feelings will often affect the personal benefit received by a decision-maker.

When an individual's interest, aptitudes, abilities, and skills make it possible to gain by exchanging low opportunity cost goods for those things that he or she could only produce at a high opportunity cost, pursuit of the potential gain will motivate the individual to trade precisely in this manner. If free exchange is allowed, it will not be necessary for people to be assigned

MYTHS OF ECONOMICS

"In exchange, when someone gains, someone else must lose."

People tend to think of making, building, and creating things as productive activities. Agriculture and manufacturing are like this. They create something genuinely new, something that was not there before. Trade, however, is only the exchange of one thing for another. Nothing is created. Therefore, it must be a zero-sum game in which one person's gain is necessarily a loss to another. So goes a popular myth.

Voluntary exchange is productive for three reasons. First, it channels goods and services to those who value them most. People have fallen into the habit of thinking of material things as wealth, but material things are not wealth until they are in the hands of someone who values them. A highly technical mathematics book is not wealth to a longshoreman with a sixth-grade education. It becomes wealth only

after it is in the hands of a mathematician. A master painting may be wealth to the collector of art, but it is of little value to the average cowboy. Wealth is created by the act of channeling goods to persons who value them highly.

Second, exchange can be advantageous to trading partners because it permits each to specialize in areas in which they have a comparative advantage. For example, exchange permits a skilled carpenter to concentrate on building house frames, while contracting for electrical and plumbing services from others who have comparative advantages in those areas. Similarly, trade permits a country such as Canada to specialize in the production of wheat, while Brazil specializes in coffee. Such specialization enlarges joint output and permits both countries to gain from the exchange of Canadian wheat for Brazilian coffee.

Third, voluntary exchange makes it possible for individuals to produce more goods through cooperative effort. In the absence of exchange, productive activity would be limited to the individual household. Self-provision and small-scale production would be the rule. Voluntary exchange permits us to realize gains derived from the division of labor and the adoption of large-scale production methods. Production can be broken down into a series of specific operations. This procedure often leads to a more efficient application of both labor and machinery. Without voluntary exchanges, these gains would be lost.

The motivating force behind exchange is the pursuit of personal gain. Unless *both* parties expect to gain from an exchange, it will not take place. Mutual gain forms the foundation for voluntary exchange. Trade is a positive-sum game.

the "right" job or to be told that, comparatively speaking, they should trade A for B because they are good at producing A but not so good at producing B. In a market setting, individuals will voluntarily specialize because they will gain by doing so. People following their own interests will produce and sell items for which they have a comparative advantage—items they can produce cheaply—and will buy those things that others can produce more cheaply.

THREE ECONOMIZING DECISIONS FACING ALL NATIONS: WHAT, HOW, AND FOR WHOM?

We have outlined several basic concepts that are important if one is to understand the economizing problem. In this section, we outline three general economizing questions that every economy, regardless of its institutions, must answer.

1. What Will Be Produced? We cannot produce as many goods as we desire. What goods should we produce and in what quantities? Should we produce more food and less clothing, more consumer durables and less clean air, more national defense and less leisure? Or, should we use up some of our productive resources, producing more consumer goods today even though it will mean fewer goods in the future? If our economy is operating efficiently (that is, on its production possibilities curve), the choice to produce more of one commodity will reduce our ability to produce others. Sometimes the impact may be more indirect. Production of some goods will not only require productive resources but may, as a by-product, reduce the actual availability of other goods. For example, production of warmer houses and more automobile travel may, as a by-product, increase air pollution, and thus reduce the availability of clean air (another desired good). Use of natural resources (water, minerals, trees, and so on) to produce some goods may simultaneously reduce the quality of our environment. Every economy must answer these and similar questions concerning what should be produced.

2. How Will Goods Be Produced? Usually, different combinations of productive resources can be used to produce a good. Education could be produced with less labor by the use of more television lectures, recording devices, and books. Wheat could be raised with less land and more fertilizer. Chairs could be constructed with more labor and fewer machines. What combinations of the alternative productive resources will be used to produce the goods of an economy?

The decision to produce does not accomplish the task. Resources must be organized and people must be motivated. How can the resources of an economy be transformed into the final output of goods and services? Economies may differ as to the combination of economic incentives, threats of force, and types of competitive behavior that are permissible, but all still face the problem of how their limited resources can be used to produce goods.

3. For Whom Will Goods Be Produced? Who will actually consume the available products? This economic question is often referred to as the distribution problem. Property rights for resources, including labor skills, might be established and resource owners might be permitted to sell their services to the highest bidder. Income from the sale of resource services would be used to bid for goods. Prices and resource ownership would be the determining factors of distribution. Alternatively, goods might be split on a strict per capita basis, with each person getting an equal share of the pie. Or, they might be divided according to the relative political influence of citizens, with larger shares going to those who are more persuasive and skillful than others at organizing and obtaining political power. They could be distributed according to need, with a dictator or an all-powerful, democratically elected legislature deciding the various "needs" of the citizens.

THE THREE DECISIONS ARE INTERRELATED

One thing is clear—these three questions are highly interrelated. How goods are distributed will exert considerable influence on the "voluntary" availability of productive resources, including human resources. The choice of what to produce will influence how resources are used. In reality, these three basic economic questions must be resolved simultaneously and all economies, whatever their other differences, must somehow answer them. There are many ways to set up the institutions—the "rules of the game"— by which an economy makes these decisions. Each will result in a different set of answers to the universal questions.

TWO METHODS OF MAKING DECISIONS— THE MARKET AND GOVERNMENT PLANNING

Market Mechanism: A method of organization that allows unregulated prices and the decentralized decisions of private property owners to resolve the basic economic problems of consumption, production, and distribution.

Two prominent ways to organize economic activity are through the **market mechanism** and **collective decision-making.** There is, of course, some overlap between these two classifications and some variation within them. The "rules of the game"—the institutions—for a market economy are established at the outset by the public decision-making process. The accepted forms of competition may vary among market economies. The rights and responsibilities of property owners can be defined differently. Once the rules are established, however, a market economy relies on the unregulated pricing mechanism to coordinate the decisions of consumers, producers, and owners of productive resources. The government will not prevent a seller from using price reductions and quality improvements to compete with other sellers. Nor will the government prevent a buyer from using a higher price to bid a product or productive resource away from another potential buyer. Legal restraints (for example, government licensing) will not be used to limit potential buyers or sellers from producing, selling, or buying in the marketplace. The free interplay and bargaining between buyers and sellers will establish the conditions of trade and answer the three basic economic questions. The government's role is secondary—that only of the referee and rule-maker.

Collective Decision-making: The method of organization that relies on public-sector decision-making (voting, political bargaining, lobbying, and so on). It can be used to resolve the basic economic problems of an economy.

As an alternative to market organization, economic decisions can be made by collective decision-making—by elected representatives, direct referendum, or other governmental mechanisms, including military force.

Central planning and political factors replace market forces. The decision to expand or contract the output of education, medical services, automobiles, electricity, steel, consumer durables, and thousands of other commodities is made by government officials and planning boards. This is not to say that the preferences of individuals are of no importance. If the government officials and central planners are influenced by the democratic process, they have to consider how their actions will influence their election prospects. If they do not, like the firm that produces a product consumers do not want, their tenure of service is likely to be a short one.

In most economies, including that of the United States, a large number of decisions are made both through the decentralized pricing system and through public-sector decision-making. Both exert considerable influence on how we solve fundamental economic problems. Although the two arrangements are different, in each case the choices of individuals acting as decision-makers are important. Economics studies how people make decisions; the tools of economics can be applied to both market- and public-sector action. Constraints on the individual and incentives to pursue various types of activities will differ according to whether decisions are made in the public sector or in the marketplace. Still, people are people; changes in personal costs and benefits will influence their choices. In turn, the acts of political participants—voters, lobbyists, and politicians—will influence public policy and its economic consequences.

LOOKING AHEAD

The next chapter presents an overview of the market sector. Chapter 4 focuses on how the public sector, the democratic collective decision-making process, functions. It is not enough merely to study how the pricing system works. To understand the forces influencing the allocation of economic resources in a country such as the United States, we must apply the tools of economics to both market- and public-sector choices.

We think this approach is important, fruitful, and exciting. How does the market sector really work? What does economics say about which activities should be handled by government? What types of economic policies are politically attractive to democratically elected officials? Is sound economic policy sometimes in conflict with good politics? We will tackle all these questions.

CHAPTER SUMMARY

1. Because of scarcity, when an individual chooses to do, to make, or to buy something, that individual must simultaneously give up something else that might otherwise have been chosen. The highest valued activity sacrificed is the opportunity cost of the choice.

2. Trade is productive. Voluntary exchange creates value by channeling goods into the hands of people who value them most. Recognition of this fact exposes the physical fallacy, which incorrectly assumes that a good or a service has a given value, regardless of who uses it and how it is used. Trade is a positive-sum game that improves the economic well-being of each voluntary participant.

3. The production possibilities curve reveals the maximum combination of any two products that can be produced with a fixed quantity of resources, assuming that the level of technology is constant. When an individual or an economy is operating at maximum efficiency, the combination of output chosen will be on the production possibilities curve. In such cases, greater production of one good will necessitate a reduction in the output of other goods.

4. The production possibilities curve of an economy can be shifted outward by (a) current investment that expands the future resource base of the economy, (b) technological advancement, and (c) the forgoing of leisure and an increase in work effort. The last factor indicates that the production possibilities constraint is not strictly fixed, even during the current time period. It is partly a matter of preference.

5. Production can often be expanded through division of labor and cooperative effort among individuals. With division of labor, production of a commodity can be broken down into a series of specific tasks. Specialization and division of labor often lead to an expansion in output per worker because they (a) permit productive tasks to be undertaken by the individuals who can accomplish those tasks most efficiently, (b) lead to improvement in worker efficiency as specific tasks are performed numerous times, and (c) facilitate the efficient application of machinery and advanced technology to the production process.

6. Joint output of individuals, regions, or nations will be maximized when goods are exchanged between parties in accordance with the law of comparative advantage. This law states that parties will specialize in the production of goods for which they are low opportunity cost producers and exchange these for goods for which they are high opportunity cost producers. Pursuit of personal gain will motivate people to specialize in those things they do best (that is, for which they are low opportunity cost producers) and sell their products or services for goods for which they are high opportunity cost producers.

7. Every economy must answer three basic questions: (a) What will be produced? (b) How will goods be produced? (c) How will the goods be distributed? These three questions are highly interrelated.

8. There are two basic methods of making economic decisions: The market mechanism and public-sector decision-making. The decisions of individuals will influence the result in both cases. The tools of economics are general. They are applicable to choices that influence both market- and public-sector decisions.

THE ECONOMIC WAY OF THINKING— DISCUSSION QUESTIONS

1. "The principle of comparative advantage gives individuals an incentive to specialize in those things they do best." Explain in your own words why this is true.

2. Economists often argue that wage rates reflect productivity. Yet, the wages of housepainters have increased nearly as rapidly as the national average, even though these workers use approximately the same methods that were applied 50 years ago. Can you explain why the wages of painters have risen substantially even though their productivity has changed so little?

3. It takes one hour to travel from New York City to Washington, D.C., by air, but it takes five hours by bus. If the air fare is $55 and the bus fare $35, which would be cheaper for someone whose opportunity cost of travel time is $3 per hour? for someone whose opportunity cost is $5 per hour? $7 per hour?

4. Explain why the percentage of college-educated women employed outside the home exceeds the percentage of women with eight years of schooling who are engaged in outside employment.

5. Explain why parking lots in downtown areas of large cities often have several decks, whereas many of equal size in suburban areas cover only the ground level.

6. Is exchange productive? If so, what does it produce? Who gains when goods are voluntarily exchanged?

7. (a) Do you think that your work effort is influenced by whether or not there is a close link between personal output and personal compensation (reward)? Explain.

   (b) Suppose the grades in your class were going to be determined by a random draw at the end of the course. How would this influence your study habits?

   (c) How would your study habits be influenced if everyone in the class were going to be given an A grade? if grades were based entirely on examinations composed of the multiple-choice questions in the *Coursebook*?

   (d) Do you think the total output of goods in the United States is affected by the close link between productive contribution and individual reward? Why or why not?

I am convinced that if it [the market system] were the result of deliberate human design, and if the people guided by the price changes understood that their decisions have significance far beyond their immediate aim, this mechanism would have been acclaimed as one of the greatest triumphs of the human mind. [1]

NOBEL LAUREATE
FRIEDRICH HAYEK

- What do economists mean when they talk about the laws of supply and demand?

- As buyers and sellers respond to changes in supply and demand, what role does time play in the adjustment process?

- How does the market process communicate information, coordinate individual decisions, and motivate the economic players?

- What happens when prices are fixed above or below the market level?

3

SUPPLY, DEMAND, AND THE MARKET PROCESS

Consider the awesome task of coordinating the economic activity of the United States, a nation with 240,000,000 people and more than 62,000,000 families. The labor force is composed of approximately 118,000,000 workers, each possessing various skills and job preferences. There are about 18,000,000 business firms, which currently produce a vast array of products ranging from hairpins to jumbo jets.

How can the actions of these economic participants be coordinated in a sensible manner? How do producers know how much of each good to produce? What keeps them from producing too many ballpoint pens and too few bicycles with reflector lights? Who directs each labor force participant to the job that best fits his or her skills and preferences? How can we be sure that business firms will choose the correct production methods? In this chapter, we analyze how a market-directed pricing system answers these questions.

In the ideal market economy, no individual or planning board tells the participants what to do. Markets are free, some would say competitive, in the sense that there are no legal restrictions limiting the entry of either buyers or sellers. The economic role of government is limited to defining property rights, enforcing contracts, protecting people from fraud, and similar activities that establish the rules of the game. Although centralized planning is absent, the participants are not without direction. As we shall see, the decentralized decision-making of market participants provides direction and leads to economic order.

In the real world, even economies that are strongly market-oriented, such as the United States economy, use a combination of market- and public-sector answers to the basic economic questions. In all economies, the institutions provide a mixture of market-sector and government allocation. Nevertheless, it is still quite useful to understand how a free-market pricing system functions, how it motivates people, and how it allocates goods and resources.

SCARCITY NECESSITATES RATIONING

Rationing: An allocation of a limited supply of a good or resource to users who would like to have more of it. Various criteria, including charging a price, can be utilized to allocate the limited supply. When price performs the rationing function, the good or resource is allocated to those willing to give up the most "other things" in order to obtain ownership rights.

When a good (or resource) is scarce, some criterion must be set up for deciding who will receive the good (or resource) and who will do without it. Scarcity makes **rationing** a necessity.

There are several possible criteria that could be used in rationing a limited amount of a good among citizens who would like to have more of it. If the criterion were first-come, first-served, goods would be allocated to those who were fastest at getting in line or to those who were most willing to wait in line. If beauty were used, goods would be allocated to those who were thought to be most beautiful. The political process might be used, and goods would be allocated on the basis of political status and ability to manip-

[1]Friedrich Hayek, "The Use of Knowledge in Society," *American Economic Review* 35, (September, 1945), pp. 519–530.

ulate the political process to personal advantage. One thing is certain: Scarcity means that methods must be established to decide who gets the limited amount of available goods and resources.

COMPETITION IS THE RESULT OF SCARCITY

Competition is not unique to a market system. Rather, it is a natural outgrowth of scarcity and the desire of human beings to improve their conditions. Competition exists both in capitalist and in socialist societies. It exists both when goods are allocated by price and when they are allocated by other means—collective decision-making, for example.

Certainly the rationing criterion will influence which competitive techniques will be used. When the rationing criterion is price, individuals will engage in income-generating activities that enhance their ability to pay the price. The market system encourages individuals to provide services to others in exchange for income. In turn, the income will permit them to procure more of the scarce goods.

A different rationing criterion will encourage other types of behavior. When the appearance of sincerity, broad knowledge, fairness, good judgment, and a positive TV image are important, as they are in the rationing of elected political positions, people will use resources to project these qualities. They will hire makeup artists, public relations experts, and advertising agencies to help them compete. We can change the form of competition, but no society has been able to eliminate it, because no society has been able to eliminate scarcity and the resulting necessity of rationing. When people who want more scarce goods seek to meet the criteria established to ration those goods, competition occurs.

The market is one method of producing and rationing scarce goods and resources. Let us investigate how it works.

CONSUMER CHOICE AND THE LAW OF DEMAND

The income of consumers is usually much too low to purchase their list of wants. The authors desire backyard tennis courts, vacations in the Far East, and summer homes in the mountains, but we have not purchased any of them. Why? Because given the restriction of limited income, our desire for other goods is even more urgent. Our incomes would allow us to purchase backyard tennis courts only if we spent less on food, trips to the beach, housing, books, clothes, and other forms of recreation. We have a choice and have chosen to sacrifice the courts instead of the other goods.

How do consumers decide which things to buy and which things to forgo? Economizing behavior suggests that to get the most satisfaction from spending their money, rational consumers will buy the things from which they expect the most satisfaction per dollar spent. Given personal tastes, they will choose the best alternatives that their limited incomes will permit. Prices influence consumer decisions. An increase in the price of a good will increase a consumer's opportunity cost of consuming it. More of other things must be given up if the consumer chooses the higher-priced commodity.

According to a basic postulate of economics, an increase in the cost of an alternative will reduce the likelihood that it will be chosen. This basic postulate implies that higher prices will discourage consumption. Lower prices will reduce the cost of choosing a good, stimulating consumption of it. This inverse relationship between the price of a good and the amount of it that consumers choose to buy is called the **law of demand.**

Law of Demand: A principle that states that there is an inverse relationship between the price of a good and the amount of it buyers are willing to purchase.

The availability of substitutes—goods that perform similar functions—helps to explain the logic of the law of demand. No single good is absolutely essential. Margarine can be substituted for butter. Wood, aluminum, bricks, and glass can take the place of steel. Car pools, slower driving, bicycling, and smaller cars are substitutes for gasoline, allowing households to reduce their gas consumption. When the price (and therefore the consumer's opportunity cost) of a good increases, people have a greater incentive to turn to substitute products and economize on their use of the more expensive good. Prices really do matter.

Exhibit 1 is a graphic presentation of the law of demand. Looking at what happened, we will assume that the price changes that occurred resulted from increasing costs facing suppliers, and that consumers did not change their desire for beef during this period. This allows us to estimate the influence of price on quantity demanded by constructing a demand curve. To do so, economists measure price on the vertical or *y*-axis, and the amount demanded on the horizontal or *x*-axis. The demand curve will slope downward to the right, indicating in this case that the amount of beef demanded will increase as price declines. During 1977–1979, the price of beef rose sharply. Consumers responded, no doubt unhappily, by using less of it. In 1977, when the average price of beef was $1.48 per pound, the average person consumed 125.9 pounds. At the higher beef price of $1.69 per pound in 1978, annual consumption dropped to 120.1 pounds. By 1979, the average price of beef had risen to $1.88 per pound; the annual

EXHIBIT 1 • The Law of Demand

As the price of beef rose during 1977–1979, consumers substituted chicken, fish, and other food products for beef. The consumption level of beef (and other products) is inversely related to its price.

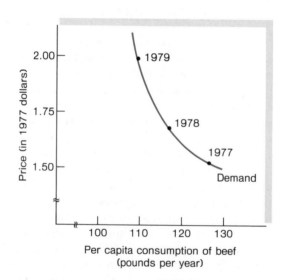

The numerical data used in this example are from *Statistical Abstract of the United States—1980* (Washington, D.C.: U.S. Government Printing Office), pp. 131, 705.

consumption of beef declined still more, to 107.6 pounds, as consumers substituted chicken, fish, and other products for the more expensive beef.

Some commodities are much more responsive to change in price than others. Consider a good for which there are several viable substitutes—a Florida vacation. If the price of a Florida vacation increases, perhaps because of higher air fares, consumers will substitute more movies, local camping trips, baseball games, TV programs, and other recreational activities for the Florida vacation. Exhibit 2 illustrates that, since good substitutes are available, an increase in the price of Florida vacations will cause a sharp reduction in quantity demanded. The quantity of Florida vacations demanded is quite responsive to a change in price.[2]

Other goods may be much less responsive to a change in price. Suppose the price of physician services were to rise 15 percent, as indicated by Exhibit 2. What impact would this price increase have on the quantity demanded? The higher prices would cause some people to prescribe their own medications for colds, flu, and minor illnesses. Others might turn to painkillers, magic potions, and faith healers for even major medical problems. Most consumers, though, would consider these to be poor substitutes for the services of a physician. Thus, higher medical prices would cause a relatively small reduction in the quantity demanded. The amount of physician services demanded is relatively unresponsive to a change in price.

However, despite differences in the degree of responsiveness, the fundamental law of demand holds for all goods. A price increase will induce consumers to turn to substitutes, leading to a reduction in the amount purchased. A price reduction will make a commodity relatively cheaper, inducing consumers to purchase more of it as they substitute it for other goods.

The demand schedule is not something that can be observed directly by decision-makers of a business firm or planning agency. Nevertheless, when

EXHIBIT 2 • Responsiveness of Demand to a Price Change

A 15 percent increase in the price of Florida vacations (D_1) caused the quantity demanded to decline from Q_0 to Q_1, a 50 percent reduction. In contrast, a 15 percent increase in the price of physician services (D_2) resulted in only a 5 percent reduction in quantity demanded (from Q_0 to Q_2).

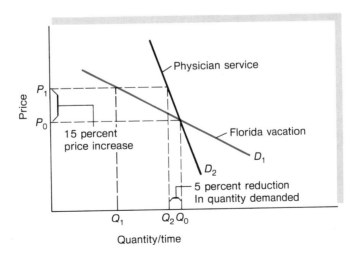

---

[2]The technical term for price responsiveness is elasticity. For those in a microeconomics course, this concept will be explored in the chapter on demand and consumer choice.

prices are used to ration goods, consumer reactions to each price communicate information about the preferences of consumers—how they value alternative commodities. The height of the unseen demand curve indicates the maximum price that consumers are willing to pay for *an additional unit* of the product. If consumers value *additional units* of a product highly, they will be willing to pay a large amount (a high price) for it. On the other hand, if their valuation of *additional units* of the good is low, they will be willing to pay only a small amount for it.

PRODUCER CHOICE AND THE LAW OF SUPPLY

How does the market process determine the amount of each good that will be produced? We cannot answer this question unless we understand the factors that influence the choices of those who supply goods. Producers of goods and services, often using the business firm:

1. organize productive inputs, such as labor, land, natural resources, and intermediate goods,
2. transform and combine these factors of production into goods desired by households, and
3. sell the final products to consumers for a price.

Production involves the conversion of resources to commodities and services. Producers have to pay the owners of scarce resources a price that is at least equal to what the resources could earn elsewhere. Stated another way, each resource employed has to be bid away from all other uses; its owner will have to be paid its opportunity cost. The sum of the amounts paid by the producer for each productive resource, including the cost of production coordination and management, will equal the product's opportunity cost. That cost represents the value of those things given up by society to produce the product.

Profit: An excess of sales revenue relative to the cost of production. The cost component includes the opportunity cost of all resources, including those owned by the firm. Therefore, profit accrues only when the value of the good produced is greater than the sum of the values of the individual resources utilized.

All economic participants have a strong incentive to undertake activities that generate profit. **Profit** is a residual "income reward" earned by decision-makers who carry out a productive activity that increases the value produced by resources. It is what is left over after all costs have been paid. If an activity is to be profitable, the revenue derived from the sale of the product must exceed the cost of employing the resources that have been diverted from other uses to make the product. Profitability indicates that consumers value the product at least as much as any others that could be produced from the resources. Sometimes decision-makers use resources unwisely. They divert resources to production of an output that consumers value less than the opportunity cost of the resources used. **Losses** result, since the sales revenue derived from the project is insufficient to pay the opportunity cost of the resources.

Loss: Deficit of sales revenue relative to the cost of production, once all the resources used have received their opportunity cost. Losses are a penalty imposed on those who misuse resources.

Losses discipline even the largest of firms. For example, in January of 1984, IBM introduced a small personal computer, the PC Jr. The company expected it to be profitable, but 15 months later, it announced that it would quit making the machines. Of IBM's $46 billion in 1984 revenue, only $150 million was accounted for by the PC Jr. Even a $40 million Christmas advertising campaign did not help. IBM could not sell enough units at a price high enough to cover its opportunity costs. So, "Big Blue," as the firm is called, threw in the towel, announcing in March of 1985 that the line had been discontinued.

As we learned in the last chapter, entrepreneurs undertake production organization, deciding what to produce and how to produce it. The business of the entrepreneur is to figure out which projects will, in fact, be profitable. Since the profitability of a project will be affected by the price consumers are willing to pay for a product, the price of resources required to produce it, and the cost of alternative production processes, successful entrepreneurs must be either knowledgeable in each of these areas or obtain the advice of others who have such knowledge.

To prosper, entrepreneurs must convert and rearrange resources in a manner that will increase their value. An individual who purchases 100 acres of raw land, puts in a street and a sewage disposal system, divides the plot into one-acre lots, and sells them for 50 percent more than the opportunity cost of all resources used is clearly an entrepreneur. This entrepreneur "profits" because the value of the resources has been increased. Sometimes entrepreneurial activity is less complex. For example, a 15-year-old who purchases a power mower and sells lawn service to the neighbors is also an entrepreneur seeking to profit by increasing the value of resources. In a market economy, profit is the reward to the entrepreneur who undertakes the project. It is also a signal to other entrepreneurs to enter a highly productive market, competing for the original entrepreneur's profit.

Law of Supply: A principle that states that there will be a direct relationship between the price of a good and the amount of it offered for sale.

How will producer-entrepreneurs respond to a change in product price? Other things constant, a higher price will increase the producer's incentive to supply the good. New entrepreneurs, seeking personal gain, will enter the market and begin supplying the product. Established producers will expand the scale of their operations, leading to an additional expansion in output. Higher prices will induce producers to supply a greater amount. The direct relationship between the price of a product and the amount of it that will be supplied is termed the **law of supply.**

Exhibit 3 presents a graphic picture of this law. The supply curve summarizes information about production conditions. Unless the profit-seeking producer receives a price that is at least equal to the opportunity

EXHIBIT 3 • The Supply Curve

As the price of a product increases, *other things constant,* producers will increase the amount of product supplied.

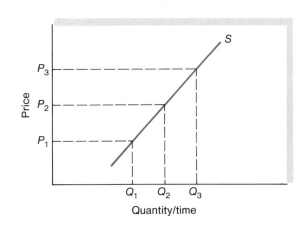

cost of the resources employed, the producer will not continue to supply the good. The height of the supply curve indicates both (a) the minimum price necessary to induce producers to supply a specific quantity and (b) the valuation of the resources used in the production of the marginal unit of the good. This minimum supply price will be high (low) if the opportunity cost of supplying the marginal unit is high (low).

MARKETS COORDINATE SUPPLY AND DEMAND ACTIVITIES

Market: An abstract concept that encompasses the trading arrangements of buyers and sellers that underlie the forces of supply and demand.

Consumer-buyers and producer-sellers make decisions independent of each other, but markets coordinate their choices and influence their actions. To the economist, a market is not a physical location. A **market** is an abstract concept that encompasses the forces generated by the buying and selling decisions of economic participants. A market may be quite narrow (for example, the market for razor blades). Alternatively, it is sometimes useful to aggregate diverse goods into a single market, such as the market for "consumer goods." There is also a broad range of sophistication among markets. The New York Stock Exchange is a highly computerized market in which buyers and sellers who never formally meet exchange shares of corporate ownership each weekday worth many millions of dollars. In contrast, the neighborhood market for lawn-mowing services may be highly informal, since it brings together buyers and sellers primarily by word of mouth.

Equilibrium: A state of balance between conflicting forces, such as supply and demand.

Equilibrium is a state in which conflicting forces are in perfect balance. When there is a balance—an equilibrium—the tendency for change is absent. Before a market equilibrium can be attained, the decisions of consumers and producers must be coordinated. Their buying and selling activities must be brought into harmony with one another.

SHORT-RUN MARKET EQUILIBRIUM

Short-Run: A time period of insufficient length to permit decision-makers to adjust fully to a change in market conditions. For example, in the short run, producers will have time to increase output by using more labor and raw materials, but they will not have time to expand the size of their plants or to install additional heavy equipment.

The great English economist Alfred Marshall pioneered the development of supply and demand analysis. From the beginning, Marshall recognized that time plays a role in the market process. Marshall introduced the concept of the **short-run,** a time period of such short duration that decision-makers do not have time to adjust fully to a change in market conditions. During the short-run, producers are able to alter the amount of a good supplied only by using more (or less) labor and raw materials with their existing plant and heavy equipment. In the short-run, there is insufficient time to build a new plant or to obtain new "made-to-order" heavy equipment for the producer's current facility.

As Exhibit 1 illustrates, the amount of a good demanded by consumers will be inversely related to its price. On the other hand, a higher price will induce producers to use their existing facilities more intensively in the short-run. As Exhibit 3 depicts, the amount of a good supplied will be directly related to its market price.

The market price of a commodity will tend to change in a direction that will bring the rate at which consumers want to buy into balance with the rate at which producers want to sell. This means that unless the quantity supplied by producers is already precisely equal to the quantity demanded by consumers, there will be a tendency for the market price to rise or fall until a balance is reached.

Exhibit 4 illustrates both supply and demand curves in the short-run for a hypothetical commodity—smoos. At a high price, $12 for example, smoo producers will plan to supply 600 units per month, whereas consumers will choose to purchase only 450. An excess supply of 150 units will result. Production exceeds sales, so inventories of smoo producers will rise. To reduce undesired inventories, some smoo producers will increase their sales by cutting their price. Other firms will have to lower their price also, or sell even fewer smoos. The lower price will make smoo production less attractive to producers. Some of the marginal producers will go out of business, and others will reduce their current output. How low will the smoo price go? When the price has declined to $10, the quantity supplied by producers and the quantity demanded by consumers will be in balance at 550 units per month. At this price ($10), coordination of buyer and seller desires is achieved. The production plans of producers are in harmony with the purchasing plans of consumers.

What will happen if the price of smoos is low—$8, for example? The amount demanded by consumers (650 units) will exceed the amount supplied by producers (500 units). An excess demand of 150 units will be present. Some consumers who are unable to purchase smoos at $8 per unit

EXHIBIT 4 · Supply and Demand

The table below indicates the supply and demand conditions for smoos. These conditions are also illustrated by the graph on the right. When the price exceeds $10, an excess supply is present, which places downward pressure on price. In contrast, when the price is less than $10, an excess demand results, which causes the price to rise. Thus, the market price will tend toward $10, at which point supply and demand will be in balance.

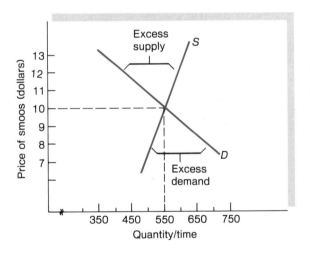

Price of Smoos (Dollars)	Quantity Supplied (Per Month)	Quantity Demanded (Per Month)	Condition in the Market	Direction of Pressure on Price
13	625	400	Excess supply	Downward
12	600	450	Excess supply	Downward
11	575	500	Excess supply	Downward
10	550	550	Balance	Equilibrium
9	525	600	Excess demand	Upward
8	500	650	Excess demand	Upward
7	475	700	Excess demand	Upward

because of the inadequate supply, would be willing to pay a higher price. Recognizing this fact, producers will raise their price. As the price increases to $10, producers will expand their output and consumers will cut down on their consumption. At the $10 price, short-run equilibrium will be restored.

LONG-RUN MARKET EQUILIBRIUM

Long-Run: A time period of sufficient length to enable decision-makers to adjust fully to a market change. For example, in the long-run, producers will have time to alter their utilization of all productive factors, including the heavy equipment and physical structure of their plants.

In the **long-run,** decision-makers will have time to adjust fully to a change in market conditions. With the passage of time, producers will be able to alter their output; not only will they use their current plant more intensively, but given sufficient time, they will be able to change the size of their production facility. The long-run is a time period long enough to permit producers to expand the size of their capital stock (the physical structure and heavy equipment of their plant).

A balance between amount supplied and amount demanded will bring about market equilibrium in the short-run. However, if the current market price is going to persist in the future, an additional condition must be present: The opportunity cost of producing the product must also be equal to the market price.

If the market price of a good is greater than the opportunity cost of producing it, suppliers will gain from an expansion in production. Profit-seeking entrepreneurs will be attracted to the industry, and output (supply) will increase until the additional supply lowers the market price sufficiently to eliminate the profits.[3] In contrast, if the market price is less than the good's opportunity cost of production, suppliers will lose money if they continue to produce the good. The losses will drive producers from the market. Supply will decline, pushing prices upward until the losses are eliminated.

SHIFTS IN DEMAND AND CHANGES IN QUANTITY DEMANDED

A demand curve isolates the impact that price has on the amount of a product purchased. Of course, factors other than price—for example, consumer income, tastes, prices of related goods, and expectations as to the future price of a product—also influence the decisions of consumers. Until now, we have assumed that these factors stay the same. If one of them changes, though, the entire demand curve will shift. Economists refer to such shifts in the demand curve as a *change in demand*.

Let us take a closer look at some of the factors that would cause the demand for a product to change. Expansion in income makes it possible for

---

[3]Bear in mind that economists use the opportunity cost concept for *all* factors of production, including those owned by the producers. Therefore, the owners are receiving a return equal to the opportunity cost of their investment capital even when profits are zero. Zero profits therefore mean that the capital owners are being paid precisely their opportunity cost, precisely what they could earn if their resources were employed in the highest valued alternative that must be forgone as the result of current use. Far from indicating that a firm is about to go out of business, zero economic profits imply that each factor of production, including the capital owned by the firm and the managerial skills of the owner-entrepreneur, is earning the market rate of return.

consumers to purchase more goods at current prices. They usually respond by increasing their spending on a wide cross-section of products. Changes in prices of closely related products also influence the choices of consumers. If the price of butter were to fall, many consumers would substitute it for margarine. The demand for margarine would decline (shift to the left) as a result. If peanut butter and jelly are frequently used together, a rise in the price of peanut butter may decrease the demand for jelly, since less peanut butter will be used.

Our expectations about the future price of a product also influence our current decisions. For example, if you think that the price of automobiles is going to rise by 20 percent next month, this will increase your incentive to buy now, before the price rises. In contrast, if you think that the price of a product is going to decline, you will demand less now, as you attempt to extend your purchasing decision into the future, when prices are expected to be lower.

Failure to distinguish between a change in *demand* and a change in *quantity demanded* is one of the most common mistakes made by introductory economics students.[4] A change in demand is a shift in the entire demand curve. A change in quantity demanded is a movement along the same demand curve.

Exhibit 5 clearly demonstrates the difference between the two. The demand curve D_1 indicates the initial demand (the entire curve) for doorknobs. At a price of $3, consumers would purchase Q_1. If the price declined to $1, there would be an increase in quantity demanded from Q_1 to Q_3. Arrow A indicates the change in quantity demanded—a movement along demand curve D_1. Now, suppose that there were a 20 percent increase in income that caused a housing boom. The demand for doorknobs would increase from D_1 to D_2. As indicated by the B arrows, the entire demand curve would shift. At the higher income level, consumers would be willing to purchase more doorknobs at $3, at $2, at $1, and at every other price than

EXHIBIT 5 • The Difference Between a Change in Demand and a Change in Quantity Demanded

Arrow *A* indicates a change in *quantity demanded,* a movement along the demand curve *D,* in response to a change in the price of doorknobs. The *B* arrows illustrate a change in *demand,* a shift of the entire curve.

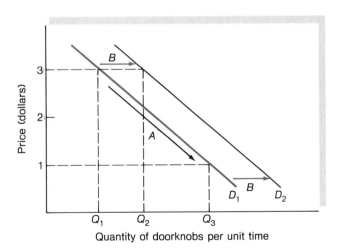

EXHIBIT 6 • A Shift in Demand

As conditions change over time, the entire demand curve for a product may shift. Facing higher gasoline prices after the large increases of 1979 and 1980, many consumers decided to purchase compact cars. The *demand* for compact cars increased, causing both an increase in price and greater sales.

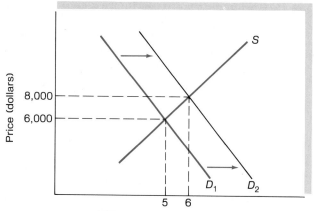

was previously true. The increase in income leads to an increase in demand—a shift in the entire curve.

How does the market react to a change in demand? What happens to price and the amount supplied of a good if demand increases? Exhibit 6 will help to answer these questions while yielding insight into real-world events. From 1970 to 1981, there was a sharp rise in the price of gasoline. Many car owners attempted to economize on their use of the more expensive fuel by substituting smaller cars for their heavier, gas-guzzling models. There was

**Alfred Marshall
(1842–1924)**

OUTSTANDING ECONOMIST

Early economists such as Adam Smith and David Ricardo thought that the price of a good was determined by its cost of production. Later, other economists, known as the "marginalists," emphasized the importance of demand and consumer preferences. They argued that goods commanded a high price, not because the goods were costly to produce, but because consumers valued *additional* units very highly. Alfred Marshall put these two ideas together in 1890 when he introduced the concept of supply and demand.

Marshall noted that "the greater the amount to be sold, the smaller must be the price at which it is offered in order that it may find purchasers." Similarly, he argued that the supply of a commodity reflects the cost of the resources required to produce the good. In turn, the price of the commodity is determined by the balancing of these two forces—supply and demand.

In a famous analogy, Marshall likened the importance of supply and demand to the blades of a pair of scissors. When discussing which was most important, he wrote:

> We might reasonably dispute whether it is the upper or the under blade of a pair of scissors that cuts a piece of paper, as whether value is governed by utility [consumer demand] or cost of production [supply].[5]

Although it is true that the blades of supply and demand operate jointly to determine price, Marshall recognized that the pasan increase in demand for compact cars. The demand curve for such cars shifted to the right (from D_1 to D_2). At the original equilibrium price ($6,000, in our example), there was an excess demand for compact cars—a shortage. This caused the price of compact cars to rise. Market forces eventually brought about a new balance between supply and demand, establishing a new equilibrium price, $8,000, at a higher sales level. The pricing system responded to the increase in demand by granting (a) producers a stronger incentive to supply more compact cars and (b) consumers an incentive to search for additional, cheaper ways to conserve gasoline other than buying compact cars.

SHIFTS IN SUPPLY

The decisions of producers lie behind the supply curve. Other things constant, the supply curve summarizes the willingness of producers to offer a product at alternative prices. Price, though, is not the only factor that producers consider. Cost is also important. Production requires the use of valuable resources—labor, machines, land, building, and raw materials. Use of these resources is costly to suppliers.

Remember that entrepreneurs will supply only those products for which they expect benefits (primarily sales revenues) to exceed their production cost. Factors that reduce the producer's opportunity cost of

sage of time affects the relative importance of the supply and demand sides of the market in its response to change. In the short-run, both supply and demand are highly significant, interacting to determine price. In contrast, in the long-run, the supply side of a market is more important. As Marshall pointed out nearly a century ago, "the longer the time period, the more important will be the influence of cost of production" on price.

Alfred Marshall's father wanted him to enter the ministry, but young Marshall turned down a theological scholarship at Oxford in order to study mathematics at Cambridge. He completed his master's degree at Cambridge and stayed on to teach mathematics for nine years. Marshall's serious study of eco-

nomics began in 1867, about the time he began teaching mathematics. After reading John Stuart Mill's *Principles*, Marshall translated the economics of Mill into mathematical equations. By 1875, Marshall's economic doctrines were well developed, and in 1885, he was appointed to the Chair of Political Economy at Cambridge, a position he occupied for almost a quarter of a century.

In his *Principles of Economics* (1890), Marshall introduced many of the concepts and tools that form the core of modern microeconomics. He pioneered the development of partial equilibrium analysis, a procedure that permits one to focus on the *primary* effects of a specific change, separating them from secondary effects that are believed to

be relatively small (and therefore unimportant). Elasticity, the short-run, the long-run, equilibrium—all of these concepts were initially developed by Marshall. More than any other English economist, Marshall turned economics into a science. His work laid the foundation for the empirical, hypothesis-testing methodology of modern economics. Marshall's influence was so great during the first 25 years of the twentieth century that this period is sometimes referred to as the "Age of Marshall." Clearly, his legacy is still accepted and honored today.

---

[5]Alfred Marshall, *Principles of Economics*, 8th ed. (London: Macmillan, 1920), p. 348.

production—lower resource prices or a technological improvement, for example—would increase the incentive to supply a larger output. Cost reductions would cause supply to increase (shift to the right). In contrast, higher input prices and changes that increase the producer's opportunity cost cause supply to decline (shift to the left).

As with demand, it is important to note the difference between (a) a change in quantity supplied and (b) a change in supply. A change in quantity supplied is a movement along the same curve in response to a change in price. A change in supply indicates a shift in the entire supply curve.

How does the market react to a change in supply? Exhibit 7 illustrates the impact of technological improvements that reduced the cost of producing video cassette recorders (VCRs) in the early 1980's. The reduction in cost made it more attractive for entrepreneurs to produce VCRs. Several new firms began production. Old firms also expanded their production, contributing to the expansion of supply. At the old $400 price, consumers would not buy the larger supply of VCRs. A reduction in price was necessary to bring the wishes of producers and consumers back into balance. By 1985, the price of video recorders had fallen to $200. At that price, coordination of buyer and seller decisions was achieved.

Sometimes political disruption or the erection of market restrictions will shift the supply curve. In 1978, during a violent political upheaval in Iran, the flow of oil from there nearly stopped, and was only partly resumed the following year. The Organization of Petroleum Exporting Countries (OPEC) used that occasion to substantially raise the price of oil sold to Western nations. Temporarily, the United States faced higher prices, no matter what quantity they wished to purchase—a higher supply curve. This led to a shortage of gasoline *at the original price.*

A market economy eliminates a shortage by allowing the price to rise. The smaller supply is rationed to those willing to pay higher prices (see Exhibit 8). Buyers save by conserving the item that has become more scarce. The rise in the price of gasoline induces consumers to use less of it. Sunday leisure trips become more expensive. Less important travel is curtailed.

EXHIBIT 7 • Improved Economy and a Shift in the Supply Curve

In 1980, video cassette recorders (VCRs) were selling for $400 each. Improved technology and manufacturing substantially reduced their production cost, shifting the supply curve to the right (from S_{80} to S_{85}). Prices declined, inducing consumers to purchase a larger quantity.

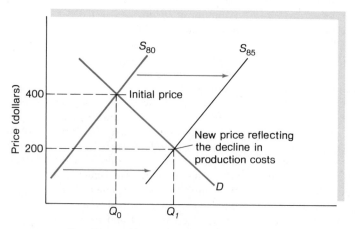

Quantity of video cassette recorders per unit time

EXHIBIT 8 • A Decrease in Supply

Following the violent political upheaval in Iran in 1978, oil production from there nearly stopped, and OPEC used the occasion to raise the price of oil sold on world markets. Supply was reduced—the supply curve shifted upwards, so that 1980 prices were considerably above those of 1978. The smaller supply was rationed to buyers willing to pay the higher prices.

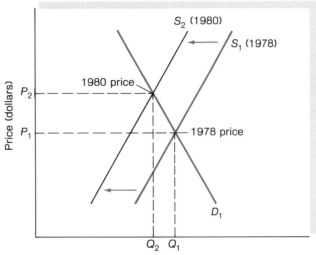

Coordination is again achieved as a new, higher equilibrium price brings the consumption decisions of consumers into harmony with the quantity supplied by producers.

THUMBNAIL SKETCH

These factors increase (decrease) the demand for a good:

1. A rise (fall) in consumer income
2. A rise (fall) in the price of a good used as a substitute
3. A fall (rise) in the price of a complementary good often used with the original good
4. A rise (fall) in the expected future price of the good

These factors increase (decrease) the supply of a good:

1. A fall (rise) in the price of a resource used in producing the good
2. A technological change allowing cheaper production of the good
3. (A disruption in supply due to political factors, weather, or war)

TIME AND THE ADJUSTMENT PROCESS

The signals that the pricing system sends to consumers and producers will change with market conditions. The market adjustment process will not be completed instantaneously, though. Sometimes various signals are sent out and understood only gradually, with the passage of time.

The response of consumers to a change in market conditions will generally be more pronounced as time passes. Consider the response of consumers when gasoline prices nearly doubled from 1978 to 1980 (corrected for inflation, gasoline prices rose more than 50 percent during the two-year period). Initially consumers responded by cutting out some unnecessary trips and leisure driving. Some drove more slowly in order to get better gasoline mileage. As Exhibit 9 illustrates, these adjustments led to some reduction in gasoline consumption. However, while the rise in gasoline prices persisted, new car purchases began to shift toward smaller cars that used less gas. Since people usually waited for their current gas-guzzler to wear out before they bought a new, smaller car, the adjustment was still taking place years later, when gasoline prices began to drop in 1982. But, while the shift to higher-mileage automobiles was taking place, there was more and more reduction in gasoline consumption. The adjustment process for gasoline is a typical one. The demand response to a price change will usually be less in the short-run than over a longer period of time.

Similarly, the adjustments of producers to changing market conditions takes time. Suppose there is an increase in demand for radios. How will this change be reflected in the market? Initially, retailers will note a decline in their inventories as radios move off their shelves more rapidly. They will increase their wholesale orders, causing producer inventories to decline. At first, producers may be unsure whether the increase in demand is a random, temporary phenomenon or a lasting change. In either case, some will use a price increase to ration their limited supplies among the increased number of buyers.

A few alert entrepreneurs may have anticipated the expansion in demand and developed plans early to increase their production. With the passage of time, other producers, initially oblivious to the increase in demand, will take note of the strong demand for radios. To bring more resources into radio production, some resource prices will have to be bid higher, raising costs. For this reason also, producers will raise their prices. Retailers will soon pass the higher prices on to consumers.

Once the increase in demand is widely perceived by suppliers, the price

EXHIBIT 9 • Time and the Buyer's Response to a Price Increase

Usually, the shorter the time period, the less responsive is consumption to a change in price. The gasoline price increases of 1979–1980 illustrate the point. Gasoline consumption declined from 7.4 millions of barrels per day to 7.0 million during the first year as the price of gasoline rose. The second year, consumption dropped to 6.6 million barrels. If the price had remained at the 1980 level for another four years, we would have expected a further decline, perhaps to Q_3, as consumers adjusted more fully. (The price fell after 1980.)

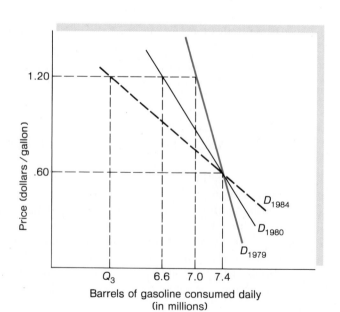

of radios will rise sharply. Profits will exist in the industry. Astute entrepreneurs who anticipated the increase in demand will have expanded their production capacity. They will be rewarded with substantial profits. Other radio suppliers will hastily attempt to expand their production in order to increase their profits. A rapid increase in production, however, will be costly for producers who failed to anticipate (and plan for) the higher level of demand. Such firms will have to resort to overtime payments, air shipments of raw materials, and/or the employment of inexperienced workers to increase their output rapidly. Producers whose apt foresight gives them more time to expand their output in an orderly fashion can do so at a lower cost.

Although producers will expand their output at different rates, the profitable opportunities will induce additional supply, which will eventually moderate the price rise needed to ration radios. All of these responses will take time, however, even though economists sometimes talk as if the process were instantaneous.

REPEALING THE LAWS OF SUPPLY AND DEMAND

Buyers often believe that prices are too high, and sellers generally perceive prices as too low. Unhappy with prices established by market forces, individuals may seek to have prices set by legislative action. Fixing prices seems like a simple, straightforward solution. Simple, straightforward solutions, though, often have unanticipated repercussions. Do not forget the secondary effects.

Price Ceiling: A legally established maximum price that sellers may charge.

Price ceilings are often popular during a period of inflation, a situation in which prices of most products are continually rising. Many people mistakenly believe that the rising prices are the cause of the inflation rather than just one of its effects. Exhibit 10a illustrates the impact of fixing a price of a product below its equilibrium level. Of course, the price ceiling does result in a lower price than market forces would produce, at least in the short-run. However, that is not the end of the story. At the below-equilibrium price, producers will be unwilling to supply as much as consumers would like to purchase. A shortage ($Q_D - Q_S$ Exhibit 10a) of the goods will result. A **shortage** is a situation in which the quantity demanded by consumers exceeds the quantity supplied by producers *at the existing price.* Normally, competing buyers would bid up the price. Fixing the price will prevent that, but will not eliminate the rationing problem. Nonprice factors will now become more important in the rationing process. Producers must discriminate on some basis other than willingness to pay as they ration their sales to eager buyers. Sellers will be partial to friends, to buyers who do them favors, and even to buyers who are willing to make illegal black-market payments.

Shortage: A condition in which the amount of a good offered by sellers is less than the amount demanded by buyers at the existing price. An increase in price would eliminate the shortage.

In addition, the below-equilibrium price reduces the incentive of sellers to expand the future supply of the good. Fewer resources will flow into the production of this good. Higher profits will be available elsewhere. With the passage of time, the shortage conditions will worsen as suppliers direct resources away from production of this commodity and into other areas.

What other secondary effects can we expect? In the real world, there are two ways that sellers can raise prices. First, they can raise their money price, holding quality constant. Or, second, they can hold the money price constant while reducing the quality of the good. Confronting a price ceiling, sellers will rely on the latter method of raising prices. Rather than do without the good, some buyers will accept the lower-quality product. It is not easy to repeal the laws of supply and demand. (See Myths of Economics.)

It is important to note that a shortage is not the same as scarcity. *Scarcity is inescapable.* Scarcity exists whenever people want more of a good than Nature has provided. This means, of course, that almost everything of value is scarce. *Shortages, on the other hand, are avoidable if prices are permitted to rise.* A higher, unfixed price (P_0 rather than P_1 in Exhibit 10a) would (a) stimulate additional production, (b) discourage consumption, and (c) ration the available supply to those willing to give up the most in exchange; that is, to pay the highest prices. These forces, an expansion in output and a reduction in consumption, would eliminate the shortage.

Exhibit 10b illustrates the case of a **price floor,** which fixes the price of a good or resource above its equilibrium level. At the higher price, sellers will want to bring a larger amount to the market, while buyers will choose to buy less of the good. A **surplus** ($Q_S - Q_D$) will result. Agricultural price supports and minimum wage legislation are examples of price floors. Predictably, nonprice factors will again play a larger role in the rationing process than would be true without a price floor. Buyers can now be more selective, since sellers want to sell more than buyers, in aggregate, desire to purchase. Buyers can be expected to seek out sellers willing to offer them favors (discounts on other products, easier credit, or better service, for example). Some sellers may be unable to market their product or service.[6] Unsold merchandise and underutilized resources will result.

Price Floor: A legally established minimum price that buyers must pay for a good or resource.

Surplus: A condition in which the amount of a good that sellers are willing to offer is greater than the amount that buyers will purchase at the existing price. A decline in price would eliminate the surplus.

EXHIBIT 10 • The Impact of Price Ceilings and Price Floors

Frame (a) illustrates the impact of a price ceiling. When price is fixed below the equilibrium level, shortages will develop. Frame (b) illustrates the effects of a price floor. If price is fixed above its equilibrium level, then a surplus will result. When ceilings and floors prevent prices from bringing about a market equilibrium, nonprice factors will play a more important role in the rationing process.

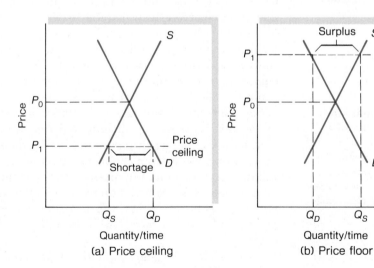

(a) Price ceiling

(b) Price floor

---

[6]Our theory indicates that minimum wage legislation (a price floor for unskilled labor) will generate an excess supply of inexperienced, low-skilled workers. The extremely high unemployment rate of teenagers—a group with little work experience—supports this view.

Note that a surplus does not mean the good is no longer scarce. People still want more of the good than is freely available from Nature, even though they desire less, *at the current price*, than sellers desire to bring to the market. A decline in price would eliminate the surplus but not the scarcity of the item.

MYTHS OF ECONOMICS

"Rent controls are an effective method of ensuring adequate housing at a price the poor can afford."[7]

When rents (a price for a good) are set below the equilibrium level, the amount of rental housing demanded by consumers will exceed the amount landlords will make available. Initially, if the mandated price is not set too much below equilibrium, the impact of rent controls may be barely noticeable. With the passage of time, however, their effects will grow. Inevitably, controls will lead to the following results.

1. *The Future Supply of Rental Houses Will Decline.* The below-equilibrium price will discourage entrepreneurs from constructing new rental housing units. Private investment will flow elsewhere, since the controls have depressed the rate of return in the rental housing market. The current owners of such housing may be forced to accept the lower price. However, potential future suppliers of rental housing have other alternatives. Many of them will opt to use their knowledge and resources in other areas.

2. *Shortages and Black Markets Will Develop.* Since the quantity of housing supplied will fail to keep pace with the quantity demanded, some persons who value rental housing highly will be unable to find it. Frustrated by the shortage, they will seek methods by which they may induce landlords to rent to them. Some will agree to prepay their rent, including a substantial damage deposit. Others will resort to tie-in agreements (for example, they might also agree to rent or buy the landlords' furniture at an exorbitant price) in their efforts to evade the controls. Still others will make under-the-table payments to secure the cheap housing.

3. *The Quality of Rental Housing Will Deteriorate.* Economic thinking suggests that there are two ways to raise prices. The nominal price can be increased, quality being held constant. Alternatively, quality can be reduced, the same nominal price being maintained. When landlords are prohibited from adopting the former, they will use the latter. They will paint rental units less often. Normal maintenance and repair service will deteriorate. Tenant parking lots will be eliminated (or rented). Cleaning and maintenance of the general surroundings will be neglected. Eventually, the quality of the rental housing will reflect the controlled price. Cheap housing will be of cheap quality.

4. *Nonprice Methods of Rationing Will Increase in Importance.* Since price no longer plays its normal role, other forms of competition will develop. Prohibited from price rationing, landlords will rely more heavily on nonmonetary discriminating devices. They will favor friends, persons of influence, and those with life-styles similar to their own. In contrast, applicants with many children, unconventional lifestyles, or perhaps dark skin will find fewer landlords who cater to their personal requirements. Since the cost to landlords of discriminating against those with characteristics they do not like has been reduced, such discrimination will become more prevalent in the rationing process.

5. *Inefficient Use of Housing Space Will Result.* The tenant in a rent-controlled apartment will think twice before moving. Why? Even though the tenant might want a larger or smaller space, or even though the tenant might want to move closer to work, he or she will be less likely to move because it is much more difficult to find a vacancy if rent control ordinances are in effect. As a result, turnover will drop somewhat, and people will end up living in apartments not quite suited to their needs.

Are conditions in the real world consistent with economic theory? More than any other major city in the United States, New York City has experimented with rent controls. The result has been an unusually large number of furniture and housing "package rentals" as both

---

[7]The information in the following section is from Peter Navarro, "Rent Control in Cambridge, Mass.," *The Public Interest*, No. 78, Winter 1985, pp. 83–100.

MYTHS OF ECONOMICS
(continued)

landlords and renters seek to avoid the impact of the controls. Complaints about the failure of landlords to undertake repairs, maintain rental units properly, and provide complimentary services such as garbage pickup and rat-control efforts are far more common in New York City than in any other place in the United States. Economic theory helps to explain why this is the case.

During the inflation-plagued 1970s, the popularity of rent controls increased. Washington, D.C., San Francisco, Los Angeles, and several other cities experimented with various types of control schemes. Studies indicated that a three-pronged pattern emerged after the imposition of rent controls.

First, investment in new construction came to a standstill after the controls were imposed. Even in cases where newly constructed buildings were exempt from the controls, construction was adversely affected; landlords feared the imposition of the controls once a new apartment dwelling was in place. Second, the rent controls induced many landlords to convert their apartment buildings to condominium complexes. In New York, for example, it was estimated that in 1984, 25,000 apartments were held off the market, or "warehoused," simply to make them more easily available for developers of condominiums and cooperative apartments. Far more than that, of course, had already been converted. Finally, vacancy rates declined as the rent-control communities began to feel the developing housing shortage.

Although rent controls may appear to be a simple solution, the truth of the matter is that a decline in the supply of rental housing, poor maintenance, and shortages are the inevitable results. Controls may initially lead to lower housing prices for some, but in the long-run the potential for the deterioration of urban life is almost unlimited. In the words of Swedish economist Assar Lindbeck: "In many cases rent control appears to be the most efficient technique presently known to destroy a city—except for bombing."[8] Though this may overstate the case somewhat, economic analysis suggests that the point is well-taken.

---

[8]Assar Lindbeck, *The Political Economy of the New Left, 1970* (New York: Harper and Row, 1972), p. 39.

HOW THE MARKET ANSWERS THE THREE BASIC ECONOMIC QUESTIONS

How does the market's pricing mechanism resolve the three basic economic questions—what goods will be produced, how will they be produced, and for whom will they be produced?

In a market economy, what will be produced is determined by the consumer's evaluation of a good (demand) relative to its opportunity cost (supply). If consumers value a good (in terms of money) more than its opportunity cost, they will choose to purchase it. Simultaneously, profit-seeking producers will supply a good as long as consumers are willing to pay a price that is sufficient to cover the opportunity cost of producing it. The result: *There is an incentive to produce those goods, and only those goods, to which consumers attach a value at least as high as the production costs of the goods.*

How goods will be produced is determined by the economizing behavior of suppliers. Suppliers have a strong incentive to use production methods that minimize costs, because lower costs will mean larger profits. Thus, producers can be expected to organize production efficiently—to use a division of labor, to discover and adapt new technologies, and to choose labor-capital combinations that will result in lower production costs.

What assurances are there that producers will not waste resources or exploit consumers by charging high prices? Competition provides the answer. Inefficient producers will have higher costs. They will find it difficult to meet the price competition of sellers who use resources wisely. Similarly, in a market with many sellers, competition among firms will, on the whole, keep prices from straying much above production costs. When prices are above the opportunity costs of a good, profits for the producers will result. As we have discussed, the profits will attract additional suppliers into the market, driving the price downward.

To whom will the goods be distributed? Goods will be allocated to consumers willing and able to pay the market price. Of course, some consumers will be better able to pay the market price—they have larger incomes (more "dollar votes") than others. The unequal distribution of income among consumers is directly related to what is produced and how. The income of individuals will reflect the extent of their provision of resources to others. Those who supply large amounts of highly valued resources—resources for which market participants are willing to pay a high price—will have high incomes. In contrast, those who supply few resources or resources that are not valued highly by others will have low incomes.

As long as the preferences and productive abilities of individuals differ, a market solution will lead to an unequal distribution of income. Many people are critical of the pricing system because of its method of distribution. But, unequal income distribution is not unique to a market economy. In virtually all systems, unequal income shares exist, and provide at least some of the incentive for individuals to undertake activities. Since efforts to alter the distribution of income will also affect supply conditions, this issue is highly complex. As we proceed, we will investigate it in more detail.

THE COMMUNICATING, COORDINATING, AND MOTIVATING FUNCTIONS OF THE MARKET

The mechanics of supply and demand are important because they help us understand forces present in the real world. However, sometimes we economists have a tendency to focus on the mechanics without fully explaining their importance. Economic activity is conducted by human decision-makers. Knowledge, coordination, and motivation are critical to the operation of every economy. If people do not know where their services are valued highly, what goods are desired by consumers, or which production methods are efficient, they cannot be expected to economize in the use of resources. Similarly, unless actions are coordinated, an economy will come to a standstill. Moreover, as many leaders of centrally planned economies have discovered, people must be motivated to act before production plans can be realized. An efficiently operating economy must communicate, coordinate, and motivate the actions of decision-makers. In this section, we will take a closer look at how the pricing system performs these functions.

COMMUNICATING INFORMATION TO DECISION-MAKERS

Communication of information is one of the most important functions of a market price. We cannot *directly* observe the preferences of consumers. How highly do consumers value tricycles relative to attic fans, television sets relative to trampolines, or automobiles relative to swimming pools? Product prices and quantities sold communicate up-to-date information about consumers' valuation of additional units of these and numerous other commodities. Similarly, we cannot turn to an engineering equation in order to calculate the opportunity cost of alternative commodities. But, resource prices tell the business decision-maker the relative importance others place on production factors (skill categories of labor, natural resources, and machinery, for example). With this information, in addition to knowledge of the relationship between potential input combinations and the output of a product, producers can make reliable estimates of their opportunity costs.

Without the information provided by market prices, it would be impossible for decision-makers to determine how intensively a good was desired relative to its opportunity costs—that is, relative to other things that might be produced with the resources required to produce the good. Markets collect and register bits and pieces of information reflecting the choices of consumers, producers, and resource suppliers. This vast body of information, which is almost always well beyond the comprehension of any single individual, is tabulated into a summary statistic—*the market price*. This summary statistic provides market participants with information on the relative scarcity of products.

When weather conditions, consumer preferences, technology, political revolution, or natural disasters alter the relative scarcity of a product or resource, market prices communicate this information to decision-makers. Direct knowledge of why conditions were altered is not necessary for making the appropriate adjustments. A change in the market price provides sufficient information to determine whether an item has become more or less scarce.[9]

COORDINATING THE ACTIONS OF MARKET PARTICIPANTS

Market prices coordinate the choices of buyers and sellers, bringing their decisions into line with each other. If suppliers are bringing more of a product to market than is demanded by consumers at the market price, thus creating a surplus, that price will fall. As the price declines, producers will reduce their output (some may even go out of business), and simultaneously the price reduction will induce consumers to use more of the good. The surplus will eventually be eliminated, and balance will be restored in the market.

Alternatively, if producers are currently supplying less than consumers are purchasing, there will be a shortage in the market. Rather than do

---

[9]The market adjustment to the destruction of the anchovy crop off the coast of Peru in 1972 provides an excellent example of the role of price as a communication signal. The normal anchovy run off the coast of Peru did not materialize in 1972. Anchovies are a major source of protein for animal feed. Soybeans are a good substitute for anchovies. It was not necessary for American farmers to know any of these things in order to make the correct response. As soybeans were used more intensively in feed grains, the price of soybeans increased during 1972–1974. Responding to the summary statistic (higher soybean prices), farmers increased their production of soybeans, which moderated the adverse effects of the anchovy destruction.

without, some consumers will bid up the price. As the price rises, consumers will be encouraged to economize on their use of the good, and suppliers will be encouraged to produce more of it. Again, price will serve to balance the scales of supply and demand. The shortage will disappear.

Prices also direct entrepreneurs to undertake the production projects that are demanded most intensely (relative to their cost) by consumers. Entrepreneurial activity is guided by the signal lights of profits and losses. If consumers really want more of a good—for example, luxury apartments—the intensity of their demand will lead to a market price that exceeds the opportunity cost of constructing the apartments. A profitable opportunity will be created. Entrepreneurs will soon discover this opportunity for gain, undertake construction, and thereby expand the availability of the apartments. In contrast, if consumers want less of a good—very large cars, for example—the opportunity cost of supplying such cars will exceed the sales revenue from their production. Entrepreneurs who undertake such unprofitable production will be penalized by losses.

An understanding of the importance of the entrepreneur also sheds light on the market adjustment process. Since entrepreneurs, like the rest of us, have imperfect knowledge, they will not be able to instantaneously identify profitable opportunities and the disequilibrium conditions that accompany them. With the passage of time, however, information about a profitable opportunity will become more widely disseminated. More and more producers will move to supply a good that is intensely desired by consumers relative to its cost. Of course, as entrepreneurs expand supply, they will eventually eliminate the profit.

The move toward equilibrium will typically be a groping process. With time, successful entrepreneurial activity will be more clearly identified. Successful methods will be copied by other producers. Learning-by-doing and trial-and-error will help producers sort out attractive projects from "losers." The process, though, will never quite be complete. By the time entrepreneurs discover one intensely desired product (or a new, more efficient production technique), change will have occurred elsewhere, creating other unrealized profitable opportunities. The wheels of dynamic change never stop.

MOTIVATING THE ECONOMIC PLAYERS

One of the major advantages of the pricing system is its ability to motivate people. Prices establish a reward-penalty system that induces the participants to work, cooperate with others, invest for the future, supply goods that are intensely desired by others, economize on the use of scarce resources, and use efficient production methods. Pursuit of personal gain is a powerful motivator.

This reward-penalty system will direct the actions of entrepreneurs. They will seek to supply goods that are intensely desired relative to their opportunity cost, because such projects are profitable. In contrast, they will try to avoid using resources to produce things that are valued less than their opportunity cost because such projects will result in losses. No government agency needs to tell decision-makers what to produce or what not to produce. No central authority forces the milkman to deliver milk, the construction firm to produce houses, the farmer to produce wheat, or the baker to produce bread. Producers choose to engage in these and millions of other productive activities because they consider them to be in their self-interest.

Similarly, no one has to tell resource suppliers to acquire, develop, and supply productive inputs. Why are many young people willing to undertake the necessary work, stress, late hours of study, and financial cost to acquire a medical or law degree, a doctoral degree in economics or physics, or a master's degree in business administration? Why do others seek to master a skill requiring an apprentice program? Why do individuals save to buy a business, capital equipment, or other assets? Although many factors undoubtedly influence one's decision to acquire skills and capital assets, the expectation of financial reward is an important stimulus. Without this stimulus, the motivation to work, create, develop skills, and supply capital assets to those productive activities most desired by others would be weakened. Market forces supply this essential ingredient so automatically that most people do not even realize it. Responding to the reward-penalty system of the market, the actions of even self-interested people will be channelled into the areas of production that are most highly desired by others, relative to their opportunity cost.

More than 200 years ago, the father of economics, Adam Smith, first articulated the revolutionary idea that competitive markets bring personal self-interest and general welfare into harmony with each other. Smith noted that the butcher, for example, supplies meat to customers, not out of benevolence, but rather out of self-interest. Emphasizing his point, Smith stated:

> Every individual is continually exerting himself to find out the most advantageous employment for whatever capital he can command. It is his own advantage, indeed, and not that of the society which he has in view. But the study of his own advantage naturally, or rather necessarily, leads him to prefer that employment which is most advantageous to society. . . . He intends only his own gain, and he is in this, as in many other cases, led by an invisible hand to promote an end which was not part of his intention. By pursuing his own interest he frequently promotes that of the society more effectually than when he really intends to promote it.[10]

Market prices coordinate the decentralized individual planning of economic participants and bring their plans (self-interest) into harmony with the general welfare. This was the message of Adam Smith in 1776. It was an idea with truly major and lasting consequences.

QUALIFICATIONS

In this chapter, we have focused on the operation of a market economy. The efficiency of market organization is dependent on (a) competitive markets and (b) well-defined private property rights. Competition, the great regulator, can protect both buyer and seller. The presence (or possible entry) of independent alternative suppliers protects the consumer against a seller who seeks to charge prices substantially above the cost of production. The

[10]Adam Smith, *An Inquiry into the Nature and Causes of the Wealth of Nations* (New York: Modern Library, 1937), p. 423.

existence of alternative resource suppliers protects the producer against a supplier who might otherwise be tempted to withhold a vital resource unless granted exorbitant compensation. The existence of alternative employment opportunities protects the employee from the power of any single employer. Competition can equalize the bargaining power between buyers and sellers.

Understanding the information, coordination, and motivation results of the market mechanism helps us see all the more clearly the importance of property rights, the things actually traded in markets. Although property rights are often associated with selfishness, they are more properly viewed as an arrangement to (a) force resource users to bear fully the cost of their actions and (b) prohibit persons from engaging in destructive forms of competition. When property rights are well-defined, secure, and tradeable, suppliers of goods and services will be required to pay resource owners the opportunity cost of each resource employed. They will not be permitted to seize and use scarce resources without compensating the owner; that is, without bidding the resources away from alternative users.

Similarly, secure property rights eliminate the use of violence as a competitive weapon. A producer you do not buy from (or work for) will not be permitted to burn down your house. Nor will a competitive resource supplier whose prices you undercut be permitted to slash your automobile tires or threaten you with bodily injury.

Lack of competition and poorly defined property rights will alter the operation of a market economy. As we proceed, we will investigate each of these problems in detail.

CHAPTER SUMMARY

1. Because people want more of scarce goods than Nature has made freely available, a rationing mechanism is necessary. Competition is the natural outgrowth of the necessity for rationing scarce goods. A change in the rationing mechanism used will alter the form of competition, but it will not eliminate competitive tactics.

2. The law of demand holds that there is an inverse relationship between price and the amount of a good purchased. A rise in price will cause consumers to purchase less because they now have a greater incentive to use substitutes. On the other hand, a reduction in price will induce consumers to buy more, since they will substitute the cheaper good for other commodities.

3. The law of supply states that there is a direct relationship between the price of a product and the amount supplied. Other things constant, an increase in the price of a product will induce established firms to expand their output and new firms to enter the market. The quantity supplied will expand.

4. Market prices will bring the conflicting forces of supply and demand into balance. If the quantity supplied to the market by producers exceeds the quantity demanded by consumers, price will decline until the surplus is eliminated. On the other hand, if the quantity demanded by consumers exceeds the quantity supplied by producers, price will rise until the shortage is eliminated.

5. When a market is in long-run equilibrium, supply and demand will be in balance and the producer's opportunity cost will equal the market price. If the opportunity cost of supplying the good is less than the market price, profits will accrue. The profits will attract additional suppliers, cause lower prices, and push the market toward an equilibrium. On the other hand, if the opportunity cost of producing a good exceeds the market price, suppliers will experience losses. The losses will induce producers to leave the market, causing price to rise until equilibrium is restored.

6. Changes in consumer income, prices of closely related goods, preferences, and expectations as to future prices will cause the entire demand curve to shift. An increase (decrease) in demand will cause prices to rise (fall) and quantity supplied to increase (decline).

7. Changes in input prices, technology, and other factors that influence the producer's cost of production will cause the entire supply curve to shift. An increase (decrease) in supply will cause prices to fall (rise) and quantity demanded to expand (decline).

8. The constraint of time temporarily limits the ability of consumers to adjust to changes in prices. With the passage of time, a price increase will usually elicit a larger reduction in quantity demanded. Similarly, the market supply curve shows more responsiveness to a change in price in the long-run than during the short-term time period.

9. When a price is fixed below the market equilibrium, buyers will want to purchase more than sellers are willing to supply. A shortage will result. Nonprice factors such as waiting lines, quality deterioration, and illegal transactions will play a more important role in the rationing process.

10. When a price is fixed above the market equilibrium level, sellers will want to supply a larger amount than buyers are willing to purchase at the current price. A surplus will result.

11. The pricing system answers the three basic allocation questions in the following manner.
    (a) What goods will be produced? Additional units of goods will be produced only if consumers value them more highly than the opportunity cost of the resources necessary to produce them.
    (b) How will goods be produced? The methods that result in the lowest opportunity cost will be chosen. Since lower costs mean larger profits, markets reward producers who discover and utilize efficient (low-cost) production methods.
    (c) To whom will the goods be distributed? Goods will be distributed to individuals according to the quantity and price of the productive resources they supplied in the marketplace. A great number of goods will be allocated to persons who are able to sell a large quantity of highly valued productive resources; few goods will be allocated to persons who supply only a small quantity of low-valued resources.

12. Market prices communicate information, coordinate the actions of buyers and sellers, and provide the incentive structure that motivates decision-makers to act. The information provided by prices instructs entrepreneurs as to (a) how to use scarce resources and (b) which

products are intensely desired (relative to their opportunity cost) by consumers. Market prices establish a reward-penalty system, which induces individuals to cooperate with each other and motivates them to work efficiently, invest for the future, supply intensely desired goods, economize on the use of scarce resources, and use efficient production methods. Even though decentralized individual planning is a characteristic of the market system, there is a harmony between personal self-interest and the general welfare, as Adam Smith noted long ago. The efficiency of the system is dependent on (a) competitive market conditions and (b) securely defined private property rights.

THE ECONOMIC WAY OF THINKING— DISCUSSION QUESTIONS

1. What is the purpose of prices? Do prices do anything other than ration goods to those with the most dollar votes? Explain. What factors determine the price of a good?

2. How many of the following "goods" do you think conform to the general law of supply: (a) gasoline, (b) cheating on exams, (c) political favors from legislators, (d) the services of heart specialists, (e) children, (f) legal divorces, (g) the services of a minister? Explain your answer in each case.

3. Which of the following do you think would lead to an increase in the current demand for beef: (a) higher pork prices, (b) higher incomes, (c) higher feed grain prices, (d) a banner-year corn crop, (e) an increase in the price of beef?

4. (a) "The motivating force behind a market economy is individual self-interest."
   (b) "Cooperation among individuals is the keystone of a market system. Without cooperation there would be no exchange and economic welfare would suffer drastically?"
   Are these statements true or false? Explain your answer.

5. "We cannot allow the price of gasoline to go any higher because it is as essential to the poor as to the rich. We cannot allow the rich to bid gasoline away from the poor. I would prefer to ration ten gallons of gas to each driver—both rich and poor." (Overhead during the gasoline shortage of 1980.)
   (a) Do you agree with this opinion? Why?
   (b) Do you think gasoline is more essential than food? Should the rich be allowed to bid food away from the poor? Should food be rationed, equal portions being granted to both rich and poor? Why or why not?
   (c) Were your answers to both (a) and (b) consistent? Explain.

6. **What's Wrong with This Way of Thinking?**
   "Economists argue that lower prices will necessarily result in less supply. However, there are exceptions to this rule. For example, in 1970, 10-digit electronic calculators sold for $100. By 1985, the price of the same type of calculator had declined to less than $15. Yet business firms produced and sold five times as many calculators in 1985 as in 1970. Lower prices did *not* result in less production and a decline in the number of calculators supplied."

7. A drought hit Brazil in 1986, damaging the coffee crop. The 1986 harvest was 16.5 million bags, down from the 1985 harvest of 33 million bags. Since Brazil is the world's leading coffee producer, there was a substantial reduction in the world supply of coffee in 1986. Use supply and demand analysis to describe:
   (a) what happened to the price of coffee in 1986,
   (b) the U.S. per capita consumption of coffee in 1986 compared to that is 1985,
   (c) the price of tea in 1986,
   (d) the revenues of coffee producers in 1986 (be careful). Coffee is allocated by the market. Did the sharp reduction in supply create a shortage? Why or why not?

Industrious students should obtain real-world data to back up their analysis. Information on coffee prices and consumption for the United States is available in the *Statistical Abstract of the United States* (annual).

- What does the economic way of thinking have to say about economic efficiency?

- When do markets fall short of the ideal of economic efficiency?

- What role does the government play in guiding economic activity?

- Why does government activity sometimes fail to meet ideal efficiency standards?

- What can economics tell us about how individuals act in the public sector?

Democracy is the worst form of government, except for all the rest.

WINSTON CHURCHILL

4 SUPPLY AND DEMAND FOR THE PUBLIC SECTOR

The economic role of government is pivotal. The government sets the rules of the game. It establishes and defines property rights, which are necessary for the smooth operation of markets. As we shall soon see, public policy is also an important determinant of economic stability. The government sometimes uses subsidies to encourage the production of some goods while it applies special taxes to reduce the availability of others. In a few cases—education, the mail service, and local electric power, for example—the government becomes directly involved in the production process.

Because of government's broad economic role, it is vital that we understand how it works and the circumstances under which it contributes to the efficient allocation of resources. Recent work in economics, particularly in the area of public choice, is relevant if we are seeking intelligent answers to the questions posed in the Chapter Focus.

In this chapter, we examine the shortcomings of the market and the potential of government policy as an alternate means for resolving economic problems. Issues involving market- and public-sector organization will be discussed repeatedly throughout this book. Political economy—how the public sector works, and how its workings compare with those of the market—is an integral and exciting aspect of economic analysis.

IDEAL ECONOMIC EFFICIENCY

Economic Efficiency:
Economizing behavior. When applied to a community, it implies that (a) an activity should be undertaken if the sum of the benefits to the individuals exceeds the sum of their costs and (b) no activity should be undertaken if the costs borne by the individuals exceed the benefits.

We need a criterion by which to judge alternative institutional arrangements—market- and public-sector policies. Economists use the standard of **economic efficiency.** The central idea is straightforward. It simply means that for any given level of effort (cost), we want to obtain the largest possible benefit. A corollary to this is that we want to obtain any specific level of benefits with the least possible effort. Economic efficiency simply means getting the most out of the available resources—making the largest pie from the available set of ingredients, so to speak.

Why efficiency? Economists acknowledge that each individual does not have the efficiency of the economy as a primary goal. Instead, each person wants the largest possible "piece of the pie." All might agree that a bigger pie is preferred, however, particularly if they and those they care most about will probably get a larger slice as a result. Not only will most people agree that efficiency is good in the abstract, but an alternative that is more efficient can potentially make more people better off than an inefficient alternative.

What does efficiency mean when applied to the entire economy? Individuals are the final decision-makers of an economy. Individuals will bear the costs and reap the benefits of economic activity. When applied to the entire economy, two conditions are necessary for ideal economic efficiency to exist:

Rule 1.   *Undertaking an economic action will be efficient if it produces more benefits than costs for the individuals of the economy.* Such actions result in gain—improvement in the well-being of at least some individuals without creating reductions in the welfare of others. Failure to undertake such activities means that potential gain has been forgone.

Rule 2. *Undertaking an economic action will be inefficient if it produces more costs than benefits to the individuals.* When an action results in greater total costs than benefits, somebody must be harmed. The benefits that accrue to those who gain are insufficient to compensate for the losses imposed on others. Therefore, when all persons are considered, the net impact of such an action is counterproductive.

When either rule 1 or rule 2 is violated, economic inefficiency results. The concept of economic efficiency applies to each and every possible income distribution, although a change in income distribution may alter the precise combination of goods and services that is most efficient. Positive economics does not tell us how income should be distributed. Of course, we all have ideas on the subject. Most of us would like to see more income distributed our way. For each kind of income distribution, though, there will be an ideal resource allocation that will be most efficient.

A closer look at supply and demand when competitive pressures are present will help you to understand the concept of efficiency. The supply curve reflects the producer's opportunity costs. Each point along the supply curve indicates the minimum price for which the units of a good could be produced without a loss to the seller. Each point along the demand curve indicates the consumer's valuation of an extra unit of the good—the maximum amount the consumer of each unit is willing to pay for the unit. Any time the consumer's valuation exceeds the producer's opportunity cost— the producer's minimum supply price—producing and selling more of the good can generate mutual gain.

When only the buyer and seller are affected by production and exchange, competitive markets directed by the forces of supply and demand are efficient. Exhibit 1 illustrates why this is true. Suppliers of a good, bicycles in this example, will produce additional units as long as the market price exceeds the production cost. Similarly, consumers will gain from the purchase of additional units as long as their benefits, revealed by the height of the demand curve, exceed the market price. Market forces will result in

EXHIBIT 1 • What is Good About Idealized Market Exchange?

When competitive forces are present, price will tend toward the supply-demand intersection *P*. At that price, the seller's opportunity cost of producing the last unit will just equal the buyer's evaluation of that unit. All potential mutual gains from production and exchange are realized.

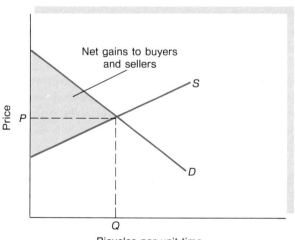

an equilibrium output level of Q: All units for which the benefits to consumers exceed the costs to suppliers will be produced. Rule 1 is met; all potential gains from exchange (the shaded area) between consumers and producers are fully realized. Production beyond Q, however, will prove inefficient. If more than Q bicycles are produced, rule 2 is violated; consumers value the additional units less than their cost. With competitive markets, suppliers will find it unprofitable to produce units beyond Q because the cost of the additional units will exceed revenues.

Consumers and producers alike will thus be guided by the pricing system to output level Q, just the right amount. The market works beautifully. Individuals, pursuing their own interests, are guided as if by an invisible hand to promote the general welfare. This was the message of Adam Smith, more than 200 years ago.

WHY MIGHT THE INVISIBLE HAND FAIL?

Is the invisible hand still working today? Why might it fail? There are four important factors that can limit the ability of the invisible hand to perform its magic.

LACK OF COMPETITION

Competition is vital to the proper operation of the pricing mechanism. It is competition that drives the prices for consumer goods down to the level of their cost. Similarly, competition in markets for productive resources prevents (a) sellers from charging exorbitant prices to producers and (b) buyers from taking advantage of the owners of productive resources. The existence of competitors reduces the power of buyers and sellers alike to rig the market in their own favor.

Modern mass production techniques, marketing, and distributing networks often make it possible for a large-scale producer to gain a cost advantage over smaller competitors. In several industries—automobiles, aircraft, and aluminum, for example—a few large firms produce the entire output. Because an enormous amount of capital investment is required to enter these industries, existing large-scale producers may be partially insulated from the competitive pressure of new rivals.

Since competition is the enemy of high prices, sellers have a strong incentive to escape from its pressures by colluding rather than competing. Competition is something that is good when the other guy faces it. Individually, each of us would prefer to be loosened from its grip. Students do not like stiff competitors at exam time, when seeking entry to graduate school, or in their social or romantic lives. Similarly, sellers prefer few real competitors.

Exhibit 2 illustrates how sellers can gain from collusive action. If a group of sellers could eliminate the competition from new entrants to the market, they would be able to raise their prices. The total revenue of sellers is simply the market price multiplied by the quantity sold. The sellers' revenues may well be greater, and their total costs would surely be lower, if the smaller, restricted output Q_2 were sold rather than the competitive output Q_1. The artificially high price P_2 is in excess of the competitive

EXHIBIT 2 • Rigging the Market

If a group of sellers can restrict the entry of competitors and connive to reduce their own output, they can sometimes obtain more total revenue by selling fewer units. Note that the total sales revenue P_2Q_2 for the restricted supply exceeds the sales revenue P_1Q_1 for the competitive supply.

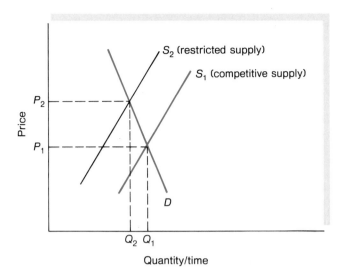

opportunity cost of supplying the good. The price of the good does not reflect its actual level of scarcity.

It is in the interest of consumers and the community that output be expanded to Q_1, the output consistent with economic efficiency. It is in the interest of sellers, though, to make the good artificially scarce and raise its price. If sellers can use collusion, government action, or other means of restricting supply, they can gain. However, the restricted output level would violate rule 2. Inefficiency would result. There is a conflict between the interests of sellers and what is best for the entire community.

When there are only a few firms in the industry and competition from new entrants can be restrained, sellers may be able to rig the market in their favor. Through collusion, either tacit or overt, suppliers may be able to escape competitive pressures. What can the government do to preserve competition? Congress has enacted a series of antitrust laws, most notably the Sherman Antitrust Act and the Clayton Act, making it illegal for firms to collude or attempt to monopolize a product market. Congress also established the Federal Trade Commission, which prohibits "unfair methods of competition in commerce," such as false advertising, improper grading of materials, and deceptive business practices.

For the most part, economists favor the principle of government action to ensure and promote competitive markets, but there is considerable debate about the effectiveness of past public policy in this area. Few economists are satisfied with the government's role as a promoter of competition.

Two general criticisms are voiced. Many economists suggest government should pursue a more vigorous antitrust policy. They believe antitrust action should be taken to expand the number of rivals in several industries—automobiles and steel, for example—that are currently dominated by a few firms. Protecting weaker competitors from stronger ones is one way to keep the weaker ones on the scene. On the other hand, other critics argue that such antitrust policy and business regulation, both past and present, have often, paradoxically, restricted competition. After all, competition can lead to low prices, and trouble for less efficient firms. Critics charge that government action has sometimes protected consumers from low prices and protected producers from new rivals. These critics argue that government regulatory policy has been part of the problem rather than part of the solution. They believe this results from an inherent flaw in the political process—the disproportionate power of special interests.

EXTERNALITIES— WHAT HAVE YOU BEEN DOING TO YOUR NEIGHBOR?

Externalities: The side effects of an action that influence the well-being of nonconsenting parties. The nonconsenting parties may be either helped (by external benefits) or harmed (by external costs).

Production and consumption of some goods will result in spillover effects that the market will fail to register. These spillover effects, called **externalities,** are present when the actions of one individual or group affect the welfare of others without their consent.

Examples of externalities abound. If you live in an apartment house and the noisy stereo of your next-door neighbors keeps you from studying economics, your neighbors are creating an externality. Their actions are imposing an unwanted cost on you. Driving your car during rush hour increases the level of congestion, thereby imposing a cost on other motorists. If an examination is graded on a curve, cheating creates an externality in as much as it raises the class average.

Not all externalities result in the imposition of a cost. Sometimes human actions generate benefits for nonparticipating parties. The homeowner who keeps a house in good condition and maintains a neat lawn improves the beauty of the entire community, thereby benefitting community members. A flood-control project that benefits the upstream residents will also generate gains for those who live downstream. Scientific theories benefit their authors, but the knowledge gained also contributes to the welfare of others.

Why do externalities create problems for the market mechanism? Exhibit 3 can help answer this question. With competitive markets in equilibrium, the cost of a good (including the opportunity cost borne by the producer) will be paid by consumers. Unless consumer benefits exceed the opportunity cost of production, the goods will not be produced. What happens, though, when externalities are present?

EXHIBIT 3 • Externalities and Problems for the Market

When external costs are present (a), the output level of a product will exceed the desired amount. In contrast, market output of goods that generate external benefits (b) will be less than the ideal level.

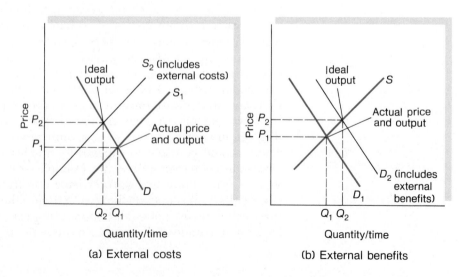

(a) External costs

(b) External benefits

Suppose that a business firm discharges smoke into the air or sewage into a river. Valuable resources, clean air and pure water, are used essentially as garbage-removal services. Neither the firm nor the consumers of its products, however, will pay for these costs. As Exhibit 3a shows, the supply curve will understate the opportunity cost of production when these external costs are present. Since the producer only has to consider the cost to the firm, and can ignore the cost imposed on secondary parties, supply curve S_1 will result. If all costs were considered, supply would be S_2. The actual supply curve S_1 will not reflect the opportunity cost of producing the good. The producer will be misled into thinking that the opportunity cost is low enough to merit an increase in supply. Output will be expanded beyond Q_2 (to Q_1), even though the community's valuation of the additional units is less than their cost. The second efficiency condition, rule 2, is violated. Inefficiency in the form of excessive air and water pollution results. In the total picture, the harm caused by the added pollution outweighs the benefits to some of the people involved.

As Exhibit 3b shows, external benefits often result in opportunities forgone. When they are present, the market demand curve D_1 will not fully reflect the total benefits, which include those going to parties who receive the benefits without payment. The secondary parties would be willing to help pay for the good. However, their preferences are not registered through the market due to the high transactions costs. Thus, output Q_1 will result. Could the community gain from a greater output of the product? Yes. The demand curve D_2 reflects both the direct benefits to paying consumers and the benefits bestowed on secondary, nonpaying parties. Expansion of output beyond Q_1 to Q_2 would result in net gain to the community. But, since neither producers nor paying consumers can capture the secondary benefits, consumption level Q_1 will result. The potential net gain from the greater output level Q_2 will be lost. Rule 1 of our ideal efficiency criterion is violated.

Competitive markets will fail to give consumers and producers the correct signals when externalities are present. The market will tend to underallocate resources to the production of goods with external benefits and overallocate resources to the production of goods that impose external costs on nonconsenting parties.

PUBLIC GOODS— MORE PROBLEMS FOR THE MARKET

Public Goods: Jointly consumed goods. When consumed by one person, they are also made available to others. National defense, poetry, and scientific theories are all public goods.

Some goods cannot be provided through the marketplace because there is no way to exclude nonpaying customers. Goods that must be consumed jointly by all are called **public goods.** National defense, the judicial and legal systems, and the monetary system are examples of public goods. The national defense that protects you also protects others. Unlike candy bars, national defense cannot be provided to some citizens but not to others. Similarly, the actions of a central monetary authority are a public good. The monetary system that influences the prices of things you buy and sell also influences the prices and incomes of others.

Why are public goods troublesome for the market? Typically, in the marketplace, there is a direct link between consumption and payment. If you do not pay, you do not consume. Similarly, the payments of consumers provide the incentive to supply products. Public goods, however, are consumed jointly. If a public good is made available to one person, it is simultaneously made available to others. Since people cannot be excluded, their incentive to pay or even to reveal their true valuation of the good is destroyed. Why would you voluntarily pay your "fair share" for national defense, the courts, or police protection if these goods were provided in the market? If others contribute a large amount, the public good will be provided pretty much regardless of what you do. If others do not pay, your actions will not make much difference anyway. Each person thus has an incentive to opt out, to refuse to help pay voluntarily for the public good.

When everybody opts out, what happens? Not very much of the public good is produced. This is precisely why the market cannot handle public goods very well. Resources will be underallocated to the production of public goods because many people, following their self-interest, will refuse to pay for them. Because of their very nature, public goods cause a conflict between self-interest and the public interest of economic efficiency.

ECONOMIC INSTABILITY

If markets are to function well, a stable monetary exchange system must be provided. Many market exchanges involve a time dimension. Houses, cars, consumer durables, land, buildings, equipment, and many other items are paid for over a period of months or even years. If the purchasing power of the monetary unit, the dollar in the United States, gyrated wildly, few would want to make transactions involving long-term commitments because of the uncertainty. The smooth functioning of the market would be retarded. Many economists believe that without the help of government, the economy would be less stable than it is.

The government's spending and monetary policies exert a powerful influence on economic stability. If properly conducted, these policies contribute to economic stability, full and efficient utilization of resources, and stable prices. Improper stabilization policies, though, can cause massive unemployment, rapidly rising prices, or both.

Economists are not in complete agreement on the extent to which public policy can stabilize the economy and promote full employment. They often debate the impact of various policy tools. All agree, however, that a stable economic environment is vital to a market economy. Those pursuing a course in macroeconomics will find both the potential and the limitations of government action as a stabilizing force in the economy discussed further in Part Two.

THE ECONOMICS OF COLLECTIVE ACTION

The pricing system will fail to meet our ideal efficiency standards if (a) markets are not competitive, (b) externalities are present, (c) public goods necessitate joint consumption, or (d) the aggregate economy is characterized by instability and the resultant uncertainty. If public sector-action can correct these deficiencies, net gains for the community are possible. Public policy does not have to be a zero-sum game.

It is important to understand that public-sector action can sometimes be expected to improve the efficiency of the market. It is also important to recognize that collective action is merely an alternative form of economic organization. Like the market, collective action is directed by human behavior and the decisions of individuals who see their own situations and interests most clearly.

If we are going to make meaningful comparisons between market allocation and collective action, we need to develop a sound theory that will help us understand both forms of economic organization. **Public choice analysis** has significantly advanced our understanding of the collective decision-making process in recent years. Something of a cross between economics and political science, public choice theory applies the principles and methodology of economics to collective choices.

In addition to their market choices, individual voters, politicans, lobbyists, and bureaucrats make "public choices" that affect many other people besides themselves. In a democratic setting, individual preferences will influence the outcome of collective decisions, just as they influence outcomes in the market. The government is *not* a supra-individual that will always make decisions in the "public interest," however that nebulous term might be defined. It is instead an institution through which individuals collectively make decisions and carry out activities.

Public choice theory postulates that individual behavior in the political arena will be motivated by considerations similar to those that influence market behavior. If self-interest is a powerful motivator in the marketplace, there is every reason to believe it will also be a motivating factor when choices are made collectively. If market choices are influenced by changes in projected personal costs relative to benefits, there is every reason to expect that such changes will also influence political choices. Public choice theory, in other words, suggests that the number of saints and sinners in the two sectors will be comparable.

In analyzing the behavior of people in the marketplace, economists develop a logically consistent theory of behavior that can be tested against reality. Through theory and empirical testing, we seek to explain various economic actions of decision-makers and, in general, how the market operates.

In the public sphere, our purpose should be the same: to explain how the collective decision-making process really operates. This means developing a logically consistent theory linking individual behavior to collective action, analyzing the implications of that theory, and testing these implications against events in the real world.

Since the theory of collective decision-making is not as well developed as our theory of market behavior, our conclusions will, of course, be less definitive. In the last 25 years, however, social scientists have made great strides in our understanding of resource allocation by the public sector.[1] Currently, this subject is often dealt with at a more advanced academic level. Even on an introductory level, though, economic tools can be used to shed light on how the public sector handles economic activities.

Public Choice Analysis: The study of decision-making as it affects the formation and operation of collective organizations, such as governments. The discipline bridges the gap between economics and political science. In general, the principles and methodology of economics are applied to political science topics.

---

[1] The contributions of Kenneth Arrow, James Buchanan, Duncan Black, Anthony Downs, Mancur Olson, and Gordon Tullock have been particularly important.

DIFFERENCES
AND SIMILARITIES
BETWEEN MARKET
AND COLLECTIVE
ACTION

There are some basic characteristics that influence outcomes in both the market and the public sectors.[2] As we have noted, there is reason to believe that the motivational factors present in both sectors are similar. There are, however, basic structural differences. Voluntary exchange coordinated by prices is the dominant characteristic of a market economy (although, of course, when externalities are present, involuntary exchange may also result). In a democratic setting, the dominant characteristic of collective action is majority rule, effective either directly or through legislative procedures. Let us take a look at both the differences and similarities between the two sectors.

1. Competitive Behavior Is Present in Both the Market and Public Sectors. Although the market sector is sometimes referred to as "the competitive sector," it is clear that competitive behavior is present in both sectors. Politicians compete with each other for elective office. Bureau chiefs

---

[2]The "Public Choice" section of this book analyzes the topics of alternative forms of economic organization—market versus collective action—in more detail.

APPLICATIONS IN ECONOMICS

Perspectives on The Cost of Political Competition

We all have our own ideas concerning how government should be run. Since government is such an extremely important force in our economy and in our lives, individuals and groups try to influence election outcomes by voting, by contributing to political campaigns, and by ringing doorbells, among other activities. In addition, legislative and executive branch decisions can be influenced directly, by lobbying.

Competition for elective office is fierce, and campaigns are expensive. For example, in 1982, the average candidate spent $1,782,000 in U.S. Senate races; House candidates spent $228,000, on average. Unlike bidders in a market auction, winners and loser alike pay the full costs of the election bid. It is common for lobbying groups to donate to opposing candidates in a close race.

During and after the election, lobbying groups compete for the attention—the ear—of elected officials. In fact, the greatest portion of campaign funds raised by incumbents is not raised at election time; rather, it accrues over their entire term in office. A large campaign contribution may not be able to "buy" a vote, but it certainly enhances the lobbyist's chance to sit down with the elected official to explain the power and the beauty of a client's position. In the competitive world of politics, the politician who does not at least listen to helpful "friends of the campaign" is less likely to survive.

Campaign contributions are only the tip of the lobbying iceberg. In Washington, D.C. alone, thousands of offices and tens of thousands of individuals, many of them extremely talented, hard-working, and well-paid, are dedicated to lobbying Congress and the executive branch of the federal government.

Trade associations, for example, have more than 3,000 offices and 80,000 employees in Washington.[3] Another indicator of the enormous amount of time and effort allocated to influencing government is that 65 percent of Fortune 200 Chief Executive Officers travel to Washington at least every two weeks, on average. Billions of dollars in budgets, in taxes, and in expenditures required by regulation are at stake, in addition to such emotional issues as gun control and abortion. The natural result is huge expenditures designed to influence governmental policy.

---

[3]More details on campaign finance can be found in Norman Ornstein *et al.*, *Vital Statistics on Congress*, 1984–85 Edition, (Washington, D.C.: American Enterprise Institute for Public Policy Research, 1984). See also David Boaz, "Spend Money to Make Money," *Wall Street Journal*, November 13, 1983.

and agency heads compete for additional taxpayer dollars. Public-sector employees, like their counterparts in the private sector, compete for promotions, higher incomes, and additional power. Lobbyists compete to secure funds, to receive favorable rulings, and to secure legislation for the interest groups they represent—including both private and governmental clients. (See boxed feature.) The nature of the competition and the criteria for success do differ between the two sectors. Nevertheless, both sectors must confront the reality of scarcity, and therefore the necessity of a rationing mechanism. Competitive behavior is an outgrowth of the need to ration scarce goods and resources.

2. Public-Sector Organization Can Break the Individual Consumption-Payment Link. In the market, a consumer who wants to obtain a commodity must be willing to pay the price. For each person, there is a one-to-one correspondence between consuming the commodity and paying the purchase price. In this respect, there is a fundamental difference between market and collective action. The government usually does not establish a one-to-one relationship between the tax bill of an individual consumer and the amount of political goods that the individual consumes.

Political Good: **Any good (or policy) supplied by the political process.**

Your tax bill will be the same whether you like or dislike the national defense, agriculture, or antipoverty policies of the government. You will be taxed for subsidies to higher education, sugarbeet growers, airlines, cultural centers, and many other **political goods**[4] regardless of whether or not you consume or use them. In some cases, you may receive very large benefits (either monetary or subjective) from a governmental action without any significant impact on your tax bill. The direct link between individual consumption of the good and individual payment for the good is not required in the public sector.

3. Scarcity Imposes the Aggregate Consumption-Payment Link in Both Sectors. Although the government can break the link between an individual's payment for a good and the right to consume the good, the reality of the *aggregate consumption-aggregate payment* link will remain. Provision of scarce goods requires sacrificing alternatives. Someone must cover the cost of providing scarce goods, regardless of the sector used to produce (or distribute) them. There are no free lunches in either the private or the public sector. Free goods provided in the public sector are "free" only to individuals. They are most certainly not free from the viewpoint of society. Taxpayers must pay for goods the government chooses to distribute free to individual consumers.

An increase in the amount of goods provided by the public sector will mean an increase in the total costs of government. More political goods will mean more taxes, either now or later. Given the fact of scarcity, the link between aggregate consumption and aggregate costs of production cannot be broken by public-sector action.

---

[4]"Political good" is a broad term used to designate any action supplied through the public sector. Note that political goods may be either private goods or public goods.

4. The Element of Compulsion is Present in the Public Sector. As we have already discussed, voluntary exchange is the dominant characteristic of market organization. Except when externalities are present, involuntary exchange is absent. In the marketplace, a minority need not yield to the majority. For example, the views of the majority, even an overwhelming majority, do not prevent minority consumers from purchasing desired goods.

Governments possess an exclusive right to the use of coercion. Large corporations like Exxon and General Motors are economically powerful, but they cannot require you to buy their products. In contrast, if the majority (either directly or through legislative process) decides on a particular policy, the minority must accept the policy and help pay for its cost, even if that minority strongly disagrees. If representative legislative policy allocates $10 billion for the development of a superweapon system, the dissenting minority is required to pay taxes that will help finance the project. Other dissenting minorities will be compelled to pay taxes for the support of welfare programs, farm subsidies, foreign aid, or hundreds of other projects on which reasonable people will surely differ. When issues are decided in the public sector, dissidents must, at least temporarily, yield to the current dominant view.

The right to compel is sometimes needed to promote social cooperation. For example, legislation compelling individuals to stop when the traffic light turns red or to drive on the right side of the road clearly enhances the safety of all. Thus, it will sometimes be possible to increase social cooperativeness and even expand the available options by public-sector actions or policies that place some limitation on our choices.

5. When Collective Decisions Are Made Legislatively, Voters Must Choose Among Candidates Who Represent a Bundle of Positions on Issues. On election day, the voter cannot choose the views of Representative Free Lunch on poverty and business welfare and simultaneously choose the views of challenger Ms. Austerity on national defense and tariffs. Inability to separate a candidate's views on one issue from his or her views on another greatly reduces the voter's power to register preferences on specific issues. Since the average representative is asked to vote on roughly 2,000 different issues during a two-year term, the enormity of the problem is obvious.

To the average individual, choosing a representative is a bit like choosing an agent who will control a substantial portion of one's income and also regulate one's activities. Even if this individual voter could personally elect the agent, it would be impossible for the voter to select one agent's views on issue X and another agent's views on issue Y. As a result of the "bundle-purchase" nature of the political process, the likelihood that a collective decision will reflect the precise views of an individual voter is low.

6. Income and Power Are Distributed Differently in the Two Sectors. Individuals who supply more highly valued resources in the marketplace have larger incomes. The number of dollar votes available to an individual reflect her or his abilities, ambitions, skills, perceptiveness, past savings, inheritance, and good fortune, among other things. An unequal distribution of consumer power is the result.

In the public sector, ballots call the tune when decisions are made democratically. One citizen, one vote is the rule. This does not mean, however, that political goods and services—those resources that make up political power or political income—are allocated equally to all citizens by the collective decision-making process. Some individuals are much more astute than others at using the political process to obtain personal advantage. The political process rewards those who are most capable of delivering votes—not only their own individual votes but those of others as well. Persuasive skills (i.e., lobbying, public speaking, public relations), organizational abilities, financial contributions, and knowledge are vital to success in politics. Persons who have more of these resources—and are willing to spend them in the political arena—can expect to benefit more handsomely, in terms of both money and power, from the political process than individuals who lack them.

THE SUPPLY OF AND DEMAND FOR PUBLIC-SECTOR ACTION

Consumers use their dollar votes to demand goods in the marketplace. Producers supply goods. The actions of both are influenced by self-interest. In a democratic political system, voters and legislators are counterparts to consumers and producers. Voters demand political goods using their political resources—votes, lobbying, contributions, and organizational abilities. Vote-conscious legislators are suppliers of political goods.

How does a voter decide which political supplier to support? Many things influence the voter's decision, but self-interest surely must be high on the list. Will the policies of Senator Snodgrass or those of the challenger, Mr. Good Deal, help me most? Where do they stand on the major issues? What are their views on those issues that may seem unimportant to others but are of vital importance to me? Are they likely to raise or lower my taxes? All of these factors influence the voter's personal benefits and costs from public-sector action. Economic theory suggests that they also influence how voters choose among the candidates.

Other things constant, voters will support those candidates whom they expect to provide them with the most benefits, net of cost. The greater the expected gains from a candidate's election, the more voters will do to ensure the candidate's success. A voter, like the consumer in the marketplace, will ask the supplier, "What can you do for me and how much will I pay?"

The goal of the political supplier is to put together a majority coalition—to win the election. Vote-seeking politicians, like profit-seeking business decision-makers, will have a strong incentive to cater to the views of politically active constituents. The easiest way to win votes, both politically and financially, is to give the constituents, or at least appear to give them, what they want. A politician who pays no heed to the views of his or her constituents is as rare as a businessperson selling bikinis in the Arctic.

There are two major reasons that voters are likely to turn to public-sector economic organization: (a) to reduce waste and inefficiency stemming from noncompetitive markets, externalities, public goods, and economic instability and (b) to redistribute income. Public-sector action that corrects, or appears to correct, the shortcomings of the market will be attractive. If properly conducted, it will generate more benefits than costs to the community. Much real-world public policy is motivated by a desire to correct the shortcomings of the market. Antitrust action is designed to promote competition. Government provision of national defense, crime prevention, a legal system, and flood-control projects is related to the public-good nature of these activities. Similarly, externalities account for public-sector action in such areas as pollution control, education, pure research, and no-fault insurance. Clearly, the tax, spending, and monetary policies of the government are used to influence the level of economic activity in most Western nations.

Demand for public-sector action may also stem from a desire to change the income distribution. There is no reason to presume that the unhampered market will lead to the most desirable distribution of income. In fact, the ideal distribution of income is largely a matter of personal preference. There is nothing in positive economics that tells us that one distribution of income is better than another. Some people may desire to see more income allocated to low-income citizens. The most common scientific argument for redistribution to the poor is based on the "public-good" nature of adequate income for all. Alleviation of poverty may help not only the poor but also those who are well-off. Middle- and upper-income recipients, for example, may benefit if the less fortunate members of the community enjoy better food, clothing, housing, and health care. If the rich would gain, why will they not voluntarily give to the poor? For the same reason that individuals will do little to provide national defense voluntarily. The antipoverty efforts of any single individual will exert little impact on the total amount of poverty in the community. Because individual action is so insignificant, each person has an incentive to opt out. When everyone opts out, the market provides less than the desired amount of antipoverty action.

Others may desire public-sector redistribution for less altruistic reasons—they may seek to enhance their own personal incomes. Sometimes redistribution will take the form of direct income transfers. In other cases, the redistribution strategy may be indirect; it may simply increase the demand for one's service. Regardless of the mechanism, higher taxes will generally accompany income redistribution.

Substantial income redistribution may adversely affect the efficiency of resource allocation and the incentive to produce. There are three major reasons why large-scale redistribution is likely to reduce the size of the economic pie.

First, such redistribution weakens the link between productive activity and reward. When taxes take a larger share of one's income, tax revenues are spread among all beneficiaries, so the benefits derived from hard work and productive service are reduced. The basic economic postulate suggests that when benefits allocated to producers are reduced (and benefits of nonproducers are raised), less productive effort will be supplied.

Second, as public policy redistributes a larger share of income, individuals will allocate more resources to **rent seeking**.[5] Rent seeking is a term used by economists to classify actions designed to change public policy—tax structure, composition of spending, or regulation—in a manner that will redistribute income to oneself. Resources used for lobbying and other

Rent Seeking: Actions by individuals and interest groups designed to restructure public policy in a manner that will either directly or indirectly redistribute more income to themselves.

---

[5]See James M. Buchanan, Robert D. Tollison, and Gordon Tullock, *Toward a Theory of the Rent-Seeking Society* (College Station: Texas A & M University Press, 1981), for additional detail on rent seeking.

means of rent seeking (perhaps "favor seeking" would be more descriptive) will not be available to increase the size of the economic pie.

Third, higher taxes to finance income redistribution and an expansion in rent-seeking activities will generate a response. Taxpayers will be encouraged to take steps to protect their income. More accountants, lawyers, and tax-shelter experts will be retained as people seek to limit the amount of their income that is redistributed to others. Like the resources allocated to rent seeking, resources allocated to protecting one's wealth from public policy will also be wasted. They will not be available for productive activity. Therefore, given the incentive structure generated by large-scale redistribution policies, there is good reason to expect that such policies will reduce the size of the economic pie.

CONFLICTS BETWEEN GOOD ECONOMICS AND GOOD POLITICS

What reason is there to believe that political action will result in economic inefficiency? Current economic and political research is continually yielding knowledge that will help us answer this question more definitively. We deal with it in more detail in a later chapter, but three important characteristics of the political process are introduced here.

THE RATIONALLY IGNORANT VOTER

Less than one half of the American electorate can correctly identify the names of their congressmen and women, much less state where their representatives stand on various issues. Why are so many people ignorant of the simplest facts regarding the political process? The explanation does not lie with a lack of intelligence on the part of the average American. The phenomenon is explained by the incentives confronting the voter. Most citizens recognize that their vote is unlikely to determine the outcome of an election. Since their vote is highly unlikely to resolve the issue at hand, citizens have little incentive to seek costly information that will help them cast an intelligent vote. Economist refer to this lack of incentive as the **rational ignorance effect**.

Rational Ignorance Effect: Voter ignorance that is present because people perceive their individual votes as unlikely to be decisive. Voters rationally have little incentive to inform themselves so as to cast an informed vote.

The rationally ignorant voter is merely exercising good judgment as to how his or her time and effort will yield the most benefits. There is a parallel between the voter's failure to acquire political knowledge and the farmer's inattention to the factors that determine the weather. Weather is probably the most important factor determining the income of an individual farmer, yet it makes no sense for the farmer to invest time and resources attempting to understand atmospheric science. An improved knowledge of how weather systems work will seldom enable the farmer to avoid their adverse effects. So it is with the average voter. The voter stands to gain little from acquiring more information about a wide range of issues that are decided in the political arena. Since the resolution of these issues, like the weather, is out of the individual voter's hands, he or she has little incentive to become more informed.

Because of this fact, most voters simply rely on information that is supplied to them freely by candidates and the mass media. Conversations with friends and information acquired at work, from newspapers, from TV news, and from political advertising are especially important because the voter has so little incentive to spend personal time and effort gathering information. It is not surprising, then, that few voters are able to accurately describe the consequences of raising tariffs on automobiles or of abolishing the farm price support program. In using their time and efforts in ways other than studying these policy issues, voters are merely responding to economic incentives.

THE PROBLEM OF SPECIAL INTEREST

Special Interest Issue: An issue that generates substantial individual benefits to a small minority while imposing a small individual cost on many other voters. In total, the net cost to the majority might either exceed or fall short of the net benefits to the special interest group.

A **special interest issue** is one that generates substantial personal benefits for a small number of constituents while imposing a small individual cost on a large number of other voters. A few gain a great deal individually, whereas a large number lose a little as individuals.

Special interest issues are very attractive to vote-conscious politicians (that is, to those most eager and most likely to win elections). Voters who have a small cost imposed on them by a policy favoring a special interest will not care enough about the issue to examine it, particularly if it is complex enough that the imposition of the cost is difficult to identify. Because information is costly, most of those harmed will not even be aware of the legislator's views on such an issue. Most voters will simply ignore special interest issues. Those representing the special interest, though, will be vitally concerned. They will let the candidate (or legislator) know how important an issue is to them. They will give financial and other help to politicians receptive to their ideas, and will oppose those who are not.

What would you do if you wanted to win an election? Support the special interest groups. Milk them for financial resources. Use those resources to "educate" the uninformed majority of voters to the fact that you support policies of interest to them. You would have an incentive to follow this path even if the total community benefits from the support of the special interest were less than the cost. The policy might cause economic inefficiency, but it could still be a political winner.

Why stand up for a large majority? Even though the total cost may be very large, each person bears only a small cost. Most voters are uninformed on the issue. They do not care much about it. They would do little to help you get elected even if you supported their best interests on this issue. Astute politicians will support the special interest group if they plan to be around for very long.

The political process tends to work in favor of special interest groups, even when their programs are inefficient. This means that there is sometimes a conflict between good politics (winning elections) and ideal public policy. Throughout, as we consider public policy alternatives, we will remind you to consider how public policy is likely to operate when special interest influence is strong.

POLITICAL GAINS FROM SHORT-SIGHTED POLICIES

The complexity of many issues makes it difficult for voters to identify the future benefits and costs. Will a tax cut reduce the long-run rate of unemployment? Are wage-price controls an efficient means of dealing with inflation? Can pro-union legislation raise the real wages of workers? These questions are complex. Few voters will analyze the short-run and long-run implications of policy in these areas. Instead, voters will have a tendency to

OUTSTANDING ECONOMIST

**James Buchanan
(1919–   )**

Thirty years ago, most economists were content to concentrate on the workings of the marketplace, its shortcomings, and what government action might do to correct these deficiencies. Political scientists and economists alike envisioned the public sector as a type of supra-individual, a creature making decisions in the public interest. James Buchanan was determined to change all this. He, perhaps more than anyone else, is responsible for what some have called the "public choice revolution." For this and related contributions, he was awarded the 1986 Nobel Prize in Economics.

Buchanan perceives government to be an outgrowth of individual behavior. Individual human beings are the ultimate choice-makers, shaping and molding group action as well as private affairs. By means of the tools of economics, theories are developed to explain how the political process works. Real-world data are used to test the theories. Buchanan's approach is that of scientific politics.

Noting that approximately 40 percent of every dollar earned in the United States is channeled through the public sector, Buchanan argues:

> It just doesn't make sense to concentrate, as traditional economic theory does, on the 60 percent of your income and product that's related to the private sector and to provide no explanation of why the remainder is used in the way it is. So the extension of the highly sophisticated tools of analysis that economics has developed over the past 200 years to the realm of political choices was a natural and logical one.[6]

In their widely acclaimed book, *The Calculus of Consent,*[7] Buchanan and Gordon Tullock develop a theory of constitutions and analyze political behavior under alternative decision rules (for example, simple majority, legislative procedure, and so on). Using the individual always as the foundation of the analysis, they develop theories concerning special interests, logrolling, and the types of activities that are most likely to be provided through the public sector. Empirical work testing many of the implications of the book continues today. In a more recent book, *The Limits of Liberty,*[8] which Buchanan considers complementary to the earlier book with Tullock, Buchanan applies his individualistic perspective to explain the emergence of property rights, law, and government itself.

A past president of the Southern Economic Association, Buchanan has also written widely on externalities, public goods, and public finance. He taught at Florida State, Virginia, UCLA, and Virginia Polytechnic Institute before accepting his present position as Distinguished Professor of Economics and general director of the Center for the Study of Public Choice at George Mason University.

---

[6]Quoted in Judith Scott-Epley, "From Constitutions to Car Inspections: Looking for a Better Way," *Virginia Tech Magazine* (September/October 1981), p. 230.

[7]J. M. Buchanan and G. Tullock, *The Calculus of Consent* (Ann Arbor: University of Michigan Press, 1962).

[8]J. M. Buchanan, *The Limits of Liberty* (Chicago: University of Chicago Press, 1975).

rely on current conditions. To the voter, the best indicator of the success of a policy is, "How are things now?"

Politicians seeking reelection have a strong incentive to support policies that generate current benefits in exchange for future costs, particularly if the future costs will be difficult to identify on election day. Public-sector action will therefore be biased in favor of legislation that offers immediate (and easily identifiable) current benefits in exchange for future costs that are complicated and difficult to identify. Simultaneously, there is a bias against legislation that involves immediate and easily identifiable costs (for example, higher taxes) while yielding future benefits that are complex and difficult to identify. Economists refer to this bias inherent in the collective decision-making process as the **shortsightedness effect.**

Shortsightedness Effect: Misallocation of resources that results because public-sector action is biased (a) in favor of proposals yielding clearly defined current benefits in exchange for difficult-to-identify future costs and (b) against proposals with clearly identifiable current costs yielding less concrete and less obvious future benefits.

The nature of democratic institutions restricts the planning horizon of elected officials. Positive results must be observable by the next election, or the incumbent is likely to be replaced by someone who promises more rapid results. Policies that will eventually pay off in the future (after the next election) will have little attractiveness to vote-seeking politicians if those policies do not exert a beneficial impact by election day. As we shall subsequently see, the shortsighted nature of the political process reduces the likelihood that governments will be able to promote economic stability and a noninflationary environment.

What if shortsighted policies lead to serious problems after an election? This can be sticky for politicians, but is it not better to be an officeholder explaining why things are in a mess than a defeated candidate trying to convince people who will not listen why you were right all the time? The political entrepreneur has a strong incentive to win the next election and worry about what is right later.

LOOKING AHEAD

In the next chapter, we will examine the government's actual spending and tax policies. In subsequent chapters, the significance of economic organization and issues of political economy will be highlighted. The tools of economics are used with a dual objective. We will point out what government ideally should do, but we will also focus on what government can be expected to do. Not surprisingly, these two are not always identical. Political economy—the use of economic tools to explain how both the market and the public sectors actually work—is a fascinating subject. It helps us to understand the "why" behind many of today's current events. Who said economics is the dismal science?

CHAPTER SUMMARY

1. Economic efficiency—creating as much value as possible from a given set of resources—is a goal by which alternative institutions and policies can be judged. Two conditions must be met to achieve economic efficiency: (a) all activities that produce more benefits than costs for the individuals within an economy must be undertaken and (b) activities that generate more costs than benefits to the individuals must not be undertaken. If only the buyer and the seller are affected, production and exchange in competitive markets are consistent with the ideal-efficiency criteria.

2. Lack of competition may make it possible for a group of sellers to gain by restricting output and raising prices. There is a conflict between (a) the self-interest of sellers that leads them to collude, restrict output, and raise product prices above their production costs and (b) economic efficiency. Public-sector action—promoting competition or regulating private firms—may be able to improve economic efficiency in industries in which competitive pressures are lacking.

3. The market will tend to underallocate resources to the production of goods with external benefits and overallocate resources to those products that generate external costs.

4. Public goods are troublesome for the market to handle because nonpaying customers cannot easily be excluded. Since the amount of a public good that each individual receives is largely unaffected by whether he or she helps pay for it, most individuals will contribute little. The market will thus tend to undersupply public goods.

5. The public sector can improve the operation of markets by providing a stable economic environment.

6. The public sector is an alternative means of organizing economic activity. Public-sector decision-making will reflect the choices of individuals acting as voters, politicians, financial contributors, lobbyists, and bureaucrats. Public choice analysis applies the principles and methodology of economics to group decision-making to help us understand collective organizations.

7. Successful political candidates will seek to offer programs that voters favor. Voters, in turn, will be attracted to candidates who reflect the voters' own views and interests. In a democratic setting, there are two major reasons why voters will turn to collective organization: (a) to reduce waste and inefficiency stemming from noncompetitive markets, externalities, public goods, and economic instability and (b) to alter the income distribution.

8. Public-sector action may sometimes improve the market's efficiency and lead to an increase in the community's welfare, all individuals considered. However, the political process is likely to conflict with ideal economic efficiency criteria when (a) voters have little knowledge of an issue, (b) special interests are strong and/or (c) political figures can gain from following shortsighted policies.

THE ECONOMIC WAY OF THINKING— DISCUSSION QUESTIONS

1. Explain in your own words what is meant by external costs and external benefits. Why may market allocations be less than ideal when externalities are present?

2. If producers are to be provided with an incentive to produce a good, why is it important for them to be able to prevent nonpaying customers from receiving the good?

3. Do you think real-world politicians adopt political positions to help their election prospects? Can you name a current political figure who consistently puts "principles above politics"? If so, check with three of your classmates and see if they agree.

4. Do you think special-interest groups exert much influence on local government? Why or why not? As a test, check the composition of the

local zoning board in your community. How many real estate agents, contractors, developers, and landlords are on the board? Are there any citizens without real estate interests on the board?

5. "Economics is a positive science. Government by its very nature is influenced by philosophical considerations. Therefore, the tools of economics cannot tell us much about how the public sector works." Do you agree or disagree? Why?

6. Which of the following are public goods: (a) an antimissile system surrounding Washington D.C.; (b) a fire department; (c) tennis courts; (d) Yellowstone National Park; (e) elementary schools?

7. "Political organization cannot reform human beings. We should not expect it to. The public sector is an alternative to the market. Political organization will influence the direction of human action primarily by modifying the incentive structure. For some types of activity, public-sector organization is likely to improve on the market, and for others, the market is likely to be superior." Do you agree or disagree? Why?

- How big is government? What goods and services do we provide through government?

- Why has the size of government grown more rapidly than our economy during the last several decades? Does government now provide more goods and services than it did in the past? Does it redistribute more income?

- What is the difference among progressive, regressive, and proportional tax structures? Is the U.S. tax structure progressive?

- How do taxes influence the choices of taxpayers? If a tax rate is increased by 10 percent, will revenue from the tax increase by 10 percent?

- How does the size of government in the United States compare with the size of government in other countries?

Our Constitution is in actual operation; everything appears to promise that it will last; but in this world nothing is certain but death and taxes.

BENJAMIN FRANKLIN
(1789)

5 GOVERNMENT SPENDING AND TAXATION

Whether the setting is the halls of Congress, the classroom, or a social gathering, a discussion of the economic role of government generally means controversy. Governments levy taxes and organize the production of goods and services. The role of government in the economy, though, is not limited to its taxation and spending activities. Governments set the rules of the game. Public policy defines property rights, enforces contracts, regulates business activities, and establishes a monetary framework. These legal and regulatory activities influence how markets work and the degree of cooperation and conflict among economic participants. In fact, the role of government as the rule-maker and referee probably exerts more influence on the economic prosperity of a nation than does its function as a producer of goods and services. Nevertheless, taxation and government expenditures are the most direct means by which the government influences the economy. Analysis of the government's taxation and spending policies will reveal a great deal about the size and economic character of government.

THE GROWTH OF GOVERNMENT

Federal, state, and local government expenditures generally amounted to less than 10 percent of gross national product (GNP) in the United States prior to the 1930s.[1] As Exhibit 1 illustrates, since 1930, the size of government has increased substantially relative to the size of the economy. In the midst of the defense effort during World War II, government expenditures

EXHIBIT 1 • The Growth of Governmental Expenditures, 1902–1985

Between 1902 and 1929, governmental spending rose from 7.7 percent to 10 percent of total output. Since 1930, governmental expenditures have increased substantially as a proportion of total output. In 1985, governmental spending summed to 35 percent of total output. Federal spending alone accounts for 24.6 percent of the total output in the United States.

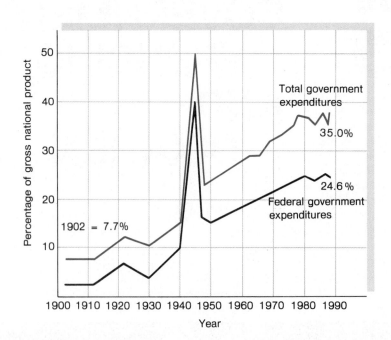

---

[1]The gross national product (GNP) is discussed in detail in Chapter 6. For now, it can be thought of as a measure of total output produced during a period.

consumed more than 50 percent of total output. At the conclusion of the war, however, they dropped back to only about 20 percent of GNP. Since the late 1940s, both the relative and absolute size of government have expanded substantially. By 1975, 34.5 percent of our total output was channelled through government, up sharply from the 21.3 percent in 1950. During the last decade, the upward trend in the size of government as a share of the economy has slowed. In fact, total government expenditures as a proportion of GNP were approximately the same in 1985 as they were in 1975.

During the 1930–1950 period, federal expenditures were the primary source of governmental growth. In recent decades, federal expenditures have generally accounted for about two thirds of the total spending by governments. State and local government spending have also expanded significantly since World War II. In 1985, state and local expenditures accounted for 10 percent of GNP, up from 2.5 percent in the late 1940s.

WHAT DO FEDERAL, STATE, AND LOCAL GOVERNMENTS DO?

The responsibilities of the three levels of government in the United States differ considerably. A breakdown of expenditures and taxes will highlight some of these differences.

Most government spending, more than two thirds of the total, takes place at the federal level. Exhibit 2 shows the broad categories of federal

EXHIBIT 2 • How the Federal Government Spends Your Tax Dollar

The breakdown of the 1985 fiscal year federal budget is presented here. Defense accounted for 30.9 percent of federal spending. Approximately 50 percent of the federal tax dollar was spent on cash income maintenance, helping people buy essentials, and manpower development.

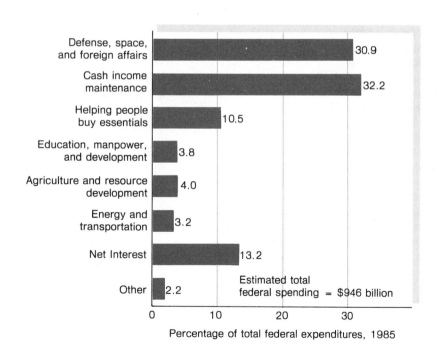

Source: *Economic Report of the President, 1986.*

expenditures for fiscal year 1985. The federal government is solely responsible for national defense. A little less than one third of federal expenditures went for defense and related areas (space, veterans' benefits, and foreign affairs) in 1985. The largest item in the federal budget was cash income maintenance—social security, unemployment payments, and public assistance to the poor and the disabled. These income transfers accounted for 32.2 percent of the total federal budget. Programs to help people buy essentials (medical care, housing, food, and so on) made up 10.5 percent of all federal spending in 1985. This category differs from cash income maintenance in that people must purchase specific goods in order to qualify for the assistance. Expenditures on education, manpower development, agriculture, energy, and transportation also constitute major items in the federal budget from year to year. Interest payments on the national debt for 1985 constituted 13.2 percent of total federal outlays.

Exhibit 3 is a graphic presentation of state and local government expenditures. In the United States, public education has traditionally been the responsibility of state and local governments. Twenty-nine percent of state and local governmental expenditures were allocated to education during the fiscal year 1984. State governments supplement federal allocations in the areas of social welfare, public welfare, and health. These social welfare expenditures composed 18 percent of the total spending of state governments during 1984. Highways, utilities, insurance trusts, law enforcement, and fire protection are other major areas of expenditure for state and local governments.

EXHIBIT 3 • What State and Local Governments Buy

Education, public welfare, and general administrative expenditures comprise the major budget items of state and local governments.

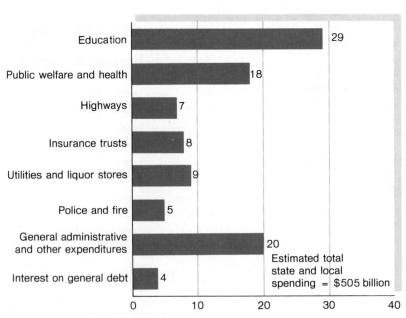

Percentage of state and local expenditures, fiscal year 1984

Source: U.S. Department of Commerce.

GOVERNMENT PURCHASES AND TRANSFER PAYMENTS

Government Purchases: Current expenditures on goods and services provided by federal, state, and local governments; it excludes transfer payments.

Transfer Payments: Payments to individuals or institutions that are not linked to the current supply of a good or service by the recipient.

It is important to distinguish between (a) government purchases of goods and services and (b) transfer payments. **Government purchases** are expenditures incurred when goods and services are supplied through the public sector. Government purchases include items such as jet planes, missiles, highway construction and maintenance, police and fire protection, and computer equipment. Governments also purchase the labor services of teachers, clerks, lawyers, accountants, and public relation experts to produce goods ranging from public education to administrative services. Since they consume resources with alternative uses, government purchases directly reduce the supply of resources available to produce private goods and services.

Transfer payments are transfers of income from taxpayers to recipients who do not provide current goods and services in exchange for these payments. Simply put, transfer payments tax income from some to provide additional income to others. Social security benefits, pensions of retired government employees, and Aid to Families with Dependent Children (AFDC) are examples of transfer payments.

Unlike government purchases, transfer payments do not *directly* reduce the resources available to the private sector. They do, however, alter the incentive structure of the economy and almost certainly exert an indirect impact on the size of the economic pie. The taxes necessary to finance transfer payments reduce the personal payoff from saving, investing, and working. If receipt of transfer payments is inversely related to income level, they will also reduce the recipient's incentive to earn taxable income. As we proceed, we will investigate the link between aggregate output and the incentive structure in more detail.

ALTERNATIVE MEASURES OF GOVERNMENT'S SIZE

Exhibit 4 presents four alternative measures of governmental size. In 1985, the purchases of federal, state, and local governments amounted to $814.6 billion, or 20.4 percent of total U.S. output. Government purchases thus consumed a little more than one fifth of our resources. Government em-

---

EXHIBIT 4 • Four Measures of the Size of Government (Federal, State and Local), 1985

1. Government purchases of goods and services	a) Billions of dollars	814.6
	b) Percentage of GNP	20.4
2. Government employment[a]	a) Millions of employees	16.0
	b) Percentage of total employment	14.8
3. Total government expenditures including transfer payments	a) Billions of dollars	1,401.2
	b) Percentage of GNP	35.0
4. Total taxes and other revenues	a) Billions of dollars	1,262.2
	b) Percentage of GNP	31.6

[a]Data are for February 1985.

Facts and Figures on Government Finance—1985 and *The Economic Report of the President, 1986* (Washington, D.C.: U.S. Government Printing Office, 1986). Intergovernmental transfer payments (i.e., federal grants to state and local governments) are not counted twice.

ployment offers a second gauge by which we can measure the size of government. In 1985, approximately one out of every seven workers (14.8 percent) was employed by a governmental unit.

As we have already pointed out, government purchases fail to tell the whole story. Governments not only employ people and provide goods and services, they also tax the income of some and transfer it to others. Once transfer payments are included (the third measure of size), total government expenditures in 1985 amounted to $1,401.2 billion, or 35.0 percent of the gross national product (GNP).[2] The total tax bill (the fourth measure of size) was slightly less, amounting to 31.6 percent of GNP. Therefore, during 1985, approximately one third of the national output was channeled through the public sector.

On a per capita basis, government expenditures were equal to $5,870 in 1985. If government expenditures in 1985 had been divided equally among the 88 million households in the United States, each household would have received $15,900.

THE CHANGING COMPOSITION OF GOVERNMENT

The federal government has traditionally been responsible for national defense in the United States. Since defense is a classic example of a public good, it is not surprising that this good is supplied through the public rather than through the private sector. Police and fire protection, road maintenance, and education have traditionally been financed and distributed by state and local governments. Each of these goods either generates external "spillover effects" or exhibits public-good characteristics. The police and fire departments available to help protect my life and property are also available for your protection. At least until congestion becomes a problem, my use of the roadways does not diminish their availability to you. Education contributes to the feasibility of a modern democratic society, thereby generating a benefit to persons other than those educated.

For many years, government has been involved in the provision of national defense, police and fire protection, roads, education, and other jointly consumed goods and services. Given the characteristics of such goods, government involvement in these areas is not surprising. Interestingly, these traditional public-sector functions are not responsible for the growth of government in recent years. As Exhibit 5a illustrates, government purchases of goods and services have fluctuated within a narrow band, around 20 percent of GNP, during the last three decades. Surprising perhaps to some, *federal* purchases of goods and services as a percent of GNP declined throughout much of the 1955–1985 period. As Exhibit 5a shows, federal purchases of goods and services as a share of GNP were 8.0 percent in 1985, down from 11.1 percent in 1955.

The expansion in the relative size of the public sector during the last three decades is almost exclusively the result of increased governmental

---

[2]The public administration costs associated with income transfer programs do involve the direct use of resources and they therefore are counted as government purchases. Only the redistribution portion is counted as a transfer payment.

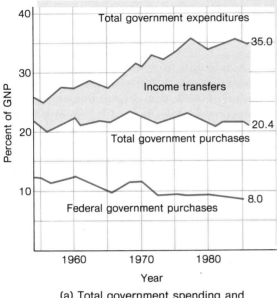

(a) Total government spending and
income transfers as a
share of GNP

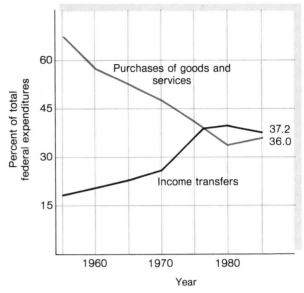

(b) Government purchases and transfers
as a share of the federal
budget

EXHIBIT 5 • Government Purchases, Transfer Payments, and the Changing Function of Government

State, local, and federal purchases of goods and services have accounted for approximately 20 percent of total output throughout the last three decades (frame a). The growth of transfer payments have accounted for the growth in the relative size of the public sector during this period. Frame b shows how government purchases and transfer payments have changed as a share of federal spending during the last three decades. Clearly, the federal government now plays a larger role as a redistributor of income and a smaller role as a producer of goods and services.

involvement in redistributive activities. The government has emerged as a major redistributor of income from one group to another—from the working population to retirees, from the employed to the unemployed, from the taxpayer to disadvantaged groups (such as female-headed households with dependent children). In 1955, income transfers were 4.5 percent of the GNP. By the mid-1970s, the government was redistributing more than 10 percent of total output away from current producers to income-transfer recipients.

Most of the expansion in the size of the transfer sector has taken place at the federal level. As a result, there has been a major change in the composition of activities undertaken by the federal government. Exhibit 5b illustrates this point. In 1985, only one third of all federal expenditures were for the purchase of goods and services, down from two thirds in 1955. On the other hand, income transfers consumed 37 percent of the federal budget in 1985, compared to less than 20 percent in 1955. It is clear that the federal government is now more heavily involved in income-redistribution activities than it is in the provision of public-sector goods and services.

TAXES TO PAY FOR A GROWING GOVERNMENT

When the government spends money and uses resources, costs are incurred. The money to cover the costs of government is collected in the form of taxes. As Exhibit 6 shows, most tax revenue comes from five sources: (a) personal income taxes, (b) payroll taxes, (c) sales taxes, (d) property taxes, and (e) corporate income taxes. Let us take a closer look at each of these major sources of tax revenue.

PERSONAL INCOME TAXES

Progressive Tax: A tax that requires those with higher taxable incomes to pay a larger percentage of their incomes to the government than those with lower taxable incomes.

Average Tax Rate: One's tax liability divided by one's taxable income.

Approximately 38 percent of the total tax dollars are raised via the personal income tax. This tax is particularly important at the federal level, where it accounts for 45 percent of the total budget receipts (Exhibit 6). Since World War II, the income tax has also become an important source of revenue at the state level, where it now accounts for almost one fifth of the tax receipts collected by the states. Only six states (Florida, Nevada, South Dakota, Texas, Washington, and Wyoming) now fail to levy a state income tax.

A distinctive characteristic of the federal income tax is its progressive structure. A **progressive tax** takes a larger percentage from high-income recipients. For example, using the rate structure applicable to income in 1986, the tax liability of a married couple with $10,000 of taxable income is $819. The **average tax rate** (ATR) can be expressed as follows:

$$\text{ATR} = \frac{\text{tax liability}}{\text{taxable income}}$$

The couple's average rate on $10,000 of income is 8.19 percent ($819/$10,000). Since the federal income tax structure is progressive, the average tax rate will increase with taxable income. For example, the tax liability (1986) of a couple with a taxable income of $20,000 is $2,461, resulting in an average tax rate of 12.3 percent, higher than the ATR for $10,000 of taxable income.

The economic way of thinking stresses that what happens at the margin is of crucial importance in personal decision-making. The **marginal tax rate** (MTR) can be expressed as follows:

Marginal Tax Rate: Additional tax liability divided by additional income. Thus, if $100 of additional earnings increases one's tax liability by $30, the marginal tax rate would be 30 percent.

$$\text{MTR} = \frac{\text{change in tax liability}}{\text{change in income}}$$

The marginal tax rate reveals both how much of one's additional income can be retained and how much must be turned over to the tax collector. For example, when the marginal tax rate is 25 percent, $25 of every $100 of additional earnings must be paid to the taxing authority. The individual is permitted to keep $75 of his or her additional income.

Under the progressive tax structure of the United States, taxpayers with larger taxable incomes pay higher marginal tax rates. Prior to 1981, the marginal tax rates on taxable income ranged from 14 percent in the lowest income bracket to 70 percent in the highest income bracket. However, 1981 tax legislation reduced the marginal tax rate in each income bracket by approximately 23 percent. Simultaneously, the top marginal tax rate was

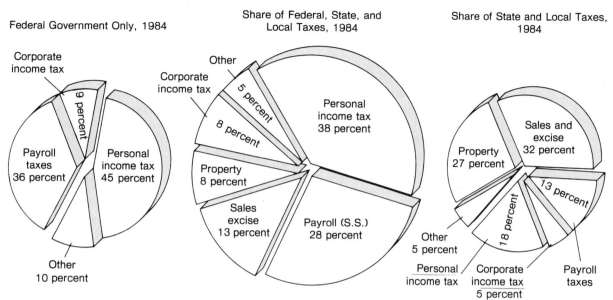

Federal Government Only, 1984

Share of Federal, State, and Local Taxes, 1984

Share of State and Local Taxes, 1984

Source: U.S. Office of Management and Budget and U.S. Department of Commerce.

EXHIBIT 6 • Paying for Government

Personal income, payroll, and corporate income taxes are the major sources of tax revenues for the federal government. Sales and property taxes are the major sources of state and local revenues.

Indexing: The automatic increasing of money values as the general level of prices increases. Economic variables that are often indexed include wage rates and tax brackets.

reduced from 70 percent to 50 percent. As we go to press in late 1986, Congress is again contemplating major tax reform.

As both money incomes and prices rose during the 1970s, many Americans were pushed into higher and higher income tax brackets even though the purchasing power of their incomes changed very little. In order to keep inflation from automatically pushing up tax rates, the 1981 legislation indexed the personal income tax structure. **Indexing** adjusts money income figures for the effects of inflation. With indexing, tax brackets are widened to compensate for the inflation-induced component of a rising money income.

Perhaps an example will help clarify how indexing works. Suppose a marginal tax rate of 10 percent is applied to the initial income bracket of $0 to $5,000, and suppose also that higher marginal tax rates are applicable at higher levels of income. In the absence of indexing, taxpayers whose incomes merely keep pace with inflation are pushed into higher tax brackets. For example, if a 10 percent inflation rate expands the taxable income of a worker from $5,000 to $5,500, it pushes that taxpayer into a higher tax bracket. Both the taxpayer's average and marginal tax rates are increased even though the expansion in income merely reflects the general rise in prices. Indexing widens the tax brackets for the effects of inflation and thereby keeps inflation from pushing taxpayers with incomes of constant purchasing power into higher tax brackets. With indexing, the $0–$5,000 income bracket would be expanded to $0–$5,500 when prices increase by 10 percent. So, when inflation increases the income of a taxpayer by 10 percent, the taxpayer's average and marginal tax rates remain constant. Indexing thus protects individuals from unlegislated tax increases that, under a progressive tax system, would otherwise be automatically imposed by inflation.

PAYROLL TAXES

Although income from all sources is covered by the income tax, only earnings derived from labor are subject to the payroll tax. Interest, dividends, rents, and other income derived from capital are not subject to payroll taxes. Payroll taxes on the earnings of employees and self-employed workers are used to finance social security (including Medicare) and unemployment compensation benefits. Payroll taxes constitute the second largest and most rapidly expanding source of tax revenue. As of 1984, 28 percent of all tax revenues originated from payroll taxes. In 1984, payroll taxes comprised 36 percent of all federal revenues, compared to only 16 percent in 1960.

    Payroll taxes are often criticized because of their regressive structure. Actually, the payroll tax encompasses proportional and regressive features. A **proportional tax** is one that takes the same percentage of income from all taxpayers, regardless of income level. Until the maximum taxable income ceiling is reached, the payroll tax is proportional. For example, in 1987, each employee pays a tax rate of 7.15 percent on earnings up to $42,600. Beyond that taxable income ceiling, no additional payroll tax is levied. So, a worker earning $10,000 incurs a payroll tax of $715, whereas one earning $20,000 is taxed twice that amount, or $1,430. Until the taxable income ceiling is met, all workers pay exactly the same tax rate.

    A **regressive tax** takes a smaller *percentage* of income from those in high earnings brackets than it does from low-income recipients. Since the social security payroll tax does not apply beyond the maximum income ceiling, it is regressive for incomes beyond that point. For example, a person with an income twice the taxable ceiling will pay exactly the same amount of payroll taxes (and only one half the average tax rate) as another individual whose earnings are equal to the taxable ceiling. All people with earnings above the taxable ceiling will pay a lower average tax rate than people with earnings below the ceiling. Thus, since the payroll tax does not apply to earnings above the ceiling, its basic structure can be considered regressive.

Proportional Tax: A tax for which individuals pay the same percentage of their income (or other tax base) in taxes, regardless of income level.

Regressive Tax: A tax that takes a smaller percentage of one's income as one's income level increases. Thus, the proportion of income allocated to the tax would be greater for the poor than for the rich.

SALES AND EXCISE TAXES

Taxes levied on the consumption expenditures for a wide range of goods and services are called sales taxes. A tax levied on specific commodities, such as gasoline, cigarettes, or alcoholic beverages, is called an excise tax. There is little difference between the two, except that one is a general tax and the other is quite specific.

    The sales tax provides the backbone for tax revenues at the state level. In 1984, 32 percent of all state tax revenues originated from this source. Even though the federal government does not levy a general sales tax, this tax still constitutes 13 percent of total tax revenue of government at all levels (Exhibit 6).

PROPERTY TAXES

Despite their unpopularity, property taxes still constitute the bulk of local tax revenues. In 1984, 76 percent of all tax revenue was generated from this source. Property taxes are often criticized because they are cumbersome. The assessor must set a value on taxable property. This generally involves a certain amount of judgment and arbitrariness. During a period of rising prices, property that has recently been exchanged is likely to command a higher valuation than similar property without an easily identifiable indicator of current value. High administration costs and problems associated with providing equal treatment for similarly situated taxpayers reduce the attractiveness of property taxes. Despite their declining importance, property taxes still constitute 8 percent of all public-sector revenues, an amount approximately equal to that generated by the corporate income tax.

CORPORATE INCOME TAX

The corporate income tax is levied on the accounting profits of the business firm. Its structure is relatively simple. In 1986, the first $25,000 of corporate profit was taxed at a rate of 15 percent. Corporate profit between $25,000 and $50,000 was taxed at 18 percent. Corporate earnings in the range from $50,000 to $75,000 were taxed at a rate of 30 percent. The rate rose to 40 percent for the profit range from $75,000 to $100,000. All corporate earnings above $100,000 were taxed at a flat rate of 46 percent. Corporate incomes in the United States have been taxed since 1909. The tax currently generates approximately 9 percent of all federal tax receipts and 8 percent of the total tax revenues for all levels of government (see Exhibit 6). In addition to the federal tax, a number of states and some local governments also levy a corporate profit tax.

Inadvertently, the corporate income tax encourages debt financing rather than equity ownership. This results because no adjustment is made for factors of production owned by the firm and the equity capital invested by the owners. A corporation that uses debt financing will incur an interest cost, which will reduce its accounting profits and tax liability. In contrast, if the same firm uses equity financing (i.e., raises financial capital by issuing additional stock), the interest cost will not appear on the firm's accounting statement. Therefore, even though there is an opportunity cost of capital, regardless of whether it is raised by equity financing or by debt, only the latter will reduce the firm's tax liability.

THE ISSUES OF EFFICIENCY AND EQUITY

There are two major factors to consider when choosing among taxation alternatives. First, taxes should be consistent with the concept of economic efficiency. Taxes should not encourage people to use scarce resources wastefully. A tax system is inconsistent with economic efficiency if it encourages individuals (a) to buy goods costing more than their value to consumers and/or (b) to channel time into tax-avoidance activities.

Ability-to-Pay Principle: The equity concept that people with larger incomes (or more consumption or more wealth) should be taxed at a higher rate because their ability to pay is presumably greater. The concept is subjective and fails to reveal how much higher the rate of taxation should be as income increases.

Second, a tax system should be equitable; that is, it should be consistent with widely accepted principles of fairness. Economists often speak of "horizontal" and "vertical" equity. Horizontal equity means equal treatment of equals. If two parties earn equal incomes, for example, horizontal equity implies that the two should be taxed equally. The corollary concept of vertical equity requires that persons who are situated differently should be taxed differently. It encompasses what economists refer to as the **ability-to-pay principle,** the seemingly straightforward idea that taxes should be levied according to the ability of the taxpayer to pay. Deciding exactly what this means, however, is at least partially subjective. Most people find it reasonable that the rich should pay more taxes than the poor. This would be in the case under a proportional tax system since high-income taxpayers would pay the flat (constant) rate on a larger tax base. Many find it reasonable that the rich should pay a *higher proportion* of their income (or wealth or consumption) in taxes than the poor. Of course, progressive taxation incorporates this concept. But, how much higher should the rate be for those with higher incomes? At this point, the consensus breaks down. There is little agreement among either laymen or professional economists about the proper degree of tax progressivity.

A tax system must take equity into account if it is to succeed. The cost of enforcing a system widely presumed to be unreasonable or unfair is certain to be extremely high. Equity, though, must be balanced with efficiency. A tax system that ignores economic efficiency will also be extremely costly to an economy.

TAXES AND ECONOMIC EFFICIENCY

Neutral Tax: A tax that does not (a) distort consumer buying patterns or producer production methods or (b) induce individuals to engage in tax-avoidance activities. There will be no excess burden if a tax is neutral.

An ideal tax system would not alter the incentive of individuals to allocate their time and income into those areas that yield them the most satisfaction. A tax of this kind is called a **neutral tax.** A neutral tax would not encourage individuals to spend more of their income on business travel, housing, medical service, or professional association publications, and less of their income on food and clothing because the former are tax-deductible and the latter are not. Similarly, a neutral tax would not encourage an individual to allocate more time and money to investments that reduce the tax burden (depreciable assets, municipal bonds, tax-free retirement plans, and so on), and less time and money to savings and work activities that generate taxable income.

Head Tax: A lump-sum tax levied on all individuals, regardless of their income, consumption, wealth, or other indicators of economic well-being.

There is a problem, though, with the concept of a neutral tax. Probably the only tax that would meet the hypothetical ideal of neutrality is a **head tax,** a tax imposing an equal lump-sum tax on all individuals. A head tax would impose the same dollar tax liability on the poor as it would on the rich (or the same liability on those who consume few goods as on those who consume many goods). Since a head tax conflicts with the concept of vertical equity—the view that persons who are situated differently should be taxed differently—it fails to pass our test of fairness.

Excess Burden of Taxation: A burden of taxation over and above the burden associated with the transfer of revenues to the government. An excess burden usually reflects losses that occur when beneficial activities are forgone because they are taxed.

Thus, we generally tax things such as income, consumption, and property. However, taxes on these items distort pricing signals and thereby cause individuals to forgo productive activities. Economists refer to this inefficiency and the accompanying reduction in private-sector output over and above the tax revenue collected as the **excess burden of taxation.** It is easy to think of cases that illustrate the excess burden of taxation. For example, if two individuals decide to forgo a mutually advantageous exchange because a tax makes the transaction unprofitable, they incur a burden from the taxation even though they do not pay a tax, because the transaction did not take place. Similarly, if a taxpayer decides to allocate more time to leisure or to household production and less time to market work—because the tax system limits the individual's ability to capture income generated by market work—a burden over and above tax revenues collected from the individual is imposed. Income from market work is lost to the individual, and whatever benefits for others that might have resulted from the work are sacrificed. Excess burdens reflect economic inefficiency, relative to our hypothetical ideal. They impose a **deadweight loss** on an economy, because they reflect a cost imposed on some individuals without any offsetting benefit to others.

Deadweight Loss: A net loss associated with the forgoing of an economic action. The loss does not lead to an offsetting gain for other participants. It thus reflects economic inefficiency.

Exhibit 7 illustrates the distinction between the tax burden associated with the transfer of purchasing power and the excess burden of taxation. Here we show the impact of a 40-cent tax imposed on each pack of cigarettes. Prior to the imposition of the tax, 35 billion packs of cigarettes were produced and sold to consumers at a market price of 80 cents per pack. The cigarette tax increases the cost of supplying and marketing cigarettes by 40 cents per pack. Thus, the supply curve of cigarettes shifts vertically by the amount of the tax. Consumers, however, would not continue to purchase as many cigarettes if the full burden of the tax were passed on to them in the form of a 40-cent increase in the per pack price. So, when the supply curve shifts vertically, the market price of cigarettes rises by less than the amount of the tax. Since the number of cigarettes demanded is thus responsive to the higher price, some of the tax burden will fall on cigarette producers. In our hypothetical example, a new equilibrium level for cigarettes will become $1 per pack, with an annual output rate of 30 billion packs of cigarettes. The tax will raise $12 billion (40 cents times 30 billion packs) of revenue. Buyers will pay 20 cents more per pack for the 30 million packs of cigarettes purchased after the tax is imposed. Simultaneously, sellers will receive 20 cents less per pack. The tax thus transfers $12 billion of revenue from cigarette buyers and sellers to the government. Note, though, that the quantity of cigarettes produced and consumed has fallen by 5 billion packs.

EXHIBIT 7 • The Impact of a Tax on Economic Activity

Here we illustrate the impact of a 40-cent tax (per pack) on cigarettes. Since the tax increases the cost of supplying cigarettes for consumption, the supply curve is shifted vertically by the amount of the tax. At the higher price, however, consumers reduce their consumption. The equilibrium price increases from 80 cents to $1 per pack. Consumers pay 20 cents more per pack and sellers receive 20 cents less as the result of the 40-cent tax. In addition, consumers and producers lose the mutual gains from exchange (triangle ABC) that would be realized if the tax did not reduce the volume of trade between cigarette producers and consumers.

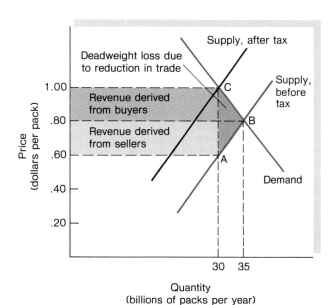

The mutually advantageous gains that would have accrued to producers and consumers (the triangle ABC) are lost. (Remember that trade is a positive-sum game, so a reduction in the volume of trade will result in economic loss.) This loss of welfare (triangle ABC) associated with the unrealized exchanges imposes an excess burden on buyers and sellers over and above the burden accompanying the transfer of revenue to the government. Clearly, the triangle ABC is a deadweight loss, since it is not accompanied by an offsetting gain in the form of additional tax revenue for the government.

In our example, the burden of the tax was divided equally between sellers and buyers. This will not always be the case. If the demand curve were steeper (and the supply curve flatter), the price of the taxed good would rise by a larger amount, imposing more of the burden on buyers. In contrast, if the demand curve were flatter (and the supply curve steeper), the market price would rise by a smaller amount, and a larger share of the tax burden would fall on sellers.

Tax Incidence: The manner in which the burden of the tax is distributed among economic units (consumers, employees, employers, and so on). The tax burden does not always fall on those who pay the tax.

The burden of taxes is not always borne by the person who writes a check to the Internal Revenue Service. Economists use the term **tax incidence** when discussing the question of how the burden of a tax is distributed among parties. Since the distribution of the tax burden is dependent on the slope of the supply and demand curves for the activity being taxed, this is not an easy question to answer.

TAX RATES, INCOME, AND WORK

As Exhibit 6 illustrates, over 60 percent of the tax revenue of the United States is derived from the taxation of personal income and work (the payroll tax). The impact of these taxes on economic efficiency and total output is one of today's most controversial economic topics. In the past, most economists believed that tax rates on income, such as those used in the United States, exerted little adverse influence on the incentive of individuals to engage in productive activity. According to this traditional view, workers lack viable alternatives to the earning of taxable income. Because of this, they will be unable, or virtually unable, to shift from current work to other income-generating activities in order to partially avoid the tax burden.

During the 1965–1980 period, marginal tax rates increased substantially. This led to a reevaluation of the traditional view. Today, many economists believe that high marginal tax rates will induce taxpayers to shift to untaxed activities such as leisure, do-it-yourself work, tax avoidance, and even tax evasion. For example, when high marginal tax rates take a major share of the income from additional work, some individuals will respond by increasing their vacation time and absenteeism, while reducing their overtime hours. Others will allocate more time to untaxed household activities, such as fixing their cars, painting their houses, and producing additional home-prepared meals, rather than to working and purchasing new cars, buying new houses, and eating meals at restaurants. Still others will take jobs with lower pay but higher nonmonetary benefits and allocate more time to real estate investments with attractive tax benefits. Business ventures designed to show an accounting loss to shelter taxable income will also flourish. These alternatives are perfectly legal. However, some individuals will also use illegal means to evade the payment of taxes. Participation in the

Underground Economy:
Unreported barter and
cash transactions that take
place outside recorded
market channels. Some are
otherwise legal activities
undertaken to evade taxes.
Others involve illegal ac-
tivities such as trafficking
in drugs, prostitution,
extortion, and similar
crimes.

underground economy is one device that many believe is widely used to avoid or reduce taxes (see "The Underground Economy"). If this view is correct—if there are fairly good, feasible alternatives to the payment of the higher tax rates—the amount of labor supplied to taxable work activities will decrease significantly as marginal tax rates rise.

Exhibit 8 illustrates the economics of this debate within the supply and demand framework. Here we consider a labor market in which workers earn an equilibrium wage of $6 per hour in the absence of income taxation. Forty hours of work per week are supplied by each worker in this market at the $6 hourly wage. Now, consider the impact of a flat 20 percent tax rate on income (or payroll). Just as the cigarette tax made it more costly to supply that product, so, too, will the income tax make it more costly to supply labor. The supply curve of labor will then decline (shift vertically) by the amount of the tax. According to the traditional view, illustrated by Exhibit 8a, the income tax will exert relatively little impact on hours worked, since the aggregate supply curve of labor is vertical (or almost vertical). The equilibrium wage, including the tax, will only be slightly higher ($6.30 per hour), and the after-tax wage rate of workers will decline substantially (to $5.04). Since the labor supply curve is almost vertical, the burden of the income tax will fall primarily on workers. Furthermore, this will be true regardless of whether the tax is paid directly by the individuals (as in the case of the personal income tax) or whether the check to the IRS is made out by their employer (as in the case of the payroll tax).

The challengers to the traditional view argue that when marginal tax rates are extremely high, say 40 percent or more, the supply curve for labor

EXHIBIT 8 • The Con-
troversy Concerning
the Incentive Effects
of the Income Tax

Here we illustrate two alternative outcomes associated with the imposition of a 20 percent tax on income. According to the traditional view (a), when the aggregate labor supply curve is vertical, or nearly vertical, the tax will result in only a small reduction in work effort (from 40 to 39 hours per week). In contrast, according to a more recent view (b), if the labor supply curve is flatter, the tax will lead to a larger reduction (from 40 to 36 hours per week) in time spent generating taxable income.

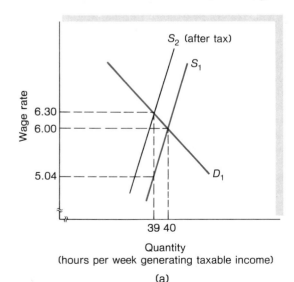

(a)

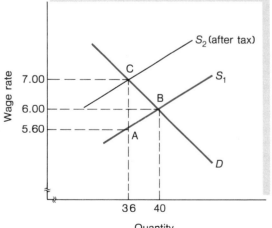

(b)

will be flatter, as illustrated by Exhibit 8b. If this is the case, the vertical shift in the labor supply curve will cause a larger decline in the work time allocated to activities that generate taxable income. For example, hours might decline from 40 per week to 36 per week (rather than to only 39 hours per week in the traditional view). Simultaneously, the higher tax rates will lead to an increase in tax-avoidance activities. Waste and sizable deadweight losses will be incurred. The triangle ABC (Exhibit 8b), which indicates only the inefficiency stemming from lost hours of work, is one measure of allocative inefficiency. However, it actually understates society's excess burden since it ignores work intensity, rent seeking, and other factors related to both the cost and value of output.

MEASURES OF ECONOMIC ACTIVITY

The Underground Economy

High marginal tax rates increase the incentive of individuals to participate in the underground economy to escape taxation. The underground economy encompasses unreported production and exchange, often conducted in cash to avoid possible detection.

There are two major components of the underground economy: (a) production and distribution of illegal goods and services and (b) the nonreporting of transactions involving legal goods and services. Drug trafficking, smuggling, prostitution, and other criminal activities are examples of the first component. Income from such activities is generally unreported to avoid detection by law enforcement authorities.

Of course, even when the work activity is legal, it is illegal to earn income and not report it to the taxing authorities. However, the likelihood of detection by the authorities is very small for certain types of activities. Since cash transactions are difficult to trace, they provide the life-blood of the underground economy. The participants in the legal-if-reported portion of the underground economy are diverse.

Taxicab drivers and waitresses may pocket fees and tips. Small-business proprietors may fail to ring up cash sales. Craft and professional workers may fail to report cash income. All of these individuals are participating in the underground economy.

In addition, it is estimated that millions of employees, ranging from farm laborers to bartenders, are paid in cash. Company books fail to record their employment. Neither income taxes nor social security deductions are withheld. The employer evades the payroll taxes, while employees pocket "tax-free" cash wage payments without endangering their eligibility for welfare or unemployment benefits.

For obvious reasons, it is difficult to accurately measure the size of the underground economy. However, most economists who have studied the issue believe that the underground economy is growing more rapidly than is reported economic activity. The rather dramatic increase in the amount of currency—particularly large-denomination bills—held by the public is consistent with this view. In addition, recent special audit procedures used by the IRS indicate that the underground economy is both large and growing. The IRS estimates that underground activities now constitute approximately 10 percent of the U.S. economy. Peter Gutmann of Baruch College believes the U.S. underground economy is even larger, closer to 15 percent.[3]

The underground economy is not a problem unique to the United States. In fact, available evidence indicates it is even more widespread in Western Europe, where tax rates are higher. The Organization for Economic Cooperation and Development estimates that between 3 and 5 percent of the total labor force in Western Europe is working "off the books" and thereby evading taxes. In Italy, Great Britain, and Sweden, the estimated size of the underground economy ranges from 10 to 30 percent of the national income. Apparently, the underground economy has become a sizable sector of Western economies.

---

[3]Peter M. Gutmann, "The Subterranean Economy," *Taxing and Spending*, April, 1979.

TAX RATES, TAX REVENUES AND THE LAFFER CURVE

Tax Rate: The per unit or percentage rate at which an economic activity is taxed.

Tax Base: The level of the activity that is taxed. For example, if an excise tax is levied on each gallon of gasoline, the tax base is the number of gallons of gasoline sold. Since higher tax rates generally make the taxed activity less attractive, the size of the tax base is inversely related to the rate at which the activity is taxed.

Laffer Curve: A curve illustrating the relationship between tax rates and tax revenues. The curve reflects the fact that tax revenues are low for both very high and very low tax rates.

It is important to distinguish between a change in **tax rates** and a change in tax revenues. The quantity or level of an activity that is taxed—the **tax base**—is inversely related to the rate at which the activity is taxed. An increase in a tax rate will lead to a less-than-porportional increase in tax revenues. Higher tax rates will make it more costly to engage in the activity, thereby inducing individuals to shift to substitutes. If there are attractive substitutes, the decline in the activity due to the tax may be substantial. Perhaps a real-world example will help clarify this point. In 1981, the District of Columbia increased the tax rate on gasoline from 10 cents to 13 cents per gallon, a 30 percent increase. Tax revenues, however, did not increase by 30 percent—they expanded by only 12 percent. Why? The higher tax rate discouraged motorists from purchasing gasoline in the District of Columbia. There was a pretty good alternative to the purchase of the more highly taxed (and therefore higher-priced) gasoline—the purchase of gasoline in Virginia and Maryland, where the tax rates (and therefore prices) were slightly lower. Because of this, the quantity of gasoline sold in Washington, D.C., declined. The revenue gains associated with the higher tax rates were partially eroded by a decline in the tax base.

Economist Arthur Laffer has popularized the idea that higher tax rates can sometimes shrink the tax base so much that tax revenues will decline despite the higher tax rates. As the result of Laffer's efforts, the curve illustrating the relationship between tax rates and tax revenues is now called the **Laffer curve.** Exhibit 9 illustrates the concept of the Laffer curve for the taxation of income-generating activity. Obviously, tax revenues would be zero if the tax rate were zero. What is not so obvious is that tax revenues would also be zero (or at least very close to zero) if the tax rate were 100 percent. Confronting a 100 percent tax rate, most individuals would go fishing or find something else to do rather than engage in productive activity that is taxed, since the 100 percent tax rate would completely remove the material reward derived from earning taxable income. Production in the taxed sector would come to a halt, and without production, tax revenues would plummet to zero.

EXHIBIT 9 • The Laffer Curve

Since taxation affects the amount of the activity being taxed, a change in tax rates will not lead to a proportional change in tax revenues. As the Laffer curve indicates, beyond some point (*B*), an increase in tax rates may actually cause tax revenues to fall. Since large tax rate increases will lead to only a small expansion in tax revenue as *B* is approached, there is no presumption that point *B* is an ideal rate of taxation.

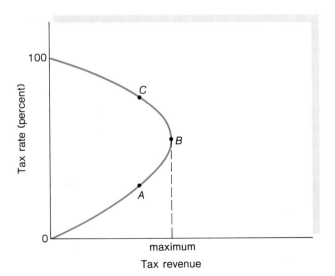

As tax rates are reduced from 100 percent, the incentive to work and earn taxable income increases, income expands, and tax revenues rise. Similarly, as tax rates increase from zero, tax revenues expand. Clearly, at some rate greater than zero but less than 100 percent, tax revenues will be maximized (point *B*, Exhibit 9). This is not to imply that the tax rate that maximizes revenue is ideal. In fact, as the maximum revenue point (*B*) is approached, relatively large tax rate increases will be necessary to expand tax revenues. In this range, the excess burden of taxation will be substantial.

Have tax rates in the United States ever been so high that we were on the backward-bending portion (the *BC* range) of the Laffer curve? A few economists have argued that this might have been the case prior to the tax cuts of 1981–1984. For the economy as a whole, however, the evidence contradicts this view. Overall tax revenue declined when tax rates were reduced in the early 1980s. There is some evidence, though, that taxpayers in the highest income (and therefore highest marginal tax) brackets may have been on the backward-bending portion of the Laffer curve. In contrast to other taxpayers, the tax revenue (adjusted for inflation) collected from the top 1.36 percent of taxpayers increased between 1981 and 1983. (See "Applications in Economics.")

APPLICATIONS IN ECONOMICS

Changes in Marginal Tax Rates and the Incentive to Earn Taxable Income[4]

The marginal tax rate is inversely related to the proportion of an additional dollar earned that a taxpayer is permitted to keep. A reduction in marginal tax rates will encourage taxpayers to earn more taxable income and will reduce their incentive to engage in tax-avoidance activities. Other things constant, lower tax rates will tend to expand the size of the taxable income base.

Interestingly, the incentive effects of a proportional rate reduction—one that reduces the tax rate in each tax bracket by the same proportion—will be greatest in the highest tax brackets. How will a reduction in a marginal tax rate from 70 percent to 50 percent influence the incentive of a high-income professional or business executive to earn *taxable* income? When confronting a 70 percent marginal rate, the taxpayer gets to keep only 30

cents of each additional dollar earned by cutting costs, producing more, or investing more wisely. After the tax cut, though, take-home pay from each dollar of taxable income jumps to 50 cents—a whopping 67 percent increase in the incentive to earn. Predictably, high-income taxpayers will spend more time finding ways to cut business costs and increase sales and less time on the golf course and on tax avoidance. Similarly, they will spend less money on tax-deductible expenditures such as plush offices and Hawaiian business conferences and more on the business of satisfying customers.

In contrast, consider the incentive effects of an *identical* percentage rate reduction in lower tax brackets. Suppose the 14 percent marginal rate was cut to 10 percent. Take-home pay, per dollar of addi-

tional earnings, expands from 86 cents to 90 cents, only a 5 percent increase. Compared to the incentive effects in the upper brackets, the same percentage tax cut in the lower tax brackets leads to a much smaller increase in take-home pay and thus a much smaller increase in the incentive to earn more taxable income.

---

[4]For additional details on this topic, see James Gwartney and Richard Stroup, "Tax Cuts: Who Shoulders the Burden?" Federal Reserve Bank of Atlanta *Economic Review* (March 1982), pp. 19–27, and James Gwartney, "Tax Rates, Taxable Income and the Distributional Effects of the Economic Recovery Act of 1981," Hearing on *Fairness and the Reagan Tax Cuts* before The Joint Economic Committee, Congress of the United States (98th Congress, 2nd Session), June 12, 1984, pp. 44–77.

APPLICATIONS IN ECONOMICS (continued)

Since most of us are motivated by after-tax earnings, proportional rate reductions will increase the incentive to earn more (and shelter less) income primarily in the upper marginal tax brackets. Predictably, the taxable income base will grow more rapidly in high than in low tax brackets when marginal tax rates are reduced proportionally. Since the lower tax rates will expand the tax base, tax revenues will decline by less than the amount of the rate reduction, particularly in the upper tax brackets.

The Kennedy-Johnson tax cut provides evidence in support of this view. The 1964 tax cut sliced the top marginal bracket from 91 percent to 70 percent, leading to a 233 percent increase (from 9 cents to 30 cents per additional dollar of earnings) in take-home pay from marginal income in this bracket. The bottom rate was cut from 20 percent

to 14 percent—about the same proportional tax reduction. But, after-tax income, per dollar of additional earnings, in the bottom bracket rose from 80 percent to 86 percent, an increase of only 7.5 percent.

Just as one would expect, given the incentive effects accompanying the rate reductions, *taxable incomes* grew rapidly in the upper tax brackets after the tax cut. This growth in the tax base partially offset the revenue losses, particularly in the highest tax brackets. Exhibit 10 presents data on tax revenue before and after the 1964 tax cut, according to percentile income groupings. For the bottom 50 percent of income earners, tax revenues (measured in 1963 dollars) declined from $5.01 billion in 1963 to $4.55 billion in 1965, a reduction of 9.2 percent. Clearly, there is no reason to think that this group is on the backward-bending portion of the Laffer curve. Revenue collections from returns in the 50th to 75th percentile and in the 75th to 95th percentile also declined, albeit by a smaller

percentage than for the lowest income grouping. In all three of these income categories, the negative impact of the rate reductions on tax revenues was dominant over the positive impact of income growth on tax revenues.

However, the picture for the top 5 percent of taxpayers was quite different. Despite the roughly 20 percent lower tax rates, measured in constant dollars, the revenues collected from the top 5 percent of earners rose from $17.17 billion in 1963 to $18.49 billion in 1965, a healthy increase of 7.7 percent. Tax revenue collected from these high-income taxpayers grew because the rapid expansion in their taxable income more than offset the loss of tax revenue associated with the rate reductions.

The 1981 tax legislation cut tax rates across the board over a 3-year period by approximately 23 percent. In addition, the top tax bracket was reduced from 70 percent to 50 percent, effective during the first year of the rate reduction. Exhibit 11 presents data on tax revenues paid according to income percentiles for 1981 and 1983. The lower rates led to substantially lower revenues for the bottom 95th percentile of taxpayers. Once again, however, the experience of the top 5 percent of taxpayers was different. Measuring in constant dollars, the tax revenue collected from the top 5 percent of taxpayers declined by only 5.6 percent, considerably less than the reduction in rates. Assuming normal personal deductions, the top 1.36 percent of taxpayers faced marginal tax rates above 50 percent prior to the 1981 legislation. Not only did these taxpayers get an across-the-board tax cut as did other taxpayers, they also benefitted dramatically from the immediate reduction in the top

EXHIBIT 10 • **The Change in Federal Income Tax Revenue Derived from Various Income Groupings, 1963–1965**

The tax revenues are ranked according to adjusted gross income prior to and subsequent to the 1964 reduction in tax rates.

Percentile of All Returns (ranked from lowest to highest income)	Tax Revenues Collected from Group (in billions of 1963 dollars)[a]		Percent Change
	1963	1965	
Bottom 50 percent	$ 5.01	$ 4.55	−9.2
50th to 75th percentile	10.02	9.61	−4.1
75th to 95th percentile	16.00	15.41	−3.7
Top 5 percent	17.17	18.49	+7.7
Total	$48.20	$48.06	−0.3

[a]These estimates were derived by interpolation.

Internal Revenue Service, *Statistics of Income: Individual Income Tax Returns* (1963 and 1965).

APPLICATIONS IN ECONOMICS
(continued)

marginal tax rate from 70 percent to 50 percent. Nevertheless, the tax revenue collected from these high-income taxpayers was 2.5 percent higher in 1983 than it was in 1981. Again, gains in tax revenues accompanying the rapid growth of the tax base more than offset the revenue losses associated with the lower rates in the highest tax brackets.

What do these data imply about the shape of the Laffer curve? First,

they indicate that most taxpayers are on the upward-sloping portion (the *AB* range of Exhibit 9) of the Laffer curve. For taxpayers confronting marginal tax rates of, say less than 30 percent, the incentive effects of rate changes are not very important. In this range, there is every reason to expect that lower tax rates will lead to an approximately proportional reduction in tax revenues. However, in the upper tax brackets (tax rates above 50 percent, for example), the incentive effects are quite important. Taxpayers in this range may well be on the

backward-bending portion of the Laffer curve. A recent study done for the National Bureau of Economic Research by Harvard professor Lawrence Lindsey indicates that marginal tax rates higher than 43 percent yielded less rather than more revenues in the early 1980s.[5] Influenced by empirical studies indicating that high tax rates do not raise much additional revenue, many western governments are now reevaluating their tax systems.

DISCUSSION

1. Do you think the rich should pay a higher percentage of their income in taxes than the poor? Why or why not?
2. Do you think the marginal earnings of persons with high incomes should be taxed at rates of 50 percent or more? Why or why not?
3. If the highest marginal rates could be reduced 10 percent without any loss of tax revenue to the Treasury, would you favor the reduction? Why or why not?

---

[5]Lawrence Lindsey, *Estimating the Revenue Maximizing Top Personal Tax Rate* (New York: National Bureau of Economic Research—Working Paper 1761, 1985).

EXHIBIT 11 • **The Change in Federal Income Tax Revenue Derived from Various Income Groups, 1981–1983**

Percentile of All Returns (ranked from lowest to highest)	Tax Revenues Collected from Group (in billions of 1983 dollars)		Percent Change
	1981	1983	
In Current Dollars			
Bottom 50 percent	23.0	19.6	− 14.8
50th to 75th percentile	63.7	53.6	− 15.9
75th to 95th percentile	115.1	97.8	− 15.0
Top 5 percent	109.3	103.2	− 5.6
Top 1.36 percent	63.3	64.9	+ 2.5
Total	311.1	274.2	− 13.5

Source: U.S. Department of Treasury, Internal Revenue Service.

WHO PAYS THE TAX BILL?

How is the burden of taxation distributed among income groupings in the United States? This is not an easy question to answer. As Exhibit 6 illustrates, we levy several different types of taxes in the United States. Economists sometimes differ in their views as to who actually bears the burden of certain taxes, particularly property and sales taxes. It should not be surprising, then, to find that disagreement exists as to precisely how the tax burden in the United States is distributed. The two most comprehensive studies concerning this issue have been conducted by Joseph Pechman of the Brookings Institution and by Edgar Browning and William Johnson of

Texas A&M and The University of Virginia, respectively.[6] Exhibit 12 illustrates the findings of these two studies.

Building on an earlier work, Pechman's study provides estimates based on a number of alternative assumptions as to the incidence of different taxes. His findings support the conclusions that the overall U.S. tax structure is within the proportional to mildly progressive range. Even Pechman's assumptions that yielded his most progressive estimates projected that high-income recipients pay only slightly higher average tax rates than households with much lower incomes.

Browning and Johnson dispute the findings of Pechman. Their study implies that the U.S. tax structure is highly progressive. Browning and Johnson draw the following conclusion:

> The overall effect of the U.S. tax system is quite progressive; the average rate of tax rises continually and substantially from 11.7 percent to 38.3 percent from the lowest income decile to the highest. Some feeling for the degree of progressivity of the tax system can be obtained by noting that the combined tax rate for the top decile is over three times the rate for the bottom decile.[7]

EXHIBIT 12 • Two Views on the Distribution of the Tax Burden in the United States

Joseph Pechman of the Brookings Institution argues that the overall U.S. tax structure is either approximately proportional or mildly progressive. Frame a illustrates Pechman's mildly progressive estimates of the average tax burden as a percent of income for each income decile. In contrast, a study by Edgar Browning and William Johnson indicates that the tax structure in the U.S. is highly progressive (frame b). Browning and Johnson estimate that the top 10 percent of earners pay an average tax rate of 38.3 percent, compared to only 11.7 percent for the bottom 10 percent of income recipients.

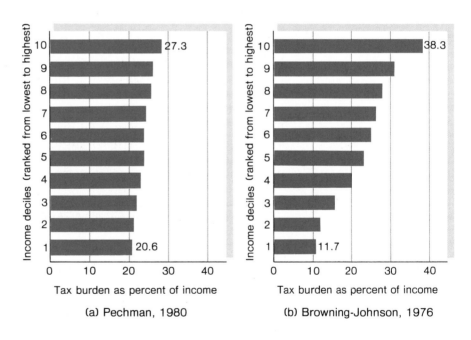

(a) Pechman, 1980

(b) Browning-Johnson, 1976

Source: Joseph Pechman, *Who Paid the Taxes, 1966–85?* (Washington, D.C.: The Brookings Institution, 1985); and Edgar K. Browning and William R. Johnson, *The Distribution of the Tax Burden* (Washington, D.C.: American Enterprise Institute, 1979).

---

[6]Joseph A. Pechman, *Who Paid the Taxes, 1966–85?* (Washington, D.C.: The Brookings Institution, 1985), and Edgar K. Browning and William R. Johnson, *The Distribution of the Tax Burden* (Washington, D.C.: American Enterprise Institute, 1979).

[7]Edgar K. Browning and William R. Johnson, *The Distribution of the Tax Burden*, p. 50.

What accounts for the difference between the findings of Pechman and Browning-Johnson? The major difference relates to different assumptions with regard to the incidence of the sales tax. Pechman assumes that the sales tax simply increases prices and he therefore allocates its incidence according to current spending. Since high-income households spend a smaller proportion of their current income, the Pechman assumption implies that the sales tax is regressive. In contrast, Browning and Johnson assume that the burden of the sales tax falls on current earnings, since transfer payments are indexed for changes in prices. According to Browning and Johnson, a higher sales tax would push up prices but would also expand the size of transfer payments, which are indexed to the price level. Browning and Johnson thus believe that income from transfer payments escapes the burden of the sales tax. If this is the case, then the burden of the sales tax would be progressive, rather than regressive as in the Pechman study.

With regard to the burden of taxation, two additional points should be noted. First, middle- and upper-middle-income taxpayers earn the bulk of income and pay the bulk of the tax bill. In 1983, 55 percent of households in the United States had incomes between $16,500 and $63,900. These households earned approximately 70 percent of the total income and they shouldered slightly more than 70 percent of the tax burden. The findings of both Pechman and Browning-Johnson are consistent with this view.

Second, people pay all taxes. Politicians sometimes speak of imposing taxes on businesses, as if part of the tax burden could be transferred from individuals to nonpersons (business firms). The assumptions of this viewpoint are incorrect. Like all other taxes, business taxes are paid by individuals. A corporation or business firm may write the tax check to the government, but it does not pay the taxes. The business firm merely collects the money from someone else—its customers, employees, or stockholders—and transfers it to the government. It makes good political rhetoric to talk about "businesses" paying taxes, but the hard facts are that individuals provide all tax revenues.

THE COST OF GOVERNMENT

Do taxes measure the cost of government? Interestingly, the answer to this question is, "Not entirely." Our old friend—the opportunity cost concept—will help us understand why. There are three types of costs incurred when governments provide goods and services.

First, there is the opportunity cost of the resources used to produce goods supplied through the public sector. When governments purchase missiles, education, highways, health care, and other goods, resources to provide these goods must be bid away from private-sector activities. If these resources were not tied-up producing goods supplied through the public sector, they would be available to produce private-sector goods. Note that this cost will be incurred regardless of whether the provision of the public-sector goods is financed by current taxes, an increase in government debt, or money creation. This cost can only be diminished by reducing the size of governmental purchases.

"THIS NEW TAX PLAN SOUNDS PRETTY GOOD... WE GET A 9% CUT AND BUSINESS PICKS UP THE BURDEN...."

BY JOHN TREVER, ALBUQUERQUE JOURNAL © BY AND PERMISSION OF NEWS AMERICA SYNDICATE.

Second, there is the cost of resources expended in the collection of the tax. Tax laws must be enforced. Tax returns must be prepared and monitored. Resources used to prepare, monitor, and enforce tax legislation are unavailable for the production of either private- or public-sector goods. In the United States, studies indicate that these compliance costs amount to between 3 and 7 percent of the tax revenue raised.

Finally, there is the excess burden cost due to price distortions emanating from the levying of taxes (and the provision of transfers). Less output will result because the tax-transfer structure will cause individuals to forgo productive activities and engage in counterproductive action (for example, tax-avoidance activities).

In essence, the cost of government activities is the sum of (a) the opportunity cost of resources used to produce government supplied goods and services, (b) the cost of tax compliance, and (c) the excess burden cost of taxation. Thus, government purchases of goods and services generally cost the economy a good bit more than either the size of the tax bill or the level of budget expenditures imply.

THE SIZE OF GOVERNMENT IN OTHER COUNTRIES

How does the size of the public sector in the United States compare with the size of the public sector in other countries? Exhibit 13 helps to answer that question. In Canada, public-sector spending accounted for 39.3 percent of total output in 1983, significantly greater than the 33 percent for the United

EXHIBIT 13 • The Size of Government— An International Comparison

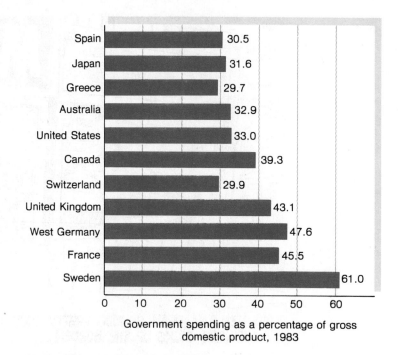

Government spending as a percentage of gross domestic product, 1983

Source: *OECD Economic Outlook* (December 1985).

States. The size of the public sectors in Japan, Switzerland, Australia, Spain, and Greece are approximately the same as in the U.S. On the other hand, compared to the U.S., government spending accounts for a substantially larger share of total output in the United Kingdom, West Germany, France, and Sweden. The higher level of government spending in these countries primarily reflects greater public-sector involvement in the provision of housing, health care, retirement insurance, and aid to the poor and unemployed. In Sweden, 61 percent of national output was either produced or channeled through the public sector in 1983, the largest figure for any democratic industrial nation.

LOOKING AHEAD

Government expenditures and tax rates are important determinants of an economy's output and employment. As we proceed, we will investigate this topic in detail. First, though, we need to develop a better understanding of how aggregate output is measured. This is the topic of the next chapter.

CHAPTER SUMMARY

1. Governmental expenditures have grown more rapidly than the U.S. economy during this century. In 1902, government spending accounted for only 7.7 percent of GNP. By 1929, the figure had risen to 10 percent. Since 1929, the relative size of government expenditures has expanded every decade. In the mid-1980s, more than one third of the total output of the United States was channeled through the public sector.

2. Government purchases of goods and services constitute approximately 20 percent of the national output. Slightly less than one out of every seven Americans works for the local, state, or federal government. Taking into account transfer payments, total government expenditures amounted to 35 percent of the gross national product in 1985.

3. During the last three decades, government expenditures in traditional areas such as national defense, highways, police and fire protection, and the provision of other goods and services has changed very little relative to the size of the economy. The growth of government in recent decades is almost exclusively the result of increased governmental involvement in the redistribution of income.

4. Personal income taxes, payroll taxes, and corporate income taxes are the major sources of federal tax revenues. Sales taxes provide the major tax base for state government, whereas local governments still rely primarily on property taxes for their revenue.

5. Payroll taxes constitute the most rapidly expanding source of tax revenues. In 1984, payroll taxes contributed 28 percent of the total tax revenue and 36 percent of the tax revenue at the federal level. The social security payroll tax is a regressive tax because it is not levied on income beyond a designated maximum.

6. As the marginal tax rates increase, the proportion of income individuals are permitted to keep for private use declines. Since it determines the share of earnings available for private expenditures, the marginal tax rate exerts a major impact on the incentive of individuals to earn taxable income.

7. Both efficiency and equity should be considered when choosing among taxation alternatives. A tax system that induces inefficient behavior will be costly to a society. Similarly, it will be costly to induce compliance with a tax system that is perceived as unreasonable or unfair.

8. Ideally, we would all prefer a neutral tax system—one that does not distort prices or induce individuals to channel scarce resources into tax-avoidance activities. However, a tax on productive activity will always alter some prices. Our goal should be to adopt an equitable system that will minimize the inefficiency effects.

9. The impact of taxes on the incentive to work is a topic of current debate among economists. The traditional view holds that since there are few good substitutes for the earning of taxable income, the aggregate labor supply curve is vertical, or nearly vertical. Taxes on income thus do not significantly reduce the quantity of labor supplied. Challengers to this view argue that leisure, household production, tax shelters, and the underground economy are fairly good substitutes for the earning of taxable income. They therefore believe that high marginal tax rates will significantly reduce productive work efforts and encourage tax avoidance, with economic inefficiency as the result.

10. It is important to distinguish between a change in tax rates and a change in tax revenues. The size of the tax base will generally be inversely related to the rate of taxation. Therefore, an increase in tax rates will lead to a less-than-proportional increase in tax revenues, particularly if there are viable substitutes for those things that are taxed.

11. At very high rates of taxation, it is possible that an increase in tax rates will cause a reduction in tax revenues, because such a large number of people will shift away from the activity that is being taxed. The Laffer curve illustrates this possibility.

12. Since a variety of taxes are levied in the United States, and since it is not easy to tell who really bears the burden of various taxes, the distribution of the tax burden among income groupings is a controversial topic. Some economists believe that the overall U.S. tax structure is appropriately proportional, while others argue that it is quite progressive.

13. The cost of government activities encompasses the following components: (a) the opportunity cost of resources used to produce public-sector goods and services, (b) the compliance costs of taxation, and (c) the excess burden costs associated with price distortions and inefficiencies emanating from taxation. Generally, these costs will exceed both the size of the government budget and the dollar amount of the tax revenue collected.

14. The size of government as a share of the economy in the United States is approximately the same as for Japan, Australia, and Switzerland, but significantly smaller than for Canada and most Western European nations.

THE ECONOMIC WAY OF THINKING— DISCUSSION QUESTIONS

1. The major categories of governmental spending are (a) national defense, (b) education, and (c) income transfers and antipoverty expenditures. Why do you think the public sector has become involved in these activities? Why not leave them to the market?

2. Do you think the tax burden in the United States is too large or too small? Explain. What policies, if any, would you advocate to change the tax burden and its distribution? Be specific and defend your position.

3. The progressive personal income tax is the major source of tax revenue in the United States. What do you think are the advantages of this tax? What are its disadvantages? What changes, if any, would you make in the nature of this tax? Why?

4. "Transfer payments exert no influence on our economy because they merely transfer income from one group of individuals to another." Evaluate.

5. Do you think the indexing of the U.S. tax structure was a good idea? Why or why not? Will indexing make it easier or more difficult for Congress to increase tax revenues without voting for a tax increase? Explain. Do you think Congress may want to repeal indexing in the future? Why or why not?

6. Do you know of anyone participating in the underground economy? Do you think as many people would participate in the underground economy if marginal tax rates were lower? Why or why not?

7. Do you believe the U.S. tax structure is equitable? Do you think it is efficient? How might it be improved? Discuss.

PART
TWO

MACRO-
ECONOMICS

The Gross National Product is one of the great inventions of the twentieth century, probably almost as significant as the automobile and not quite so significant as TV. The effect of physical inventions is obvious, but social inventions like the GNP change the world almost as much. [1]

*PROFESSOR
KENNETH BOULDING*

- **What is GNP? What does it measure?**

- **What is the difference between real and nominal GNP? Why is it important to adjust income and output data for changes in prices?**

- **How much have prices increased during the 1970s and 1980s? How do economists and statisticians measure changes in the general level of prices?**

- **Is GNP a good measure of output?**

6 TAKING THE NATION'S ECONOMIC PULSE

Ours is a society infatuated with measurement. We seek to measure everything from the figure of Miss America to the speed of an all-star pitcher's fastball. The fact that we have therefore devised methods for measuring something as important as the performance of our economy is not surprising. What is surprising is that we waited so long. In the early 1930s, Congress instructed the Department of Commerce to develop and publish data on the performance of the economy. Simon Kuznets of the National Bureau of Economic Research had been working on this topic for several years. Kuznets developed the concepts and outlined the measurement procedures that eventually led to our present-day national income accounting techniques. In 1971, Kuznets was awarded the Nobel Prize in Economics for his work on this topic.

As the opening quote from Professor Boulding indicates, the development of an economic measuring rod was an extremely important "invention." Without such an invention, it would be difficult to tell how well the economy is doing. In this chapter, we will explain how the flow of an economy's output is measured. In addition, we will analyze both the strengths and weaknesses of the measurement tools that have been developed.

THE CONCEPT OF THE GNP

The gross national product (GNP) is the most widely used measure of economic performance. Newspaper writers and television commentators report the latest GNP statistics as proudly as they announce the latest baseball scores. GNP is almost a household expression. What does it indicate? Why is it important?

Gross National Product:
The total market value of all "final product" goods and services produced during a specific period, usually a year.

The **gross national product** is a measure of the market value of goods and services produced during a specific time period. GNP is a "flow" concept. It is typically measured in terms of an annual rate. By analogy, a water gauge is a device designed to measure the amount of water that flows through a pipe each hour. Similarly, GNP is a device designed to measure the market value of production that "flows" through the economy's factories and shops each year.

WHAT COUNTS TOWARD GNP?

Since GNP seeks to measure only current production, it cannot be arrived at merely by summing the totals on all of the nation's cash registers. Many transactions have to be excluded. What does GNP include and what does it exclude?

Final Goods and Services:
Goods and services purchased by their ultimate users.

1. GNP Counts Only Final Goods and Services. A "final good" is a good in the hands of its ultimate user. As goods go through intermediate stages of production, the intermediate sales are not counted by GNP. For example, when a wholesale distributor sells steak to a restaurant, the transaction is not included in GNP. The restaurant is not the final user; it is merely buying the

---

[1]Kenneth Boulding, "Fun and Games with the Gross National Product—The Role of Misleading Indicators in Social Policy," in *The Environmental Crisis*, (ed.) Harold W. Helfrich, Jr. (New Haven, Connecticut: Yale University Press, 1970), p. 157.

Intermediate Goods:
Goods purchased for resale or for use in producing another good or service.

steak for resale. When a customer buys the steak from the restaurant, the final purchase price of steak will be added to GNP.

Goods used to produce final goods and services are called **intermediate goods.** Essentially, the value of intermediate goods (like the steak sold by the wholesaler to the restaurant) is embodied within final goods. The price of the final goods reflect their value.

Exhibit 1 will help clarify the accounting methods for GNP. Before the final good, bread, is in the hands of the consumer, it will go through several intermediate stages of production. The farmer produces a pound of wheat and sells it to the miller for 30 cents. The miller grinds the wheat into flour and sells it to the baker for 65 cents. The miller's actions have added 35 cents to the value of the wheat. The baker combines the flour with other ingredients, makes a loaf of bread, and sells it to the grocer for 90 cents. The baker has added 25 cents to the value of the bread. The grocer stocks the bread on the grocery shelves and provides a convenient location for consumers to shop. The grocer sells the loaf of bread for $1, adding 10 cents to the value of the final product. Only the market value of the final product—the $1 for the loaf of bread—is counted by GNP.

As Exhibit 1 illustrates, the price of the final product reflects the *value added* at each stage of production. Thus, the 30 cents added by the farmer, the 35 cents by the miller, the 25 cents by the baker, and the 10 cents by the grocer sums to the $1 purchase price.

EXHIBIT 1 • GNP and Stages of Production

Most goods go through several stages of production. This chart illustrates both the market value of a loaf of bread as it passes through the various stages of production (column 1) and the amount added to the bread by each intermediate producer (column 2). GNP counts only the market value of the final product. Of course, the amount added by each intermediate producer (column 2) sums to the market value of the final product.

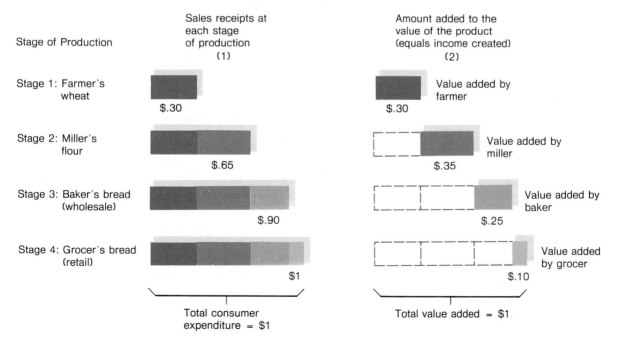

If GNP counted the sales price at each intermediate stage of production, double-counting would result. GNP would overstate the value of the final products available to users. To avoid this problem, GNP includes only the purchase price of final goods and services. Of course, as Exhibit 1 illustrates, the price of final goods is also equal to the *value added* —that is, the amount of income created at each stage of production.

2. GNP Counts Only Goods Produced During the Period. Keep in mind that GNP is a measurement of current production. Exchanges of goods or assets produced during a preceding period do not therefore contribute to current GNP.

The purchase of a used car produced last year will not enhance current GNP, nor will the sale of a "used" home, constructed five years ago. Production of these goods was counted at the time they were produced. Current sales and purchases of such items merely involve the exchange of existing goods. They do not involve current production of additional goods. Therefore, they are not counted. (Note: If a sales commission is involved in the exchange of a used car or home, the commission would add to current GNP since it involves a service during the current period.)

Since GNP counts long-lasting goods such as automobiles and houses when they are produced, it is not always an accurate gauge of what is currently being consumed. During an economic slowdown, few new durable assets will be produced. However, the consumption of durable goods that were produced and counted during an earlier period will continue. During good times, there will be a rapid expansion in the production of durable assets, but their consumption will be extended over a longer time period. Because of this cycle, GNP tends to understate consumption during a recession and overstate it during an economic boom.

GNP does not count purely financial transactions, since they do not involve current production. Purchases or sales of stocks, bonds, and U.S. securities do not count. They represent exchange of current assets, not production of additional goods. Similarly, private gifts are excluded, as are government transfer payments like welfare and social security payments. They do not enhance current production, and it would therefore be inappropriate to add them to GNP.

DOLLARS AS THE COMMON DENOMINATOR OF GNP

In grammar school, each of us was instructed about the difficulties of adding apples and oranges. Yet, this is precisely the nature of the aggregate measurement problem. Literally millions of different commodities and services are produced each year. How can the production of houses, movies, legal services, education, automobiles, dresses, heart transplants, astrological services, and many other items be added together?

These vastly different commodities and services have only one thing in common: someone pays for each of them in terms of dollars. Dollars act as a common denominator; units of each different good are weighted according to their dollar selling price. Production of an automobile adds 100 times as much to GNP as does the production of a briefcase, because the new automobile sells for $10,000 compared to $100 for the new briefcase. A heart transplant adds 50 times as much to GNP as does an appendectomy, because the heart transplant sells for $20,000 and the appendectomy for only $400. A fifth of whiskey adds more to GNP than does a week's supply of household water because the purchaser pays more for the whiskey than for the water. The total spending on all final goods produced during the year is then summed, in dollar terms, to obtain the annual GNP.

TWO WAYS OF MEASURING GNP

There are two ways of looking at and measuring GNP. The GNP of an economy can be reached either by totaling the spending on goods and services purchased, or by totaling the costs of producing and supplying those goods and services. That is, GNP can be calculated by adding the total expenditures on final goods and services supplied to purchasers. Or, alternatively, GNP can be determined by adding the total cost of supplying the goods and services, including the residual income of the producer-entrepreneurs. Either sum will equal GNP. This is true because, in simple terms, the money spent by purchasers on final goods and services can be seen as providing the wherewithal to produce and supply those goods and services.

There is a circular flow of **consumption** expenditures and resource costs illustrated for a very simple economy in Exhibit 2. There are only two

Consumption: Household spending on consumer goods and services during the current period. Consumption is a flow concept.

EXHIBIT 2 • The Circular Flow of Income

Here we illustrate two alternative ways of looking at the GNP for a simple economy consisting only of households and businesses. Households supply factor inputs in exchange for income (wages, rents, interest, and profits). These exchanges flow through the resource market (bottom loop). In turn, businesses supply final goods and services in exchange for business receipts (household spending on goods and services). These exchanges flow through the goods and services market. Both the flow of household purchases of goods and services (top loop) and the flow of factor compensation payments (bottom loop) will sum to GNP.

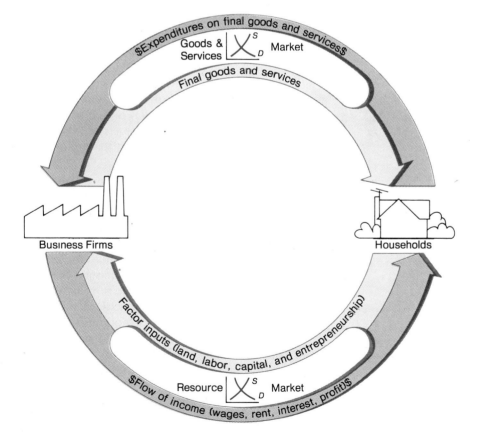

sectors—households and businesses—in this economy. The dollar flow of expenditures and receipts is indicated by the outer ring of the circular flow diagram. The flow of real products and resources is indicated by the inner ring. Goods and services produced in the business sector are sold to consumers in the household sector. Households supply the factors of production and receive income payments in exchange for their services. In turn, all the income of households is expended on the purchase of goods and services.

The bottom loop of Exhibit 2 illustrates the dollar flow of factor-cost payments (wages, rents, interest, and profits) from the business sector to the household sector in exchange for productive resources (labor, land, capital equipment, and entrepreneurship). These factor payments constitute the income of households. The price of the productive resources is determined by the forces of supply and demand operating in resource markets. Businesses use the services of the productive resources to produce goods and services.

The top loop of Exhibit 2 illustrates the dollar flow of consumer expenditures from households to businesses in exchange for goods and services. Business firms derive their revenues from the sale of products (food, clothing, medical services, and so on) they supply to households. These prices are determined in goods and services markets.

Modern economies, of course, are much more complicated than our simple two-sector circular flow model. In addition to the personal consumption expenditures of the household sector, there are governmental purchases of goods and services (for example, highways, education, warplanes, and police protection). Rather than purchase all productive inputs from households, businesses may undertake investment expenditures (business spending on machinery, production facilities, and other capital assets) out of their retained earnings, thus enhancing their future productive capabilities. In addition, foreigners both may purchase domestic goods and services and sell foreign-made products to the domestic market.

Nevertheless, the general principle still holds. Gross national product can be determined either by (a) summing the total expenditures on the "final product" goods and services produced during a period or by (b) summing the total cost incurred as a result of producing the goods and services supplied during the period. Exhibit 3 summarizes the components of GNP for both the expenditure approach and the resource cost-income approach.

It is important to note that the residual income of the producer-entrepreneur is included in the total cost of supplying goods and services, the second form of GNP measurement. Since business revenues derived from sales of goods and services will either be paid to resource suppliers or will accrue to capitalist entrepreneurs in the form of profits, the two methods of calculating GNP will yield identical outcomes. Note that profits, like contractual payments to factors of production, are considered a cost of production. Since profits are residual return, some might object to this classification. This view is incorrect. Just as wage payments induce workers to supply labor, the expectation of profit induces business decision-makers to supply capital equipment, organize production, and shoulder the risk of a residual income claimant. The latter is just as much a cost of production as the former.

From an accounting viewpoint, total payments to the factors of production, including the producer's profit or loss, must be equal to the sales price generated by the good. This is true for each good or service produced, and it is also true for the aggregate economy, as must be obvious from the previous discussion. This is a fundamental accounting identity.

$$\begin{matrix} \text{Dollar flow of expenditures} \\ \text{on final goods} \end{matrix} = \text{GNP} = \begin{matrix} \text{dollar flow of the producers' costs} \\ \text{on final goods} \end{matrix}$$

Thus, GNP obtained by adding the dollar value of final goods and services purchased will equal GNP obtained by adding the total of all "cost" items, including the producer's profits, associated with the production of final goods.

THE EXPENDITURE APPROACH

As Exhibit 3 indicates, when the expenditure approach is used to calculate GNP, four basic components of final products purchased must be considered. The left side of Exhibit 4 presents the value of these four components of GNP for 1985.

1. Consumption Purchases. Personal consumption purchases are the largest component of GNP; in 1985, they amounted to $2,582 billion. Most consumption expenditures are for nondurable goods or services. Food, clothing, recreation, medical and legal services, education, and fuel are included in this category. These items are used up or consumed in a relatively short time. Durable goods, such as appliances and automobiles, comprise approximately one eighth of all consumer purchases. These products

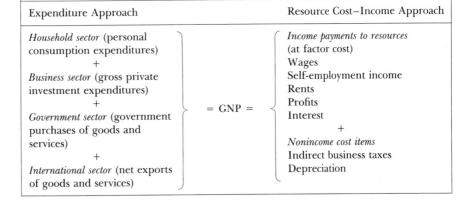

EXHIBIT 3 • The Two Ways of Measuring GNP

Even though modern economies are far more complicated than the two-sector circular flow model of Exhibit 2, there are still two methods of calculating GNP. It can be calculated either by summing the expenditures on the "final product" goods and services of each sector (left, below) or by summing the costs associated with the production of these goods and services (right, below).

Expenditure Approach		Resource Cost–Income Approach
Household sector (personal consumption expenditures)		*Income payments to resources* (at factor cost)
+		Wages
Business sector (gross private investment expenditures)		Self-employment income
	= GNP =	Rents
+		Profits
Government sector (government purchases of goods and services)		Interest
		+
+		*Nonincome cost items*
International sector (net exports of goods and services)		Indirect business taxes
		Depreciation

EXHIBIT 4 • Two Ways of Measuring GNP—1985 data (billions of dollars)[a]				
Expenditure Approach			**Resource Cost-Income Approach**	
Personal consumption		$2,582	Employee compensation	$2,373
Durable goods	$ 361		Proprietors' income	242
Nondurable goods	912			
Services	1,309		Rents	14
			Corporate profits	299
Gross private investment		670		
Fixed investment	438		Interest income	288
Inventories	232			
Government purchases		815	Indirect business taxes	
Federal	354		(includes transfers)	339
State and local	461		Depreciation (capital	
			consumption)	438
Net exports		− 74		
Gross national product		$3,993	Gross national product	$3,993

Source: U.S. Department of Commerce. These data are also available in the *Federal Reserve Bulletin,* which is published monthly.

[a]The left side shows the flow of expenditures and the right side the flow of resource costs. Both procedures yield GNP.

are enjoyed over a longer period of time even though they are fully counted at the time they are purchased.

Investment: The flow of expenditures on durable assets (fixed investment) plus the addition to inventories (inventory investment) during a period. These expenditures enhance our ability to provide consumer benefits in the future.

2. Gross Investment Purchases. Investment or capital goods provide a "flow" of future consumption or production service. Unlike food or medical services, they are not immediately "used." A house is an investment good because it will provide a stream of services long into the future. Business plants and equipment are investment goods because they, too, will provide productive services in the future. Changes in busines inventories are also classed as investment goods, since they will provide future consumer benefits.

Gross investment refers to the fact that expenditures are included both for (a) *replacement* of equipment worn out during the period and for (b) *expansion* in the supply of capital assets. In 1985, total investment expenditures were $670 billion including $438 billion for the replacement of assets worn out during the year. **Inventory investment** summed to $9 billion in 1985. The inventory component of investment varies substantially. At the beginning of an unexpected recession, inventories often rise as the result of weak demand. Later in the recession, businesses reduce their inventories in response to weak sales. In contrast, businesses generally rebuild their inventories during prosperous times when strong future sales are anticipated.

Inventory Investment: Changes in the stock of unsold goods and raw materials held during a period.

Many goods possess both consumer- and investment-good characteristics. There is not always a clear distinction between the two. National accounting procedures have rather arbitrarily classified business purchases of final goods as investment and considered household purchases, except housing, as consumption.

3. Government Purchases. In 1985, federal, state, and local government purchases were $815 billion, approximately 20 percent of total GNP. The purchases of state and local governments exceeded those of the federal government by a wide margin. The government component includes both investment and consumption services. Education, police protection, missiles, buildings, and generation of electric power, as well as medical, legal, and accounting services, are included in the government component. Since transfer payments are excluded, the size of the public sector greatly exceeds the amount counted as actually spent by the government on goods and services.

Exports: Goods and services produced domestically but sold to foreigners.

Imports: Goods and services produced by foreigners but purchased by domestic consumers, investors, and governments.

4. Net Exports. Exports are domestic goods and services purchased by foreigners. **Imports** are foreign goods and services purchased domestically. We want GNP to measure only the nation's production. Therefore, when measuring GNP by the expenditure approach, we must (a) add exports (goods produced domestically that were sold to foreigners) and (b) subtract imports (goods produced abroad that were purchased by Americans). For national accounting purposes, we can then combine these two factors into a single entry, net exports, where

$$\text{Net exports} = \text{total exports} - \text{total imports}$$

Net exports may be either positive or negative. When we sell more to foreigners than we buy from them, net exports are positive. In recent years, net exports have been negative, indicating we were buying more goods and services from foreigners than we were selling to them. In 1985, net exports were minus $74 billion.

THE RESOURCE COST-INCOME APPROACH

Exhibit 4 illustrates how, rather than summing the flow of expenditures on final goods and services, we could reach GNP by summing the flow of costs incurred in their production. Labor services play a very important role in the production process. It is therefore not surprising that employee compensation, $2,373 billion in 1985, is the largest cost incurred in the production of goods and services.

Self-employed proprietors undertake the risks of owning their own businesses and simultaneously provide their own labor services to the firm. Their earnings in 1985 contributed $242 billion to GNP, 6 percent of the total. Together, employees and self-employed proprietors accounted for approximately two thirds of GNP.

Machines, buildings, land, and other physical assets also contribute to the production process. Rents, corporate profits, and interest are payments to persons who provide either physical resources or the financial resources with which to purchase physical assets. Rents are returns to resource owners who permit others to use their assets during a time period. Corporate profits are compensation earned by stockholders, who bear the risk of the business undertaking and who provide financial resources with which the firm purchases resources. Interest is a payment to parties who extend loans to producers.

Not all cost components of GNP result in an income payment to a resource supplier. There are two major indirect costs.

1. Indirect Business Taxes. These taxes are imposed on the sale of many goods, and they are passed on to the consumer. The sales tax is a clear example. When you make a $1 purchase in a state with a 5 percent sales tax, the purchase actually costs you $1.05. The $1 goes to the seller to pay wages, rent, interest, and managerial costs. The 5 cents goes to the government. Indirect business taxes boost the market price of goods when GNP is calculated by the expenditure approach. Similarly, when looked at from the factor-cost viewpoint, taxes are an indirect cost of suppling the goods to the purchasers.

2. Depreciation. Using machines to produce goods causes the machines to wear out. Depreciation of capital goods is a cost of producing current goods, but it is not a direct cost because it reflects what is lost to the producer when machines and facilities become less valuable. Depreciation does not involve a direct payment to a resource owner. It is an estimate, based on the expected life of the asset, of the decline in the asset's value during the year. In 1985, depreciation (sometimes called capital consumption allowance) amounted to $438 billion, approximately 11 percent of GNP.

DEPRECIATION AND NET NATIONAL PRODUCT

Net National Product: Gross national product minus a depreciation allowance for the wearing out of machines and buildings during the period.

The inclusion of depreciation costs in GNP points out that it is indeed a "gross" rather than a "net" measure of economic production. Since GNP fails to allow for the wearing out of capital goods, it overstates the net output of an economy.

The **net national product** (NNP) is a concept designed to correct this deficiency. NNP is the total market value of the goods and services produced for consumers, governments, and net exports, plus any net additions to the nation's capital stock. In accounting terms, net national product is simply GNP minus depreciation.

Since NNP counts only net additions to the nation's capital stock, it is less than GNP. Net investment—the additions to capital stock—is always equal to gross investment minus depreciation. NNP counts only net investment.

THE RELATIVE SIZE OF GNP COMPONENTS

Of course, the relative importance of the components of GNP changes from time to time. Exhibit 5 shows the average proportion of GNP accounted for by each of the components during 1983–1985. When the expenditure approach is used, personal consumption expenditure is by far the largest and most stable component of GNP. Consumption accounted for 65 percent of GNP during 1983–1985, compared to only 16 percent for investment and 20 percent for government expenditures. When GNP is measured by the resource cost-income approach, compensation to employees is the dominant component (59 percent of GNP). During 1983–1985, rents, corporate profits, and interest combined to account for 16 percent of GNP.

GROSS NATIONAL PRODUCT OR GROSS NATIONAL COST?

As we have indicated, the cost and the expenditure approaches both lead to the same estimate of GNP. They are simply two ways of calculating the same thing. Considering the two approaches together helps keep the GNP in

EXHIBIT 5 • Major Components of GNP in the United States, 1983–1985

The relative sizes of the major components of GNP usually fluctuate within a fairly narrow range. The average proportion of each component during 1983–1985 is demonstrated here for both (a) the expenditure and (b) the resource cost–income approaches.

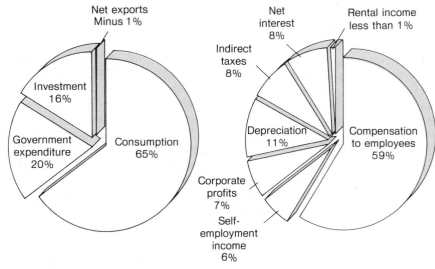

(a) Expenditure Approach

(b) Resource Cost-Income Approach

Source: *Economic Report of the President, 1986.*

perspective. From the purchaser's viewpoint, it is indeed gross national product. Good things were purchased by households, investors, governments, and foreigners. The purchasers valued the goods and services more than the purchase prices; otherwise, they would not have purchased them.

Production, though, also involves costs. The resource cost-income approach stresses the cost side of national income. The production of goods involves human toil, wear and tear on machines, sacrificing current consumption, risk, managerial responsibilities, and other of life's unpleasantries. Viewed from the producer's position, gross national cost might be a better term for GNP because resource owners had to forgo other things to produce goods and services.

As we will emphasize later, GNP is not a measure of how much "better off" we are. There are both positive and negative sides to it. Perhaps it might best be thought of as an index of current productive activity—activity that results in the goods and services that we desire, at the expense of work, waiting, risk, and depreciation, which we do not desire.

REAL AND NOMINAL GNP

Nominal Values: The value of economic variables such as GNP and personal consumption expressed in current prices. A general increase in prices will cause nominal values to rise even if there is no real change in the variable.

Real Values: The measurement of a variable after it has been adjusted for changes in the general level of prices.

It is important to distinguish between real and nominal economic values. When comparing data at different points in time, economists often use terms such as real wages, real income, or real GNP. The "real" refers to the fact that the data have been adjusted for changes in the level of prices. In contrast, **nominal values** (or *money values*, as they are often called) are expressed in current dollars. Over time, nominal values reflect changes both in (a) the real size of an economic variable and in (b) the general level of prices. In contrast, **real values** eliminate the impact of changes in the price

Real GNP: GNP in current dollars deflated for changes in the prices of the items included in GNP. Mathematically, real GNP_2 is equal to nominal GNP_2 multiplied by (GNP $Deflator_1$/GNP $Deflator_2$). Thus, if prices have risen between periods 1 and 2, the ratio of the GNP deflator in period 1 to the deflator in period 2 will be less than 1. This ratio will therefore deflate the nominal GNP for the rising prices.

GNP Deflator: A price index that reveals the cost of purchasing the items included in GNP during the period relative to the cost of purchasing these same items during a base year (currently, 1982). Since the base year is assigned a value of 100, as the GNP deflator takes on values greater than 100, it indicates that prices have risen.

Nominal GNP: GNP expressed at current prices. It is often called money GNP.

level. Stated another way, real economic data are adjusted for changes in the purchasing power of the dollar.

Perhaps an example will help clarify the difference between real and nominal values. In 1985, per capita *nominal* GNP in the United States was more than $16,800, compared to only $2,800 in 1960. Does this mean we produced almost six times as much output *per person* in 1985 as we did in 1960? Not hardly. In 1985, the general level of prices was 3.6 times the level of 1960. *Measured in terms of the price level in 1960,* **real GNP** per person in 1985 was $4,650, only about 66 percent more than GNP per person in 1960.

Nominal GNP will increase either if (a) more goods and services are produced or if (b) prices rise: Often, both (a) and (b) will contribute to an increase in GNP. Since we are usually interested in comparing only the output or actual production during two different time intervals, GNP must be adjusted for the change in prices.

How can we determine how much the prices of items included in GNP have risen during a specific period? We answer this question by constructing a price index called the **GNP deflator.** The Department of Commerce estimates how much of each item included in GNP has been produced during a year. This bundle of goods will include automobiles, houses, office buildings, medical services, bread, milk, entertainment, and all other goods included in the GNP, in the quantities actually produced during the current year. The Department then calculates the ratio of (a) the cost of purchasing this representative bundle of goods *at current prices* divided by (b) the cost of purchasing the same bundle *at the prices that were present during a designated earlier base year.* The base year chosen (currently 1982 for the GNP deflator) is assigned the value 100. The GNP deflator is equal to the calculated ratio multiplied by 100. If prices are, *on average,* higher during the current period than they were during the base year, the GNP deflator will exceed 100. The relative size of the GNP deflator is a measure of the current price level compared to the price level during the base year. (See Measures in Economic Activity for additional detail on how price indexes are constructed.)

We can use the GNP deflator to measure real GNP: GNP in dollars of constant purchasing power. If prices are rising, we simply deflate the **nominal GNP** during the latter period to account for the effects of inflation.

Exhibit 6 illustrates how real GNP is measured and why it is important to adjust for price changes. Between 1982 and 1985, nominal GNP increased 26.1 percent. However, a large portion of this increase in nominal GNP reflected higher prices rather than a larger rate of output. The GNP deflator in 1985 was 111.7, compared to 100 in 1982. Prices rose by 11.7 percent between 1982 and 1985. In determining the real GNP for 1985 in terms of 1982 dollars, we deflate the 1985 nominal GNP for the rise in prices:

$$\text{Real GNP}_{85} = \text{nominal GNP}_{85} \times \frac{\text{GNP deflator}_{82}}{\text{GNP deflator}_{85}}$$

Because prices were rising, the latter ratio is less than one. In terms of 1982 dollars, the real GNP in 1985 was $3,574 billion, only 12.9 percent more than in 1982. So, although money GNP expanded by 26.1 percent, real GNP increased by only 12.9 percent.

EXHIBIT 6 • Changes in Prices and the Real GNP

Between 1982 and 1985, GNP increased by 26.1 percent. But, when the 1985 GNP was deflated to account for price increases, real GNP increased by only 12.9 percent.

	Nominal GNP (billions of dollars)	Price Index (GNP deflator, 1982 = 100)	Real GNP (1982 dollars)
1982	$3,166	100.0	$3,166
1985	3,993	111.7	3,574
Percent increase	26.1	11.7	12.9

Source: U.S. Department of Commerce.

A change in money GNP tells us nothing about what is happening to the rate of real production unless we also know what is happening to prices. Money income could double while production actually declines, if prices more than double. On the other hand, money income could remain constant while real GNP increases, if prices fall during a time period. Data on money GNP and price changes are both essential for a meaningful comparison of real income between two time periods.

PROBLEMS WITH GNP AS A MEASURING ROD

GNP is not a perfect device for measuring current production and income. Some items are excluded, even though they would be properly classed as "current production." Sometimes production results in harmful "side effects," which are not fully accounted for. In this section, we will focus on some of the limitations and shortcomings of GNP as a measure of economic performance.

GNP DOES NOT COUNT NONMARKET PRODUCTION

The GNP fails to count household production because such production does not involve a market transaction. Because of this, the household services of millions of people are excluded. If you mow the yard, repair your car, paint your house, pick up relatives from school, or perform similar productive household activities, your labor services add nothing to GNP, since no market transaction is involved. Such nonmarket productive activities are sizable—10 or 15 percent of total GNP, perhaps more. Their exclusion results in some oddities in national income accounting.

For example, if a woman marries her gardener, and, if after the marriage the spouse-gardener works for love rather than for money, GNP will decline because the services of the spouse-gardener will now be excluded: there is no longer a market transaction. If a parent hires a baby-sitter in order to enter the labor force, these actions have a double-barreled impact on GNP. It will rise as a result of (a) the amount the baby-sitter is paid plus (b) the parent's on-the-job earnings.

MEASURES OF ECONOMIC ACTIVITY

Deriving the GNP Deflator and the Consumer Price Index

When making comparisons of output and expenditures between periods, it is important to adjust for price changes. Economists measure changes in prices by constructing a price index. A price index measures the cost (or value) of a given bundle of goods at a point in time relative to the cost of the same bundle of goods during a prior base year. The base year is assigned a value of 100. If prices are higher during the current period (that is, if the cost of purchasing the given bundle of goods has risen), the value of the price index during the current period will exceed 100.

Construction of a Price Index—Simple Illustration

A simple example can be used to illustrate the concept of a price index. Imagine that students at your college purchase only four items: hamburgers, t-shirts, blue jeans, and stereo records. In recent years, the prices of these goods have risen. Suppose we want to determine the degree to which prices rose between 1980 (the base year) and 1986. A careful sampling of prices is used to determine the average price of each item in the student's budget for both 1980 and 1986. These data are presented in Exhibit 7. Note that price changes varied among the goods. The price of hamburgers doubled between 1980 and 1986, while the price of jeans remained unchanged. T-shirt prices rose by 80 percent (from $5 to $9), but the price of stereo records declined between 1980 and 1986. How can the price data for 1980 and 1986 be used to determine the difference in the level of prices between the two years?

Method I: Using Base-Year Market Basket. A price index reveals the cost of purchasing a market basket of goods at a point in time compared to the cost of purchasing *the identical market basket* during an earlier base period. What market basket should be used? One obvious possibility would be the market basket consumed by students during the base period. Suppose a survey of the student population indicates that, on average, students purchased 60 hamburgers, four t-shirts, two pair of blue jeans and one stereo record monthly during the 1980 base year. This information permits us to determine the cost of the market basket purchased by the typical student in 1980 at both 1980 and 1986 prices. Exhibit 7 presents these calculations. The market basket consumed by the typical student in 1980 costs $100 at 1980 prices. At 1986 prices, the identical market basket costs $162.

We can now calculate the 1986 College Student Price Index (CSPI) based on the 1980 market basket.

The CSPI is:

$$\frac{\text{Cost of base-year market basket at current (1986) prices}}{\text{Cost of base-year market basket at base-year (1980) prices}} \times 100$$

The cost of the base-year market basket in 1986 was $162, compared to a cost of $100 in 1980. Thus, the 1986 CSPI *using the base-year market basket* is equal to 162 (162 ÷ 100 times 100).

Method II: Using Current-Year Market Basket. Rather than using the base-year market basket, we might use the current-year quantity of each good purchased to weight the 1980 and 1986 prices. Using this alternative, the formula for the CSPI would be:

$$\frac{\text{Cost of current-year market basket at current (1986) prices}}{\text{Cost of current-year market basket at base-year (1980) prices}} \times 100$$

EXHIBIT 7 • The 1986 Price Index (1980 = 100) Based on the Typical Market Basket Consumed by College Students in 1980 (hypothetical data)

| Monthly Purchases, 1980 | Average Price | | Cost of 1980 Market Basket | |
	1980	1986	1980 Prices	1986 Prices
60 Hamburgers	$ .80	$ 1.60	$ 48.00	$ 96.00
4 T-shirts	5.00	9.00	20.00	36.00
2 Jeans	12.00	12.00	24.00	24.00
1 Stereo record	8.00	6.00	8.00	6.00
		Total	$100.00	$162.00

Price Index in 1986 (1980 = 100) $= \frac{162}{100} = 162$

MEASURES OF ECONOMIC ACTIVITY (continued)

A 1986 survey of students indicates the quantity of each commodity purchased monthly during the year. These data are presented in Exhibit 8. They can be used to calculate the cost of purchasing the 1986 typical market basket at both 1980 and 1986 prices. As Exhibit 8 shows, the typical market basket actually purchased in 1986 would have cost $98 *at 1980 prices*. The same market basket cost $150 at 1986 prices. *Based on the current-year market basket,* then, the 1986 CSPI is equal to 153.1 (150 ÷ 98).

Why do the two alternative methods yield different values for

Consumer Price Index:
An indicator of the general level of prices. It attempts to compare the cost of purchasing the market basket bought by a typical consumer during a specific period with the cost of purchasing the same market basket during an earlier period.

the price index? The differences reflect the weights applied to 1980–1986 price changes. Method I uses the quantity purchased of each good during the earlier period (1980) to weight the price changes, while Method II uses the quantities of the current period (1986).

If the changes in purchases of goods were random, the two alternative methods would tend toward equality. However, changes in the pattern of purchases will not be random. Consumers will systematically reduce their purchases of those items that increase the most in price. Similarly, they will tend to expand their consumption of commodities that become *relatively* cheaper. The consumption patterns of Exhibits 7 and 8 illustrate this point. As the prices of hamburgers and t-shirts rose sharply between 1980 and 1986, the quantity purchased of these items declined. In contrast, the quantity of jeans and stereo records purchased increased as their *relative* prices declined between 1980 and 1986.

Since Method I assumes that consumers will purchase the base-year bundle, it makes no allowance for substitution away from those

goods (hamburgers and t-shirts in our hypothetical case) that increase most in price. So, it overstates the "true" increase in prices (and the inflation rate). In contrast, Method II imposes the current-year bundle on consumers during the base year. In reality, they would substitute away from the goods that have increased most in price. The imposition of the current-year market basket overstates the level of prices *during the base year*. It thus understates the change in prices between periods.

It was therefore no coincidence that our Method I price index (using the base-year market basket) was greater than our Method II price index (based on the current-year market basket). Method I systematically overstates the increase in prices (and the inflation rate), while Method II systematically understates it.

The Consumer Price Index
The **Consumer Price Index** (CPI) is the most widely used index of price changes over time. The CPI is prepared monthly by the Bureau of Labor Statistics of the Department of Labor. The methodology underlying the CPI is much like our Method I calculations of Exhibit 7, except that the market basket for the CPI is much broader. The CPI is designed to measure changes in the typical market basket purchased by urban consumers.[2] The composition (quantities) of that market basket is based on the Consumer Ex-

[2]Actually, the Bureau of Labor Statistics now publishes two indexes of consumer prices—one for "all urban households" and the other for "urban wage earners and clerical workers." The two differ slightly because the typical bundles of goods purchased by the two groups are not identical.

EXHIBIT 8 • The 1986 Price Index (1980 = 100) Based on Typical Market Basket Consumed by College Students in 1986 (hypothetical data)

Monthly Purchases, 1986	Average Price 1980	1986	Cost of 1986 Market Basket 1980 Prices	1986 Prices
50 Hamburgers	$ .80	$ 1.60	$40.00	$ 80.00
2 T-shirts	5.00	9.00	10.00	18.00
2 Jeans	12.00	12.00	24.00	24.00
3 Stereo records	8.00	6.00	24.00	18.00
		Total	$98.00	$150.00

Price Index in 1986 (1980 = 100) $= \frac{150}{98} = 153.1$

MEASURES OF ECONOMIC ACTIVITY (continued)

penditure Survey conducted during 1972–1973. This survey identified 382 items that comprised the typical bundle purchased by urban consumers during 1972–1973.

Each month, some 250 survey workers call or visit approximately 20,000 stores in urban areas selected to represent all urban places in the United States. All together, the CPI *each month* uses approximately 125,000 prices for the 382 food items, consumer goods and services, housing, and property taxes included in the CPI. The average price for each of the items is then weighted according to the quantity of the item purchased during 1972–1973. Just as we illustrated for the four-item market basket of Exhibit 7, the cost of purchasing the 382-item market basket *at current prices* is then compared with the cost of purchasing the same market basket *at base-year prices*. The result is a measure of current prices compared to base-year prices.

Even though the market basket for the CPI is based on 1972–1973, the base year (CPI = 100) is 1967. In 1985, the value of the CPI was 322.2, compared to the base of 100 in 1967. This indicates the price level in 1985 was more than triple the price level of 1967.

The GNP Deflator

The most general price index is the GNP deflator. The GNP deflator differs from the CPI in two important respects. First, the GNP deflator is based on the typical market basket that goes into GNP—that is, all final goods and services produced. In addition to consumer goods, the GNP deflator includes prices for goods and services pur-

chased by businesses and governments. Thus, items such as computers, airplanes, molding equipment, and office space are included in the GNP deflator. Second, the GNP deflator is calculated by Method II procedures. Prices during each period are weighted by *the current-year market basket* rather than the base-year market basket as for the CPI.

Comparison of the CPI and GNP Deflator

Exhibit 9 presents data for both the CPI and GNP deflator during the 1967–1984 period. Even though they are based on different market baskets and procedures, the two measures of the inflation rate are quite similar for most years. There were three exceptions—1974, 1979, and 1980. Since the CPI is based on the market basket of the earlier period (Method I procedure), it tends to overstate the inflation rate. The

upward bias is more important when there is substantial substitution away from items for which prices have increased sharply. Many economists believe this was the case during the 1970s, a period of sharply higher oil prices. This may well account for the differences between the CPI and GNP deflator during 1974, 1979, and 1980.

The CPI and GNP deflator were designed for different purposes. Choosing between the two depends on what we are trying to measure. If we want to determine how rising prices affect the money income of consumers, the CPI would be most appropriate since it includes only consumer goods. However, if we want an economy-wide measure of inflation with which to adjust GNP or national income data, clearly the GNP deflator is the appropriate index since it includes the price of every good and service produced.

EXHIBIT 9　•　The CPI and GNP Deflator, 1967–1985

Year	CPI (1967 = 100)	Inflation Rate (percent)	GNP deflator (1982 = 100)	Inflation Rate (percent)
1967	100.0	–	35.9	–
1968	104.2	4.2	37.7	5.0
1969	109.8	5.4	39.8	5.6
1970	116.3	5.9	42.0	5.5
1971	121.3	4.3	44.4	5.7
1972	125.3	3.3	46.5	4.7
1973	133.1	6.2	49.5	6.5
1974	147.7	11.0	54.0	9.1
1975	161.2	9.1	59.3	9.8
1976	170.5	5.8	63.1	6.4
1977	181.5	6.5	67.3	6.7
1978	195.4	7.7	72.2	7.3
1979	217.4	11.3	78.6	8.9
1980	246.8	13.5	85.7	9.0
1981	272.9	10.4	94.0	9.7
1982	289.1	6.1	100.0	6.4
1983	298.4	3.2	103.8	3.8
1984	311.1	4.3	108.1	4.1
1985	322.2	3.6	111.7	3.3

Source: *Economic Report of the President, 1986.*

The omission of many nonmarket productive activities makes comparisons over time and among countries at various stages of market development less meaningful. For example, more women are currently involved in market work than was true 30 years ago. There is widespread use of appliances today to perform functions previously performed by women at home providing unpaid household labor. This fact, along with increasing market specialization, indicates that excluded household activities are less important today than they were 30 years ago. This means the current GNP, even in real dollars, is overstated relative to the earlier period, since a larger share of total production was previously excluded.

Similarly, GNP comparisons overstate the output of developed countries when compared to underdeveloped countries. A larger share of the total production of underdeveloped countries originates in the household sector. For example, Mexican families are more likely than their U.S. counterparts to make their own clothing, raise and prepare their own food, provide their own child-rearing services, and even build their own homes. These productive labor services, originating in the household sector, are excluded from GNP. Therefore, GNP in Mexico understates output there more than GNP in the United States understates U.S. output.

GNP DOES NOT COUNT THE UNDERGROUND ECONOMY

In the preceding chapter, we indicated that many transactions go unreported because they involve either illegal activities or tax evasion (which is illegal, although the activities generating the income may not be). Many of these "underground" activities produce goods and services that are valued by purchasers. Nevertheless, since the activities are unreported, they do not contribute to GNP. Estimates of the size of the underground economy in the United States range from 10 to 15 percent of total output. Most observers, as we have noted, believe these unrecorded transactions have grown much more rapidly in recent years than has measured output. If this is true, it implies that the published GNP figures are actually understating the growth rate of output, since an expanding proportion of total output is being excluded.

GNP FAILS TO TAKE LEISURE AND HUMAN COSTS INTO ACCOUNT

Simon Kuznets, the "inventor" of GNP, suggests that the failure to fully include leisure and human costs is one of the grave omissions of national income accounting. GNP excludes leisure, a good that is valuable to each of us. One country might attain a $10,000 per capita GNP with an average work week of 30 hours. Another might attain the same per capita GNP with a 50-hour work week. In terms of total output, the first country has the greater production because it "produces" more leisure, or sacrifices less human cost. GNP, though, does not reflect this fact.

The average number of hours worked per week in the United States has declined steadily over the years. The average nonagricultural production worker spent only 35 hours per week on the job in 1985, compared to more than 40 hours in 1947: a 12 percent reduction in weekly hours worked. Clearly, this reduction in the length of the work week raised the American standard of living, even though it did not enhance GNP.

GNP also fails to take into account human costs—the physical and mental strains—associated with many jobs. On average, jobs today are less physically strenuous and less exhausting than they were 30 years ago, but they are perhaps more monotonous. These shortcomings—failure to consider leisure and the human costs of employment—reduce the significance of longitudinal GNP comparisons.

GNP DOES NOT ACCOUNT FOR SOCIAL COSTS

Production and consumption of some economic goods generate harmful side effects that either detract from current consumption or reduce our future production possibilities. For example, when property rights are defined imperfectly, air and water pollution are sometimes side effects of productive activity. Similarly, depletion of natural resources, like depreciation of capital stock, reduces our ability to produce future goods. GNP does not account for these negative side effects. It thus tends to overstate our "real output."

THE PROBLEM OF QUALITY VARIATION AND INTRODUCTION OF NEW GOODS

In a dynamic world, changes in quality and the introduction of new goods make income comparisons over time more difficult. During the last 10 or 15 years, there have been substantial changes in the quality and availability of products. Today, new automobiles are more fuel efficient and generally safer than were new automobiles 15 years ago. Dental services are generally much less unpleasant than was true 15 years ago. Some commodities—satellite television receivers, video recorders, personal computers, and heart transplants, to name a few—simply were unavailable just a few years ago. Statisticians devising price indexes attempt to make some allowance for quality improvements. Many economists believe, however, that failure to fully adjust for quality improvements and the introduction of new products result in an overestimation of the inflation rate by as much as 1 or 2 percent annually.

When the bundle of goods available each year differs substantially, the meaningfulness of income comparisons is reduced. As Exhibit 10 shows, per capita real GNP in 1930 was only about one third the figure for 1985. Does this mean that, on average, Americans produced and consumed three times more goods in 1985 than in 1930? Caution should be exercised before arriving at this conclusion. In the 1930s, there were no jet planes, electric typewriters, high speed computers, television programs, automatic dish-

---

EXHIBIT 10 • Per Capita Real GNP, 1930–1985

In 1985, per capita real GNP was 89 percent greater than in 1950, 2.56 times the 1940 level, and 2.94 times the 1930 value. How meaningful are these numbers?

Year	Per Capita Real GNP (in 1982 dollars)
1930	$ 5,085
1940	5,851
1950	7,935
1960	9,213
1970	11,785
1980	13,996
1985	14,964

Source: Derived from U.S. Department of Commerce data.

washers, or stereo records. In 1930, even a millionaire could not have purchased the typical bundle consumed by Americans in 1985. On the other hand, in 1930, there were plenty of open spaces, trees, uncongested (but rough) roads, pure-water rivers, hiking areas, and areas with low crime rates. Thus, many goods were available in 1985 that were not available in 1930, and vice versa. Under such circumstances, comparative GNP statistics lose much of their relevance.

GNP AND MEASURING ECONOMIC WELFARE

GNP means many things to many people. Some people perceive it as a measure of economic welfare, happiness, or even social progress. This is unfortunate, because GNP was never intended to measure subjective concepts that would obviously be influenced by many factors other than economic goods.

GNP focuses on the production of goods and services without making any judgments about how useful the goods are or what makes people want them. A dollar spent for the schooling of an orphan child counts no more or no less than the alcoholic's dollar spent on another bottle of cheap wine. A dollar spent on advertising counts as much as a dollar spent on a kidney machine to preserve life. A dollar spent on a ticket to a football game counts as much as a dollar spent for admission to a concert by the Boston Symphony Orchestra. GNP makes no distinction. The only criterion is whether or not someone wants the "good" or service enough to pay for it.

Might it be possible to develop a measure, if not of social progress, then of economic welfare? Some economists think so. The task is complicated by the fact that many important items that one would like to measure do not flow through markets. Because of this, there are no market prices to tell us how much they are valued by purchasers.

The work of James Tobin, the 1981 Nobel laureate, and William Nordhaus represents the most elaborate attempt to develop a broader measure of economic well-being, a measure that encompasses both the economic "goods" and "bads" generated during a period.[3] Tobin and Nordhaus refer to their measuring rod as the **measure of economic welfare** (MEW). MEW modifies the traditional GNP data in three major ways:

Measure of Economic Welfare: A new measure of economic well-being that focuses on the consumption of goods and services during a period. It differs from GNP in that (a) the estimated cost of various economic "bads" are deducted, (b) expenditures on "regrettable necessities" are excluded, and (c) the estimated benefits of leisure and various nonmarket productive activities are included.

1. The estimated cost of certain economic bads, such as pollution, litter, congestion, and noise, are subtracted from GNP.
2. Expenditures on "regrettable necessities," such as police protection and national defense, are excluded from GNP.
3. The estimated value of nonmarket goods, such as household productive activities and leisure, are added to GNP.

Tobin and Nordhaus estimate that since 1945, per capita MEW has grown less rapidly than per capita GNP. This would indicate that the growth

[3]William Nordhaus and James Tobin, "Is Growth Obsolete?" in *Economic Growth*, National Bureau of Economic Research, [Proceedings on] Fiftieth Anniversary Colloquium (New York, 1972).

of GNP in recent years may be an overstatement of our recent economic progress.

Of course, subjective judgments are involved when researchers seek to place a value on items that do not go through markets. Tobin and Nordhaus are aware that their estimates are both subjective and subject to error. Nevertheless, their work represents a challenge to other economists to develop alternative estimates based on different procedures and assumptions. The revision of our methods of measuring economic performance is clearly an exciting and potentially fertile field for tomorrow's economists.

THE GREAT CONTRIBUTION OF GNP

The great contribution of GNP (measured in constant dollars) is its precision, despite all of its shortcomings, as an indicator of short-term changes in productive activity. Current GNP provides a reasonably accurate indication of how we are doing relative to the recent past.

This is very important. If we could not accurately track the performance of the economy, we would be much less likely to adopt productive policies. This ability to identify short-run changes in economic performance is a valuable contribution. This contribution is sufficiently important to rank GNP, in Professor Boulding's words, "as one of the great inventions of the twentieth century, probably almost as significant as the automobile."

OTHER RELATED INCOME MEASURES

Exhibit 11 illustrates the relationships among five alternative measures of aggregate income. GNP, of course, is the broadest and most frequently quoted index of economic performance. As we previously discussed, NNP is simply GNP minus depreciation. Net national product measures the total flow of consumption and government expenditures plus the *net additions* to the capital stock. It values the production of goods and services of the economy at market prices. These prices, however, include indirect business taxes, which boost market prices but which do not represent the cost of using a factor of production. When economists subtract these indirect taxes from NNP, the resulting figure is called **national income.** National income thus represents net output valued at factor cost.

National income can be determined in two ways. As Exhibit 11 shows, it is NNP minus indirect business taxes, but it is also the income payments to all factors of production. So, the sum of employee compensation, interest, self-employment income, rents, and corporate profits also yields national income.

Although national income represents the earnings of all resource owners, it is not the same as personal income. **Personal income** is the total of all income received by individuals—income with which they consume goods, add to savings, and pay taxes. It differs from national income in two respects. First, some income is earned but not directly received. Stockholders do not receive all the income generated by corporations. Corporate taxes takes a share. Additional profits are channeled back into the business, remaining undistributed to the stockholder. Social security taxes are deducted

National Income: The total income payments to owners of human (labor) and physical capital during a period. It is also equal to NNP minus indirect business taxes.

Personal Income: The total income received by individuals that is available for consumption, saving, and payment of personal taxes.

from the employee's paycheck, forming a component of income earned but not directly received. These factors must be subtracted when calculating personal income.

Second, some income is received even though it was not earned *during the current period.* Government transfer payments, including social security and interest payments, are included in this category. By the same token, dividends received add to personal income, regardless of when they were earned. These components must be added to yield personal income.

As anyone who has ever worked on a job knows, the amount shown on your paycheck does not equal your salary. Personal taxes must be deducted. **Disposable income** is the income that is yours to do with as you please. It is simply personal income minus personal taxes.

There are thus five alternative measures of national product and income:

1. Gross national product
2. Net national product
3. National income
4. Personal income
5. Disposable income

Disposable Income: The income available to individuals after personal taxes. It can either be spent on consumption or saved.

EXHIBIT 11 • Five Alternative Measures of Income

The bar charts illustrate the relationship among five alternative measures of national income. The alternatives range from the gross national product, which is the broadest measure of output, to disposable income, which indicates the funds available to households for either personal consumption or saving.

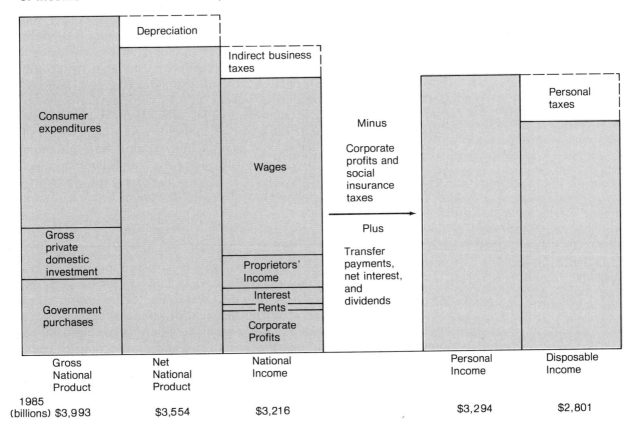

Each of the five measures something different, but they are all closely related. Movement of one of the income measures nearly always parallels movement of the other indicators. Since the five measures move together, economists often use only GNP or the terms "income," "output," or "aggregate production" when referring to the general movement of all five of the indicators of productive activity.

THE REAL INCOME-REAL OUTPUT LINK

National income accounting methods illustrate that the flow of goods and services to the household, business, government, and foreign sectors must equal the flow of income to resource suppliers (see Exhibits 2, 3, and 4). Stated another way, the actual total supply of goods and services to the various sectors of the economy must be equal to the actual total income of resource suppliers. Total output (supply) and total income are merely alternative methods of viewing the same thing. Aggregate output is the value of the "final user" goods and services supplied to the household, business, government, and foreign sectors during the period. Aggregate income is the sum of payments to resource suppliers who produced those goods. They must equal one another. Since aggregate output and aggregate income must be equal, one obviously cannot change without the other changing, too.

The only way in which a nation can increase its real income is to increase its real output. Unless there is an expansion in the production of goods and services valued by customers, businesses, governments, and foreigners, there will not be an expansion in the real income of a nation. Growth of real income is entirely dependent on the growth of real output.

When evaluating policy alternatives designed to stimulate the growth of income, one must focus clearly on the link between aggregate income and aggregate output. Proponents of policies such as tax reductions, public-sector employment, higher minimum wages, and increased unionization generally argue that their proposals will lead either to a higher level of income or to more rapid economic growth. In evaluating these and other policy alternatives, the careful researchers will ask, "How will the proposal affect output?" Unless there is reason to believe that the policy alternative will stimulate the production of desired goods and services, it will clearly not increase income.

LOOKING AHEAD

GNP and the related income concepts provide us with a measure of economic performance. In the next chapter, we will take a closer look at the movements of prices and real output in the United States and in other countries. As we proceed, we will investigate the factors that underlie these movements. Models that rely heavily on the interrelationships among household consumption, business investment, and government expenditures will be central to our analysis. As we compare the implications of our analysis with the real world, measurement of GNP and related indicators of income will help us sort out sound theories from economic nonsense.

CHAPTER SUMMARY

1. Gross national product (GNP) is a measure of the market value of final goods and services produced during a specific time period.

2. Dollars act as a common denominator for GNP. Production of each final product is weighted according to its selling price. Alternatively, GNP can be calculated by adding up the dollar factor cost of producing the final goods. The two methods sum to an identical result.

3. When the expenditure approach is used, there are four major components of GNP: (a) consumption, (b) investment, (c) government, and (d) net exports.

4. The major components of GNP, as calculated by the resource cost-income approach, are (a) wages and salaries, (b) self-employment income, (c) rents, (d) interest, (e) corporate profits, and (f) non-income expenses, primarily depreciation and indirect business taxes.

5. When comparing income and output data over time, it is important to distinguish between real and nominal values. Changes in nominal values reflect changes in the general level of prices, as well as changes in the economic variable. In constrast, data measured in real terms have been adjusted to eliminate the impact of changes in the price level. Since economics focuses primarily on real changes, economists generally use real data to measure income, output, and other variables influenced by the level of prices.

6. In effect, price indexes compare the cost of purchasing a typical bundle of goods during a time period relative to the cost of the same bundle during an earlier base year. The base-year price level is assigned a value of 100. Thus, if prices have risen relative to the base year, the price index will exceed 100. The two most widely used price indexes in the United States are the GNP deflator and the consumer price index (CPI).

7. GNP may increase because of an increase in either output or prices. The GNP deflator can be used to convert nominal GNP to real GNP. Measured in period 1 dollars,

$$\text{Real GNP}_2 = \text{nominal GNP}_2 \times \frac{\text{GNP deflator}_1}{\text{GNP deflator}_2}$$

8. GNP is an imperfect measure of current production. It excludes household production and the underground (unreported) economy. It fails to account for the negative side effects of current production, such as air and water pollution, depletion of natural resources, and other factors that do not flow through markets. It adjusts imperfectly for quality changes. GNP comparisons are less meaningful when the typical bundle of available goods and services differs widely between two time periods (or between two nations).

9. Despite all its limitations, GNP is of tremendous importance because it is an accurate tool enabling us to identify short-term economic fluctuations. Without such a reliable indicator, economic theory would be unable to determine the cause of economic slowdowns and economic policy would be less able to combat them.

10. Economists frequently refer to four other income measures that are related to GNP: net national product, national income, personal

income, and disposable income. All of these measures of income tend to move together.

11. The circular flow model illustrates that the aggregate supply of goods and services to households, businesses, governments, and foreigners, and the aggregate income of resource suppliers are merely alternative methods of viewing the same thing. Because of this, actual aggregate output and actual aggregate income will always be equal. The only way we can increase aggregate income is by increasing the aggregate supply of goods desired by economic participants.

THE ECONOMIC WAY OF THINKING— DISCUSSION QUESTIONS

1. Why does a pound of beef add more to GNP than a pound of wheat? Does it reflect demand or cost? Comment.

2. Explain why the rate of growth in GNP in current dollars can sometimes be a misleading statistic.

3. What is real GNP? How is it determined? Calculate the change in real GNP between 1970 and 1980.

4. Indicate which of the following activities are counted as part of this year's GNP:
   (a) The services of a homemaker.
   (b) Frank Murry's purchase of a 1986 Chevrolet.
   (c) Frank Murry's rental payments on a 1986 Chevrolet.
   (d) The purchase of 100 shares of AT&T stock.
   (e) Interest on a bond issued at AT&T.
   (f) Family lawn services provided by a 16-year-old.
   (g) Family lawn services purchased from the neighbor's 16-year-old, who has a lawn-mowing business.
   (h) A multibillion dollar discovery of natural gas in Oklahoma.
   (i) Deterioration of the water quality of Lake Michigan.

5. Why might the GNP be a misleading index of changes in output between 1900 and 1985 in the United States? of differences in output between the United States and Mexico?

6. "GNP counts the product of steel but not the disproduct of air pollution. It counts the product of automobiles but not the disproduct of 'blight' due to junkyards. It counts the product of cigarettes but not the disproduct of a shorter life expectancy due to cancer. Until we can come up with a more reliable index, we cannot tell whether economic welfare is progressing or regressing." Explain why you either agree or disagree with this view.

7. **What's Wrong with This Way of Thinking?**
   "An agricultural program that pays farmers to reduce their planted acreage and cut back on the production of farm products can increase everyone's income. The reduction in the supply of farm products will cause their prices to rise, which will result in an increase in the income of farmers. The higher level of farm income will cause farmers to increase their purchases of manufacturing products, which will expand the income of city dwellers. The farm subsidies will increase the income not only of farmers but also of the nation as a whole."

- What is a business cycle? How much economic instability has the United States experienced?

- Why do we experience unemployment? Are some types of unemployment worse than others?

- What do economists mean by full employment? How is full employment related to the natural rate of unemployment?

- What are some of the side effects of inflation? Does it make any difference whether or not buyers and sellers anticipate inflation? Why?

Prosperity is when the prices of the things that you sell are rising; inflation is when the prices of the things that you buy are rising. Recession is when other people are unemployed; depression is when you are unemployed.

ANONYMOUS

7 ECONOMIC FLUCTUATIONS, UNEMPLOYMENT, AND INFLATION

A stable environment is crucial to the efficient operation of an economy. The stability issue can be broken down into three specific economic goals: (a) growth of real output, (b) full employment, and (c) price stability. Obviously, these three goals are interrelated. Without full employment, the potential output of an economy will not be fully realized. Similarly, fluctuation in prices will generate uncertainty and retard economic growth. In this chapter, we will look at the stability of real output, employment, and prices. We will analyze the historical record and discuss some of the measurement problems in this area. The concept of full employment will be introduced and its meaning discussed. We will also analyze the side effects of inflation and consider how buyers and sellers adjust their choices when they anticipate rising prices in the future.

Our goal in this chapter is to provide the reader with basic knowledge about economic instability—why it is important and how it influences our lives. As we proceed, we will develop a model of our economy that will help us better understand the causes of economic instability. The government's spending and monetary policies exert an important impact on the stability of an economy. In the United States, the Employment Act of 1946 pledges that the federal government will pursue policies designed to "promote maximum employment, production, and purchasing power." In subsequent chapters, we will analyze both the potential and limitations of government as a stabilizing force.

SWINGS IN THE ECONOMIC PENDULUM

During this century, the growth rate of real GNP in the United States has averaged approximately 3.5 percent. The rate of growth, however, has not been steady. Exhibit 1 illustrates the fluctuation of real GNP, beginning with the Great Depression of the 1930s. On several occasions, the annual growth

EXHIBIT 1 • Instability in the Growth of Real GNP

Note that although fluctuations are present, the periods of positive growth outweigh the periods of declining real income. The long-run real GNP in the United States has grown approximately 3.5 percent annually.

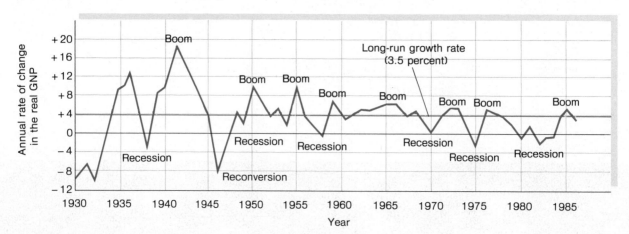

rate of real GNP has exceeded 6 percent for brief periods of time. In other instances, output as measured by real GNP actually declined. During the Great Depression, economic growth plunged. Real GNP declined by 8 percent or more each year between 1930 and 1932. Real GNP in 1933 was 30 percent smaller than it was in 1929. The 1929 level of real GNP was not reached again until 1939.

Since the 1930s, growth has been more stable. Economic booms and serious declines in the rate of output, though, continue to occur. World War II was characterized by a rapid expansion of GNP, which was followed by a decline after the war. Real GNP did not reach its 1944 level again until 1951, although the output of consumer goods did increase significantly in the years immediately following the war as the conversion was made to a peacetime economy. The years 1954, 1958, 1960, 1970, 1974, and 1979–1982 were characterized by downswings in economic activity. Upswings in real GNP came in 1950, 1955, most of the 1960s, 1972–1973, 1976–1977, and 1983–1984. During the last four decades, however, fluctuations in real GNP have fallen within the range of minus 2 percent to plus 6 percent. Compared to prior periods, this is a definite improvement.

A HYPOTHETICAL BUSINESS CYCLE

Business Cycle: Fluctuations in the general level of economic activity as measured by such variables as the rate of unemployment and changes in real GNP.

The historical data show that periods of economic expansion have traditionally been followed by economic slowdown and contraction. During the slowdown, real GNP grows at a slower rate, if at all. During the expansion phase, real GNP grows rapidly. Economists refer to these fluctuations in economic conditions as business cycles. As the term implies, a **business cycle** is a period of up-and-down motion in aggregate measures of current economic output and income. Exhibit 2 illustrates a hypothetical business cycle. When most businesses are operating at capacity level and real GNP is growing rapidly, a *business peak* or *boom* is present. A business peak is characterized by high levels of economic activity and real GNP, by way of comparison with recent years. As aggregate business conditions slow, the economy begins the contraction or recessionary phase of a business cycle. During the contraction, the sales of most businesses fall, real GNP grows at a slow rate or perhaps declines, and unemployment in the aggregate labor market

EXHIBIT 2 • The Business Cycle

In the past, ups and downs have often characterized aggregate business activity. Despite these fluctuations, an upward trend in real GNP is usually observed.

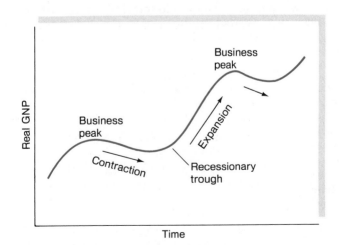

Recession: A downturn in economic activity characterized by declining real GNP and rising unemployment. In an effort to be more precise, many economists define a recession as two consecutive quarters in which there is a decline in real GNP.

Depression: A prolonged and very severe recession.

increases. The bottom of the contraction phase is referred to as the *recessionary trough*. After the downturn reaches bottom and economic conditions begin to improve, the economy enters an expansionary stage. During the expansion phase, business sales rise, GNP grows rapidly, and the rate of unemployment declines. The expansion eventually blossoms into another business peak. The peak, however, peters out and turns to a contraction, beginning the cycle anew.

The term **recession** is widely used to describe conditions during the contraction and recessionary trough phases of the business cycle. Economists define a recession as a period during which real GNP declines for two or more successive quarters. When a recession is prolonged and characterized by a sharp decline in economic activity, it is called a **depression.**

Our hypothetical business cycle of Exhibit 2 indicates steady and smooth movement from business peak to recessionary trough and back again to the peak. In the real world, cycles are not nearly so regular or predictable. As Exhibit 1 shows, various phases of the cycle have sometimes been quite lengthy. As we know, 1929–1933 was a prolonged period of economic decline that clearly deserves the title of depression. In contrast, the 1960s were characterized by lengthy expansion. Nevertheless, the phases of expansion, business peak, contraction, and recessionary trough are readily observable.

Despite these cyclical patterns, the trend in real GNP in the United States and most other industrial nations has clearly been upward. During the last 80 years, the long-run rate of growth in real GNP has been approximately 3.5 percent (see Exhibit 1). In some years, growth has been greater, and in others, less, but years of positive growth clearly outweigh the periods of falling real GNP.

Rate of Unemployment: The percent of persons in the civilian labor force who are not employed. Mathematically, it is equal to:

$$\frac{\text{Number of persons unemployed}}{\text{number in civilian labor force}} \times 100$$

Unemployed: The term used to describe a person, not currently employed, who is either (a) actively seeking employment or (b) waiting to begin or return to a job.

Labor Force: The portion of the population 16 years of age and over who are either employed or unemployed.

EMPLOYMENT FLUCTUATIONS IN A DYNAMIC ECONOMY

The **rate of unemployment** is one of the most widely used economic indicators. It is a key barometer of conditions in an important market, the aggregate labor market. This notwithstanding, the term is often misunderstood. At the most basic level, it is important to note that *unemployment* is different from *not working*. Persons may not be currently working in the marketplace for a variety of reasons. Some may have retired. Others may be attending school in order to acquire the knowledge and skills that will enhance their future livelihood. Still others may not be working as a result of illness or disability.

Only persons not working who are either looking for work or waiting to return or begin a job are counted as **unemployed.** In turn, persons must either be employed or unemployed before they are considered in the **labor force.** The rate of unemployment is the number of persons unemployed expressed as a percentage of the labor force. (See "Measures of Economic Activity" for information on how the Bureau of Labor Statistics derives the unemployment rate.)

Exhibit 3 will help explain the relationships among the important labor force classifications. We begin by grouping the noninstitutional adult popu-

**EXHIBIT 3 •
Population, Employ-
ment, and Un-
employment, 1985**

The accompanying diagram illustrates the alternative participation
status categories for the adult
population.

EXHIBIT 3 • Population, Employment, and Unemployment, 1985	
	Number of Persons, 1985[a]
Noninstitutional Population (Age 16 and over)	179.9
Not in labor force	62.7
Total labor force	117.2
Armed forces	1.7
Civilian labor force	115.5
Employed	107.2
Unemployed	8.3
Rate of labor force participation (percent)	65.1
Civilian rate of employment (as a percentage of the total noninstitutional population)	59.6
Rate of unemployment (as a percentage of the civilian labor force)	7.1

[a]Data are measured in millions, except those expressed as percentages. U.S. Department of Labor, *Monthly Labor Review* (February 1986).

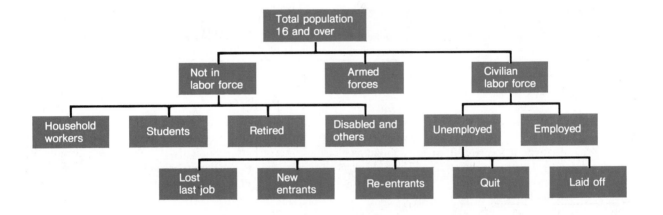

lation into three broad categories: (a) persons not in the labor force, (b) persons in the armed forces, and (c) persons either working or seeking work in the civilian labor force. In 1985, there were 62.7 million people aged 16 or over who were neither employed nor looking for market work. This is not to say these people were idle. Most were attending school, working in their households, vacationing, and/or recovering from illnesses. Nevertheless, their activities were outside the market labor force. They were not part of the labor force.

Labor force participants fall into two subgroups: the employed and the unemployed. The **rate of labor force participation** is the number of adult persons in the labor force as a percentage of the total noninstitutional population 16 years of age and over. In 1985, the rate of labor force participation was 65.1 percent, indicating that almost two out of every three adults were in the labor force.

Not all people who are unemployed lost their last job. A dynamic economy will be characterized by considerable labor mobility as workers

**Rate of Labor Force Par-
ticipation:** The number of
persons 16 years of age or
over who are either em-
ployed or actively seeking
employment as a percent-
age of the total noninstitutional population 16 years
of age and over.

move (a) from contracting to expanding industries and (b) into and out of the labor force. Spells of unemployment often accompany such changes.

As the chart of Exhibit 3 shows, there are five reasons why workers may experience unemployment. Exhibit 4 indicates the share of unemployed workers in each of these categories in 1985. Interestingly, 12.5 percent of the unemployed workers were first-time entrants into the work force. Another 27.1 percent were reentering after exiting for additional schooling, household work, or other reasons. Thus, nearly two out of five unemployed workers were experiencing unemployment as the result of entry or reentry into the labor force. A little more than 10 percent of the unemployed quit their last job. People laid off and waiting to return to their previous positions contributed 13.9 percent to the total. Workers terminated from their last job accounted for 35.9 percent of the unemployed workers.

One of the most interesting labor force developments of the post-World War II era is the dramatic increase in the labor force participation rate of women. Exhibit 5 visually illustrates this point. In 1948, the labor

MYTHS OF ECONOMICS

"Unemployed resources would not exist if the economy were operating efficiently."

Nobody likes unemployment. Certainly, extended unemployment can be a very painful experience. Not all unemployment, however, reflects waste and inefficiency. The time a person spends unemployed and in search of a job can sometimes yield a high return to both the individual and society. Since information is scarce, a person will not be aware of available opportunities as soon as he or she begins looking for a job. Information about available alternatives is acquired by shopping. One would certainly expect individuals to spend a significant amount of time shopping to seek out the best job opportunity. Often, this shopping is easiest (cheapest) if the job seeker is unemployed. Thus, job seekers usually do not take just any available job. They search, all the while acquiring valuable information, because they believe searching will lead to a preferred job opportunity.

Similarly, employers shop when they are seeking labor services. They, too, acquire information about available workers that will help them select employees who are better suited to their needs. The shopping of job seekers and employers results in some unemployment, but it also communicates information that leads to an efficient match between the characteristics of job seekers (including their preferences) and job requirements.

Parallel "unemployment" exists in the rental housing market. Dynamic factors are also present in this market. New housing structures are brought into the market; older structures depreciate and wear out. Families move from one community to another. Within the same community, renters move among housing accommodations as they seek the housing quality, price, and location that best fits their prefer-ences. As in the employment market, information is imperfect. So, renters shop among the available accommodations, seeking the most for their housing expenditures. Similarly, landlords search among renters, seeking to rent their accommodations to those who value them most highly. "Frictional unemployment" of houses is inevitable, but does it indicate inefficiency? No. It results from people's attempts to acquire information that will eventually promote an efficient match between housing units and renters.

Some unemployment, particularly cyclical unemployment, is indicative of inefficiency. However, the unemployment due to the shopping of job seekers and employers makes available more information, a scarce resource, and will eventually result in a more efficient match of applicants with job openings (and, thus, greater economic efficiency) than would be possible otherwise.

EXHIBIT 4 • Composition of the Unemployed by Reason

This chart indicates the various reasons why persons were unemployed in 1985. Only a little more than one-third (35.9%) of the persons unemployed were terminated from their last job. Nearly 40 percent of the unemployed workers were new entrants and re-entrants to the labor force.

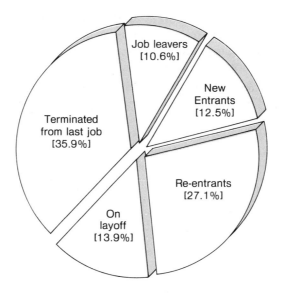

Source: *Monthly Labor Review*, February 1986.

force participation rate of women was 32.7 percent, compared to 87 percent for men. Since that time, the market work participation of women has steadily increased while the rate of men has fallen. By 1985, 54.4 percent of adult women worked outside the home. Married women accounted for most of this increase. More than half of all married women now are in the labor force, compared to only 20 percent immediately following World War II. In contrast, the labor force participation rate for men fell to 76.3 in 1985, down from 84 percent in 1960. Clearly, the composition of work force participation within the family has changed substantially during the last four decades.

EXHIBIT 5 • The Labor Force Participation of Men and Women

As the chart illustrates, the labor force participation rate for women has been steadily increasing for several decades, while the rate for men has been declining.

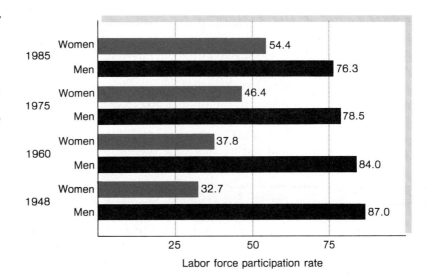

As long as workers are mobile—as long as they can voluntarily quit, switch positions from one job to another, and reallocate work responsibilities within the family—some unemployment will be present. Job switching, although it is usually accompanied by a period of unemployment, often leads to a better matching of employee job skills and preferences with the requirements of employers. Job moves of this type actually improve the efficiency of the economy and lead to a higher real income for the economy's participants (see "Myths of Economics").

Unemployment, though, can also be a sign of economic inefficiency. Unemployment may reflect demand conditions for labor, policy changes, and/or the inability or lack of incentive on the part of potential workers and potential employers to arrive at mutually advantageous agreements. To clarify matters, economists divide unemployment into three categories: frictional, structural, and cyclical. Let us take a closer look at each of these three classifications.

FRICTIONAL UNEMPLOYMENT

Frictional Unemployment: Unemployment due to constant changes in the economy that prevent *qualified* unemployed workers from being immediately matched up with existing job openings. It results from lack of complete information on the part of both job seekers and employers and from the amount of unemployed time spent by job seekers in job searches (pursuit of costly information).

Unemployment that is caused by constant changes in the labor market is called **frictional unemployment.** Frictional unemployment occurs because (a) employers are not fully aware of all available workers and their job qualifications and (b) available workers are not fully aware of the jobs being offered by employers.

The basic cause of frictional unemployment is imperfect information. The number of job vacancies may match up with the number of persons seeking employment. The qualifications of the job seekers may even meet those required by firms seeking employees. Frictional unemployment will still occur, however, because it is costly—it takes time—for qualified job seekers to identify firms demanding their services, and vice versa.

Employers looking for a new worker seldom hire the first applicant who walks into their employment office. They want to find the "best available" worker to fill their opening. It is costly to hire workers who perform poorly. It is sometimes even costly to terminate their employment. So, employers search—they expend time and resources screening applicants and choose only those who have the desired qualifications.

Similarly, persons seeking employment usually do not take the first job available. They, too, search among potential alternatives, seeking the best job available as they perceive it. They undergo search costs (submit to job interviews, use employment agencies, and so on) to uncover opportunities. As job seekers find out about more and more potential job alternatives, the benefits of additional job searches diminish. Eventually, the unemployed worker decides that the benefits of additional job searches are not worth the costs and chooses the "best" of the current alternatives. All of this takes time, and during that time the job seeker is contributing to the frictional unemployment of the economy.

Policies that influence the costs and benefits of searching will influence the level of frictional unemployment. If the job seeker's search costs are reduced, he or she will spend more time searching. For example, higher unemployment benefits make it less costly to continue looking for a preferred job. Thus, an increase in unemployment benefits would cause employees to expand their search time, thereby increasing the rate of frictional unemployment. In contrast, an improvement in the flow of information about jobs might reduce the benefits derived from additional search time. Other things constant, improved methods of disseminating job information among unemployed workers would allow workers to shop among job alternatives more quickly and effectively. Because of this, most economists believe that a national job-information data-bank would reduce search time and lower frictional unemployment.

STRUCTURAL UNEMPLOYMENT

Structural Unemployment: Unemployment due to structural changes in the economy that eliminate some jobs while generating job openings for which the unemployed workers are *not* well qualified.

Structural unemployment occurs because of changes in the basic characteristics of the economy that prevent the "matching up" of available jobs with available workers. It is not always easy to distinguish between frictional and structural unemployment. In each case, job openings and potential workers searching for jobs are present. The crucial difference between the two is that with frictional unemployment, workers possess the requisite skills to fill the job openings; with structural unemployment, they do not. Essentially, the skills of a structurally unemployed worker have been rendered obsolete by changing market conditions and technology. Realistically, the structurally unemployed worker faces the prospect of either a career change or prolonged unemployment. For older workers in particular, these are bleak alternatives.

There are many causes of structural unemployment. Dynamic change is of course at the top of the list. The introduction of new products or productive methods can substantially alter the employment and earnings opportunities of even highly skilled workers, particularly if the skills are not easily transferable to other industries. Many automobile workers experienced this reality in the early 1980s, as increased competition from foreign producers and changing technology reduced employment in the U.S. automobile industry. Shifts in public-sector priorities can also cause structural unemployment. For example, increased spending on defense and decreased spending on welfare may lead to a shortage of military scientists and unemployment among social workers. Institutional factors that reduce the ability of employees to obtain skills necessary to fill existing job openings also increase structural unemployment. For example, minimum wage legislation may reduce the incentive of business firms to offer on-the-job training, thereby contributing to structural unemployment.

CYCLICAL UNEMPLOYMENT

Cyclical Unemployment: Unemployment due to recessionary business conditions and inadequate aggregate demand for labor.

Cyclical unemployment arises when there is a general downturn in business activity. Since fewer goods are being produced, fewer workers will be required to produce them. Employers lay off workers and cut back employment.

Unexpected reductions in the general level of demand for goods and services are the major cause of cyclical unemployment. In a world of imperfect information, adjustments to *unexpected* declines in demand will be painful. When the demand for labor declines generally, workers will at first not know whether they are being laid off because of a *specific shift* in demand away from their previous employer or because of a *general decline* in aggregate demand. Similarly, they will not be sure whether their current bleak employment prospects are *temporary* or *long-term*. Workers will search for employment, hoping to find a job at or near their old wage rate. If their situation was merely the result of *shifts* among employers in demand, or, if the downturn is brief, terminated workers will soon find new employment similar to their old jobs. When there is a general decline in demand, however, workers' search efforts will be fruitless. Their duration of unemployment will be abnormally long. With time, the unemployed workers will lower their expectations and be willing to take some cut in wages. However, when the reduction in aggregate demand is substantial, the adjustment process may be lengthy and a substantial increase in the un-

MEASURES OF ECONOMIC ACTIVITY

Deriving The Unemployment Rate

Each month, the Bureau of Labor Statistics (BLS) of the U.S Department of Labor calculates the number of people employed, unemployed, and not in the labor force. Because it would be too burdensome, the BLS does not contact each person in the United States to determine each one's employment status. Instead, the employment statistics published by the BLS are based on a random sample of 59,500 households drawn from 729 different locations in the United States. The survey is conducted during the week containing the twelfth day of each month and is designed to reflect geographic and demographic groups in proportion to their representation in the nation as a whole.

Specially trained interviewers pose identical questions in the same order to each of the 59,500 households. People are classified as employed, unemployed, or not in the labor force on the basis of their responses to questions designed to elicit this information. People are considered "employed" if they (a) worked at all (even as little as one hour) for pay or profit during the survey week, (b) worked 15 hours or more without pay in a family-operated enterprise during the

week, or (c) have a job at which they did not work during the survey week because of illness, vacation, industrial disputes, bad weather, time off, or personal reasons.

People are considered unemployed if they (a) do not have a job, (b) are available for work, and (c) have actively looked for work during the past four weeks. Looking for work may involve any of the following activities: (a) registration at a public or private employment office, (b) meeting with prospective employers, (c) checking with friends or relatives, (d) placing or answering advertisements, (e) writing letters of application, or (f) being on a union or professional register. In addition, those not working are classified as unemployed if they are either waiting to start a new job within 30 days or waiting to be recalled from a layoff. Except for temporary illness, a person must be available for work to be classified as unemployed. So, students seeking summer employment prior to their availability for employment would not be counted as unemployed.

Except for people under the age of 16 and inmates of institutions, those who are neither employed nor unemployed are classified as "not in the labor force."

Major subcategories of people not in the labor force include those in school, keeping house, retired, or unable to work due to a disability.

Only people in the labor force—that is, only those classified as either employed or unemployed—enter into the calculation of the unemployment rate. The unemployment rate is the number of people unemployed divided by the number of people in the labor force. Based on its survey data, the BLS publishes the unemployment rate and other employment-related statistics monthly. Since employment and unemployment patterns vary during the year due to holidays, vacations, shifts in production schedules, and other seasonally related reasons, the unemployment data are seasonally adjusted. In addition, states use the BLS survey data and employment data from industries covered by unemployment insurance to construct state and area unemployment estimates based on BLS guidelines. The major sources of employment data are the *Monthly Labor Review* and *Employment and Earnings,* monthly publications of the U.S. Department of Labor.

employment rate is the expected result. As we proceed, we will investigate potential sources of cyclical unemployment and consider policy alternatives to reduce it.

EMPLOYMENT FLUCTUATIONS—THE HISTORICAL RECORD

Employment and output are closely linked over the business cycle. If we are going to produce more goods and services, we must either increase the number of workers or increase the *output per worker*. While output, or productivity per worker, is an important source of long-term economic growth, it changes slowly from year to year.

Thus, rapid increases in output, such as those that occur during a strong business expansion, generally require an increase in employment. As a result, output and employment tend to be positively related. Conversely, output and unemployment are inversely related—the unemployment rate generally increases when the economy dips into a recession.

The empirical evidence of Exhibit 6 illustrates the inverse relationship between output and rate of unemployment. When output plunged during the Great Depression, nearly one out of every four persons in the labor force was looking for a job and was unable to find one. As indicated in Exhibit 1, fluctuations in real output, and similarly swings in the unemployment rate, have been much less severe since World War II. Nevertheless, the impact of the business cycle is still observable. Unemployment peaks of approximately 7 percent were present during the recessions of 1958 and 1961. During the recession of 1974–1975, the unemployment rate jumped to more than 9 percent. Similarly, the unemployment rate soared to nearly 11 percent during the severe, but relatively brief recession of 1982.

EXHIBIT 6 • The Unemployment Rate, 1930–1985

The unemployment rate soared to nearly 25 percent during the Great Depression of the 1930s. During the last four decades, the unemployment rate has generally been within the 4 to 7 percent range. Note the unemployment rate increases during recessions such as those experienced in 1970, 1974–1975, and 1982. The estimated natural rate of unemployment is also indicated.

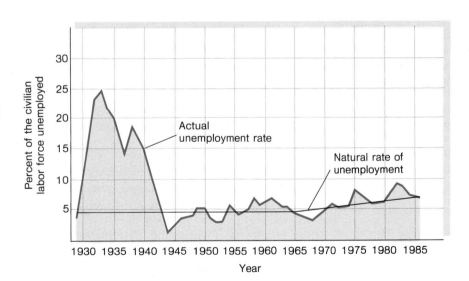

Source: *Economic Report of the President;* and Robert J. Gordon, *Macroeconomics* (Boston: Little, Brown, 1984).

THE CONCEPT OF FULL EMPLOYMENT

Full employment is a term widely used by economists and public officials alike. What does full employment mean? Clearly, full employment does not mean zero unemployment. In a world of imperfect information, employers and employees will "shop" before they buy and sell. Much of this shopping is efficient, since it leads to a better match between the skills of employees and the skills necessary to carry out productive tasks. Some unemployment is thus entirely consistent with the efficient operation of a dynamic labor market.

How much unemployment would one expect when the labor market is working well? There is not a clear answer to this question. Economists define **full employment** as the level of employment that results when the rate of unemployment is normal, considering both frictional and structural factors. Currently, most economists believe that full employment exists when approximately 94 percent of the labor force is employed.

Full employment incorporates the idea that at a given time there is some **natural rate of unemployment** in a dynamic exchange economy. This natural rate of unemployment arises from employees and employers shopping in a world of imperfect information among numerous potential alternatives. It reflects both frictional and structural factors. The natural rate of unemployment is not a temporary high or low. It is sustainable into the future. Economists sometimes refer to it as the employment rate accompanying the economy's "maximum sustainable rate of output."

The natural rate of unemployment, though, is not immutably fixed. It is influenced both by the structure of the labor force and by changes in public policy. For example, since youthful workers experience more unemployment because they change jobs and move in and out of the labor force often, the natural rate of unemployment increases when youthful workers comprise a larger proportion of the work force. This is precisely what happened during the 1960s and 1970s. In 1958, youthful workers (ages 16 to 24) constituted only 15.6 percent of the labor force. As the postwar "baby boom" generation entered the labor market, youthful workers as a share of the labor force rose dramatically. By 1980, one out of every four workers was in the youthful-worker grouping. In contrast, prime-age workers (over age 25) declined from 84.4 percent of the U.S. work force in 1958 to only 75.3 percent in 1980. Studies indicate that this increased representation of youthful workers pushed the natural rate of unemployment up by approximately 1 percent during the 1958–1980 period.

Public policies also affect the natural rate of unemployment. Policies that (a) encourage workers to reject job offers and continue to search for employment, (b) prohibit employers from offering wage rates that would induce them to employ (and train) low-skill workers, and (c) reduce the employer's opportunity cost of using layoffs to adjust rates of production will increase the natural rate of unemployment. With regard to these points, most economists believe that changes in minimum wage legislation and unemployment benefits influence the natural rate of unemployment.

Full Employment: The level of employment that results from the efficient use of the civilian labor force after allowance is made for the normal (natural) rate of unemployment due to dynamic changes and the structural conditions of the economy. For the United States, full employment is thought to exist when approximately 94 percent of the labor force is employed.

Natural Rate of Unemployment: The long-run average of unemployment due to frictional and structural conditions of labor markets. This rate is affected both by dynamic change and by public policy. It is sustainable in the future.

Exhibit 6 compares the natural rate of unemployment relative to the actual unemployment rate. Note that the actual unemployment rate fluctuates around the natural rate. The actual rate generally rises above the natural rate during a recession and falls below the natural rate when the economy is in the midst of an economic boom. As we proceed, we will often compare the actual and natural rates of unemployment. In a very real sense, macroeconomics studies why the actual and natural rates differ and the factors that cause the natural rate to change with the passage of time.

Without detracting from the importance of full employment (maximum sustainable employment), we must not overlook another vital point. Employment is a means to an end. We use employment to produce desired goods and services. Full employment is an empty concept if it means employment at unproductive jobs. The meaningful goal of full employment is productive employment—employment that will generate goods and services desired by consumers at the lowest possible cost.

THE RATE OF UNEMPLOYMENT OR THE RATE OF EMPLOYMENT— SOME STATISTIAL PROBLEMS

The definition of "unemployed" is not without ambiguity. Remember that persons are counted as unemployed only if they are (a) available for and seeking work or (b) awaiting recall from a layoff. These criteria can lead to some paradoxical outcomes. For example, a person who quit looking for work because his or her job-seeking efforts have been discouraging is not counted as unemployed. On the other hand, a welder vacationing in Florida, receiving unemployment compensation while awaiting recall to a $40,000-per-year job in the automobile industry, is considered to be among the ranks of the unemployed.

Discouraged Workers: **Persons who have given up searching for employment because they believe additional job search would be fruitless. Since they are not currently searching for work, they are not counted among the unemployed.**

One can argue that the statistical definition of "unemployment" results both in (a) people being excluded even though they would prefer to be working (or working more) and in (b) people being included who are not seriously seeking employment. **Discouraged workers** are those whose employment prospects are so bleak that they no longer consider it worthwhile to search for employment. Since they are not *actively* seeking employment, they are not counted as unemployed. Nevertheless, many discouraged workers would be willing to accept employment, were it available. When the economy turns down, the number of workers in the discouraged category rises substantially. For example, during the severe recession of 1982, the Department of Labor estimated that there were nearly 2 million (approximately 2 percent of the labor force) discouraged workers in the United States.

The method of classifying part-time workers may also result in an understatement of the number of unemployed workers. Part-time workers who desire full-time employment are classified as employed rather than unemployed if they work as much as a single hour per week. People in the latter category are certainly underemployed, if not unemployed.

On the other hand, some people may be classified as unemployed who are not seriously seeking market employment. An individual who rejects available employment because it is less attractive than the current combination of household work, continued job search, unemployment benefits, food stamps, and other governmental welfare programs is numbered among the unemployed. Required work registration in order to maintain eligibility for food stamps and assistance from Aid to Families with Dependent Children (AFDC) also adds to the ambiguity of the unemployment statistics. Some may register for employment (and therefore be numbered among the unemployed) with the primary objective of maintaining their food stamp and/or AFDC benefits.[1] People engaged in criminal activities (for example, drug pushers, gamblers, and prostitutes) or working "off the books" in the underground economy may be counted among the unemployed if they are not otherwise gainfully employed. Although estimates are difficult to project, some researchers believe that as many as a million people classified as unemployed participate in the underground economy.

As a result of these ambiguities, some economists argue that the **rate of employment** is a more objective and meaningful indicator of job availability than is the rate of unemployment. The civilian rate of employment is the number of persons employed (over the age of 16) in the civilian labor force as a percentage of the number of persons (over the age of 16) in the noninstitutional population. Both of these variables (the civilian level of employment and the noninstitutional adult population) can be readily measured. In addition, they are relatively clear. Their measurement does not require a subjective judgment as to whether a person is actually "available for work" or "actively seeking employment."

The rate of employment is relatively free of several defects that may distort the unemployment figures. For example, when a large number of discouraged job seekers stop looking for work, the rate of unemployment drops. In contrast, the rate of employment does not follow such a misleading course.

Does it make any difference which of the two figures is followed? Exhibit 7 presents data on the rates of both employment and unemployment for various years from 1950 to 1981. During the recessions that occurred in the years covered, the unemployment rate generally rose and the employment rate fell. However, the implications of the two rates as to the severity of each recession are quite different. Consider the data for 1982. The rate of unemployment for 1982 was 9.5 percent, the highest rate for any single year during the post-World War II era. This would certainly suggest that the 1982 recession was quite severe. In contrast, the rate of employment in 1982 was 57.2 percent (down from 58.4 percent in 1981), a figure that compares quite favorably with the civilian rates of employment during the relatively prosperous years of 1976 and 1977, for example.

Rate of Employment: The number of persons 16 years of age and over who are employed as a percentage of the total noninstitutional population 16 years of age and over. One can calculate either (a) a civilian rate of employment, in which only civilian employees are included in the numerator, or (b) a total rate of employment, in which both civilian and military employees are included in the numerator.

[1]See Kenneth W. Clarkson and Roger E. Meiners, "Government Statistics as a Guide to Economic Policy: Food Stamps and the Spurious Increase in the Unemployment Rates," *Policy Review* (Summer 1977), pp. 25–51, for a clear statement of this view.

EXHIBIT 7 • The Rates of Employment and Unemployment				
		Noninstitutional Population (Age 16 and Over)		
Year	Total (Millions)	Number Employed in Civilian Labor Force (Millions)	Civilian Rate of Employment (Percent)	Rate of Unemployment (Percent)
1950	106.6	58.9	55.3	5.2
1955	112.7	62.2	55.2	4.3
1960	119.8	65.8	54.9	5.4
1965	129.2	71.1	55.0	4.4
1970	140.2	78.6	56.1	4.8
1975	155.3	85.8	55.2	8.3
1976	158.3	88.8	56.1	7.6
1977	161.2	92.0	57.1	6.9
1978	164.0	96.0	58.5	6.0
1979	167.0	98.8	59.2	5.8
1980	169.8	99.3	58.5	7.0
1981	172.0	100.4	58.4	7.5
1982	173.9	99.5	57.2	9.5
1983	175.9	100.8	57.3	9.5
1984	178.1	105.0	59.0	7.4
1985 (July)	179.9	107.2	59.6	7.1

Source: U.S. Department of Labor, *Monthly Labor Review* (various issues).

Which of the two figures should the wise observer follow? The answer is both. Our economy has been undergoing several structural changes that affect both the rate of unemployment and the rate of employment. The increased incidence of working wives, the influx of a higher percentage of youthful workers into the work force, and changes in eligibility requirements for various income transfer programs—all of these factors contribute to the diversity of the unemployed population. Clearly, "the unemployed" is not a homogeneous category.

ACTUAL AND POTENTIAL GNP

Potential Output: The level of output that can be attained and sustained into the future, given the size of the labor force, expected productivity of labor, and natural rate of unemployment consistent with the efficient operation of the labor market. For periods of time, the actual output may differ from the economy's potential.

If an economy is going to realize its potential, full employment is essential. When the actual rate of unemployment exceeds the natural rate, the actual output of the economy will fall below its potential. Some resources that could be productively employed will be underutilized.

The Council of Economic Advisers defines the **potential output** as: ". . . the amount of output that could be expected at full employment. . . . It does not represent the absolute maximum level of production that could be generated by wartime or other abnormal levels of aggregate demand, but rather that which could be expected from high utilization rates obtainable under more normal circumstances."

The concept of potential output encompasses two important ideas: (a) full utilization of resources, including labor, and (b) an output constraint. Potential output might properly be thought of as the maximum sustainable output level consistent with the economy's resource base, given its institutional arrangements.

Estimates of the potential output level involve three major elements—the size of the labor force, the quality (productivity) of labor, and the natural rate of unemployment. Since these factors cannot be estimated with certainty, there is no uniform agreement among economists as to the potential rate of output for the U.S. economy. Relying on the projections of potential output developed by the Council of Economic Advisers, Exhibit 8 illustrates the record of the U.S. economy since 1950. During the 1950s, the rate of unemployment was above the natural rate. Excess capacity was present because the level of aggregate demand was insufficient to maintain full employment. The gap between potential and actual GNP was particularly large during the recessions of 1954, 1958, and 1961. During the 1960s, the gap narrowed as the economy approached and temporarily exceeded its capacity. Actual output again failed to approach its potential during the recessions of 1970, 1974–1975, and 1979–1982.

INFLATION AND THE MODERN ECONOMY

Inflation is a continuing rise in the level of prices, such that it costs more to purchase the typical bundle of goods and services chosen by consumers. Of course, even when the general level of prices is stable, some prices will be rising and others will be falling. During a period of inflation, however, the

Inflation: A continuing rise in the general level of prices of goods and services. The purchasing power of the monetary unit, such as the dollar, declines when inflation is present.

EXHIBIT 8 • Actual and Potential GNP

The graph indicates the gap between the actual and potential GNP for the period from 1950 to 1984. The presence of a gap between potential and actual GNP indicates that the resources of the economy are not being fully utilized.

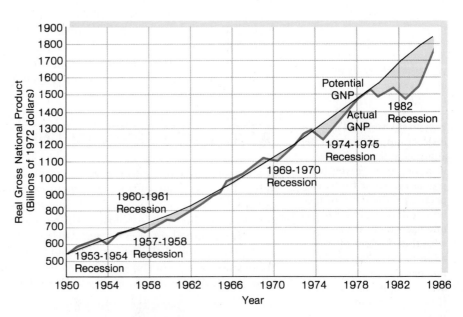

Source: President's Council of Economic Advisers.

impact of the rising prices will outweigh that of falling prices. Because of the higher prices (on average), a dollar will purchase less than it did previously. Inflation, therefore, might also be defined as a decline in the value (the purchasing power) of the monetary unit.

How do we determine whether prices, in general, are rising or falling? Essentially, we answered that question in the last chapter when we indicated how a price index is constructed. When prices are rising, on average, the price index will also rise. The annual inflation rate is simply the percent change in the price index from one year to the next. Mathematically, the inflation rate (i) can be written as:

$$i = \frac{\text{This year's PI} - \text{last year's PI}}{\text{last year's PI}} \times 100$$

So, if the price index this year was 220, compared to 200 last year, the inflation rate would equal 10 percent ([220 − 200 ÷ 200] × 100). The consumer price index and the GNP deflator are the price indices most widely used to measure the inflation rate in the United States. Since the CPI and the GNP deflator are calculated monthly and quarterly, respectively, we often compare their value during a specific month (or quarter) with their value during the same month (or quarter) one year earlier to calculate the inflation rate during the most recent 12 months.

How rapidly have prices risen in the United States? Exhibit 9 illustrates the record since 1930. Prices declined sharply during the early years of the

EXHIBIT 9 • The Inflation Rate, 1930–1985

Prices fell as the economy plunged into the Great Depression during the 1930s. World War II was characterized by high rates of inflation. During the 1952–1966 period, prices increased at an annual rate of only 1.5 percent. In contrast, the inflation rate averaged 7 percent during the 1967–1981 era, reaching double-digit rates during several years. During 1982–1984, the rate of inflation fell to approximately 4 percent annually.

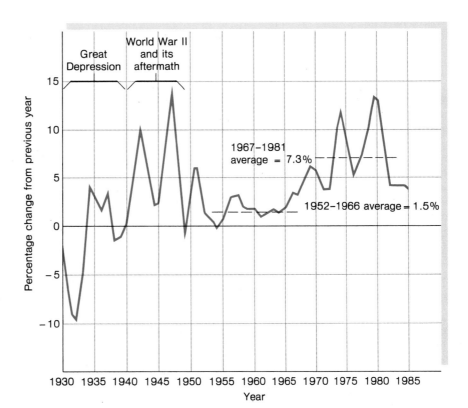

Great Depression. In contrast, World War II was characterized by a double-digit inflation rate. During the 1950s and into the mid-1960s, the annual inflation rate was usually less than 2 percent. In fact, the average inflation rate during the 1952–1966 period was 1.5 percent. Beginning in the latter half of the 1960s, inflation began to accelerate upward, jumping to 12 percent or more during 1974, 1979, and 1980. During the 1967–1982 period, the inflation rate averaged 7 percent. Price increases moderated again in the mid-1980s, as the inflation rate fell to less than 4 percent during 1983–1985.

Sometimes the focus on annual rates diverts our attention from the impact of continuous high rates of inflation. Given the lower inflation rates of the period, the price level was only 50 percent higher in 1967 than it was in 1947. In contrast, the price level tripled between 1967 and 1983.

The rate of inflation varies widely among countries. Inflation has been a way of life for many South American countries, including Argentina, Chile, Uruguay, and Brazil. Annual inflation rates of 50 percent or more have been a common occurrence in these countries. At the other end of the spectrum, the inflation rate in recent years has seldom climbed above 5 percent in Switzerland, Singapore, West Germany, and Japan. As we proceed, we will analyze why the price level has risen rapidly in some countries but not in others.

Unanticipated Inflation:
An increase in the general level of prices that was not expected by most decision-makers. Thus, it catches them by surprise.

ANTICIPATED AND UNANTICIPATED INFLATION

Before examining the effects of inflation, it is important that we distinguish between unanticipated and anticipated inflation. **Unanticipated inflation** is an increase in the price level that comes as a surprise, at least to most individuals. The unanticipated inflation rate may either exceed or fall short of the inflation rate expected by most people. For example, suppose that based on the recent past, most people anticipate an inflation rate of 4 percent. If the actual inflation rate turns out to be 10 percent, it will catch people off guard. In this instance, the actual inflation rate exceeds the expected rate. Conversely, if the actual inflation rate had been zero when 4 percent inflation was widely anticipated, the stable price level would also have caught people by surprise. In this instance, an overestimate of inflation would result.

Anticipated Inflation: An increase in the general level of prices that is expected by economic decision-makers. Past experience and current conditions are the major determinants of an individual's expectations with regard to future price changes.

Anticipated inflation is a change in the price level that is widely anticipated by decision-makers. For example, if individuals expect prices to rise 5 percent annually, the occurrence of 5 percent inflation merely fulfills their expectations. In contrast with unanticipated inflation, decision-makers are neither surprised nor caught off guard by inflation rates they anticipate.

THE EFFECTS OF INFLATION

Inflation reduces the purchasing power of money income received in the future (for example, payments from pensions, life insurance policies, and receipts from outstanding loans). When the inflation is unanticipated (or underestimated), debtors will gain at the expense of creditors. Why is this true? Inflation erodes the purchasing power of the principle and interest repayment. Thus, in terms of command over goods and services, debtors give up less (and creditors receive less) than each anticipated at the time they agreed to the loan.

Consider a simple case. Suppose you want to borrow $10,000 to start a business. Since prices have been relatively stable in the recent past, both you and the person loaning you money anticipate stable prices in the future. As a result, you both agree to a 5 percent interest rate for a 5-year loan of $10,000. At the end of five years, you will owe the lender $12,800 (the $10,000 principle plus $2,800 in compound interest over the 5-year period). Now, consider what happens if, soon after you take out the loan, the inflation rate jumps unexpectedly to 10 percent. The 10 percent inflation rate erodes the value of the principle and interest you repay when the loan comes due. In fact, your $12,800 repayment will permit the creditor to buy approximately the same market basket as could have been purchased with $7,950 at the time of the loan agreement. Far from gaining by loaning you money, the creditor ends up with even less purchasing power than his or her original principle. The unanticipated inflation redistributes income from the creditor to you. Of course, the opposite would have occurred if the inflation rate had been less than was anticipated.

When the actual inflation rate is greater than was anticipated, debtors gain at the expense of creditors. Conversely, when the inflation rate is less than was anticipated, creditors gain at the expense of debtors.

Does this mean that unanticipated inflation helps poor people? Not necessarily. We must remember that people need reasonably good credit before they can borrow money. This limits the ability of persons in the lowest income brackets to acquire debt. Most studies in this area suggest that unanticipated inflation results in a moderate redistribution from recipients of both low (less than $5,000) and high (more than $50,000) incomes to those in the middle-income groupings.

A more important redistributional effect of unanticipated inflation is the transfer of wealth among age groupings. Persons under 45 years of age are more likely to be debtors. Inflation helps them repay their housing mortgages, car loans, and other outstanding debts. In contrast, those over 50 years of age are more likely to have savings, paid-up life insurance policies, bonds, and other forms of fixed future income. Inflation erodes the purchasing power of these savings. It thus tends to redistribute income from the old to the young.

Interestingly, the biggest beneficiary of an inflation rate greater than people anticipate is the federal government. Households are net lenders, and the government is the largest debtor. Unanticipated inflation therefore tends to transfer wealth from households to the government.

It is important to recognize that past experience will influence the actions of debtors and creditors. Predictably, higher inflation rates will result in an increase in the anticipated rate of inflation. When a high rate of inflation is anticipated, lenders will demand and borrowers will grant higher interest rates on loans because both parties expect the value of the dollar to depreciate. A borrower and a lender might agree to a 5 percent interest rate if they anticipate stable prices during the course of the loan. However, if both expected prices to rise 10 percent annually, they would instead agree to a 15 percent interest rate. The higher interest rate would compensate the lender for the expected decline in the purchasing power of the dollar during the course of the loan.

When borrowers and lenders accurately anticipate an inflation rate, even high rates of inflation fail to systematically redistribute income from debtors to lenders. Debtors gain at the expense of creditors only if the actual rate of inflation exceeds the rate expected at the time the terms of the transaction are established.

When inflation is commonplace, people will adopt a variety of economic arrangements designed to protect their wealth and income against erosion by inflation. For example, collective-bargaining agreements will incorporate **escalator clauses** or contain a premium for the expected rate of inflation. Variable-rate home mortgages will be more widely used. Life and home insurance policies will be updated more often. Many long-term contracts will provide for indexing. All of these arrangements reflect the adjustments of decision-makers to an inflationary environment.

Contrary to the satirical statement at the beginning of the chapter, inflation will affect the prices of things we sell as well as the prices of goods we buy. Before we become too upset about inflation "robbing us of the purchasing power of our paychecks," we should recognize that inflation influences the size of those paychecks. The weekly earnings of employees would not have risen at an annual rate of 7 percent during the 1970s if the rate of inflation had not increased rapidly during that period. Wages are a price, also. Inflation raises both wages and prices.

> **Escalator Clause:** A contractual agreement that periodically and automatically adjusts the wage rates of a collective-bargaining agreement upward by an amount determined by the rate of inflation.

THE DANGERS OF INFLATION

Simply because money income initially tends to rise with prices, it does not follow that there is no need to be concerned about inflation, particularly high rates of inflation. Three negative aspects of inflation are particularly important.

1. Price Changes Can Frustrate the Intent of a Long-Term Contract. Since the rate of inflation varies, it cannot be predicted with certainty. Most market exchanges, including long-term contracts, are made in money terms. If unanticipated inflation takes place, it can change the result of long-term contracts, such as mortgages, life insurance policies, pensions, bonds, and other arrangements that involve a debtor-lender relationship.

2. Rapid Price Changes Cause Uncertainty. If one is not sure whether prices are going to increase, decrease, or remain the same, any contract that has a time dimension becomes hazardous because of uncertainty. The builder does not know whether to tack on a charge of 2, 5, or 10 percent to a contract, even though inflation is bound to increase building costs by some amount during the time necessary for construction. Union workers do not know whether to accept a contract calling for a 5 percent wage increase for the next two years. Inflation could partially or completely negate the increase. If price changes are unpredictable (for example, if prices rise 10 percent one year, then level off for a year or two, and then increase again by 10 or 15 percent), no one knows what to expect. Long-term money exchanges must take into account the uncertainty created by inflation.

Unfortunately, studies indicate that higher rates of inflation are associated with greater variability in the inflation rate. It becomes increasingly difficult to forecast just how much prices (and costs) will rise during the next month (or over the next several months). Therefore, the risks undertaken when entering into long-term contracts are enlarged. Given this additional uncertainty, many decision-makers will forgo exchanges involving long-term contracts. Because of this, mutually advantageous gains will be lost. The efficiency of markets is thus reduced.[2]

3. Real Resources Are Used Up As Decision-Makers Seek to Protect Themselves from Inflation. Since the failure to accurately anticipate the rate of inflation can have a substantial effect on one's wealth, individuals will divert scarce resources from the production of desired goods and services to the acquisition of information on the future rate of inflation. The ability of business decision-makers to forecast changes in prices becomes more valuable relative to their ability as managers and organizers of production. Speculative practices are encouraged as persons try to outwit each other with regard to the future direction of prices. Funds flow into speculative investments such as gold, silver, and art objects rather than into productive investments (buildings, machines, and technological research) that expand one's ability to produce goods and services. Such practices are socially counterproductive. They reduce our production possibilities.

STAGFLATION

Stagflation: A period during which an economy is experiencing both substantial inflation and a slow growth in output.

As recently as a decade ago, most economists thought that inflation was generally associated with prosperity and rapid economic growth. During the 1970s, however, the United States experienced two inflationary recessions. Economists have coined the term **stagflation** to describe the phenomenon of rapid inflation and sluggish economic growth. One of the challenges of modern economic policy is to develop a solution to the problem of stagflation—to develop economic policies that will reduce the rate of inflation, lead to a more efficient utilization of resources, and increase the future production possibilities available to economic participants. Again and again, we will return to this issue as we probe more deeply into macroeconomics.

What causes inflation? We must acquire some additional tools before we can analyze this question in detail, but we can outline a couple of theories. First, economists emphasize the link between aggregate demand and supply. If aggregate demand rises more rapidly than supply, prices will rise. Second, nearly all economists believe that a rapid expansion in a nation's stock of money causes inflation. The old saying is that prices will rise because "there is too much money chasing too few goods." The hyperinflation experienced by South American countries has mainly been the result of monetary expansion. Once we develop additional knowledge as to the operation of our economy, we will consider this issue in more detail.

---

[2]See Robert Higgs, "Inflation and the Destruction of the Free Market Economy," *The Intercollegiate Review* (Spring 1979) for an excellent discussion of this point.

**LOOKING
AHEAD**

In this chapter, we have examined the historical record for real income, employment, and prices. Measurement problems and the side effects of economic instability were discussed. In the next chapter, we will begin to develop a macroeconomic model that will help us better understand both the sources of and potential remedies for economic instability.

CHAPTER SUMMARY

1. Historically, real GNP in the United States has grown unevenly. Periods of rapid real growth have been followed by economic slowdowns. Nevertheless, the long-term trend has been upward. During the last 80 years, real GNP in the United States has grown at an average annual rate of 3.5 percent.

2. Business peak, contraction, recessionary trough, and expansion are terms used by economists to describe the four phases of the business cycle. During an expansion, output increases rapidly and unemployment declines. The highest output rate of an expansion is referred to as a business peak or economic boom. Contraction is characterized by increasing unemployment, declining business conditions, and a low rate of growth. The bottom of the contraction is referred to as the recessionary trough.

3. Officially, the Commerce Department defines a recession as two successive quarters of declining real GNP. If a recession is quite severe, it is called a depression.

4. Even an efficient exchange economy will experience some unemployment. Frictional unemployment results because of imperfect information about available job openings and qualified applicants. Structural unemployment stems from the presence of factors that prevent the "matching up" of available applicants with available jobs. Currently, frictional and structural unemployment in the United States are thought to involve approximately 6 percent of the labor force.

5. Cyclical unemployment results because aggregate demand for labor is insufficient to maintain full employment. A primary concern of macroeconomics is how cyclical unemployment can be minimized.

6. Full employment is the employment level consistent with the economy's natural rate of unemployment. The natural rate of unemployment reflects both frictional and structural factors. It is neither a temporary high or low, but rather the rate of unemployment associated with the economy's maximum sustainable rate of output. The natural rate of unemployment is not immutable. Public policies and changes in the composition of the labor force affect the natural rate.

7. Employment is a means to an end. The meaningful goal of full employment is full, productive employment—employment that produces desired goods and services.

8. The statistical definition of "unemployed" is imperfect. Some persons are not counted as unemployed because they are currently too discouraged to "actively seek employment." Others are counted even though they may be "employed" in the underground economy or only casually

seeking employment (perhaps because of the incentive structure that they confront). Because of these ambiguities, some observers believe that the rate of employment (the percentage of the noninstitutional population, age 16 and over, that is employed) may be a more objective and accurate indicator of current employment opportunities.

9. The concept of potential output encompasses two important ideas: (a) full utilization of resources and (b) a supply constraint that limits our ability to produce desired goods and services. When the resources of the economy are not fully and efficiently used, output will fall below its potential rate.

10. Inflation is a general rise in the level of prices. Alternatively, we might say that it is a decline in the purchasing power of the monetary unit— the dollar in the case of the United States. The inflation rate accelerated upward in the United States during the 1967–1982 period.

11. It is important to distinguish between anticipated and unanticipated inflation. When the actual inflation rate is greater than the anticipated rate, debtors gain at the expense of creditors. If the actual rate is less than the expected rate, creditors gain relative to debtors. In contrast, when inflation is accurately anticipated, the terms of loan agreements (particularly the interest rate) will be adjusted in a manner that eliminates the redistributive effects of inflation.

12. Inflation will have a harmful effect on an economy because it often (a) changes the intended terms of trade of long-term contracts, (b) increases the uncertainty of exchanges involving time, and (c) consumes valuable resources as individuals use their skills and talents to protect themselves from inflation.

THE ECONOMIC WAY OF THINKING— DISCUSSION QUESTIONS

1. Explain why even an efficiently functioning economic system will have some unemployed resources.

2. What is full employment? How are full employment and the natural rate of unemployment related? Indicate several factors that would cause the natural rate of unemployment to change. Is the actual rate of unemployment currently greater than or less than the natural rate of unemployment? Why?

3. How does the rate of employment differ from the rate of unemployment? Which is the better indicator of employment opportunity? Why?

4. **What's Wrong With This Way of Thinking?**
"My money wage rose by 6 percent last year, but inflation completely erased these gains. How can I get ahead when inflation continues to wipe out my increases in earnings?"

5. Does inflation help debtors relative to creditors? Why or why not? Does it help the poor relative to the rich? Explain. What is the most harmful side effect of inflation?

6. "As the inflation proceeds and the real value of the currency fluctuates widely from month to month, all permanent relations between debtors and creditors, which form the ultimate foundation of capitalism, become so utterly disordered as to be almost meaningless; and the process

of wealth-getting degenerates into a gamble and a lottery." Do you agree with this well-known economists's view? Why or why not? How high do you think the inflation rate would have to climb before these effects would become pronounced? Do you see any evidence in support of this view in the United States?

Macroeconomics is interesting . . . because it is challenging to reduce the complicated details of the economy to manageable essentials. Those essentials lie in the interactions among the goods, labor, and assets (loanable funds) markets of the economy. [1]

RUDIGER DORNBUSCH and STANLEY FISCHER

- What are the major markets that coordinate macroeconomic activities?

- Why is the aggregate demand for goods and services inversely related to the price level?

- Why is an increase in the price level likely to expand output in the short-run, but not in the long-run?

- How is the natural rate of unemployment related to the concept of long-term aggregate supply?

- What is the difference between the real interest rate and the money interest rate?

8 AN INTRODUCTION TO BASIC MACROECONOMIC MARKETS

In the last chapter, we discovered that our economy experienced ups and downs in the level of employment and growth rate of real GNP. We also found that the inflation rate varied substantially between time periods. These issues are precisely the focus of macroeconomics. Macroeconomics seeks to improve our understanding of business instability, inflation, unemployment, and related issues.

MACROECONOMIC GAME PLAN

A winning team has a successful game plan. Macroeconomics can be highly complex. If we are going to understand these complexities, we must first lay a basic foundation. In this chapter and the two that follow, we will develop a model of the basic macroeconomic markets, analyze how these markets respond to various economic changes, and consider a number of modifications to our basic model.

The operation of our basic economic model will help us accomplish an important goal: it will enhance our understanding of potential policy alternatives. Macroeconomic policy is usually divided into two components: fiscal policy and monetary policy. **Fiscal policy** entails the use of the government's taxation, spending, and debt-management policies. In the United States, fiscal policy is conducted by Congress and the President. It is thus a reflection of the collective decision-making process. **Monetary policy** encompasses actions that alter the money supply. The direction of monetary policy is determined by a nation's central bank, the Federal Reserve System in the United States. Ideally, both monetary and fiscal policy would be used to promote business stability, high employment, the growth of output, and a stable price level. It is not always easy, however, to determine which policy alternatives best serve these objectives.

After developing a basic macroeconomic model, we will analyze the impact of fiscal policy in Chapter 11. In Chapter 12, we will indicate how public policy influences the quantity of money in circulation. Chapter 13 investigates how monetary policy influences the level of prices and GNP. Finally, the last two chapters (14 and 15) of the macroeconomics section focus on the effectiveness of macroeconomic policy as a stabilization tool. Let us begin by considering the operation of three very important macroeconomic markets.

Fiscal Policy: The use of government taxation and expenditure policies for the purpose of achieving macroeconomic goals.

Monetary Policy: The deliberate control of the money supply and, in some cases, credit conditions for the purpose of achieving macroeconomic goals.

THREE KEY MARKETS: RESOURCES, LOANABLE FUNDS, AND GOODS AND SERVICES

The three basic markets of our simple macroeconomic model are: (1) resources, (2) loanable funds, and (3) goods and services. The circular flow diagram we initially introduced in Chapter 6 (Exhibit 2) will help us visual-

---

[1]Rudiger Dornbusch and Stanley Fischer, *Macroeconomics* (New York: McGraw-Hill, 1978),

ize each of the markets. In Chapter 6, we considered a strictly private economy in which households spent all of their income on consumption. We now consider an economy with a government sector in which households save as well as consume.

As before, the bottom loop of Exhibit 1 illustrates the flow of income from the business to the household sector in exchange for productive

EXHIBIT 1 • Three Key Markets and the Circular Flow of Income

A circular flow of income is coordinated by three key markets. First, the resource market (bottom loop) coordinates the actions of businesses demanding resources and households supplying them in exchange for income. Second, the loanable funds market (center) coordinates the saving choices of households and the borrowing decisions of businesses and governments. Finally, households, investors, and governments purchase products supplied by the business sector. These exchanges are coordinated in the goods and services market (top loop).

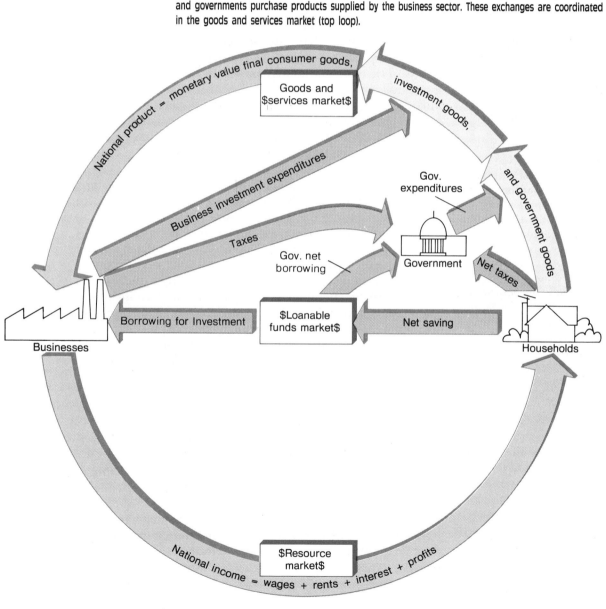

Resource Market: A highly aggregate market encompassing all resources (labor, physical capital, land, and entrepreneurship) that contribute to the production of current output. The labor market forms the largest component of this market.

Saving: Disposable income that is not spent on consumption. Saving is a "flow" concept. Thus, it is generally measured in terms of an annual rate.

Loanable Funds Market: A general term used to describe the market arrangements that coordinate the borrowing and lending decisions of business firms and households. Commercial banks, savings and loan associations, the stock and bond markets, and insurance companies are important financial institutions in this market.

Goods and Services Market: A highly aggregate market encompassing all final user goods and services during a period. The market counts all items that enter into GNP. Thus, real output in this market is equal to real GNP.

resources. Business firms demand resources such as labor and machines because of their contributions to the production of goods and services. In turn, households supply resources in order to earn wages, interest, rents, and profits. These income payments provide households with the purchasing power necessary to buy goods now and in the future. The **resource market,** an aggregate market including labor and capital submarkets, coordinates the exchange of productive inputs between the household and business sectors.

Of course, much of the income of households will still be used to purchase consumption goods and housing. As Exhibit 1 illustrates, however, there are also two indirect routes by which funds can flow from the household to the business sector. First, the net savings of households can flow through the loanable funds market to (a) business firms purchasing investment goods and (b) governments purchasing public services. **Saving** is that portion of one's disposable income that is not spent on consumption. It is income not consumed. Net saving by the household sector supplies funds to the **loanable funds market.** In turn, businesses borrow loanable funds to finance investment expenditures. In addition, governments often finance their expenditures by borrowing. When the borrowed funds are spent on investment goods and government purchases, they return to the circular flow. The price of loanable funds is the interest rate. The actions of borrowers and lenders are coordinated by the interest rate in the loanable funds market.

Second, tax revenues can flow to the government to finance government expenditures. In effect, taxes are a leakage from the circular flow that is injected back into the income stream when they are used to finance the purchase of goods and services provided by the government.

As the arrows in the top loop of Exhibit 1 illustrate, there are three major sources of expenditures on goods and services: (a) household expenditures on consumption (and new housing), (b) business investment, and (c) government purchases. Households, business investors, and governments thus demand goods and services. Purchasing resources from the household sector, businesses supply goods and services. These exchanges are coordinated in the **goods and services market** (top loop). This highly aggregated market includes items such as stereo records, movie tickets, pizza, hair styling and air travel—goods purchased primarily by households. It also includes things such as tools, trucks, houses, and even computerized robots, which either expand our ability to produce or provide us with a stream of consumer services in the future. Finally, items such as education, fire protection, and national defense, which are usually purchased by governments, are also part of the goods and services market. Obviously, these items are vastly different. They do have one thing in common, however—someone purchased them. Someone valued each item enough to give up other things that could have been purchased.

Exhibit 1 depicts the flow of income through markets for a closed economy—one that does not engage in international trade. International trade requires us to slightly modify our analysis of the goods and services market. When an economy engages in international trade, domestic businesses will export some goods and services to foreigners. Similarly, house-holds, business investors, and governments will import various goods and services. Net exports, the amount sold to foreigners minus the amount bought from them, will add to the demand for goods and services.

Thus, for an economy engaging in international trade, (a) consumption, (b) investment, (c) government purchases, and (d) net exports all contribute to the demand for goods and services.

AGGREGATE DEMAND FOR GOODS AND SERVICES

Before we proceed, we need to make an important assumption clear. Over the next several chapters we will assume that fiscal and monetary policy are unchanged. Stated another way, we will proceed as if the government's tax and spending policies are unaffected by economic circumstances. Similarly, we will assume that policy-makers maintain a constant **money supply**— that they follow policies that keep the amount of cash in our billfolds and deposits in our checking accounts constant. Of course, changes in governmental expenditures, taxes, and money supply are potentially important. We will investigate their impact in detail in subsequent chapters. For now, things will go smoother if we simply assume that policy-makers are holding governmental expenditures, taxes, and the supply of money constant.

Money Supply: The supply of currency, checking account funds, and traveler's checks. These items are counted as money since they are used as the means of payment for purchases.

What goes on in the aggregate goods and services market is vital to the health of an economy. The economy's real output, its real GNP, is merely the flow of items produced and purchased in the goods and services market during a period. The price variable in the goods and services market represents the average price of goods and services purchased during the period. It represents the economy's price level.

Just as the concepts of demand and supply enhance our understanding of markets for specific goods, they also contribute to our understanding of a highly aggregate market such as goods and services. The purchases of consumers, investors, governments, and foreigners comprise the demand for goods and services. The **aggregate demand curve** indicates the various quantities purchasers are willing to buy at different price levels. As Exhibit 2 illustrates, the aggregate demand curve slopes downward to the right, indicating an inverse relationship between the amount of goods and services demanded and the price level.

Aggregate Demand Curve: A downward sloping curve indicating an inverse relationship between the price level and the quantity of goods and services that households, business firms, governments and foreigners (net exports) are willing to purchase during a period.

In Chapter 3, we noted that the amount of a specific commodity demanded, such as television sets, is inversely related to price. This inverse relationship reflects the fact that consumers turn to substitutes when a price increase makes a good more expensive. An increase in the price level, though, indicates that the prices of all goods have risen. When all prices increase, there is no incentive to substitute among goods. Thus, the aggregate demand schedule is not simply a reflection of the negative relationship between price and quantity demanded for specific goods.

Why then, does the aggregate demand curve slope downward to the right? There are three major reasons.

EXHIBIT 2 • The Aggregate Demand Curve

There are three reasons why the quantity of goods and services purchased will decline as the price level increases: (a) an increase in the price level reduces the wealth of persons holding the nation's fixed money supply, causing them to reduce their purchases; (b) the higher price level pushes up the interest rate, which leads to a reduction in the purchases of interest-sensitive goods; and (c) net exports decline as foreigners buy less from us and we buy more from them at the higher price level.

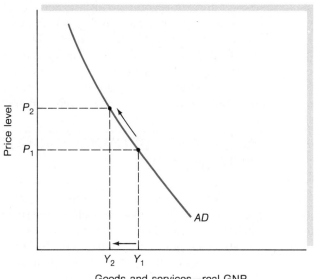

AS THE PRICE LEVEL RISES, REAL CASH BALANCES FALL, CAUSING PURCHASERS TO BUY LESS

Real Balance Effect: The increase in wealth emanating from an increase in the purchasing power of a constant money supply as the price level declines. This wealth effect leads to a negative relationship between price (level) and quantity demanded in the goods and services market.

AS THE PRICE LEVEL RISES, HIGHER INTEREST RATES REDUCE EXPENDITURES

Consider how an increase in the level of prices will influence the value of your money balances. Suppose you have a bank account of $2,000. If prices of goods and services increase by 10 percent, you will not be able to purchase as much with your $2,000. Essentially, the 10 percent increase in prices reduces your wealth because it reduces the amount of goods and services you can buy with the $2,000 in your checking account. Similarly, the real value of the money balances held by others declines.

Economists refer to the inverse relationship between the price level and the wealth of households and businesses holding a fixed supply of money as the **real balance effect.** The real balance effect helps explain the downward slope of the aggregate demand curve. People will cut back their spending on goods and services when an increase in the price level reduces the purchasing power of their money balances. In contrast, a decline in the price level will increase the wealth of people holding money balances, causing them to expand their purchases. Because of this, a negative relationship between the price level and quantity of goods and services purchased emerges from the real balance effect.

When the prices of all goods and resources increase, larger money balances will be necessary for the conduct of business. Households will try to expand their checking account funds to pay the higher prices for food, clothing, and other items regularly purchased. Similarly, businesses will want to increase their money balances to pay larger wage bills and supplier costs accompanying the higher price level. Since the supply of money is constant, it will not be possible for everybody to increase their money balances simultaneously. The additional demand for money will create a shortage. Many will try to borrow funds to increase their money balances. As they attempt to do so, they increase the demand for loanable funds and drive up the interest rate.[2]

What impact will a higher interest rate have on the demand for goods and services? Households will cut back on their purchases of interest-sensitive goods such as automobiles, consumer durables, and new homes. Similarly, firms will reduce their expenditures on business expansion and new construction. Thus, a rise in the price level leads to a higher interest rate that discourages expenditures on interest-rate-sensitive goods and services. This interest rate effect also contributes to the downward slope of the aggregate demand curve.

A HIGHER PRICE LEVEL LEADS TO A SUBSTITUTION OF FOREIGN FOR DOMESTIC GOODS

An increase in the price level will make American goods more expensive relative to foreign goods. Foreigners will reduce their purchases of American manufactured goods. Simultaneously, U.S. consumers will purchase more Japanese television sets, Korean textiles, Italian shoes, and other foreign-produced products, which are now cheaper relative to American-produced goods. Net exports will decline (or net imports rise) as foreign-produced goods are substituted for their more expensive American counterparts. Since the aggregate demand curve reflects purchases of American goods from all sources, the quantity demanded of U.S. produced goods will fall as the domestic price level increases.

SUMMARY

The accompanying thumbnail sketch indicates why the price level is inversely related to amount demanded in the aggregate goods and services market. Higher prices (a) reduce the purchasing power of the fixed money supply, (b) cause higher interest rates, and (c) reduce net exports. Each of these factors reduce the amount of goods and services demanded. So, even though the explanation differs, the aggregate demand curve, like the demand curve for a specific product, slopes downward to the right.

THUMBNAIL SKETCH

Why Aggregate Demand is Inversely Related to the Price Level

An increase in the price level leads to:

1. a reduction in the wealth of persons holding money balances,
2. a rise in the interest rate, and
3. a reduction in net exports.

Each of these factors reduce the quantity demanded of domestic goods and services.

A reduction in the price level leads to:

1. an increase in the wealth of persons holding money balances,
2. a fall in the interest rate, and
3. an increase in net exports.

Each of these factors increase the quantity demanded of domestic goods and services.

---

[2]We will provide additional detail on this topic when we analyze the demand for money in Chapter 13.

AGGREGATE SUPPLY OF GOODS AND SERVICES

As indicated in Chapter 3, an increase in the price of a specific good will give producers the incentive to expand output. However, we are now talking about an increase in the price level—an index of all prices. As with our discussion of demand, we cannot explain the shape of the aggregate supply curve by the same logic we applied to the market for a specific good.

Aggregate Supply Curve:
A curve indicating the relationship between the price level and quantity of goods supplied by producers. In the short-run, it is probably an upward sloping curve, but in the long-run most economists believe the aggregate supply curve is vertical (or nearly so).

The **aggregate supply curve** indicates the various quantities of goods and services producers will supply at different price levels. When considering aggregate supply, it is important to distinguish between the short-run and the long-run. The short-run is a time period so brief that decision-makers do not have time to fully adjust to recent *unexpected* changes, including unexpected changes in the price level. In essence, the short-run aggregate supply curve is for a specific expected price level.

Most economists believe that the short-run aggregate supply curve will slope upward to the right, as illustrated by Exhibit 3. There are two major reasons why an increase in the level of prices will, at least temporarily, lead to an increase in aggregate amount supplied. First, since the short-run aggregate supply curve is for a specific *expected* price level, an increase in the *actual* price level will improve profit margins. It is easy to see why this is the case. Important components of producers' costs will be determined by long-term contracts. Interest rates of loans, collective bargaining agreements with employees, lease agreements on buildings and machines, and other contracts with resource suppliers will influence production costs during the current period. Prices incorporated into these long-term contracts, though, will reflect the expected price level (for the current period) *at the time of the agreement.* These resource costs are temporarily fixed. If the price level

EXHIBIT 3 • The Aggregate Supply Curve, Short-Run

The aggregate supply curve shows the relationship between the price level and the production of goods and services by domestic suppliers. In the short-run, firms will generally expand output as the price level increases because the higher prices (a) improve profit margins since many components of costs are temporarily fixed and (b) lead many producers to believe the relative price of their product has increased.

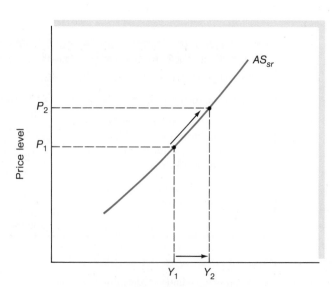

increases unexpectedly during the current period, prices of goods and services will rise relative to the temporarily fixed components of costs. Profit margins will improve and business firms will happily respond with a larger output.

Second, an increase in the general level of prices may deceive many business decision-makers into believing there has been an increase in the relative price (and demand) for their product. Fooled by the general price increase, they expand output in the expectation of strong future sales. Since all prices are rising, higher resource prices will eventually push up costs, reduce profit margins, and reduce the incentive of suppliers to continue producing the larger rate of output. Nevertheless, misled by the general increase in prices, many businesses temporarily produce more and thereby expand aggregate supply in the short-run.

Just because the aggregate supply curve has an upward slope in the short-run does not necessarily mean that it will in the long-run. The long-run is a period lengthy enough to provide sufficient time for decision-makers to adjust fully to unexpected changes. The long-run aggregate supply curve is thus indicative of the rate of output after decision-makers have had the opportunity to adjust prior commitments for any unexpected changes in the price level.

The reasons for the upward slope in the short-run shed light on the long-run aggregate supply curve. As an economy adjusts to a higher price level, costs that were temporarily fixed will eventually change. With time, long-term contracts will expire and be renegotiated. The new contracts will reflect the higher level of prices. Also with time, costs will rise and profit margins will fall to their normal levels. Similarly, business decision-makers will eventually correct errors as current sales and resource prices provide them with additional information.

Once decision-makers adjust fully to the higher price level, the factors that provided the foundation for the upward-sloping short-run aggregate supply are no longer present. An increase in the price level will not expand the economy's output capacity in the long-run. Therefore, as Exhibit 4a illustrates, the economy's long-run aggregate supply curve is vertical.

The economy's long-run aggregate supply is closely related to the concept of production possibilities, which we discussed in Chapter 2. Production of goods and services requires the application of human energy, capital resources, and knowledge. At any point in time, our production possibilities are constrained by the supply of resources, level of technology, and institutional arrangements that influence the efficiency of resource use. A higher price level will not loosen these constraints. So, there is no reason to expect aggregate supply to expand as the price level increases.

LONG-RUN AGGREGATE SUPPLY AND THE NATURAL RATE OF UNEMPLOYMENT

When an economy is operating at its long-run supply capacity, unemployment will equal its natural rate. Remember, the natural rate of unemployment is the unemployment rate that is sustainable into the future, given

EXHIBIT 4 • Aggregate Supply in the Short- and Long-Run

In the long-run, the output of goods and services is determined by factors other than the level of prices. Thus, the long-run aggregate supply *(LRAS)* curve is vertical. However, in the short-run, output may temporarily exceed or fall short of the economy's sustainable potential output. As frame b illustrates, when unemployment is *greater than* its natural rate, short-run aggregate supply *(SRAS)* will be less than its potential. In contrast, when unemployment is *less than* its natural rate, output will temporarily exceed its long-run capacity (Y_f). When output is equal to long-run capacity, unemployment will be at its natural rate.

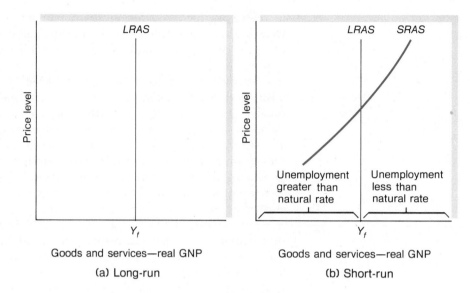

(a) Long-run

(b) Short-run

the structural and institutional characteristics of the economy. Put another way, it is an unemployment rate that is neither abnormally high nor abnormally low. When the natural rate of unemployment is present, the economy is operating at its maximum *sustainable* rate of output. Economists use the term full employment output when referring to this maximum sustainable rate.

The economy's long-run aggregate supply curve is vertical at the output rate (Y_f, Exhibit 4) attainable when unemployment is at its natural rate. Why might unemployment differ from its natural rate? Consider the following scenario. Suppose the price level had been virtually stable during recent years and that wage rates, on average, had been increasing at an annual rate of approximately 3 percent, the economy's long-term growth of real output. Reflecting these conditions, many labor-management bargaining contracts covering the next two or three years agreed to 3 percent annual wage increases. Subsequent to these agreements, wages and prices begin to rise at, say, 5 percent each year. The unanticipated inflation (increase in the price level) reduces the real wages of the workers covered by the long-term contracts.

For workers not under a contract, the process is a little different, but the result is much the same. Workers seeking better jobs when demand and prices are rising unexpectedly will not immediately realize that employers, trying hard to find additional workers, are raising wage offers everywhere. The expectations of job-seekers will lag behind reality. Their sights will be set too low, considering the new situation. Temporarily, they will be less selective in accepting jobs. Search time and unemployment will be artificially low until they realize that job offers are higher, on average, than they previously were. Thus, the unanticipated inflation reduces real wage rates for workers, whether or not they are covered by labor contracts.

How will this reduction in real wage influence employment? The lower real wage rates will improve profit margins, leading to business expansion and an increase in employment. Temporarily, unemployment will fall below its natural rate. Of course, as the long-term wage contracts expire, new labor agreements will reflect current economic conditions, including the 5 percent inflation rate. The real wages of these workers will eventually catch up with the rest of the economy. When this happens, unemployment will return to its normal level. In the short-run, though, the unanticipated general increase in prices will push unemployment below its natural rate.

Could these same factors cause unemployment to rise above its natural rate? Sure, this will happen if wages and prices rise *less* rapidly than decision-makers anticipate. Suppose prices have been increasing at an annual rate of 10 percent during the last several years. Based on the past inflation rate, many labor-management agreements will therefore provide for a 13 percent increase in money wages. Essentially, the 13 percent increase reflects a 3 percent expected improvement in productivity and a 10 percent premium for the expected general increase in prices and wages. Now, consider what would happen if the inflation rate falls to 5 percent, for example. The *real* wages of workers covered by contracts calling for 13 percent annual increases in money wages would increase sharply. The high wage rates and less-than-expected general increase in prices would squeeze the profit margin of many employers. Businesses would cut back production and workers would be laid off. Temporarily, unemployment would rise above its natural rate.

Many economists think this is precisely what happened during 1982. After inflation rates of 13 percent in 1979 and 12 percent in 1980, price increases plummeted to 4 percent in 1982. This sharp reduction in the inflation rate caught many decision-makers by surprise. Unable to pass along large increases in money wages agreed to in 1980 and 1981, employers were forced to cut back production and lay off workers. The unemployment rate soared to 10.8 percent in late 1982, up from 7.6 percent in 1981. Eventually, new agreements provided for smaller money wage increases or even wage reductions in 1983 and 1984. Unemployment fell. Nevertheless, in 1982, unemployment was well above its natural rate.

Exhibit 4b shows how the economy's employment level influences the relationship between short-run and long-run aggregate supply. When the actual and natural unemployment rates are equal, the economy will be operating at its long-run capacity (Y_f). Short-run aggregate supply ($SRAS$) is equal to long-run aggregate supply when actual unemployment is equal to the natural rate. This output rate (Y_f) is both attainable in the short-run and sustainable in the long-run.

Actual output, however, may differ from the economy's long-run potential. When unemployment rises above its natural rate, current output will be less than its potential. In this range, short-run aggregate supply will be less than long-run AS. In contrast, when unemployment is less than the natural rate, current output will exceed the economy's long-run potential (Y_f). Under these circumstances, the corresponding segment of the $SRAS$ curve will be to the right of the $LRAS$ curve.

EQUILIBRIUM IN THE GOODS AND SERVICES MARKET

Equilibrium: A balance of forces permitting the simultaneous fulfillment of plans for buyers and sellers.

When a market is in **equilibrium,** there is a balance of forces such that the actions of buyers and suppliers are consistent with one another. In addition, when long-run equilibrium is present, the conditions will persist into the future.

Two conditions are necessary for long-run equilibrium in the goods and services market. Exhibit 5 illustrates these conditions. First, aggregate demand must equal aggregate supply at the existing price level. If aggregate demand was greater than aggregate supply, purchasers would be seeking to buy more goods and services than producers were willing to supply at the current price level. This would place upward pressure on prices. On the other hand, if aggregate demand was less than aggregate supply, producers would be unable to sell all the goods produced. This would result in downward pressure on prices. So, if current price and output conditions are going to persist into the future, the amount of domestic goods demanded by consumers, investors, governments, and foreigners must equal the amount supplied.

Second, long-run equilibrium requires that the current level of prices equal the price level that buyers and sellers expected when they agreed to the price (or wage). As our analysis of the natural rate of unemployment emphasizes, decision-makers will enter into long-term contracts that they will desire to alter if future prices (or wages) are different than what was expected. Similarly, non-contracted workers seeking jobs will learn of rising wage levels, and will reject offers that do not reflect the new, higher price and wage levels. The current price level will thus persist into the future only when it is correctly anticipated by decision-makers.

EXHIBIT 5 • Long-Run Equilibrium in the Goods and Services Market

When the goods and services market is in long-run equilibrium, two conditions must be present. First, the quantity demanded must equal the quantity supplied at the current price level. Second, the price level anticipated by decision-makers must equal the actual price level. The subscripts on the *AS* and *AD* indicate that buyers and sellers alike anticipated the price level P_{100}, where the 100 represents an index of prices during an earlier base year. When the anticipated price level is actually attained, current output will equal the economy's long-run potential output (Y_f).

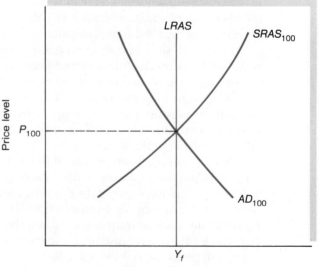

Goods and services—real GNP

As shown in Exhibit 5, we attach the subscript 100 to the aggregate demand and supply curves. The subscript implies that the choices of buyers and sellers alike were based on the anticipation of a price level P_{100}, where the 100 indicates an index of prices during an earlier base year. When an economy is in long-run equilibrium, this price level (P_{100}) will actually be attained. Thus, decision-makers have no reason to alter their views based on discovering either an underestimation or an overestimation of the current price level. When the past choices of decision-makers were based on a correct anticipation of the current price level, the economy's potential sustainable output will result. Of course, this will also be associated with unemployment equal to the natural rate.

In contrast, when decision-makers incorrectly anticipate the actual price level, many will enter into agreements they will later regret. Consider the case in which the price level increases more than was anticipated. Misled by the unexpected increase in prices, lenders in the loanable funds market agree to interest rates that are exceedingly low once the general increase in prices is taken into account. Similarly, anticipating a lower current price level, union officials accept money wage increases that end up reducing real wages during the current period. The atypically low real wage and cost conditions will stimulate output beyond the economy's long-run potential. Of course, these mistakes will be corrected in the future. The abnormally large output rate thus cannot be sustained.

Just the opposite happens if the current price level is below what was previously anticipated. Anticipating higher prices, borrowers will have agreed to interest rates that are exceedingly high in terms of current prices. Employers will agree to abnormally high real wage rates. The abnormally high costs, *relative to current prices*, will squeeze profit margins and result in an output rate below the economy's potential.

In summary, an output rate can be sustained into the future only when the prior choices of decision-makers were based on a correct anticipation of the current price level. When this is the case, the amount supplied in the short-run will equal the amount supplied in the long-run (see Exhibit 5). Correspondingly, unemployment is at its natural rate. The choices of buyers and sellers harmonize and neither has reason to alter their choices in the future. Thus, long-run equilibrium is present.

RESOURCE MARKET

The resource market encompasses the market for labor, natural resources, machines, and other factors of production. This market coordinates the choices of business firms that demand resources and resource owners who supply them.

Why do business firms demand resources? In a market economy, the demand for resources is merely a reflection of their contribution to the production of goods and services. Business firms employ labor and other resources because they contribute to the production of goods the firm believes it can sell at a profit. For example, a builder purchases resources such as lumber, cement, and glass windows, and hires the services of carpenters, bricklayers, and roofers because they are required to produce houses that the contractor hopes to sell for a profit. Other things constant, additional units add less and less to output as more of a resource is employed. Reflecting the diminishing contribution to output, the demand for resources is inversely related to price. Because of this, the demand for resources, like the demand for goods and services, slopes downward to the right.

Why are labor and other resources supplied? Most people work and supply resources to earn income. Working, though, requires us to give up something else that is valuable—leisure; time to do nonmarket work and to do other things. So, a trade-off must be made between working for income and leisure time for nonmarket activities. Higher real wages increase the opportunity cost of leisure. Because of this, as real wages increase, individuals generally make substitutions that permit them to supply more market work time. Obviously, the quantity of labor and other resources supplied expands as resource prices increase.

Exhibit 6 illustrates equilibrium in the aggregate resource market. Price coordinates the actions of buyers and sellers. In equilibrium, the market price of resources will bring the amount demanded by business firms into balance with the amount supplied by resource owners. An above-equilibrium price will result in an excess supply of resources. The excess supply will push resource prices downward toward equilibrium. In contrast, if resource prices are below equilibrium, excess demand will place upward pressure on the price of resources. Market forces will thus tend to move resource prices toward equilibrium.

The resource market and the goods and services market are highly interrelated. Changes in either one of these markets will have repercussions in the other. The demand for resources is a derived demand—it emanates from the demand for goods and services. So, there is a direct link between aggregate demand and the demand for resources. An increase in aggregate demand will increase the demand for resources. Similarly, a reduction in aggregate demand will reduce the demand for resources.

EXHIBIT 6 • Equilibrium in the Resource Market

In general, as resource prices increase, the amount demanded by employers declines and the amount supplied by resource owners expands. In equilibrium, price brings amount demanded into equality with amount supplied in the aggregate resource market. The labor market is a major component of the resource market.

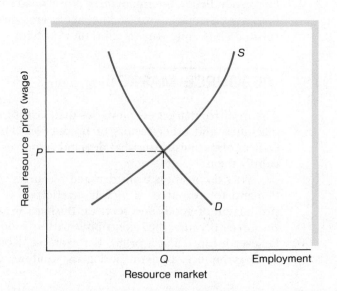

Resource market

Supply conditions in the two markets are also closely related. Resource prices and the costs of goods and services are directly related. Other things constant, a reduction in resource prices will reduce costs and improve profit margins in the goods and services markets. An increase in aggregate supply will result. Conversely, higher resource prices will increase costs and squeeze profit margins in the goods and services market. Aggregate supply will decline (shift to the left).

While it is useful to envision a heterogeneous market for resources, the labor market is the dominant resource market. In the United States, approximately 80 percent of the payments for resources go to labor, either for employees or for self-employed workers. Since this market is both large and very important, we will often focus on the labor market rather than the general resource market.

LOANABLE FUNDS MARKET

The loanable funds market coordinates the actions of borrowers and lenders. This market permits households, businesses, and governments to borrow against their assets or against future expected income. As the circular flow of income implies, households are generally *net* suppliers of loanable funds (see Exhibit 1). Businesses and governments often demand loanable funds to finance capital investment projects and other expenditures. Financial institutions, such as savings and loan associations, commercial banks, insurance companies, pension funds, and the stock and bond markets, form the core of this market.

In essence, borrowers are exchanging *future* income for purchasing power *now*. The interest rate is the price they must pay to do so. Why do you have to pay an interest premium when you borrow? Most of us are impatient. We want things now rather than in the future. Interest is the cost one pays for impatience. From the lender's viewpoint, interest is a premium one receives for waiting; for delaying possible expenditures into the future.

It is helpful to think of the interest rate in two ways. First, there is the **money interest rate,** the percentage of the amount borrowed that must be paid to the lender in the future, in addition to the principal amount borrowed. It is money interest rates that are typically quoted in newspapers and business publications. When there is inflation, the money rate of interest may be a misleading indicator of real borrowing costs. During a period of inflation, rising prices shrink the purchasing power of the loan's principal. When the principal is repaid in the future, it will not purchase as much as when the funds were initially loaned. Recognizing this fact, borrowers and lenders implicitly agree on an interest premium when they expect inflation. So, the inflation leads to a higher money interest rate, which is necessary to compensate the lender for the decline in the purchasing power of money during the lifetime of the loan.

Second, there is the **real interest rate.** The real interest rate reflects the real burden to borrowers and the payoff to lenders, in terms of command over goods and services. The real interest rate is simply the money rate of interest adjusted for inflation.

Perhaps an example will clarify the distinction between the two. Suppose a person borrows $1,000 for one year at an 8 percent interest rate.

Money Interest Rate: The interest rate measured in dollars. It overstates the real cost of borrowing during an inflation period. When inflation is anticipated, an inflationary premium will be incorporated into the nominal value of this rate.

Real Interest Rate: The interest rate adjusted for expected inflation; it indicates the real cost to the borrower (and yield to the lender) in terms of goods and services.

After a year, the borrower must pay the lender $1,080—the $1,000 principal plus the 8 percent interest. Now, suppose during the year prices rose 8 percent as the result of inflation. Because of this, the $1,080 repayment after a year commands exactly the same purchasing power as the original $1,000 did when it was loaned. In effect, the borrower pays back exactly the same amount of purchasing power as was borrowed. The lender receives nothing for making the purchasing power available to the borrower. In this case, the real interest rate was zero.

Lenders are unlikely to continue making funds available at such bargain rates. When they anticipate the 8 percent inflation rate, lenders will demand (and borrowers will agree to) a higher money interest rate to compensate for the decline in the purchasing power of the dollar. This premium for the expected decline in purchasing power of the dollar is called the **inflationary premium.** Once borrowers and lenders anticipate the inflation, they may agree to a 16 percent money interest rate, 8 percent of which reflects an inflationary premium and 8 percent a real interest return.

We can reflect the relationship between the real interest rate and the money interest rate as follows:

Real interest rate = money interest rate − inflationary premium

The size of the inflationary premium, of course, varies directly with the expected rate of future inflation. It is the real interest rate, not the money rate, that indicates the true burden of borrowers and the yield to lenders derived from a loan.

Thus, the real interest rate reflects the "true" cost of borrowing and the yield from lending. An increase in the real interest rate makes borrowing more costly. Households, investors, and governments will reduce the amount of funds demanded as the real interest rate rises. On the other hand, a higher interest rate increases the payoff derived from waiting. Lenders will therefore supply more funds as the real interest rate increases. So, as Exhibit 7 illustrates, the supply curve for loanable funds slopes upward to the right, while the demand curve has the usual downward slope.

Inflationary Premium: A component of the money interest rate that reflects compensation to the lender for the expected decrease, due to inflation, in the purchasing power of the principal and interest during the course of the loan. It is equal to the expected rate of future inflation.

EXHIBIT 7 • Equilibrium in the Loanable Funds Market

As illustrated, the quantity of loanable funds demanded is inversely related to the real interest rate. The quantity of funds lenders are willing to supply is directly related to the real interest rate. In equilibrium, the real interest rate (r) will bring the quantity demanded and quantity supplied in balance.

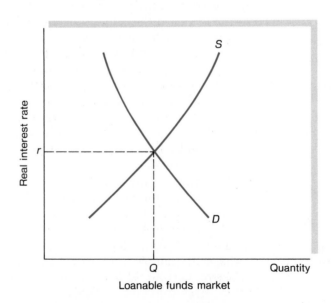

Loanable funds market

Equilibrium is present in the loanable funds market at the real interest rate when the amount of funds demanded by borrowers is equal to the amount supplied by lenders.

APPLICATIONS IN ECONOMICS

Bonds, Interest Rates, and Bond Prices

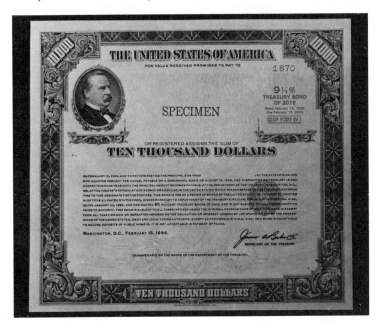

What is a Bond?

Bonds are simply IOUs issued by firms and governments. Issuing bonds is a method of borrowing money to finance economic activity. The entity issuing the bond promises to pay the bondholder the amount borrowed (called "principal") at a designated future date plus a fixed rate of interest. Some bonds pay the interest at designated intervals (i.e., on a specific date each year). Others pay both principal and interest when the bonds mature at a specified date in the future. The bond shown here is a typical government bond. The face value of the bond is $10,000 and the bond will pay the owner $9\frac{1}{4}$ percent interest paid annually (half in August and half in February) over a 30-year period. The bond matures on February 15, 2016. At that time, the owner of the bond will receive from the Treasury Department the $10,000 principal, plus the interest for the final six months.

Even though most bonds are issued for long periods of time, they can be sold to another party prior to their maturity. Each day, sales of previously issued bonds comprise the majority of bonds bought and sold on the bond market. Like most stocks traded on the stock market, new issues of bonds account for only a small portion of all bond sales.

How Does a Change in the Market Interest Rate Affect Bond Prices?

Suppose you have just bought a newly issued $1,000 bond that pays 8 percent on the $1,000 principal. As long as you own the bond, you are entitled to a fixed return of $80 per year. Let us also assume that, after you have held the bond for one year and have collected your $80 interest for that year, the market interest rate increases to 10 percent.[3] How will the increase in the interest rate affect the market price of your bond? Since bond purchasers can now earn 10 percent interest if they buy newly issued bonds, they will be unwilling to pay more than $800 for your bond, which pays only $80 interest per year. After all, why would anyone pay $1,000 for a bond that yields only $80 interest per year when the same $1,000 will now purchase a bond that yields $100 (10 percent) per year? Once the interest rate has risen to 10 percent, your 8 percent $1,000 bond will no longer sell for its original value. If potential buyers expect the new 10 percent rate to continue through 2005, the market value of your bond will fall to $800. You have experienced a $200 capital loss on the bond during the year. Rising market interest rates cause bond prices to decline.

On the other hand, falling interest rates will cause bond prices to rise. If the market interest rate had fallen to 6 percent, what would have happened to the market value of your bond? (Hint: $80 is 6 percent of $1,333.) Bond prices and interest rates are inversely linked to each other.

---

[3]The astute reader will recognize an oversimplification in this discussion. In reality, the economy supports a variety of interest rates, which usually tend to move together.

Businesses and governments often borrow funds by issuing bonds that yield an interest rate. Issuing bonds is simply a method of demanding loanable funds. In turn, the purchasers of bonds are supplying loanable funds. It is important to note that there is an inverse relationship between bond prices and interest rates. Higher bond prices are the same thing as lower interest rates (see boxed feature, "Bonds, Interest Rates, and Bond Prices").

EQUILIBRIUM IN OUR THREE MARKET MACROECONOMY

Exhibit 8 illustrates equilibrium conditions in the three basic macroeconomic markets. Aggregate demand and aggregate supply are in equilibrium at the price level P_1 and output rate Y_f (frame a). Since the P_1 price level was anticipated both by buyers and by sellers, the economy is operating at its long-run (full employment) capacity. In the resource market, price also equates amount demanded and amount supplied (frame b). Since the economy is at long-run capacity, normal unemployment is present in the labor market, an important subcomponent of the resource market. Finally, the

EXHIBIT 8 • The Three Basic Macroeconomic Markets

Here we indicate equilibrium conditions in the three basic markets that coordinate macroeconomic activity. These markets are highly interrelated. Changes in one influence equilibrium conditions in the other two. In the next chapter, we will focus on how these markets respond to changing economic conditions.

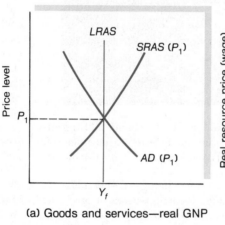

(a) Goods and services—real GNP

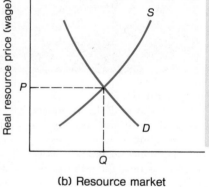

(b) Resource market

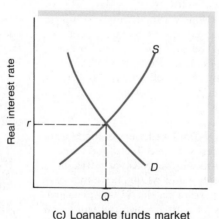

(c) Loanable funds market

real interest (*r*) has brought the amount demanded and amount supplied into balance in the loanable funds market (frame c).

When an economy is in macroeconomic equilibrium, each of the three basic macromarkets must be in equilibrium. Changes in any one of the basic macroeconomic markets will influence the equilibrium price and quantity in other markets. In fact, macroeconomics largely concerns tracing the impact of a change in one market through to other markets, particularly the goods and services market.

LOOKING AHEAD

In the next chapter, we will consider how our simple aggregate demand/ aggregate supply model adjusts to changing conditions. Factors that shift demand and supply in one or more of the markets will be analyzed. The interrelationships among the basic macroeconomic markets will be discussed in more detail. What happens when the supply of resources increases, decision-makers alter their expectations concerning the future, or the government increases its borrowing in the loanable funds market? As we proceed, we will use our model of basic macroeconomic markets to address these questions.

CHAPTER SUMMARY

1. The circular flow of income illustrates the significance of three highly aggregate markets: (a) goods and services, (b) resources, and (c) loanable funds. The resource market coordinates the exchange of labor and other inputs between the household and business sectors. The goods and services market coordinates the demand of households, business investors, governments, and foreigners with the supply of commodities produced. The loanable funds market coordinates the actions of borrowers and lenders, and thereby channels the *net* saving of households back into the flow of income as investment or government expenditures.

2. The purchases of consumers, investors, governments, and foreigners (net exports) comprise the aggregate demand for goods and services. The aggregate demand curve indicates the various quantities of goods and services purchasers are willing to buy at different price levels.

3. Assuming the money supply is constant, there are three reasons why the aggregate demand for goods and services will decline as the price level rises. First, the higher price level reduces the wealth of persons holding money balances. This reduction in wealth will induce them to cut back on their spending. Second, the higher price level will increase the demand for money relative to its fixed supply, causing households and businesses to borrow more to build up their money balances. This increased borrowing leads to higher interest rates, which discourage expenditures on interest-sensitive goods such as automobiles, homes, and investment projects. Third, a higher price level makes domestic goods more expensive and foreign goods cheaper, inducing a decline in net exports (or rise in *net* imports). Each of these factors reduces the quantity of domestic goods and services purchased as the price level rises.

4. The aggregate supply curve indicates the various quantities of goods and services suppliers will produce at different price levels. In the short-run, the aggregate supply curve will generally slope upward to the right because a higher price level (a) improves profit margins since important cost components are temporarily fixed and (b) misleads some business decision-makers into thinking there has been an increase in *relative* demand for their product.

5. Once decision-makers adjust fully to a higher price level, the factors that justified the upward sloping short-run aggregate supply curve are no longer present. Output is constrained by factors such as technology and the supply of resources. A higher price level does not loosen these restraints. Thus, the long-run aggregate supply curve is vertical.

6. Long-run aggregate supply is closely related to the natural rate of unemployment. When unemployment is at its natural rate (the rate that can be *sustained* into the future), output will also be at its maximum sustainable rate. Thus, the economy's long-run aggregate supply curve is vertical at the output rate that corresponds with the natural rate of unemployment.

7. Two conditions are necessary for long-run equilibrium in the goods and services market: (a) quantity demanded must equal quantity supplied and (b) the actual price level must equal the price level decision-makers anticipated when they made buying and selling decisions for the current period.

8. When the current price level differs from what was expected, output will differ from the economy's long-run capacity. When the current price level is *higher* than was anticipated, real wages and interest rates will be abnormally low. Unemployment will temporarily fall below its natural rate. Current output will temporarily exceed the economy's long-run capacity. In contrast, when the current price level is lower than was anticipated, real wages and interest rates will be abnormally high. Unemployment will exceed its natural rate. Under such circumstances, current output will be lower than the economy's long-run capacity.

9. Business firms demand labor and other resources because they contribute to the production of goods and services that the firms hope to sell at a profit. Individuals supply resources in order to earn income. Price in the resource market coordinates the actions of buyers and sellers. The labor market is the largest component of the general resource market.

10. The interest rate in the loanable funds market is the price borrowers pay to obtain purchasing power now rather than in the future. From the lender's viewpoint, interest is a premium one receives for delaying expenditures into the future.

11. It is important to distinguish between the real interest and money interest rates. The real interest rate reflects the real burden to borrowers and the payoff to lenders in terms of command over goods and services. In addition to this real burden, the money rate of interest also reflects the expected rate of inflation during the period the loan is outstanding. The real rate of interest is equal to the money rate of interest minus the inflationary premium.

12. The presence of macroeconomic equilibrium requires equilibrium in the (a) goods and services, (b) resource, and (c) loanable funds markets. Changes in any one of these markets will influence price and quantity in the other markets. Macroeconomics primarily concerns the adjustment of these basic aggregate markets to various changes in economic conditions.

THE ECONOMIC WAY OF THINKING— DISCUSSION QUESTIONS

1. In your own words, explain why aggregate demand is inversely related to the price level. Why isn't the aggregate demand curve simply a reflection of the downward sloping demand curve for an individual good?

2. Why does the aggregate supply curve slope upward in the short-run? Why isn't the long-run aggregate supply curve also upward sloping?

3. What is the natural rate of unemployment? Why is the natural rate of unemployment an important determinant of long-run aggregate supply?

4. Suppose prices had been rising at a 3 percent annual rate in recent years. A major union signs a 3-year contract calling for increases in money wage rates of 6 percent annually. What will happen to the real wages of the union members if the price level is stable during the next three years? If other unions signed similar contracts, what will probably happen to the unemployment rate? Why? Answer the same questions under conditions in which the price level increases at an annual rate of 8 percent during the next three years.

5. What is the current money interest rate on top-quality corporate bonds? Is this also the real interest rate? Why or why not?

6. Do you think workers are more concerned about money wages or real wages? Explain. If real wages increase, what happens to the quantity of labor supplied? The quantity demanded? Why?

- What factors will cause shifts in aggregate demand? What factors will shift aggregate supply?

- How will the goods and services market adjust to changes in aggregate demand?

- How does the economy adjust to unanticipated changes in aggregate supply?

- Does a market economy have a self-correcting mechanism that will lead it to full employment?

We might as well reasonably dispute whether it is the upper or under blade of a pair of scissors that cuts a piece of paper, as whether value is governed by [demand] or [supply]. [1]

ALFRED MARSHALL

9 WORKING WITH OUR BASIC AGGREGATE DEMAND / AGGREGATE SUPPLY MODEL

In the last chapter, we focused on the equilibrium conditions in the three basic macroeconomic markets. Equilibrium is important, but we live in a dynamic world. Predictably, changing market conditions will constantly disrupt equilibrium. Because of this, understanding how macroeconomic markets adjust to dynamic change is of crucial importance.

We are now ready to consider the determinants of aggregate demand and aggregate supply. Unanticipated changes in these factors may cause abrupt shifts in demand and supply in the goods and services market. In this chapter, we will focus on how market forces respond to such changes. As in the last chapter, we will continue to assume that the government's tax, spending, and monetary policies are unchanged. For now, we want to help the reader understand how macroeconomic markets work. Once this objective is achieved, we will be better able to understand both the potential and the limitations of macroeconomic policy.

FACTORS DETERMINING AGGREGATE DEMAND

The aggregate demand curve isolates the impact of the price level on the quantity demanded of goods and services. The price level, though, is not the only factor that influences the demand for goods and services. Several other factors, including real income, interest rates, and expectations concerning the future, also affect the choices of buyers in the goods and services market. Changes in these factors will shift the entire aggregate demand curve, altering the amount purchased at each price level. Let us take a closer look at the major factors capable of shifting the aggregate demand schedule.

REAL INCOME

If you had more income each month, what would you do with it? If you are like most people, you would spend a sizable portion of it on goods and services. In fact, most people work in order to earn income so they can buy these goods and services. Not surprisingly, there is a strong positive relationship between real income and the demand for goods and services.

Exhibit 1 illustrates the impact of a change in real income on aggregate demand. An increase in real income shifts the entire aggregate demand schedule to the right (from AD_0 to AD_1). At the higher level of income, more goods and services are purchased at each price level. Conversely, a reduction in income reduces the demand for goods and services, shifting the aggregate demand schedule to the left (to AD_2).

When considering the impact of a change in income on aggregate demand, it is important to distinguish between short-term temporary income changes and longer-term changes that one expected to be more permanent. The **permanent income hypothesis,** developed by Nobel Prize-winning economist Milton Friedman, indicates why this distinction is important. According to the permanent income hypothesis, the consumption of households is determined largely by their long-range expected or per-

Permanent Income Hypothesis: The hypothesis that consumption depends on some measure of long-run expected (permanent) income rather than on current income.

---

[1]Alfred Marshall, *Principles of Economics*, 8th ed. (London: Macmillan, 1920), p. 348.

EXHIBIT 1 • Shifts in Aggregate Demand

An expansion in real income will increase aggregate demand, shifting the entire curve to the right (from AD_0 to AD_1). In contrast, a reduction in real income decreases the demand for goods and services, causing AD to shift to the left (from AD_0 to AD_2). Changes in the real interest rate, business optimism, and expectations concerning the future rate of inflation will also shift aggregate demand.

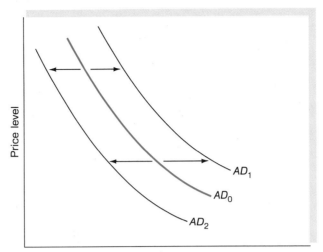

manent income. Since temporary changes in income generally do not exert much impact on long-term expected income, transitory increases or decreases in income do not exert a large impact on current consumption.

Perhaps a personal application will help explain why it is important to distinguish between temporary and long-term changes in income. Think for a moment how you would adjust your *current* spending on goods and services if an aunt left you $10,000 next month. No doubt, you would spend some of the money almost immediately. Perhaps you would buy a new stereo or take a nice vacation. However, you would probably also use a significant portion of this temporary (one-time only) increase in income to pay bills or save for future education. Now, consider how you would alter your *current* spending if your aunt indicated you were to receive $10,000 *per year* for the next 20 years. In this case, you are likely to spend most of this year's $10,000 almost immediately. You might even borrow money to buy an automobile or make some major expenditures, and thereby expand your spending on goods and services *this year* by more than $10,000.

Most people save a large portion of a temporary income gain so they can spread the benefits over a longer time period. In contrast, when an increase in income is expected to be long-term, most of this year's increase will be spent during the current period. Thus, the increase in demand for goods and services emanating from a temporary increase in income will be less than for an expansion in income that is expected to be more permanent.

REAL INTEREST RATE

As we discussed in the last chapter, the real interest rate indicates the amount of real goods and services that must be sacrificed in the future in order to consume or invest now. A lower real interest rate makes it cheaper to buy major appliances, automobiles, and houses now rather than in the future. The monthly payment necessary to finance the current purchase of these and other items decreases as the real interest rate falls. Predictably, households will demand more goods and services as the real interest rate falls.

Simultaneously, investors will find additional projects profitable as real interest rates fall. The interest rate contributes to the opportunity cost of all investment projects. If the firm must borrow, the real interest rate will contribute directly to the cost of an investment project. If the firm uses its own funds, it sacrifices real interest that could have been earned by loaning the funds to someone else rather than investing them. So, a lower real interest rate reduces the opportunity cost of a project, regardless of whether it is financed with internal funds or by borrowing. The lower opportunity cost will stimulate private investment and, therefore, aggregate demand.

A reduction in the real interest rate encourages consumers and investors alike to expand their current expenditures on goods and services. A lower real interest rate will increase aggregate demand, shifting the entire schedule to the right. In contrast, a higher real interest rate makes current consumption and investment goods more expensive. A higher real interest rate will reduce aggregate demand.

The link between real interest rates and aggregate demand highlights the interrelationships between the (a) loanable funds and (b) goods and services markets. Clearly, interest rate changes in the loanable funds market will influence equilibrium in the goods and services market.

BUSINESS EXPECTATIONS

What individuals think will happen in the future will influence current purchasing decisions. Consumers are more likely to buy big ticket items such as automobiles and houses when they expect an expanding economy to provide them with both job security and rising income in the future. Similarly, optimism concerning the future direction of the economy will stimulate current investment. Business decision-makers know that an expanding economy will mean strong sales and improved profit margins. Investment today may be necessary if one is going to benefit fully from these opportunities. So, increased optimism encourages additional expenditures by consumers and investors, increasing aggregate demand.

Of course, business pessimism exerts just the opposite impact. When consumers and investors expect a business downturn, they will cut back on their current spending for fear of becoming overextended. This pessimism leads to a decline in aggregate demand.

THE EXPECTED RATE OF INFLATION

When consumers and investors believe that prices are going to rise in the future, they have an incentive to spend more during the current period. "Buy now before prices go higher" becomes the order of the day. Thus, the expectation of an acceleration in the inflation rate will stimulate current aggregate demand, shifting *AD* to the right.

In contrast, the expectation of a deceleration in the inflation rate will discourage current spending. When prices are expected to stabilize (or at least increase less rapidly), the gain obtained by moving expenditures forward is reduced. The expectation of a deceleration in the inflation rate will thus reduce current aggregate demand (shift the *AD* curve to the left).

SUMMARY

Exhibit 2 summarizes the major factors causing shifts in aggregate demand. Shortly, we will analyze how the goods and services market adjusts to changes in demand. The government's spending, taxing, and monetary

EXHIBIT 2 • Major Factors Causing Shifts in Aggregate Demand	
Major factors causing shifts in aggregate demand are listed below. The lists exclude one important factor—macroeconomic policy. The impact of macroeconomic policy will be considered later.	
These Factors Reduce Aggregate Demand (*AD* shifts left)	**These Factors Increase Aggregate Demand (*AD* shifts right)**
Decrease in real income: Less income means less demand for goods and services. If the reduction in income is expected to be permanent (long-term), the decline in demand will be greater.	*Increase in real income:* More income leads to more demand for goods and services. If the increase in income is expected to be permanent (long-term), the increase in demand will be greater.
Higher real rate of interest retards both investment and consumption demand.	*Lower real rate of interest* stimulates both investment and consumption demand.
Increased Pessimism: Investors and consumers who expect a near-term business contraction will reduce their current demand.	*Increased optimism:* Investors and consumers who expect a near-term business expansion will increase their current demand.
Decline in the expected rate of inflation reduces the incentive to buy now before prices rise.	*Increase in the expected rate of inflation* increases the incentive to buy now before prices rise.

policies also influence aggregate demand. Knowledge of how the goods and services market works will help us better understand how fiscal and monetary policies work when we consider those topics.

FACTORS DETERMINING LONG-RUN AGGREGATE SUPPLY

Demand alone does not determine output. Goods and services must also be supplied. The aggregate supply schedule reflects the various outputs associated with alternative price levels. As we discussed previously, the long-term production possibilities of the economy are determined by the supply of resources, technology, and institutional arrangements that influence productivity and efficiency of resource use.

When focusing on the determinants of supply, it is important to differentiate between (a) changes that alter the economy's long-term production possibilities and (b) changes that only temporarily alter current output. Since their effect is long-term, the former will shift both long-run (*LRAS*) and short-run (*SRAS*) aggregate supply. In contrast, changes that lead only to temporary increases in output will shift only *SRAS*. Let us now consider the major factors that influence supply in the long-run.

SUPPLY OF LABOR AND CAPITAL

Since the Garden of Eden, resource scarcity has limited people's ability to supply goods and services. At any point in time, our production possibilities are constrained by the supply of resources—the knowledge and skills of our work force plus the availability of machines, natural resources, and capital assets. With the passage of time, the resource base can be expanded. Education, training, and skill-enhancing experience can expand the supply of human resources. Search and discovery can increase the supply of natural resources. Similarly, net investment can expand the future availability of productive equipment and physical capital.

Consider how an improvement in the skill of our work force, the discovery of a large oil pool in New Mexico, or the diversion of resources from consumption to the construction of a modern automobile plant in Tennessee influence our productive capacity. Each of these factors expands the supply of productive resources. In turn, this expansion in the resource base permits us to *produce* and *sustain* a larger rate of output. Both *LRAS* and *SRAS* shift to the right, as illustrated by Exhibit 3a. Conversely, a decline in the supply of labor and capital resources reduces both the current and long-term production capacity of the economy. A decrease in the supply of resources thus shifts both *LRAS* and *SRAS* to the left.

The direct relationship between the supply of resources and aggregate supply is generally transmitted by prices in the resource market. An increase in the supply of resources leads to lower resource prices. When resource prices are cheaper, the cost of producing goods and services declines. So, at any given price level, lower resource prices reduce costs and

EXHIBIT 3 • Shifts in Long- and Short-Run Aggregate Supply

An increase in the supply of resources or development of improved technology will expand the economy's long-term production capacity. As a result, both the long- and short-run aggregate supply curves will shift to the right (frame a, shifts to *LRAS₁* and *SRAS₁*). Conversely, factors that reduce the economy's long-term production possibilities will shift both *LRAS* and *SRAS* to the left.

Frame (b) illustrates the impact of changes such as weather conditions and inflationary expectations that alter current supply, while exerting little impact on the economy's long-term capacity. Favorable supply shocks (for example, good weather leading to a large harvest) will increase short-run aggregate supply (shift to *SRAS₁*).

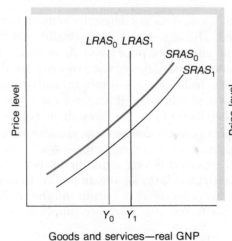 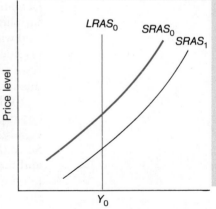

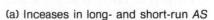

(a) Increases in long- and short-run *AS*   (b) An increase in short-run *AS*

encourage business firms to supply a larger output at each price level. As a result, the aggregate supply curve shifts to the right.

Of course, a reduction in the supply of resources exerts the opposite effect. When the supply of resources declines, resource prices rise, pushing costs upward. As costs rise, business firms will supply less at any given price in the goods and services market. Higher resource prices then shift the aggregate supply curve to the left.

TECHNOLOGY AND PRODUCTIVITY

Productivity: The average output produced per worker during a specific time period. It is usually measured in terms of output per hour worked.

Improvements in technology and productivity are closely related. Technological improvements—the discovery of economical new products or less costly ways of producing goods and services—permit us to squeeze a larger output from a specific resource supply. **Productivity** describes the amount of goods and services produced per worker, per hour. Clearly, technological advancements are an important source of higher productivity. For the most part, the enormous improvements in living standards over the last 250 years reflect changes in technology. The discovery of the steam engine, and later the internal combustion engine and the jet engine, vastly altered our energy sources. The development of the railroad, automobile, and airplane dramatically changed both the cost and speed of transportation. More recently, the discovery of a new, low-cost method of converting sand into silicon chips with a computing power a thousand times greater than the human brain is rapidly changing the way we work and play.

Improvements in technology and increases in productivity increase aggregate supply. They permit us to produce a larger output from the existing supply of resources. Thus, both *LRAS* and *SRAS* shift to the right. In contrast, a decline in productivity reduces aggregate supply, shifting the short- and long-run aggregate supply curves to the left.

INSTITUTIONAL FACTORS

Institutional factors also influence productivity and the efficiency of resource use. Institutional changes may either increase or decrease aggregate supply. Public policy that enhances economic efficiency by providing a more stable economic environment or more efficient remedies in instances where externalities would otherwise be a source of waste, increase aggregate supply. In contrast, institutional arrangements sometimes promote waste and increase production costs. For example, studies indicate that minimum wage legislation reduces employment and restricts the opportunity for training, particularly in the case of youthful workers. Output restrictions accompanying agricultural price supports generally result in inefficient production methods and reductions in output. Such arrangements reduce aggregate supply.

FACTORS DETERMINING SHORT-RUN AGGREGATE SUPPLY

As we know, the short-run aggregate supply curve indicates the GNP that business firms will supply during the current period at different price levels, holding constant the expected rate of inflation. Changes can sometimes

Supply Shock: An unexpected event that temporarily either increases or decreases aggregate supply.

influence the current output rate without altering the long-run aggregate supply curve. There are two major reasons why short-run aggregate supply may change while *LRAS* is constant.

First, supply shocks may alter current output. **Supply shocks** are surprise occurrences that temporarily increase or decrease current output. For example, adverse weather conditions, a natural disaster, or a temporary increase in the price of imports will reduce current supply, even though they do not alter the economy's long-term production capacity. They will thus decrease aggregate supply (shift *SRAS* to the left) without directly affecting *LRAS*. On the other hand, favorable weather conditions or an unexpected temporary increase in the world price of a country's export goods would increase current output, even though the economy's long-run capacity remained unchanged. As Exhibit 3b shows, favorable supply shocks increase *SRAS* (shift it to the right) without altering *LRAS*.

Second, the short-run aggregate supply curve will shift if decision-makers change their expectations with regard to the future rate of inflation. When suppliers expect less inflation, they will be more willing to supply goods and services at the current price level. So, a decline in the expected rate of inflation increases current aggregate supply (*SRAS* shifts to the right). In contrast, when business firms raise their expectations concerning future inflation, their incentive to produce and sell at the current price level is reduced. Short-run aggregate supply falls (*SRAS* shifts to the left).

Exhibit 4 summarizes the major factors influencing aggregate supply. Macroeconomic policy may also influence aggregate supply. As in the case of demand, we will consider this topic in detail in subsequent chapters.

EXHIBIT 4   •   Major Factors Causing Shifts in Aggregate Supply

Important factors that shift the long- and short-run aggregate supply curves are indicated below. As in the case of demand, we will analyze the impact of macroeconomic policy on aggregate supply later.

These factors reduce both short- and long-run aggregate supply (shift *SRAS* and *LRAS* to the left)	*These factors increase both short- and long-run aggregate supply* (shift *SRAS* and *LRAS* to the right)
Decreases in the supply of resources (higher resource prices)	Increases in the supply of resources (lower resource prices)
Decreases in productivity	Improvements in technology and increases in productivity
Institutional changes that reduce productivity and output	Institutional changes that improve productivity and expand output
These factors reduce aggregate supply in the short-run	*These factors increase aggregate supply in the short-run*
Unfavorable supply shocks	Favorable supply shocks
Increases in the expected rate of inflation	Decreases in the expected rate of inflation

EXHIBIT 5 • The Growth of Aggregate Supply

Here we illustrate impact of economic growth due to a technological advancement or discovery of an important natural resource, for example. The production capacity of the economy expands. Thus, both long- and short-run aggregate supply increase (to *SRAS₂* and *LRAS₂*). A *sustainable,* higher level of real output and real income is the result. If the money supply is held constant, a new long-run equilibrium will emerge at a larger output rate (Y_{f_2}) and lower price level (P_2).

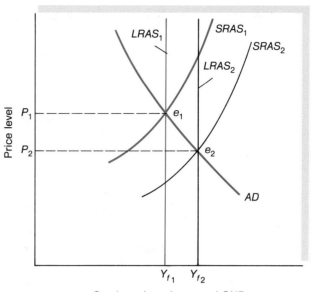

Goods and services—real GNP

ECONOMIC GROWTH AND SHIFTS IN SUPPLY AND DEMAND

We are now ready to consider how the market for goods and services adjusts to changes in demand and supply. Let us begin by considering the impact of economic growth. Suppose net investment, a technological advancement, or the discovery of an important natural resource expands our production possibilities over time. Exhibit 5 illustrates an economy initially in long-run equilibrium at price level P_1 and output Y_{f1}. Economic growth—an expansion in the economy's output potential—will shift both the long- and short-run aggregate supply curves to the right. Short-run aggregate supply expands to $SRAS_2$, while the long-run curve shifts to $LRAS_2$.

Since the economy's production possibilities have increased, it will now be possible to *produce and sustain* a higher rate of real output (Y_{f2}). The larger output rate can be achieved even while unemployment remains at its natural rate. Since the money supply is constant, the increase in aggregate supply will lead to a lower price level (P_2).[2] Given the new aggregate supply and demand conditions, the larger output and lower price level will persist into the future. Of course, changes in technology and relative resource prices will lead to movement of resources among industries. During the transition, actual unemployment may differ from its natural rate. As markets eventually adjust, though, the result will be an expansion in the economy's long-run equilibrium real income and a lower price level.

---

[2]The monetary authorities may want to maintain a stable price level as output expands. In subsequent chapters, we will explain how stable prices can be achieved as real output increases.

ANTICIPATED AND UNANTICIPATED CHANGES

Anticipated Change: A change that is foreseen by decision-makers, in time for them to adjust.

Economic growth usually takes place gradually. Because of this, decision-makers have time to anticipate changing market conditions and adjust their choices accordingly. It is important to distinguish between anticipated and unanticipated changes in markets. **Anticipated changes** are foreseen by economic participants. Decision-makers have time to adjust to anticipated changes even before they occur. For example, suppose that under normal weather conditions, a drought-resistant hybrid seed can be expected to expand the production of feed grain in the Midwest by 10 percent next year. As a result, buyers and sellers will plan for a larger supply and probable lower prices in the future. They will adjust their decision-making accordingly.

Unanticipated Change: A change that decision-makers could not reasonably foresee. Thus, choices made prior to the event did not take the event into account.

In contrast, **unanticipated changes** catch people by surprise. Our world is characterized by dynamic change. New products, crop failures, expanding markets, cheaper imports—markets are constantly changing in light of unexpected events. Economics largely concerns how markets adjust to unanticipated changes. Let us consider this issue in more detail.

UNANTICIPATED CHANGES IN AGGREGATE DEMAND

Markets do not adjust instantaneously to unanticipated changes in market conditions. For a time, it may be unclear whether a change in sales, for example, reflects a random occurrence or an actual change. It takes time to differentiate between temporary and permanent changes. Even after decision-makers are convinced market conditions have changed, it will take time to carry out decisions. In some cases, complete adjustment will also be delayed by the presence of long-term contracts. All these factors emphasize the complexity of market adjustments to unexpected events. Nevertheless, unpredictable events do occur, so the adjustment of macroeconomic markets to unanticipated change is important.

UNANTICIPATED INCREASES IN AGGREGATE DEMAND

Exhibit 6 illustrates an economy that is initially in long-run equilibrium (e_1) at output Y_f and price level P_{100}. Aggregate demand and aggregate supply are in balance. Simultaneously, decision-makers correctly anticipated the current price level. Thus, AD_1 and $SRAS_1$ intersect at the economy's full employment capacity.

What would happen if this equilibrium were disrupted by an unanticipated increase in aggregate demand? For example, suppose consumers and investors suddenly become more optimistic about future business conditions. As a result, they increase their current purchases of goods and services. Aggregate demand shifts from AD_1 to AD_2. Given the strong demand, businesses would happily expand output along $SRAS_1$. In the short-run, a new equilibrium (e_2) would result at a larger rate of output (Y_2) and a higher price level (P_{105}). Markets do not adjust instantaneously, though. Many wage rates and resource prices based on the initial weaker demand and

EXHIBIT 6 • An Un-anticipated Increase in Aggregate Demand

In response to an unanticipated increase in aggregate demand for goods and services (shift from AD_1 to AD_2), prices will rise (to P_{105}) and output will temporarily exceed full employment capability. For a time, unemployment will fall below its long-run natural rate. However, the strong demand will eventually push up resource prices, including wage rates. The higher resource prices will mean higher costs that will reduce aggregate supply (shift to $SRAS_2$). With time, a new equilibrium at a higher price level (P_{110}) and an output consistent with the economy's long-run capacity will result. Thus, the increase in demand will expand output only temporarily.

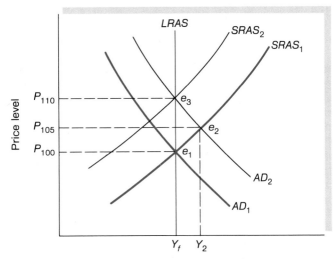

Goods and services—real GNP

lower expected price level (P_{100}) will persist for a time. Temporarily, profit margins will be highly attractive. Business firms will expand both output and employment. Unemployment will drop below its natural rate.

This is not the end of the story, however. With time, decision-makers will adjust more fully to the strong demand and higher price level. Wage rates and resource prices will rise, pushing costs upward. Aggregate supply ($SRAS$) will shift to the left as costs increase. Eventually, a new long-run equilibrium (e_3) will be established at a higher price level (P_{110}) that is correctly anticipated by decision-makers. When this happens, unemployment will return to its natural rate and output will recede to the economy's long-run potential.

Since an increase in aggregate demand does not alter the economy's productive capacity, it cannot permanently expand output (beyond Y_f). The expansion in demand temporarily expands output, but over the long-term its major effect will be higher prices (inflation).

In passing, we should also note another factor that may play a role in the adjustment process. If consumers and investors decide to spend more of their current income on goods and services, of necessity they will either have to reduce their saving or increase their borrowing. Predictably, the supply of loanable funds will decline relative to the demand. A higher real interest rate will result. How will the increase in the real interest rate influence the demand for goods and services? A higher real interest rate will make current consumption and investment spending more expensive. So, rising interest rates will limit the increased spending of consumers and investors, and thereby help to stabilize aggregate demand.

UNANTICIPATED REDUCTIONS IN AGGREGATE DEMAND

How would the goods and services market adjust to an unanticipated reduction in aggregate demand? For example, suppose decision-makers become more pessimistic about the future or suddenly expect a decline in the future price level. Exhibit 7 will help us analyze this issue. Once again, we consider an economy that is in long-run equilibrium (e_1) at output Y_f and price level

EXHIBIT 7 • An Unanticipated Reduction in Aggregate Demand

As frame a illustrates, the initial impact of an unanticipated reduction in aggregate demand (shift from AD_1 to AD_2) will be a lower price level (P_{95}) and decline in output (to Y_2). Temporarily, unemployment will rise above its natural rate. Eventually, weak demand and excess supply in the resource market will lead to lower wage rates and resource prices. This will reduce costs, leading to an expansion in short-run aggregate supply (shift to $SRAS_2$, frame b). However, this method of restoring equilibrium (e_3) may be both highly painful and quite lengthy.

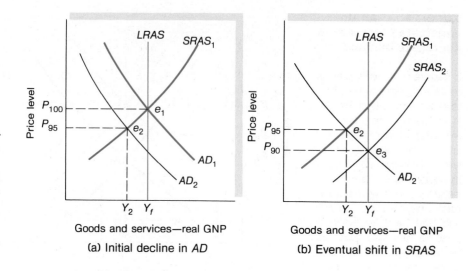

(a) Initial decline in AD

(b) Eventual shift in $SRAS$

P_{100} (frame a). Long-run equilibrium is disturbed by the reduction in aggregate demand; the shift from AD_1 to AD_2. Businesses reduce output (to Y_2) and cut prices (to P_{95}) in response to the weak demand conditions. Since many costs of business firms are temporarily fixed, profit margins will decline. Workers will be laid off, causing unemployment to increase to an abnormally high rate.

If resource prices quickly adjusted downward in response to the weak demand and rising unemployment, the decline in output to Y_2 would be brief. Lower resource prices would reduce costs and thereby increase aggregate supply (shift to $SRAS_2$). As frame b illustrates, the result would be a new equilibrium (e_3) at the economy's full employment output rate (Y_f) and a lower price level (P_{90}).

Resource prices, though, may not adjust quickly. Long-term contracts and uncertainty as to whether or not the weak demand conditions are merely temporary will slow the adjustment process. In addition, individual workers and union officials may be highly reluctant to be the first to accept lower nominal wages.

If resource prices are inflexible in a downward direction, as many economists believe, the adjustment to a reduction in aggregate demand will be both lengthy and painful. Prolonged periods of economic recession—below capacity output rates and abnormally high unemployment—may occur before long-run equilibrium is restored.

Once again, the interaction between the loanable funds and goods and services markets should be noted. If consumers and investors suddenly reduce their spending of current income, other things constant, an increase in saving is implied. The supply of loanable funds will increase relative to the demand. Real interest rates will fall, which will stimulate additional current spending. To the extent the change in aggregate demand arises from internal forces, adjustments in the loanable funds market will exert a stabilizing effect.

UNANTICIPATED CHANGES IN AGGREGATE SUPPLY

Factors that alter aggregate supply in the long-run generally take place slowly. For example, it takes time to expand the supply of capital or adopt a new, improved technology. Since long-run supply changes take place more slowly, decision-makers will be able to foresee many of the changes prior to their occurrence and adjust their choices in an orderly manner.

In contrast, changes in factors influencing the short-run aggregate supply curve are more likely to be unanticipated. By their nature, supply shocks are unpredictable. We now turn to an analysis of unexpected changes in aggregate supply.

UNANTICIPATED INCREASES IN *SRAS*

What would happen if highly favorable weather conditions or a temporary increase in the world market price of an important export commodity increased the current output and income of a nation? Since favorable supply conditions cannot be counted on in the future, they will not directly alter the economy's long-term production capacity. Exhibit 8 analyzes this issue. The favorable conditions will increase short-run aggregate supply (to $SRAS_2$). Output will temporarily expand beyond the economy's full employment constraint. The increase in current supply will place downward pressure on the price level.

As we previously discussed, people will spend only a small portion of a temporary increase in income. Since the favorable supply conditions are not

EXHIBIT 8 · An Unanticipated, Temporary Increase in Aggregate Supply

Here we illustrate the impact of an unanticipated, but temporary increase in aggregate supply such as might result from a bumper crop due to highly favorable weather conditions. The increase in aggregate supply (shift to $SRAS_2$) would lead to a lower price level (P_{95}) and an increase in current GNP (to Y_1). Since the favorable supply conditions cannot be counted on in the future, the economy's long-run aggregate supply will not increase. Predictably, decision-makers will save a large proportion of their temporarily higher real income, spreading the benefits into the future. Thus, the supply of loanable funds will increase. The real interest rate will fall (to r_2), encouraging expenditures on interest-sensitive capital goods and consumer durables.

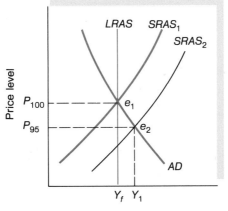

(a) Goods and services—real GNP

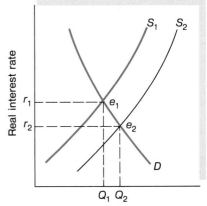

(b) Loanable funds

expected to persist in the future, a substantial share of the temporarily high income will flow predictably into savings. The supply of loanable funds will increase (to S_2, frame b), causing the real interest rate to decline. The lower real interest rate will stimulate investment and encourage the purchase of consumer durables such as automobiles and appliances.

An increase in aggregate supply that is expected to be temporary will place downward pressure on prices and reduce the real rate of interest. The lower interest rate will encourage capital formation, which will expand the resource base, permitting individuals to spread some of the benefits of the current high level of income into the future.

UNANTICIPATED DECREASES IN *SRAS*

During the 1970s, the U.S. economy was jolted by several unfavorable supply-side factors. Foremost among them was the sharp increase in the world price of crude oil, an important import commodity. The higher oil prices meant that oil-importing nations such as the United States had to give up a larger amount of other goods in exchange for each barrel of imported oil. As a result, the more expensive oil reduced the supply of goods and services in oil-importing countries. In addition, adverse weather conditions during 1974 and again in 1980 resulted in poor harvests and low agricultural output in the United States.

How will such reductions in aggregate supply influence price and output? Exhibit 9 addresses this issue. If the adverse supply shock is expected to be temporary, as would certainly be the case for a bad harvest, long-run aggregate supply would be unaffected. Short-run aggregate supply declines, as illustrated by the shift from $SRAS_1$ to $SRAS_2$. Output declines and prices rise in the goods and services market. Since people believe the lower level of output and income is only temporary, they will reduce their current saving level (and dip into past savings) to maintain a current consumption level more consistent with their longer-term perceived opportunities. But, when everyone reduces their saving level, the supply of loanable funds decreases (shifts to S_2, Exhibit 9b), causing an increase in the real interest rate (to r_2). The higher real interest rate rations funds to those willing to pay

EXHIBIT 9 • An Unanticipated Temporary Reduction in Aggregate Supply

Consider the impact of a temporary reduction in aggregate supply (shift from $SRAS_1$ to $SRAS_2$, frame a). Current output and real income will fall to Y_2, and prices will rise (to P_{105}). Many people will reduce their saving as they seek to cushion the impact of the short-term reduction in income. The supply of loanable funds will decrease (shift to S_2, frame b), pushing up the real interest rate (to r_2). Purchases of interest-sensitive goods will decline. The reduction in short-run aggregate supply leads to both a higher price level (inflation) and a higher real interest rate.

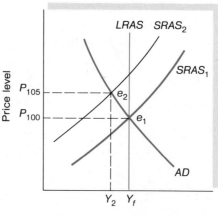

(a) Goods and services—real GNP

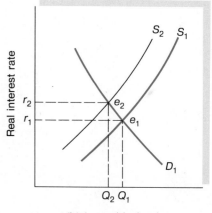

(b) Loanable funds

the most to maintain their current spending during the economic hard times. Of course, a higher real interest rate will also retard capital investment. A reduction in net investment and an accompanying decline in near-term economic growth are predictable side effects of a temporary reduction in aggregate supply.

When an adverse supply-side factor is more permanent, as in the case of a *long-term* increase in the price of oil imports, the long-run supply curve would also shift to the left. Under these circumstances, the economy would have to adjust to a lower level of real output.

Regardless of whether the decline in aggregate supply is temporary or permanent, other things constant, the price level will rise. Similarly, output will decline, at least temporarily. Theory thus indicates that the supply shocks of the 1970s contributed to the stagflation of the era.

DOES A MARKET ECONOMY HAVE A SELF-CORRECTING MECHANISM?

A market economy does possess characteristics capable of cushioning economic shocks. First, the permanent income hypothesis suggests that aggregate demand will fluctuate less than income. When incomes fall during a contraction, households will reduce their current saving to maintain a high level of current consumption. As a result, the reduction in consumer demand will be less than the reduction in aggregate income. Similarly, during an economic expansion, a substantial amount of the above-normal gains in income enjoyed by most households will be allocated to saving. So, consumption demand will increase less rapidly than income during a business expansion.

Second, changes in real interest rates will help minimize fluctuations in aggregate demand. During an economic downturn, business demand for loanable funds is generally weak. The weak demand, however, will lead to a lower real interest rate. In turn, the lower interest rate will both encourage current consumption and reduce the opportunity cost of investment projects, dampening the decline in aggregate demand. On the other hand, the real interest rate will increase as many businesses borrow in order to undertake investment projects during an economic expansion. The higher real interest rate will discourage both consumption and investment and thereby minimize the increase in aggregate demand during a business expansion. As a result, changes in the real interest rate will help stabilize aggregate demand over the course of the business cycle.

Nevertheless, various shocks may result in an output that is either greater than or less than the economy's long-run capacity. When this is the case, are market forces capable of leading the economy back to full employment capacity? Exhibit 10a illustrates demand and supply conditions in the goods and services market for an economy initially experiencing output beyond its full employment capacity. At this abnormally high level of output, unemployment will temporarily be lower than the natural rate. Similarly, supply conditions for labor and other resources will be extremely tight.

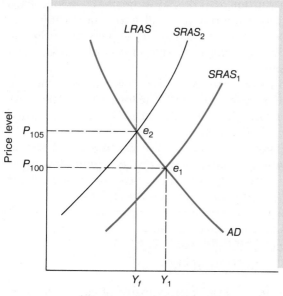

(a) Output greater than long-run
capacity

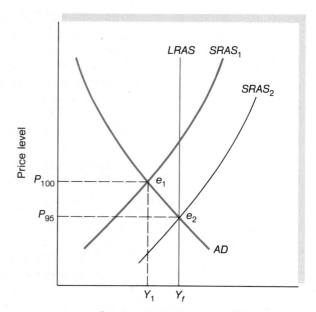

(b) Output less than long-run
capacity

EXHIBIT 10 • Adjusting to Long-Run Equilibrium

In the short-run, output may either exceed or fall short of the economy's full employment capacity (Y_f). If output is temporarily greater than the economy's potential (frame a), resource prices and production costs will rise. The higher production costs will decrease aggregate supply (to $SRAS_2$, frame a), restoring equilibrium at full employment capacity and a higher price level (P_{105}).

When an economy is temporarily operating at less than capacity (frame b), abnormally high unemployment and an excess supply in the resource market will lead to lower resource prices and production costs. The lower cost will increase aggregate supply (to $SRAS_2$, frame b). Thus, the output of a market economy will tend toward full employment capacity. However, this self-correction process will require time. As we proceed, we will consider alternative methods of attaining full employment equilibrium more rapidly.

As we discussed when considering the impact of an unanticipated increase in demand (see Exhibit 6), the abnormally high rate of output will not be sustainable. As the resource market adjusts, wage rates and other resource prices will rise, thereby increasing production costs. The higher production costs reduce *SRAS*. The economy adjusts along its aggregate demand curve, moving to a new equilibrium at full employment output (Y_f) and a higher price level. So, when unemployment is *below* its natural rate, higher wage rates and resource prices will move the economy back to long-run equilibrium.

Exhibit 10b illustrates an economy initially operating at less than its full employment capacity. Given the low rate of output (Y_1), unemployment will exceed its natural rate. The abnormally high unemployment rate and excess supply conditions in the resource market will eventually induce suppliers to accept lower wage rates and prices for other resources. With time, labor and other resource costs will fall, shifting *SRAS* to the right.[3] Eventually, lower resource prices will restore the full employment output rate at a lower price level.

Market adjustments toward full employment could best be thought of as a groping process. For example, when an economy is operating at less than full employment, indicators such as rising inventories, more lengthy job searches, and abnormally low sales send signals on current market conditions to decision-makers. Businesses will make price and output adjustments in light of the less favorable market signals. Similarly, workers will adjust their wage expectations in light of the weak demand for their services. While our analysis indicates this process will direct the economy back to full employment, it also indicates that the process will take time.

How rapidly the self-corrective process works may, in fact, be the key issue. If the self-corrective process works quite slowly, market economies will still experience prolonged periods of abnormally high unemployment and below-capacity output. Many economists believe this is the case. In turn, these economists believe that discretionary changes in fiscal and monetary policy can help keep the economy on track.

Conversely, other economists believe that the self-corrective mechanism of a market economy works reasonably well when monetary and fiscal policy follow a stable course. This latter group argues that policy mistakes are the major source of economic instability. Because of this, they call for the use of policy rules, such as a constant growth rate in the supply of money and balanced budgets, rather than discretionary use of macroeconomic policy. We will return to this debate when we consider the impact of monetary and fiscal policy.

LOOKING AHEAD

Modern macroeconomics reflects an evolutionary process. The Great Depression and the accompanying prolonged unemployment exerted an enormous impact on macroeconomics. John Maynard Keynes, the brilliant English economist, developed a theory that sheds light on the operation of an economy experiencing high rates of unemployment. The next chapter focuses on the Keynesian theory.

CHAPTER SUMMARY

1. An increase in aggregate demand involves a shift of the entire *AD* schedule to the right. Other than policy, major factors causing an increase in aggregate demand are: (a) an increase in real income, (b) a

---

[3]We have considered the self-correction mechanism within the framework of a noninflationary economy. In an inflationary setting, the reduction in real wage rates would take the form of a nominal wage increase *that is less rapid than the inflation rate.* With inflation, the real wage can fall even though nominal wage rates do not. This point, though, does not change the basic analysis. A reduction in the real wage rate, even when it takes the form of a nominal wage increase that is less than the inflation rate, would reduce real cost, increase *SRAS*, and restore full employment output.

lower real interest rate, (c) increased optimism concerning future business and employment prospects, and (d) an increase in the expected rate of inflation. Conversely, if these factors change in the opposite direction, a decrease in aggregate demand will result.

2. When considering the impact of real income on aggregate demand, it is important to distinguish between temporary and long-term changes in income. Compared with a long-term increase in income, a temporary increase in income will encourage people to save a much larger portion. Thus, the increase in aggregate demand emanating from a temporary increase in income will be substantially less than for an expansion in income that is expected to be more permanent.

3. An increase in aggregate supply involves a shift of the entire schedule to the right. The following factors will increase both long-run and short-run aggregate supply: (a) increases in the supply of labor and capital resources, (b) improvements in technology and productivity, and (c) institutional changes improving the efficiency of resource use. While these factors are the major source of long-term growth of output, they seldom lead to large increases in output and employment during a brief time period.

4. In the short-run, output may change as the result of temporary factors that do not directly alter the economy's long-run capacity. For example, a favorable supply shock or a decrease in the expected rate of inflation will increase supply during a current period, causing *SRAS* (but not *LRAS*) to shift to the right.

5. An increase in output due to economic growth (an increase in the economy's production capacity) will increase both short-run and long-run aggregate supply. The economy will now be able to produce and sustain a larger output level. If the supply of money is constant, a lower price level will result.

6. When the long-run equilibrium of an economy is disrupted by an unanticipated increase in aggregate demand, output will temporarily increase beyond the economy's long-run capacity and unemployment will fall below its natural rate. However, as decision-makers adjust to the increase in demand, resource prices will rise and output will recede to long-run capacity. In the long-run, the major impact of the increase in aggregate demand will be a higher price level (inflation).

7. An unanticipated reduction in aggregate demand will temporarily reduce output below capacity and push unemployment above its natural rate. Eventually, unemployment and excess supply in resource markets will reduce wage rates and resource prices. Costs will decline and output will return to its long-run potential. However, if wages and prices are inflexible downward, less-than-capacity output and abnormally high unemployment may persist for a long time.

8. When an economy in long-run equilibrium experiences an unanticipated favorable supply shock, output (and income) will temporarily rise above capacity and prices will decline. A lower real interest rate is also a predicted result, since a large amount of a temporary increase in

income will flow into saving. The long-run real interest rate will stimulate capital formation and, other things constant, will lead to more rapid short-run economic growth.

9. An adverse supply shock will reduce output and increase the price level. If the reduction in income is expected to be temporary, people will increase their borrowing (and reduce their saving) to maintain a consumption level more consistent with their longer-term income. As a result, the real interest rate will rise. Many economists think adverse supply shocks, particularly the sharp increase in the price of imported oil, contributed to the slow rate of growth and rapid increase in the price level during the 1970s.

10. When current output exceeds the economy's long-run capacity and unemployment is below its natural rate, wages and prices will rise until equilibrium is restored at full employment output and a higher price level. Similarly, when current output is less than the economy's long-run capacity and unemployment exceeds its natural rate, wages and prices will fall until long-run equilibrium is restored. The economy thus has a self-corrective mechanism capable of restoring full employment.

11. Many economists believe the economy's self-corrective mechanism works quite slowly and that discretionary policy changes are necessary to minimize economic instability. Others believe that the self-corrective mechanism works reasonably well and that discretionary policy is likely to do more harm than good.

THE ECONOMIC WAY OF THINKING—
DISCUSSION QUESTIONS

1. Explain in your own words how each of the following factors would influence *current* aggregate demand:
   (a) an increase in the world price of wheat, an important export commodity.
   (b) a decrease in the expected rate of inflation.
   (c) an increase in real income due to a technological improvement.
   (d) a higher price level (be careful).
   (e) an increase in the real interest rate.
2. It is often argued that if everyone simultaneously tried to save more, the result might well be a decline in real GNP. Use our basic three-market macroeconomic model to analyze the impact of an increase in thriftiness on prices, output, employment, and interest rates.
3. What impact would a sudden unexpected increase in the demand for export goods have on domestic output, price level, and unemployment?
4. What impact will each of the following have on the price level in the United States?
   (a) a reduction in the world price of oil.
   (b) a reduction in the world price of wheat.
   (c) a drought in the midwest farm belt.
   (d) a lengthy strike in the automobile industry.
   (e) a decline in the expected rate of inflation.

5. What is a supply shock? Give three examples of supply shocks.
6. Both union and management representatives expect that the price level will rise 10 percent during the next year. Explain why the unemployment rate will probably increase if the actual rate of inflation next year is only 3 percent.
7. What are the major factors influencing aggregate supply in the long-run? Why doesn't the long-run aggregate supply curve slope upward to the right like *SRAS*?

- Why did Keynes believe high rates of unemployment persisted during the Great Depression?

- What are the major components of the Keynesian model? What is the major factor that causes the level of output and employment to change?

- What determines the equilibrium level of output in the Keynesian model?

- What is the multiplier principle? Why is it important?

- Why do Keynesians believe market economies experience business instability?

I believe myself to be writing a book on economic theory which will largely revolutionize—not, I suppose, at once but in the course of the next ten years— the way the world thinks about economic problems.[1]

JOHN MAYNARD KEYNES

10 KEYNESIAN FOUNDATIONS OF MODERN MACROECONOMICS

Modern macroeconomics is the product of an evolutionary process. Prior to the Great Depression, most economists thought market adjustments would automatically guide an economy to full employment within a relatively brief time period. The prolonged, high unemployment rates during the Great Depression undermined the credibility of this view. Against the background of the 1930s, English economist John Maynard Keynes (pronounced "canes") developed a theory capable of explaining prolonged unemployment. Keynes was not only a great economist, he was also a prophet. Just as he anticipated (see chapter opening quote), the analysis of his *General Theory*, published in 1936, exerted an enormous influence on economics.[2] As he expected, it was not immediately accepted. Keynes and his followers, though, eventually won the minds of a new generation of economists seeking an explanation for the Great Depression.[3]

It is difficult to exaggerate the impact of Keynesian economics. It formed the core of macroeconomics for three decades following World War II. Several basic concepts and much of the terminology we use today can be traced to Keynes. Keynesian analysis provided the foundation for modern macroeconomics.

KEYNESIAN EXPLANATION OF THE GREAT DEPRESSION

Classical Economists: Economists from Adam Smith to the time of Keynes who focused their analyses on economic efficiency and production. With regard to business instability, they thought market prices would adjust quickly in a manner that would guide an economy out of a recession back to full employment.

Say's Law: The view that production creates its own demand. Thus, there cannot be a general oversupply because the total value of goods and services produced (income) will always be available for purchasing them.

Mainstream economists prior to the time of Keynes (often called **classical economists**) emphasized the importance of supply. In contrast, they paid little heed to aggregate demand. The disinterest of classical economists with demand issues stemmed from their adherence to Say's Law. Named for the nineteenth-century French economist J. B. Say, **Say's Law** maintains that a general overproduction of goods relative to total demand is impossible since supply (production) creates its own demand. Say's Law is based on the view that people do not work just for the sake of working. Rather, they work to obtain the income required to purchase desired goods and services. The purchasing power necessary to buy (demand) desired products is generated by production. A farmer's supply of wheat generates income to meet the farmer's demand for shoes, clothes, automobiles, and other desired goods. Similarly, the supply of shoes generates the purchasing power with which shoemakers (and their employees) demand the farmer's wheat and other desired goods.

Classicists understood that it was possible to produce too much of some goods and not enough of others. At such times, they reasoned, the prices of goods in excess supply would fall, and the prices of products in excess demand would rise. The pricing system would correct such imbalances as might temporarily exist. They did not believe, though, that a general over-

---

[1]Letter from John Maynard Keynes to George Bernard Shaw, New Year's Day, 1935.

[2]John Maynard Keynes, *The General Theory of Employment, Interest, and Money* (London: Macmillan, 1936).

[3]Keynes died rather unexpectedly in 1946, so he did not live to observe the enormous impact of his ideas on public policy, particularly during the three decades following World War II.

production of goods was possible. In aggregate, they thought demand would always be sufficient to purchase the goods produced.

Keynes rejected the classical view and offered a completely new concept of output determination. He believed that spending induced business firms to supply goods and services. From this, he argued that if total spending fell (as it might, for example, if consumers and investors became pessimistic about the future or tried to save more of their current income), business firms would respond by cutting back production. Less spending would thus lead to less output.

Of course, classical economists were aware of this possibility, but they believed the labor surplus would drive down wages, reducing costs and lowering prices until the surplus was eliminated and the economy was directed to full employment. Keynes and his followers disagreed. They argued that wages and prices are highly inflexible, particularly in a downward direction, in modern economies characterized by large business firms and powerful trade unions. Because of this, they did not believe that flexible wages and prices would direct the economy to equilibrium at full employment.

Keynesian analysis offers a completely different concept of equilibrium. In the Keynesian view, *changes in output,* rather than *changes in prices,* direct the economy to an equilibrium. Equilibrium takes place at the output rate consistent with the level of total spending at current prices. This output rate need not be associated with the full employment of resources.

The message of Keynes could be summarized as follows: Spending (demand) leads to current production. Businesses will produce only the quantity of goods and services they believe consumers, investors, governments, and foreigners will plan to buy. If these planned aggregate expenditures are less than the economy's full employment output, output will fall short of its potential. When aggregate expenditures are deficient, there are no automatic forces capable of assuring full employment. Less than capacity output will result. Prolonged unemployment will persist. Against the background of the Great Depression, this was a compelling argument.

THE BASIC KEYNESIAN AGGREGATE EXPENDITURE MODEL

As we will show, the Keynesian analysis could be presented within the framework of our *AD/AS* model. However, an alternative framework, an aggregate expenditure model, is generally used to present the Keynesian view. Equality between aggregate expenditures and output is central to the Keynesian analysis. The Keynesian aggregate expenditure model helps us visualize this point. The model will also help us better understand why Keynesians believe that changes in aggregate spending exert a powerful influence on equilibrium output and employment. The aggregate expenditure model has occupied a central position in macroeconomics for several decades. It is an integral part of the evolutionary process that led to modern macroeconomic theory.

As we develop the Keynesian aggregate expenditure model, we will make several assumptions to simplify the analysis. First, as with our *AD/AS* model, we will assume there is a specific full employment level of output. Only the natural rate of unemployment is present when full employment capacity is attained. Second, following in the Keynesian tradition, we will assume that wages and prices are completely inflexible until full employment is reached. Once full employment is achieved, though, additional demand will lead only to higher prices. Strictly speaking, these polar assumptions will not hold in the real world. They may, however, approximate conditions in the short-run. Finally, we will continue to assume that the government's taxing, spending, and monetary policies are constant.

The concept of planned aggregate expenditures is central to the Keynesian analysis. As with aggregate demand, the four components of aggregate expenditures are consumption, investment, government purchases, and net exports. The Keynesian model postulates a specific relationship between total income and each component of planned expenditures. We turn now to these issues.

PLANNED CONSUMPTION EXPENDITURES

Keynes believed that current income is the primary determinant of consumption expenditures. As he stated:

> Men are disposed, as a rule and on the average, to increase their consumption as their income increases, but not by as much as the increase in their income.[4]

According to Keynes, disposable income is by far the major determinant of current consumption. If disposable income increases, consumers will increase their planned expenditures.

Consumption Function: A fundamental relationship between disposable income and consumption. As disposable income increases, current consumption expenditures will rise, but by a smaller amount than the increase in income.

This positive relationship between consumption spending and disposable income is called the **consumption function.** Exhibit 1 illustrates this relationship for an economy. At low levels of income (less than $2 trillion), the consumption expenditures of households will exceed their disposable income. When income is low, households dissave. They either borrow or draw from their past savings to purchase consumption goods. Since consumption does not increase as rapidly as income, the slope of the consumption function will be less than one. So, the consumption schedule is flatter than the 45-degree line of Exhibit 1. As income increases, household income eventually equals and exceeds current consumption. For incomes above $2 trillion, saving increases as income rises.

PLANNED INVESTMENT EXPENDITURES

Investment encompasses (a) expenditures on fixed assets such as buildings and machines and (b) changes in the inventories of raw materials and final products not yet sold. In the short-run, Keynes argued that investment was best viewed as an **autonomous expenditure,** independent of income.

Autonomous Expenditures: Expenditures that do not vary with the level of income. They are determined by factors (such as business expectations and economic policy) that are outside the basic income-expenditure model.

Exhibit 2 illustrates an autonomous investment schedule. The flat investment schedule indicates that businesses plan to spend $400 billion on investment, regardless of current income. Planned investment is thus independent of income. In the Keynesian model, investment is primarily a function of current sales relative to plant capacity, expected future sales,

---

[4]John Maynard Keynes, *The General Theory of Employment, Interest, and Money* (London: Macmillan, 1936), p. 96.

EXHIBIT 1 • The Aggregate Consumption Function

The Keynesian model assumes that there is a positive relationship between consumption and income. However, as income increases, consumption expands by a smaller amount. Thus, the slope of the consumption function (line C) is less than one (less than the 45-degree line).

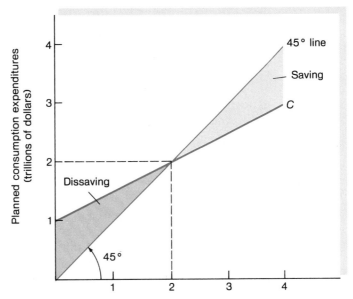

and the interest rate. Changes in these latter factors would alter investment—they would cause the entire schedule to shift either upward or downward. But, when focusing on the forces pushing an economy toward an equilibrium level of output, the basic Keynesian model postulates a constant level of planned investment expenditures.

PLANNED GOVERNMENT EXPENDITURES

As with investment, planned government expenditures in the basic Keynesian model are assumed to be independent of income. Exhibit 2 illustrates an autonomous government expenditure function of $600 billion. The combined investment and government expenditures sum to $1,000 billion.

The forces underlying government expenditures differ from those influencing private consumption and investment. Government expenditures

EXHIBIT 2 • Autonomous Investment and Government Expenditures

Within the basic Keynesian model, planned investment (line I) is autonomous of income. Investment may shift either up or down in response to changes in factors such as business optimism or the real interest rate, but it is independent of the income level. Similarly, government expenditures (line G) are a policy variable, independent of income. Thus, as income changes, planned investment and government expenditures (I + G) remain constant.

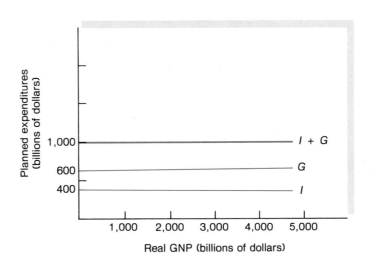

need not be constrained by income (tax revenues) or the pursuit of profit. Governments can, and often do, spend more than they receive in taxes. Planned government expenditures are best viewed as a policy variable, subject to alteration by the political process. Perceiving them as autonomous of income allows us to focus more clearly on the stability characteristics of a private economy. Later, we will analyze how changes in government expenditures influence output and employment within the framework of the Keynesian aggregate expenditure model.

PLANNED NET EXPORTS

Exports are dependent on spending choices and income levels abroad. These decisions are, by and large, unaffected by changes in a nation's domestic income level. Therefore, as Exhibit 3 illustrates, exports remain constant when income changes. In contrast, increases in domestic income will induce consumers to purchase more foreign as well as domestic goods. So, the level of imports increases as income rises.

Since exports remain constant and imports increase as aggregate income expands, net exports will decline as income expands (see Exhibit 3). From this, the Keynesian model postulates a negative relationship between income and net exports.

PLANNED VERSUS ACTUAL EXPENDITURES

It is important to distinguish between planned and actual expenditures. Planned expenditures reflect the choices of consumers, investors, governments and foreigners, *given their expectations as to the choices of other decision-makers.* Planned expenditures, though, need not equal actual expenditures. In fact, if purchasers spend a different amount on goods and services than business firms anticipated, actual expenditures will differ from what was planned. The difference will result in *un*planned changes in inventories.

What would happen if the planned expenditures of consumers, investors, and governments on goods and services were lower than producers planned? Business firms would then be unable to sell all the output produced during the period. Their *actual* inventories would increase as they unintentionally made larger inventory investments than they planned. On the other hand, consider what would happen if purchasers bought more

---

EXHIBIT 3   •   Income and Net Exports

Since exports are determined by income abroad, they are constant at $250 billion. Imports increase as domestic income expands. Thus, planned net exports fall as domestic income increases.

Total Output (Real GNP in billions)	Planned Exports (billions)	Planned Imports (billions)	Planned Net Exports (billions)
$3,400	$250	$ 50	$200
3,700	250	100	150
4,000	250	150	100
4,300	250	200	50
4,600	250	250	0

goods and services than business expected. The unexpected brisk sales would draw down inventories and result in less inventory investment than business firms planned. In this case, *actual* inventory investment would be less than they *planned*.

Actual and planned expenditures are equal only when purchasers buy the quantity of goods and services business decision-makers anticipate. Only then will the plans of buyers and sellers in the goods and services market harmonize.

KEYNESIAN EQUILIBRIUM

In our basic Keynesian model, planned expenditures on consumption, investment, government, and net exports sum to planned aggregate expenditures (*AE*). In turn, producers supply only the quantity of goods they believe consumers, investors, governments, and foreigners (net exports) plan to purchase at existing prices.

Equilibrium is present in the Keynesian model when planned aggregate expenditures equal the value of current output. When this is the case, businesses are able only to sell the amount they produce. Thus, they have no incentive to either expand or contract their output. In equation form, Keynesian macroequilibrium is attained when:

$$\underbrace{\text{total output}}_{\text{Real GNP}} = \underbrace{\text{planned } C + I + G + X}_{\substack{\text{planned aggregate} \\ \text{expenditures}}}$$

KEYNESIAN EQUILIBRIUM— TABULAR PRESENTATION

To grasp the Keynesian concept of equilibrium, it is helpful to view the major components in tabular form. Exhibit 4 presents data for planned consumption, investment, government purchases, and net exports. Investment is assumed to be determined by such factors as business expectations

---

EXHIBIT 4 • Equilibrium Level of Income, Output, and Employment

Possible Levels of Employment (Millions of Persons) (1)	Total Output (Real GNP) (Billions of Dollars) (2)	Planned Consumption (Billions of Dollars) (3)	Planned Injections ($I + G$) (Billions of Dollars) (4)	Planned Net Exports (Billions of Dollars) (5)	Planned Aggregate Expenditures (Billions of Dollars)[a] (6)	Unplanned Inventory Change[b] (Billions of Dollars) (7)	Tendency of Employment, Output, and Income (8)
90	3,400	2,500	1,000	200	3,700	−300	Increase
100	3,700	2,700	1,000	150	3,850	−150	Increase
110	4,000	2,900	1,000	100	4,000	0	Equilibrium
120[c]	4,300	3,100	1,000	50	4,150	+150	Decrease
130	4,600	3,300	1,000	0	4,300	+300	Decrease

[a]Planned $C + I + G + X$ as indicated by columns 3, 4, and 5.
[b]Total output (column 2) less planned aggregate expenditures (column 6).
[c]Full employment.

and technological change. It is thus not dependent on level of income. Similarly, government expenditures are subject to economic policy. They, too, are assumed to be independent of income. So, for all levels of income, the injections of investment and government purchases into the income streams are assumed to be constant. Within the Keynesian model, planned consumption increases with income, but it increases by a smaller amount than does income (because some of the additional income is allocated to saving and taxes). As income increases by $300 billion (from $3,400 billion to $3,700 billion, for example), consumption increases by $200 billion. While planned net exports decline with income, they fail to offset the increase in consumption since they are relatively small. Thus, aggregate expenditures increase as income expands.

For the economy illustrated by Exhibit 4, Keynesian equilibrium takes place at a GNP of $4 trillion, the income level at which planned aggregate expenditures are just equal to total output (aggregate supply). An employment level of 110 million is associated with the $4 trillion output. When GNP is equal to $4 trillion, the planned expenditures of consumers, investors, governments, and foreigners (net exports) are precisely equal to the value of the output produced by business firms. Because of this, the spending plans of purchasers mesh precisely with the production plans of business decision-makers. Given this balance, there is no reason for producers to change their plans for the next period.

At other output levels, the plans of producers and purchasers will conflict. Consider what will happen if the output of the economy temporarily expands to $4.3 trillion. Employment will increase from 110 to 120 million. At the higher income level, households will increase their spending to $3.1 trillion. When added to the $1 trillion of spending by investors or governments, and the $50 billion in net exports, total spending is equal to $4.15 trillion, $150 billion less than output. The total spending of consumers, investors, and governments will thus be insufficient to purchase the $4.3 billion of output. Unwanted and unplanned business inventories of $150 billion will arise. Of course, business firms will not continue to produce goods they cannot sell, so they will reduce production during the subsequent period. As production is cut back, output and employment will fall. The unemployment rate will rise. Given the spending plans of decision-makers, the $4.3 trillion income level cannot be maintained in the future.

What will happen if income falls temporarily below the Keynesian equilibrium? Suppose the income level of the economy pictured in Exhibit 4 were $3.7 trillion. At that income level, purchasers of goods and services would spend $3.85 billion (column 6) of current output. Business firms would be selling more than they are currently producing. Their inventories would decline below normal levels. Business firms would respond to this happy state of affairs by expanding output. Production would increase, providing jobs for previously unemployed workers. Income would rise toward the Keynesian equilibrium level of $4 trillion.

LESS THAN FULL EMPLOYMENT EQUILIBRIUM

Since Keynesian equilibrium is dependent on equality between planned aggregate expenditures and output, it need not take place at full employment. If an economy is in Keynesian equilibrium, there will be no tendency for output to change even if output is well below full employment capacity.

Exhibit 4 illustrates this point. Suppose full employment for the economy is present at an employment level of 120 million. This notwithstanding, given the current planned spending, the economy will always move toward the $4 trillion equilibrium income level. In equilibrium, employment will be 110 million, 10 million less than for full employment. More important, the excess unemployment and below-capacity output will persist into the future, as long as planned aggregate expenditures remain at $4 trillion. Insufficient spending prevents the economy from reaching its full potential.

This is precisely what Keynes thought was happening during the Great Depression. He believed that Western economies were in equilibrium at an employment rate substantially below capacity. Unless aggregate expenditures increased, the prolonged unemployment would continue. Keynesian economics provided a theory to explain the prolonged unemployment of the Great Depression.

KEYNESIAN EQUILIBRIUM— GRAPHIC PRESENTATION

The Keynesian analysis can also be presented graphically. Exhibit 5 presents a graph for which the planned aggregate consumption, investment, government, and net export expenditures are measured on the *Y*-axis and total output is measured on the *X*-axis. The 45-degree line extends from the origin and maps out all points that are equidistant from the *X*- and *Y*-axes. So, along the 45-degree line, aggregate expenditures (*AE*) are equal to total output (*GNP*).

Since aggregate expenditures equal total output for all points along the 45-degree line, the line maps out all possible equilibrium income levels. As long as the economy is operating at less than its full employment capacity, producers will produce any output along the 45-degree line they believe purchasers will buy. Producers, though, will supply a level of output only if they believe planned expenditures will be large enough to purchase it. Depending on the level of aggregate expenditures, each point along the 45-degree line is a potential equilibrium. Within the Keynesian model, then,

EXHIBIT 5 • Keynesian Equilibrium

Aggregate expenditures will be equal to total output for all points along a 45-degree line from the origin. The 45-degree line thus maps out potential equilibrium levels of output for the Keynesian model.

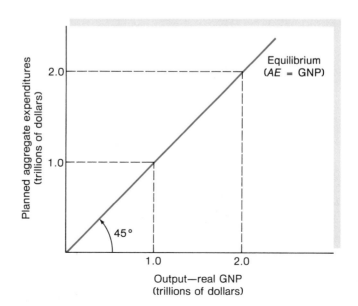

there are many possible equilibrium levels of output and employment, not just one.

Using the data of Exhibit 4, Exhibit 6 graphically depicts the Keynesian equilibrium. The $C + I + G + X$ line indicates the total planned expenditures of consumers, investors, governments, and (net) foreigners at each income level. Reflecting the consumption function, the aggregate expenditure (AE) line is flatter than the 45-degree line. Remember, as income rises, consumption also increases, but by less than the increase in income. Therefore, as income expands, total expenditures increase by less than the expansion in income.

The equilibrium level of output will be $4 trillion, the point at which the total expenditures (measured vertically) are just equal to total output (measured horizontally). Of course, the aggregate expenditure function $C + I + G + X$ will cross the 45-degree line at the $4 trillion equilibrium level of output.

As long as the aggregate expenditures function remains unchanged, no other level of output can be sustained. When total output exceeds $4 trillion (for example, $4.3 trillion), the aggregate expenditure line lies below the 45-degree line. Remember that the $C + I + G + X$ line indicates how much people want to spend at each income level. When the height of the $C + I + G + X$ line is less than the 45-degree line, total spending is less than

EXHIBIT 6 • Aggregate Expenditures and Keynesian Equilibrium

Here the data of Exhibit 4 are presented within the Keynesian cross framework. The equilibrium level of output is $4 trillion since planned expenditures ($C + I + G + X$) are just equal to output at that level of income. At a lower level of income, $3.7 trillion for example, unplanned inventory reduction would cause business firms to expand output (right-hand arrow). Conversely, at a higher income level, such as $4.3 trillion, accumulation of inventories would lead to a reduction in future output (left-hand arrow). Given current aggregate expenditures, only the $4 trillion output could be sustained. Note the $4 trillion equilibrium income level is less than the economy's potential of $4.3 trillion.

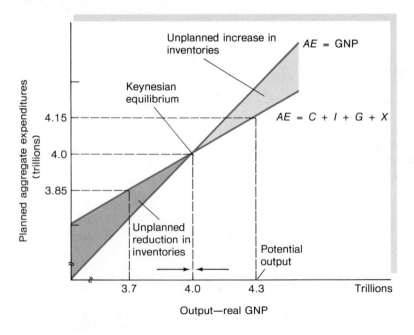

total output. Unwanted inventories will then accumulate, leading businesses to reduce their future production. Employment will decline. Output will fall back from $4.3 trillion to the equilibrium level of $4 trillion.

In contrast, if total output is temporarily below equilibrium, there is a tendency for income to rise. Suppose output is temporarily at $3.7 trillion. At that output level, the $C + I + G + X$ function lies above the 45-degree line. Aggregate expenditures exceed aggregate output. Businesses are selling more than they currently produce. Their inventories are falling. Excess demand is present. They will react to this state of affairs by hiring more workers and expanding production. Income will rise to the $4 trillion equilibrium level. Only at the equilibrium level, the point at which the $C + I + G + X$ function crosses the 45-degree line, will the spending plans of consumers, investors, and governments sustain the existing output level into the future.

As Exhibit 6 illustrates, the economy's full employment potential income level is $4.3 trillion. At this income level, though, aggregate expenditures are insufficient to purchase the output produced. Given the aggregate expenditure function, output will remain below its potential. Unemployment will persist. Within the Keynesian model, equilibrium need not coincide with full employment.

SHIFTS IN AGGREGATE EXPENDITURES AND CHANGES IN OUTPUT AND EMPLOYMENT

How could the economy reach its full employment capacity? According to the Keynesian model, it will not do so unless there is a change in the aggregate expenditure schedule. Since the Keynesian model assumes that prices are fixed until potential capacity is reached, wage and price reductions are ruled out as a feasible mechanism for directing the economy to full employment.

If consumers, investors, governments, and foreigners could be induced to expand their expenditures, output would expand to full employment capacity. Exhibit 7 illustrates this point. If additional spending shifted the aggregate expenditure schedule (AE) upward to AE_2, equilibrium output would expand to its potential capacity. At the higher level of expenditures, AE_2, total spending would equal output at $4.3 trillion.

What would happen if aggregate expenditures exceeded the economy's production capacity? For example, suppose aggregate expenditures rose to AE_3. Within the basic Keynesian model, aggregate expenditures in excess of output lead to a higher price level, once the economy reaches full employment. Nominal output will increase, but it merely reflects higher prices, rather than additional real output. Total spending in excess of full employment capacity is inflationary within the Keynesian model.

Aggregate expenditures are the catalyst of the Keynesian model. Changes in expenditures make things happen. Until full employment is attained, supply is always accommodative. An increase in aggregate expenditures will thus lead to an increase in real output and employment. Once full employment is reached, however, additional aggregate expenditures lead merely to higher prices.

The Keynesian model implies that regulation of aggregate expenditures is the crux of sound macroeconomic policy. If we could assure aggregate expenditures large enough to achieve capacity output, but not so large

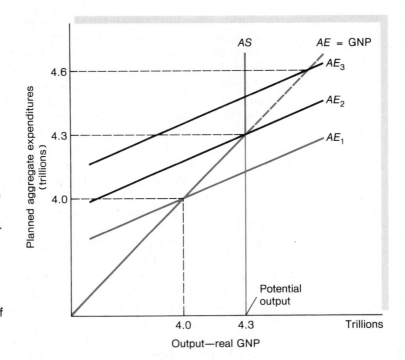

as to result in inflation, the Keynesian view implies that maximum output, full employment, and price stability could be attained.

THE KEYNESIAN MODEL WITHIN THE *AD/AS* FRAMEWORK

The Keynesian model can also be presented within the now familiar aggregate demand/aggregate supply framework. Given the polar assumptions of the model, the Keynesian supply conditions could be described as follows: Until the economy reaches its capacity, individual firms hold their price constant at the level that would be most profitable if they were operating at capacity. When demand is weak, firms simply reduce output, while maintaining the same price. Conversely, if demand increases, they will expand output while maintaining the same price until normal operating capacity is achieved. This means that the firms have a horizontal supply curve when operating below normal capacity. As a result, the short-run aggregate supply curve for the economy as a whole is perfectly horizontal until full employment capacity is attained. Once capacity is reached, firms raise their prices to ration the capacity output to those willing to pay the highest prices. Thus, the economy's *SRAS* is vertical at full employment capacity.

Exhibit 8 illustrates the shape of a Keynesian *SRAS* curve. *SRAS* is completely flat at the existing price level until potential capacity is reached. In this range, output is entirely dependent on aggregate demand. Any change in aggregate demand will lead to a corresponding change in output. Economists refer to this horizontal segment as the Keynesian range of the

EXHIBIT 8 • The Keynesian Aggregate Supply Curves

The Keynesian model implies a 90-degree angle-shaped aggregate supply curve. Since the model postulates complete wage and price inflexibility, the *SRAS* curve is flat for outputs less than potential GNP (Y_f). In this range, often referred to as the Keynesian range, output is entirely dependent on the level of aggregate demand. The Keynesian model implies that output rates beyond full employment are unattainable. Thus, both *SRAS* and *LRAS* are vertical at the economy's full employment potential output.

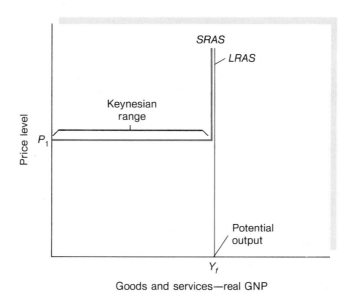

Goods and services—real GNP

aggregate supply curve. Once potential capacity is attained, output can no longer be expanded. So, both *SRAS* and *LRAS* are vertical at the capacity rate of output (Y_f).

Exhibit 9a illustrates the impact of a change in aggregate demand within the polar assumptions of the Keynesian model. When aggregate demand is less than AD_2 (for example, AD_1), the economy will languish below potential capacity. Since prices and wages are inflexible downward, below-capacity output rates (Y_1, for example) and abnormally high unemployment will persist unless there is an increase in aggregate demand. When output is below its potential, any increase in aggregate demand (for example, the shift from AD_1 to AD_2) brings previously idle resources into the productive process at an unchanged price level. In this range, the Keynesian analysis essentially turns Say's Law (supply creates an equivalent amount of demand) on its head. In the Keynesian range, an increase in demand creates its own supply.

Of course, once the economy's potential output constraint (Y_f) is reached, additional demand would merely lead to higher prices rather than to more output. Since both the *SRAS* and *LRAS* curves are vertical at capacity output, an increase in aggregate demand to AD_3 fails to expand real output.

When constructing models, we often make polar assumptions to illustrate various points. The Keynesian model is no exception. In the real world, prices will not be completely inflexible. Similarly, in the short-run, unanticipated increases in demand will not lead solely to higher prices. Nevertheless, the Keynesian model implies an important point that is illustrated more realistically by Exhibit 9b. The horizontal segment of the *SRAS* curve is an oversimplification intended to reinforce the idea that changes in aggregate demand exert little impact on prices and substantial impact on output when an economy is operating well below capacity. Thus, when

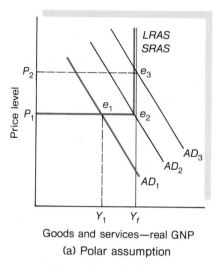

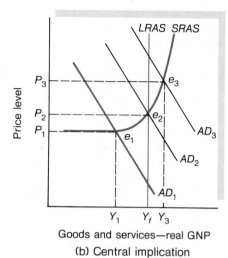

(a) Polar assumption

Goods and services—real GNP

(b) Central implication

Goods and services—real GNP

**EXHIBIT 9 • AD/AS
Presentation of
Keynesian Model**

Frame (a) illustrates the polar implications of the Keynesian model. When output is less than capacity (Y_1), an increase in aggregate demand such as illustrated by the shift from AD_1 to AD_2 will expand output without increasing prices. But, increases in demand beyond AD_2, such as a shift to AD_3, lead only to a higher price level (P_2, frame a).

Frame (b) relaxes the assumption of complete price inflexibility and short-run output inflexibility beyond Y_f. The *SRAS* therefore turns from horizontal to vertical more gradually. This would imply that unanticipated increases in aggregate demand would lead (a) primarily to increases in output when output is below capacity (for example, Y_1, frame b) and (b) primarily to increases in the price level when output is greater than capacity (for example, Y_3, frame b).

OUTSTANDING ECONOMIST

**John Maynard Keynes
(1883–1946)**

The General Theory of Employment, Interest, and Money was published in 1936. It would not be an exaggeration to rank this book alongside Adam Smith's *Wealth of Nations* and Karl Marx's *Das Kapital* as one of the most influential economic treatises ever written. In the midst of the Great Depression, Keynes provided both a plausible explanation for the massive unemployment and a strategy for ending it. He believed neither falling interest rates nor declining wages would restore full employment. Rather, additional demand was needed to put people back to work. He believed further that increases in government spending financed by budget deficits

would stimulate both demand and employment. This was the message of Keynes in the midst of the horror of the 1930s. A generation searching for answers provided a receptive audience for Keynesian analysis. Keynes married an idea with a moment in history.

Keynes was the son of John Neville Keynes, an eminent economist in his own right. The younger Keynes was educated at Cambridge, where he became a student and admirer of Alfred Marshall, the great English economist. Although he was schooled in Marshallian economics, with its emphasis on equilibrium and automatic market adjustments, he was unable to reconcile the

aggregate demand is weak (for example, AD_1), an unanticipated increase in aggregate demand will exert its primary impact on output.

On the other hand, the vertical segment of the aggregate supply curve is a simplifying assumption meant to illustrate the concept that there is an attainable output rate beyond which increases in demand will lead almost exclusively to price increases (and only small increases in real output). So, when aggregate demand is already quite strong (for example, AD_3), unanticipated increases in aggregate demand will predictably exert their primary impact on prices rather than output.

THE MULTIPLIER PRINCIPLE[5]

The multiplier principle occupies a central position in the Keynesian model. A change in autonomous expenditures, investment for example, generally leads to an even larger change in aggregate income. The **multiplier** is defined as the change in total income (equilibrium output) divided by the autonomous expenditure change that brought about the enlarged income.

The multiplier principle builds on the point that one individual's expenditure becomes the income of another. As we previously discussed,

Multiplier: The ratio of the change in equilibrium output to the independent change in investment, consumption, or government spending that brings about that change. Numerically, the multiplier is equal to 1/(1-MPC) when the price level is constant.

[5]Throughout this section, it will simplify matters if we assume a closed economy, one that does not engage in international trade. For an open economy, some of the increased spending flowing from the multiplier will be on imports. This will reduce the size of the domestic multiplier.

worldwide depression of the 1930s with the Marshallian view.

Keynes correctly anticipated that his ideas, like those of other great scholars and philosophers, would not be immediately accepted. His writings were often disorganized and confusing. Many critics thought his ideas were an attack on the puritan ethic or on the virtue of saving. Others thought that his views were a threat to the market economy. Personally, Keynes believed his ideas strengthened the case for the private sector by proposing a cure for its most serious shortcoming: the recession. He praised the virtue of profits. "The engine which drives enterprise,"

Keynes wrote, "is not thrift but profit." He was unimpressed with Marxian ideas, which he found to be "illogical and so dull."

Despite the critics, his analysis soon caught on, particularly among the new generation of economists. By the 1950s, the Keynesian analysis was dominant in academic circles throughout the Western world. By the 1960s, the Keynesian view formed the foundation for the macroeconomic policy of the United States and most other Western nations.

Keynes's personal life was full and varied. He earned millions of dollars speculating in the stock market, much of it on behalf of Cam-

bridge University. He was prominent in British social circles and was connected with the Bloomsbury group of artists and intellectuals. He married Lydia Lopokova, a ballerina in Diaghilev's Russian ballet. He enjoyed art, drama, opera, bridge, and debate with professional economists and prime ministers. In 1942, King George VI made him a lord.

The economic events of the 1970s tempered the confidence of macroeconomists in the basic analysis of Keynes. Nevertheless, his imprint is sure to endure. He revolutionized our way of thinking about macroeconomic issues.

consumption expenditures are directly related to income—an increase in income (or wealth) will lead to an increase in consumption. Predictably, income recipients will spend a portion of their additional earnings on consumption. In turn, their consumption expenditures will generate additional income for others who will also spend a portion of it.

Perhaps an example will illuminate the concept. Suppose that there were idle unemployed resources and that an entrepreneur decided to undertake a $1 million investment project. Since investment is a component of aggregate demand, the project will increase demand directly by $1 million. This is not the entire story, however. The investment project will require plumbers, carpenters, masons, lumber, cement, and many other resources. The incomes of the suppliers of these resources will increase by $1 million. What will they do with this additional income? Given the link between one's income and consumption, the resource suppliers will predictably spend a fraction of the additional income. They will buy more food, clothing, recreation, medical care, and thousands of other items. How will this spending influence the incomes of those who supply these additional consumption products and services? Their incomes will increase, also. After setting aside (saving) a portion of this additional income, these persons will also spend some of their additional income on current consumption. Their consumption spending will result in still more additional income for other product and service suppliers.

Within the Keynesian framework, an initial increase in investment (or any other autonomous shift in expenditures) expands income, which in turn leads to additional consumption spending that generates still more income. As the process moves through successive rounds, the initial spending exerts an amplified impact on income (and output). The initial investment triggers a chain reaction that causes the total increase in income to be a multiple of the initial investment. Economists refer to this process as the **multiplier principle.**

The term multiplier is also used to indicate the number by which the initial investment would be multiplied to obtain the total summation of the increases in income. If the $1 million investment resulted in $4 million of additional income, the multiplier would be 4. The total increase in income would be four times the amount of the initial increase in spending. Similarly, if total income increased by $3 million, the multiplier would be 3.

The size of the multiplier is dependent on the proportion of the additional income that households choose to spend on consumption. Keynes referred to this fraction as the **marginal propensity to consume** (MPC). Mathematically:

$$MPC = \frac{\text{additional consumption}}{\text{additional income}}$$

For example, if your income increases by $100 and you therefore increase your current consumption expenditures by $75, your marginal propensity to consume is 3/4 or .75.

Multiplier Principle: The concept that an induced increase in consumption, investment, or government expenditures leads to additional income and consumption spending by secondary parties and therefore expands total spending by a larger amount than the initial increase in expenditures.

WHAT DETERMINES THE SIZE OF THE MULTIPLIER?

Marginal Propensity to Consume: Additional current consumption divided by additional current disposable income.

EXHIBIT 10 • The Multiplier Principle

Expenditure Stage	Additional Income (Dollars)	Additional Consumption (Dollars)	Marginal Propensity to Consume
Round 1	1,000,000	750,000	3/4
Round 2	750,000	562,500	3/4
Round 3	562,500	421,875	3/4
Round 4	421,875	316,406	3/4
Round 5	316,406	237,305	3/4
Round 6	237,305	177,979	3/4
Round 7	177,979	133,484	3/4
Round 8	133,484	100,113	3/4
Round 9	100,113	75,085	3/4
Round 10	75,085	56,314	3/4
All Others	225,253	168,939	3/4
Total	4,000,000	3,000,000	

Exhibit 10 illustrates why the size of the multiplier is dependent on MPC. Suppose the MPC was equal to 3/4, indicating that consumers spend 75 cents of each additional dollar earned. Continuing with our previous example, we know that a $1 million investment would initially result in $1 million of additional income in round 1. Since the MPC is 3/4, consumption would increase by $750,000 (the other $250,000 would flow into saving), contributing that amount to income in round 2. The recipients of the round 2 income of $750,000 would spend three fourths of it on current consumption. Hence, their spending would increase income by $562,500 in round 3. Exhibit 10 illustrates the additions to income through other rounds. In total, income would increase by $4 million, given an MPC of 3/4. The multiplier is 4.

If the MPC had been greater, income recipients would have spent a larger share of their additional income on current consumption during each round. Thus, the additional income generated in each round would have been greater, increasing the size of the multiplier. There is a precise relationship between the expenditure multiplier and the MPC. The *expenditure multiplier M* is:

$$M = \frac{1}{1 - \text{MPC}}$$

Exhibit 11 indicates the size of the multiplier for several different values of MPC.

EXHIBIT 11 • A Higher MPC Means a Larger Multiplier

MPC	Size of Multiplier
9/10	10
4/5	5
3/4	4
2/3	3
1/2	2
1/3	1.5

THE MULTIPLIER PRINCIPLE AND THE KEYNESIAN AGGREGATE EXPENDITURE MODEL

Exhibit 12 illustrates the multiplier within the framework of the Keynesian aggregate expenditure model. Suppose that aggregate demand is initially equal to national income at $3.7 trillion. What will happen if business decision-makers suddenly become very optimistic about the future? Perhaps a technological breakthrough or some other event has triggered favorable business expectations. Because of this optimism, business decision-makers plan to spend an additional $50 billion on investment. This additional investment will cause the aggregate expenditure function to shift upward $50 billion. At every income level, $50 billion of additional investment is planned, as indicated by the new *AE* schedule. A new equilibrium will result in which aggregate expenditures are equal to output.

EXHIBIT 12 • The Multiplier in the Keynesian Aggregate Expenditure Model

Here we illustrate the impact of the multiplier for an economy operating below its potential capacity. An increase in planned investment triggers successive rounds of additional consumption spending, causing income to rise by a multiple of the initial increase in aggregate expenditures (shift from AE_1 to AE_2). When the MPC is 2/3, a $50 billion increase in planned investment will cause equilibrium output to expand from $3.70 trillion to $3.85 trillion, an increase of $150 billion. Hence, the multiplier is 3. Since excess capacity is present, the increase in expenditures does not lead to higher prices.

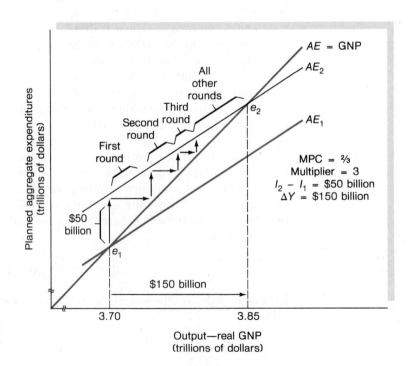

How much will equilibrium output increase? This will depend on the size of MPC. The example of Exhibit 12 illustrates the multiplier when MPC is 2/3. The $50 billion of additional investment will directly increase income by that amount (first round). Persons receiving the $50 billion will increase their spending by $33.3 billion ($50 billion multiplied by 2/3—the MPC) during the second round, causing an additional expansion in income. Of course, this additional consumption spending in round 2 will generate additional income for others. During round 3, the round-2 income recipients will increase their spending, triggering an additional expansion in income. After the process has continued through successive rounds, income will have increased by $150 billion. The $50 billion increase in initial investment eventually will thus result in a $150 billion increase in income. The multiplier is 3, since income will rise by three times the initial expansion in investment.

Although we have used an increase in investment spending to demonstrate the multiplier concept, the general principle applies to all components of aggregate expenditures. In the Keynesian model, any autonomous shift in consumption, government expenditures, or net exports will have the same amplified impact on income as we illustrated for investment.

WHY THE MULTIPLIER IS IMPORTANT

Within the framework of the Keynesian model, the multiplier is important because it explains why even small changes in investment, government, or consumption spending can induce much larger changes in output. There are both positive and negative sides to the amplified effects. On the negative side, the multiplier principle indicates that a small reduction in expenditures on investment and consumption durables, perhaps due to a decline in business and consumer optimism about the future, can be an important source of economic instability. As a result, most Keynesian economists believe that the stability of a market economy is quite fragile and constantly susceptible to even modest disruptions. On the positive side, the multiplier principle illustrates the potential of macroeconomic policy to stimulate output even if it is able to exert only a small impact on autonomous expenditures.

In evaluating the significance of the multiplier, it is important to keep two points in mind. First, it takes time for the multiplier to work. In the real world, several weeks or perhaps even months will be required for each successive round of spending. Only a fraction of the multiplier effect will be observed quickly. Most researchers believe that only about one half of the total multiplier effect will be felt during the first six months following a change in expenditures.

Second, the multiplier implies that the additional spending brings idle resources into production, leading to additional real output rather than to increased prices. When unemployment is widespread, this is a realistic assumption. However, when there is an absence of abundant idle resources, the multiplier effect will be dampened by an increase in the price level. Exhibit 13 uses the *AD/AS* framework to illustrate this point. Reflecting a total increase in expenditures accompanying a $50 billion increase in autonomous investment when MPC is equal to 2/3 (see Exhibit 12), Exhibit 13 illustrates the impact of a $150 billion increase in aggregate demand (shift

EXHIBIT 13 • The Multiplier When *SRAS* is Positively Sloped

When *SRAS* is positively sloped, equilibrium output will expand by less than the full multiplier effect. Continuing with the example of Exhibit 12, we illustrate the impact of a $50 billion increase in demand that would have expanded output by $150 billion (MPC = 2/3) *if the price level was constant*. However, some of the additional demand merely leads to higher prices. Thus, real GNP only expands from $3.70 trillion to $3.77 trillion, a $70 billion increase. The increase in the price level reduces the multiplier effect. (Note, e_2 is a short-run equilibrium. If the economy's output potential is less than $3.77 trillion, even this output rate cannot be sustained in the long-run).

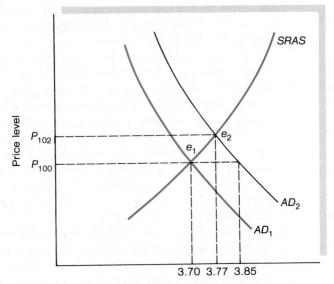

from AD_1 to AD_2). If the price level remained constant at P_{100}, real output would expand by $150 billion, implying a multiplier of 3. This will not be the case, though, when resource scarcity leads to an upward sloping *SRAS*. When the *SRAS* curve is upward sloping, part of the expansionary impact of the increase in demand is dissipated by a rise in the price level (to P_{102}). Rather than increasing by $150 billion (from $3.7 to $3.85 trillion) real output only expands by $70 billion (to $3.77 trillion). When there is an absence of abundant idle resources, the *SRAS* curve will slope upward and the multiplier will be smaller than the simple multiplier derived for a specific price level.

MAJOR INSIGHTS OF KEYNESIAN ECONOMICS

Keynesian economics dominated the thinking of macroeconomists for three decades following World War II. What are its major insights? Three points stand out.

1. *Changes in output, as well as changes in prices, play a role in the macroeconomic adjustment process, particularly in the short-run.* The classical model emphasized the role of prices in directing an economy to macroeconomic equilibrium. Keynesian analysis highlights the importance of changes in output. Modern analysis incorporates both. Market prices do not adjust instantaneously to economic change. In the short-run, changes in output and employment often signal economic change to decision-makers and provide the impetus for price adjustments. Hence, modern economists believe that both price and output conditions play a role in the adjustment process.

2. *The responsiveness of aggregate supply to changes in demand will be directly related to the availability of unemployed resources.* Keynesian analysis emphasizes that when idle resources are present, output will be highly responsive to changes in aggregate demand. Conversely, when an economy is operating at or near its capacity, output will be much less sensitive to changes in demand. So, the *SRAS* curve is relatively flat when an economy is well below capacity and relatively steep when the economy is operating near and beyond capacity (see Exhibit 9).

3. *Fluctuations in aggregate demand are an important potential source of business instability.* Abrupt changes in demand are a potential source of both recession and inflation. Policies that effectively stabilize aggregate demand—that minimize abrupt changes in demand—will substantially reduce economic instability.

Does the Keynesian model explain the prolonged unemployment of the Great Depression? Certainly the model helps us understand why markets do not adjust quickly. Closer inspection of the 1930s, though, indicates that perverse economic policies played a central role in the economic conditions of the 1930s. Markets were unable to restore full employment at least partially because policies were adopted that inadvertently turned a recession into this nation's worst depression (see Chapter 13 for details on this topic).

AD/AS OR *AE*—WHICH MODEL SHOULD WE USE?

Our three-market basic macroeconomic models featuring *AD* and *AS* and the aggregate expenditure model developed in this chapter offer alternative tools with which to analyze macroeconomic change. Which model should we use? The aggregate expenditure model has been a central focus of macroeconomics for almost four decades. We have shown that it continues to provide valuable insight in various areas. Nevertheless, we believe that reliance upon the multimarket macroeconomic model offers several advantages.

First, the simultaneous occurrence of high unemployment and inflation is easier to visualize within the *AD/AS* framework. The aggregate expenditure model makes it easy to see why an economy might experience unemployment (demand is deficient). It also offers a straightforward explanation for inflation (excess demand). But, the *AE* model does not readily explain the simultaneous occurrence of the two. Given the reliance on the *AE* model in the 1960s and 1970s, it is no coincidence that the simultaneous occurrence of inflation and unemployment during the 1970s took many macroeconomists by surprise.

Second, recent developments in macroeconomics place much more emphasis on price changes in aggregate markets, expectations, and interrelationships among macroeconomic markets. These factors are more easily visualized within the framework of the multimarket *AD/AS* model, which emphasizes *both* price and quantity (output) changes. Similarly, the *AD/AS* model enables us to see why it makes a difference whether an event is

APPLICATIONS IN ECONOMICS

The Keynesian View of the Business Cycle

Keynesian economists believe that a market economy is inherently unstable. They believe that if left to its own devices, a market economy will fluctuate between economic recession and inflationary boom.

The Keynesian view emphasizes the destabilizing potential of changes in expenditures powered by changes in optimism and the multiplier. Suppose there is an increase in income triggered by what appears to be a relatively minor disruption—a new innovation, an increase in consumer optimism, or a reduction in taxes, for example. The process of increased expansion will have a tendency to feed on itself. Higher incomes will lead to additional consumption and strong business sales. Inventories will decline and businesses will expand output (to rebuild inventories) and move investment projects forward as they become more optimistic about the future. The additional investment, magnified by the multiplier, will lead to an expansion in employment and a rapid growth of income and consumption. Unemployment will decline to a low level. Stock prices will rise as the future begins to look rosy.

Can this expansionary phase continue indefinitely? The answer is no. Eventually, full employment of both manpower and machines will result. The economy will reach its sustainable capacity. Constrained by the short supply of resources, the growth rate of the economy will have to slow. As the growth rate decelerates, business investors will become less optimistic about the future and will cut back fixed investment. The combination of a reduction in investment and increased pessimism about the future will

cause consumers to spend less, further reducing aggregate expenditures. The decline in aggregate expenditures, again magnified by the multiplier, will reduce the equilibrium level of income. As the economy plunges into a recession, inventories will rise as businesses are unable to sell their goods because of the low level of demand. Workers will be laid off. The ranks of unemployed workers will grow. Bankruptcies will become more common.

This is what Keynes perceived was happening in the 1930s. Consumers were not spending because their incomes had fallen and they were extremely pessimistic about the future. Similarly, businesses were not producing because there was little demand for their products. Investment had come to a complete standstill because underutilized resources and capacity were abundantly available. Lack of aggregate demand, the moving force of the Keynesian model, paralyzed Western economies during the 1930s. Keynes believed that his underemployment equilibrium model explained why.

Could an economy caught in the web of a depression ever turn upward? The answer is yes. Eventually, machines will wear out, and capital stock will decline to a level consistent with current income and consumption. At that point, some investment will be necessary for replacement purposes. With time, inventories will be depleted, and businesses will begin placing new orders, which will stimulate production. The gradual upturn in investment and production will generate additional income, which will stimulate consumption and start the cycle anew.

Investment Instability and the Business Cycle

Private investment is the villain in the Keynesian theory of the business cycle. An economic expansion accelerates into a boom because investment, amplified by the multiplier, stimulates other sectors of the economy. At the first sign of a slowdown, though, investment plans are sharply curtailed. The Keynesian theory implies that the investment component, responsive to even small shifts in other economic sectors, acts as the moving force behind the business cycle.

The inventory component of investment is particularly likely to fluctuate throughout the business cycle. During the expansionary phase, inventories will be reduced, since producers will be unable to keep up with the rapid expansion in demand. In contrast, during a downturn, inventories will rise sharply, reflecting the unexpectedly slow growth of aggregate demand.

Is the empirical evidence consistent with the Keynesian view? Clearly, investment is more volatile than aggregate income. Similarly, inventories tend to rise during the early phase of an economic downturn and decline to a low level during the early phase of a business expansion, just as Keynesian theory predicts. Association, however, is not the same thing as causation. Just because investment fluctuates substantially over the business cycle, it does not prove that changes in investment cause business instability. Many economists believe that economic fluctuations originate from other sources, particularly fluctuation in the supply of money. We will analyze alternative theories of the business cycle in Chapters 13 and 14.

anticipated or unanticipated. These factors are the heart of modern macroeconomics.

Finally, the *AD/AS* model makes it easier to understand and make a distinction between long-run and short-run conditions. In essence, the aggregate expenditure model is a short-run excess-capacity model. For short periods of time, prices may fail to adjust to excess demand or supply as the *AE* model postulates. In the long-run, however, this will not be the case. The *AE* model conceals the importance of the long-run. In contrast, the *AD/AS* model emphasizes the importance of both the short- and long-runs.

We believe the *AD/AS* model is more flexible and will help us better understand a broader range of economic issues. Thus, it will be our primary tool as we seek to develop more depth in our understanding of macroeconomic issues.

LOOKING AHEAD

Although Keynes emphasized that a market economy might fail to automatically reach its potential capacity, he argued that governments could use their tax and expenditure policies to stabilize aggregate demand and assure full employment. Keynes and his followers forced a reluctant economics profession to think seriously about macroeconomic policy. We turn next to this issue. We will begin by considering the potential of fiscal policy as a tool with which to promote full employment, stable prices, and the growth of real output.

CHAPTER SUMMARY

1. Classical economists emphasized the importance of supply because they believed that production created an equivalent amount of current demand (Say's Law) and that flexible wages and prices would assure full employment. The Great Depression undermined the credibility of the classical view.

2. The concept of planned aggregate expenditures is central to the Keynesian analysis. Aggregate expenditures are the sum of spending on consumption, investment, government purchases, and net exports.

3. In the Keynesian model, planned consumption expenditures are positively related to income. As income expands, though, consumption increases by a lesser amount. Both planned investment and government expenditures are independent of income in the Keynesian model. Planned *net* exports decline as income increases. The Keynesian model postulates that business firms will produce the amount of goods and services they believe consumers, investors, governments, and foreigners (net) plan to buy.

4. In the Keynesian model, equilibrium is present when planned total expenditures are equal to output. The equilibrium output level may take place at less than full employment. When it does, the high rate of unemployment will persist into the future. Unless aggregate spending (demand) increases, there is no mechanism for the restoration of full employment.

5. Planned expenditures need not equal actual expenditures. If purchasers spend less than business firms anticipate, unplanned inventories will result. Rather than continuing to accumulate undesired

inventories, businesses will cut back output. Income will recede to the equilibrium level.

6. If planned total expenditures temporarily exceed output, businesses will sell more of their products than they anticipate. An unplanned decline in inventories will result. In an effort to restore their abnormally low inventories, businesses will expand future output, and income will rise toward the equilibrium level.

7. Aggregate expenditures are the catalyst of the Keynesian model. Until full employment is attained, supply (real GNP) is always accommodative. Increases in aggregate expenditures thus lead to an expansion in both output and employment as long as the economy is operating below potential capacity. Once capacity is reached, further expansions in expenditures lead only to higher prices, without expanding real output. The Keynesian model implies that maintaining aggregate expenditures at the level consistent with full employment and stable prices is the primary function of sound macroeconomic policy.

8. According to the multiplier principle, independent changes in planned investment, government expenditures, and consumption have a magnified impact on income. Income will increase by some multiple of the initial increase in spending. The multiplier is the number by which the initial change in spending is multiplied to obtain the total amplified increase in income. The size of the multiplier increases with the marginal propensity to consume.

9. The multiplier principle indicates that small changes in spending can exert a major impact on output. In evaluating the importance of the multiplier, it is important to remember that (a) it takes time for the multiplier to work and (b) the amplified effect on real output will only be valid when the additional spending brings idle resources into production without price changes.

10. The Keynesian view of the business cycle emphasizes that market forces, once begun, tend to move together, reinforcing either expansion or contraction. Upswings and downswings feed on themselves. During a downturn, business pessimism, declining investment, and the multiplier principle combine to plunge the economy further toward recession. During an economic upswing, business and consumer optimism and expanding investment interact with the multiplier principle to propel the economy further upward. Keynesian theory suggests that a market-directed economy, left to its own devices, will be inherently unstable and fluctuate between economic recession and inflationary boom.

THE ECONOMIC WAY OF THINKING— DISCUSSION QUESTIONS

1. You have just been appointed to the president's Council of Economic Advisers. Write a short essay explaining to the president the Keynesian view concerning why a market economy may be unable to generate the full employment level of income. Be sure to explain why equilibrium may result at less than full employment.

2. How will each of the following factors influence the consumption schedule?

(a) The expectation that consumer prices will rise more rapidly in the future.

(b) Pessimism about future employment conditions.

(c) A reduction in income taxes.

(d) An increase in the interest rate.

(e) A decline in stock prices.

(f) A redistribution of income from older workers (age 45 and over) to younger workers (under 35).

(g) A redistribution of income from the wealthy to the poor.

3. Why does output change in the Keynesian model? Can the Keynesian model explain prolonged unemployment such as was present during the 1930s? How?

4. What is the multiplier principle? What determines the size of the multiplier? Does the multiplier principle make it more or less difficult to stabilize the economy? Explain.

5. "How can the Keynesian model be correct? According to Keynes, falling income, unemployment, and bad times result because people have so much income that they fail to spend enough to buy all of the goods produced. Paradoxically, rising income and good times result because people are reducing their savings, and spending more than they are making. This doesn't make sense." Explain why you either agree or disagree with this view.

6. Widespread acceptance of the Keynesian aggregate expenditure model took place during and immediately following the Great Depression. Can you explain why? The aggregate expenditure model declined in popularity when many economies experienced *both* high rates of unemployment and inflation during the 1970s. Was this surprising? Explain.

Fiscal policy has come almost full cycle in the past 50 years. From a position of no status in the classical model that dominated economic thinking until 1935, contracyclical fiscal policy reached its pinnacle in the 1960s—the heyday of Keynesian macroeconomics. It may now be on the wane as the "new macroeconomics"... replaces the Keynesian model.[1]

*PROFESSOR
J. ERNEST TANNER
TULANE UNIVERSITY*

- **How does fiscal policy affect aggregate demand? How does it affect aggregate supply?**

- **What is the Keynesian view of fiscal policy? How do the crowding-out and new classical models modify the basic Keynesian analysis?**

- **What are the components of the modern synthesis view of fiscal policy?**

- **Do budget deficits cause inflation? Do they cause high interest rates?**

- **How do budget deficits impact the welfare of future generations?**

11 MODERN MACRO-ECONOMICS: FISCAL POLICY

We are now ready to use our basic macroeconomic model to investigate the impact of fiscal policy on output, prices, and employment. Previously, we assumed that the government's taxing and spending policies remained unchanged. We will now relax that assumption. However, we want to isolate the impact of changes in fiscal policy from changes in monetary policy. Because of this, we will continue to assume that the monetary authorities maintain a constant supply of money. The impact of monetary policy will be considered beginning in Chapter 12.

BUDGET DEFICITS AND SURPLUSES

Balanced Budget: A situation in which current government revenue from taxes, fees, and other sources is just equal to current expenditures.

The government budget is a statement of its revenues and expenditures. When government revenues from all sources are equal to government expenditures (including both purchases of goods and services and transfer payments), the government has a **balanced budget.**

The budget need not be in balance, however. A **budget deficit** is present when total government spending exceeds total revenue from taxes and fees. When the government runs a budget deficit, where does it get the money to finance the excess of its spending relative to revenue? It borrows by issuing interest-bearing bonds that we refer to as the national debt. A **budget surplus** is present when government revenues from taxes and fees exceed government spending. When the government runs a surplus, revenues are used to pay some of the debt accumulated during prior periods.

Budget Deficit: A situation in which total government spending exceeds total government revenue during a specific time period, usually one year.

Budget Surplus: A situation in which total government spending is less than total government revenue during a time period, usually a year.

The federal budget is much more than merely a revenue and expenditure statement of a large organization. Of course, its sheer size means that it exerts a substantial influence on the economy. Its importance, though, emanates from its position as a policy variable. The federal budget is the primary tool of fiscal policy. In contrast with private organizations that are directed by the pursuit of income and profit, the federal government can alter its budget with an eye toward influencing the future direction of the economy.

Active Budget Deficits: Deficits that reflect planned increases in government spending or reductions in taxes designed to generate a budget deficit.

The size of the federal deficit or surplus is often used to gauge whether fiscal policy is adding demand stimulus or imposing fiscal restraint. When using it as such a gauge, however, it is important to note that changes in the size of the deficit may arise from two different sources. First, they may reflect discretionary changes in fiscal policy. That is, policy-makers may institute deliberate changes in government spending or in tax policies and thereby influence the budget deficit. Economists often refer to deficits emanating from this source as **active budget deficits.** Second, changes in the size of the deficit may merely reflect the state of the economy. During a recession, tax revenues, reflecting the decline in income, generally fall. Therefore, even if government expenditures are not increased or tax rates cut, an economic recession will tend to increase the size of the budget deficit. Deficits arising from recessionary conditions are often termed **passive**

Passive Budget Deficits: Deficits that merely reflect the decline in economic activity during a recession.

---

[1]J. Ernest Tanner, "Fiscal Policy: An Ineffective Stabilizer?" *Economic Review: Federal Reserve Bank of Atlanta*, August 1982.

budget deficits. When we speak of changes in fiscal policy, we are referring to active policy—deliberate changes in government expenditures and/or tax policy.

KEYNESIAN VIEW OF FISCAL POLICY

Prior to the 1960s, the desirability of a balanced federal budget was widely accepted among business and political leaders. Keynesian economists, though, were highly critical of this view. They argued that the federal budget should be used to promote a level of aggregate demand consistent with full employment output.

How does the federal budget influence aggregate demand? First, government purchases contribute directly to aggregate demand. The demand for goods and services expands as the government spends more on highways, education, national defense, and medical services, for example. Second, changes in tax policy also influence demand. A reduction in personal taxes increases the disposable income of households. As their after-tax income rises, individuals spend more on consumption. Similarly, a reduction in business taxes increases after-tax profitability and thereby encourages business investment spending.

According to the Keynesian view, fluctuations in aggregate demand are the major source of economic disturbances. Keynesian economists believe that a market economy tends to fluctuate between economic recession caused by too little aggregate demand and inflation emanating from excess aggregate demand. If demand could therefore be stabilized and maintained at a level consistent with the economy's full employment productive capacity, the most serious shortcoming of a market economy could be eliminated.

Keynesian theory highlights the potential of fiscal policy as a tool capable of reducing fluctuations in demand. When an economy is operating below its potential output, the Keynesian model suggests that government should institute **expansionary fiscal policy.** In other words, government purchases should be expanded and taxes should be reduced. A budget deficit should be used to finance the increased expenditures and the reduction in taxes. The government can cover its budget deficit by borrowing from individuals, insurance companies, business firms, and other suppliers of loanable funds.[2]

Exhibit 1 illustrates the case for expansionary fiscal policy when an economy is experiencing abnormally high unemployment due to deficient demand. Initially, the economy is operating at e_1. Output is below potential capacity, Y_f and unemployment is above its natural rate. As we have previously discussed, if there is no change in policy, abnormally high unemployment and excess supply in the resource market will eventually reduce

Expansionary Fiscal Policy: An increase in government expenditures and/or a reduction in tax rates such that the expected size of the budget deficit expands.

---

[2]Alternatively, the government could borrow from its central bank, the Federal Reserve Bank in the United States. However, as we will see in the following chapter, this method of financing a budget deficit would expand the money supply. Since we want to differentiate between fiscal and monetary effects, we must hold the supply of money constant. So, for now, we assume that the government deficit must be financed by borrowing from private sources.

EXHIBIT 1 • Expansionary Fiscal Policy to Promote Full Employment

Here we illustrate an economy operating at Y_1, below its potential capacity Y_f. There are two routes to a long-run full employment equilibrium. First, policy-makers could wait for lower wages and resource prices to reduce costs, increase supply to $SRAS_3$, and restore equilibrium at e_3. Keynesians believe this market adjustment method will be slow and uncertain. Alternatively, expansionary fiscal policy could stimulate aggregate demand (shift to AD_2) and guide the economy to e_2.

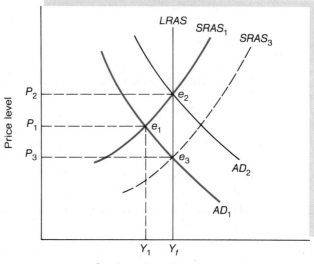

Goods and services—real GNP

Restrictive Fiscal Policy: A reduction in government expenditures and/or an increase in tax rates such that the expected size of the budget deficit declines (or the budget surplus increases).

real wages and other resource prices. The accompanying lower costs will increase supply (shift to dotted $SRAS_3$) and guide the economy to a full employment equilibrium (e_3) at a lower price level (P_3). Most Keynesian economists believe, though, that this method of adjustment will take quite a long time. They stress the potential of expansionary fiscal policy to move the economy to full employment more rapidly. An increase in government purchases coupled with a reduction in taxes would stimulate aggregate demand (shift to AD_2) and guide the economy to full employment equilibrium at e_2. So, when an economy is operating below its potential capacity, the Keynesian prescription calls for a planned budget deficit.

What would happen if a business expansion led to a level of demand that exceeds the economy's potential output? As Exhibit 2 illustrates, in the absence of a change in policy, the strong demand would push up wages and other resource prices. In turn, the higher resource prices would increase costs, reduce aggregate supply, and lead to a higher price level (P_3). The basic Keynesian model, however, indicates that **restrictive fiscal policy** could be used to reduce aggregate demand (shift to AD_2) and guide the economy to a noninflationary equilibrium (e_2). A reduced level of government purchases would diminish aggregate demand directly. Alternatively, taxes could be increased. An increase in personal taxation would reduce disposable income, causing consumption to decline. An increase in business taxes would dampen investment. Of course, the combination of reduced government expenditures and higher taxes would lead to a budget surplus (or smaller budget deficit). The Keynesian analysis indicates that this is precisely the proper policy prescription with which to combat inflation generated by excess demand.

In the Keynesian view, general economic conditions replaced the concept of the annual balanced budget as the proper criterion for determining

EXHIBIT 2 • Restrictive Fiscal Policy to Combat Inflation

Strong demand such as AD_1 will temporarily lead to an output rate beyond the economy's long-run potential (Y_f). If maintained, the high level of demand will lead to an equilibrium (e_3) at a higher price level. However, restrictive fiscal policy could restrain demand to AD_2 (or better still, prevent demand from expanding to AD_1 in the first place) and thereby guide the economy to a noninflationary equilibrium (e_2).

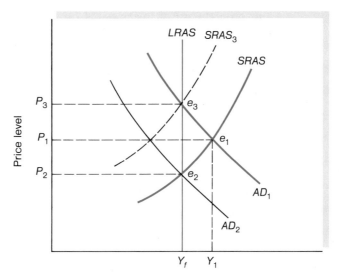

Goods and services—real GNP

Countercyclical Policy: A policy that tends to move the economy in an opposite direction from the forces of the business cycle. Such a policy would stimulate demand during the contraction phase of the business cycle and restrain demand during the expansionary phase.

the appropriateness of budgetary policy. **Countercyclical policy** suggests the government should plan a budget deficit when the economy is threatened by recession and a budget surplus (or smaller deficit) in response to the threat of inflation. Fiscal policy is a regulatory tool with which to ensure that the level of demand is sufficient to provide for full employment but not so large as to trigger an inflationary price increase.

As we emphasized in the very first chapter, it is important in economics to consider potential secondary effects of an action. Building on the basic Keynesian analysis, modern macroeconomics recognizes that budget deficits and surpluses may exert important secondary effects in other markets, particularly the loanable funds market. For an economy operating well below its potential capacity, these secondary effects may not be very important; in which case, the implications of the basic Keynesian analysis would hold. However, in the absence of excess capacity due to deficient demand, the secondary effects emanating from changes in the size of the budget deficit or surplus introduce significant modifications to the basic Keynesian analysis. We turn now to an analysis of potential important secondary effects.

FISCAL POLICY AND THE CROWDING-OUT EFFECT

Holding the supply of money constant, when the government runs a deficit, it must borrow from private lenders. Typically, the government will finance its deficit by issuing bonds. As we previously discussed, issuing bonds is simply a means of demanding loanable funds. The demand for loanable funds will increase as the government bonds compete with corporate bonds and other financial instruments for the available supply of credit. If the supply of loanable funds does not increase, government borrowing to finance a larger deficit will drive up the real rate of interest.

What impact will a higher real interest rate have on private spending? Consumers will reduce their purchases of interest-sensitive goods such as automobiles and consumer durables in response to a higher real interest rate. More importantly, a higher interest rate will increase the opportunity

OUTSTANDING ECONOMIST

**Paul Samuelson
(1915–   )**

Two generations of economists have been brought up on Paul Samuelson. His best-selling introductory text has gone through eleven editions, and literally millions of students have used it. However, as Professor Samuelson noted, "They don't give Nobel Prizes for writing textbooks." The first American to win the Nobel Prize in economics, he was so honored for "raising the level of analysis in economic science." Samuelson's earlier background was in mathematics. His book, *Foundations of Economic Analysis*,[3] gave precise mathematical meaning to much of economic reasoning. Many graduate students and faculty members have spent months poring over this masterpiece of economics.

Professor Samuelson's interests are wide-ranging, and his contributions to economics reflect this fact. International trade theory, welfare economics, theory of the firm, theory of public goods, and monetary and fiscal theory have all "felt the brush" of this master artist. His *Collected Scientific Papers* encompass three lengthy volumes.[4]

Professor Samuelson has never held a government position, although he did serve as an adviser to both President Kennedy and President Johnson. A professor of eco-

nomics at Massachusetts Institute of Technology for more than three decades, Samuelson does not believe that we will ever again experience a depression such as that of the 1930s. "It's not in the attitude of the consumer. It's not in the attitude of business. The big change since the 1930s is this: In the last analysis, we will not sit by and do nothing when a chronic slump is developing and threatens to feed upon itself. The government, in a democracy, can step in and turn the tide."[5]

Samuelson often criticizes those who perceive economics to be a precise science that yields definitive answers. He argues that economic problems are extremely complex and that generalized conclusions can seldom be drawn. Professor Samuelson is one of the few economists who is well known and respected by both professional economists and the general public. He has bridged the gap between academia and the real world.

[3]Paul Samuelson, *Foundations of Economic Analysis* (Cambridge, Massachusetts: Harvard University Press, 1947).

[4]Paul Samuelson, *Collected Scientific Papers of Paul Samuelson* (Cambridge, Mass.: MIT Press, 1966).

[5]Interview in *U.S. News and World Report*, December 14, 1964, p. 65.

cost of investment projects. Businesses will postpone spending on plant expansions, heavy equipment, and capital improvements.

Clearly, both consumers and business investors will reduce their spending in response to higher real interest rates emanating from the budget deficit. This reduction in private spending will at least partially offset additional spending induced by the deficit. Economists refer to the squeezing out of private spending by the deficit-induced rise in real interest rates as the **crowding-out effect.**

Might the higher real interest rate crowd-out an amount of private spending large enough to completely offset the expansionary effects of a budget deficit? Exhibit 3 sheds light on this question. The demand for loanable funds increases (shifts from D_1 to D_2) by the amount of the budget deficit. Exhibit 3a considers the case in which the economy was operating at capacity prior to the expansion in the deficit. So, sustainable real income does not change. The aggregate supply of loanable funds is therefore unchanged. Under these circumstances, the real interest rate increases substantially to r_2. At the higher real interest rate, private borrowing for investment and consumption decreases by Q_1Q_3. In addition, households attracted by the higher interest yield increase their saving and reduce their consumption by Q_1Q_2. The deficit is thereby entirely financed by a reduction in private spending, due either to higher borrowing cost or to a more

Crowding-Out Effect: A reduction in private spending as a result of high interest rates generated by budget deficits that are financed by borrowing in the private loanable funds market.

EXHIBIT 3 • Deficits and the Interest Rate Crowding-Out Effect

The government must borrow funds in order to finance additional spending or lower taxes (expansionary fiscal policy). If there is no sustainable increase in real income (as would be the case if the economy was operating at its potential capacity prior to the increase in the deficit), the real interest rate would increase substantially (frame a). Private spending would fall and largely offset the demand stimulus of the budget deficit in the goods and services market. Alternatively, if the economy was initially below potential capacity, the deficit would expand real output, which would stimulate additional saving (loanable funds) and thereby moderate the increase in the interest rate (frame b).

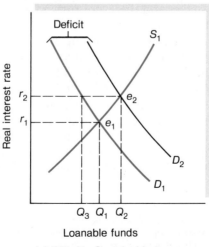

(a) With No Sustainable Increase in Real Income

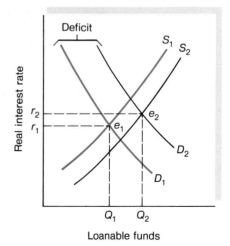

(b) With an Increase in Real Income

attractive return from saving. When this is the case, fiscal policy will exert little positive effect on aggregate demand.[6]

However, if excess capacity is present initially, the budget deficit will expand real output and income (see Exhibit 1). When this is the case, saving will expand with real income and thereby increase the supply of loanable funds (shift from S_1 to S_2, Exhibit 3b). This will moderate the increase in the real interest rate emanating from the deficit and reduce the crowding-out of private spending.

The crowding-out effect suggests that expansionary fiscal policy will exert less impact on aggregate demand than the basic Keynesian model implies. The analysis is entirely symmetrical. Restrictive fiscal policy will crowd-in private spending. If the government increases taxes and cuts back on expenditures and thereby reduces its demand for loanable funds, the real interest rate will decline. The lower real interest rate will stimulate additional private investment and consumption. So, the fiscal restraint will at least partially be offset by an expansion in private spending. As the result of this crowding-in, restrictive fiscal policy will be less potent as a weapon against inflation than the basic Keynesian model implies.

THE INTERNATIONAL LOANABLE FUNDS MARKET

Adjusted for taxes and transaction costs (including transportation), a good will tend to trade at the same price in different markets. For example, a Chevrolet automobile will sell for about the same price in Texas, California, Canada, Mexico, and other parts of the world (except for price differences related to taxes and transaction costs). After all, if General Motors could sell Chevrolets for a greater profit in one market than another, they would supply more to the profitable market (and less to other markets). Price equalization would result.

The price equilization principle also applies to the loanable funds market. Adjusted for taxes and transaction costs, the real interest rate in the United States will be approximately the same as the real interest rate in other countries with well-organized financial markets. Suppose the United States cuts taxes and therefore runs a larger budget deficit. The financing of the deficit increases the demand for loanable funds and pushes up the real interest rate as the crowding-out effect implies. How will foreigners respond to this situation? The higher after-tax real interest yield will attract funds from abroad. In turn, this in-flow of loanable funds will moderate the rise in the real interest rate in the United States.

How does the in-flow of foreign credit influence the crowding-out effect? At first glance, it appears to moderate the reduction in private demand implied by the crowding-out effect. Closer inspection, though, indicates this will not be the case. When foreigners exchange their currency for dollars in order to supply dollars to the U.S. loanable funds market, they

---

[6]Even in this polar case, there may be some increase in aggregate demand. The higher interest rate will increase the opportunity cost of holding money balances. At the higher interest rate, businesses and households will economize on their use of money to a greater degree. They will do more business with a given average money balance. Thus, they will buy (demand) more goods and services with the fixed supply of money. Nevertheless, the major point remains—the higher interest rate will crowd-out some private spending.

will bid up the price of the dollar in the international exchange market. This increase in the foreign exchange value of the dollar will make foreign goods cheaper to Americans (and U.S. goods more expensive to foreigners). The U.S. will import more and export less. Thus, some of the crowding-out of domestic demand will come in the form of a decrease in net exports (or an increase in net imports).

FISCAL POLICY—THE NEW CLASSICAL ECONOMICS MODEL

Until now, we have implicitly assumed that the current consumption and saving decisions of taxpayers are unaffected by the higher future taxes implied by budget deficits. Some economists argue that this is an unrealistic view. During the 1970s, Robert Lucas (University of Chicago), Thomas Sargent (University of Minnesota), and Robert Barro (University of Chicago) were leaders among a group of economists who argued that taxpayers would reduce their current consumption and increase saving in anticipation of higher future taxes implied by debt financing. Since this position has its foundation in classical economics, these economists and their followers are referred to as **new classical economists.**

New Classical Economists:
Modern economists who believe there are strong forces pushing a market economy toward full employment equilibrium and that macroeconomic policy is an ineffective tool with which to reduce economic instability.

When the government finances its expenditures by borrowing rather than through taxes, the *current* tax liability of citizens is reduced. However, debt financing increases their *future* tax liability. The public has to pay higher future taxes to finance the interest payments on the bonds. Thus, debt financing affects the *timing* of taxes, rather than their magnitude. It merely substitutes *higher future* taxes for *lower current* taxes.

Since debt financing does not influence the size of the overall implied tax liability, new classical economists argue that debt reduces the current wealth and therefore the current spending of taxpayers, just as surely as an equivalent amount of current taxes would. These economists therefore believe that taxes and debt financing are essentially equivalent.

Perhaps an illustration will help explain their logic. Consider the following alternative methods of paying a $10,000 liability: (a) a one-time payment of $10,000, or (b) payments of $1,000 *each year* in the future. When the interest rate is 10 percent, a $1,000 liability each year imposes a current cost of $10,000. Therefore, just as option (a) reduces current wealth by $10,000, so, too, does option (b). Now, let us consider the impact of the two options on future income. If you dip into your savings to make a one-time $10,000 payment, your future interest income will be reduced by $1,000 each year in the future (assuming a 10 percent interest rate). Just as option (b) reduces your future net income by $1,000 each year, so, too, does option (a). In both cases, current wealth is reduced by $10,000. Similarly, in both cases the flow of future net income is reduced by $1,000 each year. Because of this, the new classical economists believe the two options are essentially the same.

There is one obvious reason why debt financing may differ from the current payment of a tax liability. Since each of us has a limited life span, death means that we will not be around to pay, in full, the future tax liability implied by debt financing. Instead, debt financing will permit us, at least partially, to pass along the tax liability to future generations. New classical economists argue that this does not alter their basic analysis in a world in which the current generation is concerned about the welfare of their children and grandchildren. If parents desire to provide a given amount of *net wealth* (or after-tax future income) to their heirs, they will simply adjust their bequests and other contributions to their children in light of the expected future tax liability.

Exhibit 4 illustrates the implications of the new classical view as to the potency of fiscal policy. Suppose the fiscal authorities issue $50 billion of additional debt in order to cut taxes by an equal amount. The government borrowing increases the demand for loanable funds (shift from D_1 to D_2, frame b) by $50 billion. If the taxpayers did not recognize the higher future taxes implied by the debt, they would expand consumption in response to the lower taxes and the increase in disposable income. Under such circumstances, aggregate demand in the goods and services market would expand to AD_2. In the new classical model, though, this will not be the case. Recognizing the higher future taxes, taxpayers will cut back their spending and increase their saving by $50 billion—the amount of saving required to pay the higher future taxes on the outstanding debt. This additional saving will allow the government to finance its deficit without an increase in the real interest rate. Since debt financing, like tax financing, causes taxpayers to reduce their expenditures, aggregate demand in the goods and services market is unchanged (at AD_1). In this polar case, fiscal policy exerts no

EXHIBIT 4 • New Classical View—Higher Expected Future Taxes Crowd-out Private Spending

New classical economists emphasize that budget deficits merely substitute future taxes for current taxes. If households did not anticipate the higher future taxes, aggregate demand would increase to AD_2 (frame a). However, demand remains unchanged at AD_1 when households fully anticipate the future increase in taxes. Simultaneously, the additional saving to meet the higher future taxes will increase the supply of loanable funds to S_2 (frame b) and permit the government to borrow the funds to finance its deficit without pushing up the real interest rate. In this model, fiscal policy exerts no effect. The real interest rate, real GNP, and level of employment all remain unchanged.

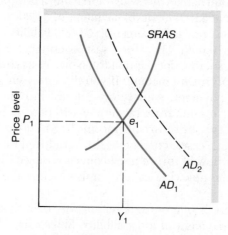

(a) Real GNP—goods and services

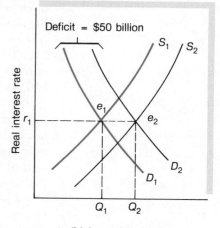

(b) Loanable funds

demand stimulus. Output, employment, and the price level are all unchanged.

The new classical view might be summarized as follows: Higher current taxes and an equivalent increase in government debt reduce the wealth (and future net income) of taxpayers by identical amounts. Substituting government debt for current taxation does not change anything. Taxpayers will recognize the higher future taxes implied by the debt and reduce their current expenditures just as if the equivalent taxes had been levied now. Thus, budget deficits do not stimulate aggregate demand. Similarly, the real interest rate is unaffected by deficits since people will save more in order to pay the higher future taxes. According to the new classical view, fiscal policy is completely impotent.

The new classical economics is controversial. Critics argue that it is unrealistic to expect taxpayers to anticipate all or even most of the future taxes implied by additional government debt. They also question whether individuals adjust their bequests to their heirs in light of expected future taxes. The debate concerning the importance of the new classical model of fiscal policy is sure to enliven macroeconomics for years to come.

DEMAND-SIDE EFFECTS OF FISCAL POLICY—A SUMMARY

Exhibit 5 summarizes the impact of the Keynesian, crowding-out, and new classical models on various economic variables. The summary highlights the significance of excess capacity when considering the potency of fiscal policy. When excess capacity is present, both the Keynesian and crowding-out models indicate expansionary fiscal policy is capable of stimulating aggregate demand, output, and employment. In the absence of excess capacity, though, both the crowding-out and new classical models indicate that fiscal policy generates secondary effects in the loanable funds market that substantially reduce its potency.

SUPPLY-SIDE EFFECTS OF FISCAL POLICY

Supply-Side Economists:
Modern economists who believe that changes in marginal tax rates exert important effects on aggregate supply.

Thus far, we have focused on the potential demand-side effects of fiscal policy. However, when fiscal changes alter *tax rates*, they may also influence aggregate supply. In the past, macroeconomists have often ignored the impact of changes in tax rates, thinking they were of little importance. In recent years, **supply-side economists** have challenged this view.[7] The supply-side argument provided the foundation for the Reagan tax policy, which led to significant reductions in marginal tax rates in the United States during the 1980s.

---

[7]See Dwight Lee (ed.), *Taxation and the Deficit Economy* (San Francisco: Pacific Institute, 1986) for an excellent set of readings providing additional detail on supply-side economics.

EXHIBIT 5 • The Potency of Fiscal Policy—A Summary of Three Models

	Keynesian Model[a]	Crowding-Out Model	New Classical Model
Impact of Expansionary Fiscal Policy (G ↑ or T ↓) on:			
real interest rate	little or no change	increase	no change
aggregate demand	increase	little change unless excess capacity is present	no change
current real output	substantial increase	little change unless excess capacity is present	little or no change
current employment	substantial increase	little change unless excess capacity is present	little or no change
price level	little or no change	little or no change	little or no change
Impact of Restrictive Fiscal Policy (G ↓ or T ↑) on:			
real interest rate	little or no change	decrease	no change
aggregate demand	decrease	little or no change	no change
current real output	substantial decrease	little or no change	little or no change
current employment	substantial decrease	little or no change	little or no change
price level	little or no change	little or no change	little or no change

[a]Assuming excess capacity is present.

From a supply-side viewpoint, the *marginal tax rate* is of crucial importance. As we discussed in Chapter 5, the marginal tax rate determines the breakdown of one's additional income between tax payments on the one hand and personal income on the other. A reduction in marginal tax rates increases the reward derived from added work, investment, saving, and other activities that become less heavily taxed. People shift into these activities away from leisure (and leisure-intensive activities), tax shelters, consumption of tax-deductible goods, and other forms of tax avoidance. These substitutions both enlarge the effective resource base and improve the efficiency with which the resources are applied (see boxed feature).

The source of the supply-side effects accompanying a change in tax rates is fundamentally different than the source of the demand-side effects. A change in tax rates affects aggregate demand through its impact on disposable income and the flow of expenditures. In contrast, it affects aggregate supply through changes in marginal tax rates, which influence the relative attractiveness of productive activity in comparison to leisure and tax avoidance.

Other things constant, lower marginal tax rates will increase the attractiveness of productive activity relative to tax avoidance. As resources shift

APPLICATIONS IN ECONOMICS

Marginal Tax Rates and Aggregate Supply

Changes in marginal tax rates influence the incentive of decision-makers to supply and effectively use productive resources. There are three major reasons why an increase (decrease) in marginal tax rates reduces (expands) aggregate supply.

First, higher marginal rates discourage work effort and reduce the productive efficiency of labor. Some individuals will substitute leisure for work. Economists refer to this as the **work-leisure substitution effect.** The higher marginal tax rates

Work-Leisure Substitution Effect: The substitution of leisure time for work time when higher tax rates reduce after-tax personal earnings. In effect, the reduction in the take-home (after-tax) portion of earnings reduces the opportunity cost of leisure, and thereby induces individuals to work less (and less intensively). Of course, lower tax rates would exert the opposite effect.

Tax Shelter Industry: Business enterprises that specialize in offering investment opportunities designed to create a short-term accounting or "paper" loss, which can then be deducted from one's taxable income; at the same time, future "capital gain" income is generated, which is taxable at a lower rate.

will induce some individuals to opt out of the labor force. Others will simply work less. Still others will decide to take more lengthy vacations, forgo overtime opportunities, retire earlier, be more particular about accepting jobs when unemployed, or forget about pursuing that promising but risky business venture. These substitutions of "leisure" for taxable work effort will reduce the available labor supply, causing aggregate supply to fall. In addition to hours of work, the effectiveness of work time can also be influenced. Since workers are unable to capture as large a proportion of a larger paycheck, they may be less willing to work intensively and productively on a job, accept additional responsibility, work under less pleasant conditions, or make similar sacrifices in order to gain a higher pay rate.

High marginal tax rates will also result in inefficient utilization of labor. Some individuals will substitute less-productive activities that are not taxed (i.e., do-it-yourself projects) or that provide the opportunity for tax avoidance (e.g., underground economy, self-employment, pleasurable business activities) for work opportunities yielding taxable income. Waste and economic inefficiency result.

Second, higher marginal tax rates also encourage investors to turn to projects that shelter current income from taxation and to turn away from projects with a higher rate of return but fewer tax-avoidance benefits. Investments in depreciable assets can often provide substantial tax advantages. Projects that supply investors with rapid depreciation write-offs and paper losses can be used to (a) push one's tax liability into the future and (b)

transform regular income into capital gains, which are often taxed at a lower rate. Resources with valuable alternative uses are channeled into the **tax shelter industry,** an industry whose prosperity, if not its existence, is solely dependent on high marginal tax rates. Investment projects that are unprofitable when pretax earnings are compared with pretax costs are undertaken because they provide tax shelter benefits. Highly productive lawyers, physicians, college professors, plumbers, and electricians, among others, spend less time working professionally and more time figuring out how to reduce their tax liability. All of this activity consumes resources that would be applied more productively were it not for the high marginal tax rates.

Third, high marginal tax rates encourage individuals to substitute less-desired tax deductible goods for more-desired, nondeductible goods. Here the inefficiency stems from the fact that individuals do not bear the full cost of tax deductible purchases. High marginal tax rates make tax deductible expenditures cheap for persons in high tax brackets. Since the personal cost, but not the cost to society, is cheap, high income taxpayers consume large amounts of deductible items (e.g., business-related lunches, vacations, luxury automobiles, medical and other fringe benefits, plush offices). Since taxpayers in high tax brackets bear only a fraction of the cost of deductible purchases, these deductible goods are substituted for more highly valued nondeductible goods whose price tags are more directly determined by production costs. Waste and inefficiency are byproducts of this incentive structure.

from the latter to the former, aggregate supply increases. Conversely, higher marginal tax rates reduce the payoff from productive activity, encourage tax avoidance, and thereby retard aggregate supply.

Exhibit 6 graphically depicts the impact of a supply-side tax cut, one that reduces marginal tax rates. The lower marginal tax rates increase aggregate supply as the new incentive structure encourages taxpayers to earn additional income and use resources more efficiently. If the tax change is perceived as long-term, both $LRAS$ and $SRAS$ will increase. Real output and income expand. Of course, the increase in real income will also increase demand (shift to AD_2). If the lower marginal rates are financed by a budget deficit, depending on the strength of the crowding-out effect and the anticipation of higher future taxes (new classical theory), aggregate demand may increase by more than aggregate supply. If this is the case, the price level will rise.

How important are the supply-side effects accompanying lower marginal tax rates? In the early 1980s, some supply-side economists argued that lower tax rates might expand output so much that tax revenues would actually increase. For taxpayers confronting exceedingly high tax rates, say marginal rates of 50 percent or more, this view may well have some validity. However, the bulk of tax revenue in the United States is derived from tax brackets of 40 percent or less. In this range, there is little evidence that lower tax rates will increase tax revenues.

When considering potential supply-side effects, it is important to keep two points in mind. First, the key relationship is between tax rates and output, not tax rates and tax revenues. If a 10 percent reduction in tax rates led to a 2 percent increase in annual output, tax revenues would decline (because the revenue loss due to the lower rates would exceed the revenue gain due to the increase in output). Nevertheless, the lower tax rates would significantly enlarge the size of the economic pie. Second, in the short-run, the demand-side effects of a tax change will generally dominate. Supply-

EXHIBIT 6 • Tax Rate Effects and Supply-side Economics

Here we illustrate the supply-side effects of a reduction in marginal tax rates. The lower marginal tax rates increase the incentive to earn and use resources efficiently. Since these effects are long-run, as well as short-run, both *LRAS* and *SRAS* increase (shift to the right). Real output expands. If the lower tax rates are financed by a budget deficit, aggregate demand may expand by a larger amount than aggregate supply, leading to an increase in the price level.

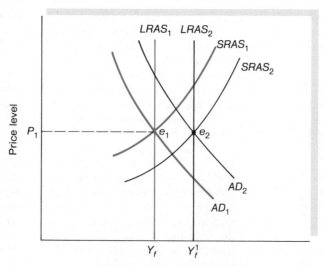

Goods and services—real GNP

side economics should not be viewed as a countercyclical device. It will take time for changing market incentives to move resources into higher-yield activities. The full positive effects of lower marginal tax rates will not be observed until labor and capital markets have time to fully adjust to the new incentive structure. Clearly, supply-side economics is a long-run strategy, not a countercyclical tool or a quick fix.

TIMING FISCAL STIMULUS AND RESTRAINT

If fiscal policy is going to reduce economic instability, stimulus and restraint must be properly timed. This is not an easy task. It takes time to institute a policy change—to revise spending programs or to change tax laws. Congress must act. A majority of the lawmakers must agree that the proposed action is in the interest of the country and that of their own districts and supporters. Even after a policy is adopted, it may be 6 to 12 months before its major impact is felt. Given our limited ability to forecast economic conditions 6 to 18 months in the future, mistakes are not only possible, they are probable.

To a large extent, macroeconomic policy-making is like shooting at a moving target you cannot see very well. Exhibit 7 illustrates this point. The use of expansionary fiscal policy to stimulate aggregate demand during an economic downturn may lead to excess demand if the economy recovers on its own by the time the fiscal stimulus exerts its major impact. Similarly, restrictive fiscal policy to cool an overheated economy may cause a recession if aggregate demand declines prior to the fiscal restraint. Since we live in a dynamic world characterized by unpredictable events, policy-makers can never be sure what macroeconomic conditions will be like 6, 12, or 18 months down the road. But, information on the state of the economy in the future is precisely what is needed if policy-makers are going to institute the proper dosage of countercyclical fiscal policy. All of this makes it exceedingly difficult to properly time discretionary changes in fiscal policy.

Fortunately, there are a few fiscal programs that tend automatically to apply stimulus during a recession and restraint during an economic boom. No discretionary legislative action is needed. The problem of proper timing is therefore minimized. Programs of this type are called **automatic stabilizers.**

Automatic Stabilizers:
Built-in features that tend automatically to promote a budget deficit during a recession and a budget surplus during an inflationary boom, even without a change in policy.

When unemployment is rising and business conditions are slow, these stabilizers automatically reduce taxes and increase government expenditures, giving the economy a shot in the arm. On the other hand, automatic stabilizers help to apply the brakes to an economic boom, increasing tax revenues and decreasing government spending. Three of these built-in-stabilizers deserve specific mention.

1. *Unemployment Compensation.* When unemployment is high, the receipts from the unemployment compensation tax will decline because of the reduction in employment. Payments will increase because more workers are now eligible to receive benefits. The program will automatically run a deficit during a business slow-down. In contrast, when the unemployment rate is low, tax receipts from the program will increase because more people are

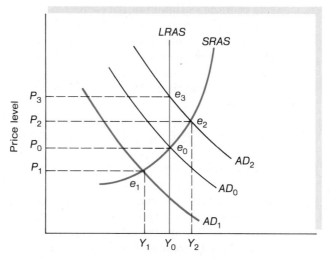

Goods and services—real GNP

EXHIBIT 7 • Why Proper Timing of Fiscal Policy is Difficult

Here we consider an economy that experiences shifts in *AD* that are not easy to forecast. Initially, the economy is in equilibrium (e_0) at price level P_0 and output Y_0. At this output, only the natural rate of unemployment is present. However, an investment slump and business pessimism shift aggregate demand to AD_1. Output falls and unemployment increases. After a time, policy-makers institute expansionary fiscal policy seeking to shift aggregate demand back to AD_0. By the time fiscal policy begins to exert its primary effect, though, private investment has recovered and decision-makers have become increasingly optimistic about the future. Thus, the expansionary fiscal policy shifts aggregate demand to AD_2, rather than AD_0. Prices rise as the economy is now overheated. Unless the expansionary fiscal policy is reversed, wages and other resource prices will eventually increase, shifting *SRAS* to the left, thus pushing the price level still higher (to P_3).

Alternatively, suppose an investment boom disrupts the initial equilibrium. The increases in investment shift aggregate demand to AD_2, placing upward pressure on prices. Policy-makers respond by increasing taxes and cutting government expenditures. By the time the restrictive fiscal policy exerts its primary impact, though, investment returns to its normal rate. As a result, the restrictive fiscal policy shifts aggregate demand to AD_1 and throws the economy into a recession. Since fiscal policy does not work instantaneously and since dynamic factors are constantly influencing private demand, proper timing of fiscal policy is not an easy task.

now working. The amount paid in benefits will decline because fewer people are unemployed. The program will automatically tend to run a surplus during good times. So, without any change in policy, the program has the desired countercyclical effect on aggregate demand.[8]

2. *Corporate Profit Tax.* Tax studies show that the corporate profit tax is the most countercyclical of all the automatic stabilizers. This results because corporate profits are highly sensitive to cyclical conditions. Under recessionary conditions, corporate profits will decline sharply and so will corporate tax payments. This sharp decline in tax revenues will tend to enlarge

---

[8]Although unemployment compensation has the desired countercyclical effects on demand, it also reduces the incentive to accept available employment opportunities. As a result, researchers have found that the existing unemployment compensation system actually increases the long-run normal unemployment rate. This issue is discussed in more detail in Chapter 14.

the size of the government deficit. During economic expansion, corporate profits typically increase much more rapidly than wages, income, or consumption. This increase in corporate profits will result in a rapid increase in the "tax take" from the business sector during expansion. Thus, corporate tax payments will go up during an expansion and fall rapidly during a contraction if there is no change in tax policy.

3. *Progressive Income Tax.* During economic expansion, the disposable income of consumers increases less rapidly than total income. This results because, with higher incomes, the progressive income tax pushes more people into the higher tax brackets. Tax revenues therefore increase because (a) income is higher and (b) tax rates on marginal income have increased. On the other hand, when income declines, many taxpayers are assigned lower tax rates, reducing the government tax take. Inflation can complicate these effects, but indexation can reduce its impact on the tax structure.

FISCAL POLICY—A MODERN SYNTHESIS

During the last two decades, we have witnessed a reevaluation of fiscal policy by macroeconomists. As the alternative theories presented in this chapter imply, disagreements in certain areas remain. It would be easy to see how one might get the idea that there is little harmony of opinion among economists concerning fiscal policy. This impression is false. Despite the differences in models, most macroeconomists accept the following synthesis position.

1. *During a depression or severe recession, expansionary fiscal policy can stimulate real output and thereby help to minimize economic instability.* During serious recessions, budget deficits stimulate aggregate demand and therefore output and employment, much as the basic Keynesian model implies. Fiscal policy is capable of preventing a recurrence of anything like the experiences of the 1930s. This is a major accomplishment that those who grew up during the *relatively* stable post-World War II era often fail to appreciate.

2. *During more normal times, the ability of fiscal policy to influence real output is far more limited than the basic Keynesian model implies, and most economists perceived during the 1960s.* The major debate among macroeconomists as to the impact of fiscal policy during normal times is not *whether* crowding-out takes place, but rather, *how* it takes place. The interest rate crowding-out and new classical models highlight this point. Both models indicate there are side effects of the deficits that substantially, if not entirely, offset increases in aggregate demand emanating from the deficits. In the one, higher real interest rates crowd-out private demand while higher anticipated future taxes accomplish the task in the other. In both cases, however, decision-makers adjust in a manner that largely offsets the potency of fiscal policy—particularly its ability to promote more rapid growth of real output.

3. *Proper timing of fiscal policy is both highly difficult to achieve and of crucial importance. Given the potential of ill-timed policy changes to add to economic instability, fiscal policy should respond only to major economic disturbances.* During the 1950s and 1960s, many macroeconomists thought that fiscal policy

changes could smooth even minor economic fluctuations. Few now adhere to that position. It is now widely recognized that in a world of dynamic change and imperfect information concerning the future, constant changes in fiscal policy in response to minor economic ups and downs can themselves become a source of economic instability.

DO DEFICITS CAUSE HIGHER INTEREST RATES AND INFLATION?

Contrary to popular opinion, the answer to this question is not obvious. With regard to the link between budget deficits and interest rates, the major models of fiscal policy differ. The crowding-out model indicates that deficits will increase the demand for loanable funds and thereby place upward pressure on the real rate of interest. On the other hand, the new classical model implies that the higher expected future taxes will stimulate additional saving and thereby permit the government to expand its borrowing at an unchanged interest rate. Which is right?

There have been a number of empirical studies in recent years. Thus far, the results are mixed. The Congressional Budget Office recently surveyed 24 studies on this topic.[9] The results of the survey indicated that while some empirical studies find a significant positive link between budget deficits and real interest rates, most of the studies indicate no statistically significant relationship. Seemingly, these findings would buttress the new classical view that deficits generate additional saving. They must, however, be interpreted with caution. Most of the studies cover the post-World War II period. As Exhibit 8 shows, *as a share of GNP,* budget deficits were rela-

EXHIBIT 8 • Deficits as a Percent of GNP, 1946–Present

During the 25 years following World War II, budget deficits were generally less than 1 percent of GNP and they were often offset by surpluses. In recent years, budget deficits have been much larger, not only in dollar terms, but more importantly, as a share of GNP. Budget deficits of between 4 and 5 percent of GNP are projected for the last half of the 1980s.

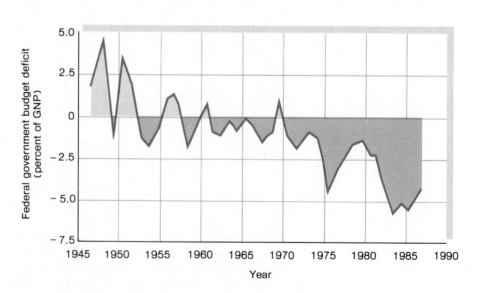

[9]Congressional Budget Office, "Deficits and Interest Rates: Empirical Findings and Selected Biography," Appendix A in *The Economic Outlook,* February, 1984, pp. 99–102. Also see Charles Plosser, "The Effects of Government Financing Decisions on Asset Returns," *Journal of Monetary Economics,* May, 1982, and Paul Evans, "Do Large Deficits Produce High Interest Rates," *American Economic Review,* March, 1985.

tively small during the 25 years following World War II. The large deficits of 1974–75 were passive deficits; they reflected recessionary conditions. Deficit running 4 to 5 percent of GNP during prosperous peacetime periods are a recent occurrence. The impact of relatively small, generally temporary deficits such as that experienced by the United States throughout most of the post-war period may be a misleading indicator of the interest rate impact of large, long-term deficits.

The behavior of the real interest rate during a period of large, long-term budget deficits in the mid-1980s is supportive of the crowding-out model. Exhibit 9 presents data on the real interest rate during the last two decades.[10] Prior to the late 1970s, the real interest rate was generally less than 2 percent. In fact, the real interest rate hovered in the 2 percent range for three decades following World War II. As Exhibit 9 shows, the real interest rate fluctuated in the 4 to 9 percent range during the period of large, long-term deficits in the 1980s.

Did the higher real interest rates in the United States attract loanable funds from abroad, as our analysis implies? Between 1980 and 1984, *real* foreign investment in the United States increased by 25 percent. The real value of the dollar in the foreign exchange market rose by more than 40 percent. The U.S. trade deficit, exports minus imports, rose from $36 billion in 1980 to $123 billion in 1984. These figures are precisely the

EXHIBIT 9 • Deficits and the Real Rate of Interest

While the real interest rate is not closely associated with year-to-year changes in the budget deficit, the persistent large deficits of the 1980s have been associated with high real interest rates.

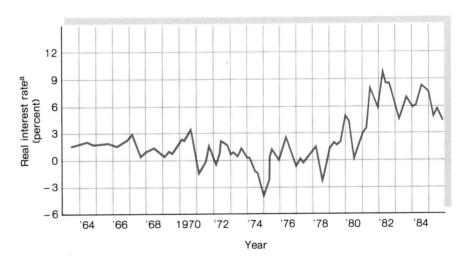

[a]We use the average quarterly interest rate on 3-month Treasury bills minus the quarterly change in the GNP implicit price deflator to approximate the real interest rate.

Source: Board of Governors, Federal Reserve System

---

[10]Of course, the real interest rate is the money interest rate minus the expected rate of inflation. Since the expected rate of inflation cannot be directly observed, it must be approximated. Exhibit 9 uses the actual change in the GNP deflator as a proxy for the expected rate of inflation.

predicted side effects of lower tax rates, large federal budget deficits, and high real interest rates.

Is there a link between deficits and expansion in saving? This link is more difficult to measure. To date, detailed statistical studies on the topic are sparse. Unfortunately, the published saving data are not really appropriate to investigate the issue. The problem is complicated by the fact that saving can take either of two forms: (a) additions to one's portfolio via new purchases of bonds, stocks, and similar assets or (b) increases in the market value of one's previous assets. The former clearly understates saving (additions to wealth), and the latter is difficult to measure. Clearly, the impact of deficits on interest rates and saving is an important topic for future research.

Finally, it should be noted that the interest rate crowding-out and new classical theories are not mutually exclusive. Both interest rates and additional saving to cover future taxes may play a role in the crowding-out process. If so, the latter would moderate the interest rate effect of the former.

What about the impact of budget deficits on inflation? Despite the continued popularity of the "budget deficits cause inflation" view, neither economic theory nor real-world data lend credence to the position. Once we consider the secondary effects, the major macroeconomic models do not imply that budget deficits will exert a significant impact on the price level.[11] The major studies in this area are consistent with this view. Independent of *monetary expansion*, the major empirical studies have failed to find a significant relationship between budget deficits and the rate of inflation.[12]

Recent economic events in the United States also illustrate the uncertainty of the oft-alleged relationship between deficits and inflation. During the last two decades, the federal government has run a budget *surplus* during only one year, 1969. This surplus was associated with an acceleration in the inflation rate from 4.7 percent in 1968 to 6.1 percent in 1969. Conversely, the largest peacetime deficits during a period of relative prosperity were experienced in the early 1980s. The budget deficit soared from $16 billion in 1980 to $179 billion in 1983 and $176 billion in 1984 (calendar year data). Meanwhile, the inflation rate decelerated from 13 percent in 1979 (and 12 percent in 1980) to 4 percent during the 1982–1984 period. This is not to say that budget deficits retard the inflation rate. Of course, other factors, including a deceleration in the growth rate of the money supply, contributed to the decline in the inflation rate during the early 1980s. Nevertheless, the evidence indicates that highly expansionary fiscal policy failed to offset the other factors. This is precisely what modern macroeconomic theory would predict.

---

[11]Some economists argue that large budget deficits will induce the monetary authorities to expand the supply of money more rapidly and thereby promote inflation. According to this theory, budget deficits are an indirect cause of inflation.

[12]For evidence on this point, see Gerald P. Dwyer, Jr., "Inflation and Government Deficits," *Economy Inquiry*, July, 1982, and Scott E. Hein, "Deficits and Inflation," *Review-Federal Reserve Bank of St. Louis*, March, 1981.

APPLICATIONS IN ECONOMICS

The National Debt: Who Owns It and Who Bears the Burden of It?

When the federal budget runs a deficit, the U.S. Treasury issues interest-bearing bonds, which are sold to financial investors. These interest-bearing bonds comprise the national debt. In effect, the national debt is a loan from financial investors to the U.S. Treasury.

Who Owns the National Debt?
As Exhibit 10 illustrates, the biggest share of the national debt, some 61.8 percent, is held internally by U.S. citizens and private institutions, such as insurance companies and commercial banks. Foreigners hold 11 percent of the total. The portion owned by foreigners is sometimes referred to as external debt. Approximately 18 percent of the debt is held by agencies of the federal government. For example, social security trust funds are often used to purchase U.S. bonds. When the debt is owned by a government agency, it is little more than an accounting transaction indicating that one government agency (for example, the Social Security Administration) is making a loan to another (for example, the U.S. Treasury).

Even the interest payments, in this case, represent little more than an internal government transfer. Approximately one tenth of the public debt is held by the Federal Reserve System. As we will see in the next chapter, this portion of the debt is an important determinant of the stock of money in the United States.

Will We Have to Pay Off the National Debt?
Borrowing is an everyday method of doing business. Many of the nation's largest and most profitable corporations continually have outstanding debts to bondholders. Yet, these corporations, particularly the profitable ones, will have no trouble refinancing the outstanding debt if they so wish. What is necessary is that the borrower have sufficient assets or income to pay both the interest and principal as they come due. As long as General Motors has billions of dollars worth of assets and corporate income, it will have no trouble borrowing a few hundred million to refinance its debt again and again, because lenders know that GM will be able to pay off the

loan. Similarly, as long as the U.S. government can raise huge revenues through taxes, lenders can be sure that the government will be able to return their money, plus interest, when due. Therefore, there is no date in the future on which the national debt must be repaid.

How Does the National Debt Influence Future Generations?
For years, laymen, politicians, and economists have debated about the burden of the national debt. One side has argued that we are mortgaging the future of our children and grandchildren. Future generations will pay the consequences of our fiscal irresponsibility. Noting that most of the national debt is held by domestic citizens, the other side has retorted, "We owe it to ourselves." Who is right? Has time, the ultimate judge, declared a winner in this debate?

Current policies affect the welfare of future generations via their impact on capital formation. If the current generation bequeaths lots of factories, machines, houses, knowledge, and other productive assets to their children, the productive potential of the next generation will be high. Alternatively, if fewer productive assets are passed along to them, their productive capability will decline accordingly. Thus, the true measure of how government debt influences future generations involves knowledge of its impact on capital formation.

Our models of fiscal policy shed light on this issue. First, when excess capacity is present, our analysis indicates that deficits during a severe recession will stimulate employment and the production of

EXHIBIT 10 · Ownership of the National Debt (1985: Q4)		
Ownership of U.S. Securities	Dollar Value (Billion)	Percentage
U.S. Government agencies	348.9	17.9
Federal Reserve Banks	181.3	9.3
Domestic investors	1201.1	61.8
Foreign investors	214.6	11.0
Total	1945.9	100.0

Board of Governors of the Federal Reserve System

both consumption and capital goods. When a deficit induces otherwise idle resources into the production of houses, factories, and other assets (as well as consumer goods), it adds to the stock of capital assets. Future generations are helped accordingly. However, during more normal times, the effect of the deficit on future generations will be determined by the relative impact of taxes and interest rates on capital formation. Suppose that the debt financing arises from lower current taxes but higher future taxes, with government expenditures remaining constant. If, as the new classical model assumes, individuals fully anticipate the added future tax liability accompanying the debt, current consumption will be unaffected by the substitution of debt for tax financing. Additional saving to cover the future tax liability will leave both the real interest rate and private investment unchanged. In this world, capital for-

mation and the welfare of future generations are unaffected by the use of debt rather than tax financing.

Now, let us consider the impact of the same deficit in a model in which decision-makers fail to anticipate the future increase in tax liability. Compared to taxes, debt financing means an increase in demand for loanable funds and a higher real interest rate. The increase in the real interest rate will crowd-out current private investment (and some consumption as well).

However, higher current taxes will also crowd-out both consumption and investment. Taxes on income streams from investments will directly reduce after-tax yields, discouraging current investment. A decline in consumption will indirectly reduce investment demand. So, both higher current taxes and higher real-interest rates adversely affect capital formation. It is not obvious that one will crowd-out more investment than the other. Therefore, the impact on future generations of substituting debt for current taxation is still ambiguous, even when decision-makers fail to

anticipate the higher future tax liabilities associated with the debt.

When an increased deficit is caused by increased spending, holding current taxes constant, then the impact on future generations depends on the quantity and quality of capital (roads, education, buildings) provided, as compared to the displaced private spending. If the government expenditures provide more valuable capital than the displaced private-sector spending would have, the added debt does not disadvantage future generations. On the other hand, if less valuable capital is provided, the debt-financed increase in government expenditures will reduce the welfare of future generations.

As Exhibit 11 illustrates, the interest cost necessary to service the national debt has grown substantially as a share of GNP in recent years. The rising interest costs mean higher tax rates and potential adverse supply-side effects. Deficit financing influences *when* the supply-side disincentive effects of higher tax rates will be imposed. Tax financing imposes these distortive effects during the current

EXHIBIT 11 • Interest Payments as a Percentage of Gross National Product

During the period from 1954 to 1973, the interest payments on the portion of the national debt held by the public comprised approximately 1.5 percent of GNP. In recent years, the percentage has risen. The interest on the national debt rose to 3.0 percent of GNP in 1984 and is projected to reach 3.5 percent of GNP in 1986.

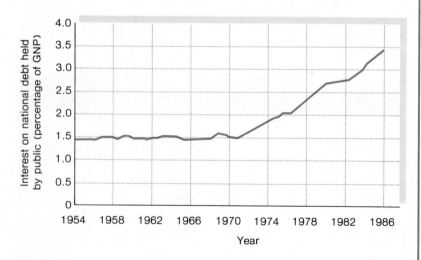

Source: Budget of the United States (annual).

**APPLICATIONS IN ECONOMICS
(continued)**

period, while deficits move them into the future. Here again, the impact on future generations is ambiguous. The higher taxes during the current period will reduce both current output and the amount of wealth passed on to future generations. By way of comparison with tax financing, a deficit would mean more capital formation (because of the less adverse *current* supply-side incentive effects associated with debt financing) during the current period, but also more severe future supply-side effects. Again, it is not obvious whether this combination either helps or hurts future generations.

In summary, theory indicates that the impact of substituting debt for tax financing exerts an ambiguous impact on the quality of productive capital passed along to future generations.

Do Deficits Make Any Difference?
If the impact of deficits on capital

formation is ambiguous, do they make any difference? There are at least two reasons why they may. First, if deficits hide the true cost of government, as they clearly do in the crowding-out model, voter-consumers may underestimate the cost of debt-financed government spending. As a result, they may support spending and accept inefficiency, which, if the cost were properly perceived, would be rejected.

Second, as the government's interest obligations become larger relative to its tax revenue potential, the risk of lending to the government increases. Lenders charge a higher interest rate—a risk premium—to borrowers who they fear may not be able to repay debt. New York City, Detroit, and other local governments have discovered this fact of life in recent years. Of course, the federal government is different in one respect: it can, in effect, pay creditors by printing money. Lenders, though, will not like being paid with dollars of declining purchasing power. Anticipation of that occurrence will increase the risk of extending loans not only to the federal government

but to other borrowers as well. Thus, to the extent that rising debt and interest costs, relative to potential tax revenue, increase the likelihood the federal government will eventually use money creation to pay off the debt, the debt breaks down the long-term capital market and increases the risk premium for all borrowers. Positive-sum exchanges that would otherwise take place will be lost as the result of uncertainty emanating from the federal debt. Such uncertainty will retard real income growth, reducing the welfare of both current and future generations.

DISCUSSION

1. Can the government or a private corporation have a continual debt outstanding? Explain.
2. Do we owe the national debt to ourselves? Does this mean that the size of the debt is of little concern? Why or why not?
3. "The national debt is a mortgage against the future of our children and grandchildren. We are forcing them to pay for our irresponsible and unrestrained spending." Evaluate.

LOOKING AHEAD

As we proceed, we will use our knowledge of fiscal policy to investigate several other issues. We are now ready, though, to integrate the monetary system into our analysis. The following chapter will focus on the operation of the banking system and the factors that determine the supply of money. In Chapter 13, we will analyze the impact of monetary policy on the real output, interest rates, and the price level. Before we move on, though, we will consider a perennial issue that is closely related to deficit finance—the impact of the national debt on our economic well-being and that of our heirs.

CHAPTER SUMMARY

1. The federal budget is the primary tool of fiscal policy. Discretionary fiscal policy encompasses deliberate changes in the government's spending and tax policies designed to alter the size of the budget deficit and thereby influence the overall level of economic activity.

2. According to the Keynesian view, fluctuations in aggregate demand are the major source of economic instability. Keynesian economists believe that discretionary fiscal policy can help stabilize aggregate demand and hasten the adjustment process to full employment equilibrium.

3. When an economy's resources are underutilized, the Keynesian model indicates that expansionary fiscal policy—that is, an increase in government spending and/or reduction in taxes—will stimulate aggregate demand and help direct the economy to its full employment capacity. Conversely, restrictive fiscal policy—higher taxes and/or a reduction in government expenditures—can be used to combat inflationary pressures due to excess aggregate demand.

4. Modern macroeconomists stress the potential importance of secondary effects that modify the basic Keynesian analysis. The crowding-out model stresses one of these effects. The crowding-out model indicates that budget deficits increase the demand for loanable funds and thereby increase the real interest rate. When excess capacity is present, demand stimulus will expand real output and income, leading to additional saving. Under these circumstances, crowding-out will be incomplete. However, when the supply of loanable funds is unchanged, higher real interest rates will crowd-out private spending and largely offset additional spending emanating from a budget deficit.

5. New classical economists argue that substitution of debt for tax financing merely changes the timing, not the level, of taxes. According to this view, taxpayers will anticipate the higher future taxes implied by additional government debt and reduce their current consumption just as if the equivalent taxes had been levied during the current period. Saving will expand, permitting the government to finance its deficit without an increase in the real interest rate. According to the new classical view, substitution of debt for tax financing will leave real interest rates, aggregate demand, output, and employment unchanged.

6. When fiscal policy changes marginal tax rates, it influences aggregate supply by altering the relative attractiveness of productive activity compared to leisure and tax avoidance. Other things constant, lower marginal tax rates will increase aggregate supply. Most economists believe that the demand-side effects of changes in taxes will dominate the supply-side effects in the short-run. Supply-side economics should be viewed as a long-run strategy, not a countercyclical tool.

7. Since dynamic change alters market conditions and our ability to forecast future macroeconomic changes is highly imperfect, it is exceedingly difficult to time discretionary changes in fiscal policy so as to reduce economic instability. The problem of proper timing is reduced in the case of automatic stabilizers, programs that apply stimulus during a recession and restraint during a boom, even though no legislative action has been taken. Unemployment compensation, corporate profit taxes, and the progressive income tax are examples of automatic stabilizers.

8. The modern synthesis of fiscal policy emphasizes three major points: (a) During a depression or severe recession, expansionary fiscal policy

can stimulate real output as the Keynesian model implies; (b) during normal times, higher real interest rates and/or higher expected future taxes substantially dampen the stimulative effects of expansionary fiscal policy; and (c) since discretionary changes in fiscal policy are difficult to time properly, fiscal policy should be altered only in response to major disturbances.

9. The weak relationship between budget deficits and real interest rates is supportive of the new classical view. However, the high real interest rate accompanying the large, long-term deficits of the 1980s is supportive of the crowding-out theory. *Independent of monetary expansion,* neither economic theory nor the empirical evidence indicates that budget deficits are a major cause of inflation.

10. The burden of the debt has long been a controversial issue. It is not true that the debt will have to be paid off sometime in the future. The debt affects future generations through its impact on capital formation. Deficits that help push the economy to its long-term capacity will increase the stock of capital assets available to future generations. During normal times, both higher current taxes and interest rates (or future taxes) crowd-out capital investment. Therefore, the impact of substituting debt for tax financing is ambiguous. Budget deficits may, however, (a) hide the true cost of government spending and thereby contribute to inefficiency and (b) lead to an expanding interest cost relative to potential tax revenues, creating uncertainty and a breakdown in the long-term capital market.

THE ECONOMIC WAY OF THINKING— DISCUSSION QUESTIONS

1. Suppose that you are a member of the Council of Economic Advisers. The president has asked you to prepare a statement on "What is the proper fiscal policy for the next 12 months?" Prepare such a statement, indicating (a) the current state of the economy (that is, unemployment rate, growth in real income, and rate of inflation) and (b) your fiscal policy suggestions. Should the budget be in balance? Present the reasoning behind your suggestions.

2. What is the crowding-out effect? How does the crowding-out effect modify the implications of the basic Keynesian model with regard to fiscal policy? How does the new classical theory of fiscal policy differ from the crowding-out model?

3. Why is it difficult to properly time discretionary changes in fiscal policy? Do you think political factors, as well as economic factors, limit the use of fiscal policy as a stabilization tool? Why or why not?

4. What are automatic stabilizers? Explain the major advantage of automatic stabilizers.

5. Which of the following would a supply-side economist be most likely to favor? Explain.
   (a) an increase in the personal exemption.
   (b) a flat-rate tax.
   (c) lower tax rates financed by elimination of various tax deductible items (interest expense, medical expenditures, and state and local taxes, for example).

6. **What's Wrong with This Way of Thinking?**
   "Keynesians argue that a budget deficit will stimulate the economy. The historical evidence is highly inconsistent with this view. A $12 billion budget deficit in 1958 was associated with a serious recession, not expansion. We experienced recessions in both 1961 and 1974–1975, despite budget deficits. The federal budget ran a deficit every year from 1931 through 1939. Yet the economy continued to wallow in the Depression. Budget deficits do not stimulate GNP and employment."

7. "The economic stimulus of deficit spending is based on money illusion. When the government issues bonds to finance its deficit, it is promising to levy future taxes so that bondholders can be paid back with interest. Bond financing is merely a substitution of future taxation for current taxation. The stimulus results because taxpayers, failing to recognize fully their greater future tax liability, are deceived into thinking that their wealth has increased. Thus, they increase their current spending." Is this view correct? Why or why not?

CHAPTER FOCUS

- What is money? How is the money supply defined?

- How have recent regulatory changes affected the banking and financial industries?

- What is a fractional reserve banking system? How does it influence the ability of banks to create money?

- What are the major functions of the Federal Reserve System?

- What are the major tools with which the Federal Reserve controls the supply of money? How do changes in Fed policy influence the supply of money?

There have been three great inventions since the beginning of time: fire, the wheel, and central banking.

WILL ROGERS

12 MONEY AND THE BANKING SYSTEM

The purposes of this chapter are to explain the operation of our banking/ finance system and to analyze the determinants of the money supply. Later, we will consider the influence of money on prices, employment, output, and other important economic variables.

To many economists, analyzing the determinants of national income without considering money is like playing football without a quarterback. The central moving force has been excluded. Although the majority would assign a somewhat lesser role to money, almost all economists believe that money, and therefore monetary policy, matters a great deal.

WHAT IS MONEY?

Money makes the world go around. Although this is an exaggeration, money is nevertheless an important cog in the wheel that makes trade go around. Without money, everyday exchange would be both tedious and costly. Of course, money is today issued and controlled by governments, but the use of money arose thousands of years ago, not because of government decree, but because money simplified exchange. Money performs three basic functions.

1. *Money Serves as a Medium of Exchange.* Without money, the gains from specialization and exchange that characterize modern economies would be impossible. Exchange would be both complicated and enormously time-consuming in a world without money. If you wanted to buy a video recorder, for example, you would first have to find someone willing to sell you the desired recorder who also wanted to purchase something you were willing to sell. Such barter transactions would be both costly and inefficient.

Money solves these problems. People simply sell their productive services or assets for money and, in turn, use the money to buy precisely the goods and services they want. For example, if a farmer wants to exchange a cow for electricity and medical services, the cow is sold for money, which is then used to buy the electricity and the medical services. Money trades in all markets, simplifying exchange and oiling the wheels of trade. Money makes it possible for each of us to specialize in the supply of those things that we do best and still purchase a broad cross-section of goods and services consistent with our individual preferences. This attribute alone would be sufficient to qualify money as one of the all-time great social inventions.

2. *Money Serves as an Accounting Unit.* Since money is widely used in exchange, it also serves as a yardstick that can be used to compare the value of goods and services. If consumers are going to spend their income wisely, they must be able to compare the value of a vast array of goods and services. Similarly, sound business decision-making will require comparisons among vastly different productive services. Money serves as a unit of account, a common denominator capable of expressing the current value of all goods and services.

3. *Money Is Used as a Store of Value.* Money is a financial asset, a form of savings. There are some disadvantages to using money as a vehicle for storing value (wealth), though. Many methods of holding money do not

Liquid Asset: An asset that can be easily and quickly converted to purchasing power without loss of value.

yield an interest return. During a time of inflation, the purchasing power of money will decline, imposing a cost on those who are holding wealth in the form of money. Money, though, has the advantage of being a perfectly **liquid asset.** It can be easily and quickly transformed into other goods at a low transaction cost and without an appreciable loss in its nominal value. Because of this, most people hold some of their wealth in the form of money because it provides readily available purchasing power for dealing with an uncertain future.

WHY IS MONEY VALUABLE?

At various times in the past, societies have used gold, silver, beads, sea shells, cigarettes, precious stones, and other commodities as money. When commodities are used as money, people use valuable resources to expand the supply of the commodity money. Because of this, the opportunity cost of commodity-based money is high.

Fiat Money: Money that has little intrinsic value; neither is it backed by or convertible to a commodity of value.

If a society uses something as money that costs little or nothing to produce, more scarce resources are available for the production of desired goods and services. Thus, most modern nations use **fiat money,** money that has little or no intrinsic value. A dollar bill is just a piece of paper. Checkable deposits are nothing more than accounting numbers. Coins have some intrinsic value as metal, but it is considerably less than their value as money.

Why is fiat money valuable? The confidence of people is important. People are willing to accept fiat money because they know it can be used to purchase real goods and services. This is partly a matter of law. The government has designated currency as "legal tender"—acceptable for payment of debts.

Money's main source of value, however, is the same as that of other commodities. Economic goods are more or less valuable because of their scarcity, relative to the amount that people desire. Money is no exception.

If the purchasing power of money is to remain stable over time, the supply of money must be controlled. The value of a dollar is measured in terms of what it will buy. Its value, therefore, is inversely related to the level of prices. An increase in the level of prices and a decline in the purchasing power of money are the same thing. Assuming a constant rate of use, if the supply of money grows more rapidly than growth in the real output of goods and services, prices will rise. This happens because the quantity of money has risen relative to the availability of goods. In layman's terms, there is "too much money chasing too few goods."

When governmental authorities rapidly expand the supply of money, the purchasing power of money deteriorates. Money is less valuable in exchange and is virtually useless as a store of value. The rapid growth in the supply of money in Germany following World War I provides a dramatic illustration of this point. During 1922–1923, the supply of German marks increased by 250 percent *per month* for a time. The German government was printing money almost as fast as the printing presses would run. Since money became substantially more plentiful in relation to goods and services, it quickly lost its value. As a result, an egg cost 80 billion marks and a loaf of bread 200 billion. Workers picked up their wages in suitcases. Shops closed at lunch hour to change price tags. The value of money had eroded.

HOW IS THE SUPPLY OF MONEY DEFINED?

Transaction Accounts: Ac-counts including demand deposits, NOW accounts, and other checkable de-posits against which the account holder is permit-ted to transfer funds for the purpose of making payment to a third party.

Demand Deposits: Non-interest-earning deposits in a bank that either can be withdrawn or made payable on demand to a third party via check. In essence, they are "check-book money" because they permit transactions to be paid for by check rather than by currency.

Money Supply (M-1): The sum of (a) currency in cir-culation (including coins), (b) demand deposits, (c) other checkable deposits of depository institutions, and (d) traveler's checks.

Determining what should be included in the money supply is not as easy as it might appear. Money is sometimes defined as anything generally accept-able as a medium of exchange. On the basis of this criterion, it is clear that currency (including both coins and paper bills) and checkable deposits should be included in the supply of money. Deposits that can be drawn from by writing a check are called **transaction accounts.** There are two general categories of transaction accounts. First, there are **demand deposits,** non-interest-earning deposits with banking institutions that are available for withdrawal ("on demand") at any time without restrictions. Demand depos-its are usually withdrawn by writing a check. Second, there are other check-able deposits that earn interest but that carry some restrictions on their transferability. Interest-earning checkable deposits generally either limit the number of checks written each month or require the depositor to main-tain a substantial minimum balance ($1,000, for example). NOW (nego-tiable order of withdrawal) accounts and ATS (automatic transfer savings) accounts are the most common types of interest-earning checking accounts. Like currency and demand deposits, interest-earning checkable deposits are available for use as a medium of exchange. Traveler's checks are also a means of payment. They can be freely converted to cash at parity (equal value).

The **money supply (M-1)** reflects the function of money as a medium of exchange. The M-1 money supply is composed of (a) currency in circu-lation, (b) demand deposits, (c) other (interest-earning) checkable deposits and (d) traveler's checks. M-1 is the narrowest and most widely used defini-tion of the money supply. (The designations M_1 and M-1 are also often used when referring to this narrow definition of the money supply.)

As Exhibit 1 shows, the total money supply (M-1) in the U.S. was $625 billion in December, 1985. Demand and other checkable deposits accounted for more than 70 percent of the M-1 money supply. This reflects that most of the nation's business—more than 75 percent—is conducted by check.

NEAR MONIES AND BROADER DEFINITIONS

Thrift Institutions: Tradi-tional savings institutions, such as savings and loan associations, mutual sav-ings banks, and credit unions.

Economists who emphasize the store-of-value function of money argue that other financial assets should also be included in the money supply. Several financial assets resemble money in many ways. Non-checkable time deposits in commercial banks and **thrift institutions** are a highly liquid means of holding purchasing power into the future. Although these deposits are not legally available on demand (without payment of a penalty), they can often be withdrawn on short notice. Some non-checkable savings accounts can even be transferred to one's checking account on request without penalty. Some forms of savings, not counted as part of M-1, even provide limited check-writing privileges. Money market mutual funds, for example, use the funds of their shareholders to purchase short-term securities. These in-vestment funds are highly liquid. As a result, shareholders are permitted to sell their shares simply by writing a check, provided the size of the check exceeds some minimum (usually $500). In addition, banks and thrift institu-tions offer money market deposit accounts, which generally pay a slightly

EXHIBIT 1 • Composition of the Money Supply in the United States (December 1985)

The size (as of December 1985) of three alternative measures of the money supply are shown above. M-1 is the narrowest and most widely used definition of the money supply. M-2, which contains M-1 plus various savings components indicated above, is approximately four times the size of M-1. The broadest measure, M-3, contains less liquid forms of savings. M-3 is more than five times the size of M-1.

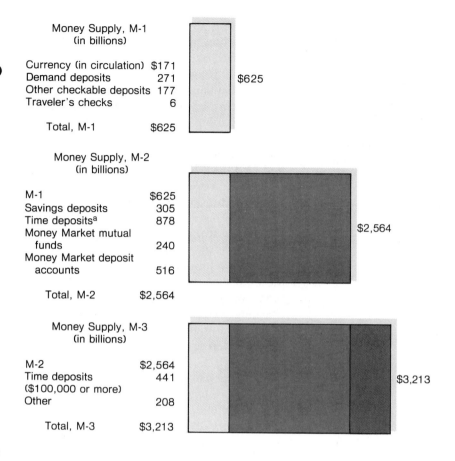

Money Supply, M-1
(in billions)

Currency (in circulation)	$171
Demand deposits	271
Other checkable deposits	177
Traveler's checks	6
Total, M-1	$625

$625

Money Supply, M-2
(in billions)

M-1	$625
Savings deposits	305
Time deposits[a]	878
Money Market mutual funds	240
Money Market deposit accounts	516
Total, M-2	$2,564

$2,564

Money Supply, M-3
(in billions)

M-2	$2,564
Time deposits ($100,000 or more)	441
Other	208
Total, M-3	$3,213

$3,213

Money Supply (M-2): Equal to M-1, plus (a) savings and time deposits (accounts of less than $100,000) of all depository institutions, (b) money market mutual fund shares, (c) money market deposit accounts, (d) overnight loans from customers to commercial banks, and (e) overnight Eurodollar deposits held by U.S. residents.

Eurodollar Deposits: Deposits denominated in U.S. dollars at banks and other financial institutions outside the United States. Although this name originated because of the large amounts of such deposits held at banks in Western Europe, similar deposits in other parts of the world are also called Eurodollars.

higher interest rate and require a larger minimum balance than do NOW accounts. Money market deposit accounts are also less liquid than NOW accounts, since depositors of the former are limited to writing only three checks per month.

Inspection of the alternative forms of saving and financial investment accounts indicates that the line between money and "near monies" is a fine one. Clearly, a broader concept of the money supply would include various highly liquid forms of savings. The most common broad definition of the money supply is M-2. The **money supply (M-2)** includes M-1, plus (a) savings and small-denomination time deposits at all depository institutions, (b) money market mutual fund shares, (c) money market deposit accounts, (d) overnight loans of customers to commercial banks (called repurchase agreements) and (e) overnight **Eurodollar deposits** of U.S. residents. In each case, these financial assets can be easily converted to checking account funds. Their owners may perceive them as funds available for use as payment. In some cases, the assets may even be directly used as a means of exchange. So, regardless of whether or not they are counted as part of the money supply, the additional assets incorporated into M-2 are close substitutes for money.

Money Supply (M-3):
Equal to M-2, plus (a) time deposits (accounts of more than $100,000) at all depository institutions and (b) longer-term (more than overnight) loans of customers to commercial banks and savings and loan associations.

There is a third method of measuring the money supply, M-3. Under this definition, the **money supply (M-3)** is composed of M-2, plus (a) large-denomination (more than $100,000) time deposits at all depository institutions and (b) longer-term (more than overnight) loans from customers to commercial banks and savings and loan associations. The additional assets included in M-3 are not quite as liquid as the items that comprise M-2.

As Exhibit 1 notes, M-2 and M-3 are roughly four to five times larger than M-1. Although all three have increased substantially in recent years, they have not always moved together. In general, the growth rates of M-2 and M-3 have been more rapid than the rate for M-1.

While we will take note of the differences between the broad and narrow definitions of the money supply, our attention will focus primarily on the narrowest definition, M-1. Unless otherwise noted, when we speak of the money supply we will be referring to the M-1 definition.

THE CHANGING NATURE OF M-1

Recent developments in financial markets have, to some extent, changed the nature of the money supply, M-1. Prior to the late 1970s, regulatory practices prohibited financial institutions from offering interest-earning checking accounts. As Exhibit 2 illustrates, during the 1970s, M-1 was almost entirely composed of currency and demand deposits, neither of which earned interest. With the financial deregulation of the 1980s, all of this changed.

Interest-earning other checkable deposits have grown rapidly during the 1980s. They now account for nearly one third of the money supply. Since other checkable deposits earn interest, they are less costly to hold than other forms of money. In contrast with currency and demand deposits, these other checkable deposits are "part transaction money" and "part savings."

EXHIBIT 2 • The Changing Nature of the Money Supply, M-1

As the result of deregulation during the 1980s, interest-earning checkable deposits are now a substantial share of the money supply. Since the opportunity cost of holding these other checkable deposits is less than for other forms of money, strictly speaking, the money supply today is not exactly comparable to the money supply prior to 1980.

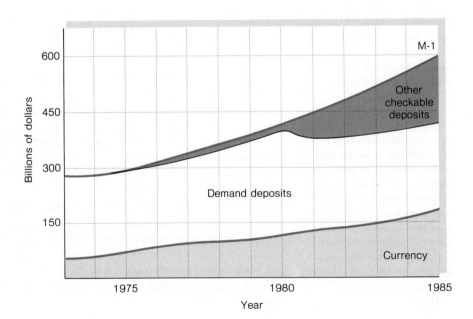

To a degree, the supply of money today is different than it was prior to 1980. This changing nature of the money supply may mean that a given growth rate in the money supply will exert a different impact on output, employment, and prices than was true prior to 1980. We will return to this issue as we analyze the impact of monetary policy in more detail.

THE BUSINESS OF BANKING

Federal Reserve System:
The central bank of the United States; it carries out banking regulatory policies and is responsible for the conduct of monetary policy.

We must understand a few things about the business of banking before we can explain the factors that influence the supply of money. The banking industry in the United States operates under the jurisdiction of the **Federal Reserve System,** the nation's central bank. Not all banks belong to the Federal Reserve, but under legislation enacted in 1980 only a nominal difference exists between member and nonmember banks.

Banks are in business to make a profit. They provide checking and savings account services to their customers. Interest-earning investments, though, are the major source of income for most banks. Banks use a sizable share of both their demand and time deposits for interest-earning purposes—primarily the extension of loans and the undertaking of financial investments.

The consolidated balance sheet for all commercial banks (Exhibit 3) illustrates the major banking functions. It shows that the major liabilities of banks are transactions, savings, and time deposits. *From the viewpoint of a bank,* these are liabilities because they represent an obligation of the bank to its depositors. Outstanding interest-earning loans comprise the major class of banking assets. In addition, most banks own sizable amounts of interest-earning securities, both government and private.

Banking differs from most businesses in that a large portion of its liabilities are payable on demand. However, even though it would be possible for all depositors to demand the money in their checking accounts on

---

EXHIBIT 3 • The Functions of Commercial Banks

Banks provide services and pay interest to attract transactions, savings, and time deposits (liabilities). A portion of their assets is held as reserves (either cash or deposits with the Fed) to meet their daily obligations toward their depositors. Most of the rest is invested and loaned out, providing interest income for the bank.

Consolidated Balance Sheet of Commercial Banks
(billions of dollars)

Assets		Liabilities	
Reserves	$ 46	Capital accounts	$ 157
Loans outstanding	1,615	Transactions deposits	536
U.S. government securities	250	Savings and time deposits	1,227
Other securities	164	Other liabilities	540
Other assets	385	Total	$2,460
Total	$2,460		

Federal Reserve Bulletin, March 1986.

Reserves: Vault cash plus deposits of the bank with Federal Reserve Banks.

RECENT CHANGES IN THE BANKING INDUSTRY

Commercial Banks: Financial institutions that offer a wide range of services (for example, checking accounts, savings, accounts, and extension of loans) to their customers. Commercial banks are owned by stockholders and seek to operate at a profit.

Savings and Loan Associations: Financial institutions that accept deposits in exchange for shares that pay dividends. Historically, these funds have been channeled into residential mortgage loans. Under recent banking legislation, S & Ls are now permitted to offer checkable deposits (NOW accounts) and extend a broad range of services similar to those of commercial banks.

the same day, the probability of this occurring is quite remote. Typically, while some individuals are making withdrawals, others are making deposits. These transactions tend to balance out, eliminating sudden changes in demand deposits.

Thus, banks maintain only a fraction of their assets in reserves to meet the requirements of depositors. As Exhibit 3 illustrates, on average, **reserves**—vault cash and deposits with the Federal Reserve—were less than 10 percent as large as the transactions deposit obligation of commercial banks at year-end 1985.

Prior to banking deregulation legislation of 1980, different types of financial institutions operated under different sets of regulations, which were designed to segment the financial market. If one wanted a checking account, a personal or business loan, or a credit card, one would go to a **commercial bank.** For maximum interest on a savings account, or to obtain funds to buy a home, one would patronize a **savings and loan association. Credit unions** specialized in small personal loans, frequently offering the advantage of automatic deductions from one's paychecks.

The Monetary Control Act of 1980 in effect restructured the banking industry, eroding the distinctions among commercial banks, savings and loan associations, credit unions, and **mutual savings banks.** The act lifted most of the restrictions on the types of loans and investments the savings and loan associations, mutual savings banks, and credit unions could make. Interest rate ceilings on time and savings deposits were phased out. All thrift institutions were permitted to offer checking account deposits. Finally, all depository institutions were placed under the jurisdiction of the Federal Reserve System, which was instructed to apply uniform reserve requirements and to offer similar services to all depository institutions. In essence, the 1980 legislation transformed savings and loan associations, credit unions, and mutual savings banks into commercial banks. All of these depository institutions now offer both checking and savings accounts, and extend a wide variety of loans to their customers. Therefore, when we speak of the banking industry, we are referring not only to commercial banks but to savings and loan associations, credit unions, and mutual savings banks as well.

Exhibit 4 provides a thumbnail sketch of the depository institutions that comprise the banking industry. The assets of commercial banks are nearly

---

EXHIBIT 4 • A Thumbnail Sketch of the Major Depository Institutions in the United States

Type of Institution	Number (Approximate)	Assets—December 1985 (billions of dollars)
Commercial banks	15,000	2,460
Savings and loan associations	4,500	1,062
Mutual savings banks	450	217
Credit unions	20,000	117

Federal Reserve Bulletin, March 1986.

twice as large as the combined total of the other three banking/depository institutions. In turn, the assets of savings and loan associations are substantially greater than those of either mutual savings banks or credit unions. Credit unions are more numerous (20,000) than any other type of depository institution, but their total assets came to only $117 billion at the beginning of 1986.

FRACTIONAL RESERVE GOLDSMITHING

Credit Unions: Financial cooperative organizations of individuals with a common affiliation (such as an employer or labor union). They accept deposits, including checkable deposits, pay interest (or dividends) on them out of earnings, and channel funds primarily into loans to members.

Mutual Savings Banks: Financial institutions that accept deposits in exchange for interest payments. Historically, home mortgages have constituted their primary interest-earning assets. Under recent banking legislation, these banks, too, are authorized to offer interest-bearing checkable accounts.

Economists often like to draw an analogy between the goldsmith of the past and our current banking system. In the past, gold was used as the means of making payments. It was money. People would store their money with a goldsmith for safekeeping, just as many of us open a checking account for safety reasons. Gold owners received a certificate granting them the right to withdraw their gold anytime they wished. If they wanted to buy something, they would go to the goldsmith, withdraw gold, and use it as a means of making a payment. Thus, the money supply was equal to the amount of gold in circulation plus the gold deposited with goldsmiths.

The day-to-day deposits of and requests for gold were always only a fraction of the total amount of gold deposited. A major portion of the gold simply "lay idle in the goldsmiths' vaults." Taking notice of this fact, goldsmiths soon began loaning gold to local merchants. After a time, the merchants would pay back the gold, plus pay interest for its use. What happened to the money supply when a goldsmith extended loans to local merchants? The deposits of persons who initially brought their gold to the goldsmith were not reduced. Depositors could still withdraw their gold anytime they wished (as long as they did not all try to do so at once). The merchants were now able to use the gold they borrowed from the goldsmith as a means of payment. As goldsmiths lent gold, they increased the amount of gold in circulation, thereby increasing the money supply.

It was inconvenient to make a trip to the goldsmith every time one wanted to buy something. Since people knew that the certificates were redeemable in gold, certificates began circulating as a means for payment. The depositors were pleased with this arrangement because it eliminated the need for a trip to the goldsmith every time something was exchanged for gold. As long as they had confidence in the goldsmith, sellers were glad to accept the certificates as payment.

Since depositors were now able to use the gold certificates as money, the daily withdrawals and deposits with goldsmiths declined even more. Local goldsmiths would keep about 20 percent of the total gold deposited with them so they could meet the current requests to redeem gold certificates in circulation. The remaining 80 percent of their gold deposits would be loaned out to business merchants, traders, and other citizens. Therefore, 100 percent of the gold certificates was circulating as money; and that portion of gold that had been loaned out, 80 percent of the total deposits, was also circulating as money. The total money supply, gold certificates plus gold, was now 1.8 times the amount of gold that had been originally deposited with the goldsmith. Since the goldsmiths issued loans and kept only a fraction of the total gold deposited with them, they were able to increase the money supply.

As long as the goldsmiths held enough reserves to meet the current requests of the depositors, everything went along smoothly. Most gold depositors probably did not even realize that the goldsmiths did not have their actual gold and that of other depositors, precisely designated as such, sitting in the "vaults."

Goldsmiths derived income from loaning gold. The more gold they loaned, the greater their total income. Some goldsmiths, trying to increase their income by extending more and more interest-earning loans, depleted the gold in their vaults to imprudently low levels. If an unexpectedly large number of depositors wanted their gold, these greedy goldsmiths would have been unable to meet their requests. They would lose the confidence of their depositors, and the system of fractional reserve goldsmithing would tend to break down.

In principle, our modern banking system is very similar to goldsmithing. The United States has a **fractional reserve banking** system. Banks are required to maintain only a fraction of their deposits in the form of cash and other reserves. Just as the early goldsmiths did not have enough gold to pay all their depositors simultaneously, neither do our banks have enough reserves to pay all their depositors simultaneously (see Exhibit 3). The early goldsmiths expanded the money supply by issuing loans. So do present-day bankers. The amount of gold held in reserve to meet the requirements of depositors limited the ability of the goldsmiths to expand the money supply. The amount of cash and other **required reserves** limits the ability of present-day banks to expand the money supply.

However, there is also an important difference between modern banking and early goldsmithing. The funds of depositors are protected both by the ability of banks to borrow from the central bank and by deposit insurance. The central bank is a lender of last resort. If all depositors suddenly attempted to withdraw their funds simultaneously, the central bank would intervene and supply the bank with enough liquid funds to meet the demand. In addition, the deposits of almost all banks—both state and national—are insured with the Federal Deposit Insurance Corporation (FDIC), an agency established in 1933. The FDIC fully insures each account up to $100,000 against losses due to bank failure. The Federal Savings and Loan Insurance Corporation and the National Credit Union Administration provide identical coverage for deposits of savings and loan associations and credit unions. In contrast with early goldsmithing, depositors with less than $100,000 in an account need not fear the loss of their funds due to the failure of their bank. Since depositors have confidence in the safety of their deposits, there is little reason for panic withdrawal of funds based on fear of possible bank failure. In turn, virtual elimination of panic withdrawals substantially reduces the likelihood of bank failures. Prior to the establishment of the FDIC in 1933, more than 10,000 banks (one third of the total) failed between 1922 and 1933. Not surprisingly, bank failures since 1933 have seldom exceeded 10 or 20 per year. Even in these cases, the funds of depositors were protected by FDIC.[1]

Fractional Reserve Banking: A system that enables banks to keep less than 100 percent reserves against their deposits. Required reserves are a fraction of deposits.

Required Reserves: The minimum amount of reserves that a bank is required by law to keep on hand to back up its deposits. Thus, if reserve requirements were 15 percent, banks would be required to keep $150,000 in reserves against each $1 million of deposits.

---

[1]In 1983, there were 50 bank failures. Most of these reflected loans that were uncollectable as the result of changing market conditions in the energy and agricultural industries. Even in these cases, however, the checking and saving accounts of depositors were protected by FDIC. The major purpose of FDIC was to eliminate panic withdrawal of funds and the accompanying financial collapses that had long plagued the economy prior to 1933. Measured by this criterion, FDIC has been enormously effective. For all practical purposes, it has eliminated bank failures due to panic withdrawals of deposits.

HOW BANKS CREATE MONEY

Under a fractional reserve system, an increase in reserves will permit banks to extend additional loans and thereby create additional transaction (checking) deposits. Since transaction deposits are money, the extension of the additional loans expands the supply of money.

To enhance our understanding of this process, let us consider a banking system without a central bank, one in which only currency acts as reserves against deposits. Initially, we will assume that all banks are required by law to maintain vault currency equal to at least 20 percent of the checking accounts of their depositors. Suppose you found $1,000 that your long-deceased uncle had apparently hidden in the basement of his house. How much would this newly found $1,000 of currency expand the money supply? You take the bills to the First National Bank, open a checking account of $1,000, and deposit the cash with the banker. First National is now required to keep an additional $200 in vault cash, 20 percent of your deposit. However, they received $1,000 of additional cash, so after placing $200 in the bank vault, First National has $800 of **excess reserves,** reserves over and above the amount they are required by law to maintain. Given their current excess reserves, First National can now extend an $800 loan. Suppose they loan $800 to a local citizen to buy a car. At the time the loan is extended, the money supply will increase by $800 as the bank adds the funds to the checking account of the borrower. No one else has less money. You still have your $1,000 checking account, and the borrower has $800 for a new car.

When the borrower buys a new car, the seller accepts a check and deposits the $800 in a bank, Citizen's State Bank. What happens when the check clears? The temporary excess reserves of the First National Bank will be eliminated when it pays $800 to the Citizen's State Bank. But, when Citizen's State Bank receives $800 in currency, it will now have excess reserves. It must keep 20 percent, an additional $160, in the reserve against the $800 checking account deposit of the automobile seller. The remaining $640 could be loaned out. Since Citizen's State, like other banks, is in business to make money, it will be quite happy to "extend a helping hand" to a borrower. When the second bank loans out its excess reserves, the deposits of the persons borrowing the money will increase by $640. Another $640 has now been added to the money supply. You still have your $1,000, the automobile seller has an additional $800, and the new borrower has just received an additional $640. Because you found the $1,000 that had been stashed away by your uncle, the money supply has increased by $2,440.

Of course, the process can continue. Exhibit 5 follows the potential creation of money resulting from the initial $1,000 through several additional stages. In total, the money supply can increase by a maximum of $5,000, the $1,000 initial deposit plus an additional $4,000 in demand deposits that can be created by extending new loans.

The multiple by which new reserves increase the stock of money is referred to as the **deposit expansion multiplier.** The amount by which additional reserves can increase the supply of money is determined by the ratio of required reserves to demand deposits. In fact, the deposit expansion multiplier is merely the reciprocal of the required reserve ratio. In our

Excess Reserves: Actual reserves that exceed the legal requirement.

Deposit Expansion Multiplier: The multiple by which an increase (decrease) in reserves will increase (decrease) the money supply. It is inversely related to the required reserve ratio.

EXHIBIT 5 • Creating Money from New Reserves

When banks are required to maintain 20 percent reserves against demand deposits, the creation of $1000 of new reserves will potentially increase the supply of money by $5000.

Bank	New Cash Deposits (Actual Reserves) (Dollars)	New Required Reserves (Dollars)	Potential Demand Deposits Created by Extending New Loans (Dollars)
Initial deposit	1000.00	200.00	800.00
Second stage	800.00	160.00	640.00
Third stage	640.00	128.00	512.00
Fourth stage	512.00	102.40	409.60
Fifth stage	409.60	81.92	327.68
Sixth stage	327.68	65.54	262.14
Seventh stage	262.14	52.43	209.71
All others	1048.58	209.71	838.87
Total	5000.00	1000.00	4000.00

---

example, the required reserves are 20 percent, or 1/5 of the total deposits. So, the potential deposit expansion multiplier is 5. If only 10 percent reserves were required, the deposit expansion multiplier would be 10, the reciprocal of 1/10.

The lower the percentage of the reserve requirement, the greater the potential expansion in the money supply resulting from the creation of new reserves. The fractional reserve requirement places a ceiling on potential money creation from new reserves.

THE ACTUAL DEPOSIT MULTIPLIER

Will the introduction of the new currency reserves necessarily have a full deposit expansion multiplier effect? The answer is no. The actual deposit multiplier may be less than the potential for two reasons.

First, the deposit expansion multiplier will be reduced if some persons decide to hold the currency rather than deposit it in a bank. For example, suppose the person who borrowed the $800 in the preceding example spends only $700 and stashes the remaining $100 away for a possible emergency. Only $700 can then end up as a deposit in the second stage of contribution to the excess reserves necessary for expansion. The potential of new loans in the second stage and in all subsequent stages will be reduced proportionally. When currency remains in circulation, outside of banks, it will reduce the size of the deposit expansion multiplier.

Second, the deposit multiplier will be less than its maximum when banks fail to use all the new excess reserves to extend loans. Banks, though, have a strong incentive to loan out most of their new excess reserves. Idle excess reserves do not draw interest. Banks want to use most of these excess reserves so they can generate interest income. Exhibit 6 shows that this is indeed the case. In recent years, excess reserves have accounted for only 1 or 2 percent of the total reserves of banks.

Currency leakages and idle excess bank reserves will result in a deposit expansion multiplier that is less than its potential maximum. However, since people generally maintain most of their money in bank deposits rather

EXHIBIT 6 • Banking and Excess Reserves

Profit-maximizing banks use their excess reserves to extend loans and other forms of credit. Thus, excess reserves are very small, approximately 1 percent of the total reserves in recent years.

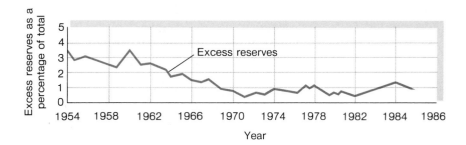

than as currency, and since banks typically eliminate most of their excess reserves by extending loans, strong forces are present that will lead to multiple expansion.

THE FEDERAL RESERVE SYSTEM

As we previously indicated, the Federal Reserve System is the central monetary authority or "central bank" for the United States. Every major country has a central banking authority. The Bank of England and the Bank of France, for example, perform central banking functions for their respective countries.

Central banks are charged with the responsibility of carrying out monetary policy. The major purpose of the Federal Reserve System (and other central banks) is to regulate the money supply and provide a monetary climate that is in the best interest of the entire economy.

The Fed, a term often used to refer to the Federal Reserve System, was created in 1913. Exhibit 7 illustrates the structure of the Federal Reserve System. While there are 12 Federal Reserve District banks, the Board of

EXHIBIT 7 • The Structure of the Federal Reserve System

The Board of Governors of the Federal Reserve System is at the center of the banking system in the United States. The board sets the rules and regulations for all depository institutions. The seven members of the Board of Governors also serve on the Federal Open Market Committee, a 12-member board that establishes Fed policy with regard to the buying and selling of government securities, the primary mechanism used to control the money supply in the United States.

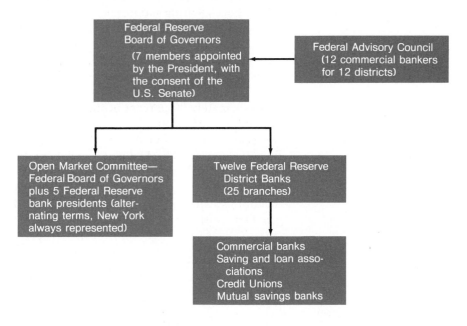

Governors is the decision-making center of the Fed. This powerful board consists of seven members, each appointed to a staggered 14-year term by the president with the advice and consent of the Senate. The president designates one of the seven members as chair for a four-year term. However, since a new member of the governing board is appointed only every other year, each president has only limited power over the Fed. Because the Fed operates with considerable independence of both Congress and the executive branch, it often becomes the "whipping boy" for legislative leaders and presidents during difficult times.

The Board of Governors establishes rules and regulations applicable to all depository institutions. It sets the reserve requirements and regulates the composition of the asset holdings of depository institutions. The board is the rule-maker, and often the umpire, of the banking industry.

The Federal Advisory Council provides the Board of Governors with input from the banking industry. The Federal Advisory Council is composed of 12 commercial bankers, one from each of the 12 Federal Reserve districts. As the name implies, this council is purely advisory.

In addition to the Board of Governors, the Federal Open Market Committee (FOMC) exerts an important influence on monetary policy. This powerful policy-making arm of the Fed is made up of (a) the seven members of the Board of Governors, (b) the president of the New York District Bank, and (c) four (of the remaining eleven) additional presidents of the Fed's District Banks, who rotate on the committee. While they do not always have a vote, all 12 presidents of the Federal Reserve regional banks attend the FOMC meetings, held every five to eight weeks. The FOMC determines the Fed's policy with respect to the purchase and sale of government bonds. As we shall soon see, this is the Fed's most frequently used method of controlling the money supply in the United States.

The 12 Federal Reserve District Banks operate under the control of the board of Governors.[2] These district banks handle approximately 85 percent of all check-clearing services of the banking system. Federal Reserve District Banks differ from commercial banks in several important respects.

1. *Federal Reserve Banks Are Not Profit-Making Institutions.* Instead, they are an arm of the government. All of their earnings, above minimum expenses, belong to the Treasury.

2. *Unlike Other Banks, Federal Reserve Banks Can Actually Issue Money.* Approximately 90 percent of the currency in circulation was issued by the Fed. Look at the dollar bill in your pocket. Chances are that it has "Federal Reserve Note" engraved on it, indicating that it was issued by the Federal Reserve System. The Fed is the only bank that can issue money.

3. *Federal Reserve Banks Act as Bankers' Banks.* Private citizens and corporations do not bank with Federal Reserve Banks. Commercial depository institutions and the federal government are the only banking customers of the Fed. Most depository institutions, regardless of their membership status

---

[2]Federal Reserve District Banks are located in Boston, New York, Philadelphia, Cleveland, Richmond, Atlanta, Chicago, St. Louis, Minneapolis, Kansas City, Dallas, and San Francisco. There are also 25 district "branch banks."

with the Fed, usually maintain some deposits with the Federal Reserve System. Of course, deposits with the Fed count as reserves. The Fed audits the books of depository institutions regularly to assure regulatory compliance and the protection of depositors against fraud. The Fed also plays an important role in the clearing of checks through the banking system. Since most banks maintain deposits with the Fed, the clearing of checks becomes merely an accounting transaction.

Initially, the Fed was made independent of the executive branch so that the Treasury would not use it for political purposes. The policies of the Treasury and the Fed, though, are usually closely coordinated. For example, the chair of the Board of Governors of the Federal Reserve, the Secretary of the Treasury, and the chair of the President's Council of Economic Advisers meet weekly to discuss and plan macroeconomic policy. In reality, it would be more accurate to think of the Fed and the executive branch as equal partners in the determinations of policies designed to promote full employment and stable prices.

HOW THE FED CONTROLS OUR MONEY SUPPLY

The Fed has three major means of controlling the money stock: (a) establishing reserve requirements for depository institutions, (b) buying and selling U.S. government securities in the open market, and (c) setting the interest rate at which it will loan funds to commercial banks and other depository institutions. We will analyze in detail how each of these tools can be used to regulate the amount of money in circulation.

Reserve Requirements. The Federal Reserve System requires banking institutions (including credit unions and savings and loan associations) to maintain reserves against the demand deposits of its customers. The reserves of banking institutions are composed of (a) currency held by the bank and (b) deposits of the bank with the Federal Reserve System. A bank can always obtain additional currency by drawing on its deposits with the Federal Reserve. So, both cash-on-hand and the bank's deposits with the Fed can be used to meet the demands of depositors. Both therefore count as reserves.

Required Reserve Ratio: A percentage of a specified liability category (for example, transaction accounts) that banking institutions are required to hold as reserves against that type of liability.

Nonpersonal Time Deposits: Time deposits owned by businesses or corporations.

Exhibit 8 indicates the **required reserve ratio**—the percentage of each deposit category that banks are required to keep in reserve (that is, their cash plus deposits with the Fed). As of January, 1986, the reserve requirement for transactions accounts was set at 3 percent for amounts under 31.7 million and 12 percent for amounts in excess of $31.7 million.[3] A reserve ratio of 3 percent is applicable for **nonpersonal time deposits** with a maturity date during the next $1\frac{1}{2}$ years. Currently, no reserves are required against nonpersonal time deposits with a maturity date of more than $1\frac{1}{2}$ years in the future. Banks are also required to maintain 3 percent in reserve against Eurodollar liabilities.

Why are commercial banks required to maintain assets in the form of reserves? One reason is to prevent imprudent bankers from overextending

[3]The $31.7 million dividing point is adjusted each year by 80 percent of the change in total transaction account deposits in all banking institutions.

EXHIBIT 8 ● The Required Reserve Ratio of Banking Institutions

Banking institutions are required to maintain 3 percent reserves against transaction-account deposits of less than $31.7 million and 12 percent reserves for transaction deposits over $31.7 million (in effect January, 1986). Other required reserve ratios are also shown below.

| | Transaction Accounts | | Nonpersonal Time Deposits | | Eurocurrency Liabilities |
| | | | | | |
	$0–31.7 million	Over $31.7 million	Less than $1\frac{1}{2}$ Years Maturity	$1\frac{1}{2}$ Years or More Maturity	All Types
Required reserves as a percent of deposits	3	12	3	0	3

Federal Reserve Bulletin, January 1986.

---

loans and thereby placing themselves in a poor position to deal with any sudden increase in withdrawals by depositors. The quantity of reserves needed to meet such emergencies is not left totally to the judgment of individual bankers, though. The Fed sets the rules.

The Fed's control over reserve requirements is important for another reason. By altering requirements, the Fed can alter the money supply. The law does not prevent commercial banks from holding reserves over and above those required by the Fed, but, as we have noted, profit-seeking banking institutions prefer to hold interest-bearing assets such as loans rather than large amounts of excess reserves. Since reserves draw no interest, banks seek to minimize their excess reserves.

Exhibit 9 shows the actual reserve position of commercial banks (see also Exhibit 6). Not surprisingly,the actual reserves of these banks are very close to the required level. Since the excess reserves of banks are very small, they respond in a manner that changes the money supply when the Fed changes the required reserve ratio.

If the Fed reduced the required reserve ratio, it would free additional reserves that banks could loan out. Profit-seeking banks would not allow these excess reserves to lie idle—they would extend additional loans. The extension of new loans would then expand the money supply.

What would happen if the Fed increased the reserve requirements? Since banks typically have very small excess reserves, they would have to extend fewer loans in the future. This reduction in loans outstanding would then cause a decline in the money supply.

Reserve requirements are an important determinant of the money supply because they influence both the availability of excess reserves and the size of the deposit expansion multiplier. Higher reserve requirements reduce the size of the deposit expansion multiplier and force banks to extend fewer loans. An increase in the required reserve ratio therefore reduces the money supply. On the other hand, a decline in the required reserve ratio

---

EXHIBIT 9 • The Reserves of Banks

The actual and required reserves of commercial banks (December 1985) are indicated below. The required reserves average approximately 9 percent against transaction deposits and 4 percent against total time deposits. Note that excess reserves of banks are exceedingly small.

	Total—Commercial Banks (December, 1985) (billions of dollars)
Total transaction deposits	536.4
Total time deposits	1227.1
Actual reserves	45.59
Required reserves	45.35
Excess reserves	.24

Federal Reserve Bulletin, March 1986.

---

increases the potential deposit expansion multiplier and the availability of excess reserves. Banks then tend to extend additional loans, thereby expanding the money supply.

In recent years, the Fed has seldom used its regulatory power over reserve requirements to alter the supply of money. Because of the deposit expansion multiplier, small changes in reserve requirements can cause large changes in the money supply. In addition, the precise magnitude and timing of a change in the money stock resulting from a change in reserve requirements are difficult to predict. For these reasons, the Fed has usually preferred to use other monetary tools.

Open Market Operations: The buying and selling of U.S. government securities (national debt) by the Federal Reserve.

Open Market Operations. The use of **open market operations,** buying and selling of U.S. securities in the open market, is by far the most important tool that the Fed uses to control the stock of money. When the Fed enters the market and buys U.S. government securities, it expands the reserves available to banking institutions. The sellers of the securities receive checks drawn on a Federal Reserve Bank. When the checks are deposited in banks, those banks acquire a deposit or credit with the Federal Reserve. The banking system has increased its reserves, and the Fed has purchased part of the national debt. Since the deposits with the Fed, like currency, count as reserves, banks can now extend more loans. The money supply will eventually increase by the amount of the securities purchased by the Fed times the actual deposit expansion multiplier.

Let us consider a hypothetical case. Suppose the Fed purchases $10,000 of U.S. securities from commercial Bank A. Bank A has fewer securities, but it now has additional excess reserves of $10,000. Put another way, $10,000 has been added to the economy's **potential reserves.** The bank can extend new loans of up to $10,000 while maintaining its initial reserve position. This $10,000 expansion of loans will contribute directly to the money supply. Part of it will eventually be deposited in other banks, and they will also be able to extend additional loans. The creation of the $10,000 of new bank

Potential Reserves: The total Federal Reserve credit outstanding. Most of this credit is in the form of U.S. securities held by the Fed.

EXHIBIT 10 • How Big is the Actual Money Deposit Multiplier?

In recent years, the actual deposit expansion multiplier has been between 2.76 and 3.11. Of course, if the reserve requirements were lowered (raised), the deposit expansion multiplier would rise (fall).

Year (December)	Money Supply (M-1) (billions of dollars)	Total Potential Reserves[a] (billions of dollars)	Money Deposit Expansion Multiplier
1970	216.6	69.7	3.11
1972	252.0	80.9	3.11
1974	277.6	94.6	2.93
1976	310.4	108.3	2.87
1978	363.1	128.0	2.84
1980	414.9	150.3	2.76
1982	480.8	170.1	2.83
1983	528.0	185.5	2.85
1984	558.5	199.0	2.81
1985	624.6	215.0	2.91

[a]Economists refer to the total potential reserves as the monetary base.

Source: Board of Governors of the Federal Reserve System and *Economic Report of the President, 1985*.

---

reserves will cause the money supply to increase by some multiple of the amount of U.S. securities purchased by the Fed.

The reserve requirements in effect in the early 1980s suggest that the potential deposit multiplier could be 9 or 10. Of course, as new reserves are injected into the banking system, there is some leakage either because of potential currency reserves circulating as cash or because some banks may be accumulating excess reserves. Exhibit 10 shows that during the 1970s, the money supply was between 2.76 and 3.11 times greater than the potential reserves,[4] suggesting that the actual deposit expansion multiplier is about 3. Therefore, when the Fed purchases U.S. securities, injecting additional reserves into the system, the money supply, on average, tends to increase by approximately $3 for each dollar of securities purchased.

Open market operations can also be used to reduce the money stock, or reduce its rate of increase. If the Fed wants to reduce the money stock, it sells some of its current holdings of government securities. When the Fed sells securities, the buyer pays for them with a check drawn on a commercial bank. As the check clears, the reserves of that bank with the Fed will decline. The reserves available to commercial banks are reduced, and the money stock falls.

Since open market operations have been the Fed's primary tool of monetary control in recent years, the money stock and the Fed's ownership of U.S. securities have followed similar paths. When the Fed increases its

---

[4]Currency in circulation plus the actual reserves of commercial banks comprise the total potential reserves. Economists often use the term "monetary base" when referring to the total potential reserves.

purchases of U.S. securities at a rapid rate, the money stock grows rapidly. A slowdown in the Fed's purchases of government bonds tends to reduce the rate of monetary expansion.

As we indicated earlier, the Federal Open Market Committee (FOMC), a special committee of the Fed, decides when and how open market operations will be used. The members meet every five or six weeks to map out the Fed's policy concerning the purchase and sale of U.S. securities.

The Discount Rate—The Cost of Borrowing from the Fed. When banking institutions borrow from the Federal Reserve, they must pay interest on the loan. The interest rate that banks pay on loans from the Federal Reserve is called the **discount rate.** Borrowing from the Fed is a privilege, not a right. The Fed does not have to loan funds to banking institutions. Banks borrow from the Fed primarily to meet temporary shortages of reserves. They are most likely to borrow from the Fed for a brief period of time while they are making other adjustments in their loan and investment portfolios that will permit them to meet their required reserves.

An increase in the discount rate makes it more expensive for banking institutions to borrow from the Fed. Borrowing is discouraged, and banks are more likely to build up their reserves to ensure that they will not have to borrow from the Fed. An increase in the discount rate is thus restrictive. It tends to discourage banks from shaving their excess reserves to a low level.

In contrast, a reduction in the discount rate is expansionary. At the lower interest rate, it costs banks less if they have to turn to the Fed to meet a temporary emergency. Therefore, as the cost of borrowing from the Fed declines, banks are more likely to reduce their excess reserves to a minimum, extending more loans and increasing the money supply.

The general public has a tendency to overestimate the importance of a change in the discount rate. Many people think an increase in the discount rate means their local banker will (or must) charge them a higher interest rate for a loan.[5] This is not necessarily so. The major source of loanable funds for commercial banks is reserves acquired through transaction and time deposits. Borrowing from the Fed amounts to less than one tenth of 1 percent of the available loanable funds of commercial banks. Since borrowing from the Fed is such a negligible source of funds, a .5 percent change in the discount rate has something less than a profound impact on the availability of credit and the supply of money. Certainly, it does not necessarily mean that your local bank will raise the rate at which it will lend to you.

If a bank has to borrow to meet its reserve requirements, it need not turn to the Fed. Instead, it can go to the **federal funds market.** In this market, banks with excess reserves extend short-term (sometimes for as little as a day) loans to other banks seeking additional reserves. If the federal funds rate (the interest rate in the federal funds market) is less than the discount rate, banks seeking additional reserves will tap this source rather

Discount Rate: The interest rate the Federal Reserve charges banking institutions for borrowing funds.

Federal Funds Market: A loanable funds market in which banks seeking additional reserves borrow short-term (generally for seven days or less) funds from banks with excess reserves. The interest rate in this market is called the federal funds rate.

---

[5]The discount rate is also sometimes confused with the prime interest rate, the rate at which banks loan money to low-risk customers. The two rates are different. A change in the discount rate will not necessarily affect the prime interest rate.

than borrow from the Fed. In recent years, the Fed has kept its loans to banking institutions at a low level by altering the discount rate to match the federal funds rate more closely. As a result, the federal funds rate and the discount rate tend to move together. If the federal funds rate is significantly higher than the discount rate, banks will attempt to borrow heavily from the Fed. Typically, when this happens, the Fed will raise its discount rate, removing the incentive of banks to borrow from the Fed rather than from the federal funds market.

Summarizing the Tools of the Fed. Exhibit 11 summarizes the monetary tools of the Federal Reserve. If the Fed wants to follow an expansionary policy, it can decrease reserve requirements, purchase additional U.S. securities, and/or lower the discount rate. If the Fed wants to reduce the money stock, it can increase the reserve requirements, sell U.S. securities, and/or raise the discount rate. Since the Fed typically seeks only small changes in the money supply (or its rate of increase), it usually uses only one or two of these tools at a time to accomplish a desired objective.

THE FED'S MONETARY GROWTH TARGETS

As the economy grows, the money supply is generally expanded, also. In a dynamic setting, therefore, the direction of monetary policy is best gauged by the rate of change in the money supply. When economists say that

---

EXHIBIT 11 • Summary of the Monetary Tools of the Federal Reserve

Federal Reserve Policy	Expansionary Monetary Policy	Restrictive Monetary Policy
1. Reserve requirements	*Reduce reserve requirements,* because this will free additional excess reserves and induce banks to extend additional loans, which will expand the money supply	*Raise reserve requirements,* because this will reduce the excess reserves of banks, causing them to make fewer loans; as the outstanding loans of banks decline, the money stock will be reduced
2. Open market operations	*Purchase additional U.S. securities,* which will expand the money stock directly, and increase the reserves of banks, inducing bankers in turn to extend more loans; this will expand the money stock indirectly	*Sell U.S. securities,* which will reduce both the money stock and excess reserves; the decline in excess reserves will indirectly lead to an additional reduction in the money supply
3. Discount rate	*Lower the discount rate,* which will encourage more borrowing from the Fed; banks will tend to reduce their reserves and extend more loans because of the lower cost of borrowing from the Fed if they temporarily run short on reserves.	*Raise the discount rate,* thereby discouraging borrowing from the Fed; banks will tend to extend fewer loans and build up their reserves so they will not have to borrow from the Fed.

monetary policy is expansionary, they mean that the rate of growth of the money stock is rapid. Similarly, restrictive monetary policy implies a slow rate of growth or a decline in the money stock.

In 1975, Congress passed legislation requiring the Federal Reserve to adopt and announce target growth rates for the money supply during the next year. At the beginning of each year, the Fed announces its target range for the growth rate of M-1, as well as for the broader definitions of the money supply. The announced targets provide the general public with information regarding the likely direction of monetary policy during the forthcoming year.

While the concept of announced monetary targets was generally applauded among economists, two significant problems have arisen. First, the Fed has often failed to follow its announced course. As Exhibit 12 shows, the actual growth rate of the money supply has generally exceeded the Fed's announced targets. For example, in 1985, the Fed indicated that it planned to expand the supply of money (M-1) between 3 percent and 8 percent during the year. In fact, the money supply grew by more than 11 percent during 1985. On a few occasions (1981, for example), the growth rate of the money supply has fallen below its target. During the 10-year period from 1976 to 1985, the Fed hit its announced target on only two occasions. Clearly, the Fed's failure to meet its targets raises questions about their importance as a guide to future monetary policy.

The second major problem relates to the changing nature of money. If a substantial component of M-1 is now used primarily as a savings device rather than for the conduct of transactions, previous relationships between

EXHIBIT 12 • The Fed's Announced Targets Compared to the Actual Path of the Money Supply

The cones indicate the target range for the growth of the money supply (M-1) as announced by the Fed at the beginning of each year. Note the actual growth rate of M-1 has generally been greater than the target range. During the 1976–1985 period, the Fed seldom hit its announced target for money growth.

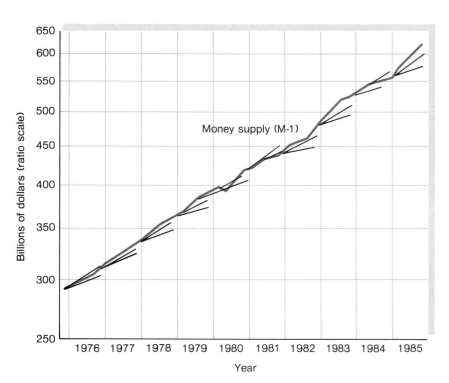

Source: *Economic Report of the President, 1985*, p. 53.

the growth of the money supply and changes in the price level may no longer hold. This is particularly true for the adjustment period during which individuals continue to restructure their holdings of money and other financial assets in light of the new opportunities, particularly the availability of interest-earning checking deposits. During this period, a rapid growth rate in the money supply (M-1) by historical standards may not be indicative of expansionary monetary policy. Clearly, the deregulation of the 1980s complicates the job of monetary policy-makers and adds to our uncertainty as to precisely what the money supply figures are telling us. After we integrate the monetary sector into our macroeconomic model, we will consider the implications of the changing nature of money in more detail.

THE FED AND THE TREASURY

Many students have a tendency to confuse the Federal Reserve and the U.S. Treasury, probably because both sound like monetary agencies. The Treasury is a budgetary agency. If there is a budgetary deficit, the Treasury will issue U.S. securities as a method of financing the deficit. Newly issued U.S. securities are almost always sold to private investors (or invested in government trust funds). Bonds issued by the Treasury to finance a budget deficit are seldom purchased directly by the Fed. In any case, the Treasury is primarily interested in obtaining funds so it can pay Uncle Sam's bills. Except for nominal amounts, mostly coins, the Treasury does not issue money. Borrowing—the public sale of new U.S. securities—is the primary method used by the Treasury to cover any excess of expenditures in relation to tax revenues.

Whereas the Treasury is concerned with the revenues and expenditures of the government, the Fed is concerned primarily with the availability of money and credit for the entire economy. The Fed does not issue U.S. securities. It merely purchases and sells government securities issued by the Treasury as a means of controlling the economy's money supply. Unlike the Treasury, the Fed can purchase government bonds by writing a check on itself without having deposits, gold, or anything else to back it up. In doing so, the Fed creates money out of thin air. The Treasury does not have this power. The Fed does not have an obligation to meet the financial responsibilities of the U.S. government. That is the domain of the Treasury. The Fed's responsibility is to provide a stable monetary framework for the entire economy. So, although the two agencies cooperate with each other, they are distinctly different institutions established for different purposes.

LOOKING AHEAD

In this chapter, we focused on the mechanics of monetary control. In the next chapter, we will analyze the impact of monetary policy on output, growth, and prices.

CHAPTER SUMMARY

1. Money is anything that is widely accepted as a medium of exchange. It also acts as a unit of account that provides a means of storing current purchasing power for the future. Without money, exchange would be both costly and tedious.

2. There is some debate among economists as to precisely how the money supply should be defined. The narrowest and most widely used defini-

tion of the money supply (M-1) includes only (a) currency in the hands of the public, (b) demand deposits, (c) other (interest-earning) checkable deposits in depository institutions, and (d) traveler's checks. None of these categories of money have significant intrinsic value. Money derives its value from its scarcity relative to its usefulness.

3. Financial deregulation in the early 1980s has, to some extent, changed the nature of money. Interest-bearing checkable deposits now account for nearly one third of the M-1 money supply. The opportunity cost of holding interest-earning money balances is less. People are motivated to hold such money balances as a form of savings, as well as for transactions purposes. Thus, the supply of money today is somewhat different than was true prior to 1980.

4. Banking is a business. Banks provide their depositors with safekeeping of money, check-clearing services on demand deposits, and interest payments on time deposits. Banks derive most of their income from the extension of loans and investments in interest-earning securities.

5. Recent legislation and regulatory changes have altered the structure of the banking industry. Currently, savings and loan associations, mutual savings banks, and credit unions offer services, including checking accounts, similar to those of commercial banks. The Federal Reserve System now regulates all of these depository institutions and is legally required to apply uniform reserve requirements to each. In essence, these changes have integrated the three classes of thrift institutions into the banking industry.

6. Under a fractional reserve banking system, banks are required to maintain only a fraction of their deposits in the form of reserves (vault cash or deposits with the Fed). Excess reserves may be invested or loaned to customers. When banks extend additional loans, they create additional deposits and thereby expand the money supply.

7. The Federal Reserve System is a central banking authority designed to provide a stable monetary framework for the entire economy. It establishes regulations that determine the supply of money. It issues most of the currency in the United States. It is a banker's bank.

8. The Fed has three major tools with which to control the money supply.

   (a) *Establishment of the Required Reserve Ratio.* Under a fractional reserve banking system, reserve requirements limit the ability of banking institutions to expand the money supply by extending more loans. When the Fed lowers the required reserve ratio, it creates excess reserves and allows banks to extend new loans, expanding the money supply. Raising the reserve requirements has the opposite effect.

   (b) *Open Market Operations.* The open market operations of the Fed can directly influence both the money supply and available reserves. When the Fed buys U.S. securities, the money supply will expand because bond buyers will acquire money and the reserves of banks will increase as checks drawn on Federal Reserve Banks are cleared. When the Fed sells securities, the money supply will contract because bond buyers are giving up money in exchange for securities. The reserves available to banks will decline, causing banks to issue fewer loans and thereby reduce the money supply.

(c) *The Discount Rate.* An increase in the discount rate is restrictive because it discourages banks from borrowing from the Fed to extend new loans. A reduction in the discount rate is expansionary because it makes borrowing from the Fed less costly.

9. For a dynamic growing economy, monetary policy can best be judged by the rate of change in the money supply. In 1975, Congress passed legislation requiring the Fed to announce targets for growth of the money supply at the beginning of each year. During the 1976–1985 period, the Fed often failed to hit its announced monetary targets. However, with the introduction of interest-earning checking accounts, the link between monetary growth and the price level may now differ from the relationship prior to 1980.

10. The Federal Reserve and the U.S. Treasury are distinct agencies. The Fed is concerned primarily with the money supply and the establishment of a stable monetary climate. The Treasury focuses on budgetary matters—tax revenues, government expenditures, and the financing of government debt.

THE ECONOMIC WAY OF THINKING— DISCUSSION QUESTIONS

1. Why can banks continue to hold reserves that are only a fraction of the demand deposits of their customers? Is your money safe in a bank? Why or why not?

2. What makes money valuable? Does money perform an economic service? Explain. Could money perform its function better if there were twice as much of it? Why or why not?

3. "People are poor because they don't have very much money. Yet, central bankers keep money scarce. If poor people had more money, poverty could be eliminated." Explain the confused thinking this statement reveals and why it is misleading.

4. Explain how the creation of new reserves would cause the money supply to increase by some multiple of the newly created reserves.

5. How will the following actions affect the money supply?
   (a) A reduction in the discount rate.
   (b) An increase in the reserve requirements.
   (c) Purchase by the Fed of $10 million of U.S. securities from a commercial bank.
   (d) Sale by the U.S. Treasury of $10 million of newly issued bonds to a commercial bank.
   (e) An increase in the discount rate.
   (f) Sale by the Fed of $20 million of U.S. securities to a private investor.

6. **What's Wrong with This Way of Thinking?**
   "When the government runs a budget deficit, it simply pays its bills by printing more money. As the newly printed money works its way through the economy, it waters down the value of paper money already in circulation. Thus, it takes more money to buy things. The major source of inflation is newly created paper money resulting from budget deficits."

7. Will individuals hold larger or smaller checking account money balances when their deposits earn interest? Why? Does this make it more difficult for policy-makers to determine the amount of money consistent with a stable price level? Explain.

CHAPTER
FOCUS

- Why do individuals and businesses hold money balances?

- How does monetary policy affect interest rates, output, and employment?

- Can monetary policy stimulate real GNP in the short-run? Can it do so in the long-run?

- Does it make any difference whether or not people quickly anticipate the effects of a change in monetary policy? Why?

- Will an increase in the stock of money cause inflation?

- Did macroeconomic policy cause the Great Depression?

In the early editions of the book, fiscal policy was top banana. In later editions that emphasis changed to equality. In this edition we've taken a stand that monetary policy is most important.

PAUL SAMUELSON
(1985 comment on the 12th edition of his classic text)

13 MODERN MACRO-ECONOMICS: MONETARY POLICY

Now that we have an understanding of the banking system and the determinants of the money supply, we can relax our prior assumption that the monetary authorities hold the supply of money constant. In this chapter, we will integrate the money market into our basic macroeconomic model. Money lubricates the wheels of exchange in all markets. Thus, changes in the supply of and demand for money exert potential important effects in all basic macroeconomic markets.

As in the case of fiscal policy, modern views on the impact of monetary policy reflect an evolutionary process. We will briefly consider the historical roots of modern monetary theory. The primary focus of this chapter is an analysis of how monetary policy works—why it sometimes influences real output, while in other situations its primary effects are on the price level.

THE DEMAND FOR MONEY

Demand for Money: At any given interest rate, the amount of wealth that people desire to hold in the form of money balances; that is, cash and checking account deposits. The quantity demanded is inversely related to the interest rate.

The amount of wealth that households and businesses desire to hold in the form of money balances is called the **demand for money.** Why do individuals and businesses want to hold cash and checking account money rather than stocks, bonds, buildings, and consumer durables?[1] Economists emphasize three major reasons why we hold money.

1. **Transactions Demand.** Money provides us with instant purchasing power. At the most basic level, we hold money so we can conduct transactions for almost any commodity quickly and easily with numerous people. Households demand money so they can pay for the weekly groceries, the monthly house payment, gasoline for the car, lunch for the kids, and other items purchased regularly. Businesses demand money so they can meet the weekly payroll, pay the utility bill, purchase supplies, and conduct other transactions. Money balances are necessary for transaction purposes because we do not always receive our income at the time we want to buy things. So, we keep a little cash or money in the bank to bridge the gap between everyday expenses and payday.

How much money will people desire in order to conduct their transactions? Other things constant, money balances for transaction purposes will increase with the nominal value of transactions. If prices remain constant, while the quantity of goods bought and sold increases, larger money balances will be required to conduct the larger volume of business. Similarly, if wages and prices increase, more money will be required by households to purchase the costlier weekly market basket and more money will be required by businesses to pay the larger wage bill. In essence, as money GNP increases as the result of either the growth of real output or higher prices, the demand for money balances will also increase.

---

[1]Be careful not to confuse (a) the demand for money balances with (b) the desire for more income. Of course, all of us would like to have more income, but we may be perfectly satisfied with our holdings of money in relation to our holdings of other goods, given our current level of wealth. When we say people want to hold more (or less) money, we mean that they want to restructure their wealth toward larger (smaller) money balances.

2. **Precautionary Demand.** Households and firms confront an uncertain future. Uncertainty produces two side effects that influence decisions: (1) risk and (2) opportunity for profit. Risk-adverse households and firms, those that are uncertain about the amount and timing of the receipt of their income, will hold additional cash or checking account balances as a precaution against unforeseen circumstances. Economists refer to the demand for money due to risk-adverse behavior associated with uncertainty over future income and expenditure patterns as the *precautionary demand for money.* While the transactions demand relates to the use of money for planned expenditures, precautionary demand stems from the recognition that unplanned expenditures may be necessary as the result of unforeseen events—a medical emergency, an unexpected decline in income, an auto accident, or such. Generally, the amount of money people wish to hold as insurance against unforeseen circumstances rises with nominal income. The precautionary demand for money balances, like transactions demand, increases with nominal GNP.

3. **Speculative Demand.** Unforeseen changes may also present decision-makers with an unexpected opportunity to purchase commodities or assets at bargain prices. Individuals and businesses may want to maintain part of their wealth in the form of money so they will be in a position to take ready advantage of opportunities to purchase desired items at very low prices. Of course, money is the most liquid form of wealth. Unlike land or houses, money places an individual (or business) in a position to respond quickly to a profit-making opportunity. Money balances maintained for this purpose are termed the *speculative demand for money.*

THE OPPORTUNITY COST OF HOLDING MONEY

The motives for holding money indicate that the demand for money is linked to money income (nominal GNP). As nominal income expands, larger money balances are required to conduct transactions and respond effectively to unforeseen events. Money balances are like other goods, though, in that price influences amount demanded. The price, or perhaps more accurately, the opportunity cost of holding money, is directly related to the nominal interest rate. Rather than maintaining $500 in cash or in a checking account that does not pay interest, you could earn interest by purchasing a $500 bond. Even if you are maintaining money balances in an interest-earning checking account, you could earn a higher rate of interest if you were willing to tie up the funds in a bond or some other less liquid form of savings.

As the nominal interest rate rises, the cost of holding money balances increases. At the higher interest rate, individuals and businesses will try to manage their affairs with smaller money balances. As Exhibit 1a illustrates, there is an inverse relationship between the quantity of money demanded and the interest rate.

With the passage of time, changes in institutional factors will influence the demand schedule for money. Both evidence and logic indicate that changes in institutional arrangements have reduced the demand for money in recent years. The widespread use of general-purpose credit cards helps households reconcile their bills with their receipt of income. Readily available short-term loans have reduced the need to maintain a substantial cash

EXHIBIT 1 · The Demand and Supply of Money

The demand for money is inversely related to the money interest rate (a). The supply of money is determined by the monetary authorities (the Fed) through their open market operations, discount rate policy, and reserve requirements (b).

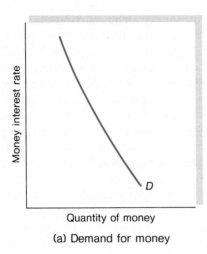

(a) Demand for money

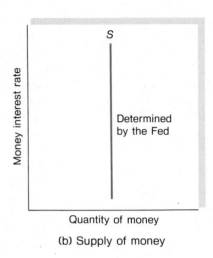

(b) Supply of money

balance for emergencies. The movement away from agriculture means that more families have a steady income every two weeks or so, rather than an unpredictable income two or three times per year. This steady income makes planning easier. These factors have reduced the need for households to maintain large cash balances (shifting the demand for money schedule to the left).

THE SUPPLY OF MONEY

Exhibit 1b illustrates the supply schedule for money. Since the money supply is determined by the monetary authorities (the Fed in the United States), the supply curve is vertical. This implies that the supply of money is insensitive to the interest rate. It is whatever the Fed decides it should be, largely independent of the interest rate. In equilibrium, the quantity of money demanded must equal the quantity supplied at the economy's money interest rate.

What impact do changes in the money supply have on price and output? Like the modern view of fiscal policy, the modern view of monetary policy is the product of an evolutionary process. Let us consider prior views that have contributed to our modern outlook on the importance of money.

Quantity Theory of Money: A theory that hypothesizes that a change in the money supply will cause a proportional change in the price level because velocity and real output are unaffected by the quantity of money.

THE QUANTITY THEORY OF MONEY

For centuries, both laymen and economists thought that increases in the money supply were a major determinant of changes in price level. Even prior to Adam Smith, early social philosophers such as David Hume argued that rapid growth in the supply of money caused inflation. Nearly a hundred years ago, the great classical economists, Englishman Alfred Marshall and American Irving Fisher, formalized a theory in support of this view. Economists refer to the theory as the **quantity theory of money.** According to the quantity theory, an increase in the supply of money will lead to a proportional increase in the price level.

The quantity theory of money can be easily understood once we recognize that there are two ways of viewing GNP. As we previously discussed, GNP is the sum of the price, P, times the quantity, Q, of each "final product" good purchased during the period. However, when the existing money stock M is multiplied by the number of times, V, that money is used to buy final products, this, too, yields the economy's GNP. Therefore,

$$PQ = \text{GNP} = MV$$

Velocity of Money: The average number of times a dollar is used to purchase final goods and services during a year. It is equal to GNP divided by the stock of money.

The **velocity of money** (V) is simply the average number of times a dollar is used to purchase a final product or service during a year. Velocity is equal to annual GNP divided by the size of the money stock. For example, in 1985, GNP was $3,993 billion and the average money supply (currency plus checkable deposits) was $593 billion. So, on average, each dollar was used 6.7 times to purchase final product goods or services included in GNP. The velocity of money was therefore 6.7.

The concept of velocity is closely related to the demand for money. When decision-makers conduct a specific amount of business with a smaller amount of money, their demand for money balances is reduced. Each dollar, though, is now being used more often. Therefore, the velocity of money is increasing. Thus, for a given income level, when the demand for money declines, the velocity of money increases.

Equation of Exchange: $MV = PQ$, where M is the money supply, V is the velocity of money, P is the price level, and Q is the quantity of goods and services produced.

The $MV = PQ$ relationship is simply an identity, or a tautology. Economists refer to it as the **equation of exchange,** since it reflects both the monetary and real sides of each final product exchange. The quantity theory of money, though, postulates that Q and V are determined by factors other than the amount of money in circulation. Classical economists believed that real output Q was determined by such factors as technology, the size of the economy's resource base, and the skill of the labor force. These factors were thought to be insensitive to changes in the money supply.

Similarly, classical economists thought the velocity of money was determined primarily by institutional factors such as the organization of banking and credit, the frequency of income payments, the rapidity of transportation, and the communication system. These factors would change quite slowly. From this, classical economists thought that for all practical purposes, the velocity or "turn over" rate of money in the short-run was constant.

If both Q and V are constant, the $MV = PQ$ relationship indicates that an increase in the money supply will lead to a proportional increase in the price level. For classical economists, the link between the money supply and the price level was quite mechanical. An increase in the quantity of money led to a proportional increase in the price level.

Of course, they recognized that the link might not always be exact. For the purposes of theory, though, it was a reasonably close approximation to reality according to the classical theory.

EARLY KEYNESIAN VIEWS ON MONEY

The Keynesian revolution emphasized the importance of demand. This notwithstanding, early Keynesians had little confidence in the ability of changes in the money supply to stimulate additional demand, particularly during an economic recession. During the 1950s, it was popular to draw an analogy between monetary policy and the workings of a string. Like a string, monetary policy could be used to pull (hold back) the economy and thereby control inflation. However, just as one cannot push with a string, monetary policy could not be used to push (stimulate) aggregate demand.

In his book, *General Theory*, Keynes offered a plausible explanation for why monetary policy might be an ineffective method of stimulating demand. What if the direction of changes in velocity were opposite to the direction of changes in the money stock? If a 5 percent increase in the supply of money led to a 5 percent reduction in velocity, monetary policy would directly influence neither real income nor the price level. Keynes himself recognized this was a highly atypical situation. He was *not* an advocate of the extreme position that held that changes in the money supply were of no consequence.[2] In the shadow of the Great Depression, though, many of his early followers took the unusual to be typical.

THE MODERN VIEW OF MONETARY POLICY

Monetarists: A group of economists who believe that (a) monetary instability is the major cause of fluctuations in real GNP and (b) rapid growth of the money supply is the major cause of inflation.

Beginning in the late 1950s, economists hotly debated the potency of changes in the supply of money. Led by Milton Friedman, later a Nobel laureate, a group of economists, subsequently called **monetarists,** challenged the existing Keynesian view. In contrast with the early Keynesians, the monetarists argued that changes in the stock of money exerted a powerful influence on both nominal and real GNP, as well as on the level of prices. As Friedman stated in his 1967 presidential address before members of the American Economic Association:

---

[2]Keynes thought that money did matter, even during a recession. He stated: "So long as there is unemployment, employment will change in the same proportion as the quantity of money, and when there is full employment, prices will change in the same proportion as the quantity of money." [*The General Theory of Employment, Interest, and Money* (New York: Harcourt, 1936), p. 296.]

Every major contraction in this country has been either produced by monetary disorder or greatly exacerbated by monetary disorder. Every major inflation has been produced by monetary expansion.[3]

After nearly two decades of debate, a modern consensus view emerged. Of course, differences remain between Keynesians and monetarists on the details of how monetary policy works. However, on the general substantive matter, both now agree that monetary policy exerts an important impact on our economy. (The quotation from Paul Samuelson introducing this chapter emphasizes this point. Winner of the 1970 Nobel prize in economics, Professor Samuelson is a long-time proponent of Keynesian theory.)

The modern view of monetary policy indicates there are two channels through which monetary policy exerts an impact on prices, output, and employment. Exhibits 2 and 3 illustrate each of the channels.

UNANTICIPATED EXPANSIONARY MONETARY POLICY

Exhibit 2 illustrates an economy initially experiencing equilibrium in the money, loanable funds, and goods and services markets. The public is just willing to hold the existing money stock (S_1) provided by the Fed at the money interest rate (i). Initially, the money interest is equal to the real interest rate (r_1), indicating that the expected rate of inflation is zero.

---

[3]Milton Friedman, "The Role of Monetary Policy," *American Economic Review* (March 1968), p. 12.

OUTSTANDING ECONOMIST

**Milton Friedman
(1912–   )**

Always provocative and audacious, Friedman is best known among the lay public for his defense of free markets. In his best selling book, *Free to Choose*, written with his wife Rose, he argues that free markets are the source of economic prosperity. Friedman, though, is far more than a libertarian economist. The 1976 recipient of the Nobel Prize, many believe he is the most creative economist of his time, if not of the 20th century.

Friedman's scholarly activity has focused on macroeconomics. He developed the permanent income hypothesis of consumption. But, his most influential work may very well be an 850-page treatise (coauthored with Anna Schwartz), entitled *A Monetary History of the United States*. The book, already a classic, is a gold mine of monetary and aggregate economic data. Based on this analysis and related work, Friedman argues that business fluctuations are the result of short-run changes in the supply of money. According to Friedman, the key to a healthy, stable economy is a constant rate of growth in the money supply.

Friedman retired from his professorship at the University of Chicago in 1977. He continues his scholarly work at Stanford's Hoover Institution, while continuing to challenge a new generation of economists with writings and lectures.

Expansionary Monetary Policy: An acceleration in the growth rate of the money supply.

Excess Supply of Money: Situation in which the actual money balances of individuals and business firms are in excess of their desired level. Thus, decision-makers will increase their spending on other assets and goods until they reduce their actual balances to the desired level.

What will happen if the Fed shifts to **expansionary monetary policy**—if it unexpectedly increases the supply of money from S_1 to S_2? The increase in the money supply leaves decision-makers with larger money balances than they desire to hold. The public will take steps to reduce the **excess supply of money.** Exhibit 2 shows how the public's response to an excess supply of money is transmitted through the interest rate to the goods and services market. To reduce their excess holdings of money balances, people will transfer funds from their checking accounts to savings accounts, money market shares, bonds, and financial assets. As they do, the supply of loanable funds will increase to S_2 (Exhibit 2, frame b). In the short-run, the real interest rate will fall to r_2.

The Fed generally pumps additional money into the economy via open market operations—the purchase of bonds in the open market. This method of increasing the money supply highlights the impact of expansionary monetary policy on the real rate of interest. When the Fed purchases bonds, it bids up bond prices and creates excess reserves for the

EXHIBIT 2 • The Short-run Effects of Monetary Policy— Interest Rate Path

Here we illustrate the short-run effects of an unanticipated increase in the supply of money as transmitted via changes in interest rates. The monetary expansion creates an excess supply of money balances, which induces individuals to purchase more bonds and thereby expand the supply of loanable funds (to S_2). The real interest rate falls (to r_2), which increases aggregate demand (to AD_2). Since the effects of the monetary expansion were unanticipated, the expansion in AD leads to both an increase in current output (to Y_2) and higher prices (inflation) in the short-run.

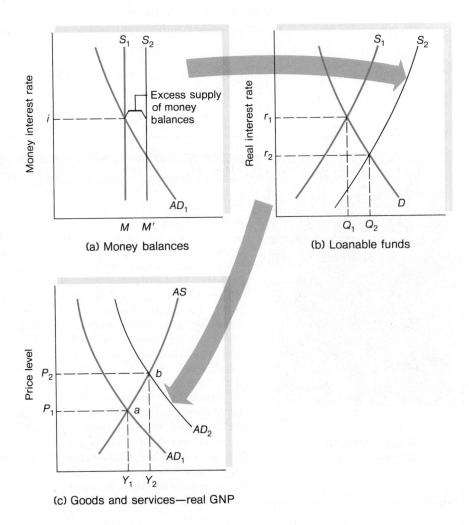

(a) Money balances

(b) Loanable funds

(c) Goods and services—real GNP

banking system. The higher bond prices directly reduce interest rates. The additional reserves will increase the incentive of banks to cut interest rates in order to extend more loans. Expansionary monetary policy thus places downward pressure on the real interest rate, at least in the short-run.

How will the lower real interest rate influence the demand for goods and services? By now the answer should be obvious. The lower real interest rate makes current investment and consumption cheaper relative to future spending. At the lower interest rate, entrepreneurs will undertake some investment projects they otherwise would have forgone. Similarly, consumers will decide to expand their purchases of automobiles and consumer durables, which can now be enjoyed with smaller monthly payments. As Exhibit 2c illustrates, aggregate demand increases to AD_2.

Since the monetary expansion was unanticipated, the increase in aggregate demand will catch many decision-makers by surprise. In the short-run, prices will rise more rapidly than costs. Profit margins will improve. Businesses will respond with an expansion in output (to Y_2). Temporarily, unemployment will recede below its natural rate.

Many economists, particularly monetarists, believe that monetary policy can also be transmitted via a more direct path. Exhibit 3 illustrates this point. Once again, an unanticipated increase in the money supply (shift from S_1 to S_2) leaves the public with an excess supply of money balances. Instead of increasing their spending exclusively or even primarily on bonds (and other saving instruments), suppose decision-makers reduce their unexpected build-up of money balances by spending more on a broad cross-section of goods and services. Households increase their spending on clothes, appliances, personal computers, automobiles and recreational activities. Businesses purchase additional machinery or add to their fixed investments. To the extent this route is chosen, there will be a direct increase in the aggregate demand for goods and services. As in the case of demand stimulus emanating from a lower real interest rate, the unanticipated increase in aggregate demand will lead to an expansion in real output (to Y_2) in the short-run.

EXHIBIT 3 • The Short-run Effects of Monetary Policy— Direct Path

Here we illustrate the direct transmission of monetary policy to the goods and services market. An unanticipated increase in the supply of money (shift to S_2, frame a) generates an excess supply of money, which causes individuals to spend more, not just on bonds, but also on goods and services directly. Aggregate demand increases. As in the case of transmission via the real interest rate, the predicted result is higher prices (inflation) and an increase in real GNP *in the short-run.*

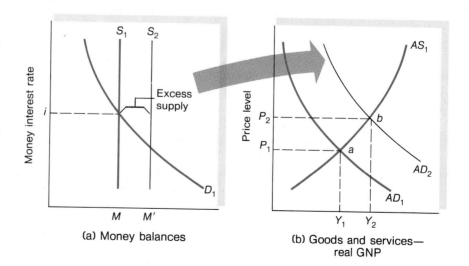

(a) Money balances

(b) Goods and services— real GNP

Modern analysis indicates that an unanticipated increase in the supply of money will lower the real interest rate and/or directly expand the demand for goods and services. As a result, aggregate demand will increase, leading to a short-run expansion in real output and employment.

How will the additional demand for goods and services affect higher prices and additional real output? While a precise answer to this question is not possible, there is good reason to believe that *in the short-run* an unanticipated increase in aggregate demand will exert its primary impact on output rather than on prices. To understand the logic of this point, it is helpful to reflect on the workings of markets when demand increases unexpectedly. Suppose you were a radio manufacturer and there was an increase in demand for your product. How would you know about it? The first indication would probably be an increase in your monthly sales. Sales, though, sometimes rise for several months and then tumble downward for a month or so. You would not want to raise prices until you were convinced that the expansion in demand for your product was permanent. An unmerited price rise would drive customers to your competitors. So, for a time at least, most businesses are likely to expand production by cutting down on maintenance time, assigning more overtime, and hiring additional workers to accommodate the strong demand and maintain their inventories.

As the strong demand persists, more and more businesses will be convinced that market conditions merit a price increase. As we discussed, though, prices initially are more likely than costs to rise rapidly. Important cost components such as lease agreements and union wage rates will be fixed in the short-run. For a time, prices will rise relative to costs. Profit margins will improve, providing an additional stimulus for production and employment. In the short-run, then, an unanticipated increase in the money supply is likely to exert its primary impact on output rather than on prices.

UNANTICIPATED RESTRICTIVE MONETARY POLICY

Restrictive Monetary Policy: A deceleration in the growth rate of the money supply.

Suppose the Fed moves toward a more **restrictive monetary policy** and reduces the money supply (or in dynamic terms, reduces its rate of growth). How would a reduction in the money supply influence our economy? To stimulate your thoughts on this topic, consider what would happen if someone, perhaps a foreign agent, destroyed half of the U.S. money stock. We simply awake one morning and find that half of the cash in our billfolds and half of the checkable deposits in our banks are gone. Ignore, for the sake of analysis, the liability of bankers and the fact that the federal government would take corrective action. Just ask yourself, "What has changed because of the drastic reduction in the money supply?" The work force is the same. Our buildings, machines, land, and other productive resources are untouched. There are no consumer durables missing. Only the money, half of yesterday's money supply, is gone.

Exhibit 4 sheds some light on the situation. To make things simple, let us assume that before the calamity, individuals and businesses were holding their desired level of money balances for current needs. The reduction in the supply of money (shift from S_1 to S_2) reduces money balances below the desired level. Excess demand is present in the money market. People will take steps designed to restore at least part of their shrunken money balances.

EXHIBIT 4 • The Short-run Effects of a Reduction in the Money Supply—The Effects are Unanticipated

A reduction in the money supply creates an excess demand for money balances. Economic agents will seek to restore their money balances by drawing on their savings, purchasing fewer bonds, and/or spending less on goods and services. As a result, aggregate demand will decline (shift to AD_2). When the reduction in aggregate demand is unanticipated, real output will decline (to Y_2) and downward pressure on prices will result.

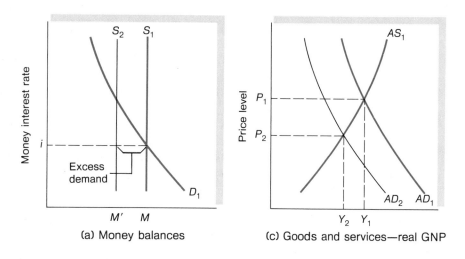

(a) Money balances

(c) Goods and services—real GNP

How do people build up their money balances? All poor, struggling college students should know the answer. They draw on past savings and cut back on current spending. As people reduce their savings and purchase fewer bonds, the supply of loanable funds will fall (relative to demand), causing the real rate of interest to increase. In turn, the higher real interest rate will induce both investors and consumers to cut back on their purchases of current goods and services. Simultaneously, others will seek to rebuild their money balances directly by spending less during the current period. Both the higher real interest rate and the direct reduction in current purchases will reduce aggregate demand (shift from AD_1 to AD_2, Exhibit 4b).

If prices and wages are perfectly flexible, as the classicists thought, the reduction in aggregate demand would not be a big problem. In the real world, however, market adjustments do not take place instantaneously. Just as unanticipated demand stimulus tends to exert its primary initial impact on output, so too, the initial effects of an unanticipated decline in aggregate demand will be on output rather than on prices.

Several months may pass before business decision-makers recognize that there has been a genuine reduction in demand for their products. Once the reduction in demand is recognized, businesses will take steps to reduce the size of rising inventories that are a side effect of weak sales. Some businesses will reduce output and layoff workers. Others will cut prices. As prices decline, profits will turn to losses since money-cost components are inflexible in the short-run. As output in the goods and services market declines, the demand for resources, including labor, will fall. Like businesses, many job seekers will fail to recognize that there has been a decline in demand for their services. They will therefore be initially reluctant to accept jobs paying a lower money wage. Anticipating that they will soon find a job at their old money wage, they will extend their employment search time and thereby increase the duration of their unemployment. Hence, neither prices nor wage rates will adjust immediately to a decline in aggregate demand accompanying an unanticipated reduction in the supply of money. In the short-run, real output will fall (to Y_2). Rising unemployment and a business slowdown will result from the restrictive monetary policy.

MONETARY POLICY IN THE LONG-RUN

In a static framework, economists sometimes equate an increase in the price level with an increase in the inflation rate. Of course, an increase in the price level does imply inflation during the period the economy moves from a lower to a higher price level. The two, though, should not be equated. Inflation is a dynamic concept—a *rate of increase* in prices, not a once-and-for-all movement to a higher price level. It is also important to distinguish between the static and dynamic with regard to the money supply. Static analysis focuses on the change in the supply of money. In a dynamic setting, though, a change in the *growth rate* of the money supply is more indicative of the direction of monetary policy.

In this section, we want to recast our analysis slightly so we can better illustrate both dynamic factors and the long-run adjustment process. Consider an economy experiencing a 3 percent growth rate of real GNP. The monetary authorities have been expanding the money supply at an annual rate of 1 percent, which is consistent with stable prices (a zero inflation rate). Since stable prices are associated with a slower rate of growth in the money supply than in the growth rate of real output, this would imply that the demand for money is decreasing. Alternatively, we could say that the velocity of money was increasing. If technological changes in financial management and various institutional changes (for example, more workers receiving a regular income, or greater use of credit cards) are consistently reducing the amount of money required to conduct a specific amount of business, the slight decline in the demand for money would be expected. Initially, the real interest rate of the economy is 3 percent. Since the inflation rate is zero, the nominal rate of interest is also equal to 3 percent. Exhibits 5 and 6 illustrate an economy initially (period 1) characterized by these conditions.

What will happen if the monetary authorities permanently increase the growth rate of the money supply from 1 percent to 6 percent annually (Exhibit 5a, beginning in period 2)? In the short-run, the expansionary monetary policy will reduce the real interest rate and stimulate aggregate demand (shift to AD_2), just as we previously explained (Exhibits 2 and 3). For a time, real output may exceed the economy's potential. However, as they confront strong demand conditions, many resource suppliers (who previously committed to long-term agreements) will wish they had anticipated the strength of demand and driven harder bargains. With the passage of time, more and more resource suppliers (including labor represented by union officials) will have the opportunity to raise prices and wages in order to rectify past mistakes. As they do so, costs will rise and profit margins will be squeezed. The higher costs will reduce aggregate supply (shift to AS_2). As the rapid monetary growth continues in subsequent periods (3, 4, 5, and so on), both AD and AS will shift upward. The price level will rise to P_{105}, P_{110}, and on to still higher levels as the money supply continues to grow more rapidly than the monetary growth rate consistent with stable prices. The rapid monetary growth leads to a continual rise in the price level—that is, a sustained inflation.

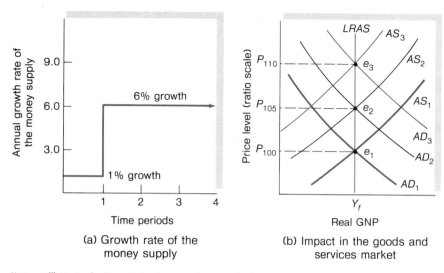

(a) Growth rate of the money supply

(b) Impact in the goods and services market

EXHIBIT 5 • The Long-run Effects of More Rapid Expansion in the Money Supply—Goods and Services Market

Here we illustrate the impact of a long-term increase in the annual growth rate of the money supply from 1 to 6 percent. Initially, prices are stable (P_{100}) when the money supply is expanding 1 percent annually. The acceleration in the growth rate of the money supply increases aggregate demand (shift to AD_2). At first, real output may expand beyond the economy's potential (Y_f). However, abnormally low unemployment and strong demand conditions will create upward pressure on wages and other resource prices, shifting aggregate supply to AS_2. Output will return to its long-run potential and the price level will increase to $P_{105}(e_2)$. If the more rapid monetary growth continues in subsequent periods, AD and AS will continue to shift upward, leading to still higher prices (e_3 and points beyond). The net result of this process is sustained inflation.

Suppose an inflation rate of 5 percent eventually emerges from the more rapid growth rate (6 percent rather than 1 percent) of the money supply. With the passage of time, more and more people will adjust their decision-making in light of the persistent 5 percent inflation. In the resource market, both buyers and sellers will eventually incorporate the expectation of the 5 percent inflation rate into long-term contracts such as collective bargaining agreements. Once that happens, resource prices and costs will rise as rapidly as prices in the goods and services market. When the inflation rate is anticipated, it will fail to either reduce real wages or improve profit margins. Unemployment will return to its natural rate.

Exhibit 6 illustrates the adjustments in the loanable funds market once borrowers and lenders expect the 5 percent inflation rate. When lenders anticipate a 5 percent annual increase in the price level, an 8 percent interest rate will be necessary to provide them with as much incentive to supply loanable funds as a 3 percent interest provided when stable prices were expected. Thus, the supply of loanable funds will shift vertically by the 5 percent expected rate of inflation. Simultaneously, borrowers who were willing to pay 3 percent interest on loans when they expected stable prices will be willing to pay 8 percent when they expect prices to increase 5 percent annually. The demand for loanable funds will therefore also increase (shift vertically) by the expected rate of inflation. Once borrowers and lenders

EXHIBIT 6 • The Long-run Effects of More Rapid Expansion in the Money Supply—Loanable Funds Market

When prices are stable, supply and demand in the loanable funds market are in balance at a real and nominal interest rate of 3 percent. If more rapid monetary expansion leads to a long-term 5 percent inflation rate (see Exhibit 5), borrowers and lenders will build the higher inflation rate into their decision-making. As a result, the nominal interest rate (*i*) will rise to 8 percent—the 3 percent real rate plus a 5 percent inflationary premium.

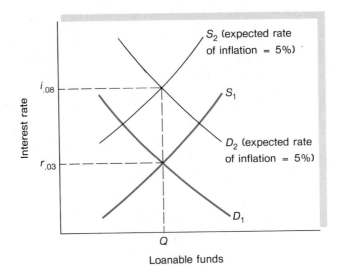

anticipate the higher (5 percent) inflation rate, the equilibrium money interest rate will rise to 8 percent. Of course, the real interest rate is equal to the money interest rate (8 percent) minus the expected rate of inflation (5 percent). In the long-run, a 3 percent real interest rate will emerge with inflation, just as it did with stable prices.[4] Inflation will fail to reduce the real interest rate in the long-run.

Modern analysis indicates that the long-run effects of rapid monetary growth differ from the short-run effects of an unanticipated move to expansionary monetary policy. In the long-run, the major consequences of rapid monetary growth are inflation and higher nominal interest rates. Rapid monetary growth will neither reduce unemployment nor stimulate real output in the long-run.

MONETARY POLICY WHEN THE EFFECTS ARE ANTICIPATED

Thus far, we have assumed that decision-makers anticipate the effects of monetary policy only *after they occur*. For example, we assumed that borrowers and lenders began to anticipate a higher inflation rate only after prices began to rise more rapidly. Similarly, resource suppliers only anticipated the inflation after its occurrence.

What if decision-makers in the market caught on to the link between expansionary monetary policy and an acceleration in the inflation rate?

---

[4]Higher rates of inflation are generally associated with an increase in the *variability* of the inflation rate. Thus, greater risk (the possibility of either a substantial gain or loss associated with a sharp change in the inflation rate) accompanies exchange in the loanable funds market when inflation rates are high. This additional risk may result in *higher* real interest rates than would prevail at lower rates of inflation. The text discussion does not introduce this consideration.

Suppose borrowers and lenders start paying attention to the money supply figures. Observing substantial increases in the money supply, they revise upward their expectation of the inflation rate. Lenders become more reluctant to supply loanable funds. Simultaneously, borrowers increase their demand for loanable funds because they also anticipate a higher rate of future inflation and they want to buy now before prices rise substantially. Under these circumstances, a reduction in supply and an increase in demand for loanable funds will quickly push up the money interest rate. If borrowers and lenders quickly and accurately forecast the future rate of inflation accompanying the monetary expansion, the real interest rate will decline only for a short period of time, if at all.

If buyers and sellers in the goods and services market also watch the money supply figures, they too may anticipate its consequences. As buyers anticipate the future inflation, they will buy now rather than later. Current aggregate demand will rise. Similarly, expecting an acceleration in the inflation rate, sellers will be reluctant to sell except at premium prices. Current aggregate supply will fall. This combination of factors will quickly push prices of goods and services upward.

Simultaneously, if buyers and sellers in the resource market believe that more rapid monetary growth will lead to a higher rate of inflation, they too will build this view into long-run contracts. Union officials will demand and employers will pay an inflationary premium for future money wages, based on their expectation of inflation. Alternatively, they may write an **escalator clause** into their collective bargaining agreements that will automatically raise money wages when the inflation transpires. If decision-makers in the resource market correctly anticipate the inflation, *real* resource prices will not decline once prices accelerate upward.

As Exhibit 7 illustrates, when individuals correctly anticipate the effects of expansionary monetary policy *prior to their occurrence,* the short-run impact of monetary policy is much like its impact in the long-run. The price level will increase, pushing up money income (P_2Y_1), but real income (Y_1)

Escalator Clause: A contractual agreement that periodically and automatically adjusts money wage rates upward as the price level rises. They are sometimes referred to as cost-of-living adjustments or COLAs.

EXHIBIT 7 • The Short-run Effects of Monetary Expansion When the Effects are Anticipated

When decision-makers fully anticipate the effects, expansionary monetary policy does not alter real output even in the short-run. Suppliers, including resource suppliers, build the expected price rise into their decisions. The anticipated inflation leads to a rise in nominal costs (and wages), causing aggregate supply to decline (shift to AS_2). While nominal wages, prices, and interest rates rise, their real counterparts are unchanged. The result: inflation without any change in real output (Y_1).

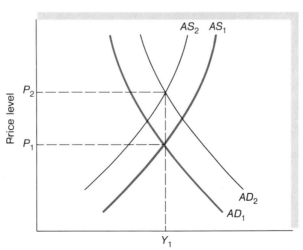

Goods and services—real GNP

will be unchanged. Nominal interest rates will rise, but real interest rates will be unchanged. Thus, when the effects of expansionary monetary policy are fully anticipated, it exerts little impact on real economic activity.

Are people likely to anticipate the effects of monetary policy? This is a topic of hot debate among economists. We will consider the topic in more detail in the next chapter. Since the effects of monetary policy differ substantially depending on whether or not they are anticipated, this is clearly a very important topic.

EFFECTS OF MONETARY POLICY— A SUMMARY

Exhibit 8 summarizes the theoretical implications of our analysis. The impact of monetary policy on major economic variables is indicated for three alternatives: (a) the short-run when the effects are unanticipated, (b) the short-run when the effects are anticipated, and (c) the long-run. Three major predictions emanate from our analysis.

1. *An unanticipated shift to a more expansionary (restrictive) monetary policy will temporarily stimulate (retard) output and employment.* As Exhibits 2 and 3 illustrate, an increase in aggregate demand emanating from an unanticipated increase in the money supply will lead to a short-run expansion in real output and employment. Conversely, as Exhibit 4 shows, an unanticipated move toward more restrictive monetary policy reduces aggregate demand and retards real output.

2. *Expansionary monetary policy will lead to inflation. Initially, the impact on prices may be small, but if rapid monetary growth persists, inflation will be the long-run result.* In the short-run, our analysis indicates that an expansion in real output may moderate the rise in prices. In the long-run, though, the

EXHIBIT 8 • Impact of Monetary Policy—A Summary			
	Short-Run, Effects Are Unanticipated	Short-Run, Effects Are Anticipated	Long-Run
Impact of expansionary monetary policy on:			
inflation rate	small increase	increases	increases
money interest rate	small increase	increases	increases
real interest rate	decreases	unchanged	unchanged
real output	increases	unchanged	unchanged
employment	increases	unchanged	unchanged
Impact of restrictive monetary policy:			
inflation rate	small decrease	decreases	decreases
money interest rate	small decrease	decreases	decreases
real interest rate	increases	unchanged	unchanged
real output	decreases	unchanged	unchanged
employment	decreases	unchanged	unchanged

major impact of expansionary monetary policy will be on prices, rather than on output.

3. *As the inflation rate rises, money interest rates will rise because both borrowers and lenders will build the expected rate of inflation into their decision-making.* As in the case of prices, monetary expansion may initially exert little upward pressure on the money interest rate. With the passage of time, though, both inflation and higher money interest rates are predictable side effects of a rapid growth rate in the money supply.

MONETARY POLICY: THE EMPIRICAL EVIDENCE

How well does our theory predict? Let us investigate the empirical evidence with regard to its consistency with our theory.

1. *Monetary Policy and Real Output.* If decision-makers, at least in the past, have failed to quickly anticipate the effects of changes in monetary policy, changes in the growth rates of the money supply and real GNP will be positively linked to each other. Monetary acceleration will lead to a rapid growth of real GNP, while a decline in the growth rate of the money supply will exert the opposite effect.

Exhibit 9 illustrates the relationship between changes in the growth rate of the money supply and real output during the last three decades. As

EXHIBIT 9 • Monetary Policy and Real Output

Periods of acceleration in the growth rate of the money supply, such as 1962–1965, 1971–1973, and 1975–1977, have generally been associated with rapid growth of real GNP. In contrast, declining growth rates in the money supply (1969–1970, 1974–1975, and 1982) have generally been associated with business contraction. Note, however, the linkage appears to have weakened during the 1980s.

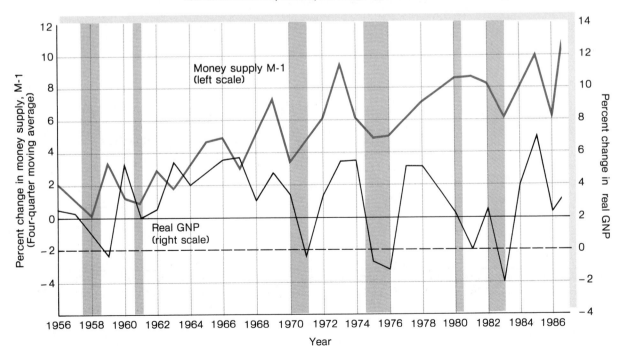

expected, the relationship is far from perfect. However, a significant positive relationship is seen. Each of the recessions (shaded periods) were preceded by monetary deceleration. On the other hand, expansionary monetary policy was present prior to and during the strong expansions of 1962–1967 and 1971–72. The recent picture is somewhat cloudier. While monetary deceleration accompanied the generally weak economy during the 1980–1982 period, the 1983–1984 recovery was much stronger than the monetary acceleration would have implied. Of course, there was a major change in fiscal policy during this period. Perhaps the reduction in tax rates contributed to the strong 1983–1984 growth. Alternatively, perhaps the recent link between monetary policy and growth has weakened in recent years because decision-makers now anticipate the effects more rapidly than was previously the case. If this is true, then the link between monetary acceleration and real GNP may be weaker in the future than has been the case in the past.

2. *Monetary Policy and Inflation.* Exhibit 10 presents a graphic picture of the relationship between monetary policy and the inflation rate for the 1956–1985 period. Our theory indicates that there may be a time lag before monetary expansion (contraction) exerts its primary impact on inflation. Thus, Exhibit 10 compares *current* money supply data with the inflation rate two years in the future.

Once again, while the linkage is far from perfect, a definite positive relationship is observable. During the 1956–1964 period, moderate mone-

EXHIBIT 10 • Changes in the Money Supply and Inflation

Here we illustrate the relationship between the rate of growth in the money supply and the annual inflation rate *two years later.* While the two are not perfectly correlated, the data do indicate that periods of monetary acceleration (for example: 1964–1968, 1970–1972, and 1976–1978) tend to be associated with an increase in the inflation rate about two years later.

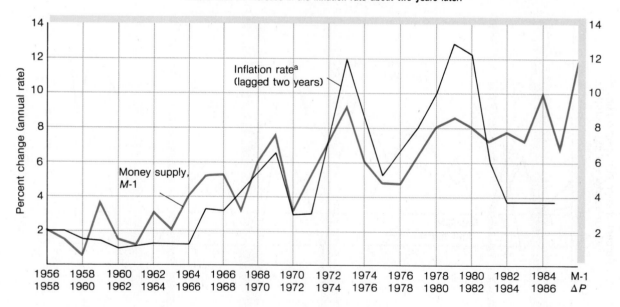

[a]As measured by CPI.

tary growth (M-1 grew at an annual rate of less than 3 percent) was associated with a low (less than 2 percent) inflation rate. The monetary acceleration of 1964–1968 was accompanied by sharply rising prices during the 1966–1970 period. Similarly, the monetary acceleration of 1971–1972 was followed by a sharply rising inflation rate during 1973–1974. Monetary acceleration during 1976–1978 was associated with a rising inflation rate during 1978–1980. Once again the relationship weakened during the 1980s. The monetary deceleration during 1981–1982 was mild, while the reduction in the inflation rate was quite sharp. The explanation of the weakening of the relationship between money, real output, and inflation is a topic of current research and debate among economists (see boxed feature).

The time series data of Exhibit 10 are consistent with the theory that expansionary monetary policy places upward pressure on prices 12 to 24 months later. Our theory, though, also indicates that the long-run impact of monetary expansion will be more predictable than its short-run effects. A major implication of our analysis is that rapid growth rates in the money supply over long periods of time will be associated with high rates of inflation.

Exhibit 11 presents data on this issue. Here we compare the rate of inflation with the growth rate of the money supply (adjusted for the nation's growth rate) for 35 countries during the 1970–1983 period. The results

EXHIBIT 11 • Money and Inflation—An International Comparison

Country (ranked according to low rate of money growth)	Average Annual Growth Rate of the Money Supply 1970–1983[a]	Average Annual Inflation Rate 1970–1983	Country (ranked according to low rate of money growth)	Average Annual Growth Rate of the Money Supply 1970–1983[a]	Average Annual Inflation Rate 1970–1983
Switzerland	3.4	4.9	United Kingdom	10.4	12.4
Norway	3.4	8.6	Spain	11.9	13.9
Singapore	3.8	5.8	Greece	12.9	14.8
Belgium	4.2	7.2	Syria	13.1	10.8
United States	4.3	7.2	Korea	15.5	13.9
Sweden	4.9	8.9	Nigeria	15.3	13.9
West Germany	5.5	5.0	Italy	15.6	14.1
Japan	5.7	7.3	Columbia	16.2	19.8
Denmark	6.0	9.3	Mexico	17.5	22.7
Canada	6.1	8.1	Turkey	23.4	27.6
Netherlands	6.4	6.6	Peru	27.6	34.2
Australia	6.4	9.9	Bolivia	30.4	31.8
New Zealand	7.6	11.9	Brazil	33.1	39.1
Honduras	7.7	7.9	Israel	33.3	45.7
India	7.7	8.2	Uruguay	34.6	44.1
France	8.1	9.6	Chile	69.1	68.1
Guatemala	9.9	9.4	Argentina	78.4	84.9

Source: United Nations, *Monthly Bulletin of Statistics* (various issues). The 35 major countries for which data were available are included.

[a]The money supply data are for the actual money supply divided by real GNP. Thus, it is the actual supply of money adjusted to reflect the country's growth rate.

illustrate that low rates of monetary growth are closely associated with low rates of inflation. The country (Switzerland) with the slowest rate of monetary growth also experienced the lowest rate of inflation. In contrast, the country (Argentina) with the highest rate of monetary growth experienced the highest inflation rate. Of 17 countries that expanded the supply of money at a single-digit rate, all but one experienced a single-digit rate of inflation. In contrast, every country that expanded the money supply at a rate of 10 percent or more experienced a double-digit inflation rate. The six countries (Bolivia, Brazil, Israel, Uruguay, Chile, and Argentina) that expanded the money supply at 30 percent or more all experienced inflation rates of 30 percent or more. Just as our theory indicates, in the long-run, inflation is closely linked with monetary expansion.

3. *Inflation and Money Interest Rates.* Exhibit 12 presents data on the inflation rate (change in CPI) and the money interest rate (the 3-month U.S. Treasury bill rate). As our theory implies, the two are closely linked. As the inflation rate rose during the 1960s, the money interest rate tracked it. During the 1970s, increases in the inflation rate (in 1973–74 and 1978–80) were associated with increases in the money rate of interest. Similarly, declines in the inflation rate during 1971–1972, 1975–1976, and 1982–1984 were all accompanied by declines in the nominal interest rate. These data provide strong evidence that, just as our theory postulates, the choices of borrowers and lenders are strongly influenced by the inflation rate.

EXHIBIT 12 • Inflation Rate and the Money Interest Rate

The expectation of inflation (a) reduces the supply and (b) increases the demand of loanable funds, causing money interest rates to rise. Note how the money rate of interest has tended to increase when the inflation rate accelerates (and decline as the inflation rate falls).

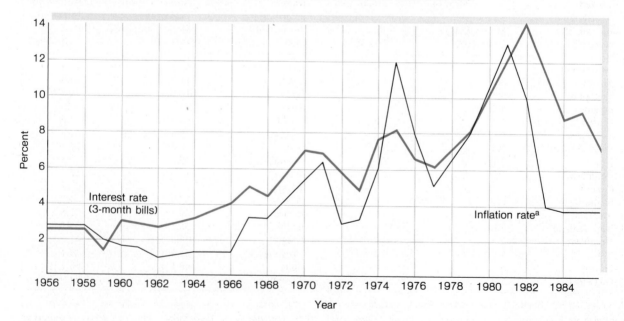

[a]As indicated by CPI.

APPLICATIONS IN ECONOMICS

"Is The Stability of Monetary Policy Breaking Down?"

As Exhibits 9 and 10 show, during the 1956–1980 period, monetary acceleration (deceleration) was closely associated with increases (decreases) in real GNP during the current period and increases (decreases) in the inflation rate 24 months later. This relationship, however, seemed to break down during the early 1980s. Only a moderate deceleration in the money supply preceded the sharp decline in the inflation rate during 1981–1983 (see Exhibit 10). Then, contrary to the predictions of several leading monetarists (including Milton Friedman), a sharp acceleration in the growth in M-1 between

mid-year 1982 and mid-year 1983 failed to re-ignite the inflation rate. As the economy rebounded from the recession of 1982, strong growth in real GNP continued during 1984 even though the growth of the money supply fell sharply.

Why did monetary policy fail to exert its usual impact in the early 1980s? Does this mean that in the future monetary policy is likely to exert a less predictable impact on output and prices? Some economists believe this is the case. Increasingly, decision-makers have become aware of the relationship between monetary policy, real

GNP, inflation, and nominal interest rates. In financial circles, weekly money supply figures are watched more closely than baseball scores. When people adjust their choices, based not only on what the Fed has done, but also on what they expect it to do in the future, the impact of monetary policy is less predictable (compare Exhibit 7 with Exhibits 2 and 3). For example, if decision-makers think a couple of months of monetary acceleration means the Fed will decelerate monetary growth in the future, they will react differently than if they believe the monetary growth is an omen of

EXHIBIT 13 • Recent Changes in the Velocity of Money

Throughout the 1960s and 1970s, the velocity of money (M-1) rose steadily. However, beginning with the financial deregulation and widespread availability of interest-earning checking accounts, the velocity of M-1 declined abruptly in the 1980s.

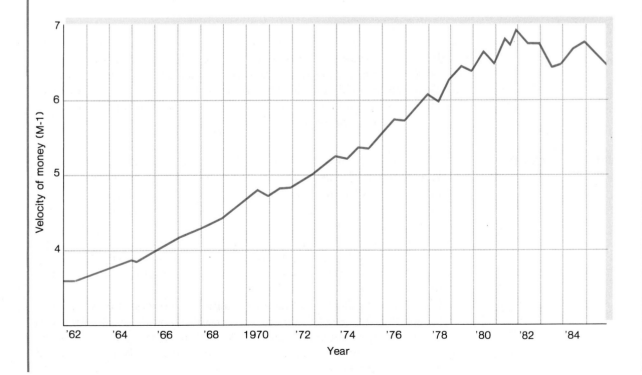

APPLICATIONS IN ECONOMICS (continued)

long-term rapid increases in the money supply. Thus, increased emphasis on the anticipated effects of monetary policy tends to weaken the link between monetary changes and other economic variables.

Other economists, particularly monetarists, argue that the weak link between the growth of the money supply, prices, and output in the 1980s is simply a temporary phenomenon related to deregulation. As we indicated in Chapter 12, deregulation has changed the nature of the measured M-1 money supply. Whereas interest-earning checking accounts were less than 5 percent of the money supply (M-1)

at the beginning of the 1980s, these funds summed to nearly one third of M-1 in early 1986 (see Exhibit 2, Chapter 12). Prior to 1980, most checking account funds did not earn interest. As a result, there was a strong incentive to transfer any temporarily idle balances into time and saving deposits that are not part of the measured money supply (M-1). This changed with the advent of deregulation and interest-earning checking accounts. Since the rate of return *differential* between interest-earning checking accounts and various types of savings deposits generally runs only about 1 percent, deregulation substantially reduced the incentive of individuals to transfer temporarily idle balances from checking accounts (that add to M-1) to savings deposits (that are excluded from M-1).

If this latter view is correct, one would expect the velocity of money to decline as deregulation reduced the opportunity cost of holding money balances (in the form of interest-earning checking deposits). As Exhibit 13 shows, the evidence is supportive of this point. While the velocity of money rose steadily throughout the 1960s and 1970s, it turned abruptly downward in the 1980s.

Does this mean that once individuals and businesses adjust fully to the new environment, a consistent link between the growth of the money supply and real output (and prices) will again emerge? This is a current topic of hot debate among economists. Since this issue is closely related to stabilization policy, it will arise again when we consider that topic in Chapter 15.

LOOKING AHEAD

Theory indicates the impact of monetary policy will be influenced by whether or not economic agents anticipate its effects. Thus far, we have said little concerning how decision-makers form expectations about the future. The next chapter will consider this important issue. Before we proceed, though, let us take a closer look at the role of monetary and fiscal policy during the Great Depression.

CHAPTER SUMMARY

1. There are three major reasons why households and businesses demand (hold) money balances. People demand money (a) in order to conduct planned transactions, (b) as a precaution against an uncertain future that may require unplanned expenditures, and (c) for speculative purposes so they can quickly respond to profit-making opportunities.

2. The quantity of money demanded is inversely related to the nominal interest rate and directly related to nominal income (GNP). The quantity of money supplied is determined by the central monetary authority (the Fed in the United States).

3. Classical economists developed the quantity theory of money that postulated that the velocity of money was constant and that real output was independent of monetary factors. According to the quantity theory, therefore, an increase in the stock of money meant only a proportional increase in prices.

APPLICATIONS IN ECONOMICS

What Caused the Great Depression?

As we previously discussed, the Great Depression exerted an enormous impact both on economic thought and on economic institutions. Prior to the Great Depression, business recessions in the United States, as well as in other countries, reversed themselves after a couple of years. The Great Depression, though, was different. Exhibit 14 presents the economic record during the period. For four successive years (1930–1933), real output fell. Unemployment soared to nearly one quarter of the work force in 1932 and 1933. Although recovery did take place during 1934–1937, the economy again fell into the depth of depression in 1938. Ten years after the catastrophe began, real GNP was virtually the same as it had been in 1929.

For years, the Great Depression was widely viewed as a failure of the market economy. In a sense that is true. The market exchange system did collapse during the 1930s. Our modern living standards—the comfortable houses, nice automobiles, permanent-press clothes, and color television sets—are largely the result of specialization, mass production, and exchange. Without an efficiently operating exchange system, production and consumption of goods and services that most of us take for granted are unattainable.

Why did the economic system break down? Analysis of the period yields some surprising answers. Armed with knowledge of how monetary and fiscal policy work, we are now in a position to understand what actually took place during the 1930s. Let us consider four important factors that contributed to the collapse of the exchange system.

1. *A sharp reduction in the supply of money during 1930–1933 reduced aggregate demand and real output.* The supply of money expanded slowly but steadily throughout the 1920s.[5] Beginning in 1930, monetary policy suddenly shifted. The supply of money declined by 6.9 percent during 1930, by 10.9 percent in 1931, and by 4.7 percent in 1932. Banks failed, and the Fed also failed to act as a lender of last resort to head off the huge decline in the supply of money. From 1929 to 1933, the quantity of money in circulation declined by 27 percent.

How will such a sharp unexpected reduction in the supply of money affect the exchange system? Our analysis indicates it will lead to reductions both in prices and in real output. As Exhibit 14 shows, prices did decline. They were 24 percent lower in 1933 than they were in 1929. Real output, though, plunged. By 1933, real GNP was 30 percent lower than the 1929 level. Changes in the purchasing power of money altered the terms of long-term contracts. During the 1930s, farmers, business people, and others who had signed long-term contracts (for example, mortgages) in the 1920s were unable to meet their fixed money commitments in an economy dominated by falling prices and wages. Bankruptcies resulted. Those trends bred fear and

	Real GNP in 1972 Dollars (billions)	Implicit GNP Deflator (1929 = 100)	Unemployment Rate	Changes in the Money Supply (M-1)
Year				
1929	315.7	100.0	3.2	+ 1.0
1930	285.6	96.8	8.7	− 6.9
1931	263.5	87.9	15.9	− 10.9
1932	227.1	78.2	23.6	− 4.7
1933	222.1	76.4	24.9	− 2.9
1934	239.1	83.0	21.7	+ 10.0
1935	260.0	84.6	20.1	+ 18.2
1936	295.5	85.0	16.9	+ 13.9
1937	310.2	89.1	14.3	+ 4.7
1938	296.7	87.0	19.0	− 1.3
1939	319.8	86.4	17.2	+ 12.1

EXHIBIT 14 • The Economic Record of the Great Depression

Source: Bureau of the Census, *The Statistical History of the United States from Colonial Times to Present* (New York: Basic Books, 1976).

[5]From 1921 through 1929, the money stock expanded at an annual rate of 2.7 percent, slightly less rapidly than the growth in the output of goods and services. Thus, the 1920s were a decade of price stability, even of slight deflation.

uncertainty, causing still more people to avoid exchanges involving long-term money commitments. Production and exchange dropped substantially. Gains previously derived from comparative advantage, specialization, and exchange were lost.[6]

2. *A large tax increase in the midst of a severe recession made a bad situation worse.* Prior to the Keynesian revolution, the dominant view was that the federal budget should be balanced. Reflecting the ongoing economic downturn, the federal budget ran a deficit in 1931 and an even larger deficit was shaping up for 1932. Assisted by the newly elected Democratic majority in the House of Representatives, the Republican Hoover administration passed the largest peacetime tax-rate increase in the history of the United States. At the bottom of the income scale, marginal tax rates were raised from 1.5 percent to 4 percent in 1932. At the top of the scale, tax rates were raised from 25 percent to 63 percent.

Our prior analysis of fiscal policy indicates the counterproductiveness of higher tax rates during a recession. Predictably, the tax increase reduced disposable income and placed still more downward pressure on aggregate demand, which had already fallen sharply in response to the monetary contraction. Simultaneously, the higher marginal tax rates reduced the incentive to earn taxable income. The restrictive fiscal policy further added to the severity of the economic decline. As Exhibit 14 shows, this is precisely what happened. As tax rates were increased in 1932, real

GNP fell by 14.8 percent. Unemployment rose from 15.9 percent in 1931 to 23.6 percent in 1932.

3. *Tariff Policy: Tariff Increases Retarded International Exchange.* Concern about low agricultural prices, an influx of imports, rising unemployment, and declining tax revenues generated public sentiment for trade restraints. Responding to this pressure, the Hoover administration pushed for a substantial increase in tariffs on a wide range of products in early 1930. The tariff legislation took effect in June of 1930. Other countries promptly responded by increasing their tariffs, further slowing the flow of goods between nations. A tariff is, of course, nothing more than a tax on exchanges between parties residing in different countries. Since the increase in tariff rates made such transactions more costly and reduced their volume, additional gains from specialization and exchange were lost.

The high tariff policy of the Hoover administration not only retarded our ability to generate output, it was also ineffective as a revenue measure. The tariff legislation increased the duty (tax) rate on imports into the United States by approximately 50 percent.[7] However, the value of the goods and services imported declined even more sharply. By 1932, the volume of imports to the United States had fallen to $2.1 billion, down from $5.9 billion in 1929. Exports declined by a similar amount. Tariff revenues fell from $602 million in 1929 to $328 million in 1932.[8] Like the monetary and fiscal policies of the era, tariff policy retarded exchange and contributed to the uncertainty of the period.

4. *The Stock Market Crash and the Business Pessimism That Followed Reduced Both Consumption and Investment Demand.* Economists gener-

ally think of the stock market as an economic thermometer. Although it may register the temperature, it is not the major cause of the fever. While historians may exaggerate the importance of the stock market crash of 1929, there is reason to believe that it was of significance. As the stock market rose substantially during the 1920s, business optimism soared. In contrast, as stock prices plummeted, beginning in October of 1929, aggregate demand fell. The falling stock prices reduced the wealth in the hands of consumers. This decline in wealth contributed to the sharp reduction in consumption expenditures in the early 1930s. In addition, the stock market crash changed the expectations of consumers and investors. Both reduced their expenditures as they became more pessimistic about the future. As spending continued to decline, unemployment rose and the situation worsened. Given the impact of both the business pessimism and the perverse policies previously discussed, a minor recession was turned into an economic debacle.

[6]For a detailed analysis of the role of monetary policy during the 1930s, see Milton Friedman and Anna J. Schwartz, *A Monetary History of the United States, 1867–1960* (Princeton: Princeton University Press, 1963), particularly the chapter entitled "The Great Contraction."

[7]The ratio of duty revenue to the value of imports on which duties were levied rose from 40.1 percent in 1929 to 59.1 percent in 1932. See U.S. Census Bureau, *The Statistical History of the United States from Colonial Times to the Present* (New York: Basic Books, 1976), p. 888.

[8]See Jude Wanniski, *The Way the World Works: How Economies Fail and Succeed* (New York: Basic Books, 1978), pp. 125–148, for additional information on the tariff policy of the period and its impact upon the economy.

APPLICATIONS IN ECONOMICS (continued)

Could It Ever Happen Again?

It is clear, with hindsight, that the Great Depression was largely a failure of macroeconomic policy. Neither economists nor politicians understood the potential destructiveness of reductions in the money supply and higher tax rates. Today that situation has changed. We have both the knowledge and the commitment to use monetary and fiscal policy in a manner at least more consistent, if not totally consistent, with economic stability.

In addition, a number of institutional changes reduce the likelihood of a repeat experience. Foremost among these is the Federal Deposit Insurance Corporation (FDIC). This government agency insures the deposits of commercial and savings banks. It provides depositors with 100 percent assurance that they will receive the money in their accounts up to the $100,000 ceiling. Since the FDIC protects the depositor, the underlying motivation for panic withdrawal of deposits is virtually eliminated. In essence, the FDIC eliminated a major source of monetary contraction and economic instability.

Today, as in the 1930s, our living standard is critically dependent on the gains from specialization and exchange. If something caused our exchange system to break down, our standard of living would plummet just as it did during the 1930s. There is no law that can guarantee we will not pursue perverse policies again. However, given our current knowledge of macroeconomics, most economists believe that the likelihood of another Great Depression is remote.

DISCUSSION

1. It is commonly held that the stock market crash caused the Great Depression. Do you think this is true? Why or why not? Why has this belief been so widely accepted?
2. Do you think our economy is "depression-proof"? Why or why not?

4. Modern economists stress that there are two channels through which monetary policy may influence the demand for goods and services: (a) an indirect path via the real interest rate and (b) a direct path through changes in spending on a broad cross-section of goods induced by an excess supply of (or demand for) money balances.

5. When monetary policy is transmitted by the interest rate, an unanticipated increase in the money supply will reduce the real interest rate and thereby cause investors and consumers to purchase more goods and services in the current period. In the short-run, the unanticipated increase in aggregate demand will expand real output, although with the passage of time more and more of the demand stimulus will be transformed into price increases. The analysis is symmetrical for an unanticipated reduction in the money supply. The restrictive policy will temporarily raise the real interest rate, reduce aggregate demand, and thereby cause a reduction in real output in the short-run.

6. Expansionary monetary policy creates an excess supply of money. In addition to buying bonds (and thereby reducing the interest rate), people may reduce their money balances by increasing their spending in several markets, including the market for goods and services. This increased spending will directly increase aggregate demand. By parallel reasoning, a reduction in the supply of money will lead to a fall in aggregate demand.

7. In the long-run, the primary impact of monetary policy will be on prices rather than on real output. When expansionary monetary policy leads to rising prices, decision-makers eventually anticipate the higher

inflation rate and build it into their choices. As this happens, money interest rates, wages, and incomes will reflect the expectation of inflation. As this happens, *real* interest rates, wages, and output will return to their long-run normal levels.

8. When the effects of expansionary monetary policy are anticipated *prior to their occurrence,* the short-run impact of an increase in the money supply is much like its impact in the long-run. Nominal prices and interest rates rise, but real output remains unchanged. Thus, theory indicates the short-run impact of monetary policy is dependent on whether or not the effects of the policy are anticipated.

9. The empirical evidence indicates that changes in monetary policy have influenced real output. Although the relationship is far from perfect, periods of monetary acceleration have been associated with rapid growth of real GNP, while monetary contraction has been associated with a slowdown in real output.

10. Both the U.S. experience and international comparisons indicate that rapid growth in the money supply is closely linked to inflation. The evidence also illustrates that inflation results in higher money interest rates.

11. Analysis of the Great Depression suggests that the depth of the economic plunge, if not its onset, was the result of perverse monetary and fiscal policies. The 27 percent reduction in the money supply between 1929 and 1933 is without parallel in United States history. It reduced aggregate demand, changed the intended real terms of the time dimension exchanges, and created enormous uncertainty. The substantial increase in tariffs (taxes on imports) in 1930 and the huge increases in tax rates in 1932 further reduced aggregate demand and the incentive to earn taxable income. Lacking understanding of monetary and fiscal tools, policy-makers followed precisely the wrong course during this period.

THE ECONOMIC WAY OF THINKING— DISCUSSION QUESTIONS

1. "One never has too much money."
   (a) Is this statement true? Explain.
   (b) Does the layperson sometimes refer to money when wealth would be more descriptive of what he or she means? Explain.

2. "Inappropriate monetary and fiscal policy was the major cause of economic instability during the 1930s, and it was the major cause of inflation in the 1970s." Evaluate this view, presenting empirical evidence to defend your position.

3. What impact will an unanticipated increase in the money supply have on the real interest rate, real output, and employment in the short-run? How will expansionary monetary policy affect the economy when the effects are widely anticipated? Why does it make a difference whether or not the effects of monetary policy are anticipated?

4. How rapidly has the money supply (M-1) grown during the last 12 months? How rapidly has the non-interest earning portion of the money supply grown during the last 12 months compared to the 1970s and the 1980–1984 period? Should the monetary authorities increase

or decrease the growth rate of the money supply during the next year? Why? (The data necessary to answer this question for the United States are available in the *Federal Reserve Bulletin.*)

5. Will a budget deficit be more expansionary if it is financed by borrowing from the Federal Reserve or from the general public? Explain.

6. Suppose that you have just been appointed Chair of the Council of Economic Advisers. Prepare a press release outlining your views on unemployment, inflation, and proper macropolicy for the next three years.

7. During the 1981–1985 period, the velocity of money (M-1) declined. Why? Has the velocity of money (M-1) continued to decline? Why do monetary policy-makers care about what happens to the velocity of money?

- Does it make any difference whether a change in macroeconomic policy is anticipated or unanticipated?

- How do individuals form expectations about what will happen in the future?

Inflation does give a stimulus ... when it starts from a condition that is noninflationary. If the inflation continues, people get adjusted to it. But when people get adjusted to it, when they expect rising prices, the mere occurrence of what has been expected is no longer stimulating.[1]

SIR JOHN R. HICKS

- Can a nation reduce its unemployment rate if it is willing to pay the price of a higher inflation rate?

- How can one explain the simultaneous occurrence of inflation and a high rate of unemployment? Is this occurrence inconsistent with economic theory?

- Can economic policy reduce the natural rate of unemployment? If so, how?

- How has the natural rate of unemployment changed in recent years? How is it likely to change during the 1990s?

14 EXPECTATIONS, INFLATION, AND UNEMPLOYMENT

People make decisions on the basis of perceptions; the perceived costs and benefits associated with choices. What individuals think is going to happen in the future is important because it affects the choices they make in the present. For example, if suppliers think the costs of producing their products are going to rise in the future, they will drive harder bargains and be more reluctant to sell at discount prices. Similarly, buyers will be more eager to buy now rather than wait until prices are higher. Our expectations about the future matter today.

Economic analysis concerns the behavior of people. In contrast with machines, people alter their choices in light of previous experience. They may be fooled from time to time, but they do learn from prior mistakes. In this chapter, we will explicitly incorporate the idea that expectations about the future influence the choices of individuals who think and learn from previous experience. We will consider alternative theories concerning how expectations are formed and investigate their implications.

Can expansionary macroeconomic policies—rapid monetary growth coupled with budget deficits, for example—reduce the unemployment rate? If so, how long can the lower unemployment rate be maintained and at what cost? Both economists and policy-makers continue to debate these questions. Expectations provide the key to the understanding of this debate. Hence, we must more fully integrate expectations into our economic way of thinking.

UNANTICIPATED AND ANTICIPATED DEMAND STIMULUS

Throughout this text, we have carefully differentiated between unanticipated and anticipated changes. Exhibit 1 illustrates why this distinction is crucial. Beginning from a position of long-run equilibrium, the impact of expansionary macropolicy is indicated under two alternative assumptions. Exhibit 1a assumes that decision-makers fail to anticipate the effects of the expansionary policies. The increase in aggregate demand therefore catches them by surprise. As we have previously discussed, unanticipated increases in aggregate demand will temporarily increase both output and employment. For a time, output will expand to a rate (Y_2) beyond the economy's long-run potential. Correspondingly, employment will expand and unemployment will recede below the economy's natural rate. In the long-run, of course, the strong demand and tight resource markets will lead to a higher price level (P_2 and beyond). Nevertheless, when the effects of expansionary policy are unanticipated, both output and employment increase in the short-run.

Exhibit 1b illustrates the impact of expansionary macroeconomic policy under the assumption that decision-makers anticipate its effects prior to their occurrence. Recognizing that expansionary policies will strengthen

---

[1]J. R. Hicks, "Monetary Theory and Keynesian Economics," in R. W. Clower (ed.), *Monetary Theory* (Harmondsworth: Penguin, 1969), p. 260.

EXHIBIT 1 • The Short-run Effects of Unanticipated Versus Anticipated Demand Stimulus Policies

When expansionary policies catch decision-makers by surprise, the increase in aggregate demand will lead to an increase in real GNP (from Y_1 to Y_2, frame a) *in the short-run.* In contrast, when suppliers correctly anticipate the inflationary impact of demand stimulus policies, nominal costs will rise, causing a decline in aggregate supply (shift $SRAS_2$, frame b). When the effects are anticipated, demand stimulus policies merely increase prices even in the short-run.

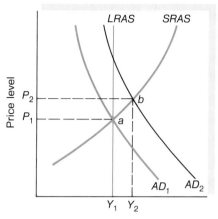

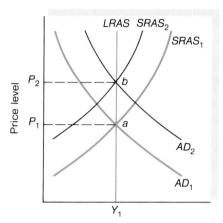

(a) Expansionary Policy Leads to Unanticipated Increase in Aggregate Demand

(b) Expansionary Policy Leads to Anticipated Increase in Aggregate Demand

demand and lead to inflation, market participants alter their choices accordingly. Agreements specifying future wage rates and resource prices immediately make allowance for an expected increase in the price level. These agreements may even include escalator clauses providing for automatic cost-of-living increases in nominal wages tied to the general price level. When buyers and sellers in the resource market fully anticipate and quickly adjust to the effects of the demand stimulus policies, wage rates and resource prices will rise as rapidly as product prices. Profit margins will fail to improve. The rising nominal costs will decrease aggregate supply, offsetting the increase in aggregate demand. The result: a higher price level, while real output is unchanged.

Thus, the impact of expansionary macroeconomic policy is dependent on whether or not decision-makers anticipate the eventual effects. If decision-makers fail to anticipate the strong demand and the increase in the price level that will eventually accompany the expansionary policy, the demand stimulus will temporarily stimulate output and reduce unemployment. In contrast, when the inflationary side effects of expansionary policies are anticipated quickly, the primary impact of the demand stimulus will be an increase in the price level (see chapter opening quote by Nobel laureate Sir John R. Hicks).

HOW ARE EXPECTATIONS FORMED?

Since expectations concerning the future exert an important impact on the effectiveness of macroeconomic policy, it is important that we understand how they are formed. There are two general theories in this area. Let us outline the essentials of each.

ADAPTIVE EXPECTATIONS

Adaptive Expectations Hypothesis: The hypothesis that economic decision-makers base their future expectations on actual outcomes observed during recent periods. For example, according to this view, the rate of inflation actually experienced during the last two or three years would be the major determinant of the expected rate of inflation for next year.

The simplest theory concerning the formulation of expectations is that people rely on the past to predict future trends. According to this theory, which economists call the **adaptive expectations hypothesis,** decision-makers believe that the best indicator of the future is what has happened in the recent past.

For example, under adaptive expectations, people would expect the price level to be stable next year if stable prices had been present during the last two or three years. Similarly, if prices had risen at an annual rate of 4 or 5 percent during the last several years, adaptive expectations implies that similar increases will be expected next year. Exhibit 2 presents a graphic illustration of the adaptive expectations hypothesis. In period 1, prices were actually stable (frame a). Therefore, on the basis of the experience of period 1, decision-makers assume that prices will be stable in period 2 (frame b). However, the actual rate of inflation in period 2 jumps to 4 percent. Continuation of the 4 percent inflation rate throughout period 2 (the periods may range from six months to several years in length) causes decision-makers to change their expectations. Relying on the experience of period 2, decision-makers anticipate 4 percent inflation in period 3. When their expectations turn out to be incorrect (the actual rate of inflation during period 3 is 8 percent), they again alter their expectations accordingly. During period 4, the actual rate of inflation declines to 4 percent, less than the expected rate. Again, decision-makers adjust their expectations as to the expected rate of inflation in period 5.

In the real world, of course, one would not expect the precise mechanical link between past occurrences and future expectations outlined in Exhibit 2. Rather than simply using the inflation rate of the immediate past period, people may use a weighted average of recent inflation rates when forming their expectations about the future. Nevertheless, the general point illustrated by Exhibit 2 remains valid.

With adaptive expectations, past experience determines the future expectations of decision-makers. If the inflation rate has been low (high) in the

EXHIBIT 2 • The Adaptive Expectations Hypothesis

According to the adaptive expectations hypothesis, the actual occurrence during the last period (or set of periods) will determine people's future expectations. The expected future rate of inflation (b) will lag behind the actual rate of inflation (a) by one period as expectations are altered over time.

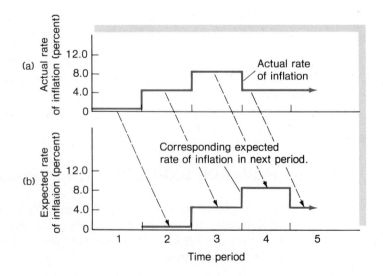

recent past, individuals will anticipate a continuation of the low (high) rate in the future.

Under adaptive expectations, forecasts of the future rate of inflation will exhibit systematic error. When the inflation rate is accelerating, decision-makers will tend to *under*estimate the future inflation rate. In contrast, when the rate of inflation is decelerating, individuals will tend to *over*estimate its future rate. We will investigate the implication of this occurrence as we proceed.

RATIONAL EXPECTATIONS

Rational Expectations Hypothesis: This viewpoint expects individuals to weigh all available evidence, including information concerning the probable effects of current and future economic policy, when they formulate their expectations about future economic events (such as the probable future inflation rate).

The idea that people form their expectations concerning what will happen in the future on all available information, including their understanding of how the economy works, is called the **rational expectations hypothesis.** Rather than merely assuming the future will be pretty much like the immediate past, people will also consider the expected effects of changes in policy. Based on their understanding of economic policy, people will alter their expectations with regard to the future when the government, for example, runs a larger deficit, expands the supply of money more rapidly, or cuts the size of its expenditures.

An important feature of the rational expectations view is its consistency with economizing behavior. When individuals economize, they will not ignore potentially valuable information—for example, the recent growth rate of the money supply—that would help them more accurately forecast the future inflation rate. According to the proponents of the rational expectations view, this is precisely the problem with adaptive expectations. The adaptive expectations theory, at least in its pure form, fails to consider the impact of current economic policy on the future direction of inflation.

Perhaps an example will help clarify the rational expectations hypothesis. Suppose prices had increased at an annual rate of 6 percent during each of the last three years. In addition, let us assume that decision-makers believe there is a relationship between the growth rate of the money supply and rising prices. Individuals note that the money stock has expanded at a 12 percent annual rate during the last nine months, up from the 7 percent rate of the past several years. According to the rational expectations hypothesis, decision-makers will integrate the recent monetary acceleration into their forecast of the future inflation rate. With rational expectations, decision-makers will project an acceleration in the inflation rate, perhaps in the 10 to 12 percent range, since they believe the future inflation rate will respond to the more rapid growth of the money supply. In contrast, the adaptive expectations hypothesis implies that people will continue to predict that the inflation rate for next period will be like it was for last period (or the last several periods).

Under rational expectations, people will consider the expected effects of macroeconomic policy when they make choices. Just as a football team alters its strategy in light of moves by an opponent, rational decision-makers alter their expectations and strategies in light of policy developments. Contrary to the views of some, the rational expectations hypothesis does not assume that people will not make forecasting errors. Rather, it implies that individuals will not continue to make the same kinds of errors. They will not continue to make systematic errors year after year.

Proponents of Rational Expectations—Robert Barro, Robert Lucas, and Thomas Sargent

OUTSTANDING ECONOMISTS

While Keynesian economists were struggling to develop policy prescriptions to reduce unemployment in the late 1960s, another group of economists was busy developing theoretical models implying that the Keynesian efforts would come to naught. The latter effort led to the theory of rational expectations, a breakthrough that vastly alters, even "revolutionizes" the way we think about macroeconomics. Foremost among the leaders of the new way of thinking about macroeconomics were Robert Barro (University of Chicago), Robert Lucas (University of Chicago), and Thomas Sargent (University of Minnesota).

While Lucas is generally given credit for the introduction of rational expectations into macroeconomics, John Muth first developed the concept in 1961. Muth, though, applied it only to commodities markets. Lucas went much further. He used the idea to analyze the operation of labor and capital markets, monetary policy, and business cycles. As the simultaneous occurrence of inflation and high unemployment led to a breakdown of the Keynesian consensus during the 1970s, Lucas' work attracted followers, particularly among youthful, mathematical economists.

Sargent and Barro have also exerted a lasting imprint on the development of rational expectations theory. Sargent, while completing his doctoral degree at Harvard (1968), first developed a discomfort with Keynesian models that assumed individuals responded passively to changes in macropolicy. Independent of Lucas, Sargent integrated the notion of rational expectations into a macroeconomic model as early as 1971. Both his theoretical and empirical work con-

tributed to the development of the rational expectations analysis during the 1970s and 1980s.

Barro also completed his doctoral degree at Harvard, just one year after Sargent. His work in the early 1970s dealt primarily with the operation of economies under conditions of extreme inflation. He is the author of a widely acclaimed intermediate text that provides a comprehensive view of new classical macroeconomics.

In the world of rational expectations, decision-makers are likened to chess players. Individuals anticipate the strategies of policy-makers and alter their behavior in light of changes in policy. As a result, the impact of the policy may differ from its intent. For example, suppose the government provides additional investment incentives (tax credits or more rapid depreciation, for example) during a recession. Initially, this strategy may stimulate investment and minimize the depth of a recession. However, once investors recognize that the government will provide tax breaks and investment subsidies during a downturn, they will delay capital improvement projects when an economy approaches a recession. The delay may permit investors to qualify for the subsidies, but it also makes the recession more likely. Once the incentives are instituted, investment will rebound more rapidly than expected as the previously delayed projects are undertaken. Once decision-makers adjust to the anticipated policy, the fluctuations of investment will be exaggerated. The policy thus fails to reduce instability.

Most of the leaders of the rational expectations school are not very interested in economic policy. This is perhaps not surprising, considering that according to the rational expectations theory, policy-makers cannot fine-tune the economy by systematically injecting stimulus during a recession and restraint during an economic boom. Rather, the proponents of rational expectations favor preannounced stable policies that remain unchanged over the business cycle. In this manner, the government can at least keep its policies from becoming a source of instability.

To date, the rational expectations view has exerted little impact on economic policy. This, however, should not be taken as evidence that the theory is unimportant. After all, nearly two decades passed after the publication of Keynes' *General Theory* before the budgetary policies of western nations began to reflect its implications.

Under rational expectations, errors will tend to be random. For example, sometimes decision-makers may overestimate the increase in the inflation rate caused by monetary expansion, and at other times they may underestimate it. However, since people learn from previous experience, they will not continue to make systematic errors.

THE PHILLIPS CURVE—THE DREAM AND THE REALITY

Phillips Curve: A curve that illustrates the relationship between the rate of change in prices (or money wages) and the rate of unemployment.

The integration of expectations into our analysis places us in a position to better understand the effects of inflation on unemployment. A curve indicating the relationship between the unemployment rate and the inflation rate is termed the **Phillips curve** after its originator, the British economist A. W. Phillips. When tracing the link between rate of change in wages (wage inflation) and unemployment over nearly a century for the United Kingdom, Phillips discovered an inverse relationship. When wage rates were rising rapidly, unemployment was low. Correspondingly, wage rates rose more slowly when the unemployment rate was high.[2]

Phillips did not draw any policy conclusions from his study, but others did. Noting that a similar inverse relationship was present between price inflation and unemployment during the post-World War II period in the United States, many economists and policy-makers concluded that demand stimulus (inflationary) policies could permanently reduce the unemployment rate. As early as 1959, Nobel prize winning economists Paul Samuelson and his MIT colleague Robert Solow argued that we could trade a little more inflation for less unemployment. Samuelson and Solow told the American Economic Association:

> In order to achieve the nonperfectionist's goal of high enough output to give us no more than 3 percent unemployment, the price index

[2]A. W. Phillips, "The Relationship between Unemployment and the Rate of Change of Money Wages in the United Kingdom, 1861–1957," *Economica*, 25 (1958), pp. 283–299.

might have to rise by as much as 4 to 5 percent per year. That much price rise [inflation] would seem to be the necessary cost of high employment and production in the years immediately ahead.[3]

Many leading economists of the 1960s concluded that a nation could reduce its unemployment rate if it was willing to pay the price of a higher rate of inflation. As Exhibit 3 indicates, even the prestigious annual Economic Report of the President argued that moderate inflation would reduce the unemployment rate. At the time, most economists thought the inflation-unemployment relationship was stable.

THE LABOR MARKET AND THE PHILLIPS CURVE UNDER ADAPTIVE EXPECTATIONS

For a while, it appeared that demand stimulus policies could reduce the unemployment rate. Both monetary and fiscal policy were more expansionary during the latter half of the 1960s. As Exhibit 3 illustrates, the unemployment rate declined while the inflation rate increased, just as the proponents of the inflation-unemployment trade-off theory anticipated.

The adaptive expectations hypothesis explains why the unemployment rate will decline when the inflation rate is accelerating due to expansionary macropolicy. Since adaptive expectations are based on past history, the theory implies the people will always *under*estimate the future inflation during a period of accelerating inflation.

When labor market participants underestimate the inflation rate, there are two reasons why inflation will stimulate employment. First, unanticipated inflation will reduce the real wages of workers employed under long-

EXHIBIT 3 • The Phillips Curve—Before the Inflation of the 1970s

This exhibit is from the *1969 Economic Report of the President,* prepared by the President's Council of Economic Advisors. The report stated that the chart "reveals a fairly close association of more rapid price increases with lower rates of unemployment." Economists refer to this link as the Phillips curve. In the 1960s, it was widely believed that policy-makers could pursue expansionary macroeconomic policies and thereby permanently reduce the unemployment rate. More recent experience has caused most economists to reject this view.

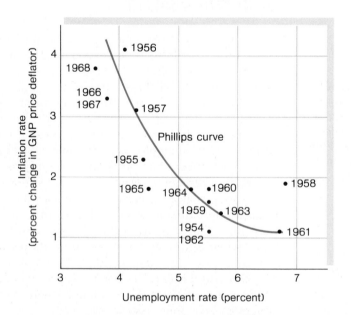

Source: *Economic Report of the President, 1969,* p. 95. The Phillips curve is fitted to the points to illustrate the relationship.

---

[3]Paul A. Samuelson and Robert Solow, "Our Menu of Policy Changes," *American Economic Review,* May 1960.

term contracts and thereby stimulate employment. Union wage contracts and other wage agreements, both explicit and implicit, often determine money wage rates over periods ranging from one to three years. Once an employer-employee agreement establishes money rates, an unexpected increase in the inflation rate will reduce the employee's real wage rate and the employer's real wage costs.

Exhibit 4 illustrates this point. Suppose that employees and employers anticipate an 8 percent inflation rate during the next year. From this, they concur on a collective bargaining agreement calling for money wages of $10 during the current year and $10.80 for the year beginning 12 months from now. If the *actual* inflation rate this year equals the 8 percent expected rate, the $10.80 money wage rate 12 months from now translates to a $10 real wage rate at today's price level. But, look what happens to the real wage rate as the inflation rate exceeds the expected rate of 8 percent. If actual inflation during the next 12 months is 12 percent, the *real wage rate* one year from now will fall to $9.64 at current prices. As Exhibit 4 shows, the higher the actual inflation rate, the lower the real wages of the employees. Unanticipated inflation tends to reduce the real wage rates of employees whose money wages are fixed by long-term contracts. At the lower real wage rate, employment will expand.

There is a second reason why underestimation of the inflation rate will tend to expand employment. When job seekers underestimate wage inflation, they will accept job offers that would otherwise be rejected if they were better informed. As we discussed in Chapter 7, a world characterized by imperfect information will lead unemployed workers to search for the job alternative that best fits their skills and preferences. Workers search because they believe their efforts will lead to a job opportunity that is superior to their best current alternative. Job search is costly, though. Job seekers incur out-of-pocket expenses (for example, the cost of transportation, telephoning, and printing of resumes) as they contact potential employers. In addition, job seekers incur the opportunity cost of potential lost earnings when

EXHIBIT 4 • Money and Real Wages Under Inflation

Actual Inflation Rate During Next 12 Months (percent) (1)	Price level one year from now (current period = 100) (2)	Money wage one year from now (expected inflation = 8%) (3)	Real Wage one year from now (current prices)[a] (4)
0	100	$10.80	$10.80
4	104	10.80	10.38
8	108	10.80	10.00
12	112	10.80	9.64
16	116	10.80	9.31
20	120	10.80	9.00

[a]Since the real wage one year from now is in terms of the current price level (equal 100), it is equal to the $10.80 money wage multiplied by 100 divided by the actual price level 12 months from now (column 2). For example, when the actual inflation rate is 12 percent, the real wage rate is equal to $10.80 × (100/112) = $9.64.

they pass up available job opportunities to search for a still better alternative. Economizing behavior indicates that workers will continue searching for employment only so long as their perceived benefits (a better eventual job) exceed their personal costs.

As inflation increases prices and money wages, information about the availability of more attractive money wage opportunities will diffuse through the economy only with the passage of time. For a while, many job seekers will be unaware of just how much inflation has improved money wage rates. They will thus accept money wage offers that would not seem as attractive if workers were fully aware of the alternatives. Misled by their underestimation of the wage inflation, job seekers reduce their search time. Correspondingly, the unemployment rate declines.

Thus, the unanticipated (or underestimated) inflation reduces the real wage rate of workers whose money wages are determined by long-term contracts and reduces the search time of job seekers. Both of these factors will expand employment and reduce the unemployment rate below its natural rate.

With adaptive expectations, though, decision-makers will eventually anticipate a higher inflation rate after it has been present for a period of time. Individuals will build the higher expected inflation rate into their decision-making. Eventually, workers and their union representatives will demand and employers will agree to money wage increases that reflect the higher current and expected future inflation wage. Similarly, job searchers will recognize that information concerning money wage rates 6, 12, or 18 months ago understates currently available money wage alternatives. So, the search time of job seekers will return to normal. Once decision-makers fully anticipate the higher rate of inflation and reflect it in their choices, the inflation will fail to depress real wage rates or reduce the search time of job seekers.[4] As this happens, employment and real output will return to their natural (long-run) rates.

Exhibit 5 illustrates what happens when one incorporates adaptive expectations into the Phillips curve analysis. Beginning from Position *A*, where stable prices are anticipated (and observed) and the natural rate of unemployment is present, expansionary policies will temporarily reduce the unemployment rate. Suppose the demand stimulus policies lead to a 4 percent inflation rate. The unemployment rate will decline to 3 percent (move to point *B*), down from the normal 5 percent rate. However, while point *B* is attainable, it is not a sustainable position. After an extended period of 4 percent inflation, decision-makers will begin to anticipate the higher rate of inflation. Workers and their union representatives will take the higher expected rate of inflation into account in their job search and collective-bargaining decision-making. Once the 4 percent rate of inflation is fully anticipated, the economy will confront a new, higher Phillips curve (the one containing points *C* and *D*). The rate of unemployment will return

---

[4]For an analysis of how rapidly these adjustments take place, see Robert J. Gordon, "Price Inertia and Policy Ineffectiveness in the United States, 1890–1980," *Journal of Political Economy*, 90, December 1982, pp. 1087–1117.

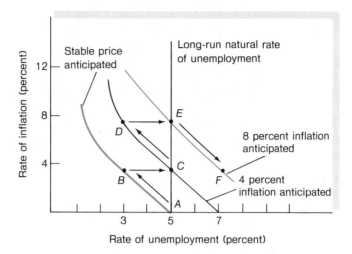

EXHIBIT 5 • Adaptive Expectations and Shifts in the Phillips Curve

With adaptive expectations, expansionary policy will temporarily reduce unemployment. When stable prices are anticipated and the unemployment rate is at its long-run natural rate (point A), demand stimulus policies will reduce unemployment while causing an increase in the inflation rate (move to B). Decision-makers, though, will eventually anticipate the higher observed inflation rate and incorporate it into their decision-making. When this happens, the Phillips curve shifts upward (to the right). Even though inflation proceeds at the expected rate (4 percent), unemployment returns to its long-run normal level (move from B to C). Once decision-makers anticipate a specific rate of inflation, policies that generate a still higher rate of inflation will be required to push the unemployment rate below its long-run, normal level. In addition, if macroplanners try to decelerate the rate of inflation, unemployment will temporarily rise above its long-run natural rate (for example, move from E to F).

to the long-run natural rate of 5 percent, even though prices will continue to rise at an annual rate of 4 percent (point C).

Once decision-makers anticipate the 4 percent rate of inflation, macroplanners can reduce the rate of unemployment only by accelerating inflation to a still higher level—that is, by providing another short-run stimulus effect. The rate of unemployment can be temporarily reduced to 3 percent only if the macroplanners are willing to tolerate 8 percent inflation (movement from C to D). Of course, once the 8 percent rate has persisted for a while, it, too, will be fully anticipated. The Phillips curve will again shift, unemployment will return to its long-run natural rate, and inflation will continue at a rate of 8 percent (point E).

Once decision-makers anticipate a higher rate of inflation (for example the 8 percent rate), what will happen if macroplanners follow a policy of deceleration to stabilize prices? When the inflation rate is declining, decision-makers will systematically *over*estimate the future inflation rate under the adaptive expectations hypothesis. Wage rates based on agreements that anticipated a continuation of the 8 percent inflation rate will be above the level consistent with full employment. Exhibit 4 illustrates this point. If the actual inflation rate falls to 4 percent when 8 percent inflation was expected, the real wages of workers will exceed the real wage present when the actual and expected rates of inflation were equal at 8 percent. The more the actual inflation rate falls short of the expected rate, the higher the real wages of workers. As real wages (and costs) rise via this method, employment will decline. Similarly, the search time of job seekers will be longer when they overestimate the impact of inflation on money wage rates. Unaware that the attractive money wage offers they seek are unavailable, job hunters will lengthen their job search. In the short-run, rising unemployment will be a side effect of the higher real wages and more lengthy job searches.

As Exhibit 5 illustrates, with adaptive expectations, once a high (8 percent) inflation rate is anticipated by decision-makers, a shift to a more restrictive policy designed to decelerate the inflation rate will cause abnormally high unemployment (the move from E to F) and economic recession. The abnormally high unemployment rate will continue until a lower rate of inflation induces decision-makers to alter their inflationary expectations downward and revise long-term contracts accordingly.

We can now summarize the implications of adaptive expectations for the Phillips curve. Under adaptive expectations, decision-makers will underestimate the future inflation rate when the rate is rising and overestimate it when the inflation rate is falling. As the result of this systematic pattern, a shift to a more expansionary policy will temporarily reduce the unemployment rate, while a move to a more restrictive policy will temporarily increase the unemployment rate. As an inflation rate persists over time, decision-makers will eventually anticipate it and unemployment will return to its natural rate. There is no long-run (permanent) trade-off between inflation and unemployment under adaptive expectations.

THE LABOR MARKET AND THE PHILLIPS CURVE UNDER RATIONAL EXPECTATIONS

What difference does it make if we assume that expectations are formed rationally, rather than adaptively? In a world of rational expectations, individuals anticipate the effects of policy changes and adjust their actions accordingly. For example, if people see a surge in the money supply or a tax cut coming, they will adjust their expectations in light of the shift toward expansionary policy. Anticipating the strong future demand, workers and union representatives will immediately press for higher wages and/or inclusion of cost-of-living provisions to prevent the erosion of their real wages by inflation. Business firms, also anticipating the increase in demand, will consent to the demands of labor, but they will also raise prices. By the time the demand stimulus arrives, it will have already been counteracted by higher money wages, costs, and product prices.[5] Rather than increasing real output and employment as intended, the demand stimulus merely leads to higher prices since it was fully anticipated by decision-makers (see Exhibit 1b).

Exhibit 6 illustrates the impact of expansionary policy on the Phillips curve when expectations are rational. Suppose an economy is initially at point A, where a 4 percent inflation rate is both observed and expected. Since the actual and expected inflation rates are equal, the long-run natural rate of unemployment is initially observed. Now, suppose policy-makers shift to a more expansionary policy; a demand stimulus policy consistent

[5]As we discussed in the last chapter, expansionary monetary policy will also increase the expected rate of inflation and lead to a higher money interest rate in the loanable funds markets. The rational expectations hypothesis also implies that money interest rates will rise quickly in response to expansionary monetary policy.

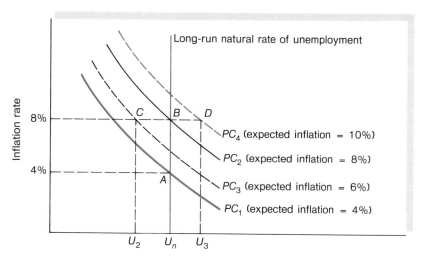

EXHIBIT 6 • Expansionary Policy with Rational Expectations

Initially, the actual and expected rates of inflation are equal at 4 percent and unemployment is equal to the economy's natural rate (point *A*). Policy-makers try to reduce unemployment by shifting to a more expansionary macropolicy consistent with an 8 percent inflationary rate. Proponents of rational explanations argue that the outcome is unpredictable. If people accurately anticipate the inflationary impact of the more expansionary course, the inflation rate will rise while unemployment remains unchanged (shift from *A* to *B*). On the other hand, if people underestimate the future inflation, unemployment will temporarily fall (as illustrated by shift from *A* to *C*). In contrast, if individuals overestimate the actual increase in the inflation rate, unemployment will rise temporarily above its long-run natural rate (shift from *A* to *D*).

with an 8 percent rate of inflation. With rational expectations, the Phillips curve will immediately shift upward as decision-makers anticipate an acceleration in the inflation rate due to the more expansionary macropolicy. If decision-makers correctly forecast the rise (to 8 percent) in the inflation rate, short-run Phillips curve PC_2 will result. Even though the inflation rate increases to 8 percent (shift from *A* to *B*), unemployment remains at its long-run natural rate.

Of course, rational expectations do not imply that decision-makers are always right. People may either underestimate or overestimate the inflationary effects of the demand stimulus. When they *under*estimate the inflationary effects, the actual inflation rate will temporarily exceed the expected rate. Suppose that even though the actual inflation rate rises to 8 percent, decision-makers only anticipate an increase to 6 percent. When this is the case, the short-run Phillips curve (PC_3, Exhibit 6) will shift out by a lesser amount than if the increase in inflation had been accurately forecast. Since individuals do not fully build the higher (8 percent) inflation rate into their decision-making, the natural unemployment rate declines to U_2 in the short-run (move from *A* to *C*).

In contrast, when individuals *over*estimate the increase in inflation, the natural unemployment rate will temporarily increase. For example, if decision-makers expect the inflation rate to rise to 10 percent while the expansionary policies only generate an increase to 8 percent, the short-run Phillips curve will shift by a larger amount (PC_4, Exhibit 6) than if the increase in inflation had been correctly forecast. In the short-run, unemployment will rise above its long-run normal rate (move from A to D).

How can policy-makers know whether rational decision-makers will over- or underestimate the effects of a policy change? According to the proponents of rational expectations, they cannot. If the errors of decision-makers are random, as the rational expectation theory implies, people will be as likely to overestimate as underestimate the inflationary impact of demand stimulus policies. Under rational expectations, then, the impact of expansionary policy on real output and employment is unpredictable, even in the short-run. If decision-makers accurately anticipate the inflationary impact of expansionary policy, the unemployment rate will remain unchanged even though the inflation rate accelerates. However, if they underestimate the future inflation impact, the unemployment rate will temporarily decline. Conversely, the unemployment rate will temporarily rise if they overestimate the inflationary impact of the policy.

The rational expectations hypothesis indicates that it will be extremely difficult for policy-makers to use demand stimulus policies to reduce the unemployment rate. Such a strategy is effective, even temporarily, only when it catches people by surprise. However, if policy-makers follow a systematic strategy, such as persistent demand stimulus or even countercyclical demand stimulus, rational human beings will catch on to the pattern. Widely anticipated policy moves will fail to exert the intended effect.

The policy implications of rational expectations are clear. The best policies are preannounced, stable policies (for example, steady growth of the money supply and a balanced federal budget). Macroeconomic policy should be long-term and changes should be weighed very carefully. Policy should not attempt to fine-tune the economy. Efforts to do so will only contribute to economic uncertainty.

On the positive side, the rational expectations hypothesis indicates that a move from inflation to stable prices can be achieved more easily than adaptive expectations imply. If policy-makers shift to a more restrictive course *and* convince the public they are going to stick to it until stable prices are achieved, the rational expectations hypothesis implies that the expected rate of inflation will decline quickly (shifting the short-run Phillips curve toward the origin). As the expectation of inflation declines, money wage rates will be scaled back. Money interest rates will fall. If a restrictive policy is really credible, the rational expectations hypothesis implies that the inflation rate can be decelerated without the economy going through a prolonged period of recession and high unemployment—a situation that is implied by the adaptive expectations hypothesis. Credibility that policy-makers will "stay the course" until inflation is brought under control, though, is absolutely essential.[6] If market participants lack confidence in the long-term anti-inflationary commitment of policy-makers, they will reduce their expectations for the future rate of inflation slowly even if current

---

[6]For evidence that even hyperinflations can be brought under control quickly (with little loss of output) when credibility is present, see Thomas Sargent, "The Ends of Four Big Inflations," in Robert E. Hall, ed. *Inflation: Causes and Effects* (Chicago: University of Chicago Press for the National Bureau of Economic Research, 1982), pp. 41–98.

policy is restrictive. When policy-makers have a past history of policy reversals and saying one thing while doing another, it will be difficult for them to establish credibility. Proponents of rational expectations are thus not surprised that restrictive policies have often led to recession and abnormally high unemployment.

EXPECTATIONS AND THE MODERN VIEW OF THE PHILLIPS CURVE

Expectations substantially alter the naive Phillips curve view of the 1960s. With regard to the Phillips curve, two major points follow from modern analysis.

1. *Demand stimulus will lead to inflation without permanently reducing the unemployment rate. Once people fully anticipate the inflationary side effects of expansionary policies, the short-run Phillips curve shifts upward to the right and employment returns to its natural rate. However, in the long-run, inflation will not reduce the unemployment rate.* Under adaptive expectations, higher inflation rates are anticipated only after they are observed for a period of time. With adaptive expectations, then, accelerating rates of inflation will temporarily reduce unemployment. With rational expectations, decision-makers respond to expansionary policies by immediately adjusting their inflationary expectations upward. So, expansionary policies fail to even temporarily reduce the unemployment rate when expectations are rational. In the long-run, though, the implications of adaptive and rational expectations are identical— persistent expansionary policy will lead to inflation without permanently reducing the unemployment rate. Neither the adaptive nor the rational expectations hypotheses indicate that expansionary policies can sustain unemployment below its natural rate.

2. *It is the difference between actual and expected rates of inflation that influences unemployment, not the magnitude of inflation as some economists previously thought.* Exhibit 7 illustrates this point by recasting the Phillips curve within

EXHIBIT 7 • The Modern Expectational Phillips Curve

It is the *differences* between the actual and expected rates of inflation that influence the unemployment rate, not the observed rate as the naive Phillips curve analysis implied. When decision-makers under- (over-) estimate the inflation rate, unemployment will fall below (rise above) the natural rate. When accurately anticipated, however, even high rates of inflation will fail to reduce unemployment below the natural rate.

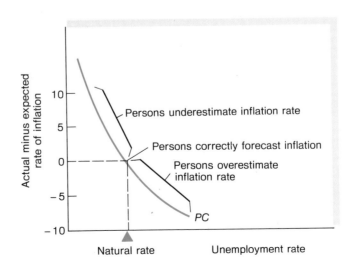

the expectations framework. When people underestimate the actual rate of inflation, abnormally low unemployment will occur. Conversely, when decision-makers expect a higher rate of inflation than what actually occurs, unemployment will rise above its natural rate. Equal changes in the actual and expected inflation rates, though, will fail to reduce the unemployment rate. If actual inflation rates of 5 percent, 10 percent, 20 percent, or even higher are *accurately anticipated*, they will fail to reduce unemployment below its natural rate.[7]

THE INFLATION/ UNEMPLOYMENT RECORD, 1961–1985

The U.S. experience during the 1960s and 1970s can now be more clearly understood. During the nearly 20 years of low inflation (and moderate monetary and fiscal policy) following World War II, decision-makers grew accustomed to relative price stability. Against this background, the *expected* rate of inflation was also low. As a result, the shift toward more expansionary policies in the mid-1960s caught people by surprise.[8] Therefore, as Exhibit 3 shows, these policies initially reduced the unemployment rate.

Contrary to the popular view of the 1960s, though, the abnormally low unemployment did not last. Exhibit 8 makes this point clear. Exhibit 8 is an updated version of Exhibit 3. Just as our theory predicts, the inflation-unemployment conditions worsened substantially as the expansionary policy persisted. The Phillips curve (PC_2) consistent with the 1970–1973 data was well to the right of PC_1. During the 1974–1982 period, still higher rates of inflation were observed. As inflation rates in the 6 to 10 percent range became commonplace in the latter half of the 1970s, the Phillips curve once again shifted upward to PC_3. The data of Exhibit 8 are highly consistent with the view that higher inflation rates fail to reduce the unemployment rate in the long-run.

THE ADAPTIVE VERSUS RATIONAL EXPECTATIONS DEBATE

Are expectations determined adaptively or rationally? This question is hotly debated among economists. The rational expectations proponents charge that the adaptive expectation hypothesis is naive. They find it difficult to accept the notion that individuals look only at past price changes while ignoring information on variables (for example, changes in the money supply, interest rates, and exchange rates) that play an important role in the actual generation of inflation.

---

[7]Empirically, higher rates of inflation are generally associated with greater *variability* in the inflation rate. Erratic variability increases economic uncertainty. It is likely to inhibit business activity, reduce the volume of mutually advantageous exchange, and cause the level of employment to fall. Thus, higher, more variable inflation rates may actually increase the natural rate of unemployment.

[8]The following data are indicative of the shift toward more expansionary macroeconomic policies beginning in the mid-1960s. Between 1965 and 1980, the money supply grew at an annual rate of 6.3 percent, compared to only 2.5 percent during the previous 15 years. Similarly, perpetual federal deficits replaced balanced budgets. During the 1950–65 period, there were 8 budget deficits and 7 surpluses. On average, the federal budget was approximately in balance during the 15 year period. During the 1965–1980 period, however, there was only one year of budget surplus, and annual deficits averaged 1.5 percent of GNP.

EXHIBIT 8 • Inflation and Real World Shifts in the Phillips Curve

The 1982 report of the Council of Economic Advisors (CEA) contained this unemployment-inflation rate chart. While the 1961–1969 data mapped Phillips curve PC_1, as demand stimulus policies led to higher inflation rates, the Phillips curve shifted out to PC_2 (for the 1970–73 period) and PC_3 (for the 1974–1983 period). In contrast with the 1969 CEA Report (see Exhibit 3), the 1982 Report stated:

> Nothing in Phillips' works or in subsequent studies showed that higher inflation was associated with sustainable lower unemployment, and nothing in economic theory gave reason to believe that the relationship uncovered by Phillips was a dependable basis for policies designed to accept more inflation or less unemployment.

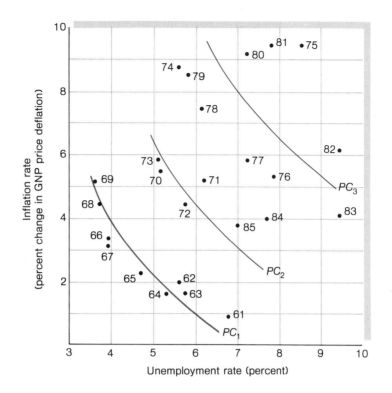

Source: *Economic Report of the President, 1982*, p. 51. The Phillips curves have been fitted and the 1982–1985 data added to the chart.

The advocates of adaptive expectations reply that the rational expectations theory implies that individuals possess an inordinate amount of information about highly complex issues. They note that the average person neither keeps up with the latest moves of the Fed nor forecasts changes in the Federal budget. The proponents of adaptive expectations charge that it is unrealistic to assume that most people will (a) develop reliable theories about the operation of a highly complex economy, (b) monitor the necessary policy variables, and (c) consistently make the implied adjustments to changes in macropolicy. They believe most people will find a simple rule of thumb such as "inflation next year will be about the same as the recent past" to be both sensible and "rational."

The proponents of rational expectations are unmoved by this argument. They believe that it overlooks several facts. After all, business firms and labor unions hire specialists to make forecasts about the future. Predictions made by prominent economists are often widely disseminated via television news and daily newspapers. Because of this, even relatively uninformed citizens, whether they realize it or not, develop a view on the expected rate of inflation.

The proponents of adaptive expectations also emphasize that long-term contracts constrain the responses of decision-makers. For example, if long-term contracts specifying nominal wages and prices cover a longer time period than it takes the monetary authorities to alter the direction of monetary policy, the authorities are in a position to reduce real wages and thereby stimulate employment.

Advocates of rational expectations respond by pointing out that the nature of contracts is influenced by macroeconomic policy. If the monetary authorities seek to exploit long-term contracts, individuals will predictably respond by including cost-of-living provisions, choosing contracts of shorter duration, and permitting renegotiation at various time intervals. According to the proponents of rational expectations, then, if expansionary policies seek to reduce *real* wages and costs, they will only induce decision-makers to alter the nature of long-term contracts. The growth of collective bargaining agreements containing escalator clauses (provisions for automatic money wage increases as the price level rises) during the 1970s is consistent with this view. As inflation accelerated upward, the number of collective bargaining agreements providing for cost-of-living wage adjustments rose from 20 percent in 1965 to nearly 70 percent in the late 1970s.

The proponents of adaptive expectations argue that the past performance of the economy is supportive of their view. For example, more rapid growth of the money supply has generally been associated with an expansion in real GNP, followed a year or two later by increases in the inflation rate. Similarly, deceleration in monetary growth has consistently led to a recession, prior to any significant reduction in the inflation rate (see Exhibits 9 and 10, Chapter 13). These findings indicate that people alter their expectations slowly as the adaptive expectations theory implies, not rapidly as suggested by the rational expectations theory.

The proponents of rational expectations remain unconvinced. They point out that a rapid change in the public's expectations in response to a policy change is dependent on confidence that the change is both real and long-term. In contrast, even rational expectations theory implies that people will respond cautiously to an *apparent change* when policy-makers have a past history of policy reversals. When the credibility of policy-makers is low, a gradual change in expectations in response to an apparent change in direction is the expected behavior. Thus, advocates of rational expectations do not believe that past evidence indicating expectations have often changed slowly is damaging to their theory.

Of course, the adaptive versus rational expectations controversy is important because the two theories have different implications for the short-run Phillips curve. We must not forget, however, that the implications of the two theories for the *long-run* Phillips curve are essentially the same. Both theories imply that expansionary macropolicy will lead to inflation without *permanently* reducing unemployment below its normal, long-run rate.

MICROECONOMICS AND REDUCING THE NATURAL RATE OF UNEMPLOYMENT

The integration of expectations into our analysis highlights the difficulties involved in the use of monetary and fiscal policy to promote employment. Can other methods be used to reduce the unemployment rate? In recent years, economists have turned to microeconomics as a means of addressing the traditional macroeconomic problem of high unemployment. The microeconomics approach to employment focuses on how the economy's natural rate of unemployment might be reduced. Remember, the natural rate of unemployment is not immutable. Among other things, it reflects the incentive structure emanating from the economy's institutional arrangements. If changes in that incentive structure could improve the efficiency of job search and remove barriers to employment, the economy's natural rate of unemployment would decline. In terms of the Phillips curve, the long-run (vertical) Phillips curve would shift to the left.

What kinds of institutional changes would be most likely to reduce the natural rate of unemployment? We will consider three changes that have been widely discussed.

REVISING THE UNEMPLOYMENT COMPENSATION SYSTEM

The unemployment compensation system was designed to reduce the hardships of unemployment. As desirable as this program is from a humanitarian standpoint, it diminishes the opportunity cost of job search, leisure, nonproductive activities, and continued unemployment. The conflict between high benefit levels and low rates of unemployment should therefore not be surprising.

The current unemployment compensation system causes the rate of unemployment to rise for two reasons. First, it greatly reduces, and in some cases virtually eliminates, the personal cost of unemployment. The benefits in most states provide covered unemployed workers with payments of 50 to 60 percent of their *previous gross earnings*. Unemployment benefits are not subject to payroll taxes (and in some cases, income taxes). In addition, unemployed workers may also qualify for other transfer benefits such as food stamps, Medicaid, and school lunch subsidies for their children. It is not unusual, then, for the benefit package of a covered unemployed worker to replace 75 percent or more of previous net earnings. Clearly, benefit levels in this range substantially reduce the incentive of individuals to search diligently for jobs and to accept employment at marginally lower wages prior to the exhaustion of their benefits.

Second, unemployment compensation acts as a subsidy to employers who offer unstable or seasonal employment opportunities. Employees would be more reluctant to work for such employers (for example, northern contractors who generally layoff workers in the winter) were it not for the fact that these employees can supplement their earnings with unemployment compensation benefits during layoffs. The system makes seasonal, temporary, and casual employment opportunities more attractive than would otherwise be the case. In essence, it encourages employers to adopt production methods and work rules that rely extensively on temporary employees and supplementary layoff benefits.

There is little doubt that the current unemployment compensation system increases the natural rate of unemployment and thereby retards aggregate supply. Most researchers in the area believe that the long-run rate of unemployment is between 0.5 and 1.0 percent higher than it would be if the negative employment effects of the system could be eliminated. Since more than 80 percent of the work force is now covered by the program, compared to 56 percent in 1960, the impact of the system on the natural rate of unemployment has probably been increasing.

How can the unemployment compensation system be reformed without undercutting the original humanitarian objectives of the program? Several policy alternatives exist. Firms that regularly terminate and lay off a high percentage of their work force might be charged a payroll tax that more accurately reflects the cost of employment instability. (The current system performs this function imperfectly.) After a specified period of time, three months, for example, unemployment compensation recipients might be required to accept available jobs (including public-sector employment) that provide wage rates equal to their unemployment compensation benefits. Alternatively, recipients' benefits might be gradually reduced as they engaged in more lengthy periods of job search and unemployment. This would reduce the incentive of individuals to wait until their benefits run out (generally 26 weeks) before accepting employment. The benefit levels of covered employees might be directly related to the stability of their work history. Conversely, a higher payroll tax rate could be imposed on workers with highly unstable work histories. Each of these proposals would increase the incentive of employers to offer stable employment and job searchers to seek out and accept employment more quickly.

REFORMING THE MINIMUM WAGE

Despite the good intentions of most of their supporters, minimum wage laws reduce the employment prospects of low-skilled, inexperienced workers. Many youthful workers fall into this category. As in the case of other price floors, minimum wages lead to an excess supply. By mandating artificially high wage rates for jobs requiring few skills, the minimum wage reduces the employment opportunities available to low-skill workers.[9]

The adverse impact of the minimum wage on the on-the-job training opportunities available to low-skill workers is also important. The legislation often makes it unfeasible for an employer to (a) provide training to inexperienced workers and (b) pay the legal minimum wage at the same time. Thus, there are few (temporarily) low-paying jobs offering a combination of informal (or formal) training and skill-building experience. This makes it difficult for low-skill workers to acquire the training and experience necessary to move up to better, higher-paying jobs.

Several proposals have been suggested to minimize these negative effects. Some economists favor abolition of the minimum wage. Others would exempt teenagers from the legislation's coverage. Still others would exempt long-term unemployed workers from the legislation. In each case, the advocates argue that the wages of low-skilled workers would settle at a market equilibrium, and the long-run employment and training opportunities available to such workers would improve.

PROVIDING TRAINING OPPORTUNITIES

Unemployment may result from mismatches between the requirements of available jobs and the skills of potential workers. Many economists believe that programs designed to improve the basic skills of workers and facilitate

[9]For additional information on this topic, see Charles Brown, Curtis Gilroy, and Andrew Cohen, "The Effect of Minimum Wage on Employment and Unemployment," *Journal of Economic Literature*, 20, June 1982, pp. 487–528.

Youth Work Scholarship:
A proposed scholarship
providing subsidies to
younger workers who
maintain jobs. Some schol-
arships would limit the
subsidies to employment
that offered on-the-job
training.

the development of new skills could reduce the natural rate of unemployment. Of course, improvement in our elementary and secondary educational system would be a step in that direction. Others believe that a vocational training loan program, similar in design to present college loan programs, would assist low and middle-income youths develop technical skills. Martin Feldstein, chairman of the Council of Economic Advisors under President Reagan, has suggested that we provide youthful workers, those under 25 years of age, for example, with a **youth work scholarship.** This plan would offer subsidies for technical training to young people who did not go on to college. Feldstein's plan would reward youthful workers for continuous employment and the acquisition of craft, clerical, operative, and perhaps even managerial skills.

The long-run goal of training programs is to improve the quality and flexibility of the labor force. Accomplishment of this objective would lead to a lower natural rate of unemployment.

DEMOGRAPHICS AND THE NATURAL RATE OF UNEMPLOYMENT

Compared to their elders, youthful workers are more likely to switch back and forth between the labor force and school. Even after they permanently enter the labor force, youthful workers are more likely to switch jobs as they search for a career path. Because of this, younger workers historically experience higher unemployment rates. In fact, the unemployment rate of persons under age 25 has typically run three times or more the rate for workers age 35 and over. For people age 25–34, the unemployment rate has generally been at least one and one-half times the rate for their older counterparts (see Exhibit 9 for 1980 data).

EXHIBIT 9 • Demographics and the Natural Rate of Unemployment, 1958–1995

Since younger workers have less stable employment patterns, the natural rate of unemployment rises when they comprise a larger share of the labor force. This was the case during the 1958–1980 period. During the next decade, however, youthful workers will become a smaller proportion of the labor force. This will reduce the natural rate of unemployment during the 1990s.

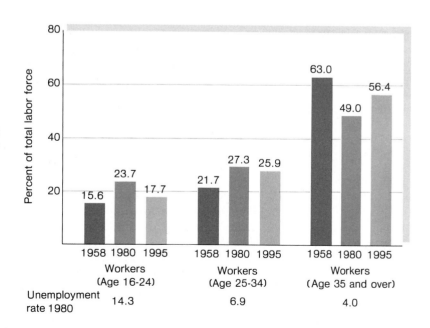

Since the employment pattern of youthful workers is less stable, the natural rate of unemployment rises as these workers make up a larger share of the labor force. As Exhibit 9 shows, this is precisely what happened during the 1958–1980 period. As those born during the "baby boom" following World War II entered the work force during the 1960s and 1970s, the labor force grew rapidly and became progressively younger. In 1958, workers age 16 to 24 constituted only 15.6 percent of the labor force. By 1980, nearly one out of every four (23.7 percent) labor force participants was in this age group. Similarly, young adults age 25 to 34 also increased as a proportion of the work force between 1958 and 1980. In contrast, workers over age 35 were a shrinking proportion of the labor force during the 1958–1980 period. As the youthful segments of the labor force grew rapidly, the natural rate of unemployment rose. Research in this area indicates that the natural rate of unemployment was between 0.5 percent and 1.5 percent higher in 1980 than in 1958 as a result of this factor. Obviously, it has contributed to the high unemployment rates of recent years.

However, this adverse demographic factor is now reversing itself. By 1995, people age 16–24 are projected to be 17.7 percent of the work force, substantially lower than the 1980 figure. Conversely, projections indicate that workers age 35 and over will comprise 56.4 percent of the labor force in 1995, up from 49 percent in 1980 (Exhibit 9). Economic theory indicates that this maturing of the U.S. work force during the next decade will reduce the natural rate of unemployment.

LOOKING AHEAD

Now that we have integrated expectations into our analysis, we are prepared to take a closer look at the potential of macroeconomic policy as a stabilization tool. The next chapter focuses on stabilization policy and related issues.

CHAPTER SUMMARY

1. The impact of demand stimulus policies is dependent on whether or not the effects are anticipated. When the effects are unanticipated, an increase in aggregate demand will temporarily expand real GNP beyond the economy's long-run output potential. In contrast, when decision-makers correctly anticipate the effects of expansionary policy, real output will remain unchanged even though the price level increases.

2. There are two major theories as to how expectations are formed: (a) the adaptive expectations hypothesis and (b) the rational expectations hypothesis.

3. According to the adaptive expectations hypothesis, individuals base their expectations for the future on observations of the recent past. Expectations for the future will lag behind observed changes.

4. The rational expectations hypothesis assumes that people use all pertinent information, including data on the conduct of current policy, when formulating their expectations about the future. While decision-makers make forecasting errors under rational expectations, the errors are not systematic. That is, they are equally likely to either overestimate or underestimate the future direction of an economic variable.

5. The Phillips curve indicates the relationship between the unemployment rate and inflation rate. Prior to the 1970s, there was a widespread belief that inflation lowered the rate of unemployment.

6. Integrating expectations into macroeconomics makes it clear that the alleged trade-off between unemployment and inflation is unstable. With adaptive expectations, expansionary policies will lead to a *short-run* trade-off of lower unemployment for an acceleration in the inflation rate. Individuals, though, will eventually come to expect the higher inflation rate and alter their decisions accordingly. This will cause unemployment to return to the natural rate.

7. With rational expectations, there is no consistent unemployment-inflation trade-off even in the short-run. The impact of expansionary macropolicy is unpredictable. If decision-makers accurately forecast the inflationary effects, expansionary policies will cause inflation while leaving the unemployment rate unchanged. However, if expansionary policy leads to an increase in inflation that exceeds (is less than) the expected increase, unemployment will temporarily fall below (rise above) its long-run normal level.

8. Contrary to the expectations of the 1960s, expansionary policy during the post-1965 period did not consistently reduce the unemployment rate. As successively higher inflation rates were observed (and anticipated) during the 1970s, the unemployment-inflation trade-off worsened.

9. In the long-run, there is no evidence that inflationary policies can reduce the unemployment rate—that inflation can be "traded off" for unemployment. Both adaptive and rational expectations theories imply that the long-run Phillips curve is vertical at the natural rate of unemployment.

10. The validity of the adaptive versus rational expectations hypotheses is hotly debated among economists. The proponents of adaptive expectations believe that the expectations used in real-world decision-making are typically based on a simple rule of thumb (the future rate of inflation will be similar to the recent past). They charge that the rational expectations hypothesis implies that people possess an unrealistic amount of knowledge about how the economy works. The proponents of rational expectations counter that it is naive to believe that decision-makers ignore information concerning how inflation is actually generated. They argue that relatively uninformed people will consult specialists and alter the nature of long-term contracts and thereby reduce the impact of inflation on real economic variables.

11. In recent years, economists have given increased attention to the importance of incentives in the determination of the natural rate of unemployment. Many economists believe that the unemployment compensation system, minimum wage legislation, and inadequate educational and training programs contribute to the high current rate of unemployment. Reform in these areas could lower the natural rate of unemployment.

12. During the 1960s and 1970s, rapid growth in the number of youthful labor force participants increased the natural rate of unemployment. This demographic factor is now reversing. As a share of the labor force,

youthful workers will decline during the next decade. This will tend to reduce the natural rate of unemployment in the 1990s.

1. Suppose the monetary authorities accelerate the annual growth rate of the money supply from a long-term trend of 5 percent to 10 percent. If decision-makers do not anticipate the effects of this policy change, how will it influence output, employment, and prices in the short-run? If the effects are anticipated, how will the expansionary policy influence output, employment, and prices in the short-run?

2. State in your own words the adaptive expectations hypothesis. Explain why adaptive expectations imply that macroacceleration will only temporarily reduce the rate of unemployment.

3. Compare and contrast the rational expectations hypothesis with the adaptive expectations hypothesis. If expectations are formed "rationally" rather than "adaptively," will it be easier or more difficult to decelerate the inflation rate without causing an economic recession? Explain.

4. How does the microeconomic approach to the problems of unemployment and economic growth differ from the traditional emphasis on monetary and fiscal policy? Is the microeconomic approach a substitute for traditional monetary and fiscal policy? Explain.

5. After a period of persistent inflation, such as was experienced in the United States during the 1974–1981 period, most economists believe that a shift to restrictive monetary policy to reduce the inflation rate will cause a recession. Why? How could the monetary authorities minimize the danger of a severe, lengthy recession?

6. Prior to the mid-1970s, many economists thought a higher rate of unemployment would reduce the inflation rate. Why? How does the modern view of the Phillips curve differ from the earlier view?

7. Why do most economists think the natural rate of unemployment rose during the 1960s and 1970s? Why do these same economists think the natural rate will fall during the next decade?

Unfortunately, policymakers cannot act as if the economy is an automobile that can quickly be steered back and forth. Rather, the procedure of changing aggregate demand is much closer to that of a captain navigating a giant super-tanker. Even if he gives a signal for a hard turn, it takes a mile before he can see a change, and ten miles before the ship makes the turn. [1]

ROBERT J. GORDON

- Historically, how much has real output fluctuated? Are economic fluctuations becoming more or less severe?

- Can macroeconomic policy moderate the business cycle?

- Why is proper timing of changes in macroeconomic policy crucial to the effectiveness of stabilization policy? Why is proper timing difficult to achieve?

- Would we have more or less instability if policy-makers simply expanded the money supply at a low, constant rate each year while balancing the federal budget?

- Should policy-makers try to smooth minor ups and downs in the growth path of real GNP?

15 STABILIZATION POLICY, OUTPUT, AND EMPLOYMENT

Activist Strategy: The view that deliberate changes in monetary and fiscal policy can be used to inject demand stimulus during a recession and apply restraint during an inflationary boom and thereby minimize economic inability.

Nonactivist Strategy: The maintenance of the same monetary and fiscal policy—that is, no change in money growth, tax rates, or expenditures—during all phases of the business cycle.

During the 1960s, economists were highly confident that macroeconomic policy could neutralize the economic ups and downs of the business cycle. Some even thought that the business cycle, like polio, would soon be banished to the pages of history. In the 1973 edition of his all-time best-selling text, Nobel laureate Paul Samuelson reflected this general optimism when he forecast that we may have to redefine "the cycle so that stagnant growth below the trend potential of growth is to be called recession even though absolute growth has not vanished."[2]

Subsequent events have tempered that optimism and led to hot debate about how best to deal with fluctuations in output, employment, and prices. Most macroeconomists, particularly those of Keynesian persuasion, favor an **activist strategy.** The activists believe that we can use monetary and fiscal policy to moderate economic fluctuations. Others favor a **nonactivist strategy.** The nonactivists believe that we can best moderate the business cycle by adopting rules and guidelines (i.e., a constant growth rate in the money supply and a balanced budget over the business cycle) that provide for stable monetary and fiscal policy, *independent of current economic conditions.*

This chapter will analyze the current debate concerning stabilization policy. The potential of monetary and fiscal policy as stabilization tools will be considered. We will also discuss various factors that limit our ability to properly apply and time macroeconomic policy. We will begin by taking a look at the historical record.

ECONOMIC FLUCTUATIONS—THE HISTORICAL RECORD

Wide fluctuations in the general level of business activity—in income, employment, and the price level—make personal economic planning extremely difficult. Such changes can cause even well-devised investment plans to go awry. The tragic stories of unemployed workers begging for food and newly impoverished investors jumping out of windows during the Great Depression vividly portray the enormous personal and social costs of economic instability and the uncertainty that it generates.

Historically, substantial fluctuations in real output have occurred. Exhibit 1 illustrates the growth record of real GNP in the United States during the last 75 years. Prior to World War II, double-digit swings in real GNP during a single year were not uncommon. Real GNP rose by more than 10 percent during World War I, during an economic boom in 1922, during a mid-1930s recovery, and again during World War II. In contrast, output fell by 5 percent or more during the 1920–21 recession, in the Depression years 1930, 1931, 1932, and 1938, and again following World War II. During the last four decades, economic ups and downs have been more moderate. Nevertheless, substantial fluctuations are still observable.

---

[1]Robert J. Gordon, *Macroeconomics* (Boston: Little, Brown, and Co., 1978), p. 334.
[2]Paul Samuelson, *Economics,* 9th edition (New York: McGraw-Hill, 1973), p. 266.

EXHIBIT 1 • The Post-World War II Decline in Economic Instability

Prior to World War II, the United States experienced double-digit increases in real GNP (in 1918, 1922, 1935–36, 1941–43) and double-digit declines in real GNP (in 1930–32 and 1946). In contrast, fluctuations in real GNP have moderated during the last four decades. Most economists believe that more appropriate macropolicy—particularly monetary policy—deserves much of the credit (see Exhibit 3).

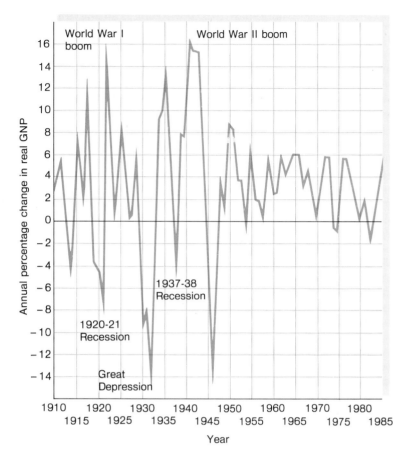

Sources: *Historical Statistics of the United States*, p. 224; *Economic Report of the President*, 1985, p. 235.

ACTIVISM VERSUS NONACTIVISM— AN OVERVIEW

How can economic fluctuations best be minimized? According to the activist's view, it is reasonable to expect that discretionary use of macroeconomic policy will reduce economic instability. Though they need not be Keynesians, activists generally reflect the Keynesian tradition. They have little confidence in the ability of a market economy to self-correct in response to inevitable economic shocks such as poor harvests, drastic changes in oil prices, or a strike in a major industry. Some activists charge that market economies are inherently unstable—that both economic expansions and contractions tend to feed on themselves. According to this view, business expansion will induce additional investment and consumption that exert a multiplier effect and lead to an inflationary boom. Resources, though, constrain the economy. Expansion in real output cannot proceed indefinitely. Growth of output will eventually slow. When this happens, optimism often turns to pessimism, which triggers a downturn. The multiplier effect also amplifies the downswing, causing unused industrial capacity and widespread unemployment. The proponents of the inherent instability view generally point to the volatile behavior of expenditures on consumer durables and private investment as supportive evidence for their position.

Other activists argue that the self-corrective mechanism of a market economy works slowly. They emphasize that restoration of full employment via lower real wage rates and interest rates is likely to be a lengthy process. They thus believe that prudent use of monetary and fiscal policy can speed the adjustment process and minimize the cost of economic instability.

Exhibit 2 illustrates the basic idea of the activists' strategy. Ideally, macroeconomic policy would apply demand restraint during an economic boom and apply demand stimulus during a recession. During an economic boom, then, proper macroeconomic policy would couple a deceleration in the growth rate of the money supply with movement toward a budget surplus (or smaller deficit). This would help restrain aggregate demand and thereby minimize the potential inflationary side effects of the boom. In contrast, when the economy dips into a recession, activist stabilization policy would shift toward stimulus. The money supply would be expanded more rapidly than normal, while budgetary policy would plan a budget deficit.

EXHIBIT 2 • Activists' Countercyclical Policy— Hypothetical Ideal

Activists believe that macropolicy based on economic conditions can help stabilize the economy. Here we illustrate the hypothetical ideal in which both monetary and fiscal policy restrain demand during an inflationary boom and add stimulus during a recession.

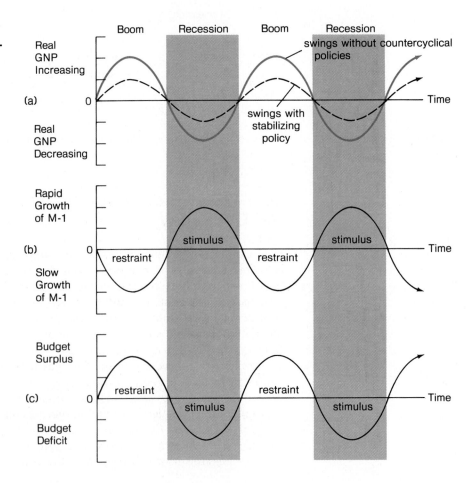

Activists believe it is feasible to apply macropolicy so that restraint will retard inflation during an economic boom and stimulus will minimize the decline in output during a recession. When macroeconomic policy is applied in this manner, it will reduce the swings in real GNP (as illustrated by the dotted line of Exhibit 2a) and employment.

In contrast with the activists' view, nonactivists argue that discretionary use of monetary and fiscal policy in response to changing economic conditions is likely to do more damage than good. They charge that erratic policy, particularly the instability of monetary policy, is a major source of economic fluctuations.

Nonactivists reject the view that minor disturbances, magnified by the multiplier, inevitably lead to either a recession or inflation boom. They emphasize that consumption, the major component of spending, is relatively stable over the business cycle. Counter to the "instability feeds on itself" view, individuals cushion the effects of a downturn by dipping into their savings and maintaining a high level of consumption during a recession. Simultaneously, lower real wages will stimulate employment and lower real interest rates will encourage the purchase of both investment goods and consumer durables during a recession. Thus, if they are not stifled by perverse macroeconomic policy, market forces will reverse a business downturn and restore full employment within a reasonable time period, according to the nonactivist position.

Nonactivists believe a market economy has self-correcting properties that work quite well. In addition, they argue that policy-makers would make fewer errors if they simply followed a stable monetary and fiscal course rather than modifying policy in response to current economic conditions.

Both activists and nonactivists agree that in the past, policy errors contributed to economic stability. Prior to the Keynesian revolution, governments often *raised* taxes to balance the budget as revenue declined during a recession. Of course, modern analysis implies that such a policy would add to the severity of the recession. Correspondingly, as Exhibit 3 illustrates, extreme gyrations in the money supply characterized monetary policy prior to World War II. Prior to 1947, sharp contractions in the money supply often accompanied major recessions. For example, the money supply *declined* at an annual rate of 9 percent during the 1920–1921 recession, and by 10 percent annually as the U.S. entered into the Great Depression; it dipped again during the 1937–1938 relapse of the depression. In contrast, double-digit growth rates in the money supply were observed during the inflationary periods of World Wars I and II. One need not be a monetarist (or nonactivist) to recognize that the erratic changes in the money supply contributed to instability prior to World War II.[3]

---

[3]Macropolicy during the heyday of classical economic theory once again illustrates that ideas have consequences "both when they are right and when they are wrong" (to quote Keynes). Since classical economists thought the budget should be balanced annually, taxes were often *raised* during recessions prior to the Keynesian revolution. Similarly, since the classists thought price adjustments were both quick and painless, they did not think changes in the supply of money affected real output. Thus, they paid little heed to monetary instability. For a detailed analysis of monetary instability, see Milton Friedman and Anna Schwartz, *A Monetary History of the United States, 1867–1960* (Princeton: Princeton University Press, 1963).

EXHIBIT 3 • The Post-World War II Decline in Monetary Instability

While fluctuations in the supply of money continue, it is clear that monetary instability has declined during the post-World War II period.

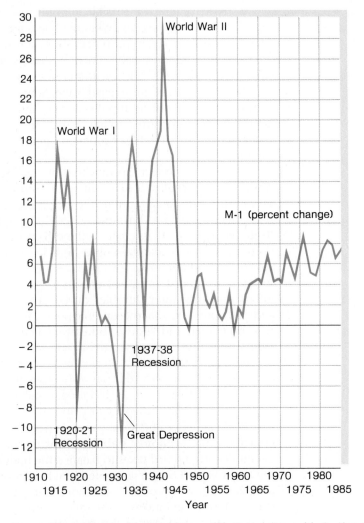

Sources: *Historical Statistics of the United States*, p. 892; *Economic Report of the President*, 1985.

While monetary fluctuations have continued since the post-World War II period, they have been much less erratic (see Exhibit 3). Correspondingly, modern governments seldom raise taxes during a business recession. As Exhibit 1 shows, more moderate swings in real output have accompanied the increased stability of monetary and fiscal policy during the post-war era. Activists and nonactivists agree that the link between the more stable macroeconomic policy and moderation of the business cycle is no coincidence.

INSTITUTING ACTIVISTS' STABILIZATION POLICY

Macroeconomic policy reduces instability only if it injects stimulus and applies restraint at the proper phase of the business cycle. Proper timing is the key to effective stabilization policy. How can policy-makers know

Industrial Capacity Utilization Rate: An index designed to measure the extent to which the economy's existing plant and equipment capacity is being used.

Index of Leading Indicators: An index of economic variables that historically has tended to turn down prior to the beginning of a recession and turn up prior to the beginning of a business expansion.

THE INDEX OF LEADING INDICATORS

whether they should be stimulating aggregate demand or applying the economic brake?

Of course, economic indicators such as the unemployment rate, growth of real GNP, and the **industrial capacity utilization rate** will provide policy-makers with information concerning the *current* state of the economy (see boxed feature). It takes time, though, for the macroeconomic policy to work. Because of this, policy-makers really need to know about the future—where the economy is going to be 6 to 12 months from now. They need to know whether a business recession or inflationary boom is around the corner. If they do not know where the economy is going, a policy change may fail to exert its primary impact quickly enough to offset a downturn or restrain future inflation.

How can policy-makers find out when the economy is about to take a turn in the macroeconomic road? The two most widely used sources of information on the future direction of the economy are the index of leading indicators and economic forecasting models.

The **index of leading indicators** is a composite statistic based on 12 key variables that generally turn down prior to a recession and turn up before the beginning of a business expansion (see boxed feature). Exhibit 4 illustrates the path of the index during the 1950–1985 period. Clearly, the index does provide information on the future direction of the economy. It forecasted each of the seven recessions during the 1950–1985 period. Generally, the index turned down 8 to 11 months prior to a recession. This would

MEASURES OF ECONOMIC ACTIVITY

The Capacity Utilization Rate

The capacity utilization rate is a ratio of actual output to capacity output. It is expressed as a percent. The utilization rate is intended to measure the extent to which industrial facilities are used to attain their potential output.

The Bureau of Economic Analysis (BEA) conducts a quarterly survey that asks a random sample of industrial firms to report their capacity utilization as a percent of practical capacity. Practical capacity is defined as the greatest level of output that the firm's *existing plant and equipment* could achieve assuming (a) the availability of labor and other variable inputs and (b) normal expected downtime for maintenance. The company utilization rates are weighted by asset size and then used to derive utilization rates for total industry and various subsectors (e.g., manufacturing, mining, and utilities).

Just as one would not expect 100 percent employment in a world of uncertainty and imperfect information, neither would one expect 100 percent utilization of plant capacity. Since the measure of capacity is based on the subjective views of firms' managers rather than actual experience, we cannot even be sure that it would be possible for a firm to achieve 100 percent capacity. It is not surprising, then, that broad capacity utilization rates are generally well below 100 percent. During the last three decades, the industrial capacity utilization rate has averaged approximately 83 percent. Utilization rates as high as 90 percent have been achieved only during wartime. Most economists interpret the significance of current capacity utilization rates by comparing them with past peaks and lows. A low utilization rate compared to the rates of recent years indicates the presence of underutilized industrial capacity, while relatively high utilization rates imply intensive use of industrial facilities. Capacity utilization rates are reported monthly in the *Federal Reserve Bulletin*.

provide policy-makers with sufficient lead time to modify policy, particularly monetary policy. There has been significant variability, however, in the lead time of the index. The downturn in the index was only three months prior to the 1982 recession and four months prior to the recession of 1954. In contrast, the index turned down 23 months prior to the recession of 1957–1958.

Unfortunately, the index is not always an accurate indicator of the future. On three occasions (1950–1951, 1962, and 1966), a downturn in the index of leading indicators forecast a future recession that did not materialize. This has given rise to the joke that the index has accurately forecast ten of the last seven recessions.

FORECASTING MODELS

Economists have developed highly complex econometric (statistical) models to improve the accuracy of macroeconomic forecasts. In essence, these models use past data on economic interrelationships to project how currently observed changes will influence the future path of key economic variables such as real GNP, employment, and the price level. The most elaborate of these models use hundreds of variables and equations to simulate the vari-

EXHIBIT 4 • The Index of Leading Indicators and the Future Direction of the Economy

The shaded periods represent business recessions. The index of leading indicators forecasted each recession during the 1955–1985 period. As the arrows show, however, the time lag between when the index turned down and when the economy fell into a recession varied. In addition, on three occasions (1950, 1962, and 1966), the index forecasted a recession that did not occur.

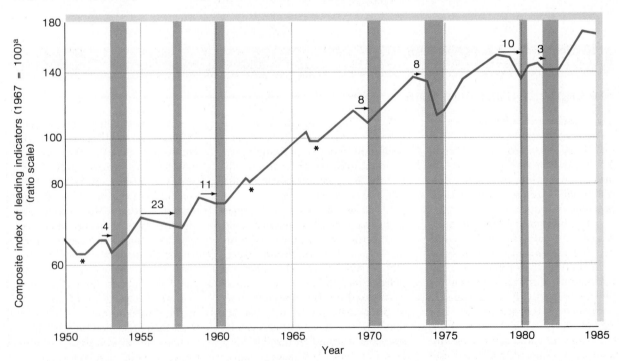

[a]The arrows indicate the number of months that the downturn in the index preceded a recession. An asterisk (*) indicates a false signal of a recession.

ous sectors and macroeconomic markets. High speed computers are employed to analyze the effects of various policy alternatives and to predict the future.

To date, the record of computer forecasting models is mixed. When economic conditions are relatively stable, the models have generally provided highly accurate forecasts for both aggregate economic variables and important subcomponents of the economy. Unfortunately, the models have been much less effective at accurately forecasting turns in the business cycle and the impact of major economic shocks. Of course, the models are only as accurate as the programmed relationships developed by their builders. Model builders are constantly restructuring their models, based on more accurate data and recent experience. Clearly, perfection must await the future. In fact, accuracy in forecasting may be beyond the reach of economics. Many economists, particularly those of rational expectations persuasion, argue this is indeed the case. (See "Can Economists Forecast the Future?")

DISCRETIONARY POLICY

Activists recognize that it is difficult to institute countercyclical macroeconomic policy. Nevertheless, they believe that discretionary action by policy-makers can help smooth business ups and downs.

MEASURES OF ECONOMIC ACTIVITY

The Index of Leading Indicators

History indicates that no single indicator is able to accurately forecast the future direction of the economy. However, several economic variables do tend to reach a high or low prior to the peak of a business expansion or the trough of an economic recession. Such variables are called leading economic indicators.

To provide more reliable information on the future direction of the economy, economists have devised an index of 12 leading economic indicators. The indicators included in the index are: (a) length of the average work week in hours; (b) average weekly claims for unemployment compensation; (c) new orders placed with manufacturers; (d) percent of companies receiving slower deliveries from suppliers; (e) net new business formations; (f) contracts and orders for plant and equipment; (g) permits for new housing starts; (h) change in manufacturing inventories; (i) change in sensitive materials prices; (j) stock prices; (k) money supply (M_2); and (l) change in credit outstanding. Each component in the series is standardized and weighted. The weight attached to each variable is based on its past performance as an indicator of macroeconomic turns.

In some cases, it is easy to see why a change in an economic indicator precedes a change in general economic activity. Consider the indicator "new orders placed with manufacturers" (measured in constant dollars). Manufacturers are usually quite willing to expand output in response to new orders. Thus, an expansion in the volume of orders is generally followed by an expansion in manufacturing output. Similarly, manufacturers will tend to scale back their future production when a decline in new orders signals the probability of weak future demand for their products.

The components of the index of leading indicators sometimes provide conflicting information. One component may be signalling continued expansion while another indicates that a recession is just around the corner. It often takes several months of continuous expansion or contraction in the index before all (or most all) of the components provide a consistent signal. Thus, an up or down turn in the index for just a few months should be interpreted with caution.

The index of leading indicators is calculated and published monthly by the Bureau of Economic Analysis of the Department of Commerce. It is reported monthly in the *Business Conditions Digest.*

APPLICATIONS IN ECONOMICS

Can Economists Forecast the Future?

Businesses and governmental units often pay thousands of dollars for the projections of highly complex computer forecasting models of the economy. Critical business and financial decisions are often based on the forecasts. In the past, persons marketing these forecasts have sometimes oversold the ability of economic theory as a tool with which to forecast the future. There are two major reasons why the ability of economists to forecast the future is extremely limited.

1. *Future changes in market conditions will primarily reflect events that cannot be foreseen at this time.* Current market prices already reflect current conditions *and* future changes that are widely anticipated. For example, today's grain prices will already reflect current and normal future weather conditions in the grain belt. Future grain prices will differ from the present primarily as the result of unanticipated future developments, such as abnormal future rainfall. The same logic also applies to macroeconomic markets. Future market conditions will differ from the present, primarily as the result of economic changes that we cannot now foresee—for example, an unexpected policy change, discovery of a new resource or technology, abnormal weather, or political upheaval in an important oil exporting nation. There is no reason to believe that economists or anyone else will be able to predict such changes with any degree of accuracy. Thus, while economic theory helps to predict the *implications* of unforeseen events, it cannot foretell what market-changing events will occur in the future.

2. *Decision-makers will often make different choices in the future because of what they learned from the past. The past is thus an imperfect indicator of the fu-*ture. Almost all forecasters, including those who rely on complex computer models, use past relationships to project the future. In a world where people learn from experience, though, forecasts based on past relationships will never fully capture the future. The experience of the 1970s illustrates this point. Prior to 1970, the unemployment rate generally declined when prices rose more rapidly. Most forecasting models in the 1970s thus assumed that a higher inflation rate would reduce unemployment. Things did not turn out that way. The 1970s were different because people adjusted their decision-making in light of past experience with inflation.

Macroeconomic forecasters have often missed major turns in the economic road. Exhibit 5 provides recent evidence on this point.

The 1980 year-end projections for 1981–1984 from five leading econometric models are presented. None of the five models forecasted the 1982 recession. In fact, the five models projected an average 1982 growth rate of 3.5 percent (with a range of 2.1 to 4.9 percent). The actual change in real GNP in 1982 was *minus* 2.1 percent. Similarly, none of the major forecasting models anticipated the sharp reduction in the inflation rate during 1981–1984. Most of the models forecasted inflation rates approximately twice the actual rate for 1982–1984.

Economic theory indicates that forecasting is a hazardous profession. The record of macroeconomic forecasters, including those who use highly sophisticated econometric models and high-speed computers, is consistent with this view.

EXHIBIT 5 • The Record of Five Major Forecasting Models During the 1980s

	1980 Year-end Forecast For:			
	1981	1982	1983	1984
Change in Real GNP				
Chase Econometrics	1.3	3.6	3.9	3.1
Data Resources	2.7	2.4	3.2	3.8
Wharton Model	2.2	2.1	3.4	3.4
Evans Econometrics	2.5	4.7	4.6	4.2
Merrill Lynch	0.6	4.9	6.0	4.3
Average of the Five Forecasts	**1.9**	**3.5**	**4.2**	**3.8**
Actual	**2.5**	**−2.1**	**3.7**	**6.8**
Inflation Rate				
Chase Econometrics	10.2	9.1	7.7	7.7
Data Resources	10.4	9.6	9.0	8.1
Wharton Model	10.3	9.6	8.3	8.0
Evans Econometrics	10.0	8.8	8.4	8.4
Merrill Lynch	9.5	7.1	6.0	6.2
Average of the Five Forecasts	**10.1**	**8.8**	**7.9**	**7.7**
Actual	**8.9**	**3.9**	**3.8**	**4.0**

Source: "Where The Big Econometric Models Go Wrong." *Business Week*, March 30, 1981.

The activist view stresses that the index of leading indicators, forecasting models, and other economic indicators provide policy-makers with an early warning system, alerting them to the likelihood of a macroeconomic change. This will provide policy-makers with sufficient time to institute moderate changes in macroeconomic policy quickly and more substantial changes with the passage of time if additional information indicates such changes are needed.

The following scenario outlines the essentials of the activists' view. Suppose the economy was about to dip into a recession. *Prior to the recession,* the index of leading indicators would almost surely alert policy-makers to the possibility of a downturn. This would permit them to shift toward macroeconomic stimulus, expanding the money supply more rapidly. Initially, the shift toward macroeconomic stimulus could be applied in moderate doses. It could then be easily offset with future action. On the other hand, if the signs of a downturn became more pronounced and *current* business conditions actually weaken, additional stimulus could be injected. Perhaps a tax reduction or a speed-up in government expenditures might be used to supplement the more expansionary monetary policy. Policy-makers can constantly monitor the situation as they inject additional stimulus. As economic indicators provide additional information with the passage of time, policy-makers can adjust their actions accordingly. If the weakness persists, the expansionary policy can be continued. Conversely, when the signs point to a strong recovery, policy-makers can move toward restraint and thereby head off potential inflationary pressure. According to the activist's view, the economy is more likely to stay on track when policy-makers are free to apply stimulus or restraint based on current information and economic conditions.

NONACTIVISTS' RESPONSE TO THE ACTIVISTS' VIEW

Until quite recently, most economists were advocates of activism. It was widely believed that countercyclical monetary and fiscal policy were both advisable and feasible. Economic events and theoretical developments alike have resulted in a reevaluation of that position. Nonactivists raise three major points in response to the activist position.

1. *Inability to forecast the future and uncertainty as to when a change in macroeconomic policy will exert its primary impact substantially reduce the potential effectiveness of discretionary stabilization policy.* If discretionary policy modifications are going to help stabilize the economy, proper timing is essential. Nonactivists believe that three time lags seriously undermine the potential of discretionary policy. First, there is the **recognition lag,** the time period between when economic conditions have changed and when policy-makers are cognizant of the change. Our ability to forecast the future is highly limited. It will even take a few months to gather and tabulate reliable information on the performance of the economy in the recent past. Predictably, it will take policy-makers a few months to recognize that the economy has dipped into a recession or that the inflation rate has accelerated.

Second, even after the need for a policy change is recognized, there is generally an additional time period before the policy change is instituted. Economists refer to this delay as **administrative lag.** In the case of monetary policy, the administrative lag is generally quite short. The Federal Open Market Committee meets monthly, and is at least potentially capable of instituting a change in monetary policy quickly. This is a major advantage

Recognition Lag: The time period between when a policy change is needed from a stabilization standpoint and when the need is recognized by policy-makers.

Administrative Lag: The time period between when the need for a policy change is recognized and when the policy is actually administered.

Impact Lag: The time period between when a policy change is implemented and when the change begins to exert its primary effects.

of monetary policy. For discretionary fiscal policy, the administrative lag is likely to be longer. Congressional committees must meet. Legislation must be proposed and debated. Congress must act and the President must consent. Each of these steps take time.

Finally, there is the **impact lag,** the time period between the implementation of a macropolicy change and when the change exerts its primary impact on the economy. While the impact of a change in tax rates is generally felt quickly, the expansionary effects of an increase in government expenditures are usually much less rapid. It will take time for the submission of competitive bids and the letting of new contracts. Several months may pass before work on a new project actually begins. Similarly, Milton Friedman argues that the impact lags of monetary policy are of significant and variable length. Friedman believes that anywhere from 6 to 18 months may pass before an acceleration in the growth rate of the economy begins to stimulate aggregate demand. The impact on the general level of prices will usually come still later.

Nonactivists argue that the time lags substantially reduce the likelihood that macropolicy can be manipulated in a manner that will provide stimulus and restraint at the proper phases of the business cycle. They argue from this that the effects of discretionary macroeconomic policy are likely to be destabilizing rather than stabilizing.

Exhibit 6 illustrates the views of activists' and nonactivists'. When the economy begins to dip into a recession, activists argue that policy-makers

EXHIBIT 6 • Time Lags and the Effects of Discretionary Policy

Beginning with A, we illustrate the path of a hypothetical business cycle. If a forthcoming recession can be recognized quickly and a more expansionary policy instituted at point B, the policy may add stimulus at point C and help to minimize the magnitude of the downturn. Activists believe that discretionary policy is likely to achieve this outcome.

However, if delays result in the adoption of the expansionary policy at C and if it does not exert its major impact until D, the demand stimulus will exacerbate the inflationary boom. In turn, an anti-inflationary strategy instituted at E may exert its primary effects at F, just in time to increase the severity of a recession beyond F. Nonactivists fear that improper timing of discretionary macropolicy will exert such destabilizing effects.

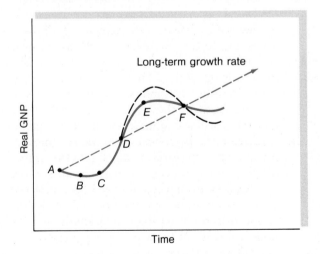

can reasonably be expected to recognize that danger and shift to a more expansionary policy at *B*. Given the expected length of the impact lag, the expansionary policy will exert its primary effects at *C*, just in time to help minimize the business downturn. In contrast, nonactivists believe the lags are likely to be more lengthy and less predictable. They fear the shift to more expansionary policy will not come until *C* and that its effects will not be significant until *D*. If this is the case, the expansionary policy will contribute to the severity of the inflationary boom (dotted line beyond *D*). Similarly, a subsequent shift to an anti-inflationary policy may begin to exert its major impact at *F*, just in time to make an oncoming recession worse (dotted line beyond *F*).

2. *Public choice analysis indicates that macropolicy may be used to pursue political objectives rather than stabilization.* Public choice analysis has led to an increased awareness of an additional pitfall that many nonactivists believe further reduces the expected effectiveness of discretionary policy. In a democracy, macropolicy will be designed by elected representatives, an elected president, and officials (such as the Board of Governors of the Federal Reserve) who are appointed by the elected president. Like other policy choices, macropolicy provides political entrepreneurs with a potential tool with which to further their political objectives. Predictably, discretionary macropolicy choices will be influenced by political considerations. It is naive to expect otherwise.

The nature of the political process, particularly the shortsightedness effect, provides politicians with little incentive to look beyond the next election. If the adaptive expectations view is correct, expansionary policies prior to an election will help bring about more favorable economic conditions—more rapid growth and lower unemployment—for a short period of time. Studies indicate that incumbents are far more successful at retaining their office when real income grows rapidly during the 12 to 18 months prior to an election.[4] Political entrepreneurs thus have a strong incentive to stimulate the economy prior to a major election. Clearly, macroeconomic policy has political, as well as economic, potential. Because of this fact, vote-maximizing political entrepreneurs, rather than using policy strictly for stabilization purposes, may use it to help make the economy look good on election day. If so, the real-world stabilizing influence of macropolicy will be further reduced.

There is some evidence that politicians have sought to use macropolicy for political gain. During the 18 months prior to the 1968 election, the unemployment rate was less than 4 percent. Nevertheless, monetary policy was quite expansionary and the Johnson Administration ran a large deficit during 1967–1968 rather than increase taxes to finance expenditures for domestic programs and the Vietnam War. Similarly, the Nixon Administration followed an expansionary monetary and fiscal course prior to the 1972 election even though real growth was strong during the 1971–1972 period. Many economists believe that the expansionary policies preceding both the

---

[4]For evidence on this point, see Ray C. Fair, "On Controlling the Economy to Win Elections," Cowles Foundation Discussion Paper No. 397, 1975.

1968 and 1972 elections laid the foundation for the inflationary instability of the 1970s.

Political scientist Edward Tufte has conducted extensive research on this issue. While reviewing evidence from 90 elections in 27 different countries, Tufte found that real disposable income accelerated in 77 percent of the election years compared to only 46 percent of the years without an election.[5] This suggests that there is at least a moderate tendency to follow more expansionary policies prior to major elections.

3. *The theory of rational expectations indicates that predictable changes in macropolicy will fail to promote economic stability.* Unlike a machine, the moving parts of our economy are living, breathing human beings, capable of altering their choices when the situation changes. As they learn from prior experience, their future response to a policy change may differ from the past.

As we have already discussed, the impact of macropolicy varies depending on whether or not it is anticipated by decision-makers (see Chapter 14, Exhibit 1). The proponents of rational expectations believe that, sooner or later, the public will figure out any systematic policy, including countercyclical stabilization policy. However, once a policy is widely anticipated and individuals adjust their decision-making in light of the expected effects (for example, rising prices or higher interest rates), the policy no longer exerts the predicted impact on real output and employment. Economists refer to this phenomenon as the **policy ineffectiveness theorem.**

Policy Ineffectiveness Theorem: The proposition that any systematic policy will be rendered ineffective once decision-makers figure out the policy pattern and adjust their decision-making in light of its expected effects. The theorem is a corollary of the theory of rational expectations.

Perhaps an example will illustrate why rational expectations economists have little confidence that even properly timed macropolicy will be effective. Suppose it is widely anticipated that the government will employ expansionary macropolicy in response to a recession. As the signs of an economic slowdown appear, the public anticipates that policy-makers will increase the growth of the money supply and cut taxes (perhaps by allowing a more attractive depreciation allowance or increasing the investment tax credit) to spur business investment. It makes sense, once this strategy is anticipated, for investors to delay investment projects and wait for the expected lower interest rates and investment tax incentives. This delay, though, only increases the severity of the current downturn and leads to pent-up investment demand. Once the anticipated expansionary policy is instituted, investment expenditures will tend to grow more rapidly than past experience indicated would be the case (and more rapidly than is desirable from a stabilization viewpoint). In essence, once decision-makers adjust their choices in light of the anticipated countercyclical policy, the policy fails to exert the desired stabilizing effects.

The logic of the analysis applies symmetrically to an economic boom. If the public anticipates slower money growth, higher interest rates, and higher taxes will be used to restrain an economic boom, they will spend and invest *more* prior to the expected restrictive policy. In turn, the increase in spending will contribute to the development of an economic boom.

---

[5]Edward R. Tufte, *Political Control of the Economy* (Princeton, N.J.: Princeton University Press, 1978).

The message of rational expectations theory to stabilization policy-makers is clear. Human decision-makers will foil your good intentions. Countercyclical macropolicy will fail because once people expect your systematic response to recessions and booms, it will be in their personal interest to respond in a manner that will undermine the policy.

In the long-run, of course, rational expectations theory also suggests that the intentions of political entrepreneurs seeking to "hype" the economy prior to election time will be undermined. If the public expects expansionary policy during a pre-election period, the primary impact of the policy will be on prices (inflation) and nominal interest rates, not real output and employment.

NONACTIVISTS' STABILIZATION POLICY

Led by Milton Friedman, the monetarists have consistently argued that activism will contribute to economic instability because we are incapable of timing policy changes properly. Public choice economists now question the likelihood that vote-conscious politicians will consistently follow a stabilization strategy. Finally, proponents of rational expectations conclude that even if it were possible to time and execute countercyclical policy properly, it would fail to accomplish the desired objective. While the logic of each of these three groups differs, they all arrive at the same conclusion: nonactivism, a stable, predictable macropolicy, is the best strategy.

Nonactivists recommend that policy-makers choose a long-run policy path (for example, 3 percent monetary growth and no change in tax rates or real government expenditures) and inform the public of this choice. This course should then be pursued regardless of cyclical ups and downs. As policy-makers stay on course, they will gain credibility. The public will develop confidence in the future stability of the policy. Uncertainty will be reduced, thereby increasing the efficiency of private decision-making. Nonactivists are confident this strategy would result both in less instability and in more rapid growth than Western economies have experienced in the past.

Suppose we were going to adopt a nonactivist strategy. What rules or guidelines would we choose? Nonactivists are not of uniform opinion as to what constitutes the best strategy. Let us consider a number of alternatives.

NONACTIVIST MONETARY POLICY

The most widely advocated nonactivist monetary policy is the constant money growth rule long championed by Milton Friedman. Under this plan, the money supply would be expanded continuously at an annual rate (3 percent, for example) that approximates the long-run growth of the U.S. economy. During a period of rapid growth, the money supply would expand less rapidly than would goods and services. Because of this, it would automatically exert some restraint. In contrast, during a recession, the constant money growth rate would exceed the growth of real output, offsetting any tendency toward a downward spiral. More importantly, once decision-makers developed confidence in the steady growth strategy, they could make their plans based on the expected steady course. No longer would they have to worry about and hedge against a possible monetary surge or plunge.

How does the steady growth rule differ from the monetary targets currently employed by the Fed? According to the nonactivists, the problem with the monetary targets is that the Fed does not take them very seriously. The Fed did not choose to adopt the targets. Rather, Congress imposed them. The Fed responded by adopting target ranges that are wide enough to provide substantial variability. Finally, if the Fed wants to change policy course, it simply changes the targets. Nonactivists believe the targets are more cosmetic than real. Thus, they fail to exert the stabilizing effects of a constant growth rule.

Recent changes in the banking industry and fluctuations in the velocity of money have caused some economists to question the wisdom of the

**Martin Feldstein
(1939–   )**

OUTSTANDING ECONOMIST

In 1982, President Reagan tapped Martin Feldstein for the chairmanship of the Council of Economic Advisors, a position he occupied for two years. His tenure as chairman was sometimes stormy. Feldstein argued that higher taxes were necessary to reduce the mounting budget deficit. This often placed him at odds with tax-cutting supply-side economists within the administration.

Feldstein's scholarly record could only be described as remarkable. In 1977, he received the John Bates Clark Medal, an award presented by The American Economic Association to the most outstanding economists under age 40. During the last two decades, he has published hundreds of articles, primarily dealing with the impact of government programs on the incentive to work, save, and invest. He is president of the National Bureau of Economic Research, the nation's most prestigious "think tank." At Harvard, he presides over the university's best-enrolled course, Social Analysis 10, a survey of economic principles.

Feldstein is a leader among the expanding group of economists who believe the tools of microeconomics shed considerable light on the traditional macroeconomic problems of sluggish growth and inflation. His research on the effects of unemployment benefits indicates that the system causes workers to lengthen their job search time and induces employers to make more extensive use of temporary layoffs. The result: a higher rate of unemployment. Feldstein argues that "there is a growing recognition that our high permanent rate of unemployment cannot be lowered by expansionary demand policies." He believes the solution will be found through policies that "correct labor market disincentives and distortions."[6] As we search for solutions, the work of this outstanding economist is sure to play an important role.

[6]Martin Feldstein, "The Retreat from Keynesian Economics," *The Public Interest* (Summer 1981), p. 97.

simple money growth rule. The introduction of various types of interest-earning checking accounts complicates the precise definition of money. Perhaps as a result of these changes, the velocity of money declined substantially during 1982 and 1983, after increasing at a moderate rate continuously throughout the post-World War II period. Critics argue that this development illustrates the impracticality of a monetary rule.

Nonactivists believe that these problems can be worked out. Allan Meltzer of Carnegie Mellon University is a long-time advocate of a monetary rule that many believe would solve problems created both by changes in the nature of money and by fluctuations in velocity. Rather than expanding M-1 by a constant amount, Meltzer advocates that the money supply be increased a constant amount equal to the long-run growth of real GNP (approximately 3.5 percent), *minus* the change in the velocity of money. Under Meltzer's monetary rule, the price level would be stable and nominal GNP would expand at the long-run growth rate of the economy. In effect, Meltzer's modified money growth rule adjusts the growth rate of the money supply in light of how money is defined and used by the public. If the velocity of M-1 fell, perhaps because of an increase in demand for money balances or a change in the nature of M-1 such as we experienced during the financial deregulation of the 1980s, the money supply would grow more rapidly under Meltzer's rule. On the other hand, if the velocity of M-1 was increasing, the money supply would grow more slowly. The Meltzer policy thus adjusts the monetary growth rate to offset fluctuations in velocity (the demand for money).

From the viewpoint of nonactivists, the important point is not the precise rule, but rather the removal of monetary policy from the hands of activist policy-makers. If left to their own discretion, policy-makers will inevitably make destabilizing errors, according to nonactivists.

NONACTIVIST FISCAL POLICY

In the area of fiscal policy, the simplest rule would require that the budget be balanced annually. Since revenues and expenditures fluctuate over the business cycle, however, a balanced budget rule would require tax increases and/or expenditure reductions during a recession. The opposite changes would be required during a period of rapid growth. Such changes are inconsistent with the nonactivist pursuit of stable (unchanged) policies.

In theory, the proper nonactivist fiscal strategy is a balanced budget over the business cycle. Under this plan, the same tax rates and expenditure policies would remain in effect during both booms and recessions. Surpluses would result during periods of prosperity, while deficits would accrue during recessions. The problem with this strategy is that it fails to provide a precise indicator revealing how well the policy-makers are adhering to the steady course. Thus, nonactivists, particularly those with a public choice background, recognize that a "balance the budget over the business cycle" rule is unlikely to impose a steady course on policy-makers.

Some nonactivists believe that a constitutional amendment limiting both government spending and budget deficits is a necessary ingredient for stable fiscal policy. These nonactivists believe pressure from special interests and the short-time horizon of political officials elected for limited terms biases the political process toward expansionary fiscal policy (expanding debt and spending increases). Because of this, they favor a constitutional amendment that would require supramajority (for example, 60 percent) Congressional approval for either (a) deficit-financed government spending or (b) rapid increases (more rapid than the growth of national income) in federal spending.

It is one thing to favor a general strategy and another to develop a practical, workable policy to implement the strategy. Clearly, the non-activists have not yet arrived at a detailed fiscal policy program that would command wide acceptance among even the proponents of nonactivism.

IS THERE AN EMERGING CONSENSUS?

The major area of disagreement between activists and nonactivists involves the merits of a policy response to changing circumstances. Activists fear that, if strictly followed, a stable policy strategy would prevent appropriate responses to economic shocks, particularly if the strategy was institution-alized. In their view, failure to respond to a major shock, perhaps stemming from war, another oil price run, or a collapse of investment, might well result in a major economic disaster.

On the other hand, the nonactivists fear that discretion will consistently be abused. They point to Federal Reserve policy since 1979 as evidence of this point. In October of 1979, the Fed announced that increased weight would be given to monetary targets and the path of the aggregate money supply. Many interpreted this to mean that the Fed would follow a mon-etarist strategy—a low, stable growth rate of the money supply. A check of the record reveals that this was not the case. The growth rate of the money supply continued bouncing around pretty much as it had done prior to October, 1979. To nonactivists, this illustrates that unless you tie the hands of policy-makers, they will inevitably pursue an activist strategy. Counter to the intent, the result will be more instability, according to nonactivists.

While stressing the fundamental differences, however, we must not fail to recognize emerging points of agreement. Similarly, we must not forget that most economists are hybrids. They are influenced by the analysis of alternative schools of thought.

Activists, as well as nonactivists, are aware of the difficulties involved in the proper timing of macropolicy. Fine-tuning, the idea that policy-makers can successfully promote stability by responding to each short-term bump in the economic road, has lost most of its luster. Recognizing that fine-tuning is beyond our current knowledge and capability, most activists now favor a policy response only in the case of major cyclical disturbances.

Both activists and nonactivists also recognize that policy instability is a potential source of economic instability. Both are sensitive to the potential destructiveness of erratic policy swings. Monetary and fiscal policy blunders of the magnitude committed prior to 1945 are thus unlikely to be repeated.

Activists and nonactivists actually share a great deal of common ground. Their differences primarily concern the proper amount of policy-making flexibility. Activists favor substantial flexibility so that policy-makers can respond to *major* economic disturbances. Nonactivists favor little flexibility because they fear it will be abused by policy-makers. Perhaps some combination of inflexible rules that would apply during relatively normal times and policy-maker discretion to override the rules in response to a major economic swing will emerge as a point of consensus between activism and nonactivism.

CONCLUDING THOUGHT

Economists who pronounced the death of business instability during the 1960s clearly underestimated the difficulties involved in steering a stable economic course. Unfortunately, economic bumps in the road are likely to continue in the foreseeable future. Recent economic instability must be placed in perspective, though. We must not allow failure to achieve perfection to conceal progress that has already been made.

As Exhibit 1 clearly shows, economic fluctuations have been much less pronounced since World War II. Sensible macroeconomic policy deserves most of the credit for this increased stability (see Exhibit 3). The Keynesian revolution convinced economists and policy-makers alike that macroeconomic policy mattered—that it was too important to be left to fate. Beginning with the Keynesian revolution, fiscal and monetary policy has been instituted in a manner that prevented economic disturbances from becoming catastrophic depressions. This is an important achievement to which macroeconomists can point with a sense of pride.

CHAPTER SUMMARY

1. Historically, the United States has experienced substantial swings in real output. Prior to World War II, year-to-year changes in real GNP of 5 to 10 percent were experienced on several occasions. Since World War II, the fluctuations in real output have been more moderate.

2. Macropolicy activists believe that a market economy is inherently unstable or that the market's self-corrective process works slowly. They are confident that discretionary monetary and fiscal policy will promote economic stability.

3. Nonactivists believe that a market economy has self-correcting tendencies that work quite well during a stable policy environment. They argue that policy-makers would make fewer errors if they merely instituted stable monetary and fiscal policies, rather than altering policy in response to current economic conditions.

4. The index of leading indicators and other forecasting devices warn policy-makers when a turn in the economic road is just ahead. While recognizing that forecasting devices sometimes give false signals, activists argue that policy-makers can initially respond cautiously to signals indicating the need for a policy change and then act more aggressively if the situation requires it. Activists thus believe that discretionary macroeconomic policy can effectively restrain the economy during an inflationary boom and stimulate output during a business recession.

5. Nonactivists stress that inability to accurately forecast the future and quickly modify macroeconomic policy, along with uncertainty as to when a policy change will exert its primary impact, substantially reduce the effectiveness of discretionary policy as a stabilization tool.

6. Public choice theory indicates that politicians have a strong incentive to follow an expansion course prior to major elections. Political use of macropolicy reduces its effectiveness as a stabilization tool.

7. The theory of rational expectations argues that even properly timed countercyclical policy will fail to reduce instability once decision-makers figure out the systematic pattern and adjust their choices in light of the expected effects. According to rational expectations theory, any systematic policy that is widely anticipated will fail to exert a predictable impact on real output and employment once the public adjusts to the policy.

8. Rather than attempting countercyclical policies, nonactivists believe the economy would be more stable if policy-makers simply (a) increase the money supply at a low, constant rate and (b) maintain a stable tax and expenditure policy.

9. The major disagreement between activists and nonactivists involves the merits of a policy response to changing circumstances. Activists fear that strict adherence to a policy such as the constant (fixed) money growth rule will prevent policy-makers from responding correctly to major recessions and inflations. Correspondingly, nonactivists fear that policy-maker discretion will result in destabilizing policies.

10. Despite their differences, activists and nonactivists agree on several important points. Both agree that (a) it is more difficult to properly time stabilization policy than was generally perceived during the 1960s, (b) past errors have contributed to economic instability, and (c) it is a mistake for policy-makers to respond to minor changes in economic indicators.

11. While stabilization policy has not eliminated economic ups and downs, it has virtually eliminated the likelihood that an economic disturbance will become a catastrophic depression. This is an important achievement that is often overlooked today.

THE ECONOMIC WAY
OF THINKING—
**DISCUSSION
QUESTIONS**

1. Compare and contrast the views of activists and nonactivists with regard to the following points: (a) the self-stabilizing characteristics of a market economy; (b) the ability of policy-makers to forecast the future; (c) the validity of the rational expectations hypothesis; and (d) the use of rules versus discretion in the institution of monetary and fiscal policy.

2. What is the index of leading indicators? Evaluate its potential usefulness to policy-makers.

3. Do you think more detailed computer models of the economy will enhance the ability of economists to forecast future economic changes more accurately? Why or why not?

4. How does economic instability during the last four decades compare with instability prior to World War II? Is there any evidence that stabilization policy has either increased or decreased economic stability during the post–World War II period?

5. Why do most nonactivists favor a monetary rule such as expansion of the money supply at a constant annual rate? What are some of the

potential problems with a monetary rule? Do you think a monetary rule could be devised that would reduce economic instability? Why or why not?

6. The Chair of the Council of Economic Advisors has requested that you write a short paper indicating how economic policy can be used to stabilize the economy and achieve a high level of economic growth during the next five years. Be sure to make specific proposals. Indicate why your recommendations will work. You may submit your paper to your instructor.

7. Evaluate the effectiveness of monetary and fiscal policy during the last three years. Has it helped to promote stable prices, rapid growth, and high unemployment? Do you think policy-makers have made mistakes during this period? If so, indicate why.

MICRO-ECONOMICS

- How do economists analyze consumer choice? What assumptions do they make?

- What role does time play in the consumption of goods?

- What factors will cause a demand curve to shift?

- What is demand elasticity, and why is it a useful concept? What factors determine the elasticity of demand for a good?

- What determines the demand for a specific item? Is advertising effective? Is it useful, or just misleading?

Wisdom, whose lessons have been represented as so hard to learn by those who were never at her school, only teaches us to extend a simple maxim universally known. And this is, not to buy at too dear a price. [1]

HENRY FIELDING

16 DEMAND AND CONSUMER CHOICE

Macroeconomics focuses on aggregate markets—the big picture. Aggregate outcomes are, of course, the result of many individual decisions. We cannot understand or successfully influence the big picture without a solid knowledge of how microeconomic decisions are made. In this section, we will break down the aggregate product market into microeconomic markets for specific products.

Microeconomics focuses on how changes in *relative* prices influence consumer decisions. As we stressed in Chapter 3, the price system guides individuals in their production and consumption decisions.[2] Prices coordinate the vast array of individual economic activities by signaling relative wants and needs, and by motivating market participants to bring their own activities into harmony with those of others. Changes in one market affect conditions in others. In this chapter, we take a closer look at (a) the interrelationships among markets and (b) the factors underlying the demand for specific products.

CHOICE AND INDIVIDUAL DEMAND

Exhibit 1 shows how consumers allocated their spending among alternative goods in 1950 and 1984. Why did consumers spend more on transportation than on medical care, or more on alcoholic beverages than on religious and welfare activities? Why have consumer expenditures on food declined (as a percentage of the total), while spending on housing has expanded? If we are to answer these questions, we will need to know something about the factors that influence the behavior of consumers.

When analyzing the choices of consumers, economists usually make the following assumptions.

1. *Limited Income Necessitates Choice.* Most of us are all too aware that our desire for goods far exceeds our limited incomes. People do not have enough resources to produce everything they would like. A limited income forces each of us to make choices. When one good or service is purchased, many others must be sacrificed.

2. *Consumers Make Decisions Purposefully.* Consumption decisions are made with the desire to upgrade one's personal welfare in mind. A foolish purchase means giving up something more worthwhile. The purpose or goal behind a consumer decision can usually be met in many different ways, so that careful consideration of alternatives is useful. Consumers generally choose the alternative that is expected to enhance their personal welfare the most, relative to cost. They do not *consciously* choose a lesser-valued alternative when another of equal cost but projected greater benefit is available.

3. *One Good Can Be Substituted for Another.* Consumers have many goals, each with alternative means of satisfaction. No single good is so precious

---

[1] Henry Fielding, *Tom Jones,* Book VI, Chapter III.

[2] You may want to review Chapter 3 before beginning the study of microeconomics.

EXHIBIT 1 • How Consumers Spent their Income, 1950 and 1984

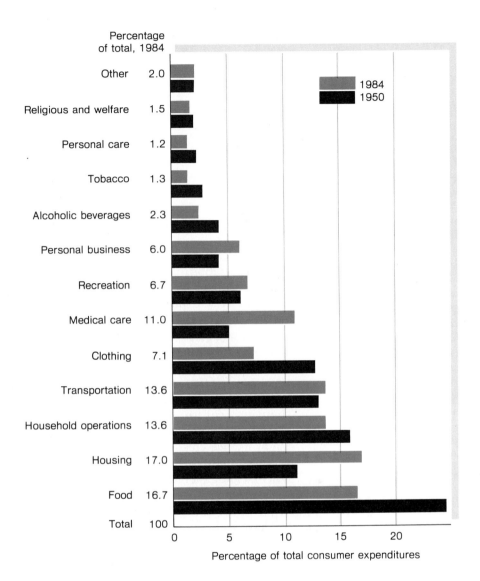

Percentage of total, 1984

Other	2.0
Religious and welfare	1.5
Personal care	1.2
Tobacco	1.3
Alcoholic beverages	2.3
Personal business	6.0
Recreation	6.7
Medical care	11.0
Clothing	7.1
Transportation	13.6
Household operations	13.6
Housing	17.0
Food	16.7
Total	100

Percentage of total consumer expenditures

U.S. Department of Commerce.

that some of it will not be given up in exchange for a large enough quantity of other goods. For example, consumers will give up some fried chicken to have more pizza, hamburgers, fish, ham sandwiches, or apple pie. Similarly, reading, watching movies and television, or playing cards can be substituted for playing football. How about our "need" for basic commodities such as water or energy? The "need" of a person for an item is closely related to its cost—what must be given up to obtain the item. Southern California residents "need" water from the north, but the individual resident, when faced with a high water cost, finds that cactus gardens can be substituted for lawns, a plumber's bill for a faucet drip, and flow constrictors for full-force showers. The need for water depends on its cost. People living in Montana, where household electricity costs about twice as much as in nearby Washington, use half as much electricity per household. Montanans reduce their "need" for electricity by substituting gas, fuel oil, insulation, and wool sweaters.

4. *Consumers Must Make Decisions without Perfect Information, but Knowledge and Past Experience Will Help.* No human being has perfect foresight. Napoleon did not anticipate Waterloo; Julius Caesar did not anticipate the actions of Brutus. Consumers will not always correctly anticipate the consequences of their choices.

Consumer choices, however, are not made in a vacuum. You have a pretty good idea of what to expect when you buy a cup of coffee, five gallons of gasoline, or lunch at your favorite diner. Why? Because you have learned from experience—your own and that of others. When you buy a product, your expectations may not be fulfilled precisely (for example, the coffee may be stronger than expected or the gasoline may make your car knock), but even these experiences will give you valuable information that can be used in making future decisions.

5. *The Law of Diminishing Marginal Utility Applies: As the Rate of Consumption Increases, the Utility Derived from Consuming Additional Units of a Good Will Decline.* Utility is a term economists use to describe the subjective personal benefits that result from an action. The **law of diminishing marginal utility** states that the **marginal** (or additional) **utility** derived from consuming successive units of a product will *eventually* decline as the rate of utilization increases. For example, the law implies that even though you might like ice cream, your marginal satisfaction from *additional* ice cream will eventually decline. Ice cream at lunchtime might be great. An additional helping for dinner might be even better. However, after you have had it for evening dessert and a midnight snack, ice cream for breakfast will begin to lose some of its attraction. The law of diminishing marginal utility will have set in, and thus the marginal utility derived from the consumption of additional units of ice cream will decline.

Law of Diminishing Marginal Utility: A basic economic principle, which states that as the consumption of a commodity increases, the marginal utility derived from consuming more of the commodity (per unit of time) will eventually decline. Marginal utility may decline even though total utility continues to increase, albeit at a reduced rate.

Marginal Utility: The additional utility received by a person from the consumption of an additional unit of a good within a given time period.

MARGINAL UTILITY AND CONSUMER CHOICE

Consumer choices, like other decisions, are influenced by changes in benefits and costs. If a consumer wants to get the most out of his or her expenditures, how much of each good should be purchased? As more of a good is consumed per unit of time, the law of diminishing marginal utility states that the consumer's marginal benefit per unit of time will decline. A consumer will gain by purchasing more of a product as long as the benefit, or marginal utility (MU), derived from the consumption of an additional unit exceeds the costs of the unit (the expected marginal utility from other consumption alternatives that must now be given up).

Given a fixed income and specified prices for the commodities to be purchased, consumers will maximize their satisfaction (or total utility) by ensuring that the last dollar spent on each commodity purchased yields an equal degree of marginal utility. If consumers are to get the most for their money, the last dollar spent on product A must yield the same utility as the last dollar spent on product B (or any other product).[3] After all, if tickets for football games, for example, yielded less marginal utility *per dollar* than did opera tickets, the obvious thing for a consumer to do would be to cut back spending on football games and allocate more funds for opera tickets. If people really attempt to spend their money in a way that yields the greatest amount of satisfaction, the applicability of the consumer decision-making theory outlined above is difficult to question.

PRICE CHANGES AND CONSUMPTION DECISIONS

Demand is the schedule of the amount of a product that consumers would be willing to purchase at alternative prices during a specific time period. The first law of demand states that the amount of a product purchased is inversely related to its price. Why? First, as the price of a product declines, the opportunity cost of consuming it will fall. The lower opportunity cost will induce consumers to buy more of it. What will happen to the marginal utility derived from the product, though, as they increase their rate of consumption? It will fall. Thus, as more of the product is consumed, a point is reached where the benefits (marginal utility) derived from the consumption of still more units will again be less than the cost. Purposeful decision-makers will not choose such units. A price reduction will thus induce consumers to purchase more of a product, but the response will be limited because of the law of diminishing marginal utility. Economists refer to this tendency to substitute a *relatively* cheaper product for goods that are now more expensive as the **substitution effect.**

Substitution Effect: That part of an increase in amount consumed that is the result of a good being cheaper in relation to other goods because of a reduction in price.

Second, since the money income of consumers is constant, a reduction in the price of a product will increase their real income—the amount of goods and services they are able to purchase. Typically, consumers will respond by purchasing more of the cheaper product (as well as other products) because they can now better afford to do so. This factor is referred to as the **income effect.** (Both the income and substitution effects are derived graphically in the addendum to this chapter, entitled "Consumer Choice and Indifference Curves.")

Income Effect: That part of an increase in amount consumed that is the result of the consumer's real income (the consumption possibilities available to the consumer) being expanded by a reduction in the price of a good.

Of course, the substitution and income effects will generally induce consumers to purchase less of a good if its price rises. Why will consumers curtail their consumption of a product that has risen in price? They will do so because the opportunity cost of consuming the product has risen, making it a less attractive buy. As consumption is reduced, however, the consumer's

---

[3]Mathematically, this implies that the consumer's total utility is at a maximum when limited income is spent on products such that

$$\frac{\mathrm{MU_a}}{P_a} = \frac{\mathrm{MU_b}}{P_b} = \cdots = \frac{\mathrm{MU_n}}{P_n}$$

where MU represents the marginal utility derived from the last unit of a product, and P represents the price of the good. The subscripts a, b, . . . , n indicate the different products available to the consumer. In the continuous case, the above expression implies that the consumer will get the most for his or her money when the consumption of each product is increased only to the point at which the marginal utility from one more unit of the good is equal to the marginal utility obtainable from the best alternative purchase that must now be forgone. For more advanced students, this proposition is developed in an alternative, more formal manner in the Addendum on indifference curves.

marginal utility derived from the product will rise. If the price increase is not so great as to price the consumer out of the market completely, a sufficient fall in the rate of consumption will raise the product's marginal utility enough so that it will again equal its new, higher opportunity cost. With moderate increases in price, the consumer's reduction in consumption will be limited. We must also bear in mind that if the consumer's money income is constant, the price increase reduces the individual's real income. A reduction in real income will tend to result in a reduction in the consumption of many goods, generally including the good that has increased in price.

Exhibit 2 illustrates the adjustment of consumers to a higher price. During 1985–1986, gasoline prices fell rapidly in the United States. As demand theory would predict, consumers increased their rate of consumption. As gasoline prices fell from $1.20 to $.80, Jones's average weekly consumption rose from 16 gallons to 20 gallons. The availability of less expensive fuel resulted in his postponement of a costly tuneup on his car, which would have saved some fuel. He went to the grocery store a little more often, rather than waiting as usual to combine shopping trips with other business near the shopping center. He and his family took a vacation by car, which would have been much more expensive at the 1985 gasoline price level. At the higher rate of use, the marginal utility of gasoline fell, bringing it into line with the lower price.

Still lower gasoline prices would cause an even greater increase in consumption. The additional decline in price would allow consumers to enjoy still more slightly lower valued uses of gasoline. Lower prices bring on further consumption increases, but the response is limited because the marginal utility of gasoline falls as consumption rises.

TIME COST AND CONSUMER CHOICE

The monetary price of a good is not always a complete measure of its cost to the consumer. Consumption of most goods requires time as well as money. Time, like money, is scarce to the consumer. A lower time cost, like

EXHIBIT 2 • Gas Prices, Consumption, and Marginal Utility

An individual, Jones in this case, will increase his rate of consumption of a product as long as MU exceeds its opportunity cost (principally the price of the good). Higher prices will induce him to consume less, but the reduction in consumption will be limited because the MU of the product will rise as consumption falls.

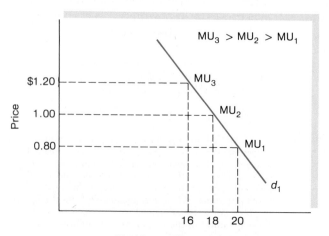

a lower money price, will make a product more attractive to consumers.[4]

Some commodities are demanded primarily because of their ability to reduce the consumer's time cost. Consumers are often willing to pay higher money prices for such goods. The popularity of automatic dishwashers, electric razors, prepared foods, air travel, and taxi service is based on their low time cost in comparison with substitutes.

What is the cost of a college education? Tuition payments and the price of books comprise only a small component. The major cost of a college education is the time cost—approximately 4000 hours. If a student's time is valued at only $3 per hour, the time cost of a college education is $12,000!

Time costs, unlike money prices, differ among individuals. They are higher for persons with greater earning power. Other things being equal, high-wage consumers choose fewer time-intensive (and more time-saving) commodities than persons with a lower time cost. High-wage consumers are overrepresented among air and taxicab passengers but underrepresented among television watchers, chess players, and long-distance automobile travelers. Can you explain why? You can, if you understand how both money and time cost influence the choices of consumers.

CONSUMER CHOICE AND MARKET DEMAND

The market demand schedule is the amount demanded by all the individuals in the market area at various prices. Since individual consumers purchase less at higher prices, the amount demanded in a market area is also inversely related to price.

Exhibit 3 illustrates the relationship between individual demand and market demand for a hypothetical two-person market. The individual demand curves for both Jones and Smith are shown. Jones and Smith each consume 20 gallons of gasoline weekly at 80 cents per gallon. The amount

EXHIBIT 3 • Individual and Market Demand Curves

The market demand curve is merely the horizontal sum of the individual demand curves. The market demand curve will slope downward to the right just as the individual demand curves do.

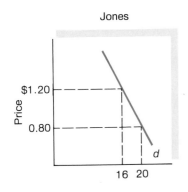
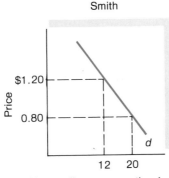
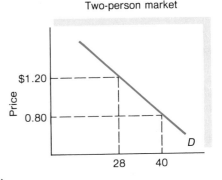

Weekly gasoline consumption (gallons)

---

[4]For a technical treatment of the importance of time as a component of cost from the vantage point of the consumer, see Gary Becker, "A Theory of the Allocation of Time," *Economic Journal* (September 1965), pp. 493–517.

demanded in the two-person market is 40 gallons. If the price rises to $1.20 per gallon, the amount demanded in the market will fall to 28 gallons, 16 demanded by Jones and 12 by Smith. The market demand is simply the horizontal sum of the individual demand curves.

Market demand reflects individual demand. Individuals buy less as price increases. Therefore, the total amount demanded in the market declines as price increases.

CONSUMER SURPLUS

Consumer Surplus: The difference between the maximum amount a consumer would be willing to pay for a unit of a good and the payment that is actually made.

The demand curve reveals how many units consumers will purchase at various prices. In so doing, it reveals consumers' evaluation of units of a good. The height of the demand curve indicates how much consumers value an added unit. The difference between the amount that consumers would be willing to pay and the amount they actually pay for a good is called **consumer surplus.** As Exhibit 4 illustrates, it is measured by the area under the demand curve but above the market price.

Previously, we indicated that voluntary exchange is advantageous to buyer and seller alike. Consumer surplus is a measure of the net gain to the buyer/consumer. Consumer surplus also reflects the law of diminishing marginal utility. Consumers will continue purchasing additional units of a good until the marginal utility is just equal to the market price. Up to that point, however, consumption of each unit generates a surplus for the consumer, since the value of the unit generally exceeds the market price. In aggregate, the total value (utility) to consumers of a good may be far greater than the total cost to them.

The size of the consumer surplus is determined by the market price. Reducing the market price will increase the consumer surplus; increasing the market price will cause the surplus to decline.

WHAT CAUSES THE DEMAND CURVE TO SHIFT?

The demand schedule isolates the impact of price on the amount purchased, assuming other factors are held constant. What are these "other factors"? How do they influence demand?

EXHIBIT 4 • Consumer Surplus

As the shaded area indicates, the difference between the amount consumers would be willing to pay and the price they actually pay is called consumer surplus.

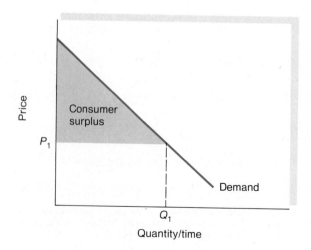

Changes in the Income of Consumers Influence the Demand for a Product.[5] The demand for most products is positively related to income. As their income expands, individuals typically spend more on consumption. The demand for most products increases. Conversely, a reduction in consumer income usually causes the demand for a product to fall.

Changes in the Distribution of Income Influence the Demand for Specific Products. If more income were allocated to alcoholics and less to vegetarians, the demand for liquor would increase, whereas the demand for vegetables would fall. Consider another example. Suppose a law were passed that taxed all inheritances over $500,000 at a 90 percent rate. If the law effectively reduced the income of sons and daughters of the wealthy, it would also reduce their demand for yachts, around-the-world cruises, diamonds, and perhaps even Harvard educations. If the revenues from the tax were redistributed to persons with incomes below $5000, the demand for hamburgers, used cars, moderately priced housing, and other commodities that low-income families purchase would increase relative to yachts, cruises, and diamonds.

Substitutes: Products that are related such that an increase in the price of one will cause an increase in demand for the other (for example, butter and margarine, Chevrolets and Fords).

The Prices of Closely Related Goods Influence the Demand for a Product. Related goods may be either substitutes or complements. When two products perform similar functions or fulfill similar needs, they are **substitutes.** There is a direct relationship between the price of a product and the demand for substitutes. For example, margarine is a substitute for butter. Higher butter prices will increase the demand for margarine as consumers substitute it for the more expensive butter. Similarly, higher coffee prices will increase the demand for such substitutes as cocoa and tea. On the other hand, if technology, good weather, or some other factor reduces the price of a good, then the demand for its substitutes will decline. A substitute relationship exists between beef and pork, pencils and pens, apples and oranges, and so forth.

Complements: Products that are usually consumed jointly (for example, lamps and light bulbs). An increase in the price of one will cause the demand for the other to fall.

Other closely related products are consumed jointly. Goods that "go together," so to speak, are called **complements.** With complements, there is an inverse relationship between the price of one and the demand for the other. For example, as the experiences of the 1970s illustrate quite well, higher gasoline prices cause the demand for large automobiles to decline. Gasoline and large automobiles are complementary. Similarly, lower prices in 1985 for compact disc players increased the demand for compact discs and for high quality speaker systems. Ham and eggs are complementary items, as are tents and camping equipment.

Changes in Consumer Preferences Influence Demand. Why do preferences change? Preferences change because people change. New information, for example, might change their valuation of a good. How did

---

[5]Do not forget that a change in *quantity demanded* is a movement along a demand curve in response to a change in price, but a change in *demand* is a shift in the entire demand curve. Review Chapter 3 if you find this point confusing.

consumers respond to new information linking cigarette smoking to cancer in the mid-1960s? They responded by purchasing and smoking fewer cigarettes. Annual per capita consumption, which had been increasing, fell more than 6 percent between 1965 and 1970. As more consumers learned that cigarettes were "cancer sticks," many of them changed their preferences.

Changes in Population and Its Composition Influence the Demand for Products. The demand for products in a market area is directly related to the number of consumers. Because of this, changes in the composition of the population may also have an impact on demand. If a higher percentage of the population is between 16 and 21 years of age, the demand for movies, stereo equipment and records, sports cars, and college educations will be positively affected. An increase in the number of elderly people will positively affect the demand for medical care, retirement housing, and vacation travel.

Expectations Influence Demand. When consumers expect the future price of a product to rise (fall), their current demand for it will expand (decline). "Buy now, before the price goes even higher" becomes the order of the day. When the price of coffee rose sharply in 1986, how did shoppers respond? Initially, current sales increased; consumers hoarded the product because they expected its price to continue rising. Conversely, if consumers thought the price of automobiles, for example, would be 10 percent lower next year, would their actions be influenced? Yes. Many consumers would defer their automobile purchases until next year, waiting for bargain prices.

An economist constructing a demand schedule for a product assumes that factors other than the price of the product are held constant. As Exhibit 5 shows, a change in any of the factors that influence consumer decisions will cause the entire demand curve to shift. The accompanying Thumbnail Sketch (a) points out that *quantity demanded* (but not demand) will change in response to a change in the price of a product and (b) summarizes the major factors that cause a change in *demand* (a shift of the entire curve.)

THUMBNAIL SKETCH

Change in Quantity Demanded and Change in Demand

A change in this factor will cause the quantity demanded (but not demand) to change:

1. The current price of the product

Changes in these factors will cause the entire demand curve to shift:

1. Consumer income
2. The distribution of consumer income
3. Price of related products (substitutes and complements)
4. Consumer preferences
5. Population in the market area
6. Expectations about the future price of the product

EXHIBIT 5 • Price is Not All That Matters

Other things constant, the demand schedule will slope downward to the right. However, changes in income and its distribution, the prices of closely related products, preferences, population, and expectations about future prices will also influence consumer decisions. Changes in these factors will cause the entire demand curve to shift (for example, increase from D_1 to D_2).

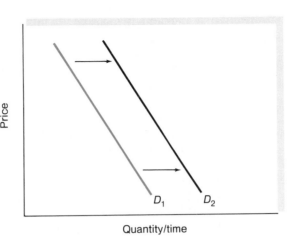

THE ELASTICITY OF DEMAND

If the tuition charges at your school go up 50 percent next year, how many of your classmates will be back? If the price of salt doubles, how much less will you purchase? These are questions about price elasticity of demand.

Price Elasticity of Demand[6] is defined as:

$$\frac{\text{Percent change in quantity demanded}}{\text{percent change in price}}$$

Price Elasticity of Demand: The percent change in the quantity of a product demanded divided by the percent change in its price. Price elasticity of demand indicates the degree of consumer response to variation in price.

This ratio is called the elasticity coefficient. Elasticity of demand refers to the flexibility of consumers' desires for a product—the degree of their responsiveness to a change in a product's price. If a small rise in price causes consumers to choose a much smaller amount of a product, the demand for the product is elastic. In contrast, if a substantial increase in price results only in a small reduction in quantity demanded, the demand is inelastic. On an elastic demand curve, the quantity demanded is highly sensitive to a change in price. In contrast, an inelastic demand curve indicates inflexibility or little consumer response to variation in price.

The precise distinction between elastic and inelastic can be determined by the elasticity coefficient. When the elasticity coefficient is greater than 1 (ignoring the sign), demand is elastic. An elasticity coefficient of less than 1

---

[6]You might want to distinguish between (a) the elasticity at a point on the demand curve and (b) the *arc* elasticity *between* two points on the demand curve. The formula for point elasticity is:

$$\frac{\text{Change in quantity demanded}}{\text{Initial quantity demanded}} \div \frac{\text{Change in price}}{\text{Initial price}}$$

The formula for arc elasticity is:

$$[(q_0 - q_1)/\tfrac{1}{2}(q_0 + q_1)] \div [(P_0 - P_1)/\tfrac{1}{2}(P_0 + P_1)]$$

where the subscripts 0 and 1 refer to the respective prices and amounts demanded at two alternative points on a specific demand curve. The arc elasticity is really an average elasticity between the two points on the curve.

means that demand is inelastic. "Unitary elasticity" is the term used to denote a price elasticity of 1. The sign of the elasticity coefficient is negative, since a change in price causes the quantity demanded to change in the opposite direction.

GRAPHIC REPRESENTATION OF DEMAND ELASTICITY

Exhibit 6 presents demand curves of varying elasticity. A demand curve that is completely vertical is termed "perfectly inelastic." The addict's demand for heroin or the diabetic's demand for insulin might *approximate* perfect inelasticity over a wide range of prices, although no demand curve will be perfectly inelastic at all prices (Exhibit 6a).

The more inelastic the demand, the steeper the demand curve *over any specific price range.* Inspection of the demand for cigarettes (Exhibit 6b), which is highly inelastic, and the demand for portable television sets (Exhibit 6d), which is relatively elastic, indicates that the inelastic curve tends to be steeper. When demand elasticity is unitary, as Exhibit 6c illustrates, a

EXHIBIT 6 • Demand Elasticity

(a) *Perfectly inelastic*—Despite an increase in price, consumers still purchase the same amount. The price elasticity of an addict's demand for heroin or a diabetic's demand for insulin might be approximated by this curve.

(b) *Relatively inelastic*—A percent increase in price results in a smaller percent reduction in sales. The demand for cigarettes has been estimated to be highly inelastic.

(c) *Unitary elasticity*—The percent change in quantity demanded is equal to the percent change in price. A *curve* of decreasing slope results. Sales revenue (price times quantity sold) is constant.

(d) *Relatively elastic*—A percent increase in price leads to a larger percent reduction in purchases. Consumers substitute other products for the more expensive good.

(e) *Perfectly elastic*—Consumers will buy all of farmer Jones's wheat at the market price, but none will be sold above the market price.

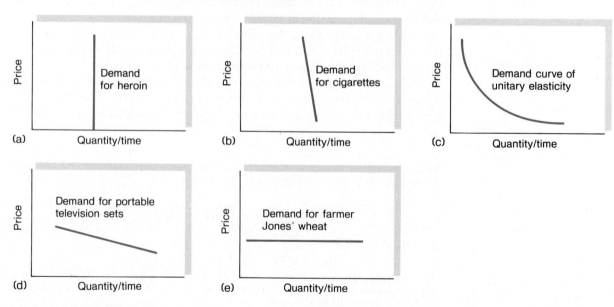

demand curve that is convex to the origin will result. When a demand curve is completely horizontal, an economist would say that it is perfectly elastic. Demand for the wheat of a single wheat farmer, for example, would approximate perfect elasticity (Exhibit 6e).

Since elasticity is a relative concept, the elasticity of a straight-line demand curve will differ at each point along the line. As Exhibit 7 illustrates, the elasticity of a straight-line demand curve (one with a constant slope) will range from highly elastic to highly inelastic. For Exhibit 7, when the price rises from $10 to $11, sales decline from 20 to 10. According to the arc elasticity formula, the price elasticity of demand is −7.0. Demand is very elastic in this region. In contrast, demand is quite inelastic in the $1 to $2 price range. As the price increases from $1 to $2, the amount demanded declines from 110 to 100. The arc elasticity of demand in this range is only −0.14; demand is highly inelastic.

Why do we bother with elasticity? Why not talk only about the slope of a demand curve? We use elasticities because they are independent of the units of measure. Whether we talk about dollars per gallon or cents per quart, the elasticities, given in percentages, remain the same. This is appropriate because people do not care what units of measurement are used; they care about what they receive for their money.

DETERMINANTS OF ELASTICITY OF DEMAND

Economists have estimated the price elasticity of demand for many products. Exhibit 8 presents some of these estimates, which vary a great deal. The demand for several products—salt, toothpicks, matches, light bulbs, and newspapers, for example—is highly inelastic. On the other hand, the demand for fresh tomatoes, Chevrolet automobiles, and fresh green peas is highly elastic. What factors explain this variation? Why is demand highly responsive to changes in price for some products but not for others?

EXHIBIT 7 • The Slope of a Demand Curve is Not the Same as the Price Elasticity

With this straight-line (constant-slope) demand curve, demand is more elastic in the high-price range. The formula for arc elasticity (see footnote 6) shows that when price rises from $1 to $2 and quantity falls from 110 to 100, demand is inelastic. A price rise of the same magnitude (but of a smaller percentage), from $10 to $11, leads to a decline in quantity of the same size (but of a larger percentage), so that elasticity is much greater. (Price elasticities are negative, but we typically ignore the sign and look only at the absolute value.)

The Availability of Substitutes. This factor is the most important determinant of demand elasticity. When good substitutes for a product are available, a price rise simply induces consumers to switch to other products. Demand is elastic.

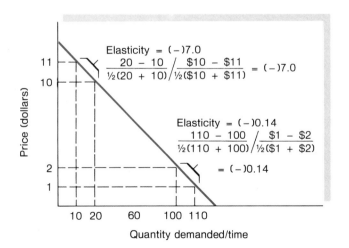

EXHIBIT 8 • The Estimated Price Elasticity of Demand for Selected Products

Inelastic	
Salt	0.1
Matches	0.1
Toothpicks	0.1
Airline travel, short run	0.1
Gasoline, short run	0.2
Gasoline, long run	0.7
Residential natural gas, short run	0.1
Residential natural gas, long run	0.5
Coffee	0.25
Tobacco products, short run	0.45
Legal services, short run	0.4
Physician services	0.6
Taxi, short run	0.6
Automobiles, long run	0.2
Approximate unitary elasticity	
Housing, owner occupied, long run	1.2
Private education	1.1
Tires, short run	0.9
Tires, long run	1.2
Radio and television receivers	1.2
Elastic	
Fresh Tomatoes	4.6
Foreign travel, long run	4.0
Airline travel, long run	2.4
Fresh green peas	2.8
Automobiles, short run	1.2–1.5
Chevrolet automobiles	4.0

Hendrik S. Houthakker and Lester D. Taylor, *Consumer Demand in the United States*, (Cambridge, Massachusetts: Harvard University Press, 1966, 1970); Douglas R. Bohi, *Analyzing Demand Behavior* (Baltimore: Johns Hopkins University Press, 1981); and U.S. Department of Agriculture.

For example, if the price of fountain pens increased, many consumers would simply switch to pencils, ballpoint pens, and felt-tip pens. If the price of Chevrolets increased, consumers would substitute Fords, Volkswagens, and other cars.

When good substitutes are unavailable, the demand for a product tends to be inelastic. Medical services are an example. When we are sick, most of us find witch doctors, faith healers, palm readers, and cod-liver oil to be highly imperfect substitutes for a physician. Not surprisingly, the demand for physician services is inelastic.

The availability of substitutes increases as the product class becomes more specific, thus enhancing price elasticity. For example, as Exhibit 8 shows, the price elasticity of Chevrolets, a narrow product class, exceeds that of the broad class of automobiles in general.

The Share of Total Budget Expended on the Product. If the expenditures on a product are quite small relative to the consumer's budget, demand tends to be more inelastic. Compared to one's total budget, expenditures on some commodities are almost inconsequential. Matches, toothpicks, and salt are good examples. Most consumers spend only $1 or $2 per year on each of these items. A doubling of their price would exert little influence on the family budget. Therefore, even if the price of such a product were to rise sharply, consumers would still not find it in their interest to spend much time and effort looking for substitutes.

Time and Adjustment to a Price Change. It takes time for consumers to recognize and to respond fully to a change in the price of a product. Initially, all consumers may not be aware of the price change; more will become aware of it as the price change persists into the future. Consumer response to a price change can also be slow because rapid adjustment of individual consumption patterns is often costly.

Generally, the longer a price change persists, the greater the price elasticity of demand. The direct relationship between the elasticity coefficient of demand and the length of the time period allowed for consumer adjustment is often referred to as the second law of demand. According to this law, the elasticity of demand for a product is generally greater in the long-run than in the short-run.

Gasoline consumption patterns in the 1970s and 1980s provide a vivid illustration of the second law of demand. When gasoline prices rose from 35 cents to 60 cents during 1973–1975, did consumers *immediately* stop driving their 350-horsepower, gas-guzzling automobiles? No. When their full-sized cars wore out, though, many consumers did switch to compact cars giving higher gas mileage. In the short-run, consumers responded to higher gas prices by reducing speeds, forming car pools, and driving less often. Given more time, however, they also substituted compact cars for full-sized models, reducing gasoline consumption even more. As Exhibit 8 shows, then, the long-run demand for gasoline (0.7) proved more elastic than the short-run demand (0.2).

The same process occurred in reverse when gasoline prices fell from $1.20 to 80 cents during 1985–1986. Cheaper fuel allowed consumers to pay more attention to convenience and speed, and less attention to carpools and gas mileage. With time, people gradually replaced many small cars with larger cars that delivered more performance and more comfort.[7] Once again, the response was greater after consumers had more time to react to the price change.

Even though the demand for most products will be more elastic in the long-run than in the short-run, there can be some exceptions, primarily among durable consumer goods. Often, such purchases can initially be delayed into the future as prices rise. Repairs to existing goods can at first

---

[7]Since drivers had become accustomed to the parking convenience and handling of small cars, and since technology had been concentrated on building more comfort and performance into fuel-efficient cars, the years of high gasoline prices following 1973 probably had a lasting impact on consumer preferences (increasing the demand for small autos, and thus decreasing the demand for gasoline) and on the auto technology (again decreasing the demand for gasoline).

be a substitute for a purchase; repairing the old washing machine one more time, for example. Thus, higher prices result in a greater reduction in quantity demanded in the short-run than is possible over an extended time period.

ELASTICITY AND TOTAL EXPENDITURES

Price elasticity establishes the relationship between a change in price and the corresponding change in total expenditures on the product. Let us examine how this relationship works. When demand is inelastic, the percent change in price exceeds the percent reduction in sales. The price effect dominates. Suppose that when the price of beef rises from $2 to $2.40 (a 20 percent increase), the quantity demanded by an average consumer falls from 100 pounds to 90 pounds (a 10 percent reduction) per year. Since the percent increase in price exceeds the percent reduction in quantity demanded, we know that demand is inelastic.[8] At the $2 price, the average person spends $200 annually on beef. When the price rises to $2.40, the average annual expenditures rise to $216. The higher beef prices cause total expenditures to increase because demand is inelastic.

When demand is elastic, on the other hand, the percent decline in quantity demanded will exceed the percent increase in price. The loss of sales will exert a greater influence on total expenditures than the rise in price. Total revenues will therefore fall.

Exhibit 9 summarizes the relationship between changes in price and total expenditures for demand curves of varying elasticity. When demand is inelastic, a change in price will cause total expenditures to change in the same direction. If demand is elastic, price and total expenditures will change in opposite directions. For unitary elasticity, total expenditures will remain constant as price changes.

HOW DOES INCOME INFLUENCE DEMAND?

As income expands, the demand for most goods will increase. **Income elasticity** indicates the responsiveness of the demand for a product to a change in income. It is defined as:

Income Elasticity: The percent change in the quantity of a product demanded divided by the percent change in consumer income. It measures the responsiveness of the demand for a good to a change in income.

EXHIBIT 9 • Demand Elasticity, Change in Price, and Change in Total Expenditures

Price Elasticity of Demand	Numerical Elasticity Coefficient[a]	The Impact of a Change in Price on Total Expenditures (and Sales Revenues)
Elastic	1 to ∞	Price and total expenditures change in opposite directions
Unitary	1	Total expenditures remain constant as price changes
Inelastic	0 to 1	Price and total expenditures change in the same direction

[a]The sign of the elasticity coefficient is negative.

---

[8]Calculate the elasticity coefficient as an exercise. Is it less than 1?

$$\frac{\text{Percent change in quantity demanded}}{\text{Percent change in income}}$$

As Exhibit 10 shows, the income elasticity coefficients for products vary; they are normally positive, however. In general, goods that people regard as "necessities" will have a low income elasticity of demand. Therefore, it is understandable that items such as fuel, electricity, bread, tobacco, economy clothing, and potatoes have a low income elasticity. A few commodities, such as navy beans, low-quality meat cuts, and bus travel have a negative income elasticity. Economists refer to goods with a negative income elasticity as **inferior goods.** As income expands, the demand for inferior goods will decline.

Goods that consumers regard as "luxuries" generally have a high (greater than 1) income elasticity. For example, private education, new automobiles, recreational activities, expensive foods, swimming pools, and air travel are all income-elastic. As income increases, the demand for these products thus expands rapidly.

Inferior Goods: Goods for which the income elasticity is negative. Thus, an increase in consumer income causes the demand for such a good to decline.

DETERMINANTS OF SPECIFIC PREFERENCES—WHY DO CONSUMERS BUY *THAT*?

Did you ever wonder why a friend spent hard-earned money on something that you would not have even if it were free? Tastes differ, and as we have already shown, they influence demand. What determines preferences? Why do people like one thing but not another? Economists have not been able to explain very much about how preferences are determined. The best strategy has generally been to take preferences as given, using price and other

EXHIBIT 10 • The estimated income elasticity of demand for selected products

Low income elasticity	
Margarine	−0.20
Fuel	0.38
Electricity	0.20
Fish (Haddock)	0.46
Food	0.51
Tobacco	0.64
Hospital care	0.69
High income elasticity	
Private education	2.46
New cars	2.45
Recreation and amusements	1.57
Alcohol	1.54

Hendrik S. Houthakker and Lester D. Taylor, *Consumer Demand in the United States, 1929–1970* (Cambridge, Massachusetts: Harvard University Press, 1966); L. Taylor, "The Demand for Electricity: A Survey," *Bell Journal of Economics* (Spring 1975); F. W. Bell, "The Pope and the Price of Fish." *American Economic Review*, vol. 58 (December 1968).

demand-related factors to explain and predict human behavior. Still, there are some observations about consumer preferences worth noting.

First, the preferences behind any one choice are frequently complex. The person looking for a house wants far more than just a shelter: an attractive setting, a convenient location, quality of public services, and a great many other factors will enter the housing decision. Each person may evaluate the same attribute differently. Living near a school may be a high priority for a family with children but a nuisance to a retired couple.

Second, the individual consumer's choice is not always independent of other consumers. Not wanting to be left out, a person might buy an item to "get on the bandwagon"—just because others are buying the same item. Or, a good may have "snob appeal," setting owners apart from the crowd or elevating them into an exclusive group. Even relatively inexpensive items may have this appeal.[9]

A third factor influencing consumer choice is advertising. Advertisers would not spend tens of billions of dollars each year if they did not get results. How does advertising affect consumers? Does it simply provide valuable information about product quality, price, and availability? Or, does it use repetition and misleading information to manipulate consumers? Economists are not of one opinion. Let us take a closer look at this important issue.

ADVERTISING—HOW USEFUL IS IT?

What does advertising do for Americans? What were the results of the $95 billion spent on advertising in 1985? Advertising is often used as a sponsoring medium; it reduces the purchase price of newspapers, magazines, and, most obviously, television viewing. It is the consumer of the advertised products who indirectly pays for these benefits, though. Advertising thus cannot be defended solely on the basis of its sponsorship role.

Advertising does convey information about product price, quality, and availability. New firms or those with new products, new hours, new locations, or new services use advertising to keep consumers informed. Such advertising facilitates trade and increases efficiency. But, what about those repetitious television commercials that offer little or no information? Critics charge that such advertising is wasteful, misleading, and manipulative. Let us look at each of these charges.

Is Advertising Wasteful? A great deal of media advertising simply seems to say "We are better" without providing supportive evidence. An advertiser may wish to take customers from a competitor or establish a brand name for a product. A multimillion-dollar media campaign by a soap, cigarette, or automobile manufacturer may largely be offset by a similar campaign waged by a competitor. The consumers of these products end up paying the costs of these battles for their attention and their dollars. We must remember, however, that consumers are under no obligation to purchase adver-

---

[9]See Harvey Leibenstein, "Bandwagon, Snob, and Veblen Effects in the Theory of Consumer Demand," *Quarterly Journal of Economics* (May 1950), pp. 183–207; and R. Joseph Monsen and Anthony Downs, "Public Goods and Private Status," *Public Interest* (Spring 1971), pp. 64–76, for a more complete discussion of bandwagon and snob effects.

tised products. If advertising results in higher prices with no compensating benefits, consumers can turn to cheaper, nonadvertised products.

A brand name in which people have confidence, even if it has been established by advertising, is an asset at risk for the seller. People value buying from sellers in whom they have confidence, and will pay a premium to do so. If something happens to damage a brand name, the willingness of consumers to pay falls, and the value of the brand name falls, too. When brand names are not allowed, as in the case of alcoholic beverages during the Prohibition era, consumers often suffer. Without brand names to protect, anonymous moonshiners sometimes were careless and allowed dangerous impurities into the moonshine. Some consumers of moonshine were blinded, and others died. Today the situation is different. Those who buy Jack Daniels or Jim Beam whiskey know that besides skill and integrity, the distillers have an enormous sum of money tied up in their brands. A brand-name distiller would spend a large amount of money to avoid even one death from an impure batch. Is a brand name, promoted by costly advertising, worthwhile to the customer? The customer must decide.

Is Advertising Misleading? Unfair and deceptive advertising—including false promises, whether spoken by a seller or packaged by an advertising agency—is illegal under the Federal Trade Commission Act. The fact that a publicly advertised false claim is easier to establish and prosecute than the same words spoken in private is an argument for freedom in advertising. But, what about general, unsupported claims that a product is superior to the alternative or that it will help one enjoy life more? Some believe that such noninformational advertising should be prohibited. They would establish a government agency to evaluate the "informativeness" of advertising. There are dangers in this approach, however. Someone would have to decide what was informative and what was not, or what was acceptable and what was not. If we could be assured that the special agency would be staffed by "regulatory saints" (borrowing a phrase from George Stigler), it would make sense to follow this course. Past experience, however, indicates that this would not be the case. Eventually, the regulatory agency would most likely be controlled by established business firms and advertising interests. Firms that played ball with the political bloc controlling the agency would be allowed to promote their products. Less powerful and less political rivals would be hassled. Costs would rise as a result of paperwork created by compliance procedures. If consumers are misled by slick advertisers to part with their money without good reason, might they not also be misled by a slick media campaign to support politicians and regulatory policies that are not in their interest? Why should we expect consumers to make poor decisions when they make market choices, but wise decisions when they act in the political (and regulatory) arena? Clearly, additional regulation is not a cure-all. Like freedom in advertising, it has some defects.

Does Advertising Manipulate the Preferences of Consumers? The demand for some products would surely be much lower without advertising. Some people's preferences may, in fact, be shaped by advertising. However, in evaluating the manipulative effect of advertising, we must keep two things in mind. First, business decision-makers are likely to choose the simplest route to economic gain. Generally, it is easier for business firms to cater to the actual desires of consumers than attempt to reshape their preferences or persuade them to purchase an undesired product. Second, even if advertising does influence preferences, does it follow that this is bad? Economic theory cannot provide an answer. Economic theory does not rank people's desires; it does not assign different values to a person's desires before and after a change in preferences. Suppose several students of classical music spend an evening at a disco and suddenly find that they like disco music more than they like Brahms. Were the students' tastes "more natural" or better before being shaped by the disco? Economists may have an opinion, but they have no analytical answer to that question.

LOOKING AHEAD

In this chapter, we outlined the mechanism by which consumers' wants and tastes are communicated to producers. Consumer choices underlie the market demand curve. Discovering the market demand for a product tells producers how strongly consumers desire each commodity relative to others. In the following chapter, we turn to costs of production, which arise because resources have alternative uses. In fact, the cost of producing a good tells the producer how badly the resources are desired in *other* areas. An understanding of these two topics—consumer demand and cost of production—is essential if we are to understand how markets allocate goods and resources.

CHAPTER SUMMARY

1. The demand schedule indicates the amount of a good that consumers would be willing to buy at each potential price. The first law of demand states that the quantity of a product demanded is inversely related to its price. A reduction in the price of a product reduces the opportunity cost of consuming it. At the lower price, many consumers will substitute the now cheaper good for other products. In contrast, higher prices will induce consumers to buy less as they turn to substitutes that are now *relatively* cheaper.

2. The market demand curve reflects the demand of individuals. It is simply the horizontal sum of the demand curves of individuals in the market area.

3. In addition to price, the demand for a product is influenced by the (a) level of consumer income, (b) distribution of income among consumers, (c) price of related products (substitutes and complements), (d) preferences of consumers, (e) population in the market area, and (f) consumer expectations about the future price of the product. Changes in any of these six factors will cause the *demand* for the product to change (the entire curve to shift).

4. Consumers usually gain from the purchase of a good. The difference between the amount that consumers would be willing to pay for a good and the amount they actually pay is called consumer surplus. It is measured by the area under the demand curve but above the market price.

5. Time, like money, is scarce for consumers. Consumers consider both time and money costs when they make decisions. Other things constant, a reduction in the time cost of consuming a good will induce consumers to purchase more of the good.

6. Price elasticity reveals the responsiveness of the amount purchased to a change in price. When there are good substitutes available and the item forms a sizable component of the consumer's budget, its demand will tend to be more elastic. Typically, the price elasticity of a product will increase as more time is allowed for consumers to adjust to the price change. This direct relationship between the size of the elasticity coefficient and the length of the adjustment time period is often referred to as the second law of demand.

7. Both functional and subjective factors influence the demand for a product. Some goods are chosen because they have "snob appeal." Goods may also have a "bandwagon effect," fulfilling a consumer's desire to be fashionable. Observation suggests that goods are demanded for a variety of reasons.

8. The precise effect of advertising on consumer decisions is difficult to evaluate. The magnitude of advertising by profit-seeking business firms is strong evidence that it influences consumer decisions. Advertising often reduces the amount of time consumers must spend looking for a product and helps them make more informed choices. However, a sizable share of all advertising expenditures is largely for noninformational messages. Although this is a controversial area, it is clearly much easier to point out the shortcomings of advertising than to devise an alternative that would not have similar imperfections.

THE ECONOMIC WAY OF THINKING— DISCUSSION QUESTIONS

1. What impact did the substantially lower gasoline prices of the mid-1980s have on (a) the demand for big cars, (b) the demand for small cars, (c) the incentive to experiment and develop electric and other non-gas-powered cars, (d) the demand for gasoline (*Be careful*), and (e) the demand for vacations by automobile in Florida?

2. "As the price of beef rises, the demand of consumers will begin to decline. Economists estimate that a 5 percent rise in beef prices will cause demand to decline by 1 percent." Indicate the two errors in this statement.

3. The following chart presents data on the price of fuel oil, the amount of it demanded, and the demand for insulation. (a) Calculate the price elasticity of demand for fuel oil as its price rises from 30 cents to 50 cents; from 50 cents to 70 cents. (b) Are fuel oil and insulation substitutes or complements? How can you tell from the figures alone?

	Fuel Oil	*Insulation*
Price per Gallon (cents)	Quantity Demanded (millions of gallons)	Quantity demanded (millions of tons)
30	100	30
50	90	35
70	60	40

4. What are the major factors that influence a product's price elasticity of demand? Explain why these factors are important.

5. Do you think that television advertising—as it is conducted by the automobile industry, for example—is wasteful? If so, what would you propose to do about it? Indicate why your proposal would be an improvement over the current situation.

6. Residential electricity in the state of Washington costs about half as much as in nearby Montana. A study showed that in Washington, the average household used about 1200 kilowatt-hours per month, whereas Montanans used about half that much per household. Do these data provide us with two points on the average household's demand curve for residential electricity in this region? Why or why not?

7. **What's Wrong with This Way of Thinking?**
   "Economics is unable to explain the value of goods in a sensible manner. A quart of water is much cheaper than a quart of oil. Yet water is essential to both animal and plant life. Without it, we could not survive. How can oil be more valuable than water? Yet economics says that it is."

ADDENDUM

Consumer Choice and Indifference Curves

In the text of this chapter, we used marginal utility analysis to develop the demand curve of an individual. In developing the theory of consumer choice, economists usually rely on a more formal technique—indifference curve analysis. Since this technique is widely used at a more advanced level, many instructors like to include it in their introductory course. In this addendum, we use indifference curve analysis to develop the theory of demand in a more formal—some would say more elegant—manner.

WHAT ARE INDIFFERENCE CURVES?

There are two elements in every choice: (a) preferences (the desirability of various goods) and (b) opportunities (the attainability of various goods). The **indifference curve** concept is useful for portraying a person's preferences. An indifference curve simply separates better (more preferred) bundles of goods from inferior (less preferred) bundles. It provides a diagrammatic picture of how an individual ranks alternative consumption bundles.

In Exhibit A-1, we assume that Robinson Crusoe is initially consuming 8 fish and 8 breadfruit per week (point *A*). This initial bundle provides him with a certain level of satisfaction (utility). He would, however, be willing to trade this initial bundle for certain other consumption alternatives if the opportunity presented itself. Since he likes both fish and breadfruit, he would especially like to obtain bundles to the northeast of *A*, since they represent more of both goods. However, he would also be willing to give up some breadfruit if in return he received a compensatory amount of fish. Similarly, if the terms of trade were right, he would be willing to exchange

Indifference Curve: A curve, convex from below, that separates the consumption bundles that are more preferred by an individual from those that are less preferred. The points *on* the curve represent combinations of goods that are equally preferred by the individual.

EXHIBIT A-1 • The Indifference Curve of Robinson Crusoe

The curve generated by connecting Crusoe's "I do not care" answers separates the combinations of fish and breadfruit that he prefers to the bundle *A* from those that he judges to be inferior to *A*. The *I* points map out an indifference curve.

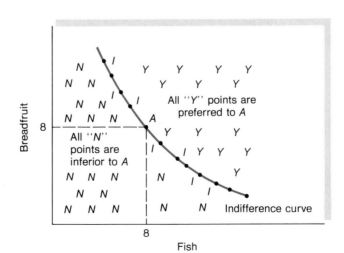

fish for breadfruit. The trade-offs he is just willing to make lie *along* the indifference curve. Of course, he is quite willing to move to any bundle on a higher indifference curve.

Starting from point *A* (8 fish and 8 breadfruit), we ask Crusoe if he is willing to trade that bundle for various other bundles. He answers "Yes" (*Y*), "No" (*N*), or "I do not care" (*I*). Exhibit A-1 illustrates the pattern of his response. Crusoe's "I do not care" answers indicate that the original bundle (point *A*) and each alternative indicated by an *I* are valued equally by Crusoe. These *I* points, when connected, form the indifference curve. This line separates the preferred bundles of fish and breadfruit from the less valued combinations. Note that such a curve may be entirely different for any two people. The preferences of different individuals vary widely.

We can establish a new indifference curve by starting from any point not on the original curve and following the same procedure. If we start with a point (a consumption bundle) to the northeast of the original indifference curve, all points on the new curve will have a higher level of satisfaction for Crusoe than any on the old curve. The new curve will probably have about the same shape as the original.

CHARACTERISTICS OF INDIFFERENCE CURVES

In developing consumer theory, economists assume that the preferences of consumers exhibit certain properties. These properties enable us to make statements about the general pattern of indifference curves. What are these properties, and what do they imply about the characteristics of indifference curves?

1. More Goods Are Preferable to Fewer Goods—Thus, Bundles on Indifference Curves Lying Farthest to the Northeast Are Always Preferred. Assuming the consumption of only two commodities, since *both* commodities are desired, the individual will always prefer to have more of at least one of the goods without loss of any of the others. This means that combinations to the northeast of a point on the diagram will always be preferred to points lying to the southwest.

2. Goods Are Substitutable—Therefore, Indifference Curves Slope Downward to the Right. As we indicated in the text of this chapter, individuals are willing to substitute one good for another. Crusoe will be willing to give up some breadfruit if he is compensated with enough fish. Stated another way, there will be some amount of additional fish such that Crusoe will stay on the same indifference curve, even though his consumption of breadfruit has declined. However, in order to remain on the same indifference curve, Crusoe must always acquire more of one good to compensate for the loss of the other. The indifference curve for goods thus will always slope downward to the right (run northwest to southeast).

3. The Valuation of a Good Declines As It Is Consumed More Intensively—Therefore, Indifference Curves Are Always Convex When Viewed from Below. The slope of the indifference curve represents the willingness of the individual to substitute one good for the other. Economists refer to the amount of one good that is just sufficient to compensate

Marginal Rate of Substitution: The change in the consumption level of one good that is just sufficient to offset a unit change in the consumption of another good without causing a shift to another indifference curve. At any point on an indifference curve, it will be equal to the slope of the curve at that point.

the consumer for the loss of a unit of the other good as the **marginal rate of substitution.** The marginal rate of substitution is equal to the slope of the indifference curve. Reflecting the principle of diminishing marginal utility, the marginal rate of substitution of a good will decline as the good is consumed more intensively relative to other goods. Suppose Crusoe remains on the same indifference curve while continuing to expand his consumption of fish relative to breadfruit. As his consumption of fish increases (and his consumption of breadfruit declines), his valuation of fish relative to breadfruit will decline. It will take more and more units of fish to compensate for the loss of still another unit of breadfruit. The indifference curve will become flatter and flatter, reflecting the decline in the marginal rate of substitution of fish for breadfruit as Crusoe consumes more fish relative to breadfruit.

Of course, just the opposite will happen if Crusoe's consumption of breadfruit increases relative to that of fish—if he moves northwest along the same indifference curve. In this case, as breadfruit is consumed more intensively, Crusoe's valuation of it will decline relative to that of fish, and the marginal rate of substitution of fish for breadfruit will rise (the indifference curve will become steeper and steeper). Therefore, since the valuation of each good declines as it is consumed more intensively, indifference curves must be convex when viewed from the origin.

4. Indifference Curves Are Everywhere Dense. We can draw an indifference curve through any point on the diagram. This simply means that any two bundles of goods can be compared by the individual.

5. Indifference Curves Cannot Cross—If They Did, Rational Ordering Would Be Violated. If indifference curves crossed, our postulate that more goods are better than fewer goods would be violated. Exhibit A-2 illustrates

EXHIBIT A-2 • Indifference Curves Cannot Cross

If the indifference curves of an individual crossed, it would lead to the inconsistency pictured here. Points X and Y must be equally valued, since they are both on the same indifference curve (i_1). Similarly, points X and Z must be equally valued, since they are both on indifference curve i_2. If this is true, Y and Z must also be equally preferred, since they are both equally preferred to X. However, point Y represents more of both goods than Z, so Y has to be preferred to Z. When indifference curves cross, this type of internal inconsistency always arises.

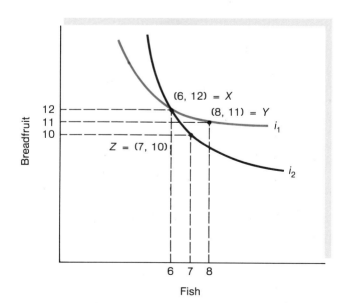

this point. The crossing of the indifference curves implies that points Y and Z are equally preferred, since they both are on the same indifference curve as X. Consumption bundle Y, though, represents more of both fish and breadfruit than bundle Z, so Y must be preferred to Z. Whenever indifference curves cross, this type of internal inconsistency (irrational ranking) will arise. So, the indifference curves of an individual must not cross.

THE CONSUMER'S PREFERRED BUNDLE

Consumption Opportunity Constraint: The constraint that separates the consumption bundles that are attainable from those that are unattainable. In a money income economy, it is usually called a budget constraint.

Together with the opportunity constraint of the individual, indifference curves can be used to indicate the most preferred consumption alternatives available to an individual. The **consumption opportunity constraint** separates consumption bundles that are attainable from those that are unattainable.

Assuming that Crusoe would produce only for himself, his consumption opportunity constraint would look like the production possibilities curves discussed in Chapter 2. What would happen if natives from another island visited Crusoe and offered to make exchanges with him? If a barter market existed that permitted Crusoe to exchange fish for breadfruit at a specified exchange rate, his options would resemble those of the market constraint illustrated by Exhibit A-3. First, let us consider the case in which Crusoe inhabits a barter economy in which the current market exchange rate is 2 fish equal 1 breadfruit. Suppose as a result of his expertise as a fisherman, Crusoe specializes in this activity and is able to bring 16 fish to the market per week. What consumption alternatives will be open to him? Since 2 fish can be bartered in the market for 1 breadfruit, Crusoe will be able to consume 16 fish, or 8 breadfruit, or any combination on the market constraint indicated by the line between these two points. For example, if he trades 2 of his 16 fish for 1 breadfruit, he will be able to consume a bundle consisting of 14 fish and 1 breadfruit. Assuming that the set of indifference curves of Exhibit A-3 outline Crusoe's preferences, he will choose to con-

EXHIBIT A-3 • Consumer Maximization—Barter Economy

Suppose that the set of indifference curves shown here outline Crusoe's preferences. The slope of the market (or budget) constraint indicates that 2 fish trade for 1 breadfruit in this barter economy. If Crusoe produces 16 fish per week, he will trade 8 fish for 4 breadfruit in order to move to the consumption bundle (8 fish and 4 breadfruit) that maximizes his level of satisfaction.

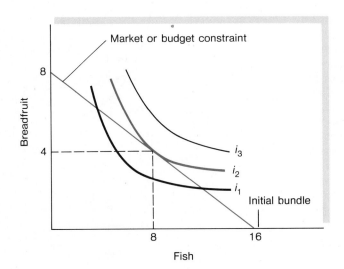

sume 8 fish and 4 breadfruit. Of course, it would be possible for Crusoe to choose many other combinations of breadfruit and fish, but none of the other attainable combinations would enable him to reach as high a level of satisfaction. Since he is able to bring only 16 fish to the market, it would be impossible for him to attain an indifference curve higher than i_2.

Crusoe's indifference curve and the market constraint curve will coincide (they will be tangent) at the point at which his attainable level of satisfaction is maximized. At that point (8 fish and 4 breadfruit), the rate at which Crusoe is *willing* to exchange fish for breadfruit (as indicated by the slope of the indifference curve) will be just equal to the rate at which the market will *permit* him to exchange the two (the slope of the market constraint).[10] If the two slopes differ at a point, Crusoe will always be able to find an attainable combination that will permit him to reach a *higher* indifference curve. He will always move down the market constraint when it is flatter than his indifference curve, and up if the market constraint is steeper.[11]

CRUSOE IN A MONEY ECONOMY

Budget Constraint: The constraint that separates the bundles of goods that the consumer can purchase from those that cannot be purchased, given a limited income and the prices of products.

As far as the condition for maximization of consumer satisfaction is concerned, moving from a barter economy to a money income economy changes little. Exhibit A-4 illustrates this point. Initially, the price of fish is $1, and the price of breadfruit $2. The market therefore permits an exchange of 2 fish for 1 breadfruit, just as was the case in Exhibit A-3. In Exhibit A-4, we assume Crusoe's money income is $16. At this level of income, he confronts the same market constraint (usually called a **budget constraint** in an economy with money) as for Exhibit A-3. Given the product prices and his income, Crusoe can choose to consume 16 fish, or 8 breadfruit, or any combination indicated by a line (the budget constraint) connecting these two points. Given his preferences, Crusoe will again choose the combination of 8 fish and 4 breadfruit if he wishes to maximize his level of satisfaction. As was true for the barter economy, when Crusoe maximizes his satisfaction (moves to the highest attainable indifference curve), the rate at which he is willing to exchange fish for breadfruit will just

---

[10]This actually is required only if the two goods are available in completely divisible amounts, not just as whole fish or whole breadfruit. For simplicity, we assume here that fractional availability is not a problem.

[11]Mathematically, the satisfaction of the consumer is maximized when the marginal rate of substitution of fish for breadfruit is equal to the price ratio. In utility terms, the marginal rate of substitution of fish for breadfruit is equal to the MU of fish divided by the MU of breadfruit. Therefore, the following expression is a condition for maximum consumer satisfaction:

$$\frac{MU_f}{MU_b} = \frac{P_f}{P_b}$$

This can be rewritten as follows:

$$\frac{MU_f}{P_f} = \frac{MU_b}{P_b}$$

Note that this is precisely the condition of consumer maximization that we indicated earlier in this chapter (see footnote 3).

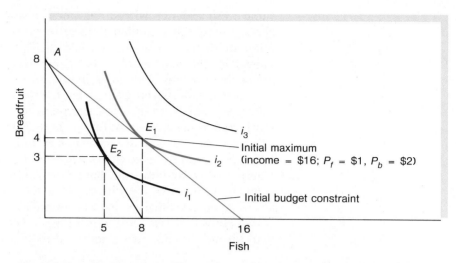

EXHIBIT A-4 • Consumer Maximization— Money Income Economy

Suppose that Crusoe's income is $16-per day, the price of fish (P_1) is $1, and the price of breadfruit (P_b) is $2. Thus, Crusoe confronts exactly the same price ratio and budget constraint as in Exhibit A-3. Assuming that his preferences are unchanged, he will again maximize his satisfaction by choosing to consume 8 fish and 4 breadfruit. What will happen if the price of fish rises to $2? Crusoe's consumption opportunities will be reduced. His budget constraint will turn clockwise around point A, reflecting the higher price of fish. Crusoe's fish consumption will decline to 5 units. (Note: since Crusoe's real income has been reduced, his consumption of breadfruit will also decline.)

equal the rate at which the market will permit him to exchange the two goods. Stated in more technical terms, when his level of satisfaction is at a maximum, Crusoe's marginal rate of substitution of fish for breadfruit, as indicated by the slope of the indifference curve at E_1, will just equal the price ratio (P_f/P_b, which is also the slope of the budget constraint).

What will happen if the price of fish increases? Exhibit A-4 also answers this question. Since the price of breadfruit and Crusoe's money income are constant, a higher fish price will have two effects. First, it will make Crusoe poorer, even though his *money* income will be unchanged. His budget constraint will turn clockwise around point A, illustrating that his consumption options are now more limited—that is, his real income has declined. Second, the budget line will be steeper, indicating that a larger number of breadfruit must now be sacrificed to attain an additional unit of fish. It will no longer be possible for Crusoe to attain indifference curve i_2. The best he can do is indifference curve i_1, which he can attain by choosing the bundle of 5 fish and 3 breadfruit.

Using the information supplied by Exhibit A-4, we can now locate two points on Crusoe's demand curve for fish. When the price of fish was $1, Crusoe chose 8 fish; when the price rose to $2, Crusoe reduced his consumption to 5 (see Exhibit A-5). Of course, other points on Crusoe's demand curve could also be located if we considered other prices for fish.

The demand curve of Exhibit A-5 is constructed on the assumption that the price of breadfruit remains $2 and that Crusoe's money income remains constant at $16. If either of these factors were to change, the entire demand curve for fish, illustrated by Exhibit A-5, would shift.

EXHIBIT A-5 • Crusoe's Demand for Fish

As Exhibit A-4 illustrates, when the price of fish is $1, Crusoe chooses 8 units. When the price of fish increases to $2, he reduces his consumption to 5 units. This gives us two points on Crusoe's demand curve for fish. Other points on the demand curve could be derived by confronting Crusoe with still other prices of fish. [Note: Crusoe's money income ($16) and the price of breadfruit ($2) are unchanged in this analysis.]

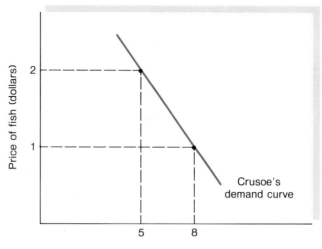

The indifference curve approach is a useful way to illustrate how a person with a fixed budget chooses between two goods. In the real world, of course, people have hundreds, or even thousands, of goods to choose from, and the doubling of only one price usually has a small impact on a person's overall consumption and satisfaction possibilities. In our simple example, the twofold increase in the price of fish makes Crusoe much worse off, since he spends a larger portion of his budget on the item.

THE INCOME AND SUBSTITUTION EFFECTS

In the text, we indicated that when the price of a product rises, the amount consumed will change as a result of both an "income effect" and a "substitution effect." Indifference curve analysis can be used to separate these two effects. Exhibit A-6 is similar to Exhibit A-4. Both exhibits illustrate Crusoe's response to an increase in the price of fish from $1 to $2 when money

EXHIBIT A-6 • The Income and Substitution Effects

Here we break down Crusoe's response to the rise in the price of fish from $1 to $2 (see Exhibit A-4) into the substitution and income effects. The move from E_1 to F illustrates the substitution effect, whereas the move from F to E_2 reflects the income effect.

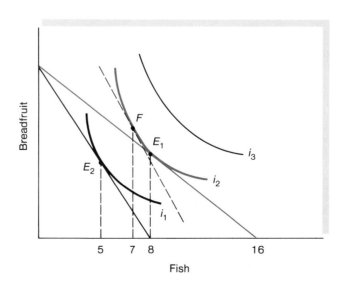

income ($16) and the price of breadfruit ($2) are held constant. Exhibit A-6 however, breaks down his total response into the substitution effect and the income effect. The reduction in the consumption of fish solely because of the substitution (price) effect, holding Crusoe's income (level of satisfaction) constant, can be found by constructing a line tangent to Crusoe's original indifference curve (i_2), the slope of which indicates the higher price of fish. This line (the broken line of Exhibit A-6), which is parallel to Crusoe's actual budget constraint (the line containing point E_2), reflects the higher price of fish. It is tangent to the original indifference curve i_2, so Crusoe's real income is held constant. As this line indicates, Crusoe's consumption of fish will fall from 8 to 7, due strictly to the fact that fish are now more expensive. This move from E_1 to F is a pure substitution effect.

Real income, though, has actually been reduced. As a result, Crusoe will be unable to attain point F on indifference curve i_2. The best he can attain is point E_2, which decreases his consumption of fish by another 2 units to 5. Since the broken line containing F and the budget constraint containing E_2 are parallel, the relative prices of fish and breadfruit are held constant as Crusoe moves from F to E_2. The move from F to E_2 is thus a pure income effect. The reduction in the consumption of fish (and breadfruit) is due entirely to the decline in Crusoe's real income.

Indifference curve analysis highlights the assumptions and considerations that enter into consumer decisions. The logic of the proof that there is an inverse relationship between the price and the amount demanded is both elegant and reassuring. It is elegant because of the internal consistency of the logic and the precision of the analysis. It is reassuring because it conforms with our expectations, which are based on the central postulate of economics—that incentives matter in a predictable way.

CHAPTER
FOCUS

Opportunity cost is the value of the best alternative that must be sacrificed in order to engage in an activity. This is the only relevant cost in economic analysis because it is based on the very nature of the science—the formulation of principles for maximum satisfaction of human wants and scarce resources. The supply curve of any commodity or service consequently reflects opportunity costs which are determined indirectly by consumers clamoring for a myriad of goods. [1]

MARSHALL COLBERG

- Why are business firms used by societies everywhere to organize production?

- How are firms organized in market economies?

- What are explicit and implicit costs, and what role do they play in guiding the behavior of the firm?

- How does economic profit differ from accounting profit? What is the role of profit for a firm, and for an industry?

- How do short-run costs differ from long-run costs for the firm?

- What factors can shift the firm's cost curves?

17 COSTS AND THE SUPPLY OF GOODS

Demand and supply interact to determine the market price of a product. In the last chapter, we illustrated that the demand for a product reflects the preferences of consumers. In this chapter, we focus on costs of production, which are the major determinants of both the nature and the position of the supply curve for a good. If the cost of producing a good exceeds its price, producers will not continue to supply it. Most persons recognize that supply and cost of production are closely linked. For example, if it costs $400 to produce a stereo set, manufacturers will not supply the sets, at least not for very long, at a price of $200. In the long-run, the sets will be supplied only if they can command a price of at least $400.

In this chapter, we lay the foundation for a detailed investigation of the link between costs and market supply. The nature and function of costs are central to economic analysis. The economist's use of the term "costs" differs sometimes from that of business decision-makers and accountants. What do economists mean by costs? Why are costs so important? What is the function of costs in a market economy? We discuss these and related questions in this chapter.

ORGANIZATION OF THE BUSINESS FIRM

The business firm is an entity designed to organize raw materials, labor, and machines with the goal of producing goods and/or services. Firms (a) purchase productive resources from households and other firms, (b) transform them into a different commodity, and (c) sell the transformed product or service to consumers.

Economies may differ in the amount of freedom they allow business decision-makers. They may also differ in the incentive structure used to stimulate and guide business activity. Nevertheless, every society relies on business firms to organize resources and transform them into products. In Western economies, most business firms choose their own price, output level, and productive techniques. In socialist countries, government policy often establishes the selling price and constrains the actions of business firms in various other ways. In any case, the central position of the business firm as the organized productive unit is universal to capitalist and socialist economies alike.

INCENTIVES, COOPERATION, AND THE NATURE OF THE FIRM[2]

Most firms are privately owned in capitalist countries. The owners, who may or may not act as entrepreneurs, are the individuals who risk their wealth on the success of the business. If the firm is successful and makes profits, these financial gains go to the owners. Conversely, if things go badly and the firm suffers losses, the owners must bear the consequences. Thus, the

---

[1]Marshall R. Colberg, Dascomb R. Forbush, and Gilbert R. Whitaker, *Business Economics* (Homewood, Illinois: Irwin, 1980), p. 12.

[2]A classic article on this topic is Ronald Coase, "The Nature of the Firm," *Economica*, (1937), pp. 386–405. See also Armen Alchian and Harold Demsetz, "Production, Information Costs, and Economic Organization," *American Economic Review*, (Dec. 1972), pp. 777–795.

wealth of the owners is directly influenced by the success or failure of the firm.

Business firms rely primarily on two organizational methods when producing a good or service: team production and contracting. In team production, employees work together under the supervision of the owner, or the owner's representative. The owner must direct the efforts of the employees, provide an incentive system (including the maintaining of morale), and monitor the work of each to prevent shirking. Team members are **shirking** if they are reducing output by working at less than a normal rate of productivity. Taking long work breaks, paying more attention to worker convenience than to results, and "horsing around" when diligence is called for are examples of shirking. A worker will shirk more when the costs of doing so are shifted to other members of the team. It is not easy to prevent shirking, but the owner's gains from the firm depend directly on successful monitoring and incentive management, as well as on wise choices of outputs and production techniques. The owner is a **residual claimant,** receiving the excess of revenues over costs. If costs exceed revenues, however, the value of the firm and the owner's wealth are reduced.

Many firms make extensive use of contracting when producing goods or services. The Boeing Company, for example, hires many employees, but when it builds a giant 747 airliner, it also contracts with hundreds of other firms to provide many of the needed parts and services. This reduces the employee monitoring problem for Boeing. The company only has to monitor the product of the contractor supplying the jet engines, rather than monitor all the engine-building workers. This adds some additional transactions costs, though, since it must search out reliable suppliers, and negotiate and enforce contracts.

How do owners share the risks and liabilities of the firm? How do they carry out or participate in the decision-making? There are three major legal structures under which business firms may be organized—proprietorships, partnerships, or corporations. The role of residual claimants (owners), and the liability faced by them, differs in each of the three structures.

Shirking: Working at less than a normal rate of productivity, thus reducing output. Shirking is more likely when workers are not monitored, so that the cost of lower output falls on others.

Residual Claimant: Individual in a firm who receives the excess of revenues over costs. A residual claimant gains if the firm's costs are reduced and if revenues are increased.

PROPRIETORSHIPS

A proprietorship is a business firm that is owned by a single individual who is fully liable for the debts of the firm. In addition to assuming the responsibilities of ownership, the proprietor often works directly for the firm, providing managerial and other labor services. Many small businesses, including neighborhood grocery stores, barbershops, and farms, are business proprietorships. As Exhibit 1 shows, proprietorships comprised 70 percent of all business firms in 1982. Because most proprietorships are small, however, they generated only 6 percent of all business receipts for that year.

PARTNERSHIPS

A partnership consists of two or more persons acting as co-owners of a business firm. The partners share risks and responsibilities in some prearranged manner. There is no difference between a proprietorship and a partnership in terms of owner liability. In both cases, the owners are fully liable for all business debts incurred by the firm. Many law, medical, and accounting firms are organized along partnership lines. This form of business structure accounts for only 10 percent of the total number of firms and 4 percent of all business receipts.

EXHIBIT 1 • How Business Firms Are Organized

Nearly three out of every four firms is a proprietorship, but only 6% of all business revenues are generated by proprietorships. Corporations are only one out of every five firms, but generate 90% of all revenues.

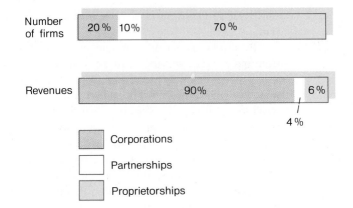

Source: Statistical Abstract of the United States: 1986, Table 876 (Data are for 1982).

CORPORATIONS

Measured in terms of business receipts, the corporate business structure is by far the most important. Even though corporations comprised only 20 percent of all business firms in 1982, they accounted for 90 percent of all business receipts. What are the distinctive characteristics of the corporation? What accounts for its attractiveness?

First, the stockholders of the corporation are the legal owners of the firm. Any profits of the firm belong to them. Their liability, however, is strictly limited. They are liable for corporate debts only to the extent of their explicit investment. If a corporation owes you money, you cannot directly sue the stockholders. You can, of course, sue the corporation. But, what if it goes bankrupt? You and others to whom the firm owes money will simply be out of luck.

Second, the limited liability makes it possible for corporations to attract investment funds from a large number of "owners" who do not participate in the day-to-day management of the firm. The stockholders of many large corporations simply hire managers to operate the firm. Corporations are thus often characterized by a separation of ownership and operational management.

Third, ownership can easily be transferred. The shares, or ownership rights, of an owner who dies can be sold by the heirs to another owner without disrupting the business firm. Because of this, the corporation is an ongoing concern. Similarly, any stockholders who become unhappy with the way a corporation is run can bail out merely by selling their stock.

The managers of a large corporation might be thought of as trained experts hired by the stockholders to run the firm. The decisions of stockholders to buy and sell shares of stock mirror the confidence of investors in the management of the firm. If current and prospective stockholders alike come to believe that the managers will do a good job, the demand for the firm's stock will increase. Rising stock prices will reflect this increase in demand. Conversely, when a large number of the current stockholders want to sell their shares because they are dissatisfied with the current management, the supply of the firm's stock put up for sale increases, causing its price to tumble. Falling stock prices will often lead to a shake-up in the management of the firm.

If an outside person or group believes their own managerial strategy would be better, they can try to purchase enough stock to gain control of the corporation and replace the current management. Such a "takeover" is usually resisted by the management, but it often raises the value of the stock, suggesting that others in the market also believe the new management would improve the corporation's performance.

THE ROLE OF COSTS

Consumers would like to have more economic goods, but resources are scarce. We cannot produce as much of all goods as we would like. The use of resources to produce one commodity leaves fewer resources with which to produce other desired goods. Thus, the desire for product A must be balanced against the desire for other items that must now be sacrificed because resources have been consumed by the production of A. Every economic system must balance the desire for each good against the scarcity of resources required to produce the good. When decisions are made in the political arena, the budget process performs this balancing function. Congress (or the central committee, or the king) decides how much each good is valued relative to every other good. Taxes and budgets are set accordingly.

In a market economy, consumer demand and cost of production are central to the performance of this balancing function. The desire of consumers for a specific good must be balanced against the *desire for other goods* that could be produced with the resources. Since resources have alternative uses, certain goods that could be produced with these resources are lost. It is these forgone opportunities that give rise to costs of production. Resources employed in the production of a good must be paid an amount that will draw them away from their alternative employment opportunities. As resources are bid away from their alternative employment opportunities, costs of production are incurred. Costs of production reveal the value of the resources in their alternative uses.

The demand for a product can be thought of as the voice of consumers instructing firms to produce a good. On the other hand, costs of production represent the voice of consumers saying that other items that could be produced with the resources are also desired. The demand for a product indicates the intensity of consumers' desires for the item. The cost of producing a product indicates the desire of consumers for other goods that must now be forgone because the necessary resources have been employed in the production of the first item.

CALCULATING ECONOMIC COSTS AND PROFITS

Business firms, regardless of their size, give primary attention to profits. What is profit? Most people, including many businesspeople, think of profit as that portion of their sales revenues that remains after they have paid for raw materials, labor, machines, and similar inputs. Unfortunately, this concept of profit, which stems from accounting procedures, generally ignores some of the firm's costs.

Explicit Costs: Money paid by a firm to purchase the services of productive resources.

Implicit Costs: The opportunity costs associated with a firm's use of resources that it owns. These costs do *not* involve a direct money payment. Examples include wage income and interest forgone by the owner of a firm who also provides labor services and equity capital to the firm.

The key to understanding the economist's concept of profit is our old friend—opportunity cost. The firm incurs a cost whenever it uses a resource, thereby requiring the resource owner to forgo the highest valued alternative. These costs may either be explicit or implicit. **Explicit costs** result when the firm makes a monetary payment to resource owners. Money wages, interest, and rental payments are a measure of what the firm gives up to employ the services of labor and capital resources. Firms also usually incur **implicit costs**—costs associated with the use of resources owned by the firm. Since implicit costs do not involve a direct money or contractual payment, they are often excluded from accounting statements. For example, the owners of small proprietorships often supply labor services to their businesses. There is an opportunity cost associated with the use of this resource; other opportunities have to be given up because of the time spent by the owner in the operation of the business. The highest valued alternative forgone is the opportunity cost of the labor service provided by the owner. The **total cost** of production is the sum of the explicit and implicit costs incurred by the employment of all resources involved in the production process.

PROFIT AND THE OPPORTUNITY COST OF CAPITAL

Total Cost: The costs, both explicit and implicit, of all the resources used by the firm. Total cost includes an imputed normal rate of return for the firm's equity capital.

The most important implicit cost generally omitted from accounting statements is the cost of capital. Persons who supply equity capital to a firm expect their financial investment to yield at least a normal rate of return, which could be derived from other investment opportunities. If investors do not earn this normal rate of return on their investment, they will not continue to supply financial capital to the business.

This normal rate of return is the **opportunity cost of capital.** If the normal rate of return on equity capital is 10 percent, investors will not continue to supply funds to firms unable to earn a 10 percent rate of return on capital assets. As a result, earning the normal rate of return—that is, covering the opportunity cost of capital—is vital to the survival of a business firm.

ACCOUNTING PROFIT AND ECONOMIC PROFIT

Opportunity Cost of Capital: The implicit rate of return that must be paid to investors to induce them to continuously supply the funds necessary to maintain a firm's capital assets.

Economic Profit: The difference between the firm's total revenues and total costs.

Since economists seek to measure the opportunities lost due to the production of a good or service, they include both explicit and implicit costs in total cost. **Economic profit** is equal to total revenues minus total costs, including both the explicit and implicit cost components. Economic profits will be present only if the earnings of a business are in excess of the opportunity cost of using the assets owned by the firm. Economic losses result when the earnings of the firm are insufficient to cover explicit and implicit costs. When the firm's revenues are just equal to its costs, both explicit and implicit, economic profits will be zero.

Remember that zero economic profits do not imply that the firm is about to go out of business. On the contrary, they indicate that the owners are receiving exactly the market rate of return on their investment (assets owned by the firms).

Since accounting procedures often omit implicit costs, such as those associated with owner-provided labor services or capital assets, the accounting costs of the firm generally understate the opportunity costs of production. This understatement of cost leads to an overstatement of profits. Therefore, the **accounting profits** of a firm are generally greater than the

Accounting Profits: The sales revenues minus the expenses of a firm over a designated time period, usually one year. Accounting profits typically make allowances for changes in the firm's inventories and depreciation of its assets. No allowance is made, however, for the opportunity cost of the equity capital of the firm's owners, or other implicit costs.

Short-Run (in Production): A time period so short that a firm is unable to vary some of its factors of production. The firm's plant size typically cannot be altered in the short-run.

firm's economic profits (see boxed feature). When the omission of the costs of owner-provided services is unimportant, as is the case for most large corporations, accounting profits approximate what we refer to as the normal rate of return. High accounting profits (measured as a rate of return on a firm's assets), relative to the average for other firms, suggest that a firm is earning an economic profit. Correspondingly, a low accounting rate of profit implies economic losses.

SHORT-RUN AND LONG-RUN

A firm cannot instantaneously adjust its output. Time plays an important role in the production process. Economists often speak of the **short-run** as a time period so short that the firm is unable to alter its present plant size. In the short-run, the firm is "stuck" with its existing plant and heavy equipment. They are "fixed" for a given time period. The firm can alter output, however, by applying larger or smaller amounts of variable resources, such as labor and raw materials. The firm's existing plant capacity can thus be used more or less intensively in the short-run.

In sum, we can say that the short-run is that period of time during which at least one factor of production, usually the size of the firm's plant, cannot be varied.

How long is the short-run? The length varies from industry to industry. In some industries, substantial changes in plant size can be accomplished in

APPLICATIONS IN ECONOMICS

Economic and Accounting Cost—A Hypothetical Example

The revenue-cost statement for a corner grocery store owned and operated by Terry Smith is presented below.

Terry works full-time as the manager, chief cashier, and janitor. Terry has $30,000 worth of refrigeration and other equipment invested in the store. Last year, Terry's total sales were $85,000; suppliers and employees were paid $50,000. Terry's revenues exceed explicit costs by $35,000. Did Terry make a profit last year? The accounting statement for the store will probably show a net profit of $35,000. However, if Terry did not have a $30,000 personal investment in equipment, these funds could be collecting 10 percent interest. Thus, Terry is forgoing $3000 of interest

each year. Similarly, if the building that Terry owns was not being used as a grocery store, it could be rented to someone else for $500 per month. Rental income thus forgone is $6000 per year. In addition, since Terry is tied up working in the grocery story, a $28,000 managerial position with the local A&P is forgone. Thus, when one considers the interest, rental, and salary income that Terry had to forgo in order to operate the grocery store last year, Terry's implicit costs were $37,000. The total costs were $87,000. The total revenue of Terry's grocery store was less than the opportunity cost of the resources utilized. Terry incurred an economic loss of $2000, despite the accounting profit of $35,000.

Total revenue		**$85,000**
Sales (groceries)		
Total (explicit costs)		
Groceries, wholesale	$38,000	
Utilities	2,000	
Taxes	3,000	
Advertising	1,000	
Labor services (employees)	6,000	
Total (explicit) costs		$50,000
Net (accounting) profit		$35,000
Additional (implicit) costs		
Interest (personal investment)		$ 3,000
Rent (Terry's building)		6,000
Salary (Terry's labor)		28,000
Total implicit costs		$37,000
Total explicit and implicit costs		**87,000**
Economic profit (**total revenue minus explicit and implicit costs**)		**−2,000**

a few months. In other industries, particularly those that use assembly lines and mass production techniques (for example, aircraft and automobiles), the short-run might be a year or even several years.

Long-Run (in Production): A time period long enough to allow the firm to vary all factors of production.

The **long-run** is a time period of sufficient length to allow a firm the opportunity to alter its plant size and capacity and all other factors of production. All resources of the firm are variable in the long-run. In the long-run, from the viewpoint of an entire industry, new firms may be established and enter the industry; other firms may dissolve and leave the industry.

Perhaps an example will help to clarify the distinction between the short- and long-run time periods. If a battery manufacturer hired 200 additional workers and ordered more raw materials to squeeze a larger output from the existing plant, this would be a short-run adjustment. In contrast, if the manufacturer built an additional plant (or expanded the size of its current facility) and installed additional heavy equipment, this would be a long-run adjustment.

COSTS IN THE SHORT-RUN

We have emphasized that in the short-run some of a firm's factors of production, such as the size of the plant, will be fixed. Other productive resources will be variable. In the short-run, then, we can break the firm's costs into these two categories—fixed and variable.

Fixed Cost: Cost that does not vary with output. However, fixed cost will be incurred as long as a firm continues in business and the assets have alternative uses.

Fixed costs will remain unchanged even though output is altered. A firm's insurance premiums, its property taxes, and, most significantly, the opportunity cost of using its fixed assets will be present whether the firm produces a large or a small rate of output. Nor will costs vary with output. These costs are "fixed" as long as the firm remains in business. Fixed costs will be present at all levels of output, including zero. They can be avoided only if the firm goes out of business.

Average Fixed Cost: Fixed cost divided by the number of units produced. It always declines as output increases.

What will happen to **average fixed cost** (AFC) as output expands? Remember that the firm's fixed cost will be the same whether output is 1, 100, or 1000. The average fixed cost is simply fixed cost divided by output. AFC will decline as output is increased (see Exhibit 2a).

EXHIBIT 2 • General Characteristics of the Short-run Cost Curves

Average fixed costs (a) will be high for small rates of output, but they will always decline as output expands. Marginal cost (b) will rise sharply as the plant's production capacity q is approached. As graph (c) illustrates, ATC will be a U-shaped curve, since AFC will be high for small rates of output and MC will be high as the plant's production capacity is approached.

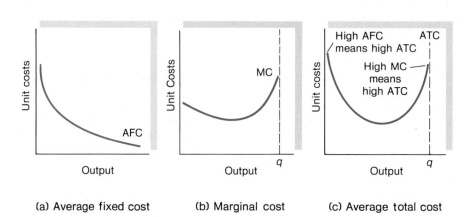

(a) Average fixed cost   (b) Marginal cost   (c) Average total cost

Variable Costs: Costs that vary with the rate of output. Examples include wages paid to workers and payments for raw materials.

Average Variable Cost: The total variable cost divided by the number of units produced.

Average Total Cost: Total cost divided by the number of units produced. It is sometimes called per unit cost.

Marginal Cost: The change in total cost required to produce an additional unit of output.

Variable costs are those costs that vary with output. For example, additional output can usually be produced by hiring more workers and expending additional funds on raw materials. Variable costs involve expenditures on these and other variable inputs. At any given level of output, the firm's **average variable cost** is the total variable cost divided by output.

We have noted that total cost includes explicit and implicit costs. The total cost of producing a good is also the sum of the fixed and variable costs at each output level. At zero output, total cost will equal fixed cost. As output expands from zero, variable cost and fixed cost must be added to obtain total cost. **Average total cost** (ATC), sometimes referred to as "unit cost," can be found by dividing total cost by the total number of units produced. Average total cost is also equal to the sum of the average fixed and average variable costs.

The economic way of thinking emphasizes the importance of what happens "at the margin." How much does it cost to produce an additional unit? **Marginal cost** is the change in total cost that results from the production of one additional unit. In the short-run, as illustrated by Exhibit 2, marginal costs will generally decline if output is increased, then eventually reach a minimum, and then increase. The rising marginal costs simply reflect the fact that it becomes increasingly difficult to squeeze additional output from a plant as the facility's management capacity (the dotted line of Exhibit 2b) is approached. The Thumbnail Sketch summarizes the interrelationships among a firm's various costs.

THUMBNAIL SKETCH

Relationships among a Firm's Costs

1. Total cost includes both explicit and implicit costs.
2. Total cost = fixed cost + variable cost.
3. Marginal cost = change in total cost per added unit of output.
4. Average total cost = total cost ÷ output.
5. Average fixed cost = fixed cost ÷ output.
6. Average variable cost = variable cost ÷ output.
7. Average total cost = average fixed cost + average variable cost.

As a firm alters its rate of output in the short-run, how will unit cost be affected? First, let us look at this question intuitively. In the short-run, the firm can vary output by using its fixed plant size more (or less) intensively. As Exhibit 2 illustrates, there are two extreme situations that will result in a high unit cost of output. First, when the output rate of a plant is small relative to its capacity, it is obviously being underutilized. Under these circumstances, average fixed cost will be high, and therefore average total cost will also be high. It will be costly and inefficient to operate a large plant substantially below its production capacity. At the other extreme, overutilization can also result in high unit cost. An overutilized plant will mean congestion, waiting time for machines, and similar costly delays. As output approaches the maximum capacity of a plant, overutilization will lead to high marginal costs, and therefore to high average total costs.

Thus, the average total cost curve will be U-shaped, as pictured in Exhibit 2c. Average total cost will be high for both an underutilized plant (because AFC is high) and an overutilized plant (with a high MC).

DIMINISHING RETURNS AND PRODUCTION IN THE SHORT-RUN

Our analysis of the link between unit cost and output rate is corroborated by a long-established economic law, the law of diminishing returns. The **law of diminishing returns** states that as more and more units of a variable factor are applied to a fixed amount of other resources, output will eventually increase by smaller and smaller amounts. Therefore, in terms of their impact on output, the returns to the variable factor will diminish.

The law of diminishing returns is as famous in economics as the law of gravity is in physics. The law is based on common sense. Have you ever noticed that as you apply a single resource more intensively, the resource eventually tends to accomplish less and less? Consider a farmer who applies fertilizer more and more intensively to an acre of land (a fixed factor). At some point, the application of additional 100-pound units of fertilizer will expand the wheat yield by successively smaller amounts.

Essentially, the law of diminishing returns is a constraint imposed by nature. If it were not valid, it would be possible to raise all the world's foodstuffs on an acre of land, or even in a flowerpot. Suppose we did *not* experience diminishing returns when we applied more labor and fertilizer to land. Would it ever make sense to cultivate any of the less fertile land? Of course not. We would be able to increase output more rapidly simply by applying another unit of labor and fertilizer to the world's most fertile flowerpot! But, of course, that would be a fairy tale; the law of diminishing returns applies in the real world.

Exhibit 3 illustrates the law of diminishing returns numerically. Col-

Law of Diminishing Returns: The postulate that as more and more units of a variable resource are combined with a fixed amount of other resources, employment of *additional* units of the variable resource will eventually increase output only at a decreasing rate. Once diminishing returns are reached, it will take successively larger amounts of the variable factor to expand output by one unit.

EXHIBIT 3 • The Law of Diminishing Returns (hypothetical data)			
(1) Units of the Variable Resource, Labor (per Day)	(2) Total Product (Output)	(3) Marginal Product	(4) Average Product
0	0		—
1	8	8	8.0
2	20	12	10.0
3	34	14	11.3
4	46	12	11.5
5	56	10	11.2
6	64	8	10.7
7	70	6	10.0
8	74	4	9.3
9	75	1	8.3
10	74	−1	7.4

Total Product: The total output of a good that is associated with alternative utilization rates of a variable input.

umn 1 indicates the quantity of the variable resource, labor in this example, that is combined with a specified amount of the fixed resource. Column 2 shows the **total product** that will result as the utilization rate of labor increases. Column 3 provides data on the **marginal product,** the change in total output associated with each additional unit of labor. Without the application of labor, output would be zero. As additional units of labor are applied, total product (output) expands. As the first three units of labor are applied, total product increases by successively larger amounts (8, then 12, then 14). Beginning with the fourth unit, however, diminishing returns are confronted. When the fourth unit is added, marginal product—the change in the total product—declines to 12 (down from 14, when the third unit was applied). As additional units of labor are applied, marginal product continues to decline. It is increasingly difficult to squeeze a larger total product from the fixed resources (for example, plant size and equipment). Eventually, marginal product becomes negative (beginning with the tenth unit).

Marginal Product: The increase in the total product resulting from a unit increase in the employment of a variable input. Mathematically, it is the ratio of (a) change in total product divided by (b) change in the quantity of the variable input.

Column 4 of Exhibit 3 provides data for the **average product** of labor. The average product is simply the total product divided by the units of labor applied. Note the average product increases as long as the marginal product is greater than the average product. This is true through the first four units. The marginal product of the fifth unit of labor, though, is 10, less than the average product for the first four units of labor (11.5). Therefore, beginning with the fifth unit, average product declines as additional labor is applied.

Average Product: The total product (output) divided by the number of units of the variable input required to produce that output level.

Using the data from Exhibit 3, Exhibit 4 illustrates the law of diminishing returns graphically. Initially, the total product curve (Exhibit 4a) increases quite rapidly. As diminishing marginal returns are confronted (beginning with the fourth unit of labor), total product increases more slowly. Eventually, a maximum output (75) is reached with the application of the ninth unit of labor. The marginal product curve (Exhibit 4b) reflects

EXHIBIT 4 · The Law of Diminishing Returns

As units of variable input (labor) are added to a fixed input, total product will increase, first at an increasing rate and then at a declining rate (graph a). This will cause both the marginal and average product curves (graph b) to rise at first and then decline. Note that the marginal product curve intersects the average product curve at its maximum.

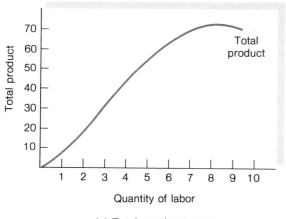

(a) Total product curve

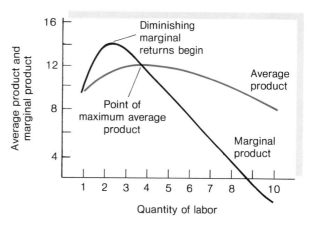

(b) Average and marginal product curve

the total product curve. Geometrically, marginal product is the slope—the rate of increase—of the total product curve. That slope, the marginal product, reaches its maximum with the application of three units of labor. Beyond three units, diminishing returns are present. Eventually, at ten units of labor, the marginal product become negative. When marginal product becomes negative, total product is necessarily declining. The average product curve rises as long as the marginal product curve is above it, since each added unit of labor is raising the average. The average product reaches its maximum at four units of labor. Beyond that, each additional unit of labor brings down the average product, and the curve declines.

DIMINISHING RETURNS AND COST CURVES

What impact will diminishing returns have on a firm's costs? Once a firm confronts diminishing returns, larger and larger additions of the variable factor are required to expand output by one unit. Marginal costs rise until, eventually, they exceed average total cost. When marginal costs are greater than ATC, ATC increases. It is easy to see why. What happens when an above-average student is added to a class? The class average goes up. What happens if a unit of above-average cost is added to output? Average total cost would rise. The firm's marginal cost curve therefore crosses the ATC curve at the ATC's lowest point. For output rates beyond the minimum ATC, the rising marginal cost causes average total cost to increase. Again, the average total cost curve is U-shaped.

Exhibit 5 numerically illustrates the implications of the law of diminishing returns for a firm's short-run cost curve. Here, we assume that Royal Roller Skates, Inc., combines units of a variable input with a fixed factor to produce units of output (skates). Columns 2, 3, and 4 indicate how total cost schedules vary as output is expanded. Total fixed costs, representing the

EXHIBIT 5 • Numerical Short-Run Cost Schedules of Royal Roller Skates, Inc.

	Total Cost Data (per Day)			Average/Marginal Cost Data (per Day)			
(1)	(2)	(3)	(4)	(5)	(6)	(7)	(8)
Output per Day	Total Fixed Cost	Total Variable Cost	Total Cost, (2) + (3)	Average Fixed Cost, (2) ÷ (1)	Average Variable Cost, (3) ÷ (1)	Average Total Cost, (4) ÷ (1)	Marginal Cost, Δ(4) ÷ Δ(1)
0	$50	$ 0	$ 50	—	—	—	—
1	50	15	65	$50.00	$15.00	$65.00	$15
2	50	25	75	25.00	12.50	37.50	10
3	50	34	84	16.67	11.33	28.00	9
4	50	42	92	12.50	10.50	23.00	8
5	50	52	102	10.00	10.40	20.40	10
6	50	64	114	8.33	10.67	19.00	12
7	50	79	129	7.14	11.29	18.43	15
8	50	98	148	6.25	12.25	18.50	19
9	50	122	172	5.56	13.56	19.11	24
10	50	152	202	5.00	15.20	20.20	30
11	50	202	252	4.55	18.36	22.91	50

opportunity cost of the fixed factors of production, are $50 per day. For the first four units of output, total variable costs increase at a *decreasing rate*. Why? In this range, there are increasing returns to the variable input. Beginning with the fifth unit of output, however, diminishing marginal returns are present. From this point on, total variable costs and total costs increase by successively larger amounts as output is expanded.

Columns 5 through 8 of Exhibit 5 reveal the general pattern of the average and marginal cost schedules. For small output rates, the average total cost of producing skates is high, primarily because of the high AFC. Initially, marginal costs are less than ATC. When diminishing returns set in for output rates beginning with five units, however, marginal cost rises. Beginning with the sixth unit of output, marginal cost exceeds average variable cost, causing AVC to rise. Beginning with the eighth unit of output, MC exceeds ATC, causing it also to rise. ATC thus reaches a minimum at seven units of output. Observe the data of Exhibit 5 carefully to ensure that you fully understand the relationships among the various cost curves.

Using the numeric data of Exhibit 5, Exhibit 6 graphically illustrates both the total and the average/marginal cost curves. Note that the marginal cost curve intersects both the average variable cost and average total cost curves at the minimum points (Exhibit 6b). As marginal costs continue to rise above average total cost, unit costs rise higher and higher as output increases beyond seven units.

In sum, the firm's short-run cost curves are merely a reflection of the law of diminishing marginal returns. Assuming that the price of the variable resource is constant, marginal costs decline so long as the marginal product of the variable input is rising. This results because, in this range, smaller and smaller additions of the variable input are required to produce each extra unit of output. This situation is reversed, however, when diminishing returns are confronted. Once diminishing returns set in, more and more units

EXHIBIT 6 • Costs in the Short-run

Using data of Exhibit 5, graph (a) illustrates the general shape of the firm's short-run total cost curves; graph (b) illustrates the general shape of the firm's average and marginal cost curves. Note that when output is small (for example, 2 units), average total cost will be high because the average fixed costs are so high. Similarly, when output is large (for example, 11 units) per unit cost (ATC) will be high because it is extremely costly to produce the marginal units. Thus, the short-run ATC curve will be U-shaped.

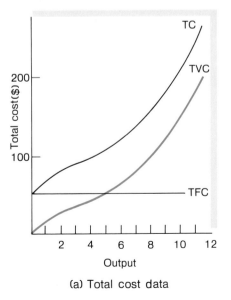

(a) Total cost data

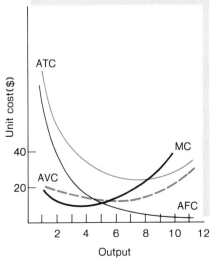

(b) Average/marginal cost data

of the variable factor are required to generate each additional unit of output. Marginal cost will rise, because the marginal product of the variable resources is declining. Eventually, marginal costs exceed average variable and average total costs, causing these costs also to rise. A U-shaped short-run average total cost curve results.

COSTS IN THE LONG-RUN

The short-run analysis relates costs to output *for a specific size of plant.* Firms, though, are not committed forever to their existing plant. In the long-run, a firm can alter its plant size and all other factors of production. All resources used by the firm are variable in the long-run.

How will the firm's choice of plant size affect production costs? Exhibit 7 illustrates the short-run average total cost curves for three plant sizes, ranging from small to large. If these three plant sizes were the only possible choices, which one would be best? The answer depends on the rate of output the firm expects to produce. The smallest plant would have the lowest cost if an output rate of less than q_1 were produced. The medium-sized plant would provide the least-cost method of producing output rates between q_1 and q_2. For any output level greater than q_2, the largest plant would be the most cost-efficient.

The long-run average total cost curve shows the minimum average cost of producing each output level when the firm is free to choose among all possible plant sizes. It can best be thought of as a "planning curve," because it reflects the expected per unit cost of producing alternative rates of output while plants are still in the blueprint stage.

Exhibit 7 illustrates the long-run average total cost curve when only three plant sizes are possible. The planning curve *ABCD* is mapped out. Given sufficient time, of course, firms can usually choose among many plants of various sizes. Exhibit 8 presents the long-run planning curve under these circumstances. A smooth planning curve results. Each short-run average total cost curve will be tangent to the long-run planning curve.

EXHIBIT 7 • The Long-run Average Cost

The short-run average cost curves are shown for three alternative plant sizes. If these three were the only possible plant sizes, the long-run average curve would be *ABCD*.

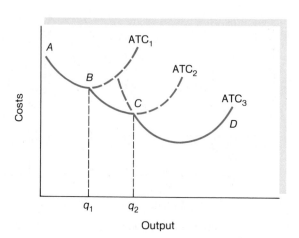

EXHIBIT 8 • The Planning Curve

When many alternative plant sizes are possible, the long-run average total cost curve LRATC is mapped out.

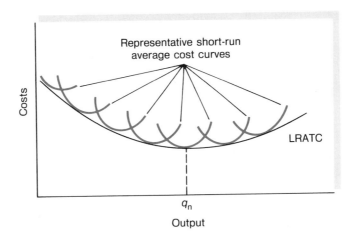

The tangency, though, will occur at the least-cost output level for the short-run curve only when the long-run curve is parallel to the x-axis (for example, q_n, Exhibit 8).

No single plant size could produce the alternative output rates at the costs indicated by the planning curve. The long-run average total cost curve merely outlines the expected average costs of production for each of a large number of plants that differ in size.

SIZE OF FIRM AND UNIT COST IN THE LONG-RUN

Do larger firms have lower minimum unit costs than smaller ones? The answer to this question depends on which industries are being considered. There is a sound basis, though, for **initially** expecting some cost reductions from large-scale production methods. Why? Large firms typically produce a large total volume of output.[3] Volume of output denotes the total number of units of a product that the firm expects to produce.[4] There are three major reasons why unit costs initially decline as firms plan a larger total volume of output (and a larger size of plant).

1. Adoption of Mass Production Techniques. Large firms are often able to use mass production techniques that are economical *only* when large volumes of output are planned. Mass production usually involves large development and setup costs. Once the production methods are established,

---

[3]Throughout this section, we assume that firms with larger plants necessarily plan a larger volume of output than do their smaller counterparts. Reality approximates these conditions. Firms choose large plants because they are planning to produce a large volume.

[4]Note the distinction between rate and volume of output. *Rate* of output is the number of units produced during a specific period (for example, the next six months). *Volume* is the total number of units produced during all time periods. For example, Boeing might produce two 747 airplanes per month (rate of output) while planning to produce a volume of one hundred 747s during the expected life of the model. Increasing the rate (reducing the time period during which a given output is produced) tends to raise costs, whereas increasing the volume (total amount produced) tends to lower costs. For additional information on production and costs, see Armen Alchian, "Costs," in *International Encyclopedia of the Social Sciences* (New York: Macmillan, 1968), pp. 404–415, and Jack Hirshleifer, "The Firm's Cost Function: A Successful Reconstruction," *Journal of Business* (July 1962), pp. 235–255.

though, marginal costs are low. Because of the large setup costs, mass production techniques are uneconomical for small volumes of output. For example, the use of molds, dies, and assembly line production methods reduce the per unit cost of automobiles only when the planned volume is in the millions. In contrast, these methods would result in high per unit costs if they were used to produce only a few thousand automobiles.

2. Specialization. Large-scale operation results in greater opportunity for specialized use of labor and machines. Adam Smith noted 200 years ago that the output of a pin factory is much greater when one worker draws the wire, another straightens it, a third cuts it, a fourth grinds the point, a fifth makes the head of the pin, and so on.[5] In economics, the whole can sometimes be greater than the sum of the parts. Specialization provides the opportunity for people to become exceptionally proficient at performing small but essential functions. When each of them acts as a specialist, more is produced than if each made the final product from start to finish.

3. Learning by Doing. Workers and managers in a firm that has made more units have probably learned more from their experience. Improvements in the production process result. Baseball players improve by playing, and musicians improve by performing. Similarly, workers and management improve their skills as they "practice" productive techniques. This factor has been found to be tremendously important in the aircraft and automobile industries, among others.

ECONOMIES AND DISECONOMIES OF SCALE

Economies of Scale: Reductions in the firm's per unit costs that are associated with the use of large plants to produce a large volume of output.

Economic theory suggests that compared to smaller firms, larger firms have lower unit costs. When unit cost declines as output expands, **economies of scale** are present over the initial range of outputs. The long-run average total cost curve is falling.

Are diseconomies of scale possible—that is, are there ever situations in which the long-run average costs are greater for larger firms than they are for smaller ones? The economic justification for diseconomies of scale is less obvious (and less tenable) than that for economies of scale. However, as a firm gets bigger and bigger, bureaucratic inefficiencies *may* result. Codebook procedures tend to replace managerial genius. Problems associated with monitoring performance, coordinating activities, conveying information, and carrying out managerial directives may multiply. These factors combine to cause rising long-term average total cost in some, although certainly not all, industries.

---

[5]Smith went on to state: "I have seen a small manufactory of this kind where ten men only were employed, and where some of them consequently performed two or three distinct operations. Those ten persons, therefore, could make among them upwards of forty-eight thousand pins in a day. But if they had all wrought separately and independently, and without any of them having been educated to this peculiar business, they certainly could not each of them have made twenty, perhaps not one pin in a day." (Adam Smith, *An Inquiry into the Nature and Causes of the Wealth of Nations*, 1776 [Cannan's edition, Chicago: University of Chicago Press, 1976], pp. 8–9).

Economies and diseconomies of scale stem from different sources than do increasing and diminishing returns. Economies and diseconomies of scale are long-run concepts. They relate to conditions of production when all factors are variable. In contrast, increasing and diminishing returns are short-run concepts. They are applicable only when the firm has a fixed factor of production.

Exhibit 9 outlines three different long-run average total cost (LRATC) curves that describe real-world conditions in differing situations. For Exhibit 9a, both economies and diseconomies of scale are present. Higher per unit costs will result if the firm chooses a plant size other than the one that minimizes the cost of producing output q, the ideal size of plant in this situation. If each firm in an industry faces the same cost conditions, we can generalize and say that any plants that are larger or smaller than this ideal size will experience higher unit costs. A very narrow range of plant sizes would be possible in industries with the LRATC depicted by Exhibit 9a. Some lines of retail sales and agriculture might approximate these conditions.

Exhibit 9b demonstrates the general shape of the LRATC that economists believe is present in most industries. Initially, economies of scale exist, but once a minimum efficient scale is reached, wide variation in firm size is possible. Firms smaller than the minimum efficient size would have higher per unit costs, but firms larger than that would not gain a cost advantage. **Constant returns to scale** are present for a broad range of output rates (between q_1 and q_2). This situation is consistent with real-world conditions in many industries. For example, small firms can be as efficient as larger ones in such industries as apparel, lumber, shoes, publishing, and in many lines of retailing.

Constant Returns to Scale: Unit costs are constant as the scale of the firm is altered. Neither economies nor diseconomies of scale are present.

EXHIBIT 9 · Three Different Types of Long-run Average Cost Curves

Graph (a) indicates that for output levels less than q, economies of scale are present. Immediately beyond q, diseconomies of scale dominate. Graph (b) indicates that economies of scale are important until some minimum output level q_1 is attained. Once the minimum has been attained, there is a wide range of output levels (q_1 to q_2) that are consistent with the minimum ATC for the industry. Graph (c) indicates that economies of scale exist for all relevant output levels. As we will see later, this type of long-run ATC curve has important implications for the structure of the industry.

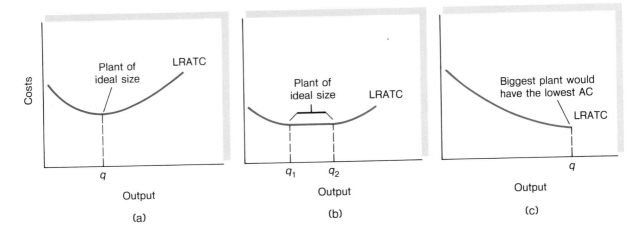

Exhibit 9c indicates that economies of scale exist for all relevant output levels. The larger the firm size, the lower the per unit cost. The LRATC in the telephone service industry may approximate the curve of Exhibit 9c.

WHAT FACTORS CAUSE THE FIRM'S COST CURVES TO SHIFT?

In outlining the general shapes of a firm's cost curves in both the long- and the short-runs, we assumed that certain other factors remained constant, not changing with the firm's output. What are those other factors, and how will they affect production costs?

1. *Prices of Resources.* If the price of resources used should rise, the firm's cost curves will shift upward. Higher resource prices will increase the cost of producing each alternative output level. As Exhibit 10 illustrates, the firm's cost curves will shift upward. For example, what happens to the cost of producing automobiles when the price of steel rises? The cost of producing automobiles also rises. Conversely, lower resource prices will result in cost reductions. Thus, the cost curves for any specific plant size will shift downward.

2. *Taxes.* Taxes are a component of the firm's cost. Suppose that an excise tax of 20 cents were levied on each gallon of gasoline sold by a service station. What would happen to the seller's costs? They would increase, just as they did in Exhibit 10. The firm's average total and marginal cost curves would shift upward by the amount of the tax.

3. *Technology.* Technological improvements often make it possible to produce a specific output with fewer resources. For example, the printing press drastically reduced the number of labor-hours required to print newspapers and books. The spinning wheel reduced the labor-hours necessary to weave cotton into cloth. More recently, computers and robots have reduced costs in many industries. As Exhibit 11 shows, a technological improvement will shift the firm's cost curves downward, reflecting the reduction in the amount of resources used to produce alternative levels of output.

EXHIBIT 10 • Higher Resource Prices and Cost

An increase in resource prices will cause the firm's cost curves to shift upward.

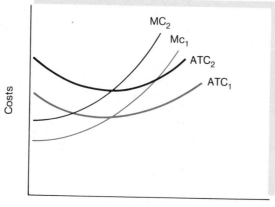

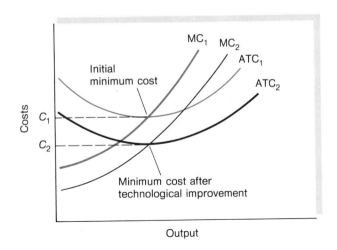

COSTS AND THE ECONOMIC WAY OF THINKING

When analyzing the firm's costs, economists often present a highly mechanical—some would say unrealistic—view. The role of personal choice tends
to be glossed over.

It is important to keep in mind that costs are incurred when choices are
made. When business decision-makers choose to purchase raw materials,
hire new employees, or renew the lease on a plant, they incur costs. All these
decisions, like other choices, must be made under conditions of uncertainty.
Of course, past experience acts as a useful guide, yielding valuable information. Because of this, business decision-makers will have a good idea of the
costs that will be associated with alternative decisions.

Opportunity costs are usually "expected costs"—they represent that
which the decision-maker expects to give up as the result of a choice. Think
for a moment of what the cost curves developed in this chapter really mean.
The firm's short-run marginal cost curve represents the opportunity cost of
expanding output, *given the firm's current plant size.* The firm's long-run
average total cost curve represents the opportunity cost per unit of output
associated with varying plant sizes and rates of output, *given that the alternative plants are still on the drawing boards.* Opportunity costs look forward,
reflecting expectations—often based on the past record—as to what will be
forgone as a result of current decisions. At decision time, neither the short-
run marginal cost nor the long-run average total cost can be determined
from accounting records. Accounting costs look backward. They yield valuable information about historical costs.

**Sunk Costs: Costs that
have already been in-
curred as a result of past
decisions. They are some-
times referred to as historical costs.**

SUNK COSTS

Historical costs associated with past decisions—economists call them **sunk
costs**—should exert no direct influence on current choices. The outcome of
past choices will provide knowledge relevant to current decisions, but the
specific costs themselves are no longer relevant. Past choices cannot be
reversed; money that has been spent is gone for good. Current choices

should be based on the costs and benefits expected in relation to *current* market conditions.

If they are to minimize costs, business decision-makers must recognize the irrelevance of sunk costs. Let us consider a simple example that emphasizes this point. Suppose that the firm of Exhibit 5 pays $100,000 to purchase and install a skate-producing machine. The machine is expected to last ten years. The company's books record the cost of the machine as $10,000 each year under the heading of depreciation. The machine can be used only to make roller skates. Since dismantling and reinstallation costs are high, the machine cannot be leased or sold to another firm. It has no scrap value. In other words, there are no alternative uses for the machine. The machine's annual production of roller skates will generate $50,000 of revenues for the firm when it is employed with raw materials and other factors of production that cost $45,000.

Should the firm continue to use the machine? The annual depreciation cost of the machine suggests that the firm loses $5000 annually on the output of the machine. The depreciation cost, however, is a sunk cost. It was incurred when the machine was installed. The current opportunity cost of the machine is precisely zero. The firm is not giving up anything by con-

MYTHS OF ECONOMICS

"A good business decision-maker will never sell a product for less than its production costs."

This statement contains a grain of truth. A profit-seeking entrepreneur would not *undertake* a project knowing that the costs could not be covered. However, this view fails to emphasize (a) the time dimension of the production process and (b) the uncertainty associated with business decisions. The production process takes time. Raw materials must be purchased, employees hired, and plants equipped. Retailers must contract with suppliers. As these decisions are made, costs result. Many of the firm's costs of production are incurred long before the product is ready for marketing.

Even a good business decision-maker is not always able to predict the future correctly. Market condi-

tions may change in an unexpected manner. At the time the product is ready for sale, buyers may be unwilling to pay a price that will cover the seller's past costs of production. These past costs, however, are now sunk costs and no longer relevant. Current decisions must be made on the basis of current cost and revenue considerations.

Should a grocer refuse to sell oranges that are about to spoil because their wholesale cost cannot be covered? The grocer's current opportunity cost of selling the oranges may be nearly zero. The alternative may be to throw them in the garbage next week. Almost any price, even one far below past costs, would be better than letting the oranges spoil.

Consider another example. Suppose a couple who own a house

plan to relocate temporarily. Should they refuse to rent their house for $200 (if this is the best offer available) because their monthly house payment is $240? Of course not. The house payment will go on, regardless of whether or not they rent the house. If the home-owners can cover their opportunity costs, perhaps a $60 monthly fee for a property management service, they will gain by renting rather than leaving the house vacant.

Past mistakes provide useful lessons for the future, but they cannot be reversed. Bygones are bygones, even if they resulted in business loss. Only current revenue and cost considerations are relevant to current decisions about price levels and profitability. There is no need to fret over spilt milk, burnt toast, or yesterday's business losses.

tinuing to operate it. Since the machine generates $5000 of additional net revenue, the firm should continue using it. Of course, if current market conditions are expected to continue, the firm will not purchase a similar machine or replace the machine when it wears out, but this should not influence the decision of whether or not to continue operating the current one. The irrelevance of sunk costs helps explain why it often makes sense to continue operating older equipment (it has a low opportunity cost), even though it might not be wise to purchase similar equipment again.

COST AND SUPPLY

Economists are interested in cost because they seek to explain the supply decisions of firms. A strictly profit-maximizing firm will compare the expected revenues derived from a decision or a course of action with the expected costs. If the expected revenues exceed costs, the course of action will be chosen because it will expand profits (or reduce losses).

In the short-run, the marginal cost of producing additional units is the relevant cost consideration. A profit-maximizing decision-maker will compare the expected marginal costs with the expected additional revenue from larger sales. If the latter exceeds the former, output (the quantity supplied) will be expanded.

Whereas marginal costs are central to the choice of short-run output, the expected average total cost is vital to a firm's long-run supply decision. *Before entry into an industry*, a profit-maximizing decision-maker will compare the expected market price with the expected long-run average total cost. Profit-seeking potential entrants will supply the product if, and only if, they expect the market price to exceed their long-run average total cost. Similarly, existing firms will continue to supply a product only if they expect the market price will enable them at least to cover their long-run average total cost.

LOOKING AHEAD

In this chapter, we outlined several basic principles that affect costs for business firms. We will use these basic principles when we analyze the price and output decisions of firms under alternative market structures in the chapters that follow.

CHAPTER SUMMARY

1. The business firm is used to organize productive resources and transform them into goods and services. There are three major business structures—proprietorships, partnerships, and corporations. Proprietorships are the most numerous, but most of the nation's business activity is conducted through corporations.
2. The demand for a product indicates the intensity of consumers' desires for the item. The (opportunity) cost of producing the item indicates the desire of consumers for other goods that must now be given up because the necessary resources have been used in the production of the item. In a market economy, these two forces—demand and costs of production—balance the desire of consumers for more of a good against the reality of scarce resources, which requires that other goods be forgone as more of any one specific item is supplied.

3. Economists employ the opportunity cost concept when figuring a firm's costs. Therefore, total cost includes not only explicit (money) costs but also implicit costs associated with the use of productive resources owned by the firm.

4. Since accounting procedures often omit costs, such as the opportunity cost of capital and owner-provided services, accounting costs generally understate the opportunity cost of producing a good. As a result of these omissions, the accounting profits of a firm are generally larger than the firm's economic profits.

5. Economic profit (loss) results when a firm's sales revenues exceed (are less than) its total costs, both explicit and implicit. Firms that are making the market rate of return on their assets will therefore make zero economic profit. Firms that transform resources into products of greater value than the opportunity cost of the resources used will make an economic profit. On the other hand, if the opportunity cost of the resources used exceeds the value of the product, losses will result.

6. The firm's short-run average total cost curve will tend to be U-shaped. When output is small (relative to plant size), average fixed cost (and therefore ATC) will be high. As output expands, however, AFC (and ATC) will fall. As the firm attempts to produce a larger and larger rate of output using its fixed plant size, diminishing returns will eventually set in, and marginal cost will rise quite rapidly as the plant's maximum capacity is approached. Thus, the short-run ATC will also be high for large output levels because marginal costs are high.

7. The law of diminishing returns explains why a firm's short-run marginal and average costs will eventually rise as the rate of output expands. When diminishing marginal returns are present, successively larger amounts of the variable input will be required to increase output by one more unit. Thus, marginal costs will eventually rise as output expands. Eventually, marginal costs will exceed average total costs, causing the latter to rise, also.

8. The ability to plan a larger volume of output often leads to cost reductions. These cost reductions associated with the scale of one's operation result from (a) a greater opportunity to employ mass production methods, (b) specialized use of resources, and (c) learning by doing.

9. The LRATC reflects the costs of production for plants of various sizes. When economies of scale are present (that is, when larger plants have lower per unit costs of production), LRATC will decline. When constant returns to scale are experienced, LRATC will be constant. A rising LRATC is also possible. Bureaucratic decision-making and other diseconomies of scale may in some cases cause LRATC to rise.

10. In analyzing the general shapes of a firm's cost curves, we assumed that the following factors remained constant: (a) resource prices, (b) technology, and (c) taxes. Changes in any of these factors would cause the cost curves of a firm to shift.

11. In any analysis of business decision-making, it is important to keep the opportunity cost principle in mind. Economists are interested in costs primarily because costs affect the decisions of suppliers. Short-run marginal costs represent the supplier's opportunity cost of producing addi-

tional units with the existing plant facilities of the firm. The long-run average total cost represents the opportunity cost of supplying alternative rates of output, given sufficient time to vary all factors, including plant size.

12. Sunk costs are costs that have already been incurred. They should not exert a *direct* influence on current business choices. However, they may provide a source of information that will be useful in making current decisions.

THE ECONOMIC WAY OF THINKING— DISCUSSION QUESTIONS

1. What is economic profit? How might it differ from accounting profit? Explain why firms that are making zero economic profit are likely to continue in business.

2. Which of the following do you think reflect sound economic thinking? Explain your answer.
   (a) "I paid $200 for this economics course. Therefore, I'm going to attend the lectures even if they are useless and boring."
   (b) "Since we own rather than rent, housing doesn't cost us anything."
   (c) "I own 100 shares of stock that I can't afford to sell until the price goes up enough for me to get back at least my original investment."
   (d) "It costs to produce private education, whereas public schooling is free."

3. Suppose a firm produces bicycles. Will the firm's accounting statement reflect the opportunity cost of producing bicycles? Why or why not? What costs would an accounting statement reveal? Should current decisions be based on accounting costs? Explain.

4. Explain in your own words why a firm's short-run average total costs will decline initially but eventually increase as the rate of output is expanded.

5. Which of the following are relevant to a firm's decision to increase output: (a) short-run average total cost; (b) short-run marginal cost; (c) long-run average total cost? Justify your answer.

6. Economics students often confuse (a) diminishing returns to the variable factor and (b) diseconomies of scale. Explain the difference between the two and give one example of each.

7. **What's Wrong with This Way of Thinking?**
   "The American steel industry cannot compete with German and Japanese steel producers. After World War II, these countries rebuilt modern, efficient mills that made use of the latest technology. In contrast, American mills are older and less efficient. Our costs are higher because we are stuck with old facilities."

CHAPTER
FOCUS

Competition is conducive to the continuous improvements of industrial efficiency. It leads some producers to eliminate wastes and cut costs so that they may undersell others. It compels others to adopt similar measures in order that they may survive. It weeds out those whose costs remain high and thus operates to concentrate production in the hands of those whose costs are low. [1]

CLAIR WILCOX

- What does the term "competition" mean in economics?

- What is the purely competitive model and why is it important?

- What determines the output of a competitive firm?

- How do competitive firms change their output when price changes, in the short-run? In the long-run?

- What is the role of time in determining the elasticity of supply?

- How is the competitive model related to economic efficiency?

18 THE FIRM UNDER PURE COMPETITION

In the last chapter, we outlined some basic principles that determine the general relationship between output and costs of production for any firm. Of course, a firm's output decisions will be influenced by its costs and its revenues. In this and the next two chapters, we will illustrate how the structure of an industry affects the revenues and output levels of firms. We will analyze four models of industrial structure: (a) pure competition, (b) monopoly, (c) monopolistic competition, and (d) oligopoly. These models will help us understand the role of competitive forces under various market conditions. This chapter focuses on pure competition.

THE PROCESS OF COMPETITION

Competition as a Dynamic Process: A term that denotes rivalry or competitiveness between or among parties (for example, producers or input suppliers), each of which seeks to deliver a better deal to buyers when quality, price, and product information are all considered. Competing implies a lack of collusion among sellers.

Before we introduce the model of pure competition, a few comments about the use of the term "competition" are in order. It is important not to lose sight of the function of **competition as a dynamic process** to explain the mechanics of alternative forms of industrial structure. The competitive process emphasizes the rivalry among firms—the effort on the part of a seller to outperform the alternative suppliers. Competing firms may use a variety of methods—quality of product, style, convenience of location, advertising, and price—to attract consumers. Independent action and rivalry are the essential ingredients of the competitive process.

Rivalry among sellers serves consumers well because sellers are under intense pressure to cater to consumers' preferences. Producers who offer only low quality at a high price find that their customers turn to rival sellers.

As the introductory quotation from Professor Wilcox indicates, competition also places pressure on producers to operate efficiently and to avoid waste. Competition weeds out the inefficient—those who are incapable of providing consumers with quality goods at low prices. Competition also keeps producers on their toes in other areas. The production techniques and product offerings that lead to success today will not necessarily pass the competitive market test tomorrow. Producers who survive in a competitive environment cannot be complacent. They must be forward-looking and innovative. They must be willing to experiment and quick to adopt improved methods.

Each competitor is, of course, in business to make a profit. Rival firms struggle for the dollar votes of consumers. Competition, though, is the taskmaster that forces producers to serve the interests of consumers and to do so at the lowest possible level of profit. As Adam Smith noted more than 200 years ago, competition harnesses the profit motive and puts it to work, elevating our standard of living and directing our resources toward the production of those goods that we desire most intensely relative to their cost. Smith pointed out that aggregate output would be vastly expanded if individuals specialized in those things they did best and cooperated with others desirous of their services. He believed that self-interest directed by competitive markets would generate precisely these two ingredients—spe-

---

[1]Clair Wilcox, *Competition and Monopoly in American Industry,* Monograph no. 21, Temporary National Economic Committee, Investigation of Concentration of Economic Power, 76th Congress, 3rd session (Washington, D.C.: U.S. Government Printing Office, 1940).

cialization and cooperation. Smith emphasized this theme in Book 1 of *The Wealth of Nations*:

> It is not from the benevolence of the butcher, the brewer, or the baker, that we expect our dinner, but from their regard to their own self-interest. We address ourselves, not to their humanity but to their self-love, and never talk to them of our own necessities, but of their advantages.[2]

In Smith's time, as today, many thinkers erred because they did not understand that productive action and voluntary exchange offer the potential for mutual gain. Both parties to an economic exchange generally gain (see "Myths of Economics," p. 45). Bridled by competition, self-interest leads to economic cooperation and provides a powerful fuel for the benefit of humankind. Paradoxical as it seems, even though benevolence may be the more admirable attitude, it cannot generate the cooperative effort that is a natural outgrowth of self-interest directed by competition. Unilateral giving does not generate the information and feedback to buyers and sellers inherent in the competitive market process. Thus, the competitive process occupies center stage in economic analysis, which seeks to explain the forces that direct the economic behavior of human beings.

Before we move on to more technical material, two additional points should be addressed. First, a dual usage of the term "competition" has evolved through the years. The term is used to describe a rivalry or competitiveness among sellers, as we have already noted. In addition, the term "competition," or more precisely, "pure competition," is used to describe a hypothetical model of industrial structure characterized by independent firms and a large number of sellers. This dual usage can sometimes be confusing. It is important to recognize that firms can be competitive in the sense of rivalry even though they may not be competitive in the industrial structure sense. To avoid confusion, we will use the complete expression "pure competition" when we discuss the competitive model of industrial structure.

Second, we have emphasized the role of competition as the taskmaster forcing sellers to obey the desires of consumers. As is generally the case with those under the thumb of a tough taskmaster, sellers have a strong incentive to escape the discipline imposed by competitive forces. Business participants often try to avert the discipline of competition. Much of the material on industrial structure will provide a framework within which to analyze both the likelihood of a business firm escaping the directives of competition and the economic implications of its doing so.

Pure Competition: A model of industrial structure characterized by a large number of small firms producing a homogeneous product in an industry (market area) that permits complete freedom of entry and exit.

Homogeneous Product: A product of one firm that is identical to the product of every other firm in the industry. Consumers see no difference in units of the product offered by alternative sellers.

THE PURELY COMPETITIVE MODEL

Pure competition presupposes that the following conditions exist in a market.

1. *All Firms in the Market Are Producing a **Homogenous Product**.* The product of firm A is identical to the product offered by firm B and all other

---

[2]Adam Smith, *An Inquiry into the Nature and Causes of the Wealth of Nations* (1776; Cannan's ed., Chicago: University of Chicago Press, 1976), p. 18.

firms. This presupposition rules out advertising, locational preferences, quality difference, and other forms of nonprice competition.

2. *A Large Number of Independent Firms Produce the Product.* The independence of the firms rules out joint actions designed to restrict output and raise prices.

3. *Each Buyer and Seller Is Small Relative to the Total Market.* Therefore, no single buyer or seller is able to exert any noticeable influence on the market supply and demand conditions. For example, a wheat farmer selling 5000 bushels annually would not have a noticeable impact on the U.S. wheat market, in which 2,500,000,000 bushels are traded annually.

Barriers to Entry: Obstacles that limit the freedom of potential rivals to enter an industry.

4. *There Are No Artificial **Barriers to Entry** into or Exit from the Market.* Under pure competition, any entrepreneur is free either to produce or fail to produce in the industry. New entrants need not obtain permission from the government or the existing firms before they are free to compete. Nor does control of an essential resource limit market entry.

The purely competitive model, like other theories, is abstract. Keep in mind that the test of a theory is not the realism of its assumptions but its ability to make *predictions* that are consistent with the real world (see Chapter 1). Assumptions are made and ideas are simplified so that we can better organize our thoughts. Models, based on simplifications and assumptions, can often help us develop the economic way of thinking.

WHY IS PURE COMPETITION IMPORTANT?

Previously, we discussed how supply and demand jointly determine market price. The model of pure competition is another way of looking at the operation of market forces. This model will help us understand the relationship between the decision-making of individual firms and market supply. If we familiarize ourselves with the way in which economic incentives influence the supply decisions of firms within the competitive model, we will be better able to understand the behavior of firms in markets that are less than purely competitive.

There are other reasons for the model's importance. Its conditions are approximated in a few important industries, most notably agriculture. The model will help us understand these industries. In addition, as we will show later, the equilibrium conditions in the competitive model yield results that are identical to ideal static efficiency conditions. Many economists thus use the competitive model as a standard by which to judge other industrial structures.

Price Takers: Sellers who must take the market price in order to sell their product. Because each price taker's output is small relative to the total market, price takers can sell all of their output at the market price, but are unable to sell any of their output at a price higher than the market price. Thus, they face a horizontal demand curve.

THE WORKINGS OF THE COMPETITIVE MODEL

Since a competitive firm by itself produces an output that is small relative to the total market, it cannot influence the market price. A purely competitive firm must accept the market price if it is to sell any of its product. Competitive firms are sometimes called **price takers,** because they must take the market price in order to sell.

Exhibit 1 illustrates the relationship between market forces [graph (b)] and the demand curve facing the purely competitive firm [graph (a)].

EXHIBIT 1 • The Firm's Demand Curve Under Pure Competition

The market forces of supply and demand determine price (b). Under pure competition, individual firms have no control over price. Thus, the demand for the product of the firm is perfectly elastic (a).

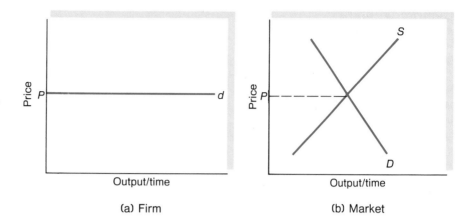

(a) Firm   (b) Market

If a pure competitor sets a price above the market level, consumers will simply buy from other sellers. Why pay the higher price when the identical good is available elsewhere at a lower price? For example, if the price of wheat were $4 per bushel, a farmer would be unable to find buyers for wheat at $4.50 per bushel. A firm could lower its price, but since it is small relative to the total market, it can already sell as much as it wants at the market price. A price reduction would merely reduce revenues. A purely competitive *firm* thus confronts a perfectly elastic demand for *its* product.

DECIDING HOW MUCH TO PRODUCE—THE SHORT-RUN

The firm's output decision is based on comparison of benefits with costs. If a firm produces at all, it will continue expanding output as long as the benefits (additional revenues) from the production of the additional units exceed their marginal costs.

How will changes in output influence the firm's costs? In the last chapter, we discovered that the firm's short-run marginal costs will *eventually* increase as the firm expands its output by working its fixed plant facilities more intensively. The law of diminishing marginal returns assures us that this will be the case. *Eventually*, both the firm's short-run marginal and average total cost curves will turn upward.

What about the benefits or additional revenues from output expansion? **Marginal revenue** (MR) is the change in the firm's total revenue per unit of output. It is the additional revenue derived from the sale of an additional unit of output. Mathematically,

Marginal Revenue: The incremental change in total revenue derived from the sale of one additional unit of a product.

$$MR = \frac{\text{change in total revenue}}{\text{change in output}}$$

Since the purely competitive firm sells all units at the same price, its marginal revenue will be equal to the market price.

In the short-run, the purely competitive firm will expand output until marginal revenue (its price) is just equal to marginal cost. This decision-making rule will maximize the firm's profits (or minimize its losses).

Exhibit 2 helps explain why. Since the firm can sell as many units as it would like at the market price, the sale of one additional unit will increase revenue by the price of the product. As long as price exceeds marginal cost,

EXHIBIT 2 • Profit Maximization and the Purely Competitive Firm

The purely competitive firm would maximize profits by producing the output level *q*, where *P* = MC.

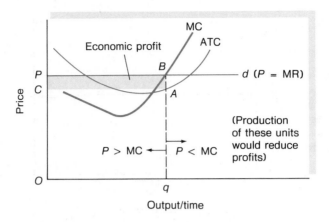

revenue will increase more than cost as output is expanded. Since profit is merely the difference between total revenue and total cost, profit will increase as output is expanded as long as price exceeds MC. For the pure competitor, profit will be at a maximum when P = MR = MC. This would be the output level q for the firm of Exhibit 2.

Why would the firm not expand output beyond q? The cost of producing such units is given by the height of the MC curve. The sale of these units would increase revenues only by P, the price of the product. Production of units beyond q would add more to cost than to revenue. Therefore, production beyond q, the P = MC output level, would reduce the firm's profits.

A profit-maximizing firm with the cost curves indicated by Exhibit 2 would produce exactly q. The total revenue of the firm would be the sales price P multiplied by output sold q. Geometrically, the firm's total revenues would be $POqB$. The firm's total cost would be found by multiplying the average total cost by the output level. Geometrically, total costs are represented by $COqA$. The firm's total revenues exceed total costs, and the firm is making short-run economic profit (the shaded area).

In the real world, of course, decisions are not made by entrepreneurs who sit around drawing curves labeled MC and P. Many have not even heard of these concepts. Our model also ignores the problem of uncertainty. Very often, businesspeople must make decisions without complete knowledge of what costs or product price will be. In addition, there may be problems of "lumpiness." The manager may prefer to use 1.7 machines and 2.5 people to carry out a production process. Managers, however, know that machines and people alike come in discrete "lumps," or whole units. They may not be able to approximate what they want even by renting, or changing the machine size they use, or hiring part-time employees.

Despite the inconvenient and uncertain facts of real life, our simple model does make fairly accurate predictions. A business decision-maker who has never heard of the P = MC rule for profit maximization probably has another rule that yields approximately the same outcome. For example, the rule might be: Produce those units, and only those units, that add more to revenue than to cost. This ensures maximum profit (or minimum loss). It also takes the firm to the point at which P = MC. Why? To stop short of that point is to fail to produce units that add more (the sales price) to revenue than they do to cost. Similarly, refusal to produce units that cost more than they add to revenue ensures that production will not exceed the $P = MC$ output level. This commonsense rule thus leads to the same outcome as the competitive model, even when the decision-maker knows none of the technical jargon of economics. This shows why economics is often described as organized common sense.

Exhibit 3 uses numeric data to illustrate profit-maximizing decision-making for a competitive firm. The firm's short-run total and marginal cost schedules have the general characteristics we discussed in the previous chapter. Since the firm confronts a market price of $5 per unit, its marginal revenue is $5. Total revenue thus *increases* by $5 per additional unit of output. The firm maximizes its profit when it supplies an output of 15 units.

There are two ways of viewing this profit-maximizing output rate. First, we could examine the difference between total revenue and total cost, identifying the output rate at which this difference is greatest. Column 6, the profit data, provides this information. For small output rates (less than 11), the firm would actually experience losses. But, at 15 units of output, an $11 profit is earned ($75 total revenue minus $64 total cost). Inspection of the profit column indicates that it is impossible to earn a profit larger than $11 at any other rate of output.

EXHIBIT 3 • Profit Maximization of a Competitive Firm— A Numeric Illustration					
(1) Output (per Day)	(2) Total Revenue	(3) Total Cost	(4) Marginal Revenue	(5) Marginal Cost	(6) Profit (TR − TC)
0	$ 0.00	$ 25.00	$0.00	$ 0.00	− 20.00
1	5.00	29.80	5.00	4.80	− 24.80
2	10.00	33.75	5.00	3.95	− 23.75
3	15.00	37.25	5.00	3.50	− 22.25
4	20.00	40.25	5.00	3.00	− 20.25
5	25.00	42.75	5.00	2.50	− 17.75
6	30.00	44.75	5.00	2.00	− 14.75
7	35.00	46.50	5.00	1.75	− 11.50
8	40.00	48.00	5.00	1.50	− 8.00
9	45.00	49.25	5.00	1.25	− 4.25
10	50.00	50.25	5.00	1.00	− 0.25
11	55.00	51.50	5.00	1.25	3.50
12	60.00	53.25	5.00	1.75	6.75
13	65.00	55.75	5.00	2.50	9.25
14	70.00	59.25	5.00	3.50	10.75
15	75.00	64.00	5.00	4.75	11.00
16	80.00	70.00	5.00	6.00	10.00
17	85.00	77.25	5.00	7.25	7.75
18	90.00	85.50	5.00	8.25	4.50
19	95.00	95.00	5.00	9.50	0.00
20	100.00	108.00	5.00	13.00	− 8.00
21	105.00	125.00	5.00	17.00	− 20.00

Exhibit 4a presents the total revenue and total cost approach in graph form. Profits will be maximized when the total revenue line exceeds the total cost curve by the largest vertical amount. That takes place, of course, at 15 units of output.

The marginal approach can also be used to determine the profit-maximizing rate of output for the competitive firm. Remember, as long as price (marginal revenue) exceeds marginal cost, production and sale of additional units will add to the firm's profit (or reduce its losses). Inspection of columns 4 and 5 of Exhibit 3 indicates that MR is greater than MC for the first 15 units of output. Production of these units will expand the firm's profit. In contrast, the production of each unit beyond 15 adds more to cost than to revenue. Profit will therefore decline if output is expanded beyond 15 units. Given the firm's cost and revenue schedule, the profit-maximizing manager will choose to produce 15, and only 15, units per day.

Exhibit 4b graphically illustrates the marginal approach. Note here that the output rate (15 units) at which the marginal cost and marginal revenue curves intersect coincides with the output rate in Exhibit 4a at which the total revenue curve exceeds the total cost curve by the largest amount.

EXHIBIT 4 • Profit Maximization—The Total and Marginal Approaches

Utilizing the data of Exhibit 3, here we provide two alternative ways of viewing profit maximization. As graph (a) illustrates, the profits of the competitive firm are maximized at the output level at which total revenue exceeds total cost by the maximum amount. Graph (b) demonstrates that the maximum-profit output can also be identified by comparing marginal revenue and marginal cost.

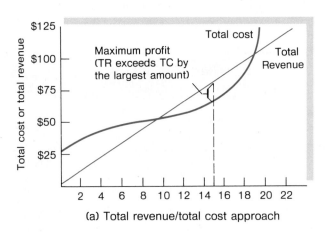

(a) Total revenue/total cost approach

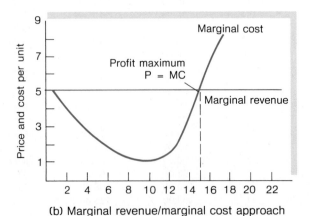

(b) Marginal revenue/marginal cost approach

LOSSES AND GOING OUT OF BUSINESS

Suppose changes take place in the market that depress the price below a firm's average total cost. How will a profit-maximizing (or loss-minimizing) firm respond to this situation? The answer to this question depends on both the firm's current sales revenues relative to its *variable cost* and its expectations about the future. The firm has three options—it can (a) continue to operate in the short-run, (b) shut down temporarily, or (c) go out of business.

If the firm anticipates that the lower market price is temporary, it may want to continue operating in the short-run as long as it is able to cover its variable cost.[3] Exhibit 5 illustrates why. The firm shown in this exhibit would minimize its loss at output level q, where $P = $ MC. At q, total revenues ($OqBP_1$) are, however, less than total costs ($OqAC$). The firm confronts short-run economic losses. Even if it shuts down completely, it will still incur fixed costs, *unless it goes out of business*. If the firm anticipates that the market price will increase enough that it will be able to cover its average total costs in the future, it may not want to sell out. It may choose to produce q units in the short-run, even though losses are incurred. At price P_1, production of output q is clearly more advantageous than shutting down, because the firm is able to cover its variable costs and pay some of its fixed costs. If it were to shut down, *but not sell out*, the firm would lose the entire amount of its fixed cost.

EXHIBIT 5 • Operating with Short-run Losses

A firm making losses will operate in the short run if it (a) can cover its variable costs now and (b) expects price to be high enough in the future to cover all its costs.

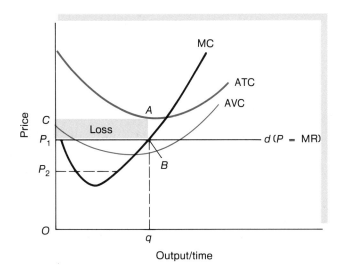

---

[3]When discussing this issue, it is vital that we keep the opportunity cost concept in mind. The firm's fixed costs are opportunity costs that do not vary with output. However, they can be avoided if, and only if, the firm goes out of business. Fixed costs are *not* (as some economics texts have stated) the depreciated value of the firm's fixed assets. Accounting depreciation "costs" may bear little resemblance to the firm's actual fixed cost. The proper specification of fixed cost relates (a) to how much the firm's assets would bring if they were sold or rented and (b) to other costs, such as operating license fees and debts, which could be avoided if the firm declared bankruptcy and/or went out of business. Since fixed costs can be avoided if the firm goes out of business, the firm will not operate even in the short-run if it does not anticipate that market conditions will improve. See Marshall Colberg and James King, "Theory of Production Abandonment," *Revista Internazionale di Scienze Economiche e Commerciali* 20 (1973), 961–1072.

Shutdown: A temporary halt in the operation of a business. The firm does *not* sell its assets. Its variable cost will be eliminated, but the firm's fixed costs will continue. The shut-down firm anticipates a return to operation in the future.

What if the market price declines below the firm's average variable cost (for example, P_2)? Under these circumstances, a temporary **shutdown** is preferable to short-run operation. If the firm continues to operate in the short-run, operating losses merely supplement losses resulting from the firm's fixed costs. Therefore, even if the firm expects the market price to increase, enabling it to survive and prosper in the future, it will shut down in the short-run when the market price falls below its average variable cost.

The firm's third option is **going out of business** immediately. After all, even the losses resulting from the firm's fixed costs (remember that if they are costs of doing business, they must be avoidable by not doing business) can be avoided if the firm sells out. If it does not expect market conditions to change for the better, this is the preferred option.

THE COMPETITIVE FIRM'S SHORT-RUN SUPPLY CURVE

The competitive firm that intends to stay in business will maximize profits (or minimize losses) when it produces the output level at which $P = MC$ and variable costs are covered. Therefore, the portion of the firm's short-run marginal cost curve that lies above its average variable cost is the short-run supply curve of the firm.

Going Out of Business: The sale of a firm's assets, and its permanent exit from the market. By going out of business, a firm is able to avoid fixed cost, which would continue during a shutdown.

Exhibit 6 illustrates that as the market price increases, the competitive firm will expand output along its MC curve. If the market price were less than P_1, the firm would shut down immediately because it would be unable to cover even its variable costs. If the market price is P_1, however, a price equal to the firm's average variable cost, the firm may supply output q_1 *in the short-run.* Economic losses will result, but the firm would incur similar losses if it shut down completely. As the market price increases to P_2, the firm will happily expand output along its MC curve to q_2. At P_2, price is also equal to average costs. The firm is making a "normal rate of return," or zero economic profits. Higher prices will result in a still larger short-run output. The firm will supply q_3 units at market price P_3. At this price, economic profits will result. At still higher prices, output will be expanded even more. As long as price exceeds average variable cost, the firm will expand supply along its MC curve, which therefore becomes the firm's short-run supply curve.

EXHIBIT 6 • The Supply Curve for the Firm and the Market

The short-run market supply is merely the sum of the supply produced by all the firms in the market area (b).

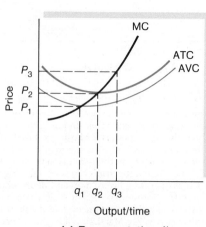
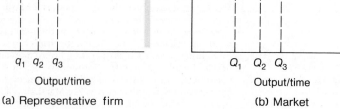

(a) Representative firm

(b) Market

THE SHORT-RUN MARKET SUPPLY CURVE

The short-run market supply curve corresponds to the total amount supplied by all of the firms in the industry. For a purely competitive industry, the short-run market supply curve is the horizontal summation of the marginal cost curves (above the level of average variable cost) for all firms in the industry. Since individual firms will supply a larger amount at a higher price, the short-run market supply curve will slope upward to the right.

Exhibit 6 illustrates this relationship. As the price of the product rises from P_1 to P_2 to P_3, the individual firms expand their output along their marginal cost curves. Since the individual competitive firms supply a larger output as the market price increases, the total amount supplied to the market also expands.

Our construction of the short-run market supply curve assumes that the prices of the resources used by the industry are constant. When the entire industry (rather than just a single firm) expands output, resource prices may rise. If this does happen, the short-run market supply curve will be just slightly more inelastic (steeper) than the sum of the supply curves of the individual firms.

The short-run market supply curve, together with the demand curve for the industry's product, will determine the market price. At the short-run equilibrium market price, each of the firms will have expanded output until marginal costs have risen to the market price. They will have no desire to change output, *given their current size of plant.*

OUTPUT ADJUSTMENTS IN THE LONG-RUN

In the long-run, firms have the opportunity to alter their plant size and enter or exit from an industry. As long-run adjustments are made, output in the whole industry may either expand or contract.

LONG-RUN EQUILIBRIUM

In addition to the balance between quantity supplied and quantity demanded necessary for short-run equilibrium, the firms in a competitive industry must earn the normal rate of return, and only the normal rate, before long-run equilibrium can be attained. If economic profit is present, new firms will enter the industry, and the current producers will have an incentive to expand the scale of their operations. This will lead to an increase in supply, placing downward pressure on prices. In contrast, if firms in the industry are suffering economic losses, they will leave the market. Supply will decline, placing upward pressure on prices.

Therefore, as Exhibit 7 illustrates, when a competitive industry is in long-run equilibrium, (a) the quantity supplied and the quantity demanded will be equal at the market price, and (b) the firms in the industry will be earning normal (zero) economic profit (that is, their minimum ATC will just equal the market price).

ADJUSTING TO AN EXPANSION IN DEMAND

Suppose a purely competitive market is in equilibrium. What will happen if there is an increase in demand? Exhibit 8 presents an example. An entrepreneur introduces a fantastic new candy product. Consumers go wild over it. However, since it sticks to one's teeth, the market demand for toothpicks

EXHIBIT 7 • Long-run Equilibrium in a Competitive Market

The two conditions necessary for equilibrium in a competitive market are depicted here. First, quantity supplied and quantity demanded must be equal in the market (b). Second, the firm must earn zero economic profit, that is, the "normal rate of return," at the established market price (a).

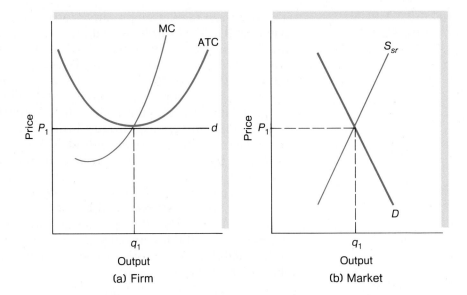

(a) Firm

(b) Market

increases from D_1 to D_2. The price of toothpicks rises from P_1 to P_2. What impact will the higher market price have on the output level of toothpick-producing firms? It will increase (from q_1 to q_2, Exhibit 8) as the firms expand output along their marginal cost curves. In the short-run, the toothpick producers will make economic profits. The profits will attract new

EXHIBIT 8 • How the Market Responds to an Increase in Demand

The introduction of a new candy product that sticks to one's teeth causes the demand for toothpicks to increase to D_2 [graph (b)]. Toothpick prices rise to P_2, inducing firms to expand output. Toothpick firms make short-run profits [graph (a)], which draw new competitors into the industry. Thus, the toothpick supply expands (shifts from S_1 to S_2). If cost conditions are unchanged, the expansion in supply will continue until the market price of toothpicks has declined to its initial level P_1.

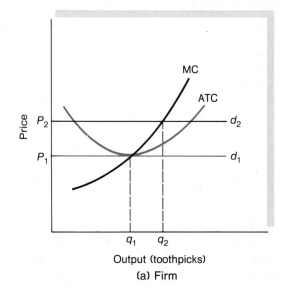

(a) Firm

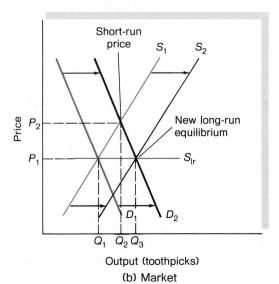

(b) Market

toothpick producers to the industry and cause the existing firms to expand the scale of their plants.[4] Hence, the market supply will increase (shift from S_1 to S_2) and eventually eliminate the short-run profits. If cost conditions are unchanged in the industry, the market price for toothpicks will return to its initial level, even though output has expanded to Q_3.

ADJUSTING TO A DECLINE IN DEMAND

Economic profits attract new firms to an industry; economic losses (those expected to continue) encourage capital and entrepreneurship to move out of the industry and into other areas where the profitability potential is more favorable. Economic losses mean that the owners of capital in the industry are earning less than the market rate of return. The opportunity cost of continuing in the industry exceeds the gain.

Exhibit 9 illustrates how market forces react to economic losses. Initially, an equilibrium price exists in the industry. The firms are just able to cover their average costs of production. Now, suppose there is a reduction in consumer income, causing the market demand for the product to decrease and the market price to decline. At the new, lower price, firms in the industry will not be able to cover their costs of production. In the short-run, they will reduce output along their MC curve. This reduction in output by the individual firms results in a reduction in the quantity supplied in the market.

In the face of short-run losses, there will be a reduction even in replacement capital into this industry. Some firms will leave the industry. Others

EXHIBIT 9 • Impact of a Decline in Demand

A reduction in market demand will cause price to fall and short-run losses to occur. The losses will cause some firms to go out of business and others to reduce their scale. Thus, the market supply will fall, causing market price to rise. The supply will continue to decline and price will continue to rise until the short-run losses have been eliminated (S_2).

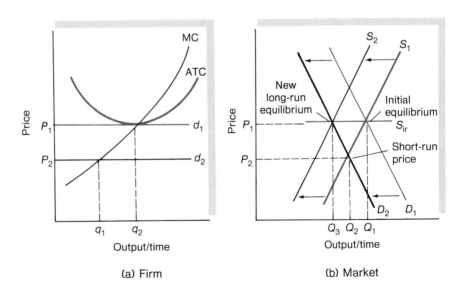

(a) Firm

(b) Market

---

[4]If the *long-run* average total cost curve results in only one possible minimum-cost output level (see Exhibit 9a of the previous chapter), the expansion in the long-run supply will be generated entirely by the entry of new firms. However, when the long-run average total cost is such that a wide range of minimum-cost output levels is possible (see Exhibit 9b of the previous chapter), both the entry of new firms and expansion by the established firms will contribute to the increase in supply.

will reduce the scale of their operations. These factors will cause the industry supply to decline, to shift from S_1 to S_2. What impact will this have on price? It will rise. In the long-run, the market supply will decline until the price rises sufficiently to permit "normal profits" in the industry.

THE LONG-RUN SUPPLY CURVE

The long-run market supply curve indicates the minimum price at which firms will supply various market output levels, given sufficient time both to adjust plant size (or other fixed factors) and to enter or exit from the industry. The shape of the long-run market supply curve is dependent on what happens to the cost of production as the output of an industry is

APPLICATIONS IN ECONOMICS

A Shift in Demand—the Impact of Papal Decree on the Price of Fish[5]

Sometimes changes in institutions, legal restrictions, or regulatory policies influence the demand for a product. The 1966 papal decree lifting the Catholic Church's ban on the eating of meat on Fridays provides an interesting illustration of this point. Prior to the lifting of the ban, most of the nearly 600 million Roman Catholics consumed fish on Fridays. After the decree, many shifted to substitute goods such as beef, pork, and chicken. The demand for fish therefore declined. As our analysis indicates, a decline in demand will lead to a lower market price in the short-run.

Economist Frederick Bell of Florida State University estimated the impact of the reduction in demand on the market price of fish in the Northeast United States, an area where Catholics comprise a large proportion of the total population. As we discussed earlier, changes in personal income and the price of related commodities (beef, pork, and poultry in this case) will influence the demand for a good. Bell utilized statistical techniques to adjust for these factors. This permitted him to isolate the independent effect of the papal decree on the price of fish.

Bell estimated the impact of the decree on the price of seven different species of fish during the period following the decree. As Exhibit 10 shows, his analysis indicates that the price of each variety of fish fell. In the case of large haddock, the price was 21 percent lower after the papal decree than for the 10 years prior to the lifting of the ban. In other instances, the decline in price was smaller. On average, Bell estimates,

the price of fish in the Northeastern United States fell by 12.5 percent as the result of the papal decree. Just as economic theory indicates, a reduction in demand for a product leads to a lower price in the short-run (see Exhibit 9).

---

[5]Frederick W. Bell, "The Pope and The Price of Fish," *American Economic Review,* 58 (December 1968), pp. 1346–1350.

EXHIBIT 10 • The Papal Decree and the Price of Fish

The papal decree lifting the ban against the eating of meat on Fridays reduced the demand for fish and resulted in lower prices for fish.

Species	Percent Change in the Price of Fish After Papal Decree
Sea scallops	−17
Yellowtail flounder	−14
Large haddock	−21
Small haddock (scrod)	−2
Cod	−16
Ocean perch	−10
Whiting	−20
All species (average)	−12.5

Source: F. W. Bell, "The Pope and The Price of Fish," *American Economic Review* (December, 1968).

altered. Three possibilities emerge, although one is far more likely than the other two.

Constant Cost Industry: An industry for which factor prices and costs of production remain constant as market output is expanded. Thus, the long-run market supply curve is horizontal.

If factor prices remain unchanged, the long-run market supply curve will be perfectly elastic. In terms of economics, this describes a **constant cost industry.** Exhibits 8 and 9 both picture constant cost industries. As Exhibit 8 illustrates, an expansion in demand causes prices to increase *temporarily.* The high prices and profits stimulate additional production. The short-run market supply continues to expand until the market price returns to its initial level and profits return to their normal level. In the long-run, the larger supply will not require a permanent price increase. The *long-run* supply curve is thus perfectly elastic. Exhibit 9 illustrates the impact of a decline in demand in a constant cost industry. Again, the long-run supply curve is perfectly elastic, reflecting the basically unchanged cost at the lower rate of industry output.

A constant cost industry is most likely to arise when the industry's demand for the resources is quite small relative to the total demand for these resources. For example, since demand of the matches industry for wood, chemicals, and labor is so small relative to the total demand for these resources, doubling the output of matches would exert only a negligible impact on the price of the resources used by the industry. Matches therefore approximate a constant cost industry.

INCREASING COST INDUSTRIES

Increasing Cost Industries: Industries for which costs of production rise as the industry output is expanded. Thus, the long-run market supply is directly related to price.

For most industries, called **increasing cost industries** by economists, an expansion in total output causes a firm's production cost to rise. As the output of an industry increases, demand for resources used by the industry expands. This usually results in higher resource prices, which cause the firm's cost curves to shift upward. For example, an increase in demand for housing places upward pressure on the prices of lumber, roofing, window frames, and construction labor, causing the cost of housing to rise. Similarly, an increase in demand (and market output) for beef may cause the prices of feed grains, hay, and grazing land to rise. Thus, the production costs of beef rise as more of it is produced.

In some industries, additional demand may lead to industrial congestion, which will reduce the efficiency of the industry and cause costs to rise, even though resource prices are constant. For example, as the demand for lobster increases, additional fishermen are attracted to the industry. However, the increase in the number of fishermen combing lobster beds typically leads to congestion, which reduces the catch per hour of individual fishermen. The production cost in the lobster industry therefore rises as output per labor-hour declines.

For an increasing cost industry, an expansion in market demand will bid up resource prices and/or lead to industrial congestion, causing the per unit cost of the firms to rise. As a result, a larger market output will be forthcoming only at a higher price. The long-run market supply curve for the product will therefore slope upward.

Exhibit 11 depicts an increasing cost industry. An expansion in demand causes higher prices and a larger market output. The presence of short-run profit attracts new competitors to the industry, expanding the market output even more. *As the industry expands,* factor prices rise and congestion costs

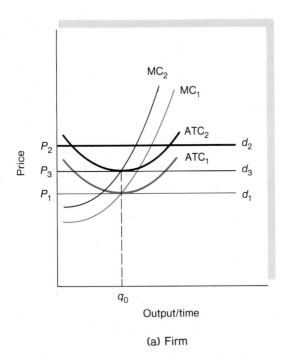

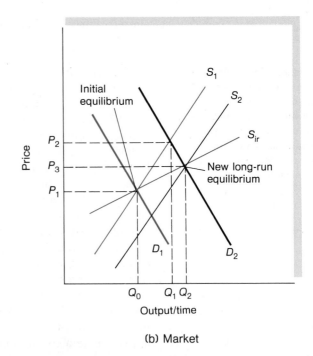

(a) Firm

(b) Market

EXHIBIT 11 • **Increasing Costs and the Long-run Supply**

Most often, higher factor prices and industrial congestion will cause costs to rise as the *market* output increases. For such increasing cost industries, the long-run supply curve (S_{lr}, graph b) will slope upward to the right.

increase. What happens to the firm's cost curves? Both the average and marginal cost curves rise (shift to ATC_2 and MC_2). This increase in production cost necessitates a higher long-run price. Hence, the long-run supply curve slopes upward to the right.

DECREASING COST INDUSTRIES

Decreasing Cost Industries: Industries for which costs of production decline as the industry expands. The market supply is therefore inversely related to price. Such industries are atypical.

Conceivably, factor prices could decline if the market output of a product were expanded. Since a reduction in factor prices would lead to a lower long-run competitive market price for the product, economists refer to such industries as **decreasing cost industries.** The long-run (but not the short-run) market supply curve for a decreasing cost industry would slope downward to the right. For example, as the electronics industry expands, suppliers of components may be able to adopt large-scale techniques that will lead to lower component prices. If this occurs, the cost curves of the electronics firms may drift downward, causing the industry supply curve for electronics products to slope downward to the right (at least temporarily). However, since expansion of an industry is far more likely to cause rising rather than falling input prices, decreasing cost industries are atypical.

MARKET ADJUSTMENTS TO CHANGING COSTS OF PRODUCTION

We have analyzed the impact that changes in market demand conditions have on both the short- and long-run market price. Often, disequilibrium is the result of changes in costs of production. Suppose a technological advancement makes it possible for the firms of an industry to produce a given output level with fewer inputs. Costs are therefore reduced. The market price will decline, but in the short-run, price will decline less than cost. The firms will make short-run economic profits. The profits, however, will attract new firms into the industry, and the short-run market supply curve will continue shifting to the right until the profits have been eliminated. Price will decline. In long-run equilibrium, firms are just able to cover their average (and marginal) costs.

An increase in costs of production can be traced in a similar manner. Higher costs of production will cause an increase in the short-run market price, but the immediate increase will be insufficient to cover the higher per unit cost of production completely. Short-run losses will result. Some firms will exit from the industry. This exodus of industry resources will continue until the reduction in market supply is sufficient to push the market price upward to the long-run normal profit equilibrium.

Can you graphically depict the market adjustment that would result from a reduction (or increase) in costs or production? Try it and see. (Remember to assume that demand is unchanged.)

SUPPLY ELASTICITY AND THE ROLE OF TIME

The market supply curve is more elastic in the long-run than in the short-run because the firm's short-run response is limited by the "fixed" nature of some of its factors. The short- and long-run distinction offers a convenient two-stage analysis, but in the real world there are many intermediate production "runs." Some factors that could not be easily varied in a one-week time period can be varied over a two-week period. Expansion of other factors might require a month, and still others, six months. To be more precise, the cost penalty for quicker availability is greater for some production factors than for others. In any case, a faster expansion usually means that greater cost penalties are necessary to provide for an earlier availability of productive factors.

When a firm has a longer time period to plan output and adjust all of its productive inputs to the desired utilization levels, it will be able to produce any specific rate of output at a lower cost. Because it is less costly to expand output slowly, the expansion of output by firms will increase with time, as long as price exceeds cost and up to the point at which returns begin to diminish. Therefore, the elasticity of the market supply curve will increase as more time is allowed for firms to adjust control.

Exhibit 12 illustrates the important effect of time on the supply response of producers. When the price of a product increases from P_1 to P_2, the *immediate* supply response of the firms is small because it is costly to expand output hastily. After one week, firms are willing to expand output only from Q_1 to Q_2. After one month, due to cost reductions possible because of the longer production planning period, firms are willing to offer Q_3 units at the price P_2. After three months, the rate of output expands to Q_4. In the long-run, when it is possible to adjust all inputs to the desired utilization levels (within a six-month time period, for example), firms are willing to supply Q_5 units of output at the market price of P_2. The supply curve for products is typically more elastic over a longer time period than for a shorter period. The length of time necessary to bring about large changes in quantity supplied can vary dramatically across industries. The

EXHIBIT 12 · Time and the Elasticity of the Supply

The elasticity of the market supply curve usually increases as more time is allowed for adjustment to a change in price.

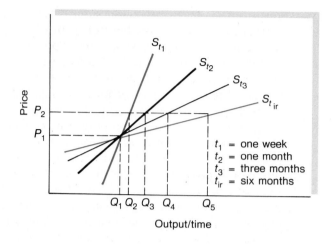

t_1 = one week
t_2 = one month
t_3 = three months
t_{ir} = six months

boxed feature on the dairy industry shows that the adjustment process there takes many years.

THE ROLE OF PROFITS IN THE COMPETITIVE MODEL

In the competitive model, profits and losses are signals sent to producers by consumers. Economic profits will be largest in those areas in which consumer wants at the margin are greatest *relative to costs of production*. Profit-seeking entrepreneurs will guide additional resources into these areas. Supply will increase, driving prices down and eliminating the profits. Free entry and the competitive process will protect the consumer from arbitrarily high prices. In the long-run, competitive prices will reflect costs of production.

Economic profits result because a firm or entrepreneur increases the value of resources. The successful business decision-maker combines resources into a product that consumers value more than the sum of the resources used to produce it. That is why consumers are willing to pay a price in excess of the cost of producing the good. In contrast, losses result when the actions of a producer reduce the value of resources. The value of the resources used up by such unsuccessful firms exceeds the price consumers are willing to pay for their product. Losses and bankruptcies are the market's way of bringing such wasteful activities to a halt.

Producers, like other decision-makers, of course, confront uncertainty and dynamic change. Entrepreneurs, at the time they must make investment decisions, cannot be sure of either future market prices or costs of production. They must base their decisions on expectations. Within the framework of the competitive model, however, the reward-penalty system is clear. Firms that efficiently produce and correctly anticipate the products and services for which future demand will be most urgent (relative to production cost) will make economic profits. Those that are inefficient and incorrectly allocate resources into areas of weak future demand will be penalized with losses.

EFFICIENCY AND THE COMPETITIVE MODEL

Economists often seem to be enchanted by the purely competitive model. They sometimes use it as the standard by which to judge other models. What accounts for the special significance of pure competition? Most economists agree that under rather restrictive assumptions resource allocation within the purely competitive model is ideal from society's viewpoint. In what sense can we say that it is "ideal"?

PRODUCTION EFFICIENCY (P = ATC)

In the long-run, competition forces firms to minimize their average total cost of production and to charge a price just sufficient to cover production costs. Competitive firms must use production methods that minimize costs if they are going to survive. In addition, they must choose a scale of operation that minimizes their long-run average total cost of production. Consumers of competitively produced goods will benefit, since they will receive the largest quantity at the lowest possible price, given the prevailing cost

APPLICATIONS IN ECONOMICS

Increasing Milk Supplies—Slowly

When milk prices rise and are expected to remain higher, other things equal, dairies will expand their output of milk. They will retain more older cows past their prime—cows that would have been sent to slaughter. New dairy cows will be added to the herd, and more expensive feed rations may be used to boost milk output from each cow in the herd. Genetically advanced cows capable of producing more milk, will be sought. New firms will enter the dairy business.

Some of these changes will begin immediately. Others, though, especially those that change the size and composition of dairy herds, will take years to complete. Similarly, a decrease in milk production will take many years, if milk price falls.

Just how slow is the response in the dairy industry? The supply elasticity numbers that follow, from a study published in 1985 at the University of Wisconsin, indicate that even after 25 years, some of the long-run effects of a milk price increase are felt. A 10 percent increase in the price of milk will, after one year, lead to only a 1.2 percent increase in the quantity of milk supplied. But, after six years, the same price increase would lead to a 12 percent quantity increase, and after 10 years, the response would be 25 percent. Given 20 years to react, dairies would provide a 50 percent increase in the quantity of milk supplied, in response to the same 10 percent price increase. After 30 years, the response would be greater still. On the dairy farm, at least, changes can take a great deal of time.

Supply Elasticities for Milk	
Length of Run (Years)	Percent Change in the Quantity of Milk Supplied Due to a 10% Rise in the Price of Milk
1	1.2
3	2.3
6	11.7
10	24.6
15	39.0
20	50.3
25	59.5
30	67.0

Source: Richard Klemme and Jean-Paul Chavas, "The Effects of Changing Milk Price on Milk Supply and National Dairy Herd Size," *Economic Issues*, University of Wisconsin, June 1985.

conditions. Competitive markets will eliminate waste and production ineffi-ciency. Inefficient, high-cost producers will confront economic losses and be driven from a competitive industry.

ALLOCATIVE EFFICIENCY (P = MC)

Allocative Efficiency: The allocation of resources to the production of goods and services most desired by consumers. The allocation is "balanced" in such a way that realloca-tion of resources could not benefit anyone without hurting someone else.

Allocative efficiency refers to the balance achieved by the allocation of available resources to the production of goods and services most desired by consumers, given their incomes. Allocative efficiency is present when all markets are in long-run competitive equilibrium. Each good is produced as long as consumers value it more than the alternative goods that might be produced with the same resources. No unit of the good is produced if a more valuable alternative must be forgone, and if any reallocation of re-sources toward different goods or different combinations of goods—any disturbance of the allocative balance—would not benefit any one person without hurting someone else.

The profit-maximization rule (P = MC) assures allocative efficiency within the competitive model. The market demand (price) reflects con-sumers' valuation of an additional unit of a good. The seller's marginal cost indicates the value of the resources (in their alternative uses) necessary to produce an additional unit of the good. When the production of each good is expanded so long as price exceeds marginal cost, each good will be produced if, and only if, consumers value it more than the alternatives that might have been produced. In purely competitive markets, therefore, profit-maximizing producers will be led to produce the combination of goods most desired by consumers.

PURE COMPETITION AND THE REAL WORLD

In the purely competitive model, the "invisible hand" that Adam Smith spoke of does its job very well indeed. Producers who are motivated purely by the desire to make a profit act no differently than they would if they cared only about the efficient satisfaction of consumers' desires. Because of the resulting price structure, even the desire of a very selfish consumer for a consumption item is balanced against the value of the good (price relative to that of other goods) to other people. In other words, prevailing prices provide each person with the information and incentive to heed the wishes of others. An incredibly complex array of consumer desires, production possibilities, and resource availabilities can be optimally coordinated in the model. No central person or group need know or understand all the aspects of the model. A few market prices condense the needed information and convey it to each decision-maker.

However, pure competition is merely a hypothetical model. It can only exist under very restrictive conditions. For better or for worse, these condi-tions are often absent in the real world, for several reasons. First, in many industries, the production costs of large firms are less than those of small firms, due to economies of scale. Under these circumstances, it is neither feasible nor economical to have the industry's output divided among a larger number of small producers. Second, the preferences of consumers differ widely with regard to such factors as product design, quality, and location of purchase. In short, consumers desire variety, not the homoge-neous products implied by the purely competitive model. Third, we live in a dynamic world. Changes in knowledge and technology often alter both the availability and cost of alternative products. Disequilibrium, rather than a stable, purely competitive equilibrium, is the dominant characteristic. The purely competitive hypothetical ideal loses some of its relevance in a world characterized by rapid technological change, constant introduction of new products, and continual discovery of new information. Fourth, competition (in the rivalry sense) is multidimensional. Pure competition emphasizes one

OUTSTANDING ECONOMIST

Friedrich A. von Hayek (1899–   )

For six decades, Professor Hayek has been a consistent and eloquent defender of classical liberalism, even when most of the world was moving toward central planning and big government. Born in Vienna, Hayek was a lecturer in Austria during the 1920s. In 1931, he accepted a professorship of economics at the London School of Economics. After World War II, he joined the faculty of the University of Chicago, where he taught for many years. He is currently Distinguished Senior Fellow at the CATO Institute, a libertarian think tank in Washington, D.C. In 1979, Hayek was the joint recipient (along with Gunnar Myrdal) of the Nobel Prize in economics.

Hayek studied under Ludwig von Mises at the University of Vienna. The two eventually became the most powerful proponents in this century for what is known as the "Austrian school" of economics. Hayek has made important contributions in areas as diverse as monetary theory, markets and knowledge, capital theory, and the theory of business cycles.

Hayek believes the meaning of competition is a major source of confusion among economists. Many economists classify markets as either perfectly or imperfectly competitive. Perfect competition is believed to be both "ideal" and rarely achievable, and imperfect competi-

tion is viewed as both widespread and undesirable. Hayek argues that markets will be competitive when the government does not create artificial obstacles restricting the entry of firms. According to Hayek, competition is a process that "creates the views people have about what is best and cheapest." In the absence of entry barriers created by government, the lowest possible price will exist in markets—that is, prices will be driven down to the level of production costs. Producers will be unable to take advantage of consumers. "The practical lesson of all this," Hayek states, "is that we should worry much less about whether competition in a given case is perfect and worry much more whether there is competition at all."[6]

His most recent publications include a three-volume work entitled *Law, Legislation, and Liberty*, in which he articulates his views on the importance of rules over discretionary authority, the interrelationship of economic and political freedom, and the illusory concept of social justice. Hayek is much more than an economist—he is a social critic, philosopher, political theorist, and scholar.

[6]Friedrich A. Hayek, *Individualism and Economic Order* (Chicago: University of Chicago Press, 1948), pp. 105–106.

of the dimensions—price. But, competition for the approval of consumers based on product quality, producer reliability and honesty, convenience of location, and quickness of service is also of tremendous importance. This nonprice competition may be just as intense as the price competition of the purely competitive model.

**LOOKING
AHEAD**

Pure competition is important because it can help us understand real-world markets characterized by low barriers to entry and a substantial number of independent sellers. At the opposite end of the spectrum lie markets characterized by high barriers to entry and a single seller. The following chapter focuses on the hypothetical model developed by economists to analyze markets of this type—pure monopoly.

CHAPTER SUMMARY

1. Competition as a process should not be confused with pure competition, a model of industrial structure. Competition as a process implies rivalry. Rival firms use quality, style, location, advertising, and price to attract consumers. Pure competition, on the other hand, is a model of industrial structure that assumes the presence of a large number of small (relative to the total market) firms, each producing a homogeneous product in a market for which there is complete freedom of entry and exit.

2. The competitive process places producers under strong pressure to operate efficiently and heed the views of consumers. Those who do not offer quality goods at economical prices lose customers to rivals. As Adam Smith recognized long ago, self-interest is a powerful motivator of human beings. If it is bridled by competition, self-interest leads to economic cooperation and productive effort.

3. Under pure competition, firms are price takers—they face a perfectly elastic demand curve. Profit-maximizing (or loss-minimizing) firms will expand output as long as the additional output adds more to revenues than to costs. Therefore, the competitive firm will produce the output level at which marginal revenue (and price) equals marginal cost.

4. The firm's short-run marginal cost curve (above its average variable cost) is its supply curve. Under pure competition, the short-run *market* supply curve is the horizontal sum of the marginal cost curves (when MC is above AVC) for all firms in the industry.

5. If a firm (a) is covering its average variable cost and (b) anticipates that the price is only temporarily below average total cost, it may operate in the short-run even though it is experiencing a loss. However, even if it anticipates more favorable market conditions in the future, loss minimization will require the firm to shut down if it is unable to cover its average variable cost. If the firm does not anticipate that it will be able to cover its average total cost even in the long-run, loss minimization requires that it immediately go out of business (even if it is covering its average *variable* cost) so that it can at least avoid its fixed cost.

6. When price exceeds average total cost, a firm will make economic profits. Under pure competition, profits will attract new firms into the

industry and stimulate the existing firms to expand. The market supply will increase, pushing price down to the level of average total cost. Competitive firms will be unable to make long-run economic profits.

7. Losses exist when the market price is less than the firm's average total cost. Losses will cause firms to leave the industry or reduce the scale of their operations. Market supply will decline until price rises sufficiently, so firms can earn normal (that is, zero economic) profits.

8. As the output of an industry expands, marginal costs will increase in the short-run, causing the short-run market supply curve to slope upward to the right. If cost conditions to the industry remain unchanged, as the market output is expanded, the long-run supply curve will be perfectly elastic. However, as the output of an industry expands, rising factor prices and industrial congestion will normally cause the firm's cost curve to shift upward. The long-run market supply curve for such an increasing cost industry will slope upward to the right.

9. Within the framework of the purely competitive model, firms that efficiently produce and correctly anticipate those goods for which future demand will be most urgent (relative to costs of production) will make profits. Firms that inefficiently produce and incorrectly allocate resources to the production of goods for which future demand turns out to be weak (relative to costs of production) will be penalized with losses. In the short-run, firms might make either profits or losses, but in the long-run, competitive pressures will eliminate economic profits (and losses).

10. Economists often argue that pure competition leads to ideal economic efficiency because (a) average costs of production are minimized and (b) output is expanded to the level at which the consumer's evaluation of an additional unit of a good is just equal to its marginal cost.

THE ECONOMIC WAY OF THINKING— DISCUSSION QUESTIONS

1. Farmers are often heard to complain about the high cost of machinery, labor, and fertilizer, suggesting that these costs drive down their profit rate. Does it follow that if, for example, the price of fertilizer fell by 10 percent, farming (a highly competitive industry with low barriers to entry) would be more profitable? Explain.

2. If the firms in a competitive industry are making short-run profits, what will happen to the market price in the long-run? Explain.

3. What factors will cause the supply curve for a product to slope upward in the long-run? Be specific.

4. A sales tax, collected from the seller, will shift the firm's cost curves upward. Outline the impact of a sales tax within the framework of the competitive model. Use diagrams to indicate both the short-run and long-run impact of the tax. Who will bear the burden of the sales tax?

5. What do economists mean when they say that resource allocation is ideal or efficient? Why is it sometimes argued that a purely competitive economy will allocate goods ideally? Explain.

6. The following table presents the expected cost and revenue data for the Tucker Tomato Farm. The Tuckers produce tomatoes in a greenhouse and sell them wholesale in a purely competitive market. (a) Fill in the firm's marginal cost, average variable cost, average total cost, and profit

schedules. (b) If the Tuckers are profit maximizers, how many tomatoes should they produce when the market price is $500 per ton? Indicate their profits. (c) Indicate the firm's output level and maximum profit if the market price of tomatoes increases to $550 per ton. (d) How many units would the Tucker Tomato Farm produce if the price of tomatoes declined to $450? Indicate the firm's profits. Should the firm continue in business? Explain.

Cost and Revenue Schedules—Tucker Tomato Farm, Inc.

Output (Tons per Month)	Total Cost	Price per Ton	Marginal Cost	Average Variable Cost	Average Total Cost	Profits (Monthly)
0	$1000	$500	—	—	—	—
1	1200	500	_____	_____	_____	_____
2	1350	500	_____	_____	_____	_____
3	1550	500	_____	_____	_____	_____
4	1900	500	_____	_____	_____	_____
5	2300	500	_____	_____	_____	_____
6	2750	500	_____	_____	_____	_____
7	3250	500	_____	_____	_____	_____
8	3800	500	_____	_____	_____	_____
9	4400	500	_____	_____	_____	_____
10	5150	500	_____	_____	_____	_____

Competitive industries have their monopolistic aspects; monopolized industries have their competitive aspects. The most that can be said today is that competition is far too common to justify the thesis that the competitive system is approaching extinction, and that monopoly is far too common to justify its treatment as an occasional exception to the general rule. [1]

CLAIR WILCOX

- • **What, exactly, is a monopoly? What are the barriers that allow monopoly to exist?**

- • **What price will a monopolist set?**

- • **Why is monopoly a problem?**

- • **What are the reasons for trying to regulate monopolies? What problems occur when we do regulate monopolies?**

- • **In dealing with monopoly, what are the policy alternatives, and what can we expect from each one?**

- • **What impact does dynamic change have on a monopoly situation?**

19 MONOPOLY AND HIGH BARRIERS TO ENTRY

In the last chapter, we analyzed pure competition, a hypothetical market structure characterized by numerous sellers. We now turn to the other extreme of market structure—pure monopoly. The word "monopoly," derived from two Greek words, means "single seller." When only a single seller for a product exists, the firm will exert more control over price and output. This does not mean that the monopolist is completely free from competitive pressures. As Professor Wilcox implies, varying degrees of competition are present even under conditions of monopoly.

The absence of numerous rivals and the existence of substantial barriers to those rivals will influence the nature of a market. The profit-maximizing price for a monopolist, the impact of monopoly on the efficiency of the market, and potential gains from policies to improve the expected outcome of free markets in these circumstances will be discussed in this chapter.

DEFINING MONOPOLY

Monopoly: A market structure characterized by a single seller of a well-defined product for which there are no good substitutes and by high barriers to the entry of any other firms into the market for that product.

We will define **monopoly** as a market structure characterized by (a) high barriers to entry and (b) a single seller of a well-defined product for which there are no good substitutes. Even this definition is ambiguous because "high barriers" and "good substitutes" are both relative terms. Are the barriers to entry into the automobile or steel industries high? Many observers would argue that they are. After all, it would take a great deal of financial capital to successfully compete in these industries. There are no *legal* restraints, however, that prevent you or anyone else from producing automobiles or steel. In addition, if you can convince even a small percentage of capital market investors that you are likely to be successful in any industry, it will be possible to raise large amounts of financial capital. The concept of barriers to entry is, in part, subjective.

Similarly, there is always some substitutability among products, even those produced by a monopolist. Is a letter a good substitute for telephone communication? For some purposes, legal correspondence for example, a letter is a very good substitute. In other cases, when the speed of communication and immediacy of response are important, telephone communication has a tremendous advantage over letter writing. Are there any good substitutes for electricity? Most of the known substitutes for electric lighting (candles, oil lamps, and battery lights, for example) are inferior to electric lights. Natural gas, fuel oil, and wood, though, are often excellent substitutes for electric heating.

Monopoly, then, is always a matter of degree. Pure monopoly, like pure competition, is a rare phenomenon. Nevertheless, there are two reasons why it is important to understand how markets work under pure monopoly. First, the monopoly model will help us understand markets dominated by only a few sellers. A dominant firm in an industry often has a tendency to

---

[1]Clair Wilcox, *Competition and Monopoly in American Industry*, Monograph no. 21, Temporary National Economic Committee, Investigation of Concentration of Economic Power, 76th Congress, 3rd session (Washington, D.C.: U.S. Government Printing Office, 1940), p. 8.

behave like a monopolist. When there are only two or three producers in a market, they may seek to collude rather than compete with each other and thus together behave like a monopoly. Second, there is only a single producer in a few important industries. Local telephone and electricity services provide examples. The monopoly model will illuminate the operation of such markets.

BARRIERS TO ENTRY

What makes it difficult for potential competitors to enter a market? Three factors are of particular importance.

1. Legal Barriers. Legal barriers are the oldest and most effective method of protecting a business firm from potential competitors. Kings once granted exclusive business rights to favored citizens or groups. Today, governments continue to establish barriers, restricting the right to buy and sell goods. To compete in the communications industry in the United States (for example, in order to operate a radio or television station), one must obtain a government franchise. The Post Office, a government corporation, is granted the exclusive right to deliver first-class mail, although this is sometimes challenged. Potential private competitors are eliminated by law. Shops at airports frequently have exclusive franchises, as do local public utilities in most areas of the United States.

Licensing, a process by which one obtains permission from the government to enter a specific occupation or business, often limits entry. In many states, a person must obtain a license before operating a liquor store, barbershop, taxicab, funeral home, or drugstore. Sometimes, these licenses cost little and are designed to ensure certain minimum standards. In other cases, they are expensive and designed primarily to limit competition.

Patent: The grant of an exclusive right to use a specific process or produce a specific product for a period of time (17 years in the United States).

Another legal barrier to entry is a **patent,** which grants the owner a legal monopoly on the commercial use of a newly invented product or process for a limited period of time; 17 years in the United States. Once a patent has been granted, other persons are prevented from using the procedures or producing the product unless they obtain permission from the patent holder. Essentially, the patent system is designed to permit inventors to reap the benefits of their inventions. Nevertheless, patents are often used to restrict the entry of rivals into a broad market area. For example, Polaroid's control over patent rights enabled it to exclude all rivals from the instant-picture market for years, until Eastman Kodak developed a new process. Polaroid went to court, however, and forced Eastman Kodak to withdraw from that market. The new process was judged to be an infringement on Polaroid's patent.

2. Economies of Scale. In some industries, a firm is unable to produce at a low cost unless it is quite large, both in absolute terms and relative to the market. Under these circumstances, economies of scale prevent small firms from entering the market, building a reputation, and competing effectively with large firms. The existing firms are thus protected from potential competitors.

3. Control over an Essential Resource. If a single firm has sole control over a resource essential for entry into an industry, it can eliminate potential competitors. The famous DeBeers Company of South Africa is a classic case. Since this company has almost exclusive control over all of the world's diamond mines, it can effectively prevent other firms from entering the diamond-producing industry. Its ability to raise the price of new diamonds is limited only by the availability of substitute gems, and by the potential sales by current owners of previously produced diamonds.

THE HYPOTHETICAL MODEL OF MONOPOLY

Suppose you invent, patent, and produce a microwave device that locks the hammer of any firearm in the immediate area. This fabulous invention can be used to immobilize potential robbers or hijackers. Since you own the exclusive patent right to the device, you are not concerned about a competitive supplier in the foreseeable future. Although other products are competitive with your inventions, they are poor substitutes. In short, you are a monopolist.

What price should you charge for your product? Like the purely competitive firm, you will want to expand output as long as marginal revenue exceeds marginal cost. Unlike the purely competitive firm, however, you will face a downward-sloping demand curve. Since you are the only firm in the industry, the industry demand curve will coincide with your demand curve. Consumers will buy less of your product at a higher price. At high prices, even a monopolist will have few customers.

TOTAL REVENUE, MARGINAL REVENUE, AND ELASTICITY OF DEMAND

Since the demand curve of a monopolist slopes downward, there are two conflicting influences on total revenue when the seller reduces price in order to expand output and sales. As Exhibit 1 illustrates, the resultant increase in sales (from q_1 to q_2) will probably influence the total revenue of

EXHIBIT 1 • The Effect of Increases in Sales on Revenue

When a firm faces a downward-sloping demand curve, a price reduction that increases sales will exert two conflicting influences on total revenue. First, total revenue will rise because of an increase in the number of units sold (from q_1 to q_2). However, revenue losses from the lower price (P_2) on units that could have been sold at a higher price (P_1) will at least partially offset the additional revenues due to increased sales. Therefore, the marginal revenue curve will lie inside the firm's demand curve.

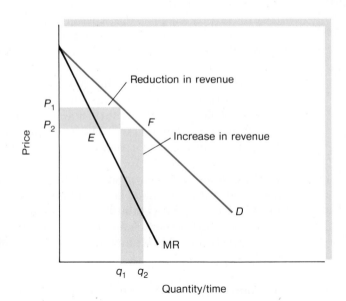

the monopolist; additional units can now be sold at the lower price that could not have been sold at the higher price. The sale of these units will increase total revenue. However, a price reduction will also tend to *lower* the monopolist's total revenue, simply because the units of the product that *could* have been sold at the higher price are now sold at a lower price (P_1 rather than P_2, as illustrated). The marginal revenue derived from the additional sales will be less than the sales price. Thus, as shown in Exhibit 1, the marginal revenue curve of the monopolist will lie inside (below) the demand curve of the firm.[2]

While the demand curve shows the number of units that can be sold at different prices, it also reveals how revenues vary as price and output are altered. Using a straight-line demand curve, Exhibit 2 illustrates how total

EXHIBIT 2 • Price, Total Revenue, and Marginal Revenue of a Monopolist

In the elastic portion of the monopolist's demand curve (prices greater than $10), a price reduction will be associated with rising total revenue (frame b) and positive marginal revenue. At unitary elasticity (output of 50 units), total revenue will reach a maximum. When the monopolist's demand curve is inelastic (output beyond 50 units), lower prices will lead to declining total revenue and negative marginal revenue.

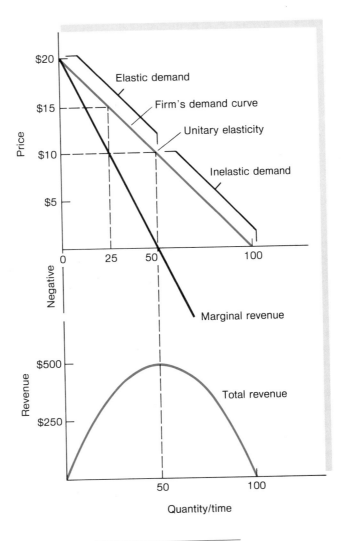

---

[2]For a straight-line demand curve, the marginal revenue curve will bisect any line parallel to the x-axis. For example, the MR curve will divide the line P_2F into two equal parts, P_2E and EF.

and marginal revenue are related to elasticity of demand. At very high prices, the sales of the monopolist will be small. As price is reduced and output is expanded on the elastic portion of the monopolist's demand curve, total revenue will rise. Marginal revenue will be positive. Suppose the monopolist charged $15 for a product and sold 25 units, yielding a total revenue of $375. If the monopolist cut the price to $10, sales would expand to 50 units. Total revenue would rise to $500. A price reduction from $15 to $10 would thus increase the total revenue of the monopolist.

Consider the output rate at which elasticity of demand is equal to unity. At that point, total revenue reaches its maximum. Marginal revenue is equal to zero. As price falls below $10 into the inelastic portion of the monopolist's demand curve, total revenue declines as output is expanded. For this range of price and output, marginal revenue will be negative. Thus, marginal revenue goes from positive to negative as the elasticity of demand changes from elastic to inelastic (at output 50 of Exhibit 2).

This analysis has obvious implications. For a monopolist operating on the inelastic portion of its demand curve, a price increase would lead to more total revenue *and* less total cost (since fewer units would be produced and sold). Because of this, we would never expect a profit-maximizing monopolist to push the sales of a product into the range in which the product's demand curve becomes inelastic.

THE PROFIT-MAXIMIZING OUTPUT

Both costs and revenues must be considered when we analyze the profit-maximizing decision rule for the monopolist. The profit-maximizing monopolist will continue expanding output until marginal revenue equals marginal cost. The price at which that output level can be sold is given by the demand curve of the monopolist.

Exhibit 3 provides a graphic illustration of profit maximization. The monopolist will continue to expand output as long as marginal revenue exceeds marginal cost. Therefore, output will be expanded to Q, where MR = MC. The monopolist will be able to sell the profit-maximizing output Q for a price indicated by the height of the demand curve. At any output

EXHIBIT 3 • The Short-run Price and Output of a Monopolist

The monopolist will reduce price and expand output as long as MR exceeds MC. Output Q will result. When price exceeds average cost at any output level, profit will accrue at that output level.

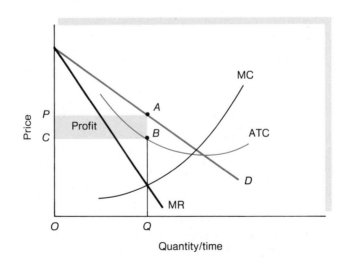

less than Q, the benefits (marginal revenue) of producing the *additional* units will exceed their costs. The monopolist will gain by expanding output. For any output greater than Q, the monopolist's costs of producing *additional* units will be greater than the benefits (marginal revenue). Production of such units will reduce profits.

Exhibit 3 also depicts the profits of a monopolist. At output Q, the monopolist would charge price P. Price times the number of units sold yields the firm's total revenue ($PAQO$). The firm's total cost would be $CBQO$, the average per unit cost multiplied by the number of units sold. The firm's profits are merely total revenue less total cost, the shaded area of Exhibit 3.

Even though competitive and monopolistic firms alike expand output until MR = MC, there is one important difference. For the competitive firm, price will also equal marginal cost at the maximum-profit output. This will not be true for the monopolist. A profit-maximizing monopolist will choose an output rate at which price is greater than marginal cost. We will consider the implications of this difference later.

Exhibit 4 provides a numeric illustration of profit-maximizing decision-making. At low output rates, marginal revenue exceeds marginal cost. The monopolist will continue expanding output as long as MR is greater than MC. Thus, an output rate of eight units per day will be chosen. Given the demand for the product, the monopolist can sell eight units at a price of $17.25 each. Total revenue will be $138, compared to a total cost of $108.50. The monopolist will make a profit of $29.50. The profit rate will be smaller at all other output rates. For example, if the monopolist reduces the price to $16 in order to sell nine units per day, marginal revenue will increase by $6. However, the marginal cost of producing the ninth unit is $6.25. Since the cost of producing the ninth unit is greater than the revenue it brings in, profits will decline.

EXHIBIT 4 • Profit Maximization for a Monopolist

Rate of Output (per Day) (1)	Price (per Unit) (2)	Total Revenue (1) × (2) (3)	Total Cost (per Day) (4)	Profit (3) − (4) (5)	Marginal Cost (6)	Marginal Revenue (7)
0	—	—	$ 50.00	$ −50.00	—	—
1	$25.00	$ 25.00	60.00	−35.00	$10.00	$ 25.00
2	24.00	48.00	69.00	−21.00	9.00	23.00
3	23.00	69.00	77.00	− 8.00	8.00	21.00
4	22.00	88.00	84.00	4.00	7.00	19.00
5	21.00	105.00	90.50	14.50	6.50	17.00
6	19.75	118.50	96.75	21.75	6.25	13.50
7	18.50	129.50	102.75	26.75	6.00	11.00
8	17.25	138.00	108.50	29.50	5.75	8.50
9	16.00	144.00	114.75	29.25	6.25	6.00
10	14.75	147.50	121.25	26.25	6.50	3.50
11	13.50	148.50	128.00	20.50	6.75	1.00
12	12.25	147.00	135.00	12.00	7.00	− 1.50
13	11.00	143.00	142.25	.75	7.25	− 4.00

Can the monopolist gan by *raising* the price, to $18.50 for example? It may surprise some that the answer is no. If price is increased to $18.50, only seven units will be sold, for a total revenue of $129.50. The cost of producing seven units will be $102.75. The output of seven units will generate a profit of $26.75, less than could be attained at the lower price ($17.25) and larger output (eight). The highest price is not always the best price for the monopolist. Sometimes a price reduction will increase the firm's total revenue more than its total cost.

MARKET FORCES AND THE MONOPOLIST

Can market forces eliminate the profits of a monopolist? It is possible—technological change, for example, may provide low-cost substitutes for consumers. High barriers to market entry, though, insulate a monopolist from direct competitive pressures, which would otherwise lead to expanded output and reduced prices.

Does this mean that a monopolist can be assured of economic profit? Not necessarily. A monopolist's ability to make profits is limited by the demand for whatever product is produced. In some cases, even a monopolist may be unable to sell for a profit. For example, there are thousands of clever, patented items that are never produced because demand—cost conditions are not favorable. Exhibit 5 illustrates this possibility. When the average cost curve of a monopolist is always above its demand curve, economic losses will result. Even a monopolist will not want to operate under these conditions. If market conditions are expected to improve, the monopolist will produce output Q (at which MR = MC) and charge price P, *operating in the short-run* as long as variable cost can be covered. If the loss-producing conditions persist, however, the monopolist will discontinue production.

REALITY AND THE MONOPOLY MODEL

Thus far, we have proceeded as if monopolists always knew exactly what their revenue and cost curves looked like. Of course, this is not true in the real world. A monopolist cannot be sure of the demand conditions for a

EXHIBIT 5 • When a Monopolist Incurs Losses

Even a monopolist will incur short-run losses if the average cost curve lies above the demand curve.

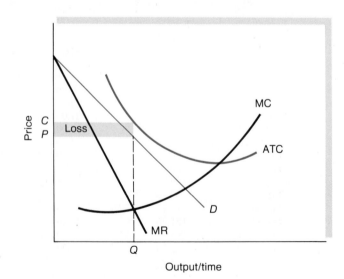

Price Searcher: A seller with imperfect information, facing a downward sloping demand curve, who trys to find the price that maximizes profit.

product. Demand curves frequently shift, and choices must be made without the benefit of perfect knowledge.

The monopolist is, in fact, a **price searcher;** a seller trying to find the price at which profit will be maximized. How many sales will be lost if the price is raised? How many sales will be added if the price is lowered? Trial and error are often necessary to learn the answers. A firm that is a price searcher must set a price on the basis of what it *expects* to happen if the price is changed.

The revenue and cost data illustrated in Exhibits 3, 4, and 5 might be thought of as representing *expected* revenues and costs associated with various output levels. A monopolist, of course, seldom calculates what we have called demand, marginal revenue, and cost curves. Even so, the same questions are asked: Would a lower price add more to revenue than to cost? Would a higher price decrease revenue more than cost? The profit-maximizing price is usually just approximated. When the monopolist who *is* maximizing profits acts *as if* MR and MC had been calculated, however, our model of monopoly shows what the monopolist is trying to do.

PRICE DISCRIMINATION

Price Discrimination: A practice whereby a seller charges different consumers different prices for the same product or service.

Thus far, we have assumed that all sellers of a product will charge each customer the same price. Sometimes, though, sellers can increase their revenues (and profits) by charging different prices to different groups of consumers. This practice is called **price discrimination.**

If price discrimination is going to be beneficial to a seller, three conditions must be met. First, the firm must confront a downward-sloping demand curve for its product. A monopolist will meet this criterion; a pure competitor will not. Second, there must be at least two identifiable groups of consumers whose price elasticities of demand for the firm's product differ. The seller must be able to identify and separate these consumers at a low cost. Third, the sellers must be able to prevent the customers who are charged a low price from reselling the product to customers who are charged higher prices.

Exhibit 6 illustrates why sellers can sometimes gain from price discrimination. Here, there are two groups of customers for the firm's product. The demand of the first group is less elastic (a) than the demand of the second group. In each market, the seller will maximize profit by equating marginal cost and marginal revenue. The best price for the group with the less elastic demand is P_a, associated with the output rate at which $MR_a = MC$. Since the amount purchased by this group is not very sensitive to an increase in price, the higher price (P_a) will generate more revenues (and profit) from this group. In contrast, the demand of the second group (b) is more sensitive to price. When the price charged the second group decreases, the group purchases substantially more units. The lower price P_b thus maximizes the profit from this group.

What easily identifiable characteristics might be linked to the customer's elasticity of demand? Factors such as age, income, and sex will sometimes influence elasticity of demand. For example, the demand of

EXHIBIT 6 • Price Discrimination

Sometimes the demand of some consumers is less elastic than that of other consumers. When this is true, a firm may be able to gain by segmenting its market and charging a higher price to the consumers with a less elastic demand (a) and a lower price to consumers whose demand is more elastic (b).

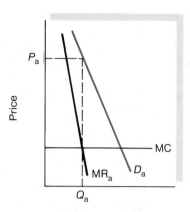

(a) Consumers with less elastic demand

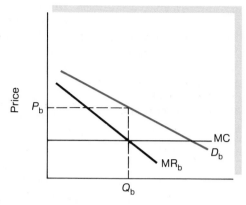

(b) Consumers with more elastic demand

children for movies, airline tickets, and football games is often believed to be more elastic than the demand of adults.

Can you think of any example of price discrimination? Airlines often offer discount fares to individuals willing to travel during off-peak hours, make reservations well in advance, or travel with another person paying a full fare. The demand of these consumers is thought to be more elastic than that of other customers, such as business travelers. Because of this, the group with the more elastic demand is given the discount, while other customers are required to pay the full fare. Why do the producers of professional journals usually charge individual subscribers lower rates than libraries? They generate more revenue by charging higher prices to subscribers with an inelastic demand (libraries). Why are women often charged lower prices for attending nightclubs and baseball games? Again, price discrimination apparently leads to greater increases in revenues than in costs.

A seller need not be a pure monopolist to gain from price discrimination. Any firm that faces a downward-sloping demand curve for its product may employ the technique. In fact, competitive weapons such as discounts and economy fares are often indicative of price discrimination. We introduce the concept while discussing monopoly merely to illustrate the general point.

DEFECTS AND PROBLEMS OF MONOPOLY

Monopolists, by keeping the market constantly understocked, by never fully supplying the effectual demand, sell their commodities much above the natural price, and raise their emoluments, whether they consist of wages or profit, greatly above their natural rate. [3]

---

[3] Adam Smith, *An Inquiry into the Nature and Causes of the Wealth of Nations* (1776; Cannan's ed., Chicago: University of Chicago Press, 1976), p. 69.

"*And though in 1969, as in previous years, your company had to contend with spiralling labor costs, exorbitant interest rates, and unconscionable government interference, management was able once more, through a combination of deceptive marketing practices, false advertising, and price fixing, to show a profit which, in all modesty, can only be called excessive.*"

Drawing by Lorenz © 1970 The New Yorker Magazine, Inc.

What types of problems arise under monopoly? Can public policy improve resource allocation in markets characterized by monopoly?

FOUR DEFECTS OF MONOPOLY

From Adam Smith's time to the present, economists have generally considered monopoly a necessary evil at best. There are four major reasons for this view.

1. *Monopoly Severely Limits the Options Available to Consumers.* If you do not like the food at a local restaurant, you can go to another restaurant. If you do not like the wares of a local department store, you can buy good substitutes somewhere else. The competition of rivals protects the consumer from the arbitrary behavior of a single seller. What, though, are your alternatives if you do not like the local telephone service? You can send a letter or deliver your message in person, or you can write to your legislative representative and complain. These are not very satisfactory alternatives to the service of the monopolist, however. If the monopolist "pushes you around," you often have no feasible alternative but to accept poor service, rude treatment, or high prices.

In the absence of monopoly, the consumer can buy a product either from firm A or from another firm. In the presence of monopoly, the option is to buy from the monopolist or do without. This reduction in the options available to the consumer greatly reduces the consumer's ability to discipline monopolists.

2. *Monopoly Results in Allocative Inefficiency.* Allocative efficiency requires a community to undertake an activity when it generates additional

benefits that are in excess of costs. This requires that a firm expand output as long as price exceeds marginal cost. A profit-maximizing monopolist, however, would restrict output below this level, in order to maintain marginal revenue in excess of marginal cost. Marginal cost would be equal to marginal revenue, maximizing profits for the monopolist, at a *lower* level of output than that at which price would be equal to marginal cost.

The logic of this criticism is pictured in Exhibit 7. Demand is a measure of the degree to which consumers value additional units of a product. The marginal cost curve represents the opportunity cost of the resources used to produce the additional units. Ideally, economic efficiency would require output to be expanded as long as the height of the demand curve exceeded the marginal cost. From the viewpoint of the entire community, output level Q_i would be best.

The monopolist, however, would produce only Q_m units, the profit-maximizing output rate. If output were expanded beyond Q_m to Q_i, how much would consumers gain? The area under the demand curve, ABQ_iQ_m, reveals the answer. How much would it cost the monopolist to produce these units? CBQ_iQ_m reflects the monopolist's costs. The benefits of expanding output from Q_m to Q_i exceed the costs by ABC. The monopolist, though, would not produce these additional units because they would add less to the monopoly's revenues (assuming that all consumers are charged the same price) than to its costs. Potential gains represented by ABC are lost under monopoly. As Adam Smith observed 200 years ago, the monopolist understocks the market and charges prices that are too high.

3. *Under Monopoly, Profits and Losses Do Not Properly Induce Firms to Enter and to Exit from Industries.* When barriers to entry are low, profits induce firms to produce goods for which consumers are willing (because of the expected benefits) to pay prices sufficient to cover costs of production. Inefficient firms face competition and are unable to cover their costs. They

EXHIBIT 7 • Understocking in the Market

A monopolist will produce only output Q_m, even though Q_i is best for the entire community. If output were expanded from Q_m to Q_i, the benefits *to the community* would exceed the costs by *ABC*. However, since the profit of the monopolist is a maximum at Q_m, units beyond Q_m will not be produced. What is best for the monopolist (output Q_m) conflicts with what is best for the community (output Q_i).

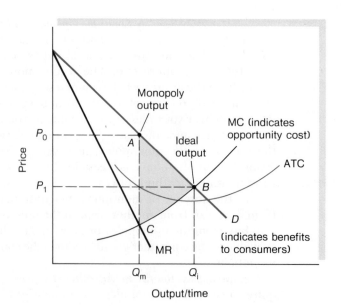

are forced to become efficient or leave the market. Losses also constrain firms from producing goods for which consumers are not willing to cover costs of production. Profits and losses direct resources into those activities for which consumer valuation is highest.

For the monopolist, profits play a smaller role because entry barriers are high. The discipline of close competition is missing. Even though losses will induce exit from the market, some of the cost of inefficiency or some degree of monopoly profits are a premium enjoyed at the consumer's expense.

4. *Legal Protection for Monopolies Encourages Rent-Seeking Activities.* We pointed out in Chapter 4 that governmental policies can be used to transfer income to organized groups and individuals. If a legally protected monopoly can raise the rate of profit above normal, we should expect potential monopolists to seek to establish such monopolies, and to be willing to compete, if necessary, to obtain the monopoly rights.

Gordon Tulluck, in a classic 1967 article[4], pointed out that when the government restricts entry into a market, potential monopolists will compete for exclusive franchises or for other such awards of monopoly power. For example, suppose the government issues a license providing a seller with the exclusive right to sell liquor in a specific market. If this grant of monopoly power permits the licensee to earn monopoly profit, potential suppliers will expend resources trying to convince government officials that they should be granted the license. The potential monopolists will lobby government officials, make political contributions, hire representatives to do consulting studies, and undertake other action designed to convince politicians that they can best "serve the public interest" as a monopoly supplier. Any firm that expects its rent-seeking activities to be successful will be willing to spend up to the present value of the future expected monopoly profits, if necessary, to obtain the monopoly protection. Other suppliers, of course, may also be willing to invest in rent-seeking activities. When several suppliers believe they can win, the total expenditures of all firms on rent-seeking activities may actually consume resources worth more than the economic profit expected from the monopoly enterprise.

Rent seeking does not increase the size of the economic pie. From an efficiency standpoint, rent-seeking activities are pure waste. Thus, the major social cost of legal monopolies may well be the rent-seeking activities they encourage.

WHEN CAN A MONOPOLIZED INDUSTRY BE COMPETITIVE?

The most serious problems raised by a monopoly would be avoided if the monopolist faced the threat of rivals producing the same product or even close substitutes. The presence of competitors would prevent independent firms from restricting output and raising prices.

Why not break up the monopoly into several rival units, substituting competition for monopoly? If it were not for economies of scale, this would be a very good strategy.

---

[4]See Gordon Tullock, "The Welfare Costs of Tariffs, Monopolies, and Theft," *Western Economic Journal* 5 (June 1967), 224–232.

Exhibit 8 compares competition and monopoly, assuming that economies of scale are unimportant in the industry. The minimum-cost output conditions for purely competitive firms thus would not differ from those of monopolists. If the industry were purely competitive, price would be determined by supply and demand. As Exhibit 8a illustrates, under these conditions, competition would drive price down to P_c in the long-run. An industry output of Q_c would result. The market price would just equal the *marginal* opportunity costs of production.

In contrast, if the industry were monopolized, the profit-maximizing monopolist would equate marginal revenue with marginal cost (Exhibit 8b). This would lead to an output level of Q_m. The monopolist would charge P_m, a price higher than would exist in a competitive industry. When economies of scale are unimportant, imposition of competitive conditions on a monopolized industry would result in lower prices, a larger output, and improved economic efficiency.

ECONOMIES OF SCALE AND NATURAL MONOPOLY

Unfortunately, it is often unrealistic to expect similar cost conditions for pure competition and monopoly. Economies of scale are often the reason that certain industries tend to be monopolized. If economies of scale are important, larger firms will have lower per unit cost than smaller rivals. Sometimes economies of scale may be so important that per unit cost of production will be lowest when the entire output of the industry is produced by a single firm. In the absence of government intervention, the "natural" tendency will then be toward monopoly, because increases in firm size through merger, or "survival of the fittest," will lead to lower per unit cost.

Exhibit 9 depicts the **natural monopoly** case. The long-run average cost in the industry declines and eventually crosses the demand curve. To take full advantage of the economies of scale, given the demand for the product, the total output of the industry would have to be produced by a single firm. If the firm were an unregulated monopolist, it would produce output Q_m and charge price P_m. The firm would realize economic profits, because average cost would be less than price at the profit-maximizing output level. It would be very difficult for any firm to begin to compete with the natural

EXHIBIT 8 • Pure Competition and Pure Monopoly in the Absence of Economies of Scale

Here we assume that a product can be produced by either numerous small firms or a monopolist at the same average total and marginal costs. When there are no cost disadvantages for small-scale production, competition serves to reduce price. For a purely competitive industry (a), supply and demand would dictate price P_c. The firms would just be able to cover their cost. If all the firms merged into a monopoly and *cost conditions remained the same,* the monopolist would restrict output to Q_m (where MC would equal MR). Price would rise to P_m.

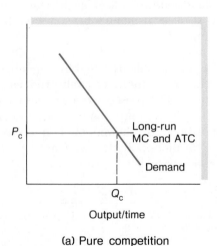

(a) Pure competition

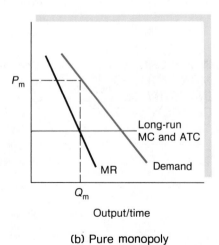

(b) Pure monopoly

EXHIBIT 9 • Monopoly and Competition with Economies of Scale

EXHIBIT 9 • Monopoly and Competition with Economies of Scale

When economies of scale are important, efforts to impose a competitive market structure are self-defeating. For an industry with cost (and demand) curves like those indicated here, prices (and costs) would be lower under monopoly than if there were ten competitors of size Q_c.

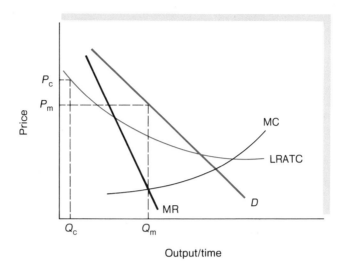

monopolist; initially, while the new competitor was still small, it would have very high costs of production and would be unable to make profits at price P_m. The "natural" monopoly conditions of the industry would act as an entry barrier to potential competitors.

Therefore, when "natural" monopoly exists, a "competitive" market structure will be both costly and difficult to maintain. Suppose the output of an industry were divided among ten firms of size Q_c (see Exhibit 9). These small firms would have per unit average costs of P_c. Even if they charged a price equal to their average cost, the price would be higher than the monopolistic price P_m. In addition, since firms larger than Q_c would always have lower per unit costs, there would be a strong tendency for firms to merge and become larger. Imposition of a competitive structure would be self-defeating in cases in which monopoly "naturally" exists because of the economies of scale.

In what situations are substantial economies of scale present? It is difficult for an observer to know, especially when technology is constantly changing. Existing and potential suppliers sometimes have different opinions as to the importance of scale economies, at a given time and place. However, it is commonly assumed that delivery of local telephone service, water, and electricity exhibit natural monopoly conditions. If there were several telephone companies operating in the same area, each with its own lines and transmission equipment, the resulting duplication would be costly. In such industries, a large number of firms might not be feasible.

POLICY ALTERNATIVES TO NATURAL MONOPOLY

When monopoly or near monopoly results from economies of scale, there are three policy alternatives. First, monopolists could be permitted to operate freely. We have already pointed out that this option limits consumer choice and results in a higher product price (and smaller output) than is consistent with ideal economic efficiency. Second, government regulation could be imposed on the monopolists. Third, the government could completely take over production in the industry. Government operation is an alternative to private monopoly. Let us take a closer look at the last two alternatives, and compare them with private monopoly.

REGULATING THE MONOPOLIST

Can government regulation improve the allocative efficiency of unregulated monopoly? In theory, the answer to this question is clearly yes. Government regulation *can* force the monopoly to reduce its price; at the lower government-imposed price ceiling, the monopolist will voluntarily produce a larger output.

Exhibit 10 illustrates why ideal government price regulation would improve resource allocation. The profit-maximizing monopolist sets price at P_0 and produces output Q_0, where MR = MC. Consumers, however, would value *additional* units more than the opportunity cost. How can the regulatory agency improve on the situation that would result from unregulated monopoly?

1. Average Cost Pricing. If a regulatory agency forces the monopolist to reduce price to P_1, at which the firm's ATC curve intersects with the market (and firm) demand curve, the monopolist will expand output to Q_1. Since the firm cannot charge a price above P_1, it cannot increase revenues by selling a smaller output at a higher price. Once the price ceiling is instituted, the firm can increase revenues by P_1, and by only P_1, for each unit it sells. The regulated firm's MR is constant at P_1 for all units sold until output is increased to Q_1. Since the firm's MC is less than P_1 (and therefore less than MR), the profit-maximizing, regulated monopolist will expand output from Q_0 to Q_1. The benefits from the consumption of these units (ABQ_1Q_0) clearly exceed their costs (CEQ_1Q_0). Social welfare has improved as a result of the

EXHIBIT 10 • **Regulation of a Monopolist**

If unregulated, a profit-maximizing monopolist with the costs indicated here would produce Q_0 units and charge P_0. If a regulatory agency forced the monopolist to reduce price to P_1, the monopolist would expand output to Q_1. Ideally, we would like output to be expanded to Q_2, where P = MC, but regulatory agencies usually do not attempt to keep prices as low as P_2. Can you explain why?

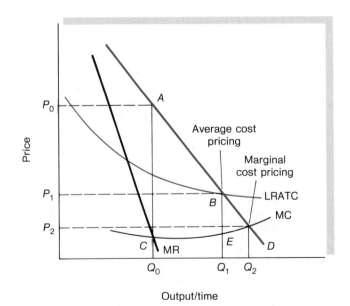

regulative action (we will ignore the impact on the distribution of income). At that output level, revenues are sufficient to cover costs. The firm is making zero economic profit (or "normal" accounting profit).

2. Marginal Cost Pricing. Ideally, since even at the Q_1 output level marginal cost is still less than price, additional welfare gains are possible if output is increased to Q_2. However, if a regulatory agency forced the monopolist to reduce price to P_2 (so that price would equal marginal cost at the output level Q_2), economic losses would result. Even a monopolist, unless subsidized, would not undertake production if the regulatory agency set the price at P_2 or any price below P_1. Usually, problems associated with determining and allocating the necessary subsidy would make this option infeasible.

WHY REGULATION MAY GO ASTRAY

Analysis of economic incentives suggests that government regulation of monopolies will usually not be an ideal solution. Why?

Lack of Information. In discussing ideal regulation, we assumed that we knew what the firm's ATC, MC, and demand curves looked like. In reality, of course, this would not be the case. The firms themselves have difficulty knowing their costs, and especially their demand curves, with any precision.

Because estimates of demand and marginal costs are difficult to obtain, regulatory agencies usually use profits (or rate of return) as a gauge to determine whether the regulated price is too high or too low. The regulatory agency, guarding the public interest, seeks to impose a "fair" or "normal" rate of return on the firm. If the firm is making profits (that is, an abnormally high rate of return), the price must be higher than P_1 and should be lowered. If the firm is incurring losses (less than the fair or normal rate of return), the regulated price must be less than P_1, and the firm should be allowed to increase price.

The actual existence of profits, though, is not easily identified. Accounting profit, even allowing for a normal rate of profit, is not the same as economic profit. In addition, regulated firms have a definite incentive to adopt reporting techniques and accounting methods that conceal profits. This will make it difficult for a regulatory agency to identify and impose the price consistent with allocative efficiency.

Cost Shifting. To a large degree, the owners of the regulated firm can expect the long-run rate of profit to be essentially fixed regardless of whether efficient management reduces costs or inefficient management allows costs to increase. If costs decrease, the "fair return" rule imposed by the regulatory agency will force a price reduction; if costs increase, the fair return rule will allow a price increase. Thus, the *owners* of the regulated firm have less incentive to be concerned about costs than the owners of unregulated firms. Managers will have a freer hand to pursue personal objectives. They will be more likely to fly first-class, entertain lavishly on an expense account, give their relatives and friends good jobs, grant unwarranted wage increases, and in general make decisions that increase costs, but yield personal benefits to the managers. Since monopoly means that buyers do not have a close substitute to turn to, they will bear the burden of managerial inefficiency. Normally, wasteful activities would be policed by the owners, but since the firm's rate of return is set by the regulatory agency, the owners have little incentive to be concerned.

Exhibit 11 demonstrates the impact of inefficient management. If the firm's costs were effectively policed, average total cost curve ATC_1 would result. Because of production inefficiency, however, the firm's average total cost curve shifts to ATC_2. A regulatory agency, granting the firm a fair return, would then allow a price increase to P_2.[5] Even though P_2 might still be less than the unregulated profit-maximizing monopolist would charge, some of the gains of the regulatory policy would be lost.[6]

The Impact of Inflation. Regulation based on normal rate of return will encounter serious difficulties during inflationary times. If the costs of labor, energy resources, and other factors of production rise along with other prices, the cost of producing the product or service of the regulated firm will increase during the period of inflation. A rate structure based on *last year's cost figures* will not permit the firm to earn a normal rate of return. Of course, as its rate of return drops below normal, the firm's case for a rate increase *next* year will be strengthened. If the inflation continues, however, the regulated firm's rate of return will continue to be below normal. The firm will be unable to earn the normal rate of return during inflationary times as long as its rate structure is based on historical costs. As a result of low earnings, the regulated firm will have difficulty raising funds in the capital market. If the normal rate of return on capital is 12 percent, who will want

EXHIBIT 11 • Cost Shifting and Monopoly Regulation

Managers of a regulated firm have a greater incentive to follow policies that yield personal gain at the expense of higher cost. With time, this may cause the cost curves of the regulated monopolistic firm to rise, resulting in higher prices even though monetary profits are still normal.

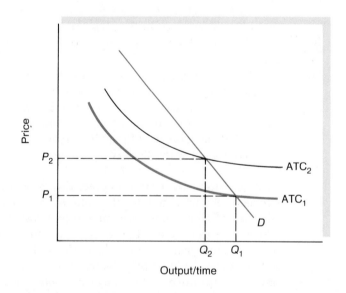

---

[5]Alternatively, the situation might be such that the regulatory agency simply permits the firm to maintain price P_2 because the firm's costs are ATC_2, even though ATC_1 could be attained with efficient operation.

[6]If the regulatory agency did not *immediately* force the monopolist to reduce prices after a cost reduction, the incentive of the monopolist to operate efficiently would be increased, since any improvement in operational efficiency would then result in *short-run* economic profits.

to invest with a firm that is able to earn only 9 percent? Many regulated utilities were caught in precisely this cost-regulated price squeeze as the price of energy and other resources soared during the inflation of the 1970s.

Quality Regulation. It is much easier to regulate product price than to regulate quality. Regulated firms desiring to raise the price of their product can often do so by taking cost-reducing steps that result in quality deterioration. Consider the quality dimension of a seemingly uniform good such as telephone service. The speed at which your call goes through, the likelihood that you will have to redial the desired number, how often your phone is out of order, and how quickly you can get it repaired are included in the quality of telephone service. Since these factors are hard to control, it is extremely difficult for a regulatory agency to impose a price *per constant quality unit.* During inflationary times, regulated firms caught in a cost-regulated price squeeze may be particularly tempted to lower the quality of their product.

Special Interest Effect. The difficulties of government regulation discussed thus far are practical limitations that a regulatory agency, seeking to perform its duties efficiently, would confront. But, the special interest effect suggests that regulatory authorities cannot necessarily be expected to pursue only efficiency. Regulated firms have a strong incentive to see that "friendly," "reasonable" people serve as regulators, and they will invest political and economic resources to this end. Just as rent seeking activities intended to obtain monopoly privileges can be expected, so can activities to influence regulatory decisions.

What about consumer interests? Do you know who serves on the Interstate Commerce Commission or the public utility regulatory boards? Do you know any consumer who voted against a politician because of his or her appointments to a regulatory commission? Chances are that you do not. Consumer interests are widely dispersed and disorganized. Ordinarily, consumers cannot be expected to invest time, resources, votes, and political contributions to ensure that a particular regulatory commission represents their views. The firms that are regulated can, however, be expected to make such investments.[7] Even though the initial stimulus for a regulating agency might come from consumer interests, economic theory suggests that such agencies will eventually reflect the views of the business and labor interests they are supposed to regulate.

THE GOVERNMENT-OPERATED FIRM

Government-operated firms—socialized firms such as the Post Office, the Tennessee Valley Authority, and many local public utilities—present an alternative to both private monopoly and regulation. How do socialized firms operate in the real world? The decision-makers of firms owned by the government are influenced by political and economic factors alike. With the rise of public-sector action, economists have recently expressed renewed interest in the socialized firm.

---

[7]The special interest effect will be weaker when regulatory commissions are elected rather than appointed, allowing the voter to separate this issue from other issues of greater importance.

The ideal theoretical solution is straightforward. The socialized firm should (a) operate efficiently and (b) set price equal to marginal cost. When cost conditions are like those illustrated by Exhibit 7, the government-operated monopoly firm will ideally expand output to Q_i (where $P = MC$) and charge price P_1. The firm will make profits that can be channeled into the public treasury. On the other hand, marginal cost pricing may sometimes result in economic losses, requiring a subsidy for the government-operated firm. Exhibit 10 illustrates this possibility. Output should be expanded to Q_2 if the potential marginal welfare gains are to be fully realized. Price P_2 will be charged. The consumer's valuation of the marginal unit (P_2) will equal its marginal cost. Since losses result at this price and output, it will be necessary to subsidize the public enterprise.

This analysis assumes that the socialized firm will both operate efficiently and set the proper price. How realistic are these assumptions? The same "perverse" managerial incentives—incentives to ignore efficiency and pursue personal or professional objectives at the firm's expense—that regulated firms confront also tend to plague the government-operated firm. Professor John Kenneth Galbraith and others have argued that dispersed corporate ownership rights limit the ability of poorly informed stockholders to police management inefficiency. Managers have more freedom to pursue their own objectives at the expense of "owners." The socialized firm presents the extreme case of disorganized, uninformed "owners" who are in a weak position to assert their ownership rights. No small group of owners will be able to increase its wealth if the public enterprise operates more efficiently. The disorganized owners (voters and taxpayers) will have neither the incentive nor the information to police the managerial decision-making of public enterprises effectively—to reward efficiency and penalize inefficiency. Higher costs results.

In much the same way, special interests also affect incentives—usually in terms of political or group gain—and result in inefficiency. The managers, employees, and specialized users of public enterprises often comprise special interest groups, particularly if the employees are well organized (for example, unionized) for political action. Should the wages of public-sector employees be raised and their working conditions improved? Should comfortable offices, lengthy coffee breaks, and lucrative fringe benefits be provided to employees? Should attractive positions in the public enterprise be provided to the politically faithful? Should management resist pressure to lay off unneeded workers (particularly at election time), abandon unprofitable service areas, and charge users low prices (that is, less than the marginal cost) when the opportunity cost of providing the service is high? On all these issues, the interests of special interest groups involved with public-sector production and its consumption, will be in conflict with the interests of the disorganized, uninformed taxpayers. Under these circumstances, economic theory suggests that the views of the special interest groups will usually dominate, even when inefficiency and higher costs result.

Public enterprises can thus be expected to use at least some of their monopoly power, not to benefit the wide cross-section of disorganized taxpayers and consumers, but as a cloak for inefficient operation and actions that advance the personal and political objectives of those who exercise control over the firm. Government ownership, like unregulated monopoly and government regulation, is a less than ideal solution. It is not especially surprising that those who denounce monopoly in, for instance, the telephone industry seldom point to a government-operated monopoly—such as the Post Office—as an example of how an industry should be run.

SUMMARY

The policy implications that can legitimately be drawn from an analysis of monopoly are more limited than might initially appear. We may not like monopolistic power or its effects, but the alternatives are not terribly attractive. Monopoly power based on economies of scale poses a particularly troublesome problem. When average total costs decline with the size of firm, per unit costs will be minimized if a single firm produces the entire market output. However, if a monopolist is permitted to dominate the market, inefficiency will arise because a monopolist will restrict output and charge a price in excess of marginal cost. Since smaller firms have higher per unit costs, restructuring the industry to increase the number of firms is unattractive. Neither is regulation an ideal solution. Since regulators do not possess the information necessary to impose an efficient outcome and since the special interest effect indicates that regulators are susceptible to manipulation by the industrial interests, regulation is unlikely to achieve our hypothetical ideal efficiency conditions. Finally, since public-sector managers are likely to pursue political objectives at the expense of economic efficiency, public ownership is also a less than ideal solution. Thus, economic theory indicates that there are no ideal solutions when natural monopoly is present. Choices must be made among alternatives, all of which are imperfect.

DYNAMIC CHANGE, MONOPOLY POWER, AND RESOURCE ALLOCATION

We have analyzed monopoly within a static framework and emphasized the lack of competition (sellers of alternative products) *within the industry*. No firm, though, is an island unto itself. Each firm competes with every other firm for the dollar votes of consumers. Dynamic change is present in the real world and the expectation of monopoly profit may influence its speed. Competitors will seek to develop and market substitutes for products offered by profitable firms. If a monopoly is profitable, it will attract rivals that produce substitute products. Actual and potential substitutes exist for almost every product. With the passage of time, the development of substitutes is a threat to the market power of even an entrenched monopoly.

High monopoly prices will encourage development of substitutes. For example, the high price of natural rubber spurred the development of synthetic rubber. High rail-shipping rates accelerated the development of long-distance trucking. The strong exercise of monopoly power by the Organization of Petroleum Exporting Countries (OPEC) subjected oil to vastly intensified competition from coal, solar energy, and other nonpetroleum energy sources, as well as from greatly expanded exploration efforts. The result was a long tumble in the price OPEC could charge for its oil. What seemed to be a secure monopoly position for OPEC turned out to be something very different.

This dynamic competition from substitute products and suppliers, both actual and potential, is important for two reasons. First, a monopolist will sometimes choose to produce a larger output and charge a lower price—lower than the short-run profit-maximizing price—to discourage potential rivals from developing substitutes. When this happens, the allocative inefficiency associated with monopoly will be less than our static model implies. Second, the expectation of monopoly profits may spur product development. In fact, the patent system is based on this premise. When a new product or production method is patented, monopoly power is granted to the patent owner for a period of 17 years. Others are prohibited from copying the product or technique. If this "reward" of temporary monopoly power and profit did not exist, businesses would be less inclined to undertake research designed to reduce costs and improve product quality (see Applications in Economics on product obsolescence). Thus, even though these dynamic competitive forces will operate more slowly than when barriers to entry into an industry are low, the development of substitutes will nonetheless tend with the passage of time to erode the market power of a monopolist.

LOOKING AHEAD

Most markets do not fit neatly into either the pure competition or pure monopoly models. Many markets are characterized by low barriers to entry and competition on the basis of product quality, design, convenience of location, and producer reliability. Other markets involve a small number of rival firms, operating under widely varying entry conditions. In the next chapter, we will investigate market structures that lie between pure competition and monopoly.

CHAPTER SUMMARY

1. Pure monopoly is a market structure characterized by (a) high barriers to entry and (b) a single seller of a well-defined product for which there are no good substitutes. Pure monopoly is at the opposite end of the market-structure spectrum from pure competition.
2. Analysis of pure monopoly is important for two reasons. First, the monopoly model will help us understand the operation of markets dominated by a few firms. Second, in a few important industries, such as telephone services and utilities, there is often only a single producer in a market area. The monopoly model will help us understand these markets.
3. The three major barriers to entry into a market are legal restrictions, economies of scale, and control of an essential resource.
4. The monopolist's demand curve is the market demand curve. It slopes downward to the right. The marginal revenue curve for a monopolist will lie inside the demand curve because of revenue losses from the lower price for units that could have been sold at a higher price.
5. For the elastic portion of a monopolist's demand curve, a lower price will increase total revenue. For the inelastic portion of the monopolist's demand curve, a price reduction will cause total revenue to decline. A profit-maximizing monopolist will not operate on the inelastic portion

of the demand curve because in that range it is always possible to increase total revenue by raising the price and producing fewer units.

6. A profit-maximizing monopolist will lower price and expand output as long as marginal revenue exceeds marginal cost. At the maximum-profit output, MR will equal MC. The monopolist will charge a price along its demand curve for that output rate.

7. If losses occur in the long-run, a monopolist will go out of business. If profit results, high barriers to entry will shield a monopolist from competitive pressures. Therefore, *long-run* economic profits for a monopoly are sometimes possible.

8. Economists are critical of a monopoly because (a) it severely limits the role of demand in the market for a good and thus consumers' "control" over the producer; (b) the unregulated monopolist produces too little output and charges a price in excess of the marginal cost; (c) profits are less able to stimulate new entry, which would expand the supply of the product until price declined to the level of average production costs; and (d) legal monopoly encourages rent-seeking activity.

9. Natural monopoly exists when long-run average total costs continue to decline as firm size increases (economies of scale). Thus, a larger firm always has lower costs. Cost of production will be lowest when a single firm generates the entire output of an industry.

10. In the presence of natural monopoly, there are three policy alternatives: (a) private, unregulated monopoly; (b) private, regulated monopoly; and (c) government ownership. Economic theory suggests that each of the three will fail to meet our criteria for ideal efficiency. Private monopoly will result in higher prices and less output than would be ideal. Regulation will often fail to meet our ideal efficiency criteria because (a) the regulators will not have knowledge of the firm's cost curves and market demand conditions; (b) firms have an incentive to conceal their actual cost conditions and take profits in disguised forms; and (c) the regulators often end up being influenced by the firms they are supposed to regulate. Under public ownership, managers often can gain by pursuing policies that yield them personal benefits and by catering to the views of special interest groups (for example, well-organized employees and specialized customers) who will be able to help them further their political objectives.

11. Even a monopolist is not completely free from competitive pressures. All products have some type of substitute. Monopolists who raise the price of their products provide encouragement for other firms to develop substitutes, which may eventually erode the market power of the monopolist. Some monopolists may charge less than the short-run, profit-maximizing price to discourage *potential* competitors from developing substitute products.

12. Monopoly profits derived from patents have two conflicting effects on resource allocation. *Once a product or process has been discovered,* the monopoly rights permit the firm to restrict output and raise price above the current marginal (and average) cost of production. However, the possibility of future monopoly rights granted by a patent encourage entrepreneurs to improve products and develop lower-cost methods of production.

APPLICATIONS IN ECONOMICS

Product Obsolescence, Monopoly Power, and the Dynamics of Product Development

Many Americans believe that business firms can gain by producing shoddy merchandise that wears out quickly. It is often charged that business firms, over the objections of consumers, produce goods with a short life expectancy so they can sell replacements. Economists have sometimes been at the forefront of those deploring such planned obsolescence.

Yet, a solid majority of economists believe that price indexes overstate the measured rate of inflation because they fail to make an adequate allowance for actual observed improvements in product quality. Why has the quality of products, on the average, risen, if firms have an incentive to produce shoddy, nondurable goods?

Should a Car Last a Lifetime?
There are three important points to keep in mind. First, the production of longer-lasting, higher-quality goods will increase costs. There are no free lunches. A car that lasts 15 years will be more expensive than one with a shorter life expectancy. We should expect consumers to trade off lower prices for more durability. At some point, the greater durability will not be worth the price.

Second, "newness," product variability, and style changes are often valued by consumers. For example, operational reliability aside, many consumers would prefer three differently styled, new-model cars lasting 5 years each to a single car of equal cost that lasts 15 years. *Under these conditions*, the production of goods with less than maximum life expectancy is perfectly consistent with consumer tastes.[8]

Third, goods engineered to last a relatively short time put their owners in a more adaptable position. For example, buyers of new American cars in 1971–1972 preferred large cars. At the time, this made good sense because gasoline prices were low and had been falling in real terms for many years. The value of large, gas-guzzling cars dropped sharply in 1974, though, as gasoline prices soared and spot shortages developed. Years later, in the mid-1980s, the reverse happened: gasoline prices fell sharply, and buyers found it economical to buy cars with more size, comfort, and safety. If those who bought large cars in 1971–1972 and small cars in the early 1980s had paid for years of extra durability, their losses (and the nation's) would have been greater. In a dynamic world, one decision every ten years is less flexible (and, if wrong, more costly to correct) than a decision every five years.

Durability of Products and Producer Choices
In a competitive environment, producers have a strong incentive to cater to the preferences of consumers. Product quality, including durability, is a competitive weapon. If customers really want longer-lasting products, competitive firms have a strong incentive to introduce them. If consumers are willing to pay the price for greater durability, firms that cater to their views can gain. Durability, however, is only one facet of a product that is attractive to consumers. Low prices, newness, and product variation are also preferred by many people. Much of our planned obsolescence undoubtedly stems from the choice of consumers to give up some of the former (durability) to have more of the latter.

The Monopolist and the Durability of Products
Will a monopolist ever introduce a new, improved, longer-lasting product, even if the new product is expected to drive the existing profitable product off the market? Strange as it may seem, a monopolist will introduce the new product if two conditions are met.

1. The product must be a genuine improvement—it must give the consumer more service per dollar of opportunity cost (to the monopolist) than the monopolist's current product.

2. The monopolist must be able to enforce property rights over gains from the new product. A patent preventing others from copying the innovative idea serves this purpose.

If these two conditions are met, the monopolist will be able to price the new product such that it will be profitable to introduce, even though it may eventually replace the monopolist's current product line. Two examples will help to clarify this point.

Super Sharp: The Better Blade
Suppose Super Sharp Razor, Inc., has a monopoly on razor blades,

---

[8]Both the authors and reader may disagree with such "vulgar taste." We should be aware, however, that such disagreement stems from our views about how consumers should behave and does not necessarily mean that the system that caters to that taste is defective.

APPLICATIONS IN ECONOMICS (continued)

which sell for 5 cents and give one week of comfortable shaves. Currently, Super Sharp makes a 3-cent profit (return above opportunity cost) on each blade. Assume the firm discovers (and quickly patents) a blade made with the same machines at the same cost but with a slightly different metal alloy.[9] It gives two weeks of comfortable shaves instead of one. Will the firm market the new blade, even though it will lose one half of its weekly sales of blades? Yes! Customers will gladly pay up to 10 cents per blade for the new blades, which last twice as long. Instead of making 3 cents per customer per week, the firm now will make up to 8 cents per customer every two weeks. Profits will rise. In fact, a price of 9 cents per blade will benefit the buyer *and* Super Sharp alike.

Would Monopoly Oil Sell the Miracle Carburetor?

For years, it has been rumored that a much more efficient "miracle carburetor" for automobiles has been discovered, but that the big oil companies have plotted to keep it off the market because it would reduce their profits from the sale of gasoline.

Suppose an oil cartel, Monopoly Oil, sells all the oil and gasoline in the world. This hypothetical organization has also obtained the patent on a miracle carburetor. The real improvement is simply a little plastic gizmo that can be inserted

into ordinary carburetors. The gizmo can be made in quantity for 1 cent each, and each gizmo lasts just long enough (one year, on average) to save its buyer 1000 gallons of gas. If Monopoly Oil makes 5 cents per gallon economic profit on each gallon of gasoline, the sale lost *per gizmo* will cost the firm $50 per year. Will Monopoly Oil sell the gizmo? Of course! If gas sells for 95 cents per gallon (but the opportunity cost of crude oil, refining, and so on is only 90 cents), the cartel will *increase* its profit by selling the gizmo (cost 1 cent), which replaces 1000 gallons of gasoline, as long as the price of the gizmo exceeds $50.01. The consumer would certainly pay far more than $50.01 to save 1000 gallons of gas. Indeed, any price below $950 per gizmo would help the motorist.[10]

Do Patents Help or Hurt the Consumer?

A patent right is crucial, of course, to both of the above examples. If firms could not at least partially capture the gains to be made from introducing a new product, they might prefer to keep it off the market and thereby prevent other firms from cutting into their profits by copying the new idea.

The patent system has a dual impact on the allocation of resources. First, the patent monopoly grants, as any monopoly does, the patent owner the ability (for a limited time) to keep the price of the patented item higher than costs of production warrant. Thus, *for patented inventions that have already been introduced,* consumers would be bet-

ter off if competition replaced patent monopolies.

There is also, however, a second effect. The fact that one can patent a new product or production process encourages the development of improved, lower-cost goods. Public policy in the United States allows temporary patent monopolies, which are costly to consumers in the short-run, in order to provide firms (and individuals) with a strong incentive to undertake the risk and effort involved in the development of technological improvements, which may lead to lower costs and greater efficiency in the long-run.

---

[9]If the blade requires new and different machines that render the firm's current machines obsolete, the firm will still introduce the product. It will do so, however, at a slower pace, because the cost associated with new machines is higher than the zero *opportunity cost* (assuming the old machines have no alternative use) of using existing machines. Phasing in the new product so that the existing machines may be more fully used could be a cheaper alternative for Super Sharp. If so, it will also be cheaper for society.

[10]If the gizmo were invented by someone other than Monopoly Oil, the inventor would have an even stronger incentive to introduce the product. However, the introduction of the product *by someone else* would detract from the net profit of Monopoly Oil. The latter would have an incentive to suppress the product, if possible. The cartel might attempt to use political power or extra-legal methods to keep the product off the market. Of course, these two actions could well lead to counterproductive economic activity.

THE ECONOMIC WAY OF THINKING— DISCUSSION QUESTIONS

1. Which of the following are monopolists: (a) your local newspaper, (b) Boston Celtics, (c) General Motors, (d) U.S. Postal Service, (e) Johnny Carson, (f) American Medical Association? Is the definition of an industry or market area important in the determination of a seller's monopoly position? Explain.

2. What are barriers to entry? Give three examples. Why are barriers to entry essential if a firm is to make profits in the long-run?

3. Do monopolists charge the highest prices for which they can sell their products? Do they maximize their average profit per sale? Are monopolistic firms always profitable? Why or why not?

4. The retail liquor industry is potentially a competitive industry. However, the liquor retailers of a southern state organized a trade association that sets prices for all firms. For all practical purposes, the trade association transformed a competitive industry into a monopoly. Compare the price and output policy for a purely competitive industry with the policy that would be established by a profit-maximizing monopolist or trade association. Who benefits and who is hurt by the formation of the monopoly?

5. Does economic theory indicate that a monopoly forced by an ideal regulatory agency to set prices according to either marginal or average cost would be more efficient than an unregulated monopoly? Explain. Does economic theory suggest that a regulatory agency *will* follow a proper regulation policy? What are some of the factors that complicate the regulatory function?

6. Is a monopolist subject to any competitive pressures? Explain. Would an unregulated monopolist have an incentive to operate and produce efficiently? If so, why?

7. What is the purpose of the patent system? Is the patent system efficient or inefficient? Explain.

8. United Airlines has a monopoly on the food and drinks served on its flights. Why have they for many years given meals away on their flights? Why does People Express Airline charge for its food and drinks? Why does it advertise Dom Perignon champagne at only $48 per bottle (in 1986) on its flights when the same bottle costs much more in wine stores?

9. How can a firm, through rent-seeking activities, hope to "buy" monopoly profits? Is there competition for monopoly-seller positions? How does competition among rent seekers for monopoly profit influence the efficiency of resource allocation?

- What are the characteristics of monopolistic competition?

- How do consumers fare, under monopolistic competition? How large should we expect producer profits to be?

- How is oligopoly different from monopolistic competition?

- Why have economists been unable to construct a general theory of oligopoly?

- What is the theory of contestable markets? What can we say about the outcomes in such markets?

- What do we know about competitiveness in the U.S. economy, and how it has changed over the last several decades?

- What is the role of accounting profits in the economy? How large are accounting profits, and what changes have occurred in profit levels over the years?

Difference in tastes, desires, incomes and locations of buyers, and differences in the uses which they wish to make of commodities all indicate the need for variety and the necessity of substituting for the concept of a "competitive ideal" an ideal involving both monopoly and competition.[1]

EDWARD H. CHAMBERLIN

20 THE INTERMEDIATE CASES: MONOPOLISTIC COMPETITION AND OLIGOPOLY

Most real-world firms operate in markets that fall between the extremes of pure competition and pure monopoly. These firms do not confront numerous competitors all producing a homogeneous product sold at a single price; neither do most firms produce a good or service that is unavailable from other sellers. Instead, most firms face varying degrees of competition. In some cases, there are competitors offering roughly the same product; in other instances, the competitor's product is merely an attractive substitute. There may be numerous competitors, or there may be only a few other sellers in a given market. The models of monopolistic competition and oligopoly have been developed by economists to describe markets that are neither purely competitive nor purely monopolistic.

Monopolistically competitive and oligopolistic firms have different degrees of freedom in setting prices, altering quality, and choosing a marketing strategy than do firms in purely competitive or purely monopolistic markets. Most firms, unlike those under purely competitive conditions, will lose some *but not all* of their customers when they increase the price of their product. These firms face a downward-sloping demand curve. Like monopolists, they are price searchers: they must search for the price most consistent with their overall goal—maximum profit, for example. As we have indicated, though, just as they are not pure competitors, most price searchers are not monopolists, either. Thus, their freedom to raise prices is limited by the existence of actual and potential competitors offering similar products. The difference between monopolistic competition and oligopoly is in one sense a difference in the degree to which a price searcher is limited by competition.

CHARACTERISTICS OF MONOPOLISTIC COMPETITION

Monopolistic Competition:
A situation in which there are a large number of independent sellers, each producing a differentiated product in a market with low barriers to entry. Construction, retail sales, and service stations are good examples of monopolistically competitive industries.

During the 1920s, many economists believed that neither pure competition nor pure monopoly was descriptive of markets such as retail sales, construction, service businesses, and small manufacturing, which were generally characterized by numerous firms offering different but closely related products or services. The need for a more accurate model for markets of this type led to the theory of **monopolistic competition.** The theory was developed independently by Joan Robinson, a British economist, and Edward Chamberlin, an American economist. The major works of Robinson and Chamberlin were both published in 1933.[2] These economists outlined three distinguishing characteristics of monopolistic competition.

---

[1]Edward H. Chamberlin, *The Theory of Monopolistic Competition* (Cambridge, Massachusetts: Harvard University Press, 1948), p. 214.

[2]See Joan Robinson, *The Economics of Imperfect Competition* (1933, reprint ed., New York: St. Martin's, 1969), and Edward H. Chamberlin, *The Theory of Monopolistic Competition* (Cambridge, Massachusetts: Harvard University Press, 1933).

PRODUCT DIFFERENTIATION

Differentiated Products: Products distinguished from similar products by such characteristics as quality, design, location, and method of promotion.

Monopolistic competitors offer **differentiated products** to consumers. Goods and services of one seller are differentiated from those of another by convenience of location, product quality, reputation of the seller, advertising, and various other product characteristics.

Since the product of each monopolistic competitor is slightly different from that of its rivals, the individual firm faces a downward-sloping demand curve. A price reduction will enable the firm to attract new customers. Alternatively, the firm will be able to increase its price by a small amount and still retain many of its customers, who prefer the location, style, dependability, or other product characteristics offered by the firm. The demand curve confronted by the monopolistic competitor is highly elastic, however. Even though each firm has some control over price, that control is extremely limited, since the firm faces competition from rivals offering very similar products. The availability of close substitutes and the ease with which consumers can turn to rival firms (including new firms that are free

Joan Robinson (1903–1983)

OUTSTANDING ECONOMIST

Along with Edward Chamberlin, Joan Robinson is given credit for developing the theory of monopolistic competition. In her book *The Economics of Imperfect Competition* (1933), she redefined the market demand curve to account for interdependence among firms. Following Alfred Marshall, she used differences among products to define an industry. Essentially, she viewed each firm as a monopolist facing a downward-sloping demand curve that is affected by the behavior of other "monopolists" in the industry. Unlike Chamberlin, she did not introduce product differentiation and quality competition *within an industry* into her analysis.

Professor Robinson's contribution to economics goes far beyond her role in developing the theory of monopolistic competition. A long-time professor emerita of economics at Cambridge University, she was one of a select group of economists who worked with Keynes during the developmental stage of

his *General Theory*. She fully accepted the Keynesian view that the market economy is inherently unstable. Furthermore, she argued that market economies suffer from other serious defects—income inequality, pollution, business concentration, and manipulation of demand.

During the latter years of her life, Professor Robinson was a vocal critic of the capitalist system. Nevertheless, her scholarly work was highly acclaimed by economists of all persuasions. The *Collected Economic Papers* of Professor Robinson fill four volumes.[3] Her work in economics ran the gamut. Capital theory, international trade, Marxian economics, growth theory, and comparative systems are among the many areas that felt the touch of her pen.

---

[3]Joan Robinson, *Collected Papers*, 4 vols. (New York: Humanities Press, 1960–1972).

to enter the market) force a monopolistically competitive firm to think twice before raising its price.

**LOW BARRIERS
TO ENTRY**

Under monopolistic competition, firms are free to enter into or exit from the market. There are neither legal barriers nor market obstacles hindering the movement of competitors into and out of a monopolistically competitive market. Monopolistic competition resembles pure competition in this respect; firms in both these types of markets confront the constant threat of competition from new, innovative rivals.

**MANY INDEPENDENT
FIRMS**

A monopolistic competitor faces not only the potential threat posed by new rivals but competition from many current sellers as well. Each firm is small relative to the total market. No single firm or small group of firms is able to dominate the market.

Retailing is perhaps the sector of our economy that best typifies monopolistic competition. In most market areas, there are a large number of retail stores offering similar products and services. Rivalry is intense, and stores are constantly trying new combinations of price and quality of service (or merchandise) to win customers. The *free entry* that typifies most retailing makes for rapid change. Yesterday's novelty can quickly become obsolete as new rivals develop still better (or more attractive) products and marketing methods.

PRICE AND OUTPUT UNDER MONOPOLISTIC COMPETITION

How does a monopolistic competitor decide what price to charge and what level of output to produce? Like a pure monopolist, a monopolistic competitor will face a downward-sloping demand curve for its product. Additional units can be sold only at a lower price. Therefore, the marginal revenue curve of the monopolistic competitor will always lie below the firm's demand curve.

Any firm can increase profits by expanding output as long as marginal revenue exceeds marginal cost. Therefore, a monopolistic competitor will lower its prices and expand its output until marginal revenue is equal to marginal cost.

Exhibit 1 illustrates the profit-maximizing price and output under monopolistic competition. A profit-maximizing monopolistic competitor will expand output to q, where marginal revenue is equal to marginal cost. It will charge price P, the highest price at which output q can be sold. For any output level less than q (for example, R), a price reduction and sales expansion will add more to total revenues than to total costs. At output R, marginal revenues exceed marginal costs. Thus, profits will be greater if price is reduced so output can be expanded. On the other hand, if output exceeds q (for example, S), sale of additional units beyond q will *add* more to costs (MC) than to revenues (MR). The firm will therefore gain by raising the price to P, even though the price rise will result in the loss of customers.

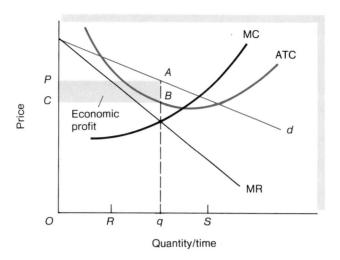

Profits will be maximized by charging price P and producing the output level q, where MC = MR.

The firm pictured by Exhibit 1 is making economic profit. Total revenues $PAqO$ exceeds the firm's total costs $CBqO$ at the profit-maximizing output level. Since barriers to entry in monopolistically competitive markets are low, profits will attract rival competitors. Other firms will attempt to duplicate the product (or service) offered by the profit-making firms.

What impact will the entry of new rivals have on the demand for the products of profit-making firms already in the market? These new rivals will draw customers away from existing firms. As long as monopolistically competitive firms can make economic profits, new competitors will be attracted to the market. This pressure will continue until the competition among rivals has shifted the demand curve for monopolistic competitors inward far enough to eliminate economic profits. In the long-run, as illustrated by Exhibit 2, a monopolistically competitive firm will just be able to cover its production costs. It will produce to the MR = MC output level, but the entry of new competition will force the price down to the average per unit cost.

If losses exist in a monopolistically competitive industry, some of the existing firms in the industry will go out of business over a period of time. As firms leave the industry, some of their previous customers will buy from other firms. The demand curve facing the remaining firms in the industry will shift out until the economic losses are eliminated and the long-run, zero-profit equilibrium illustrated by Exhibit 2 is again restored.

Under monopolistic competition, profits and losses play precisely the same role as they do under pure competition. Economic profits will attract new competitors to the market. The increased availability of the product (and similar products) will drive the price down until the profits are eliminated. Conversely, economic losses will induce competitors to exit from the market. The decline in the availability of the product (supply) will allow the price to rise until firms are once again able to cover their average cost.

EXHIBIT 2 • Monopolistic Competition and Long-run Normal Profit

Since entry and exit are free, competition will eventually drive prices down to the level of average total cost.

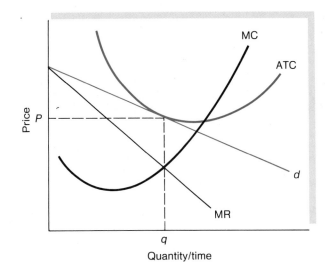

In the short-run, a monopolistic competitor may make either economic profits or losses, depending on market conditions. In the long-run, however, only a normal profit rate (that is, zero economic profits) will be possible because of competitive conditions and freedom of entry.

COMPARING PURE AND MONOPOLISTIC COMPETITION

As you can see, determination of price and output under monopolistic competition is in some ways very similar to that under pure competition. Also, since the long-run equilibrium conditions under pure competition are consistent with ideal economic efficiency, it is useful to compare and contrast other market structures with pure competition. There are both similarities and differences between pure and monopolistic competition.

SIMILARITIES BETWEEN PURE AND MONOPOLISTIC COMPETITION

Since barriers to entry are low, neither pure nor monopolistic competitors will be able to earn long-run economic profit. In the long-run, competition will drive the price of pure and monopolistic competitors down to the level of average total cost.

In each case, entrepreneurs have a strong incentive to manage and operate their businesses efficiently. Inefficient operation will lead to losses and forced exit from the market. Pure and monopolistic competitors alike will be motivated to develop and adopt new cost-reducing procedures and techniques because lower costs will mean higher profits (or at least smaller losses).

The response of pure and monopolistic competitors to changing demand conditions is very similar. In both cases, an increase in market demand leads to higher prices, short-run profits, and the entry of additional firms. With the entry of new producers, and the concurrent expansion of existing firms, the market supply will increase. The process will continue until the market price falls to the level of average total cost, squeezing out all economic profit. Similarly, a reduction in demand will lead to lower prices and short-run losses, causing output to fall and some firms to exit. The remaining firms can raise prices until short-run losses are eliminated.

Profits and losses will direct the activities of firms under both pure and monopolistic competition.

DIFFERENCES BETWEEN PURE AND MONOPOLISTIC COMPETITION

As Exhibit 3 illustrates, the pure competitor confronts a horizontal demand curve; the demand curve faced by a monopolistic competitor is downward-sloping. This is important because it means that the marginal revenue of the monopolistic competitor will be less than, rather than equal to, price. So, when the profit-maximizing monopolistic competitor expands output until MR = MC, price will still exceed marginal cost (Exhibit 3b). In contrast, in long-run equilibrium, the price charged by the pure competitor will *equal* marginal cost (Exhibit 3a). Also, for a firm in monopolistic competition, unlike one in pure competition, the equilibrium (zero economic profit) output· rate fails to minimize the firm's long-run average total cost, as Exhibit 3 illustrates. The monopolistic competitor would have a lower per unit cost if a larger output were produced.

ALLOCATIVE EFFICIENCY UNDER MONOPOLISTIC COMPETITION

The efficiency of monopolistic competition has been the subject of debate among economists for years. At one time, the dominant view seemed to be that allocative inefficiency results because monopolistic competitors fail to operate at an output level that minimizes their long-run average total cost. Due to the proliferation in the number of monopolistic competitors, the sales of each competitor fall short of their least-cost capacity level. The potential social gain associated with the expansion of production to the P = MC output rate is lost. The advocates of this view point out that if there were fewer producers, they would each be able to operate at a minimum-cost output rate. Instead, there is wasteful duplication—too

EXHIBIT 3 • Comparing Pure and Monopolistic Competition

The long-run equilibrium conditions of firms under pure and monopolistic competition are illustrated here. In both cases, price is equal to average total cost, and economic profit is absent. However, since the monopolistically competitive firm confronts a downward-sloping demand curve for its product, its equilibrium price exceeds marginal cost, and equilibrium output is not large enough to minimize average total cost. *For identical cost conditions,* the price of the monopolistic competitor will be slightly higher than that of the pure competitor. Chamberlin referred to this slightly higher price as the premium a society pays for variety and convenience (product differentiation).

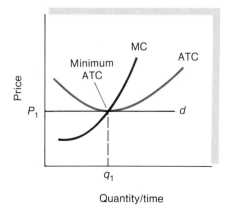

(a) Pure competition

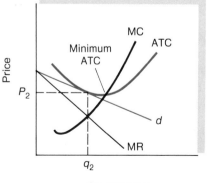

(b) Monopolistic competition

many producers each operating below their minimum-cost output capacity. According to this traditional view, the location of two or more filling stations, restaurants, grocery stores, or similar establishments side by side is indicative of the economic waste generated by monopolistic competition.

In addition, the critics of monopolistic competition argue that it often leads to self-defeating, wasteful advertising. Firms have an incentive to use advertising to promote artificial distinctions between similar products. Each firm bombards consumers with advertisements proclaiming (or implying) that its own product is fancier, has greater sex appeal, and/or brings quicker relief than any product of rival firms. Firms that do not engage in such advertising can expect their sales to decline. Advertising, though, results in higher prices for consumers and thus is costly from society's point of view.

In recent years, this traditional view has been seriously challenged. Many economists now believe that such a view is mechanistic and fails to take into account the significance of dynamic competition. Most important, the traditional view assumes that consumers place no value on the wider variety of qualities and styles that results from monopolistic competition. Prices might very well be slightly lower if there were fewer gasoline stations, located farther apart, and offering a more limited variety of service and credit plan options. Similarly, the prices of groceries might very well be slightly lower if there were fewer supermarkets, each a bit more congested and located less conveniently for some customers. However, since customers value product diversity as well as lower prices, they might be better off under the conditions created by monopolistic competition. Edward Chamberlin, one of the developers of the theory, argues that higher prices (and costs) are simply the premium consumers pay for variety and convenience. When consumers receive utility from product diversity, one cannot conclude that pure competition, with lower price but reduced diversity also, would be preferable to monopolistic competition.

The defenders of monopolistic competition also deny that this leads to excessive, wasteful advertising. They point out that advertising often reduces the consumer's search time and provides valuable information on prices. If advertising really raises prices, it must provide the consumer with something valuable. Otherwise, the consumer will purchase lower-priced, nonadvertised goods. When consumers really prefer lower prices and less advertising, firms offering that combination do quite well. In fact, proponents argue that monopolistic competitors actually do often use higher-quality service and lower prices to compete with rivals who advertise heavily.

The debate among economists has helped clarify this topic's issues. Nevertheless, the efficiency of monopolistic competition continues to be one of the unresolved issues of economics.

REAL-WORLD MONOPOLISTIC COMPETITORS

In our model, we assume that firms have perfect knowledge of their costs and demand conditions. Real-world firms do not have such information. They must rely on past experience, market surveys, experimentation, and other business skills when they make price, output, and production decisions.

Could profits be increased if prices were raised, or would lower prices lead to larger profits? Real-world business decision-makers cannot go into the back room and look at their demand-cost diagram to answer these questions. They must search. They might raise prices for a time and see what happens to their sales. Or, they might lower prices to see if additional sales will expand revenues more than costs. Note that prices that are too high, as well as prices that are too low, can reduce profit. The astute, successful business decision-maker will search and find the profit-maximizing price—the MR = MC output level—that our model assumes is common knowledge.

For real-world entrepreneurs, the problem of uncertainty goes well beyond setting the profit-maximizing price. When considering entry into a monopolistically competitive field, how can entrepreneurs decide whether demand and cost conditions will permit them to make a profit? Just what combination of qualities should be built into the firm's product or service? What location will be best? What forms of advertising will be most effective? Again, past experience, trial and error, and business skill will guide profit-seeking entrepreneurs. Those who have exhibited skill on the basis of past successful experiences will be encouraged to stay and expand. Newcomers can learn by working with others, hiring expert help, or contracting with existing firms, perhaps on a franchise basis.

Despite their high hopes, many firms go out of business every year. In recent years, among corporate establishments alone, the number of firms going out of business has generally exceeded 200,000 annually. A great many of these unsuccessful businesses are small, monopolistically competitive firms that are forced out of business by losses stemming from market competition.

Why do losses occur in the real world? Since business decisions must be made with imperfect information, mistakes sometimes result. A firm may mistakenly produce a good for which consumers are unwilling to pay a price that will enable the producer to cover the costs of production. Losses are the market's method of bringing such activities to a halt. Economic losses signal that the resources would be valued more highly if they were put to other uses. That is, the opportunity cost of production exceeds the value of the output. Losses also provide the incentive to correct this allocative inefficiency.

CHARACTERISTICS OF OLIGOPOLY

Oligopoly: A market situation in which a small number of sellers comprise the entire industry. It is competition among the few.

"Oligopoly" means "few sellers." When there are only a few firms in an industry, the industrial structure is called an **oligopoly.** In the United States, the great majority of output in such industries as automobiles, steel, cigarettes, and aircraft is produced by five or fewer dominant firms. In addition to a small number of producers, there are several other characteristics that oligopolistic industries have in common.

INTERDEPENDENCE AMONG FIRMS

Since the number of sellers in an oligopolistic industry is small, each firm must take the potential reactions of rivals into account when it makes business decisions. The decisions of one seller often influence the price of products and the profits of rival firms. In an oligopoly, the welfare of each seller is dependent on the policies followed by its major rivals.

SUBSTANTIAL ECONOMIES OF SCALE

In an oligopolistic industry, large-scale production (relative to the total market) is necessary to attain a low per unit cost. Economies of scale are significant. A small number of the large-scale, cost-efficient firms will meet the demand for the industry's product.

Using the automobile industry as an example, Exhibit 4 illustrates the importance of economies of scale as a source of oligopoly. It has been estimated that each firm must produce approximately one million automobiles annually before its per unit cost of production is minimized. However, when the selling price of automobiles is barely sufficient for firms to cover their costs, the total quantity demanded from these producers is only six million. To minimize costs, then, each firm must produce at least one sixth (one million of the six million) of the output demanded. In other words, the industry can support no more than five or six firms of cost-efficient size.

SIGNIFICANT BARRIERS TO ENTRY

As with monopoly, barriers to entry limit the ability of new firms to compete effectively in oligopolistic industries. Economies of scale are probably the most significant entry barrier. A potential competitor will be unable to start out small and gradually grow to the optimal size, since a firm in an oligopolistic industry must gain a large share of the market before it can minimize per unit cost. Patent rights, control over an essential resource, and government-imposed restraints may also prevent additional competitors from entering oligopolistic industries. Without substantial barriers to entry, oligopolistic competition would be similar to monopolistic competition.

PRODUCTS MAY BE EITHER HOMOGENEOUS OR DIFFERENTIATED

The products of sellers in an oligopolistic industry may be either homogeneous or differentiated. When firms produce identical products, there is less opportunity for nonprice competition. On the other hand, rival firms producing differentiated products are more likely to use style, quality, and advertising as competitive weapons.

EXHIBIT 4 • Economies of Scale and Oligopoly

Oligopoly exists in the automobile industry because firms do not fully realize the cost reductions from large-scale output until they produce approximately one sixth of the total market.

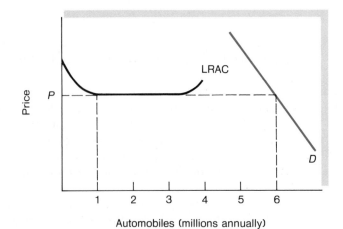

PRICE AND OUTPUT UNDER OLIGOPOLY

Unlike a monopolist or a pure competitor, an oligopolist cannot determine the product price that will deliver maximum profit simply by estimating market demand and cost conditions. An oligopolist must also predict how rival firms (that is, the rest of the industry) will react to price (and quality) adjustments. Since each oligopolist confronts such a complex problem, it is impossible to determine the precise price and output policy that will emerge in oligopolistic industries. Economics does, however, indicate a potential range of prices, and the factors that will determine whether prices in the industry will be high or low relative to costs of production.

Consider an oligopolistic industry in which seven or eight rival firms produce the entire market output. Substantial economies of scale are present. The firms produce identical products and have similar costs of production. Exhibit 5 depicts the market demand conditions and long-run costs of production of the individual firms for such an industry.

What price will prevail? We can answer this question for two extreme cases. First, suppose that each firm sets its price independently of the other firms. There is no collusion, and each competitive firm acts independently, seeking to maximize profits by offering consumers a better deal than its rivals. Under these conditions, the market price would be driven down to P_c. Firms would be just able to cover their per unit costs of production. What would happen if a *single firm* raised its price? Its customers would switch to rival firms, which would now expand to accommodate the new customers. The firm that raised its price would lose out. It would be self-defeating for any one firm to raise its price if the other firms did not raise theirs.

What would happen if supply conditions were such that the market price was above P_c? Since the demand curve faced by each *individual firm* is highly elastic, rival sellers would have a strong incentive to reduce their price. Any firm that reduced its price slightly, by 1 percent, for example,

EXHIBIT 5 • The Range of Price and Output under Oligopoly

If oligopolists competed with one another, price-cutting would drive price down to P_c. In contrast, perfect cooperation among firms would lead to a higher price P_m and a smaller output (Q_m rather than Q_c). The shaded area shows profit if firms collude.

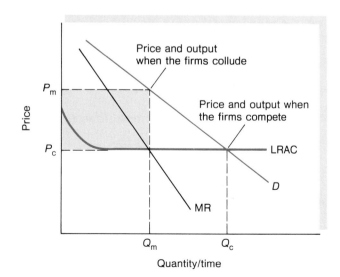

would gain numerous customers. The price-cutting firm would attract some new buyers to the market, but, more important, that firm would also lure many buyers away from rival firms charging higher prices. Total profit would expand as the price-cutter gained a larger share of the total market. But, what would happen if all firms attempted to undercut their rivals? Price would be driven down to P_c, and the economic profit of the firms would be eliminated.

When rival oligopolists compete (pricewise) with one another, they drive the market price down to the level of costs of production. This is not always the case, however. There is a strong incentive for oligopolists to collude, raise price, and restrict output.

Cartel: An organization of sellers designed to coordinate supply decisions so that the joint profits of the members will be maximized. A cartel will seek to create a monopoly in the market.

Suppose the oligopolists, recognizing their interdependence, acted cooperatively to maximize their joint profit. They might form a **cartel,** such as OPEC, to accomplish this objective. Alternatively, they might collude without the aid of a formal organization. Under federal antitrust laws, collusive action to raise price and raise the joint profit of the firms would, of course, be illegal. Nevertheless, let us see what would happen if oligopolists followed this course. Exhibit 5 shows the marginal revenue curve that would accompany the market demand D for the product. Under perfect cooperation, the oligopolists would refuse to produce units for which marginal revenue was less than marginal cost. Thus, they would restrict joint output to Q_m, where MR = MC. Market price would rise to P_m. With collusion, substantial joint profits (the shaded area of Exhibit 5) could thus be attained. The case of perfect cooperation would be identical with the outcome under monopoly.

Collusion: Agreement among firms to avoid various competitive practices, particularly price reductions. It may involve either formal agreements or merely tacit recognition that competitive practices will be self-defeating in the long-run. Tacit collusion is difficult to detect. The Sherman Act prohibits collusion and conspiracies to restrain interstate trade.

In the real world, however, the outcome is likely to fall between the extremes of price competition and perfect cooperation. Oligopolists generally recognize their interdependence and try to avoid vigorous price competition, which would drive price down to the level of per unit costs. But, there are also obstacles to collusion. Thus, prices in oligopolistic industries do not rise to the monopolistic level. Oligopolistic prices are typically above the purely competitive level but below that for pure monopoly.

OBSTACLES TO COLLUSION

Collusion is the opposite of competition. It involves cooperative actions by sellers to turn the terms of trade in favor of the group, and against buyers. Since oligopolists can profit by colluding to restrict output and raise price, economic theory suggests that they will have a strong incentive to do so.

Each *individual* oligopolist, though, also has an incentive to cheat on collusive agreements. Exhibit 6 will help us understand why. An undetected price cut will enable a firm to attract (a) customers who would not buy from any firm at the higher price *and* (b) those who would normally buy from other firms. The demand facing the oligopolistic *firm* will thus be considerably more elastic than the industry demand curve. As Exhibit 6 shows, the price P_i that maximizes the industry's profits will be higher than the price P_f that is best for each individual oligopolist. If a firm can find a way to undercut the price set by the collusive agreement, while other sellers maintain the higher price, expanded sales will more than make up for the reduction in per unit profit margin.

In oligopolistic industries, there are two conflicting tendencies. An oligopolistic firm has a strong incentive to cooperate with its rivals so that

EXHIBIT 6 • Gaining from Cheating

The industry demand (D_i) and marginal revenue curves are shown in graph (b). The joint profits of oligopolists would be maximized at Q_i, where $MR_i = MC$. Price P_i would be best for the industry as a whole. However, the demand curve (d_f) facing each firm (graph a) would be much more elastic than D_i. Given the greater elasticity of its demand curve, an individual firm would maximize its profit by cutting its price to P_f and expanding output to q_f, where $MR_f = MC$. Thus, individual oligopolists could gain by secretly shaving price and cheating on the collusive agreement.

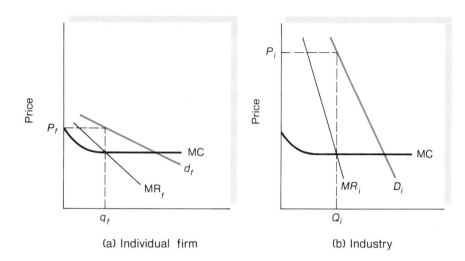

(a) Individual firm   (b) Industry

joint profit can be maximized. However, it also has a strong incentive to cheat secretly on any collusive agreement to increase its share of the joint profit. Oligopolistic agreements therefore tend to be unstable. This instability exists whether the cooperative behavior is formal, as in the case of a cartel, or informal.

There are certain situations in which it is difficult for oligopolists to collude. Five major obstacles can limit collusive behavior.

When the Number of Oligopolists Is Larger, Effective Collusion Is Less Likely. Other things constant, as the number of major firms in an industry increases, it becomes more costly for the oligopolists to communicate, negotiate, and enforce agreements among themselves. Developing and maintaining collusive agreements become more difficult. In addition, the greater the number of firms, the more likely it is that the objectives of individual firms will conflict with those of the industry. Each firm will want a bigger slice of the pie. Opinions about the best collusive price arrangement will differ because marginal costs, unused plant capacity, and estimates of market demand elasticity are likely to differ among firms. Aggressive, less mature firms may want to expand their share of total output. These conflicting interests contribute to the breakdown of collusive agreements.

When It Is Difficult to Detect and Eliminate Price Cuts, Collusion Is Less Attractive. Unless a firm has a way of policing the pricing activities of its rivals, it may be the "sucker" in a collusive agreement. Firms that secretly cut prices may gain a larger share of the market, while others maintain their higher prices and lose customers and profits. Price-cutting can sometimes be accomplished in ways that are difficult for the other firms to identify. For example, a firm might provide better credit terms, faster delivery, and other related services "free" to improve slightly the package offered to the consumer.[4]

---

[4]See Marshall R. Colberg, Dascomb Forbush, and Gilbert R. Whitaker, *Business Economics,* 5th ed. (Homewood, Illinois: Irwin,1975), for an extensive discussion of the alternative methods by which business firms are able to alter price.

When firms sell a differentiated product, improvements in quality and style can be used as competitive weapons. "Price cuts" of this variety are particularly attractice to an oligopolist because they cannot be easily and quickly duplicated by rivals. Competitors can quickly match a reduction in money price, but it will take time for them to match an improvement in quality. When firms can freely use improvements in quality to gain a larger share of the market, collusive agreements on price are of limited value. When cheating (price-cutting) is profitable and difficult for rivals to police, it is a good bet that oligopolistic rivals will be induced to cheat.

Low Entry Barriers Are an Obstacle to Collusion. Unless potential rivals can be excluded, oligopolists will be unable to make unusually large profits. Successful collusion will merely attract competitors into the industry, which will eliminate the profits. Even with collusion, long-run profits will not be possible unless entry into the industry can be blocked.

Local markets are sometimes dominated by a few firms. For example, many communities have only a small number of ready-mix concrete producers, bowling alleys, accounting firms, and furniture stores. In the absence of government restrictions, however, entry barriers into these markets are often low (see Boxed Feature on Contestable Markets). The threat of potential rivals reduces the gains from collusive behavior under these conditions.

Unstable Demand Conditions Are an Obstacle to Collusion. Demand instability tends to increase the honest differences of opinion among oligopolists about what is best for the industry. One firm may want to expand because it anticipates a sharp increase in future demand, while a more pessimistic rival may want to hold the line on existing industrial capacity. Greater differences in expectations about future demand create greater conflict among oligopolistic firms. Successful collusion is more likely when demand is relatively stable.

Vigorous Antitrust Action Increases the Cost of Collusion. Under existing antitrust laws, collusive behavior is prohibited. Secret agreements are, of course, possible. Simple informal cooperation might be conducted without discussions or collusive agreements. However, like other illegal behavior, all such agreements are not legally enforceable by any firm. Vigorous antitrust action can discourage firms from making such illegal agreements. As the threat of getting caught increases, participants will be less likely to attempt collusive behavior.

**THE KINKED
DEMAND CURVE**

As we noted earlier, the demand for an oligopolistic firm's product depends not only on market conditions but also on the reaction of rival firms, so the oligopolist must predict the reactions of rivals. How will rivals react to a price change? When there is a dominant firm in an industry, rivals may be willing to follow the leadership of the larger firm. For example, if General Motors raises its prices by 5 percent, the other major automobile manufacturers might cooperate by raising their prices by a similar amount. Oligopolists, though, can never be sure what rivals will do. Sometimes prospective price increases are announced simply to observe the reactions of competitors.

The response of rivals is more difficult to predict when there is no single dominant firm in an industry. However, it may be that rivals are more likely to match a price reduction than a price increase. If a nondominant firm increases its price, other firms could expand their market shares by maintaining their current prices. The sales of the firm that increases its price may fall substantially. On the other hand, when a single oligopolist lowers its price, it seems likely that rivals will respond. If they do not, their

---

APPLICATIONS IN ECONOMICS

Contestable Markets: Low Entry Barriers May Yield Competitive Results

Markets with few sellers are sometimes more competitive than they seem. Consider the case of the airline route between Salt Lake City, Utah, and Albuquerque, New Mexico. Only two airlines serve this route directly, since it has so little traffic. Further, there would seem to be high barriers to entry, since it takes multimillion dollar airplanes to compete, as well as facilities for reservations, ticketing, baggage handling and so on. The two airlines are well aware of the rivalry (with or without competition) between them, and they both charge the same price. One might expect that price to be high, perhaps close to the monopoly level. But, there is reason to believe that the two airlines, much as they would like to collude and drive up the price, will not be able to do so, as long as other airlines are free to enter this market.

Contestable Market: A market in which the costs of entry and exit are low, so that a firm risks little by entering. Efficient production and zero economic profits should prevail in a contestable market. A market can be contestable even if capital requirements are high.

To compete on an airline route may require millions of dollars in equipment, but the barriers to entry are much lower than that fact suggests. The Salt Lake City—Albuquerque market, for example, can be entered simply by shifting aircraft, personnel, and equipment from other locations. The aircraft can even be rented or leased. By the same token, if a new entrant (or an established firm) wants to leave that market, nearly all the invested capital values can be recovered, through shifting the aircraft and other capital equipment to other routes, or leasing them to other firms. An airline route then, in the absence of legal barriers, is a classic case of a **contestable market:** the costs of entry and exit are low, so that a firm risks little by entering.[5] If entry is later judged to be a mistake, exit is relatively easy because fixed costs are not sunk costs, but are instead recoverable. Entry into a contestable market may require the use of large amounts of capital, but so long as the capital is recoverable, and not a sunk cost, the large capital requirement is not a high barrier to entry.

In a contestable market, potential competition, as well as actual entry, can discipline firms selling in the market. When entry and exit are not expensive, even a single seller in a market faces the serious

prospect of competition. Contestable markets yield two important results: (a) prices will not for long be higher than the level necessary to achieve zero economic profits, and (b) least-cost production will occur. The reason is that either inefficiency or prices above costs represent a profitable opportunity for new entrants. Potential competitors who see an opportunity for economic profit can be expected to enter and move the market toward the perfectly competitive result.

These results do have a policy implication: if policy-makers want to correct an oligopoly (or monopoly) situation, they should consider what might be done to make the market in question contestable. Much of the enthusiasm of economists for deregulation can be traced to the fact that regulation often is the primary restraint to entry. Many economists believe that deregulation permitting new entry can make many markets contestable, achieving lower prices and more efficiency than can direct regulation of producers. We will have more to say about this in the next chapter.

---

[5]The classic article on this topic is William J. Baumol's "Contestable Markets: An Uprising in the Theory of Industry Structure," *American Economic Review* 72 (March, 1982), pp. 1–15.

Kinked Demand Curve: A demand curve that is highly elastic for a price *increase* but inelastic for a price *reduction*. These differing elasticities are based on the assumption that rival firms will match a price reduction but not a price increase.

sales may fall sharply. If the price reduction is matched by the other firms of the industry, however, it is not likely to increase sales substantially for any single firm.

The hypothesis of the **kinked demand curve** is based on these assumptions about the reactions of rival firms. The essential idea of the kinked demand curve is that the oligopolist's demand curve will be (a) very *elastic* for a price increase because other firms will maintain their prices but (b) very inelastic for a price reduction because the other firms will respond by reducing their prices also. The kinked demand curve hypothesis thus implies that prices in oligopolistic industries are likely to be quite stable.

Exhibit 7 illustrates the kinked demand curve. Since the demand curve is kinked at output Q, the marginal revenue curve will be discontinuous. This means that marginal costs could vary substantially at output Q while continuing to equal marginal revenue. For example, both MC_1 and MC_2 intersect the MR curve at output Q. Therefore, despite these changes in cost, the profit-maximizing price of the oligopolist will remain at P. When the demand curve of a firm is kinked, the firm's profit-maximizing price may remain unchanged despite substantial changes in cost conditions.

Economists continue to debate the importance of the kinked demand curve hypothesis. Initially, the widespread use of price lists and categories that established prices in oligopolistic industries for a significant time period was thought to be consistent with the concept of a kinked demand and stable prices. Recent studies suggest, however, that price stability in oligopolistic industries may be more apparent than real. These studies have found that even when the *list* price of a product is stable, firms use such factors as discounts, credit terms, and delivery conditions to alter "price" in response to changing market conditions. In any event, it is clear that the kinked demand theory does not offer a complete explanation of price determination. Even though the theory predicts tendencies *once a price is established*, it does not explain how the initial price is set.

EXHIBIT 7 • The Kinked Demand Curve

Here we illustrate the demand curve of an oligopolist when rivals match a price reduction but fail to respond to a price increase. Under these assumptions, if an oligopolistic firm increases its price, it will lose many customers to rival firms. In contrast, a price reduction, since it will be matched by competitors, will lead to few additional customers. Thus, the oligopolist's demand curve is kinked, and the corresponding MR curve is discontinuous, as shown. The oligopolist will not change price even if MC fluctuates between E and F.

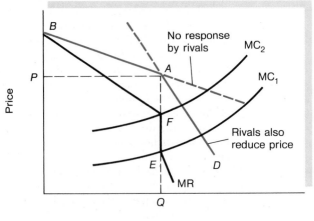

LIMITS OF THE OLIGOPOLY MODEL

Market Power: The ability of a firm that is not a pure monopolist to earn unusually large profits, indicating that it has some monopoly power. Because the firm has few (or weak) competitors, it has a degree of freedom from the discipline of vigorous competition.

Uncertainty and imprecision characterize the theory of oligopoly. We know that firms will gain if they can successfully agree to restrict output and raise price. However, collusion also has its costs. We have outlined some of the conflicts and difficulties (costs) associated with the establishment of perfect cooperation among oligopolistic firms. In some industries, these difficulties are considerable, and the **market power** of the oligopolists is therefore relatively small. In other industries, oligopolistic cooperation, although not perfect, may raise prices significantly. Economists would say that such firms have market power, indicating that even though these firms are not pure monopolists, they do have some monopoly power. Analysis of the costs and benefits of collusive behavior, while it does not yield precise predictions on oligopoly pricing, at least allows us to determine when discipline by competitive pressures is more likely for an oligopolist.

CONCENTRATION AND REAL-WORLD OLIGOPOLISTIC POWER

Concentration Ratio: The total sales of the four (or sometimes eight) largest firms in an industry as a percentage of the total sales of the industry. The higher the ratio, the greater is the market dominance of a small number of firms. The ratio can be seen as a measure of oligopolistic power.

Which industries are dominated by a small number of firms? How important is oligopoly? Economists have developed a tool, the concentration ratio, to help answer these questions.

The **concentration ratio** is the percentage of total industry sales made by the four (or sometimes eight) largest firms of an industry. This ratio can vary from nearly zero to 100, with 100 indicating that the sales of the four largest firms comprise those of the entire industry.

The concentration ratio can be thought of as a broad indicator of competitiveness. In general, the higher (lower) the concentration ratio, the more (less) likely that the firms of the industry will be able to successfully collude against the interests of consumers. This ratio, though, is by no means a perfect measure of competitiveness. Since the sales of foreign producers are excluded, it overstates the degree of concentration in industries in which foreign firms compete. Neither does the concentration ratio reveal the elasticity of demand for products, even though concentration is not as great a problem if good substitutes for a product are available. For example, the market power of aluminum producers is partially limited by competition from steel, plastics, copper, and similar products. Similarly, the monopoly power of commercial airlines is substantially reduced by the availability of automobiles, buses, chartered private flights, and even conference telephone calls. Concentration ratios tend to conceal such competitiveness among products.

The concentration ratio can also overstate the competitiveness in instances in which the relevant market area is a city or region. For example, consider the case of newspaper publishing companies. In 1982, there were more than 7500 such companies in the United States. Sales of the four largest companies amounted to only 22 percent of the national market. Most cities, however, were served by only one or two newspapers. In most market areas, newspaper publishing is a highly concentrated industry, even though this is not true nationally. In this instance, the concentration ratio for the nation in the newspaper publishing industry probably overstates the actual competitiveness of the industry.

What do concentration ratios reveal about the U.S. economy? Exhibit 8 presents concentration data for several manufacturing industries in 1947 and in 1982, the most recent year for which the Census Bureau calculated concentration ratios for industries economy-wide. Several industries, including the automobile, steel, aircraft, telephone and telegraph, computer equipment, and soap industries, are dominated by a few firms. They are oligopolistic. At the other end of the spectrum, the "big four" accounted for less than 20 percent of the sales of sporting goods, saw mill products, bottled and canned soft drinks, and commercial printing.

Most research suggests that there has been, if anything, an increase in business competitiveness over the last several decades. *Within specific industries,* there are cases of both increases and decreases in the degree of concentration. For example, concentration increased in the motor vehicle, farm machinery, and photographic equipment industries between 1947 and 1982. On the other hand, the degree of concentration in aircraft, computer equipment, steel, telephone and telegraph equipment, and meat packing has declined significantly in recent years.

EXHIBIT 8 • Concentration Ratios for Selected Manufacturing Industries in 1947 and 1982

Industry	1947	1982	Change
High concentration (40 or more)			
Motor vehicles and car bodies	71	92	+21
Blast furnaces and steel mills	50	42	− 8
Tires and inner tubes	70[a]	66	− 4
Aircraft and parts	72	64	− 8
Telephone and telegraph	92	76	−16
Farm machinery	36	53	+17
Soap and other detergents	72[a]	60	−12
Photographic equipment and supplies	61	74	+13
Electronic computing equipment	66[a]	43	−23
Medium concentration (20–39)			
Petroleum	37	28	− 9
Bread, cake, and related products	16	34	+18
Periodicals	34	20	−14
Gray iron foundries	16	29	+13
Toilet preparations	24	34	+10
Pharmaceuticals	28	26	− 2
Newspapers	21	22	+ 1
Meat packing	41	29	−12
Low concentration (less than 20)			
Bottled and canned soft drinks	12[a]	14	+ 2
Commercial printing	13[a]	7	− 6
Sporting and athletic goods	24	17	− 7
Sawmills	11[a]	17	+ 6

[a]Data are for 1963.

U.S. Bureau of the Census, *Census of Manufacturing, 1947* and *1982.*

CONCENTRATION AND MERGERS

Horizontal Merger: The combining under one ownership of the assets of two or more firms engaged in the production of *similar products*.

At some points in American history, especially during the early developmental stages of American manufacturing, mergers had an important influence on the structure of our economy. The desire of oligopolistic firms to merge is not surprising. A **horizontal merger,** the combining of two or more firms' assets under the same ownership, provides the firms with an alternative to both the rigors of competition and the insecurity of collusion.

There have been two great waves of horizontal mergers. The first occurred between 1887 and 1904; the second between 1916 and 1929. Many corporations whose names are now household words—U.S. Steel, General Electric, Standard Oil, General Foods, General Mills, and American Can, for example—are products of mergers formed during these periods. Mergers led to a dominant firm in manufacturing industries such as steel, sugar refining, agricultural implements, leather, rubber, distilleries, and tin cans.

Analysis of these horizontal mergers leads to two interesting observations. First, horizontal mergers can create a highly profitable dominant firm, even if there is freedom of entry into an industry. The entry of new competitors takes time. A firm formed by merger that controls a substantial share of the market for a product can often realize oligopolistic profits for a period of time before the entry of new firms drives prices back down to the level of average cost. Of course, if entry barriers can be established to limit or retard the entry of new rivals, the incentive to merge is further strengthened.[6] Second, with the passage of time, competitive forces have generally eroded the position of the dominant firms created by horizontal mergers. Almost without exception, the market share of the dominant firms created by horizontal mergers began to decline soon after the mergers were consummated. Smaller firms gained ground relative to the dominant firm. This suggests that temporary profits stemming from market power, rather than economies of scale, were the primary motivation for the horizontal mergers. In 1950, the Celler-Kefauver Act made it substantially more difficult to use horizontal mergers as a means of developing oligopolistic power. Today, mergers involving large firms seldom involve former competitors.

Vertical Merger: The creation of a single firm from two firms, one of which was a supplier or customer of the other—for example, a merger of a lumber company with a furniture manufacturer.

Another type of merger, the **vertical merger,** joins a supplier and a buyer—for example, an automobile maker and a steel producer. A vertical merger might simplify the long-range planning process for both firms and reduce the need for costly legal contracting between the two. Even though vertical mergers generally do not increase concentration within industries, some economists are concerned that such mergers may reduce competition if either the buyer or the supplier grants a market advantage to the other.

Conglomerate Merger: The combining under one ownership of two or more firms that produce *unrelated products*.

A **conglomerate merger** combines two firms in unrelated industries. The stated intent is usually to introduce new and superior management into the firm being absorbed. This type of merger results in increased size but not necessarily in reduced competition. Since the 1960s, when some very large corporations were formed by conglomerate merger, some observers have expressed concern that the concentration of political power created by

---

[6]See George Stigler, "Monopoly and Oligopoly by Merger," *American Economic Review* (May 1950), pp. 23–24, for a detailed analysis of this issue.

such mergers and the enormous financial assets available to the operating units may be potentially dangerous. Others have argued that conglomerate mergers often lead to more efficient management and increased competitiveness within specific industries.

CONCENTRATION AND PROFITS

The model of oligopoly implies that if the firms in concentrated industries cooperate with one another, they can *jointly* exercise monopoly power. Is there a relationship between industrial concentration and profitability in the real world? Researchers in this area have not been able to arrive at a definite conclusion. An early study by Joe Bain showed a distinctly positive relationship between concentration and profitability. George Stigler, in a detailed study of manufacturing industries, found that from 1947 to 1954 "the average [profit] rate in the concentrated industries was 8.00 percent, while that in the unconcentrated industries was 7.16 percent." Later, both a study by William Shepherd covering the period from 1960 to 1969 and the White House Task Force on Antitrust Policy presented evidence that the rate of profitability is higher in concentrated industries.

Nevertheless, other researchers remain unconvinced. Sam Peltzman argues that the alleged link "between profitability and concentration is, in fact, attributable to other factors which happen to be correlated with concentration." Yale Brozen argues that the proper test is between concentration and future (not past) profitability. His work indicates that "rates of returns in concentrated industries at a later time . . . turn out to be insignificantly different from those in less concentrated industries."[7]

The weight of the evidence on this topic suggests that the profit rate of firms in concentrated industries is just slightly higher than the profit rate of other firms. The link between industrial concentration and profitability is a weak one. Other factors, such as demand conditions, management efficiency, and entrepreneurship, are the major determinants of business profitability. Thus, the odds are only a little better than 50-50 that a more concentrated industry will be more profitable than a less concentrated one.

MARKET POWER AND PROFIT—THE EARLY BIRD CATCHES THE WORM

In the last chapter, we saw that under certain conditions an unregulated monopolist can earn economic profit, even in the long-run. Similarly, our analysis of oligopoly suggests that if barriers to entry are high, firms might be consistently able to earn above-average profits, even in the long-run. Suppose a well-established firm, such as Exxon or General Motors, is able to use its market power to earn consistent economic profits. Do its current

---

[7]For a detailed analysis of this issue, see Joe S. Bain, "Relation of Profit Rate to Industry Concentration: American Manufacturing 1936–40," *Quarterly Journal of Economics* (August 1951); Yale Brozen, "Concentration and Profits: Does Concentration Matter?" in *The Impact of Large Firms on the U.S. Economy,* ed. J. Fred Weston and Stanley I. Ornstein (Lexington, Massachusetts: Heath, 1973); George Stigler, *Capital and Rates of Return in Manufacturing Industries* (Princeton, New Jersey: Princeton University Press, 1963); H. M. Mann, "Seller Concentration, Barriers to Entry, and Rates of Return in Thirty Industries, 1950–1960," *Review of Economics and Statistics* (August 1966); Sam Peltzman, "Profits, Data, and Public Policy," in *Public Policies Toward Mergers,* ed. J. Fred Weston and Sam Peltzman (Pacific Palisades, California: Goodyear, 1967); W. G. Shepherd, "Elements of Market Structure," *Review of Economics and Statistics* (February 1972); and "White House Task Force on Antitrust Policy," Report 1, in *Trade Regulation Reports,* Suppl. 415 (May 26, 1969).

MYTHS OF ECONOMICS

"The prices of most goods are unnecessarily inflated by at least 25 percent as a result of the high rate of profit of producers."

Profits are about as popular with consumers as failing grades are with students at the end of a term. When food prices rise, the profits of farmers, meat processors, and food store chains are heavily publicized by the news media. If gasoline prices jump, many people believe that they are being pushed up by greedy profiteering on the part of the major oil companies. The casual observer might easily be left with the impression that large profits are the major source of the high cost of living.

This issue is clouded by the fact that both the size of profits and their function are largely misunderstood by most people. Surveys show that young people believe the after-tax profits of corporations comprise between 25 and 30 percent of sales. A national sample poll of adults conducted by Opinion Research of Princeton found that the average person thought profits comprised 29 cents of every dollar of sales in manufacturing. In reality, as Exhibit 9b shows, the after-tax accounting profits of manufacturing corporations are about 4 to 5 percent of sales. Thus, the public believes that the rate of profit as a percentage of sales is nearly six times as great as the actual figure!

Why are people so misinformed on this issue? The popular media are one source of confusion. They nearly always report the accounting profits of firms in dollar terms, instead of comparing them to sales, stockholder equity, or the value of the firms' assets. A favorite device is to report that profits, either annually or quarterly, were up by some astonishing percentage.[8]

---

[8]This is equally true for large wage increases. Apparently, the extreme example rather than the norm helps to sell newspapers. We should note that such reports do not imply an antibusiness bias. The *Wall Street Journal*, not noted for such bias, regularly headlines its stories in the same manner.

EXHIBIT 9 • How Great are Profits?

After-tax corporate profits average about 12 percent of stockholder equity and 5 percent of sales in the United States.

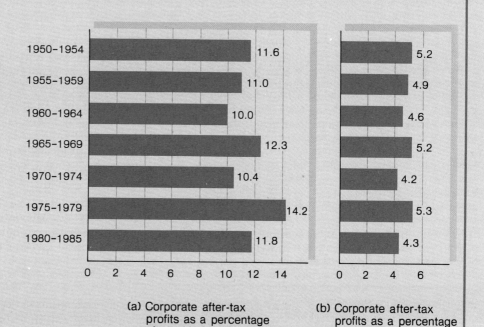

(a) Corporate after-tax profits as a percentage of stockholder equity

(b) Corporate after-tax profits as a percentage of corporate sales

Economic Report of the President, 1986. As the result of changes in definitions and accounting procedures, the data for one period may not be perfectly comparable to the figures for other periods.

Unless we know whether profits were high, normal, or low during the previous period, this type of statement tells little or nothing about the firm's earnings rate on its capital assets. For example, suppose a corporation with $100 million of assets earned a profit of $2 million last year, a 2 percent rate of return on its capital assets. Now, suppose the firm's earnings this year are $4 million, generating only a 4 percent rate of return. It would not be unusual for the popular media to report, "The profits of corporation X soared to $4 million, a 100 percent increase over last year." What this statement conceals is that the profits of the firm as a percentage of its capital assets were less than one

could earn on a savings account.

Not only is the average person misinformed about the size of profits, but most people do not understand their function. Many believe that if profits were eliminated, our economy would continue to operate as if nothing had happened. This erroneous view indicates a misunderstanding of what accounting profits are. Accounting profits are primarily a monetary return to those who have invested in machines, buildings, and nonhuman productive resources. Investment in physical capital involves both risk and the forgoing of current consumption. If profits were eliminated, the incentive of persons to invest and provide the tools that make the American worker the most productive in the world would be destroyed. Who would invest in either physical or human capital (for example, education) if such in-

vestments did not lead to an increase in future income—that is, if investment did not lead to accounting profit?

Profits play an important role in our economy. People who increase the value of resources—who produce something that is worth more than the resources that went into it—are rewarded with economic profit (and generally an above-average accounting profit). Those who allocate resources to a venture producing outputs that consumers value less than the venture's opportunity cost will experience economic losses (below-average accounting profits). Without this reward-penalty system, individuals (and firms) would have neither the information nor the incentives to use resources wisely and produce the goods that consumers desire most, relative to the goods' opportunity costs.

stockholders gain because of its monopoly power? Surprisingly, the answer is no. The ownership value of a share of corporate stock for such a corporation long ago began to reflect its market power and profitability. Many of the *present* stockholders paid high prices for their stock because they expected the firm to be highly profitable. In other words, they paid for any above-normal economic profits that the firm was expected to earn because of its monopoly power.

Do not expect to get rich buying the stock of monopolistic or oligopolistic firms known to be highly profitable. You are already too late. The early bird catches the worm. Those who owned the stock when these firms initially developed their market position have already captured the gain. The value of their stock increased at that time. After a firm's future prospects are widely recognized, subsequent stockholders fail to gain a higher-than-normal rate of return on their financial investment.

LOOKING AHEAD

The competitiveness of a market economy is influenced not only by the various market structures operating within it but also by public policy. Business activity is often directly regulated by the government. In the next chapter, we will investigate the business structure of the U.S. economy and consider the impact of regulatory activities.

CHAPTER SUMMARY

1. The distinguishing characteristics of monopolistic competition are (a) firms that produce differentiated products, (b) low barriers to entry into and exit from the market, and (c) a substantial number of independent, rival firms.

2. Monopolistically competitive firms face a gently downward-sloping demand curve. They often use product quality, style, convenience of location, advertising, and price as competitive weapons. Since all rivals within a monopolistically competitive industry are free to duplicate another's products (or services), the demand for the product of any one firm is highly elastic.

3. A profit-maximizing firm will expand output as long as marginal revenue exceeds marginal cost. Thus, a firm under monopolistic competition will lower its price so that output can be expanded until MR = MC. The price charged by the profit-maximizing monopolistic competitor will be greater than its marginal cost.

4. If monopolistic competitors are making economic profits, rival firms will be induced to enter the market. They will expand the supply of the product (and similar products), enticing some customers away from established firms. The demand curve faced by an individual firm will fall (shift inward) until the profits have been eliminated.

5. Economic losses will cause monopolistic competitors to exit from the market. The demand for the products of each remaining firm will rise (shift outward) until the losses have been eliminated.

6. Since barriers to entry are low, firms in a monopolistically competitive industry will make only normal profits in the long-run. In the short-run, they may make either economic profits or losses, depending on market conditions.

7. Traditional economic theory has emphasized that monopolistic competition is inefficient because (a) price exceeds marginal cost at the long-run equilibrium output level; (b) long-run average cost is not minimized; and (c) excessive advertising is sometimes encouraged. However, other economists have argued more recently that this criticism is misdirected. According to the newer view, firms under monopolistic competition have an incentive to (a) produce efficiently; (b) undertake production if and only if their actions will increase the value of resources used; and (c) offer a variety of products.

8. Oligopolistic market structure is characterized by (a) an interdependence among firms, (b) substantial economies of scale that result in only a small number of firms in the industry, and (c) significant barriers to entry. Oligopolists may produce either homogeneous or differentiated products.

9. There is no general theory of price, output, and equilibrium for oligopolistic markets. If rival oligopolists acted totally independently of their competitors, they would drive price down to the level of cost of production. Alternatively, if they used collusion to obtain perfect cooperation, price would rise to the level that a monopolist would charge. The actual outcome lies between these two extremes.

10. Collusion is the opposite of competition. Oligopolists have a strong incentive to collude and raise their prices. However, the interests of

individual firms will conflict with those of the industry as a whole. Since the demand curve faced by individual firms is far more elastic than the industry demand curve, each firm could gain by cutting its price (or raising product quality) by a small amount so that it could attract customers from rivals. If several firms tried to do this, however, the collusive agreement would break down.

11. Oligopolistic firms are less likely to collude successfully against the interests of consumers if (a) the number of rival firms is large; (b) it is costly to prohibit competitors from offering secret price cuts (or quality improvements) to customers; (c) entry barriers are low; (d) market demand conditions tend to be unstable; and/or (e) the threat of antitrust action is present.

12. Competition can come from potential, as well as actual rivals. If entry and exit are not expensive, and if there are no legal barriers to entry, the theory of contestable markets indicates that competitive results may occur even if only one or a few firms are actually in the market.

13. The kinked demand curve helps explain why oligopolistic prices may tend to be inflexible. Under the basic assumption of the kinked demand curve—rivals will match price reductions but not increases—a firm's price rise leads to a sharp reduction in its sales, but a price reduction attracts a few new customers. Thus, once a price is established, it remains inflexible for extended periods of time.

14. Analysis of concentration ratios suggest that, on balance, there has been an increase in the competitiveness of the U.S. economy in recent decades.

15. Accounting profits as a share of stockholder equity are probably slightly greater in highly concentrated industries than in those that are less concentrated. The relationship between profits and concentration, however, is not a close one. This suggests that several other factors, such as changing market conditions, quality competition, risk, and ability to exclude rivals, are the major determinants of profitability.

16. The after-tax accounting profits of business firms average about 5 cents of each dollar of sales, substantially less than most Americans believe to be the case. Accounting profits average approximately 12 percent of stockholder equity. This rate of return (accounting profit) provides investors with the incentive to sacrifice current consumption, assume the risk of undertaking a business venture, and supply the funds to purchase buildings, machines, and other assets.

THE ECONOMIC WAY OF THINKING— DISCUSSION QUESTIONS

1. Explain in your own words the meaning of product differentiation. What tactics might be used to differentiate one's product?

2. Why do many economists argue that monopolistic competition is inefficient? If there were fewer small firms in a monopolistically competitive industry (for example, retail groceries) would the *average* selling prices in the industry decline? Why or why not? Would convenience, location, and other quality factors change? Why or why not? Do you think monopolistic competition is inefficient? Explain.

3. It is often charged that competitive advertising among monopolistically competitive firms is wasteful. (a) Do you think that advertising in the following industries is wasteful: retail grocery sales, retail furniture sales, cigarettes, local restaurants, cosmetics, movie theaters, retail department stores? Explain. (b) Does this advertising result in high prices? (c) Is the advertising valuable to consumers? Explain. (d) Why is it that more firms do not compete by eliminating their advertising and charging lower prices?

4. Explain why decision-makers for firms in an oligopolistic industry have an incentive to collude. What are the factors that influence the success or failure of their collusive efforts?

5. "Effective collusion requires firms to agree on both price and quality. A firm can lower price by raising quality, or it can raise price by lowering quality, even without changing the actual monetary sales price. Unless a firm can keep its competitors from adjusting quality, the gains from price collusion will be short-lived." Do you agree? Why or why not?

6. "High concentration leads to either overt or tacit collusion. Thus, prices in oligopolistic industries will almost surely be rigged against the consumer and to the benefit of the producer." Do you agree? Why or why not?

7. Are profits important in a market economy? Why or why not? Can you think of policies designed to reduce profitability that are consistent with economic efficiency? Explain. Do not forget to consider any secondary effects.

8. **What's Wrong with These Ways of Thinking?**
   (a) "Firms such as General Motors, AT & T, and General Electric have been using their monopoly power to realize economic profit for years. These high profit rates are benefitting the stockholders of these corporations at the expense of the consumers."
   (b) "Our town has only one rental car company. I'll bet they charge monopoly prices. There is no way we can expect competitive prices with only one seller in the market."

CHAPTER
FOCUS

- How is the U.S. economy structured? In particular, what role does big business play? How important is competition?

- What forms of antitrust legislation are important? What are its policy objectives? How effective has it been?

- What new directions have appeared for antitrust policy in recent years?

- What theories do economists put forth to explain and predict government regulation of business?

- What has been the history of traditional economic regulation? What changes have been occurring?

- What is "the new social regulation," and how does it differ from traditional economic regulation? What can we say about its costs and benefits?

If we can avoid the creation of undue market power, by and large we expect to achieve better market performance— better in terms of lower prices, higher quality products and innovations both in product and technology. [1]

DONALD F. TURNER, FORMER CHIEF OF THE ANTITRUST DIVISION

21 BUSINESS STRUCTURE, REGULATION, AND DEREGULATION

Most contemporary economists believe, just as Adam Smith did, that competition and rivalry among business firms provide benefits to consumers and workers alike. Competition forces producers to operate effciently and to supply consumers with the goods they most intensely desire (relative to costs). Similarly, competition for resources forces each producer to treat workers and other resource suppliers fairly, offering them pay rates and work environments that are attractive relative to those available elsewhere.

But, despite widespread agreement on the desirability of competition, there are two major aspects of competition about which there is a great deal of disagreement: the strength and extent of real-world competitive pressures and the actual effectiveness of governmental regulatory policy. As we have discussed, both the nature of competition and its intensity vary according to the structure of the industry under consideration. For example, as we have seen, competitive elements will eventually be introduced into even highly concentrated oligopolistic industries; at the same time, tendencies toward collusion must also be considered. Economists often disagree on the ability of unregulated markets to provide for a strong competitive environment.

As for the argument concerning the effects of regulation on competition, some economists point out that regulatory policy, by limiting various types of noncompetitive behavior, effectively increases the discipline of the market. Others charge that past regulatory policies have often reduced market competitiveness, contributed to economic inefficiency, and in general, ignored major concerns of consumers and workers. In this chapter, we will analyze the structure of the U.S. economy and consider the effects of regulatory policy on economic behavior in the light of these controversies.

THE STRUCTURE OF THE U.S. ECONOMY

The structure of the U.S. economy is extremely diverse. There are approximately 18 million business firms in the United States. Owner-operated farming and service businesses alone account for more than 6 million firms. These businesses are, of course, quite small. In contrast, there are roughly 440,000 corporations with annual business receipts in excess of $1 million. Some of these are giants with thousands of employees and annual sales running into the billions of dollars.

The structure of our economy has changed significantly over the years. A century ago, over half of all workers were employed in agriculture, and fewer than 20 percent worked in manufacturing. Throughout the first half of this century, the relative size of the agricultural sector declined steadily and manufacturing output increased, as a share of total output. By 1950, the manufacturing sector accounted for 30 percent of total U.S. output; agriculture had declined to less than 10 percent.

Since 1950, a new trend in industrial structure has evolved. The relative sizes of *both* the agricultural and manufacturing sectors have declined, and

---

[1]Donald F. Turner, "The Antitrust Chief Dissents," *Fortune* (April 1966), p. 113.

the government and service sectors (for example, health care, education, professional, and repair workers) have expanded. As a share of the total, employment in the government and service sectors rose from 25 percent to more than 39 percent between 1950 and 1985. In contrast, manufacturing employment fell from 34 percent in 1950 to less than 20 percent in 1985.

Industry has shifted geographically, and the composition of the labor force has also changed. During the 1960s and 1970s, there was a movement of industry from the northeast urban centers to the Sunbelt. Fewer than a third of all workers in 1960 were female; by 1985, women accounted for 44 percent of the total work force.

HOW MUCH OF OUR ECONOMY IS COMPETITIVE?

The question, "how much of our economy is competitive," is a difficult one to answer. In a very real sense, every firm competes with every other one for the consumer's additional dollar of spending. Competition is everywhere; the seller of compact disks, for example, competes with the book store and the local restaurant for our entertainment budgets.

As we have discussed, competition, even within an industry, is multi-dimensional. Dynamic innovation, entrepreneurship, and product-quality competition may be important even in highly concentrated industries. The concentration ratio of an industry, as we found in the previous chapter, provides an indication of competitiveness, but it is an imperfect measure. Available substitutes reduce the monopoly power of firms in some concentrated industries. Other firms are restrained by the threat of entry from potential rivals. Still others face stiff competition from foreign producers.

The relative importance of competitive and noncompetitive sectors within the economy changes with time. Moreover—and perhaps most important—it is not clear where the line should be drawn between competitive and noncompetitive industries. Most economists would probably classify unregulated industries in which the four largest firms produce less than 20 or 25 percent of the market as competitive. On the other hand, industries in which the largest firms produce more than half of the output would generally be classified as oligopolistic, suggesting the presence of non-competitive elements. These categories, however, are arbitrary.

Exhibit 1 sheds some light on the competitiveness of the U.S. economy. The table breaks down our gross national product by sector and industrial concentration. Agriculture, construction, wholesale and retail trade, and service industries have traditionally been characterized by small firms and low barriers to entry.[2] These sectors, in addition to manufacturing industries with four-firm concentration ratios of less than 20 percent, accounted for more than two fifths of the total national output in 1983. They now comprise roughly one half of the private sector. This suggests that competitive forces play a highly important role in our economy.

On the other hand, business concentration and regulated sectors are also important. Regulated industries and government generate well over

---

[2]In 1971, proprietorships, partnerships, and corporations with sales of less than $1 million accounted for 81 percent of the income generated by agriculture, 64 percent of income from service, 44 percent of construction income, and 25 percent of wholesale and retail trade income.

EXHIBIT 1 • The Competitiveness of the U.S. Economy, 1983

National Income Originating from:	Billions of Dollars	Percentage of Total
Low barriers to entry	1114	42
Agriculture, forestry, and fisheries	61	
Construction	112	
Wholesale and retail trade	386	
Service	427	
Manufacturing (industries with concentration ratios of less than 20 percent)[a]	128	
Medium barriers to entry	137	5
Manufacturing (industries with concentration ratios between 20 and 40 percent)[a]	137	
High barriers to entry (unregulated)	355	13
Manufacturing (industries with concentration ratios greater than 40 percent)[a]	315	
Mining	40	
Primarily regulated industries	606	23
Transportation, communications, and utility	212	
Finance, insurance, and real estate	394	
Government	392	15
All other	48	2
Total	2652	100

[a]The concentration ratios were for the U.S. Bureau of the Census' two-digit industrial classification. The following industries had four-firm concentration ratios of greater than 40 percent: tobacco, chemicals, rubber products, stone, clay, and glass products, primary metals, electrical equipment, transportation equipment (aircraft and automobiles), machinery (except electrical), and instruments and related products.

Derived from the *Statistical Abstract of the United States–1985* Tables 727, 1342, and 1362.

one third of our total output. Highly concentrated manufacturing industries such as tobacco, chemicals, automobiles, aircraft, primary metals, and electrical equipment accounted for 13 percent of our national income in 1983. Most economists believe that firms in these industries are best capable of escaping the discipline of competition. Of course, many of these concentrated industries confront stiff foreign competition. For example, even though only a few firms account for all *domestic production,* more than one out of every four automobiles sold in the United States is bought from a foreign producer. Foreign competition is also important in other industries. Imports accounted for only 6.5 percent of industrial shipments in 1975, but in 1984, the figure had risen to 10.9 percent.

Product-quality competition may also account for strong rivalry even among a limited number of competitors. Moreoever, in a firm as big as General Motors, even the rivalry among divisions (Buick versus Oldsmobile, for example) may be intense. Direct price competition within the firm is presumably controlled, but competition involving quality remains. Leaders in each division compete for recognition and advancement, and each is judged by monthly sales and profit figures. Thus, competitive forces are not entirely absent even in a concentrated industry.

These data on the U.S. industrial structure indicate that competitive, concentrated, and highly regulated sectors are all sizable. More than two fifths of our national output is generated by roughly competitive industries—that is, industries in which rivalry exists among a substantial number of firms. Another one fifth of our output originates from industries characterized by a significant degree of industrial concentration. Highly regulated industries account for nearly a quarter of the total output. The government sector generates the remainder of the total output.[3]

Over the past several decades, the competitive portion of the economy has been expanding relative to the less competitive portion. Exhibit 2 reports some of the findings of William G. Shepherd, showing that firms in competitive industries have produced a rising percentage of national income, while monopolies have produced a falling share. The intermediate categories have also declined in importance. Shepherd attributes the sharp increase in competition from 1958 to 1980 to antitrust policy, increased import competition, and deregulation.

Exhibit 3 provides another view of the recent time trend in concentration, looking at the share of assets controlled by the largest firms, rather than at market shares. By this criterion, the biggest nonfinancial firms have

---

EXHIBIT 2 • The Increasing Competitiveness of the U.S. Economy, 1939–1980

This chart presents the findings of a recent study by William Shepherd, an industrial economist from the University of Michigan. Shepherd found that the share of national income produced by the competitive sectors of the U.S. economy has been rising for several decades, while the share produced in less competitive markets has been falling. The "single dominant firm" here is one with more than a 50 percent market share, high barriers to entry, and the ability of the dominant firm to control pricing and to influence innovation. A "tight oligopoly" means a 4-firm concentration ratio above 60 percent and stable market shares, or government-regulated firms with the ability to strongly influence the regulated prices, such as milk markets.

Market Structure Category	Percentage Shares of National Income Produced in Each Category,		
	1939	1958	1980
1. Pure Monopoly	6.2	3.1	2.5
2. Single Dominant Firm	5.0	5.0	2.8
3. Tight Oligopoly	36.4	35.6	18.0
4. Effectively Competitive	52.4	56.3	76.7
Total	100.0	100.0	100.0

Source: William G. Shepherd, "Causes of Increased Competition in the U.S. Economy, 1939–1980," *Review of Economics and Statistics*, November 1982, p. 618.

---

[3]These data reflect the research on this topic. For additional detail, see George Stigler, *Five Lectures on Economic Problems* (New York: Longman, 1949); G. Warren Nutter and Henry A. Einhorn, *Enterprise Monopoly in the United States: 1899–1958* (New York: Columbia University Press, 1969); and Solomon Fabricant, "Is Monopoly Increasing?" *Journal of Economic History* (Winter 1953).

EXHIBIT 3 • Concentration of Assets among America's Biggest Firms

The shares of tangible assets held by the largest nonfinancial business corporations declined during the 1970–1984 period.

Asset Size Group	Percent of tangible assets of nonfinancial corporations held by the largest firms						
	1970	1977	1978	1979	1980	1981	1984
Top 50	NA	22.7	22.3	21.9	22.4	22.2	NA
Top 100	32.1	29.7	29.2	28.9	29.4	28.8	28.0
Top 200	40.0	38.3	37.7	37.4	37.7	36.9	34.0

Source: Economic Report of the President, 1985 (p. 200), and *Statistical Abstract of the United States, 1986*.

---

decreased in size relative to the rest of the economy in recent years. The share of tangible assets owned by the largest 200 firms fell from 40 percent in 1970 to 34 percent in 1984. The relative size of assets owned by the top 100 firms also fell during this period.

PUBLIC POLICY AND BIG BUSINESS IN THE U.S. ECONOMY

The stated objective of public policy has been to restrain various aspects of big business activity, especially when competition seems threatened. Many believe that antitrust action can help promote efficiency and keep political power and income more equally distributed. To what extent does the economic and political power of large corporations threaten competitiveness? To what extent does this power need to be restrained? Some observers argue that large firms threaten our decentralized economic institutions and our democratic political structure. Certainly, public choice theory indicates that concentrated business interests, like other special interest organizations, often exert a disproportional influence on the political process. This notwithstanding, we should keep three points in mind as we evaluate this issue and the effectiveness of the government's antitrust policies.

First, bigness and absence of competition are not necessarily the same thing. A firm can be big and yet function in a highly competitive industry. For example, Sears and Montgomery Ward are both large, but they are also part of a highly competitive industry—retail sales.

Second, large size does not ensure greater profitability. The real-world data indicate that profits as a percentage of stockholder equity are unrelated to corporate size.[4] Many of the companies formed by conglomerate mergers discovered this when their earnings took a nose dive during the 1970s.

Third, the firms that comprise the largest 100 or 200 corporations are heterogeneous and constantly changing. As successful management and the vagaries of business fortune exert their influences, some firms are pushed

---

[4]See William G. Shepherd, *The Economics of Industrial Organization* (Englewood Cliffs, New Jersey: Prentice-Hall), pp. 270–272, for evidence on this issue. Shepherd found that large corporate size had a mild *negative* impact on the rate of profit of firms during the period from 1960 to 1969.

out of the top group and others enter. Of the 100 largest manufacturing corporations in 1909, only 36 remained on the list in 1948. Of the 50 largest manufacturing firms in 1947, only 25 remained in that category in 1972. Of those that dropped out during the period from 1947 to 1972, 5 failed to make even the top 200. With time, even giants stumble and fall, and new competitors arise to take their place. In a world of changing technology and consumer preferences, bigness guarantees neither success nor sticking power.

ANTITRUST LEGISLATION—THE POLICY OBJECTIVES

Predatory Pricing: The practice by which a dominant firm in an industry temporarily reduces price to damage or eliminate weaker rivals, so that prices can be raised above the level of costs at a later time.

Antitrust legislation seeks to (a) ensure that the economy is structured such that competition exists among firms in the same industry (or market area) and to (b) prohibit business practices that tend to stifle competition. Once these objectives are accomplished, it is assumed that market forces can be relied on to allocate goods and services.

Exclusive Contract: An agreement between manufacturer and retailer that prohibits the retailer from carrying the product lines of firms that are rivals of the manufacturer. Such contracts are illegal under the Clayton Act when they "lessen competition."

There are numerous tactics business entrepreneurs might use to avoid the rigors of competition. We have already stressed that collusion and price agreements are potential weapons with which to turn trade in favor of the seller. Potential competitors might also decide to divide a market geographically, agreeing not to compete in certain market areas. Large, diversified firms might use **predatory pricing,** a practice by which a firm *temporarily* reduces its price below cost in certain market areas in order to damage or eliminate weaker rivals. Once the rivals have been eliminated, the firm uses its monopoly power to raise prices above costs. A competitor might also use exclusive contracts and reciprocal agreements to maintain an advantage over rivals. An **exclusive contract** (or dealership) is an arrangement whereby the manufacturer of a line of products prohibits retailers from selling any of the products of rival producers. An established firm offering many product lines might use this tactic to limit the entry by rivals into retail markets offering only narrow product lines. A **reciprocal agreement** is a situation in which the buyer of a product requires the seller to purchase another product as a condition of sale. For example, General Motors was charged in 1963 with telling railroads that if they did not buy GM locomotives, GM would not ship its automobiles by rail. These business practices involve the use of market power rather than superior performance to gain at the expense of rivals. In one form or another, they are all illegal under current antitrust legislation.

Reciprocal Agreement: An agreement between firms whereby the buyer of a product requires the seller to purchase another product as a condition of sale. The practice is illegal under the Clayton Act when it substantially reduces competition.

MAJOR ANTITRUST LEGISLATION

A society that organizes economic activity on the basis of competitive markets rather than on detailed regulation or socialized planning may need to pursue an antitrust policy. The United States, to a greater extent than most Western countries, has adopted antitrust legislation designed to promote competitive markets. Three major legislative acts—the Sherman Act, the Clayton Act, and the Federal Trade Commission Act—form the foundation of antitrust policy in the United States.

The Sherman Act. The Sherman Act was passed in 1890, largely in response to a great wave of mergers. The infamous tobacco, sugar, and Standard Oil trusts enraged Congress and the American people. Action against business concentration was necessary. The most important provisions of the act are the following:

Section 1: Every contract, combination in the form of trust or otherwise, or conspiracy, in restraint of trade or commerce among the several states or with foreign nations, is hereby declared illegal.

Section 2: Every person who shall monopolize, or conspire with any other person or persons to monopolize any part of the trade or commerce among the several states, or with foreign nations, shall be guilty of a misdemeanor.

The language of the Sherman Act is vague and subject to interpretation. What does it mean "to attempt to monopolize" or "combine or conspire with another person"? Initially, the courts were hesitant to apply the act to manufacturing corporations. In 1911, however, the Supreme Court ruled that Standard Oil and American Tobacco had used "unreasonable" tactics to restrain trade. At the time, the Standard Oil trust controlled 90 percent of the country's refinery capacity. American Tobacco controlled three fourths of the tobacco manufacturing market. Both firms were broken up into several smaller rival firms.

The Supreme Court, however, did not prohibit monopoly *per se*. It was the tactics used by Standard Oil and American Tobacco that caused the Court to rule against them. In later cases, the Supreme Court refused to break up other trusts (U.S. Steel and American Can, for example) because it could not be proved that they had followed "unfair or unethical" business practices. The Sherman Act, though, does not clearly define unfair or unethical business practices, and the courts were reluctant to enforce it. The act was ineffective, and two other antitrust laws were passed in 1914.

The Clayton Act. The Clayton Act was passed in an effort to spell out and prohibit specific business practices. The following are prohibited by the Clayton Act when they "substantially lessen competition or tend to create a monopoly": (a) *price discrimination*—charging purchasers in different markets different prices that are unrelated to transportation or other costs; (b) *tying contracts*—a practice whereby the seller requires the buyer to purchase another item; (c) *exclusive dealings*—agreements whereby the seller of a good is forbidden to sell to a competitor of the purchaser; (d) *interlocking stockholding*—one firm purchasing the stock of a competing firm; (e) *interlocking directorates*—the same individual(s) serving on the boards of directors of competing firms.

Although somewhat more specific than the Sherman Act, the Clayton Act is still vague. At what point do the prohibited actions actually become illegal? Under what circumstances do these actions "substantially lessen competition"? The task of interpreting this ambiguous phrase still remains with the courts.

The Federal Trade Commission Act. The Federal Trade Commission Act declared unlawful all "unfair methods of competition in commerce." The Federal Trade Commission (FTC), composed of five members appointed by the president to seven-year terms, was established to determine the exact meaning of "unfair methods." However, a 1919 Supreme Court decision held that the courts, not the FTC, had the ultimate responsibility for interpreting the law. Today, the FTC is concerned primarily with (a) enforcing consumer protection legislation, (b) prohibiting deceptive advertising, a power it acquired in 1938, and (c) preventing overt collusion.

When a complaint is filed with the FTC, usually by a third party, the commission investigates. If there is a violation, the FTC initially attempts to settle the dispute by negotiation between the parties. If the attempts to negotiate a settlement fail, a hearing is conducted before one of the commission's examiners. The decision of the hearing examiner may be appealed to the full commission, and the FTC's decision may later be appealed to the U.S. Court of Appeals. The great majority of cases brought before the FTC are now settled by mutual consent of the parties involved.

MORE RECENT ANTITRUST LEGISLATION

Additional antitrust legislation was passed in the 1930s. The Robinson-Patman Act of 1936 prohibits selling "at unreasonably low prices" when such practices reduce competition. The section of the Clayton Act dealing with price discrimination was aimed at eliminating predatory pricing. The Robinson-Patman Act went beyond this. It was intended to protect competitors not just from stronger rivals who might temporarily sell below cost but also from more efficient rivals who were actually producing at a lower cost. Chain stores and mass distributors were the initial targets of the legislation. Economists have often been critical of the Robinson-Patman Act, since it has tended to eliminate price competition and protect inefficient producers.

In 1938, Congress passed the Wheeler-Lea Act, which was designed to strengthen sectors of the Federal Trade Commission Act that had been weakened by restrictive court decisions. Before the passage of the act, the courts were reluctant to prohibit unfair business practices, such as false and deceptive advertising, unless there was proof of damages to either consumers or rival firms. The Wheeler-Lea Act removed this limitation and gave the FTC extended powers to prosecute and ban false or deceptive advertising.

In 1950, Congress passed the Celler-Kefauver Act (sometimes referred to as the antimerger act), which prohibits a firm from acquiring the assets of a competitor if the transaction substantially lessens competition. The Clayton Act, though it prohibits mergers through stock acquisition, proved unable to prevent business combinations from being formed by sale of assets. The Celler-Kefauver Act closed this loophole, further limiting the ability of firms to combine to escape competitive pressures.

Since the intent of the Celler-Kefauver Act is to maintain industrial competition, its applicability to mergers between large firms in the same industry is obvious. The act also prohibits vertical mergers between large firms if competition is reduced by such mergers. For example, the merger of a publishing company with a paper producer is now illegal if the courts find that it lessens competition. However, the applicability of the Celler-Kefauver Act to conglomerate mergers remains ambiguous, primarily because there has not been a clear-cut court decision in this area.

THUMBNAIL SKETCH

Antitrust Legislation

Antitrust laws prohibit the following:

1. Collusion—contracts and conspiracies to restrain trade (Sherman Act, Sec. 1)
2. Monopoly and attempts to monopolize any part of trade or commerce among the several states (Sherman Act, Sec. 2)
3. Persons serving on the board of directors of competing firms with more than $1 million of assets (Clayton Act, Sec. 8)
4. Unfair and deceptive advertising (Federal Trade Commission Act as amended by Wheeler-Lea Act)
5. Price discrimination if the intent is to injure a competitor (Robinson–Patman Act)

The following practices are also illegal when they substantially lesson competition or tend to create a monopoly:

1. Tying contracts (Clayton Act, Sec. 3)
2. Exclusive dealings (Clayton Act, Sec. 3)
3. Interlocking stockholdings and horizontal mergers (Clayton Act, Sec. 7, as amended by Celler-Kefauver Act)
4. Interlocking directorates (Clayton Act, Sec. 8)

THE EFFECTIVENESS OF ANTITRUST POLICY—THE DOMINANT VIEW

Few economists are completely satisfied with all aspects of antitrust policy, but most observers believe it has exerted a positive, though probably not dramatic, influence on competitive markets. The Sherman and Clayton Acts prohibit the most efficient methods of collusion (for example, mergers, interlocking boards of directors, and interlocking stockholdings) and thereby raise the costs of colluding. Also, since current collusive agreements must thus be tacit and unenforceable, rivals are more likely to cheat. The expected benefits of collusion have been effectively reduced, and economic theory suggests that the magnitude of anticompetitive collusive business practices should therefore be reduced. In addition, counterproductive (from the viewpoint of society) competitive tactics—exclusive contracts, price discrimination, and tying contracts, for example—have been made more costly. Prohibiting such practices has probably served to reduce entry barriers into markets. Since the passage of the Celler-Kefauver Act, most observers believe that antitrust legislation has effectively limited the power of firms to reduce competition *within an industry* through merger. Today, in contrast with earlier periods in American history, the probability of mergers contributing to industrial concentration—and hindering the competition that tends to erode it—is substantially lower.

ANTITRUST POLICY— THE DISSENTING VIEW

Antitrust, like most other areas of policy, has its critics. Some of the dissenting views are only partially critical. Many economists, though in agreement with overall objectives, disagree with specific aspects of antitrust policy. Many people in business argue that current legislation is vague and that it is therefore difficult to determine whether or not a firm is in compliance.

There are three major dissenting schools of thought on antitrust policy, which include (a) those individuals who would like deconcentration policies to be pursued more vigorously, (b) those who believe that the strength of competitiveness renders antitrust policy unnecessary, and (c) those who believe that antitrust policy is simply incapable of attacking industrial concentration. We will look briefly at each of these views.

Antitrust Policies Should Be More Vigorously Enforced. The proponents of this position argue that greater effort is required to ensure the existence of competitive markets. They often point out that antitrust policy has functioned primarily as a holding action. That is, it prevents large firms from *increasing* their market share, but it is ineffective as a means for *reducing* industrial concentration. Policy can end up working against its own objectives. For example, an established firm controlling 50 or 60 percent of a market is generally left untouched, whereas two smaller firms with a combined market share of as little as 10 percent may be prohibited from merging. Current policy, therefore, often protects strong, established firms while weakening their smaller rivals. Those who view current policy as self-defeating typically favor an antitrust policy that would more thoroughly restructure concentrated industries, dividing large firms into smaller, independent units.

Antitrust Policy Is Unnecessary. The advocates of this position argue that antitrust legislation places too much emphasis on the number of competitors without recognizing the positive role of dynamic competition. They believe an antitrust policy that limits business concentration will often promote inefficient business organization and will therefore encourage higher prices. They reject the notion that pure competition is a proper standard of economic efficiency.[5] As Joseph Schumpeter, an early proponent of this view of competition and regulation, emphasized two decades ago: *It . . . is a mistake to base the theory of government regulation of industry on the principle that big business should be made to work as the respective industry would work in perfect competition.*[6]

Like Schumpeter, current advocates of this position believe innovative activity is at the heart of competition. An ingenious innovator may forge ahead of competitors, but competition from other innovators will always be present. Competition is a perpetual game of leapfrog, not a process that is dependent on the number of firms in an industry. Bigness is a natural outgrowth of efficiency and successful innovation. One of the leading proponents of this position, John McGee, of the University of Washington, argues that concentration is neither inefficient nor indicative of a lack of competition:

> *Take an industry of many independent producers, each of which is efficiently using small scale and simple methods to make the same product. . . . Suppose that a revolution in technology or management techniques now occurs, so that there*

---

[5]See Dominick T. Armentano, *Antitrust and Monopoly: Anatomy of a Policy Failure* (New York: John Wiley, 1982), for an excellent presentation of this viewpoint.

[6]Joseph Schumpeter, *Capitalism, Socialism and Democracy* (New York: Harper Torchbooks, 1950), p. 106.

is room in the market for only one firm using the new and most efficient methods. Whether it occurs quickly through merger or gradually through bankruptcy, an atomistic industry is transformed into a "monopoly," albeit one selling the same product at a lower price than before. If expected long-run price should rise, resort can still be had to the old and less efficient ways, which were compatible with . . . small firms. It would be incomplete and misleading to describe that process as a "decline of competition." [7]

Antitrust Policy Is Incapable of Dealing with Big Business. The third group of critics argues that antitrust policy is simply incapable of dealing with a modern economy already dominated by a few hundred industrial giants. The leading proponent of this position, John Kenneth Galbraith, charges that monopoly power is far too prevalent for one to expect that market forces could be imposed on large corporations. Galbraith argues that even if this were possible, competition would hinder, not help, economic development. Galbraith states his case against antitrust and competition as follows:

But it will also be evident that the antitrust laws, if they worked as their proponents hoped, would only make problems worse. Their purpose is to stimulate competition, lower prices, otherwise unshackle resource use and promote a more vigorous expansion of the particular industry. But the problem of the modern economy is not inferior performance of the planning system—of the monopolistic or oligopolistic sector, to revive the traditional terminology. The problem is the greater development here as compared with the market system. And the greater the power, the greater the development. Where the power is least— where economic organization conforms most closely to the goals envisaged by the antitrust laws—the development is least. If they fulfilled the hopes of their supporters and those they support, the antitrust laws would make development more unequal by stimulating development further in precisely those parts of the economy where it is now greatest. [8]

NEW DIRECTIONS IN ANTITRUST POLICY— THE AT&T AND IBM CASES

Since the days of the Standard Oil trust nearly a century ago, antitrust policy has been strongly influenced by the notion that ideal competitive conditions are characterized by a large number of small firms. This emphasis on the number and size of rival firms has sometimes been pursued with little regard as to how well the interests of consumers are served by a given industry or firm. The Reagan administration altered the course of antitrust policy, taking the position that bigness does not necessarily mean badness or absence of competition. In the enforcement of antitrust legislation, the Reagan administration has placed more emphasis on business efficiency and consumer welfare, and less emphasis on industrial concentration and size of firm.

The thrust of the Reagan policy became clear with the settlements in the IBM and AT&T cases on the same day: January 8, 1982. In both cases, the government sought to break the firms into a large number of small firms. Both cases had dragged on for years. The filing of the case against

[7]John S. McGee, *In Defense of Industrial Concentration* (New York: Praeger, 1971), pp. 21–22.
[8]John Kenneth Galbraith, *Economics and the Public Purpose* (Boston: Houghton Mifflin, 1973), pp. 216–217.

IBM in 1969 was one of the last significant acts of the Johnson administration. The AT&T case was filed in 1975 by the Ford administration. The estimated combined costs of these suits to the government and the companies ran in excess of $500 million.

APPLICATIONS IN ECONOMICS

AT&T and Cross-subsidies

Cross-subsidies are a perennial issue in regulation. When a regulated firm serves more than one market, regulators must allocate fixed costs to each market if they are to set prices according to the average (or total) costs of production. In economics, there is no logical way to allocate such joint costs between the two markets. An unregulated firm has no need to do so. Based on marginal costs and marginal revenues, the firm charges a price to maximize profit (or minimize loss) in each market. Any economic profit leads to more entry, until the price is driven down to average cost. When price (and entry) are regulated, however, the arbitrary division of joint costs is necessary, and consumers in one market may be required to subsidize those in the other market. So it was in the case of telephones.

Local telephone lines are a fixed cost of providing both local and long-distance services. Until the AT&T divestiture settlement in 1982, state and federal regulators had agreed to load much of the fixed cost of the local lines onto the long-distance bills, which were charged according to minutes of use by customers. Rather than recognize the fixed nature of these costs (the same wires had to be in place and maintained regardless of how many minutes they were used, or whether or not any long-distance calls were made) and charge each customer the true (fixed) cost, fixed charges were kept low. Long-

distance rates were set high enough to make up the difference.

The result of this system was to provide large subsidies to local service at the expense of long-distance telephone customers. Those who used more than 50 minutes per month[9] of long-distance service paid more than their share of the combined system's costs, while those using less than 50 minutes (a large majority) paid less than the costs they generated. In general, businesses and a few other users paid far more than their share.

The system was politically very popular at the state and local level, because as telephone customers paid their bills each month, they had detailed information before them. Seldom was there a situation in which consumers knew just who to blame in case of a rate increase. In large numbers, they complained to their state regulatory commissions whenever commissioners allowed those bills to rise. The large users were unable to counter the popular pressure on politically selected commissioners. The majority was understandably less upset when others paid the higher bills. This system was very inefficient, however. Long-distance calls costing only 7 to 9 cents a minute at the margin were charged at 30 to 40 cents, so everyone used far less than the optimal amount of long-distance service. The net result was an estimated loss to the economy of $10 to $14 billion. AT&T did not mind the cross-subsidy of local ser-

vice by long distance, since it provided both, and was assured a fixed rate of return by the regulators.

When technological advances made it possible for new suppliers to enter the industry and serve large customers at a lower rate, the system began to come apart. If the new services could offer a better deal to the biggest customers, the source of the cross-subsidies would disappear. Regulators could keep newcomers out, but now the really huge size of the penalties paid by large users was becoming obvious, and the politics of continuing the system of cross-subsidies became less attractive.

Following the divestiture agreement, AT&T continued to provide long-distance service at rates regulated by the Federal Communications Commission, but MCI, GTE Sprint, and other competitors were also allowed into the market. State regulators still would like to keep local rates low and load costs onto long-distance users, but now AT&T and the other long-distance suppliers, not owning the local firms, are hurt by such an arrangement and will fight it. Lower long distance rates and a higher fixed cost for local service are likely outcomes of the competitive forces now in place.

---

[9]This estimate, and the others in this feature, were reported by Professor John T. Wenders in ". . . And Now Learn to Love the Chaos," *Wall Street Journal*, Nov. 29, 1985.

As part of its settlement, AT&T agreed to divest itself of its 22 local telephone companies with assets of $80 billion. These companies continued to operate as regulated public utilities. In return, AT&T was permitted to enter the fast-growing electronic data and computer fields, from which it had been barred since 1956.

In the early 1980s, new competitors were severely testing the dominance of AT&T in the telecommunications industry. Even though AT&T had maintained substantial market power in the telephone communications industry, technological developments were eroding its position in the broader electronic communications area. Thus, under the terms of the settlement, the research and development arm of AT&T began to operate within the forces of market pressure, while the telephone communication arm separated and continued to operate in the regulated sector. (See "AT&T and Cross-subsidies.")

While AT&T operated as a regulated utility, IBM did not. By the late 1960s, IBM was far and away the dominant firm in the computer-manufacturing industry. Like AT&T, IBM had established an image as an aggressive, innovative company. According to the government's position, IBM was hindering competition by charging prices that were too low for the corporation's smaller rivals to meet. The government, though, failed to adequately prove that consumers had been harmed by IBM's dominant share of the market.

The passage of time and the competitive process played important roles in the resolution of both of these cases. In the late 1960s, it was quite possible that the competitiveness of the computer-manufacturing industry was being endangered by the near-monopoly position of IBM; by the latter half of the 1970s, this was no longer true. Technological innovations, foreign competition, and the presence of strong rivals (Prime Computer, Wang, Digital, Control Data, Fujitsu, Hitachi, Burroughs, Cray Research, Olivetti, Siemens, and Philips, for example) were eroding IBM's market position. It was not even clear that any American firm would be the leader in the future computer-manufacturing market. It was against this background that the Reagan administration laid the IBM case to rest.

THEORIES OF REGULATION AND REGULATORY POLICY

Antitrust policy seeks to assure that the structure of an industry is competitive. Regulatory policies tend to be somewhat more direct and specific, often dictating pricing or operational policies for business firms. What does economics tell us about how regulation can be expected to work? To date, economists have been unable to develop a complete theory of regulation. Given the complex array of political and economic factors involved, this should not be surprising. In regulated markets, predicting what sellers will offer and how much consumers will be willing to buy at various prices is not enough. The regulatory process also must take account of (a) buyers who are unwilling to pay the full cost, (b) sellers who are inefficient producers, (c) politicians who are simultaneously considering thousands of pieces of legislation, and (d) voters, many of whom are "rationally uninformed" on regulatory issues. It is not easy to predict how such a complex system will deal with economic problems.

We can, however, facilitate our discussion of regulation by breaking it down into two major types: traditional economic regulation and the newer social regulation. We can also draw some conclusions about the decision-making of economic and political participants in the regulatory process. Economic analysis indicates that decision-makers in the regulatory process, like those in other areas, respond to incentives. There are three incentive-related characteristics of the regulatory process that should be kept in mind.

1. *The Demand for Regulation Often Stems from the Special Interest Effect and Redistribution Considerations Rather Than from the Pursuit of Economic Efficiency.* The wealth of an individual (or business firm) can be increased by an improvement in efficiency and an expansion in production. Regulation introduces another possibility. Sellers can gain if competition in their market is restricted. Buyers can gain, at least in the short-run, if a legal requirement forcing producers to supply goods below cost is passed. Regulation opens up an additional avenue whereby those most capable of bending the political process to their advantage can increase their wealth.

Our earlier analysis suggested that special interest groups, such as well-organized, concentrated groups of buyers or sellers, exert a disproportionate influence on the political process. In addition, the regulators themselves often comprise a politically powerful interest group. Bureaucratic entrepreneurs are key figures in the regulatory process. Their cooperation is important to those who are regulated. In exchange for cooperation, politicians and bureaucrats are offered all manner of political support.

These factors suggest that there will be demand for economic regulation even if it contributes to economic inefficiency. The wealth of specific groups of buyers, sellers, and political participants may be enhanced, even though the total size of the economic pie is reduced. This is particularly true if the burden of economic inefficiency is widely dispersed among rationally uninformed taxpayers and groups of consumers.

2. *Regulation Is Inflexible—It Often Fails to Adjust to Changing Market Conditions.* Dynamic change often makes regulatory procedures obsolete. The introduction of the truck vastly changed the competitiveness of the ground transportation industry (previously dominated by railroad interests). Nevertheless, the regulation of price, entry, and routes continued for years, even though competitive forces had long since eliminated the monopoly power of firms in this industry. Similarly, city building codes that may have been appropriate when adopted have become obsolete and now retard the introduction of new, more efficient materials and procedures. In many cities, for example, regulatory procedures have prevented builders from introducing such cost-saving materials as plastic pipes, preconstructed septic tanks, and prefabricated housing units. Why does the process work this way? In contrast with the market process, regulatory procedures generally grant a controlling voice to established producers. The introduction of new, more efficient products would reduce the wealth of the existing producers of protected products. The political (regulatory) process is often responsive to these producers' charges that substitute materials (or new producers) would create unfair competition, violate safety codes, or generally be unreliable. Hearings are held. Lawsuits are often filed. Regulatory

commissions meet and investigate—again and again. These procedures result in cost, delay, and inflexibility.

3. *With the Passage of Time, Regulatory Agencies Often Adopt the Views of the Business Interests They Are Supposed to Regulate.* Although the initial demand for regulatory action sometimes originates with disorganized groups seeking protection from practices they consider unfair or indicative of monopolistic power, forces are present that will generally dilute or negate the impact of such groups in the long-run. Individual consumers (and taxpayers) have little incentive to be greatly concerned with regulatory actions. Often, they are lulled into thinking that since there is a regulatory agency, the "public interest" is served. In contrast, firms (and employees) in regulated industries are vitally interested in the structure and composition of regulatory commissions. Favorable actions by the commission could lead to larger profits, higher-paying jobs, and insulation from the uncertainties of competition. Thus, firms and employee groups, recognizing their potential gain, invest both economic and political resources to influence the actions of regulatory agencies. (See the "The High Cost of Dairy Regulation.")

How do vote-maximizing political entrepreneurs behave under these conditions? The payoffs from supporting the views of an apathetic public are small. Clearly, the special interest effect is present. When setting policy and making appointments to regulatory agencies, political entrepreneurs have a strong incentive to support the position of well-organized business and labor interests—often the very groups the regulatory practices were originally designed to police.

Regulatory activity in the United States has expanded substantially since the mid-1960s. As Exhibit 4 illustrates, the number of employees involved in the regulatory process increased rapidly in the 1970s, peaking in 1980. Murray Weidenbaum, former chairman of the Council of Economic Advisers, estimated that the various forms of regulation imposed a cost of approximately $500 per person on the U.S. economy during 1979.

TRADITIONAL ECONOMIC REGULATION

Regulation of business activity is not a new development. In 1887, Congress established the Interstate Commerce Commission (ICC), providing it with the authority to regulate the railroad industry and, later, the trucking industry. Commissions were established to regulate the commercial airline and

APPLICATIONS IN ECONOMICS

The High Cost of Dairy Regulation

Economic regulation is usually justified on the grounds that it provides benefits to the consumer. Because of the special interest effect, though, the outcome is often quite different: consumers pay more than they otherwise would, and producers benefit. More surprising is the fact that even producers often receive just a fraction of the dollars spent as a result of these programs.

Proponents of farm legislation argue that government action is needed to assure consumers of a steady supply of food. Largely because of changes in the weather, food prices sometimes swing widely. Proponents say that if farm incomes fall drastically because of short-term price declines, farmers may go out of business, leading to food shortages. According to this view, government stabilization of food prices can help assure a steady supply of food for the consumer.

Federal farm programs cost the taxpayer billions of dollars. The farm bill passed by Congress in late 1985 was expected to cost more than $50 billion in direct costs over three years. Let us examine just one of its components—the dairy program.

The government uses price supports and marketing orders to maintain prices. Price supports guarantee farmers a minimum price for their milk. If consumers do not buy all the milk available at that price, the government buys the surplus in the form of butter, nonfat dry milk, and cheese.

Federal marketing orders also affect the price of milk. These orders set minimum prices just for Grade A milk, the highest quality milk. The minimum prices vary depending on where the milk is sold. The highest price is set for people who buy milk for drinking, while lower prices are set for commercial markets—producers of ice cream, butter, and cheese.

Economists Jeffrey LaFrance of Montana State University and Harry de Gorter of Agriculture Canada (Canada's counterpart to the U.S. Agriculture Department) estimate that between 1980 and 1984, the cost of U.S. dairy programs to consumers and taxpayers averaged $2.22 billion per year (in 1984 dollars). But, they also conclude that of this total, farmers received only $270 million!

Where did the money go? About $1.3 billion was direct government outlays for buying and storing dairy surpluses—not count-

ing the cost of buying products the government later donated to domestic food-aid programs.

A large part of the cost occurred because the dairy program changed relative prices, and this changed incentives for producers and consumers. The guaranteed support price encouraged excess production of milk, as farmers spent resources on dairy barns, milking equipment, and feed that they would not have spent if they had received the correct market signal. A study by Richard Klemme and Jean-Paul Chavas of the University of Wisconsin at Madison concluded that a sustained increase in the price of milk leads to a slow but steady increase in milk production. By their estimate, a 10 percent increase in the price of milk leads to an 8.9 percent increase in milk production over five years, and a 24.6 percent increase after ten years.

Furthermore, marketing orders encourage farmers to expand production of the more expensive Grade A milk, the only milk that can be sold at the highest regulated price. Since the consumer demand for drinking milk is less elastic than the commercial demand, farmers can sell a large quantity of Grade A milk even at a high regulated price. The high regulated price, however, encourages farmers to produce more Grade A milk than consumers of drinking milk are willing to purchase. Since the government buys milk only at the lower "commercial use" price support and then only after it has been converted to cheese, butter, or nonfat dry milk, the excess supply of Grade A milk cannot be directly sold to the government.

To dispose of all they have produced, farmers must divert the excess supply of Grade A milk to commercial markets, for the production of ice cream, cheese, butter,

and nonfat dry milk. Here, demand is more elastic—when the price goes up, customers buy significantly less milk; when it goes down, they buy significantly more. So, the price they pay moves toward the lowest legal price for milk—the government support price. This is true even though much of what these commercial users are buying is the expensively produced Grade A milk. While Grade B milk is cheaper to produce and would be satisfactory for commercial uses, farmers produce very little of it.

According to LaFrance and de Gorter, after paying the extra costs to produce the extra Grade A milk that is then diverted to the commercial market, farmers net only 1 percent more per year for milk than they would without price supports or marketing orders. To achieve this modest gain for farmers, taxpayers shell out $1.3 billion a year for the program, while fresh milk consumers pay an additional $1.3 billion more than they otherwise would for milk. LaFrance and de Gorter estimate that in 1984, people who drank fresh milk paid about 24 cents more per gallon than they would have in a nonregulated market. The only beneficiaries other than farmers are consumers of cheese and other related dairy products, who are paying $160 million less than they would otherwise.

All together, the benefits of the program—the farmers' gains plus the savings to consumers of cheese, butter, and ice cream—amount to only 16 percent of the loss to taxpayers and fresh milk consumers. Without a dairy program, consumers and taxpayers would be better off, and farmers would be in nearly the same position as they are today.

By Jane S. Shaw, Senior Writer
Political Economy Research Center
Bozeman, Montana

EXHIBIT 4 • Staffing for Regulatory Agencies

Regulatory employment increased rapidly in the 1970s, and peaked in 1980. In the face of deregulation and the Reagan administration's drive to cut the size of government, it fell in the early 1980s.

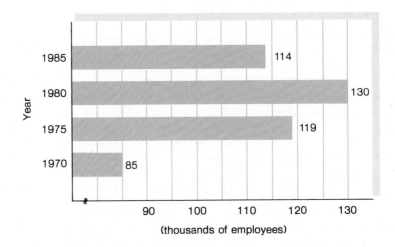

(thousands of employees)

Source: Tramontozzi, Paul M., "Regulatory Cutbacks Resume: Reagan's 1986 Plans For the Regulatory Agencies". Occasional Paper 441 Center for the Study of American Business, Washington University, St. Louis, Missouri.

Economic Regulation: Regulation of product price or industrial structure, usually imposed on a specific industry. By and large, the production processes used by the regulated firms are unaffected by this type of regulation.

broadcasting industries (the Civil Aeronautics Board and the Federal Communications Commission, respectively). State commissions have regulated the generation of electrical power for many years. These activities focus on what has been called **economic regulation.**

There are several important elements of traditional economic regulation. First, it is generally industry-specific. For whatever reason, it has been deemed that unregulated market forces create various problems in an industry. Sometimes the problem is monopoly. In other cases, excess supply stemming from "cutthroat" competition is alleged to be a problem. In general, it is believed that regulation of the industry is necessary to protect the interests of the public and to provide for orderly competition. Second, traditional regulation often involves *both* the fixing of price (rates) and the protection of existing firms from potential rivals. Third, as the regulation evolves, it often takes on a cartel-like structure. This is not surprising. As we have discussed, two factors limit the effectiveness of collusive agreements among cartel members. Means must be found to (a) block the entry of potential new competitors and (b) prevent cartel members from cheating on agreements to fix prices. Regulatory agencies are sometimes used to help business firms in a specific industry accomplish both of these objectives.

During the 1970s, widespread dissatisfaction with the traditional regulatory approach developed in several industries. Major steps toward deregulation were taken in the ground and air transportation industries.

Deregulation in the Trucking Industry. The ICC was initially established to regulate rates in the railroad industry. Actually, much of the railroad industry supported the ICC's establishment. For many years, the commission regulated rates and allocated hauls to various rail shippers. Beginning in the 1930s, however, the railroads began to confront stiff competition from the developing trucking industry. Since the trucking industry could be entered with relative ease, competitive forces were pushing rates downward.

8-18

"OF COURSE YOU MAY REGISTER A COMPLAINT ABOUT ALL THE GOVERNMENT PAPERWORK, SIR... BUT IT HAS TO BE IN WRITING."

DUNAGIN'S PEOPLE BY RALPH DUNAGIN © FIELD ENTERPRISES, INC. 1977. PERMISSION OF NEWS AMERICA SYNDICATE.

In response to the demands of railroad and large trucking interests, in 1935, the regulatory control of the ICC was extended to include the trucking industry.

The ICC influenced the structure of the ground transportation industry in several ways. First, it limited the number of shippers in interstate commerce. Rail and truck shippers were required to obtain licenses from the ICC before they were permitted to compete in the interstate transportation industry. The ICC issued such licenses only when the proposed new service was deemed "necessary for the public convenience." Established shippers were granted the opportunity to present the ICC with counter-evidence attesting that the entry of a new shipper was unnecessary or even harmful. The ICC's policies severely limited entry into the trucking industry.

Second, the ICC regulated shipping rates and permitted the rail and truck industries to establish price-fixing rate bureaus. Competitors who wanted to *reduce* their prices below the schedule established by the rate bureau had to ask the ICC to hear their cases. Typically, it would take six to eight months to obtain a ruling from the ICC. These arrangements strongly discouraged price competition in interstate shipping.

Third, the ICC limited the products that carriers could haul, the routes they could travel, and the number of cities along the route they could serve. Carriers were prohibited from using price reductions as a means to arrange a "return haul." A carrier that was granted a license to haul from St. Louis to Denver might simultaneously have been prohibited from hauling a return shipment along the way, from Kansas City. A carrier's assigned route from New Orleans to Chicago might have required an intermediate stop in

Atlanta. The result: miles of wasteful travel and trucks that were empty nearly 40 percent of the time.

The ICC's strict regulation of the trucking industry has been relaxed considerably in recent years. The Motor Carrier Act of 1980 allows freer entry. The number of ICC-authorized carriers rose from about 18,000 in 1980 to 33,548 in 1984. Generally, the act permits competitors to reduce rates as much as 10 percent without obtaining the ICC's approval. The ICC was instructed to eliminate its prohibition on carriers from serving intermediate points along a route and its restrictions that limited the ability of carriers to arrange return-trip haulage. The antitrust immunity of the rate-setting bureaus was removed.

A study by the Federal Trade Commission indicates that the relaxation of entry barriers and rate-fixing policies has exerted a significant impact on the trucking industry.[10] During the first year after passage of the trucking deregulation legislation, the ICC granted 27,960 additional routes to new and existing carriers, compared to only 2710 during fiscal year 1976. Some 2452 new firms entered the trucking industry. Discount rates were widespread, and in general, freight rates fell between 5 and 20 percent during 1980–1981. Non-price competition also occurred, as schedule reliability increased, and truckers made more specialized equipment available. There was an influx of small, primarily nonunion carriers into the industry. Price competition led to the acceptance of a temporary wage freeze by the Teamsters union. The influx of competition led to a shakeout in the trucking industry. As the profitability rates of trucking firms fell sharply, failure rates increased. According to the American Trucking Associations, 1400 trucking companies failed in 1984, more than four times the annual rate that occurred in the 1970s.[11]

Deregulation in the Airline Industry. The history of the airline industry has followed a similar pattern. For decades, the airline business was operated under the close supervision of the Civil Aeronautics Board (CAB).[12] In effect, the regulatory powers of the CAB imposed a monopolistic structure on the industry. The CAB blocked competitive entry and outlawed competitive pricing. Any carrier that wanted to compete in an interstate route had to convince the CAB that its services were needed. To say that the CAB limited entry on major routes would be an understatement. Despite more than 150 requests, the CAB did not grant a single trunk (long-distance) route to a new carrier between 1938 and 1978. CAB policy also stifled price competition. Carriers that wanted to lower prices were required to present an application to the CAB. A hearing would be held, at which time the firm's competitors would have ample opportunity to indicate why the impending rate reduction was unfair or potentially harmful to their operations.

---

[10]A summary of deregulation results, including trucking deregulation, is provided in the *Economic Report of the President—1986*, Ch. 5.

[11]See Daniel Machalaba, "More Companies Push Freight Haulers to get Better Rates, Service" *Wall Street Journal*, December 18, 1985.

[12]Many people incorrectly associate the CAB with regulation of air safety, a function that it did perform in the past. However, since 1958, the Federal Aviation Agency has been responsible for air safety rules.

At least partially in response to evidence that regulatory policies were leading to excessive fares, half-empty planes, and a uniform product offering, airline regulatory policies in the United States were substantially relaxed in the late 1970s. Under the direction of economist Alfred Kahn, the CAB moved toward deregulation. Carriers were permitted to raise prices by as much as 10 percent and lower them by as much as 70 percent merely by giving the CAB notice 45 days in advance. In 1978, Congress passed the Airline Deregulation Act, which reduced the restrictions on price competition and entry into the industry.

What has been the result of the move toward deregulation? The number of special plans (night-coach discount fares, preplanned charters, seasonal discounts, and so on) has vastly increased. During 1978, on average, air fares dropped an estimated 20 percent, and the number of passenger-miles traveled shot up by nearly 40 percent. From 1979 to 1984, fares fell an additional 13 to 15 percent.[13] Passenger convenience also increased, as a higher percentage of passengers did not have to change planes on their flights. With easier entry into markets, small cities in particular were served by more flights, though smaller planes were sometimes used to provide the more flexible and cheaper service.

Deregulation substantially increased airline efficiency. With higher, regulated fares, airlines competed partly by increased frequency of flights on lucrative routes. This meant that planes flew nearly half empty on those flights. After deregulation, however, lower fares and new entrants were allowed, and efficiency became critical to each firm's survival. The average passenger load factor (percent of seats filled) increased from about 54 to about 60 percent. The loads hauled per employee rose nearly 20 percent on the major airlines.

THE NEW SOCIAL REGULATION

Social Regulation: **Legislation designed to improve the health, safety, and environmental conditions available to workers and/ or consumers. The legislation usually mandates production procedures, minimum standards, and/or product characteristics to be met by producers and employers.**

Along with movement toward deregulation of industrial structure and prices, there has been a sharp increase in what economists call **social regulation.** In the late 1960s and early 1970s, people had great faith in the ability of government to improve the quality of life. The economy was prospering, and people turned their attention more toward reducing health hazards, preserving the environment, and reducing the negative impacts of new technologies and the booming economy. The new social regulation was one result. It consists of a body of laws in the areas of health, safety, and the environment. Agencies such as the Occupational Safety and Health Administration (OSHA), Consumer Product Safety Commission (CPSC), Food and Drug Administration (FDA), and Environmental Protection Agency (EPA) grew rapidly. These new agencies as a group are now larger, in terms of number of employees and size of budgets, than the older regulatory agencies.

There are several significant differences between the two types of regulation. The older economic regulation focuses on a specific industry,

---

[13]See Joseph P. Schweiterman, "Fare is Fair in Airline Deregulation," *Regulation*, July/August 1985, pp. 32–38 for a discussion of special fares and overall fare reductions.

whereas the new social regulation applies to the entire economy. Also, though more broadly based, social regulation is much more involved than economic regulation in the actual details of an individual firm's production. Economic regulation confines its attention to price and product quality—the final outcomes of production. The social regulatory agencies, on the other hand, frequently specify in detail the engineering processes to be followed by regulated firms and industries.

The major cost of social regulation is generally felt in the form of higher production costs and higher prices. Social regulation requires producers to alter production techniques and facilities in accordance with dictated standards—to install more restrooms, to emit less pollution, or to reduce noise levels, for example—and most of the mandated changes increase costs. Of course, there are costs associated with the process of regulation itself; employment and operating costs of regulatory agencies must be met, which means higher taxes. The higher cost stemming from mandated regulations can also be seen as a tax. As Exhibit 5 illustrates, the higher cost shifts the supply curve for a good affected by the regulation to the left. Higher prices and a decline in the output of the good result.

Who pays the cost? As with any tax, the burden is shared by buyers and sellers according to the elasticity of supply and demand. When consumers have more options to the taxed good, so that their demand is more elastic, they will pay a smaller portion of the tax. In Exhibit 5, the new price $(P_2 + t)$ will be closer to P_1 when demand is more elastic. Sellers will pay a smaller portion when the supply curve is more elastic, meaning that they have other options. In the short-run, suppliers of goods may have capital committed to the production process with little option, so that the short-run supply is likely to be inelastic. In the long-run, of course, capital is quite mobile among uses, and the supply should be more elastic.

One estimate of pollution control costs, in terms of dollar outlays, suggests that for at least the first several years following 1973 (the first year

EXHIBIT 5 • The Regulation "Tax"

Regulation that requires businesses to adopt more costly production techniques is similar to a tax. If the regulation increases per unit costs by t, the supply curve shifts upward by that amount. Higher prices and a smaller output result.

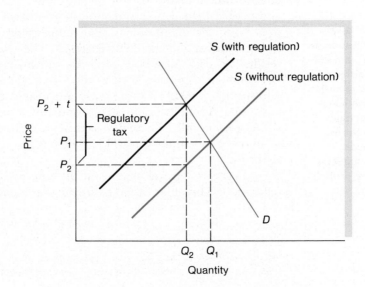

that estimated outlays exceeded $20 billion), businesses paid much more than households.[14] In 1982, out of a total of $56.6 billion spent, the estimate was that households paid $9 billion, businesses paid $34.2 billion, and government paid $13.4 billion.

In other cases, some of the key opportunity costs are not cash outlays, and are nearly impossible to calculate. For example, the FDA often bans the sale of a new drug until years of tests costing millions of dollars are completed, demonstrating that the drug is safe. Two important costs of this regulation, if the drug finally proves (or would have proven) to be safe, are: (a) some drugs are never developed because of the expensive tests and delays, and (b) people who could have been helped by the drug cannot have it for those years. These opportunity costs may be very large, but they do not show up as expenditures.

Even when the costs of a regulation are measurable largely in cash, it is frequently difficult to assess the costs per unit of results. For example, proponents of mandatory airbags to reduce passenger injuries in auto crashes estimate that the bags can be produced for $200 to $300 per car, while automakers say the cost would be $700 to $800. Perhaps more important (since lives, not airbags are fundamentally at stake) is the cost per life saved. Those estimates range from $0.5 million to $5 million per life.[15] Who is right? And, is the cost worthwhile? One important question becomes: are there cheaper ways to save lives on the highway?

While there is strong disagreement about the costs and benefits of proposed new regulations for automobile safety, a new study by the Brookings Institution[16] indicates that the auto safety regulations prevailing in the early 1980s probably provided enough benefits to at least offset their costs. The same study, however, concluded that regulations requiring emission controls to reduce air pollution, and requiring increases in fuel efficiency for automobiles have been very costly, while yielding few, if any benefits. An unintended result of the increased regulatory costs of buying and operating new automobiles has been to reduce their sales, keeping older cars on the road longer. The earlier design of these older cars, and the wear they have experienced, increase the pollution they emit while decreasing the safety and fuel efficiency they provide. The study criticizes the lack of coordination among the many regulations on automobiles. Rules requiring greater fuel economy, for example, make cars smaller, lighter, and less safe. Emission controls often reduce fuel economy, while safety requirements increase weight and decrease performance and fuel economy. Yet, each regulation is established with little regard to these conflicting impacts on the desirability of autos.

[14]These estimates, converted to the 1982 price level, are from Kit D. Farber, et al., "Pollution Abatement and Control Expenditures, 1972–82," *Survey of Current Business*, February 1984, p. 28.

[15]These estimates are reported in John D. Graham, "Secretary Dole and the Future of Automobile Airbags," *The Brookings Review*, Vol. 15, No. 4 (Summer, 1985), pp. 10–15.

[16]See Robert W. Crandall, Howard K. Gruenspecht, Theodore E. Keeler, and Lester B. Lave, *Regulating the Automobile* (Washington, D.C.: The Brookings Institution, 1986).

The new social regulation is costly, but it can have important benefits. The primary goal of social regulation is the attainment of a cleaner, safer, healthier environment. Nearly everyone agrees that this is a worthy objective. There is, however, considerable disagreement about the procedures that are most likely to accomplish this objective and the price that should be paid to make improvements. Resources are scarce. More social regulation will mean less of other things.

It should not be any more surprising that people differ with regard to the proper consumption level of environmental amenities than it is that they differ with regard to the proper consumption level of ice cream, for example. If 100 people were asked the best rate of consumption for strawberry ice cream, there would be a wide variety of answers. Similarly, the extent to which we should bear costs to make our air and water cleaner, and drugs safer, for example, is a question that each person may answer quite differently. One's preferred consumption rate for these benefits, like the preferred rate for strawberry ice cream, will depend in part on the expected cost and who pays that cost. Those who expect others to foot the bill will naturally prefer more of any valued good, whether it is ice cream or safety.

Differing preferences as to how many other goals should be given up to attain a safer, cleaner, healthier environment comprise only part of the problem faced by regulators. An important characteristic of most socially regulated activities is a lack of information about their effects. This is not a coincidence. In most cases, the lack of information contributes directly to the demand for the regulation. For example, if consumers knew exactly what the effect of a particular drug would be, there would be little need for the FDA to make that drug unavailable. Many people, though, are unaware of the precise effects of drugs, air pollution, or work-place hazards, even when the information is available to experts. It is costly to communicate information, particularly highly technical information. A case can be made, therefore, that we should let the experts decide which drugs, how much air pollution, and what forms of work-place safety should be sought. A lack of solid information generates much of the demand for social regulation. Of course, the lack of information also makes it difficult to evaluate the effectiveness of the regulatory activity.

Future Directions. Most people concede that regulation, both economic and social, is an imperfect solution. It is quite difficult, however, to separate beneficial regulations from those that are counterproductive. Even though there is strong support for the continuation and expansion of social regulatory activities, recent experience indicates forces favoring deregulation are also present. Improved empirical evidence on the effectiveness of specific social regulation programs may very well emerge during the next decade.

CHAPTER SUMMARY

1. During the first 50 years of this century, the relative size of the manufacturing sector consistently increased, while the agricultural sector declined. Since 1950, a new trend has developed. The relative sizes of both the service and government sectors have increased, while agricul-

ture and manufacturing have generated a shrinking share of our national income.

2. It is not easy to categorize each industry as competitive or noncompetitive. Nevertheless, empirical research on industrial structure suggests that roughly 40 to 50 percent of our economy is highly competitive, in the sense of rivalry. Another 20 percent of our output is generated by unregulated firms in industries of medium or high concentration. Highly regulated industries account for nearly one quarter of our total output; public-sector firms generate the remainder.

3. Foreign imports are an important and growing competitor in many industries. Import penetration increased from 6.5 percent in 1975 to 10.9 percent in 1984.

4. Antitrust legislation seeks to (a) maintain a competitive structure in the unregulated private sector and (b) prohibit business practices that are thought to stifle competition.

5. The Sherman, Clayton, and Federal Trade Commission Acts form the foundation of antitrust policy in the United States. The Sherman Act prohibits conspiracies to restrain trade and/or monopolize an industry. The Clayton Act prohibits specific business practices, such as price discrimination, tying contracts, exclusive dealings, and mergers and acquisitions (as amended), when they "substantially lessen competition or tend to create a monopoly." As it has evolved through the years, the Federal Trade Commission is concerned primarily with enforcing consumer protection legislation, prohibiting deceptive advertising, and investigating industrial structure.

6. Most economists believe that antitrust policy in the United States has promoted competition and reduced industrial concentration, but not to any dramatic extent.

7. The breakup of AT&T reduced the cross-subsidy of local telephone service by long-distance ratepayers, although the dispute about how much fixed cost should be paid by long-distance users remains unsettled.

8. To date, economists have been unable to develop a complete theory of regulation. However, economic analysis does suggest that: (a) the demand for regulation often stems from special interest and redistribution considerations rather than from the pursuit of economic efficiency; (b) regulation often fails to adjust to changing market conditions; and (c) with the passage of time, regulatory agencies are likely to adopt the views of the interest groups they are supposed to regulate.

9. Traditional economic regulation has generally sought to fix prices and/or influence industrial structure. During the 1970s, changing market conditions and empirical studies generated widespread dissatisfaction with economic regulation. Significant moves toward deregulation were made in the late 1970s, particularly in the trucking and airline industries. New entrants, intense competition, and discount prices have accompanied the deregulation of these industries.

10. In recent years, economic regulation has been relaxed, and social regulatory activities have expanded rapidly. Social regulation seeks to

provide a cleaner, safer, healthier environment for workers and consumers. Pursuit of this objective is costly—higher product prices and higher taxes accompany such regulation. Since the costs and particularly the benefits are often difficult to measure and evaluate, the efficiency of social regulatory programs is a controversial topic, and the topic of much current research.

THE ECONOMIC WAY OF THINKING— DISCUSSION QUESTIONS

1. "Big business dominates the U.S. economy. Big business uses its power to decide what products we purchase, what jobs we hold, what kind of homes we live in, and even what political candidates we vote for." Evaluate.

2. Do you think that competition can be counted on to discipline the industrial business firms of a modern economy? Explain.

3. Currently, antimerger policy does not restrict conglomerate mergers between large firms if such mergers do not reduce competition in a specific market. Do you think such mergers should be prohibited? Why or why not?

4. "Efficiency requires large-scale production. Yet, big businesses mean monopoly power, high prices, and market inefficiency. We must choose between production efficiency and monopoly." Evaluate.

5. Legislation mandating automobiles to be installed with stronger bumpers has presumably made cars both safer and more expensive. Do you think this social regulation has been beneficial? Why or why not? Similar legislation requiring that new automobiles be fully equipped with air bags that would automatically open on impact would have the same effects on safety and price. Do you think this regulation should be imposed? Why or why not?

6. Is there any reason to believe that consumer choice and free markets would provide less than the amount of safety desired by purchasers of a product—lawn mowers, for example? Why or why not?

7. Will social legislation mandating work places and products to be safer reduce the profitability of the regulated firms? Who bears the cost of such legislation? Who receives the primary benefits of the legislation?

8. Some economists argue that if the government lowered the trade barriers that limit the sale of foreign-produced goods in our domestic market, the need for antitrust action would be reduced. Do you agree or disagree? Explain your answer.

9. Why do you think AT&T, which still is in the long-distance telephone business but no longer in the local service business, now opposes the high long-distance rates it previously supported?

FACTOR MARKETS AND INCOME DISTRIBUTION

- Why do business firms demand labor, machines, and other resources?

- Why is the demand for a productive resource inversely related to its price?

- How do business firms decide how many skilled laborers, unskilled laborers, machines, and other factors of production to employ?

- How is the quantity supplied of a resource related to its price in the short-run? . . . in the long-run?

- What determines the market price in resource markets?

It is . . . necessary to attach price tags to the various factors of production . . . in order to guide those who have the day-to-day decisions to make as to what is plentiful and what is scarce.[1]

PROFESSOR JAMES MEADE

22 THE SUPPLY OF AND DEMAND FOR PRODUCTIVE RESOURCES

Thus far we have focused on markets for consumer goods and services. These markets (a) allocate goods and services among competing consumers and (b) determine which consumer goods will be produced. We now turn to an analysis of **resource markets,** or, as they are sometimes called, factor markets. Resource markets coordinate the choices of business employers and resource suppliers. Prices in resource markets provide individuals with an incentive to engage in productive activity and allocate productive resources among competing employers.

Resource Markets: Markets in which business firms demand factors of production (for example, labor, capital, and natural resources) from household suppliers. The resources are then used to produce goods and services. These markets are sometimes called factor markets.

As in consumer-good markets, the interplay of supply and demand determine prices in resource markets. Resources are demanded because they contribute to the production of goods and services. Since resources must be bid away from competitive firms seeking to put them to alternative uses, costs are incurred whenever resources are employed. Profit-seeking firms will find it advantageous to hire a resource if it adds more to the firm's revenue than it does to costs. Conversely, income payments motivate individuals to supply resources. When choosing among alternative employment opportunities, utility-maximizing resource suppliers will seek out those options they believe to be most advantageous.

HUMAN AND NONHUMAN RESOURCES

Broadly speaking, there are two different types of productive inputs—nonhuman and human resources. **Nonhuman resources** are further broken down into the categories of physical capital, land, and natural resources. Capital consists of man-made goods used to produce other goods. Tools, machines, and buildings are part of the capital stock.

Nonhuman Resources: The durable, nonhuman inputs that can be used to produce both current and future output. Machines, buildings, land, and raw materials are examples. Investment can increase the supply of nonhuman resources. Economists often use the term "physical capital" when referring to nonhuman resources.

Net investment can increase the supply of nonhuman resources. Increasing the available stock of nonhuman resources, though, involves the sacrifice of current consumption goods. Resources that are used to produce machines, upgrade the quality of land, or discover natural resources could be used to produce current goods and services directly. Why take the roundabout path? The answer is that sometimes indirect methods of producing goods are less costly in the long-run. Robinson Crusoe found he could catch more fish by taking some time off from hand-fishing to build a net. Even though his initial investment in the net reduced his current catch, once the net was completed he was able to more than make up for his earlier loss of output.

Additions to capital stock, whether they are fishing nets or complex machines, involve current sacrifices. Capital-intensive methods of production are adopted only when decision-makers expect the benefits of a larger future output to more than offset the current reduction in the production of consumption goods.

Just as the supply of machines can be increased, so too can wise land-clearing and soil conservation practices be used to upgrade both the quantity and quality of land. Similarly, the supply of natural resources can be

---

[1]James E. Meade, "Economic Efficiency and Distributional Justice," in *Comtemporary Issues in Economics*, ed. Robert W. Crandall and Richard S. Eckaus (Boston: Little, Brown, 1972), p. 319.

Human Resources: The abilities, skills, and health of human beings that can contribute to the production of both current and future output. Investment in training and education can increase the supply of human resources.

Investment in Human Capital: Expenditures on training, education, and skill development designed to increase the productivity of an individual.

increased (within limits) by the application of more resources to discovery and development.

The future productivity of **human resources** can also be increased. Investment in such things as education, training, health, skill-building experience, and migration to areas where jobs are more readily available involves current sacrifices to increase future productivity (and income). Economists refer to such activities as **investment in human capital.**[2]

Decisions to invest in human capital involve all the basic ingredients of other investment decisions. Consider the decision of whether or not to go to college. For most people, it is partly an investment decision. As many of you will testify, an investment in a college education requires the sacrifice of current earnings as well as payment for direct expenses such as tuition and books. The investment is expected to lead to a better job, considering both monetary and nonmonetary factors, and other benefits associated with a college education. The rational investor will weigh the current costs against the expected future benefits. College will be chosen only if the latter are greater than the former.

Some may find it offensive to refer to human beings as though they were machines. Nothing unethical is implied in the term "human capital." Men and women are, of course, not factors of production. They are human beings. However, the effort, skill, ability, and ingenuity of individuals can be applied productively. They can be used to improve human welfare. It is these productive resources that we refer to as human resources, or human capital.

Human resources differ from nonhuman resources in two important respects. First, human capital is embodied in the individual. Choices concerning the use of human resources are vitally affected by working conditions, location, job prestige, and similar nonpencuniary factors. Although monetary factors influence human capital decisions, individuals have some leeway in trading off money income for better working conditions. Second, human resources cannot be bought and sold in nonslave societies. Although the services of human resources are bought and sold daily, the right to quit, to sell one's services to another employer, or use them in an alternative manner, always exists.

In competitive markets, the price of resources, like the price of products, is determined by supply and demand. To develop the theory of price for resource markets, we must first develop a theory for each of these determining factors. Let us begin by focusing on the demand for resources, both human and nonhuman.

THE DEMAND FOR RESOURCES

Producers employ laborers, machines, raw materials, and the other resources required to produce goods and services firms hope to sell for a profit. The demand for a resource exists because there is a demand for

---

[2]The contributions of T. W. Schultz and Gary Becker to the literature on human capital have been particularly significant. See B. F. Kiker, ed., *Investment in Human Capital* (Columbia: University of South Carolina Press, 1971), for an excellent collection of readings in this area.

Derived Demand: Demand for an item based on the demand for products the item helps to produce. The demand for resources is a derived demand.

goods that the resource helps to produce. The demand for each resource is thus a **derived demand;** it is derived from consumers' demands for products.

For example, a service station hires mechanics because customers demand repair service, not because the service station owner receives benefits simply from having mechanics around. If customers did not demand repair service, mechanics would not be employed for long. Similarly, the demand for such inputs as carpenters, plumbers, lumber, and glass windows is derived from the demand of consumers for houses and other consumer products these resources help to make.

Most resources contribute to the production of numerous goods. For example, glass is used to produce windows, ornaments, dishes, light bulbs, and mirrors, among other things. The total demand for a resource is the sum of the derived demand for it in each of its uses. Consequently, when economists study the demand for factors of production, they must trace changes in resource prices to their impact in the product market.

How will firms respond to an increase in the price of a resource? In the long-run, the higher price of a resource will lead to two distinct adjustments, which will ensure an inverse relationship between price and the amount of the resource demanded. First, firms will seek to reduce their use of the now more expensive input by substituting other resources for it. Second, the increase in the price of the resource will lead to both higher costs and higher product prices. Consumers will buy less of the higher-priced product and substitute other goods for it, leading to a decline in the demand for resources used to make it. Therefore, the amount demanded of a factor of production will decline as its price increases. The demand curve for a resource will slope downward.

Let us look a little more closely at both of these adjustments.

1. *Substitution in Production.* Firms will use the input combination that minimizes their costs. When the price of a resource goes up, cost-conscious firms will use lower-cost substitutes. The degree to which such substitution can take place will vary. Resources that are good substitutes may exist even though they are not currently being used. Sometimes the style and dimensions of a product can be altered in a manner that will conserve on the use of a more expensive input. The presence of good substitutes in production ensures not only that quantity demanded will be inversely related to price but also that the demand for the resource will be highly elastic.

2. *Substitution in Consumption.* An increase in the price of a resource will lead to higher prices for products that the input helps to produce. The higher product prices will encourage consumers to purchase substitute goods, reducing the consumption of the more expensive product. When less of that product is produced, however, producer demand for resources (including the one that has risen in price) will decline. The recent experience of the American automobile industry illustrates the point. Throughout much of the 1970s, wages in the U.S. automobile industry increased quite rapidly. The higher wages placed upward pressure on the prices of American-made automobiles. However, as auto prices rose, many consumers switched to substitute products. American auto sales declined, causing a reduction in quantity of labor demanded in the automobile industry and therefore widespread layoffs.

Other things constant, the more elastic the demand for the product, the more elastic the demand for the resource. This relationship stems from the derived nature of resource demand. An increase in the price of a product for which the demand is highly elastic will cause a sharp reduction in the sales of the good. There will thus also be a relatively sharp decline in the demand for the resources used to produce the good.

TIME AND THE DEMAND FOR RESOURCES

It will take time for producers to adjust fully to a change in the price of a resource. Typically, a producer will be unable to alter a production process or the design of a product immediately to conserve on the use of a more expensive input or to use more efficiently an input whose price has declined. Similarly, consumers may be unable to alter their consumption patterns immediately in response to price changes. Thus, the short-run demand for resources is typically less elastic than the demand in the long run.

Using steel as an example, Exhibit 1 illustrates the relationship between time and the demand for resources. Initially, higher steel prices may lead to only a small reduction in usage. If the high price of steel persists, however, automobile manufacturers will alter their designs, moving toward lighter-weight cars that require less steel. Architectural firms will design buildings that permit more substitution of plastics, wood, aluminum, glass, and other resources for steel. Products made with steel will increase in price, which will encourage consumers to find more and more ways to cut back on their use. However, these adjustments will not take place instantaneously. Therefore, the demand (D_{sr}) for steel, like that for most other products, will be more inelastic in the short-run than in the long-run.

SHIFTS IN THE DEMAND FOR RESOURCES

The entire demand curve for a resource, like that for a product, may shift, for one of three reasons.

1. *A Change in the Demand for a Product Will Cause a Similar Change in the Demand for the Resources Used to Make the Product.* Anything that increases the demand for a consumer good simultaneously increases the demand for

EXHIBIT 1 • Time and the Demand Elasticity of Resources

An increase in the price of steel will lead to a much larger reduction in consumption in the long run than in the short run. Typically, the demand for resources will be more inelastic in the short run.

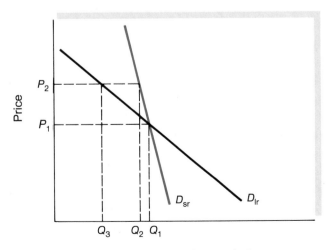

Quantity of steel per unit time

resources required to make it; a decline in product demand and price will reduce the demand for resources embodied in the product. During the 1970s, the demand for small automobiles increased sharply, primarily because of higher gasoline prices. The increase in demand for small cars led to an increase in demand for workers to produce them. Employment at plants producing small cars expanded during the 1970s, even while auto workers were being laid off at plants producing large cars. Falling gasoline prices in the mid-1980s reversed this situation. Propelled by lower gasoline prices, the demand for larger automobiles increased, while the demand for small cars declined. Reflecting the demand in product markets, employment at automobile plants making full-size cars expanded, while employment at plants producing small cars fell.

2. *Changes in the Productivity of a Resource Will Alter the Demand for the Resource.* The higher the productivity of a resource, the greater the demand for it. Several factors combine to determine the productivity of a resource. First, the **marginal product** of any resource will depend on the amount of other resources with which it is working. In general, additional capital will tend to increase the productivity of labor. For example, someone with a lawn mower can mow more grass than the same person with a pair of shears. A student working with a textbook, class notes, and tutor can learn more economics than the same student without these tools. The quantity and quality of the tools with which we work significantly affects our productivity.

Second, technological advances can improve the productivity of resources, including labor. Advances in the computer industry illustrate this point. Working with computer technology, an accountant and a data-entry person can maintain business records and create bookkeeping reports that previously would have required 10 to 15 workers. Similarly, computers have vastly increased the productivity of typesetters, telephone operators, quality-control technicians, and workers in many other occupations.

Third, improvements in the quality (skill level) of a resource will increase productivity and therefore the demand for the resource. As workers obtain valuable new knowledge and/or upgrade their skills, they enhance their productivity. In essence, such workers move into a different skill category, where demand is greater.

All these factors help explain why wage rates in the United States, Canada, Western Europe, and Japan are higher than in most other areas of the world. Given the skill level of workers, the technology, and the capital equipment with which they work, individuals in these countries produce more goods and services per hour of labor. The demand for labor (relative to supply) is greater because of labor's increased productivity. Essentially, the workers' greater productivity leads to higher wage rates.

3. *A Change in the Price of a Related Resource Will Affect the Demand for the Original Resource.* An increase in the price of a substitute resource will lead to an increase in demand for the given resource. For example, when the wage rates of unionized workers in a given field or industry increase, demand for nonunion workers will expand. Conversely, an increase in the price of a resource that is a complement to a given resource will decrease the demand for the given resource. For example, higher prices for computers would most likely cause the demand for computer programmers to fall.

Marginal Product: The change in total output that results from the employment of one additional unit of a factor of production—one workday of skilled labor, for example.

MARGINAL PRODUCTIVITY AND THE FIRM'S HIRING DECISION

How does a producer decide whether or not to employ additional units of a resource? We noted previously that the marginal product of a resource is the increase in output that results when the employment of a resource is expanded by one unit. The resource's marginal product multiplied by the marginal revenue of the product being produced yields what is known as the **marginal revenue product,** or MRP. The MRP is simply the change in the firm's total revenue brought about by the employment of one extra unit of a resource. It reveals how much the employment of the resource adds to revenues.

A profit-maximizing firm will, of course, continue to expand output as long as marginal cost is less than marginal revenue. This rule can be generalized to include the firm's employment of resources. Since firms are usually price takers when they buy resources, the price of a resource is its marginal cost. When a firm has a fixed factor of production—its plant size, for example—the marginal product of a resource will decline as its employment increases, according to the law of diminishing returns. To maximize profit, employment of a resource should be expanded as long as MRP exceeds the price of the resource.

Thus, a profit-maximizing firm will hire units of a variable resource up to the employment level at which the price of the resource (its marginal cost) is just equal to the marginal revenue product of the resource. This decision rule applies to all firms, pure competitors and price searchers alike.

The marginal product of a resource multiplied by the selling price of the product yields the resource's **value marginal product** (VMP). When a firm sells its product in a competitive market, the selling price and the marginal revenue of the product are equal. Under pure competition, therefore, the marginal revenue product of a resource is equal to its value marginal product.

Exhibit 2 illustrates how a firm decides how much of a resource to employ. Compute-Accounting Inc. uses computer equipment and data-entry operators to supply clients with monthly accounting statements. The firm sells its service in a competitive market for $200 per statement. Given the fixed quantity of computer equipment owned by Compute-Accounting, column 2 relates the employment of data-entry operators to the expected total output (quantity of accounting statements). One data-entry operator can process five statements per week. When two operators are employed, nine statements can be completed. Column 2 indicates how total output is expected to change as additional data-entry operators are employed. Column 3 presents the marginal product schedule for data-entry operators. Column 6, the marginal revenue product schedule, shows how the employment of each additional operator affects total revenues.

Since Compute-Accounting sells its service competitively, both the marginal revenue product and the value marginal product of labor equal MP (column 3) times the sales price per accounting statement (column 4). What if the firm is not a perfect competitor? The marginal revenue product must

Marginal Revenue Product: The change in the total revenue of a firm that results from the employment of one additional unit of a factor of production. The marginal revenue product of an input is equal to its marginal product multiplied by the marginal revenue (price) of the good or service produced.

Value Marginal Product: The marginal product of a resource multiplied by the selling price of the product it helps to produce. Under perfect competition, a firm's marginal revenue product will be equal to the value marginal product.

EXHIBIT 2 • The Short-run Demand Schedule of a Firm

Compute-Accounting Inc. uses computer technology and data-entry operators to provide accounting services in a competitive market. For each accounting statement processed, the firm receives a $200 fee (column 4). Given the firm's current fixed capital, column 2 shows how total output changes as additional data-entry operators are hired. The marginal revenue product schedule (column 6) indicates how hiring an additional operator affects the total revenue of the firm. Since a profit-maximizing firm will hire an additional employee if, and only if, the employee adds more to revenues than to costs, the marginal revenue product curve is the firm's short-run demand curve for the resource (see Exhibit 3).

Units of the Variable Factor (data-entry operators) (1)	Total Output (Accounting Statements Processed per week) (2)	Marginal Product Change in (2) / Change in (1) (3)	Sales Price Per Statement (4)	Total Revenue (2)×(4) (5)	Marginal Revenue Product (3)×(4) (6)
0	0.0	—	$200	$ 0	—
1	5.0	5.0	200	1,000	$1,000
2	9.0	4.0	200	1,800	800
3	12.0	3.0	200	2,400	600
4	14.0	2.0	200	2,800	400
5	15.5	1.5	200	3,100	300
6	16.5	1.0	200	3.300	200
7	17.0	0.5	200	3,400	100

always equal MR multiplied by MP. When the firm confronts a downward-sloping demand curve for its product, the marginal revenue of the product will be less than its price. When this is the case, the marginal revenue product of a resource will be less than its value marginal product.

How does Compute-Accounting decide how many operators to employ? Additional operators will increase output, which will expand total revenue (column 5). Employment of additional operators, though, will also add to production costs since the operators must be paid. If Compute-Accounting is going to maximize profit, it will hire additional operators as long as their employment adds more to revenues than to costs. Thus, as Exhibit 3 illustrates, the marginal revenue product curve of operators (Exhibit 2, column 6) is also the firm's short-run demand curve for the resource.[3] At a weekly wage of $1,000, Compute-Accounting would hire only one operator. If the weekly wage dropped to $800, two operators would be hired. At still lower wage rates, additional operators would be hired.

The location of the firm's MRP curve depends on (a) the price of the product, (b) the productivity of the resource, and (c) the amount of other resources with which the resource is working. Changes in any one of these three factors will cause the MRP curve to shift. For example, if Compute-Accounting obtained additional computer equipment that made it possible

---

[3]Strictly speaking, this is true only for a variable resource that is employed with a fixed amount of another factor.

EXHIBIT 3 • The Firm's Demand Curve for a Resource

The firm's demand curve for a resource will reflect the marginal revenue product of the resource. In the short run, it will slope downward because the marginal product of the resource will fall as more of it is used with a fixed amount of other resources. The location of the MRP curve will depend on (a) the price of the product, (b) the productivity of the resource, and (c) the quantity of other factors working with the resource.

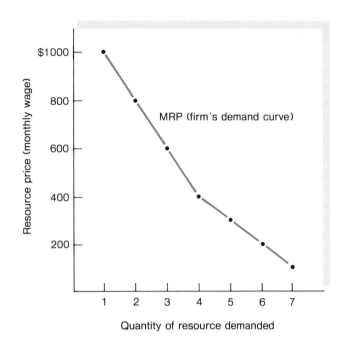

Quantity of resource demanded

for the operators to complete more statements each week, the MRP curve for labor would increase. This increase in the quantity of the other resources working with labor would increase labor's productivity.

ADDING OTHER FACTORS OF PRODUCTION

Thus far, we have analyzed the firm's hiring decision, assuming that it employed one variable resource (labor) and one fixed resource. Production, though, usually involves the use of many resources. When a firm employs multiple resources, how should the resources be combined to produce the product? We can answer this question by considering either the conditions for profit maximization or the conditions for cost minimization.

Profit Maximization When Multiple Resources Are Employed. The same decision-making considerations apply when the firm employs several factors of production. The profit-maximizing firm will expand its employment of a resource as long as the marginal revenue product of the resource exceeds its employment cost. If we assume that resources are perfectly divisible, the profit-maximizing decision rule implies that, in equilibrium, the marginal revenue product of each resource will be equal to the price of the resource. Therefore, the following conditions will exist for the profit-maximizing firm:

MRP of skilled labor $= P_{SL}$ (wage rate of skilled labor)

MRP of unskilled labor $= P_{UL}$ (wage rate of unskilled labor)

MRP of machine $= P_{M}$ (explicit or implicit rental price of machine A)

and so on, for all other factors.

Cost Minimization When Multiple Resources Are Employed. If the firm is maximizing profits, clearly it must produce the profit-maximizing output at the least possible cost. If the firm is minimizing costs, the marginal dollar expenditure for each resource will have the same impact on output as every other marginal resource expenditure. Factors of production will be employed such that the marginal product per last dollar spent on each factor is the same for all factors.

Suppose that a dollar expenditure on labor caused output to rise by ten units, whereas an additional dollar expenditure on machines generated only a five-unit expansion in output. Under these circumstances, five more units of output would result if the firm spent $1 less on machines and $1 more on labor. The firm's total (and per unit) cost would be reduced if it substituted labor for machines.

If the marginal dollar spent on one resource increases output by a larger amount than a dollar expenditure on other resources, costs can always be reduced by substituting resources with a high marginal product per dollar for those with a low marginal product per dollar expenditure. This substitution should continue until the marginal product per dollar expenditure is equalized—that is, until the resource combination that minimizes cost is attained. When this is true, the proportional relationship between the price of each resource and its marginal product will be equal for all resources.

Therefore, the following condition exists when per unit costs are minimized:

$$\frac{\text{MP of skilled labor}}{\text{price of skilled labor}} = \frac{\text{MP of unskilled labor}}{\text{price of unskilled labor}}$$

$$= \frac{\text{MP of machine A}}{\text{price (rental value) of machine A}}$$

and so on, for the other factors.

In the real world, it is sometimes difficult to measure the marginal product of a factor. Businesspeople may not necessarily think in terms of equating the marginal product/price ratio for each factor of production. Nevertheless, if they are minimizing cost, this condition will be present. Real-world decision-makers may use experience, trial and error, and intuitive rules but the question always is: "Can we reduce costs by using more of one resource and less of another?" However, when profits are maximized and the cost-minimization method of production is attained, regardless of the procedures used, the outcome will be as if the employer had followed the profit-maximization and cost-minimization decision-making rules just discussed.

MARGINAL PRODUCTIVITY, DEMAND, AND ECONOMIC JUSTICE

According to the law of diminishing marginal returns, as the employment level of a resource increases, other things constant, the marginal product (and marginal revenue product) of the resource will decline. As we have just seen, a profit-maximizing employer will expand the use of a resource until its marginal revenue product is equal to the price of the resource. If the price of the resource declines, employers will increase their utilization level of that resource. Therefore, as Exhibit 4 shows, the marginal productivity approach can be used to illustrate the inverse relationship between quantity demanded and resource price.

Some observers, noting that under pure competition the price of each resource is equal to the value of what it produces (that is, input price equals the marginal product of the input multiplied by the price of the product), have argued that competitive markets are "just" or "equitable" because each resource gets paid exactly what it is worth. There is a major defect in this line of reasoning, however. The "marginal productivity" of labor (or any other factor) cannot be determined independently of the contribution of other factors. When a product is produced by a combination of factors, as is almost invariably the case, it is impossible to assign a specific proportion of the total output to each resource. For example, if one uses a tractor, an acre of land, and seed to produce wheat, one cannot accurately state that labor (or the seed or the land) produced one half or any other proportion of the output. Hence, those who argue that the factor payments generated by competitive markets are just, because each resource gets paid according to its productive contribution, are assuming one can assign a specific proportion of the total output to each resource, which is not possible. The marginal product can be used as a measure of the change in total output associated with the use of an additional unit of a resource, but this measurement does not directly link one resource with one segment of output.

The marginal productivity theory is really a theory about the demand for resources. The central proposition of the theory is that profit-maximizing employers will never pay more for a unit of input, whether it is skilled labor, a machine, or an acre of land, than the input is worth to them. The worth of a unit of input to the firm is determined by how much additional revenue (marginal revenue product) is generated (or seems to be generated) when the unit is used. That is, pursuit of profit will induce

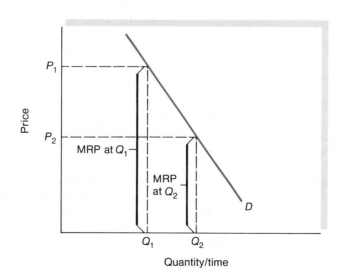

EXHIBIT 4 • Marginal Productivity and Demand

Other things constant, an increase in the employment level will cause the MRP of a resource to decline. The larger quantity of the resource can be employed only at a lower price.

employers to hire additional units of each resource as long as the units' marginal productivity generates revenues in excess of costs. Resource prices will tend to reflect—though somewhat roughly in the real world—the marginal productivity of the resource.

However, the price of each resource is determined by conditions of supply as well as conditions of demand. Even though marginal productivity theory helps us understand the demand side of the market, it reveals nothing about the share of the total product produced by a resource or the justice of a resource price. We must analyze the supply of resources to factor markets in order to complete the picture.

THE SUPPLY OF RESOURCES

As in the case of demand, the supply response in resource markets may vary between the short-run and long-run. The short-run is a period so brief that there is insufficient time to alter the availability of a resource through investment in human and physical capital. In contrast, in the long-run, resource suppliers have time to fully adjust their investment choices to a change in resource prices. Let us begin by focusing on supply in the short-run.

SHORT-RUN SUPPLY

Resource Mobility: A term that refers to the ease with which factors of production are able to move among alternative uses. Resources that can easily be transferred to a different use or location are said to be highly mobile. In contrast, when a resource has few alternative uses, it is immobile. For example, the skills of a trained rodeo rider would be highly immobile, since they cannot be easily transferred to other lines of work.

Most resources have alternative uses; they can be used to perform a variety of functions. The principle of utility maximization implies that resource owners will use their factors of production in a manner that leads to their greatest net advantage. As a result, prices will influence the quantity of a resource applied to a specific use.

An increase in the price of a resource will attract potential resource suppliers into the market. In contrast, resource suppliers will shift into other activities when the price of a resource falls. Thus, the supply curve for a specific resource (for example, engineering services, craft labor, or wheat farm land) will slope upward to the right in the short-run.

The elasticity of supply to a particular use will be dependent on **resource mobility.** Resources that can be easily transferred from one use to another in response to changing price incentives (in other words, those resources with a great many alternative uses or locations) are said to be highly mobile. The supply of such factors to any specific use will be elastic. Factors that have few alternative uses are said to be immobile and will have an inelastic short-run supply.

What can we say about resource mobility in the real world? First, let us consider the mobility of labor. When labor skills can be transferred easily and quickly, human capital is highly mobile. Within skill categories (for example, plumber, store manager, accountant, and secretary), labor will be highly mobile within the same geographical area. Movements between geographical areas and from one skill category to another are more costly to accomplish. Labor will thus be less mobile for movements of this variety.

What about the mobility of land? Land is highly mobile among uses when location does not matter. For example, the same land can often be used to raise either corn, wheat, soybeans, or oats. Thus, the supply of land allocated to production of each of these commodities will be highly responsive to changes in their relative prices. Undeveloped land on the outskirts of cities is particularly mobile among uses. In addition to its value in agriculture, such land might be quickly subdivided and used for a housing development or a shopping center. However, since land is totally immobile physically, supply is unresponsive to changes in price that reflect the desirability of a location.

Machines are typically not very mobile among uses. A machine developed to produce airplane wings is seldom of much use in the production of automobiles, appliances, or other products. Steel mills cannot easily be converted to produce aluminum. There are, of course, some exceptions. Trucks can typically be used to haul a variety of products. Building space can often be converted from one use to another. In the short-run, however, immobility and inelasticity of supply are characteristic of much of our physical capital.

LONG-RUN SUPPLY

In the long-run, the supply of resources can change substantially. Machines wear out, human skills depreciate, and even the fertility of land declines with use and erosion. These factors reduce the supply of resources. Through investment, though, the supply of productive resources can be expanded. Current resources can be invested to expand the stock of machines, buildings, and durable assets. Alternatively, current resources can be used to train, educate, and develop the skills of future labor force participants. The supply of both physical and human resources in the long-run is determined primarily by investment and depreciation.

Price incentives will, of course, influence the investment decisions of firms and individuals. Considering both monetary and nonmonetary factors, investors will choose those alternatives they believe to be most advantageous. Higher resource prices will induce utility-maximizing individuals to undertake investments that will permit them to supply more of the higher priced resource. In contrast, other things constant, lower resource prices will reduce the incentive of individuals to invest and expand the future supply of a resource. Thus, resource prices will influence the incentive to invest and acquire resources and thereby lead to an inverse relationship between the price of a resource and quantity supplied in the long-run.

The theory of long-run resource supply is general. The expected payoff from an investment alternative will influence the decisions of investors in human, as well as physical, capital. For example, the higher salaries of physical and space scientists employed in the expanding space program during the early 1960s induced an expanding number of college students to enter these fields. Similarly, attractive earning opportunities in accounting and law led to an increase in investment and quantity supplied in these areas during the period from 1965 to 1975. During the last decade, job opportunities for computer programmers, systems analysts, and computer technicians have been highly attractive as the computer revolution spread throughout our economy. As salaries in these areas rose, the number of students in computer science and technology courses expanded substantially. As in other markets, suppliers respond to changing incentives in resource markets.

Considering both monetary and nonmonetary factors, investors will not knowingly invest in areas of low return when higher returns are available elsewhere. Of course, since human capital is embodied in the individual, nonpecuniary considerations will typically be more important for human than for physical capital. Nevertheless, expected monetary payoffs will influence investment decisions in both areas.

The long-run, of course, is not a specified length of time. Investment can increase the availability of some resources fairly quickly. For example, it does not take very long to train additional bus drivers. Thus, in the absence of barriers to entry, the quantity of bus drivers supplied will expand rapidly in response to higher wages. However, the gestation period between expansion in investment and an increase in quantity supplied is substantially longer for some resources. It takes a long time to train physicians, dentists, lawyers, and pharmacists. Higher earnings in these occupations may have only a small impact on their current availability. Additional investment will go into these areas, but it will typically be several years before there is any substantial increase in the quantity supplied in response to higher earnings for these resources.

Because supply can be substantially expanded over time by investment, the supply of a resource will be much more elastic in the long-run than in the short-run. This is particularly true when there is a lengthy gestation period between an increase in investment and an actual increase in the availability of a resource.

Using engineering services as an example, Exhibit 5 illustrates the relationship between the short- and long-run supply of resources. An increase in the price of engineering services (the wage rate of engineers) will result in some immediate increase in quantity supplied. Persons currently employed as engineers may choose to work more hours. In addition, the higher wage rates may induce workers with engineering skills currently

EXHIBIT 5 • Time and the Elasticity of Supply for Resources

The supply of engineering services (and other resources that require a substantial period of time between current investment and expansion in the future quantity supplied) will be far more inelastic in the short-run than in the long-run.

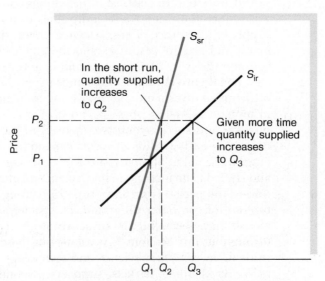

Quantity of engineering services per unit time

employed in mathematics, physics, or similar fields to switch to engineering. While these adjustments are important, they may fail to substantially increase the quantity supplied in the short-run. With time, however, the more attractive earning opportunities in engineering will raise the level of investment in human capital in this area. More students will enter engineering programs. It takes time, though, to acquire an engineering degree. Several years may pass before the additional newly acquired engineering degrees exert a major impact on supply. Nevertheless, the expanded human capital investments will eventually exert important effects. Thus, in the long-run, the quantity of engineering services may be quite elastic, even though supply is highly inelastic in the short-run.

OUTSTANDING ECONOMIST

**Gary Becker
(1930–   )**

This innovative economist is perhaps best known for his ingenious application of economics to several areas that many had previously considered noneconomic by nature. Before his pioneering book, *The Economics of Discrimination*,[4] research by economists in this area was scanty. Apparently, many felt that something as irrational as prejudice was beyond the realm of a rational science like economics. Becker's book proved otherwise. In it, he developed a general theory that could be used to analyze (and measure) the impact of discrimination in several areas on the status of minorities and women. His work laid the foundation for the burgeoning of research interest in the economics of discrimination that took place during the 1960s and 1970s.

Later, Becker applied economic analysis to such seemingly noneconomic subjects as crime prevention, family development, an individual's allocation of time, and even the selection of a marriage partner.[5] The human capital approach underlies much of Becker's research. His widely acclaimed book, *Human Capital*,[6] is already a classic. The work developed a the-oretical foundation for human investment decisions in education, on-the-job training, migration, and health. Becker looks at the individual as a "firm" that will invest in human resources if it is "profitable" to do so. Considering both monetary and nonmonetary factors, the human capital decisions of these profit-maximizing (or utility-maximizing) individuals will be based on the attractiveness (rate of return) of alternative investment opportunities. High rates of return will attract human capital investment to an area, whereas low rates of return will repel it.

His imaginative work earned him the J. B. Clark Award (1967), granted by the American Economic Association to the "outstanding economist under 40."

---

[4]Gary Becker, *The Economics of Discrimination* (Chicago: University of Chicago Press, 1957).

[5]Gary Becker, *The Economic Approach to Human Behavior* (Chicago: University of Chicago Press, 1976), and Gary Becker and W. M. Landes, *Essays in the Economics of Crime and Punishment* (New York: Columbia University Press, 1974).

[6]Gary Becker, *Human Capital* (New York: Columbia University Press, 1964).

SUPPLY, DEMAND, AND RESOURCE PRICES

The theories of supply and demand for resources have been analyzed. This is all we need to develop the theory of resource pricing in competitive markets. When factor prices are free to vary, resource prices will bring the choices of buyers and sellers into line with each other. Continuing with our example of engineers, Exhibit 6 illustrates how the forces of supply and demand push the market price toward equilibrium, where quantity demanded and quantity supplied are equal. Equilibrium is achieved when the price (wage) of engineering services is P_1. Given the market conditions illustrated by Exhibit 6, excess supply is present if the price of engineering services exceeds P_1. Some resource owners are unable to sell their services at the above-equilibrium price. Responding to this situation, they will cut their price (wage) and thereby push the market toward equilibrium. In contrast, if the resource price is less than P_1, excess demand is present. Employers are unable to obtain the desired amount of engineering services at a below-equilibrium resource price. Rather than doing without the resource, employers will bid the price up to P_1 and thereby eliminate the excess demand.

How will a resource market adjust to an unexpected change in market conditions? As is true for product markets, adjustment to changes do not take place instantaneously in resource markets. Our analysis of short-run and long-run responses makes the nature of the adjustment process clear. Suppose there is an unanticipated increase in demand for a resource. As Exhibit 7 illustrates, an increase in market demand (from D_1 to D_2) initially leads to a sharp rise in the price of the resource (from P_1 to P_2), particularly if the short-run supply is quite inelastic. However, at the higher price, the quantity of the resource supplied will expand with time. If it is a natural resource, individuals and firms will put forth a greater effort to discover and develop the now more valuable productive factor. If it is physical capital, a building or machine, current suppliers will have greater incentive to work

EXHIBIT 6 • Equilibrium in a Resource Market

The market demand for a resource such as engineering services is a downward sloping curve reflecting the declining marginal revenue product of the resource. The market supply slopes upward since higher resource prices (wage rates) will induce individuals to supply more of the resource. Resource price P_1 brings the choices of buyers and sellers into harmony. At the equilibrium price (P_1), the quantity demanded will just equal the quantity supplied.

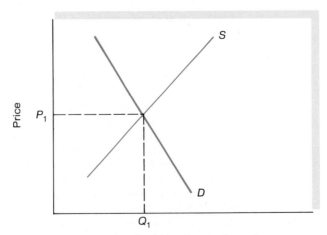

Quantity of engineering services—hours

EXHIBIT 7 • Adjusting to Dynamic Change

An increase in demand for a resource will typically cause price to rise more in the short run than in the long run. Can you explain why?

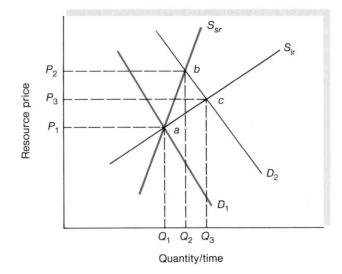

intensively to expand production. New suppliers will be drawn into the market. Higher prices for human capital resources will also lead to an expansion in the quantity supplied. With time, more people will acquire the training, education, and experience necessary to supply the service that now commands a higher price. The expansion of the supply will eventually moderate the price rise. Because of these forces, as Exhibit 7 illustrates, the long-run price increase will be less than the short-run increase.

The market adjustment to an unexpected reduction in demand for a resource is symmetrical. A reduction in demand will cause the price of the resource to fall further in the short-run than over a longer period of time. At the lower price, some resource suppliers will use their talents in other areas. The incentive for potential new suppliers to offer the resource will be reduced by the fall in price. With time, the quantity of the resource supplied will decline, making the long-run decline in price more moderate. Those with the poorest alternatives (that is, lowest opportunity cost) will continue to provide the resource at the lower prices. Those with better alternatives will move to other areas.

LOOKING
AHEAD

Now that we have outlined the theoretical underpinnings of factor markets, we can apply the analysis to a broad range of economic issues. The next chapter will focus on the labor market and the determination of wage rates. Later, we will focus on the capital market and the allocation of resources over time. The operation of these two markets plays an important role in determining the distribution of income, a topic that will also be analyzed in detail in a subsequent chapter.

CHAPTER SUMMARY

1. Factor markets, where productive resources and services are bought and sold, help to determine what is produced, how it is produced, and how the distribution of income (output) is accomplished. There are two

broad classes of productive resources—nonhuman capital and human capital. Both are durable in the sense that they will last into the future, thereby enhancing future productive capabilities. Both yield income to their owners. Investment can expand the future supply of both.

2. The demand for resources is derived from demand for products that the resources help to produce. The quantity of a resource demanded is inversely related to its price. There are two reasons why if the price of a resource increases, less of it will be used. First, producers will substitute other resources for the now more expensive input (substitution in production). Second, the higher resource price will lead to higher prices for products that the resource helps to make, inducing consumers to reduce their purchases of those goods (substitution in consumption).

3. The short-run market demand curve will be more inelastic than the long-run curve. It will take time for producers to adjust their production process to use more of the less expensive resources and less of the more expensive resources.

4. The demand curve for a resource, like the demand of a product, may shift. The major factors that can increase the demand for a resource are (a) an increase in demand for products that use the resource, (b) an increase in the productivity of the resource, and (c) an increase in the price of substitute resources.

5. Profit-maximizing firms will hire additional units of a resource as long as the marginal revenue product of the resource exceeds its hiring cost, usually the price of the resource. If resources are perfectly divisible, firms will expand their usage of each resource until the marginal revenue product of each resource is just equal to its price.

6. When a firm is minimizing its costs, it will employ each factor of production up to the point at which the marginal product per last dollar spent on the factor is equal for all factors. This condition implies that the marginal product of labor divided by the price of labor must equal the marginal product of capital (machines) divided by the price of capital, and that this ratio (MP_i/P_i) must be the same for all other inputs used by the firm. When real-world decision-makers minimize per unit costs, the outcome will be as if they had followed these mathematical procedures, even though they may not consciously do so.

7. Resource owners will use their factors of production in the manner that they consider most personally advantageous. Many resources will be relatively immobile in the short-run. The less mobile a resource, the more inelastic its short-run supply. There will be a positive relationship between amount supplied and resource price even in the short-run.

8. In the long-run, investment and depreciation will alter resource supply. Resource owners will shift factors of production toward areas in which resource prices have risen and away from areas in which resource prices have fallen. Thus, the long-run supply will be more elastic than the short-run supply.

9. The prices of resources will be determined by both supply and demand. The demand for a resource will reflect the demand for products that it helps make. The supply of resources will reflect the human and physical capital investment decisions of individuals and firms.

10. Changing resource prices will influence the decisions of users and suppliers alike. Higher resource prices give users a greater incentive to turn to substitutes and stimulate suppliers to provide more of the resource. Since these adjustments take time, when the demand for a resource expands, the price will usually rise more in the short-run than in the long-run. Similarly, when there is a fall in resource demand, price will decline more in the short-run than in the long-run.

THE ECONOMIC WAY OF THINKING— DISCUSSION QUESTIONS

1. What is the meaning of the expression "invest in human capital"? In what sense is the decision to invest in human capital like the decision to invest in physical capital? Is human capital investment risky? Explain.
2. (a) "Firms will hire a resource only if they can make money by doing so."
   (b) "In a market economy, each resource will tend to be paid according to its marginal product. Highly productive resources will command high prices, whereas less productive resources will command lower prices."
   Are (a) and (b) both correct? Are they inconsistent with each other? Explain.
3. Use the information of Exhibit 2 to answer the following:
   (a) How many employees (operators) would Compute-Accounting hire at a weekly wage of $250 if it were attempting to maximize profits?
   (b) What would the firm's maximum profit be if its fixed costs were $1,500 per week?
   (c) Suppose there was a decline in demand for accounting services, reducing the market price per monthly statement to $150. At this demand level, how many employees would Compute-Accounting hire at $250 per week in the short-run? Would Compute-Accounting stay in business at the lower market price? Explain.
4. Are productivity gains the major source of higher wages? If so, how does one account for the rising real wages of barbers, who by and large have used the same technique for half a century? (Hint: Do not forget opportunity cost and supply.)
5. "However desirable they might be from an equity viewpoint, programs designed to reduce wage differentials will necessarily reduce the incentive of people to act efficiently and use their productive abilities in those areas where demand is greatest relative to supply." Do you agree or disagree? Why?
6. **What's Wrong with This Way of Thinking?**
   "The downward-sloping marginal revenue product curve of labor shows that better workers are hired first. The workers hired later are less productive."

- Why do some people earn more than others?

- Why are wages higher in the United States than they are in India or China? Why are the wages of Americans higher today than they were 50 years ago?

- How is our national income divided between labor and capital?

- Does automation destroy jobs? Does it harm workers?

- Can we legislate higher wages?

- Why are the earnings of whites greater than the earnings of minorities? Why are the earnings of men greater than the earnings of women?

A fair day's-wages for a fair day's-work; it is as just a demand as governed men ever made of governing. It is the everlasting right of man.

THOMAS CARLYLE

23 EARNINGS, PRODUCTIVITY, AND THE JOB MARKET

The major source of income for most people is labor earnings; income derived from current work. The earnings of U.S. workers are among the highest in the world and they have been increasing. The earnings of individuals, however, vary widely. An unskilled laborer may earn the $3.35 minimum wage, or something close to it. Lawyers and physicians often earn $75 per hour. Dentists and even economists might receive $50 per hour. This chapter focuses on earnings—the source of high earnings, the explanation of why earnings vary, and the reasons why some groups earn more than others.

WHY DO EARNINGS DIFFER?

The earnings of paired individuals in the same occupation or with the same amount of education very often differ substantially. The earnings of persons with the same family background also vary widely. For example, one researcher found that the average earnings differential between brothers was $5,600, compared to $6,200 for men paired randomly.[1] In addition, the earnings of persons with the same IQ, level of training, or amount of experience typically differ. How do economists explain these variations? Several factors combine to determine the earning power of an individual. Some seem to be the result of good or bad fortune. Others are clearly the result of conscious decisions made by individuals. In the previous chapter, we analyzed how the market forces of supply and demand operate to determine resource prices. The subject of earnings differentials can be usefully approached within the framework of this model.

If (a) all individuals were homogeneous, (b) all jobs were equally attractive, and (c) workers were perfectly mobile among jobs, the earnings of all employees in a competitive economy would be equal. If, given these conditions, higher wages existed in any area of the economy, the supply of workers to that area would expand until the wage differential was eliminated. Similarly, low wages in any area would cause workers to exit until wages in that area returned to parity. However, the conditions necessary for earnings equality do not exist in the real world. Thus, earnings differentials are present.

EARNINGS DIFFER-ENTIALS DUE TO NONHOMOGENEOUS LABOR

All workers are clearly not the same. They differ in several important respects, which influence both the supply of and demand for their services.

Worker Productivity and Specialized Skills. The demand for employees who are highly productive—those with a higher marginal revenue product—will be greater than the demand for those who are less productive. Persons who can operate a machine more skillfully, hit a baseball more consistently, or sell life insurance policies with greater regularity will have a higher marginal revenue product than their less skillful counterparts. Because they are more productive, their services will command a higher wage from employers.

---

[1]Christopher Jencks, *Inequality* (New York: Basic Books, 1972), p. 220.

Workers can increase their productivity by investment in human capital. When education, vocational training, and other investments in human capital increase productivity, they will lead to higher earnings. In fact, the higher earnings provide individuals with the incentive to invest in themselves and thereby upgrade their knowledge and skills. If additional worker productivity did not lead to higher earnings, individuals would have little incentive to incur the direct and indirect cost of productivity-enhancing educational and training programs.

Of course, native ability and motivation will influence the rate at which an individual can transform educational and training experience into greater productivity. Individuals differ in the amount of valuable skills they develop from a year of education, vocational school, or on-the-job training. We should not expect a rigid relationship to exist between years of training (or education) and skill level.

Nevertheless, detailed empirical studies indicate that investment in human capital leads to higher earnings *once the person enters the labor force full-time.* For example, in 1984, the median income of college graduates age 25 and over was $15,871, compared to $12,769 for high school graduates. Some of the additional earnings of college graduates may reflect native ability, intelligence, and motivation. Research, however, indicates that a large proportion of the additional earnings also reflects knowledge and skills acquired through investment and human capital. Similarly, economic research has shown that training enhances the earnings of workers.

Investment in human capital and development of specialized skills can protect high-wage workers from the competition of others willing to offer their services at a lower price. Few persons could develop the specialized skills of a Barbara Mandrell or a Bill Cosby. Similarly, skill (and human capital) factors also limit the supply of heart surgeons, trial lawyers, engineers, and business entrepreneurs. As Exhibit 1 illustrates, when the demand for a specialized resource is great relative to its supply, the resource will be able to command a high wage. In 1983, the average earnings level of engineers was $32,300, more than three times the figure for laborers. Since engineers possess specialized skills developed by both formal education (usually between 16 and 18 years) and experience, laborers are unable to compete directly in the engineering market. In contrast, the training and skill requirements for laborers are possessed by many. Since the supply of laborers is large relative to the demand, their earnings are substantially less.

It is important to keep in mind that wages are determined by demand relative to supply. Other things constant, a skilled specialist will command a higher wage than one with less skill, but high skill will not guarantee high wages in the absence of demand. For example, expert harness makers and blacksmiths typically command low wages today, even though the supply of these workers is small—because demand even for the services of experts in these areas is low.

Worker Preferences. This very important source of earnings differentials is sometimes overlooked. People have different objectives in life. Some want to make a great deal of money. Many are willing to work long hours,

EXHIBIT 1 • Supply, Demand, and Wage Differentials

The mean number of years of education for engineers is 17.0 compared to 12.0 for laborers. Because of their specialized skills, high-wage engineers are protected from direct competition with laborers and other persons who do not possess such skills.

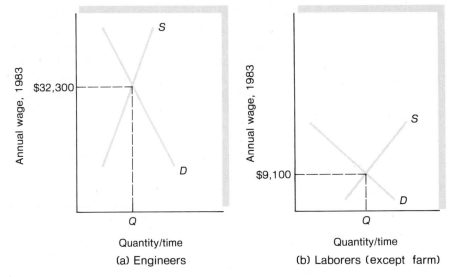

(a) Engineers

(b) Laborers (except farm)

Earnings data are from the U.S. Department of Commerce.

undergo agonizing training and many years of education, and sacrifice social and family life to make money. Others may be "workaholics" because they enjoy their jobs. Still others may be satisfied with enough money to get by on, preferring to spend more time with their family, the Boy Scouts, the television, or the local tavern keeper.

Economics does not indicate that one set of worker preferences is more desirable than another, any more than it suggests that people should eat more spinach and less pastrami. Economics does indicate, however, that these factors contribute to differences in wages and earnings. Other things constant, persons who are more highly motivated by monetary objectives will be more likely to do the things necessary to command higher wage rates.

Race and Sex. Discrimination on the basis of race or sex contributes to earnings differences among individuals. Employment discrimination may directly limit the earnings opportunities of minorities and women. **Employment discrimination** exists when minorities or women employees are treated in a manner different from similarly productive whites or men. Of course, the earnings of minority employees, for example, may differ from whites for reasons other than employment discrimination. Nonemployment discrimination may limit the opportunity of minority groups and women to acquire human capital (for example, quality education or specialized training) that would enhance both their productivity and earnings. To isolate the impact of current employment discrimination, we must (a) adjust for the impact of education, experience, and skill factors and (b) then make comparisons between similarly qualified groups of employees who differ with regard to race (or sex) only. (See Measures of Economic Activity for additional detail on this topic.)

There are two major forms of employment discrimination—wage rates and employment restrictions. Exhibit 2 illustrates the impact of wage dis-

Employment Discrimination: Unequal treatment of persons on the basis of their race, sex, or religion, which restricts their employment and earnings opportunities compared to others of similar productivity. Employment discrimination may stem from the prejudices of employers, consumers, and/or fellow employees.

crimination. When majority employees are preferred to minority and female workers, the demand for the latter two groups is reduced. The wages of blacks and women decline relative to those of white men.

Essentially, there is a dual labor market—one market for the favored group and another for the group toward whom discrimination is directed. The favored group, such as whites, is preferred, but the less expensive labor of minority workers is a substitute productive resource. Both white and minority employees are employed, but the whites are paid a higher wage rate.

Exclusionary practices may also be an outlet for employment discrimination. Either in response to outside pressure or because of their own views, employers may primarily hire whites and males for certain types of jobs. When minority and female workers are excluded from a large number of occupations, they are crowded into a smaller number of remaining jobs and occupations. If entry restraints prevent people from becoming supervisors, bank officers, plumbers, electricians, and truck drivers, they will be forced to accept alternatives. The supply of labor in the restricted occupations will increase, causing wage rates to fall. The exclusionary practices will result in higher wages for white males holding jobs from which blacks and females are excluded. The outcome will be an overrepresentation of white males in the higher paying occupations, while a disproportionate number of blacks and women will occupy the lower-paying, nonrestricted positions. The impact will be a reduction in the earnings of minorities and women relative to white males.

While employment discrimination undoubtedly influences earning opportunities available to minorities and women, economic theory implies that discrimination is costly to employers when they are merely reflecting their own prejudices. If employers can hire *equally productive* minority employees (or women) at a lower wage than whites (or men), the profit motive gives them a strong incentive to do so. An employer who continues to hire high-wage whites, when similar minority employees are available at a lower wage,

EXHIBIT 2 • The Impact of Direct Wage Discrimination

If there is employment discrimination against blacks or women, the demand for their services will decline, and their wage rate will fall from W_w to W_b.

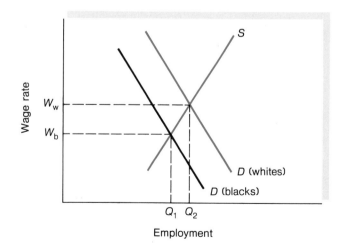

will have higher costs and lower profits than nondiscriminative employers. Since competition forces an employer to pay for prejudice with lower profits, it tends to moderate discriminatory actions.[2] Regardless of whether employers are motivated by goodwill or pursuit of profit, when a substantial proportion (it need not be all) of employers follow a nondiscriminatory policy, the wages of equally productive minority (women) and white (men) employees will approach parity.

EARNINGS DIFFERENTIALS DUE TO NON-HOMOGENEOUS JOBS

Nonpecuniary Job Characteristics: Working conditions, prestige, variety, location, employee freedom and responsibilities, and other nonwage characteristics of a job that influence how employees evaluate the job.

When individuals evaluate employment alternatives, they consider working conditions as well as wage rates. Is a job dangerous? Does it offer the opportunity to acquire the experience and training that will enhance future earnings? Is the work strenuous and nerve-racking? Are the working hours, job location, and means of transportation convenient? These factors are what economists call **nonpecuniary job characteristics.** Workers are willing to trade off higher wage rates for more favorable nonpecuniary job characteristics. There are numerous examples of this. Because of the dangers involved, aerial window washers (those who hang from windows 20 stories up) earn higher wages than other window washers. Sales jobs involving a great deal of out-of-town travel typically pay more than similar jobs without such inconvenience. Electricians in contract construction are paid more than equally skilled electricians with jobs in which the work and pay are more steady. Because the majority of economists prefer the more independent work environment and intellectual stimulation offered by colleges and universities, the earnings of economists in academia are typically lower than those of economists in business.

Substantial wage differentials exist between similar jobs in (a) large and small firms and (b) urban and rural areas. Nonpecuniary factors, such as transportation costs and locational preferences, help explain these differentials. Large firms must typically draw their labor force from a wider geographical area, resulting in longer average travel time to and from work. Congestion problems are more severe. These factors make employment with large firms less desirable. Because of this, they must pay higher wage rates to attract the desired size of labor force. Similarly, the lower wages in rural areas probably reflect, at least partially, employees' willingness to trade off higher wages for jobs in preferred living areas. These differences in the nonpecuniary characteristics of jobs contribute to earnings differences among individuals.

EARNINGS DIFFERENTIALS DUE TO IMMOBILITY OF LABOR

It is costly to move to a new location or train for a new occupation in order to obtain a job. Such movements do not take place instantaneously. In the real world, labor, like other resources, does not possess perfect mobility. Some wage differentials thus result from an incomplete adjustment to change.

---

[2]For empirical evidence that competition reduces the effects of employer discrimination, see James Gwartney and Charles Haworth, "Employer Cost and Discrimination: The Case of Baseball," *Journal of Political Economy* (June 1974).

Since the demand for labor resources is a derived demand, it is affected by changes in product markets. An expansion in the demand for a product causes a rise in the demand for specialized labor to produce the product.

MEASURES OF ECONOMIC ACTIVITY

Earnings Differentials According to Race Corrected for Differences in Productivity-Related Factors

Earnings may differ among groups for reasons other than employment discrimination. If we want to isolate the impact of employment discrimination, earnings comparisons must be made between similarly productive groups. A recent study by Leonard Carlson and Carol Swartz of Emory University uses statistical techniques to "correct" the earnings of minorities for productive characteristics that obviously affect earnings, independent of employment discrimination.[3] In essence, Carlson and Swartz calculated what the earnings of white men would be if they had the same average education, age, language (English), marital status, native birth, annual hours worked, and regional location as minority men. The actual earnings of minority men were then compared to the "corrected" (productivity adjusted) earnings of white men.

Exhibit 3 summarizes the findings of Carlson and Swartz. The actual earnings of black men were only 67 percent the earnings of white men in 1979. However, when the work force characteristics (education, age, language, marital status, and so on) of black men were taken into account, the corrected earnings of black men rose to 84 percent of the white male earnings. Thus, productivity-related factors accounted for approximately half of the earnings differential between white and black men. Mexican-Americans constitute the second largest minority group in the United States. Even though the actual earnings of Mexican-American men were only 66 percent of the earnings for white men, their "corrected" earnings were almost equal (97 percent) to the white earnings.

This implies that if Mexican-American men possessed the same worker characteristics as white men, their earnings would be very close to parity with their white counterparts. The actual and corrected earnings for other minority groups are also presented in Exhibit 3. Interestingly, both the actual and corrected earnings of Japanese-American men were slightly greater than for their white counterparts. The two most recent arrivals among the minority groups—Cubans and Vietnamese—appear to be doing quite well, given their worker characteristics. The corrected relative wage of both groups was 98 percent of the white wage in 1979. Clearly, differences in worker characteristics as well as employment discrimination, contribute to earnings differences between white and minority men.

EXHIBIT 3 • The Actual and Productivity Corrected Wages of Minority Males Compared to White Males, 1979

	The Wage of Minority Men Relative to White Men, 1979	
	Actual	Corrected
White	100	100
Black	67	84
Mexican American	66	97
Japanese American	105	101
Chinese American	89	89
Puerto Rican	63	95
American Indian	74	90
Cuban	64	98
Vietnamese	64	98

Source: Leonard A. Carlson and Carol Swartz, "The Relative Earnings of Blacks and Other Minorities, 1980," Economics Department Working Paper, Emory University, 1986. The estimates are based on 1980 census data.

[3]Leonard A. Carlson and Carol Swartz, "The Relative Earnings of Blacks and Other Minorities, 1980," Economics Department Working Paper, Emory University, 1986.

Since resources are often highly immobile (that is, the supply is inelastic) in the short-run, the expansion in demand may cause the wages of the specialized laborers to rise sharply. This is what happened in the oil-drilling industry in the late 1970s. An expansion in demand triggered a rapid increase in the earnings of petroleum engineers, oil rig operators, and other specialized personnel. Falling oil prices triggered the opposite effect in the mid-1980s. The demand and employment opportunities of specialized resources declined substantially as output in the oil industry fell during 1985–1986. Demand shifts in the product market favor those in expanding industries but work against those in contracting industries.

Institutional barriers may also limit the mobility of labor. Licensing requirements limit the mobility of labor into many occupations—medicine, taxicab driving, architecture, and mortuary science among them. Unions may also follow policies that limit labor mobility and alter the free-market forces of supply and demand. Minimum wage rates may retard the ability of low-skill workers to obtain employment in certain sectors of the economy. These restrictions on labor mobility will influence the size of wage differentials among workers.

SUMMARY OF WAGE DIFFERENTIALS

As the Thumbnail Sketch shows, wage differentials stem from many sources. Many of them play an important allocative role, compensating people for (a) human capital investments that increase their productivity or (b) unfavorable working conditions. Other wage differentials reflect, at least partially, locational preferences or the desires of individuals for higher money income rather than nonmonetary benefits. Still other differentials, such as those related to discrimination and occupational restrictions, are unrelated to worker preferences and are not required to promote efficient production.

THUMBNAIL SKETCH

Sources of Earnings Differentials

Differences in workers:

1. Productivity and specialized skills (for example, human capital, native ability, motivation)
2. Worker preferences (trade-off between money earnings and other things)
3. Race and sex discrimination

Differences in jobs:

1. Location of jobs
2. Nonpecuniary job characteristics (for example, convenience of working hours, job safety, likelihood of temporary layoffs, and working conditions)

Immobility of resources:

1. Temporary disequilibrium resulting from dynamic change
2. Institutional restrictions (for example, occupational licensing and union-imposed restraints)

PRODUCTIVITY AND THE GENERAL LEVEL OF WAGES

It is also important to understand why the general level of wages varies from one country to another and from one period of time to another within the same country. Real earnings are vastly greater in the United States than they are in India or China. In addition, the average real earnings per hour in the United States have approximately doubled during the past 25 years. What factors account for these variations in the general level of wages?

Differences in labor productivity—output produced per worker-hour—are the major source of variation in real wages between nations and between time periods. When the amount produced per worker-hour is high, real wages will be high.

Exhibit 4 illustrates the relationship between real wages and output per worker-hour since World War II. Between 1947 and 1985, output per worker-hour rose 103 percent in the nonfarm private sector. What happened to employee compensation? During the same time period, the hourly compensation of employees, measured in constant 1972 dollars, increased from $1.94 to $3.90, an increase of 101 percent.

The close relationship between amount produced and real wages should not be surprising. Do not forget that real income and real output are simply two ways of viewing the same thing. Expansion in real income is totally dependent on expansion of output. Without expansion of output, our money incomes, whatever they may be, will not enable us to purchase more goods and services in aggregate.

EXHIBIT 4 • Productivity and Employee Compensation, 1947–1985

As the diagram illustrates, productivity of employees per worker-hour is closely related to earnings.

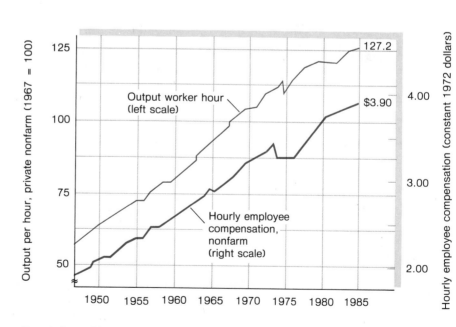

Economic Report of the President, 1986.

In the last chapter, we showed that the productivity of a resource, including labor, is dependent on the amount of other resources with which it works. Contrary to what many believe, physical capital (for example, modern labor-saving machines) is not the enemy of high real wages (see Myths of Economics, "Automation is the major cause of unemployment"). In fact, just the opposite is true.

Machines make it possible for labor to produce more per worker-hour. Are jobs destroyed in the process? Specific jobs are sometimes eliminated, but this merely releases human resources so they can be used to expand output in other areas. Output and productivity, not jobs, are the source of high real wages.

MYTHS OF ECONOMICS

"Automation is the major cause of unemployment. If we keep allowing machines to replace people, we are going to run out of jobs."

Machines are substituted for people if, and only if, the machines reduce costs of production. Why has the automatic elevator replaced the operator, the tractor replaced the horse, and the power shovel replaced the ditch digger? Because each is a cheaper method of accomplishing a task.

The fallacy that **automation** causes unemployment stems from a failure to recognize the secondary effects. Employment may decline in a specific industry as the result of automation. However, lower per

Automation: A production technique that reduces the amount of labor required to produce a good or service. It is beneficial to adopt the new labor-saving technology only if it reduces the cost of production.

unit costs in that industry will lead to either (a) additional spending and jobs in other industries or (b) additional output and employment in the specific industry as consumers buy more of the now cheaper good.

Perhaps an example will help illustrate the secondary effects of automation. Suppose someone develops a new toothpaste that actually prevents cavities and sells it for half the current price of Colgate. At last, we have a toothpaste that really works. Think of the impact the invention will have on dentists, toothpaste producers and their employees, and even the advertising agencies that give us those marvelous toothpaste commercials. What are these people to do? Haven't their jobs been destroyed?

These are the obvious effects; they are seen to be the direct result of the toothpaste invention. What most people do not see are the additional jobs that will indirectly be created by the invention. Consumers will now spend less on toothpaste, dental bills, and pain relievers. Their real income will be higher. They will now be able to spend

more on other products they would have forgone had it not been for the new invention. They will increase their spending on clothes, recreation, vacations, swimming pools, education, and many other items. This additional spending, which would not have taken place if dental costs had not been reduced by the technological advancement, will generate additional demand and employment in other sectors.

It is undeniable that jobs have been eliminated in the toothpaste and dental industries because of a reduction in consumer spending in these areas. However, new jobs have been created in other industries and consumers have increased their spending as a result of the savings attributable to the new invention.

When the demand for a product is elastic, a cost-saving invention can even generate an increase in employment in the industry affected by the invention. This was essentially what happened in the automobile industry when Henry Ford's mass production techniques reduced the cost (and price) of cars. When the price of automobiles fell

MYTHS OF ECONOMICS (continued)

50 percent, consumers bought three times as many cars. Even though the worker-hours per car decreased by 25 percent between 1920 and 1930, employment in the industry increased from 250,000 to 380,000 during the period, an increase of approximately 50 percent.

Even if the demand for automobiles had been inelastic, automation would not have caused long-run unemployment. When demand is inelastic, less will be spent on the lower-cost, lower-priced commodity, leaving more to be spent on other goods and services. This spending on other products, which would not have resulted without the new invention, will ensure that there is not a net reduction in employment.

Of course, technological advances that release labor resources may well harm specific individuals or groups. Automatic elevators reduced the job opportunities of elevator operators. Computer technology has reduced the demand for telephone operators. In the future, videotaped lectures may even reduce the job opportunities available to college professors. Thus, the earnings opportunities of specific persons may, at least temporarily, be adversely affected by cost-reducing automated methods. It is understandable why groups directly affected fear and oppose automation.

Focusing on jobs alone, though, can lead to a fundamental misunderstanding about the importance of machines, automation, and technological improvements. Automation neither creates nor destroys jobs. The real impact of cost-reducing machines and tech-nological improvements is an increase in production. Technological advances make it possible for us to produce as much with fewer resources, thereby releasing valuable resources so that production (and consumption) can be expanded in other areas. Other tasks can be accomplished with the newly available resources. Since there is a direct link between improved technology and rising output, automation exerts a positive influence on economic welfare from the viewpoint of society as a whole. In aggregate, running out of jobs is unlikely to be a problem. Jobs represent obstacles, tasks that must be accomplished if we desire to loosen the bonds of scarcity. As long as our ability to produce goods and services falls short of our consumption desires, there will be jobs. A society running out of jobs would be in an enviable position: It would be nearing the impossible goal—victory over scarcity.

Increasing productivity is brought about by a cooperative process. Investment, both in human and nonhuman capital, is vital to the growth of productivity. For several decades, the educational level of members of the work force in the United States has steadily increased. The median number of years of schooling of persons in the labor force in 1984 was 12.9, compared to 10.6 years in 1949. Simultaneously, the nonhuman capital per worker has expanded (although the growth rate of capital investment per worker has slowed considerably in recent years). Both the development and innovative application of improved technological methods are also important determinants of the growth of productivity. Technological improvements make it possible to obtain a larger output from the same resource base. Of course, modern technological advancements are often linked to investments in both physical and human capital.

During the last two decades, there has been a vast influx of workers into the labor force as the rate of labor force participation among women increased, and as the children of the post-World War II "baby boom" came of working age. Simultaneously, inflation and high real interest rates dampened investment in physical capital. Economics suggests that a rapid growth in the labor force, accompanied by a sagging rate of capital formation, will adversely affect worker productivity and compensation per worker-hour.

As Exhibit 5 shows, this has been precisely the case. During the period from 1948 to 1965, both output per hour and hourly compensation grew annually at a rate slightly in excess of 3 percent. Since 1974, there have been sharply lower increases in productivity. As the growth rate of output per hour declines, increases in worker compensation per hour must also decline. Real incomes cannot continually increase faster than the expansion in the production of goods and services. As the growth of productivity sagged during the 1974–1985 period, growth in real worker compensation per hour also sagged (Exhibit 5). This lag in the growth rate of productivity is a serious matter. Several leading economists believe that unless the United States begins to allocate a somewhat larger share of its national output to investment, worker productivity and the growth of real income will continue to stagnate.

HOW IS THE ECONOMIC PIE DIVIDED?

We have emphasized that wage rates generally reflect the availability of tools (physical capital) and the skills and abilities of individual workers (human capital). Wages tend to be high when physical capital is plentiful, technology is advanced, and the work force is highly skilled. When the equipment available to the typical worker is primitive and most workers lack education and skills, wages are low. Human capital and physical capital alike contribute to the productive process.

How is the pie divided between these two broad factors of production in the United States? Exhibit 6 provides an answer. In 1950, approximately 81 percent of the national income was earned by employees and self-employed proprietors, the major categories reflecting the earnings of human capital. In 1985, the share of national income allocated to human capital was also 81 percent. Income earned by nonhuman capital—rents, interest, and corporate profits—currently comprises 18 to 20 percent of the national income.

EXHIBIT 5 • The Sagging Growth of Productivity in the United States		
Period	Increase in Output per Hour, Private Business Sector (Average Annual Rate)	Increase in Real per Hour Compensation, Private Business Sector (Average Annual Rate)
1948–1955	3.7	3.4
1956–1965	3.0	3.1
1966–1973	2.2	2.0
1974–1985	0.8	0.2

Derived from *Economic Report of the President, 1986*. Table B-44.

EXHIBIT 6 • The Shares of Income Going to Physical and Human Capital

Including self-employment income, approximately four fifths of the national income is earned by owners of human capital.

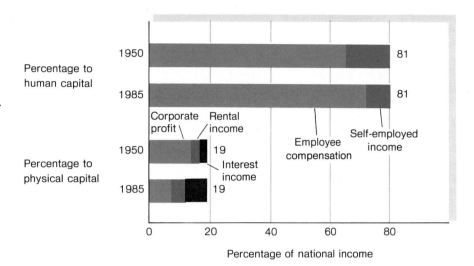

Economic Report of the President, 1986, Table B-23.

CAN HIGHER WAGES BE LEGISLATED?

Minimum Wage Legislation: Legislation requiring that all workers in specified industries be paid at least the stated minimum hourly rate of pay.

In 1938, Congress passed the Fair Labor Standards Act, which provided for a national **minimum wage** of 25 cents per hour. Approximately 43 percent of the private, nonagricultural work force was covered by this legislation. During the last 40 years, the minimum wage has been increased several times, and coverage now extends to 84 percent of the nonagricultural labor force. Currently, federal legislation requires most employers to pay wage rates of at least $3.35 per hour.

Minimum wage legislation is intended to help the working poor. There is good reason to believe, however, that such legislation has the opposite effect. Economic theory indicates that the quantity demanded of labor, particularly a specific skill category of labor, will be inversely related to its wage rate.

If a higher minimum wage increases the wage rates of unskilled workers above the level that would be established by market forces, the quantity of unskilled workers employed will fall. The minimum wage will price the services of the least productive (and therefore lowest-wage) workers out of the market.

Exhibit 7 provides a graphic illustration of the direct effect of a $3.35 minimum wage on the employment opportunities of a group of low-skill workers. Without a minimum wage, the supply of and demand for these low-skill workers would be in balance at a wage rate of $2.50. The $3.35 minimum wage makes the low-skill labor service more expensive. Employers will substitute machines and highly skilled workers (whose wages have not been raised by the minimum) for the now more expensive low-productivity employees. Jobs in which low-skill employees are unable to produce a marginal revenue product equal to or greater than the minimum

EXHIBIT 7 • Employment and the Minimum Wage

If the market wage of a group of employees were $2.50 per hour, a $3.35-per-hour minimum wage would (a) increase the earnings of persons who were able to maintain employment and (b) reduce the employment of others (E_0 to E_1), pushing them onto the unemployment rolls or into less-preferred jobs.

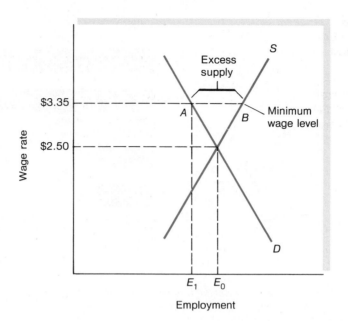

will be eliminated. As the cost (and price) of goods and services produced by low-skill employees rises, consumers will rely more heavily on substitute goods produced by highly skilled labor and foreign markets. The net effect of this substitution process will be a reduction in the quantity demanded of low-skill labor.

Of course, some low-skill workers will be able to maintain their jobs, but others will be driven into sectors not covered by the legislation or onto the unemployment and welfare rolls. Workers who retain their jobs will gain. The most adverse effects will fall on those workers who are already most disadvantaged—those whose market earnings are lowest relative to the minimum wage—because it will be so costly to bring their wages up to the minimum.

The direct results of minimum wage legislation are clearly mixed. Some workers, most likely those whose previous wages were closest to the minimum, will enjoy higher wages. Others, particularly those with the lowest prelegislation wage rates, will be unable to find work.[4] They will be pushed into the ranks of the unemployed or out of the labor force.

THE MINIMUM WAGE, EXPERIENCE, AND JOB TRAINING

The minimum wage also affects the training opportunities and types of jobs available to low-skill workers. Many inexperienced workers face a dilemma. They cannot find a job without experience (or skills), but they cannot obtain

---

[4]The impact of minimum wage legislation could differ from the theoretical results we have outlined if labor markets were dominated by a single buyer. Economists refer to this situation as "monopsony." We choose not to present the monopsony model here because (a) in a modern society, where labor is highly mobile, the major assumptions of the model are seldom met; and (b) the bulk of the empirical evidence in this area is consistent with the competitive model.

experience without a job. This is particularly true for youthful workers. Employment experience obtained at an early age, even on seemingly menial tasks, can help one acquire work habits (for example, promptness and self-confidence), skills, and attitudes that will enhance one's value to employers in the future. Since minimum wage legislation prohibits the payment of even a temporarily low wage, it substantially limits the employer's ability to offer employment to inexperienced workers.

Minimum wage legislation also limits the range of jobs available to low-skill workers. Consider a construction firm that hires "helpers" at $2.50 per hour to work with carpenters and electricians. Since the helpers require close supervision, often make mistakes, and are used on odd jobs during slack periods, they are initially able to command only a low wage. After the minimum wage is introduced, the contractor will receive more applications—including those of workers with experience and past training—but will hire fewer workers at the higher wage. The contractor, now able to be more selective, will hire and train fewer inexperienced helpers. Some **entry-level jobs** will be eliminated.

As entry-level jobs that offer training opportunities to low-productivity workers are eliminated in many sectors of the economy, the positions available to inexperienced workers will be primarily **dead-end jobs.** As Martin Feldstein has pointed out, the minimum wage acts as an institutional barrier limiting the opportunity to acquire on-the-job training.[5] Many leading economists believe that minimum wage legislation is the major reason for the almost complete lack of skill-building jobs at the lower end of the wage spectrum.

Some people incorrectly argue that inexperienced, low-skill workers have few employment opportunities because they have so few qualifications. Low productivity (skill level) results in low wages, but, in the absence of legal barriers, it need not result in high levels of unemployment. No worker is either qualified or unqualified in an absolute sense. One's qualifications must be considered in relation to one's wage rate. For example, a carpenter may be "qualified" and in great demand at an hourly wage rate of $5. The same carpenter, though, may be "unemployable" at $10 per hour. A $10 minimum wage rate would obviously make many workers unemployable, since many would lack the qualifications (skills) necessary to command such high wages. Even though the effects are less widespread, a $3.35 minimum wage does precisely the same thing to low-skill workers; it makes them unqualified, that is, unemployable, at such a high wage rate.

Entry-Level Jobs: Jobs that require little training or experience and therefore allow untrained or inexperienced job seekers to enter the work force. These jobs frequently are stepping stones to better jobs.

Dead-End Jobs: Jobs that offer the employee little opportunity for advancement or on-the-job training.

MINIMUM WAGE AND TEENAGE UNEMPLOYMENT

Most empirical studies of the minimum wage in the United States have focused on teenagers, since there is a higher proportion of low-wage workers (reflecting their lack of skill-building experience) in this age group. There have been several studies of the impact of the minimum wage on the employment opportunities of youth. Most of these studies indicate that a 10

---

[5]It is ironic that although we subsidize formal education, we establish barriers that restrict a worker's ability to acquire training. See Martin Feldstein, "The Economics of the New Unemployment," *Public Interest* (Fall 1973), pp. 3–42.

percent increase in the minimum wage reduces teenage employment by 1 to 3 percent.[6]

The impact of the minimum wage on the employment opportunities of youthful blacks is particularly severe. Since a higher minimum wage leads to an excessive supply of unskilled workers, employers have the opportunity to choose among a surplus of applicants for each opening. They generally choose those workers, within the low-productivity group, who have the most skill, experience, and education. These are generally not youthful blacks. In addition, since all workers must be paid the minimum, the employer's incentive to hire less skilled and less favored groups is destroyed.

Exhibit 8 shows how the unemployment rate of black teenagers has changed following increases in the minimum wage during the last three decades. In March 1956, the minimum wage was increased from 75 cents to $1. During the 12 months following this increase in the minimum wage, the overall unemployment rate averaged 4.1 percent, compared to 4.2 percent for the 12 months prior to the jump in the minimum wage. In contrast, the unemployment rate of black teenagers rose from 15.8 percent to 18.1 percent during the 12 months following the increase. A similar pattern was present for increases in the minimum wage during 1961–1963 and 1967–1968. In both of these cases, the unemployment rate of black teenagers rose during the period after the increase in the minimum wage even though the unemployment rate for all workers fell. During the 1974–1981 period, the minimum wage was increased seven different times, almost every year. In addition, the number of workers covered was expanded. During the 1974–1981 period, the unemployment rate of both the general labor force and black teenagers rose substantially. Nevertheless, the differential between the two continued to widen.

Much of the research documenting the adverse impact of the minimum wage on the employment opportunities of blacks has been done by black economists. Andrew Brimmer, a former member of the Federal Reserve Board, has been among the leading critics of the minimum wage. Brimmer argues:

> A growing body of statistical and other evidence accumulated by economists shows that increases in the statutory minimum wage dampen the expansion of employment and lengthen the lineup of those seeking jobs. Advances in the minimum wage have a noticeably adverse impact on young people—with the effects on black teenagers being considerably more severe.[7]

---

[6]See Jacob Mincer, "Unemployment Effects of Minimum Wages," *Journal of Political Economy,* vol. 84 (August 1976); James Ragan, "Minimum Wages and the Youth Labor Market," *Review of Economics and Statistics,* vol. 59 (May 1977); Finis Welch, *Minimum Wages: Issues and Evidence* (Washington: American Enterprise Institute, 1978); Charles L. Betsey and Bruce H. Dunson, "Federal Minimum Wage Laws and the Employment of Minority Youth," *American Economic Review,* vol. 71 (May 1981); and Charles Brown, Curtis Gilroy, and Andrew Kohen, "The Effect of the Minimum Wage on Employment and Unemployment," *Journal of Economic Literature,* vol. 20 (June 1982).

[7]Andrew Brimmer, quoted in Louis Rukeyser, "Jobs Are Eliminated," Naught News Service (August 1978).

EXHIBIT 8 • Changes in the Minimum Wage and the Unemployment of Black Teenagers

12 Months Prior to and Subsequent to Change in Minimum Wage	Minimum Wage	Percent of Workers Covered	Unemployment Rate	
			All Workers	Black Teenagers
March 1955–Feb. 1956	$0.75	—	4.2	15.8
March 1956–Feb. 1957	1.00	53	4.1	18.1
Sept. 1960–Aug. 1961	1.00	—	6.6	27.4
Sept. 1963–Aug. 1964[a]	1.25	62	5.4	28.4
Feb. 1966–Jan. 1967	1.25	—	3.8	25.1
Feb. 1968–Jan. 1969[a]	1.60	73	3.6	25.4
May 1973–Apr. 1974	1.60	—	4.9	30.3
Jan. 1981–Dec. 1981[a]	3.35	84	7.9	37.8

[a]The minimum wage was increased in stages. The time period is the 12 months following the final increase in the minimum wage called for by the legislation.

Source: U.S. Department of Labor, *Monthly Labor Review* (various issues).

Several bills currently before Congress would provide for a lower minimum wage for teenagers. These proposals would permit employers to pay teenagers wage rates of between 60 percent and 75 percent of the adult minimum wage. Advocates believe this type of legislation would help alleviate an important side effect of the minimum wage—the low availability of training and employment opportunities for youthful, inexperienced workers. The major opposition to this legislation comes from labor organizations. This should not be surprising. Low-skill—often nonunion—labor is a substitute for high-skill, (union) labor; a lower minimum wage would enhance the attractiveness of substitute, nonunion labor. Stated another way, the demand for union workers might not be as strong if low-skilled labor were not priced out of the market by the minimum wage.

LOOKING AHEAD

Payments to resources are of vital importance because individual incomes are determined by (a) resource prices and (b) the amount of resources that one owns. However, the purchasing power of the income received by resource owners is dependent on productivity. There is nothing magical about the growth of real income; it is dependent on the growth of real output. The real output of a nation is strongly influenced by the capital equipment with which people work. The next chapter analyzes the factors that underlie the availability of capital and the investment choices of decision-makers.

APPLICATIONS IN ECONOMICS

Employment Discrimination and the Earnings of Women

Since World War II, there has been a dramatic shift in the household/work force role of women, particularly married women. In 1984, more than half of the *married* women were in the labor force, up from less than one fourth in 1949. As Exhibit 9 shows, in the aggregate the labor force participation rate of women has risen from 37.6 percent in 1960 to 54.7 percent in 1984.

While more women were working, their earnings changed little relative to men. In fact, the female/male earnings ratio for *full-time workers* was approximately 60 percent throughout the 1950–1980 period. As Exhibit 9 shows, the earnings of women have improved relative to men in the 1980s. Nevertheless, women working full-time earned only 64 percent as much as their male counterparts in 1984.

Employment Discrimination and Family Specialization
Why are the earnings of women so low compared to men? Most people

blame employment discrimination. A Presidential Task Force in the 1970s concluded that widespread and pervasive discrimination accounted for the lower earnings of women relative to men. There is substantial evidence supportive of this view. In contrast with minorities relative to whites, the age, education, marital status, language, and regional locational characteristics of men and women are similar. Even after correcting for these factors, the earnings of women are only about two thirds as great as those of men. Occupational data are consistent with the view that women are crowded into a few low-paying jobs. Until recently, more than half of all women were employed in just four occupations—clerical workers, teachers, nurses, and food service workers. High-paying professional, managerial, and craft occupations, particularly occupations where on-the-job experience leads to upward mobility, appear to be reserved primarily for men.

Despite this evidence, the case that employment discrimination is the sole or even the major source of the earnings differential between men and women is less than airtight. First, the size of even the adjusted differential should cause one to pause. If an employer could really hire women who were *willing and able to do the same work as men* for 35 percent less, the profit motive would provide the employer with a strong incentive to do so. Remember, the average business earns a profit of about 5 percent on total sales (or total cost). If an employer could really cut labor cost 35 percent merely by hiring women (primarily) rather than men, surely many less "sexist" employers, perhaps even women employers, would jump at the chance. Of course, as more and more employers substituted women for men workers, the earnings ratio of women to men would move toward parity. This is not what is observed in the real world. There is little evi-

EXHIBIT 9 • The Labor Force Experience of Females, 1960–1985

Between 1960 and 1985, the labor force participation of females rose from 35 to 55 percent. However, the F/M earning ratio fluctuated around 60 percent during the 1960–1980 period, before climbing to 64.2 percent in 1985.

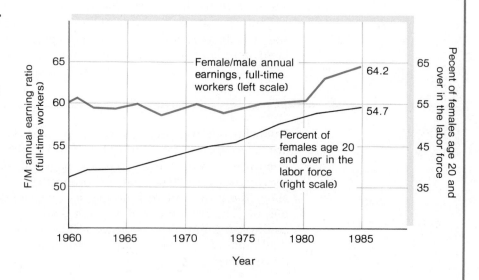

APPLICATIONS IN ECONOMICS (continued)

dence that the 35 percent earnings differential is attracting many profit-seeking employers to substitute women for men in their work force.

Second, it is important to recognize that *married* men and women have different areas of traditional specialization within the family. Married men typically pursue paid employment aggressively because they are expected to be the family's primary breadwinner. Since men envision continuous labor force participation, they are more likely to make a geographic move to improve their earnings and choose jobs for which employment experience leads to higher earnings. Given their traditional responsibility for monetary earnings, men are also more likely to accept jobs

with long hours, uncertain schedules, and out-of-town travel.

In contrast, married women have generally had the primary responsibility for operating the household and caring for children. Given these areas of specialization, many women anticipate intermittent labor force participation. Thus, women seek different sorts of jobs than men. They seek jobs with less travel time, flexible hours, and those that are complementary with household responsibilities. Similarly, women seek jobs that will (a) be available wherever the primary earner (the husband) might locate, and (b) allow them to reenter the labor force with only a small reduction in earning power.[8] Viewed in this light, it is not particularly surprising that women find nursing, teaching, secretarial, and other jobs with easily transportable skills highly attractive.

Is there evidence in support of the view that differing areas of spe-

cialization within the family are an important source of earnings differences according to sex? Since preferences cannot be directly observed, the family specialization theory is difficult to test. However, Exhibit 10 sheds some light on its importance. Here we illustrate the median annual earnings of women relative to men, *according to marital status.* Clearly, married women earn substantially less than married men. Even when working full-time, year-round, married women earn only

[8]For an analysis of how family specialization influences the employment and earnings of women, see Solomon Polachek, "Discontinuous Labor Force Participation and its Effect on Women's Market Earnings," in Cynthia B. Lloyd (ed.)., *Sex Discrimination and the Division of Labor* (New York: Columbia University Press, 1975), and James Gwartney and Richard Stroup, "Measurement of Employment Discrimination According to Sex," *Southern Economic Journal* (April, 1973).

EXHIBIT 10 • Female/ Male Earnings According to Marital Status— 1984

Although the female/male earnings ratio varies considerably according to marital status and time worked, the earnings of single women relative to the earnings of single men are much higher than the earnings of women in other marital status groupings. Source: U.S. Department of Commerce, *Current Population Reports,* Series P-60, no. 143 (Table 9).

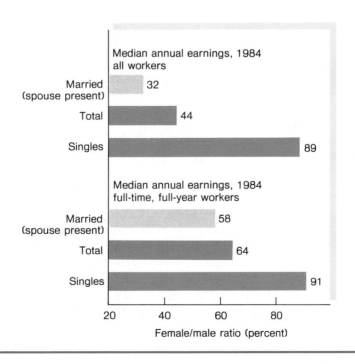

APPLICATIONS IN ECONOMICS (continued)

58 percent as much as men. However, the earnings gap between men and women is substantially less for singles, the group least influenced by actual and potential differences in specialization within the traditional family. In 1984, the female/male annual earning ratio for full-time, full-year workers was 91 per-

cent for singles. Thus, while a huge earning disparity exists between the earnings of married men and married women, the differential is much smaller for singles. This pattern of earnings differences according to marital status implies that, although employment discrimination may well be a contributing factor, family specialization may also be an important determinant of the overall earnings differential between men and women.

The Future

What can we say about the future direction of earnings according to sex? Since women are now participating more fully in the labor force, their work experience is becoming more similar to men. Perhaps anticipating more lengthy (and less interrupted) labor force participation, there has been a rather dramatic change in the educational choices of women. Exhibit 11 illustrates this point. Increasingly, women are preparing for the professions, rather than for the office. For example, women earned 45.4 percent of the accounting degrees in 1982–1983, up from only 10.1 percent during 1970–1971. Similar advances were made in medicine, veterinary medicine, law, architecture, pharmacy, and economics. With the passage of time, this increased concentration on continuous labor force participation and professional skills will push the female/male earnings ratio upward.[9] In all likelihood, the growth of the female/male ratio in the early 1980s (see Exhibit 9) is the beginning of a trend that will continue in the years ahead.

EXHIBIT 11 • Women as a Proportion of Persons Earning Selected Professional Degrees, 1970–1971 and 1982–1983

Field of Study	Women as a Percentage of Persons Earning First Professional Degree in the Field	
	1970–71	1982–83
Accounting	10.1	45.4
Medicine	9.2	26.7
Dentistry	1.2	15.6
Optometry	2.4	22.0
Veterinary Medicine	7.8	40.9
Law	7.3	36.2
Architecture	12.0	34.8
Pharmacy	25.2	49.4
Economics	11.2	33.3
Engineering	0.8	13.3

Source: Commission on Professionals in Science and Technology, *Professional Women and Minority* (Washington, D.C., CPST, 1986).

[9]James P. Smith and Michael P. Ward, *Women's Wages and Work in the Twentieth Century* (Los Angeles: Rand Foundation, 1984).

CHAPTER SUMMARY

1. There are three major sources of wage differentials among individuals: differences in workers, differences in jobs, and degree of labor mobility. Individual workers differ with respect to productivity (skills, human capital, motivation, native ability, and so on), specialized skills, employment preferences, race, and sex. These factors influence either the demand for or the supply of labor. In addition, differences in nonpecuniary job characteristics, changes in product markets, and institutional restrictions that limit labor mobility contribute to variations in wages among workers.

2. Productivity is the ultimate source of high wages. Workers in the United States, Canada, Japan, and other industrial countries earn high wages because their output per hour is high as the result of (a) worker knowledge and skills (human capital) and (b) the use of modern machinery (physical capital).

3. During the last two decades, the size of the U.S. work force has grown rapidly. This rapid growth in the labor force, coupled with a sagging rate of capital formation, has adversely affected the growth rate of worker productivity and real compensation per worker-hour.

4. Approximately 80 percent of national income in the United States is allocated to human capital (labor); 20 percent is allocated to owners of physical (nonhuman) capital.

5. Automated methods of production will be adopted only if they reduce costs. Although automation might reduce revenues and employment in a specific industry, the lower cost of production will increase real income, causing demand in other industries to expand. These secondary effects will cause employment to rise in other industries. Improved technology expands our ability to produce. It is expanded production, not the number of jobs, that contributes to our economic well-being.

6. Both employment discrimination and differences in employability characteristics (the quality and quantity of schooling, skill level, prior job experience, and other human capital factors) contribute to earnings differentials among groups. Economic research indicates that approximately half of the earnings disparity between whites and blacks is due to differences in employability (productivity) characteristics rather than employment discrimination.

7. In the mid-1980s, women working full-time, year-round, earned only about 65 percent as much as men. Some of this differential may emanate from discrimination in the labor market. However, differences between men and women in areas of specialization within the family may also contribute to the earnings differential.

8. Minimum wage legislation increases the earnings of some low-skill workers, but others are forced to accept inferior employment opportunities, join the ranks of the unemployed, or drop out of the labor force completely. Minimum wage legislation reduces the ability of employers to offer (and low-skill employees to find) work with on-the-job training and skill-building experience. Thus, the jobs available to low-skill workers tend to be primarily dead-end jobs. The minimum wage exerts its most adverse affects on the employment and training opportunities of teenagers, particularly minority teenagers.

THE ECONOMIC WAY OF THINKING— **DISCUSSION QUESTIONS**

1. What are the major reasons for the differences in earnings among individuals? Why are wages in some occupations higher than in others? How do wage differentials influence the allocation of resources? How important is this function? Explain.

2. Why are real wages in the United States higher than in other countries? Is the labor force itself responsible for the higher wages of American workers? Explain.

3. What are the major factors that would normally explain earnings differences between (a) a lawyer and a minister, (b) an accountant and an elementary school teacher, (c) a business executive and a social worker, (d) a country lawyer and a Wall Street lawyer, (e) an experienced, skilled craftsperson and a 20-year-old high school dropout, (f) a fire fighter and a night security guard, and (g) an upper-story and a ground-floor window washer?

4. Is employment discrimination the major cause of earnings differences between whites and blacks? Is it the cause of earnings differences between males and females? Carefully justify your answer.

5. **What's Wrong with This Way of Thinking?**

   "Higher wages help everybody. Workers are helped because they can now purchase more of the things they need. Business is helped because the increase in the workers' purchasing power will increase the demand for products. Taxpayers are helped because workers will now pay more taxes. Union activities and legislation increasing the wages of workers will promote economic progress."

6. **What's Wrong with This Way of Thinking?**

   "Jobs are the key to economic progress. Unless we can figure out how to produce more jobs, economic progress will be stifled."

- Why are people willing to pay interest to obtain loanable funds? How does the interest rate bring the choices of borrowers and lenders into harmony?

- How does inflation influence the interest rate? What are the three components of the money interest rate?

- How does an investor decide if an investment project is profitable?

- What are the sources of economic profit? How does expected profitability influence investment decisions?

- What role do interest and profit play in the allocation of resources?

A greater result is obtained by producing goods in round-about ways than by producing them directly. . . . That round-about methods lead to greater results than direct methods is one of the most important and fundamental propositions in the whole theory of production. [1]

EUGEN VON BOHM-BAWERK

24 CAPITAL, INTEREST AND PROFIT

Roundabout Method of Production: The use of productive effort to make tools and other capital assets, which are then used to produce the desired consumer good.

Consumption is the objective of all production. We undertake the production of goods because we wish either to consume the good directly or use the service the good provides. All goods and services are produced by changing the form, condition, or location of raw materials through the application of human energy (human capital) and tools (physical capital).

As the Austrian economist Eugen von Bohm-Bawerk pointed out in 1884, physical capital can magnify the productivity of human beings. We can often produce a larger amount of a product with the same quantity of labor (or the same amount of a product with a lesser quantity of labor) if we first apply human energy and ingenuity to the construction of tools, machines, and even factories, and later use these constructed capital resources to produce the desired product. Economists refer to this procedure as a **roundabout method of production.**

Through the ages, human beings have expanded both their use of tools (physical capital) and their use of knowledge about how tools can be developed and applied. This combination—more (and better) tools and the development of superior methods of production—has made it possible for us to attain the standard of living we enjoy today.

In order to use tools and innovative methods of production to expand total production in the future, we are required to make current sacrifices. Generally speaking, we must divert resources from the production of current consumption goods to expand the availability of capital goods and knowledge in the future. Roundabout production methods thus require the sacrifice of current consumption. Economic efficiency requires that these costs be balanced against future expected benefits. This chapter focuses on how a market economy directs the physical and human capital investment decisions of individuals.

THE INTEREST RATE

Interest is the additional amount a person is willing to pay to obtain a good or resource now rather than later. People generally acquire goods earlier by borrowing from a third party and making an immediate payment, rather than by simply paying the seller a larger amount at a designated date in the future. Because of this, the interest rate is often defined as the price of loanable funds. This definition is entirely proper. We should keep in mind, however, that it is the earlier availability of goods and services that can be purchased with money, not the money itself, that is desired. Willingness to pay an interest premium for loanable funds is evidence of one's desire (preference) for earlier availability.

Interest would exist even in a nonmonetary economy. Consider the economic life of a primitive economy. Suppose Robinson Crusoe wanted to obtain additional breadfruit now. If the price of breadfruit were 2 fish, Crusoe could obtain 5 breadfruit now in exchange for 10 fish. Alternatively,

---

[1]Eugen von Bohm-Bawerk, "A Capitalist Production," in *The Capitalist Reader,* ed. Lawrence S. Stepelevich (New Rochelle, New York: Arlington House, 1977), pp. 26–27.

suppose some natives from another island would be willing to supply Crusoe the 5 breadfruit now in exchange for some amount of fish (let's say 11 fish) to be supplied one year from now. In effect, Crusoe would be paying 11 fish one year from now, rather than 10 fish now, to obtain the 5 breadfruit. Implicitly, he would be paying interest at a rate of 10 percent, since the breadfruit seller would not require him to pay the price (10 fish) now if he were willing to pay the price plus a 10 percent premium one year from now.

LOANABLE FUNDS: DEMAND AND SUPPLY

Positive Rate of Time Preference: The desire of consumers for goods now rather than in the future.

The demand of consumers and investors alike forms the basis of the market demand for loanable funds. Consumers demand loanable funds because they prefer earlier availability of goods. On average, individuals possess a **positive rate of time preference.** By this we mean that people subjectively value goods obtained in the immediate or near future (including the present) more highly than goods obtained in the distant future. Most people would rather have a new automobile now rather than the same automobile ten years from now.

There may be some exceptions. For example, a person with a large quantity of a perishable good, bananas, for example, might be willing to exchange 100 bananas now for fewer bananas in the future. In a modern economy, though, perishable goods can be exchanged for money, a nonperishable commodity.[2]

There is nothing irrational or even shortsighted about a positive rate of time preference. Given the uncertainties of the world in which we live, it is perfectly reasonable to prefer the reality of current consumption to the uncertainty of some larger amount (in physical or monetary terms) of future consumption. As the saying goes, "A bird in the hand is worth two in the bush." Of course, the premium that one must pay for earlier availability—the interest rate—will influence the relative amounts of current and future consumption.

Investors demand loanable funds so that they can invest in capital goods and finance roundabout methods of production that are potentially productive. Since roundabout methods of production often make it possible to produce a larger output at a lower cost, decision-makers can gain even if they have to pay an interest premium to purchase the machines, buildings, and other resources required by the production process.

Perhaps a simple example will clarify the link between the demand for loanable funds and the productivity of capital. Robinson Crusoe could pursue his fishing occupation by either (a) combining his labor with natural resources (direct production) or (b) constructing a net and eventually combining his labor with this tool (a roundabout method of production). Let us assume that Crusoe could catch 2 fish per day by hand fishing, but could catch 3 fish per day if he constructed and used a net that would last for 360 days. Suppose it would take Crusoe 5 days to build the net. The opportunity cost of constructing the net would be 10 fish (2 per day for each of the 5 days

---

[2]Of course, inflation may cause the purchasing power of money to diminish. The impact of inflation on the interest rate is discussed later in this chapter.

Crusoe spent building the net). If Crusoe used the roundabout method of production, his output during the next year (including the 5 days required to build the net) would be 1,080 fish (3 per day for 360 days). Alternatively, hand fishing during the year would lead to an output of only 730 (2 fish per day for 365 days). The capital-intensive, indirect method of production would be highly productive. Total output during the year would be expanded by 350 fish if the roundabout method of production were used.

Crusoe's fish production, though, would decline during the time he was constructing the net. Crusoe might be on the verge of starvation. Suppose a fishing crew from a neighboring island visited Crusoe and offered to lend him 10 fish so that he could undertake the capital investment project (building the net). Crusoe could gain. If Crusoe could borrow the 10 fish (the principal) in exchange for, say, 20 fish (a 100 percent interest rate) a year later, the investment project would be highly profitable.

Crusoe's—or the investor's—demand for loanable fish (or funds) stems from the productivity of the capital investment. Since construction of the net enables Crusoe to expand his total output during the year, he is willing to pay an interest premium for current availability. Crusoe's willingness to pay an interest premium for earlier availability stems directly from the productivity of capital.

An increase in the interest rate is, in essence, an increase in the cost of earlier availability. As Exhibit 1 illustrates, consumers and investors alike will curtail their borrowing in response to this increase in costs (higher interest rates). Some consumers will reduce their current consumption rather than pay the higher premium for earlier availability of consumer goods. In addition, some investment projects that would lead to gain at a lower interest rate will not be profitable at higher rates. Therefore, the amount of funds demanded is inversely related to the interest rate.

Even though higher interest rates cause the amount of borrowing to decline, they encourage lenders to provide a larger supply of funds to the market. Even individuals with a positive rate of time preference will give up current consumption to supply funds to the loanable funds market if the price is right—that is, if the interest rate is attractive. While people generally prefer earlier consumption, they also prefer more goods to fewer goods.

EXHIBIT 1 • The Determination of the Interest Rate

The demand for loanable funds stems from the consumer's desire for earlier availability and the productivity of capital. As the interest rate rises, current goods become more expensive in comparison with future goods. Therefore, borrowers will reduce the amount of loanable funds demanded. On the other hand, higher interest rates will stimulate lenders to supply additional funds to the market.

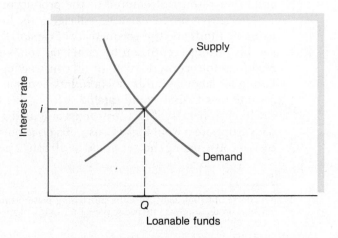

A rise in the interest rate increases the quantity of future goods available to persons willing to sacrifice current consumption. This increase in the quantity of future goods that can be obtained for each dollar supplied to the loanable funds market will result in a supply curve that slopes upward to the right.

The interest rate brings the plans of borrowers into harmony with the plans of lenders. In equilibrium, the quantity of funds demanded by borrowers is equal to the amount supplied by lenders, as Exhibit 1 shows.

MONEY RATE OF INTEREST AND REAL RATE OF INTEREST

Money Rate of Interest: The rate of interest in monetary terms that borrowers pay for borrowed funds. During periods when borrowers and lenders expect inflation, the money rate of interest exceeds the real rate of interest.

Real Rate of Interest: The money rate of interest minus the expected rate of inflation. The real rate of interest indicates the interest premium, in terms of real goods and services, that one must pay for earlier availability.

We have emphasized that the interest rate is a premium borrowers are willing to pay for earlier availability. During periods of inflation, the **money rate of interest,** determined by the forces of supply and demand in the loanable funds market, may be a misleading indicator of how much borrowers give up to obtain earlier availability. Suppose the money rate of interest is 10 percent at a time when prices are rising at an annual rate of 5 percent. A person borrowing $100 will have to pay back $110 one year later. During that year, however, the level of prices will have increased by 5 percent. The $110 paid to the lender one year later will not buy 10 percent more goods. Instead, it will buy only 5 percent more goods than the $100 provided to the borrower one year earlier. Therefore, when the rate of inflation is taken into account, the **real rate of interest** is only 5 percent.

Once decision-makers anticipate rising prices, the money rate of interest will include an inflationary premium compensating lenders for the expected decline in the purchasing power of their principal and interest over the duration of the loan. The real rate of interest is equal to the money rate of interest minus the premium for the expected rate of inflation.

Recognizing the decline in the purchasing power of the dollars with which they will be repaid, lenders will reduce the amount of money supplied to the loanable funds market unless they are compensated for the anticipated rate of inflation. Simultaneously, once borrowers become fully aware that they will be paying back their loans with dollars of less purchasing power, they will be willing to pay the inflationary premium as well as the real rate of interest. If borrowers and lenders fully anticipate a 5 percent rate of inflation, for example, they will be just as willing to agree on a 10 percent interest rate as they were to agree on a 5 percent interest rate when both anticipated stable prices. Under inflationary conditions, the money rate of interest will therefore incorporate an inflationary premium reflecting the expected future increase in prices. An increase in the expected rate of inflation in the future will cause money interest rates to rise. It should not be surprising, then, that higher money interest rates are often associated with high rates of inflation. The U.S. experience during the 1970s illustrates the point. Money interest rates soared to historical highs as double-digit inflation rates were observed during the period.

THE MULTIPLICITY OF INTEREST RATES

So far, we have proceeded as though there is a single interest rate. In the real world, of course, there are many interest rates. There is a mortgage rate, a prime interest rate (the rate charged to business firms with strong credit ratings), a consumer loan rate, and a credit card rate, to name only a few. These interest rates generally differ.

The interest rate on a given loan is influenced by (a) the cost of processing, (b) the risk associated with the borrower, and (c) the duration of the loan. The accounting costs associated with a loan of several hundred thousand dollars may actually be smaller than those for a consumer loan of a few hundred dollars, if, for example, the large loan is repaid in a lump sum at a designated time in the future and the small loan is repaid monthly. Since the bookkeeping costs per dollar loaned are generally higher for small loans, interest rates will be higher for such loans.

The interest rate on a loan is also influenced by the credit standing of the borrower and the risk associated with lending to that borrower. Banks are likely to charge an unemployed worker a higher interest rate than they charge General Motors. Since the probability of default is considerably greater for the unemployed worker than for General Motors, the former will have to pay a risk premium, which will be incorporated into the interest rate of the loan. Similarly, the interest rate on a "secured loan," such as a mortgage on a house, will be less than that on a unsecured loan, such as a credit card purchase.

The degree of risk involved in a loan also varies with the loan's duration. Lenders usually require higher interest rates for longer-term loans since they involve greater risk. The longer the time period, the more likely that the financial standing of the borrower will deteriorate substantially or that market conditions will change dramatically. Also, unless rates are believed to be unusually high, borrowers are willing to pay a premium to keep the funds for a longer period of time. Thus, long-term loans usually carry a premium that compensates for the additional uncertainties and additional benefits of the longer time period.

THE COMPONENTS OF AN INTEREST RATE—A SHORT SUMMARY

As Exhibit 2 illustrates, the money rate of interest on a loan has three components. The pure interest component is the market price one must pay for earlier availability. The inflationary premium component reflects the expectation that the loan will be repaid with dollars of less purchasing power as the result of inflation. The third component—the risk premium—reflects the risk imposed on the lender by the possibility the borrower may be unable to repay the loan. The risk premium, therefore, is directly related to the probability of default by the borrower.

EXHIBIT 2 • Three Components of the Money Interest

The money interest rate reflects the following three components: (a) pure interest, (b) inflationary premium, and (c) risk premium. When decision-makers expect a high rate of inflation during the period the loan is outstanding, the inflationary premium will be substantial. Similarly, the risk premium will be large when probability of default by the borrower is substantial.

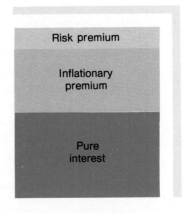

Risk premium

Inflationary premium

Pure interest

THE VALUE OF FUTURE INCOME

Suppose one year from now, you will have $100 in receipts. How much would that $100 be worth today? Clearly, it would be worth less than $100. If you deposited $100 today in a savings account earning 6 percent interest, you would have $106 one year from now. The interest rate connects the value of dollars (and capital assets) today with the value of dollars (an expected streams of receipts) in the future. The interest rate is used to discount the value of a dollar in the future so that its present worth can be determined today.

Net Present Value: The current worth of future income after it is discounted to reflect the fact that revenues in the future are valued less highly than revenues now.

The **net present value** (NPV) of a payment received one year from now can be expressed as follows:

$$NPV = \frac{\text{receipts one year from now}}{1 + \text{interest rate}}$$

If the interest rate is 6 percent, the current value of the $100 to be received one year from now is:

$$NPV = \frac{\$100}{1.06} = \$94.34$$

If one invested $94.34 in a savings account yielding 6 percent interest, the account would be valued at $100 one year from now.

Discounting: The procedure used to calculate the present value of future income. The present value of future income is inversely related to both the interest rate and the amount of time that passes before the funds are received.

Economists use the term **discounting** to describe this procedure of reducing the value of a dollar to be received in the future to its present worth. Clearly, the value of a dollar in the future is inversely related to the interest rate. For example, if the interest rate were 10 percent, the net present value of $100 received one year from now would be only $90.91 ($100 divided by 1.10).

The net present value of $100 received two years from now is:

$$NPV = \frac{\$100}{(1 + \text{interest rate})^2}$$

If the interest rate were 6 percent, $100 received two years from now would be equal to $89 today ($100 divided by 1.06^2). In other words, $89 invested today would yield $100 two years from now.

The net present value procedure can be used to determine the current value of any future income stream. If R represents receipts received at the end of the year and i represents the interest rate, the net present value of the future income stream[3] is:

$$NPV = \frac{R_1}{(1 + i)} + \frac{R_2}{(1 + i)^2} + \cdots + \frac{R_n}{(1 + i)^n}$$

Exhibit 3 shows the net present value of $100 received at various times in the future at several different discount rates. The chart clearly illustrates two points. First, the present value of the $100 received one year from now, when discounted at a 4 percent interest rate, is $96.15, compared to $98.04

---

[3]For a specific annual income stream in perpetuity, the net present value is equal simply to R/i, where R is the annual revenue stream and i the interest rate. For example, if the interest rate is 10 percent, the NPV of a $100 income stream in perpetuity is equal to $100/.10, or $1,000.

EXHIBIT 3   •   The Net Present Value of $100 to be Received in the Future

The columns indicate the net present value of $100 to be received a designated number of years in the future for alternative interest rates. For example, at a discount rate of 2 percent, the net present value of $100 to be received five years from now is $90.57. Note that the net present value of the $100 declines as either the interest rate or the number of years in the future increases.

Net Present Value of $100 to Be Received a Designated Number of Years in the Future for Alternative Interest Rates

Years in the Future	2 Percent	4 Percent	6 Percent	8 Percent	12 Percent	20 Percent
1	98.04	96.15	94.34	92.59	89.29	83.33
2	96.12	92.46	89.00	85.73	79.72	69.44
3	94.23	88.90	83.96	79.38	71.18	57.87
4	92.39	85.48	79.21	73.50	63.55	48.23
5	90.57	82.19	74.73	68.06	56.74	40.19
6	88.80	79.03	70.50	63.02	50.66	33.49
7	87.06	75.99	66.51	58.35	45.23	27.08
8	85.35	73.07	62.74	54.03	40.39	23.26
9	83.68	70.26	59.19	50.02	36.06	19.38
10	82.03	67.56	55.84	46.32	32.20	16.15
15	74.30	55.53	41.73	31.52	18.27	6.49
20	67.30	45.64	31.18	21.45	10.37	2.61
30	55.21	30.83	17.41	9.94	3.34	0.42
50	37.15	14.07	5.43	2.13	0.35	0.01

when a 2 percent discount rate is applied. Second, the present value of the $100 declines as the date of its receipt is set farther into the future. If the applicable discount rate is 6 percent, the present value of $100 received one year from now is $94.34, compared to $89 if the $100 is received two years from now. If the $100 is received five years from now, its current worth is only $74.43. So, the present value of a future dollar payment is inversely related to both the interest rate and how far in the future the payment will be received.

MAKING INVESTMENT DECISIONS

Since investment projects (roundabout methods of production) involve a current sacrifice to generate a flow of output (and revenue) in the future, the discounting procedure is particularly important for investors. The value of net receipts derived from an investment project over the years can be estimated and receipts discounted to determine their current worth. This determination of the net present value of the project provides the decision-maker with an estimate of how much the project is worth now.

A worthwhile investment project must be expected to yield a rate of return equal to or greater than the opportunity cost of loanable funds. The investment discount rate, the rate at which the firm can borrow and lend funds, represents the opportunity cost of funds to the firm. If the current estimated worth (present value) of the project exceeds its cost, it would make sense to undertake the project. On the other hand, if the cost of the project exceeds the discounted value of the future net receipts, a profit-seeking firm should reject the prospective project.

Let us consider an example. Suppose a truck rental firm is contemplating the purchase of a new $40,000 truck. Past experience indicates that after the operational and maintenance expenses have been covered, the firm can rent the truck for $12,000 per year (received at the end of each year) for the next four years, the expected life of the vehicle.[4] Since the firm can borrow and lend funds at an interest rate of 8 percent, we will discount the future expected income at an 8 percent rate. Exhibit 4 illustrates the calculation. Column 4 shows how much $12,000 available at year-end for each of the next four years is worth today. In total, the net present value of the expected rental receipts is $39,744—less than the purchase price of the truck. The project should therefore not be undertaken.

The decision to accept or reject a prospective project is highly sensitive to the discount rate. If the discount rate in our example had been 6 percent, reflecting lower interest rates, the net present value of the future rental income would have been $41,580.[5] Since it pays to purchase a capital good whenever the net present value of the income generated exceeds the purchase price of the capital good, the project would have been profitable at the lower interest rate.

After allowance is made for risk factors, the competitive process tends to equalize the net present value of a machine (or some other capital investment project) and the purchase price of the machine (or the cost of the

EXHIBIT 4 • The Discounted Present Value of $12,000 of Truck Rental for Four Years

Year (1)	Expected Future Income (Received at Year-End) (2)	Discounted Value (8 Percent Rate) (3)	Present Value of Income (4)
1	$12,000	0.926	$11,112
2	12,000	0.857	10,284
3	12,000	0.794	9,528
4	12,000	0.735	8,820
			$39,744

[4]For the sake of simplicity, we assume that the truck has no scrap value at the end of four years.
[5]The derivation of this figure is shown in the following tabulation:

Year	Expected Future Income (dollars)	Discounted Value per Dollar (6% rate)	Present Value of Income (dollars)
1	12,000	0.943	11,316
2	12,000	0.890	10,680
3	12,000	0.840	10,080
4	12,000	0.792	9,504
			41,580

investment project). If the net present value of an investment project exceeds its current cost, the investor will make a profit. As more and more business decision-makers learn about the attractive opportunities for profit, they will enter the market as competitors. The entry of new competitors generally results in an increase in the price of the investment project and/or a reduction in the price of the service it provides. As we discussed previously, this process tends to erode the economic profit and equalize the net present value of the expected future revenues and the current price (or cost) of the investment.

INVESTING IN HUMAN CAPITAL

In earlier chapters, we discussed the concept of human capital. A decision to invest in human capital—to continue in school, for example—involves all the ingredients of other investment decisions. Since the returns and some of the costs normally accrue in the future, the discounting procedure helps one to assess the present value of expected costs and revenues associated with a human capital investment.

Exhibit 5 illustrates the potential human capital decision confronting Susan, an 18-year-old high school graduate contemplating the pursuit of a bachelor's degree in business administration. Just as the investment in the truck involves a cost in order to generate a future income, so too, does a degree in business administration. If Susan does not go to college, she will be able to begin work immediately at an annual earnings of E_1. Alternatively, if she goes to college, she will incur direct costs (C_d) in the form of tuition, books, transportation, and related expenses. She will also bear the opportunity cost (C_o) of lower earnings while in college. However, the study of business will expand Susan's knowledge and skills, and thereby enable her to earn a higher future income (E_2 rather than E_1). Will the higher future income be worth the cost? To answer this question, Susan must discount each year's additional income stemming from completion of the business degree and compare that with the discounted value of the cost, including the opportunity cost of earnings lost during the period of study.

EXHIBIT 5 • Investing in Human Capital

Here we illustrate the human capital investment decision confronting Susan, an 18-year-old who just finished high school. If Susan goes to college in business administration, she will incur the direct cost (C_d) of the college education (tuition, books, transportation, and so on) plus the opportunity cost (C_o) of earnings forgone while in college. However, with a business degree, she can expect higher future earnings (B) during her career. If the discounted present value of the additional future earnings exceeds the discounted *value* of the direct and indirect cost of a college education, the business degree will be a profitable investment for Susan.

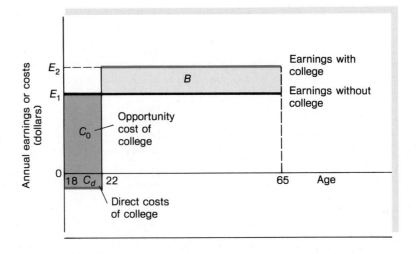

If the discounted value of the additional future income exceeds the discounted value of the cost, acquiring the degree is a worthwhile human capital investment.

Of course, nonmonetary considerations may also be important, particularly for human capital investment decisions, since human capital is embodied in the individual. For example, Susan's preferences might be such that she would really prefer working as a college graduate in the business world (rather than in the jobs available to high school graduates) even if she did not make more money. Thus, the nonpecuniary attractiveness of business may induce her to pursue the business degree even if the monetary rate of return is low (or even negative).

Even though human capital investments can be analyzed in the same terms as any other investment, the analysis is likely to be less precise, since it is difficult to isolate the nonmonetary aspects of these decisions. However, the same methods—the discounting procedures and the comparison of the present value of future revenues (or benefits) with costs—can apply to both human and physical capital investment decisions.

ECONOMIC PROFIT AND INVESTMENT

Why do individuals purchase long-lasting capital assets? Why do they invest in education, training, and other forms of human capital? They do so because they expect to profit—to do better than if they simply invested the funds at the market rate of interest.

Economic profit is a return to investment in excess of the opportunity cost of loanable funds. There are three basic sources of economic profit: (a) uncertainty, (b) entrepreneurial alertness, and (c) monopoly.

Economic Profit: A return to investors that exceeds the opportunity cost of financial capital.

PROFIT AND UNCERTAINTY

In a world of perfect knowledge and communication and no uncertainty, profits (and losses) would be completely absent. The real world, though, is one of change, disequilibrium markets, uncertainty, and imperfect knowledge. No one can predict the future with certainty. Unanticipated shifts in market prices or costs can cause the rate of return derived by investors to rise or fall. Investments (ownership of physical and human capital) expose one to additional uncertainty. In a sense, investing resembles a game of chance. Unanticipated changes, changes that no one could have foreseen, create winners and losers. If people did not care whether their income experienced substantial variability or not, the uncertainty accompanying investment projects would not affect the average rate of return. Most people, though, dislike uncertainty. They prefer the certain receipt of $1,000 to a 50-50 chance of receiving either nothing or $2,000. Therefore, people must be paid a premium if they are going to willingly accept the uncertainty that necessarily accompanies investments. This premium is a source of economic profit.

PROFIT AND ENTREPRENEURSHIP

While the world is characterized by uncertainty, some individuals are better than others at identifying potentially profitable opportunities. At any given time, there is virtually an infinite number of potential investment projects. Some will increase the value of resources and therefore lead to a handsome rate of return on capital. Others will reduce the value of resources, generating economic losses.

Alertness to potential opportunities to combine resources in a manner that increases their value is a source of economic profit. Economists refer to this source of profit as a return to entrepreneurship.

This component of profit reflects the ability of astute entrepreneurs to recognize and undertake economically beneficial projects that have gone unnoticed by others. Discovery of a lower-cost method of production, introduction of a new product highly valued relative to cost, development of an improved marketing technique, or the correct anticipation of a future market change provide examples of entrepreneurial behavior that markets reward with economic profit. Originality, quickness to act, and imagination are important aspects of entrepreneurship. Successful entrepreneurship involves leadership; most profits will be gone by the time the imitators arrive on the scene.

The great Harvard economist Joseph Schumpeter believed that entrepreneurship and innovative behavior were the moving forces behind capitalism. According to Schumpeter, this entrepreneurial discovery of new, improved ways of doing things led to a nation's continual improvement in its standard of living:

> The fundamental impulse that sets the capitalist engine in motion comes from the new consumer's goods, the new methods of production or transportation, and new markets, and the new forms of industrial organization that capitalist enterprise creates.[6]

Of course, entrepreneurial decision-making is always conducted in an atmosphere of uncertainty. It is important to be first and to be innovative, but it is also important to be correct. Frequently, the entrepreneur's vision turns out to have been a mirage. What appeared to be a profitable opportunity often turns out to have been an expensive illusion.

Entrepreneurship, like other resources, is scarce. Just as people differ with regard to other skills, so, too, do they possess differing amounts of entrepreneurial ability. Potential entrepreneurs are confined to using their own wealth and that of co-venturers, in addition to whatever can be borrowed. Entrepreneurs with a past record of success will be able to attract funds more readily for investment projects. Therefore, in a market economy, previously successful entrepreneurs will exert a disproportionate influence over decisions as to which projects will be undertaken and which will not.

MONOPOLY PROFIT

As we discussed in previous chapters, profits may also originate from sole ownership of a key resource (as in the diamond industry), government regulation (as in the taxicab market of many cities), or a legally granted property right to a technical innovation (as for patented products). In such cases, the monopoly rights to the key resource, privileged license, or patent

---

[6]Joseph A. Schumpeter, *Capitalism, Socialism, and Democracy* (New York: Harper Torchbooks, 1950), p. 83.

OUTSTANDING ECONOMIST

**Joseph Schumpeter
(1883–1950)**

Born in Austria, Schumpeter began his career practicing law, but soon turned to the teaching of economics. After a brief term (1919–1920) as the Austrian Minister of Finance, he taught economics during the 1920s at several European universities and was a visiting professor at Harvard University in 1927–1928 and again in 1930. In 1932, he emigrated to the United States, accepting a professorship at Harvard.

Although Schumpeter was widely respected for his scholarly achievements, he was a maverick among economists. He rejected the view that pure competition was the proper standard by which to judge the economic efficiency of markets. At a time when mathematical economics was asserting itself, he had little use for analysis that reduced economic decision-making to a set of mathematical equations. During the "Age of Keynes," Schumpeter was an unabashed non-Keynesian.

A former president of the American Economic Association (1949), Schumpeter is perhaps best known for his views on entrepreneurship and the future of capitalism. He believed that the progressive improvement in the economic well-being of the masses was the result of the creative and innovative behavior of business entrepreneurs. Schumpeter believed that in the early stages of its development, capitalism provided an almost ideal environment for the innovator. Entrepreneurs willing to risk their livelihood to pursue an innovative idea could be counted on to provide a steady stream of improved products at a reduced cost. Profits would accrue to those who successfully instituted innovative ideas. Losses would eliminate the less capable.

These forces would generate widespread prosperity. As Schumpeter put it:

> Queen Elizabeth owned silk stockings. The capitalist achievement does not typically consist in providing more silk stockings for queens but in bringing them within the reach of factory girls in return for steadily decreasing amounts of effort.[7]

Despite his admiration for a dynamic capitalist system, Schumpeter thought that the system would generate the seeds of its own destruction. Unlike Marx, who argued that capitalism would break down under the weight of its own failures, Schumpeter thought that the success of capitalism would eventually "undermine the social institutions which protect it."[8] He believed that the growth of large, technologically efficient organizations would dampen innovative zeal. The daring entrepreneur would be replaced by the organization person, the committee, and the board of directors.

In addition, the affluence produced by a capitalist system would generate the wealth necessary to support a large intellectual class, which would neither understand nor appreciate the system. It would also breed a generation of flabby business leaders incapable of defending the system against its intellectual critics, who would turn the masses toward socialism. Is Schumpeter's indictment of capitalism correct? Only the future will tell.

---

[7]Schumpeter, *Capitalism, Socialism, and Democracy*, p. 67.

[8]Ibid., p. 61.

"My ambition is to get so good at growing things that the government will pay me not to."

GRIN AND BEAR IT BY FRED WAGNER © BY AND PERMISSION OF NEWS AMERICA SYNDICATE.

are worth the present value of the future return that is in excess of what could be earned in competitive markets. In contrast with the transitory profits earned in markets with low entry restraints, monopoly profit may persist over a lengthy time period. What does economics say about monopoly profit? Two factors must be considered. First, as we pointed out previously, monopolists can gain from a "contrived" scarcity. They may choose to supply less of a product so that the price can be raised and profits increased. They may well forgo the production of units even though their marginal cost is less than the product price. If one considers only the static economic effects, allocative inefficiency will result.

Second, monopoly profit does not exist in a vacuum. In a dynamic economy, potential monopoly profit will induce competitors to follow pathways that lead to monopoly profit. If dynamic efficiency indicates that the investment resulting in monopoly profit is actually beneficial, this advantage must be weighed against the static allocative inefficiency. The protection of property rights to inventions, new products, and innovative production techniques falls in this category—economic activities of this variety, though they result in monopoly profits, can clearly lead to improvements in economic welfare. To encourage innovative activities, most countries have established a patent system, even though a temporary grant of monopoly power results.

Regardless of their source, the present value of future monopoly profits is incorporated into the value of the assets that provide the "monopoly rights." Licenses that protect their owners from competitors command high prices if they guarantee an above-market rate of return. Similarly, the market value of patent rights and specialized resources incorporates the present value of any future monopoly profits these assets might bestow on their owners. Once the monopoly profits are recognized by others, the market value of the monopoly-granting asset will rise until the monopoly profits have been eliminated.

INTEREST, PROFIT, AND RESOURCE ALLOCATION

Both interest and profit perform important allocation functions.[8] Interest induces people to forgo current consumption, a sacrifice that is a necessary ingredient for capital formation. Economic profit provides both human and physical capital decision-makers with the incentive to (a) undertake investments yielding an uncertain return and (b) discover and develop beneficial and productive investment opportunities.

Although nonmonetary factors are more important in human capital decision-making, opportunity cost and the pursuit of profit guide human capital investors just as they guide physical capital investors. As with choosing to purchase a new machine, choosing a human capital investment project (obtaining a law degree, for example) involves cost, the possibility of profit, and uncertainty. In both instances, the expected return will influence the investor. Giving due consideration to nonmonetary factors, physical and human capital investors alike seek to undertake only those projects they anticipate will yield benefits in excess of costs. To the extent they are correct, their actions will increase the value of resources—that is, they will create wealth.

LOOKING AHEAD

The agricultural price support program illustrates the importance of many of the concepts incorporated into this chapter. The competitive process and the normal rate of return, the relationship between the expected future income and the present value of an asset, and capitalization of the future value of monopoly profit—these concepts will help us understand the impact of agricultural price supports. We conclude this chapter with an analysis of this issue.

---

[8]In addition to wages, interest, and profits, economists often discuss "rent" as a return to a factor of production. Economists define rent as a return to a factor the supply of which is perfectly inelastic. We have not included this discussion for two reasons. First, one can legitimately argue that the supply of all factors of production has some elasticity. After all, even the supply of usable land can be expanded through drainage, clearing, and conservation. Therefore, rent is always a matter of degree. Second, the term "rent" is used in a variety of ways, even by economists. The macroeconomic usage differs substantially from the usage in microeconomics. The term is sometimes used to define the returns to a specialized resource, such as an actor's talent, even though training plays an integral part in the supply of the resource. Rent is also sometimes applied to a factor the supply of which is temporarily fixed, even though it can clearly be expanded in the future. Since the returns to capital can be adequately discussed without introducing rent, we concluded that the cost of the ambiguity of the term exceeded the benefits of an extended discussion.

APPLICATIONS IN ECONOMICS

"Can Agricultural Price Supports Make Farming More Profitable?"

Price Support Programs:
Legislative action establishing a minimum price for an agricultural product. The government pledges to purchase any surplus of the product that cannot be sold to consumers at the support price.

Acreage Restriction Program: A program designed to raise the price of an agricultural product by limiting the acreage planted with the product.

Since the 1930s, the government has instituted various types of **price support programs** for agricultural products. Price supports are designed to increase the prices of crops such as wheat, cotton, tobacco, peanuts, rice, and feed grains and thereby increase farmers' incomes. However, there is good reason to question the programs' effectiveness.

Using wheat as an example, Exhibit 6 illustrates the nature of the early price support programs. These programs established a price floor (support) for wheat above the market equilibrium level and pledged that any wheat that could not be sold at the support price would be purchased by the government. Of course, the above-equilibrium price led to an excess supply of wheat. As Exhibit 6a illustrates, the excess supply was initially relatively small (A_1B_1), since both the demand for and the supply of wheat were highly inelastic in the short-run. With the passage of time, however, both the demand and supply curves became more elastic. Given sufficient time to adjust,

farmers both cultivated wheat land more intensively and increased the amount of land allotted to wheat. Therefore, the excess supply the government had pledged to purchase continued to increase. (Compare the size of the excess supply of Exhibit 6b and 6a.)

The costs of storing the excess supply expanded rapidly. In fact, during the 1950s, these storage costs became a national scandal. The public outcry over the huge costs, economic waste, spoilage, and fraud eventually led to an alteration of the program.

In an effort to maintain a policy of support for farmers without creating surplus crops and the attendant problems, Congress adopted an **acreage restriction program** designed to reduce the output of agricultural products. Under this plan, price is still fixed above the market equilibrium, but the number of acres that farmers can plant is reduced to decrease supply and bring it into balance with demand at the above-equilibrium support price. Each farm is granted an acreage allotment of wheat (and other sup-

EXHIBIT 6 • Impact of Agricultural Price Supports

When a price support program pushes the price of an agricultural product, such as wheat, above the market equilibrium, an excess supply of the product results. Initially, the excess supply may be small $(A_1B_1$ of frame (a)). However, as farmers adjust their planting and cultivation, the long-run supply of wheat becomes increasingly elastic, causing the excess supply to expand (to A_2B_2, frame (b)).

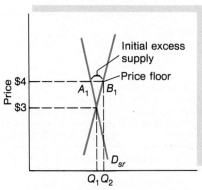

Bushels of wheat per year

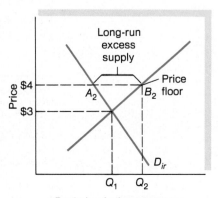

Bushels of wheat per year

APPLICATIONS IN ECONOMICS (continued)

ported products), based on the acres planted during a base year. The allotments are attached to the farm. Owners of farms are prohibited from planting more than the specified number of acres for each product.

Exhibit 7 illustrates the economics of the acreage restriction program. By restricting the number of acres planted, the supply of the product is reduced until the price of the product rises to the support level. If the government has to purchase the product at the support price, it can reduce the acreage allotments of farmers during the next period. In contrast, if the market price rises above the support level, the government can relax the allotment a little during the next period. In this manner, the government is able to bring the amount demanded and amount supplied into balance at the supported price level (for example, as Exhibit 7 illustrates, at the $4 price floor for wheat).

The acreage restrictions make

it more costly to grow any given amount of a product. Normally, farmers would minimize their cost of growing more wheat (or any other product) by using a little more of each of the factors of production (land, labor, fertilizer, machinery, and so on). The acreage restriction program prohibits them from using more land. The support price provides farmers with an incentive to produce more wheat, for example, but they must do so by using factors of production other than land more intensively. Higher costs result, shifting the supply curve of Exhibit 7 to the left (to S_2). Supply curve S_1 is unattainable once the acreage restrictions are imposed, since it would require a larger amount of land than is permissible under the allotment program.

Is farming more profitable in the long-run after the imposition of the acreage restrictions and price support programs? Surprisingly, the answer is no. To the extent that price supports make farming more profitable in the short-run, the demand for land with acreage allotments increases (see Exhibit 8). Competition bids up the price of land with acreage allotments until

the investors receive only the normal rate of return. Just as one cannot earn an abnormally high rate of return by purchasing stock ownership rights of a firm already earning monopoly profit, neither can a farmer earn an abnormally high rate of return by purchasing the ownership rights of farms with acreage allotments.

Suppose the price support program permitted wheat growers to earn an additional $100 each year from an acre of land planted in wheat. If that were true, the net present value (NPV) of the land with a wheat allotment would rise by $100 divided by the interest rate. At a 10 percent rate of interest, the value of the additional $100 per year would equal $1,000 (NPV = R/i = $100/.10 = $1,000). The value of an acre of land with a wheat allotment would rise by $1,000. Essentially, the value of the monopoly-profit income stream derived from the price support program would be capitalized into the value of land with a wheat allotment.

The major beneficiaries of the price support/acreage restriction program have been the owners of land with an allotment at the time of

EXHIBIT 7 • Acreage Restrictions and Limiting Output

Rather than permit farmers to raise an amount of wheat that would generate an excess supply at the support price, under the acreage restriction program the government restricts the number of acres allocated to the growing of wheat, causing the supply of wheat to decline to S_2. With the acreage restrictions, the excess supply is eliminated, and the $4 support price is maintained.

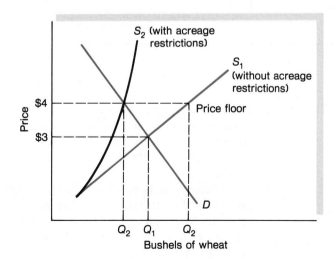

APPLICATIONS IN ECONOMICS (continued)

EXHIBIT 8 • Rising Land Values and Capitalizing Profit

Since land with an acreage allotment permits one to plant wheat and sell it at the above-market-equilibrium price, the price support program makes such land more valuable. Competition drives the price of land *with an allotment* upward until the higher land values fully capture the larger profits resulting from the program. But once land values have risen, the farmer's rate of return on investment is no higher with the program than it was prior to the program's establishment. The major beneficiaries of price support programs have been those who owned land with acreage allotments *at the time the programs were established.*

the program's establishment. Competition for land with acreage allotments has driven the price of such land up until the rate of return on agricultural land with allotments is equal to the market rate of return. Thus, the profit rate of the current owners of the land is no higher than it would have been had Congress never adopted any kind of price support system in the first place.

DISCUSSION

1. Suppose the current price support/acreage allotment program for wheat were abolished. What would be the impact on (a) the value of land with wheat allotments, (b) the cost of producing wheat, (c) the market price of wheat, and (d) the profitability of wheat farming?

2. Farmers are often heard to complain that they are not helped by the price support/acreage allotment program, and yet they oppose its repeal. Explain why these seemingly contradictory views are not surprising.

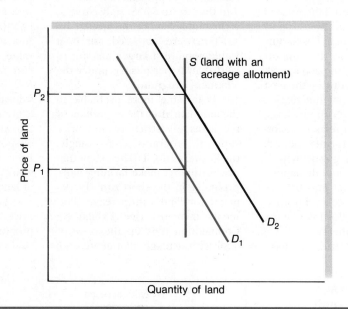

CHAPTER SUMMARY

1. The extensive use of tools, machinery, and other forms of physical capital sets human beings apart from other animals. An increase in the quantity (and quality) of tools and the adoption of innovative, roundabout methods of production have made our current standard of living possible.

2. Roundabout methods of production require the sacrifice of current production because resources that might otherwise be used to produce consumption goods directly are employed in the construction of tools, machines, and other constructed capital assets designed to increase future productive capability.

3. Interest is the price people are willing to pay to obtain goods and services now rather than in the future. Since earlier availability is usu-

ally attained through borrowing in the loanable funds market, the interest rate is often defined as the price of loanable funds.

4. Consumers and investors alike demand loanable funds and are willing to pay the price—the interest rate. This is so because consumers have a positive rate of time preference, and investors are willing to pay a premium for the loanable funds required to undertake potentially productive capital investment projects. If consumers did not prefer earlier availability and if capital investments were not productive, there would be no reason to expect a positive interest rate.

5. During inflationary times, the money rate of interest incorporates an inflationary premium reflecting the expected future increase in the price level. Under these circumstances, the money rate of interest exceeds the real rate of interest.

6. The money rate of interest on a specific loan reflects three basic factors—the pure interest rate, an inflationary premium, and a risk premium that is directly related to the probability of default by the borrower.

7. Since a dollar in the future is valued less than a dollar today, the value of future receipts must be discounted to calculate their current worth. The discounting procedure can be used to calculate the net present value of an expected income stream from a potential investment project. A project should be undertaken only if the net present value of the expected income from the project exceeds its current cost (purchase price).

8. The expectation of economic profit influences investment decisions in both human and physical capital. Other things constant, the higher the expected profit, the more attractive the project to an investor.

9. There are three basic sources of economic profit: (a) uncertainty, (b) entrepreneurial alertness, and (c) monopoly.

10. Since the future is uncertain, investors must expose themselves to uncertainty arising from unanticipated shifts in market demand and costs. Since most people dislike uncertainty, investors must be paid a premium (a return in excess of the interest rate) to induce them to accept the uncertainty that necessarily accompanies investment. This uncertainty premium is a source of economic profit.

11. Astute entrepreneurs are able to recognize and undertake economically beneficial investment opportunities that have gone unnoticed by others. Entrepreneurial alertness to potential opportunities to combine resources in a manner that increases their value is a source of economic profit.

12. Profits may also emanate from monopoly power—entry barriers that shield suppliers from competitive pressure. Sole ownership of a vital resource, legal restraint of entry, and patents can bestow monopoly rights on owners of assets. Monopoly profits encourage entrepreneurs to invest resources to acquire a monopoly privilege.

THE ECONOMIC WAY OF THINKING—
DISCUSSION QUESTIONS

1. Suppose U.S. investors are considering the construction of bicycle factories in two different countries, one in Europe and the other in Africa. Projected costs and revenues are at first identical, but the chance of guerilla warfare (and possible destruction of the factory) is suddenly

perceived in the African nation. In which country will the price of bicycles (and the current rate of return to bicycle factories) probably rise? Will the investors be better off in the country with the higher rate of return? Why or why not?

2. How would a change in each of the following factors influence the rate of interest in the United States?
   (a) The time preference of lenders.
   (b) The time preference of borrowers.
   (c) An increase in domestic inflation.
   (d) Increased uncertainty about a nuclear war.
   (e) Improved investment opportunities in Europe.

3. Can you discover ways to make pure economic profits from an investment by reading about currently profitable investments in the *Wall Street Journal*? Why or why not?

4. "Any return to capital above the pure interest yield is unnecessary. The pure interest yield is sufficient to provide capitalists with the earnings necessary to replace their assets and to compensate for their sacrifice of current consumption. Any return above that is pure gravy; it is excess profit." Do you agree with this view? Why or why not?

5. How are human and physical capital investment decisions similar? How do they differ? What determines the profitability of a physical capital investment? Do human capital investors make profits? If so, what is the source of profit? Explain.

6. Suppose you are contemplating the purchase of a minicomputer at a cost of $1,000. The expected lifetime of the asset is three years. You expect to lease the asset to a business for $400 annually (payable at the end of each year) for three years. If you can borrow (and lend) money at an interest rate of 8 percent, will the investment be a profitable undertaking? Is the project profitable at an interest rate of 12 percent? Provide calculations in support of your answer.

7. How do the accounting profits of corporations differ from economic profits? Do corporate profits incorporate an interest return? A risk return? A pure profit return? A monopoly profit return? As a percentage of corporate assets, how large do you think each of these returns is in most manufacturing industries? Explain.

CHAPTER
FOCUS

If one talks to any worker long enough, and candidly enough, one discovers that his loyalty to the union is not simply economic. One may even be able to show him that, on a strictly cost-benefit analysis, measuring income lost from strikes and jobs lost as a result of contract terms, the cumulative economic benefits are delusions. It won't matter. In the end, he will tell you, the union is the only institution that ensures and protects his "dignity" as a worker. [1]

IRVING KRISTOL

- How much of the U.S. work force is unionized?

- How does the collective bargaining process work? How important is the "strike" in the bargaining process?

- Can unions increase the wages of their members? What makes a union strong? What factors limit the power of a union?

- Can unions increase the share of income going to labor?

- Do unions cause inflation?

- What impact have unions had on the legal structure of worker-management relations?

25 LABOR UNIONS AND COLLECTIVE BARGAINING

Labor Union: A collective organization of employees who bargain as a unit with employers.

In an earlier chapter, we mentioned that labor unions may be able to establish institutional arrangements that will affect supply and demand, and therefore alter wage rates. We are now prepared to examine the labor market effects of unions. A **labor union** is an organization of employees usually working either in the same occupation or industry, who have consented to joint bargaining with employers concerning wages, working conditions, grievance procedures, and other elements of employment. The primary objective of a labor union is to improve the welfare of its members.

Unions have historically been controversial. Some believe that labor unions are a necessary shield protecting workers from the beast of employer greed. Others charge that unions are monopolies seeking to provide their members with benefits at the expense of economic efficiency, consumers, and other workers. Still others argue that the economic influence of unions—both for good and for bad—is vastly overrated. This chapter will enhance our understanding of labor unions and the economic factors that influence their ability to achieve desired objectives.

UNION MEMBERSHIP AS A SHARE OF THE WORK FORCE

Historically, the proportion of the U.S. labor force belonging to a labor union has fluctuated substantially. In 1900, less than 3 percent of the U.S. work force belonged to a labor union. From this low level, union membership expanded during the 1900–1920 period. By 1920, 12 percent of the work force was unionized. In the aftermath of World War I, union membership declined, falling to less than 7 percent of the work force in 1935. Favorable legislation adopted during the Depression of the 1930s encouraged unions. Union membership as a share of the labor force grew rapidly during 1935–1955, reaching a peak in the mid-1950s.

During the last three decades, union membership has waned. As Exhibit 1 shows, union workers in 1984 accounted for only 17.1 percent of the nonfarm labor force, down from 33.2 percent in 1955.

Why have union members declined as a share of the U.S. work force in recent decades? Several factors have contributed to the decline. First, most of the recent growth in employment has been with relatively small firms (less than 100 employees) in service and high-tech industries. Small firms are costly to organize and unions have traditionally been weak in service and high-tech industries. Second, competition has eroded union strength in several important industries. Foreign producers have increased their market share in steel, mining, automobiles, and other heavy manufacturing industries. Employment has thus been shrinking in these areas of traditional union strength. Deregulation in transportation and communication industries has also reduced the effectiveness of unions. As these industries have become more competitive, unionized firms have faced increased competition from nonunion producers. Finally, even regional growth patterns

---

[1] Irving Kristol, "Understanding Trade Unionism," *Wall Street Journal* (October 23, 1978). Reprinted with permission of the *Wall Street Journal*.

EXHIBIT 1 • The Slide in Union Membership as a Share of Nonagricultural Employment

As a proportion of nonfarm employment, union membership has declined from 33.2 percent in 1955 to 17.1 percent in 1984.

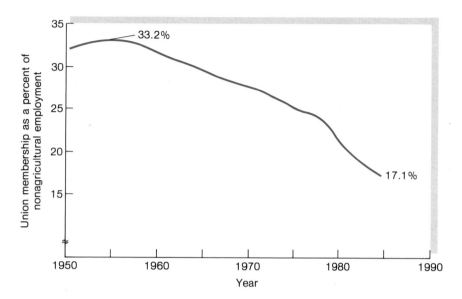

Source: *Statistical Abstract of the United States: 1981* (p. 412), and *The Monthly Labor Review* (February 1985), pp. 26 and 68.

have adversely affected union strength. During the 1960s and 1970s, population and employment grew rapidly in the sunbelt, while stagnating in the northeast and upper middle west. Since the former is an area of union weakness and the latter an area of strength, this pattern also retarded the growth of union membership.

All of these factors, of course, have to some extent been caused by union success in raising union wages. Wages higher than productivity alone would retard the growth of employment in the geographic areas, the industries, and the classes of firms employing the high wage workers. In contrast, where wages are low relative to productivity, business investment and the growth of employment are encouraged.

THE COLLECTIVE BARGAINING PROCESS

Collective Bargaining Contract: A detailed contract between (a) a group of employees (a labor union) and (b) an employer. It covers wage rates and conditions of employment.

Each year, **collective bargaining contracts** covering wages and working conditions for six to nine million workers are negotiated. A collective bargaining contract is a union-management agreement prescribing the conditions of employment. Union negotiators, acting as agents for a group of employees, bargain with management about the provisions of a labor contract. If the union representatives are able to obtain a contract they consider acceptable, they will typically submit it to a vote of the union members. If approved by the members, the contract establishes in detail wage rates, fringe benefits, and working conditions for a future time interval, usually the next two or three years. During that time interval, union and management alike must abide by the conditions of the contract. While the labor contract is between management and union, it also applies to the nonunion bargaining unit members who are employed by the firm or industry.

Union Shop: The requirement that all employees join the recognized union and pay dues to it within a specified length of time (usually 30 days) after their employment with the firm begins.

Right-to-Work Laws: Laws that prohibit the union shop—the requirement that employees must join a union (after 30 days) as a condition of employment. Each state has the option to adopt (or reject) right-to-work legislation.

THE STRIKE AND COLLECTIVE BARGAINING

Strike: An action of unionized employees in which they (a) discontinue working for the employer and (b) take steps to prevent other potential workers from offering their services to the employer.

Some labor-management contracts contain a **union shop** provision. A union shop contract requires all workers to join the union after a specified length of employment, usually 30 days. Union proponents argue that since all workers in the bargaining unit enjoy the benefits of collective bargaining, all should be required to join and pay dues. In the absence of a union shop, individual workers might reap gains brought about by the union without incurring the costs.

Opponents of the union shop argue that all employees are not helped by a union. Some unions lack the necessary power to obtain wage increases. Some employees may feel that they would be better off if they could bargain for themselves. In addition, unions often engage in political activities, either directly or indirectly. These activities may run counter to the views of individual employees. Why should an employee be forced, as a condition of employment, to support activities he or she does not approve? In 1947, Congress passed the Taft-Hartley Act; Section 14-B allows states to enact **right-to-work laws** prohibiting union shop contracts. Thus, when a state has a right-to-work statute, a union-management contract cannot require a worker to join a union as a condition of employment. Currently, some 20 states, most of them in the sunbelt, have adopted right-to-work legislation.

Typically, management and labor negotiators begin the bargaining process for a new labor contract several months, or even a year, before the termination of the current agreement. The new contract is usually approved before the old contract has terminated. However, at the termination of the old labor-management agreement, if the bargaining process has broken down and there is no agreement on a new contract, either side may use its economic power to try to bring the other to terms.

Employers can withhold employment from workers at the expiration of the old contract. However, since employers can unilaterally announce their terms for continued employment, they seldom discontinue operations.

The major source of work stoppage is the strike. A **strike** consists of two major actions by a union: (a) employees, particularly union employees, refuse to work, and (b) steps are taken to prevent other employees from working for the employer. Both conditions are essential to a strike. Without efforts to prevent other employees, often referred to as "scabs" or "strike-breakers," from accepting jobs with the employer, a strike would merely be a mass resignation. A strike also involves picketing to restrict and discourage the hiring of other workers, actions to prevent free entry and exit from a plant, and perhaps even violence or the threat of violence against workers willing to cross the picket lines.

The purpose of a strike is to impose economic costs on an employer so that the terms proposed by the union will be accepted. When the strike can be used to disrupt the production process and interfere with the employer's ability to sell goods and services to customers, it is a very powerful weapon. Under such conditions, the employer may submit to the wage demands of the union, as a means of avoiding the costs of the strike.

Given the nature of the strike, it is not surprising that the "right to strike" has had an uneven history. At times, striking was prohibited because it was thought to interfere with the rights of nonunion workers. Before the passage of legislation in the early 1900s clearly establishing the right to strike, courts were sometimes willing to intervene and limit certain types of strikes. The role of law enforcement in strikes also has had a mixed history. In some areas, the police have given nonstrikers, who desire to continue working, protection to and from their jobs. In other cases, they have permitted pickets to block entry and have turned their backs on violence between strikers and nonstrikers. Even today, the protection a nonstriker can expect from the police varies from location to location.

The United States has established some limitations on the right to strike. Several states limit the right of public employees to strike. The Taft-Hartley Act allows the president to seek a court injunction prohibiting a strike for 80 days when it is believed that the strike would create a "national emergency." During the 80-day period, work continues under the conditions of the old contract. If a settlement has not been reached during this "cooling-off" period, however, employees again have the option of using the strike weapon. Strikes by federal employees are also prohibited by law. When the air-traffic controllers' union called a strike during the summer of 1981, striking workers who refused to return to work were fired and eventually replaced.

THE COST OF A STRIKE

A strike can be costly to both union and management. From the firm's viewpoint, a work stoppage may mean that it will be unable to meet the current demand for its product. It may lose customers, and they may be difficult to win back once they have turned to competitors during the strike. A strike will be more costly to the firm when (a) demand for its product is strong, (b) it is unable to stockpile its product, and (c) its fixed costs are high even during the strike. If the firm can stockpile its product in anticipation of a strike, a work stoppage may not have much impact on current sales. For example, automobile producers, particularly during slack times, often have an inventory of new cars that allows them to meet current demand during a 60- or even 90-day strike. In contrast, the shipping revenues of a trucking firm may be completely eliminated by a truckers' strike. The firm would be unable to deliver its service because of the strike, and potential customers would therefore turn to rail, air, postal, and other forms of shipping. The firm could suffer a permanent loss of sales.

Careful timing can also magnify the cost of a strike. Agricultural unions can threaten farmers with the loss of an entire year's income by striking at harvest time. Similarly, major league umpires can strengthen their position by striking at World Series time.

The nature of the product, the level of current demand, and the ability of the firm to continue to meet the requests of its customers during a strike all influence the effectiveness of the strike as a weapon. The more costly a work stoppage would be to a firm, the greater the pressure on it to yield to the demands of the union.

Strikes, particularly if they are long, are also quite costly to employees. Although a carnival attitude often prevails during the early days of a strike, a few weeks without paychecks impose an extreme hardship on most families. Strike funds are usually inadequate to deal with a prolonged strike. In recent years, welfare benefits have been used to reduce the cost imposed on workers by the strike.[2] Temporary employment in other areas can sometimes be arranged, but as a strike continues, pressures build on the union to arrive at a settlement.

Strikes sometimes exert a substantial impact on secondary parties who are unable to influence union-management relations. For example, a prolonged strike in the steel industry might cause a loss of work time in automobile, construction, and other industries. A teachers' strike might force a working parent to quit his or her job to care for the children. A public transit strike in New York can paralyze Fun City. A coal miners' strike can leave Londoners without heat. Should third parties be protected when strikes involve the public interest? Many would answer this question in the affirmative. But, how can the public be protected without interfering with the bargaining process? These questions have not yet been fully answered.

KEEPING WORK STOPPAGES IN PERSPECTIVE

Since a strike is news, work stoppages receive considerable media exposure. Nevertheless, work stoppages due to strikes must be placed in proper perspective. The strike, or the threat of it, forces both management and labor to bargain seriously. Both have a strong incentive to settle without a work stoppage. This is usually what happens. Each year an estimated 120,000 labor contracts are terminated. Thus, during the course of a year, 120,000 labor and management bargaining teams sit across the bargaining table from each other. They deal with the important issues of wages, fringe benefits, grievance procedures, and conditions of employment. More than 97 percent of the time, labor-management contracts are agreed to without the use of strikes. One seldom hears about these contracts because peaceful settlements are back-page news, at best. It is the strikes that rate the headlines.

As Exhibit 2 illustrates, very little potential work time is lost as the result of strikes. During the last 35 years, the number of worker-hours lost because of strikes was less than three tenths of 1 percent of the total working time—and the proportion has been falling. During 1981–85, less than one tenth of 1 percent of the total work time was lost due to strikes, substantially less than the amount of work time lost because of absenteeism.

HOW CAN UNIONS INFLUENCE WAGES?

The collective-bargaining process often gives one the impression that wages are established primarily by the talents of the union-management representatives who sit at the bargaining table. It might appear that market forces play a relatively minor role. However, as both union and management are well aware, market forces provide the setting in which the bargaining process is conducted. They often tip the balance of power one way or the other.

High wages increase the firm's costs. When union employers face stiff competition from nonunion producers or foreign competitors, they will be less able to pass along higher wage costs to their customers. Competition in

---

[2]The availability of welfare benefits to strikers varies among areas.

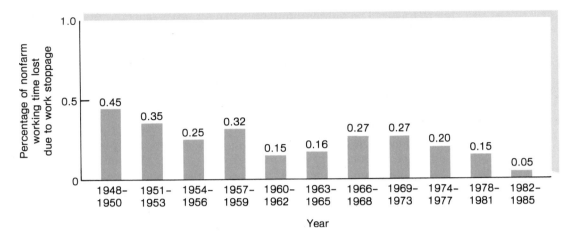

Employment and Training Report of the President—1981 and *Monthly Labor Review* (March 1986).

EXHIBIT 2 • The Percentage of Work Time Lost Due to Strikes, 1948–1981

Since 1960, less than three-tenths of 1 percent of nonfarm working time has been lost due to labor disputes.

the product market thus limits the bargaining power of a union. Changing market conditions also influence the balance of power between union and management. When the demand for a product is strong, the demand for labor will be high, and the firm will be much more willing to consent to a significant wage increase. When demand is weak, however, the product inventory level of the firm (or industry) is more likely to be high. The firm's current demand for labor will be weakened. It will be much less vulnerable to a union work stoppage. Under such conditions, wage increases will be much more difficult to obtain.

As we have already indicated, collective-bargaining agreements cover wages and fringe benefits (vacation time, sick leave, accident benefits, and so on). Fringe benefits are an indirect component of employee compensation. So, when we speak of wage rates, we include direct money wages as well as employer-provided fringe benefits.

A union can use three basic strategies to increase the wages of its members: supply restrictions, bargaining power, and increase in demand. We will examine each of these in turn.

SUPPLY RESTRICTIONS

If a union can successfully reduce the supply of competitive labor, higher wage rates will automatically result. Licensing requirements, long apprenticeship programs, immigration barriers, high initiation fees, refusal to admit new members to the union, and prohibition of nonunion workers from holding jobs are all practices that unions have used to limit the supply of labor to various occupations and jobs. Craft unions, in particular, have often been able to obtain higher wages because of their successful effort to limit the entry of competitive labor. In the 1920s, unions successfully lobbied for legislation that reduced the torrent of worker-immigrants from abroad to a mere trickle. The tighter immigration laws considerably reduced the influx of new workers, reducing the growth of supply in U.S. labor markets and thus causing higher wages to prevail.

Exhibit 3a illustrates the impact of supply restrictions on wage rates. Successful exclusionary tactics will reduce supply, shifting the supply curve from S_0 to S_1. Facing the supply curve S_1, employers will consent to the wage rate W_1. Compared with a free-entry market equilibrium, the wage rate has increased from W_0 to W_1, but employment has declined from E_0 to E_1. At the higher wage rate, W_1, an excess supply of labor, AB, will result. The restrictive practices will prevent this excess supply from undercutting the above-equilibrium wage rate. Because of the exclusionary practices, the union will be able to obtain higher wages for E_1 employees. Other employees who would be willing to accept work even at wage rate W_0 will now be forced into other areas of employment.

BARGAINING POWER

Must unions restrict entry? Why can they not simply use their bargaining power, the strike threat, as a vehicle for raising wages? If they have enough economic power, this will be possible. A strike by even a small percentage of vital employees can sometimes halt the flow of production. For example, a work stoppage by airline mechanics can force major airlines to cancel their flights. Because the mechanics perform an essential function, an airline cannot operate without their services, even though they constitute only 10 percent of all airline employees.

If the union is able to obtain an above-free-entry wage rate, the impact on employment will be similar to a reduction in supply. As Exhibit 3b illustrates, employers will hire fewer workers at the higher wage rate obtained through bargaining power. Employment will decline below the free-entry level (from E_0 to E_1) as a result of the rise in wages. An excess supply

EXHIBIT 3 • Supply Restrictions, Bargaining Power, and Wage Rates

The impact of higher wages obtained by restricting supply is very similar to that obtained through bargaining power. As illustrated by graph (a), when union policies reduce the supply of one type of labor, higher wages result. Similarly, when bargaining power is used in order to obtain higher wages (graph b), employment declines and an excess supply of labor results.

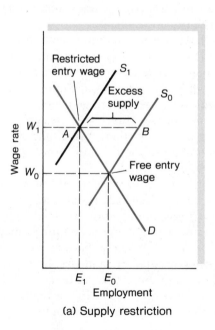

(a) Supply restriction

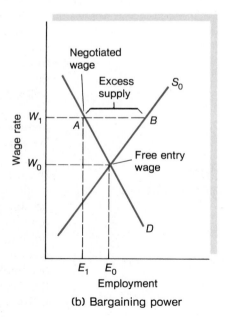

(b) Bargaining power

of labor, *AB* , will exist, at least temporarily. More employees will seek the high-wage union jobs than employers will choose to hire. Nonwage methods of rationing jobs will become more important.

**INCREASE
IN DEMAND**

The demand for union labor is usually determined by factors outside the union's direct control, such as the availability of substitute inputs and the demand for the product. Unions, though, can sometimes use their political power to increase the demand for their services. They may be able to induce legislators to pass laws requiring the employment of certain types or amounts of labor for a task (for example, unneeded firemen on trains, allegedly for safety reasons, or a certain number of stage engineers). Unions often seek import restrictions as a means of increasing the demand for domestic labor. For example, automobile workers strongly support high tariffs and import quotas for foreign-made atuomobiles. Garment workers have used their political muscle to raise tariffs and reduce import quotas for clothing goods produced abroad. Such practices increase the demand for domestic automobiles and clothing, thereby increasing the demand for domestic auto and garment workers. It is not surprising that the management and union representatives of a specific industry often join hands in demanding government tariff protection from foreign competition. As Exhibit 4 illustrates, successful union actions to increase demand for the services of union members result in both higher wages and an expansion in employment, usually at the expense of consumers.

A union in a strong bargaining position may shift the firm off its demand curve. This can happen if the union offers an "all-or-none" settlement in which the union specifies both wage and the quantity of labor (or restrictive work rules). To get any labor at all in this case, the firm must hire more labor at the union wage than it wants. For example, the International Typographical Union has stipulated that after a page of newspaper type has

**EXHIBIT 4 • Rising
Demand and Wage
Increases**

If a union can follow policies that will lead to an increase in the demand for its services, wages will rise automatically.

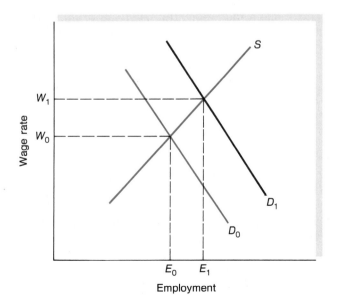

been set and run automatically (to save time and to get late news in before a deadline), the same page must later be set, proofread, and corrected in the newspaper's composing room. This is called "bogus type" and is discarded. If the newspaper wants any work—and no picket lines—from typesetters, it must either pay them to do "bogus" work or make other bargaining concessions that will induce the union to withdraw the rule. This type of "make-work rule" is another way in which a union may be able to loosen the connection between higher wages and lower levels of employment.

UNION POWER, EMPLOYMENT, AND MONOPSONY

Is unionization necessary to protect employees from the power of employers? When there are a large number of employers in a market area, the interest of employees will be protected by competition among employers. Under these circumstances, each employer must pay the market wage to employees to keep them from shifting to higher-paying alternative employers. In a modern society, labor is highly mobile. Most employees work in a labor market in which there are many employers. However, a few workers may confront a situation in which there is only a single employer of labor, at least for the specific skill category of labor supplied by the workers. For example, if a single large employer—perhaps a textile manufacturer or lumber mill—dominates the labor market of a small town, local workers may have few alternative employment opportunities.

Monopsony: A market in which there is only one buyer. The monopsonist confronts the market supply curve for the resource (or product) bought.

Analysis of resource markets under conditions of **monopsony** will help us understand situations in which the market is dominated by a single employer or a small number of employers. Monopsony refers to a market situation in which there is a single buyer for a specific resource; for example, a specific skill category of labor. As we previously discussed, when the seller has a monopoly, the seller can profit by restricting output and charging a price above the marginal cost of production. Under monopsony, the buyer has a monopoly. Since the alternatives available to sellers are limited, the monopsonist-buyer will be able to profit by restricting the purchase of the resource and paying a price (wage rate) that is less than the marginal revenue generated by the resource.

Marginal Factor Cost: The cost of employing an additional unit of a resource. When the employer is small relative to the total market, the marginal factor cost is simply the price of the resource. In contrast, under monopsony, marginal factor cost will exceed the price of the resource, since the monopsonist faces an upward-sloping supply curve for the resource.

Exhibit 5 illustrates the impact of monopsony in the labor market. Since the monopsonist is the only employer (purchaser of labor), its supply curve for the resource in question will coincide with the market supply curve for that resource. The supply curve for the resource will slope upward to the right because higher wages are necessary to attract the additional workers desired. For now, we will assume that both the old and new employees will be paid the higher wage rates if employment is expanded. The **marginal factor cost** (MFC) curve indicates the marginal cost of labor to the monopsonist. The marginal factor cost of labor will exceed the wage rate because the higher wages necessary to attract each additional worker must be paid to all employees. As illustrated by Exhibit 5, this means that the monopsonist's marginal factor cost curve will be steeper than the labor supply curve.

EXHIBIT 5 • Labor Market Monopsony and Unionization

As frame (a) illustrates, the monopsonist's supply curve for labor will slope upward to the right. The marginal factor cost curve for labor will be steeper than the labor supply curve. The monopsonist will hire E_1 units of labor and pay a wage rate, W_1, along its labor supply curve. If a union establishes a wage floor, W_2 of frame (b), for example, the monopsonist may hire additional workers (E_2 rather than E_1) at the higher wage rate.

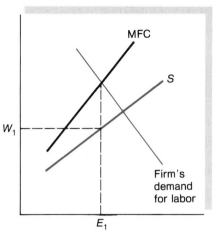

(a) Monopsony (without unionization)

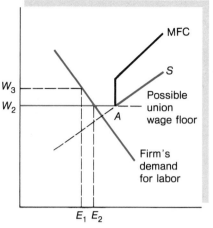

(b) Monopsony (with unionization)

How many workers should a profit-maximizing monopsony employ? The monopsonist's demand curve for labor indicates how much each additional worker adds to the firm's total revenue. The monopsonist will continue to expand employment as long as hiring additional workers adds more to total revenues than to total costs. This means that the monopsonist will choose employment level E_1, where the firm's demand curve, reflecting the marginal revenue product of labor, is just equal to the marginal factor cost of labor. A wage rate of W_1 will be sufficient to attract E_1 employees. For employment levels beyond E_1, it would cost (MFC) the monopsonist more to hire an additional worker than that worker would add to total revenue. As the result of this cost, the monopsonist firm will hire fewer employees than it would if it were not the only buyer in the labor market.

Exhibit 5b illustrates what would happen if a union established a wage floor—W_2, for example—for a monopsonist. The wage floor would prohibit the monopsonist from paying low wages even if employment dropped. The union would confront the employer with the supply curve W_2AS. In essence, the wage floor would become the firm's marginal factor cost curve until the wage floor intersected the labor supply curve at A. As long as the marginal factor cost of additional units of labor was less than the firm's demand curve, additional workers would continue to be employed. Thus, if a union imposed wage rate W_2, the monopsonist would expand employment to E_2. In this case, unionization would result in both higher wages and an expansion in employment. If the union expanded the wage rate above W_3, employment would fall below E_1, the level employed by a nonunion monopsonist. But, for any wage floor less than W_3, the monopsonist would expand employment beyond E_1.

While this analysis is sound as far as it goes, there are three additional factors that should be considered.[3] First, a higher wage rate will obviously

---

[3]See Armen Alchian and William Allen, *Exchange and Production: Competition, Coordination, and Control* (Belmont, California: Wadsworth, 1983), pp. 334–339, for additional theoretical analysis of monopsony.

increase the firm's total costs of production. In the long-run, when the firm sells its product in a competitive market, higher per unit costs will almost certainly force the firm to raise its price. A decline in the firm's market share and output is a likely result. As the firm's market share declines, employment of all factors of production, including labor, will fall.

Second, a monopsonist will often be able to confine the higher wage rates to new employees only. When this is the case, the marginal factor cost curve of the monopsonist will not differ from its labor supply curve. Rather than restricting employment to keep wages low, the firm may simply offer new employees (but not old ones) higher job classifications and more attractive employment conditions to obtain their services.

Third, given the speed of transportation, employers often draw workers from 30 to 50 miles away. In addition, many employees (particularly skilled workers, professionals, and managers) compete in a much broader labor market, a national labor market in some cases. Over a period of time, such workers will flow into and away from local labor markets. Given the mobility of labor, then, most employers will be small relative to their labor market, and their decisions to expand or contract their work force will not exert much impact on the market wage rate. Under these circumstances, marginal factor cost is nearly the same as the wage rate in the competitive market model. A rise in the wage rate will therefore almost certainly reduce employment.

The strength of these factors is enough to substantially reduce monopsony power. When economic researchers have compared the predictive power of the monopsony model with the competitive model, the latter has generally been shown to perform better. Empirical evidence thus indicates that unions normally operate in labor markets characterized by competition rather than monopsony.

WHAT GIVES A UNION STRENGTH?

Not all unions are able to raise the wages of their workers. What are the factors that make a union strong? Why are some unions able to maintain employee wages above free-entry level, while others have a negligible impact on wage rates?

Simply stated, if a union is to be strong, the demand for its labor must be inelastic. This will enable the union to obtain large wage increases while suffering only modest reductions in employment. In contrast, when the demand for union labor is quite elastic, a substantial rise in wages will mean few, if any, jobs.

There are four major determinants of the demand elasticity for a factor of production: (a) the availability of substitutes, (b) the elasticity of product demand, (c) the share of the input as a proportion of total cost, and (d) the supply elasticity of substitute inputs.[4] We now turn to the importance of each of these conditions as a determinant of union strength.

---

[4]Alfred Marshall, *Principles of Economics*, 8th ed. (New York: Macmillan, 1920).

THE AVAILABILITY OF GOOD SUBSTITUTE INPUTS

When it is difficult to substitute other inputs for unionized labor when producing a good, the union is strengthened. Since nonunion labor is a good substitute for union labor, the power of unions to exclude nonunion labor is an important determinant of union strength. Unless a union can prevent nonunion employees from entering an occupation and cutting wages below the union level, it will be unable to raise wages significantly above the free-entry level.

Even if a union can successfully restrict competition from nonunion employees, the availability of machines that are good substitutes for labor will greatly reduce the power of the union. Wage increases will induce employers to mechanize. A substantial wage increase can thus mean a sharp reduction in employment. Many workers may be laid off.

A comparison of the experiences of elevator operators and airline pilots highlights the importance of substitute inputs. When the elevator operators of many large cities unionized and negotiated substantial wage increases, their gains were short-lived. Employers quickly turned to automated elevators, and the employment of elevator operators fell drastically. Airline pilots, however, are able to maintain above-free-entry wage rates without much substitution in production. People do not object to riding an automated elevator, but they are not likely (at least not in the foreseeable future) to tolerate an automated airplane. Because a low-cost substitute was available for elevator operators, their union was weakened. In contrast, there have historically been few substitutes for unionized airline pilots. Until the recent growth of nonunion airlines, the pilots' union was one of the strongest unions in the United States.

ELASTICITY OF DEMAND FOR THE PRODUCTS OF UNIONIZED FIRMS

Wages are a component of costs. An increase in the wages of union members will almost surely lead to higher prices for goods produced with union labor. Unless the demand for the good produced by union labor is inelastic, the output produced by unionized firms will decline if the union pushes up wages (and costs). If a union is going to have a significant impact on wages, it must produce a good for which the demand is inelastic.

Our analysis implies that a union will be unable to significantly increase wages above the free market rate when producing a good that competes with similar (or identical) goods produced by nonunion labor or foreign producers. The demand for the good produced by union labor will almost surely be highly elastic when the same product is available from nonunion and foreign producers. Thus, if the union pushes up wages and costs, the market share of unionized firms will shrink and the employment of union labor will fall substantially.

Both past history and recent events are consistent with this view. In the 1920s, the United Mine Workers obtained big wage gains in unionized coal fields. The union was unable to halt the growth of nonunion mining, though, particularly in the strip mines of the West. The unionized mines soon lost the major share of their market to nonunionized fields, leading to a sharp reduction in the employment of union members.

More recently, the strength of the Teamster's union was substantially eroded when deregulation subjected the unionized segment of the trucking industry to much more intense competition from nonunion firms in the early 1980s. With deregulation, nonunion firms with lower labor costs entered the industry. Given their labor-cost advantage, many of the new entrants cut prices to gain a larger share of the market. The market share of the unionized firms declined. More than 100,000 Teamsters lost their jobs. Given the sharp reduction in the employment of their members, the Teamsters eventually agreed to wage concessions and a reduction in their fringe-benefit package.

Unions sometimes negotiate substantial wage increases, even though they may eventually result in significant reductions in employment. This appears to be the case in both the steel and automobile industries. As Exhibit 6 shows, the hourly earnings of production workers in these two industries rose sharply compared to other workers in the private sector during the 1970s. By 1982, the average hourly earnings of steel workers were 74 percent greater than for all private-sector workers, up from a 19 percent premium in 1969. The parallel wage premium in the automobile industry was 51 percent in 1982, up from 21 percent in 1969.

No doubt partially as the result of the wage and cost increases during the 1970s, foreign producers were able to expand their share of both the steel and automobile manufacturing markets in the United States. The employment of unionized labor in both industries declined. Between 1978 and 1982, membership in the United Steel Workers Union fell by 45 percent. Between 1978 and 1980, the United Automobile Workers (UAW) lost 142,000 members, nearly a 16 percent decline. Eventually, major unions representing steel and automobile workers agreed to several concessions, including the loss of various paid vacation days and scheduled cost-of-living wage increases. In addition, the UAW applied pressure that led to a reduction in Japanese imports. This combination of factors arrested, at least temporarily, the employment decline in the U.S. automobile industry. Nevertheless, the experience of steel and automobile workers during the last decade once again reveals that product market competition significantly reduces the bargaining power of even the strongest unions.

UNION LABOR AS A SHARE OF COST OF PRODUCTION

If the unionized labor input comprises only a small share of total production cost, demand for that labor will tend to be relatively inelastic. For example, since the wages of plumbers and pilots comprise only a small share of the

EXHIBIT 6	• Average Hourly Earnings of Nonsupervisory Production Workers in the Steel and Automobile Industries Compared to Other Private-Sector Workers				
	Average Hourly Earnings (nonsupervisory production workers)				
Year	Private Sector	Steel Industry	Automobile Industry	Percent Premium in Steel	Percent Premium in Automobile
1969	$3.38	$ 4.02	$ 4.10	+19	+21
1975	5.15	6.94	6.44	+34	+25
1982	7.68	13.35	11.62	+74	+51
1985	8.58	13.35	13.44	+56	+57

Source: U.S. Department of Labor, *Monthly Labor Review.*

total cost of production in the housing and air travel industries, respectively, a doubling or even tripling of the wages of plumbers or airline pilots would result in only a 1 or 2 percent increase in the cost of housing or air travel. A large increase in the price of such inputs would have little impact on product price, output, and employment. This factor has sometimes been called "the importance of being unimportant," because it is important to the strength of the union.

THE SUPPLY ELASTICITY OF SUBSTITUTE INPUTS

We have just explained that if wage rates in the unionized sector are pushed upward, firms will look for substitute inputs, and the demand for these substitutes will increase. If the supply of these substitutes (such as nonunion labor) is inelastic, however, their price will rise sharply in response to an increase in demand. The higher price will reduce the attractiveness of the substitutes. An inelastic supply of substitutes will thus strengthen the union by making the demand for union labor more inelastic.

WAGES OF UNION AND NONUNION EMPLOYEES

The precise impact of unions on the wages of their members is not easy to determine. Nevertheless, several studies have examined the effect of unionism on wages.[5] H. Gregg Lewis, in a pioneering study published in 1963, estimated that, on average, union workers received wages between 10 and 15 percent higher than those of nonunion workers with similar productivity characteristics. Of course, some unions had an even greater impact. Lewis estimated that strong unions, such as the electricians', plumbers', tool and die-makers', metal craft workers', truckers' (this was prior to moves toward deregulation), and commercial airline pilots' unions, were able to raise the wages of their members by 25 percent or more. In general, Lewis's evidence indicates that craft unions are stronger than industrial unions. From the standpoint of economic theory, this is not surprising. Craftworkers usually perform a vital service for which there are few good substitutes.

Unionization appears to have had the least impact on the earnings of cotton textile, footwear, furniture, hosiery, clothing, and retail sales workers. In these areas, the power of the union has been substantially limited by the existence of readily available nonunion workers. Even when a union shop exists, the demands of the union are moderated by the fear of placing the unionized employer at a competitive disadvantage in relation to the nonunion employers of the industry.

The data for Lewis's study were gathered primarily in the 1940s and 1950s. More recent studies suggest the union-nonunion wage differential may have widened during the 1960s and 1970s. Frank Stafford estimated that when employee characteristics were held constant, the annual earnings of unionized craft and operative workers were 25 percent greater than those

[5]See H. Gregg Lewis, *Unionism and Relative Wages in the United States* (Chicago: University of Chicago Press, 1963), for a discussion of many of these studies. Also see Albert Rees, *The Economics of Trade Unions* (Chicago: University of Chicago Press, 1967).

of their nonunion counterparts. Michael Boskin, using 1967 data, placed the union-nonunion differential at between 15 and 25 percent. In a more recent study, Paul Ryscavage estimated that, in 1973, the wages of union workers exceeded those of nonunion workers with similar productivity characteristics by more than 25 percent. Ryscavage placed the union-nonunion wage differential at 29 percent for craft workers, 23 percent for operatives, 44 percent for truck drivers (primarily Teamsters), and 36 percent for laborers.[6]

Above and beyond wage differences for union and nonunion workers, it is important to note that higher wages for union members do not necessarily mean an increase in the share of income going to labor in general—in other words, higher union wages do not necessarily benefit all workers. (The featured Myths of Economics addresses this issue.)

In the final analysis, a general increase in the level of wages is dependent on an increase in productivity per hour. Of course, improvements in (a) technology, (b) the machines and tools available to workers (physical capital), (c) worker skills (human capital), and (d) the efficiency of economic organization provide the essential ingredients for higher levels of productivity. Higher real wages can be obtained only if the production of goods and services is expanded. Although unions can increase the wages of union workers, they cannot increase the wages of all workers unless their activities increase the total productivity of labor.

DO UNIONS CAUSE INFLATION?

Labor unions are often accused of pushing up wages and thereby triggering price increases that cause inflation. Inspection of this view, however, indicates that it suffers from a major defect; it fails to incorporate the secondary effects of higher union wages. Let us consider this issue in more detail.

Suppose an economy were initially experiencing stable prices and the normal (natural) rate of unemployment. What would happen if a major union, that of the automobile workers, for example, used its economic power and the threat of a strike to obtain a very substantial increase in wages? The higher wages would trigger both direct and secondary effects. The increased labor costs would push up the prices of automobiles, trucks, and buses, particularly if imports could also be restrained. The direct effect of the higher automobile prices would be an increase in the consumer price index.

However, there would also be important secondary effects that are often overlooked. Confronting the higher automobile prices, consumers must either (a) purchase significantly fewer automobiles (quality-constant units) or (b) increase their expenditures on automobiles. To the extent that consumers purchased fewer (or less expensive) automobiles, the amount of

---

[6]F. P. Stafford, "Concentration and Labor Earnings: Comment," *American Economic Review* (March 1968), pp. 174–181; M. J. Boskin, "Unions and Relative Wages," *American Economic Review* (June 1972), pp. 466–472; and P. M. Ryscavage, "Measuring Union-Nonunion Earnings Differences," *Monthly Labor Review* (December 1974), pp. 3–9.

labor services required by the automobile industry would decline. Automotive employment would fall (or at least expand by an abnormally small amount). Some workers who would have been able to find jobs in the automobile industry will now be forced into other lines of employment. The labor supply in these alternative employment areas would increase, placing *downward* pressure on wages and costs in these sectors.

On the other hand, if consumers increased their expenditures on automobiles, they would have less income to spend on other things. Consumers would be forced to cut back their spending in other areas. The demand for products, the consumption of which must now be forgone as a result of the increase in expenditures on automobiles, would decline. Market adjustments would place downward pressure on prices in these areas.

Clearly, neither of these secondary effects would trigger an inflationary spiral. In fact, quite the opposite is true. Both (a) and (b) would place downward pressure on costs and prices outside of the automobile industry, which would, at least partially, offset the impact of higher automobile prices on the general price level. Of course, relative prices would change. The prices of goods requiring the services of automobile workers would rise, but the prices (and costs) of other goods would decline (or rise less rapidly). Once we consider the secondary effects, there is no reason to expect that an increase in the wages of automobile or other unionized workers would trigger a sustained increase in the general price level.

THE CONTRIBUTION AND SIGNIFICANCE OF UNIONS

Economists generally focus on wages and employment when discussing the impact of unions. The data suggest that many unions are able to raise the wages of their members, but, as we have seen, there is little evidence that unions have been able to significantly influence labor's share of total income. It is also clear that rising production, not union power, is the primary source of the increasing real wages of modern industrial society.

Yet, the union movement continues to be almost sacrosanct in the minds of many workers, particularly blue-collar workers. Even workers who belong to a weak union, as determined by its impact on wage rates, often have a strong loyalty to the union. Older workers, in particular, often spin stories about how things used to be. Are they wrong? Would the American economy be different if there were no unions? Wage and income data cannot give full answers to these questions. In perhaps the most important sense, the contribution of unions to American life cannot be statistically measured.

The great contribution of unions in the United States has been their role in defending employees against a sense of powerlessness, unimportance, alienation, and insecurity. The union movement has established a system of on-the-job civil rights and what Summer Slichter has called "industrial jurisprudence" to protect workers' rights.

A union provides the worker with a strong defense against the whim, arbitrary actions, and excesses of a foreman or management representative.

Because of the power of the union, even in cases where only a portion of the workers are unionized, management has a greater incentive to treat workers with dignity and to grant them a sense of individual importance. These worker benefits are, for the most part, nonpecuniary and difficult to measure, but they are nevertheless extremely important.

In an industrial society, it is easy to see how individual employees could acquire a sense of helplessness. After all, what does one employee mean to General Motors, General Electric, or Boeing? If workers were unorganized, foremen, supervisors, and personnel managers would possess a great deal of power. In such a case, it would not be difficult to believe stories about employees being fired because they refused to contribute to the foreman's personal Christmas fund or because they won half of their supervisor's paycheck on a lunch-hour craps game. Analysis of economic incentives suggests that when the foreman is king and the worker is a replaceable cog in the wheel, management arbitrariness, worker insecurity, and alienation will result.

The union movement set out nearly a century ago to relieve the helplessness of the individual worker. Today, labor contracts define a worker's civil rights and provide the worker with a series of industrial appeal courts. Specifically, a worker cannot be fired without good cause, which must be proved to the satisfaction of his or her union representative. Actions the worker considers arbitrary or unfair can be taken to a shop steward, appealed through labor-management channels, and eventually brought to an objective outside arbitrator. When a union brings a grievance to the attention of management, management listens. Production at multimillion-dollar plants has been brought to a halt because a single worker's civil rights, as specified by the labor contract, were violated. Collective bargaining gives

MYTHS OF ECONOMICS

"Unions have increased the wages of workers and thereby expanded the share of income going to labor."

It is one thing for unions to increase the wages of *union members*. It is quite another for them to increase the wages of *all workers*, both nonunion and union. Neither economic theory nor empirical evidence indicates unions are able to increase the general level of wages. If unions were the primary source of high

wages, the real wages of workers would be higher in highly unionized countries such as Australia, the United Kingdom, and most European countries than they are in the United States. But, this is not what we observe. For example, real wages are at least 40 percent lower in the United Kingdom than they are in the United States, even though nearly half of the work force is unionized in the United Kingdom compared to less than 20 percent in

the United States. The real source of high wages is high productivity, not labor unions. In turn, high productivity depends on abundant physical capital, the knowledge and skill of the work force, and institutional arrangements that encourage the creation of wealth.

To the extent unions increase the wages of union members, there is good reason to believe they do so primarily at the expense of nonunion workers. Higher union wages

MYTHS OF ECONOMICS (continued)

(and costs) will lead to a reduction in the output of products that intensively use union labor. This factor, along with the substitution of physical capital for labor at the higher wage rate, will cause employment in the unionized sectors to fall. What will happen to employees who are unable to find jobs in the unionized sector? They will compete for nonunion jobs, increasing supply and depressing nonunion wages. Labor economist Gregg Lewis has estimated that the real wages of nonunion workers, four fifths of the labor force, are 3 to 4 percent lower than they would be in the absence of unionism.[7]

If labor unions increased the wages of all workers and therefore the share of income going to labor, we would expect labor's share of income to be directly related to union membership. Again, the evidence is inconsistent with this view. Exhibit 7 presents data on labor's share of income since 1930. Total employee compensation (including the social security contribution of the employer) has increased slightly since World War II. However, this is primarily a reflection of the decline in the number of self-employed persons in agriculture and the corresponding increase in the proportion of employed workers. Since the earnings of self-employed proprietors such as farmers, sales personnel, accountants, and small business operators emanates primarily from their labor services, a clearer picture of the labor-property-owner components of income emerges when self-employment income is added to employee compensation. As Exhibit 7 shows, this measure of labor's share has been amazingly constant. Between 81 and 83 percent of national income in the United States has gone to labor during each five-year period since 1935. The share of national income going to labor did not rise as union membership grew as a proportion of the labor force during the 1935–1955 period. Neither has it fallen as union membership has declined since 1955. In conclusion, while there is evidence that unions sometimes increase the wages of their members, there is no evidence that they are able to increase the general level of real wages or the share of income earned by labor relative to physical capital.

---

[7]H. Gregg Lewis, *Unionism and Relative Wages in the United States* (Chicago: University of Chicago Press, 1963).

EXHIBIT 7 • Labor's Share of National Income, 1930–1984

As a share of the nonfarm work force, union membership increased from less than 10 percent in the 1930s to nearly 35 percent in the mid-1950s. Since 1960, union membership declined substantially as a proportion of the U.S. labor force (see Exhibit 1). Despite these fluctuations, the share of national income allocated to labor (employee compensation and self-employment income) has been virtually constant throughout the 1930–1984 period.

Source: Derived from the national estimates of the U.S. Department of Commerce published in *Survey of Current Business.*

management a greater incentive to see that supervisors use discretion in dealing with each worker.[8]

This is not to say that the worker is always right in disputes involving labor and management. But, it is important for the self-esteem, morale, and human dignity of workers that they are able to have their say, that they are not powerless, and that they can take their grievances to a neutral third party. Unions have played a vital role in establishing these worker rights and in promoting a sense of community among workers.

LOOKING AHEAD

The previous four chapters have analyzed markets for human and physical resources. Wages, prices, and employment levels in these markets determine our personal incomes. The next chapter will focus on the distribution of income among individuals.

CHAPTER SUMMARY

1. Union membership grew rapidly during the 1935–55 period. In 1955, approximately one out of three nonfarm workers in the United States belonged to a union. During the last three decades, union membership has waned. In 1984, only one in six nonfarm workers were union members.

2. The strike is a major source of union power. A strike can cause the employer to lose sales while incurring continuing fixed cost. The threat of a strike, particularly when inventories are low, is an inducement for the employer to consent to the union's terms.

3. A strike is also costly to employees. Strike funds are usually inadequate to deal with a prolonged strike. The loss of just a few paychecks can impose extreme hardship on most families. The potential cost of a strike to both union and management provides each with an incentive to bargain seriously to avoid a work stoppage.

4. Agreement on most collective bargaining contracts is reached without a work stoppage. Since World War II, the number of work hours lost due to strikes is less than three tenths of the total work time—and the proportion of work time lost due to strikes has been declining.

5. There are three basic methods a union can use to increase the wages of its members: (a) restrict the supply of competitive inputs, including nonunion workers; (b) apply bargaining power enforced by a strike or threat of one; and (c) increase the demand for the labor service of union members.

6. When there are a large number of employees competing for labor services, each employer will have to pay the market wage rate to keep

---

[8]Of course, when a union is large enough to deal effectively with management and the government, individual workers may not exert much control within the union. There are occasional problems with corrupt and arbitrary actions by union officials, at both the local and the national levels. Opposition to union leadership from within the union is sometimes risky. On the whole, however, unions have worked effectively to give their members a greater voice in determining how their place of work is managed. For a discussion of these problems and how they are handled, see Lloyd G. Reynolds, *Labor Economics and Labor Relations*, 7th ed. (Englewood Cliffs, New Jersey: Prentice-Hall, 1978), Chapter 16.

employees from shifting to higher-wage alternatives. However, when monopsony is present, the single purchaser of labor may be able to profit by restricting employment and paying a wage rate that is less than the marginal revenue generated by the labor. Under these circumstances, a wage floor established by a union can result in both higher wages and increased employment.

7. If a union is going to increase the wages of its members without experiencing a significant reduction in employment, the demand for union labor must be inelastic. The strength of a union is enhanced if (a) there is an absence of good substitutes for this service, (b) the demand for the good it produces is highly inelastic, (c) the union labor input is a small share of the total cost of production, and/or (d) the supply of any available substitute is highly inelastic. An absence of these conditions weakens the power of the union.

8. Studies suggest that the earnings of union members exceed those of similar nonunion members by between 10 and 25 percent. Research using data from the 70s tends to place the differential closer to the higher figure. The most powerful unions have been able to obtain even larger wage gains for their members. Some weaker unions, unable to restrict the supply of nonunion workers (or products made by them), have had little impact on wages. Most of the real wage increases of union workers have probably been obtained at the expense of nonunion workers and consumers.

9. There is no indication that unions have significantly increased the share of national income going to labor in general. The real wages of workers are a reflection of their productivity rather than the result of union action or power. There is little reason to believe that unions enhance worker productivity—they may even retard it.

10. An increase in the wages of union members will either reduce expenditures on goods produced by nonunion labor or increase the supply of nonunion labor. In either case, the secondary effects of higher union wages will tend to reduce prices in the nonunion sector. Thus, there is no reason to believe that unions cause sustained increases in the general price level (inflation).

11. Unions in the United States have helped defend employees against a sense of powerlessness, unimportance, alienation, and insecurity, and against arbitrary behavior by management. The union movement is primarily responsible for our system of "industrial jurisprudence." Many think these nonpecuniary factors are far more important than the impact of unions on wages.

THE ECONOMIC WAY OF THINKING—
DISCUSSION QUESTIONS

1. Assume that the primary objective of a union is to raise wages. (a) Discuss the conditions that will help the union achieve this objective. (b) Why might a union be unable to meet its goal?

2. Suppose that Florida migrant farm workers are effectively unionized. What will be the impact of the unionization on (a) the price of Florida oranges, (b) the profits of Florida fruit growers in the short-run and in the long-run, (c) the mechanization of the fruitpicking industry, and (d) the employment of fruit pickers?

3. Unions in the North have been vigorously involved in efforts to organize lower-wage workers in the South. Union leaders often express their compassion for the low-money-wage southern workers. Can you think of a reason, other than compassion, for northern union leaders' (and workers') interest in having the higher union scale extended to the South? Explain.

4. "Unions have brought a decent living to working men and women. Without unions, employers would still be paying workers a starvation wage." Analyze.

5. (a) "An increase in the price of steel will be passed along to consumers in the form of higher prices of automobiles, homes, appliances, and other products made with steel." Do you agree or disagree?

   (b) "An increase in the price of craft-union labor will be passed along to consumers in the form of higher prices of homes, repair and installation services, appliances, and other products that require craft-union labor." Do you agree or disagree?

   (c) Are the interests of labor unions in conflict primarily with the interests of union employers? Explain.

6. "The purpose of unions is to push the wage rate above the competitive level. By their very nature, they are monopolists. Therefore, they will necessarily cause resources to be misallocated." Do you agree or disagree? Explain.

7. "If a union is unable to organize all the major firms in an industry, it is unlikely to exert a major impact on the wages of union members." Indicate why you either agree or disagree.

CHAPTER FOCUS

We can compare two countries with relatively similar income distributions. If the first keeps most families in their economic place while the second allows much shifting of places, the second is surely more equal, even in strictly economic terms. But the international statistics all economists use from the UN or OECD—cannot report this simple, crucial economic fact. [1]

MARK LILLA

- How unequal are incomes in the United States? How does income inequality in the United States compare with that of other countries?

- How much income mobility is there in the United States—do the rich remain rich while the poor remain poor?

- What are the characteristics of the poor? Have they changed in recent decades?

- How is the poverty rate derived? Have income transfers reduced the poverty rate?

- Is social security an insurance program? Who is helped and who is hurt by social security?

26 INEQUALITY, INCOME MOBILITY, AND THE BATTLE AGAINST POVERTY

In a market economy, the distribution of income is determined by the sale price of factor services, the resources of individuals, and the choices of individuals as to how their resources are to be employed. Because market income stems from the productive contribution of one's human and physical resources, owners have an incentive to employ their resources efficiently. When resources are allocated by market prices, there is no central distributing agency that carves up the economic pie and allocates slices to various individuals. The income of each person (or household) is determined by what they receive from others in exchange or as a gift. Since the basic abilities, opportunities, and preferences of individuals differ, income inequality will result.

Economics does not tell us that one distribution of income is better than another. It does help us better understand the process, however. It also sheds light on how policy alternatives designed to alter the distribution of income can be expected to work. This chapter focuses on these issues and related topics.

INCOME INEQUALITY IN THE UNITED STATES

Money income is only one component of economic well-being. Such factors as leisure, the nonpecuniary advantages and disadvantages of a job, and the expected stability of future income are also determinants of economic welfare. Nevertheless, since income represents command over market goods and services, it is highly significant. Moreover, it is readily observable. It is the most widely used measure of economic well-being and degree of inequality.

Exhibit 1 indicates the share of before-tax annual income received by quintile—that is, by each fifth of families ranked from the lowest to the

EXHIBIT 1 • Income Inequality of Families—Selected Years 1952–1983					
	Percentage of Before-Tax Aggregate Income Received by:				
	Lowest 20 Percent of Recipients	Second Quintile	Third Quintile	Fourth Quintile	Top 20 Percent of Recipients
1952	4.9	12.3	17.4	23.4	41.9
1962	5.0	12.1	17.6	24.0	41.3
1972	5.4	11.9	17.5	23.9	41.4
1976	5.4	11.8	17.6	24.1	41.1
1983	4.7	11.1	17.1	24.4	42.7

Source: Bureau of the Census, *Current Population Reports*, Series P-60, No. 146, Table 17.

---

[1]Mark Lilla, "Why the 'Income Distribution' Is So Misleading," *The Public Interest*, 77 (Fall 1984): 63–76.

highest. If there were total equality of annual income, each quintile (fifth) of the population would have received 20 percent of the aggregate income. Clearly that was not the case. In 1983, the bottom 20 percent of family income recipients received 4.7 percent of the total income. At the other end of the spectrum, the 20 percent of families with the highest annual incomes received 42.7 percent of the total income in 1983. The top quintile of income recipients thus received approximately nine times as much income • as the bottom quintile of recipients.

Exhibit 1 also illustrates that there was little change in the distribution of pre-tax family income in the United States between 1952 and 1983. Throughout the 1952–1983 period, the bottom 20 percent of family income recipients received approximately five percent of the aggregate money income. In contrast, the 20 percent of families with the highest annual incomes earned slightly more than 40 percent of the total.

Two points emerge from Exhibit 1. First, there is a great deal of inequality in annual income in the United States. Second, the degree of inequality in annual money income has remained virtually unchanged during the last several decades.

IS ANNUAL INCOME A GOOD MEASURE OF ECONOMIC STATUS?

How meaningful are the data of Exhibit 1? If all families were similar except in the amount of income received, the use of annual income data as an index of inequality would be far more defensible. However, this is not the case. The aggregate data lump together (a) small and large families, (b) prime-age earners and elderly retirees, (c) multi-earner families and families without any current earners, and (d) husband-wife families and single-parent families. Even if individual incomes over a lifetime were exactly equal, these factors would result in substantial inequality in annual income data.

Consider just one factor, the impact of age, on the pattern of lifetime income. Typically, the annual income of young people is low, particularly if they are going to school or acquiring training. Many persons under 25 years of age studying to be lawyers, doctors, engineers, and economists will have a low annual income during this phase of their life. This does not mean they are poor, however, at least not in the usual sense. After completing their formal education and acquiring work experience, individuals move into their prime working years. During this phase of life, annual income is generally quite high, particularly for families in which both husband and wife work. It is, however, also a time period when families are purchasing houses and providing for children. All things considered, annual income during the prime working years tends to overstate the economic well-being of most households. Finally, there is the retirement phase, characterized by less work, more leisure, and smaller family size. Even families that are quite well off tend to experience income well below the average for the entire population during the retirement phase.

Exhibit 2 highlights major differences between high- and low-income families that underlie the distributional data of Exhibit 1. The typical high-income family (top 20 percent) was headed by a well-educated person in the prime working-age phase of life whose income was supplemented with the earnings of other family members, particularly working wives. In contrast, persons with little education, nonworking retirees, youthful workers, and

EXHIBIT 2 • The Differing Characteristics of High- and Low-Income Families, 1983		
	Bottom 20 Percent of Income Recipients, 1983	Top 20 Percent of Income Recipients, 1983
Mean years of schooling (household head)	10.1	14.3
Age of household head (percent distribution)		
Under 35	44	16
35–64	32	77
65 and over	24	7
Family status (percent distribution)		
Married-couple family	58	94
Single-parent family	42	6
Percent of married couple families in which wife works	26	66
Percent of total earners supplied by group	10	29
Percent of total weeks worked supplied by group	7	31

Source: U.S. Department of Commerce, *Money Income of Households, Families, and Persons in the United States: 1983*, Washington, D.C.: U.S. Government Printing Office, 1985.

single-parent families are substantially overrepresented among low-income families (bottom 20 percent of income recipients). The mean number of years of schooling for the household heads of high-income families was 14.3 years, compared to only 10.1 years for heads of families with low annual incomes. Seventy-seven percent of the high-income families had household heads in the prime working age category (age 35 to 64), compared to only 32 percent of the low-income families. Only one parent was present in 42 percent of the low-income families, whereas 94 percent of the high-income group were husband-wife families.

At least partially reflecting the overrepresentation of prime working age households, there was a striking difference in work time between low- and high-income families. Sixty-six percent of the high-income married couple families were characterized by a working wife, compared to only 26 percent for low-income married families. The top 20 percent of income recipients contributed 31 percent of the total number of weeks worked, while the low-income group contributed only 7 percent of the total work time.

Exhibit 2 sheds substantial light on the distributional data of Exhibit 1. The high-income recipients were better educated, more likely to be in their prime working years, and they worked approximately 4.5 times as many weeks as low-income families in 1983. Given these factors, it is not surprising that the top 20 percent of recipients earned approximately 9 times the annual income of the bottom quintile.

FAMILY SIZE, AGE, AND THE INEQUALITY OF INCOME AFTER TAXES AND TRANSFERS

The income data of Exhibit 1 represent income *before taxes*. Noncash income transfers are excluded. Families of varying size and at various stages of their lifetime earnings are lumped together. Suppose these factors were taken into account—that income comparisons were made *after taxes and transfers* for families of the same size and age of household head. How much inequality would still be present?

A detailed study by Edgar Browning and William Johnson addresses this question. Browning and Johnson investigated the distribution of annual income in 1976 for three-person households headed by a 35- to 44-year-old.[2] Exhibit 3 presents their findings. As column 3 shows, the distribution of pre-tax market income was highly unequal, not unlike the distribution of income presented in Exhibit 1. The top fifth of the households surveyed, the high-income households, received 41.0 percent of the aggregate income, compared to only 5.3 percent for the lowest one fifth (column 3). However, the low-income families paid fewer taxes on their income and received more income transfers as supplements.

Once adjustment was made for cash and in-kind transfers, as well as for income tax, the distribution of net income was considerably more equal. As Exhibit 3 (column 6) shows, the top group of income recipients received 36.3 percent of the aggregate net income, compared to 9.2 percent for the bottom quintile. Thus, after taxes and transfers, the top quintile received approximately 4 times the annual income of the bottom 20 percent of recipients, compared to 8 times the amount of their income prior to taxes and transfers (column 3).

EXHIBIT 3 • The Distribution of Income Among Three-person Households, 1976

Household heads in these data were 35 to 44 years old.

Income Grouping (1)	Market Income (in Billions) (2)	Percent Distribution of Market Income (3)	Cash and In-Kind Transfers minus Taxes (in Billions) (4)	Net Income (in Billions) (5)	Percent Distribution, Net Income (6)	Net Income per Hour (7)
Lowest fifth	2.29	5.3	+ 0.73	3.02	9.2	5.78
Second fifth	5.42	12.6	− 0.86	4.56	13.8	5.77
Third fifth	7.76	18.1	− 1.84	5.92	17.9	5.68
Fourth fifth	9.90	23.0	− 2.34	7.56	22.9	6.66
Top fifth	17.60	41.0	− 5.61	11.99	36.3	9.82

Edgar K. Browning and Jacquelene M. Browning, *Public Finance and the Price System* (New York: Macmillan, 1983), p. 244.

---

[2]See Edgar K. Browning and William R. Johnson, *The Distribution of the Tax Burden* (Washington, D.C.: American Enterprise Institute, 1979).

Perhaps even more surprising, Browning and Johnson found that most of the difference in the net income of three-person households headed by a 35- to 44-year-old reflects hours of work. The net income per hour of work for the top quintile was $9.82, compared to $5.78 for the bottom quintile (column 7). According to Browning and Johnson, the net income per hour worked of the top 20 percent of households was less than twice the net income of the bottom 20 percent of households. In fact, the net income per hour of work was almost identical for the bottom 60 percent of households. Just as Exhibit 2 implies, the findings of Browning and Johnson illustrate why it is important to consider the significance of family size, age, hours worked, and taxes and transfers when interpreting data on income inequality.

INCOME INEQUALITY IN OTHER COUNTRIES

How does income inequality in the United States compare with that in other nations? Exhibit 4 presents a summary of household income data compiled by the World Bank. These data indicate that the distribution of income in the United States, Canada, Australia, and France is quite similar. The degree of income inequality in Sweden and the United Kingdom is slightly less

EXHIBIT 4 • **Equality and Inequality Around the World**			
	Percentage Share of Household Income Received by:		
Country (Year)	Bottom 20 Percent	Middle Three Quintiles	Top 20 Percent
Developing Nations			
India (1975–76)	7.0	43.6	49.4
Kenya (1976)	2.6	37.0	60.4
Indonesia (1976)	6.6	44.0	49.4
Thailand (1975–76)	5.6	44.6	49.8
Brazil (1972)	2.0	31.4	66.6
South Korea (1976)	5.7	49.0	45.3
Mexico (1977)	2.9	39.4	57.7
Yugoslavia (1978)	6.6	54.7	38.7
Israel (1979–80)	6.0	54.1	39.9
Hong Kong (1980)	5.4	47.6	47.0
Developed Nations			
United Kingdom (1979)	7.0	53.3	39.7
Japan (1979)	8.7	53.8	37.5
France (1975)	5.3	48.9	45.8
Australia (1975–76)	5.4	47.5	47.1
Canada (1981)	5.3	54.7	40.0
Sweden (1981)	7.4	50.9	41.7
United States (1980)	5.3	54.8	39.9

Source: The World Bank, *World Development Report*, 1985, Table 28.

than in the United States. In light of their welfare-state policies and relative homogeneous populations—that is, uniformity with respect to race and ethnicity—the lesser inequality of income in Sweden and the United Kingdom is not surprising.

The share of income going to the wealthy is usually greater in less developed countries. According to the World Bank study, the top 20 percent of income recipients received 66.6 percent of the aggregate income in Brazil, 60.4 percent in Kenya, and 57.7 percent in Mexico. Although the degree of inequality was less pronounced in India, Indonesia, and Thailand, it was still substantially more unequal than for developed nations. Among the developing nations of Exhibit 4, only South Korea, Yugoslavia, Israel, and Hong Kong were marked by a degree of inequality similar to that of developed nations. A side effect of the greater inequality of most developing nations is the absence of a strong middle-income group. Note the middle three quintiles (Exhibit 4, middle column) generally received less income in developing than developed nations.

INCOME MOBILITY—DO THE POOR STAY POOR AND THE RICH STAY RICH?

Income Mobility: Movement of individuals and families either up or down income distribution rankings when comparisons are made at two different points in time. When substantial income mobility is present, one's current position will not be a very good indicator as to what one's position will be a few years in the future.

The distribution of annual income is like a snapshot. It presents a picture at a moment in time. However, since the picture does not reveal the degree of movement across income groupings, it may be misleading. Consider two countries with identical distributions of annual income.[3] In both cases, the annual income of the top quintile of income recipients is 8 times greater than the bottom quintile. Now, suppose that in the first country—we will refer to it as Static—the same people are at the top of the income distribution year after year. Similarly, the poor people of Static remain poor year after year. Static is characterized by an absence of **income mobility.** In contrast, earners in the second country, which we will call Dynamic, are constantly changing places. Indeed, every five years, each family spends one year in the upper-income quintile, one year in each of the three middle-income quintiles, and one year in the bottom-income quintile. In Dynamic, no one is rich for more than one year (out of each five) and no one is poor for more than a year. Obviously, the degree of economic inequality in Static and Dynamic is vastly different. You would not know it, though, by looking at their annual income distributions. In fact, the annual income distributions in the two countries are identical.

The contrast between Static and Dynamic indicates why it is important to consider income mobility when addressing the issue of economic inequality. Until recently, detailed data on income mobility were sparse. Fortunately, this situation is changing, primarily as the result of a group of researchers at the University of Michigan's Survey Research Center. Under the direction of James Morgan and Greg Duncan, the Center collects detailed socioeconomic data on a representative sample of the U.S. population

---

[3]The authors are indebted to Mark Lilla from whom this illustrative method was drawn.

and tracks the same individuals and their families each year. With these data, it is now possible to see how income and other indicators of economic status change with time.

A detailed study of the University of Michigan panel data was published in 1984.[4] Exhibit 5 summarizes the major findings of the study with regard to income mobility. After grouping families by their income in 1971, the table then looks at the relative income position of the families seven years later. For example, the first row indicates the relative income position in 1978 of families who were in the top quintile of income recipients in 1971. Surprisingly, only 48.5 percent of the Americans who were best off (the top quintile) in 1971 were able to retain the same position in 1978. More than 20 percent fell to the bottom three quintiles of the 1978 income distribution. The bottom row of Exhibit 5 tracks the experience of families in the lowest-income quintile in 1971. A little more than half (55.5 percent) of the families in the bottom-income quintile in 1971 remained there in 1978. In contrast, 22.5 percent of the families at the bottom in 1971 were able to move into one of the top three income quintiles by 1978. Six percent of the poor in 1971 moved to the top quintile seven years later.

The diagonal (color) numbers of Exhibit 5 provide a measure of income mobility. If there was little or no income mobility within the American system, each diagonal number would be close to 100 percent. For the three middle-income quintiles, the diagonal numbers are approximately 33 percent, indicating that only one third of the persons in each of these quintiles remained in the same quintile. Two thirds moved either up or down the income ladder between 1971 and 1978. Of those at the top or bottom in 1971, only about half remained in the same position in 1978.

The data of Exhibit 5 focus on changes in the income of families. What

---

EXHIBIT 5 • Income Mobility—Family Income Ranking in 1978 Compared to Ranking in 1971

Family Income Quintile, 1971	Family Income Quintile, 1978					
	Highest	Second	Third	Fourth	Lowest	Total
Highest	48.5	29.5	14.0	4.5	3.5	100%
Second	22.0	31.5	25.5	15.0	6.0	100%
Third	14.0	18.5	30.5	23.5	13.5	100%
Fourth	9.0	13.5	21.5	34.5	21.5	100%
Lowest	6.0	7.0	9.5	22.0	55.5	100%

Source: Derived from Greg J. Duncan et al., *Years of Poverty, Years of Plenty* (Ann Arbor: Institute of Social Research, 1984).

---

[4]Greg J. Duncan et al., *Years of Poverty, Years of Plenty: The Changing Fortunes of American Workers and Families* (Ann Arbor: Institute for Social Research, University of Michigan, 1984). Also see Bradley R. Schiller, "Relative Earnings Mobility in the United States," *American Economic Review*, vol. 67, no. 5 (1977), pp. 926–939 for an earlier pioneer study of income mobility.

can we say about income mobility across generations? If your parents are poor (or wealthy), does it mean you will be poor (or wealthy)? The Michigan panel data are just now starting to yield information related to this issue. Nearly 1,500 young adults in the study have now left their parents and formed families of their own. Among those who came from families with incomes in the top quintile, 36 percent were able to attain this lofty ranking relative to the other newly formed families. In contrast, 41 percent of the offspring of families in the highest-income quintile fell to the bottom three income quintiles among the newly formed families. Among the offspring of poor families, less than half (44 percent) remained in the bottom quintile among the newly formed families. For middle-income families (the three middle quintiles), offspring were spread almost evenly among the five quintiles of the income distribution for newly formed families.

The data thus indicate that while high-income families are able to influence the economic status of their offspring, they are unable to pass along their lofty income position to most of their children. Similarly, the children of low-income families face disadvantages but they frequently attain income well above that of the parents. For the three middle-income quintiles, parents fail to exert a systematic impact on the success or failure of their children. Thus, the *intergenerational* distribution of income approaches perfect mobility among the middle-income groupings.

The findings of the Michigan panel data are highly consistent with the findings of Christopher Jencks, based on a less detailed, but much earlier study by the Center for Educational Policy Research at Harvard. Writing in 1972, Jencks stated:

> Among men born into the most affluent fifth of the population . . . we estimate that less than half will be part of the same elite when they grow up. Of course, it is also true that very few will be in the bottom fifth. Rich parents can at least guarantee their children that much. Yet, if we follow families over several generations, even this will not hold true. Affluent families often have at least one relatively indigent grandparent in the background, and poor families, unless they are black or relatively recent immigrants, have often had at least one prosperous grandparent.[5]

Our analysis indicates that drawing conclusions from *annual* income data must be done with care. The annual data camouflage the fact that many high-income earners had much lower incomes just a few years before. Similarly, many with low current incomes have attained significantly higher incomes previously (and they can be expected to do so again in the future). Panel income data indicate that the inequalities observed at a point in time are substantially reduced over time as individuals and families exchange relative economic positions. This income mobility is particularly important across generations. The ability of American parents to pass along their economic status to their children is quite limited.

---

[5]Excerpt from *Inequality: Reassessment of the Effect of Family and Schooling in America*, p. 216, by Christopher Jencks et al., copyrighted by Basic Books, Inc., Publishers, New York.

POVERTY IN THE UNITED STATES

In an affluent society such as the United States, income inequality and poverty are related issues. Poverty could be defined in strictly relative terms—the bottom one fifth of all income recipients, for example. However, this definition would not be very helpful, since that would mean that poverty could never decline.

The official definition of poverty in the United States is based on the perceived minimum income necessary to provide food, clothing, shelter, and basic necessities economically for a family. This **poverty threshold income level** varies with family size and composition. The poverty threshold income is adjusted annually for changes in prices. For purposes of determining whether or not income is above the poverty threshold, the official poverty rate considers only money income. (See Measures of Economic Activity for additional details on how the poverty rate is measured.)

How many people are poor? According to the official definition of poverty, there were 33.7 million poor people and 7.3 million poor families in 1984. As Exhibit 6 indicates, 14.4 percent of the population (11.6 percent of the families) was officially classified as poor in 1984. During the 1950s and 1960s, the poverty rate declined substantially. By 1970, the official poverty rate for families had fallen to 10.1 percent, down from 18.1 percent in 1960 and 32.0 percent in 1947. During the 1970s, the overall poverty rate changed little. In fact, the official poverty rate was slightly higher in 1980 than it was in 1970. During the early 1980s, the poverty rate rose. Most commentators point to the stagnating economy during 1979–1982 and to cutbacks in transfer programs during the early years of the Reagan Administration as the source of the rising poverty rates in the 1980s. As we proceed, we will investigate the link between poverty and income transfers in more detail.

In recent years, the composition of the poverty population has changed substantially. As Exhibit 7 indicates, elderly persons and the working poor formed the core of the poverty population in 1959. Twenty-two percent of

Poverty Threshold Income Level: The level of money income below which a family is considered to be poor. It differs according to family characteristics (for example, number of family members) and is adjusted when consumer prices change.

EXHIBIT 6 • The Poverty Rate of Persons and Families in the United States, 1960–1984

Year	Poverty Rate (Percent)	
	Persons	Families
1947	n.a.	32.0
1960	22.2	18.1
1970	12.6	10.1
1980	13.0	10.3
1984	14.4	11.6

Source: Bureau of the Census, *Money Income and Poverty Status of Families and Persons in the United States: 1984* (Table 15), and *Economic Report of the President 1964* (Table 7).

the poor families were headed by an elderly person in 1959. Most poor people (70 percent) worked at least some part of the year. By 1984, the picture had changed dramatically. In 1984, only 10 percent of the poor families were headed by an elderly person. The poverty rate among husband-wife families also declined sharply between 1959 and 1984. In the 1980s, the problem of poverty is interwoven with family instability. Nearly half (48 percent) of the poor families were headed by a female in 1984, up from 23 percent in 1959. Many of these women were not in the work force. As a result, only 49 percent of the poor household heads worked at all during the year in 1984, compared to 70 percent who worked in 1959.

MEASURES OF ECONOMIC ACTIVITY

Determining the Poverty Rate

Families and individuals are classified as poor or nonpoor based on the poverty threshold income level originally developed by the Social Security Administration (SSA) in 1964. Since consumption survey data indicated that low- and median-income families of three or more persons spent approximately one third of their income on food, the SSA established the poverty threshold income level at three times the cost of an economical, nutritionally adequate, food plan. A slightly larger multiple was used for smaller families and individuals living alone. The poverty threshold income varies according to family size, because the food costs vary by family size and composition. The poverty threshold income level is adjusted annually to account for rising prices. The chart below illustrates how the poverty threshold for a family of four has increased as prices have risen:

Year	Poverty Threshold Income Level for a Family of Four
1959	$ 2,973
1970	3,968
1980	8,414
1984	10,609

Even though the poverty threshold income level is adjusted for prices, it is actually an *absolute* measure of economic status. As real income increases, the poverty threshold income will decline relative to the income of the general populace.

The official poverty rate is the *number of persons or families* living in households with a money income *below* the poverty income threshold *as a proportion of the total*. When determining a person's or family's income, the official poverty rate considers only money income. Income received in the form of *noncash* benefits such as food stamps, medical care, and housing subsidies, is completely ignored in the calculation of the official poverty rate.

Since noncash benefits targeted for low-income households have grown rapidly since the late 1960s, the failure of the official poverty rate to count this "income" reduces its accuracy as a measurement tool. To remedy this deficiency, Congress instructed the Bureau of Census to develop a poverty index that included noncash benefits as income. In addition to the official poverty rate, the Bureau now pub-

lishes annual data for three "adjusted" poverty rates based on alternative methods of accounting for noncash benefits. Economists generally favor the use of the recipient value-adjusted poverty rate. This method values noncash benefits at the equivalent amount of cash income a recipient would be willing to exchange for the noncash benefits. It thus takes into account the possibility that recipients might rather have cash than the in-kind benefits.

When the value of noncash benefits is added to money income, the *adjusted* poverty rate for all age groups is reduced. For example, while the official poverty rate for families was 11.6 percent in 1984, the adjusted poverty rate based on the recipient value method of evaluating food, housing, and medical benefits was only 9.8 percent.

The poverty rate is calculated each year based on a current population survey of nearly 60,000 households designed to reflect the population of the United States. The most comprehensive source for detailed data on this topic is the Bureau of Census publication, "Characteristics of the Population Below the Poverty Level" (annual).

EXHIBIT 7 • The Changing Composition of the Poor

	1959	1984
Number of Poor Families (in millions)	8.3	7.3
Poverty Rate (Percent)	18.5	11.6
Percent of Poor Families Headed by:		
Female	23	48
Nonwhite	26	32
Elderly person (age 65 and over)	22	10
Prime working-age (25–64) person	57	67
Person who worked at least some during the year	70	49

Source: U.S. Department of Commerce, *Characteristics of the Population Below the Poverty Level: 1982* (Table 5), and *Money Income and Poverty Status of Families and Persons in the United States: 1984* (Table 18).

TRANSFER PAYMENTS AND THE POVERTY RATE

In the mid-1960s, it was widely believed that an increase in income transfers directed toward the poor would substantially reduce, if not eliminate, the incidence of poverty. The *1964 Economic Report of the President* (p. 77) presented the dominant view. The report stated:

> Conquest of poverty is well within our power. About $11 billion (approximately $36 billion measured in 1984 dollars) a year would bring all poor families up to the $3,000 income level we have taken to be the minimum for a decent life. The majority of the nation could simply tax themselves enough to provide the necessary income supplements to their less fortunate citizens. The burden—one fifth of the annual defense budget, less than 2 percent of GNP—would certainly not be intolerable.

The 1965–1975 period was characterized by a rapid growth in income transfer programs. Overall transfers, including those directed toward the elderly, approximately doubled *as a proportion of personal income* between 1965 and 1975. As the War on Poverty programs of the Johnson administration were put in place, income transfers directed toward the poor also grew rapidly. Measured in 1984 dollars, **means-tested income transfers** tripled, expanding from $24 billion in 1965 to $73 billion in 1975 (Exhibit 8). As a proportion of personal income, means-tested transfers jumped from 1.6 percent in 1965 to 3.2 percent in 1975.

Means-tested Income Transfers: Transfers that are limited to persons or families with an income below a certain cut-off point. Eligibility is thus dependent on low-income status.

Did the expansion in government income transfers reduce the poverty rate as the *1964 Economic Report of the President* anticipated? Exhibits 9 and 10 shed light on this question. Continuing the trend of the post-World War II era, the official poverty rate fell throughout the 1960s. During the 1970s, however, the rate leveled off. By 1980, the official poverty rate was 10.3 percent, virtually unchanged from the 1968 rate.

		Means-Tested Transfer Payments	
Year	Total Transfer Payments as a Percent of Personal Income	Total (Billions of 1984 dollars)	As a Percent of Personal Income
1965	8.5	25.6	1.6
1975	18.2	72.7	3.2
1980	17.3	81.3	3.0
1984	17.6	80.3	2.6

EXHIBIT 8 • The Path of Government Income Transfers, 1965–1984[a]

[a]Includes noncash transfers such as food stamps, school lunch subsidies, public housing and other housing subsidies, and medicaid.

Source: *Economic Report of the President: 1985* (Table 22), and Department of Commerce, *Estimates of Poverty Including the Value of Noncash Benefits: 1984* (Table 14).

Aggregate poverty rate data as presented in Exhibit 9 conceal an important difference between the experience of the elderly and nonelderly that has largely gone unnoticed. Exhibit 10 highlights this point. The poverty rate for the elderly continued to decline throughout the 1970s. By 1984, the official poverty rate of the elderly had fallen to 7.3 percent, down from 17.0 percent in 1968 and 30.0 percent in 1959 (Exhibit 10a). The experience of working-age Americans, however, was vastly different. After falling for several decades, the official poverty rate of nonelderly families bottomed in 1968 and has been rising ever since (Exhibit 10b).

Why has so little progress been made against poverty—particularly poverty among the nonelderly—during the War on Poverty era? For a time, it was widely believed that the stagnating poverty rate of the 1970s reflected the failure of the official data to count noncash benefits derived from programs such as Medicare, Medicaid, food stamps, public housing, and school

EXHIBIT 9 • The Poverty Rate, 1947–1984

The official poverty rate of families declined sharply during the 1950s and 1960s, changed little during the 1970s, and rose during the early 1980s. The shaded area of the bars indicates the additional reduction in the poverty rate when noncash benefits are counted as income. In 1984, the poverty rate adjusted for noncash benefits (recipient value method) was 9.8 percent, compared to the official rate of 11.6 percent.

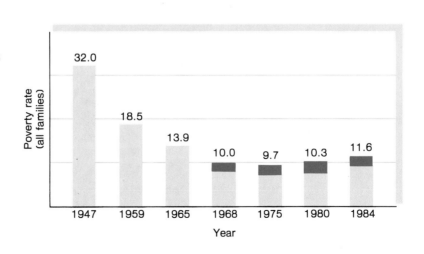

EXHIBIT 10 • Changing Poverty Rates, the Differing Experience of the Elderly and Nonelderly, 1959–84

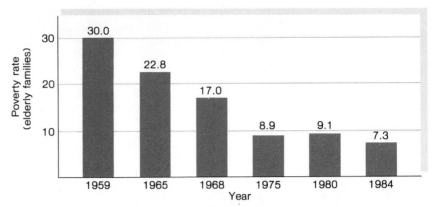

(a) The official poverty rate for elderly families has declined sharply since 1959.

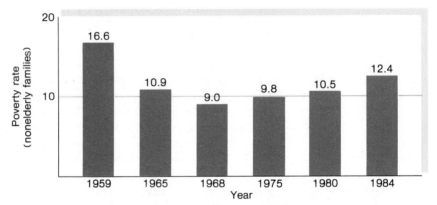

(b) In contrast, the official poverty rate for nonelderly families has been rising since the late 1960s.

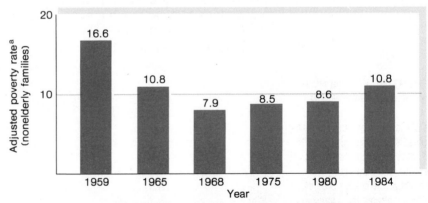

(c) Adjusting for noncash transfers reduces the poverty rate of the nonelderly but it does not alter the basic pattern.

[a]The recipient value method was used to adjust the poverty rate for noncash food, housing, and medical benefits.

Source: Derived from Department of Commerce, *Money Income and Poverty Status of Families and Persons in the United States: 1984* and *Estimates of Poverty Including the Value of Noncash Benefits: 1984*. See James Gwartney and Thomas S. McCaleb, "Have Antipoverty Programs Increased Poverty?" *The Cato Journal* (Summer/Spring, 1985).

lunches. Since in-kind transfers have grown rapidly since 1970, this is a potential source of bias. Addressing this issue, the Department of Commerce now publishes adjusted poverty rates that count the in-kind benefits. Given the size of noncash transfers, it is now possible to reconstruct adjusted poverty rate data for earlier time periods.[6]

As Exhibit 9 illustrates, once noncash benefits are counted, the poverty rate is reduced. Adjusting the poverty rate for the value of noncash benefits to recipients reduces the poverty rate of families to 9.8 percent in 1984, compared to the official rate of 11.6 percent. However, as Exhibit 10c illustrates, adjustment for noncash benefits does not significantly alter the picture for working-age Americans. Even after accounting for noncash benefits, the poverty rate of working-age families has been rising since 1968. By 1984, it had risen to 10.8 percent, the exact poverty rate of working-age families in 1965.

Economic and social changes have retarded progress against poverty. While the employment rate has increased during the last 15 years, real wage rates have stagnated. The failure of real wage increases during the 1970–1985 period to match their growth during the 1960s has contributed to the poverty of *working* Americans. In addition, increases in the divorce rate, births to unwed mothers, and the incidence of female-headed households have contributed to the problem. Nonetheless, the results achieved from expanded expenditures (compared to the mid 1960s) on transfer programs have been disappointing. Whether one looks at the official or adjusted poverty rates, the picture is the same. Except for the elderly, the steady progress of the 1950s and 1960s came to a halt during the 1970s and 1980s.

FACTORS LIMITING THE EFFECTIVENESS OF TRANSFER PROGRAMS

How can one explain the relative ineffectiveness, at least compared to what was expected, of income transfer as a weapon against poverty? Analysis of the impact of transfers on the incentive structure confronting the poor enhances our understanding of this issue. While government transfers improved the living standards of many poor people, the programs also severely penalized self-improvement efforts of low-income Americans.

It is important to recognize that the poor are not a monolithic group. In fact, the poor consist of at least two rather distinct groups. There is a hardcore group characterized by individuals who are generally victims of debilitating disease, or physical, mental, or emotional disability. The hardcore poor remain poor during both the good times and the bad. There is also a second group, which might be called the marginal poor. The periods of poverty experienced by the marginal poor reflect factors such as loss of job, change in family status, premature termination of schooling (or training), or choice of a high-risk lifestyle. In contrast with the hardcore poor,

---

[6]See James Gwartney and Thomas S. McCaleb, "Have Antipoverty Programs Increased Poverty?" *The CATO Journal* (Spring/Summer, 1985), for additional details on this topic.

the personal choices of the marginal poor exert an impact on the incidence and duration of their periods of poverty.

There are three major secondary effects that reduce the ability of transfer programs to uplift the living standards of the poor, particularly the marginally poor.

Marginal Tax Rate: The amount of one's additional (marginal) earnings that must be paid explicitly in taxes or implicitly in the form of a reduction in the level of one's income supplement. Since it establishes the fraction of an additional dollar earned that an individual is permitted to keep, it is an important determinant of the incentive to work.

1. *High implicit* **marginal tax rates** *reduce the incentive of the poor to earn. The net increase in income of the poor is thus much smaller than the transfer.* When the size of the transfer payments to the poor is linked to income, an increase in redistribution results in an increase in the implicit marginal tax rate of the poor. As the incomes of the poor rise, they qualify for fewer programs and the size of their income transfers is reduced. For the poor, higher earnings mean less transfer income. Under these circumstances, therefore, the link between additional earnings and additional net income is weakened for the income transfer recipient.

Transfer benefits derived from Aid for Families with Dependent Children (AFDC), food stamps, Medicaid, school lunch subsidies, rent supplements, and housing subsidies decline as income rises. The implicit marginal tax rate associated with individual programs appears to be quite reasonable. For example, food stamp benefits are reduced by $30 for each $100 of monthly earnings up to a monthly earnings of $800 for a family of four. The implicit marginal tax rate for AFDC is higher, usually in the 50 percent range. The real problem arises, though, when the potential benefits from several programs are considered. Exhibit 11 illustrates this point for a mother with two children residing in Pennsylvania. If she earned no income, she would be eligible for annual cash and in-kind benefits of $7,568 from AFDC, food stamps, Medicaid, and the Earned Income Tax Credit. If the family's earnings rose to $2,000, transfer benefits would be reduced and taxes increased, leaving the family with spendable income of $8,391. Additional earned income of $2,000 thus generates only $823 in additional

EXHIBIT 11 • The Effect of Transfer Benefits and Taxes on the Incentive of A Pennsylvania Mother with Two Children to Earn Income (September 1983)

Annual Gross Wage	Transfer Benefits[a]	Income and Employment Taxes[b]	Spendable Income	Implicit Marginal Tax Rate
$ 0	$7568	$ 0	$7568	—
2000	6525	134	8391	58.8
4000	5482	268	9214	58.8
5000	3040	346	7694	252.0
6000	2059	611	7448	124.6
7000	1719	810	7909	53.9
8000	1378	1021	8357	55.2
9000	1038	1240	8798	55.9
10000	698	1469	9229	56.9

[a]The following benefits are included: AFDC, Earned Income Tax Credit, food stamps and Medicaid. The Medicaid benefits were valued at the 1978 national average adjusted for inflation between 1978 and 1982.

[b]Includes social security and federal and state income taxes.

Source: Data are derived from U.S. House of Representatives Committee on The Ways and Means, *Background Material on Poverty* (Washington D.C.: Government Printing Office, 1983) Table 10, page 89.

spendable income, equivalent to a marginal tax rate of 58.8 percent. At higher levels of earned income, this implicit marginal tax rate is even greater. If earned income rose from $4,000 to $5,000, spendable income would *decrease* from $9,214 to $7,694, an implicit marginal tax rate of 252 percent. If income increased further to $6,000, the family would lose eligibility for AFDC, and its after-tax-and-transfer income would decrease again, this time by $246. In fact, a family earning $6,000 has less spendable income than a family with no earned income, and a family earning $10,000 each year (equivalent to a full-time year-round job paying $5 an hour) would have spendable income of $9,299, just $1,661 more than a family with no earned income at all. The loss in transfer benefits and the increased taxes when earnings rise from zero to $10,000 is equivalent to a tax rate of 83 percent on earned income.

Such extremely high marginal tax rates severely retard the incentive of persons with low income to earn. Many transfer recipients who would otherwise engage in market work decide to work fewer hours or not all all. (Note Exhibit 7 indicates that the family head of one half the poor families did not work at all during 1984.) As a result, some portion of the transfer income is merely replacement income; it simply replaces income the recipient would have earned in the absence of the transfer. Thus, the net income of recipients increases by less than the amount of the transfer.

2. *The skills of the poor depreciate when they opt out of the labor force due to the high implicit marginal tax rates. Declining skills further limit their ability to escape poverty.* Individuals who do not use their skills for extended periods of time will find it difficult to compete with otherwise similar individuals with continuous labor force participation. The long-term consequences of an incentive structure that encourages nonwork is even more destructive than the short-term effects. As marginal poor people opt for nonwork, their work record deteriorates. With the passage of time, they become less and less able to support themselves. As the length of time out of the work force expands, marginally poor individuals move into the hardcore poor category.

3. *Some economists believe that transfer programs may encourage individuals to engage in behavior that can lead to poverty.* By insuring against adversity, these economists suggest, transfer programs reduce the opportunity costs of such activities as dropping out of school or drug and alcohol dependence. Furthermore, the detailed rules and guidelines intended to limit abuse of transfer programs tend to reduce the possibility of individually tailored solutions for recipients. Potential recipients may alter their behavior in order to meet program eligibility requirements, rather than take steps to reduce the likelihood of personal adversity and welfare dependence.

Negative Income Tax: A system of transferring income of the poor, whereby a minimum level of income would be guaranteed by the provision of income supplements. The supplement would be reduced by some fraction (less than 1) as the family earned additional income. An increase in earnings would always cause the disposable income available to the family to rise.

THE MECHANICS OF A SIMPLE NEGATIVE INCOME TAX

Would it be possible to devise an income transfer system that would avoid at least the most extreme disincentive effects associated with the current system? Some economists, most notably Milton Friedman, believe that the cost of redistribution would be substantially reduced if a simple **negative income tax** were substituted for the current jungle of complex and sometimes conflicting welfare programs.

How would the negative income tax work? To begin with, a base income level would be established. This guaranteed income level would reflect family size, with larger families receiving greater income supplements. As income was earned, the base income supplement would be reduced by a fraction of the family's outside income. This fraction would be the *marginal tax rate*. A family would always face a marginal tax rate of substantially less than 100 percent. (Most plans suggest a 33 or 50 percent rate.) Recipients would always get to keep a significant amount of any additional earnings.

Exhibit 12 illustrates the mechanics of a negative income tax. Under this plan, a family of four would be guaranteed an income of $3,200 and a marginal tax rate of 33 percent. As outside income rises, the family's disposable income increases by two thirds of the amount earned. For example, initial earnings of $1,200 would increase the family's disposable income by $800, from $3,200 to $4,000. The family would receive more in supplementary income than it would pay in taxes until income reached $9,600, the **break-even point.** At the break-even point, the family's tax bill would equal the income supplement; beyond the break-even point, the family would face a positive tax bill.

Would a negative income tax help the poor without generating major counterproductive side effects? During the 1968–1982 period, the United States government funded a number of negative income tax experiments in New Jersey, rural Iowa, Gary (Indiana), Seattle, and Denver. The data generated by these experiments have been extensively analyzed by economists. The results indicate that even a negative income tax transfer program would result in a significant reduction in work effort by the poor. Philip Robins, of the University of Miami, summarizes the findings in the following manner:

> The labor supply responses from the four NIT experiments are remarkably consistent. On average, husbands reduced labor supply by about the equivalent of two weeks of full-time employment. Wives and single female heads reduced labor supply by about the equivalent of three weeks of full-time employment. Youth reduced labor supply by about the equivalent of four weeks of full-time employment. Because women and youth work fewer hours per year than do husbands, their

Break-Even Point: Under a negative income tax plan, the income level at which one neither pays taxes nor receives supplementary income transfers.

EXHIBIT 12 • The Mechanics of the Negative Income Tax

The graph illustrates how a negative income tax with a 33 percent marginal tax rate and a minimum income of $3200 for a family of four would work. If the family had zero earnings during the year, it would receive a $3200 annual subsidy. As earnings rose, the family's after-tax income would increase by 67 cents (and the subsidy would decline by 33 cents) for every dollar of income earned, until the break-even income level of $9600 was attained.

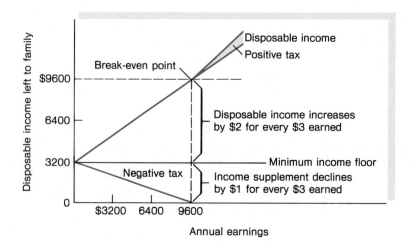

effects are correspondingly much larger in percentage terms. All of these responses may be viewed as those forthcoming from a fairly generous NIT program—one having a guarantee level equal to the poverty level and a tax rate equal to 50 percent.[7]

Once again, the NIT experiments indicate that in economics there are no solutions, only trade-offs.

ESTIMATING THE COSTS OF REDISTRIBUTION

Estimating the loss of output emanating from redistributive activities is a highly complex issue. Income transfers from the rich to the poor will increase the marginal tax rates (either explicit or implicit) of both. High marginal tax rates reduce the effectiveness of markets to allocate resources efficiently. They also tend to reduce labor supply. A recent study by Edgar Browning and William Johnson sought to measure the loss of output due to the reduction in the supply of labor associated with the rise in marginal tax rates accompanying income transfers.[8] Browning and Johnson estimated that it would cost $3.49 in terms of lost output to transfer an additional $1 from the top 60 percent to the bottom 40 percent of recipients under a negative income tax plan.

---

[7]Philip K. Robins, "A Comparison of the Labor Supply Findings from Four Negative Income Tax Experiments," *Journal of Human Resources* (Fall, 1985), p. 580.

[8]See Edgar K. Browning and William Johnson, "The Trade-off Between Equality and Efficiency," *Journal of Political Economy* (April, 1984).

APPLICATIONS IN ECONOMICS

Social Security and the Intergenerational Redistribution of Income

"Social security"—officially known as Old Age, Survivors, Disability and Health Insurance (OASDHI)—is the largest federal program providing for income redistribution. It offers protection against the loss of income that usually accompanies old age or death or dismemberment of a breadwinner. Its Medicare provisions are designed to offset the heavier health care expenses often incurred by the elderly and the disabled. In 1985, more than $250 billion was paid out to 40 million recipients under the various provisions of OASDHI.

Social Security is Not an Insurance Program

When social security legislation was passed in 1935, it was envisioned by many as a kind of compulsory national retirement insurance that would operate much like a pension program. Even today, many people believe that their social security tax contributions go into an actuarially sound reserve fund, where these payments are set aside for their retirement. This is not the case. In contrast with private insurance programs, the tax revenues paid into the OASDHI trust fund are not set aside or invested to pay for the contributor's future benefits. The social security system operates on a "pay-as-you-go" basis. The tax revenues paid into the system are distributed almost immediately to retirees and other beneficiaries of the program. The present social security system is an intergenerational income transfer program. It collects tax revenues from the present generation of workers and redistributes the money to current retirees. Each worker must trust that the next generation will bear the future tax burden necessary to keep the system going.

The Financial Problems of Social Security

The social security system is financed by a payroll tax, of which the employer and the employee each pay half. The tax is levied on the earnings of employees up to a maximum limit. In 1960, employees and their employers each paid a 3 percent tax on the first $4,800 of employee earnings. The maximum combined employee-employer tax was $288.

APPLICATIONS IN ECONOMICS (continued)

By 1985, both employee and employer were paying a 7.05 percent tax rate on a tax base of approximately $39,600. The maximum employee-employer tax in 1985 was $5,584. *Measured in real dollars*, the maximum social security tax in 1985 was more than five times the amount of 1960.

Despite huge tax increases, the social security system has experienced almost constant financial trouble in recent years. Predictably, the situation will get much worse after the turn of the century unless the structure of the program is altered. The source of the problem is not a mystery. There are two major factors contributing to the financial troubles of the system.

First, the number of beneficiaries has risen substantially relative to the number of workers. As with any new retirement program, only a few persons reached retirement age in the years just after social security was initiated (1935). As the social security system matured, however, more and more of the nation's retired workers became eligible for payments. The declining birth rate after the post-World War II baby boom and the increased life expectancy of retirees also contributed to the decline in the number of workers paying taxes to finance each social security beneficiary. As Exhibit 13 illustrates, in 1950, there were 16 taxpaying workers to finance the benefits of each social security beneficiary. By 1970, there were only 4 workers per social security recipient. The ratio of workers per social security beneficiary has now fallen to 3.

Demographic factors indicate that the situation will worsen. When the generation born during the post-World War II baby boom reaches retirement soon after the year 2010, the number of workers per retiree is expected to be about 2.

Second, the level of social security retirement benefits have risen more rapidly than the earnings base that supports them. Between 1970 and 1983, the *real* average monthly benefits of social security recipients rose by 46 percent, far more rapidly than real earnings of the workers who support the system (Exhibit 14). Therefore, by 1983, the ratio of average retirement benefits to average gross earnings had risen to 36 percent, up from 23 percent in 1970. Unless this trend is halted, the system will experience additional financial troubles.

Winners and Losers Under Social Security

The primary beneficiaries of social security were persons close to retirement during periods when benefits

EXHIBIT 13 • The Declining Number of Workers per Social Security Recipient

In 1950, there were 16 workers for each Social Security beneficiary.

In 1970, there were 4 workers for each Social Security beneficiary.

In 1985, there were 3 workers for each Social Security beneficiary.

By 2025, there will be just 2 workers for each Social Security beneficiary.

Result: An increasing burden on each worker whose Social Security taxes support the program.

APPLICATIONS IN ECONOMICS (continued)

were increased substantially. These workers paid lower tax rates (or higher rates for only brief periods of time). Yet, they received the higher benefits. Today's social security retirees are receiving real benefits of four or five times the amount they paid into the system. The return on the social security taxes they paid generally exceeds 25 percent, much better than they could have done had they invested the funds privately.

In contrast, studies indicate the workers paying for these large benefits will not do nearly as well. For example, those now at age 35 can expect to earn a real rate of return of only 2 or 3 percent on their social security tax dollars, less than what they could earn from personal investments. For two-earner couples just entering the labor force, the expected return from social security taxes is negative.

In summary, social security has been a good deal for current and past retirees. But, it is not a very good deal for younger workers. Workers now entering the labor force would probably be better off if they could invest their tax dollars elsewhere.

Fairness and Social Security

Fairness is not an economic concept. Nevertheless, economics does reveal information about benefits and costs that allow individuals to make more informed, subjective judgments. Three characteristics of the current social security system are important in this regard.

1. *The elderly are no longer the least well-off age group.* In the 1950s, the income status and poverty rate of the elderly indicated that they were significantly less well-off than the rest of the population. In the 1980s, this is not the case. Adjusted for family size, the income of the elderly is now higher than for any other age grouping. The wealth holdings (ownership of houses, stocks, bonds, and so on) of the elderly are much higher than for the rest of the population. The official poverty rate of the elderly in 1984 was 7.3 percent, compared to 12.4 percent for nonelderly families (Exhibit 10). If the value of in-kind benefits were included, the adjusted poverty rate of the elderly would be even lower compared to the rest of the population. In contrast with the situation two decades ago, the social security system today transfers income from persons who are, on average, less well-off (current workers) to people who are better off (current retirees).

2. *The social security retirement system transfers income from blacks to whites.* This is not the intent of the program. Nevertheless, it is a result. Since blacks generally begin working earlier and have a lower life expectancy, their tax payments relative to retirement benefits will be substantially greater than for whites. Consider the case of two 25-year-old men, one white and the other black. Given his life expectancy, the

average 25-year-old black male who works and pays social security taxes can expect to receive only five months of benefits before his death. The white male of the same age can expect to draw benefits for 73 months, nearly 15 times longer than his black coworker. Similarly, a black female at age 25 can expect to draw social security benefits for 8.3 years, compared to 13.0 years for her white counterpart.[9] Given the expected low or negative rate of return of youthful workers in general, the program clearly imposes a major net cost on blacks in general, and youthful workers in particular.

3. *The social security system taxes working wives while providing them little or no additional benefits.* The social security system was designed in the 1930s when few wives were in the labor force. Women are thus permitted to draw benefits based on either the earnings of their husband or their personal earnings. Generally, the benefits based on the work

---

[9]National Center for Policy Analysis, *The Effect of the Social Security System on Black Americans* (Dallas: National Center for Policy Analysis, 1983).

EXHIBIT 14 • The Rising Social Security Benefits and the Earnings that Support Them

Year	Average Monthly Benefits—Retired Worker (1983 dollars)	Average Monthly Benefits as a Percent of Gross Average Monthly Earnings[a]
1950	181	19
1960	248	21
1970	302	23
1980	411	33
1983	441	36

[a]The gross average earnings are for production employees in the private sector.

Source: *Economic Report of the President: 1985* (Tables 5-6 and B-39).

**APPLICATIONS IN ECONOMICS
(continued)**

history of the husband are greater. When this is the case, the working wife pays taxes into the system and receives no additional retirement benefits in return.

The Politics of Social Security

The early popularity of social security is easy to understand. Before the program "came of age"—while there were still 10 to 20 taxpayers for each recipient—pay-as-you-go financing enabled Congress to grant substantial benefits to retired and near-retired workers while increasing taxes by only very small amounts at the time of passage. Whenever coverage was expanded or benefits increased, future benefits were financed by writing future tax increases into the law. The added benefits were usually scheduled to begin accruing just before election time, and the tax increases were postponed until after the election. In addition, the growing numbers of workers entering the system added immediately to the pool of taxpayers but did not increase the drain on the trust funds until later. The political gains were enormous, since Congress could grant immediate benefits to a relatively concentrated group (composed primarily of older people, who are quite likely to vote in an election), while the cost of the program was widely dispersed and would be incurred (or at least felt) primarily in the future.

The political profiteering of earlier Congresses, though, has exacted its price from present and future legislators. By now, the inevitable tax increases have become very large. There is no big trust fund from which benefits for the increasing number of social security participants can be paid. The work force is not growing in size (or productivity) as rapidly as before. Taxes must be increased still further if past promises of benefits are to be kept. A program that was a boon to political careers is now a serious political problem. Sizable tax increases without the promise of larger real benefits are a politician's nightmare.

The Future of Social Security

Given its financial condition and structure, future changes in social security are a likely occurrence. Three major changes have been widely discussed.

1. *Raise the normal eligibility age with life expectancy and remove the full indexing of future benefits.* The retirement age is already scheduled to rise to age 67 after the turn of the century. Linking it to life expectancy would provide for additional increases in the eligibility age. Removal of full indexing of future benefits would gradually reduce *real* benefits. Proponents of this reform argue that the current level of benefits cannot be justified given the current economic status of the elderly.

2. *Gradually phase the system into an insurance program.* This idea, suggested by Michael Boskin of Stanford, would require still higher taxes so that a trust fund could accumulate to finance earmarked future benefits for current taxpayers. Instead of taking a chance that future generations will levy higher taxes to pay for benefits, current taxpayers would be paying earmarked funds into a trust system to finance their own retirement benefits. If this plan were in place, no big leap in taxes would be necessary when the post-World War II baby boom generation reaches retirement around 2010. The trust fund would add to the nation's savings, eliminating one of the defects of the current system.

3. *Allow people to substitute, at least partially, individual retirement accounts (IRAs) and/or the purchase of government bonds for social security taxes.* Essentially, this plan would permit individuals to use their social security tax dollars to acquire a property right to either a private investment fund or a government bond. Should the individual die prior to retirement, the property could be passed on to his or her heirs. As more people opt for this alternative plan over time, the provision of retirement benefits would shift away from social security and toward private investments and government bonds. This plan would also alleviate the adverse impact of the current system on blacks and working women. Interestingly, the United Kingdom has recently modified its social retirement system in this direction.

DISCUSSION

1. Explain the major problems confronting the social security system. What solutions would you suggest?

2. Why do you think the social security system is operated by the government? Could a private insurance company establish the same type of plan? Why or why not?

Transferring income from producers to nonproducers is an expensive undertaking. Perhaps a negative income tax might be able to reduce the loss of output compared to the current system. However, both the NIT experiments and the work of Browning and Johnson indicate that it is not a cure-all.

Are redistribution programs worth the cost? Economics cannot answer that question. It can only help identify and quantify the possibilities for redistributing income in relation to the total amount of income available to be distributed—the economic pie. Social Security is the largest single income redistribution program. We will conclude this chapter by taking a closer look at this important income transfer program.

CHAPTER SUMMARY

1. The annual income data before taxes and transfers indicate that the bottom 20 percent of families receive approximately 5 percent of the aggregate income, while the top 20 percent receive slightly more than 40 percent. There has been little change in the distribution of annual money income during the past three decades. Adjustment for taxes and noncash transfer benefits reduces the differential between high and low earners. However, recent research indicates that for persons of similar age the net income of the top quintile is approximately 4 times that of the bottom quintile after accounting for taxes and transfers.

2. A substantial percentage of the inequality in annual income distribution reflects differences in age, education, family status and time worked. Youthful inexperienced workers, students, and retirees are overrepresented among those with low incomes. Persons in their prime working years are overrepresented among high-income recipients. Persons with high incomes have substantially more years of schooling. Married-couple families with multi-earners are overrepresented among the high-income recipients, while single-parent families with few earners make up a large share of the low-income recipients. The weeks worked contributed by the top quintile of families was 4.5 times the number worked by the bottom 20 percent of income recipients.

3. Differences in the after-tax and transfer income per hour of work for persons of the same age are small. For example, the *net income per hour* of the top quintile of earners was less than twice the *net income per hour* of the bottom quintile for three-person households headed by a 35- to 44-year-old.

4. In general, income is distributed more equally in the advanced industrial nations than in less developed nations. The degree of income equality is similar for the United States, Canada, Australia, and France. Compared to these nations, there is slightly less income inequality in welfare states, such as Sweden and the United Kingdom.

5. In interpreting the significance of the annual income distribution, it is important to recognize that the annual data camouflage the movement of persons up and down the distribution over time. Many persons with middle and high current income had substantially lower incomes just a few years ago. Similarly, many low-income recipients have attained significantly higher incomes in the past (and many will do so again in the future).

6. There is substantial intergenerational income mobility in the United States. Of the children born to parents who are in the top 20 percent of all income recipients, studies indicate that fewer than half are able to attain this high-income status themselves. Similarly, approximately half

of the children of families in the bottom quintile of the income distribution attain a higher relative position during their lifetimes.

7. According to the official data, approximately 12 percent of the families in the United States were poor in 1984. Those living in poverty were generally younger, less educated, less likely to be working, and more likely to be living in families headed by a female than those who were not poor.

8. During the 1965–1975 period, transfer payments—including means-tested transfers—increased quite rapidly in both real dollars and as a share of personal income. As income transfers expanded, the poverty rate of the elderly continued to decline. However, beginning in the late 1960s, the poverty rate for working-age Americans began to rise. By 1984, the official poverty rate of nonelderly families was well above the rate of the mid-1960s, prior to the expansion in War on Poverty transfer programs. Even after adjustment for in-kind food, housing, and medical benefits, the poverty rate of working-age Americans has been rising since the late 1960s.

9. When considering the impact of current income transfer programs on the poverty status of working-age persons, it is important to recognize the following points:

   (a) When the transfer benefits of low-income families decline with income, the incentive of the poor to earn personal income is reduced. Thus, means-tested transfers tend to increase the *net* income of the poor by less than the amount of the transfer.

   (b) When high marginal tax rates accompanying transfers induce the poor to opt out of the labor force, their skills depreciate, further limiting their ability to escape poverty.

   (c) The effectiveness of transfers may also be limited as the result of the tendency of programs designed to protect against adversity to encourage choices that actually increase the occurrence of the adversity.

10. Some economists believe that the cost of redistribution could be substantially lowered if the negative income tax were substituted for current social welfare programs. The major advantages of the negative income tax (relative to present programs) are (a) its simplicity and (b) its provision for the transfer of income to people because they are poor, rather than on the basis of other selective characteristics. However, the results of the negative income tax experiments indicate that it is no cure-all. Even transfers based on a negative income tax would reduce work effort and real output.

11. The social security program is, by far, the largest single transfer program. It is not an insurance program. The taxes levied on the current generation are paid out, almost immediately, to current recipients. The number of workers per social security recipient has been declining and, in recent years, benefit levels have been increasing more rapidly than the income base that supports them. Trends have thus led to higher taxes and financial troubles for the system. Given the current relatively high economic status of the elderly, and the adverse impact of the social security system on blacks and working wives, future changes in the system are likely.

**THE ECONOMIC WAY
OF THINKING—
DISCUSSION
QUESTIONS**

1. Do you think the current distribution of income in the United States is too unequal? Why or why not?

2. Do you think it is proper for a tax-transfer system to redistribute income from (a) households making between $25,000 to $30,000 per year to (b) households with incomes between $12,000 and $15,000 per year? Suppose the high-income household head is a prime-earning-age construction worker and the low-income household head is a retired medical doctor. How would this affect your answer?

3. "Welfare is a classic case of conflicting goals. Low welfare payments continue to leave people in poverty, but high welfare payments attract people to welfare roles, reduce work incentives, and cause higher rates of unemployment" (quoted from the *There Is No Free Lunch Newsletter*).
   (a) Evaluate. (Hint: apply the opportunity cost concept.)
   (b) Can you think of a plan to resolve the dilemma? Is the dilemma resolvable? Why or why not?

4. Since income transfers to the poor typically increase the marginal tax rate confronted by the poor, does a $1,000 additional transfer payment necessarily cause the income of poor recipients to rise by $1,000? Why or why not?

5. Consider a table such as Exhibit 5 in which the family income of parents is grouped by quintiles down the rows and the family income of their offspring is grouped by quintiles across the columns. If there were no intergenerational mobility in this country, what pattern of numbers would be present in the table? If the nation had attained complete equality of opportunity, what pattern of numbers would emerge? Explain.

6. "Means-tested transfer payments reduce the current poverty rate. However, they also create an incentive structure that discourages self-provision and self-improvement. Thus, they tend to increase the future poverty rate. Welfare programs essentially purchase a lower poverty rate today in exchange for a higher poverty rate in the future." Evaluate.

CHAPTER
FOCUS

- Can people "create" natural resources? What role does human knowledge, ingenuity, effort and culture play in determining our stock of energy and other natural resources?

- How important are substitutes in the case of natural resources?

- What are proved reserves, and how can they expand over time?

- How is benefit-cost analysis done, and why is it important in natural resource economics?

- What does the energy crisis of the 1970s tell us about natural resource markets? What was the role of the Organization of Petroleum Exporting Countries (OPEC) in the crisis? What was the role of U.S. energy policy?

- Why do we periodically see "doomsday" projections about natural resources? How accurate have they been?

- Why are property rights important for natural resource management?

"Barren timber for building is of great value in a populous and well-cultivated country, and the land which produces it affords a considerable rent. But in many parts of North America the landlord would be much obliged to any body who would carry away the greater part of his large trees."[1]

ADAM SMITH

27 ENERGY AND NATURAL RESOURCE ECONOMICS

The value of a resource depends very much on the situation in which it is found and on the people who have access to it. When Adam Smith wrote the sentences in the chapter-opening quote, and published them in 1776, large trees had great value in the British Isles, where the labor to use wood was cheap and trees were scarce. Large trees were a nuisance in America, though, where labor was scarce and trees were plentiful. It was costly even to remove the trees to make way for crops. In America today, workers armed with chain saws, lumber mills, and woodworking tools help make the big trees very valuable, and cleared farmland abounds. For these reasons, trees have increased in value over the years.

Natural resources, unlike manufactured items, are in one sense "gifts of nature." Crude oil, water, virgin forests, and native animal populations are examples of natural resources. They are not created by human hands. In most cases, though, their value (including even our esthetic appreciation of them) depends on human effort, technology, culture, and ingenuity. Wilderness, for example, was not appreciated by most people until recent decades. It was instead a problem to be overcome; now, wilderness is eagerly pursued by those in search of solitude and a pristine natural setting. Crude oil was simply bothersome—a sticky mess wherever it surfaced—until imagination and technology transformed it into "black gold."

In this chapter we will examine the production and use of energy and other natural resources. As we will see, the economic principles of earlier chapters are helpful in understanding people's choices and their decisions about natural resources. Economic principles apply here, just as they do in other decision-making situations.

The economic way of thinking can help us investigate and understand a great many issues and answer a great many questions. How responsive are petroleum supplies and demands when petroleum prices change? As demands for water increase, will we have enough? What can we say about the long-run availability of minerals, which are in finite supply on earth? What pressures will population growth put on resource supplies? What roles can markets play in producing and allocating natural resources? What difficulties are there for such markets? What can economic thinking tell us about governmental policy toward natural resources? We will focus on these and related questions in this chapter.

IN NATURAL RESOURCE MARKETS, INCENTIVES MATTER

As in all markets, the quantity of a natural resource demanded will fall, and the quantity supplied will rise, when its price rises (other things constant). The higher price provides users with the incentive to conserve and to find substitutes for the newly expensive resource. The higher price also brings forth extra production, providing additional supplies. Lower prices have

[1]Adam Smith, *Wealth of Nations*, Edwin Cannan, ed. (New York: The Modern Library, 1937), p. 163.

the opposite effect, reducing the quantity supplied of the resource, and increasing the quantity demanded.

The use of water by industry, as illustrated in Exhibit 1, provides some good examples of the results of substitution. When automakers, steel producers, or oil refineries need water for their production processes, the amount they use will depend on the price they must pay to get the water. Some processes use much more water than others, and where water costs are high, producers use processes requiring less water. The same is true for any other industry and any other resource. Consumers will respond in the same way.

As in most markets, time is an important factor in determining the responsiveness of producers and users to a price change—the price elasticities of demand and supply. A consideration of energy markets will help us illustrate these points.

RESOURCE DEMAND IS FAR MORE ELASTIC IN THE LONG-RUN THAN IN THE SHORT-RUN

The *immediate* response of consumers to higher energy prices is likely to be relatively weak. In the short-run, individuals will find it costly to reduce their consumption of electricity, fuel oil, and gasoline by a large amount, even if the prices of these energy products rise sharply. Of course, some

---

EXHIBIT 1 • How Water "Requirements" Can Vary

When the use of water is expensive, people find ways to use less of it. These numbers, all from actual industrial plants, demonstrate the wide variations possible, even within a specific industrial use. How much water is needed to generate a unit of electricity? That depends very much on how costly water is, as the table shows. The "need" can vary from 1.32 gallons to 170 gallons.

Product or User and Unit	Draft (in gallons) Maximum	Typical	Minimum
Steam-electric power (kw-h.)	170	80	1.32
Petroleum refining (gallon of crude oil)	44.5	18.3	1.73
Steel (finished ton)	65,000	40,000	1,400
Soaps, edible oils (pound)	7.5	—	1.57
Carbon black (pound)	14	4	0.25
Natural rubber (pound)	6	—	2.54
Butadiene (pound)	305	160	13
Glass containers (ton)	667	—	118
Automobiles (per car)	16,000	—	12,000
Trucks, buses (per unit)	20,000	—	15,000

Source: H. E. Hudson and Janet Abu-Lughod, "Water Requirements," *Water for Industry*, Jack B. Graham and Meredith F. Burrill, eds. Publication no. 45 (Washington, D.C.: American Association for the Advancement of Science, 1956), pp. 19–21.

energy-saving measures can be adopted immediately. More care can be taken to turn off the lights in unoccupied rooms. Warmer clothing can be substituted for heating oil in the winter, and fans can replace air conditioning in the summer. Nonessential driving can be curtailed. These adjustments, though, will be small *compared to the potential reduction over a longer period of time.*

Consumption adjustments that would be very costly in the short-run become easier with time. Old and new houses will be better insulated. Higher gasoline prices will induce new car buyers to exchange some power and size for more fuel economy, and auto makers will design more economical cars. Home appliances, farming, industrial processes, and vacation trips will become less energy intensive over time. Several years will pass, however, before old habits, old techniques, old buildings, and old machinery are completely replaced.

As Exhibit 2 illustrates, the demand for energy products can be highly inelastic in the short-run. In the long-run, though, energy-saving adjustments are more attractive. As our theory predicts, and as the boxed feature "Prices and Quantities: How Energy Buyers Respond" verifies, the demand for energy will be much more elastic in the long-run than in the short-run.

THE SHORT-RUN SUPPLY WILL BE INELASTIC DUE TO THE LENGTHY PRODUCTION CYCLE

New energy sources generally take years of development. Crude oil is a case in point. Oil companies will search more diligently for additional crude oil supplies when they believe the oil they find will be sold for a higher price. The search will take time, however. Promising areas must be tested, exploratory wells must be drilled, and production equipment must be put in place. These are time-consuming processes. It usually takes more than three

EXHIBIT 2 • Supply and Demand in the Energy Market

As Exhibit 2a illustrates, both the supply of and demand for energy products tend to be highly inelastic during the short run. However, as Exhibit 2b shows, both supply of and demand for energy products will be considerably more elastic in the long run.

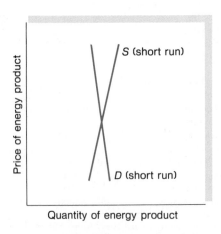

(a) Supply and demand in short run

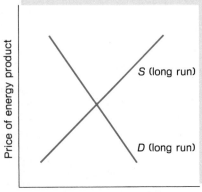

(b) Supply and demand in long run

years from the time the search begins until the refined product can be brought to market. Even though development and delivery can be somewhat accelerated (at a cost), higher product prices will have only a small effect on output in the short-run.

As Exhibit 2b indicates, the supply response to an increase in price expands with time. Not only will more exploration and development of new wells occur, but further extraction of oil from existing wells will be more

APPLICATIONS IN ECONOMICS

Prices and Quantities: How Energy Buyers Respond

Economic theory tells us that the demand for a commodity depends on the price of the commodity, the income of buyers, and the price of substitutes. The theory is demonstrated clearly in energy markets.

Consumers determine how much electricity, gas, or other energy form is used. For example, in the case of electricity they choose whether or not to use electric heat and how high to set the thermostat. But they also decide how much aluminum (made with large quantities of electricity) to buy and which producers (those using more electricity per ton of aluminum, or less per ton) to buy from. Higher electricity prices raise aluminum prices relative to the prices of substitute metals and increase costs more significantly for producers using more electricity per ton. Producers using techniques and equipment that are rising less rapidly in price will enjoy a competitive advantage. Thus, even with very little knowledge of how or why electricity prices are rising throughout the economy, consumers make choices that move sales away from the energy form rising fastest in cost, and toward conservation, other energy sources, and other means of satisfying their wants.

How much less will be consumed when the price of an energy form rises? Exhibit 3, summarizing the results of several statistical studies, provides some answers in the form of estimated price elasticities. For residential electricity, a 10 percent rise in price would lead to a 2 percent short-run reduction in quantity demanded. The short run here means one year. When buyers have up to 10 years to respond, the long-run elasticity indicates that the same 10 percent price rise would cause a 7 percent decline in residential use of electricity, other factors held constant.

Price elasticities are useful in predicting fuel usage as fuel prices change. However, other factors, such as income and the price of substitutes, will also influence consumption. In addition, we cannot expect the same reaction to a price change from people in different situations. Once auto manufacturers have spent years in researching and developing techniques to save fuel, for example, even a return to the much lower gasoline prices of years past would not bring back the previous level of gas guzzling. Measured elasticities reflect history, but history can never be retraced exactly, even if the path of prices is somehow repeated. Estimated price elasticities are a rough but often useful guide to buyer behavior when prices of an important commodity like energy change.

EXHIBIT 3 • Price responsiveness of energy forms: estimated price elasticities

Fuel	Estimated Elasticity[a]	
	Short Run	Long Run
Residential electricity	0.2	0.7
Residential natural gas	0.1	0.5
Gasoline	0.2	0.7

[a]When income and other factors such as other fuel prices are held constant, the elasticities indicate the ratio of percent change in quantity to the percent change in price causing the quantity change. Each elasticity is actually a negative number, since price and quantity demanded move in opposite directions.

Douglas R. Bohi, *Analyzing Demand Behavior* (Baltimore: Johns Hopkins University Press, 1981), p. 159.

economical at the higher price. On average, about two thirds of a well's oil is left in an oil pool when the well is abandoned. Extracting the rest is too expensive. But, when oil prices rise, wells are not abandoned so quickly. The oil field can be flooded with water, or injected with steam or chemicals to increase total recovery. These measures take time and money, but higher production will result.

INFORMATION IS SCARCE AND COSTLY, SO INFORMATION IS IMPERFECT

What will be the long-run future availability of energy and other natural resources? This information is difficult to obtain. Natural resources are different from manufactured goods, whose long-run availability depends mainly on the size of the work force and the factories we choose to build and maintain. In the short-run, manufactured inventories determine what can be supplied. For a natural resource such as a mineral, long-run availability depends not only on "factories" (mining equipment and refining capacity built and maintained) but also on reserves of the raw material, such as ore, or crude oil reserves in the ground, needed for production.

Mineral reserves are frequently misunderstood by observers outside the industry. They often confuse total reserves that *can become* available with the reserves we know about now. Known reserves are naturally much smaller in quantity.

Why do we not know more about reserves that might eventually be made available? To find oil or other mineral reserves not only takes time, but also requires the use of valuable equipment, skilled labor, and other factors of production. In other words, known, or "proved" reserves are expensive. **Proved reserves** are the discovered and verified quantity of resources that producers believe they can recover *at current prices and levels of technology*. To find and prove reserves too many years in advance would be wasteful, just as producing automobiles years before their use would be wasteful. Proved reserves, in fact, are similar to inventories in any other industry. To produce inventories too soon costs more than it is worth, and would reduce profits. Just as an auto dealer might hold a 2- to 3-month inventory of cars, oil and gas producers commonly hold a 10- to 15-year supply of oil and gas reserves. And, just as we do not worry about running out of cars in 2 to 3 months, both logic and the available evidence indicate that we need not fear running out of oil in 10 to 15 years.

Proved Reserves: The verified quantity of a resource that can be recovered at current prices and levels of technology.

RESOURCE DECISIONS ARE MADE AT THE MARGIN

In natural resource markets, as in all markets, decisions concern actions taken at the margin. In fact, two natural resources, diamonds and water, provide a classic way to explain the concept of marginal values. Writing before the discovery of the marginal principle, Adam Smith was puzzled by the fact that water, which is so valuable and necessary for life itself, is much cheaper than natural diamonds, which normally are "useless baubles." Modern economists know that price and market value are determined by the value of marginal units, rather than by the average value to buyers or sellers. Since the supply of water is very great compared to the supply of diamonds, the value of an *extra* unit of water is relatively small (at most times and in most places), even though the total value of the world's supply of water is far greater than the total value of it's diamond supply.

Crude oil wells provide another example. As we said earlier, each well is abandoned when the marginal cost of pumping becomes greater than the value of the oil extracted. This typically occurs when about two thirds of the oil in the pool remains. But, when the price of oil is high, additional expenses to extract more of the oil are justified.

Various uses of water provide yet another useful application of the marginal principle. The willingness of a farmer or a municipality to pay for water reflects the *marginal* value of the water in farming or in the city. In the water-short American west, the marginal values can be high, and the differences quite large. Demand for water by residential, commercial, and industrial users in cities is growing, and 90 percent of the water is used by farmers. Consider the San Joaquin Valley of California, where cotton farmers typically use 2.5 feet of irrigation water on their land in the course of a year. Cities in the area would very much like to buy some of this water, and would pay farmers handsomely for it. A not-yet-published study by economists for the Environmental Defense Fund (EDF) indicates that the cotton land, with the water rights, is worth about $2000 per acre, but that the water rights alone for each acre would be worth between $3000 and $11,000 if they could be sold to municipalities and other water users. The marginal value of water clearly is higher in non-agricultural uses, so we would expect trade (sales) to move water to the higher-valued uses. In addition, EDF points out that diverting some of the water from farming uses in that location would reduce important water pollution problems there. Laws currently prevent trades in many cases, however, so the large increases in the value of water that could be created by trades are still just potential gains from trade.

If the sales were allowed, would the cities drain agriculture of all its water? Once again, remember the marginal principle! Only at the margin is water worth the very high amounts, in the cities. Since agriculture has 90 percent of the water, all other users could double their use (from 10 to 20 percent) and agriculture would lose only one ninth of its water. Any large increase in the amount of water in non-agricultural uses would greatly reduce the value of water *at the margin* to those users, while increasing the marginal value of water on farms. The sale of water by farmers would only continue so long as the falling marginal value of water outside of agriculture remained higher than its rising marginal value on farms.

In considering the problems and policy options for natural resources, it is essential to keep the marginal principle in mind. Prices and values are determined at the margin, and good decisions are made considering the marginal effects of alternative choices.

OPPORTUNITY COSTS ARE THE RELEVANT COSTS

Effective natural resource management requires the recognition of opportunity costs. This may seem obvious, at this stage in your studies. But, governmental resource policy often makes it difficult or unattractive for decision-makers to learn or to use opportunity costs in their decision-making. Consider the case of federally owned hydropower—electricity generated by water falling through turbines in a dam built across a river. By law, such federally owned power must be sold "at cost," meaning the out-of-pocket costs of generating and delivering the electricity, not its opportunity cost. This electric power is usually generated and sold at a price far below the cost of power from other generating plants selling electricity. Power that is available at such low prices, which cannot be sold to others at a profit, is used even where it has very little value. The opportunity cost of the power is ignored.

Pacific Northwest electricity sold by the federal Bonneville Power Administration provides an example. It has been sold in recent years at prices far lower than other power in the region. Users pay only a fraction of the value of that power in other potential uses (a fraction of its opportunity cost). Yet, if they were permitted to trade electricity rights at a profit, they would try hard to economize on its use to gain by selling it to utilities, who could then avoid buying higher cost power from newer, more expensive power plants. Fewer new generating plants would be needed. Conservation by users of the cheap power could make some of that cheaper power available for use by others. The opportunity cost of the "cheap" hydropower is high, but users now have little incentive to recognize and act on that fact.

National Forests provide another example. What is the cost of keeping a portion of a National Forest in its current use? One measure of the opportunity cost is the rental or lease payments that timber companies, recreation clubs, preservation groups, or others might offer to obtain primary use of that portion of the forest. Such offers are not made, though, except when the Forest Service has already decided the forest's use, and has called for bids from certain categories of commercial users. Even then, only one category of users, loggers for example, can bid. And, the value to them is learned only after the decision has been made. Most users pay little or nothing and have an incentive to claim that there will be huge benefits if their own use is favored, as they lobby for just that outcome.

Benefit-cost Analysis (B-C): A process used to determine the efficiency of a project by estimating each benefit and each cost. A project is said to be efficient if it generates more benefits than costs.

OPPORTUNITY COST AND BENEFIT-COST ANALYSIS

When economists look at a project to judge whether or not it is an efficient use of resources, they analyze benefits and opportunity costs. **Benefit-cost analysis** (B-C) is a process to determine the efficiency of a project by estimating every benefit and every cost. The project is said to be efficient if benefits exceed costs. The benefit-cost ratio is often calculated by simply dividing total benefits by total costs. An efficient project has a benefit-cost ratio greater than one.

The purpose of using B-C is to separate efficient projects from inefficient ones, and to avoid the latter. Inefficient projects move resources from higher-valued uses to lower-valued ones. To do its job, B-C must correctly measure all of the benefits and all of the costs (present and future), implied by the choice being analyzed, and compare them properly. Then, the B-C must be used by decision-makers. There are thus three major reasons why even B-C may go astray:

1. *Measurement assigning a dollar amount to the costs and benefits can be very difficult.* Goods and services involved in natural resource projects often are unpriced. They frequently involve publicly provided goods and services, which are not marketed. Because of this, it is difficult to determine their value and their opportunity cost. Costs and values are subjective, so when preferences are not revealed by offers to buy and to sell, objective estimates may be almost impossible. In recent years, some especially difficult issues have arisen regarding the preservation of natural areas. (See the boxed

APPLICATIONS IN ECONOMICS

Tough Issues in Natural Resource Preservation

Some values claimed for natural resources are by their nature difficult to measure. An example of this is the **existence value** of a natural wonder, such as the Grand Canyon. Some people derive satisfaction just from knowing that the Grand Canyon exists in its unspoiled state. A few years ago, a dam for water storage and power generation to be built in the canyon was proposed. Some of the grandeur would be lost if the dam were built. The dam, like

Existence Value: The satisfaction people can derive simply from knowing that something—the Grand Canyon or Hoover Dam, for example—exists. It is extremely difficult to measure existence values.

Irreversibility: Once an action is taken, some physical effects may not be reversible—the prior physical conditions cannot be restored. Such a situation involves an irreversibility.

Hoover dam farther west on the same river, would have a grandeur of its own, but it would certainly not be the same. Building the dam and harnessing the wild river would create existence value for some people and would destroy it for others. Since many of those who would appreciate the existence of either the unspoiled canyon or the dam would never visit the Grand Canyon, how can we take their evaluations into account? How can we estimate that component of the opportunity cost of building (or not building) the dam?

Voluntary organizations, such as those organized to preserve the Statue of Liberty, or the Hawk Mountain Sanctuary provide one way that existence values are expressed. People who never visit the sites contribute to their preservation. But, each of us who enjoys such value may choose to "free ride," leaving the cost of providing the existence value to others. In the end, existence values that individuals refuse to voluntarily support might have to be ignored. While existence values are everywhere, they are nearly impossible to estimate.

Another difficult issue in resource management is the problem

of irreversible decisions. A dam built in the Grand Canyon would have some permanent physical effects. **Irreversibility** means that once the action is taken, some physical effects could not be reversed. Once the dam is built, even removing it would not restore the original beauty of the Grand Canyon, because the water behind the dam would permanently change the appearance of its walls. Opponents of such a project argue that irreversibility puts the project in a special category, so that postponing the project to preserve the option for the future is an especially attractive option. Unfortunately, the situation is not so easy to analyze.

Suppose the project were actually beneficial, producing $1 million of net benefits in electricity and water storage services per year. To delay the project 5 years would mean giving up $5 million in benefits, and giving them up forever. At an interest rate of 10 percent, $5 million is equivalent to $500,000 per year forever. What permanent conservation (or other) goals could be purchased with that permanent stream of income? While a delay can preserve an option, the delay itself may have irreversible effects.

feature, "Tough Issues in Natural Resource Preservation.") But, economists and other policy analysts work hard to approximate willingness-to-pay or opportunity costs, since rational governmental decisions and policies may depend on the resulting imperfect estimates.

2. *An inappropriate rate of interest may be used when calculating the benefits and costs.* The chapter on "Capital, Interest, and Profit," explained why comparing present and future dollar amounts requires the use of an interest rate and a discounting procedure. A dollar in benefits (or costs) today is worth more than a dollar next year. The choice of the appropriate interest rate can strongly influence estimated costs and benefits. That choice is not a simple one, however, and economists have long debated how the correct rate should be chosen. Projects involving natural resources have often been the stage for those debates.

3. *Policymakers may fail to use the B-C analysis when making decisions on resource use.* Supporters of a project will usually lobby for it and opponents will lobby against it, regardless of the B-C results. Political considerations, rather than economics, may determine the outcome of the issue. Efficiency has no political constituency, and the success of political decision-makers depends more on pleasing politically effective interest groups than on making efficient decisions.

In discussing the application of economic principles to natural resource issues, we have frequently used energy market examples. Bearing in mind these principles, we turn now to a description of energy markets and energy policy. Public policy always involves politics as well as economics. Nowhere has that been more important in the last 15 years than in energy markets.

POLITICS, POLICY, AND ENERGY

The most headlined development affecting the worldwide petroleum market during the 1970s was the emergence of the Organization of Petroleum Exporting Countries (OPEC) as a strong producer cartel. OPEC, which had been formed in 1960, had tried in the 1960s to bring about the production controls needed to drive prices up. It did not succeed at first, but by 1970 the stage was set for some dramatic price increases.

The increases, which began in 1970 and accelerated after the Arab embargo of 1973, did not reflect any major rise in worldwide costs of producing oil. Rather, forces developing over several decades had created a new petroleum market environment in which OPEC countries found themselves able to raise prices substantially.

Long before OPEC, governments in many oil-producing countries had begun seizing a larger role in production and pricing decisions. Most imposed higher taxes and forced changes in the agreements by which oil companies developed petroleum resources within their borders. Some simply nationalized the oil companies in their countries. As oil companies saw their revenues taken increasingly by taxes, and their contracts for future oil development changed to give the governments more control, they began to pump oil very rapidly. Between 1960 and 1970, world oil production more than doubled, even as world oil prices dropped. (See Applications in Economics: "Politics, Property Rights, and Pumping Rates.")

Falling world petroleum prices encouraged users of gasoline and other oil products to buy cars and install long-lived capital facilities that, reflecting low oil prices, used oil in large quantities. As a result, the world demand for oil would be high for several years.

By 1970, however, excess capacity to produce oil for world markets had disappeared. Oil production in the United States, the world's largest producer, had peaked.

The world had already begun to realize that falling oil prices could not continue, and that prices were likely to rise at some point in the future. Price increases, especially the quadrupling of the world price of crude oil during 1973–1974, led by OPEC, signaled that the time had arrived.

Acting together, the 13 OPEC nations were in a position to exert an important influence on the world oil market. They produced about 40 percent of the world's oil and held over two thirds of the proved reserves. OPEC members were not forced to curtail output very much at first, since the demand for energy is relatively inelastic in the short-run.

Expectations of future price increases spurred buyers to "stock up now, before prices go up," increasing current demand. The expectation of future price increases provided an incentive for all oil producers to raise their current prices, producing less oil now and more in the future, when it would

APPLICATIONS IN ECONOMICS

Politics, Property Rights, and Pumping Rates

In petroleum exporting countries, most of the exploration, development, and production of oil has been done by private oil companies. The companies signed contracts, called concession agreements, with the exporting nations, agreeing to explore for oil and produce it in exchange for royalty payments and the payment of taxes. Huge oil fields were discovered, and a great deal of oil flowed from them. Over the years the exporting countries changed the terms of the agreements by raising their tax rates, and occasionally by nationalizing the company properties, as Iran did in 1951. Competition increased worldwide, though, and oil prices fell from 1957 to 1970.

OPEC was formed in 1960 to try to seize some control over world markets. During the 1960s, OPEC members gradually increased tax rates, made modest attempts at reducing production growth, and took some steps toward nationalization of the concessions. In 1968, OPEC formally announced its intent to maximize tax revenues and, over time, to nationalize company operations. It became clear to the companies that even if they escaped nationalization, future production would mean much higher payments to the governments. Companies facing such probabilities increased their pumping rates in the 1960s, contributing to the 118 percent increase in world crude oil production from 1960 to 1970.

One result was that each company in that situation faced a strong incentive to pump oil very rapidly, since oil left in the ground would probably not be theirs in the future anyway. There was little incentive for the companies to conserve for future production, since their rights to the oil under the existing contractual arrangements were coming to an end. The rapid production of oil during the 1960s was one result, and this helped push world oil prices down until 1970. When OPEC raised oil prices beginning in 1970, the starting point was an artificially low price.

bring higher prices. Investors began to search for more oil, and took steps to make existing wells produce more, but it would take years for those investments to increase world oil supplies.

It appeared that the OPEC cartel had the world by the tail. During 1978–1980, OPEC again sharply increased the export price of oil. By the early 1980s, though, world consumption and production of petroleum had responded. The OPEC share of world production fell from about 40 percent in 1972 to less than 33 percent by 1985. The price of crude oil in the United States, having risen from less than $4 per barrel in 1973 to its high of $32 in 1981, dropped briefly to around $10 in 1986.

To see why these changes were possible, we need to examine United States energy policy. These policies, together with OPEC activities, provided "laboratory conditions" for anyone interested in observing economic theory in action.

ENERGY POLICY AND THE ENERGY CRISIS IN THE UNITED STATES

Real Price: The cost of an item, corrected for inflation. For example, if the price of oil doubles while the prices of all other goods also double, the real price of oil is unchanged. Decisions are generally based on real prices, rather than the uncorrected prices.

For Americans, the energy crisis of the 1970s resulted partly from world market conditions, and partly from domestic policies of the 1950s and 1960s. From 1950 to 1972, just before the energy crisis began, the **real price** of energy to the American consumer had fallen substantially. In that time, gasoline prices fell 22 percent, residential electricity fell 54 percent, and residential natural gas fell 19 percent, all in real terms. Price declines of that size stimulated more consumption. From 1950 to 1970, energy use in the United States doubled. Much of the world had a similar experience.

Low and falling energy prices meant that homes and office buildings were being designed to emphasize uniqueness, style, and living space, rather than energy conservation. Automobiles were being built to provide more power and comfort, but with less attention to fuel economy. These and other capital items were being constructed to reflect the falling energy prices and the rising incomes of the period. This had the effect of locking in a higher demand for the following decade. After all, energy prices had been falling for more than 20 years. Energy users wanted to take advantage of that fact. In doing so, they committed themselves to higher energy consumption for years to come.

Against this backdrop of falling prices and rapid expansion in energy use, public policy in three important areas—price regulation, import restrictions, and tighter environmental regulation—added to the forces that culminated in the energy crisis.

ENERGY SHORTAGES AND THE REGULATION OF NATURAL GAS PRICES

Another important factor in the energy market was the regulation of natural gas prices. Beginning in 1954, the Federal Power Commission (forerunner of today's Federal Energy Regulatory Commission) regulated the well-head price of natural gas. At first the commission allowed the real price of gas to rise, but in 1961, it began to use a pricing formula that substantially reduced the price. Throughout most of the 1960s and well into the 1970s, the FPC fixed the price of natural gas at about one third the price of its energy equivalent in crude oil. This below-equilibrium price encouraged consumers to use more natural gas, and at the same time, it greatly reduced the incentive of producers to discover and produce more natural gas.

Needless to say, encouraging consumption while retarding production is the perfect formula for creating a shortage. By 1974, the ratio of proved reserves/consumption for natural gas had fallen to 10, from over 20 in 1961. The nation's inventory of known gas reserves had been cut in half, relative to annual consumption. Natural gas shortages put upward pressure on the demand for electricity and oil, raising costs and prices in those markets. The OPEC cartel could hardly ask for better cooperation.

IMPORT RESTRIC-TIONS, THE ORIGIN OF OPEC, AND DECLINING OIL RESERVES

After World War II, an increase in world-wide discovery and production of low cost crude oil turned the United States from a net exporter of oil to a net importer, and put downward pressure on oil prices. In 1959, a coalition of domestic oil companies lobbied successfully for mandatory import quotas, limiting the import of cheap foreign oil. This policy contributed to falling world oil prices at the time, and had the unplanned side effect of increasing the desire of oil exporting nations to form a cartel. In 1960, OPEC was formed. The "drain America first" policy of the United States government boosted production of increasingly expensive domestic crude, at the expense of consumers. This helped flood the world market with surplus oil, and world oil prices continued to decline through the 1960s. Domestic reserves declined, relative to consumption. American producers knew that as domestic oil became more expensive, there would be increasing pressure over time to import more foreign crude at very low prices. Once again, American policy was helping to set the stage for large OPEC price increases.

ENERGY MARKETS AND ENVIRONMEN-TAL REGULATIONS

Beginning in the late 1960s, the United States began to take steps to preserve air and water quality. Increasingly stringent emission standards for automobiles resulted in a substantial decline in the miles per gallon of fuel for the average auto. Together with rising incomes, a growing population, and expectations caused by falling real gasoline prices, this trend generated a strong increase in the demand for gasoline.

Simultaneously, the United States began to crack down on air and water pollution from oil refineries. New refineries had to meet tougher, more expensive standards. In many places, permission to build added refinery capacity was simply denied. Uncertainty about the future of import quotas—when and where might cheap foreign oil be allowed into the United States in the future—further reduced incentives to meet the growing demand for gasoline by adding refinery capacity.

THE ENERGY CRISIS AND OUR POLICY RESPONSE

The outbreak of the Middle East War in 1973, and the oil embargo that accompanied it, provided the backdrop for the energy crisis of the 1970s. Declining domestic prices had encouraged domestic energy consumption and led to the construction of energy-intensive capital assets that would continue to promote energy consumption in the future. Import restrictions encouraged the rapid drain of U.S. domestic oil reserves, and the apparent abundance of cheaply available foreign reserves, kept out only by import quotas, discouraged domestic exploration. Price controls on natural gas were depleting our proved gas reserves, while new environmental regulations were increasing the demand and reducing the supply of refinery facilities. The Nixon price freeze of 1971–1973 further aggravated the situation.

In October 1973, the U.S. domestic consumption of energy was at a high level and could not be reduced easily. Simultaneously, the domestic supply of proved petroleum reserves had dwindled to a low level. Given the long production lags and the demand for energy by owners of cars, houses, and buildings designed for cheap energy, both the supply and the demand for crude oil were highly inelastic in the short run.

So, when OPEC raised the price of crude oil from $2.50 to over $10.00 in less than two years, strong conservation efforts were needed, along with vigorous efforts to call forth the most efficient additional energy supplies. A substantially higher price for petroleum and its products, which would naturally emerge in the market without price controls, would have brought both of these about. The price controls stifled these forces.

ENERGY CRISIS: THE MYTHICAL ENERGY GAP

In the national debate following the OPEC price increases of 1973–1974, many public leaders pointed out that while higher prices would provide the incentive for added petroleum production, they also would give "windfall gains" to those already holding proved reserves. Also, users of petroleum products could face hardships from the higher prices.

Many leaders also doubted that there would be large buyer and seller responses to changes in price. They simply ignored existing economic studies, which showed that, over time, price would exert a great impact on the production and allocation of energy. Most news reports referred to energy "needs" and "requirements" as if these grew in fixed proportion to population or to GNP, without regard to energy prices and responses to price changes. Exhibit 4 illustrates this mistaken view. Although the events since

EXHIBIT 4 • The Mythical Vertical Demand and Supply Curves for Energy

Leaders of popular opinion often assume that the demand and supply curves for energy resources resemble those presented here. Both economic reasoning and real-world data indicate that this view is incorrect.

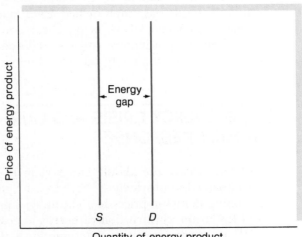

1973 have clearly disproven this view, similar misconceptions are seen constantly in regard to other natural resources, such as water in the arid west. It is worthwhile to examine why such a way of thinking is misleading.

The "energy gap" notion overlooks the fact that energy is not desired for itself, but rather to produce other goods and services. Gasoline, for example, is used to produce transportation. The gasoline cannot be more indispensable than the transportation it helps make possible. Giving up the least important third of one's auto travel saves a third of one's gasoline use. Car pooling, shorter vacation trips, and Sunday excursions on bicycles instead of by car come quickly to mind.

The impact of price on energy supplies is also disregarded in the "gap" theory. Thus, data on *proved* reserves were mistakenly taken to indicate *absolute* reserves; Americans were warned that the supply of fossil fuels was sufficient to last only 10 to 15 years.

This grim view of our energy future was widely accepted. Fears that an uncontrolled market price would lead to extremely high prices without bringing forth much greater supplies led to the imposition of price controls. Low prices, however, meant that users had less incentive to conserve, and producers had less incentive to supply more oil. There was indeed an "energy gap"—caused by price controls!

PRICE CONTROLS—WINNERS AND LOSERS

Whenever a price is legally set below the market clearing level, shortages of course result. So it was with energy in the 1970s. As we have seen, natural gas consumers lucky enough to own natural gas hook-ups got a bargain. They could keep their houses warm and take long, hot showers cheaply, since the price was kept low by regulation. But, many who wanted to hook-up their homes or apartments to natural gas lines were out of luck. For many utilities, not enough gas was available to serve additional customers.

There was another unwanted side effect of price controls: the demand for heating oil and electricity (much of it generated by oil-fired generators) increased. Consumers who could not get natural gas had to buy the much more expensive substitutes, which were often based on petroleum. In some neighborhoods, people in the newer houses had to pay much more for heating and cooling energy than did their luckier neighbors across the street, who happened to already have gas hook-ups. What about poor people? If they rented their housing, instead of owning it, they did not necessarily benefit from the low gas price. Owners of rental housing with gas hook-ups could now charge higher rents than their competitors who could not offer gas hook-ups in their rental units. Whenever price controls are effective, they keep prices below market-clearing levels. This means a shortage, and only those with access during the shortage can gain from the low price. Just as poor people lack access to goods via cash, they often lack non-money access. In this case, access meant ownership of a gas hook-up. It was the owners of the hook-ups, not necessarily the ones paying the gas bill, who benefitted from the cheap natural gas.

One clear beneficiary of natural gas price controls was the OPEC cartel. The demand for their oil was increased by American price controls on natural gas, since fuel oil and electricity made with petroleum products had to be used due to the natural gas shortage brought on by price controls.

CRUDE OIL AND THE ENTITLEMENT PROGRAM

Controlling the price of domestic crude oil also became a serious problem. At the low controlled price, old wells would be abandoned too early, and new drilling would be much slower than if prices were allowed to rise. Recognizing this, the federal government set up a very complex set of prices, so that oil from wells with very low production, newly discovered oil, or oil from wells needing expensive special treatment to keep pumping could be sold at higher prices. The idea was to allow the oil companies to charge higher prices for oil more costly to produce.

However, since estimating the cost of oil from a particular well was an impossible task in Washington, a complex set of prices, each applied in a different kind of situation, was put in place. It was an enormous regulatory problem. The nation's top energy administrator testified that it took the full-time efforts of 4000 workers at a cost of $100 million annually just to regulate the domestic price of crude oil.[2]

Much of the effort had to go toward keeping the companies from classifying each well in a higher-priced category than it "deserved" according to the rules set by Congress. For oil companies, the process meant that it paid them to put some of their best people to work in Washington, D.C., making the case that various wells belonged in higher price categories. Much talent, money, and time were diverted away from discovering and producing oil, and into finagling within the regulatory system.

There were additional problems. Who would get the lower-priced crude oil? Which refiners would be the lucky ones? Would it be the ones who had the foresight (or luck) to have found or paid for the wells? These were billion dollar questions. To see that no company benefitted more than another from higher world petroleum prices, a system of subsidies and taxes called an **entitlement allocation program** was instituted in 1974. Rights (entitlements) to use cheap, price-controlled oil were decreed not to belong to the owner of the oil, even if the owner had a refinery in which to use the oil. Instead, whoever used the oil had to buy the entitlement from the government. Money from the entitlements went to subsidize the import of expensive foreign oil. In 1981, for example, a typical refinery using domestic oil might have paid $24 per barrel plus an additional $6 per barrel for the entitlement to do so. A typical East Coast refinery, buying OPEC oil at $36 that year, received $6 per barrel in subsidy. One effect, then, was to subsidize firms that had not borne the risk and cost of developing oil reserves, at the expense of firms that had done so. Another effect was to make the average cost of oil to both refineries $30 in 1981, even though the cost to the economy for each barrel imported was $36.

The entitlement program meant that OPEC was subsidized by a tax on American oil producers. It also meant that American users of petroleum products failed to get the true price signal that conservation was really worth $36 per barrel of oil saved, rather than the subsidized $30 price paid

Entitlement Allocation Program: A system of subsidies and taxes instituted in the mid-1970s. Refiners were taxed for each barrel of price-controlled domestic oil they used, and the proceeds were used to subsidize refiners for each barrel of imported and new (more costly) domestic oil they processed. The program increased the demand for imported oil.

---

[2]Frank G. Zarb, quoted in *Federal Energy Administration Regulation*, ed. Paul W. MacAvoy (Washington, D.C.: American Enterprise Institute, 1978), p. 54. Eventually, the Department of Energy was established to handle the regulatory problems. By fiscal year 1981, approximately 100,000 people were employed by the department, which had an annual budget of more than $10 billion.

by the refineries and passed on to consumers. Energy conservation was held back, and the demand for OPEC oil was further increased by the price control and entitlement programs.

Price controls and the entitlement program, with their unintended side effects of reducing energy conservation and subsidizing the import of oil, strengthened the demand for imported oil. The Shah of Iran was overthrown in 1978, and oil production there slowed. World oil prices jumped again. The Middle East showed further signs of political unrest. Iraq invaded Iran, and that war further reduced oil production in both countries. From about $13 per barrel in 1978, the price rose to $34 in 1981. However, in early 1981, the United States removed all price controls on domestic oil products. This provided oil refiners with an incentive to search for the cheapest oil wherever it could be found. The demand for OPEC oil fell. The cartel cut its production to try to keep the price high. At the high price, though, output in the rest of the world was increasing. The price fell from its 1981 high to as low as $10 in early 1986.

WAS THE ENERGY CRISIS CONTRIVED?

As we noted earlier, the dramatic oil price increases of 1973–74 and 1979–81 were not caused by huge increases in the average cost of producing crude oil. Many observers attributed the price increases simply to OPEC and/or the oil companies exercising their monopoly power. But, how much power does OPEC have? Clearly, it pursues agreement among its members on the price for oil, and tries to exercise monopoly power by limiting each member to a specified share of a total production rate low enough to support the OPEC target price. Has it been effective?

The collapse of world prices in the mid-1980s confirmed the suspicions of economists skeptical of the power of OPEC. They had pointed out that OPEC members were frequently unable to agree even on what the price should be. Members with the largest reserves, such as Saudi Arabia, recognized that very high current prices would stimulate competitive supply sources and long-term conservation investments, reducing the future demand for their product. Members with much smaller oil reserves, such as Algeria, had less concern about future oil prices, and wanted more for their oil immediately. Further, even if the group agreed on a price and the limits on each member's output needed to maintain the cartel price, it would be very difficult for them to police the agreement. A price above the marginal cost of producing oil gives each member an incentive to cheat by offering better terms "under the table" to buyers.

Economists recognize that a cartel arrangement is extremely difficult to administer and police, without a single governmental authority to control all members. Not all economists agree on whether or not the cartel in fact has had a major influence on world oil prices. But, if the price increases were not caused by the cartel's use of monopoly power, what did cause them? How can the huge price increases of 1973–74 and 1979–81 be explained?

A number of important factors, apart from monopoly power, can help explain the two big price hikes. We have touched on each of them:

1. The world's demand for oil had been increasing during the 1950s and 1960s due to rising incomes and a capital stock that reflected expectations of falling oil prices, which had been present in both decades.

2. The world was gradually coming to recognize, in the 1960s, that oil prices would eventually rise, as demand continued to grow. Ordinarily, this would have caused a rising oil price, as some oil field owners cut back production to produce more later, at the expected higher price.

3. Production of oil in the 1950s and 1960s had been artificially stimulated by the anticipation of more governmental seizures of oil fields in many oil producing countries. This caused companies to pump very rapidly, to get what they could before their contracts in the oil fields ran out, or were simply taken away from them (as indeed happened in several cases). This rapid pumping had ended by 1973, as the oil companies had largely lost their properties in those countries where that danger existed.

4. By 1970, excess capacity had disappeared, and increased demand was pushing against short-run supply. Since it is marginal cost, not average-cost, that sets a competitive market price, and since the artificially high pumping rates in some countries had just about stopped, the price increases of 1970–1973 are not hard to explain, even without a cartel. The far steeper increases of 1973–74 and of 1979–1981 are another matter.

5. The two really steep price increases have followed political and military crises. The first was due, at least in part, to the 1973 war in the Middle East, and the ensuing Arab oil embargo applied to the United States and several other western nations. The second followed the overthrow of the Shah in Iran and greatly reduced oil production there. This was accompanied by the outbreak of trouble in a number of Middle East locations, each signalling potential trouble for oil production.

But, were the price increases larger because the cartel helped enforce them? Clearly, most people *believed* that OPEC had monopoly power and was capable of using it to bring about higher future prices. Remember, a price increase that is expected to stick, rather than be reversed, will increase demand in the short-run. The view of OPEC as a strong cartel certainly was widespread when the steepest price advances occurred. Undoubtedly, this view contributed to the rising prices.

WAS BIG OIL RIPPING OFF THE CONSUMER?

Surveys taken during the 1970s indicated a belief by the general public that more than 40 cents of every sales dollar in the petroleum industry was accounting profit. In reality, the figure was about 5 cents. The profit rates of firms in the petroleum industry differ little, on average, from those of other types of firms. During 1974–1981, the peak "energy crisis" years, the rate of return on stockholder equity was 18.0 percent, compared to 15.6 percent for all manufacturing. Only during 1974 and 1979–1981 were oil industry profits substantially greater than for other firms. Those added profits, of course, drew large investments into the industry, making possible an increased supply of petroleum products. In the years before 1974 and after 1981, the profits of large oil companies were slightly less than for manufacturing firms in general.

Since total profits were around 5 cents per sales dollar, the higher profits that did occur accounted for only a tiny part of petroleum product price increases. Profits had little to do with the energy crisis, aside from their normal and constructive role of encouraging investment where the additional investment would create the largest return for the economy. To blame oil company profits for the oil price increases after 1970 got the cart before the horse. It also ignored the important information and incentives passed along to investors by even small changes in profit rates.

THE FUTURE OF NATURAL RESOURCE MARKETS

Is the world running out of natural resources? (See "Myths of Economics.") Can we forecast future supply and scarcity? What factors will determine the future of natural resource availability?

As we noted at the beginning of this chapter, the value of a resource depends on the knowledge and ingenuity possessed, and the circumstances faced by its potential users. In a very real sense, humankind creates resources, even though the physical resource is a gift of nature. The challenge, then, is to see that knowledge is created in a timely way, and ingeniously applied in a manner appropriate to the circumstances. Historically, the price system has provided information on approaching resource scarcity, and supplied inventors, innovators, and investors with the proper incentives to deal appropriately with the situation. For that to happen,

MYTHS OF ECONOMICS

"We are running out of energy, minerals, timber and other non-renewable natural resources. Doomsday is just around the corner."

The first recorded doomsday forecast, says J. Clayburn LaForce,[3] was the fifteenth century prediction that England would run out of wood. "At the time, wood was the main source of fuel, and terrible consequences were expected. What happened? The price of that resource gradually rose as forests around urban centers receded. In response to higher prices, people gradually began to substitute coal for charcoal [a wood derivative] in both personal and commercial uses. England en-

tered its greatest period of economic growth and that 'sceptered isle' still has forests."

Doomsday forecasts have been made ever since, often by very responsible people. In 1865, the noted economist William Jevons argued that the industrial growth of that century could not be maintained far into the future because the world was running out of coal, the primary energy resource at the time.[4]

Governments have made some of the worst forecasts. In 1905, Theodore Roosevelt predicted a timber famine if present rates of cutting continued. In 1914, the Bureau of Mines reported that the total U.S.

supply of crude oil was approximately 6 million barrels. We now produce that much every 20 months.

---

[3]Quoted from J. Clayburn LaForce, "The Energy Crisis: The Moral Equivalent of Bamboozle," International Institute for Economic Research, Original Paper 11 (Los Angeles, April 1978).

[4]In his book, *The Coal Question* (London: Macmillan, 1865), Jevons stated: "We cannot long maintain our present rate of increase of consumption; the cost of fuel must rise, perhaps within a lifetime, to a rate injurious of our commercial and manufacturing supremacy; and the conclusion is inevitable, that our present happy progressive condition is a thing of limited duration."

MYTHS OF ECONOMICS
(continued)

A major energy crisis occurred in the United States in the early 1800s, when home lighting depended on lamps that burned whale oil, especially from the sperm whale. "As population rose," LaForce relates, "demand for this resource increased, and many predicted that soon there would be no more whales and that we would be faced with darkness during the winter nights."

The price of whale oil rose. Over some 30 to 40 years, the price of sperm whale oil rose from 43 cents per gallon to $2.55 a gallon, while the price of other whale oil rose from 23 cents to $1.42 a gallon. Higher prices motivated consumers and entrepreneurs to seek alternatives, LaForce explains, including distilled vegetable oils, lard oil, and coal gas. By the early 1850s, coal oil (kerosene) had won out. And very soon thereafter, a new substitute appeared: petroleum replaced coal oil as the source of kerosene. A new industry was born.

As for whale oil, by 1896, its price had fallen to 40 cents per gallon, and even at that price few people used it. The whale oil crisis had passed.

"All this happened," says LaForce, "with no pretense of a national energy (or lighting) plan. There were no price controls. . . . Each change had been guided and coordinated by 'the invisible hand' of the market: the price mechanism."

Dire predictions about our natural resource future became a fad during the 1970s. The "year of exhaustion" of important natural resources, especially crude oil, was a popular news item. The arithmetic of the doomsday calculations was unassailable. One simply divided the current annual consumption rate (averaged over, say, the last two decades) and divided that number into the quantity of proved reserves of the resource. That provided the years of the resource remaining. Add that number to the current date, and we have the "year of exhaustion."

Why then have the years to exhaustion projections proved to be so wrong? There are two major reasons for their inaccuracy. First, "proved reserves" of a mineral resource are an inventory. *Proved reserves are costly to find and verify, so we do not want to bear the cost of "proving" a mineral deposit too many years in advance.* We want to produce inventories, including proved reserves, only a few weeks, months, or years ahead of the time we need them. The size of currently proved reserves says nothing at all about the sufficiency for the future of absolute reserves.

Second, doomsday predictions have generally failed to consider the role of price changes and technology. Both consumption rates and the expected recoverable supply are projected *assuming current technology and prices.* But, when a resource becomes more scarce, its price rises. This provides additional incentive for innovators, engineers, and inventors to alter technology in a manner that will (a) conserve on direct use of the resource, (b) provide substitutes for the resource, and (c) develop new methods of discovering and recovering larger quantities of the resource. In resource economics, it is critical to remember that we want the services gained by using the resource, not the resource itself. There are very few services that we could not find substitutes for, if we really needed to. For all these reasons, the cost of most natural resources has remained constant or fallen for decades, and in most cases, for centuries.

The classic study of Harold Barnett and Chandler Morse illustrates this point. Using data from 1870 to 1963, Barnett and Chandler found that resource costs declined during that long period.[5] Far from suggesting that doomsday was around the corner, the facts of natural resource availability tell a much more optimistic story. Relative price data indicate that technology and the ever-increasing availability of substitutes have outrun our ability to use up scarce natural resources. When price changes are allowed to reflect changing scarcities, constructive human responses to specific scarcities is an understandable and predictable occurrence. Just as they have been wrong in the past, future doomsday forecasts that fail to incorporate human response to relative price changes will prove to be wrong in the future.

[5]See Harold Barnett and Chandler Morse, *Scarcity and Growth: The Economics of Natural Resource Availability*, (Baltimore: The Johns Hopkins University Press for Resources for the Future, 1963). An update and extension of the data, reaching similar conclusions, is in Manuel H. Johnson, Fredrick W. Bell, and J. T. Bennett, "Natural Resource Scarcity: Empirical Evidence and Public Policy," *Journal of Environmental Economics and Management*, 7, (September 1980); 258–269. Not all economists fully accept this view, however. See V. Kerry Smith, ed., *Scarcity and Growth Reconsidered* (Baltimore; Johns Hopkins University Press for Resources for the Future, 1979).

Goosemyer

by parker and wilder

GOOSEMYER BY PARKER AND WILDER © FIELD ENTERPRISES, INC. 1983. PERMISSION OF NEWS AMERICA SYNDICATE.

however, prices must reflect the opinions of buyers and sellers, including speculators, on current and coming resource scarcities. Appropriate price signals, in turn, depend on the existence of well-defined, secure, and transferrable property rights.

PROPERTY RIGHTS AND NATURAL RESOURCE CONSERVATION

There is every reason to believe that resource markets will send both users and producers the proper signals, should proved reserves fall to dangerous levels. Owners of petroleum resources will make the decision to extract oil on the basis of the expected future price. If they believe petroleum is going to be worth 10 percent more next year, and if their best alternative investment yields less than 10 percent, they will hold their reserves. Of course, if property rights are not secure, as in the case of oil reserves in the 1960s that were about to be nationalized, then markets will not convey the proper signal, and proper resource allocation may not take place. That oil was pumped too rapidly. Or, if rights to the resource are not transferrable (cannot be traded for profit), as in the case of some water rights, then once more, markets do not provide the proper incentives. The water may be used in low-valued uses, and in effect, be wasted. Only when property rights exist, can be easily protected, and can be traded, will markets provide to owners of the resources the information and incentives to see that the resources are properly cared for and used.

LOOKING AHEAD

We have seen that natural resource markets frequently can do far more than people realize, but only when property rights are appropriately defined, secure, and transferable. In the next chapter, we will return in more depth to our discussion from Chapter 4 on market failure. Natural resources for which property rights are not properly defined, such as water and air, are especially vulnerable to abuse, and play a prominent role in most discussions of market failure.

CHAPTER SUMMARY

1. Natural resources are "gifts of nature," but their value depends on human effort, knowledge, culture, and ingenuity, and on the circumstances in which people have access to the resources.

2. As with other markets, incentives matter in resource markets. Both the quantity demanded of a resource, and the quantity supplied, depend on the resource price. Substitutes can be found everywhere. Both the demand and the supply curves will be more elastic when buyers and sellers have more time in which to respond to a price change.

3. Information about the future availability of a natural resource is costly, and proved reserves of a mineral resource are equivalent to an inventory. It is not desirable to discover and verify an oil field or a mineral deposit too far in advance of when it will be used.

4. Resource values are determined at the margin, rather than by the average usefulness or average cost of the resource. When a resource is worth more at the margin in one use than in another, gains from trade are possible.

5. The opportunity cost of a resource is its relevant cost. Non-marketed resources, and projects involving those resources, are difficult to evaluate. Benefit-cost analysis is a process to conduct project evaluation.

6. The Organization of Petroleum Exporting Countries was formed in 1960, and appeared to have control of the world oil market in the 1970s. But, economists are now uncertain as to how much of the large price increases were brought about by the cartel's manipulations of supply and price, and how much was the result of normal market forces in the presence of wars and other disturbances in oil producing regions. United States energy policy has frequently strengthened the demand for OPEC oil.

7. Recent history shows us that energy markets react like other markets to changes in price. Responses are stronger over time. Profits in the oil industry are approximately the same as profits elsewhere in the economy, and like other profit levels, they fluctuate.

8. Minerals in general have not been rising in cost over the past several decades, even though we continue to use more of them from a fixed physical stock available from nature. The availability of substitutes and the development of new technologies have protected humankind from any lasting shortages.

9. In a market setting, the existence of secure, transferable property rights is a key to proper conservation and wise use of natural resources, as with all other goods and services.

THE ECONOMIC WAY OF THINKING— DISCUSSION QUESTIONS

1. In what sense are crude oil and other natural resources "gifts of nature"? In what sense are they not?

2. Why is the price elasticity of demand for electricity, natural gas and other energy products greater in the long-run than in the short-run? Can you give some examples of responses that will be more complete after one year than after one week?

3. Why will more oil *in total* be produced from an oil well, when the price of crude oil is higher?

4. What is the difference between the total reserves of a mineral, and the proved reserves of the same mineral? Which is more important in the short-run? in the long-run?

5. Why is the marginal principle so important in natural resource management decisions? Give some examples of mistakes one might make by ignoring the importance of marginal costs and marginal benefits.

6. If a resource is not owned, and therefore is not priced, does it have a zero opportunity cost? Might it be treated as if it did?

7. What is benefit-cost analysis, and what are some of the reasons that it is difficult to use?

8. What were the circumstances leading up to the oil crisis of 1973? Did U.S. policymakers' actions help solve the energy crisis, from an economic point of view? Explain. What was the role of environmental policy?

9. Are energy consumers "winners" when energy price ceilings are put in place? Who wins and who loses?

10. In the 1970s, it was widely believed that "Big Oil" had created the oil crisis, and that their profits were the major reason for the large increases in gasoline prices. Comment.

11. Is there any natural resource that we might run out of? Why would almost any economist disagree with a positive answer to that question? Does that mean that economists believe that no resource will become more scarce? Explain.

PUBLIC
CHOICE

- **Why do market decision-makers face inappropriate incentives when an externality is present?**

- **What role do imperfect information and imperfect property rights play in causing externalities?**

- **What can we learn from the theory of external effects about pollution problems and alternative solutions? Why are some solutions to pollution problems less effective than others?**

- **What is the "free rider" problem? What kinds of goods are likely to be susceptible to this problem?**

- **What can we say about consumers' lack of knowledge in the market, and when is this problem likely to be most serious?**

Thus, from the beginning, capitalism has been character-ized by a tension between laissez-faire and interven-tion—laissez-faire representing the expression of its economic drive, intervention of its demo-cratic political orientation. That tension continues today, a deeply imbedded part of the historic character of the capi-talist system.[1]

ROBERT HEILBRONER and LESTER THUROW

28 PROBLEM AREAS FOR THE MARKET

Market Failure: The failure of the market system to attain hypothetically *ideal* allocative efficiency. This means that potential gain exists that has not been captured. However, the cost of establishing a mechanism that could *potentially* capture the gain may exceed the benefits. Therefore, it is not always possible to improve the situation.

We have emphasized that a properly functioning market system uses prices to coordinate the decisions of buyers and sellers. Market prices give each decision-maker the information needed to make intelligent decisions, while weighing the relative desires of others. Equally important, prices provide the incentive to use that information. Even when they think only of themselves, decision-makers facing appropriate prices act as if they care about others. For example, to personally gain the largest return, resource owners have an incentive to move their resources to where others value them most. Producers want to get the most highly valued production from the bundle of resources they use, and to minimize the cost (the value to others) of those resource inputs. Buyers have an incentive to economize on their consumption of goods and services to get as much satisfaction as possible from their limited budgets.

In short, the "invisible hand" of Adam Smith provides each decision-maker in the market economy with the information and incentive to act as if others matter. However, as we pointed out in Chapter 4, the invisible hand can slip. (At this point, the reader should review Chapter 4.) There are several potential causes of **market failure,** economic activity that results in allocative inefficiency relative to the hypothetical ideal of economists. The causes of market failure can be grouped into four general classes: (a) externalities, (b) public goods, (c) poorly informed buyers or sellers, and (d) monopoly.

In this chapter, we will delve more deeply into market failure and the possible responses to it, especially government responses. Since the impact of monopoly on the product and factor markets has already been investigated, this chapter will emphasize the other three categories of market failure.

Keep in mind that market failure is merely a failure to attain conditions of *ideal* efficiency. Alternative forms of economic organization will also have defects. Market failure creates an opportunity for government to improve the situation. In some circumstances, however, public-sector action will not be corrective. Sometimes there may even be good reason to expect it will be counterproductive. We will analyze market failure in this chapter and focus on the operation of the public sector in the next chapter.

EXTERNAL EFFECTS AND THE MARKET

External Costs: Harmful effects of an individual's or a group's action on the welfare of nonconsenting secondary parties. Litterbugs, drunk drivers, and polluters, for example, create external costs.

The genius of a market exchange system lies in its ability to bring personal and social welfare into harmony. When two parties trade, and only they are affected, production and voluntary exchange also promote the *social* welfare. When externalities are present, though, production and exchange affect the welfare of nonconsenting secondary parties. The external effects may be either positive or negative.

If the welfare of nonconsenting secondary parties is adversely affected, the spillover effects are called **external costs.** A steel mill that belches smoke

---

[1]See Robert Heilbroner and Lester Thurow, *Economics Explained* (Englewood Cliffs, New Jersey: Prentice-Hall, 1982), p. 17.

into the air imposes an external cost on surrounding residents who prefer clear air. A junkyard creates an eyesore, making an area less pleasant for passersby. Similarly, litterbugs, drunk drivers, muggers, and robbers impose unwanted costs on others. If the spillover effects enhance the welfare of secondary parties, they are called **external benefits.** A beautiful rose garden provides external benefits for the neighbors of the gardener. A golf course generally provides spillover benefits to surrounding property owners.

When external costs and external benefits are present, market prices will not send the proper signals to producers and consumers. This situation results in market failure.

External Benefits: Beneficial effects of group or individual action on the welfare of non-paying secondary parties.

External Costs. From the viewpoint of economic efficiency, an action should be undertaken only if it generates benefits in excess of its social costs. **Social costs** include (a) the private cost borne by the consenting parties and (b) any external cost imposed on nonconsenting secondary parties.

When external costs are present, market prices understate the social cost generated by the use of resources or consumption of products. Decision-makers are not forced to fully bear the cost associated with their actions. Motivated by self-interest, they may undertake actions that generate a net loss to the community. The harm done to the secondary parties may exceed the net private gain. In such circumstances, private interest and economic efficiency are in conflict.

Social Costs: The sum of (a) the private costs that are incurred by a decision-maker and (b) any external costs of the action that are imposed on nonconsenting secondary parties. If there are no external costs, private and social costs will be equal.

"In other words, what you'll have us believe, sir, is that all the fish in the river next to your plant suddenly died of old age."

External Costs and Ideal Output. Externalities may result from the actions of either consumers or producers. When the actions of a producer impose external costs on others, the costs of the firm, reflecting only private costs, are not an accurate indicator of the total social costs of production.

Exhibit 1 illustrates the impact of external costs on the socially desirable price and output. Suppose there are a large number of copper-producing firms. They are able to discharge their waste products (mainly sulfur dioxide) into the air without charge, even though the pollution damages people and property downwind from the discharge. These air pollution costs are external to the copper producers. If allowed to operate freely, the producers have little incentive to adopt either cleaner production techniques or control devices that would limit the costs inflicted on others. These alternatives would only increase their private production cost.

Since pollutants can be freely discharged into the atmosphere, each copper producer expands output as long as marginal private costs (MC_p) are less than price. This leads to market supply curve S_1, the horizontal summation of the *private* marginal cost curves of the copper producers. Given the demand, the equilibrium market price for copper is P_1. Producers

EXHIBIT 1 • Supply, Externalities, and Minimum-cost Production

The dashed supply curve, S_2, is the ideal, reflecting the social and private cost of producing copper, *and* incorporating production techniques that are chosen to minimize the *sum* of those costs. S_1, however, reflects purely the private costs, and production techniques chosen to minimize only the private costs. The latter production techniques result in S_3, the actual sum of private and social costs when social costs are being ignored by the producer. Thus, the ideal output is Q^* and the optimal cost (and price) is P^*. But, when the producer is not forced to be responsible for social costs, we can expect the larger output Q_1, and the much larger marginal cost MC_s, even though buyers only pay P_1 for copper output.

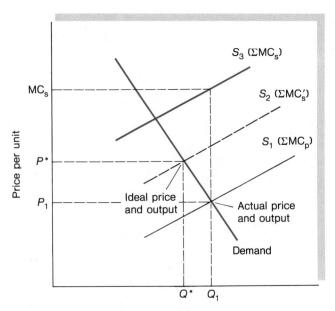

Quantity of goods (tons of copper)

supply Q_1 units of copper. At output level Q_1, however, the *social* marginal cost of copper is MC_s, an amount substantially in excess of both the private cost and the consumer's valuation (as indicated by the height of the demand curve at Q_1) of copper. As a result of the external costs, output is expanded beyond the ideal efficiency level. From the standpoint of efficiency, the market price, which fails to reflect the external cost, is too low. Additional units of copper are produced even though the value of the resources, as measured by the social marginal costs (and supply curve S_3) required to produce the units, exceeds the consumer's valuation of the units. A deterioration in air quality is a by-product.

If, on the other hand, copper producers used different production techniques, including efficient pollution control methods, supply curve S_2 (Exhibit 1) would result. Ideal output would be Q^* at price P^*. Customers would buy only the copper for which they were willing to pay all the costs, including the costs imposed on third parties. Since the consumer benefit derived from the marginal units of copper would be equal to the marginal cost to society of producing copper ($P^* = MC_s'$), production would be socially efficient.

When a producer's action imposes external costs on secondary parties, the producer's marginal costs will be understated. Therefore, the producer will choose to produce more of a good, charge less for it, and probably use different techniques to produce it, as compared to outcomes consistent with ideal economic efficiency.

External Costs and Property Rights. Clearly defined and enforced property rights are essential for the efficient operation of a market economy. The problems caused by externalities stem from a failure (or an inability) to clearly define and enforce property rights. Property rights help determine how resources will be used and who will be allowed to use them. **Private property rights** give owners the exclusive right to control and benefit from their resources as long as their actions do not harm others. It is important to recognize that private property rights do not include the right to use one's property in a manner that will injure others. For example, property rights do not grant the owners of rocks the right to throw them at automobiles.

Property rights also provide individuals with legal protection against the actions of parties who might damage, abuse, or steal their property. While property rights are often associated with selfishness on the part of owners, they could more properly be viewed as a means by which owners (including corporate owners) are protected against the selfishness of others. If adequately compensated, though, property owners often allow others to use their assets, even though the value of the assets will become consequently lower. Rental car firms sell individuals the right to use their automobiles despite the reduction in the resale value of the car. Housing is often rented, even though normal use by the renter imposes a maintenance and upkeep cost on the homeowner. Since property rights are clearly defined and enforceable in these cases, the market exchange system induces people who use the property (including the owner, whose wealth is tied up in the value of the property) to fully consider the costs of their actions.

Private Property Rights: A set of usage and exchange rights held *exclusively* by the owner(s).

ENFORCEABLE PROPERTY RIGHTS AND INFORMATION

To legally enforce property rights, the owner must be able to show in court that those rights have in fact been violated. If John runs into Mary's car, the case is often fairly simple, and the parties may not even have to go to court. When John knows that Mary can prove him at fault and quantify the damages, he (or his insurance company) will simply compensate Mary for the damage done. (If John was insured, his rates will likely rise.) But, consider the case of Mr. Steel, the factory owner whose smoke fouls the air at Mary's home. Mary may have a right to clean air, which is violated by Mr. Steel's smoke. To receive compensation, however, she must be able to demonstrate in court: (a) the extent of the damage inflicted by the pollution, (b) that the pollutant in question actually caused the damage, and (c) that the pollutant came from Mr. Steel's plant. It is likely to be very costly, or even impossible, for her to do so. Her property rights, then, although defined, are probably not enforceable. They are useless, in effect, and the market therefore does not lead to an efficient solution.

The high cost (or the unavailability) of information can make property rights unenforceable, and bring about market failure. Unfortunately, the same lack of information may prevent governmental solutions from improving the situation. If we cannot estimate the consequences of certain actions, such as the emission of certain amounts of a pollutant at a specific time in a specific place, this lack of information will prevent any rational approach, private or public, to the problem.

COMMUNAL PROPERTY RIGHTS AND EFFICIENCY

Communal Property Rights: Rights to property that can be used by all citizens as intensively as they desire. No one has the right to exclude another from the use of such property. These rights are sometimes referred to as common property rights.

Some people argue that property should be owned communally. **Communal property rights** (sometimes called common property rights) grant anyone the right to use a resource that is not currently being used by someone else. The rights to use highways, city parks, rivers, and the atmosphere are effectively held communally. If there is more of a resource than people wish to use, communal property rights work well enough. However, problems arise when scarce resources are owned jointly by all. Since no one has exclusive ownership rights, all individuals (and firms) are free to use communal property as intensively as they wish. Communal property rights generally lead to the overutilization of scarce resources (see "The Importance of Communal and Private Property Rights").

The problems of air and water pollution stem from the nature of the ownership rights to these resources. Since the atmosphere, rivers, streams, and many lakes are, in effect, owned communally, the users of these resources have little incentive to practice conservation or to use less pollution-intensive methods of production. Any *single user* of our commonly owned air and water resources would gain little by voluntarily incurring control costs to reduce pollutants that the particular user puts into the air (or water). The general level of pollution would virtually be unaffected by one user's actions. However, when *all* users fail to consider how their actions affect air and water quality, the result is overutilization, excessive pollution, and economic inefficiency.

The characteristics of some commodities make it costly or nearly impossible for the government to establish property rights in a manner that will ensure that private parties bear the entire cost or reap all the benefits of an activity. Exclusive ownership can easily be granted for such commodities as apples, cabbages, waterbeds, cars, and airline tickets, but how would one assign property rights to salmon or whales, which travel thousands of miles each year? Similarly, who owns an oil pool that is located on the property of hundreds of different landowners? In the absence of clearly assigned property rights, spillover costs and overutilization are inevitable. Certain whales have been on the verge of extinction because no single individual (or small group) has an incentive to reduce its own current catch so that the future catch will be larger. Each tries to catch as many whales as possible now; someone else will catch those whales, the argument goes, if the first person (or group) does not. The same principle applies to oil-pool rights when many well owners can draw from the same pool and no single owner can control the rate of withdrawal. In the absence of regulation, each oil-well operator has an incentive to draw the oil *from a common pool* as rapidly as possible. When all operators do so, though, the commonly owned oil is drawn out too rapidly and the total amount that can be withdrawn falls.

EXTERNAL BENEFITS AND MISSED OPPORTUNITIES

Spillover effects are not always harmful. Sometimes the actions of an individual (or firm) generate external benefits; gains that accrue to nonparticipating (and nonpaying) secondary parties. When external benefits are present, the personal gains of the consenting parties understate the total social gain, including that of secondary parties. Activities with greater social benefits than costs may not be undertaken because no single decision-maker will be able to fully capture all the gains. Considering only personal net gains, decision-makers will allow potential social gains to go unrealized.

As in the case of external costs, external benefits occur when property rights are undefined or unenforceable. Because of this, it is costly—or impossible—to withhold these benefits from secondary parties and retain them for oneself at the same time. The producer of a motion picture has

APPLICATIONS IN ECONOMICS

The Importance of Communal and Private Property Rights

What is common to many is taken least care of, for all men have greater regard for what is their own than for what they possess in common with others.[2]

Aristotle

The point made by Aristotle more than 2000 years ago is as true now

as it was then. It is as important in primitive cultures as it is in developed ones. When the property rights to a resource are communally held, the resource invariably is abused. In contrast, when the rights to a resource are held by an individual (or family), conservation and wise utilization generally result. The following examples from six-

teenth-century England, nineteenth-century American Indian cultures, and modern Russia illustrate the point.

_____
[2]Aristotle, as quoted by Will Durant in *The Life of Greece* (New York: Simon and Schuster, 1939), p. 536.

APPLICATIONS IN ECONOMICS (continued)

Cattle Grazing on the English Commons

Many English villages in the sixteenth century had commons, or commonly held pastures, which were available to any villagers who wanted to graze their animals. Since the benefits of grazing an additional animal accrued fully to the individual, whereas the cost of overgrazing was an external one, the pastures were grazed extensively. Since the pastures were communal property, there was little incentive for an *individual* to conserve grass in the present so that it would be more abundant in the future. When everyone used the pasture extensively, there was not enough grass at the end of the grazing season to provide a good base for next year's growth. What was good for the individual was bad for the village as a whole. In order to preserve the grass, pastures were fenced in the enclosure movement. After the enclosure movement established private property rights, owners and managers saw to it that overgrazing no longer occurred.

The Property Rights of American Indians

Among American Indian tribes, common ownership of the hunting grounds was the general rule. Because the number of native Americans was small and their hunting technology was not highly developed, hunted animals seldom faced extinction. However, there were at least two exceptions.

One was the beaver hunted by the Montagnais Indians of the Labrador Peninsula. When the French fur traders came to the area in the early 1600s, the beaver increased in value and therefore became increasingly scarce. Recognizing the depletion of the beaver population and the animal's possible extinction, the Montagnais began to institute private property rights. Each beaver-trapping area on a stream was assigned to a family, and conservation practices were adopted. The last remaining pair of beavers was never trapped, since the taker would only be hurting his own family the following year. For a time, the supply of beavers was no longer in jeopardy. However, when a new wave of European trappers invaded the area, the native Americans, because they were unable to enforce their property rights, abandoned conservation to take the pelts while they could.[3] Individual ownership was destroyed, and conservation disappeared with it.

The second animal that faced extinction was the communally owned buffalo. Once native Americans gained access to both the gun and the white man's market for hides, their incentive and ability to kill the buffalo increased. By 1840, Indians had emptied portions of the Great Plains of the area's large buffalo population.[4] In this case, the communal property problem could not be solved by the Indians. Unlike the beaver, the buffalo ranged widely over the Great Plains. Individual, family, and even tribal rights were impossible to establish and enforce. Like oil in a common pool or the sperm whale on the high seas, buffalo were a "fugitive resource," the mobility of which made property rights (and therefore sound management) unattainable. Only the later fencing of the range solved the problem, after most buffalo herds had already been destroyed by both Indians and whites.

Property Rights in the Soviet Union

In the Soviet Union, 97 percent of the farmland is cultivated collectively. The output of the collective farms goes to the state. As a result, most of the benefits derived from wise conservation practices and efficient production techniques accrue to secondary parties (the state) rather than to the individual workers. Families living on collective farms are permitted to cultivate a private plot, the area of which is not to exceed one acre. The "owners" of these private plots are allowed to sell their produce in a relatively free market. Although these private plots constitute approximately 1 percent of the land under cultivation in the Soviet Union, the Communist press reported that about one quarter of the total value of agricultural output was generated by these plots in 1980. The productivity per acre on the private plots was approximately 33 times higher than that on the collectively farmed land![5] Property rights make a difference even in the Soviet Union. Clearly, the farm workers take better care of the plots they own privately than the land they own communally. Aristotle would surely be satisfied with the long-range accuracy of his observation.

---

[3]For an economic analysis of the Montagnais management of the beaver, together with historical references, see Harold Demsetz, "Toward a Theory of Property Rights," *American Economic Review* (May 1967), pp. 347–359.

[4]This fascinating part of native American history has been recorded in Francis Haines, *The Buffalo* (New York: Crowell, 1970).

[5]See Hedrick Smith, *The Russians* (New York: New York Times Book Co., Quadrangle, 1976), pp. 199–214, for an informative account of the life on collective farms in the Soviet Union.

rights to the film and can collect a fee from anyone who sees or rents it. In contrast, a person who produces a beautifully landscaped lot that is visible from the street cannot collect a fee for the enjoyment that others derive from it. Some of the benefits of the landscaper's efforts accrue to secondary parties who probably will not help cover the cost.

Why should we be bothered if others benefit from our actions? Most of us are not, although it is quite possible, for example, that more people would better maintain their property if those who derived benefits from it helped pay for it. Generally, external benefits become important only when our inability to capture these potential gains forces us to *forgo* a socially beneficial activity. Exhibit 2 illustrates this point. Education adds to students' productivity, preparing them to enjoy higher future earnings. In addition, at least certain types of education reduce the future cost of welfare, generate a more intelligent populace, and perhaps even lower the crime rate. Some of the benefits of education, then, particularly elementary and secondary education, accrue to the citizenry as a whole. The private market demand curve understates the total social benefits of education. In the absence of government intervention, as shown in Exhibit 2, Q_1 units of education result from market forces. However, when external benefits MB are added to private benefits, the social gain from additional units of education exceeds the cost until output level Q_s is produced. Social welfare could thus be improved if output were expanded beyond Q_1 to Q_s, but since educational consumers cannot capture these external gains, they fail to purchase units beyond Q_1. The free market output is too small. A subsidy is required if the ideal output level Q_s is to be achieved.

When external benefits are present, the market demand curve understates the social gains of conducting the beneficial activity. Potential social gains go unrealized because no single decision-maker can fully appropriate or capture the gains; they are seen as "lost" when bestowed on nonpaying secondary parties. Decision-makers thus lack the incentive to carry an activity far enough to capture the potential social gains.

EXHIBIT 2 • Adding External Benefits

The demand curve *D*, indicating only private benefits, understates the social benefits of education. At output Q_1, the social benefit of an additional unit of education exceeds the cost. Ideally, output should be expanded to Q_s, where the social benefit of the marginal unit of education would be just equal to its cost. A public subsidy of *AB*, per unit of education, would lead to this output level.

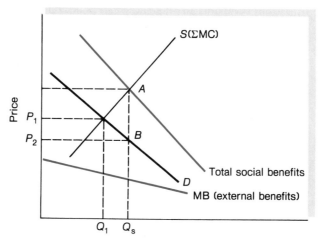

PUBLIC-SECTOR RESPONSES TO EXTERNALITIES

What can the government do to improve the efficiency of resource allocation when externalities are present? Sometimes private property rights can be more clearly defined and more strictly enforced. The granting of property rights to ranchers and homesteaders greatly improved the efficiency of land use in the Old West. More recently, the establishment of enforceable property rights to the oyster beds of the Chesapeake Bay improved the efficiency of oyster farming in the area. In many instances, however, it is difficult to delineate boundaries for a resource, determine who owns what portion, and enforce those rights. This is clearly the case with air and water rights. The clean-air rights of property owners often lack enforcement due to the high cost of information. In most states, water itself is not individually owned, although the right to use the water in certain ways may be privately held. Thus, the market process often fails to give good information and incentives to water users. External costs frequently result.

Why not simply prohibit activities that result in external cost? After all, why should we allow nonconsenting parties to be harmed? This approach has a certain appeal, but closer inspection indicates that it is often an unsatisfactory solution. Automobile exhaust imposes an external cost on bicyclists and, for that matter, on everyone who breathes. Dogs are notorious for using the neighbor's lawn for bone burying and relief purposes. Motorboats are noisy and frighten fish, much to the disgust of fishermen. Few people, though, would argue that we should do away with cars, dogs, and motorboats. From a social viewpoint, prohibition is often a less desirable alternative than tolerating the inconvenience of the external costs. The gains from the activity must be weighed against the costs imposed on those who are harmed, as well as against practical problems associated with controlling the activity.

When we cannot establish and enforce property rights, as in the case of our air resources, but we do not want simply to prohibit an activity, an alternative control strategy may be necessary. There are three general approaches that government might take. First, a government agency might act as a resource manager, charging the users of the resource a fee. Second, a regulatory agency might establish a maximum pollution emission standard and require that polluters attain at least that standard. Third, the agency might specify exactly what pollution control steps each polluter must take. We will consider each of these alternatives.

THE POLLUTION TAX APPROACH

Economists often favor a user's charge, which we will call a pollution tax. Exhibit 3 uses actual cost estimates from a copper smelter to illustrate the economics of this approach. The copper-producing firm has minimum costs of production when it spends nothing on pollution control. The marginal control cost curve reveals the cost savings (control costs avoided) that accrue to the firm when it pollutes. The marginal damage cost curve shows the cost ($32.50 per ton) imposed on parties downwind from the smelter. Without any tax or legal restraints, the smelter would emit 190,000 tons of sulfur

EXHIBIT 3 • Taxing a Smelter's Emissions

The marginal control cost curve shows that the firm, if it pays no damage costs itself, will emit 190,000 tons per year while spending nothing on control costs. However, if taxed according to the marginal damages it imposes ($32.50 per ton), it will voluntarily cut back its emissions to 17,100 tons per year, which is the socially efficient level. Further control would cost more than its social benefit.

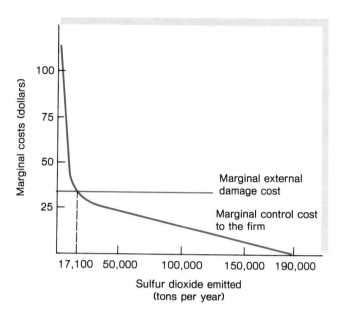

Richard L. Stroup, "The Economics of Air Pollution Control" (Ph.D. diss., University of Washington, 1970).

dioxide into the air per year, causing $6.2 million in damage. A tax equal to the marginal damage cost of $32.50 per ton emitted would cause the firm to reduce its emissions to 17,100 tons per year and reduce pollution damage from $6.2 million to about $0.6 million per year. The control cost of reducing emissions to this level would be about $2.9 million per year. Total social costs each year would fall from $6.2 million (all borne by those suffering pollution damage) to $3.5 million (combined costs of pollution damage and control, paid entirely by the firm and its customers). The net social gain would be $2.7 million.

The tax approach would promote efficient resource allocation by altering several economic incentives in a highly desirable way. First, the pollution tax would increase the cost of producing pollution-intensive goods, causing the supply in these industries to decline. A properly set tax would approximate the ideal price and output conditions illustrated by Exhibit 1. The revenues generated by the tax could be used to compensate secondary parties harmed by the pollutants or to finance a wide range of projects, including applied research on alternative methods of improving air quality. Second, the pollution tax would give firms an economic incentive to use methods of production (and control technology) that would create less pollution. As long as it was cheaper for the firm to control harmful emissions than to pay the emission fee (tax), the firm would opt for control. Third, since firms would be able to lower their tax bills by controlling pollution, a market for innovative emission-control devices would exist. Entrepreneurs would be induced to develop low-cost control devices and market them to firms that would now have a strong incentive to reduce their levels of emissions.

The pollution tax is appealing, since it can, at least in theory, be efficient. But, it is seldom even discussed seriously by policy-makers. There are three common objections: first, an efficient tax is one based on damage costs of the emissions. Without knowing what the damage costs are, an efficient tax cannot be stated or implemented. To determine the damage costs is difficult, yet any efficient control strategy an agency might choose will require a good estimate. This, then, is hardly a valid objection. A second objection is that an emission tax requires monitoring of the effluent. But, once again, any efficient strategy requires the agency to know what is being emitted, so the objection does not weaken the tax relative to other strategies. A more telling objection is a political one: to switch from a situation in which the polluter does not pay any damages to one in which all (estimated) damages are paid to the tax collector by polluters would involve a huge wealth transfer. Whole industries would be shaken up, some of them dramatically. Some firms might be put out of business. Lobbyists for polluters have kept the tax strategy from being seriously considered by policy-makers.

Given the damage and control cost estimates of Exhibit 3, the pollution tax approach does not fully eliminate pollution emissions. Should it? Clearly, the answer is no. At pollution emission levels of less than 17,100 tons per year, the marginal costs of pollution control would exceed the marginal benefits of the control. In cases such as that illustrated by Exhibit 3, substantial improvement can be made at a modest cost. At some point, however, it will become extremely costly to make additional improvements.

The pollution tax approach recognizes that cleaning up the environment is like squeezing water from a wet towel. Initially, a great deal of water can be squeezed from the towel with very little effort, but it becomes increasingly difficult to squeeze out still more. So it is with the environment. At some point, the benefit of a cleaner environment simply becomes less than its cost.

People want clean air and water. However, since they want other things as well, those entrusted with the authority to control pollution should ask themselves two crucial questions: How many other goods and services are we willing to give up to fight each battle against pollution? And, how much would the public like us to spend, from its own pockets, to achieve additional freedom from pollution? Since we all want to obtain the maximum benefit from expenditures on pollution control, it is important that these questions be answered carefully, no matter which control strategy we adopt.

Maximum Emission Standard: The maximum amount of pollution that a polluter is permitted to emit, established by the government or a regulatory authority. Fines are generally imposed on those who are unwilling or unable to comply.

THE MAXIMUM EMISSION STANDARD APPROACH

Although economics suggests that the pollution tax approach would be much more efficient, a **maximum emission standard** is more often imposed. In this case, the regulatory agency forces all producers to reduce their emissions to a designated level. Producers who are unable to meet the standard are required to terminate production.

The problem with this approach is that the costs of eliminating pollution emissions generally vary widely among polluters. Some can control pollution much more cheaply than others, but the maximum emissions standard approach fails to use this fact to get more control per dollar of expenditure in control costs. It thus results in less efficient pollution control per dollar than, for example, the pollution tax strategy.

Exhibit 4 illustrates why the standard emissions approach is an inefficient method of reducing the pollution level. Estimated minimum costs of added control by three particulate pollution emitters are listed. Suppose the regulatory agency wants to reduce the total particulate emissions from the three firms by three tons. The emission standards approach might accomplish this simply by requiring each firm to reduce its particulate emissions by one ton. The cost of these equal reductions will differ substantially among the firms; it will cost the electric utility $80, the steel plant $990, and the petroleum refiner $573. If this method is adopted, it will cost society $1643 in control cost to meet the new maximum pollution standard, which is three tons below the previous level of emissions.

Alternatively, the regulatory agency might levy a pollution tax and eliminate the same amount of pollution for much less. If we assume that a 3-ton reduction is small for each producer, so that each additional ton of pollution reduction raises control costs only by one dollar, then a tax of just $82.50 per ton would cause the electric utility to reduce particulate emissions by 3 tons, at a total cost of $243 ($80 + $81 + $82 = $243). That would allow the utility to escape 3 × $82.50 = $247.50 in added tax. The other polluters would not cut back emissions, but would choose to pay the tax, which is cheaper for them than the control costs. With the tax approach, which causes the cheapest control to take place, society buys the 3-ton reduction in pollution for $243, about one seventh the cost incurred in the

EXHIBIT 4 • Controlling Pollution—Cheaper For Some Than for Others

Some polluters face much higher control costs than others. If the authorities' control strategy does not properly take this into account, control may be needlessly expensive and opposition to control needlessly strong. If each polluter were required to reduce particulate pollution by one ton, total control costs for that change would be $80 + $990 + $573 = $1643. But, if a pollution tax of $82.50 were levied, the steel and petroleum plants would pay it, while the electric utility would find it cheaper to control some of its particulate pollution, and a reduction of 3 tons of emissions would cost roughly $240 instead of more than $1640.

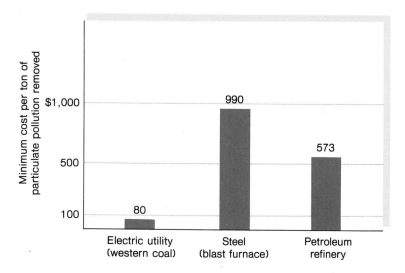

Source: EPA reports, summarized by Robert Crandall in *Controlling Industrial Pollution,* The Brookings Institution, Washington, DC, 1983, (page 36).

elimination of the same amount of pollution under the maximum emission control strategy.

A much more efficient form of the maximum emission strategy is to require the same one-ton-per-firm reduction, but allow the remaining rights to pollute (their original pollution rate, minus one ton each) to be traded among the three. In this case, the electric utility would sell two tons of its rights-to-pollute, one to each of the other two firms. Why? It can profit by reducing its pollution by 3 tons for $243, then selling its "excess" pollution rights to the other two firms, saving the steel firm $990 and the refinery $573. The amount paid by the two firms to the utility for its service (added pollution control, beyond its own requirement) would be more than $80 per ton, but no higher than the $990 plus $573 saved by the other two. The net savings to society in getting the full 3-ton reduction in pollution is again the same as in the pollution tax case. The emission rights trading strategy also has an important political advantage: no large payments (or small ones either) would have to be made by the firms to the tax collector.

Since each polluter has a different control cost schedule, either the pollution tax strategy or the emission rights trading strategy would result in the most pollution control per control dollar spent, and reach any desired pollution level at the lowest possible price. Some people object to the emissions trading strategy because pollution emitted at one location may cause more damage or less damage than the same pollution at another place. This is true, but any efficient strategy would have to make adjustments to recognize this fact. The emissions trading strategy might allow polluters in densely populated areas to exchange their pollution rights with polluters in a sparsely populated area with a bonus. Two tons of pollution rights in Manhattan might trade for three tons on a sparsely populated part of the coast, where the winds usually blow the particulates out to sea with much less damage.

The emissions trading strategy is being seriously considered for adoption in many areas of the United States. One version of it, the "bubble concept," allows limited tradeoffs among pollution sources only within a plant or group of plants within a small area, for a single pollutant, holding total emissions constant within the plants. Rather than forcing each component of a single plant to meet the particulate emission standard, the bubble concept allows the plant manager to meet an overall emission standard within an imaginary bubble surrounding his or her plant. A highly restricted version of the bubble concept was instituted by the Environmental Protection Agency in 1979. In its 1984 annual report (released in February of 1986), the President's Council on Environmental Quality stated that by October of 1984, the EPA had approved 37 bubbles and proposed 9 others, for a total estimated saving of $200 million compared to the traditional control approach. Over half of the plants affected would reduce emissions by more than would be required under the traditional approach. Such sizable savings make this strategy seem worthy of further consideration!

THE SPECIFIC PRESCRIPTION APPROACH

We have shown how the emission standard approach (without emissions trading) is less efficient than the pollution tax. Even less efficient is the approach taken by Congress in requiring the EPA to implement the Clean

Air Act in the case of coal-burning electric power plants. Rather than set emission standards, Congress ordered the EPA to require that new plants use specific kinds of pollution control apparatus—giant "scrubbers" to clean exhaust gases from new coal-burning electric power plants. Even though cheaper and more reliable means are frequently available to produce electricity with the same or less pollution, especially the use of clean coal, the far more expensive scrubbers are required. This favors certain regions of the country over others, and delays the construction of newer, cleaner power plants, so that the air is dirtier than it would be with the cheaper control methods. As ironic and as well known as this situation is,[6] more efficient approaches have not proven to be politically feasible. For reasons that we will explore more fully in the next chapter, the government solution to market failure is often itself rather inefficient.

SHOULD THE GOVERNMENT ALWAYS TRY TO CONTROL EXTERNALITIES?

When an externality is present, ideal efficiency of resource allocation may not be attained. It does not follow, though, that the government can always improve the situation and bring the economy closer to its ideal allocation level. In evaluating the case for a public-sector response to externalities, one should keep in mind the following three points.

1. *Sometimes the Economic Inefficiency Resulting from Externalities Is Small. Therefore, Given the Cost of Public-Sector Action, Net Gain from Intervention Is Unlikely.* The behavior of individuals often influences the welfare of others. The length of hair, choice of clothing, and personal hygiene of some individuals may affect the welfare of secondary parties. Should an agency in charge of personal appearance and hygiene be established to deal with externalities in these areas? Persons who value personal freedom would answer with a resounding no. From the standpoint of economic efficiency, their view is correct. The effects of externalities in these and similar areas are small. Since the costs of correcting the externalities would often be larger, the misallocation that results is usually the smallest attainable.

Government intervention requires the use of scarce resources. Regulatory agencies must be established; suits and countersuits are typically filed. These actions require the use of scarce legal resources. Most public-sector decision-makers lack the information necessary to determine which activities should be taxed and which should be subsidized. Administrative problems such as these greatly reduce the attractiveness of public-sector action. When the external effects are small, the cost of government intervention is likely to exceed the loss due to market inefficiency, *relative to the hypothetical ideal.* Under these circumstances, the best approach is usually to do nothing.

2. *The Market Often Finds a Reasonably Efficient Means of Dealing with Externalities.* The existence of externalities implies the presence of *potential* gain. If the external effects are significant, market participants have an incentive to organize economic activity in a manner that will enable them to

---

[6]For fascinating accounts of the politics and economics of this situation, see Bruce A. Ackerman and William T. Hassler, *Clean Coal/Dirty Air* (New Haven: Yale University Press, 1981), and Robert Crandall, *Controlling Industrial Pollution: The Economics and Politics of Clean Air* (Washington, D.C., The Brookings Institution, 1983).

capture the potential gain. If the number of parties affected by the externality is small, they may be able to arrive at a multi-party bargain that will at least partially negate the inefficiency and loss resulting from the externality.

Some entrepreneurs have devised ingenious schemes to capture benefits that were previously external to private parties. Private developers of country clubs and golf courses can capture the amenity benefits of locating houses nearby. They can charge more for the lots, since the buyers will benefit from trees, gardens, manicured lawns, and so on. If consumers are willing to pay for these amenities, as they often are, the first developers who provide such services will gain profits from the higher prices on the sale of surrounding lots.[7] Other developers will soon follow suit, trying to gain by also providing amenities. Thus, market forces sometimes devise efficient arrangements for dealing with external effects.

3. *Government Action May Also Impose an External Cost on Secondary Parties.* We have already mentioned that government intervention designed to correct the inefficiencies created by externalities is costly. Often, the costs of public-sector intervention exceed the benefits. Therefore, on efficiency grounds, intervention should be rejected. In addition, we should recognize that even democratic public-section action results in the imposition of an externality—the majority imposes an external cost on the minority, which is opposed to the action. Just as an individual may carry an activity too far when some of the costs are borne by others, a majority may also carry an action beyond the point of ideal efficiency. The gains that accrue to the majority may be less than the costs imposed on the minority. So, even though the government can potentially take corrective measures, counter-productive economic action by the democratic majority may result if the external costs imposed on the minority are not fully considered. (Limits to the effectiveness of government action will be discussed more fully in the next chapter.)

MARKET FAILURE: PUBLIC GOODS

Public goods comprise the extreme case of commodities, the consumption of which results in spillover benefits to secondary parties. In the original formulation by Paul Samuelson, there are two distinctive characteristics of public goods. First, the availability of a public good to one person makes it

---

[7]The development of Disney World in Florida is an interesting case in which entrepreneurial ingenuity made it possible to capture external benefits more fully. When Walt Disney developed Disneyland in California, the market value of land in the immediate area soared as a result of the increase in demand for services (food, lodging, gasoline, and so on). Since the land in the area was owned by others, the developers of Disneyland were unable to capture these external benefits. However, when Disney World was developed near Orlando, Florida, the owners purchased an enormous plot of land, far more than was needed for the amusement park. As was the case with Disneyland in California, the operation of Disney World caused land values in the immediate area to rise sharply. However, since the developers of Disney World initially purchased a large amount of land near the attraction, they were able to capture the external benefits by selling prime property to hotels, restaurants, and other businesses desiring a nearby location.

equally available to all others. Public goods must therefore be consumed jointly by all. Second, because of this joint consumption, it may be impossible to exclude nonpayers from the receipt of public goods.

Examples of *pure* public goods are scarce. National defense is one. The defense system that protects you provides similar protection to all other citizens. Our legal and monetary systems are also public goods. The laws and individual rights available to one citizen are also provided to others. The policies of the Federal Reserve are provided equally to all citizens. The quality of the atmosphere, and, to a lesser extent, that of rivers and waterways can also be classified as public goods.

THE FREE RIDER PROBLEM

Free Rider: One who receives the benefit of a good without contributing to its costs. Public goods and commodities that generate external benefits offer people the opportunity to become free riders.

Since nonpaying consumers cannot be excluded (at a reasonable cost), a sufficient amount of public goods may not be provided by the market mechanism. If public goods were provided through the market, each of us would have an incentive to become a **free rider,** one who receives the benefits of a good without paying toward its costs. Why contribute to the cost of supplying a public good? Your actions will have a negligible impact on the supply of clean air, pure water, national defense, and legal justice. The sensible path will lead you to do nothing. As long as you travel that path alone, you will ride along, free and easy. If everyone else joins you, however, the aggregate lack of action will lead to an insufficient quantity of public goods.

Suppose national defense were provided entirely through the market. Would you voluntarily help to pay for it? Your contribution would have a negligible impact on the total supply of defense available to each of us, even if you made a *large personal* contribution. Many citizens, even though they might value defense highly, would become free riders, and few funds would be available to finance the necessary supply. If the military-industrial complex were dependent on market forces, it would be small indeed!

The harmony between private and social interests tends to break down for public goods. The amount of a public good available to an individual (and others) will be virtually unaltered by whether or not the individual pays for it. Each individual thus has an incentive to become a free rider. When numerous individuals become free riders, however, less than the ideal amount of the public good is produced.

NEAR PUBLIC GOODS

Few commodities are pure public goods, but a much larger set of goods are jointly consumed even though nonpaying customers can be excluded. For example, such goods as radio and television broadcasts, national parks, interstate highways, movies, and football games are jointly consumed. Assuming no congestion problem, additional consumption of these "near public goods," *once they are produced,* is costless to society.

Should nonpaying customers be excluded when the marginal cost of providing the good to them is zero? Many economists argue that such near public goods as highways, national parks, and television programming should be provided free to consumers, at the expense of the taxpayer. Why exclude people from the consumption of these near public goods when their use of the goods does not add to the costs? The argument has a certain appeal.

We must be careful, however. Television programs, highways, parks, and other public goods are scarce. The consumption of other products must be sacrificed to produce such goods. If a zero price is charged, how does one determine whether or not consumers value additional units enough to cover their opportunity cost? How can an intensely concerned minority communicate its views as to the types of near public goods that should be produced? Taxes will be necessary to cover the costs of making near public goods freely available. Will such taxes lead to inefficiency? These factors reduce the attractiveness of public-sector provision of jointly consumed commodities when exclusion of nonpaying consumers is possible.

APPLICATIONS IN ECONOMICS

Private Provision of Public Goods

An excellent example of a public good is the preservation of a locally or nationally significant form of wildlife. Hawks, sea lions, and wild geese belong to no one, but their survival keeps ecosystems in balance and intact. We all benefit when habitats are kept available to ensure that such species do not become extinct. Despite the fact that each of us can be a free rider if others make the effort and sacrifice needed to bring about such preservation, successful voluntary efforts in the private sector have done just that: thousands of organizations, each defying the free rider problem, have for many decades led the conservation movement, privately establishing successful conservation projects.

Some of these groups are very large. The Nature Conservancy owns and manages a national system of nearly 800 sanctuaries and has preserved some 2.4 million acres since 1951. The 1984 Annual Report of the President's Council of Environmental Quality reports that the National Audubon Society has a sanctuary system of over 63 units totalling over 250,000 acres. Others are small—a local garden club might own and manage two acres to preserve a particular wild flower.

Private groups have often been leaders in educating the public, and have been well ahead of government in providing their particular public good. Two examples involve hawks and sea lions.

Example 1: The Hawk Mountain Sanctuary

In the 1930s, hawks were considered a nuisance or worse, since they killed certain other birds, including domestic chickens. There was often a bounty on them—the government would pay people who killed hawks. Conservationists, however, had begun to worry about the declining numbers of hawks, pointing out that among other things, hawks ate rodents, keeping down the grain losses experienced by farmers. The environmental movement was still very weak, however, and the slaughter of hawks continued.

In one area in particular, Hawk Mountain of eastern Pennsylvania, thousands of hawks were killed on certain days each year. So upset was Rosalie Edge, an early conservationist (and leading suffragist) that when reasoning with governmental authorities failed, she organized a small group of conservationists who simply bought Hawk Mountain for $3500. They prevented further shooting from that critical spot, and established a nonprofit educational and conservation group—the Hawk Mountain Sanctuary Association. Seven thousand members from all over the nation, in addition to admission fees paid by 50,000 visitors per year, support a visitor and education center at the mountain where previously the hawks were slaughtered by the thousands each year.

Example 2: Sea Lion Caves, Inc.

Like hawks, sea lions on the Oregon coast were formerly hunted, and bounties were paid to those who killed them. Sea lions feed on fish, and during the 1920s the state of Oregon paid $5 per sea lion killed. Several bounty hunters made their living in this fashion. The intent was to reduce sea lion consumption of coastal salmon. Earlier, commercial fishing interests hired professional hunters to exterminate the sea lion. However, one important area of the sea lion's Oregon habitat was privately owned and used as a tourist attraction—Sea Lion Caves, where the animals could be viewed up close, in a natural setting. The owners of the caves had to spend a good deal of time driving off bounty hunters. By 1931, conservation legislation was passed to protect sea lions in most areas of the Oregon coast, but while the extermination pressure was on, the profit-seeking Sea Lion Cave operation had played an important part in the survival of

**PRIVATE PROVISION
OF PUBLIC GOODS
(continued)**

the sea-going mammals. The sea lions themselves are not owned, and their survival is largely a public good. But, private ownership of the habitat had concentrated enough of the benefits in the hands of a tourist-based business to help guarantee the survival of the endangered animals at a critical time.

Can private clubs and businesses eliminate the public goods problem? Not necessarily, since there is no guarantee that the optimal amount of public goods will be provided. The problem continues to exist and to be an important source of market failure. However, these private-sector philanthropic and entrepreneurial solutions to certain public goods problems do remind us that whenever the will exists to solve such problems, government action is not the only possible way. The same sort of informed and determined efforts needed to convince government to do the right thing can frequently find private solutions more quickly and cheaply.

MARKET FAILURE: POOR INFORMATION

In the real world, market choices, like other decisions, are made with incomplete information. Consumers do not have perfect knowledge about the quality of a product, the price of alternative products, or side effects that may result from a product. They may make incorrect decisions, decisions they will later regret, because they do not possess good information.

The reality of imperfect knowledge is not, of course, the fault of the market. In fact, the market provides consumers with a strong incentive to acquire information, and producers providing consumers with the best deal with an incentive to advertise that fact. Because consumers must bear the consequences of their mistakes, they certainly will seek to avoid the deliberate purchase of "lemon" products.

**GETTING YOUR
MONEY'S WORTH**

**Repeat-Purchase Item: An
item purchased often by
the same buyer.**

The consumer's information problem is minimal if the item is purchased regularly. Consider the problem of purchasing a brand of soap. There is little cost associated with trying out brands. Since soap is a regularly purchased product, trial-and-error is an economical means of determining which brand is most suitable to one's needs. It is a **repeat-purchase item.** The consumer can use past experience to good advantage when buying repeat-purchase items such as soap, toothpaste, most food products, lawn service, and gasoline.

What incentive does the producer have to supply accurate information that will help the customer make a satisfying long-run choice? Is there a conflict between consumer and producer interests? The answers to these questions are critically affected by the seller's dependence on return customers.

If dissatisfaction on the part of *current* customers is expected to have a strong adverse effect on *future* sales, a business entrepreneur will attempt to provide accurate information to help customers make wise choices. The future success of business entrepreneurs who sell repeat-purchase products is highly dependent on the future purchases of currently satisfied customers. There is a harmony of interest because buyer and seller alike will be better off if the customer is satisfied with the product purchased.

LET THE BUYER BEWARE

Major problems of conflicting interests, inadequate information, and unhappy customers arise when goods either (a) are difficult to evaluate on inspection and are seldom repeatedly purchased from the same producer or (b) are potentially capable of serious and lasting harmful side effects that cannot be detected by a layperson. Under these conditions, human nature being what it is, we would expect some unscrupulous producers to sell low-quality, defective, and even harmful goods.

When customers are unable to distinguish between high-quality and low-quality goods, their ability to police quality and price is weakened. When this is the case, business entrepreneurs have a strong incentive to cut costs by reducing quality. Consumers get less for their dollars. Since sellers are not dependent on repeat customers, they may survive and even prosper in the marketplace. The probability of customer dissatisfaction is thus increased because of inadequate information and poor quality. Accordingly, the case for an unhampered market mechanism is weakened.

Consider the consumer's information problem when an automobile is purchased. Are most consumers capable of properly evaluating the safety equipment? Except for a handful of experts, most people are not. Some consumers might individually seek expert advice. It may be more efficient, though, to prevent market failure by having the government regulate automobile safety and require certain safety equipment.

As another example of the problem of inadequate consumer information, consider the case of a drug manufacturer's exaggerated claims for a new product. Until consumers have had experience with the drug or have listened to others' experiences, they might make wasteful purchases. Government regulation might benefit consumers by forcing the manufacturer to modify its claims.

ENTREPRENEURS AND INFORMATION

Consumers have the incentive to seek good information, but that can be very expensive. Entrepreneurial sellers, when they are in fact providing good value, have an incentive to bridge the information gap, and to let consumers know it. How? As we mentioned in Chapter 4, franchises are one way to accomplish this. The tourist traveling through an area for the first time—and very possibly the last—may find that eating at a franchised food outlet and sleeping at a franchised motel is the cheapest way to avoid costly mistakes. Franchise operations are policed by the national office that sells the franchises. Their incentive is to maintain the franchise reputation for quality, because if it declines, their ability to sell new franchises is hurt. Even though the tourist may visit a particular establishment only once, the franchise turns that visit into a "repeat purchase," since the reputation of the entire national franchise operation is at stake.

Similarly, the advertising of a brand name nationally develops a reputation that is at stake when purchases are made. How much would the Coca Cola Company pay to avoid a dangerous bottle of Coke being sold? Surely, it would be a large sum. The company's reputation is a hostage to quality control. Advertising investments act as a signal that the firm is serious about its future business, and has something important to lose if it cheats customers.

Johnson & Johnson's experience with Tylenol capsules is a concrete example of how far a company is willing to go to protect a brand name. In 1982, seven people died as a result of taking Tylenol capsules that had been laced with cyanide. Even though Johnson & Johnson, the producer of the capsules, was not at fault, the company spent at least $60 million to recall 31 million bottles of Tylenol, provide consumers and retailers with refunds, and introduce a new triple-sealed bottle of Tylenol. Although Tylenol's share of the market dropped to below 7 percent immediately following the tragedy, by 1984, its share was almost as high as the 35 percent it had before the deaths occurred, according to *Business Week* magazine.

In early 1986, though, Johnson & Johnson faced a replay of the situation when a woman died after taking cyanide-laced capsules. This time the company decided to stop making Tylenol capsules, because it was unable to ensure their safety. It recalled existing bottles of Tylenol capsules and offered to replace them with more tamper-resistant Tylenol "caplets." *The New York Times* estimated that this move to protect the reputation of Tylenol would cost Johnson & Johnson $100 to $150 million.

As this example indicates, entrepreneurial measures such as assuring the quality of a franchiser or protecting a brand name can be expensive. They cannot, however, guarantee that customers will never be cheated or disappointed after a transaction. Despite the best efforts of entrepreneurs, the lack of consumer information will continue to assure that the market will remain imperfect relative to the economists' ideal, and that government will have a potential role to play in improving on the market's results.

LOOKING AHEAD

In this chapter, we focused on the failures of the market. In the next chapter, we will use economic analysis to come to a better understanding of the workings of the public sector. We will also discuss some of the expected shortcomings of public-sector action. Awareness of both the strengths and weaknesses of alternative forms of economic organization will help us to make more intelligent choices in this important area.

CHAPTER SUMMARY

1. The sources of market failure can be grouped into four major categories: (a) externalities, (b) public goods, (c) poor information, and (d) monopoly.
2. When externalities are present, the market may fail to confront decision-makers with the proper incentives. Since decision-makers are not forced to consider external cost, they may find it personally advantageous to undertake an economic activity even though it generates a net loss to the community. In contrast, when external benefits are present, decision-makers may fail to undertake economic action that would generate a net social gain.

3. When external costs originate from the activities of a business firm, the firm's cost curve will understate the social cost of producing the good. If production of the good generates external costs, the price of the product under competitive conditions will be too low and the output too large to meet the *ideal requirements* of economic efficiency.

4. External costs result from the failure or inability of a society to establish private property rights. Clearly established private property rights enable owners to prohibit others from using or abusing their property. In contrast, communal property rights normally result in overutilization, since most of the cost of overutilization (and misuse) is imposed on others.

5. When external benefits are present, the market demand curve will understate the social gains of conducting the activity. The consumption and production of goods that generate external benefits will tend to be lower than the socially ideal levels.

6. The efficient use of air and water resources is particularly troublesome for the market because it is often impossible to apportion these resources and determine ownership rights. A system of emission charges (a pollution tax) is capable of inducing individuals to make wiser use of these resources. Emission charges (a) increase the cost of producing pollution-intensive goods, (b) grant firms an incentive to use methods of production that create less pollution, and (c) provide producers with an incentive to adopt control devices when it is economical to do so.

7. When the marginal benefits (for example, cleaner air) derived from pollution control are less than the social gains associated with a pollution-generating activity, prohibition of the activity that results in pollution (or other external cost) is not an ideal solution.

8. When the control costs of firms vary, the emission charge (pollution tax) approach will permit society to reduce pollution by a given amount at a lower cost than will the maximum emission standard method, which is currently widely used. The marginal cost of attaining a cleaner environment will rise as the pollution level is reduced. At some point, the economic benefits of a still cleaner environment will be less than the costs.

9. In evaluating the case for government intervention in situations involving externalities, one must consider the following factors: (a) the magnitude of the external effects relative to the cost of government action; (b) the ability of the market to devise means of dealing with the problem without intervention; and (c) the possibility that the political majority may carry the government intervention too far if the external costs imposed on the minority are not fully considered.

10. When it is costly or impossible to withhold a public good from persons who do not or will not help pay for it, the market system breaks down because everyone has an incentive to become a free rider. When everyone attempts to ride for free, production of the public good will be lower than the socially ideal level.

11. The market provides an incentive for consumers to acquire information. When a business is dependent on repeat customers, it has a strong

incentive to promote customer satisfaction. However, when goods are either (a) difficult to evaluate on inspection and seldom purchased repeatedly from the same producer or (b) have potentially serious and lasting harmful effects, consumer trial and error may be an unsatisfactory means of determining quality. Franchising and brand names often communicate reliable information on product quality to consumers and thereby reduce the likelihood that consumers will be cheated or misled, even in cases when the specific item is not purchased regularly.

THE ECONOMIC WAY
OF THINKING—
**DISCUSSION
QUESTIONS**

1. Why may external cost be a cause of economic inefficiency? Why is it important to define property rights clearly? Explain.
2. Devise a tax plan that would (a) reduce the extent of automobile pollution, (b) provide an incentive for entrepreneurs to develop new products that would limit pollution, and (c) permit continued automobile travel for those willing to bear the total social costs. Explain how your plan would influence incentives and why it would work.
3. "When goods generate external benefits, the market is unable to produce an adequate supply. This is why the government must provide such goods as police and fire protection, education, parks, and vaccination against communicable diseases."
   (a) Do you agree? Explain.
   (b) Does governmental provision necessarily ensure "an adequate supply"? How would you define "adequate supply"?
   (c) Such goods as golf courses, shopping centers, country clubs, neckties, and charity also generate some spillover external benefits. Do you think the government should provide these goods in order to ensure an adequate supply?
4. Which of the following goods are most likely to result in a large number of dissatisfied customers: (a) light bulbs, (b) food at a local restaurant, (c) food at a restaurant along an interstate highway, (d) automobile repair service, (e) used cars, (f) plumbing services, (g) used automatic dishwashers, (h) used sofas, (i) television repair service? Explain your answer.
5. What are public goods? Why does a decentralized pricing system have trouble producing an adequate amount of public goods?
6. Are people more likely to take better care of an item they own jointly (communally) or one they own privately? Why? Does the presence of private property rights affect the behavior of persons in noncapitalist nations? Why or why not?
7. **What's Wrong with This Way of Thinking?**
   "Corporations are the major beneficiaries of our lax pollution control policy. Their costs are reduced because we permit them free use of valuable resources—clean water and air—in order to produce goods. These lower costs are simply added to the profits of the polluting firms."
8. **What's Wrong with This Way of Thinking?**
   "Private property rights are a gamble. What if the owner doesn't take

good care of what he owns? Communal property rights are better—
there are more people to take care of what they own. Surely someone
will exercise the needed care." (Hint: What was Aristotle's position on
this issue?)

9. Can you think of any public goods, or near public goods, that are
   supplied privately? Do such examples show that there is no such thing
   as a free rider problem?

CHAPTER
FOCUS

- What are the major reasons that voters seek government action?

- When can governmental action be socially efficient, so that the benefits to those who gain are larger than the costs to others?

- Why might antipoverty programs improve efficiency, while also redistributing income?

- Can we expect citizens to promote governmental programs that are not efficient? What role do constitutional rules play in limiting this behavior?

- What is self-interest redistribution? Why might politicians find such redistribution politically attractive?

- How do incentives for government agencies to operate efficiently compare with those in the private sector?

We no longer expect results from government. What was a torrid romance between the people and government for so long has now become a tired middle-aged liaison which we do not quite know how to break off. [1]

PETER DRUCKER

29 PUBLIC CHOICE: UNDERSTANDING GOVERNMENT AND GOVERNMENT FAILURE

In the previous chapter, we learned more about the imperfections of market decision-making in coordinating production and exchange among individuals. There, and in earlier chapters, we have seen the constructive role government can play in improving situations where the market fails. The collective decision-making process, though, is not a flawless mechanism that automatically corrects the inefficiencies of the market. A painful lesson of history is that government action often does not have the hoped-for and planned-for results. Even well-designed programs based on humanitarian principles sometimes fail to meet their initial objectives. The chapter-opening quotation, from Peter F. Drucker, reveals a cynicism that grew during the 1970s, replacing the optimism of the 1960s. The great hopes of many Americans during that decade for extensive social improvements through public-sector action were to a large extent unfulfilled. The cynicism is to some degree a reaction to that disappointment.

Traditionally, economists have focused on market failure and what ideal public policy might do to improve on those failures, virtually ignoring the actual operation of the public sector. This traditional neglect, however, has become less and less satisfactory. Approximately two fifths of our national income is channeled through the various governmental departments and agencies. One third of the nation's land is owned by the federal government alone, in addition to holdings of state and local governments. Also, the legal framework establishes the "rules of the game" for the market sector. The government's role in defining property rights, enforcing contracts, fixing prices, and regulating business and labor practices has a tremendous impact on the operation of an economy, as we have seen in previous chapters. To understand our economy, it is necessary that we understand governmental decision-making.

Building on our discussions of Chapter 4 (many students may want to review Chapter 4 at this time), this chapter analyzes the political process and how it deals with economic issues. In studying collective decision-making, we seek to understand the link between individual preferences and political outcomes. The political process is simply an alternative method of making economic decisions. Like the market, it is likely to have defects. When we evaluate the costs and benefits of public-sector action, we must also realistically compare the likely results of collective action with the expected outcome of market allocation. In other words, for any economic activity, we must ask ourselves: In which sector will the defects stand least in the way of our goals?

Most political decisions in Western countries are made legislatively. We will focus on a system in which voters choose legislators, who in turn institute public policy. Let us see what the tools of economics reveal about the political process.

HOW VOTERS DECIDE

Individuals express their preferences for types of action primarily through the voting process. In a legislative system, citizens must express their views

---

[1]Peter F. Drucker, "The Sickness of Government," *Public Interest* (Winter 1969), p. 5.

through a representative. Voters influence the quantity of political goods and the prices to users indirectly, by voting on the composition of the body of elected representatives.

How do voters decide whom to support? Many factors no doubt influence their decisions. Which candidate is the most persuasive, and which presents the best television image? Who appears to be honest? Many subjective judgments on questions of this sort can be important.

The perceived views of candidates on issues, especially the issues most important to the individual voter, will also influence the voter's decision. According to economic theory, other things constant, each voter will support the candidate who offers the voter the greatest expected net subjective benefits. Factors other than expected direct economic gain will make a difference, but perceived personal gain will certainly be an important component.

The greater the net personal economic gain to a voter from a particular candidate's platform, as that voter perceives it, the more likely it is that the voter will favor that candidate. The greater the perceived net economic cost imposed on that voter by a candidate's positions, the less inclined the voter will be to support the candidate. "Perceived" is an important word here, since voters will not be fully informed on most issues.

As we discussed in Chapter 4, when decisions are made collectively, the direct link between the individual's choice and the outcome of the issue is broken. The choice of a single voter is seldom decisive when the decision-making group is large. Recognizing that the outcome will not depend on one vote, the individual voter has little incentive to seek information (which is costly) on issues and candidates in order to cast a more informed vote. The result is called the rational ignorance effect. (See Chapter 4, pp. 93–94.)

Even a voter who knows the candidates and their previous stands on the hundreds of issues arising each year cannot anticipate all the issues to be faced by elected candidates during their next term in office. In this complex situation, labels such as liberal, conservative, Democrat, and Republican become attractive to the voter. Although oversimplified, such categories allow the rationally ignorant voter to hazard a guess as to a candidate's stand on future issues. In the world of politics, a candidate's "image", however vague or incorrect, is very important to political success. The details of a politician's stand on particular issues are simply not known to most voters. That fact strongly influences the actions of suppliers in the political marketplace.

SUPPLY, PROFITS, AND THE POLITICAL SUPPLIER

The entrepreneur is a dynamic force in the private sector. The entrepreneur seeks to gain by undertaking potentially profitable projects. In the competitive market process, business entrepreneurs produce commodities that are intensely desired relative to their supply. Similarly, the political supplier (politician) is a dynamic force in the collective decision-making process. The political supplier seeks to offer voters an image and a bundle of political goods that will increase the chances of his or her winning elections. Those who are successful survive and may achieve private power, fame, and even fortune. These goals are as important in the political arena as they are in the private sector. To increase the chance of being elected, the political supplier must be alert to the political goods and services that can attract the most voters. Put another way, politicians have a strong incentive to supply political goods, when the costs, measured in votes lost, are smaller than the benefits—the votes gained.

This does not mean that politicians always favor the viewpoint of the majority on a *specific* issue. In some cases, a candidate may gain more votes among an intensely active minority of people, willing to vote for or against the candidate on this one issue, than from a dispassionate (and rationally uninformed) majority opposed to that position.

MONEY, POLITICAL ADVERTISING, AND THE SUCCESSFUL POLITICIAN

Votes win elections, but rationally uninformed voters must be convinced to "want" a candidate. Perceptions, not just realities, influence decisions. What is required to win the support of voters? Both the candidate's positive attributes (for example honesty, compassion, and effectiveness) and his or her position on issues, as we have stressed, are important. However, candidates must bring their strengths to the attention of the voters. Money, staff, and expertise are required to promote a candidate among the voting population.

The important role of product advertising and the media in determining consumer preferences has been stressed by John Kenneth Galbraith, among others. Since voters have little incentive to acquire information on most issues prior to voting, the impact of advertising and the media is even more important in affecting political decisions than private-sector market decisions. The buyer or seller in a market personally reaps the benefit from a more informed decision, and must live with the results of each choice, because it is decisive for the individual. In the public sector, by contrast, advertising and favorable attention in the media are more important due to the strength of the rational ignorance effect.

BEING SUCCESSFUL MEANS BEING POLITICAL

What does our analysis suggest about the motivation of political decision-makers? Are we implying that they are highly selfish, that they consider only their own pocketbooks and ignore the public interest? The answer is no. When people act in the political sphere, they may genuinely want to help their fellow citizens. Factors other than personal political gain, narrowly defined, influence the actions of many political suppliers. On certain issues, one may feel strongly that one's position is best for the nation, even though it may not be currently popular. The national interest as perceived by the political supplier may conflict with the position that would be most favorable to reelection prospects. Some politicians may opt for the national interest even when it means political defeat. None of this is inconsistent with an economic view of political choice.

However, the existence of political suicide does not change the fact that *most* politicians prefer political life. There is a strong incentive for political suppliers to stake out positions that will increase their vote total in the next election. A politician who refuses to give major consideration to electoral gain increases the risk of replacement by a more astute (and less public-minded) politician. Competition—the competition of vote-maximizing political candidates—presents even the most public-spirited politician with a strong incentive to base his or her decisions primarily on political considerations. Just as neglect of economic profit is the route to market oblivion, neglect of potential votes is the route to political oblivion.

THE DEMAND FOR PUBLIC-SECTOR ACTION

People participate in market activity to obtain more goods and services. People turn to the government for much the same reason. Most voters demand public-sector action for two major reasons: (a) to improve economic efficiency and thus capture potential gains lost to market failure and (b) to redistribute income.

PUBLIC-SECTOR ACTIONS TO CORRECT MARKET FAILURE

There is potential social gain—and potential political profit—in correcting problems and providing benefits where markets have failed. Corrective action can increase the size of the economic pie, generating personal benefits for individual voters. Each form of market failure discussed in the previous chapter provides potential opportunities for government to improve efficiency by actions which result in more total benefits than total costs.

Where external costs exist, regulation or taxation can reduce the negative side effects for which markets do not hold private decision-makers accountable. When there are external benefits of activities insufficiently provided by private means, regulation and tax policy again can intervene. For example, sidewalks can be required in residential neighborhoods, and owners can be compelled to keep them snow-free, in order to provide external benefits to pedestrians. Similarly, tax breaks can be provided for nonprofit organizations that fight diseases, preserve natural area, art, or architecture, or do other charitable works generating benefits for individuals who do not pay for them.

When markets have not provided sufficient public goods, government can tax the public to provide them. Police protection against criminal activity is an example of a public good often provided with far greater benefits than costs. We all gain when each of us is free from serious worry that a criminal can threaten, injure, or rob us at will. Political suppliers respond strongly to voter's views that protecting the civil liberties and the property of individuals is a high priority, and one that would be underprovided by the market. Few politicians argue against the provision by government of effective law enforcement.

On a larger scale, national defense is a classic public good. Whoever protects the nation against foreign threats or invasion provides a service to all, including those who would try to be free riders and let others pay for defense. Government is able to tax everyone and use the revenue to provide defensive protection. There is net political gain available for politicians who support the provision by government of important public goods not provided sufficiently in markets.

Poorly informed consumers can also be helped by government action. Government certification or licensure of accountants, doctors, and lawyers can protect uninformed consumers from those who would practice without the training and experience necessary to perform effectively. Building codes can protect people against unsafe building practices, and so on. When the cost of informed choices is high, and the cost of consumer protection is low, appropriate government action can create net benefits for individuals at large, and for politicians who provide these services through government action.

When monopoly power causes output to be lower, and prices to be higher than they would be in competitive markets, several government policies can potentially help the consumer and the economy as a whole. Anti-trust activities, regulation of monopoly prices, and governmental provision in place of market provision all have some potential for providing net gains to society and political "profit"—a net gain of votes—to political suppliers of these services.

INCOME REDISTRIBUTION AND THE DEMAND FOR GOVERNMENT ACTION

While public policy sometimes inadvertently results in income transfers, in other cases public-sector programs are specifically designed to redistribute income, either because of a demand for a more equal distribution of income among *all* citizens or because of a demand for more income by and/or for a specific group of citizens. As Exhibit 1 illustrates, direct income transfers through the public sector have increased substantially during recent decades. Income transfer payments constituted only 6.3 percent of national income in 1959; they had risen to 14.9 percent by 1985.

EXHIBIT 1 • The Growth of Government Transfer Payments

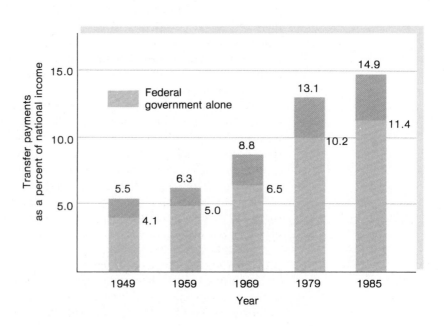

Economic Report of the President, 1986.

Public-Good Effects of Income Redistribution. Some redistribution of income may stem from the public-good characteristics of antipoverty efforts. The welfare of many citizens may be adversely affected by the hardship and poverty of others. For example, the economic conditions of ill-clothed children, street beggars, and the elderly poor may impose a cost on many of their fellow citizens. However, private antipoverty efforts, like private-sector national defense, have public-good characteristics. Even though the welfare of a person may be improved if there are fewer poor people, the amount that any one individual contributes to the antipoverty effort exerts little impact on the overall status of the poor. Since the number of poor people, like the strength of our national defense, is largely independent of one's *personal* contribution, individuals motivated by the desire to reduce poverty in general, not the desire personally to help, may simply become free riders. When a large number of people become free riders, though, less than the desired amount of antipoverty effort will be voluntarily supplied.

Under these circumstances, collective action against poverty may improve the general welfare of the community. If everyone is required to contribute through the tax system, the free-rider problem can be overcome. Effective antipoverty efforts may not only help the poor but may also help donors willing to give their fair share if others will do likewise.

Self-Interest Redistribution. Collective action to redistribute income does not always stem from the public-good nature of antipoverty efforts. Rather than seek to correct what economists call market failure, people would sometimes much rather correct what they see as the market's failure to make them as wealthy as they would like to be. Redistribution motivated solely by the desire of its supporters to help themselves is called **self-interest redistribution** by economists. It is quite common, but it is almost never called income redistribution by those who seek it. When farmers lobby for farm subsidies, they may argue that agricultural price supports are in our national interest, or that supports are needed to preserve the family farm. When college administrators (and professors) ask for government funds, they typically make their requests on behalf of students or in the name of scientific advances. Yet, in each case, it is more than a happy coincidence that the desired program also redistributes income to those making the requests. Clearly, a strong element of self-interest is involved.

When are politicians most likely to favor self-interest redistribution? We have seen that transfers to the poor, as a public good, might produce benefits greater than their costs. At best, self-interest redistribution results in equally balanced benefits and costs. Politicians, however, may be able to gain from such transfers. If transfers are made to well-organized and clearly defined groups, such as the elderly, union members, or auto producers, strong political support can be obtained from these groups. The special interest effect is important here. If those who pay are a large, unorganized group (for example, taxpayers in general, or all who buy autos) and the costs are diffused, few votes are lost. This is especially true if the costs can be hidden. Complex programs, debt financing, and money creation are all ways of hiding the cost of providing the redistribution of benefits.

Self Interest Redistribution: **Redistribution motivated solely by the desire of the members of a group to help themselves. Nonrecipients do not gain from an improvement in the welfare of the recipients.**

Many who gain the most from self-interest redistribution never receive a check from the government. Others get only part of their benefits via direct payments. Dairy producers have successfully invested large sums to obtain and maintain federal and state regulation of fresh-milk markets. Most of their estimated $270 million in annual benefits are not in the form of direct payments from the government, but in the form of prices set far above competitive levels. Consumers bear the burden of high prices, and even pay amounts over and above the redistributed income. Since the artificial prices and regulations are inefficient, those who gain receive less than the losers pay.

As both the budget and the regulatory powers of government grow, individuals, firms, and unions will find it in their interest to spend more time looking for ways to capture gains bestowed by the government (see "Rent Seeking and the Constitution"). By the same token, less effort will be devoted to production activities.

VOTERS' DEMANDS AND POLITICAL OUTCOMES: WHY GOVERNMENT ALSO IS IMPERFECT

Voters' lives can often be improved by appropriate governmental policy. When markets fail, or when voters simply want to redistribute income, government is a powerful tool. However, it is simply an alternative method of economic organization, not an automatic corrective mechanism. Government action may sometimes go awry.

Why might government action go in directions that will fail to benefit most citizens? There are several reasons to expect that it will fall short of both the ideal efficiency criteria of economists and of the more general responsiveness to "the public interest," a criteria often stressed by non-economists. **Government failure** results when public policy promotes economic inefficiency. Chapter 4 began our exploration into the reasons for government failure. We will now explain more fully the various causes of government failure.

Government Failure: Failure of government action to meet the criteria of ideal economic efficiency.

GOVERNMENT FAILURE: UNINFORMED VOTERS

The rational ignorance effect indicates that when voters go to the polls, they will not be fully informed on the issues, nor on the candidates' positions on the issues. How strong is the rational ignorance effect? As Exhibit 2 shows, fewer than half of all Americans of voting age can name their Congressmen. Through the years, many polls have been taken on the information possessed by voters. The results are always similar. Just as economic theory predicts, voters are generally uninformed about political candidates and specific issues.

Does this rational ignorance cause problems? As the result of the rational ignorance effect, the political process is biased against proposals with elusive benefits and easily identified costs. Anthony Downs states the argument for this viewpoint:

EXHIBIT 2 • Political Knowledge and Rational Ignorance

Rational ignorance is widespread in politics, as these numbers suggest. Also, political knowledge and influence are not distributed equally. Since knowledge is important to the exercise of influence, the figures imply that it is unlikely that poor people, city people, or black people will use government to help themselves at the expense of rich, rural, or white people.

		Percentage of Voters Who Know Their Congressmen					
		Location		Race		Income	
	Total	City	Rural	White	Black	Under $5000	Over $15,000
Correctly identified their congressmen	46	37	55	50	17	38	50
Did not know or failed to identify their congressmen correctly	54	63	45	50	83	62	50

Source: Louis Harris Poll, conducted for the U.S. Senate, Committee on Governmental Operations. Published as *Confidence and Concern: Citizens View American Government* (Part 2) (Washington, D.C.: U.S. Government Printing Office, December 1973), pp. 215–216.

Benefits from many government actions are remote from those who receive them, either in time, space or comprehensibility. Economic aid to a distant nation may prevent a hostile revolution there and save millions of dollars and even the lives of American troops, but because the solution is remote, the average citizen—living in rational ignorance—will not realize he is benefiting at all.[2]

Rational ignorance may also lead to the adoption of other proposals that cost more than they are worth. Counterproductive proposals tend to be accepted when the benefits are clearly recognizable and the costs are partially concealed and difficult for voters to identify. In fact, politicians will often attempt to conceal the cost of their programs. For example, politicians will tend to favor taxes that are difficult for voters to identify rather than direct tax levies. The splitting of payroll taxes between employer and employee, when the burden does not depend on who formally pays, suggests that legislators can gain by deceiving voters as to their personal share of the cost of government. Similarly, the continued popularity of deficit spending and money creation is consistent with the theory. When these methods of gaining control over private resources are substituted for direct taxation, voters are less likely to be fully aware of their individual tax burden. As a result, the incentive of politicians to support measures that are in the long-run best interests of voters is reduced.

The low probability that one's vote will make any difference explains more than rational ignorance; it also explains why many citizens fail to vote.

---

[2]Anthony Downs, "Why the Government Budget Is Too Small in a Democracy," *World Politics* 12, no. 4 (1960), p. 551.

Even when there is a presidential election, only about half of all voting age Americans take the time to register and vote. Given the low probability one's vote will be decisive, this low voter turnout should not be surprising. The rationality of voters is further indicated by the fact that when elections are close, turnouts are larger, but they are smaller when the margin of victory for the winner is large.[3] A vote in a close election has a greater chance of actually making a difference.

GOVERNMENT FAILURE: THE SPECIAL INTEREST EFFECT

Many people think of government as the great equalizer, a tool to be used in controlling powerful economic interests. In reality, the relationship often seems to run the other way—strong interest groups seem to control the government. Can economic tools help to explain this phenomenon?

---

[3]This and other results consistent with the rational actions of voters can be found in Yoram Barzel and Eugene Silberberg, "Is the Act of Voting Rational?" *Public Choice*, Vol. XVI, (Fall 1973) pp. 51–58.

APPLICATIONS IN ECONOMICS

Why General Motors Receives Better Signals Than Congress

Most Americans are frustrated in their dealings with large, centralized organizations. The individual has very little impact on the decision-making of General Motors or Congress. One person's vote (or, in the case of a car purchase, even several thousand "dollar votes") will count very little. *Yet, taken together, the votes of millions of people do determine future policy choices and directions.* When we send a large corporation or Congress a message, how strong is the signal? How carefully are individual decisions made when dollar votes are cast by consumers or when political votes are cast by citizens?

There is good reason to believe that a giant corporation, such as General Motors, is voted for (or against) after a much more careful process of individual decision-making than goes into the choice of representatives for Congress. How can this be? After all, Congress controls a larger part of our earnings than General Motors. Why spend more time and effort in choosing a car than in choosing a congressional candidate? Since time and effort are scarce, an individual spends them in a manner that will yield the greatest personal payoff. An extra hour of time will result in larger payoff if the individual spends it on an auto purchase decision. Why? There are two major reasons.

1. The individual's "dollar vote" is always decisive (one gets one's choice), but a political vote is seldom decisive. An individual must live with, and pay for, his or her own private choice, but one usually lives with, and pays for, the political choices of others, regardless of one's own vote.

2. Careful research by a voter on political issues may be largely fruitless at election time, since a vote must be cast for a single bundle of political stands (one candidate among two or three). When purchasing a car, the individual can choose trunk size, upholstery, en- gine size, and passenger room from among many combinations *and get what she or he wants.* The time spent comparing each alternative yields a clear payoff.

With these factors in mind, we can easily understand why the average person may know more about a car (or television set, golf clubs, or calculator) at purchase time than about congressional candidates at election time. In both cases, personal choices have minimal impact on society. However, the *personal* payoff derived from a careful purchase choice is very different. A person receives most of the benefit from a better market choice. A better political choice, however, is a public good. It is ironic that decisions determining which automobile executives prosper (or which lead their companies into financial trouble) are made more carefully than those that determine the makeup of Congress.

A special interest issue is one for which a small number of voters *individually* acquire large gains at the expense of a large number of citizens who *individually* suffer small losses. The rational unawareness of intelligent voters with regard to (a) the relevance of most issues to their personal welfare and (b) the position of their elected representatives on the issues enhances the power of special interests. Voters are generally uninformed on most issues. Typically, most of us decide to vote for or against a political candidate on the basis of the few issues that are of substantial importance to us. We ignore numerous other issues that *individually* exert (or seem to exert) little impact on our well-being.

For example, despite their importance to the nation as a whole, the views of political decision-makers on such things as Japanese fishing rights, appointments to the Interstate Commerce Commission, and allocation of licenses for the operation of television stations do not command the scrutiny of most citizens. Generally, these issues fail to influence most voters' choices. The same is not true, however, for small groups whose welfare is substantially affected by the resolution of these issues. When most voters are uninformed and do not vote on the basis of a special interest issue, the special interest can be influential far beyond what its numbers would indicate.

An additional factor enhancing the power of special interest groups is the importance of special interest groups as a source of the funds critical to political campaigns. If a politician wants to win the support of voters who have little incentive to study the issues, free information must be provided to them. Further, it is not enough simply to provide the information. Like advertising of any kind, the message must normally be short and entertaining to attract attention. The voter is seldom in the mood to study a dry presentation of the complex facts and logic behind most issues. Newspaper ads, printed materials, television spots, and other advertising techniques are needed to create a positive image—and all of these cost money. Candidates without the financial resources to provide high quality television and other media advertising to rationally ignorant voters are seriously handicapped.[4] Similarly, candidates who are not effective in dealing with the major communications media face a severe disadvantage. Professional coaching and the services of an effective public relations staff can help, but are costly. Money can be made available, however. Since special interest groups feel strongly about certain issues, they offer candidates who will listen to—and especially those who will support—their position a ready source of campaign contributions.[5]

---

[4]Political expenditures on advertising and other persuasion techniques indicate that candidates are fully aware of the importance of media exposure. On average, candidates in races for the U.S. Senate or House of Representatives spend between 70 and 80 percent of their campaign resources in this area.

[5]Abundant evidence documents the importance of special interest campaign contributions. Senators, congressmen, and presidents have long benefited from the financial assistance of businesses, unions, and other interest groups that are in a position to be rewarded by public-sector decisions. Congressional committee chairs are, more often than not, well cared for by the industrial and labor interests that stand to benefit from the committee's actions. Analysis of state government reveals the existence of similar pressures. A study of political contributions in Florida indicated that the lion's share comes from special interest groups that are state regulated. A study in Illinois revealed a similar pattern.

"It's good to be back where I can spend somebody else's money!"

GRIN AND BEAR IT BY FRED WAGNER © BY AND PERMISSION OF NEWS AMERICA SYNDICATE.

Enterprising politicians can often conceal their support of special interests by "packaging" issues so that it is more difficult for even alert voters to recognize the cost imposed on them. The more complex the policy under question, the more difficult it is for the average voter to figure out how he or she would be affected. There is an incentive for politicians to make special interest issues very complex. The special interest group will most assuredly figure out that it stands to gain from a given proposal, but the typical voter will find it difficult to determine the seemingly complex proposal's actual impact.[6]

Frequently, political suppliers (politicians) can reap political gain by supporting special interest legislation, even if such legislation is economically inefficient. Since most voters will be uninformed on any given special interest issue, political suppliers have a strong incentive to (a) support the views of a special interest group, (b) solicit from it both votes and money, (c) make the consequences of the special interest issue difficult for the average voter to understand (for example, by making the issue a part of a complex policy proposal), and (d) use funds obtained from the special interest group to promote their candidacy. In other words, political suppliers have an incentive to solicit resources from special interests and use the resources obtained from them to run, not as a special interest candidate, but as the "candidate of the people." Politicians who refuse to follow this strategy run the risk of losing elections to those who accept such a course as a fact of political life.

The special interest effect helps explain the presence of legislation that appears to reflect neither a desire for economic efficiency nor a desire for

---

[6]Gordon Tullock, in *Toward a Mathematics of Politics* (Ann Arbor: University of Michigan Press, 1966), emphasizes this point.

more income equality. For example, consider tariff trade restrictions on such commodities as steel and automobiles. For years, economists have pointed out that tariff or quota protection, particularly for firms that possess substantial market power, leads to an inefficient allocation of resources. It would be difficult to find an issue on which there is more general agreement among economists. However, the benefits of the repeal of such legislation would be widely dispersed and difficult for consumers to perceive. The costs of the repeal imposed on automobile and steel manufacturers and employees would be highly concentrated.

Despite the fact that political figures argue from time to time that automobile and steel prices are not sufficiently competitive, political protection of domestic producers and workers at the expense of consumers remains in force. Usually, the reason given for protection is "jobs." Protection of an industry may increase employment in that industry, or at least keep employment from falling. What, though, is the cost to the rest of the economy, including all other workers, of protecting a specific industry and specific jobs from foreign competition? The Applications in Economics feature provides a case study of the auto industry, indicating that the costs are enormous. Yet, the policies persist. Politicians obviously perceive that greater political gains can be obtained from a continuation of the present quota and tariff protection policy on autos, steel, and many other commodities, than from the repeal of such inefficient policies.

APPLICATIONS IN ECONOMICS

The Cost of Special Interest Protection: A Case Study

How costly are protectionist measures to consumers, and what are they worth to domestic workers? The American automobile industry provides a case study. Falling sales of domestically produced cars and rising import sales led to demands by U.S. carmakers and the United Auto Workers for protection in the early 1980s. The U.S. government reached an agreement with Japan that Japanese imports to the U.S. would be limited to 1.68 million units per year beginning in 1981. That quota was raised slightly in 1984, and in 1985, it rose to 2.25 million on a "voluntary" basis—the U.S. government would not enforce it, officially. The quotas had a strong effect, as the economy recovered in 1983 and 1984, and the demand for automobiles soared. There were often waiting lists for Japanese cars, and auto dealers increased car prices.

Robert Crandall of the Brookings Institution estimated that in the 1981–1983 period, the quotas raised the prices of American cars by an average of about $400, and the price of Japanese cars by about $1000 each, costing American consumers about $4.3 billion in 1983.[7] He also estimated that if every sale lost by the Japanese had gone to American producers, about 46,000 U.S. jobs would have been preserved. But, the American cars also went up in price, of course, so the estimate of *net* jobs saved fell to 26,000. Each job, then, cost U.S. consumers an estimated $165,000. The U.S. International Trade Commission did a separate study resulting in an estimate of $193,000 per job saved. Since the jobs paid far less than that, and most of the workers could have found other jobs (usually at lower pay), the cost of the quota policy far outweighed the benefits to workers. The losers (consumers) lost substantially more than the winning workers gained.

---

[7]See Robert W. Crandall, "Import Quotas and the Automobile Industry: The Costs of Protectionism," *Brookings Review*, Summer 1984, pp. 8–16.

Why is it that politicians who support inefficient special interest legislation are not removed from office by taxpayers? There is some incentive to do this, but it is greatly reduced for the individual because of the high cost of forming coalitions, particularly among a loosely knit group.[8] Each taxpayer has a strong incentive to "let the others do it"; that is, to act as a free rider in the effort to hold politicians accountable. When everyone decides to ride free, though, nothing is accomplished.

GOVERNMENT FAILURE: IMPRECISE REFLECTION OF CONSUMER PREFERENCES

The collective process is likely to be imprecise in reflecting the wishes of "consumers" (voters) because they can usually express their wishes only through a broker (legislator) who represents a "bundle" of political goods and tax prices. The voter either gets the bundle of political goods offered by candidate A or the bundle offered by candidate B. Neither of these bundles of political goods necessarily represents what a specific consumer would like to have. The political consumer does not have the freedom to "shop around" on each issue, but must accept the bundle favored by the majority coalition. It should come as no surprise that voters often cannot find a candidate they can wholeheartedly support. It is hardly the fault of the politician, who must try to please a majority of the voters, and who cannot cater to a small minority on a wide variety of issues.

In sharp contrast to the market, the consumer's ability to make discriminating choices is very limited in the public sector. Circumstances change, new information becomes available, and relative prices change, but the political consumer has little opportunity to respond by making marginal adjustments. Approximately two fifths of our economic resources are channeled through the public sector. Yet, during a single year, each of us makes perhaps 1000 times as many market as public-sector decisions.

GOVERNMENT FAILURE: THE SHORTSIGHTEDNESS EFFECT

The shortsightedness effect results because the complexity of an issue may make it extremely difficult for the voter to accurately anticipate *future* benefits and costs. Thus, voters tend to rely mainly on current conditions. Candidates and legislators seeking to win the current election have a strong incentive to stress public-sector action that yields substantial current benefits relative to costs. Therefore, public-sector action is biased in favor of legislation that offers immediate (and easily identified) current benefits at the expense of future costs that are complex and difficult to identify. Similarly, there is a bias against legislation that involves immediate and easily identifiable costs (for example, higher taxes) while yielding future benefits that are complex and difficult to identify. Government action on issues whose future consequences are unclear tends to be shortsighted.

Short-Term Costs and Government Inaction. It has been noted that public-sector action is "crisis-oriented." In recent years, we have experienced a welfare crisis, a poverty crisis, an environmental crisis, an energy

---

[8]Sometimes intense publicity will make the support of a specific piece of special interest legislation temporarily unpopular. In this case, entrepreneurs will take special care to modify or disguise their support of vested interest groups.

crisis, and an inflation crisis. One reason for this is that planning for the future tends to be unrewarding for those in government. Future costs and benefits are difficult for voters to identify. In addition, many of those who will be affected in the future are not current voters. Given the public-sector bias against proposals with current costs and difficult-to-identify future benefits, the government's crisis orientation is understandable. The vote-maximizing politician has an incentive to follow a policy of minimum current expenditures until the crisis point is reached, all the while paying lip service to the problem. Economics suggests that democratic decision-making is often inconsistent with sensible *long-range* planning.

Short-Term Benefits and Government Action. While proposals with future benefits difficult to perceive are usually delayed, proposals with immediate benefits, at the expense of complex future costs—costs that will accrue after the next election—are very attractive to political entrepreneurs. Office-holders and candidates alike have a strong incentive to support such proposals and emphasize the immediate voter benefits.

Is there any evidence that the pursuit of short-term political gains has led to inappropriate public-sector action? Consider the issue of macro-economic instability. In the 1960s and 1970s, inflationary expectations were relatively low, and slow to change. Expansionary monetary and fiscal policy could be used to "heat up" the economy and reduce the rate of un-employment in the short-run. An overheated economy, though, leads to inflation. The shortsightedness effect predicts that the party in power would, in those circumstances, tend to follow an expansionary policy in the 12 to 24 months before an election, even if these policies would result in future inflation. The "stabilization" policies preceding the presidential elections of those two decades suggest that incumbent political suppliers made a substantial effort to give voters the impression that the economy was strong on election day. There is little doubt, however, that expansionary macropolicy overheated the economy in each case, causing a post-election increase in the rate of inflation. Once people begin to recognize the inflationary effects of expansionary policy, the political profit from the policy fell. Expectations of inflation adjusted more quickly, and the expansionary portion of the cycle became more brief.

The shortsightedness effect can be a source of conflict between good politics and sound economics. Policies that are efficient from the standpoint of social benefits and costs are not necessarily the policies that will enhance a politician's election prospects. As a result, grossly inefficient projects may be undertaken and potentially beneficial projects may be ignored.

GOVERNMENT FAILURE: FEW INCENTIVES FOR INTERNAL EFFICIENCY

Government has often been charged with inaction, duplication, delays, frivolous work, and general inefficiency. These charges are difficult to document or prove. How does government compare with the private sector? Certainly a great deal of seemingly meaningless activity goes on in the private sector as well, but private firms, even those with monopoly power, can gain from actions that improve operational efficiency. There is an incentive to produce efficiently because lower costs will mean higher profits. Even though the stockholders of a private firm can seldom identify good and bad individual decisions, they can easily observe a "bottom line" index of efficiency—the firm's rate of profit. In the private sector, the possibility of bankruptcy, falling stock prices, and/or a takeover bid by the management of another firm are deterrents to economic inefficiency.

Public-sector decision-makers, both political and bureaucratic, confront an incentive structure that is less conducive to operational efficiency. Since there is no easily identified index of performance analogous to the profit rate, public-sector managers can often gloss over economic inefficiency. If a public-sector decision-maker spends money unwisely or uses resources primarily for personal benefit (for example, plush offices, or extensive "business travel"), the burden of this inefficiency will fall on the taxpayer. The notorious and persistent cost overruns in the Pentagon are just one example of the difficulty inherent in cost control without a profit motive and without vigorously competing firms. The public sector is also not subject to the test of bankruptcy, which tends to eliminate inefficient operations in the private sector. Political finesse is far more important to success in the public sector than operational efficiency. At election time, political candidates and parties must offer something more impressive than efficiency in government if they expect to win.

Taxpayers would be the major beneficiaries of reduced costs and an improvement in public-sector efficiency. A public-sector manager seldom reaps personal reward by saving the taxpayers money. In fact, if an agency fails to spend this year's allocation, its case for a larger budget next year is weakened. Agencies typically go on a spending spree at the end of a budget period if they discover that they have failed to spend all of this year's appropriation.

Insofar as political officials are interested in efficiency, they will tend to choose ways of improving efficiency that are visible and simple to communicate. A well-publicized campaign to save a few dollars by eliminating limousine service for high government officials can produce greater political benefits than a complex government reorganization plan that would save taxpayers millions of dollars. The latter idea is too complex and the outcome too difficult for voters to identify.

It is important to note that the argument of internal inefficiency is not based on the assumption that employees of a bureaucratic government are necessarily lazy or incapable. Rather, the emphasis is on the structure of information and incentives under which managers and other workers toil. No individual or relatively small group of individuals has much incentive to ensure efficiency. Their performances cannot readily be judged, and without private ownership their personal wealth would not be significantly increased or reduced by changes in the level of efficiency. Since public officials and bureau managers spend other people's money, they are likely to be less conscious of cost than they would be with their own resources. Attempts to control waste and abuse are made through rules that try to anticipate problems, rather than by an owner's drive toward profit and away from loss. Without a need to compare sales revenues to costs, there is no test by which to define economic inefficiency clearly or measure it accurately, much less eliminate it. The perverse incentive structure of a bureaucracy is bound to have an impact on its internal efficiency. The boxed feature on private fire protection reports on one among many studies that tend to confirm this result.

THE ECONOMIC ANALYSIS OF THE PUBLIC SECTOR

Most economic texts make only brief reference to the major issues discussed in this chapter. Our purpose has been to analyze how we would *expect* the public sector to handle various classes of economic issues.

In the past, economists were usually content with a discussion of what the government *should* do, regardless of how unrealistic that solution might be. Without ignoring government's ideal activities, we have extended our analysis to what, in fact, government is *likely* to do and what the outcomes

APPLICATIONS IN ECONOMICS

Private- Versus Public-Sector Production of Fire Protection

Is private-sector production actually more efficient than public-sector production of the same service? A number of economic studies have been done that seem to confirm that it frequently is. One example is the case of the Scottsdale, Arizona, fire department. Scottsdale funds its fire protection publicly, through taxation, but purchases the protection from a private firm. It puts the contract out for bid, and the winning bidder provides the service.

Economist Roger Ahlbrandt did an extensive economic study of the Scottsdale fire service and its cost, comparing it with fire services in 49 other cities.[9] He concluded that governmental provision (rather than just government funding) of the service would cost Scottsdale 89 percent more than private provision. Was the private service effective? Did the cost reductions occur at the expense of effective fire control? Insurance rates are one indi-rect measure of the effectiveness of the service. Insurance companies have strong incentives to adjust rates properly to fit the circumstances, since each insurance company needs low rates to be competitive, but rates set too low would not pay for fire damage claims. Scottsdale rates are the same as those in similar cities using governmental provision of the services. The same level of services are apparently being provided, at a lower cost.

Why does the private, for-profit firm cut costs? To win the bidding, the firm must keep its price down. To make a profit, then, the service company has a strong incentive to be innovative and efficient. The firm serving Scottsdale—Rural/Metro, Inc.—has pioneered several techniques to reduce costs without reducing service. Among its innovations have been robot fire-fighting equipment, high-visibility paint on fire trucks, and a high-capacity fire hose. It has also used creative staffing patterns, including a mix of full-time and "reserve" firefighters to cut labor costs. The reservists are on call one week a month, are less intensively trained, and are used only on certain types of fires.

In the case of the Scottsdale fire service, as in many others, economic logic seems to be supported: when owners and managers are spurred on by the hope of profit and the fear of loss, and are guided by the price system, buyers gain. It is extremely difficult, and perhaps impossible to duplicate the information and in-centives of the private sector in a governmental setting.

---

[9]This and many other studies are sum-marized in E. S. Savas, *Privatizing the Public Sector* (Chatham, N.J., Chatham House, 1982) Ch. 6.

of its intervention are likely to be. The broad relevance of economic tools has helped us explain the real-world influence of public-sector action on an economy's efficiency.

IS ECONOMIC ANALYSIS TOO CYNICAL?

We have discussed how economic factors influence the workings of the public sector. Our analysis may differ considerably from that presented in a typical political science course. Some of you may object that our approach is cynical, that not enough emphasis has been given to the dedicated public servants who devote all of their energy to the resolution of complex public-sector issues. Our analysis does not deny the existence of such individuals. They exist in government just as they do in the private sector. We merely emphasize that in a legislative democracy, the pressures at work typically fail to reward and encourage (or sometimes even to allow) the initiatives they might want to take. In fact, it is often difficult for these individuals to survive without compromising.

One might also argue that voters are more public spirited than we have indicated. They may be willing to sacrifice their personal welfare for the public good. However, if voters are motivated primarily by what is in the public interest, how then does one account for the behavior of trade associations, business lobbyists, labor unions, public employee groups, lawyers, physicians, teachers, developers, and hundreds of other organized groups, all attempting to shape the rules and regulations of the public sector to their own advantage?

The test of any theory is its consistency with events in the real world. Certainly, we have not outlined a complete theory of the public sector. Casual observation of current events, though, should give one sufficient cause to question the validity of theories that emphasize only the public interest, equal power, and the humanitarian nature of governmental action. Democratic governments are a creation of the interactions of imperfect human beings. A growing number of economists believe that economic theory has a great deal to say about the types of public-sector actions that will result from these interactions.

THE PUBLIC SECTOR VERSUS THE MARKET: A SUMMARY

Throughout this text, we have argued that theory can explain why both market forces and public-sector action sometimes break down—that is, why they sometimes fail to meet the criteria for ideal efficiency. The deficiencies of one or the other sector will often be more or less decisive depending on the type of economic activity. Nobel laureate Paul Samuelson has stated, "There are not rules concerning the proper role of government that can be established by a prior reasoning."[10] This does not mean, however, that economics has nothing to say about the *strength* of the case for either the market or the public sector in terms of specific classes of activities. Nor does it mean that social scientists have nothing to say about institutional arrange-

---

[10]P. A. Samuelson, "The Economic Role of Private Activity," in *The Collected Scientific Papers of Paul A. Samuelson*, ed. J. E. Stiglitz, vol. 2 (Cambridge, Massachusetts: MIT Press, 1966), p. 1423.

ments for conducting economic activity. It merely indicates that each issue and type of activity must be considered individually.

The case for government intervention is obviously stronger for some activities than for others. For example, if an activity involves substantial external effects, market arrangements often result in economic inefficiency, and public-sector action may allow for greater efficiency. Similarly, when compatititive pressures are weak or when there is reason to expect consumers to be poorly informed, market failure may result, and again government action may be called for. (See the Thumbnail Sketch for a summary of factors that influence the case for market or for public-sector action.)

THUMBNAIL SKETCH

These factors weaken the case for market-sector allocation:

1. External costs
2. External benefits
3. Public goods
4. Monopoly
5. Uninformed consumers

These factors weaken the case for public-sector intervention:

1. Voter ignorance, inability to recognize costs and benefits fully, and cost concealment
2. The power of special interests
3. The shortsightedness effect
4. Little incentive for operational efficiency
5. Imprecision in the reflection of consumer preferences

The identical analysis holds for the public sector. When there is a good reason to believe that special interest influence will be strong, the case for government action to correct market failures is weakened. Similarly, the lack of a means of identifying and weeding out public-sector inefficiency weakens the case for government action. More often than not, the choice of proper institutions may be a choice among evils. For example, we might expect private-sector monopoly if an activity is left to the market and perverse regulation due to the special interest effect if we turn to the public sector. Understanding the shortcomings of both the market and the public sectors is important if we are to improve our current economic institutions.

At one time, economists assumed that the private sector operated according to the perfectly competitive model. In the past, some economists have assumed that government operates so as to fulfill the conditions of ideal allocative efficiency. Both assumptions are, of course, simplistic. The application of economics to public choice helps us understand why public policy sometimes goes astray and how public-sector incentives might be altered to improve the efficiency of government action.

LOOKING AHEAD

Once we understand the sources of potential government failure, we are in a better position to suggest potential remedies. We close this section with a perspective that considers a remedy for dealing with potential problems of political power—a very useful remedy installed in the United States two centuries ago.

APPLICATIONS IN ECONOMICS

Rent Seeking and the Constitution: A Perspective

Well-defined and transferrable property rights are critical in the market setting because they make productive trades both easier and more attractive. People will pay for something (or work to create it) only if they believe they will continue to have it, or will gain from trading it to others. Government plays an important role in keeping property rights secure from thieves and marauders. However, when government takes a larger role and begins to tax, subsidize, and regulate, there is an unwanted side effect: property rights are effectively jeopardized. They become less secure.

The active involvement of government in economic endeavors means that buyers, sellers, and outsiders can change the terms of trade, or simply obtain the wealth of others, through the political process. Dairy farmers do this through politically-set minimum prices, and subsidies from taxpayers. Auto companies and unions do it through trade restrictions and "bailout" schemes when their high prices and wages cause consumers to prefer foreign autos. Thousands of special interest groups pursue their goals not just through voluntary transactions, which only take place when all trading parties gain, but also through political means using the coercive powers of government. One result is that even those

who wish only to protect their own positions must fight to do so in the political arena. Only with good organization and costly effort can individuals and groups hope to keep from being subject to adverse regulation to benefit others, or taxes to subsidize others.

Actions taken to seek government favors, or to defend against losses in the political process are called "rent seeking," as we explained in Chapter 4. As we indicated there (see p. 88), lobbying and other rent-seeking activities are expensive. In fact, lobbyists and other rent seekers might be compared to "hired guns." If government prevents hired guns from committing crimes, individuals do not need the services of hired guns. But, if the hired guns of some people are allowed to take away the rights and property of others, then we all need to hire guns, even though they are expensive and the community as a whole loses from the proliferation of hired guns. Similarly, when a citizen who is not represented by strong lobbying efforts finds some of his or her rights and property threatened by legal restrictions or taxation, the need to find one's own "hired gun" (lobbyist) for protection may seem strong indeed. And, those who do invest in such a lobbying machine will be tempted to use it "offensively" (to

gain from restrictions or taxes placed on others.)

It is exactly to stop this kind of legal, but chaotic and wasteful rent-seeking activity, that our Constitution was designed and enacted. The Constitution is a set of "rules for making rules," limiting what politicians can do in the way of taking rights and wealth from some in order to bestow them on others. The United States Constitution, which will be 200 years old in 1988, recognized the dangers inherent in a strong central government. It established the legislative, executive, and judiciary branches, giving each of them countervailing powers to help keep the others in check. It put limits on what government as a whole could do.

Private property rights were made more secure by the Constitution, so that citizens were encouraged to look to voluntary exchange, and away from government compulsion, as the best way to prosper as individuals. Activities intended merely to redivide the pie were discouraged in favor of pie-enlarging activities. It is largely under that regime that the nation has prospered enormously for more than two centuries.

Recent decades have seen a movement away from Constitutional constraints on transfer activities. Some scholars date the move

APPLICATIONS IN ECONOMICS (continued)

from 1913, when the sixteenth amendment to the Constitution was passed, allowing our current progressive income tax and putting the federal government explicitly in the business of redistributing income.[11] Others stress the importance of the depression era of the 1930s, when many social programs redistributing income were put into place. Still others point to the acceptance in the 1960s of large and continuing federal deficits. These came to be considered tolerable because Keynesian economic analysis suggested that deficits could, in some circumstances, encourage growth. The result was that large transfer expenditures no longer had to be accompanied by current tax increases. Transfer expenditures rose rapidly in the late 1960s and through the 1970s, in any case.

As we pointed out in Chapter 4 (Applications in Economics, "The Cost of Political Competition"), firms and industry associations have been allocating more and more resources to the political and bureaucratic arenas, at the expense of productive activity. Observers who believe that Constitutional limits to government control and transfers and the resulting rent-seeking activities are critical to economic growth are worried by these trends. Time will tell whether their concerns are well-founded.

---

[11]Terry L. Anderson and Peter J. Hill, *The Birth of a Transfer Society* (Hoover Institution Press, 1980).

CHAPTER SUMMARY

1. It is fruitful to analyze the public sector in the same way in which we analyze the private sector. Collective action, through government, has the potential for correcting market failures and redistributing income. The public sector is an alternative to the market—it provides an alternative means of organizing production and/or distributing output.

2. Voters cast ballots, make political contributions, lobby, and adopt other political strategies to demand public-sector action. Other things constant, voters have a strong incentive to support the candidate who offers them the greatest personal gain relative to personal costs. Obtaining information is costly. Since group decision-making breaks the link between the choice of the individual and the outcome of the issue, it is rational for voters to remain uninformed on many issues. Candidates are generally evaluated on the basis of a small subset of issues that are of the greatest personal importance to individual voters.

3. Market failure presents government with an opportunity to undertake action that will result in additional benefits relative to costs. Other things constant, the greater the social loss resulting from the market failure, the stronger is the incentive for public-sector action.

4. Positive economics cannot tell us whether an action should be conducted in the public or in the market sector. However, analysis of how both sectors operate does help build the case for conducting any given activity in either sector. When market failure is prevalent, the case for public sector action is strengthened. On the other hand, expectation of government failure reduces the strength of the argument for government intervention.

5. There is a strong incentive for political entrepreneurs to support special interest issues and to make the issues difficult for the unorganized, largely uninformed majority to understand. Special interest groups

supply both financial and direct elective support to the politician. Constitutional rules are one way to limit the power of special interests to use the political process to achieve their interests at the expense of the group as a whole.

6. Because of imperfect voter information, proposals whose benefits are elusive and whose costs are clear-cut tend to be rejected, even though they might promote the community's welfare. Counterproductive policies whose benefits are easily recognizable and whose costs are difficult to identify tend to be accepted. There is a strong incentive for politicians to package public policy in a manner that amplifies the benefits and conceals the costs imposed on voters.

7. The shortsightedness effect is another potential source of conflict between good politics and sound economics. Both voters and politicians tend to support projects that promise substantial current benefits at the expense of difficult-to-identify future costs. There is a bias against legislation that involves immediate and easily identifiable costs but complex future benefits.

8. The economic incentive for operational efficiency is small for public sector action. No individual or relatively small group of individuals can capture the gains derived from improved operational efficiency. There is no force analogous to the threat of bankruptcy in the private sector that will bring inefficient behavior to a halt. Since public sector resources, including tax funds, are communally owned, their users are less likely than private resource owners to be cost conscious.

9. A growing portion of public-sector activity involves income redistribution. Economic analysis indicates two potential sources of pressure for income redistribution: (a) the public-good nature of antipoverty efforts and (b) self-interest. From the viewpoint of a vote-maximizing politician, there is incentive to support redistribution from unorganized to well-organized groups. Considerable income redistribution in the United States is of this type.

THE ECONOMIC WAY OF THINKING—
DISCUSSION QUESTIONS

1. Do you think that advertising exerts more influence on the type of car chosen by a consumer than on the type of politician chosen by the same person? Explain your answer.

2. Do you think that the political process works to the advantage of the poor? Explain. Are the poor well organized? Do they make substantial campaign contributions to candidates? Are they likely to be well informed? Is it surprising that a large amount of the approximately $300 billion of cash income transfer payments in the United States does not go to the poor? Explain.

3. Which of the following public-sector actions are designed primarily to correct "market failure": (a) laws against fraud, (b) truth-in-lending legislation, (c) rate regulation in the telephone industry, (d) legislation setting emission control standards, (e) subsidization of pure research, (f) operation of the Post Office? Explain your answer.

4. Do political suppliers ever have an incentive to deceive voters about the cost of legislation? If so, when? Can you give any examples of cases in which this has happened?

5. The liquor industry contributes a large share of the political funds to political contests on the state level. Yet its contributions to candidates for national office are minimal. Why do you think this is true? (*Hint:* Who regulates the liquor industry?)

6. One explanation for the shortsightedness effect in the public sector is that future voters cannot vote now to represent their future interests. Are the interests of future generations represented in market decisions? For example, if the price of chromium were expected to rise rapidly over the next 30 years due to increased scarcity, how could speculators grow rich while providing the next generation with more chromium at the expense of current consumers?

7. **What's Wrong with This Way of Thinking?**
"Public policy is necessary to protect the average citizen from the power of vested interest groups. In the absence of government intervention, regulated industries, such as airlines, railroads, and trucking, would charge excessive prices, products would be unsafe, and the rich would oppress the poor. Government curbs the power of special interest groups."

PART SIX

INTERNATIONAL ECONOMICS AND COMPARATIVE SYSTEMS

- How large is the international sector in the United States? What are the major import and export products of the U.S.? Which countries are the major trading partners of the U.S.?

- Under what conditions can a nation gain from international trade?

- How do trade restrictions affect the welfare of a nation?

- Why do nations erect trade barriers? Are there valid arguments in support of trade restrictions?

- Do trade restrictions create (or save) jobs?

- Will free trade with low-wage countries cause wage rates in high-wage countries to decline?

If a foreign country can supply us with a commodity cheaper than we ourselves can make it, [we had] better buy it of them with some part of our own industry, employed in a way in which we have some advantage. The general industry of the country will not thereby be diminished, but only left to find out the way in which it can be employed with the greatest advantage.[1]

ADAM SMITH

30 GAINING FROM INTERNATIONAL TRADE

We live in a shrinking world. Wheat raised on the flatlands of western Kansas may be processed into bread in a Russian factory. The breakfast of many Americans might include bananas from Honduras, coffee from Brazil, or hot chocolate made from Nigerian cocoa beans. The volume of international trade, enhanced by improved transportation and communications, has grown rapidly in recent years. In 1984, the total trade among nations was approximately $3.5 trillion. Approximately 16 percent of the world's total output is now sold in a country other than that in which it was produced—double the figure of two decades ago.

Although we speak of international trade, exchanges, for the most part take place between individuals (or business firms) that happen to be located in different countries. International trade, like other voluntary exchange, results because both the buyer and the seller gain from it. If both parties did not expect to gain, there would be no trade.

THE COMPOSITION OF THE INTERNATIONAL SECTOR

As Exhibit 1 shows, the size of the trade sector varies among nations. International trade comprises more than one half of the GNP of the Netherlands and approximately one quarter of the GNP in Sweden, Canada, West Germany, and the United Kingdom. The relative size of the trade sector is smaller for Japan, Australia, and the United States. Approximately 8 percent of the GNP in the United States results from trade.

However, the size of the international sector relative to GNP may actually understate the importance of trade. Many of the products we purchase from foreigners would be much more costly if we were dependent solely on

EXHIBIT 1 • The Size of the Trade Sector for Selected Countries, 1984	
Country	International Trade as a Percentage of GNP
Netherlands	52
Sweden	29
West Germany	26
Canada	24
United Kingdom	24
France	20
Australia	13
Japan	12
United States	8
Source: U.S. Department of Commerce.	

[1]Adam Smith, *An Inquiry into the Nature and Causes of the Wealth of Nations* (1976; Cannan's ed., Chicago: University of Chicago Press, 1976), pp. 478–479.

our domestic production. We are dependent on foreign producers for several products, including almost all of our coffee and bananas, more than 90 percent of the bauxite we use to make aluminium, all of our chromium, diamonds, and tin, and most of our cobalt, nickel, manganese, and asbestos. The life-style of Americans (as well as that of our trading partners) would change dramatically if international trade were halted.

Exhibit 2 summarizes the leading products exported and imported by the United States. Motor vehicles, computers, aircraft, scientific equipment, and grain products are among the major export products of the United States. Petroleum, automobiles, clothing, footwear, coffee, and diamonds are among our major imports.

The structure of U.S. trade has changed in recent years. Agricultural products (wheat, corn, and soybeans) and high-technology manufacturing products (for example, aircraft, computers, telecommunication equipment, and machine tools) have comprised an increasing share of our total exports. On the other hand, foreign producers have supplied more and more import products to our domestic markets in such established industries as steel, textiles, automobiles, and, of course, crude petroleum.

With which countries does the United States trade? As Exhibit 3 shows, Canada heads the list. In 1984, approximately one fifth of the total U.S. volume of trade was with Canada. Japan, Mexico, and the nations of the European Economic Community (particularly West Germany, the United Kingdom, France, and Italy) were also among the leading trading partners

---

EXHIBIT 2 • The Major Export and Import Products of the United States

Exports	Value (in billions)	Percentage of Total Exports	Imports	Value (in billions)	Percentage of Total Imports
Motor vehicles and parts	17.7	8.3	Petroleum	55.9	17.2
Computers	13.5	6.4	Automobiles	45.3	13.9
Aircraft	10.9	5.1	Clothing	13.5	4.1
Power generating machinery	9.1	4.3	Iron and steel	10.2	3.1
Corn	7.1	3.3	Office machines	10.8	3.3
Wheat	6.7	3.2	Footwear	5.0	1.5
Scientific instruments	6.2	2.9	Natural gas	4.9	1.5
Soybeans	5.4	2.5	Fish	3.7	1.1
Coal	4.1	1.9	Paper	3.3	1.0
Plastic materials	4.1	1.9	Coffee	3.1	1.0
Telecommunications equipment	3.9	1.8	Diamonds	2.9	0.9
Total	212.1	—	Total	325.7	—

Source: *Statistical Abstract of the United States, 1986*, pp. 656–657.

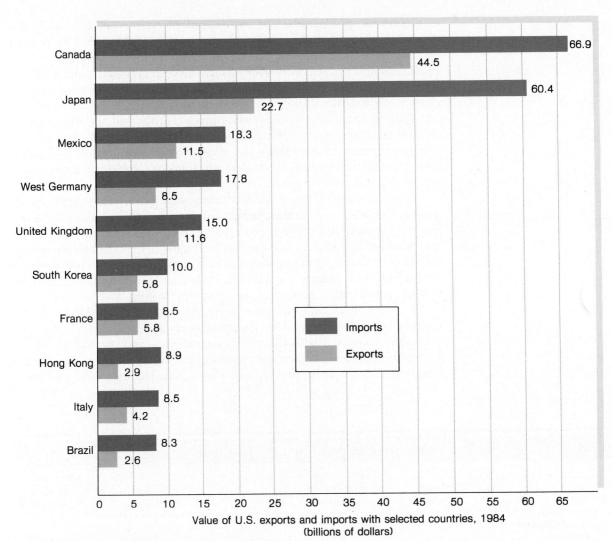

Value of U.S. exports and imports with selected countries, 1984
(billions of dollars)

Source: U.S. Department of Commerce.

EXHIBIT 3 • The Leading Trading Partners of the United States, 1984

Canada, Japan, Mexico, and Western European countries are the leading trading partners of the United States. In recent years, South Korea, Hong Kong, and Brazil have also emerged as important trading partners of the U.S.

of the United States. More than half of the U.S. trade in 1984 was with Canada, Japan, and the industrial nations of Western Europe. During the 1970s, U.S. trade with petroleum-exporting countries such as Saudi Arabia and Venezuela grew rapidly. However, the volume of trade with these nations declined as the price of crude oil declined in the 1980s. South Korea, Hong Kong, and Brazil emerged as major trading partners of the U.S. during the 1980s.

GAINS FROM SPECIALIZATION AND TRADE

The law of comparative advantage, which we discussed in Chapter 2, explains why mutual gains arise from specialization and exchange. According to the law of comparative advantage, trading partners gain by specializing in the production of goods for which they are low opportunity cost producers and by trading for those goods for which they are high opportunity cost producers. Specialization in the area of one's comparative advantage minimizes the cost of production and leads to maximum joint output between trading partners.

International trading partners can gain if they specialize in those things they do best. We know that the resource base varies among nations. Countries with warm, moist climates such as Brazil and Colombia specialize in the production of coffee. Land is abundant in sparsely populated nations such as Canada and Australia. These nations tend to specialize in land-intensive products, such as wheat, feed grains, and beef. In contrast, land is scarce in Japan, a nation with a highly skilled labor force. The Japanese therefore specialize in manufacturing, using their comparative advantage to produce cameras, automobiles, and electronic products for export.

It is easy to see why trade and specialization expand joint output and lead to mutual gain when the resource bases of regions differ substantially. However, even when resource differences among nations are less dramatic, mutual gain is possible. Since failure to comprehend the principle of mutual gains from trade is often a source of "fuzzy thinking," we will take the time to illustrate the principle in detail.

Suppose that the United States and Japan produce two products: food and clothing. Consider a case in which the output per worker of both food and clothing is higher for Japan than for the United States. Perhaps due to its previous experience or natural endowments, Japan has an **absolute advantage** in the production of both commodities. Using hypothetical data, Exhibit 4 illustrates this situation. Japanese workers can produce 3 units of food per day, compared to only 2 units per day for U.S. workers. Similarly, Japanese workers are able to produce 9 units of clothing per day, compared to only 1 unit of clothing per day for U.S. workers.

Given that the Japanese workers are more efficient at producing *both* food and clothing than their American counterparts, are gains from trade possible? Perhaps surprising to some, the answer is yes. As long as *relative* production costs of the two goods differ between Japan and the United States, gains from trade are possible. Exhibits 5 and 6 illustrate this point.

Given the size of the labor force and the productivity of workers in each country, Exhibit 5 illustrates the pre-trade production and consumption possibilities for the United States and Japan. (For simplicity, we will assume that the relative cost of food and clothing in each country is independent of output. Relaxation of this assumption would not alter the basic analysis.) First, let us consider the pre-trade situation in the United States. The 200 million worker-days could be applied entirely to the production of food. In this instance, the U.S. could produce 400 million units of food (2 units per

Absolute Advantage: A situation in which a nation, as the result of its previous experience and/or natural endowments, can produce a product with fewer resources than another nation.

EXHIBIT 4 • The Relative Cost and Production Possibilities of Food and Clothing in the United States and Japan—Hypothetical Data

Gains from exchange depend on comparative advantage, not absolute advantage. Here we illustrate a case in which U.S. workers are able to produce 2 units of food per day, compared to 3 units per day for Japanese workers. Similarly, U.S. workers are able to produce only 1 unit of clothing per day, compared to 9 units per day for Japanese workers. However, even though it is at an absolute disadvantage in the production of both goods, the U.S. has a *comparative* advantage in the production of food. The opportunity cost of producing a unit of food in the U.S. is one half unit of clothing, compared to an opportunity cost of food in Japan of 3 units of clothing. Thus, the U.S. is the low opportunity cost producer of food. The table also illustrates various production possibilities for both the United States and Japan, given the size of their labor forces (200 million worker days for the U.S. and 50 million worker days for Japan) and their production efficiency. Exhibit 5 translates the data for each country into a pre-trade production possibilities curve.

	Units of Output from Per Worker Day	Production Possibilities millions of units (at full employment)				
		P_1	P_2	P_3	P_4	P_5
United States (200 million worker days)						
Food	2	400	300	200	100	0
Clothing	1	0	50	100	150	200
Japan (50 million worker days)						
Food	3	0	50	75	100	150
Clothing	9	450	300	225	150	0

---

day) and zero units of clothing. Of course, clothing output could be expanded if labor were allocated from food to clothing production. However, the U.S. would have to sacrifice 2 units of food production for each unit of clothing produced. Thus, if clothing output in the U.S. is expanded from zero to 50 million, in the absence of trade, U.S. food output will have to be cut back by 100 million units—from 400M to 300M. Given the productivity of its workers in both food and clothing, Exhibit 5 outlines the various combinations of food and clothing that could be produced with the 200 million worker-days available in the United States.

Exhibits 4 and 5 also indicate the pre-trade production possibilities of Japan. If Japan uses all of its 50 million worker-days to produce clothing, 450 million units (9 per day times 50 million days) of clothing could be produced. It would thus be possible for Japan to produce the output combination of 450 million units of clothing and zero units of food. In the absence of trade, Japan must sacrifice 9 units of clothing for each 3 units of food it produces. A unit of food thus costs the Japanese 3 times as much as a unit of clothing. For example, if the Japanese want to produce 50 million units of food, they must be willing to sacrifice 150 million units of clothing, cutting clothing output from 450 million to 300 million. In the absence of

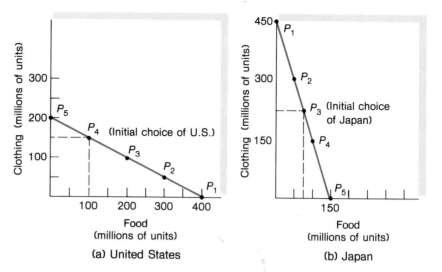

EXHIBIT 5 • The Production Possibilities of the United States and Japan Before Specialization and Trade

Based on the data of Exhibit 4, the production possibilities constraints of the U.S. and Japan prior to trade are illustrated here. The slope of the production possibilities constraint reflects the opportunity cost of food relative to clothing. Since Japan is the high opportunity cost producer of food, its production possibilities constraint is steeper than the constraint for the U.S. In the absence of trade, consumption in each country will be restricted by the country's production possibilities constraints. Prior to trade, the U.S. chooses combination P_4 (100M food, 150M clothing) and Japan chooses P_3 (75M food and 225M clothing).

trade, Exhibit 5b graphically illustrates the various combinations of food and clothing that the Japanese could produce with the employment of 50 million worker-days.

DIFFERENCES IN OPPORTUNITY COST—THE SOURCE OF GAINS FROM TRADE

As long as the opportunity cost of production of the two goods differs between Japan and the United States, trade will lead to mutual gain. Consider the opportunity cost of food in each of the two countries. If Japanese workers produce 1 additional unit of food, they sacrifice the production of 3 units of clothing. In Japan, the opportunity cost of 1 unit of food is 3 units of clothing. On the other hand, 1 unit of food can be produced in the U.S. at an opportunity cost of only 1/2 unit of clothing. U.S. workers are therefore the low opportunity cost producers of food, even though they cannot produce as much food per day as the Japanese workers. Both countries can gain if the U.S. trades food to Japan for clothing at a trading ratio greater than 1 food = 1/2 clothing (the U.S. opportunity cost of food) but less than 1 food = 3 clothing (the Japanese opportunity cost of food). Any intermediate trading ratio between these two extremes would permit the U.S. to acquire clothing cheaper than it can be produced in the U.S. and simultaneously permit Japan to acquire food at a lesser sacrifice than it can be produced in Japan.

Suppose the two countries agree to a trading ratio (an "intermediate price") in which 1 unit of food exchanges for 1 unit of clothing. This would allow each country to specialize in the area of its comparative advantage—food for the U.S. and clothing for the Japanese—while trading for the commodity for which it is a high opportunity cost producer. As Exhibit 6 shows, specialization and trade benefits both countries. Rather than producing and consuming its initially preferred combination of 150M clothing and 100M food (M refers to millions of units), the U.S. could produce 400M food and import 200M clothing from Japan in exchange for 200M food. This would permit the U.S. to consume the combination 200M units of food and 200M units of clothing. Following trade, the U.S. is able to consume a larger quantity of both food and clothing than the preferred bundle in the absence of trade.

Similarly, the Japanese benefit from specialization and exchange. Prior to trade, the preferred bundle in Japan was 225M clothing and 75M food. With trade, the Japanese could specialize in the production of clothing. If the Japanese produce 450M units of clothing and export 200M to the U.S. in exchange for 200M units of food, they would be left with the combination

EXHIBIT 6 • **The Effects of Trade on Production and Consumption Possibilities of the United States and Japan**

Prior to trade, the two countries produce and consume the combinations represented by US$_1$ (P_4 of Exhibit 5a) and J$_1$ (P_3 of Exhibit 5b). When trade takes place at an exchange ratio of one unit of food equals one unit of clothing, both countries gain by specializing in their area of comparative advantage. The U.S. specializes in the production of food, produces 400M units, and exports 200M units of food to Japan in exchange for 200M units of clothing. This permits the U.S. to consume the combination 200M food and 200M clothing (imported from Japan). Compared to the no trade option chosen (150M clothing and 100M food), the U.S. is able to consume a larger quantity of both goods after trade.

Simultaneously, Japan can also increase its consumption of both goods. When Japan specializes in the production of clothing, it can produce 450M units, and export 200M units to the U.S. in exchange for 200M units of food. This permits Japan to consume 250M units of clothing and 200M units of food, compared to its initial preferred bundle of 225M clothing and 75M food. Specialization and trade thus expands the consumption possibilities of both countries.

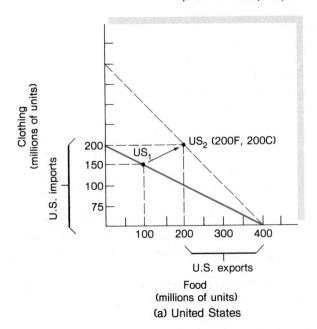

(a) United States

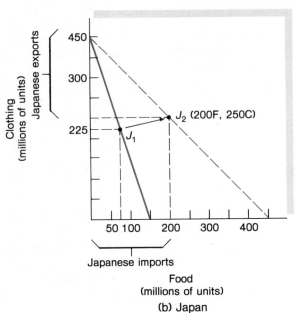

(b) Japan

200M units of food (imported from the U.S.) and 250M units of clothing. As was the case for the U.S., the exchange permits the Japanese to consume a larger quantity of both commodities relative to their preferred pre-trade output combination.

Specialization and exchange leads to an expansion in the joint output of the two countries. Prior to trade, the two countries produced 375M units of clothing (150M in the U.S. and 225M in Japan) and 175M units of food (100M in the U.S. and 75M in Japan). With specialization and trade, clothing production expands to 450M units, an increase of 75M. Similarly, food production jumps to 400M, an increase of 225M over the pre-trade output level.

Mutual gains accrue to trading partners when each nation specializes in the production of those products for which it is a low opportunity cost producer and trades them for those goods for which it is a high opportunity cost producer. Such specialization and exchange will permit nations to maximize their joint output. A country can gain from trade even when it is at an absolute disadvantage in the production of all goods. It is comparative advantage, not absolute advantage, that is the source of gains from trade.

While our hypothetical example illustrates the case of complete specialization, a country need not specialize in the production of just a few products to realize gains from trade. The example of complete specialization was used for illustrative purposes only. Similarly, we ignored the potential importance of transportation costs. Of course, transportation costs reduce the potential gains from trade. Sometimes transportation costs, both real and artificially imposed, exceed the mutual gain. (See "Frederic Bastiat on Obstacles to Gains from Trade.") When this is so, exchange does not occur. However, this does not negate the basic point; the potential realization of gains from specialization and exchange implied by the law of comparative advantage.

THE EXPORT-IMPORT LINK

Confusion about the merit of international trade often results because people do not consider all the consequences. Why are other nations willing to export their goods to the United States? So they can obtain dollars. Yes, but why do they want dollars? Would foreigners be willing to continue exporting oil, radios, watches, cameras, automobiles, and thousands of other valuable products to us in exchange for pieces of paper? If so, we could all be semiretired, spending only an occasional workday at the dollar printing press office! Of course, foreigners are not so naive. They trade goods for dollars so they can use the dollars to import goods and purchase ownership rights to U.S. assets.

Exports provide the buying power that makes it possible for a nation to import other goods. Nations export goods so that they will be able to import foreign products. If a nation does not import goods from foreigners, foreigners will not have the purchasing power to buy that nation's export products. Thus, the exports and imports of a nation are closely linked.

SUPPLY, DEMAND, AND INTERNATIONAL TRADE

How does international trade affect prices and output levels in domestic markets? Supply and demand analysis will help us answer this question. High transportation costs and the availability of cheaper alternatives elsewhere diminish the attractiveness to foreigners of some U.S. products. In some cases, U.S. producers will be unable to produce, transport, and market a product competitively. In other instances, however, U.S. producers will be able to sell profitably to foreigners even when transportation costs are considered.

Given our modern transportation and communication networks, the market for many commodities is worldwide. When a product can be transported long distances at a low cost (relative to its value), the price of the

APPLICATIONS IN ECONOMICS

Frédéric Bastiat on Obstacles to Gains from Trade

Since voluntary exchange is a positive-sum economic activity, obstacles to mutually advantageous exchange are costly. As Frédéric Bastiat notes in the following essay,[2] like bad roads and high transportation costs, tariffs limit the gains from voluntary exchange. Best known for his cutting satire, Bastiat chastises French legislators for spending tax funds to reduce the transport costs of goods and then turning around and erecting tariff barriers that, in effect, increase transportation costs. Even though it was written in 1845, the thrust of Bastiat's message remains valid today.

The illusions of inventors are proverbial, but I am positively certain that I have discovered an infallible means of bringing products from every part of the world to France, and vice versa, at a considerable reduction in cost.

It requires neither plans, estimates, preparatory study, engineers, mechanists, contractors, capital, shareholders, or government aid.

Why does an article manufactured at Brussels, for example, cost dearer when it comes to Paris?

Between Paris and Brussels *obstacles* of many kinds exist. First of all, there is distance, which entails loss of time, and we must either submit to this ourselves or pay another to submit to it. Then comes [sic] rivers, marshes, accidents, bad roads, which are so many difficulties to be surmounted. We succeed in building bridges, in forming roads, and making them smoother by pavement, iron rails, etc. But all this is costly, and the commodity must be made to bear the cost.

Now, among these obstacles there is one which we have ourselves set up.... There are men who lie in ambush along the frontier, armed to the teeth, and whose business it is to throw difficulties into the way of transporting merchandise from the one country to another. They are called customs officials, and they act in precisely the same way as ruts and bad roads....

I often seriously ask myself how anything so whimsical could ever have entered into the human brain, as first of all to lay out many millions for the purpose of removing *natural obstacles* which lie between France and other countries, and then to lay out many more millions for the purpose of substituting *artificial obstacles* ... so that the obstacle created and the obstacle removed neutralize each other.

[The] problem is resolved in three words: Reduce your tariff. You will then have done what is equivalent to constructing the Northern Railway without cost... (emphasis in the original).

---

[2]Frédéric Bastiat, *Economic Sophisms*, trans. Patrick James Stirling (London: Unwin, 1909), pp. 68–70. Reprinted with permission of T. Fisher Unwin, Ltd./Ernest Benn, Ltd., London.

product is in effect determined by the forces of supply and demand in a worldwide market. If domestic producers have a comparative advantage in the production of the product, they will be able to compete effectively in the world market.

Using soybeans as an example, Exhibit 7 illustrates the relationship between the domestic and world markets for an internationally traded commodity. Worldwide market conditions determine the price of soybeans. In an open economy, domestic producers are free to sell and domestic consumers are free to buy the product at the world market price (P_w). At the world market price, U.S. producers will supply Q_p, while U.S. consumers will purchase Q_c. Reflecting their comparative advantage, U.S. soybean producers will export $Q_p - Q_c$ units at the world market price.

Let us compare the open economy outcome with the situation in the absence of trade. If U.S. producers were not allowed to export soybeans, the domestic price would be determined by the domestic supply (S_d) and demand (D_d) only. A lower "no-trade" price (P_n) would emerge. Who are the winners and losers as the result of free trade in soybeans? Clearly, soybean producers gain. Free trade allows domestic producers to sell a larger quantity (Q_p rather than Q_n). As a result, the *net* revenues of soybean producers will rise by $P_w bc P_n$. On the other hand, domestic consumers of soybeans will have to pay a higher price under free trade. Consumers will lose both (a) because they have to pay P_w rather than P_n for the Q_c units they purchase, and (b) because they lose the consumer surplus on the $Q_n - Q_c$ units not purchased at the higher price. Thus, free trade imposes a net cost of $P_w ac P_n$ on consumers. Nevertheless, free trade leads to a net welfare gain. The gains of producers outweigh the losses to consumers by the triangle *abc*.

When one focuses only on an export product, it appears that free trade benefits producers relative to consumers. As Exhibit 7 illustrates, that view is correct as far as it goes. It is potentially misleading however, because it ignores the secondary effects. How will foreigners generate the dollars they will need to purchase soybeans and other export products of the United

EXHIBIT 7 • Producer Benefits from Exports

As frame (b) shows, the price of soybeans and other internationally traded commodities is determined by the forces of supply and demand in the world market. If U.S. soybean producers were prohibited from selling to foreigners, the domestic price would be P_n (frame a). Free trade permits the U.S. soybean producers to sell Q_p units at the higher world price (P_w). The quantity $Q_p - Q_c$ is exported abroad. Compared to the no-trade situation, the producers' gain from the higher price ($P_w bc P_n$) exceeds the cost imposed on domestic consumers ($P_w ac P_n$) by the triangle abc.

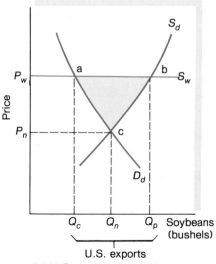

(a) U.S. market for soybeans

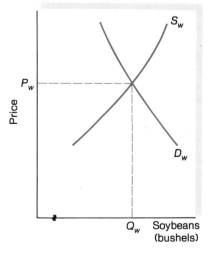

(b) World market for soybeans

States? Remember, imports and exports are linked. If foreigners do not sell goods to us, they will not have the purchasing power necessary to purchase goods from us. U.S. imports—that is, the purchase of goods from low-cost foreign producers—provides foreigners with the dollar purchasing power necessary to buy U.S. exports. As the domestic supply of imported goods (used to pay for exports such as soybeans) expands, prices in import-competitive markets will decline. Of course, the lower prices in the import-competitive markets will benefit the U.S. consumers who appeared at first glance to be harmed by the higher prices (compared to the no-trade situation) in export markets.

Exhibit 8 illustrates the impact of imports, using shoes as an example. In the absence of trade, the price of shoes in the domestic market would be P_n, the intersection of the domestic supply and demand curves. However, the world price of shoes is P_w. In an open economy, many U.S. consumers would take advantage of the low shoe prices available from foreign producers. At the lower world price, U.S. consumers would purchase Q_c units of shoes, importing $Q_c - Q_p$ from foreign producers.

Compared to the no-trade situation, free trade in shoes results in lower prices and an expansion in domestic consumption. The lower prices lead to a net consumer gain of $P_n abP_w$. Domestic producers lose $P_n acP_w$ in the form of lower sales prices and reductions in output. However, the net gain of consumers exceeds the net loss of producers by *abc*.

For an open economy, international competition directs the resources of a nation toward the areas of their comparative advantage. When domestic producers have a comparative advantage in the production of a good, they will be able to compete effectively in the world market and profit from the export of goods to foreigners. In turn, the exports will generate the purchasing power necessary to buy goods that foreigners can supply more economically than we can produce. Relative to the no-trade alternative, international trade and specialization result in lower prices (and higher

**EXHIBIT 8 •
Consumer Benefits
from Imports**

In the absence of trade, the domestic price of shoes would be P_n. Since many foreign producers have a comparative advantage in the production of shoes, trade leads to lower prices. At the world price P_w, U.S. consumers will demand Q_c units, of which $Q_c - Q_p$ are imported. Compared to the no-trade situation, consumers gain $P_n abP_w$, while domestic producers lose $P_n acP_w$. A net gain of abc results.

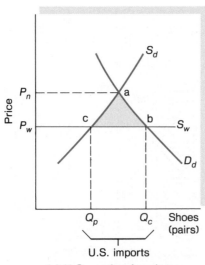

(a) U.S. market for shoes

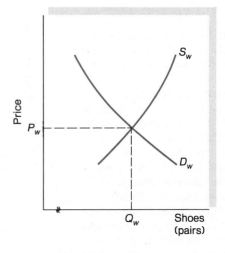

(b) World market for shoes

consumption levels) for imported products and higher prices (and lower consumption levels) for exported products. More importantly, trade permits the producers of each nation to concentrate on the things they do best (produce at a low-cost), while trading for those things which they do least well. The result is an expansion in both output and consumption compared to what could be achieved in the absence of trade.

The pattern of U.S. exports and imports is consistent with this view. The United States is a nation with a technically skilled labor force, fertile farm land, and substantial capital formation. Thus, we export computers, aircraft, power generating equipment, scientific instruments, and land-intensive agricultural products—items we are able to produce at a comparatively low cost. Simultaneously, we import substantial amounts of petroleum, textile (clothing) products, shoes, coffee, and diamonds—goods for which it is costly to produce additional units domestically. Clearly, trade permits us to specialize in those areas in which our comparative advantage is greatest and trade for those products we are least suited to produce.

THE ECONOMICS OF TRADE RESTRICTIONS

Tariff: A tax levied on goods imported into a country.

Despite the potential benefits from free trade, almost all nations have erected trade barriers. What kinds of barriers are erected? Tariffs and quotas are the two most commonly used trade-restricting devices. A **tariff** is nothing more than a tax on foreign imports. As Exhibit 9 shows, tariff barriers in the United States have fluctuated. Until the 1940s, tariffs of between 30 and 50 percent of product value were often levied. In recent years, the average tariff rate has been approximately 10 percent.

Exhibit 10 illustrates the impact of a tariff on automobiles. In the absence of a tariff, the world market price of P_w would prevail in the domestic market. At that price, U.S. consumers purchase Q_1 units. Domestic

EXHIBIT 9 • How High are U.S. Tariffs?

Tariff rates in the United States fell sharply during the period from 1930 to 1950. Subsequently, they leveled off at approximately 10 percent of duty-eligible imports.

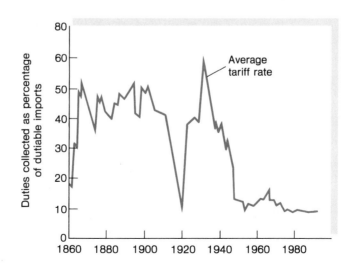

Source: U.S. Department of Commerce.

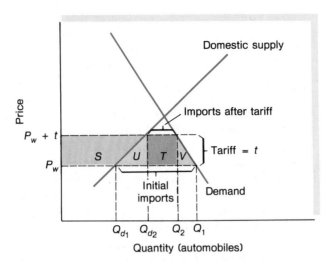

Here we illustrate the impact of a tariff on automobiles. In the absence of the tariff, the world price of automobiles is P_w: U.S. consumers purchase Q_1 units (Q_{d1} from domestic producers plus $Q_1 - Q_{d1}$ from foreign producers). The tariff makes it more costly for Americans to purchase automobiles from foreigners. Imports decline and the domestic price increases. Consumers lose the sum of the areas S + U + T + V in the form of higher prices and reduction in consumer surplus. Producers gain the area S and the tariff generates T tax revenues for the government. The areas U and V are deadweight losses due to a reduction in allocative efficiency.

producers supply Q_{d1}, while foreigners supply Q_1 minus Q_{d1} units to the U.S. market. When the United States levies a tariff t on automobiles, Americans can no longer buy cars at the world price. U.S. consumers have to pay $P_w + t$ to purchase an automobile from foreigners. The market price thus rises to $P_w + t$. At that price, domestic consumers demand Q_2 units (Q_{d2} supplied by domestic producers and $Q_2 - Q_{d2}$ supplied by foreigners). The tariff results in a higher price and lower level of domestic consumption.

The tariff benefits domestic producers and the government at the expense of consumers. Since they do not pay the tariff, domestic producers will expand their output in response to the higher (protected) market price. In effect, the tariff acts as a subsidy to domestic producers. Domestic producers gain the area S (Exhibit 10) in the form of additional net revenues. The tariff raises revenues equal to the area T for the government. The areas U and V represent costs imposed on consumers that do not benefit either producers or the government. Simply put, U and V represent a deadweight loss due to loss of efficiency as the result of the tariff.

The story does not end here, however. Since foreigners are unable to sell goods for which they are low-cost producers in the U.S. market, they acquire fewer dollars. Foreign demand for U.S. exports, products for which we are low-cost producers, declines because our trade restrictions have diminished the ability of foreigners to acquire the dollars necessary to buy our goods. Because of this, we end up producing less in areas where we have a comparative advantage and more in areas where we are high-cost producers. Potential gains from specialization and trade go unrealized.

Import Quota: A specific quantity (or value) of a good permitted to be imported into a country during a given year.

An **import quota,** like a tariff, is designed to restrict foreign goods and protect domestic industries. A quota places a ceiling on the amount of a product that can be imported during a given period (typically a year). Many products, ranging from steel to brooms, are subject to import quotas.

Since quotas reduce the foreign supply to the domestic market, the price of quota-protected products is higher than that which would result from free trade. In many ways, quotas are more harmful than tariffs. With a quota, additional foreign supply is prohibited regardless of how low the prices of foreign products are. With a tariff, products are at least supplied to the domestic market if the cost advantage of foreign producers is sufficient to overcome the tariff.

How much do tariffs and quotas cost the American consumer? Several researchers have attempted to answer this question. Most estimates indicate that consumers paid between $50 billion and $100 billion more for goods—approximately 2 percent of our aggregate output—in the early 1980s as the result of tariffs and quotas.[3] The primary beneficiary of these protective measures were producers of textiles, carbon steel, automobiles, and dairy products.

WHY DO NATIONS ADOPT TRADE RESTRICTIONS?

If trade restrictions promote inefficiency and reduce the potential gains from specialization and trade, why do nations adopt them? Three factors contribute to the existence of trade barriers: partially valid arguments for the protection of specific industries under certain circumstances; economic illiteracy—ignorance as to who is helped and who is harmed by trade restrictions; and, the special interest nature of trade restrictions. We now turn to a consideration of each of these factors.

PARTIALLY VALID ARGUMENTS FOR RESTRICTIONS

There are four major, at least partially valid, arguments for protecting certain domestic industries from foreign competitors.

1. *National Defense Argument.* Certain industries—aircraft, petroleum, and weapons, for example—are vital to national defense. A nation might want to protect such industries from foreign competitors so that a domestic supply of these materials would be available in case of an international conflict. Would we want to be entirely dependent on Arabian or Russian petroleum? Would complete dependence on French aircraft be wise? Most Americans would answer no, even if trade restrictions were required to preserve these domestic industries.

The national defense argument is sound; however, it is often abused. Relatively few industries are truly vital to our national defense. Partial reliance on foreign producers during peacetime may not weaken the capacity of certain domestic industries, particularly those that extract raw materials, to supply the nation's needs in case of war. When the merits of protecting a domestic industry are analyzed, the costs and benefits involved in the national defense argument must be weighed carefully.

---

[3]See Murray Weidenbaum and Michael Munger, "Protection At Any Price," *Regulation,* July/August 1983.

2. *The Industrial Diversity Argument.* Economies that are largely dependent on the revenues from a few major export products or raw materials are characterized by instability. If a domestic economy specializes in the production of only one or two major goods, changes in world demand can exert a drastic influence on domestic economic conditions. Brazil's coffee-dominated economy is an example. Protection of domestic industries would encourage diversity. Clearly, this argument does not apply to the U.S. economy, which is already highly diversified.

3. *The Infant-Industry Argument.* The advocates of this view hold that new domestic industries should be protected from older, established foreign competitors. As the new industry matures, it will be able to stand on its own feet and compete effectively with foreign producers. The infant-industry argument has a long and somewhat notorious history. Alexander Hamilton used it to argue for the protection of early U.S. manufacturing. While it is clearly an argument for temporary protection, the protection, once granted, is often difficult to remove. Nearly a century ago, this argument was used to gain tariff protection for the young steel industry in the United States. Surely, today, steel is a very mature industry. Nevertheless, public policy has failed to remove the tariff.

Dumping: The sale of a good by a foreign supplier in another country at a price lower than the supplier sells it in its home market.

4. *Anti-dumping Argument.* **Dumping** is the sale of goods abroad at a price below their cost (and below their price in the domestic market of the exporting nation). In some cases, dumping merely reflects the exporter's desire to penetrate a foreign market. In other instances, dumping may emanate from export subsidies of foreign governments. At various times in the past, it has been alleged that Argentina has dumped textiles, Korea has dumped steel, and Canada has dumped radial tires onto the U.S. market. Dumping is illegal. The Trade Agreements Act of 1979 provides for special anti-dumping duties (tariffs) when a good is sold in the United States at a price lower than that found in the domestic market of the exporting nation.

As in the case of imports, dumping generally benefits domestic consumers and imposes costs on domestic producers. The lower prices of the "dumped" goods permit consumers to obtain the goods more economically than they are available from domestic producers. Simultaneously, the lower prices make it more difficult for domestic producers to compete. Predictably, domestic producers (and their employees) are the major source of the charges that dumping is unfair.

Economists generally emphasize two points with regard to dumping. First, dumping can, in a few instances, be used as a weapon to gain monopoly power. For example, if the foreign firm temporarily cuts its price below cost, it might eliminate domestic competition and later raise its price to a higher level after the domestic competitors have been driven from the market. However, this is usually not a feasible strategy. After all, domestic producers may re-enter the market if price is raised in the future. In addition, alternative foreign suppliers limit the monopoly power of a producer attempting this strategy. Even though the charge that foreigners are attempting to monopolize the U.S. market is often made by producers, economists are generally skeptical. Before accepting this conclusion, economists believe that one would do well to consider whether the dumping charge might merely be a "red herring" reflecting the desire of domestic producers to reduce competition from abroad.

Second, the law of comparative advantage indicates that a country (as a whole) can gain from the purchase of foreign-produced goods when they are cheaper than domestic goods. This is true regardless of whether the low price of foreign goods reflects comparative advantage, subsidies by foreign governments, or poor business practices. Unless the foreign supplier is likely to monopolize the domestic market, there is little reason to believe that dumping harms the economy.

TRADE BARRIERS AND JOBS

Part of the popularity of trade restrictions stems from their ability to protect or create easily identifiable jobs. Whenever foreign competitors begin to make inroads into markets that have traditionally been supplied by domestic producers, the outcry for "protection to save jobs" is sure to be raised. Many politicians will recognize the potential gain from a protectionist policy and respond accordingly.

The recent history of the automobile industry in the United States illustrates this point. During the 1970s, imported automobiles gained a larger and larger share of the U.S. market. There were several reasons for these gains. High wages in the U.S. auto industry, improved efficiency of foreign producers, excessive government regulation of the domestic auto industry, and failure of U.S. producers to offer high performance small cars when gasoline prices soared during the 1970s were all contributing factors. The increased competition from imports encouraged both management and labor to seek trade restrictions.

The Reagan administration, firmly on record as favoring free trade, was reluctant to request either tariffs or quotas. Nevertheless, the administration bargained with the Japanese government, which eventually agreed to restrict "voluntarily" the number of Japanese automobiles sold in the U.S. market to 1.6 million. As is the case with quotas, voluntary restrictions push up prices in the domestic market. When foreign producers limit their sales to the U.S. market, they will be able to sell the restricted quantity at a higher *per unit* price. The voluntary restrictions of the Japanese illustrate this point. Prior to the restrictions, the price differential between a Toyota Corolla or a Nissan Sentra sold in Japan and the same automobiles sold in the U.S. was less than $500. After the restrictions, the Japanese-U.S. price differential for these automobiles jumped to approximately $3,000.[4] In a large measure, Japanese producers were primary beneficiaries of voluntary restrictions.

The restrictions will also exert a secondary effect that usually goes unnoticed. Since the Japanese will be selling fewer automobiles in the U.S. market, they will earn fewer dollars with which to purchase grains, lumber, chemicals, and other U.S. export products. Workers in export industries will be hurt as the Japanese demand for their products declines. Jobs in these industries will be destroyed. Interestingly, the wage rates in most of these American export industries are approximately half the wage rates of the automobile workers helped by the restrictions.

---

[4]See Robert W. Crandall, "Detroit Rode Quotas to Prosperity," *The Wall Street Journal*, January 29, 1986.

In the long-run, trade restrictions such as quotas, tariffs, and allegedly voluntary limitations can neither create nor destroy jobs. Jobs protected by import restrictions will be offset by jobs destroyed in export industries. The choice is not whether automobiles (or some other product) will be produced in the United States or Japan. The real question is (a) whether our resources will be used to produce automobiles and other products for which we are a high opportunity cost producer or (b) whether the resources will be used for agriculture, high-technology manufactured goods, and other products for which we are a low cost producer.

What about industries that are long-time recipients of protection? Of course, sudden and complete removal of trade barriers would harm producers and workers. It would be costly to effect an immediate transfer of the protected resources to other areas and industries. Gradual removal of such barriers would minimize the cost of relocation and eliminate the shock effect. The government might also cushion the burden by subsidizing the retraining and relocation costs of displaced workers.

SPECIAL INTERESTS AND THE POLITICS OF TRADE RESTRICTIONS

Protectionism is a politican's delight because it delivers visible benefits to the protected parties while imposing the costs as a hidden tax on the public.

Murray L. Weidenbaum
(former Chairman of the Council of Economic Advisors)

Even when trade restrictions promote inefficiency and harm economic welfare, political entrepreneurs may be able to reap political gain from their enactment. Those harmed by a protectionist policy for industry X will individually bear a small and difficult-to-identify cost. Consumers who will pay higher prices for the products of a protected industry are an unorganized group. Most of them will not associate the higher product prices with the protectionist policy. Similarly, numerous export producers (and their employees) will individually be harmed only slightly. The rational ignorance effect implies that those harmed by trade restrictions are likely to be uninformed and unconcerned about our trade policy.

General Agreement on Tariffs and Trade (GATT): An organization composed of most non-Communist countries designed to set the rules for the conduct of international trade and reduce barriers to trade among nations.

In contrast, special interest groups—specific industries, unions, and regions—will be very concerned with the protection of their industries. The benefits they derive will be quite visible. Thus, they will be ready to aid political entrepreneurs who support their views and penalize those who do not. Clearly, vote-seeking politicians will be sensitive to the special interest views.

Often, there will be a conflict between sound economics and good politics on trade restriction issues. Real-world public policy will, of course, reflect the politics of the situation.

EFFORTS TO LIMIT PROTECTIONISM

After high tariffs restricted international trade during the early 1930s, Congress in 1934 adopted legislation authorizing the President to negotiate limited reductions in trade restrictions in exchange for similar concessions from our trading partners. Concern about the impact of trade restrictions on international economic health eventually led to the development of a multination organization called **General Agreement on Tariffs and Trade**

(GATT) shortly after World War II. GATT has grown from 22 members to an international organization of 87 members representing nations that conduct approximately 80 percent of the world trade. GATT spells out the rules for international trade and oversees bargaining among nations designed to reduce trade barriers.

MYTHS OF ECONOMICS

"Free trade with low-wage countries such as China and India would cause the wages of U.S. workers to fall."

Many Americans believe that trade restrictions are necessary to protect U.S. workers from imported goods produced by cheap foreign labor. How can U.S. labor compete with Indian and Chinese workers receiving $1 per hour? The fallacy of this argument stems from a misunderstanding of both the source of high wages and the law of comparative advantage.

High hourly wages do not necessarily mean high per unit labor cost. Labor productivity must also be considered. For example, suppose a U.S. steel worker receives an hourly wage rate of $15. A steel worker in India receives only $1.50 per hour. Given the capital and production methods used in the two countries, however, the U.S. worker produces 20 times as many tons of steel per worker-hour as the Indian worker. Because of the higher productivity per worker-hour, *per unit* labor cost is actually lower in the United States than in India!

Labor in the United States possesses a high skill level and works with large amounts of capital equipment. These factors contribute to the high productivity and the high hourly wages of American workers. Similarly, low productivity per worker-hour is the primary reason

for low wages in such countries as India and China.

When analyzing the significance of wage and productivity differentials across countries, one must remember that gains from trade emanate from *comparative advantage,* not *absolute* advantage (see Exhibits 4, 5, and 6). The United States cannot produce everything cheaper than China or India merely because U.S. workers are more productive and work with more capital than workers in China and India. Neither can the Chinese and Indians produce everything cheaper merely because their wage rates are low compared to the U.S. When resources are directed by relative prices and the principle of comparative advantage, *both* high-wage and low-wage countries gain from the opportunity to specialize in those activities that, *relatively speaking,* they do best. The comparative advantage of low-wage countries is likely to be in the production of labor-intensive goods such as wigs, rugs, toys, textiles, and assembled manufactured products. On the other hand, the comparative advantage of the United States, a country with a highly skilled labor force and an abundance of fertile farm land, lies in the production of high-technology manufacturing products (computers, aircraft, and scientific instruments, for example) and land-intensive agricultural

products (wheat, corn, and soybeans). The pattern of U.S. exports and imports confirms this point (see Exhibit 2). Trade permits both high- and low-wage countries to reallocate their resources away from productive activities in which they are inefficient (relative to foreign producers) to activities in which they are highly efficient. The net result is an increase in output and consumption opportunities for both trading partners.

If foreigners, even low-wage foreigners, will sell us a product cheaper than we ourselves could produce it, we can gain by using our resources to produce other things. Perhaps an extreme example will illustrate the point. Suppose a foreign producer, perhaps a Santa Claus who pays workers little or nothing, were willing to supply us with free winter coats. Would it make sense to enact a tariff barrier to keep out the free coats? Of course not. Resources that were previously used to produce coats could now be freed to produce other goods. Output and the availability of goods would expand. The real wages of U.S. workers would rise. National defense aside, it makes no more sense to erect trade barriers to keep out cheap foreign goods than to keep out the free coats of a friendly, foreign Santa Claus.

Modern U.S. trade policy conducted within the framework of GATT has substantially reduced tariffs. Under the Trade Expansion Act of 1962, Congress authorized the President to reduce tariffs by up to 50 percent and to completely eliminate duties of less than 5 percent. This led to the Kennedy Round of GATT negotiations that reduced tariffs on several industrial commodities. Legislation adopted in 1974 provided the President with similar authority and led to the Tokyo Round of tariff reductions which was completed in 1979. Authorizing the President to reduce tariffs within the framework of GATT without additional Congressional action limits the ability of special interests to erect and maintain overt trade barriers. Thus, tariffs have declined substantially during the post World War II period (see Exhibit 9).

Paradoxically, while tariffs have been reduced, various nations have established price controls and regulatory policies that also limit the freedom of international trade. An important feature of the Tokyo Round of GATT negotiations was an agreement to limit the growth of nontariff barriers. Whether this agreement will eventually lead to meaningful reductions in nontariff barriers is dependent on the continuing bargaining processes within the framework of GATT.

LOOKING AHEAD

There are many similarities between trade within national borders and trade across national boundaries. However, there is also a major difference. In addition to the exchange of goods for money, trade across national borders generally involves the exchange of national currencies. The next chapter deals with the financial arrangements under which international trade is conducted.

CHAPTER SUMMARY

1. The volume of international trade has grown rapidly in recent decades. In the mid-1980s, approximately 16 percent of the world's output was sold in a different country than that in which it was produced.

2. The trade sector comprises approximately 8 percent of the U.S. GNP. More than half of all U.S. trade is with Canada, Japan, and the developed nations of Western Europe.

3. Comparative advantage rather than absolute advantage is the source of gains from trade. As long as the *relative* production costs of goods differ between nations, the nations will be able to gain from trade.

4. Mutual gains from trade accrue when each nation specializes in the production of goods for which it is a low opportunity producer and trades for goods for which it is a high opportunity cost producer. This pattern of specialization and trade will allow trading partners to maximize their joint output and expand their consumption possibilities.

5. Exports and imports are closely linked. The exports of a nation are the primary source of purchasing power used to import goods. When a nation restricts imports, it simultaneously limits the ability of foreigners to acquire the purchasing power necessary to buy the nation's exports.

6. International competition directs the resources of a nation toward their areas of comparative advantage. In an open economy, when domestic

producers have a comparative advantage in the production of a good, they will be able to export their product and compete effectively in the world market. On the other hand, for commodities for which foreign producers have the comparative advantage, a nation could import the goods more economically (at a lower opportunity cost) than they can be produced domestically.

7. Relative to the no-trade alternative, international exchange and specialization result in lower prices for products that are imported and higher domestic prices for products that are exported. However, the net effect is an expansion in the aggregate output and consumption possibilities available to a nation.

8. The application of a tariff, quota, or other import restriction to a product reduces the amount of the product that foreigners supply to the domestic market. As a result of diminished supply, consumers face higher prices for the protected product. Essentially, import restrictions are subsidies to producers (and workers) in protected industries at the expense of (a) consumers and (b) producers (and workers) in export industries. Restrictions reduce the ability of domestic producers to specialize in those areas for which their comparative advantage is greatest.

9. Both high-wage and low-wage countries gain from the opportunity to specialize in the production of goods that they produce at a low opportunity cost. If a low-wage country can supply a good to the United States cheaper than the U.S. can produce it, the U.S. can gain by purchasing the good from the low-wage country and using the scarce resources of the United States to produce other goods for which it has a comparative advantage.

10. National defense, industrial diversity, and the infant-industry arguments can be used to justify trade restrictions for specific industries under certain conditions. It is clear, though, that the power of special interest groups and voter ignorance about the harmful effects offer the major explanations for real-world protectionist public policy.

11. In the long-run, trade restrictions do not create jobs. A decline in our imports from other nations leads to a reduction in those nations' purchasing power and thus to a reduced demand for our export products. Jobs protected by import restrictions are offset by jobs destroyed in export industries. Since this result of restrictions often goes unnoticed, their political popularity is understandable. Nevertheless, the restrictions are inefficient, since they lead to the loss of potential gains from specialization and exchange.

12. Even though trade restrictions promote economic inefficiency, they are often attractive to politicians because they generate visible benefits to special interests—particularly business and labor interests in protected industries—while imposing costs on consumers and taxpayers that are *individually* small and largely invisible.

THE ECONOMIC WAY OF THINKING—
DISCUSSION QUESTIONS

1. Suppose at the time of the Civil War the United States had been divided into two countries and that through the years no trade existed between the two. How would the standard of living in the "divided" United States have been affected? Explain.

2. Do you think the United States could benefit if all barriers to trade among North American nations were eliminated? Would Canada gain? Mexico? Why or why not?

3. Can both (a) and (b) be true? Explain.
   (a) "Tariffs and import quotas promote economic inefficiency and reduce the real income of a nation. Economic analysis suggests that nations can gain by eliminating trade restrictions."
   (b) "Economic analysis suggests that there is good reason to expect trade restrictions to exist in the real world.

4. "Tariffs and quotas are necessary to protect the high wages of the American worker." Do you agree or disagree? Why?

5. **What's Wrong with This Economic Experiment?**
   A researcher hypothesizes that higher tariffs on imported automobiles will cause total employment in the United States to increase. Automobile tariffs are raised and the following year employment in the U.S. auto industry increases by 100,000, compared to a three-year annual increase of 50,000 before the higher tariff legislation was passed. The researcher concludes that the higher tariffs on imported automobiles increased total domestic employment by creating approximately 50,000 jobs in the U.S. automobile industry.

6. It is often alleged that Japanese producers receive subsidies from their government that permit them to sell their products at a low price in the U.S. market. Do you think we should erect trade barriers to keep out cheap Japanese goods if the source of their low price is governmental subsidies? Why or why not?

7. How do tariffs and quotas differ? Can you think of any reason why foreign producers might prefer a quota rather than a tariff? Explain.

- What determines the exchange rate value of the dollar relative to other currencies?

- How does a system of flexible exchange rates work?

- How does a system of fixed exchange rates work?

- How do monetary and fiscal policy influence the exchange rate?

- What information is included in the balance of payments accounts of a nation? Why are these accounts important?

- What are the advantages and disadvantages of the current international monetary system?

Over the past 20 years, economic relationships among countries have been marked by an increasing degree of interdependence.[1]

DONALD KOHN

31 INTERNATIONAL FINANCE AND THE FOREIGN EXCHANGE MARKET

Since World War II, the volume of international exchange has grown rapidly. As we discussed in the last chapter, specialization and trade enable the countries of the world to expand their joint output, since the production of each good is undertaken by those producers who are most efficient. Like voluntary exchange within domestic markets, voluntary exchange between persons of different nations is mutually advantageous to the trading partners. Since international trade fosters a more efficient use of resources, the world has benefited substantially from its growth.

International trade is complicated by the fact that it generally involves two different currencies. Farmers in the United States want dollars, not some foreign currency, when they sell their wheat. Therefore, foreign purchasers must exchange their currency for dollars before they buy U.S. wheat. Similarly, French wine makers want to be paid in francs, not dollars. Therefore, U.S. importers must exchange dollars for francs when they purchase French wines (or French exporters must obtain francs before they pay the winemakers).

In this chapter, we analyze how international currencies are linked and how the rates for their exchange are determined. Between 1944 and 1971, most nations linked their currencies to a fixed exchange rate system. The price of each national currency was fixed with respect to other currencies. Since many businesspeople and some economists favor a return to this type of system, we will analyze its operation. Since 1971, most Western nations have permitted the value of their monetary unit relative to other currencies to be determined largely by market forces. Let us begin our consideration of international finance with an analysis of how markets determine the value of one currency relative to another.

THE FOREIGN EXCHANGE MARKET

Foreign Exchange Market:
The market in which the currencies of different countries are bought and sold.

If a U.S. buyer wants to purchase a good or service from a seller in another country, the buyer can exchange dollars for the currency of the seller's country in the foreign exchange market. The **foreign exchange market** is a widely disperse, highly organized market in which the currencies of different countries are bought and sold. Commercial banks and currency brokers around the world are primary organizers of the market.

Suppose you own a shoe store in the United States and are preparing to place an order for sandals from a manufacturer. You can purchase the sandals from a domestic manufacturer and pay for them with dollars. Alternately, you can buy them from a British manufacturer, in which case they must be paid for in pounds because the employees of the British manufacturer must be paid with pounds. If you buy from the British firm, either you will have to change dollars into pounds at a bank and send them to the British producer, or the British manufacturer will have to go to a bank and change your dollar check into pounds. In either case, purchasing the British sandals will involve an exchange of dollars for pounds.

---

[1]Donald Kohn, "Interdependence, Exchange Rates, Flexibility and National Economies," Federal Reserve Bank of Kansas City *Monthly Review* (April 1975), p. 3.

The British producer sells sandals for 10 pounds per pair. How can you determine whether the price is high or low? To compare the price of the sandals produced by the British firm with the price of domestically produced sandals, you must know the exchange rate between the dollar and the pound. The **exchange rate** is simply the price of one national currency (the pound, for example) in terms of another national currency (such as the U.S. dollar). Exchange rates enable consumers in one country to translate the prices of foreign goods into units of their own currency. When the exchange rate is expressed in terms of dollars per unit of the foreign currency, the dollar price is merely the foreign price multiplied by the exchange rate. For example, if it takes 1.50 dollars to obtain 1 pound, then the British sandals priced at 10 pounds would cost $15.00 (10 times the 1.50 dollar price of the pound).

Suppose the dollar pound exchange rate is $1.50 = 1 pound and that you decide to buy 200 pairs of sandals from the British manufacturer at 10 pounds ($15) per pair. You will need 2,000 pounds in order to pay the British manufacturer. If you contact an American bank that handles exchange rate transactions and write the bank a check for $3,000 (the 1.50 exchange rate multiplied by 2,000), it will supply the 2,000 pounds. The bank will typically charge a small fee for handling the transaction.

Where does the American bank get the pounds? The bank obtains the pounds from British importers who want dollars to buy things from Americans. Note, the U.S. demand for foreign currencies (such as the pound) comes from the demand of Americans for things purchased from foreigners. On the other hand, the U.S. supply of foreign exchange comes from the demand of foreigners for things bought from Americans.

Exhibit 1 presents data on the exchange rate between the dollar and selected foreign currencies during the 1973–1986 period. Under the current flexible system, the exchange rate between currencies changes from

Exchange Rate: The domestic price of one unit of foreign currency. For example, if it takes $1.50 to purchase one English pound, the dollar-pound exchange rate is 1.50.

EXHIBIT 1 • Foreign Exchange Rates, 1973–1986 (U.S. cents per unit of foreign currency)

Year	French Franc	German Mark	Japanese Yen	British Pound	Canadian Dollar
1973	22.5	37.8	0.369	245.10	99.98
1974	20.8	38.7	0.343	234.03	102.26
1975	23.4	40.7	0.337	222.16	98.30
1976	20.9	39.7	0.337	180.48	101.41
1977	20.3	43.1	0.373	174.49	94.11
1978	22.2	49.9	0.480	191.84	87.73
1979	23.5	54.6	0.458	212.24	85.39
1980	23.7	55.1	0.443	232.58	85.53
1981	18.5	44.4	0.454	202.43	83.41
1982	15.3	41.2	0.403	174.80	81.08
1983	13.2	39.2	0.421	151.59	81.13
1984	11.5	35.2	0.421	133.56	77.24
1985	11.2	34.3	0.422	129.56	73.23
1986 (May)	14.5	45.9	0.606	154.39	72.72

Source: Council of Economic Advisers, *Economic Report of the President* (Washington, D.C.: U.S. Government Printing Office, 1986) and *The Wall Street Journal*, May 6, 1986.

day to day and even from hour to hour. Thus, the annual exchange rate data given in Exhibit 1 are really averages for each year.

Between 1980 and 1985, the exchange rate value of the dollar appreciated against the major foreign currencies. An **appreciation** in the value of a nation's currency means that fewer units of the currency are now required to purchase one unit of a foreign currency. For example, in 1985, only 34 cents were required to purchase a German mark, down from 55 cents in 1980.[2] As the result of this appreciation in the value of the dollar relative to the mark, West German goods became less expensive to Americans. The direction of change in the prices that West Germans paid for American goods was just the opposite. An appreciation of the U.S. dollar in terms of the mark is the same thing as a depreciation in the mark relative to the dollar.

A **depreciation** makes foreign goods more expensive, since it decreases the number of units of the foreign currency that can be purchased with a unit of domestic currency. As Exhibit 1 shows, the number of cents required to purchase a French franc, German mark, Japanese yen, or British pound rose substantially in 1986. The dollar thus depreciated against these currencies, increasing the price of goods purchased by Americans from producers in these countries in 1986.

Appreciation: An increase in the value of a domestic currency relative to foreign currencies. An appreciation increases the purchasing power of the domestic currency over foreign goods.

Depreciation: A reduction in the value of a domestic currency relative to foreign currencies. A depreciation reduces the purchasing power of the domestic currency over foreign goods.

EXCHANGE RATES UNDER A FLEXIBLE EXCHANGE RATE SYSTEM

What determines the exchange rate between two currencies? Under a system of **floating** or **flexible exchange rates,** the value of currencies in the exchange rate market is determined by market forces. Just as the forces of supply and demand determine other prices, so too, they determine the exchange rate value of currencies in the absence of government intervention.

To simplify our explanation of how the exchange rate market works, let us assume that the United States and England are the only two countries in the world. Under these circumstances, the supply and demand for pounds is the supply and demand for foreign exchange.

In our two-country world, the demand for pounds in the exchange rate market originates from the demand of Americans for British goods, services, and assets (either real or financial). For example, when U.S. residents purchase men's suits from a British manufacturer, travel in the United Kingdom, or purchase the stocks, bonds, or physical assets of British business firms, they demand pounds from (and supply dollars to) the foreign exchange rate market to pay for these items. On the other hand, the supply

Flexible Exchange Rates: Exchange rates that are determined by the market forces of supply and demand. They are sometimes called "floating exchange rates."

---

[2]Since an appreciation means a *lower* price of foreign currencies, some may think it looks like a depreciation. Just remember that a lower price of the foreign currency means that one's domestic currency will buy more units of the foreign currency and thus more goods and services from foreigners. For example, if the dollar price of the pound falls, this means that a dollar will buy more pounds and thus more goods and services from the British. Therefore, a lower dollar price of the pound means the dollar has appreciated relative to the pound.

of pounds (and demand for dollars) in the exchange rate market comes from the demand of the British for items supplied by Americans. When the British purchase goods, services, or assets from Americans, they supply pounds to (and demand dollars from) the exchange rate market.

Exhibit 2 illustrates the demand and supply curves of Americans for foreign exchange; British pounds in our two-country case. The demand for pounds is downward sloping because a lower dollar price of the pound—this means a dollar will buy more pounds—makes British goods cheaper for American importers and investors. The goods produced by one country are generally good substitutes for the goods of another country. This means that when foreign (British) goods become cheaper, Americans will increase their expenditures on imports (and therefore the quantity of pounds demanded will increase). It will take time for American consumers to respond fully to the price of British goods. *Initially,* Americans may not increase their expenditures on British goods in response to the lower dollar price of the pound. However, with time, the American demand for British goods will be highly elastic. Thus, Americans will eventually increase their expenditures on the lower-priced (in dollars) British goods and therefore they will demand more pounds as the pound's dollar price declines.

The supply curve for pounds is dependent on the purchases of American goods by the British. An increase in the dollar price of the pound means that a pound will purchase more dollars and more goods priced in

EXHIBIT 2 • Equilibrium in the Foreign Exchange Market

The dollar price of the pound is measured on the vertical axis. The horizontal axis indicates the flow of pounds to the foreign exchange market. The equilibrium exchange rate is $1.50 = 1 pound. At the equilibrium price, the quantity demanded of pounds just equals the quantity supplied. A higher price of pounds such as $1.80 = 1 pound would lead to an excess supply of pounds, causing the dollar price of the pound to fall. On the other hand, a lower price, for example $1.20 = 1 pound, would result in an excess demand for pounds, causing the pound to appreciate.

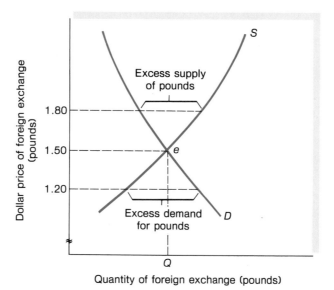

terms of dollars. The price (in terms of pounds) of American goods, services, and assets *to British consumers* declines as the dollar price of the pound increases. The British will purchase more from Americans and therefore supply more pounds to the exchange rate market as the dollar price of the pound rises. Because of this, the supply curve for pounds slopes upward to the right.

As Exhibit 2 shows, equilibrium is present at $1.50 = 1 pound—the dollar price of the pound that brings the quantity demanded and quantity supplied of pounds into balance. The market-clearing price of $1.50 per pound not only equates demand and supply in the exchange rate market; it also equates (a) the value of U.S. purchases on items supplied by the British with (b) the value of items sold by U.S. residents to the British. Demand and supply in the currency market are merely the mirror image of (a) and (b).

What would happen if the price of the pound was above equilibrium—$1.80 = 1 pound, for example. At the higher dollar price of the pound, British goods would be more expensive for Americans. Americans would cut back on their purchases of English shoes, glassware, textile products, financial assets, and other items supplied by the British. Reflecting this reduction, the quantity of pounds demanded by Americans would decline. Simultaneously, the higher dollar price of the pound would make U.S. exports cheaper for the British. For example, a $15,000 American automobile would cost British consumers 10,000 pounds when one pound trades for $1.50, but it would cost only 8,333 pounds when one pound exchanges for $1.80. If the price of the pound was $1.80, the British would supply more pounds to the exchange rate market to purchase the cheaper American goods. Thus, at the $1.80 = 1 pound price, the quantity of pounds demanded by Americans falls and the quantity supplied by the British increases. An excess supply of pounds results, causing the dollar price of the pound to decline until equilibrium is restored at the $1.50 = 1 pound price.

At a below-equilibrium price such as $1.20 = 1 pound, an opposite set of forces would be present. The lower dollar price of the pound would make English goods cheaper for Americans and American goods more expensive for the British. The quantity demanded of British goods and pounds by Americans would increase. Simultaneously, the quantity of American goods demanded and pounds supplied by the British would decline. An excess demand for pounds would result at the $1.20 = 1 pound price. The excess demand would cause the dollar price of the pound to rise until equilibrium was restored at $1.50 = 1 pound.

CHANGING MARKET CONDITIONS AND EXCHANGE RATES

When exchange rates are free to fluctuate, the market value of a nation's currency will appreciate and depreciate in response to changing market conditions. Any change that alters the quantity of goods, services, or assets bought from foreigners relative to the quantity sold to foreigners will also alter the exchange rate. What types of changes will alter the exchange rate value of a currency?

Differential Growth Rates of Income. An increase in domestic income will encourage the nation's residents to spend a portion of their additional income on imports. Thus, when the income of a nation grows rapidly relative to its trading partners, the nation's imports tend to rise relative to exports. As Exhibit 3 illustrates, an increase in imports also increases the demand for foreign exchange, the pound in our two-country case. As the demand for pounds increases, the dollar price of the pound rises (from $1.50 to $1.80). The appreciation in the value of the pound (and depreciation in the value of the dollar) will reduce the incentive of Americans to import British goods, while increasing the incentive of the British to purchase U.S. exports. These two forces will restore equilibrium in the exchange market at a new, higher dollar price of the pound.

Just the opposite happens when the income of a nation lags. A slow growth of domestic income coupled with rapid growth of income abroad will lead to a decline in imports relative to exports. The *relative* strength of the nation's exports will cause the demand for the currency of the slow-growth nation to rise. Paradoxical as it may seem, *other things constant*, sluggish growth of income relative to one's trading partners causes the slow-growth nation's currency to appreciate, since the nation's imports decline relative to exports.

Differential Rates of Inflation. Other things constant, domestic inflation will cause a nation's currency to depreciate on the exchange market, whereas deflation will result in appreciation. Suppose prices in the United States rise by 50 percent, while our trading partners are experiencing stable prices. The domestic inflation will cause U.S. consumers to increase their demand for imported goods (and foreign currency). In turn, the inflated domestic prices will cause foreigners to reduce their purchases of U.S. goods, thereby reducing the supply of foreign currency to the exchange market. As Exhibit 4 illustrates, the exchange rate will adjust to this set of circumstances. The dollar will depreciate relative to the pound.

Exchange rate adjustments permit nations with even high rates of inflation to engage in trade with other countries experiencing relatively

EXHIBIT 3 • The Growth of Income and the Growth of Imports

Other things constant, if incomes grow more rapidly in the United States than in England, U.S. imports will grow relative to exports. The increase in the imports will increase the demand for pounds, causing the dollar price of the pound to rise (from $1.50 to $1.80).

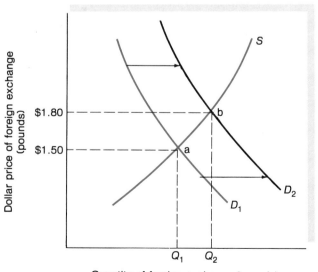

EXHIBIT 4 • Inflation with Flexible Exchange Rates

If prices were stable in England while the price level increased 50 percent in the United States, the U.S. demand for British products (and pounds) would increase, whereas U.S. exports to Britain would decline, causing the supply of pounds to fall. The dollar would depreciate relative to the pound. When the dollar price of the pound has risen to $2.25 = 1 pound (rather than $1.50 = 1 pound), the original price of U.S. goods to British consumers is restored.

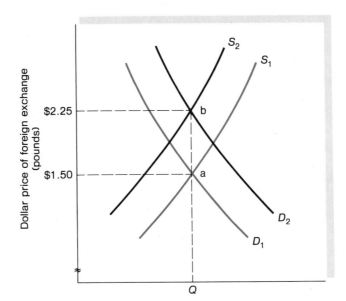

Quantity of foreign exchange (pounds)

stable prices. A depreciation in a nation's currency in the exchange rate market compensates for the nation's inflation rate. For example, if the annual inflation rate in the United States is 50 percent and the value of the dollar in exchange for the pound depreciates 50 percent annually, then the prices of American goods measured in pounds is unchanged to British consumers. Thus, when the exchange rate value of the dollar changes from $1.50 = 1 pound to $2.25 = 1 pound, the depreciation in the dollar restores the original prices of U.S. goods to British consumers even though the price level in the U.S. has increased by 50 percent.

What if prices in both England and the United States are rising at an annual rate of 10 percent? The prices of imports (and exports) will remain unchanged relative to domestically produced goods. Equal rates of inflation in each of the countries will not cause the value of exports to change relative to imports. Identical rates of inflation will not disturb an equilibrium in the exchange market. Inflation contributes to the depreciation of a nation's currency only when a country's rate of inflation is more rapid than that of its trading partners.

Changes in Interest Rates. Short-term financial investments will be quite sensitive to changes in real interest rates—that is, interest rates adjusted for the expected rate of inflation. International loanable funds will tend to move toward areas where the expected real rate of return (after compensation for differences in risk) is highest. If real interest rates increase in the United States relative to Western Europe, British, French, and West German borrowers will demand dollars (and supply their currencies) in the exchange rate market to purchase the high yield American assets. The increase in demand for the dollar and supply of European currencies will cause the dollar to appreciate relative to the British pound, French franc, and German mark.

In contrast, when real interest rates in other countries are high relative to the United States, short-term financial investors will move to take advantage of the improved earnings opportunities abroad. As investment funds move from the United States to other countries, there will be an increase in the demand for foreign currencies and an increase in the supply of dollars. A depreciation in the dollar relative to the currencies of countries experiencing the high real interest rates will be the result.

MACROECONOMIC POLICY AND THE EXCHANGE RATE

The thumbnail sketch summarizes the major forces that cause a nation's currency to appreciate or depreciate when exchange rates are determined by market forces. Since monetary and fiscal policy exert an impact on income growth, inflation, and real interest rates, they also influence the exchange rate.

THUMBNAIL SKETCH

Currency Appreciation and Depreciation with Freely Fluctuating Exchange Rates

These factors will cause a nation's currency to appreciate:

1. A slow rate of growth in income that causes imports to lag behind exports.
2. A rate of inflation that is lower than one's trading partners.
3. Domestic real interest rates that are greater than real interest rates abroad.

These factors will cause a nation's currency to depreciate:

1. A rapid rate of growth in income that stimulates imports relative to exports.
2. A rate of inflation that is higher than one's trading partners.
3. Domestic real interest rates that are lower than real interest rates abroad.

Monetary Policy and the Exchange Rate. Suppose the United States began to follow a more expansionary monetary policy. How would the more expansionary monetary policy influence the exchange rate market? When the effects are not fully anticipated, expansionary monetary policy will lead to more rapid economic growth, an acceleration in the inflation rate, and lower real interest rates.[3] As the thumbnail sketch shows, each of these factors will increase the supply of dollars (and the demand for foreign exchange), causing the dollar to depreciate. The rapid growth of income will stimulate imports. Similarly, the acceleration in the U.S. inflation rate (relative to our

---

[3]A complete analysis would show that neither growth nor the real interest rate will change if people fully anticipate the effects of the change in monetary policy on the price level. In this chapter, we assume for simplicity that the price level effects of monetary policy are unanticipated. This clearly is more relevant in the short-run rather than in the long-run.

trading partners) will make U.S. goods less competitive abroad, causing a decline in exports. Simultaneously, the lower real interest rate will encourage the flow of capital abroad. The expected outcome of a more expansionary monetary policy is a depreciation in the exchange rate value of the dollar.

The effects of a switch to a more restrictive monetary policy will be just the opposite. The restrictive monetary policy will retard economic growth, decelerate the inflation rate, and push real interest rates upward. Exports will grow relative to imports. Investment funds from abroad will be drawn by the high real interest rates in the United States. Foreigners will demand more dollars with which to purchase goods, services, and real assets in the United States. The strong demand for the dollar will cause it to appreciate.

Fiscal Policy and the Exchange Rate. Fiscal policy tends to generate conflicting influences on the exchange rate market. Suppose the United States shifts toward a more restrictive fiscal policy, planning a budget surplus or at least a smaller deficit. Just as with restrictive monetary policy, the restrictive fiscal policy may cause a reduction in aggregate demand, an economic slowdown, and a decline in the rate of inflation. These factors will discourage imports and stimulate exports, causing an appreciation in the exchange rate value of the dollar. However, restrictive fiscal policy will also mean less government borrowing, which will place downward pressure on real interest rates in the United States. The lower real interest rates will cause financial capital to flow from the United States. The supply of dollars to the exchange market will increase, placing downward pressure on the exchange rate value of the dollar. The final outcome is uncertain. If the impact of the reduction in imports dominates, the dollar will appreciate. On the other hand, if the impact of the low real interest rate dominates, the dollar will depreciate.

The analysis of expansionary fiscal policy is symmetrical. To the extent that an increase in the size of the deficit stimulates aggregate demand, income, and prices, it will stimulate imports relative to exports. This will cause the dollar to depreciate. However, to the extent it causes higher real interest rates in the United States, foreign investment will flow to the U.S., causing the dollar to appreciate. Thus, the net impact of expansionary fiscal policy on the value of a nation's currency in the foreign exchange market is indeterminate.

THE APPRECIATION AND DEPRECIATION IN THE DOLLAR, 1973–1986

As Exhibit 1 shows, the dollar depreciated against the German mark and Japanese yen during the latter half of the 1970s. In turn, it appreciated against most major currencies during the first half of the 1980s. We are now in a position to better understand these fluctuations in the exchange rate value of the dollar. During the late 1970s, the annual inflation rate of the United States was generally 3 or 4 percent higher than the rate for West Germany and Japan. Simultaneously, real interest rates in the U.S. were lower. As our analysis indicates, a high inflation rate and low real interest rate will cause a nation's currency to depreciate in the exchange rate market.

These forces reversed during the 1980s, as the U.S. moved toward a more restrictive monetary policy and expansionary fiscal policy. Beginning in 1981, the more restrictive monetary policy retarded the inflation rate. The U.S. inflation rate plunged from double-digit levels in 1979–1980 to 3.2 percent in 1983. Simultaneously, pushed along by both the restrictive monetary policy and huge budget deficits, real interest rates in the United States rose to historic highs. This combination of forces—a low inflation coupled with a high real rate of return on financial investments—increased the demand for the dollar. As a result, the dollar appreciated against most major currencies during the first half of the 1980s.

In 1986, the situation changed again. Real interest rates declined in the United States, reducing the attractiveness of U.S. investments to foreigners. Simultaneously, U.S. imports expanded sharply relative to exports during the strong recovery of 1983–1985 and the appreciation of the dollar during the first half of the 1980s. Thus, when real interest rates fell in 1986, the excess of imports relative to exports caused the dollar to depreciate in the exchange rate market.

THE OPERATION OF A FIXED EXCHANGE RATE SYSTEM

Fixed Exchange Rate System: An international monetary system in which each country's currency is set at a fixed rate relative to all other currencies and governmental policies are used to maintain the fixed rate.

Between 1944 and 1971, most of the world operated under a system of fixed exchange rates. Under a **fixed exchange rate system,** each nation "pegs" the price of its currency to another currency, such as the dollar (or gold), for long periods of time. Governments intervene in the foreign exchange market or alter their economic policies in an effort to maintain the fixed value of their currency.

Fixing the price of a currency in the exchange market, like fixing other prices, results in surpluses and shortages. As market conditions change, the exchange rate that equates the quantity supplied of each currency with the quantity demanded also changes. What happens when the fixed rate differs from the equilibrium rate? Building on the analysis of Exhibit 2, suppose the equilibrium exchange rate was $1.50 = 1 pound. If the price of the pound is fixed at $1.80 = 1 pound, an excess supply of pounds will result. At the $1.80 = 1 pound fixed rate, the pound is overvalued (and the dollar undervalued). At the $1.80 per pound exchange rate, the U.S. will persistently export more to the British than the British will import from the United States. The central bank in the United States will have to continually increase its holdings of pounds—that is, buy the excess supply of pounds, to maintain the above-equilibrium price of the pound. In essence, this situation leads to a surplus of exports over imports for the United States in its trade with England.

What would happen if the dollar price of the pound was set below equilibrium, such as $1.20 = 1 pound (Exhibit 2)? The below-equilibrium price of the pound would lead to an excess demand for pounds. Since the pound is undervalued (and the dollar overvalued) at the $1.20 per pound price, British imports are cheap to Americans (and U.S. exports expensive for the British). In its trade with the British, the U.S. would persistently buy (import) more than it sells (export). To defend the $1.20 per pound fixed rate, the U.S. central bank would have to draw down its holdings of pounds, balances that were perhaps built up during periods when the dollar price of the pound was above equilibrium.

To make a fixed rate system work, each country must maintain a reserve balance of other currencies that will permit it to weather temporary periods of excess demand relative to supply. When the fixed rate system was put in place at the end of World War II, the **International Monetary Fund** (IMF) was established to perform this function. The IMF required each of its more than 100 member countries to deposit a specified amount of its currency into a reserve fund held by the IMF. Thus, it possessed substantial holdings of dollars, francs, pounds, marks, and other currencies of the participating nations. As the need arose, these reserves were loaned to nations experiencing difficulties with their balance of payments.

The premise of a fixed rate system is that a nation ordinarily pays for its imports with exports. Of course, countries may temporarily experience periods where imports exceed exports. During such periods, nations can draw down their reserve balance. However, chronic debtor nations— nations persistently importing more than they export—must take corrective action designed to bring exports and imports into balance. During the 1944–1971 period, the IMF provided discipline to the system by encouraging and in some cases requiring member nations to adopt policies that would bring their exports and imports into balance.

What steps can a nation experiencing an excess of imports over exports take to remedy this situation under a fixed rate system? Basically, there are three alternatives.

1. *A Nation Can Devalue Its Currency.* **Devaluation** is a one-step reduction in the value of a nation's currency under a fixed rate system. When a currency is overvalued, a devaluation can restore equilibrium between the demand and supply of the currency in the exchange market. For example, if there is an excess supply of dollars (excess demand for pounds) in the exchange market when the fixed exchange rate is $1.20 = 1 pound, a devaluation of the dollar (perhaps to $1.50 = 1 pound) could restore balance. A devaluation makes imports more expensive to domestic consumers, while encouraging exports. It thus tends to correct an excess of imports relative to exports.

2. *A Nation Can Heighten Trade Barriers, Adopting Tariffs and Quotas in an Effort to Reduce Imports and Bring the Value of Its Currency on the Foreign Exchange Market into Equilibrium.* This strategy is in conflict with economic efficiency and the promotion of the free flow of trade between nations. Nevertheless, it was often adopted during the period from 1944 to 1971. Once a nation's exchange rate was established, it tended to become sacred. Politicians during that period, including many in the United States, frequently argued that even though they did not like to impose trade restrictions, the barriers were necessary to avoid devaluation. The balance of payments issue was an excellent excuse to promote trade restrictions— which were advocated by special interests—against low-cost foreign goods.

3. *A Nation Can Follow Restrictive Macroeconomic Policy Designed to Promote Deflation (or at least Retard Inflation) and High Interest Rates.* Policymakers might use restrictive monetary and fiscal policy to attract an excess of imports relative to exports. Restrictive monetary policy and fiscal policy would

International Monetary Fund: An international banking organization, with more than 100 nation members, designed to oversee the operation of the international monetary system. Although it does not control the world supply of money, it does hold currency reserves for member nations and make currency loans to national central banks.

Devaluation: An official act that changes the level of the "fixed" exchange rate in a downward direction. In essence, it is a one-step depreciation of a currency under a fixed exchange rate system.

retard inflation and increase interest rates. A slower rate of inflation relative to one's trading partner would encourage exports and discourage imports. Higher domestic real interest rates would attract foreign investment and thereby increase the nation's supply of foreign exchange.

When a nation uses macroeconomic policy to restore balance in the exchange market, an important point emerges. This method of bringing about equilibrium in the exchange market attempts to manipulate the level of all other prices to maintain one price—the fixed exchange rate. In contrast, a flexible exchange rate system changes one price, the foreign exchange rate—to restore balance between what is bought from and what is sold to foreigners.

THE BALANCE OF PAYMENTS

Balance of Payments: A summary of all economic transactions between a country and all other countries for a specific time period—usually a year. The balance of payments account reflects all payments and liabilities to foreigners (debits) and all payment and obligations (credits) received from foreigners.

Just as countries calculate their gross national product so that they have a general idea of the domestic level of production, most countries also calculate their balance of international payments in order to keep track of their transactions with other nations. The **balance of payments** account is a periodic report that summarizes the flow of economic transactions with foreigners. It provides information on the nation's exports, imports, earnings of domestic residents on assets located abroad, earnings on domestic assets owned by foreigners, international capital movements, and official transactions by central banks and governments.

Balance of payments accounts are kept according to the principles of double-entry bookkeeping. Each entry on the debit (−) side of the ledger implies an identical entry on the credit side (+). Any transaction that supplies the nation's domestic currency (or creates a demand for foreign currency) in the foreign exchange market is recorded as a debit, or minus, item. Imports are an example of a debit item. Transactions that create a demand for the nation's currency (or a supply of foreign currency) on the foreign exchange market are recorded as a credit, or plus item. Exports are an example of a credit item.

The balance of payments transactions can be grouped into three basic categories: current account, capital account, and official reserve account. Let us take a look at each of these.

CURRENT ACCOUNT TRANSACTIONS

Current Account: The record of all transactions with foreign nations that involve the exchange of merchandise goods and services or unilateral gifts.

All payments (and gifts) that are related to the purchase or sale of goods and services during the designated period are included in the **current account.** In general, there are three major types of current account transactions: the exchange of merchandise goods, the exchange of services, and unilateral transfers.

Merchandise Trade Transactions. The export and import of merchandise goods comprise by far the largest portion of a nation's balance of payments account. As Exhibit 5 shows, in 1984, the United States imported $340.5 billion of merchandise goods and exported only $230.4 billion. When Americans import goods from abroad, they also supply dollars to the foreign exchange market. Imports are recorded as debits in the balance of

EXHIBIT 5 • U.S. Balance of Payments, 1984		
Item		Amount (billions of dollars)
Current Account		
1. Exports of goods and services		+ 362.4
a. Merchandise exports (including military sales)	+ 230.4	
b. Services	+ 44.4	
c. Income from U.S. assets abroad	+ 87.6	
2. Imports of goods and services		− 452.5
a. Merchandise imports (including military purchases)	− 340.5	
b. Services	− 43.6	
c. Income from foreign assets in U.S.	− 68.5	
3. Net unilateral transfers abroad		− 11.4
a. U.S. government grants and pensions	− 8.5	
b. Private remittances	− 2.9	
Current Account Balance		− 101.5
Capital Account		
4. Outflow of U.S. capital		− 17.3
a. U.S. direct investment abroad	− 4.5	
b. Loans to foreigners	− 12.8	
5. Inflow of foreign capital		+ 93.9
a. Foreign direct investments in U.S.	+ 22.5	
b. Loans from foreigners	+ 71.4	
6. Statistical discrepancy		+ 24.6
Capital Account Balance		+ 101.2
Official Reserve Account		
7. Increase (−) in U.S. official reserve assets		− 3.1
8. Increase (+) in foreign official asset in U.S.		+ 3.4
Official Reserve Balance		+ 0.3
TOTAL	0.0	0.0

Source: U.S. Commerce Department, *Survey of Current Business,* June 1985.

Balance of Merchandise Trade: The difference between the value of merchandise exports and the value of merchandise imports for a nation. The balance of trade is only one component of a nation's total balance of payments.

payments accounts. In contrast, when U.S. producers export their products, foreigners demand dollars on the exchange market to pay for the U.S. exports. Exports are the credit item.

The difference between the value of a country's merchandise exports and the value of its merchandise imports is known as the **balance of merchandise trade.** If the value of a country's merchandise exports falls short of (exceeds) the value of its merchandise imports, it is said to have a balance of trade deficit (surplus). In 1984, the United States ran a balance of merchandise trade deficit of $110.1 billion. Although trade deficit has generally been given a negative connotation by the news media, it is not clear whether a country receiving more goods from foreigners than it exports necessarily finds itself in an unfavorable position. The negative view of a trade deficit undoubtedly stems from its impact on the value of the dollar on the foreign exchange market. Other things constant, a U.S. trade deficit implies that

Americans are supplying more dollars to the exchange market than foreigners are demanding for purchase of American goods. If the trade deficit were the only factor influencing the value of the dollar on the exchange market, one could anticipate a decline in the foreign exchange value of the U.S. currency. However, several others factors also affect the supply of and demand for the dollar on the exchange market.

Service Exports and Imports. The export and import of "invisible services," as they are sometimes called, also exert an important influence on the foreign exchange market. The export of insurance, transportation, and banking services generates a demand for dollars by foreigners just as the export of merchandise does. A French business that is insured with an American company will demand dollars with which to pay its premiums. When foreigners travel in the United States or transport cargo on Mexican ships, they will demand dollars with which to pay for these services. Similarly, income earned by U.S. investments abroad will cause dollars to flow from foreigners to Americans. These service exports are thus entered as credits on the current account.

On the other hand, the import of services from foreigners expands the supply of dollars to the exchange market. Therefore, service imports are entered on the balance of payments accounts as debit items. Travel abroad by U.S. citizens, the shipment of goods on foreign carriers, and income earned by foreigners on U.S. investments are all debit items, since they supply dollars to the exchange market.

These service transactions are substantial. As Exhibit 5 indicates, in 1984, the U.S. service exports were $44.4 billion, compared to service imports of $43.6 billion.

Unilateral Transfers. Monetary gifts to foreigners, such as U.S. aid to a foreign government or private gifts from U.S. residents to their relatives abroad, supply dollars to the exchange market. These gifts are debit items in the balance of payments accounts. Monetary gifts to Americans from foreigners are credit items. Gifts in kind are more complex. When products are given to foreigners, goods flow abroad, but there is no offsetting influx of foreign currency—that is, a demand for dollars. Balance of payments accountants handle such transactions as though the United States had supplied the dollars with which to purchase the direct grants made to foreigners. So, these items are also entered as debits. Because the U.S. government (and private U.S. citizens) made larger grants to foreigners than we received, net unilateral transfers of $11.4 billion were entered as a debit item on the current accounts for 1984.

Balance on Current Account. The difference between (a) the value of a country's exports of goods and services and (b) the value of its imports of goods and services plus net unilateral transfers is known as the **balance on current account.** This is a summary statistic for all current account transactions. As with the balance of trade, if the value of the exports is less than (exceeds) the value of the imports plus the unilateral transfers, the country

---

Balance on Current Account: The import-export balance of goods and services plus net private and government transfers. If a nation's export of goods and services exceeds (is less than) the nation's import of goods and services plus net unilateral transfers to foreigners, a current account surplus (deficit) is present.

is said to be experiencing a deficit (surplus) on current account transactions. In 1984, the United States ran a $101.5 billion deficit on current account transactions.

CAPITAL ACCOUNT TRANSACTIONS

Capital account transactions are composed of (a) direct investments by Americans in real assets abroad (or by foreigners in the United States) and (b) loans to and from foreigners. If a U.S. investor purchases a shoe factory in Mexico, the Mexican seller will want to be paid in pesos. The U.S. investor will supply dollars (and demand pesos) on the foreign exchange market. U.S. investment abroad is thus entered on the balance of payments accounts as a debit item. On the other hand, foreign investment in the United States creates a demand for dollars on the exchange market. Therefore, it is entered as a credit.

Investment abroad can be thought of as the import of a bond or ownership right. Importing ownership of a financial (or real) asset from abroad has the same effect on the balance of payments as importing goods from abroad. Therefore, both are recorded as debits. Similarly, in a sense, we are exporting bonds and ownership of capital when foreigners invest in the United States. These transactions enter as a credit.

As for domestic markets, many international transactions are conducted on credit. When a U.S. banker loans $100,000 to a foreign entrepreneur for the purchase of U.S. exports, the banker is in effect importing a foreign bond. Since the transaction supplies dollars to the exchange market, it is recorded as a debit. On the other hand, when Americans borrow from abroad, they are exporting bonds. Since this transaction creates either a demand for dollars on the part of the foreign lender (in order to supply the loanable funds) or a supply of foreign currency, it is recorded as a credit in the U.S. balance of payments account.

In 1984, both the direct investments of foreigners in the United States and the loans from foreigners were substantially larger than U.S. direct investments and loans abroad. As a result, the U.S. ran a capital account surplus of $101.2 billion.

THE OFFICIAL RESERVE ACCOUNT

Special Drawing Rights: Supplementary reserves, in the form of accounting entries, established by the International Monetary Fund (also called "paper gold"). Like gold and foreign currency reserves, they can be used to make payments on international accounts.

Governments maintain official reserve balances in the form of foreign currencies, gold, and **special drawing rights** (SDRs) with the International Monetary Fund, a type of international central bank. Countries running a deficit on their current and capital account balance can draw on their reserves. Similarly, countries running a surplus can build up their reserves of foreign currencies and reserve balances with the IMF. Under the fixed exchange system present during 1944–1971, these reserve transactions were highly significant. Countries experiencing balance of payments difficulties were forced to draw on their reserves to maintain their fixed exchange rate. Countries that were selling more to foreigners than foreigners were buying from them accumulated the currencies of other nations.

However, under the current (primarily) flexible rate system, nations permit a rise or fall in the foreign exchange value of their currency to bring about equilibrium in the exchange rate market. Thus, changes in the official reserve account are generally quite small. In 1984, the net change in the U.S. official reserve position was $0.3 billion.

BALANCING THE
ACCOUNTS

Reflecting double-entry bookkeeping procedures, the aggregated balance of payments accounts must balance. The following balance of payments' identity must hold:

$$\underset{\text{balance}}{\text{current account}} + \underset{\text{balance}}{\text{capital account}} + \underset{\text{account balance}}{\text{official reserve}} = 0$$

However, the specific components of the accounts need not balance. For example, the debit and credit items of the current account need not be equal. Specific components may run either a surplus or a deficit. Nevertheless, since the balance of payments as a whole must balance, a deficit in one area implies a surplus in another.

If a nation is experiencing a deficit on its current account balance, it must experience an offsetting surplus on the sum of its capital account and official reserve account balances. Under a pure flexible exchange system, official reserve transactions are zero. Therefore, under a flexible rate system, a current account deficit implies a capital account surplus. Similarly, under a flexible rate system, a current account surplus would imply a capital account deficit.

What is the meaning of a current account deficit? If a nation buys more goods and services from foreigners than it sells to foreigners, it must cover this excess of purchases compared to sales in precisely the same way an individual would do so. It must borrow or sell ownership rights to foreigners. This was the situation of the United States in 1984. As Exhibit 5 shows, including unilateral transfers, U.S. citizens bought $452.5 billion of goods and services from foreigners while selling them only $362.4 billion. Because of this, the U.S. experienced a current account deficit of $101.5 billion. To fill the gap between their current expenditures and recipients, U.S. citizens and the government sold ownership rights and borrowed from foreigners. As a result, the capital account of the U.S. ran a $101.2 billion surplus, approximately the current account deficit.

Should a nation be concerned when it is running a current account deficit under a flexible rate system? When thinking about this question, it is important to recognize that the U.S. deficit or surplus on current account depends on how foreigners spend the dollars they acquire from the sales of goods, services, and ownership rights to the United States. If foreigners spend these dollars only on current goods and services (U.S. exports), the U.S. will run a current account surplus. On the other hand, if foreigners find investment opportunities attractive in the United States and therefore spend a large share of their acquired dollars on real and financial investments in the United States, the U.S. will run a current account deficit (and a capital account surplus). In either case, both countries benefit from specialization and gains from trade. After all, if the dollars come back in the form of an inflow of foreign capital, lower domestic interest rates and an increase in capital formation will result.

Interestingly, an economy that offers more attractive investment opportunities than its trading partners can expect to run a current account deficit under a flexible exchange rate system. The attractive investment opportunities will lead to a net inflow of foreign capital and a capital account surplus. But, a capital account surplus implies a current account deficit under a flexible exchange rate system. Foreigners will have to sell more goods and services than they buy abroad in order to acquire the funds necessary to finance their net capital investments.

THE CURRENT INTERNATIONAL MONETARY SYSTEM

The international monetary system in effect since 1973 might best be described as a managed flexible rate system. The system qualifies as a flexible rate system because all of the major industrial countries allow the exchange rate value of their currencies to float. Many small countries maintain fixed exchange rates against the dollar, the English pound, or some other major currency. Therefore, the exchange rate value of these currencies rises and falls with the major currency to which they are tied. The system is managed because the major industrial nations have from time to time altered their official reserve holdings in an effort to moderate major swings—say, swings of 20 percent or more within six months—in exchange rates. For example, the Carter administration intervened with international reserves and loans from West Germany and Japan to moderate the fall of the dollar in 1978. Similarly, the Reagan administration sought to halt the appreciation of the dollar in 1985.

Recent intervention has often involved coordinated efforts on the part of the major industrial nations. The macroeconomic policies and the purchases and sales of currency reserves of the Group of Seven (United States, Japan, France, United Kingdom, West Germany, Canada, and Italy) have been conducted with an eye for exchange rate stability in recent years.

ADVANTAGES OF THE CURRENT SYSTEM

The proponents of the current system stress three major advantages of the structure. We will discuss each of these in turn.

1. *The current system is flexible enough to adjust to major shocks that influence the value of currencies.* The system of floating exchange rate handled the inflation and soaring oil prices of the 1970s and the unanticipated plunge in oil prices in the 1980s with a minimum of difficulty. The volume of international trade continued to rise even during the period of instability.

2. *The current system allows countries to pursue independent macroeconomic policies.* When inflation rates and growth rates vary across nations, a change in only one price—the exchange rate—will bring the flow of international transactions into balance. In contrast, countries often had to follow macropolicy designed to deflate or inflate their economies in order to solve trade imbalances under a fixed rate system. Clearly, it is less painful to alter one price rather than the level of all prices.

3. *The current structure solves trade imbalances without trade restrictions.* Under the fixed rate system, nations often raised tariffs and imposed quotas in an attempt to maintain the fixed exchange rate. Such policies retarded the potential gains from international exchange.

DISADVANTAGES OF THE CURRENT SYSTEM

The current system is not without its critics. The critics of the system stress the following problems:

1. *The current system leads to volatile rate changes which create uncertainty.* Between 1980 and 1985, the dollar appreciated by 50 percent or more

against major currencies such as the French franc, German mark, and British pound. In contrast, the dollar depreciated by nearly a third against several leading currencies in 1986 (see Exhibit 1). Critics of the current system argue that fluctuations of this type make it difficult for exporters and importers to plan for the future.

When evaluating the merit of this charge, one should keep in mind that futures markets allow buyers and sellers to hedge against currency fluctuations when they engage in long-term contracts in another currency. For example, an American business contracting to purchase Japanese houseware products to be delivered in six months can arrange now *at a designated current price* for the delivery of the yen needed to complete the transaction. Thus, if international traders want to avoid the uncertainty implied by potential fluctuations in the exchange rate, futures markets in currencies permit them to do so at a moderate cost.

2. *Since the current system fails to impose macroeconomic policy discipline, we can expect more inflation than under a fixed rate system.* Under a fixed rate system, inflationary policies lead to balance of payments deficits. Since policymakers will not want to devalue the nation's currency, proponents of this view charge that fixed rates restrain policymakers more than a flexible rate system. In essence, this view stresses the cost of providing macroeconomic policymakers with greater independence—they are likely to abuse it.

3. *Changes in exchange rates alter trade balances slowly, only after the passage of time.* In the short-run, the demand for imports may be highly inelastic. When a nation's currency depreciates, it will take time for American consumers to revise purchasing agreements and find alternatives for foreign goods that now cost more in terms of dollars. As a result, a depreciation in the dollar may *initially* increase the total spending on imports. *For a time*, it may expand rather than restrict the size of a balance of trade deficit. Thus, changes in exchange rates are a crude instrument with which to deal with trade imbalances, according to this view.

APPLICATIONS IN ECONOMICS

The Gold Standard International Monetary System

Throughout history, gold has played an important role in monetary matters. The gold standard is an international monetary system under which the value of each nation's currency (for example, the dollar, pound, or mark) is defined in terms of gold. Most recently, the world economy operated on a gold standard during the period from the 1870s until World War I.

When each currency is linked to gold, in essence, the precious metal becomes a world currency. Suppose the U.S. pledged it would buy and sell gold from both domestic citizens and foreigners at a price of 1/20 of an ounce = $1. Simultaneously, suppose other countries set the value of their currencies in terms of gold. Perhaps the English would set the value of a pound equal to 1/10 of an ounce of gold and the French would set the value of the franc at 1/40 of an ounce of gold. Under these circumstances,

when each country sets the value of its currency in terms of gold, the countries also establish a system of fixed exchange rates. For example, if a pound traded for twice as much gold (1/10 of an ounce rather than 1/20 of an ounce) as the dollar, the fixed exchange rate value of the pound would be 1 pound = $2. No one would ever pay more for a pound than $2 because they could always buy 1/10 of an ounce of gold for $2 and then use the gold to buy

APPLICATIONS IN ECONOMICS (continued)

a pound. Similarly, the exchange rate between the French franc and the dollar would be $0.50 = 1$ franc because the dollar exchanges for twice as much gold (1/20 versus 1/40 of an ounce) as the franc. Since each currency is readily redeemable in gold, the currency of each nation is little more than a gold certificate under a gold standard system.

How did an economy adjust to the flow of international trade under a gold standard? Since domestic citizens could redeem gold for money, an inflow of gold, in effect, increased the nation's money supply. Under a gold standard system, the flow of gold among countries tended to bring imports and exports of nations into balance. If a nation's imports exceed its exports, the differential was paid in gold. Thus, "trade-deficit" nations exported gold to "trade-surplus" nations. These gold transfers caused the money supply of trade-deficit nations to fall and the money supply of trade-surplus countries to rise. Prices soon reflected these changes in the supply of money. Prices declined in the trade-deficit nations as a result of the shrinking supply of money. The price reductions made the goods of the trade-deficit nations cheaper on in-

ternational markets, stimulated exports, and thereby restored the balance of trade. Similarly, prices in the trade-surplus nations rose as these countries acquired gold and expanded their money supply. The price inflation in the trade-surplus nations made their products less competitive. Exports declined, moving the trade balance of these countries toward equilibrium.

Despite the beauty of the system's simplicity, the gold standard had a number of drawbacks. First, real resources were tied up in the mining of gold so that it could be transferred between trading nations. Second, as the international sector grew in importance, the demand for exchange currency expanded. Since the supply of gold was virtually fixed, this expanding demand could not be satisfied. Third, with gold-backed currency used for both domestic and foreign transactions, the system placed a stranglehold on monetary planners. While this might be considered an advantage during periods of inflation, dissatisfaction arose when a reduction in a nation's gold stock (as a result of a trade deficit) not only placed downward pressure on prices but also caused a decline in employment and income. As the result of these disadvantages, the gold standard was abandoned in 1914.

While the gold standard is very much like a fixed exchange rate system, a fixed system can be main-

tained without linking currencies to gold. To make a fixed rate system work, countries must conduct their monetary policy *as if* they are on a gold standard. When a country runs a trade surplus, it should increase the growth rate of its money supply more rapidly. This will cause the domestic price level to rise, making its exports less competitive. Eventually, balance between what is sold to foreigners and what is bought from them will be restored. On the other hand, a country that is running a trade deficit should reduce its rate of monetary growth in order to reduce the domestic price level and make its goods and services more competitive in the world market. The more restrictive monetary policy will eventually restore balance in the trade sector.

Despite the similarities, there is one crucial difference between a pure gold standard and a fixed rate system such as was present during the 1944–1971 period. The gold standard does not allow policymakers a choice with regard to altering monetary policy. Under a pure gold standard, the money supply of nations experiencing a trade surplus increases automatically, while the money supply of trade deficit nations declines. The gold standard eliminates the discretion of the policymakers. Proponents of the gold standards usually find this to be one of its most attractive features.

CONCLUDING REMARKS

The current international monetary system is the product of an evolutionary process. Future modifications are likely. Perhaps more than ever, there is a widespread recognition that the economic health of nations is influenced by the flow of international trade. This may lead, either formally or informally, to a joint determination of monetary and fiscal policies among western nations. The annual economic summit of the major industrial nations is a step in that direction.

CHAPTER SUMMARY

1. The foreign exchange market is a highly organized market in which currencies of different countries are bought and sold. The exchange rate is the price of one national currency in terms of another. The exchange rate permits consumers in one country to translate the prices of foreign goods into units of their own currency.

2. When international trade takes place, it is usually necessary for one country to convert its currency to the currency of its trading partner. Imports of goods, services, and assets (both real and financial) by the United States generate a demand for foreign currency with which to pay for these items. On the other hand, exports of goods, services, and assets supply foreign currency to the exchange market because foreigners exchange their currency for the dollars needed to purchase the export items.

3. The value of a nation's currency on the exchange market is in equilibrium when the supply of the currency (generated by imports—the sale of goods, services, and assets to foreigners) is just equal to the demand for the currency (generated by exports—the purchasing of goods, services, and assets from foreigners).

4. Under a flexible rate system, if there is an excess supply of dollars (excess demand for foreign currencies) on the foreign exchange market, the value of the dollar will depreciate relative to other currencies. A depreciation will make foreign goods more expensive to U.S. consumers and U.S. goods cheaper to foreigners, reducing the value of our imports and increasing the value of our exports until equilibrium is restored. On the other hand, an excess demand for dollars (excess supply of foreign currencies) will cause the dollar to appreciate, stimulating imports and discouraging exports until equilibrium is restored.

5. With flexible exchange rates, a nation's currency tends to appreciate when (a) rapid economic growth *abroad* (and slow growth at home) stimulates exports relative to imports, (b) the rate of domestic inflation is below that of the nation's trading partners, and (c) domestic real interest rates increase relative to one's trading partners. The reverse of these conditions will cause a nation's currency to depreciate.

6. Unanticipated restrictive monetary policy will raise the real interest rate, reduce the rate of inflation, and, at least temporarily, reduce aggregate demand and the growth of income. These factors will in turn cause the nation's currency to appreciate on the foreign exchange market. In contrast, expansionary monetary policy will result in a currency depreciation.

7. Fiscal policy tends to generate conflicting influences on the exchange rate. To the extent that expansionary fiscal policy (larger budget deficits) stimulates income, it promotes imports relative to exports, causing a currency to depreciate. However, to the extent expansionary fiscal policy increases the real interest rate of a nation, it causes an appreciation of a nation's currency due to an inflow of foreign investment. The analysis is symmetrical for restrictive fiscal policy.

8. During the period from 1944 to 1971, most of the nations of the free

world operated under a system of fixed exchange rates. Under this system, if the value of the goods, services, and capital assets exported to foreigners is less than the value of the items imported, there is an excess supply of the country's currency on the foreign exchange market. When this happens, the country must (a) devalue its currency, (b) take action to reduce imports (for example, heighten its trade barriers), or (c) pursue a restrictive macropolicy designed to increase interest rates and retard inflation. During the period when the fixed rates were in effect, corrective action taken to maintain the rates was often in conflict with the goals of maximum freedom in international markets and the macropolicy objective of full employment.

9. Prior to World War I, most countries set the value of their currency in terms of gold. When trade was conducted under the gold standard, the gold stock of a nation would fall if it imported more than it exported. The decline in the stock of gold would decrease the nation's money supply, causing prices to fall and making the nation's goods more competitive on the international market. In contrast, if a nation was a net exporter, its stock of gold would rise, causing inflation and making the nation's goods less competitive on the international market. However, alterations in the supply of gold often caused abrupt shifts in income and employment. The gold standard was abandoned in 1914.

10. The balance of payments accounts record the flow of payments between a country and other countries. Transactions (for example, imports) that supply a nation's currency to the foreign exchange market are recorded as debit items. Transactions (for example, exports) that generate a demand for the nation's currency on the foreign exchange market are recorded as credit items.

11. In aggregate, the balance of payment accounts must balance since the accounts are kept according to the principles of double-entry bookkeeping. Thus, (a) the current acount balance plus (b) the capital account balance plus (c) the official reserve account balance must equal zero. However, the individual components of the accounts need not balance. A deficit in one area implies an offsetting surplus in other areas.

12. Under a pure flexible rate system, there will not be any official reserve account transaction. Under these circumstances, a current account deficit implies a capital account surplus (and vice versa). Interestingly, an economy offering attractive investment opportunities to foreigners will tend to run a capital account surplus, which also implies a current account deficit under a flexible rate system.

13. Since 1973, most countries have operated under a managed flexible rate system. It is a managed system because the major industrial nations have used their official reserve balances in an effort to moderate swings in exchange rates. Nevertheless, market forces now play the major role in the determination of exchange rates among the major industrial nations. Given the severe shocks that international markets have suffered since it was instituted in 1973, the current system appears to be working reasonably well.

THE ECONOMIC WAY
OF THINKING—
**DISCUSSION
QUESTIONS**

1. During the early 1980s, the United States shifted toward a more restrictive monetary policy that sharply decelerated the domestic inflation rate. Simultaneously, the federal government was running a large budget deficit. Explain how this policy mix influences the value of the dollar in the exchange rate market.

2. How do flexible exchange rates bring about balance in the exchange rate market? Do flexible exchange rates lead to a balance between exports and imports? Do you think the United States should continue to follow a policy of flexible exchange rates? Why or why not?

3. "If a current account deficit means that we are getting more items from abroad than we are giving to foreigners, why is it considered a bad thing?" Comment.

4. Suppose the exchange rate between the United States and Mexico freely fluctuated in the open market. Indicate which of the following would cause the dollar to appreciate (or depreciate) relative to the peso.

   (a) An increase in the quantity of drilling equipment purchased in the United States by Pemex, the Mexican oil company, as a result of a Mexican oil discovery.

   (b) An increase in the U.S. purchase of crude oil from Mexico as a result of the development of Mexican oil fields.

   (c) Higher interest rates in Mexico, inducing U.S. citizens to move their financial investments from U.S. to Mexican banks.

   (d) Lower interest rates in the United States, inducing Mexican investors to borrow dollars and then exchange them for pesos.

   (e) Inflation in the United States and stable prices in Mexico.

   (f) Ten percent inflation in both the United States and Mexico.

   (g) An economic boom in Mexico, inducing Mexicans to buy more U.S.-made automobiles, trucks, electric appliances, and television sets.

   (h) Attractive investment opportunities, inducing U.S. investors to buy stock in Mexican firms.

5. The chart below indicates the actual newpaper quotation of the 1986 exchange rate of various currencies:

	U.S. Dollar Equivalent	
	May 1	May 2
British pound	1.526	1.523
French franc	.1419	.1420

   On May 2, did the dollar appreciate or depreciate against the British pound? How did it fare against the French franc?

6. **What's Wrong with This Way of Thinking?**
   "The government can change from fixed to flexible exchange rates, but we will continue to run a balance of payments deficit because foreign goods, produced with cheap labor, are simply cheaper than goods produced in the United States."

7. "A nation cannot continue to run a deficit on current account. A healthy growing economy will not persistently expand its indebtedness to foreigners. Eventually, the trade deficits will lead to national bankruptcy." Evaluate this view.

Development is not purely an economic phenomenon. Ultimately it must encompass more than the material and financial side of people's lives. Development should therefore be perceived as a multidimensional process involving the reorganization and reorientation of entire economic and social systems.[2]

MICHAEL P. TODARO

- How do economists differentiate between developed and less developed countries?

- How wide is the economic gap between rich and poor nations?

- Are economic growth and development the same thing?

- Why do some nations grow while others stagnate? What are the major obstacles that retard economic progress?

- Is the economic gap between rich and poor nations narrowing or widening?

32 ECONOMIC DEVELOPMENT AND THE GROWTH OF INCOME[1]

Throughout history, economic growth and income levels substantially greater than those required for survival have been rare. In the battle with Nature for survival, human beings have usually had to struggle and toil merely to eke out a minimal living. The wheels of progress have moved forward slowly. Economic growth and the rising standard of living taken for granted by much of the Western world did not exist for extended periods of recorded history and still do not exist for many non-Western countries. For example, Phelps Brown showed that the real income of English building trade workers was virtually unchanged between 1215 and 1798, a period of nearly six centuries. The living conditions of peasants in such countries as India and Pakistan are not much different from those of their ancestors 1000 years ago.

Against this background of poverty and stagnation, the economic record of the Western world during the last 250 years is astounding. In 1750, people all over the world struggled 50, 60, and 70 hours per week to obtain the basic necessities of life—food, clothing, and shelter. Manual labor was the major source of energy. Animals provided the means of transportation. Tools and machines were primitive by today's standards.

In the last two centuries, petroleum, electricity, and nuclear power have replaced human and animal power as the major sources of energy. Automobiles, airplanes, and trains are now the major means of transportation. Subsistence levels of food, shelter, and clothing are taken for granted, and the typical Western family worries instead about financing summer vacations, obtaining video cassette recorders, and providing for the children's college educations. For the first time in history, economic growth is such that subsistence-level living standards have been far surpassed in many parts of the world.

DEVELOPED AND LESS DEVELOPED COUNTRIES

Less Developed Countries: Low income countries characterized by rapid population growth, an agriculture-household sector that dominates the economy, illiteracy, extreme poverty, and a high degree of inequality.

Like the rich nations, the poor countries of the world differ from each other in many respects. Some have grown rapidly in recent years; others have continued to stagnate. War and political upheaval have contributed to the poverty of some; cultural and tribal stability dominate others. There is no sharp division between developed and **less developed countries.** If per capita income were used to distinguish between the two, there would be no significant difference between the income level of the wealthiest less developed country and that of the poorest developed nation. In many respects, the division between the developed and less developed countries is arbitrary. However, there is a set of characteristics generally shared by the less developed countries.

---

[1]The authors would like to thank James Cobbe for his helpful suggestions that contributed to the development of this chapter.

[2]Michael P. Todaro, *Economics for a Developing World* (London: Longman, 1977), p. 87.

1. *The Most Obvious Characteristic of Less Developed Nations Is Low Per Capita Income.* Extreme poverty, hunger, and filth are a way of life throughout much of India, Pakistan, most of Asia, Africa, and much of Latin America. Exhibits 1 and 2 present the harsh statistics. In 1983, per capita *annual* income was $120 in Ethiopia, $130 in Bangladesh, and $260 in India. Approximately 2.3 billion people—45.4 percent of the world's population—lived in the 35 poorest countries with a 1983 annual income per person of less than $400. Another 22.7 percent of the world's population lived in countries where the per capita GNP was between $400 and $1,500 in 1983. Even though these poor countries (the two poorest groups of Exhibits 1 and 2) contained more than two thirds of the world's total population, they generated only 15.9 percent of the world's output. In contrast, 29 countries with a per capita GNP of $5,000 or more (the high-income countries) accounted for one fifth of the world's population in 1983, but they generated almost three fourths of the world's output. The low-income status of the poor countries of Exhibits 1 and 2 reflects the absence of economic development. By the same token, the standard of living of the wealthy nations is the fruit of past economic development.

2. *The Agriculture-Household Sector Dominates the Economy of Less Developed Nations.* Nearly two thirds of the labor force of the low-income countries of Asia, Africa, and South America is employed in agriculture. In contrast, 2 percent of the U.S. labor force is employed in this sector. The size of the household (nonmarket) sector in less developed countries is generally far greater than that in developed nations. Most households in less developed nations raise their own food, make much of their clothing, and construct the family shelter. The specialization and exchange that dominate developed economies are largely absent in less developed countries.

3. *Rapid Population Growth Generally Characterizes Less Developed Nations.* The population of the poor countries of Asia, Africa, and South America

---

EXHIBIT 1 • Annual Per Capita Output of Nations, 1983

Poorest Countries (Annual Output Less than $400)		Poor Countries (Annual Output $400 to $1500)		Middle-Income Countries (Annual Output $1500 to $5000)		High-Income Countries (Annual Output Greater than $5000)	
Selected Countries	Per Capita GNP, 1983	Selected Countries	Per Capita GNP, 1983	Selected Countries	Per Capita GNP, 1983	Selected Countries	Per Capita GNP, 1983
Ethiopia	$120	Bolivia	$ 510	Chile	$1,870	Hong Kong	$ 6,000
Bangladesh	130	Indonesia	560	Brazil	1,880	Italy	6,400
Zaire	170	Egypt	700	South Korea	2,010	United Kingdom	9,200
Uganda	220	Philippines	760	Argentina	2,070	Japan	10,120
India	260	Nigeria	770	Mexico	2,240	France	10,500
Haiti	300	Thailand	820	South Africa	2,490	West Germany	11,430
China	300	Peru	1,040	Yugoslavia	2,570	Australia	11,490
Ghana	310	Turkey	1,240	Greece	3,920	Canada	12,310
Pakistan	390	Columbia	1,430	Spain	4,780	United States	14,110

Source: The World Bank, *World Development Report, 1986* (Table 1).

EXHIBIT 2 • World Population and Output in 1983 by Income Level of Countries

The 72 countries with per capita annual output of less than $1,500 accounted for 68.1 percent of the world's population but only 15.9 percent of the world GNP in 1983. In contrast, the 20 percent of the world's population living in countries with a per capita output of more than $5,000 produced 74.9 percent of the world GNP in 1983.

Category	Percent of World's Population	Percent of World GNP
35 Poorest Countries (Per capita output less than $400)	45.4	4.5
37 Poor Countries (Per capita output $400 to $1,500)	22.7	11.4
25 Middle-Income Countries (Per capita output $1,500 to $5,000)	11.9	9.2
29 High-Income Countries (Per capita output greater than $5,000)	20.0	74.9

Source: The World Bank, *World Development Report, 1986* (Table 1). The GNP figures were converted to U.S. dollars using the exchange rate method.

---

has been expanding at an average annual rate of approximately 2.5 percent. The population of these nations doubles every 25 or 30 years. In contrast, the population growth of the developed nations of Europe and North America is generally less than 1 percent each year.

4. *Income Is Usually More Unequally Distributed in Less Developed Countries.* Not only is the average income low in less developed countries, but most of the available income is allocated to the wealthy. The top 10 percent of all income recipients usually receives a larger proportion of the aggregate income in less developed countries than in developed nations. Often, this reflects the existence of a two-sector economy—a trade and financial sector linked to the developed world and an agriculture-household sector bound by tradition. The incomes of persons employed in the trade and financial sectors may be comparable to those of individuals in developed nations, but most of the population belong to the dominant agriculture-household sector and languish in poverty.

5. *Inadequate Health Care, Poor Educational Facilities, and Illiteracy Are Widespread in Less Developed Nations.* While nearly all school-age children attend primary school in North America and the European nations, less than half do so in many less developed countries. One third or less of the adult population is literate in such countries as Bangladesh, Ethiopia, Pakistan, and India. Physicians and hospitals are unavailable in many parts of the less developed world. Most of the resources of these nations are allocated to the provision of basic necessities—food and shelter. Health care and education are luxuries most people cannot afford.

HOW WIDE IS THE ECONOMIC GAP BETWEEN THE DEVELOPED AND LESS DEVELOPED NATIONS?

Most countries of the continents of Asia, Africa, and South America possess the characteristics of less developed nations. Per capita income is low. The agriculture-household sector dominates the economy. Rapid population growth, economic inequality, and poverty abound. On the other hand, these indicators of underdevelopment are generally absent from North America, Europe, Oceania, Japan, and the Soviet Union. Although there are a few exceptions, these areas by and large comprise the developed nations of the world.

How wide is the economic gap between the developed and less developed world? This is a difficult question to answer. The gross national product per capita is a measure of the goods and services available to individuals, but how can we draw meaningful comparisons when Mexico's GNP is measured in pesos, Brazil's GNP is measured in cruzeiros, Australia's GNP is measured in pounds, and so on?

Exchange Rate Conversion Method: Method that uses the foreign exchange rate value of a nation's currency to convert that nation's GNP to another monetary unit, such as the U.S. dollar.

The simplest method used to deal with this problem is the **exchange rate conversion method.** This method uses the value of each nation's currency in the exchange rate market to convert the nation's GNP to a common currency, such as the U.S. dollar. For example, if the British pound is worth 1.5 times as much as the U.S. dollar *in the foreign exchange market,* then the GNP of the United Kingdom is converted to dollars by multiplying the British GNP *in pounds* by 1.5. Similarly, the exchange rate value of the currency of other nations is used to convert their GNP to dollars. Since the procedure is relatively simple, most international income comparisons are based on this technique.

According to the exchange rate conversion method, the per capita GNP of the market economies of North America, Europe, Oceania, and Japan was $11,060 in 1983, compared to only $850 for the less developed countries of the world. This exchange rate conversion income comparison implies that the per capita GNP of developed nations was approximately 13 times the comparable figure for less developed countries in 1983.

Although the exchange rate conversion method is simple and straightforward, it may be a misleading indicator of differences in living standards among nations. The exchange rate of a currency reflects the relative purchasing power of the currency for goods traded in international markets. However, it may not be a reliable indicator of the relative purchasing power of the currency for goods and services not exchanged in international markets. For example, merely because a pound purchases 1.5 dollars in the foreign exchange market, it does not follow that it will purchase 1.5 times as much housing, education, recreation, childcare service, and similar items in the United Kingdom as a dollar will purchase in the United States. Since many items are not traded in international markets, the *domestic* purchasing power of a currency may be either more or less than its purchasing power in the exchange market.

The quality of comparative international income data would be greatly improved if the conversion ratio between currencies were expressed in terms of the ability of the currencies to purchase a typical bundle of goods and services in the country of their origin. The United Nations International Comparison Project study begun in 1968 by the United Nations

Purchasing Power Parity Method: Method for determining the relative purchasing power of different currencies by comparing the amount of each currency required to purchase a typical bundle of goods and services in domestic markets. This information is then used to convert the GNP of each nation to a common monetary unit.

Statistical Office, the University of Pennsylvania, and the World Bank, has devised such a purchasing power index for several currencies. The **purchasing power parity method** compares the costs of purchasing a typical bundle of goods and services in the domestic markets for various nations. Each category in the bundle is weighted according to its contribution to GNP. The cost of purchasing the typical bundle in each nation is then compared to the dollar cost of purchasing the same bundle in the United States. Once the purchasing power of each nation's currency (in terms of the typical bundle) is determined, this information can be used to convert the GNP of each country to a common monetary unit (for example, the U.S. dollar).

The purchasing power parity method has been used to compare the output of 34 developed and less developed countries. In general, income comparisons based on the purchasing power parity method indicate that the exchange rate conversion method overstates the income of developed nations relative to less developed countries. As Exhibit 3 illustrates, the per capita GNP of developed countries is estimated to be five times the per capita GNP of less developed countries when the purchasing power parity method was used, compared to 13 times for estimates based on the exchange rate conversion method.

Estimates based on the purchasing power of currencies in the country of their origin are almost certainly a more accurate indicator of international differences in per capita GNP than the more widely circulated estimates based on exchange rate conversions. Nevertheless, even the purchasing power parity method indicates the economic gap between developed and less developed countries is extremely large.

EXHIBIT 3   •   **Measuring the Economic Gap Between Developed and Less Developed Countries**

If the per capita GNP of industrial, market-economy nations is estimated by the exchange rate conversion method, it is 13 times greater than that of less developed countries. However, if the more accurate purchasing power parity procedure is used, the gap narrows, indicating that the GNP per capita is approximately 5 times greater for industrial nations than for less developed countries.

	Per Capita GNP	
	Industrial Countries[a]	Less Developed Countries[b]
Exchange rate method		
1983 U.S. dollars	$11,060	$850
1983 (industrial countries = 100)	100	8
Purchasing power parity method		
1980 (industrial countries = 100)	100	20

[a]North America, Europe, Japan, and Oceania. The Soviet Union and other centrally planned economies of Eastern Europe are not included in these data.
[b]Asia, Africa, South America, and Central America.

Source: The World Bank, *World Development Report, 1981 and 1986.*

ARE GROWTH AND DEVELOPMENT THE SAME THING?

During the two decades following World War II, economists failed to draw a clear distinction between growth and development. Development was deemed present if a country was able to generate and sustain a significant rate of increase in GNP—for example, 5 percent or more. In recent years, it has become increasingly popular to define growth in strictly positive terms—the rate of change in GNP. Development is now widely perceived as a normative concept, encompassing not only growth but also distributional and structural changes that imply an improvement in the standard of living for most of the populace.

It is important to understand the distinction between two types of growth—extensive and intensive growth. **Extensive economic growth** is present when the output of a nation, as measured by real GNP, for example, is expanding. A nation may experience extensive growth even though the output per person is not rising. Since economists are interested primarily in the well-being of individuals, they generally focus on **intensive economic growth,** the expansion in the availability of goods and services per person. Per capita real output (or income) is a measure of intensive economic growth. If a society's production of goods and services is expanding more rapidly than is its population, per capita real income will rise. On average, the economic well-being of people will improve, reflecting the intensive economic growth. Conversely, if the population of the nation is expanding more rapidly than is production, per capita real income will decline. Economic regression, the opposite of intensive growth, will be the result.

Growth focuses on changes in output. The "new" view of economic development is concerned with the structure and division of the fruits of growth. In this normative view, development requires not only growth in output per person but also an improvement in the availability of consumption goods for a wide spectrum of the populace, including those people in the bottom half of the income distribution. Some economists adhere to the **trickle-down theory**—the view that intensive growth will, with time, lead to an improvement in the standard of living for all major segments of the society. They argue that the enlarged output and higher level of income will eventually "trickle down," bringing improvements in economic opportunity, education, and living standards to the masses.

The trickle-down theory is not without critics. Opponents of the theory argue that growth does not necessarily lead to an improvement in the status of those in the lower half of the economic spectrum. They refer to the experience of such countries as Brazil as evidence supporting their position. Since the mid-1960s, Brazil has achieved substantial economic growth. However, the distribution of income in Brazil is highly skewed. More than 60 percent of the aggregate income is allocated to the wealthiest 20 percent of the population. By way of comparison, the wealthiest one fifth of the population receives between 40 and 45 percent of the aggregate income in the developed countries of Europe and North America. Many development economists charge that the rapid growth of Brazil has failed to significantly

Extensive Economic Growth: An expansion in the total output of goods and services, regardless of whether or not output per capita increases.

Intensive Economic Growth: An increase in output per person. When intensive economic growth is present, output is growing more rapidly than population.

Trickle-Down Theory: The theory that intensive economic growth will eventually lead to an improvement in the standard of living of the entire society, even for persons at the bottom of the economic spectrum.

alter the economic status of the overwhelming majority of its citizens. Perhaps this situation will change in the future, but the Brazilian experience has shaken the faith of many economists in the trickle-down theory.

Even though economic growth and development can be distinguished, it is obvious that growth is necessary for development. Without sustained economic growth, continuous improvement in the economic opportunities and status of a nation's populace, including those at the bottom of the economic spectrum, will be impossible.

SOURCES OF ECONOMIC GROWTH

Why do some countries grow rapidly while others stagnate? Lay persons often argue that natural resources are the key ingredient of economic growth. Of course, other things constant, countries with abundant natural resources do have an advantage. It is clear, though, that natural resources are neither a necessary nor sufficient condition for economic growth. Japan has few natural resources and imports almost all of its industrial energy supply. Similarly, Hong Kong has practically no raw materials, very little fertile soil, and no domestic sources of energy. Yet, the growth records of these two countries are envied throughout the world. In contrast, such resource-rich nations as Ghana, Kenya, and Bolivia are poor and experiencing only slow growth. Physical resources are not the key to economic progress.

If natural resources are not the key to growth, what is? Thus far, economists have been unable to construct a general theory of growth and development. Therefore, we cannot fully determine the essential ingredients necessary for the transition from stagnation to economic progress and development. Economics is nevertheless capable of pinpointing certain important determinants. Three factors stand out. Clearly, (a) investment in physical and human capital, (b) technological advances, and (c) improvement in economic organization play important roles in the growth process.

INVESTMENT IN PHYSICAL AND HUMAN CAPITAL

Machines can have a substantial impact on a person's ability to produce. Even Robinson Crusoe on an uninhabited island can catch far more fish with a net than he can with his hands. Farmers working with modern tractors and plows can cultivate many more acres than their great-grandfathers, who probably worked with hoes. Similarly, education and training that improve the knowledge and skills of workers can vastly improve their productivity. For example, a cabinetmaker, skilled by years of training and experience, can build cabinets far more rapidly and efficiently than can a lay person. Both physical capital (machines) and human capital (knowledge and skills) expand the productive capacity of a worker.

The acquisition of physical and human capital, though, involves an opportunity cost. When time and effort are expended on the production of machines or the development of skills, fewer resources are available for current production. There are no free lunches. The cost of additions to a nation's stock of physical and human capital is a reduction in current consumption, either domestically or abroad if the investment is financed by borrowing.

As we discussed in Chapter 2, nations that allocate a larger share of their resources to investment expand their productive base more rapidly. Stated another way, a nation's investment rate affects the growth rate of the nation's resource base and thereby affects its rate of economic growth. Other things constant, nations that invest more in human and physical capital tend to grow more rapidly.

TECHNOLOGICAL PROGRESS

Technological Advancement: The introduction of new techniques or methods of production that enable a greater output per unit of input.

Technological improvement makes it possible to generate additional output with the same amount of resources. **Technological advancement**—the adoption of new techniques or methods of production—enables workers to produce goods at a fraction of their former cost. Less human and physical capital per unit of output is required.

Technological advancement is brought about by capital formation and research investments. Modern technological breakthroughs are generally the result of systematic investments in research and development. Thus, advancements in science and technology, like other improvements requiring investment expenditures, necessitate the sacrifice of current consumption.

When analyzing the phenomenal growth of Western nations during the nineteenth century, economic historians often point to dramatic technological advancements as the major source of economic progress. This view certainly has some merit. From a technological viewpoint, a person living in 1750 would probably have felt more at home in the world at the time of Christ than in today's society. During the last 250 years, technology has radically altered our way of life. The substitution of power-driven machines for human labor, the development of new sources of energy (for example, the steam engine, the internal combustion engine, hydroelectric power, and nuclear power), and developments in transportation and communications are the foundation of modern society. Without them, the growth and development of the last 250 years would have been impossible.

Of course, technological progress did not originate in the middle of the eighteenth century. The development of basic tools, the control of fire, the domestication of animals, and the development of bronze, pottery, and even iron, all of which represent fundamental technological progress, were accomplished before 1750. It is the rapidity and depth of recent technological progress that account for its uniqueness.

Invention: The discovery of a new product or process, often facilitated by the knowledge of engineering and scientific relationships.

Innovation: The successful introduction and adoption of a new product or process; the economic application of inventions.

Obviously, technological progress encompasses **invention,** the discovery of new products or processes. But, it also includes **innovation,** the practical and effective adoption of new techniques. It is sometimes easy to overlook the significance of innovation, but it is crucial to economic development. Many innovators were not involved in the discovery of the products for which they are now famous. Henry Ford played a minor role in the discovery and development of the automobile. His contribution was an innovative one—the adoption of mass production techniques, which facilitated the low-cost production of reliable automobiles. J. C. Penney played an important role in American economic progress, not because he invented anything, but because he effectively introduced the department store. Inventions are important, but without innovators, inventions are merely ideas waiting to be exploited.

Although technological advancement has played an important role in the promotion of material progress, it is clearly not a sufficient condition for sustained economic growth. Modern technology is available to all, including the less developed nations. If technology were the only requirement for economic growth, the less developed nations would be growing rapidly.

Before modern technology can set growth in motion, the work force of a nation must be sufficiently knowledgeable to operate and maintain complex machines. Innovative entrepreneurs who are capable of adapting technology to the needs (and price structure) of a nation must be available and have access to resources. This means that capital investment and savings are required. Among less developed nations, these conditions generally do not exist. Poverty and primitive methods of production thus survive in the modern world despite the availability of advanced technology.

EFFICIENT ECONOMIC ORGANIZATION

Allocative Inefficiency: The use of an uneconomical combination of resources to produce goods and services that are not intensely desired relative to their opportunity cost.

The efficiency with which the economic activity of a country is organized will influence the country's output and growth rate. If the economic organization of a nation encourages waste and fails to reward the creation of wealth, economic growth will be stunted. Regardless of the form of economic organization present, certain basic conditions must be met if waste and inefficiency are to be avoided. The incentive structure must encourage production of goods and services most desired by people. **Allocative inefficiency** results when a nation's resources are used to produce the wrong products. For example, waste results when a nation whose people intensely desire more food and better housing, uses valuable resources to produce unwanted national monuments and luxurious vacations for political leaders. In the same way, waste results when a nation ill-equipped to manufacture steel and automobiles insists on using resources that could be productive in other areas (for example, agriculture) to produce these prestige goods.

Efficient economic organization must also encourage producers to choose low opportunity cost methods of production. Regardless of whether an economy is centrally planned or market directed, efficient production requires that the marginal productive contribution of each resource reflect its opportunity cost. Waste results when producers are discouraged from the adoption of the least-cost resource combination. For example, if unfavorable tax treatment or interest rate controls discourage the use of capital, economic waste and higher production costs will result.

Infrastructure: The provision of a legal, monetary, educational, transportation, and communication structure necessary for the efficient operation of an exchange economy.

The supply of public goods and goods that generate substantial external benefits is also an important ingredient of efficient economic organization. Broadly speaking, this issue relates to the provision of an economic infrastructure. **Infrastructure** is a term used by economists to describe the economy's legal, monetary, educational, transportation, and communication structure. The provision of an adequate infrastructure involves several things, including a legal system that clearly defines property rights and a monetary system that encourages the wise use of resources across time periods (i.e., something approximating price stability). It also involves the provision of an educational system that encourages children of all social classes to develop their skills and abilities.

Finally, an efficient economy requires the development of highways, telephones, and power sources necessary for the realization of gains from specialization, division of labor, and mass production methods—the "heart and soul" of a modern exchange system. These networks often are provided by government, but each has also been provided privately since users can be made to pay for the benefits they receive through tolls and user charges. However they are provided, a sound infrastructure is an integral part of efficient economic organization.

WHY POOR NATIONS REMAIN POOR: SOURCES OF ECONOMIC STAGNATION

During the last 200 years, sustained growth has taken place throughout most of Europe, North America, and Oceania. More recently, living standards have improved substantially in Japan, the Soviet Union, and several small countries in Asia. At the same time, poverty, subsistence-level living standards, and malnutrition have persisted throughout much of Asia, Africa, South America, and Central America. In these places, most people continue to live and die in a world of poverty, malnutrition, and disease, just as they have done for thousands of years.

Why have industrialization and economic growth bypassed these people? There is no single, comprehensive answer to this question. However, we can point to several obstacles to economic growth.

Obstacle 1: A Low Savings Rate Contributes to the Vicious Circle of Underdevelopment. Capital formation is an important potential stimulus to economic growth. Investment, though, necessitates saving. Resources used to enhance a nation's future productive capacity are unavailable for the production of food, shelter, and other necessities of life.

Exhibit 4 illustrates the dilemma faced by underdeveloped nations. They are caught in a **vicious circle of underdevelopment.**[3] Since living standards are barely above the subsistence level, these countries use most of their resources for the provision of current consumption goods, such as food, clothing, and housing. Little is left for investment. Nations that invest (and save) little grow slowly. Since most underdeveloped nations have a low savings (and therefore low investment) rate, their growth rate is slower than that of advanced nations that invest a larger share of their GNP.

Vicious Circle of Underdevelopment: A pattern of low income and low economic growth, which tends to perpetuate itself. Since the current consumption demands of poor nations are large in proportion to available income, the savings and investment rates of these nations are low. In turn, the low investment rate retards future growth, causing poor nations to remain poor.

[3]Ragnar Nurkse provides a clear statement of the vicious circle of underdevelopment:

In discussions of the problem of economic development, a phrase that crops up frequently is "the vicious circle of poverty."

A situation of this sort [the vicious circle of underdevelopment] relating to a country as a whole can be summed up in the trite proposition: "A country is poor because it is poor".... The supply of capital is governed by the ability and willingness to save; the demand for capital is governed by the incentives to invest.

On the supply side, there is the small capacity to save, resulting from the low level of real income....

On the demand side, the inducement to invest may be low because of the small buying power of the people, which is due to their small real income, which again is due to low productivity.

See Ragnar Nurkse, *Problems of Capital Formation in Underdeveloped Countries* (New York: Oxford University Press, 1953), pp. 4–5.

EXHIBIT 4 • The Vicious Circle of Underdevelopment

Since incomes are low in underdeveloped nations, savings and investment rates are also low. Low rates of investment retard the future growth of income. Thus, underdevelopment is self-perpetuating. The circle is complicated by the population bomb, which often explodes when a country begins to break out of the pattern.

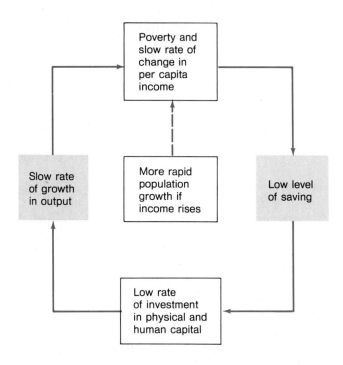

Real-world data are consistent with the vicious circle of underdevelopment. The saving rate in most countries of Africa and Southeast Asia is between 5 and 15 percent of GNP. In contrast, the saving rate for industrial nations is between 20 and 25 percent.[4] The low saving rate of underdeveloped nations undermines capital formation and thereby limits the economic growth of poor countries.

Obstacle 2: The Population Bomb May Explode as Soon as Growth Improves Living Standards. In 1798, Thomas Malthus argued that living standards would never climb much above subsistence level because an improvement in economic well-being would cause people to have more children. From this, any temporary improvement in economic welfare would cause the population to increase until per capita income returned to subsistence levels. Therefore, according to Malthus, economic growth would trigger a population explosion, which would eradicate the temporary gains associated with growth.

The experience of Europe and North America during the last 250 years is clearly inconsistent with the crude Malthusian theory. Recent historical data on income and population, however, have encouraged some development economists to reevaluate the relevance of Malthus's ideas. High rates of population growth do appear to retard economic growth in some coun-

---

[4]See the World Bank, *World Development Report, 1985* (Washington, D.C.: International Bank for Reconstruction and Development, 1985), Table 5, for detailed evidence that saving rates are positively linked to the income level of a nation.

tries. The rate of population growth in the poor countries of Asia, Africa, and South America is typically two or three times the rate in wealthy industrial nations. Poor countries would thus theoretically have to grow substantially more rapidly than industrial nations merely to maintain the same rate of growth of per capita income.

Rapid population growth in underdeveloped nations is also likely to increase the **dependency ratio,** the number of children and older persons in a society divided by the total population. Improvements in health associated with economic growth usually lead to a decline in the rate of infant mortality and an increase in the proportion of older people as a share of the total population. With more young children and elderly nonworkers, the burden imposed on the productive working-age population is compounded. The experiences of such countries as India, Bangladesh, Burma, and Egypt, all of which have a rapid rate of population expansion, suggest that the population bomb complicates the growth process.[5]

Obstacle 3: Political Instability May Discourage Investment and Retard Growth. Suppose in a certain country, a political revolution resulting in government expropriation of land holdings, buildings, and other business assets seemed imminent. Or, suppose you feared the rise of a new regime that would impose punitive taxes on interest income, profits, and/or capital assets. Would you want to invest your savings in such a country? Most people would not.

As a rule of thumb, the more securely present and future property rights are defined, the more capital formation there will be. In contrast, insecurely defined property rights and a potentially volatile political climate will repel capital investment and retard economic growth.

Dependency Ratio: The number of children (under a specific age—14, for example) and the number of the elderly (age 65 and over) living in a country, divided by the total population. An increasing ratio indicates that a larger burden is being placed on the productive-age work force.

---

[5]The dependency ratio for a typical group of less developed and developed countries is presented below.

	Dependency Ratio, 1983 (Percentage of Population under the Age of 14 or over the Age of 64)
Less developed countries	
Bangladesh	44
India	43
Burma	45
Egypt	43
Developed countries	
United States	33
Canada	32
Japan	32
United Kingdom	35
West Germany	31

Although the productive contribution and consumption burden of children and the elderly differ among countries, it is clear that the prime-working-age population of the developed nations has fewer nonproducers to support than that of the less developed nations. See the World Bank, *World Development Report, 1985,* Table 21, for more extensive data.

Unfortunately, the political climate of many underdeveloped nations is highly unstable. Prejudice and injustice, a highly unequal distribution of wealth, and a history of political favoritism to a ruling class make political upheaval a distinct possibility. Wise investors, both domestic and foreign, avoid investment in real assets under these conditions. Those who do undertake business ventures find it advantageous to seek favors (and assurances) from the military and ruling classes. This may aggravate the situation in the long-run. Unquestionably, several Latin American countries have suffered because of their political instability. Nationalization and the threat of expropriation have discouraged both domestic and foreign investment. Continued poverty and economic stagnation have been the results.

Again, many underdeveloped nations are caught in a vicious cycle. The level of poverty is such that many are willing to support political revolution in the hope that it will better their lot. As the possibility of political upheaval increases, however, the investment necessary to improve the economic welfare of the citizenry comes to a standstill. In turn, the low rate of investment and accompanying economic stagnation make political revolution still more likely. Many underdeveloped nations will be unable to improve their economic conditions until they solve the problem of political instability.

Obstacle 4: Public Policy in Many Less Developed Countries Distorts Prices and Promotes Economic Inefficiency. Prices direct resources. If resources are going to be allocated efficiently, the relative prices of products and factors must reflect their relative scarcity and true value. Inappropriate pricing signals are a potential source of inefficiency for market and centrally planned economies alike—and for developed and less developed countries.

Unfortunately, public policy in less developed countries has often distorted pricing signals and directed resources away from areas of high productivity. For example, several less developed nations (particularly African countries) have adopted price controls on agricultural commodities that have depressed agricultural prices below world market levels, made farming unprofitable, and driven investment from agriculture. While the intent was to help urban consumers, the result was a decline in agricultural output and widespread food shortages. Similarly, high marginal tax rates have often reduced the incentive to earn and have driven the most productive people away from less developed nations. (See "Do High Marginal Tax Rates Retard the Economic Growth of Less Developed Countries?") Strict business and occupational licensing, often administered for political purposes, has been a source of inefficiency, protected markets, and high costs in many less developed countries. Official exchange rates have often been set so high that they have eliminated the competitiveness of a nation's export goods and necessitated the adoption of import restrictions. Interest rate controls have often discouraged savings and driven financial capital abroad.

Less developed nations do not, of course, have a monopoly on foolish economic practices. Developed nations do silly things, too. However, the effects of policies that distort prices, impede business activity, and discourage production are more pronounced in the less developed world. Here, the results are sometimes catastrophic.

Since price distortions emanate from a variety of sources, it is not easy to quantify their effects. Economists are just now beginning to undertake research in this area. To date, the most comprehensive study of price distortions on the growth of less developed countries has been undertaken by the World Bank.[6] The World Bank study focused on price distortions during the 1970s arising from foreign exchange controls, trade restrictions, wage, price, and interest rate controls, and inflation. A price distortion index for 31 less developed countries was derived. In turn, the price distortion index was related to economic growth. Exhibit 5 summarizes the findings of the World Bank study. Nine "low-distortion," less developed countries were

---

[6]The World Bank, *World Development Report: 1983*, Chapter 6.

APPLICATIONS IN ECONOMICS

Do High Marginal Tax Rates Retard the Economic Growth of Less Developed Countries?[7]

Less developed countries of Asia, Africa, and South America have often levied high tax rates to raise revenue to finance government-directed projects. When high tax rates take a large share of the fruits generated by productive activities, the incentive of individuals to work and undertake business projects is reduced. High tax rates may also drive a nation's most productive citizens to other countries where taxes are lower. They also discourage foreigners from financing domestic investment projects. In short, economic theory indicates that high marginal tax rates will retard productive activity, capital formation, and economic growth.

To date, the most detailed study of the impact of high marginal tax rates on the economic growth of less developed countries has been conducted by Alvin Rabushka of Stanford University. Rabushka undertook the tedious task of reconstructing the 1960–1982 tax structure for 54 less developed countries for which data could be obtained. He found that some countries levied very high marginal tax rates, which took effect only at very high income thresholds. Oth-

ers levied high marginal rates on even modest levels of income. A few countries imposed only low or medium tax rates.

Rabushka used the tax structure data to classify each country as a low, medium, or high tax rate nation. Exhibit 6 presents Rabushka's data on tax rates and economic growth for both low and high tax countries among the 54 less developed nations. The data show that lower tax rates were generally associated with more rapid rates of growth. The lowest tax country among the 54 less developed countries was Hong Kong, which levied a flat tax rate of 15 percent on all income above a modest level ($6,410 in 1983). Only one of the 54 countries, Singapore, which was also a low tax nation, was able to exceed the 7.0 annual increase in per capita income achieved by Hong Kong during the 1960–1982 period.

The average growth rate of per capita income for the eight countries classified as low tax was 3.7 percent annually. In contrast, economic growth was much slower in the 10 countries that levied top marginal tax rates ranging from 50 to 70 percent *on incomes of less than*

$10,000. Among the 10 high tax countries, only two (Pakistan and Turkey) were able to attain an annual growth rate in excess of 1.3 percent during the 1960–1982 period. The average growth rate of the 10 high tax countries was 0.7 percent, less than one fifth the average growth rate for the eight low tax countries.

Summarizing the findings of this study, Rabushka concluded:

> Good economic policy, including tax policy, fosters economic growth and rising prosperity. In particular, low marginal income tax rates, or high thresholds for medium- and high-rate tax schedules, appear consistent with higher growth rates. The key in any system of direct taxation is to maintain low tax rates or high (income) thresholds.[8]

---

[7]This feature is based on the work of Alvin Rabushka of Stanford University.

[8]Alvin Rabushka, "Taxation and Liberty in the Third World," paper presented to a conference on Taxation and Liberty held in Santa Fe, New Mexico, September 26–27, 1985.

APPLICATIONS IN ECONOMICS
(continued)

EXHIBIT 5 • Marginal Tax Rates and Economic Growth

	Highest Marginal Tax Rate[a]	Income at which The Top Rate Takes Effect[a]	Growth Rate of Per Capita Income, 1960–1982
Low Tax Rate Countries			
Hong Kong	15	6410	7.0
Paraguay	30	31,250	3.7
Indonesia	35	50,000	4.2
Argentina	45	36,377	1.6
Ivory Coast	45	24,119	2.1
Solomon Islands	42	3699	1.3
Singapore	45	355,450	7.4
Venezuela	45	804,020	1.9
Average Growth Rate			**3.7**
High Tax Rate Countries[b]			
Bangledesh	60	7890	0.3
Chile	58	3671	0.6
Ghana	60	450	− 1.3
India	67.5	9434	1.3
Jamaica	57.5	4242	0.7
Pakistan	60	7407	2.8
St. Vincent	55	5555	0.6
Turkey	60	8929	3.4
Uganda	70	4277	− 1.1
Zaire	50	1986	− 0.3
Average Growth Rate			**0.7**

[a]Marginal tax rates in effect in the early 1980s. However, a similar pattern of marginal tax rates was also present during the 1960s and 1970s. The income threshold of each country was converted to U.S. dollars at the exchange rate as of December 31, 1983.
[b]Developing countries with top marginal tax rates of less than 50 percent were classified as low tax rate countries. Countries with top marginal tax rates of 50 percent or more that apply to income levels of less than $10,000 were classified as high tax rate countries.

Source: Alvin Rabushka, "Taxation and Liberty in The Third World." Paper presented to a conference on Taxation and Liberty held in Santa Fe, New Mexico, September 26–27, 1985.

able to achieve an average annual growth rate of 6.8 percent during the 1970s. In contrast, the average growth rate of the eleven "high-distortion" less developed countries was only 3.1 percent. In terms of *per capita* GNP, the growth rate of the low-distortion countries was 4.5 percent, compared to only 0.8 percent for the high-distortion countries. While the results of this study must be considered tentative at this point, they do imply that price distortions emanating from unwise public policy are a major obstacle to economic progress in many less developed countries.

EXHIBIT 6 • *Price Distortions and Economic Growth— The Result of the World Bank Study*

	Annual Growth of Real GNP 1970–1979	
	Aggregate	Per Capita
Low-distortion countries[a]	6.8	4.5
Median-distortion countries[b]	5.7	2.9
High-distortion countries[c]	3.1	0.8

[a]The low-distortion countries were: Malawi, Thailand, Cameroon, South Korea, Malaysia, Philippines, Tunisia, Kenya, Yugoslavia, and Columbia.
[b]The median-distortion countries were: Ethiopia, Indonesia, India, Sri Lanka, Brazil, Mexico, Ivory Coast, Egypt, and Turkey.
[c]The high-distortion countries were: Senegal, Pakistan, Jamaica, Uruguay, Bolivia, Peru, Argentina, Chile, Tanzania, Bangladesh, Nigeria, and Ghana.
Source: The World Bank, *The World Development Report, 1983*, Table 6.1 and Table 19.

LOOKING AHEAD

In the next chapter, we will use economic tools to analyze different economic systems. First, however, we will consider the diversity of economic records among the less developed countries.

APPLICATIONS IN ECONOMICS

Rich and Poor Nations—Are They Two Worlds Drifting Apart?

Since almost everyone was poor 250 years ago, people did not worry much about subsistence-level living standards and starvation in other countries. Of course, there were rich nations and poor nations, but the per capita income of the rich was seldom more than twice that of the poor.

During the eighteenth century, sustained economic growth took place throughout much of Europe and North America. By 1850, there was a virtual explosion of economic development, and it soon spread to Oceania, Russia, and Japan. Not only did industrial nations grow rapidly during this period, but the fruits of growth were also widely dispersed. The living standards of the well-off and those not so well-off increased substantially. Today, even poor people in North Amer-

ica, Europe, Oceania, and Japan are far better off than most citizens of an underdeveloped nation. The present level of affluence in the developed nations is unprecedented.

Economic growth over the last century has created an enormous gulf between developed and less developed countries. While the per capita income of wealthy nations in 1800 was approximately twice that of the poor countries, the average income of people in developed nations today is probably five times greater (see Exhibit 2). Some observers have argued that the world is comprised of growing industrial nations on the one hand and stagnating, less developed countries on the other. According to this view, the widening gap between rich and poor nations threatens to plunge the world into crisis. Evidence indi-

cates this view is an oversimplification. The less developed countries are not a monolithic block of humanity condemned forever to poverty and stagnation, but rather are nearly 100 nations with widely varying growth rates and records. Exhibit 7 highlights this diversity.

The less developed nations of the mid-1980s can be broken down into several groups. (Even with this analysis, there will of course be some oversimplification.) First, there are the densely populated nations that can be said to be barely winning the battle for economic survival. The per capita incomes of Ethiopia, Zaire, Uganda, Ghana, Bolivia, and Peru in fact declined during the 1973–1983 period. The growth of per capita income in several other very poor nations—including India, Somalia,

APPLICATIONS IN ECONOMICS:
(continued)

Guinea, Haiti, Afghanistan, Zimbabwe, and Jamaica—was insignificant or, in several cases, nonexistent during the 1970s and early 1980s. Approximately one quarter of the world's population lives in these very poor, stagnating nations. The twentieth century has passed them by. They eke out a subsistence-level living, while the economic development of their countries falls farther and farther behind that of the more developed nations.

Most of these nations face the obstacles to growth just described. Relentless poverty keeps their saving and investment rates very low.

EXHIBIT 7 • Wealth of Nations—Growth of Population and Income

Selected Countries	Per Capita GNP, 1983 (U.S. Dollars)	Percentage of World Population 1983	Average Annual Growth Rate 1973–1983 (Percent)		
			GNP	Population	GNP per Capita
Poor country (slow growth in per capita income)					
Ethiopia	120	0.8	2.3	2.7	−0.4
Zaire	170	0.6	−1.0	2.5	−3.5
Uganda	220	0.3	−2.1	2.8	−4.9
India	260	14.3	4.0	2.3	1.7
Ghana	310	0.3	−1.3	3.1	−4.4
Bolivia	510	0.1	1.5	2.6	−1.1
Peru	1,040	0.3	1.8	2.4	−0.6
Poor country (rapid growth in per capita income)					
China	300	19.9	6.0	1.5	4.5
Indonesia	560	3.0	7.0	2.3	4.7
Egypt	700	0.9	8.8	2.5	6.3
Thailand	820	1.0	6.9	2.3	4.6
Paraguay	1,410	0.1	8.2	2.5	5.7
Brazil	1,880	2.5	4.8	2.3	2.5
South Korea	2,010	0.8	7.3	1.6	5.7
Hong Kong	6,000	0.1	9.3	2.5	7.8
Singapore	6,620	0.1	8.2	1.3	6.9
Rich country					
United Kingdom	9,200	1.1	1.1	0.0	1.1
Japan	10,120	2.3	4.3	0.9	3.4
France	10,500	1.1	2.5	0.4	2.1
West Germany	11,430	1.2	2.1	−0.1	2.2
Australia	11,490	0.3	2.4	1.3	1.1
Canada	12,310	0.5	2.3	1.2	1.1
Sweden	12,470	0.2	1.3	0.2	1.1
United States	14,110	4.6	2.3	1.0	1.3

Source: The World Bank, *World Development Report, 1986.*

**APPLICATIONS IN ECONOMICS:
(continued)**

Political instability and insecure property rights discourage investment. High tax rates, trade restrictions, price controls, and government imposed red tape limit exchange. As a result of the population bomb, there are more and more people for the productive members of the population to feed. The future of these nations is bleak.

Fortunately, there is a second group of less developed countries that has achieved a very impressive growth record. As Exhibit 7 illustrates, during the 1973–1983 period, the growth of per capita income in China, Indonesia, Egypt, Thailand, South Korea, Hong Kong, and Singapore was substantially more rapid than the growth of the richer industrial nations. Even among this group, there is considerable diversity. Some are large, while others are small. Some (China and Indonesia) are rich with minerals, but others (Hong Kong, Singapore, and Egypt) have few natural resources.

Nevertheless, the high growth countries do have several things in common. During the last decade, property rights have been relatively secure in each of the less developed countries experiencing rapid growth, and as a result, each has attracted substantial foreign private investment. Interestingly, with the possible exception of Egypt, aid from foreign governments has played little part in the rapid growth of these nations. Finally, the high growth nations have moved toward an incentive structure that encourages farmers and business entrepreneurs to produce and earn income. Several of them (Hong Kong, Paraguay, Indonesia, and Singapore) are characterized by low marginal tax rates. Even in China, recent reforms have increased the ability of agricultural workers to capture the benefits of increases in production. The data of Exhibit 7, along with that of Exhibits 5 and 6, indicate that incentives matter—they affect the economic progress of nations.

Exhibit 7 also highlights differences between developed and less developed nations in the rate of population growth. Compared to industrial nations, the population growth of poor nations—both those achieving economic growth as well as those stagnating—has been quite rapid. While the population of the United States, Japan, and the developed nations of Europe has been expanding less than 1 percent an-nually, the population growth rate of the less developed countries has generally exceeded 2.5 percent annually.

For less developed countries, the rapid population growth is both a problem and an opportunity. It is a problem because population expansion is clearly running a tight race with economic growth. However, it also presents an opportunity. If less developed countries can reduce their birth rates, the initial impact on their growth rates is likely to be quite positive. A reduction in a nation's birth rate will result in a smaller number of dependents per working-age adult, which would stimulate the growth in per capita income. The rising real income would in turn generate additional savings and the investment necessary to sustain a more rapid rate of economic growth. Nations currently experiencing rapid growth in aggregate GNP can expect a period of very rapid growth in *per capita* income if they are able to reduce their birth rates. If this happens, less developed countries such as South Korea, Egypt, Thailand, Indonesia, Brazil, and perhaps China may well follow in the footsteps of Japan and by the turn of the century begin to move rapidly up the ladder of economic development.

CHAPTER SUMMARY

1. For the first time in history, economic growth is such that per capita income far surpasses the subsistence level in most of Europe, North America, Oceania, Japan, and the Soviet Union. Living conditions have been transformed for the one fifth of the world's population that reside in these regions.
2. In contrast, two thirds of the world's population maintain a bare subsistence level of income in countries with a per capita GNP of less than $1,500 per year. These countries generate only a little more than 15 percent of the world's GNP.

3. The major characteristics of less developed countries are (a) low per capita income, (b) a large agriculture-household sector, (c) rapid population growth, (d) inequality of income distribution, and (e) widespread illiteracy coupled with poor educational and health facilities.

4. Although there is no sharp dividing line between developed and less developed countries, the nations of North America, Europe (including the Soviet Union) and Oceania, as well as Japan, can be classified as developed countries. In contrast, most of the countries of Asia, Africa, South America, and Latin America exhibit the characteristics of underdevelopment.

5. When estimated by the exchange rate conversion method, the per capita GNP of developed countries is approximately 13 times the comparable figure for less developed countries. Since the exchange rate conversion method does not reflect the relative purchasing power of currencies for goods not traded in international markets, it may be a misleading indicator of living standards across countries. Income comparisons based on the purchasing power parity method indicate that the exchange rate conversion method overstates the relative income of developed nations. When measured by the purchasing power parity method, the per capita GNP of developed countries is estimated to be five times that of less developed countries.

6. Economic growth is a positive concept. Extensive growth is present when the real GNP of a nation expands. Intensive growth requires an increase in output per person. Economic development is a normative concept, encompassing distributional and structural factors as well as higher per capita income. Economic development implies an advance in the standard of living for a broad cross-section of a nation's population, including those people in the bottom half of the income distribution.

7. The availability of domestic natural resources is not the major determinant of growth. Countries such as Japan and Hong Kong have impressive growth rates without such resources, while many resource-rich nations continue to stagnate.

8. While economists have been unable to develop a general theory of economic growth and development, several important determinants of economic progress have been pinpointed. The following factors have played an important role in the economic progress of developed nations: (a) investment in physical and human capital, (b) development and dissemination of technologically improved production methods and products, and (c) efficient economic organization.

9. The major obstacles to economic development among poor nations of the world are (a) low savings and investment rates that reflect the vicious circle of underdevelopment; (b) rapid population growth; (c) political instability, which reduces the security of property rights and thereby retards investment; and (d) waste and inefficiency arising from public policy that distorts pricing signals and promotes economic inefficiency. Recent economic research indicates policies that depress agricultural prices, impose high marginal tax rates, limit international trade, and generate high rates of inflation retard the economic progress of less developed countries.

10. The economic growth record of less developed countries is mixed. Approximately one quarter of the world's inhabitants live in countries characterized by both extreme poverty and per capita real income that is either stagnating or falling. The rates of population growth in these countries are among the highest in the world. Their economic prospects are bleak. In contrast, the recent economic growth record in other less developed countries, including Egypt, Hong Kong, Indonesia, Singapore, South Korea, Thailand, Brazil, Paraguay, and more recently China, has been highly impressive. These countries may well duplicate the post-World War II "Japanese miracle" of economic development and join the developed world in the near future, particularly if they are able to reduce their rates of population growth.

THE ECONOMIC WAY OF THINKING— DISCUSSION QUESTIONS

1. Imagine you are an economic adviser to the president of Mexico. You have been asked to suggest policies to promote economic growth and a higher standard of living for the citizens of Mexico. Outline your suggestions and discuss why you believe they would be helpful.

2. Explain the logic of the vicious circle of underdevelopment. How can a poor nation break out of this circle?

3. It is often argued that the rich nations are getting richer and the poor are getting poorer. Is this view correct? Is it an oversimplification? Explain.

4. As the people of a nation become wealthier, do you think they will save a larger percentage of their income? Why or why not? As a nation becomes wealthier, do you think that length of the average workweek will decline? Why or why not? Does the experience of the United States support your answer? Explain.

5. The size of the population in some countries may partially reflect the desire of some people for additional security in the form of children to support them in their old age. Is this method of providing for one's retirement inferior to our system of compulsory social security? Why or why not?

6. Discuss the importance of the following as determinants of economic growth: (a) natural resources; (b) physical capital; (c) human capital; (d) technical knowledge; (e) attitudes of the work force; (f) size of the domestic market; (g) economic policy.

CHAPTER
FOCUS

- Are there basic economic principles that apply to all economies?

- What are the distinguishing characteristics of capitalism and socialism?

- How is the Soviet economy organized? How does the economic record of the Soviet Union compare with market-directed economies?

- What are the distinguishing characteristics of the Yugoslavian economy? In what ways is the economy of Yugoslavia unique?

- How rapidly has the Japanese economy grown since 1950? How does the economic organization of Japan differ from that of other market economies?

Since the activities of individuals in the use of the means of production are regulated, at any given time and place, through the institutions then and there prevailing, the precise manner in which society will use its means of production will depend upon and be determined by the character of its economic institutions.[1]

HOWARD R. BOWEN

33 COMPARATIVE ECONOMIC SYSTEMS

The institutions and organizations of an economy influence economic outcomes. In previous chapters, we have focused our analysis on the operation of mixed capitalistic economies such as those that exist in the United States, Canada, Australia, Japan, and throughout most of Western Europe. Market forces play an important role in the allocation of resources in these countries. Government action is also important. Private industries are often regulated by government. Government ownership and operation of utilities, transportation, communication, and educational facilities are not uncommon, even in Western countries. In addition, taxes and government subsidies are sometimes used to alter market outcomes. Throughout this book, we have used economic tools to help us understand the incentives and expected results of governmental policy that redirects market forces.

Today, nearly one third of the world's population lives in the Soviet Union, Eastern Europe, and China. The economies of these countries are organized along socialist lines. They are characterized by central planning and government ownership. Market-directed capitalism and centrally planned socialism are two systems of economic organization. There are, however, many variations of each. For example, the economic organization of Yugoslavia differs substantially from that of the Soviet Union. The Japanese economy differs somewhat from the capitalist organization of the United States and Western European countries. After examining the general institutional arrangements of socialist and capitalist systems, we will take a closer look at the economic organization and performance of three interesting economies—those of the Soviet Union, Yugoslavia, and Japan.

GENERAL APPLICATION OF BASIC ECONOMIC PRINCIPLES

All economic systems, despite their differences, face similar constraints. Scarcity of economic goods confronts individuals and nations alike with budgetary problems. No nation is able to produce as much as its citizenry would like to consume. Therefore, regardless of economic organization, choices must be made. The decision to satisfy one desire leaves many other desires unsatisfied. All economic systems are constrained by the bonds of scarcity.

Many other economic concepts that have been discussed throughout this book apply to all economic systems. Let us reconsider and summarize four of these basic ideas.

1. *Opportunity Cost.* An economy can be organized so that various goods can be provided without charge to the consumer, but economic organization cannot eliminate the opportunity costs associated with the provision of goods. The provision of additional medical services, even if distributed free, necessitates the use of resources that could have been used to produce other things. Similarly, if there is an expansion of the national defense sector, there must be a contraction of other sectors. Whenever productive resources have alternative uses, as they almost always

---

[1]Howard R. Bowen, *Toward Social Economy* (New York: Holt, 1946), p. 52.

do, the production of goods is costly, regardless of the form of economic organization.

2. *Diminishing Marginal Returns.* According to the law of diminishing marginal returns, increased application of a variable resource to a fixed factor of production, such as land or natural resources, will expand output by a smaller and smaller amount. Other things being equal, a nation cannot continue to expand output proportionally by simply using more labor with the current stock of physical capital. Neither can proportional increases in agricultural output be achieved by using more and more fertilizer with the current stock of land. The law of diminishing returns limits the ability of both the Soviet Union and the United States to expand output from a given resource base. It is applicable to all economies. With the passage of time, of course, capital formation (an expansion in the resource base) and improved technology will permit us to loosen the bonds of scarcity. Without capital formation and improvements in technical knowledge, growth of output in capitalist and socialist countries alike will be severely retarded.

3. *Comparative Advantage and Efficiency.* Total production is greatest when each good is generated by the low opportunity cost producer. The assignment of a productive task to a high opportunity cost producer is inefficient (that is, output will be below its potential level), regardless of whether the activity takes place in a capitalist or a socialist economy. No matter what the type of economic organization, the goal of efficient production can best be attained by heeding the principle of comparative advantage.

4. *The Law of Demand.* Reflecting the law of diminishing marginal utility, the law of demand states that the quantity demanded of a good will be inversely related to its price. The law of demand is just as relevant in socialist countries as it is in capitalist countries. High prices will discourage consumption in both. For example, if socialist planners set the price of color television sets quite high, few will be purchased. On the other hand, if planners set zero or extremely low prices for medical services or basic housing, the quantity demanded will be large—often greater than the supply. Waiting lines and other forms of nonprice rationing will result.

INCENTIVES MATTER

Changes in the structure of incentives alter human behavior in both capitalist and socialist countries. For example, at one time in the Soviet Union, the managers of glass plants were rewarded according to the tons of sheet glass produced. Not surprisingly, most plants produced sheet glass so thick that one could hardly see through it. The rules were changed so that the managers were rewarded according to the square meters of glass produced. The managers reacted in a predictable way. Under the new rules, Soviet firms produced very thin glass that easily broke. Incentives matter, even to the managers of Soviet firms.

In our analysis of alternative economic systems, we will focus on how economic organization affects people's motivations. Marxists often argue that communism will eventually alter basic human motivations. They believe that people will cease to respond in predictable, traditional ways to changes in personal costs and benefits. Perhaps this is so, but the experiences of the Soviet Union and other Communist countries have produced little evidence thus far to support this view. Therefore, until human nature

Socialism: A system of economic organization in which (a) the ownership and control of the basic means of production rest with the state and (b) resource allocation is determined by centralized planning rather than by market forces.

does change radically, an analysis based on the postulate that incentives do affect human decisions is most relevant. This is not to say that only economic considerations matter. Religious, cultural, and political factors can and do influence economic behavior. The economic approach does not deny their importance.

CONTRASTING CAPITALISM AND SOCIALISM

Joseph Schumpeter, the renowned Harvard economist, defined **socialism** as:

> ... an institutional pattern in which the control over means of production and over production itself is vested with a central authority—

OUTSTANDING ECONOMIST

Karl Marx (1818–1883)

Karl Marx was much more than an economist. He was a philosopher, a historian, a sociologist, a political scientist—and a revolutionary. More has been written about Marx than about any other economist. His most famous work, written with Friedrich Engels, is *The Communist Manifesto* (1848). The most complete statement of Marx's economic views is contained in his monumental *Das Kapital* (1867). Like other socialists, Marx advocated collective ownership and control of factories and other capital assets. But, unlike most socialist theoreticians, Marx advocated a mass working-class movement to overthrow capitalism and usher in a new socialist world order.

While studying at the University of Berlin, Marx developed an interest in the philosophy of Hegel that was to influence his own work considerably. Marxian theory applies Hegel's dialectical method of logic (thesis-antithesis-synthesis) to the observable, concrete phenomena of nature and society. To Marx, history was perceived of as a dynamic, dialectical process characterized by the struggle between social

classes. Each ruling class becomes outmoded with time, reactivating the struggle with other classes, causing political and economic crises, and eventually leading to the overthrow of the existing social structure and the creation of a new structure. Marx used the decline and fall of feudalism and the rise of capitalism and the bourgeoisie in Europe as an illustration of his theory. He stressed that the transition periods are sometimes violent, as in the case of the Enclosure Movement (in which English peasants were driven from the land) and the 1789 French Revolution.

Marx predicted that the capitalist ruling class, having fulfilled its economic functions, would eventually fall. He believed that capitalist growth would depress the rate of profit, causing severe economic crises (recessions and depressions) and forcing capitalists to oppress the working class further in order to maintain their own standard of living. This would not only encourage the workers to take power but would allow them to do so, because the capitalist class would grow weaker and weaker. Although Marx

or, as we may say, in which, as a matter of principle, the economic affairs of society belong to the public and not the private sphere.[2]

As Schumpeter's definition implies, capitalist and socialist economic organizations differ in two important respects—ownership of physical capital and resource allocation.

OWNERSHIP OF PHYSICAL CAPITAL— PRIVATE OR GOVERNMENT

Every economic system has a legal framework within which the rights of resource owners are defined. Practically all economic systems guarantee the rights of individuals to sell their own human capital—their labor—to the highest bidder. Earnings are derived from the sale of labor services in

---

[2]Joseph A. Schumpeter, *Capitalism, Socialism, and Democracy*, 3rd ed. (New York: Harper, 1950), p. 167.

---

believed the final victory of the industrial proletariat over the bourgeoisie was inevitable, he advocated revolutionary activity to accelerate the process and prepare the working class for its future role. Once the revolution became a reality, the ruling proletariat would "centralize all instruments of production in the hands of the state," which Marx believed would lead to a rapid increase in production and efficiency. But, Marx emphasized that workers must directly control not only the means of production but also the political process.

Marx argued that a workers' government would dismantle the existing state institutions and set up a new, fundamentally more democratic system, even if violence were required to do so. The successful revolution would thoroughly eliminate the bourgeoisie and culminate in a classless society, to which all individuals would voluntarily contribute "according to their abilities" and by which they would be rewarded "according to their needs."

Much of Marx's economic analysis attacked the ideas of the classical economists, led by Adam Smith,

whose defense of capitalism Marx found untenable. Smith believed that market coordination brought individual self-interest and economic progress into harmony; Marx viewed history, including the economic activities that shaped it, as characterized by conflict and class struggle. Smith believed that market exchange would release individuals from the oppression of government. Marx, on the other hand, believed capitalist economic activity to be the oppressor from which people should (and would) be freed. Harmony would exist only in the classless socialist state.

Marx's ideas began to attract worldwide attention in the late nineteenth century. The Social Democratic Party of Germany, a large political party, declared itself Marxist in 1875. Marx's ideas influenced Eugene V. Debs, the Socialist Party candidate for the U.S. presidency who received nearly 1 million votes in 1920. Today, many governments claim to be Marxist, but Marx's prescription for worker democracy is seldom actually followed.

World history since Marx's

time has validated some of his predictions and disproved others. Marx foresaw the advent of large corporations, the worldwide expansion of capitalism, and the rise of large working-class organizations. There have been, as Marx predicted, severe economic and political crises, such as the Great Depression of the 1930s, but contrary to his expectations, capitalism has always (so far) recovered. Marx believed that proletarian revolutions would take place first in the most developed countries. Thus, he surely would have been surprised to find that the major socialist revolutions have occurred in Russia and China—countries that at the time of their revolutions were underdeveloped and largely agricultural, with only a small industrial working class.

The postrevolutionary stage is a troublesome area for modern followers of Marx. Contrary to Marx's views, there is little evidence that the state will eventually wither away after capitalism is abolished. In fact, the all-powerful bureaucratic state is most imposing in the Soviet Union, the most highly developed of the existing communist societies.

capitalist and socialist societies alike. Under socialism, however, the rewards obtained from the use of physical capital (machines, buildings, and so on) in the production process accrue to the state. If the state actually owns the nonhuman productive resources, the earnings they generate go directly to the state. The state can also use taxation to gain at least partial control over earnings that would otherwise accrue to other owners of physical capital. In either case, under socialism, investment in physical capital reflects the views of those who control the state.

RESOURCE · ALLOCATION— MARKETS OR CENTRAL PLANNING

Capitalism: An economic system based on private ownership of productive resources and allocation of goods according to the signals provided by free markets.

Every economy must have a mechanism that coordinates the economic activity of microunits—business firms, individual resource owners, and consumers. The mechanism must solve such problems as the use of resources, the selective production of goods, and the distribution of income.

Under market-directed **capitalism,** economic activity is coordinated by contractual agreements between private parties who possess property rights to products and resources. There is no central planning mechanism. Market prices direct the actions of decentralized decision-makers. The forces of supply and demand push prices up or down in response to the decisions of individual buyers and sellers.

Under a socialist economic organization, resources are used and allocated in accordance with a centrally determined and administered scheme. Economic decisions, such as what and how much will be produced, what the relative proportions of investment and consumption will be, how resources will be used in production, and to whom the product will be distributed, are made by a central authority. The central plan may also include decisions on quantities of raw materials and inputs, techniques of production, prices, wages, locations of firms and industries, and the employment of labor. Socialist economic objectives generally reflect the preferences and value judgments of central planners. These objectives may or may not reflect the views of consumers.

Exhibit 1 summarizes the distinctive characteristics of capitalist and socialist economic organization. Capitalist economies are characterized by private ownership of physical assets and the use of market forces to coordinate the actions of buyers and sellers and thereby determine the allocation of goods and resources. Markets also coordinate employment and investment decisions and determine the distribution of income under capitalism. In contrast, government ownership (or control) of physical assets and the allocation of resources by central planning are the distinctive characteristics of socialist economic organization. Under socialism, the central planners also determine the patterns of employment and investment as well as the distribution of income.

CLASSIFYING REAL- WORLD ECONOMIES

In reality, all modern economies use some combination of capitalist and socialist economic organization. Exhibit 2 classifies several economies according to their reliance on (a) private ownership or public ownership of assets and (b) market allocation compared to central planning. Economies characterized by both private ownership and market allocation best fit pure capitalism. Hong Kong, Japan, the United States, and Canada fall at the capitalism end of the spectrum (the southwest corner of Exhibit 2). On the

EXHIBIT 1 • Contrasting Capitalism and Socialism

	Capitalism	Socialism
Property rights	Nonhuman resources are owned by private parties (that is, individuals or corporations)	Nonhuman resources are owned by the government
Allocation of goods and resources	Determined by market forces	Determined by centralized planning
Employment	Workers are self-employed or employed by private firms	Workers are employed by the government or government-controlled cooperatives
Investment	Undertaken by private parties seeking profits and higher future incomes	Undertaken by the government in accordance with the objectives of the planners
Income distribution	Determined by market forces that reward productivity and owner-ship of economic resources	Determined by central planners who may seek to promote equality or any other desired pattern of income distribution

other hand, economies characterized by government ownership of assets and central planning approximate pure socialism (the northeast corner of Exhibit 2). The Soviet Union, China, and most of the centrally planned economies of Eastern Europe fall into this category.

EXHIBIT 2 • The Classification of Economies

The Soviet Union and China most closely approximate pure social-ism, while Hong Kong, and the United States come closest to pure capitalism. The Yugoslavian econ-omy is characterized by govern-ment ownership coupled with substantial reliance on markets. Thus, it lies in the southeast corner of the diagram. On the other hand, Sweden has only modest govern-ment ownership, but government planning plays a major role in the allocation of resources. Therefore, it lies toward the northwest corner.

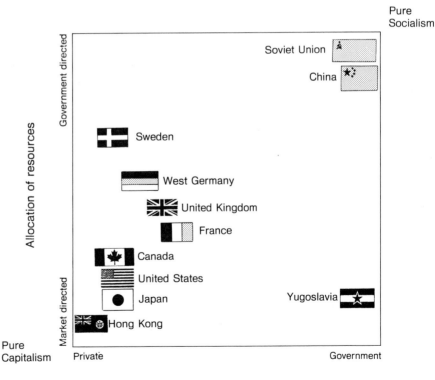

Yugoslavia and Sweden are interesting exceptions to the pure capitalism or pure socialism classifications. In Yugoslavia, most of the means of production are owned by the government. Market prices, though, are widely used to allocate goods and resources. Thus, the Yugoslavian economy is something of a hybrid. In Sweden, most physical assets are owned by private individuals and corporations. Nevertheless, the government uses taxes, subsidies, and regulatory powers to shape the allocation of resources. More than half of the national income of Sweden is channelled through government, a significantly larger proportion than for France, West Germany, or the United Kingdom, for example. The Swedish economy, too, is something of a cross between capitalism and socialism.

THE SOVIET ECONOMY

Command Economy: An authoritarian socialist economy characterized by centralized planning and detailed directives to productive units. Individual enterprises have little discretionary decision-making power.

The Soviet Union is the largest socialist economy in the world. Since Soviet planning relies heavily on central directives, the economy is also sometimes referred to as a command economy. A **command economy** is characterized by detailed directives—detailed instructions to productive agents concerning what they are to do and how they are to do it.

The Soviet government owns and operates almost all of the business-industrial sector, including manufacturing firms, the wholesale and retail network, and the banking, finance, transportation, communications, and agricultural sectors. Organizationally, the state-operated Soviet economy is a giant vertically and horizontally integrated corporation, with Communist party members acting as stockholders. The party establishes the economic policy objectives, strives to ensure their execution and oversees the bureaucracy necessary to carry out the details of the planning directives. Much like individual factories (or other subunits) of a large U.S. corporation, Soviet business firms ("enterprises") are supposed to implement the directives of the central planning authorities.

Gosplan: The central planning agency in the Soviet Union.

The **Gosplan,** the government's central planning agency, is directly responsible to Communist party officials. The Gosplan drafts the basic plan for the entire economy, which takes on the force of law when it is approved by the Soviet government. At present, both a five-year plan (which focuses on long-range objectives) and a one-year plan are constructed by the Gosplan. The central planning agency supplies each of the more than 200,000 Soviet enterprises with a thick document outlining their available resources and production targets. This planning document tells each enterprise what commodities are to be produced, the amounts of labor and raw materials it is allocated, new machinery that should be installed, the timing of available credit, and other operational details. The problem of the enterprise is to transform its allotted inputs into the target output. The operational targets of the annual plan are used as criteria in evaluating the performance of a firm at the end of the planning period and in rewarding it accordingly.

COORDINATION UNDER CENTRAL PLANNING

Under Soviet planning, commodities and raw materials are centrally rationed in physical terms. The central planners decide how much of each good will be produced and the quantity of resources, including intermediate

Material Balance Method:
A method of central planning employed in the Soviet Union and other Eastern European countries whereby the planning agency keeps track of the physical unit of resources and allocates them among state enterprises in a manner that will permit each enterprise to achieve its targeted output and thereby lead to the fulfillment of the economy's central plan.

goods, that will be used to produce the final output. How do Soviet planners accomplish this task? Essentially, they use the **material balance method** to reconcile the supply and demand for resources. Under this method, the central planning agency prepares a balance sheet of all available resource supplies and sources of resource demand. Beginning with the total supply of all productive resources—labor, raw materials, minerals, imports, and so on—the planning agency allocates these resources to individual enterprises in the quantities it believes will be necessary to produce the enterprise's targeted output. Simultaneously, the central planners assign each enterprise output targets that, when fulfilled, will produce the quantity of each good called for by the central plan. Of course, the Gosplan must ensure that the total quantity of each input allocated to the enterprises (the total demand for the input) balances with the total supply of the input.

Under the material balancing system, the output of one enterprise (steel, for example) is generally the input of another enterprise (a tractor-producing firm, for example). The failure of one firm to meet its production quota sets off a domino effect. Firms that are not supplied with adequate inputs fail to meet their production quotas unless they make adjustments.

Consider the problem that arises if the target output for, say, trucks is increased by 20 percent. The planners must take additional steps to ensure that the truck-producing enterprises receive the right amount of labor, capital equipment, component parts manufactured by other enterprises, and raw materials such as steel, aluminum, glass, and copper. If other suppliers fail to meet their quotas to truck-manufacturing enterprises, the truck manufacturers will also fail to meet their quotas.

The Soviet planners confront an enormous coordination problem in ensuring that each enterprise receives just the right amount of labor and materials at just the right time to keep things moving smoothly. Literally billions of interrelated planning decisions must be made.

Of course, with mathematical techniques and computer technology, it is theoretically possible to arrive at a solution that will provide the right amount of each input to each enterprise so that quotas can be met. What happens, though, when there is an unexpected change—perhaps adverse weather conditions or equipment failure? Bottlenecks will develop. Confronted with an input shortage, enterprise managers often cut corners to meet their production quotas. For example, they may use less than the specified amount of the input in short supply.[3] Alternatively, they may attempt to make a deal with other enterprise managers to supply the input in exchange for a similar future or past favor. An informal system of connections exists among successful enterprise managers in the Soviet Union.

[3]Technically, an enterprise can sue a supplier that fails to deliver inputs according to the specifications of the plan. However, since the procedures are cumbersome and unlikely to bring satisfactory results quickly, most enterprise managers find it easier to make an exchange with other managers, use less than the specified amount of ingredients to stretch out supplies, and/or follow other, more direct procedures in order to meet their production targets. See Hedrick Smith, *The Russians* (New York: Quadrangle/The New York Times Book Co., Inc., 1976), for several interesting accounts of how Soviet plant managers react to material shortages.

It is interesting to compare the response of a market system and a material balance planned system to an imbalance between supply and demand in the resource market. Under market allocation, if there is an excess supply of steel and excess demand for lumber, steel prices will fall and lumber prices will rise until the imbalances are corrected. Changes in relative prices will motivate literally millions of producers and users of steel and lumber to take the steps needed to restore balance between supply and demand in the two markets. Under material balance planning, an imbalance will trigger administrative action. In response to an excess demand for lumber, the planners could either increase their output target of enterprises producing lumber or reduce the allocation of lumber to enterprises using lumber. If the lumber output targets are increased, then inputs will have to be reallocated from other industries, such as steel, to lumber producers. On the other hand, if the allocation of lumber to users is reduced, planners will have to reduce the output targets of enterprises using lumber. In either case, the plans of numerous enterprises will have to be altered. Each revision will require administrative action at several different levels. Clearly, the correction of even a simple supply and demand imbalance is a formidable task, one unlikely to be accomplished quickly.

MOTIVATING SOVIET MANAGERS

Although the central plan is composed by the planners, it is the responsibility of the enterprise managers to carry out the plan. An incentive structure combining the "carrot" and the "stick" is used to motivate enterprise managers. Both pecuniary and nonpecuniary factors play a role. Managers who meet their production quotas are rewarded with bonuses, promotions, and medals. When the output of an enterprise is falling short of the production quotas, it is up to the manager to exhort the employees to work longer and harder, to obtain additional labor and material inputs, or to persuade the higher authorities that the production quota should be lowered. If these efforts are insufficient and the enterprise fails to meet its production target, the manager can expect demotion.

How do the planning authorities know how much an enterprise is capable of producing? Just as a government bureau in the United States has an incentive to confront legislative authorities with the image of an overworked agency squeezing the maximum output from an unrealistically small budget, so too, do Soviet enterprise managers have an incentive to project this image to the central planners. From the viewpoint of an enterprise manager, the ideal plan is one that provides a quantity of resources such that the firm's output target can be easily achieved. Managers thus have an incentive to provide the central planners with misleading and even false information with regard to the actual productive capability of the firm. Since high-level central planners have limited knowledge of the real output that an efficiently operated firm can achieve in its particular circumstances, they are in a weak position to control the actions of the enterprise managers.

If an enterprise manager is able to persuade the planners to provide sufficient resources for the easy achievement of the plan, they are unlikely to exceed the targeted output by much. After all, a large output relative to the target will reveal the true potential of the enterprise and lead to a substantially larger output target next year. Shrewd enterprise managers will prefer to stockpile resources or trade them to other enterprises for future favors, while exceeding this year's target by only a modest margin.

Of course, Soviet leaders are not unaware of these problems. Stiff penalties are applied to persons who fail to carry out their assigned responsibilities. Procedures designed to provide more accurate information and limit collusion have been established. Both economic and noneconomic incentives are used by the Soviet government to motivate managers and workers to meet the targets of the central plan. However, the system itself makes it difficult to detect misrepresentation and collusive behavior (the Russians call it "familyness") among enterprise managers and low-level planners.

Perhaps even more significant, the Soviet enterprise manager has little incentive to innovate, improve product quality, or experiment with alternative production techniques. The potential gains associated with the discovery of a better way of doing things are small, while the risks are great if an innovative method proves to be a failure. In addition, resource combinations supplied by the central planning authority often limit the adoption of innovative production methods. Since quantifying the gains from quality improvements and innovative achievements is difficult, the Soviet reward system emphasizes *quantity rather than quality* of output. Predictably, innovative behavior and product quality suffer as a result of this incentive structure.

PRIORITIES UNDER SOVIET PLANNING

With central planning, the allocation of resources is in accordance with the preferences of the planners. In the past, Soviet planners have consistently emphasized two priorities. First, heavy industries such as steel, mining, and military hardware have been favored over light industries such as textiles and household goods. Second, investment goods have been emphasized relative to consumption goods. As Exhibit 3 shows, the Soviet Union allocates a much larger share of its GNP to investment (and a much smaller share to consumption) than does the United States. In fact, the investment rate of the Soviet Union is among the highest in the world. Centralized

---

EXHIBIT 3 • The Functional Use of GNP in the United States and the Soviet Union

The Soviet economy, responding to the views of the planners, allocates a much larger share of GNP to investment and defense.

	Percent Share of Total GNP	
	United States	Soviet Union
Consumption	72	56
Defense	6	12
Investment	19	29
Government administration	3	3

The World Bank, *World Development Report, 1981*, and Svetozor Pejovich, *A Report Card on Socialism—Life in the Soviet Union* (Dallas: The Fisher Institute, 1979), pp. 65 and 98.

economic organization enables the planners to emphasize industrialization and capital accumulation, even though this may not reflect the views of the citizens. Current consumption, of course, is sacrificed as a result.

PRICES AND THE ALLOCATION OF SOVIET GOODS

The Soviet Union does use prices to ration goods among consumers. However, the central planners determine both the aggregate quantity of each consumer good and its price. When the supply of a product is exhausted, there is no pricing system that will induce producers to supply a larger amount. Thus, as Exhibit 4 illustrates, the supply curve for each good is independent of its price. However, the demand curve for consumer goods does obey the law of demand. Like their counterparts in other countries, Soviet consumers will want to buy more at lower prices.

In most instances, Soviet planners try to set the price of goods at the level that will bring the quantity demanded into line with the available supply (for example, P_1 of Exhibit 4). However, this is not always true. In some cases, the price of a good is deliberately set below the market equilibrium for reasons of income distribution. When this happens, shortages develop and waiting lines form when the good is available. On the other

EXHIBIT 4 • The Use of Prices in the Soviet Union

The supply of each good is determined in accordance with the priorities of the central plan. Thus, the quantity supplied of a good, shoes for example, is unresponsive to a change in price. However, the demand curve for shoes and other consumer goods does obey the law of demand. Soviet central planners also set the price of goods. In many cases, they will attempt to establish a price (such as P_1) that will equate amount demanded with the available supply. In other cases, the price may be set either below or above equilibrium. Below equilibrium prices such as P_2 will result in shortages and waiting lines, while above equilibrium prices will lead to surpluses. Note that under the Soviet planning system an increase in demand (shift to D_2, for example) does not lead to increased availability of the good.

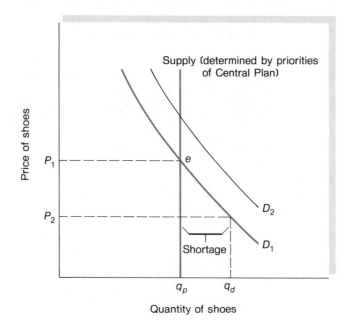

hand, planners will sometimes overestimate the demand for a good and therefore set its price above the equilibrium. Unsold goods are the result.

The results of Soviet price-setting policies are easily observable. Western tourists are often puzzled by the simultaneous occurrence of lengthy waiting lines as consumers seek to purchase goods in short supply and state-operated stores overflowing with unpurchased goods, particularly items that are less desired because of their poor quality or high price. Hedrick Smith paints a vivid picture of the plight of the Soviet consumer:

> I had heard about consumer shortages before going to Moscow but at first it seemed to me that the stores were pretty well stocked. Only as we began to shop in earnest as a family did the Russian consumer's predicament really came through to me. First, we needed textbooks for our children (who went to Russian schools) and found that the sixth-grade textbooks had run out. A bit later, we tried to find ballet shoes for our 11-year-old daughter, Laurie, only to discover that in this land of ballerinas, ballet shoes size 8 were unavailable in Moscow. . . . Goods are produced to fill the Plan, not to sell. Sometimes the anomalies are baffling. Leningrad can be overstocked with cross-country skis and yet go several months without soap for washing dishes. In the Armenian capital of Yenevan, I found an ample supply of accordians but local people complained they had gone weeks without ordinary kitchen spoons or tea samovars. In Rostov, on a sweltering mid-90s day in June, the ice cream stands were all closed by 2 p.m. and a tourist guide told me that it was because the whole area had run out of ice cream, a daily occurrence.[4]

These results are not surprising. They are a natural outgrowth of a *centrally-imposed* pricing structure.

THE PRIVATE SECTOR IN THE SOVIET UNION

Soviet law prohibits (a) a private person from acting as a trade middleman and (b) the hiring of an employee for the purpose of making a profit. However, there are two major areas in which private enterprise is permitted—personal services and a portion of agriculture. Soviet professionals (for example, physicians and teachers) and craft laborers (for example, tailors, shoe repairers, and painters) are free to sell their services to consumers. Often, these "self-employed" workers are moonlighters. They work regularly for a state enterprise but also provide their services to private consumers during nonworking hours.

The agricultural sector has consistently been a problem for the Soviet economy. Initially, there was substantial opposition to collectivization. Crop failures and low productivity (in comparison with that of other advanced economies) have been commonplace for years. Peasants on the collective farms are permitted to grow products on a small assigned plot—usually one acre in size. Products raised on the private plots may be consumed or sold in the market for prices determined by the fluctuations of supply and demand. In total, these private plots constitute slightly more than 1 percent

---

[4]*Ibid.*, p. 60. Reprinted by permission of Times Books, a division of Quadrangle/The New York Times Book Co., Inc., New York.

of the total agricultural land under cultivation. Nevertheless, as Exhibit 5 illustrates, they accounted for 25 percent of the total agricultural output in 1980. A major share of the total output of such products as eggs, potatoes, vegetables, fruits, meat, and dairy products is derived from these private plots.[5] Despite their less than optimal size, these private plots are an important source of agricultural production.

THE DISTRIBUTION OF INCOME IN THE SOVIET UNION

Wages are the major source of income in the Soviet Union. Despite the ideal communist distributional ethic put forth by Karl Marx ("From each according to his ability, to each according to his need"), substantial occupational wage differentials exist in the Soviet Union. The earnings of skilled craft workers are generally two to four times those of unskilled laborers. The

EXHIBIT 5 • Agriculture Production on Private Plots in the Soviet Union, 1980

Although the private agriculture plots constituted only 1.5 percent of the land under cultivation, output on these plots accounted for 25 percent of the total value of agriculture production in 1980. Each year a large share of the aggregate output of several products is produced on these private plots.

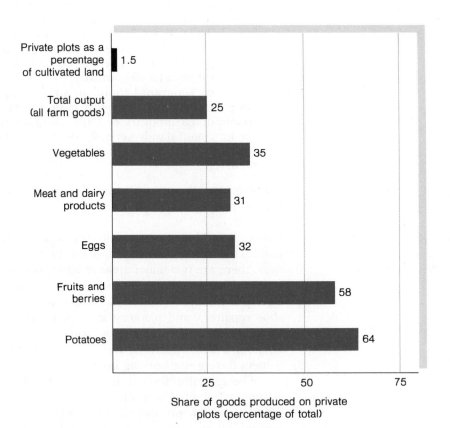

U.S. News and World Report, November 9, 1981, p. 41. Also see A. Yemelyanov, "The Agrarian Policy of the Party and Structural Advances in Agriculture," *Problems of Economics* (March 1975), pp. 22–34.

---

[5]The fact that more land-intensive agricultural products—grains and cotton, for example— are grown on the collective farms partially accounts for the fact that the productivity of these farms (measured in terms of value per acre) is lower than that of the private plots. However, the large disparity strongly suggests that incentives matter. Apparently, Soviet farmers cultivate the private plots, which generate personal gain, much more intensively than the collective farms, where most of the gains from efficiency accrue to others.

earnings of scientists, engineers, journalists, athletes, and high-level central planners are several times greater than the national average.

How does income inequality in the Soviet Union compare with that in Western nations? Comparable data are difficult to obtain. Exhibit 6 presents data on income shares of low- and high-income households for several countries. These data imply that the degree of income inequality in the Soviet Union is somewhat less than for the United States. After taxes, the bottom 20 percent of households received 8.7 percent of the aggregate personal income in the Soviet Union (1972–1974), compared to only 6.2 percent in the United States (1976). Correspondingly, the top quintile of households received a smaller share of the aggregate income in the Soviet Union than in the United States. However, the distribution of income in the Soviet Union is apparently not much different than several Western market economies. Perhaps surprising to some, the degree of income inequality in Sweden appears to be somewhat less than for the Soviet Union. The distribution of income in Japan and the United Kingdom is quite similar to the Soviet Union.

Income inequality data in the Soviet Union, though, should be interpreted with caution. The prices of many products purchased intensively by the poor (medical service, clothing, and food) are, relatively speaking, cheaper in the Soviet Union than they are in most Western economies. In contrast, most luxury goods, such as automobiles and air travel, are relatively more expensive in the Soviet Union. As the result of these structural factors, data on income inequality may overstate differences in economic status between the rich and the poor in the Soviet Union. Opposite biases,

EXHIBIT 6 • The Distribution of Income Shares in the Soviet Union Compared to Selected Market Economies

	Percentage of Aggregate Income Received		
Country and Year	Bottom 20% of Households	Top 20% of Households	Top 10% of Households
(After Taxes)			
Soviet Union, 1972–1974[a]	8.7	38.5	24.1
United States, 1976	6.2	42.0	—
Sweden, 1972	9.3	35.2	20.5
(Before Taxes)			
United States, 1980	5.3	39.9	23.3
Canada, 1981	5.3	40.0	23.8
Japan, 1979	8.7	37.5	22.4
United Kingdom, 1979	7.0	39.7	23.4

[a]For urban households only.

Source: The after-tax data for the Soviet Union (1972–1974) and Sweden (1972) are from Abram Bergson, "Income Inequality Under Soviet Socialism," *Journal of Economic Literature, 22* (September 1984). The after-tax data for the United States (1976) are from Edgar K. Browning and Jacquelene M. Browning, *Public Finance and the Price System* (New York: MacMillian Publishing Co., 1983 (Table 8–7). The before-tax data are from *The World Development Report: 1985* (Table 28).

however, are also present. Soviet elites are often presented with special privileges that do not show up in the income statistics. Automobiles can usually be easily obtained by upper-level bureaucrats and Communist party members. Soviet officials and members of favored groups, such as scientists, writers, actors, ballet stars, and economic managers, are granted the right to shop in special stores that offer goods at cut-rate prices and that stock many items unavailable to other citizens. Such products as choice meats, fine wines, fresh fruits and vegetables, French perfumes, Japanese electronic equipment, American cigarettes, and imported clothing are sold in these stores.[6] Since income data do not incorporate privileges of this type, they understate economic inequality in the Soviet Union.

INCOME AND GROWTH IN THE SOVIET UNION

It is interesting to compare the size and growth record of the Soviet economy with Western market economies, particularly the United States. In terms of development, the Soviet's economy lags well behind the Western industrial nations. Nearly one quarter of the Soviet labor force is still involved with agriculture, compared to only 3 percent in the United States. As Exhibit 7 illustrates, the *per capita* GNP of the Soviet Union is less than one half that of the United States and only about two thirds the *per capita* GNP

EXHIBIT 7 • The Gross National Product of the Major Economic Powers

The per capita GNP of the Soviet Union lags well behind that of the United States, the EEC countries, and Japan. In aggregate, output in the Soviet Union is a little more than one half as great as that of the United States and approximately two thirds that of the EEC countries. The countries of the European Economic Community (EEC) are Belgium, France, West Germany, Italy, Greece, the Netherlands, Denmark, Ireland, and the United Kingdom.

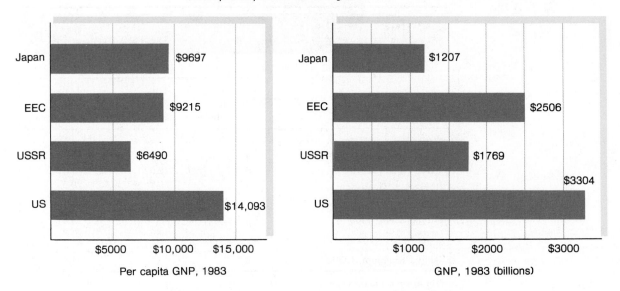

Per capita GNP, 1983

GNP, 1983 (billions)

Source: *Statistical Abstract of the United States—1986* (Tables 1472 and 1473) and *The World Development Report, 1985* (Table 1).

[6]See Hedrick Smith, *The Russians*, pp. 26–30.

of Western Europe and Japan. Of course, both the land area and population of the Soviet Union exceed the United States. Thus, the *aggregate* GNP of the Soviet Union is approximately 54 percent as large as for the United States. While the total size of the Soviet economy is substantially larger than Japan, it is smaller than the combined size of the economies of the European Economic Community (Exhibit 7).

In many respects, the growth record of the Soviet economy has been quite impressive, particularly during the 25 years following World War II. Spurred on by its high investment rate, the Soviet annual growth rate averaged approximately 7 percent during the 1950s and 5 percent during the 1960s, according to most analysts. Among Western industrial nations, only Japan was able to chalk up a more impressive record during the 1950–1970 period. As Exhibit 8 shows, Soviet economic growth has slowed in recent years. In fact, during the most recent decade (1976–1985), the Soviet growth rate has converged with that of Western economies.

The decline in the growth of the Soviet economy is not surprising. During the 1950s and 1960s, the Soviet growth rate was enhanced by the borrowing of more advanced technology from the West. As the technological gap between Western economies and the Soviet Union narrows, economic growth emanating from this factor dissipates. Innovation and entrepreneurship are important ingredients of growth for modern economies. These are not strengths of a socialist planned economy. If the Soviet economy is going to duplicate its impressive growth rate of the 1950–1970 period, Soviet planners will have to find a way of building more incentives for innovative behavior into the system. If they are unable to overcome this deficiency, the Soviet economy is unlikely to exceed the growth of the more advanced Western industrial economies.

EXHIBIT 8 • The Average Annual Growth Rate in Real Gross National Product, Major Industrial Nations, 1966–1985

	Annual Growth Rate of GNP	
Countries	1966–1975	1976–1985
Soviet Union	4.5	2.6
United States	2.6	2.9
Japan	8.0	4.7
Canada	3.6	2.1
France	4.7	2.2
West Germany	3.2	2.3
Italy	4.3	2.2
United Kingdom	2.3	1.7
Sweden	2.9	1.2[a]
Australia	4.0	2.3[b]
Yugoslavia	5.3	3.2[b]

[a]Data are for the 1976–1984 period.
[b]Data are for the 1976–1983 period.

Source: *Economic Report of the President, 1986*, Table B–110 and United Nations Statistical Office, *Monthly Bulletin of Statistics* (various issues).

YUGOSLAVIA—SOCIALISM OR THE MARKET

Before World War II, Yugoslavia had a free-market, capitalist economy. After the war (and the civil war that followed), the country became part of the Communist bloc with a government headed by Marshal Josip Tito. Initially, Tito organized the Yugoslav economy along Soviet lines. Central planning organs prescribed the quantity and quality of production, determined the methods and techniques of production, allocated inputs, set prices, and decided on the distribution of the national income. Within the framework of a five-year plan, these decisions were translated into output targets and input allocations that were handed down to the socialist managers of individual firms. Tito, however, was unwilling to accept Soviet domination. In addition, the Yugoslav economy stagnated under detailed central planning. In the early 1950s, Yugoslavia moved toward a decentralized economy that permitted market forces to play a significant role in the allocative process.

Today, the Yugoslavian economy is a hybrid economy characterized by both government ownership of the major physical assets and considerable reliance on market prices. The bulk of economic activity—estimates range from 80 to 90 percent—is conducted by worker-managed, socially owned business firms. In contrast with the Soviet Union, however, these socialist enterprises are not run by state-appointed managers following a central plan. Instead, enterprise managers in Yugoslavia are chosen by the employees of the firm and they are expected to pursue profits.

The organization of small businesses and agriculture in Yugoslavia also differs substantially from that of the Soviet Union. In Yugoslavia, citizens are permitted to own and operate small-scale enterprises, employing a maximum of five workers. In agriculture, peasants can privately own up to 25 acres. In addition, certain business firms, such as law firms, hotels, restaurants, and craft shops, are operated by private entrepreneurs, much as they are in Western countries.

THE YUGOSLAVIAN BUSINESS FIRM

Even though the government maintains ownership of the firm's assets, the management of individual enterprises in Yugoslavia is turned over to the employees. The employees of each firm elect a workers' council, which manages the firm. Each employee has one vote, and the workers' council is elected by secret ballot. The council, like a manager of a Western firm, purchases raw materials and determines the quantity and quality of goods produced, the level of employment, the method of production, and even the price charged for finished products. When the firm's revenues exceed costs, the firm's net profits go, with no strings attached, to the employees (including managers) of the firm.

As in the capitalist West, Yugoslavian business firms that satisfy consumers—that provide them with goods highly valued relative to their costs—will earn profits. The "employee owners" divide the firm's profit among themselves in a manner prescribed by the workers' council. When a worker retires, leaves his or her job, or is fired (by a vote of all employees), the worker's rights to any profits from the firm expire.

What impact does this form of economic organization have on economic incentives and production methods? Since the income of employees is directly affected by the firm's profit level, they have an incentive to elect managers who will operate the firm efficiently. In a sense, the position of the employees of the firm is parallel to that of stockholders in the West. The employees, like stockholders, seek efficient operation and a high level of profits because they are residual income recipients (in addition to wage recipients). However, unlike stockholders, individual workers in Yugoslavia can neither hold on to these rights when no longer attached to the firm nor sell them. Only current workers, collectively, are allowed to own factors of production.

There are several important ramifications of the Yugoslavian form of economic organization.

1. *Since the employees of the firm are also, at least indirectly, involved in the management of the firm, no separation between "labor" and "management" is present.* According to the Yugoslav view, capitalist relations in production and distribution are characterized not only by private ownership but also by separation of labor and management. Since capitalist workers do not participate in the firm's decision-making, they become disillusioned with the production process and dissatisfied with the income distribution. This is unlikely to happen under the Yugoslavian system. After all, the workers are management. Since employees have a direct stake in the profits of the firm, they will support management that pursues profits and seeks to avoid waste and other activities that increase the firm's costs.

2. *The Yugoslavian form of economic organization encourages workers to push for an immediate distribution of profits among themselves rather than for the allocation of profits to investment or future fringe benefits (for example, fancier offices or a company recreation center).* This is perfectly rational behavior because present capitalization of future profit-sharing rights cannot be realized through the private sale of ownership rights. Unlike stockholders in the West, Yugoslav workers can ill afford not to declare dividends every year. Postponed dividends may be lost forever for those with the likelihood of departing from the firm. In contrast, Western stockholders can always sell their shares whenever they are dissatisfied with the dividend policy of the management.

3. *Predictably, Yugoslavian enterprises will be constantly plagued by shortages of funds for both working capital and fixed investment.* The workers' tendency to allocate larger shares of the enterprise profits for purposes of wage and salary augmentation puts a continual strain on the firm's liquidity. Consequently, many enterprises have to resort to heavy borrowing and are thus forced to operate under perpetual indebtedness.

4. *Yugoslav firms have a strong tendency to substitute capital goods for labor.* The workers' profit-sharing right increases the cost, as seen by current employees, of hiring additional units of labor (that is, additional profit-sharing partners). Other things constant, increasing the size of the firm's work force will reduce the size of the profit share granted to each current employee. The employee's share of the firm's profit will be smaller as one of 1100 workers than as one of 1000 workers. Consequently, Yugoslav enterprises tend to use highly capital-intensive techniques of production. As

a result, many laborers, both skilled and unskilled, have been forced to emigrate to other countries to find work.

5. *Yugoslav enterprises have little or no pecuniary incentive to invest their funds in the establishment of new enterprises.* Even though money invested in new ventures can draw interest, investors have no claim to management rights or dividends. These are reserved exclusively for the workers of the new enterprise. Consequently, the financing of new enterprises comes primarily from governmental authorities, either through direct investment or by guaranteeing bank loans. Here, the gains of the public authority are basically twofold. First, it secures a dominating influence over the firm's management and its policies. Second, it obtains a certain return on its investment through taxation. Taxes levied on the enterprise profits generate a major portion of state revenues in Yugoslavia.

THE YUGOSLAVIAN ECONOMIC RECORD

The transition of the Yugoslav economy to market socialism was accompanied by remarkable changes elsewhere in the economy. First, there was a shift of labor out of the agricultural sector and into the manufacturing and services sectors. In 1945, approximately 75 percent of the population was employed in agriculture; in 1981, only 29 percent of the work force was working in the agriculture sector. At the same time, there was a change in exports from agriculture and mining to a highly diversified export pattern. More than 75 percent of the value of exports in 1981 was generated by the export of manufactured goods.

Second, the growth of real output and income per capita has been remarkable despite erratic fluctuations. Under centralized command planning, the Yugoslav real output was at a virtual standstill before 1952. Between 1952 and 1960, real GNP in Yugoslavia grew at an annual rate of nearly 10 percent. Since that time, the annual rate of growth of industrial production has averaged approximately 6 percent. During the 1966–1975 period, the real GNP of Yugoslavia expanded at a 5.3 percent rate, one of the more impressive growth records in the world (see Exhibit 8). Since 1976, the growth of the Yugoslavian economy has apparently slowed. Nevertheless, it continues to expand at an impressive rate.

In current years, however, the Yugoslavian economy has experienced relatively high rates of unemployment. In the early 1980s, unemployment in Yugoslavia was estimated to be in excess of 10 percent. The continuous influx of peasants from rural to urban areas has created a persistent excess supply of unskilled workers. In addition, semiskilled and skilled workers often cannot find employment because of the desire of firms to use capital-intensive production techniques. Consequently, approximately 1 million Yugoslavs, 5 percent of the total population, have sought jobs in neighboring Western European countries.

THE JAPANESE "MIRACLE"

By American and European standards, the Japanese people in 1950 were poor and their methods of production primitive. Forty-two percent of the Japanese labor force was employed in agriculture, compared to 12 percent in the United States.[7] The per capita GNP of Japan was one eighth that of the United States.

The transformation of the Japanese economy during the last three decades is the success story of the postwar era. Today, the Japanese economy is the third largest in the world, ranking after the U.S. and Soviet

---

[7]By 1981, the percentage of the Japanese work force employed in agriculture had declined to 12 percent. Since labor productivity is generally higher in manufacturing than in agriculture, this shift from agriculture contributed to the rapid growth of Japan.

APPLICATIONS IN ECONOMICS

Recent Economic Reforms in China

Like the Soviet Union, the Chinese economy is characterized by detailed central planning. In recent years, though, China has adopted economic reforms that allow market exchange to play a more significant role in the allocation of goods and resources. To date, the reforms have exerted their primary impact on the agriculture sector.

Under the reforms first adopted in 1978, responsibility for collectively owned farms is allocated to individuals and households (or a small group of farmers) who enter into long-term contracts with the commune (the state). The contracts specify the land to be cultivated, payments to be made for the use of agricultural equipment, and a specific amount of produce the "farmers" will deliver to the commune. Amounts produced over and above the required quota belong to the contractual farmers. This produce in excess of the production quota may either be consumed or sold in free markets. Restriction on individual stock breeding, household side-line occupations, transport of agricultural goods, and rural trade fairs have been removed. Farmers can even own their own tractors and trucks and hire laborers to work in their "leased" fields. As a result, a

thriving quasi free-market agricultural economy has developed in China.[8]

The early returns indicate that these reforms have substantially stimulated agricultural output. During the 1981–1984 period, overall agricultural production expanded at a 9 percent annual rate. The output of grains jumped from 305 million tons in 1978 to more than 400 million tons in 1984, an increase of more than 30 percent. China is now a grain exporter, rather than importer. Output of several other commodities, including meat products, rose even more rapidly than grain output during 1978–1984.

The success of the agricultural reforms appears to be laying the foundation for decentralization in other sectors. Measures incorporated into the Seventh Five-Year Plan (1986–1990) call for prices— whether state-controlled or not— that reflect production costs. The plan recognizes this will mean increased prices for some commodities that are currently subsidized. In other cases, prices of commodities that are currently taxed heavily will decline. If effectively instituted, this plan would mean greater emphasis on markets and less on the prefer-

ences of the planners.

It is not clear where this process of economic reform will lead. Clearly, there are strong forces that stand to lose from movements toward decentralized decision-making. The state bureaucracy that has dominated economic decision-making for several decades cannot be expected to relinquish its power without a struggle. Communist ideology, with its emphasis on egalitarianism rather than economic efficiency, can be expected to retard the move toward greater reliance on markets. Appearances, though, are sometimes more important than reality. Clearly, the Chinese leaders want to maintain the appearance of socialist (Communist) economic organization. Like the Yugoslavs of the 1950s, they appear to be searching for a socialist system that accommodates decentralized (market) decision-making. It will be interesting to follow this experiment in comparative economics.

---

[8]See Luc DeWulf, "Economic Reform in China," *Finance and Development*, March 1985, and Alvin Rabushka, *Does the World Need More Capitalism?* Center for Economic Education, University of Tennessee at Chattanooga, 1985.

economies. Adjusted for inflation, the GNP of Japan grew approximately 9.5 percent annually between 1950 and 1980. During that period, the income of the typical Japanese family, measured in dollars of constant purchasing power, doubled every eight years!

The data of Exhibit 9 illustrate the phenomenal economic growth of Japan. In 1950, the *per capita* GNP of Japan was only one eighth that of the United States. Measured in inflation-adjusted 1982 U.S. dollars, the Japanese per capita GNP in 1950 was $1,004, compared to $7,950 for the United States. During the 1950–1983 period, the real per capita GNP of Japan increased almost tenfold. By 1983, it was nearly 70 percent that of the United States, compared to only 12.7 percent in 1950.

The land area of Japan is 10 percent smaller than that of California. Its population is approximately one half as great as that of the United States. It lacks natural resources; almost all of Japan's petroleum is imported. On the surface, it would appear to be an overpopulated nation, lacking energy and natural resources. How can we explain the economic performance of Japan?

Several factors underlie the Japanese "miracle." Japan's economy is primarily a capitalist market economy. Nevertheless, it differs in several important respects from the market economies of Western Europe and North America. Let us consider some of the unique features of the Japanese economy.

THE JAPANESE LABOR MARKET

In contrast with laborers in most market economies, Japanese workers are intensely loyal to the firms in which they are employed. Two factors appear to explain this loyalty. First, the large Japanese firms make a **lifetime em-**

EXHIBIT 9 • The Japanese "Miracle"

	United States (1982 dollars)	Japan[a] (1982 dollars)	Japan as a Percentage of United States
Gross National Product (in billions)			
1950	1204	82	6.8
1960	1665	191	11.5
1970	2416	529	21.9
1980	3187	1029	32.3
1983	3278	1198	36.5
Gross National Product per capita			
1950	7905	1004	12.7
1960	9215	2046	22.2
1970	11782	5007	42.5
1980	13995	8803	62.9
1983	13976	9616	68.8

[a]The Japanese data were converted to U.S. dollars by the exchange rate method.

Source: U.S. Department of Commerce.

Lifetime Employment Commitment: An arrangement offered by most large firms in Japan whereby employees are guaranteed employment until the age of 55 unless guilty of misconduct.

ployment commitment to their employees. After a probationary period, which is usually less than one year, employees acquire tenure. Henceforth, they cannot be discharged except for misconduct (for example, excessive absenteeism, commission of a crime, or fighting on the job). Since seniority largely determines the wage scales of blue- and white-collar workers, the lifetime employment commitment system provides workers with economic security. As long as the firm is able to meet its economic obligations, the employee need not worry about layoffs, unemployment, or loss of income. Of course, the employee may resign, but this is unusual. The tenure of the employee is maintained until he or she reaches the age of 55, when retirement is compulsory.

Second, employee unions in Japan are almost exclusively company unions, and they represent both white- and blue-collar workers rather than particular types of jobs, as in the United States. For this reason, national federations of unions in Japan have little to do with the establishment of compensation and working conditions; these matters are dealt with by labor and management on the company, not the national, level. Approximately one third of the Japanese labor force is unionized, compared to one sixth in the United States. In contrast to U.S. labor-management relations, however, the union-management relationship in Japan is characterized by cooperation rather than conflict. Japanese unions often support wage reductions as a means of avoiding employment cutbacks during periods of weak demand for the product of their firm. Thus, unemployment in Japan is substantially lower than it is the United States.[9] In contrast to the United States and Western European economies, the proportion of managers who are experienced union leaders is high in Japan. Consultation between management and employee representatives is an integral part of Japanese industrial relations. Each has certain areas of control: Unions play an important role in the establishment of wage differentials among jobs; management is given a great deal of flexibility in the assignment of employees, and the movement of employees among positions in the firm is seldom resisted by the union. Areas of joint labor-management consultation include future production plans, projected technological changes, and the transfer of personnel to new plants. Since the long-run economic prospects of employees, including provisions for retirement, are closely tied to the success of the firm, it is not unusual for management and the union to work out a temporary reduction in wages during an economic slowdown or in order to enable the firm to expand into a new market.

Ichiro Nakayama, a senior Japanese labor economist, summed up the labor-management relationship as follows:

> One of the facts that is frequently referred to as the most marked characteristic of labor-management relations in Japan is the relative absence of conflict between employer and worker in all phases of industrial relations. . . . This manifests in various features of the trade union organization known as the enterprise-wide union—for example, the

---

[9]For example, the Japanese unemployment rate in 1984 was 2.8 percent compared to 7.5 percent in the United States.

lack of a strong feeling of confrontation at the collective bargaining table, the ambiguous distinction between union membership and employee's status . . . and the importance attached to the system of life-long employment. When compared with those in Western countries, labor-management relations in Japan are conspicuous, in the last analysis, by the common characteristic of a close human relationship between employers and employees.[10]

SAVINGS AND INVESTMENT

The savings and investment rates of Japan are much higher than those of other market economies. Urban workers in Japan save approximately 20 percent of their disposable income. Not surprisingly, the major share of corporate profits is rechanneled into investment. During the 1960s and 1970s, nearly one third of the GNP of Japan was allocated to investment, substantially more than the share allocated to investment in other industrial market economies. No democratic market economy has ever chosen to allocate such a large share of its output to capital formation during peacetime.

The Japanese tax structure is at least partially responsible for these high rates of saving and investment. Capital gains derived from the sale of securities are not taxed in Japan. Businesses and land capital gains are taxed at much lower rates than they are in Western countries. Interest and dividends are taxed at a maximum rate of 25 percent, compared to marginal tax rates of 50 percent and more for income derived from interest and dividends in most western nations. A system of tax credits encourages various forms of saving.

TAXES IN JAPAN

Although the Japanese tax structure is progressive, there are so many exemptions that high marginal rates can generally be avoided, particularly if one is willing to save. Until recent years, taxes were substantially lower in Japan than in the United States, Canada, and Western Europe. During the past decade, the size of the public sector has grown rapidly in Japan. Thus, the "tax gap" between other industrial nations and Japan has narrowed. As Exhibit 10 illustrates, however, taxes still consume a smaller share of GNP in Japan than in other market-directed economies. In 1982, tax revenues accounted for 27.2 percent of GNP in Japan, compared to 30.5 percent in the United States, 39.6 percent in the United Kingdom, and 50.3 percent in Sweden. Many believe that low tax rates, particularly during the 1950–1976 period, have contributed to the impressive growth record of Japan.

THE ECONOMIC FUTURE OF JAPAN

In recent years, the phenomenal growth rate of Japan has slowed. The Japanese real GNP expanded at an annual rate of 4.7 percent during 1976–1985, compared to 8.0 percent during 1966–1975. Nevertheless, Japan is still growing more rapidly than any other major industrial nation (see Exhibit 8).

The slowdown of the Japanese economy from the lofty growth records of 1950–1975 period was expected. During the 1950s and 1960s, Japan, like

[10]As quoted in Hugh Patrick and Henry Rosovsky, eds., *Asia's New Giant* (Washington, D.C.: Brookings Institution, 1976), p. 639.

EXHIBIT 10 • Taxes in Selected Western Countries, 1978	
Country	Tax Revenues as a Percentage of GNP, 1982
Sweden	50.3
West Germany	37.3
France	43.7
United Kingdom	39.6
United States	30.5
Japan	27.2

Source: *Facts and Figures on Government Finance, 1986* (Washington, D.C.: Tax Foundation, 1986), Table A33.

the Soviet Union, was able to profit by drawing on the technology and methods of production of more advanced countries.[11] Since Japanese manufacturing is now as modern as that of other industrial economies, this potential source of growth is no longer present. Since the Japanese import 100 percent of their oil, the higher crude oil prices of the 1970s also retarded the growth of the Japanese economy.

While world oil prices have now reversed, there is still reason to question whether the Japanese growth rate will return to the levels of the 1960s. As real incomes of Japanese workers continue to expand, they are likely to opt for a shorter work week and longer vacations in the future. An increase in environmental pollution has accompanied Japan's rapid growth. The Japanese will probably allocate more resources to pollution control as their standard of living rises. These factors will most likely cause the growth rate of the Japanese GNP to fall below the rate of the 1950–1975 period.

SOCIALISM OR CAPITALISM?

Which form of economic organization is best? Economics cannot provide a definitive answer to this question. Both philosophical and economic factors must be considered. It is clear that some socialist economies have impressive growth records. Socialism need not fall victim to its own economic inefficiency, as some observers once argued was inevitable. However, the economic achievements under capitalism have been highly impressive. No socialist country provides either the abundance or diversity of goods and services available to consumers in the high-tech, industrial, market economies of North America, Western Europe, and Japan. Neither has any less-developed socialist economy been able to equal the impressive growth rates of the market-directed economies of Hong Kong, Singapore, South Korea,

---

[11]A study by the Brookings Institution found that the major determinants of the growth rate differential between Japan and other major market economies were (a) rapid capital formation, (b) advances in knowledge and technology, and (c) economies of scale. See Edward F. Denison and William K. Chung, "Economic Growth and Its Source," in Patrick and Rosovsky, *Asia's New Giant.*

and Indonesia during the 1973–1983 period, to say nothing of the post-1950 record of Japan.

In summary, the record indicates that economic progress can occur under both capitalism and socialism. The choice of an economic system, though, involves much more than material goods and economic data. One's view of human nature, freedom, and equality are also important considerations. At the individual level, the choice is yours.

CHAPTER SUMMARY

1. Basic economic concepts, such as opportunity cost, diminishing marginal returns, comparative advantage, and the law of demand apply to socialist and capitalist economies alike. Different forms of economic organization can change the incentives faced by decision-makers (for example, managers and workers), but basic economic principles do not differ from one type of economy to another.

2. Capitalist economies are characterized by private ownership of productive assets and the use of markets to allocate goods and resources. The distinguishing characteristics of socialist economies are government ownership of physical capital and resource allocation by central planning.

3. Central planning is the dominant characteristic of the Soviet economy. The Gosplan, a central planning agency, presents state enterprises with an allocation of inputs and target levels for output. Key commodities and raw materials are centrally rationed in physical terms. The rewards of managers and workers are affected by their success at meeting the targets of the central planning authority. Pecuniary as well as non-pecuniary incentives are used to motivate managers and workers to carry out the directives of the central planners.

4. Central planning in the Soviet Union has stressed heavy industries and capital investment. The share of GNP allocated to investment in the Soviet Union is substantially higher than that in the United States.

5. The supply of each consumer good is determined by the priorities of the central planners. Just as for market economies, however, the quantity demanded by Soviet consumers is inversely related to price. Soviet planners generally use prices to allocate the centrally determined supply among consumers. However, shortages and surpluses often occur when the planners set the prices of various goods either below or above the market-clearing price.

6. Even though small, private plots constitute slightly more than 1 percent of the land under cultivation in the Soviet Union, they have accounted for approximately one fourth of the total value of Soviet agricultural production in recent years.

7. The distribution of income in the Soviet Union is probably less unequal than for the United States. The distribution of income shares in Japan, the United Kingdom, and Sweden, however, appears to be quite similar to that of the Soviet Union. Comparisons of income inequality of market-directed economies with the Soviet Union may be misleading. The prices of many items purchased intensively by the poor, including medical service, basic food products, and housing, are low in the Soviet

Union. This, of course, is beneficial to low-income families. On the other hand, the state provides privileges—such as the use of automobiles and the right to shop at stores where high-quality goods are sold at low prices—only to government officials and other members of the Soviet elite. Such benefits are an important source of economic inequality in the Soviet Union.

8. The per capita GNP of the Soviet Union is substantially less than that of Japan, the United States, and the countries of the European Economic Community. Nevertheless, the economic growth record of the Soviet economy has been impressive, particularly during the 1950s and 1960s. During the last decade, the growth of real GNP in the Soviet Union has converged with the rate of growth of the major Western industrial nations. Many observers believe that the future growth of the Soviet Union is vitally dependent on the development of an incentive system capable of stimulating experimentation and innovation.

9. The Yugoslavian economy combines socialist and capitalist economic organization. Central planning directs the economy and channels capital investment into designated areas. However, business firms have a great deal of discretionary decision-making authority. Employees of each firm elect a workers' council, which manages the firm. The firm is usually free to decide what products it will produce, the production techniques to be used, the employment level, and even product prices. As in market economies, business firms in Yugoslavia pursue profits that are then distributed to employees according to their wishes. Despite high rates of unemployment, the growth record of the Yugoslav economy has been impressive.

10. The growth record of Japan has been the most impressive of the major industrial nations during the postwar period. The following factors have contributed to this rapid growth: (a) institutional arrangements that have encouraged harmonious labor-management relations, (b) very high rates of saving and capital formation, and (c) low tax rates.

11. Economics does not tell us which form of economic organization is best. However, economic analysis can reveal a great deal about how alternative systems will operate in reality.

THE ECONOMIC WAY OF THINKING—
DISCUSSION QUESTIONS

1. Compare and contrast the role of business managers of firms in the United States, the Soviet Union, and Yugoslavia. In which country would managers have the greatest incentive to operate the firm efficiently?

2. What do you think are the major advantages of a centrally planned economy? What are the major disadvantages? Do you believe that market allocation is superior or inferior to centralized planning? Explain your answer.

3. How does Yugoslav socialism differ from socialism as practiced in the Soviet Union? Which system do you think is better? Why?

4. "Socialism means production for use, not for profit. Workers contribute according to their qualifications, and they are rewarded according to egalitarian principles. Socialism takes power from the business

elite and grants it to the workers, who, after all, produce the goods."
Analyze this point of view.

5. What major factors have contributed to the rapid economic growth of Japan? Do you think the Japanese economy will grow as rapidly in the future as it has in the past? Why or why not?

6. Do you think the United States should encourage firms to adopt the lifetime employment commitment offered by the major firms in Japan? Why or why not? What are the advantages and disadvantages of this system?

7. **What's Wrong with This Way of Thinking?**
"Central planning makes it possible for an economy to invest more and to expand at a more rapid rate. Consumer incomes, stimulated by the high rates of capital formation, also increase rapidly. Thus, the consumer is the major beneficiary of central planning, which stresses a rapid rate of capital formation."

A PRODUCTION THEORY AND ISOQUANT ANALYSIS

When analyzing production theory and input utilization, economists often rely on isoquant analysis. Since the technique is widely used at the intermediate level, some instructors explain the concept in their introductory course.

WHAT ARE ISOQUANTS?

Isoquant: A curve representing the technically efficient combinations of two inputs that can be used to produce a given level of output.

Generally, several alternative input combinations can be used to produce a good. For example, 100 bushels of wheat might be produced with 2 acres of land, 5 bushels of seed, and 100 pounds of fertilizer. Alternatively, the wheat could be produced with more land and less fertilizer, or more seed and less land, or more fertilizer and less seed. Many input combinations could be used to produce 100 bushels of wheat.

The word "isoquant" means "equal quantity." An **isoquant** is a curve that indicates the various combinations of two inputs that could be used to produce an equal quantity of output. Exhibit 1 provides an illustration. The isoquant labeled "100 units of cloth" shows the various combinations of capital and labor that a technically efficient producer could use to produce 100 units of cloth. Every point on a isoquant is technically efficient. By that we mean that it would not be possible, given the current level of technology, to produce a larger output with the input combination. If a producer wanted to produce a larger output, 140 units of cloth, for example, it would be necessary to use more of at least one of the resources. Since larger output levels require additional resources, isoquants representing larger levels of output always lie to the northeast of an isoquant diagram.

CHARACTERISTICS OF ISOQUANTS

Isoquant analysis must be consistent with the laws of production. What do the laws of production imply about the characteristics of isoquants?

1. *Isoquants Slope Downward to the Right.* Within the relevant range of utilization, an increase in the usage level of an input makes it possible to

EXHIBIT 1 • The Isoquant

An isoquant represents all input combinations that, if used efficiently, will generate a specific level of output. As illustrated here, 100 units of cloth could be produced with the input combinations L_1K_1 or L_2K_2 or any other combination of labor and capital that lies on the isoquant representing 100 units of cloth.

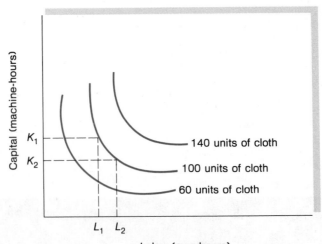

expand output. If, for example, the use of the labor input is expanded, it is possible to produce the same output level (stay on the same isoquant) with a smaller quantity of capital. Since both labor and capital can be used to increase production, they can be substituted for each other. Constant output can be maintained either by (a) using more labor and less capital or (b) by using more capital and less labor. Thus, every isoquant runs from the northwest to the southeast, as illustrated by Exhibit 1.

2. *Isoquants Are Convex When Viewed from the Origin.* The convexity of isoquants is related to the law of diminishing marginal returns. As one continues to substitute labor for capital, larger and larger amounts of labor are required to maintain output at a constant level. The law of diminishing marginal returns implies that as labor is used more intensively, it becomes increasingly difficult to substitute labor for each additional unit of capital. Since larger and larger amounts of labor are required to compensate for the loss of each additional unit of capital (and thus maintain the constant level of output), the isoquant becomes flatter as labor is used more intensively (see Exhibit 2, point B).

On the other hand, when capital is used more and more intensively, larger and larger amounts of capital are required to compensate for the loss of a unit of labor. Thus, an isoquant becomes steeper as capital (the y factor) is used more intensively (see Exhibit 2, point A). Since the marginal returns to each factor decrease as the factor is used more intensively, an isoquant is convex when viewed from the origin.

3. *The Slope of the Isoquant Is the Marginal Product of Labor Divided by the Marginal Product of Capital.* The slope of the isoquant is determined by the amount of labor that must be added to maintain a constant level of output when one uses one less unit of capital. This slope is dependent on the marginal productivity of labor relative to capital. When labor is used intensively relative to capital, its marginal product is low, relative to capital. Under these circumstances, as Exhibit 2 (point B) illustrates, the slope of the isoquant is small (the isoquant is flat). In contrast, when capital is used

EXHIBIT 2 • Convexity and the Slope of the Isoquant

When labor is used intensively relative to capital (point *B*), the shape of the isoquant is much flatter than it is when capital is used more intensively (point *A*). The slope of an isoquant is the ratio of the marginal products of the two factors (MP$_L$ divided by MP$_K$). When labor is used intensively relative to capital, its marginal product falls (and that of capital increases). Since the marginal product of labor is low (and the marginal product of capital is high) when labor is used intensively (as at point *B*), the isoquant is relatively flat.

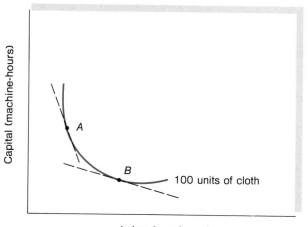

intensively (Exhibit 2, point A), the marginal product of labor is high, relative to capital. The steepness of the isoquant reflects this fact. At any point on the isoquant, the slope of the isoquant is equal to MP_L/MP_K.

THE ISOCOST LINE

A set of isoquants outlines the technically efficient input combinations that could be used to produce alternative levels of output. Before we can determine the economically efficient input combination for producing a level of output, we must also incorporate information about cost and resource prices.

Firms generally can purchase inputs at a fixed price per unit. The **isocost line** shows the alternative combinations of inputs that can be purchased with a given outlay of funds. As the term implies, the cost of purchasing an input combination on the isocost line is equal to the cost of purchasing every other input combination on the same line. To construct an isocost line, two pieces of information are required: (a) the prices of the resources and (b) the specific outlay of funds. Exhibit 3 illustrates the construction of three different isocost lines, assuming that the price of labor is $5 per unit and that the price of capital is $10 per unit. Consider the $500 isocost line. If all funds were spent on labor, 100 units of labor could be purchased. Alternatively, if the entire $500 were expended on capital, 50 units of capital could be purchased. It would be possible to purchase any input combination between these two extremes—for example, 80 units of labor and 10 units of capital—with the $500. The input combinations are represented by a line connecting the two extreme points, 100 units of labor on the x-axis and 50 units of capital on the y-axis. Note that the slope of the isocost line is merely the price of labor divided by the price of capital (P_L/P_K).

If the outlay of funds was to increase, it would be possible to purchase

Isocost Line: A line representing the various combinations of two factors that can be purchased with a given money budget (cost).

EXHIBIT 3 · The Isocost Line

The isocost line indicates the alternative combinations of the resources that can be purchased with a given outlay of funds. When the price of a unit of labor is $5 and that of a unit of capital is $10, the three isocost lines shown here represent the alternative combinations of labor and capital that could be purchased at costs of $500, $1000, and $1500. The slope of the isocost line is equal to P_L/P_K ($5/$10 = ½ in this case).

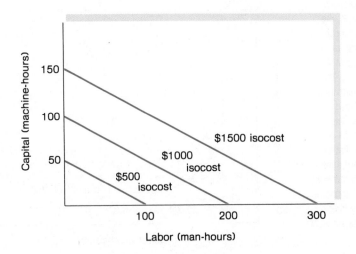

more of both labor and capital. Thus, as Exhibit 3 illustrates, the isocost lines move in a northeast direction as the size of the outlay of funds increases.

MINIMIZING THE COST OF PRODUCTION

A profit-seeking firm will want to choose the minimum-cost method of production. We can combine isoquant analysis and the isocost line to derive the minimum-cost input combination for producing a given output level. As Exhibit 4 illustrates, the minimum-cost input combination for producing 100 units of cloth is represented by the point at which the lowest isocost line just touches (is tangent to) the isoquant for 100 units of cloth. At that point (A of Exhibit 4), the producer will be able to combine 120 units of labor purchased at a cost of $600 ($5 per unit) with 40 units of capital purchased at a cost of $400 ($10 per unit) to produce 100 units of cloth. The total cost of the 100 units is $1000 ($10 per unit).

Of course, other input combinations could be used to produce the 100 units of cloth. However, they would be more costly, given the current prices of labor and capital. For example, if the input combination B were used to produce the 100 units, the total cost would be $1250 ($12.50 per unit).

When costs are at a minimum, the isoquant is tangent to the isocost line. The slopes of the two are equal at that point. In other words, when the cost of producing a specific output is at a minimum, the MP_L/MP_K (the slope of the isoquant) will be equal to P_L/P_K (the slope of the isocost line). Since:

$$\frac{MP_L}{MP_K} = \frac{P_L}{P_K}$$

then:

$$\frac{MP_L}{P_L} = \frac{MP_K}{P_K}$$

EXHIBIT 4 • The Cost-Minimization Resource Combination

When the cost of producing an output level (for example, 100 units of cloth) is minimized, the isoquant is tangent to the isocost line. At that point (A), $MP_L/MP_K = P_L/P_K$.

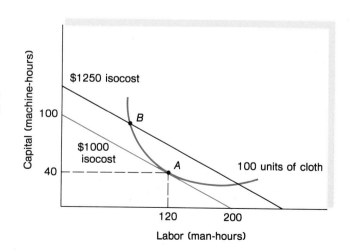

The latter equation represents precisely the condition that our earlier analysis, in the chapter devoted to supply of and demand for productive resources, indicated would be present if the cost of production were at a minimum.

The isoquant analysis indicates that when a firm chooses the minimum-cost method of production, the ratio of the price of labor to the price of capital will equal the ratio of the marginal productivities of the factors. This makes good economic sense. It implies, for example, that if capital is twice as expensive per unit as labor, the firm will want to substitute the cheaper labor for capital until the marginal product of capital is twice that of labor.

COST MINIMIZATION AND CHANGES IN RESOURCE PRICES

The minimum-cost input combination is dependent on both (a) the technical relationship between the productive inputs and output, as illustrated by the isoquant, and (b) the price of the factors, represented by the isocost line. If the ratio of the price of labor to the price of capital changes, the minimum-cost input combination will be altered.

Exhibit 5 illustrates this point. Exhibit 4 shows that if the price of labor were $5 and the price of capital were $10, the minimum-cost input combination to produce 100 units of cloth would be 120 units of labor and 40 units of capital. The total cost of the 100 units would be $1000. Exhibit 5 indicates what would happen if the price of labor increased from $5 to $10. At the higher price of labor, a $1000 outlay of funds would now purchase only 100 units of labor (rather than 200). As a result of the increase in the price of labor, the isocost line would become steeper, as indicated by the lines *MN* and *OP*. The lowest isocost line that is tangent to the isoquant for 100 units would now be *OP*. The new minimum-cost input combination would be 90 units of labor and 60 units of capital. Cost-minimizing producers would substitute capital for labor. The cost of producing the 100 units would rise (from $1000 to $1500).

THE SIGNIFICANCE OF ISOQUANT-ISOCOST ANALYSIS

Isoquant-isocost analysis is most applicable in the long-run, when all factors are variable and the possibilities for substitution are greatest. It is a conceptual tool, more suitable for illustrating principles than for solving manage-

EXHIBIT 5 • **The Impact of an Increase in the Price of a Resource**

The slope of the isocost line increases as the price of a unit of labor rises from $5 to $10. As a result of the increase in the price of labor, (a) cost-minimizing producers substitute capital for the more expensive labor, and (b) the minimum cost of producing 100 units of cloth rises.

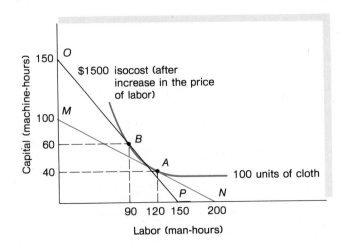

ment problems. Few firms would try to design their production activities by drawing isoquants, although some managers might make mental use of the model to design numerical techniques for minimizing costs. In any case, firms that do maximize profits behave as though they were using the analysis.

Isoquant-isocost analysis helps clarify the production conditions that must be met if a firm is to minimize its production cost and get the largest possible output from a specific outlay of funds.

B GENERAL BUSINESS AND ECONOMIC INDICATORS

SECTION 1 • National Income and Product Accounts*

	The Sum of These Expenditures				EQUALS	LESS	EQUALS	LESS	EQUALS
	Personal Consumption Expenditure	Gross Private Domestic Investment	Government Purchases of Goods and Services	Net Export of Goods and Services	Gross National Product (GNP)	Capital Consumption Allowances	Net National Product (NNP)	Indirect Business Taxes	National Income
Year					Billions of Dollars				
1929	77.3	16.7	8.9	1.1	103.9	9.9	94.0	7.1	84.7
1930	69.9	10.3	9.2	1.0	90.4	8.0	82.4	7.2	75.4
1932	48.6	1.0	8.1	0.4	58.0	7.4	50.7	6.8	42.8
1933	45.8	1.6	8.3	0.4	56.0	7.6	48.4	7.1	39.4
1934	51.3	3.3	9.8	0.6	65.1	6.8	58.2	7.8	49.5
1936	61.9	8.5	12.0	0.1	82.5	7.0	75.4	8.7	65.0
1938	63.9	6.5	13.0	1.3	84.7	7.3	77.4	9.2	67.4
1939	67.0	9.5	13.6	1.2	91.3	9.0	82.3	9.4	71.2
1940	71.0	13.4	14.2	1.8	100.4	9.4	91.1	10.1	79.6
1941	80.8	18.3	25.0	1.5	125.5	10.3	115.3	11.3	102.8
1942	88.6	10.3	59.9	0.2	159.0	11.3	147.7	11.8	136.2
1943	99.5	6.2	88.9	− 1.9	192.7	11.6	181.1	12.8	169.7
1944	108.2	7.7	97.1	− 1.7	211.4	12.0	199.4	14.2	182.6
1945	119.6	11.3	83.0	− 0.5	213.4	12.4	201.0	15.5	181.6
1946	143.9	31.5	29.1	7.8	212.4	14.2	198.2	17.1	180.7
1947	161.9	35.0	26.4	11.9	235.2	17.6	217.6	18.4	196.6
1948	174.9	47.1	32.6	7.0	261.6	20.4	241.2	20.1	221.5
1949	178.3	36.5	39.0	6.5	260.4	22.0	238.4	21.3	215.2
1950	192.1	55.1	38.8	2.2	288.3	23.6	264.6	23.4	239.8
1951	208.1	60.5	60.4	4.5	333.4	27.2	306.2	25.3	277.3
1952	219.1	53.5	75.8	3.2	351.6	29.2	322.5	27.7	291.6
1953	232.6	54.9	82.8	1.3	371.6	30.9	340.7	29.7	306.6
1954	239.8	54.1	76.0	2.6	372.5	32.5	340.0	29.6	306.3
1955	257.9	69.7	75.3	3.0	405.9	34.4	371.5	32.2	336.3
1956	270.6	72.7	79.7	5.3	428.2	38.1	390.1	35.0	356.3
1957	285.3	71.1	87.3	7.3	451.0	41.1	409.9	37.4	372.8
1958	294.6	63.6	95.4	3.3	456.8	42.8	414.0	38.6	375.0
1959	316.3	80.2	97.9	1.5	495.8	44.6	451.2	41.7	409.2
1960	330.7	78.2	100.6	5.9	515.3	46.4	468.9	45.3	424.9
1961	341.1	77.1	108.4	7.2	533.8	47.8	486.1	48.0	439.0
1962	361.9	87.6	118.2	6.9	574.6	49.4	525.2	51.5	473.0
1963	381.7	93.1	123.8	8.2	606.9	51.4	555.5	54.6	500.3
1964	409.3	99.6	130.0	10.9	649.8	53.9	595.9	58.7	537.6
1965	440.7	116.2	138.6	9.7	705.1	57.4	647.7	62.5	585.2
1966	477.3	128.6	158.6	7.5	772.0	62.1	709.9	65.2	642.0
1967	503.6	125.7	179.7	7.4	816.4	67.4	749.0	70.1	677.7
1968	552.5	137.0	197.7	5.5	892.7	73.9	818.7	78.7	739.1
1969	597.9	153.2	207.3	5.6	963.9	81.4	882.5	86.3	798.1
1970	640.0	148.8	218.2	8.5	1015.5	88.8	926.6	94.0	832.6
1971	691.6	172.5	232.4	6.3	1102.7	97.5	1005.1	103.4	898.1
1972	757.6	202.0	250.0	3.2	1212.8	107.9	1104.8	111.1	994.1

*Details may not add to totals due to rounding and to minor statistical discrepancies.

SECTION 1 • National Income and Product Accounts* (continued)								
The Sum of These Expenditures				EQUALS	LESS	EQUALS	LESS	EQUALS
Personal Consumption Expenditure	Gross Private Domestic Investment	Government Purchases of Goods and Services	Net Export of Goods and Services	Gross National Product (GNP)	Capital Consumption Allowances	Net National Product (NNP)	Indirect Business Taxes	National Income
Year				Billions of Dollars				
1973	837.2	238.8	266.5	16.8	1359.3	118.1	1241.2	120.8	1122.7
1974	916.5	240.8	299.1	16.3	1472.8	137.5	1335.4	129.0	1203.5
1975	1012.8	219.6	335.0	31.1	1598.4	161.8	1436.6	140.0	1289.1
1976	1129.3	277.7	356.9	18.8	1782.8	179.2	1603.6	151.7	1441.4
1977	1257.2	344.1	387.3	1.9	1990.5	201.5	1789.0	165.7	1617.8
1978	1403.5	416.8	425.2	4.1	2249.7	229.9	2019.8	178.1	1838.2
1979	1566.8	454.8	467.8	18.8	2508.2	265.8	2242.4	189.4	2047.3
1980	1732.6	437.0	530.3	32.1	2732.0	303.8	2428.1	213.3	2203.5
1981	1915.1	515.5	588.1	33.9	3052.6	347.8	2704.8	251.5	2443.5
1982	2050.7	447.3	641.7	26.3	3166.0	383.2	2782.8	258.8	2518.4
1983	2229.3	501.9	675.7	− 5.3	3401.6	399.6	3002.0	282.5	2718.3
1984	2423.0	674.0	736.8	−59.2	3774.7	418.9	3355.8	310.6	3039.3
1985	2581.9	670.4	814.6	−74.4	3992.5	438.2	3554.3	328.5	3215.6

Source: *Economic Report of the President, 1986* and *Economic Report of the President, 1970.*

SECTION 2 • Real Output and Prices

| | GROSS NATIONAL PRODUCT, 1929–1985 | | | PRICE INDEXES: 1929–1985 | | | |
| | | | | GNP Deflator | | Consumer Price Index | |
Year	1982 Prices (billions of dollars)	Annual Real Rate of Growth	Real GNP Per Capita (1982 dollars)	Index (1982 = 100)	Annual Percentage Change	Index (1967 = 100)	Annual Percentage Change
1929	709.6	—	5828	14.6	—	51.3	0.0
1930	640.0	− 9.8	5243	14.2	− 3.2	50.0	− 2.5
1931	587.2	− 8.2	4735	12.9	− 9.2	45.6	− 8.8
1932	503.3	−14.3	4111	11.5	−11.0	40.9	−10.3
1933	496.4	− 1.0	3952	11.2	− 2.3	38.8	− 5.1
1934	538.8	8.5	4276	12.2	8.6	40.1	3.4
1935	589.4	9.4	4632	12.4	1.9	41.1	2.5
1936	673.9	14.3	5216	12.5	0.4	41.5	1.0
1937	706.0	4.8	5481	13.1	4.8	43.0	3.4
1938	673.9	− 4.5	5164	12.8	− 2.4	42.2	− 1.9
1939	726.4	7.8	5554	12.7	− 0.7	41.6	1.4
1940	772.9	6.4	5850	13.0	2.0	42.0	1.0
1941	909.4	17.7	6817	13.8	6.2	44.1	5.0
1942	1080.3	18.8	8011	14.7	6.6	48.8	10.7
1943	1276.2	18.1	9333	15.1	2.6	51.8	6.1
1944	1380.6	8.2	9976	15.3	1.4	52.7	1.7
1945	1354.8	− 1.9	9682	15.7	2.9	53.9	2.3
1946	1096.9	−19.0	7758	19.4	22.9	58.5	8.7
1947	1066.7	− 2.8	7401	22.1	13.9	66.9	14.4
1948	1108.7	3.9	7561	23.4	7.0	72.1	2.7
1949	1109.0	0.0	7434	23.5	− 0.5	71.4	− 1.8
1950	1203.7	8.5	7905	23.9	2.0	72.1	5.8
1951	1328.2	10.3	8576	24.9	4.8	77.8	5.9
1952	1380.0	3.9	8759	25.4	1.5	79.5	0.9
1953	1435.3	4.0	8960	25.9	1.6	80.1	0.6
1954	1416.2	− 1.3	8687	26.3	1.6	80.5	− 0.5
1955	1494.9	5.6	9009	27.2	3.2	80.2	0.4
1956	1525.6	2.1	9032	28.1	3.4	81.4	2.9
1957	1551.1	1.7	9019	29.1	3.6	84.3	3.0
1958	1539.2	− 0.8	8801	29.7	2.1	86.6	1.8
1959	1629.1	5.8	9161	30.4	2.4	87.3	1.5
1960	1665.3	2.2	9217	30.9	1.6	88.7	1.5
1961	1708.7	2.6	9302	31.2	1.0	89.6	0.7
1962	1799.4	5.3	9646	31.9	2.2	90.6	1.2
1963	1873.3	4.1	9899	32.4	1.6	91.7	1.6
1964	1973.3	5.3	10284	32.9	1.5	92.9	1.2
1965	2087.6	5.8	10744	33.7	2.7	94.5	1.9
1966	2208.3	5.8	11235	34.9	3.6	97.2	3.4
1967	2271.4	2.9	11431	35.9	2.6	100.0	3.0
1968	2365.6	4.1	11786	37.7	5.0	104.2	4.7
1969	2423.3	2.4	11956	39.8	5.6	109.8	6.1
1970	2416.2	− 0.3	11783	42.0	5.5	116.3	5.5
1971	2484.8	2.8	11966	44.4	5.7	121.3	3.4

SECTION 2 • Real Output and Prices (continued)

| | GROSS NATIONAL PRODUCT, 1929–1985 | | | PRICE INDEXES: 1929–1985 | | | |
| | | | | GNP Deflator | | Consumer Price Index | |
Year	1982 Prices (billions of dollars)	Annual Real Rate of Growth	Real GNP Per Capita (1982 dollars)	Index (1982 = 100)	Annual Percentage Change	Index (1967 = 100)	Annual Percentage Change
1972	2608.5	5.0	12428	46.5	4.7	125.3	3.4
1973	2744.1	5.2	12949	49.5	6.5	133.1	8.8
1974	2729.3	− 0.5	12762	54.1	9.1	147.7	12.2
1975	2695.0	− 1.3	12478	59.3	9.8	161.2	7.0
1976	2826.7	4.9	12964	63.1	6.4	170.5	4.8
1977	2958.6	4.7	13434	67.3	6.7	181.5	6.8
1978	3115.2	5.3	13996	72.2	7.3	195.4	9.0
1979	3192.4	2.5	14185	78.6	8.9	217.4	13.3
1980	3187.1	− 0.2	13995	85.7	9.0	246.8	12.4
1981	3248.8	1.9	14123	94.0	9.7	272.4	8.9
1982	3166.0	− 2.5	13626	100.0	6.4	289.1	3.9
1983	3277.7	3.5	13975	103.8	3.8	298.4	3.8
1984	3492.0	6.5	14754	108.1	4.1	311.1	4.0
1985	3573.5	2.3	14963	111.7	3.3	322.2	3.8

Source: *Economic Report of the President, 1986* and *The Statistical History of the United States.*

SECTION 3 • Population and Employment

	POPULATION AND LABOR FORCE				UNEMPLOYMENT RATES			
Year	Civilian Noninstitutional Population Age 16 and over[a] (Millions)	Civilian Labor Force (Millions)	Civilian Labor Force Participation Rate	Employment/ Population Ratio (Including Armed Forces)	All Workers	Both Sexes, Age 16–19 Years	Men Age 20+	Women Age 20+
1929	85.6	49.2	57.5	55.9	3.2	—	—	—
1930	87.1	49.8	57.2	52.5	8.7	—	—	—
1931	88.2	50.4	57.1	48.4	15.9	—	—	—
1932	89.3	51.0	57.1	43.8	23.6	—	—	—
1933	90.5	51.6	57.0	43.1	24.9	—	—	—
1934	91.7	52.2	56.9	44.9	21.7	—	—	—
1935	92.9	52.9	56.9	45.8	20.1	—	—	—
1936	94.1	53.4	56.7	47.5	16.9	—	—	—
1937	95.2	54.0	56.7	49.0	14.3	—	—	—
1938	96.5	54.6	56.6	46.2	19.0	—	—	—
1939	97.8	55.2	56.4	47.2	17.2	—	—	—
1940	100.4	55.6	55.4	47.8	14.6	—	—	—
1941	101.5	55.9	55.0	51.2	9.9	—	—	—
1942	102.6	56.4	55.0	56.3	4.7	—	—	—
1943	103.7	55.5	53.5	61.2	1.9	—	—	—
1944	104.6	54.6	52.2	62.5	1.2	—	—	—
1945	105.6	53.9	51.0	60.9	1.9	—	—	—
1946	106.5	57.5	54.0	55.1	3.8	—	—	—
1947	101.8	59.4	58.3	58.3	3.9	—	—	—
1948	103.1	60.6	58.8	58.4	3.8	9.2	3.2	3.6
1949	104.0	61.3	58.9	57.7	5.9	13.4	5.4	5.3
1950	105.0	62.2	59.2	57.2	5.2	12.2	4.7	5.1
1951	104.6	62.0	59.3	59.4	3.2	8.2	2.5	4.0
1952	105.2	62.1	59.0	59.5	2.9	8.5	2.4	3.2
1953	107.1	63.0	58.8	59.2	2.8	7.6	2.5	2.9
1954	108.3	63.6	58.7	57.5	5.4	12.6	4.9	5.5
1955	109.7	65.0	59.3	56.7	4.3	11.0	3.8	4.4
1956	111.0	66.6	60.0	59.3	4.0	11.1	3.4	4.2
1957	112.3	66.9	59.6	58.3	4.2	11.6	3.6	4.1
1958	113.7	67.6	59.5	57.1	6.6	15.9	6.2	6.1
1959	115.3	68.4	59.3	57.6	5.3	14.6	4.7	5.2
1960	117.2	69.6	59.4	57.7	5.4	14.7	4.7	5.1
1961	118.8	70.5	59.3	57.0	6.5	16.8	5.7	6.3
1962	120.1	70.6	58.8	57.2	5.4	14.7	4.6	5.4
1963	122.4	71.8	58.7	57.0	5.5	17.2	4.5	5.4
1964	124.5	73.0	58.6	57.3	5.0	16.2	3.9	5.2
1965	126.5	74.5	58.9	57.7	4.4	14.8	3.2	4.5
1966	128.1	75.8	59.2	58.6	3.7	12.8	2.5	3.8
1967	130.0	77.3	59.5	59.0	3.7	12.9	2.3	4.2
1968	132.0	78.7	59.6	59.2	3.5	12.7	2.2	3.8
1969	134.3	80.7	60.1	59.7	3.4	12.2	2.1	3.7

[a]Prior to 1947 the data are for persons age 14 and over

SECTION 3 • Population and Employment (continued)

	POPULATION AND LABOR FORCE				UNEMPLOYMENT RATES			
Year	Civilian Noninstitutional Population Age 16 and over[a] (Millions)	Civilian Labor Force (Millions)	Civilian Labor Force Participation Rate	Employment/ Population Ratio (Including Armed Forces)	All Workers	Both Sexes, Age 16–19 Years	Men Age 20+	Women Age 20+
1970	137.1	82.8	60.4	58.9	4.8	15.3	3.5	4.8
1971	140.2	84.4	60.2	58.0	5.8	16.9	4.4	5.7
1972	144.1	87.0	60.4	58.3	5.5	16.2	4.0	5.4
1973	147.1	89.4	60.8	59.0	4.8	14.5	3.3	4.9
1974	150.1	91.9	61.2	59.0	5.5	16.0	3.8	5.5
1975	153.2	93.8	61.2	57.1	8.3	19.9	6.8	8.0
1976	156.2	96.2	61.6	57.9	7.6	19.0	5.9	7.4
1977	159.0	99.0	62.3	58.9	6.9	17.8	5.2	7.0
1978	161.9	102.3	63.2	60.3	6.0	16.4	4.3	6.0
1979	164.9	105.0	63.7	60.9	5.8	16.1	4.2	5.7
1980	167.7	106.9	63.7	60.2	7.0	17.8	5.9	6.4
1981	170.1	108.7	63.9	60.0	7.5	19.6	6.3	6.8
1982	172.3	110.2	64.0	58.7	9.5	23.2	8.8	8.3
1983	174.2	111.6	64.1	58.8	9.5	22.4	8.9	8.1
1984	176.4	113.5	64.3	60.5	7.4	18.9	6.6	6.8
1985	178.2	115.5	64.8	61.1	7.1	18.6	6.2	6.6

Source: *Economic Report of the President*, 1986 and 1967 and *The Statistical History of the United States*.

SECTION 4 • Money Supply, Interest Rates, and Federal Finances

Year	Money Supply M−1 (billions of dollars)	Annual Change In M−1	Interest Rate of Corporate Bonds (Moody, Aaa Percent)	Federal Budget Totals (billions of dollars)			National Debt	
				Fiscal Year Outlays	Fiscal Year Receipts	Surplus or Deficit (−)	Billions of Dollars	As a Percent of GNP
1929	26.5	—	4.73	3.1	3.9	0.7	16.9	16.3
1930	25.4	− 4.2	4.56	3.3	4.1	0.8	16.1	17.8
1931	23.6	− 7.1	4.58	3.6	3.1	− 0.5	16.8	22.2
1932	20.7	−12.3	5.01	4.7	1.9	− 2.7	19.5	33.6
1933	19.5	− 5.8	4.49	4.6	2.0	− 2.6	22.5	40.5
1934	21.5	0.3	4.60	6.6	3.0	− 3.6	27.7	42.5
1935	25.6	19.1	3.60	6.5	3.7	− 2.8	28.7	39.8
1936	29.1	13.7	3.24	8.4	4.0	− 4.4	38.5	46.7
1937	30.3	4.1	3.26	7.7	5.0	− 2.8	41.3	45.7
1938	30.1	− 0.7	3.19	6.8	5.6	− 1.2	42.0	50.0
1939	33.6	11.6	3.01	9.1	6.3	− 3.9	45.0	49.7
1940	39.0	16.1	2.84	9.5	6.5	− 2.9	48.5	48.3
1941	45.4	16.4	2.77	13.7	8.7	− 4.9	55.3	44.1
1942	55.2	21.6	2.83	35.1	14.6	− 20.5	77.0	48.4
1943	72.3	31.0	2.73	78.6	24.0	− 54.6	140.8	73.1
1944	86.0	18.9	2.72	91.3	43.7	− 47.6	202.6	95.8
1945	99.2	15.3	2.62	92.7	45.2	− 47.6	259.1	121.4
1946	106.0	6.9	2.53	55.2	39.3	− 15.9	269.9	127.1
1947	113.1	6.7	2.61	34.5	38.5	4.0	258.4	109.0
1948	111.5	− 1.4	2.82	29.8	41.6	11.8	252.4	96.5
1949	111.2	− 0.3	2.66	38.8	39.4	0.6	252.8	97.1
1950	116.2	4.5	2.62	42.6	39.4	− 3.1	257.4	89.3
1951	122.7	5.6	2.86	45.5	51.6	6.1	255.3	76.6
1952	127.4	3.8	2.96	67.7	66.2	− 1.5	259.2	73.7
1953	128.8	1.1	3.20	76.1	69.6	− 6.5	266.1	71.6
1954	132.3	2.7	2.90	70.9	69.7	− 1.2	271.3	72.8
1955	135.2	2.2	3.06	68.4	65.5	− 3.0	274.4	67.6
1956	136.9	1.3	3.36	70.6	74.6	3.9	272.8	63.7
1957	135.9	− 0.7	3.89	76.6	80.0	3.4	270.6	60.0
1958	141.1	3.8	3.79	82.4	79.6	− 2.8	276.4	60.5
1959	141.0	0.1	4.38	92.1	79.2	− 12.8	284.8	57.4
1960	141.8	0.6	4.41	92.2	92.5	0.3	286.5	55.6
1961	146.5	3.3	4.35	97.7	94.4	− 3.3	289.2	54.2
1962	149.2	1.8	4.33	106.8	99.7	− 7.1	298.6	52.0
1963	154.7	3.7	4.26	111.3	106.6	− 4.8	306.5	50.5
1964	161.9	4.7	4.40	118.5	112.6	− 5.9	312.5	48.1
1965	169.5	4.7	4.49	118.2	116.8	− 1.4	317.9	45.1
1966	173.7	2.5	5.13	134.5	130.8	− 3.7	320.0	41.5
1967	185.1	6.6	5.51	157.5	148.8	− 8.6	322.3	39.5
1968	199.4	7.7	6.18	178.1	153.0	− 25.2	344.4	38.6
1969	205.8	3.2	7.03	183.6	186.9	3.2	351.7	36.5
1970	216.6	5.2	8.04	195.6	192.8	− 2.8	369.0	36.3
1971	230.8	6.6	7.39	210.2	187.1	− 23.0	396.3	35.9

SECTION 4 · Money Supply, Interest Rates, and Federal Finances (continued)

Year	Money Supply M–1 (billions of dollars)	Annual Change In M–1	Interest Rate of Corporate Bonds (Moody, Aaa Percent)	Federal Budget Totals (billions of dollars)			National Debt	
				Fiscal Year Outlays	Fiscal Year Receipts	Surplus or Deficit (−)	Billions of Dollars	As a Percent of GNP
1972	252.0	9.2	7.21	230.7	207.3	− 23.4	425.4	35.1
1973	265.9	5.5	7.44	245.7	230.8	− 14.9	456.4	33.6
1974	277.5	4.4	8.57	269.4	263.2	− 6.1	473.2	32.1
1975	291.1	4.9	8.83	332.3	279.1	− 53.2	532.1	33.3
1976	310.3	6.6	8.43	371.8	298.1	− 73.7	619.2	34.7
1977	335.3	8.1	8.02	409.2	355.6	− 53.6	697.6	35.0
1978	363.0	8.3	8.73	458.7	399.7	− 59.0	767.0	34.1
1979	389.0	7.2	9.63	503.5	463.3	− 40.2	819.0	32.7
1980	414.8	6.6	11.94	590.9	517.1	− 73.8	906.4	33.2
1981	441.8	6.5	14.17	678.2	599.3	− 78.9	996.5	32.6
1982	480.8	8.8	13.79	745.7	617.8	−127.9	1140.9	36.0
1983	528.0	9.8	12.04	808.3	600.6	−207.8	1375.8	40.4
1984	558.5	5.8	12.71	851.8	666.5	−185.3	1559.6	41.3
1985	624.7	11.9	11.37	946.3	734.1	−212.2	1821.0	45.6

Source: *Economic Report of the President* (various years).

SECTION 5	•	Size of Government as a Share of GNP, 1929–1985			
FEDERAL, STATE, AND LOCAL GOVERNMENT					
Year	Expenditures (Percent of GNP)	Revenues (Percent of GNP)	Purchase of Goods and Services (Percent of GNP)	Non Defense Purchases of Goods and Services (Percent of GNP)	Transfer Payments to Persons (Percent of GNP)
1929	10.0	11.9	8.2	—	0.9
1933	19.2	16.7	14.4	—	3.8
1937	16.6	17.0	13.2	—	2.7
1939	19.3	16.9	14.9	13.3	2.8
1940	18.4	17.7	14.1	11.8	2.7
1941	22.9	19.9	19.9	8.8	2.1
1942	40.3	20.6	37.6	6.5	1.7
1943	48.4	25.5	46.1	4.6	1.2
1944	48.8	24.2	45.9	4.3	1.4
1945	43.5	25.0	38.9	4.2	2.8
1946	22.2	24.8	13.7	5.9	6.2
1947	18.5	24.6	11.2	7.0	5.6
1948	19.5	22.8	12.5	8.1	5.5
1949	23.0	21.7	15.0	9.6	6.5
1950	21.3	24.1	13.5	8.4	6.2
1951	23.8	25.7	18.1	7.8	4.4
1952	26.8	25.7	21.6	8.3	4.1
1953	27.4	25.6	22.3	9.1	4.1
1954	26.2	24.3	20.4	9.2	4.6
1955	26.5	25.0	18.6	8.9	4.6
1956	24.5	25.7	18.6	9.1	4.3
1957	25.7	25.9	19.4	9.5	4.9
1958	28.1	25.3	20.9	10.8	5.8
1959	26.6	26.3	19.7	10.5	5.6
1960	26.6	27.2	19.5	10.9	5.7
1961	28.1	27.3	20.3	9.7	6.3
1962	28.1	27.5	20.6	11.7	6.1
1963	27.9	28.0	20.4	12.1	6.1
1964	27.4	27.0	20.0	12.2	5.9
1965	26.9	27.0	19.7	12.4	5.9
1966	27.9	27.8	20.5	12.5	6.0
1967	30.0	28.3	22.0	13.0	6.7
1968	30.5	29.8	22.1	13.3	7.0
1969	30.1	31.1	21.5	13.3	7.2
1970	31.3	30.2	21.5	13.9	8.3
1971	31.5	29.7	21.1	14.4	9.1
1972	31.1	30.8	20.6	14.2	9.2
1973	30.3	30.9	19.6	13.9	9.3
1974	31.7	31.4	20.3	14.7	10.2
1975	34.1	30.0	21.0	15.4	11.9
1976	34.0	30.8	20.0	14.8	11.6
1977	31.9	31.0	19.5	14.4	11.1

SECTION 5 • Size of Government as a Share of GNP, 1929–1985 (continued)				
FEDERAL, STATE, AND LOCAL GOVERNMENT				
Year	Expenditures (Percent of GNP)	Revenues (Percent of GNP)	Purchase of Goods and Services (Percent of GNP)	Non Defense Purchases of Goods and Services (Percent of GNP)	Transfer Payments to Persons (Percent of GNP)
1978	30.9	30.9	18.9	14.1	10.6
1979	30.6	31.1	18.7	13.8	10.7
1980	32.6	31.3	19.4	14.2	11.7
1981	33.0	32.0	19.3	13.8	11.9
1982	35.1	31.6	20.3	14.1	12.8
1983	35.0	31.2	19.9	13.5	12.8
1984	33.9	31.0	19.5	13.2	11.9
1985	35.1	31.6	20.4	13.8	12.0

Source: *Economic Report of the President* (various years)

SECTION 6 • International Comparisons, Income, Growth, and Prices

Country (ranked according to GNP per capita)	Population (millions) mid-1983	GNP per capita			Adjusted Average Annual Growth Rate of the Money Supply 1970–83*	Average Annual Inflation Rate 1970–83
		Dollars 1983	Average Annual Growth Rate (percent) 1965–83			
Switzerland	6.5	16,290	1.4		3.4	4.9
United States	234.5	14,110	1.7		4.3	7.2
Norway	4.1	14.020	3.3		3.4	8.6
Sweden	8.3	12,470	1.9		4.9	8.9
Canada	24.9	12,320	2.5		6.1	8.1
Denmark	5.1	11,570	1.9		6.0	9.3
Australia	15.4	11,490	1.7		6.4	9.9
West Germany	61.4	11,430	2.8		5.5	5.0
France	54.7	10,500	3.1		8.1	9.6
Japan	119.3	10,120	4.8		5.7	7.3
Netherlands	14.4	9,890	2.3		6.4	6.6
United Kingdom	56.3	9,200	1.7		10.4	12.4
Belgium	9.9	9,170	3.1		4.2	7.2
New Zealand	3.2	7,730	1.2		7.6	11.9
Singapore	2.5	6,620	7.8		3.8	5.8
USSR	272.5	6,490	2.8		—	—
Italy	56.8	6,400	2.8		15.6	14.1
Hong Kong	5.3	6,000	6.2		—	8.6[a]
Spain	38.2	4,780	3.0		11.9	13.9
Greece	9.8	3.920	4.0		12.9	14.8
Yugoslavia	22.8	2,570	4.7			20.0[a]
Uruguay	3.0	2,490	2.0		34.6	44.1
Mexico	75.0	2,340	3.2		17.5	22.7
Argentina	29.6	2,070	0.5		78.4	84.9
Korea, Rep. of	40.0	2,010	6.7		15.5	13.9
Brazil	129.7	1,880	5.0		33.1	39.1
Chile	11.7	1,870	−0.1		69.1	38.1
Syria	9.6	1,760	4.9		13.1	10.8
Columbia	27.5	1,430	3.2		16.2	19.8
Paraguay	3.2	1,410	4.5		—	12.7
Turkey	47.3	1,240	3.0		23.4	27.6
Guatemala	7.9	1,120	2.1		9.9	9.4
Peru	17.9	1,040	0.1		27.6	34.2
Thailand	49.2	820	4.3		—	9.7[a]
Nigeria	93.6	770	3.2		15.3	13.9
Egypt	45.2	700	4.2		—	11.9[a]
Honduras	4.1	670	0.6		7.7	7.9
Indonesia	155.7	560	5.0		—	19.9[a]
Bolivia	6.0	510	0.6		30.4	31.8
China	1,019.1	300	4.4		—	—
India	733.2	260	1.5		7.7	8.2

Source: United Nations, *Monthly Bulletin of Statistics* (various issues).

*The money supply data are for the actual money supply divided by real GNP. Thus, it is the actual supply of money adjusted to reflect the country's growth rate.

[a]1970–1982

GLOSSARY

Ability-to-Pay Principle: The equity concept that people with larger incomes (or more consumption or more wealth) should be taxed at a higher rate because their ability to pay is presumably greater. The concept is subjective and fails to reveal how much higher the rate of taxation should be as income increases.

Absolute Advantage: A situation in which a nation, as the result of its previous experience and/or natural endowments, can produce a product with fewer resources than another nation.

Accounting Profits: The sales revenues minus the expenses of a firm over a designated time period, usually one year. Accounting profits typically make allowances for changes in the firm's inventories and depreciation of its assets. No allowance is made, however, for the opportunity cost of the equity capital of the firm's owners, or other implicit costs.

Acreage Restriction Program: A program designed to raise the price of an agricultural product by limiting the acreage planted with the product.

Active Budget Deficits: Deficits that reflect planned increases in government spending or reductions in taxes designed to generate a budget deficit.

Activist Strategy: The view that deliberate changes in monetary and fiscal policy can be used to inject demand stimulus during a recession and apply restraint during an inflationary boom and thereby minimize economic inability.

Adaptive Expectations Hypothesis: The hypothesis that economic decision-makers base their future expectations on actual outcomes observed during recent periods. For example, according to this view, the rate of inflation actually experienced during the last two or three years would be the major determinant of the expected rate of inflation for next year.

Administrative Lag: The time period between when the need for a policy change is recognized and when the policy is actually administered.

Aggregate Demand Curve: A downward sloping curve indicating an inverse relationship between the price level and the quantity of goods and services that households, business firms, governments and foreigners (net exports) are willing to purchase during a period.

Aggregate Supply Curve: A curve indicating the relationship between the price level and quantity of goods supplied by producers. In the short-run, it is probably an upward sloping curve, but in the long-run most economists believe the aggregate supply curve is vertical (or nearly so).

Allocative Inefficiency: The use of an uneconomical combination of resources to produce goods and services that are not intensely desired relative to their opportunity cost.

Anticipated Change: A change that is foreseen by decision-makers, allowing them time to adjust.

Anticipated Inflation: An increase in the general level of prices that is expected by economic decision-makers. Past experience and current conditions are the major determinants of an individual's expectations with regard to future price changes.

Appreciation: An increase in the value of a domestic currency relative to foreign currencies. An appreciation increases the purchasing power of the domestic currency over foreign goods.

Automatic Stabilizers: Built-in features that tend automatically to promote a budget deficit during a recession and a budget surplus during an inflationary boom, even without a change in policy.

Automation: A production technique that reduces the amount of labor required to produce a good or service. It is beneficial to adopt the new labor-saving technology only if it reduces the cost of production.

Autonomous Expenditures:
Expenditures that do not
vary with the level of
income. They are
determined by factors (such
as business expectations and
economic policy) that are
outside the basic income-
expenditure model.

Average Fixed Cost: Fixed
cost divided by the number
of units produced. It always
declines as output increases.

Average Product: The total
product (output) divided by
the number of units of the
variable input required to
produce that output level.

Average Tax Rate: One's tax
liability divided by one's
taxable income.

Average Total Cost: Total cost
divided by the number of
units produced. It is sometimes called per unit cost.

Average Variable Cost: The
total variable cost divided by
the number of units
produced.

**Balance of Merchandise
Trade:** The difference
between the value of
merchandise exports and the
value of merchandise
imports for a nation. The
balance of trade is only one
component of a nation's total
balance of payments.

Balance of Payments: A
summary of all economic
transactions between a
country and all other
countries for a specific time
period—usually a year. The
balance of payments account
reflects all payments and
liabilities to foreigners

(debits) and all payment and
obligations (credits) received
from foreigners.

Balance on Current Account:
The import-export balance
of goods and services plus
net private and government
transfers. If a nation's export
of goods and services
exceeds (is less than) the
nation's import of goods and
services plus net unilateral
transfers to foreigners, a
current account surplus
(deficit) is present.

Balanced Budget: A situation
in which current government
revenue from taxes, fees,
and other sources is just
equal to current
expenditures.

Benefit-cost Analysis (B-C): A
process used to determine
the efficiency of a project by
estimating each benefit and
each cost. A project is said to
be efficient if it generates
more benefits than costs.

Break-Even Point: Under a
negative income tax plan,
the income level at which
one neither pays taxes nor
receives supplementary
income transfers.

Budget Constraint: The
constraint that separates the
bundles of goods that the
consumer can purchase from
those that cannot be
purchased, given a limited
income and the prices of
products.

Budget Deficit: A situation in
which total government
spending exceeds total
government revenue during
a specific time period,
usually one year.

Budget Surplus: A situation in
which total government
spending is less than total
government revenue during
a time period, usually a
year.

Business Cycle: Fluctuations
in the general level of
economic activity as
measured by such variables
as the rate of unemployment
and changes in real GNP.

Capital Formation: The
production of buildings,
machinery, tools, and other
equipment that will enhance
the ability of future
economic participants to
produce. The term can also
be applied to efforts to
upgrade the knowledge and
skill of workers and thereby
increase their ability to
produce in the future.

Capitalism: An economic
system based on private
ownership of productive
resources and allocation of
goods according to the
signals provided by free
markets.

Cartel: An organization of
sellers designed to
coordinate supply decisions
so that the joint profits of
the members will be
maximized. A cartel will seek
to create a monopoly in the
market.

Choice: The act of selecting
among alternatives.

Classical Economists:
Economists from Adam
Smith to the time of Keynes
who focused their analyses
on economic efficiency and
production. With regard to

business instability, they thought market prices would adjust quickly in a manner that would guide an economy out of a recession back to full employment.

Collective Bargaining Contract: A detailed contract between (a) a group of employees (a labor union) and (b) an employer. It covers wage rates and conditions of employment.

Collective Decision-making: The method of organization that relies on public-sector decision-making (voting, political bargaining, lobbying, and so on). It can be used to resolve the basic economic problems of an economy.

Collusion: Agreement among firms to avoid various competitive practices, particularly price reductions. It may involve either formal agreements or merely tacit recognition that competitive practices will be self-defeating in the long-run. Tacit collusion is difficult to detect. The Sherman Act prohibits collusion and conspiracies to restrain interstate trade.

Command Economy: An authoritarian socialist economy characterized by centralized planning and detailed directives to productive units. Individual enterprises have little discretionary decision-making power.

Commercial Banks: Financial institutions that offer a wide range of services (for example, checking accounts, savings accounts, and extension of loans) to their customers. Commercial banks are owned by stockholders and seek to operate at a profit.

Communual Property Rights: Rights to property that can be used by all citizens as intensively as they desire. No one has the right to exclude another from the use of such property. These rights are sometimes referred to as common property rights.

Complements: Products that are usually consumed jointly (for example, lamps and light bulbs). An increase in the price of one will cause the demand for the other to fall.

Concentration Ratio: The total sales of the four (or sometimes eight) largest firms in an industry as a percentage of the total sales of the industry. The higher the ratio, the greater is the market dominance of a small number of firms. The ratio can be seen as a measure of oligopolistic power.

Conglomerate Merger: The combining under one ownership of two or more firms that produce *unrelated products*.

Constant Returns to Scale: Unit costs are constant as the scale of the firm is altered. Neither economies nor diseconomies of scale are present.

Consumer Price Index: An indicator of the general level of prices. It attempts to compare the cost of purchasing the market basket bought by a typical consumer during a specific period with the cost of purchasing the same market basket during an earlier period.

Consumer Surplus: The difference between the maximum amount a consumer would be willing to pay for a unit of a good and the payment that is actually made.

Consumption: Household spending on consumer goods and services during the current period. Consumption is a flow concept.

Consumption Function: A fundamental relationship between disposable income and consumption. As disposable income increases, current consumption expenditures will rise, but by a smaller amount than the increase in income.

Consumption Opportunity Constraint: The constraint that separates the consumption bundles that are attainable from those that are unattainable. In a money income economy, it is usually called a budget constraint.

Contestable Market: A market in which the costs of entry and exit are low, so that a firm risks little by entering. Efficient production and zero economic profits should prevail in a contestable market. A market can be contestable even if capital requirements are high.

Countercyclical Policy: A policy that tends to move the economy in an opposite direction from the forces of the business cycle. Such a policy would stimulate demand during the contraction phase of the business cycle and restrain demand during the expansionary phase.

Credit Unions: Financial cooperative organizations of individuals with a common affiliation (such as an employer or labor union). They accept deposits, including checkable deposits, pay interest (or dividends) on them out of earnings, and channel funds primarily into loans to members.

Crowding-Out Effect: A reduction in private spending as a result of high interest rates generated by budget deficits that are financed by borrowing in the private loanable funds market.

Current Account: The record of all transactions with foreign nations that involve the exchange of merchandise goods and services or unilateral gifts.

Cyclical Unemployment: Unemployment due to recessionary business conditions and inadequate aggregate demand for labor.

Dead-End Jobs: Jobs that offer the employee little opportunity for advancement or on-the-job training.

Deadweight Loss: A net loss associated with the forgoing of an economic action. The loss does not lead to an offsetting gain for other participants. It thus reflects economic inefficiency.

Demand Deposits: Non-interest-earning deposits in a bank that either can be withdrawn or made payable on demand to a third party via check. In essence, they are "checkbook money" because they permit transactions to be paid for by check rather than by currency.

Demand for Money: At any given interest rate, the amount of wealth that people desire to hold in the form of money balances; that is, cash and checking account deposits. The quantity demanded is inversely related to the interest rate.

Dependency Ratio: The number of children (under a specific age—14, for example) and the number of the elderly (age 65 and over) living in a country, divided by the total population. An increasing ratio indicates that a larger burden is being placed on the productive-age work force.

Deposit Expansion Multiplier: The multiple by which an increase (decrease) in reserves will increase (decrease) the money supply. It is inversely related to the required reserve ratio.

Depreciation: A reduction in the value of a domestic currency relative to foreign currencies. A depreciation reduces the purchasing power of the domestic currency over foreign goods.

Depression: A prolonged and very severe recession.

Derived Demand: Demand for an item based on the demand for products the item helps to produce. The demand for resources is a derived demand.

Devaluation: An official act that changes the level of the "fixed" exchange rate in a downward direction. In essence, it is a one-step depreciation of a currency under a fixed exchange rate system.

Differentiated Products: Products distinguished from similar products by such characteristics as quality, design, location, and method of promotion.

Discount Rate: The interest rate the Federal Reserve charges banking institutions for borrowing funds.

Discounting: The procedure used to calculate the present value of future income. The present value of future income is inversely related to both the interest rate and the amount of time that passes before the funds are received.

Discouraged Workers: Persons who have given up searching for employment because they believe additional job search would be fruitless. Since they are not currently searching for work, they are not counted among the unemployed.

Disposable Income: The income available to individuals after personal taxes. It can either be spent on consumption or saved.

Division of Labor: A method that breaks down the production of a commodity into a series of specific tasks, each performed by a different worker.

Dumping: The sale of a good by a foreign supplier in another country at a price lower than the supplier sells it in its home market.

Economic Efficiency: Economizing behavior. When applied to a community, it implies that (a) an activity should be undertaken if the sum of the benefits to the individuals exceeds the sum of their costs and (b) no activity should be undertaken if the costs borne by the individuals exceed the benefits.

Economic Good: A good that is scarce. The desire for economic goods exceeds the amount that is freely available from Nature.

Economic Profit: A return to investors that exceeds the opportunity cost of financial capital.

Economic Regulation: Regulation of product price or industrial structure, usually imposed on a specific industry. By and large, the production processes used by the regulated firms are unaffected by this type of regulation.

Economic Theory: A set of definitions, postulates, and principles assembled in a manner that makes clear the "cause and effect" relationships of economic data.

Economies of Scale: Reductions in the firm's per unit costs that are associated with the use of large plants to produce a large volume of output.

Economizing Behavior: Choosing the objective of gaining a specific benefit at the least possible cost. A corollary of economizing behavior implies that when choosing among items of equal cost, individuals will choose the option that yields the greatest benefit.

Employment Discrimination: Unequal treatment of persons on the basis of their race, sex, or religion, restricting their employment and earnings opportunities compared to others of similar productivity. Employment discrimination may stem from the prejudices of employers, consumers, and/or fellow employees.

Entitlement Allocation Program: A system of subsidies and taxes instituted in the mid-1970s. Refiners were taxed for each barrel of price-controlled domestic oil they used, and the proceeds were used to subsidize refiners for each barrel of imported and new (more costly) domestic oil they processed. The program increased the demand for imported oil.

Entrepreneur: A profit-seeking decision-maker who decides which projects to undertake and how they should be undertaken. A successful entrepreneur's actions will increase the value of resources.

Entry-Level Jobs: Jobs that require little training or experience and therefore allow untrained or inexperienced job seekers to enter the work force. These jobs frequently are stepping stones to better jobs.

Equation of Exchange: $MV = PQ$, where M is the money supply, V is the velocity of money, P is the price level, and Q is the quantity of goods and services produced.

Equilibrium: A balance of forces permitting the simultaneous fulfillment of plans for buyers and sellers.

Escalator Clause: A contractual agreement that periodically and automatically adjusts money wage rates upward as the price level rises. They are sometimes referred to as cost-of-living adjustments or COLAs.

Eurodollar Deposits: Deposits denominated in U.S. dollars at banks and other financial institutions outside the United States. Although this name originated because of the large amounts of such deposits held at banks in Western Europe, similar deposits in other parts of the world are also called Eurodollars.

Excess Burden of Taxation: A burden of taxation over and above the burden associated with the transfer of revenues to the government. An excess burden usually reflects losses that occur when beneficial activities are forgone because they are taxed.

Excess Reserves: Actual reserves that exceed the legal requirement.

Excess Supply of Money: Situation in which the actual money balances of individuals and business firms are in excess of their desired level. Thus, decision-makers will increase their spending on other assets and goods until they reduce their actual balances to the desired level.

Exchange Rate: The domestic price of one unit of foreign currency. For example, if it takes $1.50 to purchase one English pound, the dollar-pound exchange rate is 1.50.

Exchange Rate Conversion Method: Method that uses the foreign exchange rate value of a nation's currency to convert that nation's GNP to another monetary unit, such as the U.S. dollar.

Exclusive Contract: An agreement between manufacturer and retailer that prohibits the retailer from carrying the product lines of firms that are rivals of the manufacturer. Such contracts are illegal under the Clayton Act when they "lessen competition."

Existence Value: The satisfaction people can derive simply from knowing that something—the Grand Canyon or Hoover Dam, for example—exists. It is extremely difficult to measure existence values.

Expansionary Fiscal Policy: An increase in government expenditures and/or a reduction in tax rates such that the expected size of the budget deficit expands.

Expansionary Monetary Policy: An acceleration in the growth rate of the money supply.

Explicit Costs: Money paid by a firm to purchase the services of productive resources.

Exports: Goods and services produced domestically but sold to foreigners.

Extensive Economic Growth: An expansion in the total output of goods and services, regardless of whether or not output per capita increases.

External Benefits: Beneficial effects of group or individual action on the welfare of non-paying secondary parties.

External Costs: Harmful effects of an individual's or a group's action on the welfare of nonconsenting secondary parties. Litterbugs, drunk drivers, and polluters, for example, create external costs.

Externalities: The side effects of an action that influence the well-being of nonconsenting parties. The nonconsenting parties may be either helped (by external benefits) or harmed (by external costs).

Fallacy of Composition: Erroneous view that what is true for the individual (or the part) will also be true for the group (or the whole).

Federal Funds Market: A loanable funds market in which banks seeking additional reserves borrow short-term (generally for seven days or less) funds from banks with excess reserves. The interest rate in this market is called the federal funds rate.

Federal Reserve System: The central bank of the United States; it carries out banking regulatory policies and is responsible for the conduct of monetary policy.

Fiat Money: Money that has little intrinsic value; neither is it backed by or convertible to a commodity of value.

Final Goods and Services: Goods and services purchased by their ultimate users.

Fiscal Policy: The use of government taxation and expenditure policies for the purpose of achieving macroeconomic goals.

Fixed Cost: Cost that does not vary with output. However, fixed cost will be incurred as long as a firm continues in business and the assets have alternative uses.

Fixed Exchange Rate System: An international monetary system in which each country's currency is set at a fixed rate relative to all other currencies and governmental policies are used to maintain the fixed rate.

Flexible Exchange Rates: Exchange rates that are determined by the market forces of supply and demand. They are sometimes called "floating exchange rates."

Foreign Exchange Market: The market in which the currencies of different countries are bought and sold.

Fractional Reserve Banking: A system that enables banks to keep less than 100 percent reserves against their deposits. Required reserves are a fraction of deposits.

Free Rider: One who receives the benefit of a good without contributing to its costs. Public goods and commodities that generate external benefits offer people the opportunity to become free riders.

Frictional Unemployment: Unemployment due to constant changes in the economy that prevent *qualified* unemployed workers from being immediately matched up with existing job openings. It results from lack of complete information on the part of both job seekers and employers and from the amount of unemployed time spent by job seekers in job searches (pursuit of costly information).

Full Employment: The level of employment that results from the efficient use of the civilian labor force after allowance is made for the normal (natural) rate of unemployment due to dynamic changes and the structural conditions of the economy. For the United States, full employment is thought to exist when between 94 and 95 percent of the labor force is employed.

General Agreement on Tariffs and Trade (GATT): An organization composed of most non-Communist countries designed to set the rules for the conduct of international trade and reduce barriers to trade among nations.

GNP Deflator: A price index that reveals the cost of purchasing the items included in GNP during the period relative to the cost of purchasing these same items during a base year (currently, 1982). Since the base year is assigned a value of 100, as the GNP deflator takes on values greater than 100, it indicates that prices have risen.

Goods and Services Market: A highly aggregate market encompassing all final user goods and services during a period. The market counts all items that enter into GNP. Thus, real output in this market is equal to real GNP.

Gosplan: The central planning agency in the Soviet Union.

Government Failure: Failure of government action to meet the criteria of ideal economic efficiency.

Government Purchases: Current expenditures on goods and services provided by federal, state, and local governments; it excludes transfer payments.

Gross National Product: The total market value of all "final product" goods and services produced during a specific period, usually a year.

Head Tax: A lump-sum tax levied on all individuals, regardless of their income, consumption, wealth, or other indicators of economic well-being.

Horizontal Merger: The combining under one ownership of the assets of two or more firms engaged in the production of *similar products.*

Human Resources: The abilities, skills, and health of human beings that can contribute to the production of both current and future output. Investment in training and education can increase the supply of human resources.

Impact Lag: The time period between when a policy change is implemented and when the change begins to exert its primary effects.

Implicit Costs: The opportunity costs associated with a firm's use of resources that it owns. These costs do *not* involve a direct money payment. Examples include wage income and interest forgone by the owner of a firm who also provides labor services and equity capital to the firm.

Import Quota: A specific quantity (or value) of a good permitted to be imported into a country during a given year.

Imports: Goods and services produced by foreigners but purchased by domestic consumers, investors, and governments.

Income Effect: That part of an increase in amount consumed that is the result of the consumer's real income (the consumption possibilities available to the consumer) being expanded by a reduction in the price of a good.

Income Elasticity: The percent change in the quantity of a product demanded divided by the percent change in consumer income. It measures the responsiveness of the demand for a good to a change in income.

Income Mobility: Movement of individuals and families either up or down income distribution rankings when comparisons are made at two different points in time. When substantial income mobility is present, one's current position will not be a very good indicator as to what one's position will be a few years in the future.

Index of Leading Indicators: An index of economic variables that historically has tended to turn down prior to the beginning of a recession and turn up prior to the beginning of a business expansion.

Indexing: The automatic increasing of money values as the general level of prices increases. Economic variables that are often indexed include wage rates and tax brackets.

Indifference Curve: A curve, convex from below, that separates the consumption bundles that are more preferred by an individual from those that are less preferred. The points *on* the curve represent combinations of goods that are equally preferred by the individual.

Industrial Capacity Utilization Rate: An index designed to measure the extent to which the economy's existing plant and equipment capacity is being used.

Inferior Goods: Goods for which the income elasticity is negative. Thus, an increase in consumer income causes the demand for such a good to decline.

Inflation: A rise in the general level of prices of goods and services. The purchasing power of the monetary unit, such as the dollar, declines when inflation is present.

Inflationary Premium: A component of the money interest rate that reflects compensation to the lender for the expected decrease, due to inflation, in the purchasing power of the principal and interest during the course of the loan. It is equal to the expected rate of future inflation.

Infrastructure: The provision of a legal, monetary, educational, transportation, and communication structure necessary for the efficient operation of an exchange economy.

Innovation: The successful introduction and adoption of a new product or process; the economic application of inventions.

Intensive Economic Growth: An increase in output per person. When intensive economic growth is present, output is growing more rapidly than population.

Intermediate Goods: Goods purchased for resale or for use in producing another good or service.

International Monetary Fund: An international banking organization, with more than 100 nation members, designed to oversee the operation of the international monetary system. Although it does not control the world supply of money, it does hold currency reserves for member nations and make currency loans to national central banks.

Invention: The discovery of a new product or process, often facilitated by the knowledge of engineering and scientific relationships.

Inventory Investment: Changes in the stock of unsold goods and raw materials held during a period.

Investment: The flow of expenditures on durable assets (fixed investment) plus the addition to inventories (inventory investment) during a period. These expenditures enhance our ability to provide consumer benefits in the future.

Investment in Human Capital: Expenditures on training, education, and skill development designed to increase the productivity of an individual.

Irreversibility: Once an action is taken, some physical

effects may not be reversible —the prior physical conditions cannot be restored. Such a situation involves an irreversibility.

Kinked Demand Curve: A demand curve that is highly elastic for a price *increase* but inelastic for a price *reduction*. These differing elasticities are based on the assumption that rival firms will match a price reduction but not a price increase.

Labor Force: The portion of the population 16 years of age and over who are either employed or unemployed.

Labor Union: A collective organization of employees who bargain as a unit with employers.

Laffer Curve: A curve illustrating the relationship between tax rates and tax revenues. The curve reflects the fact that tax revenues are low for both very high and very low tax rates.

Law of Comparative Advantage: A principle that states that individuals, firms, regions, or nations can gain by specializing in the production of goods that they produce cheaply (that is, at a low opportunity cost) and exchanging those goods for other desired goods for which they are high opportunity cost producers.

Law of Demand: A principle that states that there is an inverse relationship between the price of a good and the amount of it buyers are willing to purchase.

Law of Diminishing Marginal Utility: A basic economic principle that states that as the consumption of a commodity increases, the marginal utility derived from the consuming more of the commodity (per unit of time) will eventually decline. Marginal utility may decline even though total utility continues to increase, albeit at a reduced rate.

Law of Diminishing Returns: The postulate that as more and more units of a variable resource are combined with a fixed amount of other resources, employment of *additional* units of the variable resource will eventually increase output only at a decreasing rate. Once diminishing returns are reached, it will take successively larger amounts of the variable factor to expand output by one unit.

Law of Supply: A principle that states that there will be a direct relationship between the price of a good and the amount of it offered for sale.

Less Developed Countries: Low income countries characterized by rapid population growth, an agriculture-household sector that dominates the economy, illiteracy, extreme poverty, and a high degree of inequality.

Lifetime Employment Commitment: An arrangement offered by most large firms in Japan whereby employees are guaranteed employment until the age of 55 unless guilty of misconduct.

Liquid Asset: An asset that can be easily and quickly converted to purchasing power without loss of value.

Loanable Funds Market: A general term used to describe the market arrangements that coordinate the borrowing and lending decisions of business firms and households. Commercial banks, savings and loan associations, the stock and bond markets, and insurance companies are important financial institutions in this market.

Long-Run: A time period of sufficient length to enable decision-makers to adjust fully to a market change. For example, in the long-run, producers will have time to alter their utilization of all productive factors, including the heavy equipment and physical structure of their plants.

Long-run (in Production): A time period long enough to allow the firm to vary all factors of production.

Loss: Deficit of sales revenue relative to the cost of production, once all the resources used have received their opportunity cost. Losses are a penalty imposed on those who misuse resources.

Macroeconomics: The branch of economics that focuses on how human behavior affects outcomes in highly aggregated markets, such as the markets for labor or consumer products.

Marginal: Term used to describe the effects of a change, given the current situation. For example, the marginal cost is the cost of producing an additional unit of a product, given the producer's current facility and production rate.

Marginal Cost: The change in total cost required to produce an additional unit of output.

Marginal Factor Cost: The cost of employing an additional unit of a resource. When the employer is small relative to the total market, the marginal factor cost is simply the price of the resource. In contrast, under monopsony, marginal factor cost will exceed the price of the resource, since the monopsonist faces an upward-sloping supply curve for the resource.

Marginal Product: The increase in the total product resulting from a unit increase in the employment of a variable input. Mathematically, it is the ratio of (a) change in total product divided by (b) change in the quantity of the variable input.

Marginal Propensity to Consume: Additional current consumption divided by additional current disposable income.

Marginal Rate of Substitution: The change in the consumption level of one good that is just sufficient to offset a unit change in the consumption of another good without causing a shift to another indifference curve. At any point on an indifference curve, it will be equal to the slope of the curve at that point.

Marginal Revenue Product: The change in the total revenue of a firm that results from the employment of one additional unit of a factor of production. The marginal revenue product of an input is equal to its marginal product multiplied by the marginal revenue (price) of the good or service produced.

Marginal Tax Rate: The amount of one's additional (marginal) earnings that must be paid explicitly in taxes or implicitly in the form of a reduction in the level of one's income supplement. Since it establishes the fraction of an additional dollar earned that an individual is permitted to keep, it is an important determinant of the incentive to work.

Marginal Utility: The additional utility received by a person from the consumption of an additional unit of a good within a given time period.

Market: An abstract concept that encompasses the trading arrangements of buyers and sellers that underlie the forces of supply and demand.

Market Failure: The failure of the market system to attain hypothetically *ideal* allocative efficiency. This means that potential gain exists that has not been captured. However, the cost of establishing a mechanism that could *potentially* capture the gain may exceed the benefits. Therefore, it is not always possible to improve the situation.

Market Mechanism: A method of organization that allows unregulated prices and the decentralized decisions of private property owners to resolve the basic economic problems of consumption, production, and distribution.

Market Power: The ability of a firm that is not a pure monopolist to earn unusually large profits, indicating that it has some monopoly power. Because the firm has few (or weak) competitors, it has a degree of freedom from the discipline of vigorous competition.

Material Balance Method: A method of central planning employed in the Soviet Union and other Eastern European countries whereby the planning agency keeps track of the physical unit of resources and allocates them among state enterprises in a manner that will permit each enterprise to achieve its targeted output and thereby lead to the fulfillment of the economy's central plan.

Maximum Emission Standard: The maximum amount of pollution that a polluter is permitted to emit, established by the government or a regulatory authority. Fines are generally imposed on those who are unwilling or unable to comply.

Means-tested Income Transfers: Transfers that are limited to persons or families with an income below a certain cut-off point. Eligibility is thus dependent on low-income status.

Measure of Economic Welfare: A new measure of economic well-being that focuses on the consumption of goods and services during a period. It differs from GNP in that (a) the estimated cost of various economic "bads" are deducted, (b) expenditures on "regrettable necessities" are excluded, and (c) the estimated benefits of leisure and various nonmarket productive activities are included.

Microeconomics: The branch of economics that focuses on how human behavior affects the conduct of affairs within narrowly defined units, such as individual households or business firms.

Middleman: A person who buys and sells, or who arranges trades. A middleman reduces transactions costs, usually for a fee or a markup in price.

Minimum Wage Legislation: Legislation requiring that all workers in specified industries be paid at least the stated minimum hourly rate of pay.

Monetarists: A group of economists who believe that (a) monetary instability is the major cause of fluctuations in real GNP and (b) rapid growth of the money supply is the major cause of inflation.

Monetary Policy: The deliberate control of the money supply and, in some cases, credit conditions for the purpose of achieving macroeconomic goals.

Money Rate of Interest: The rate of interest in monetary terms that borrowers pay for borrowed funds. During periods when borrowers and lenders expect inflation, the money rate of interest exceeds the real rate of interest.

Money Supply: The supply of currency, checking account funds, and traveler's checks. These items are counted as money since they are used as the means of payment for purchases.

Money Supply (M-1): The sum of (a) currency in circulation (including coins), (b) demand deposits, (c) other checkable deposits of depository institutions, and (d) traveler's checks.

Money Supply (M-2): Equal to M-1, plus (a) savings and time deposits (accounts of less than $100,000) of all depository institutions, (b) money market mutual fund shares, (c) money market deposit accounts, (d) overnight loans from customers to commercial banks, and (e) overnight Eurodollar deposits held by U.S. residents.

Money Supply (M-3): Equal to M-2, plus (a) time deposits (accounts of more than $100,000) at all depository institutions and (b) longer-term (more than overnight) loans of customers to commercial banks and savings and loan associations.

Monopolistic Competition: A situation in which there are a large number of independent sellers, each producing a differentiated product in a market with low barriers to entry. Construction, retail sales, and service stations are good examples of monopolistically competitive industries.

Monopoly: A market structure characterized by a single seller of a well-defined product for which there are no good substitutes and by high barriers to the entry of any other firms into the market for that product.

Monopsony: A market in which there is only one buyer. The monopsonist confronts the market supply curve for the resource (or product) bought.

Multiplier: The ratio of the change in equilibrium output to the independent change in investment, consumption, or government spending that brings about that change. Numerically, the multiplier is equal to $1/(1-MPC)$ when the price level is constant.

Multiplier Principle: The concept that an induced increase in consumption, investment, or government expenditures leads to additional income and consumption spending by secondary parties and therefore expands total spending by a larger amount than the initial increase in expenditures.

Mutual Savings Banks: Financial institutions that accept deposits in exchange for interest payments. Historically, home mortgages have constituted their primary interest-earning assets. Under recent banking legislation, these banks, too, are authorized to offer interest-bearing checkable accounts.

National Income: The total income payments to owners of human (labor) and physical capital during a period. It is also equal to NNP minus indirect business taxes.

Natural Monopoly: A market situation in which the average costs of production continually decline with increased output. Thus, a single firm would be the lowest-cost producer of the output demanded.

Natural Rate of Unemployment: The long-run average of unemployment due to frictional and structural conditions of labor markets. This rate is affected both by dynamic change and by public policy. It is sustainable in the future.

Negative Income Tax: A system of transferring income of the poor, whereby a minimum level of income would be guaranteed by the provision of income supplements. The supplement would be reduced by some fraction (less than 1) as the family earned additional income. An increase in earnings would always cause the disposable income available to the family to rise.

Net National Product: Gross national product minus a depreciation allowance for the wearing out of machines and buildings during the period.

Net Present Value: The current worth of future income after it is discounted to reflect the fact that revenues in the future are valued less highly than revenues now.

Neutral Tax: A tax that does not (a) distort consumer buying patterns or producer production methods or (b) induce individuals to engage in tax-avoidance activities. There will be no excess burden if a tax is neutral.

New Classical Economists: Modern economists who believe there are strong forces pushing a market economy toward full employment equilibrium and that macroeconomic policy is an ineffective tool with which to reduce economic instability.

Nominal GNP: GNP expressed at current prices. It is often called money GNP.

Nominal Values: The value of economic variables such as GNP and personal consumption expressed in current prices. A general increase in prices will cause nominal values to rise even if there is no real change in the variable.

Nonactivist Strategy: The maintenance of the same monetary and fiscal policy—that is, no change in money growth, tax rates, or expenditures—during all phases of the business cycle.

Nonhuman resources: The durable, nonhuman inputs that can be used to produce both current and future output. Machines, buildings, land, and raw materials are examples. Investment can increase the supply of nonhuman resources. Economists often use the term "physical capital" when referring to nonhuman resources.

Nonpecuniary Job Characteristics: Working conditions, prestige, variety, location, employee freedom and responsibilities, and other nonwage characteristics of a job that influence how employees evaluate the job.

Nonpersonal Time Deposits: Time deposits owned by businesses or corporations.

Normative Economics: Judgments about "what ought to be" in economic matters. Normative economic views cannot be proved false, because they are based on value judgments.

Oligopoly: A market situation in which a small number of sellers comprise the entire industry. It is competition among the few.

Open Market Operations: The buying and selling of U.S. government securities (national debt) by the Federal Reserve.

Opportunity Cost: The highest valued benefit that must be sacrificed (forgone) as the result of choosing an alternative.

Opportunity Cost of Capital: The implicit rate of return that must be paid to investors to induce them to continuously supply the funds necessary to maintain a firm's capital assets.

Passive Budget Deficits: Deficits that merely reflect the decline in economic activity during a recession.

Patent: The grant of an exclusive right to use a specific process or produce a specific product for a period of time (17 years in the United States).

Permanent Income Hypothesis: The hypothesis that consumption depends on some measure of long-run expected (permanent) income rather than on current income.

Personal Income: The total income received by individuals that is available for consumption, saving, and payment of personal taxes.

Phillips Curve: A curve that illustrates the relationship between the rate of change in prices (or money wages) and the rate of unemployment.

Policy Ineffectiveness Theorem: The proposition that any systematic policy will be rendered ineffective once decision-makers figure out the policy pattern and adjust their decision-making in light of its expected effects. The theorem is a corollary of the theory of rational expectations.

Political Good: Any good (or policy) supplied by the political process.

Positive Economics: The scientific study of "what is" among economic relationships.

Positive Rate of Time Preference: The desire of consumers for goods now rather than in the future.

Potential Output: The level of output that can be attained and sustained into the future, given the size of the labor force, expected productivity of labor, and natural rate of unemployment consistent with the efficient operation of the labor market. For periods of time, the actual output may differ from the economy's potential.

Potential Reserves: The total Federal Reserve credit outstanding. Most of this credit is in the form of U.S. securities held by the Fed.

Poverty Threshold Income Level: The level of money income below which a family is considered to be poor. It differs according to family characteristics (for example, number of family members) and is adjusted when consumer prices change.

Predatory Pricing: The practice by which a dominant firm in an industry temporarily reduces price to damage or eliminate weaker rivals, so that prices can be raised above the level of costs at a later time.

Price Ceiling: A legally established maximum price that sellers may charge.

Price Discrimination: A practice whereby a seller charges different consumers different prices for the same product or service.

Price Elasticity of Demand: The percent change in the quantity of a product demanded divided by the percent change in its price. Price elasticity of demand indicates the degree of consumer response to variation in price.

Price Floor: A legally established minimum price that buyers must pay for a good or resource.

Price Searcher: A seller with imperfect information, facing a downward sloping demand curve, who tries to find the price that maximizes profit.

Price Support Programs: Legislative action establishing a minimum price for an agricultural product. The government pledges to purchase any surplus of the product that cannot be sold to consumers at the support price.

Private Property Rights: Property rights that are exclusively held by an owner, and that can be transferred to others at the owner's discretion.

Production Possibilities Curve: A curve that outlines all possible combinations of total output that could be produced, assuming (a) the utilization of a fixed amount of productive resources, (b) full and efficient use of those resources, and (c) a specific state of technical knowledge.

Productivity: The average output produced per worker during a specific time period. It is usually measured in terms of output per hour worked.

Profit: An excess of sales revenue relative to the cost of production. The cost component includes the opportunity cost of all resources, including those owned by the firm. Therefore, profit accrues only when the value of the good produced is greater than the sum of the values of the individual resources utilized.

Progressive Tax: A tax that requires those with higher taxable incomes to pay a larger percentage of their incomes to the government than those with lower taxable incomes.

Property Rights: The rights to use, control, and obtain the benefits from a good or service.

Proportional Tax: A tax for which individuals pay the same percentage of their income (or other tax base) in taxes, regardless of income level.

Proved Reserves: The verified quantity of a resource that can be recovered at current prices and levels of technology.

Public Choice Analysis: The study of decision-making as it affects the formation and operation of collective organizations, such as governments. The discipline bridges the gap between economics and political science. In general, the principles and methodology of economics are applied to political science topics.

Public Goods: Jointly consumed goods. When consumed by one person, they are also made available to others. National defense, poetry, and scientific theories are all public goods.

Purchasing Power Parity Method: Method for determining the relative purchasing power of different currencies by comparing the amount of each currency required to purchase a typical bundle of goods and services in domestic markets. This information is then used to convert the GNP of each nation to a common monetary unit.

Quantity Theory of Money: A theory that hypothesizes that a change in the money supply will cause a proportional change in the price level because velocity and real output are unaffected by the quantity of money.

Rate of Employment: The number of persons 16 years of age and over who are employed as a percentage of the total noninstitutional population 16 years of age and over. One can calculate either (a) a civilian rate of employment, in which only civilian employees are included in the numerator, or (b) a total rate of employment, in which both civilian and military employees are included in the numerator.

Rate of Labor Force Participation: The number of persons 16 years of age or over who are either employed or actively seeking employment as a percentage of the total noninstitutional population 16 years of age and over.

Rate of Unemployment: The percent of persons in the civilian labor force who are not employed. Mathematically, it is equal to:

$$\frac{\text{Number of persons unemployed}}{\text{number in civilian labor force}} \times 100$$

Rational Expectations Hypothesis: This viewpoint expects individuals to weigh all available evidence, including information concerning the probable effects of current and future economic policy, when they formulate their expectations about future economic events (such as the probable future inflation rate).

Rational Ignorance Effect: Voter ignorance that is present because people perceive their individual votes as unlikely to be decisive. Voters rationally have little incentive to inform themselves so as to cast an informed vote.

Rationing: An allocation of a limited supply of a good or resource to users who would like to have more of it. Various criteria, including charging a price, can be utilized to allocate the limited supply. When price performs the rationing function, the good or resource is allocated to those willing to give up the most "other things" in order to obtain ownership rights.

Real Balance Effect: The increase in wealth emanating from an increase in the purchasing power of a constant money supply as the price level declines. This wealth effect leads to a negative relationship between price (level) and quantity demanded in the goods and services market.

Real GNP: GNP in current dollars deflated for changes in the prices of the items included in GNP. Mathematically, real GNP_2 is equal to nominal GNP_2 multiplied by (GNP $Deflator_1$/GNP $Deflator_2$). Thus, if prices have risen between periods 1 and 2, the ratio of the GNP deflator in period 1 to the deflator in period 2 will be less than 1. This ratio will therefore deflate the nominal GNP for the rising prices.

Real Interest Rate: The interest rate adjusted for expected inflation; it indicates the real cost to the borrower (and yield to the lender) in terms of goods and services. It is equal to the money rate of interest minus the expected rate of inflation.

Real Price: The cost of an item, corrected for inflation. For example, if the price of oil doubles while the prices of all other goods also double, the real price of oil is unchanged. Decisions are generally based on real prices, rather than the uncorrected prices.

Real Values: The measurement of a variable after it has been adjusted for changes in the general level of prices.

Recession: A downturn in economic activity characterized by declining real GNP and rising unemployment. In an effort to be more precise, many economists define a recession as two consecutive quarters in which there is a decline in real GNP.

Reciprocal Agreement: An agreement between firms whereby the buyer of a product requires the seller to purchase another product as a condition of sale. The practice is illegal under the Clayton Act when it substantially reduces competition.

Recognition Lag: The time period between when a policy change is needed from a stabilization standpoint and when the need is recognized by policy-makers.

Regressive Tax: A tax that takes a smaller percentage of one's income as one's income level increases. Thus, the proportion of income allocated to the tax would be greater for the poor than for the rich.

Rent Seeking: Actions by individuals and interest groups designed to restructure public policy in a manner that will either directly or indirectly redistribute more income to themselves.

Repeat-Purchase Item: An item purchased often by the same buyer. Examples would

include products like soap, toothpaste, potato chips, milk, and butter.

Required Reserve Ratio: A percentage of a specified liability category (for example, transaction accounts) that banking institutions are required to hold as reserves against that type of liability.

Required Reserves: The minimum amount of reserves that a bank is required by law to keep on hand to back up its deposits. Thus, if reserve requirements were 15 percent, banks would be required to keep $150,000 in reserves against each $1 million of deposits.

Reserves: Vault cash plus deposits of the bank with Federal Reserve Banks.

Residual Claimant: Individual in a firm who receives the excess of revenues over costs. A residual claimant gains if the firm's costs are reduced and if revenues are increased.

Resource: An input used to produce economic goods. Land, labor skills, natural resources, and capital are examples.

Resource Market: A highly aggregate market encompassing all resources (labor, physical capital, land, and entrepreneurship) that contribute to the production of current output. The labor market forms the largest component of this market.

Resource Mobility: A term that refers to the ease with which factors of production

Resource Mobility (Cont.) are able to move among alternative uses. Resources that can easily be transferred to a different use or location are said to be highly mobile. In contrast, when a resource has few alternative uses, it is immobile. For example, the skills of a trained rodeo rider would be highly immobile, since they cannot be easily transferred to other lines of work.

Restrictive Fiscal Policy: A reduction in government expenditures and/or an increase in tax rates such that the expected size of the budget deficit declines (or the budget surplus increases).

Restrictive Monetary Policy: A deceleration in the growth rate of the money supply.

Right-to-Work Laws: Laws that prohibit the union shop—the requirement that employees must join a union (after 30 days) as a condition of employment. Each state has the option to adopt (or reject) right-to-work legislation.

Roundabout Method of Production: The use of productive effort to make tools and other capital assets, which are then used to produce the desired consumer good.

Saving: Disposable income that is not spent on consumption. Saving is a "flow" concept. Thus, it is generally measured in terms of an annual rate.

Savings and Loan Associations: Financial institutions that accept deposits in exchange for shares that pay dividends. Historically, these funds have been channeled into residential mortgage loans. Under recent banking legislation, S & Ls are now permitted to offer checkable deposits (NOW accounts) and extend a broad range of services similar to those of commercial banks.

Say's Law: The view that production creates its own demand. Thus, there cannot be a general over-supply because the total value of goods and services produced (income) will always be available for purchasing them.

Scarcity: Fundamental concept of economics which indicates that less of a good is freely available than consumers would like.

Scientific Thinking: Development of theory from basic postulates and the testing of the implications of that theory as to their consistency with events in the real world. Good theories are consistent with and help explain real-world events. Theories that are inconsistent with the real world are invalid and must be rejected.

Secondary Effects: Economic consequences of an initial economic change, even though they are not immediately identifiable. Secondary effects will be felt only with the passage of time.

Self Interest Redistribution: Redistribution motivated solely by the desire of the members of a group to help themselves. Non-recipients do not gain from an improvement in the welfare of the recipients.

Shirking: Working at less than a normal rate of productivity, thus reducing output. Shirking is more likely when workers are not monitored, so that the cost of lower output falls on others.

Shortage: A condition in which the amount of a good offered by sellers is less than the amount demanded by buyers at the existing price. An increase in price would eliminate the shortage.

Short Run: A time period of insufficient length to permit decision-makers to adjust fully to a change in market conditions. For example, in the short run, producers will have time to increase output by using more labor and raw materials, but they will not have time to expand the size of their plants or to install additional heavy equipment.

Short Run (in Production): A time period so short that a firm is unable to vary some of its factors of production. The firm's plant size typically cannot be altered in the shortrun.

Shortsightedness Effect: Misallocation of resources that results because public-sector action is biased (a) in favor of proposals yielding clearly defined current benefits in exchange for difficult-to-identify future costs and (b) against proposals with clearly identifiable current costs yielding less concrete and less obvious future benefits.

Social Costs: The sum of (a) the private costs that are incurred by a decision-maker and (b) any external costs of the action that are imposed on nonconsenting secondary parties. If there are no external costs, private and social costs will be equal.

Social Regulation: Legislation designed to improve the health, safety, and environmental conditions available to workers and/or consumers. The legislation usually mandates production procedures, minimum standards, and/or product characteristics to be met by producers and employers.

Socialism: A system of economic organization in which (a) the ownership and control of the basic means of production rest with the state and (b) resource allocation is determined by centralized planning rather than by market forces.

Special Drawing Rights: Supplementary reserves, in the form of accounting entries, established by the International Monetary Fund (also called "paper gold"). Like gold and foreign currency reserves, they can be used to make payments on international accounts.

Special Interest Issue: An issue that generates substantial individual benefits to a small minority while imposing a small individual cost on many other voters. In total, the net

cost to the majority might either exceed or fall short of the net benefits to the special interest group.

Stagflation: A period during which an economy is experiencing both substantial inflation and a slow growth in output.

Strike: An action of unionized employees in which they (a) discontinue working for the employer and (b) take steps to prevent other potential workers from offering their services to the employer.

Structural Unemployment: Unemployment due to structural changes in the economy that eliminate some jobs while generating job openings for which the unemployed workers are *not* well quaiified.

Substitutes: Products that are related such that an increase in the price of one will cause an increase in demand for the other (for example, butter and margarine, Chevrolets and Fords).

Substitution Effect: That part of an increase in amount consumed that is the result of a good being cheaper in relation to other goods because of a reduction in price.

Sunk Costs: Costs that have already been incurred as a result of past decisions. They are sometimes referred to as historical costs.

Supply Shock: An unexpected event that temporarily either increases or decreases aggregate supply.

Supply-Side Economists: Modern economists who

believe that changes in marginal tax rates exert important effects on aggregate supply.

Surplus: A condition in which the amount of a good that sellers are willing to offer is greater than the amount that buyers will purchase at the existing price. A decline in price would eliminate the surplus.

Tariff: A tax levied on goods imported into a country.

Tax Base: The level of the activity that is taxed. For example, if an excise tax is levied on each gallon of gasoline, the tax base is the number of gallons of gasoline sold. Since higher tax rates generally make the taxed activity less attractive, the size of the tax base is inversely related to the rate at which the activity is taxed.

Tax Incidence: The manner in which the burden of the tax is distributed among economic units (consumers, employees, employers, and so on). The tax burden does not always fall on those who pay the tax.

Tax Rate: The per unit or percentage rate at which an economic activity is taxed.

Tax Shelter Industry: Business enterprises that specialize in offering investment opportunities designed to create a short-term accounting or "paper" loss, which can then be deducted from one's taxable income; at the same time, future "capital gain" income is generated, which is taxable at a lower rate.

Technological Advancement: The introduction of new techniques or methods of production that enable a greater output per unit of input.

Technology: The body of skills and technological knowledge available at any given time. The level of technology establishes the relationship between inputs and the maximum output they can generate.

Thrift Institutions: Traditional savings institutions, such as savings and loan associations, mutual savings banks, and credit unions.

Total Cost: The costs, both explicit and implicit, of all the resources used by the firm. Total cost includes an imputed normal rate of return for the firm's equity capital.

Total Product: The total output of a good that is associated with alternative utilization rates of a variable input.

Transaction Accounts: Accounts including demand deposits, NOW accounts, and other checkable deposits against which the account holder is permitted to transfer funds for the purpose of making payment to a third party.

Transaction Costs: The time, effort, and other resources needed to search out, negotiate, and consummate an exchange.

Transfer Payments: Payments to individuals or institutions that are not linked to the current supply of a good or service by the recipient.

Trickle-Down Theory: The theory that intensive economic growth will eventually lead to an improvement in the standard of living of the entire society, even for persons at the bottom of the economic spectrum.

Unanticipated Change: A change that decision-makers could not reasonably foresee. Thus, choices made prior to the event did not take the event into account.

Unanticipated Inflation: An increase in the general level of prices that was not expected by most decision-makers. Thus, it catches them by surprise.

Underground Economy: Unreported barter and cash transactions that take place outside recorded market channels. Some are otherwise legal activities undertaken to evade taxes. Others involve illegal activities such as trafficking in drugs, prostitution, extortion, and similar crimes.

Unemployed: The term used to describe a person not currently employed, who is either (a) actively seeking employment or (b) waiting to begin or return to a job.

Union Shop: The requirement that all employees join the recognized union and pay dues to it within a specified length of time (usually 30 days) after their employment with the firm begins.

Utility: The benefit or satisfaction expected from a choice or course of action.

Value Marginal Product: The marginal product of a resource multiplied by the selling price of the product it helps to produce. Under perfect competition, a firm's marginal revenue product will be equal to the value marginal product.

Variable Costs: Costs that vary with the rate of output. Examples include wages paid to workers and payments for raw materials.

Velocity of Money: The average number of times a dollar is used to purchase final goods and services during a year. It is equal to GNP divided by the stock of money.

Vertical Merger: The creation of a single firm from two firms, one of which was a supplier or customer of the other—for example, a merger of a lumber company with a furniture manufacturer.

Vicious Circle of Under-development: A pattern of low income and low economic growth, which tends to perpetuate itself. Since the current consumption demands of poor nations are large in proportion to available income, the savings and investment rates of these nations are low. In turn, the low investment rate retards future growth, causing poor nations to remain poor.

Work-Leisure Substitution Effect: The substitution of leisure time for work time when higher tax rates reduce after-tax personal earnings. In effect, the reduction in the take-home (after-tax) portion of earnings reduces the opportunity cost of leisure, and thereby induces individuals to work less (and less intensively). Of course, lower tax rates would exert the opposite effect.

Youth Work Scholarship: A proposed scholarship providing subsidies to younger workers who maintain jobs. Some scholarships would limit the subsidies to employment that offered on-the-job training.

CREDITS

INDEX

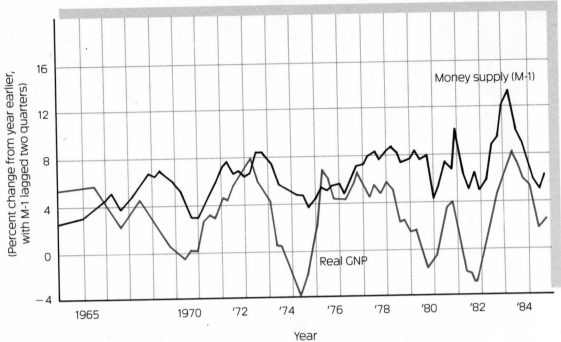

EXHIBIT E: The Growth Rate of the Money Supply (M-1) and Real GNP, 1965–1985

The money supply and real GNP often move together.

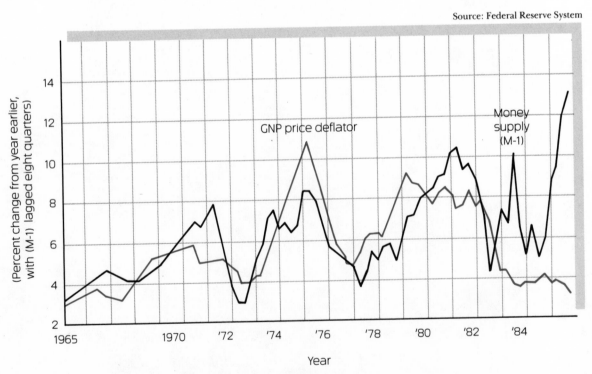

EXHIBIT F: The Growth Rate of the Money Supply and Inflation

As the 1965–1985 data illustrate, rapid growth in the money supply (M-1) has often been associated with an acceleration in the inflation rate in the past.